FILM DIRECTORS

A COMPLETE GUIDE

Compiled and Edited by Michael Singer

LONE EAGLE

This book is dedicated to the memory of
FRANÇOIS TRUFFAUT

Photographs by Toris Von Wolfe. Black and white photos printed by Isgo Lepejian, Custom Black & White Photo Lab, Burbank, CA.

FILM DIRECTORS: A Complete Guide

LONE EAGLE PUBLISHING
9903 Santa Monica Blvd., Suite 204
Beverly Hills, CA 90212

Printed in the United States of America

Book designed by Liz Vietor

ISBN 0-943728-15-0
ISSN 0740-2872

NOTE: We have made every reasonable effort to ensure that the information contained herein is as accurate as possible. However, errors and omissions are sure to occur. We would appreciate your notifying us of any which you find.

*Lone Eagle Publishing is a division of Lone Eagle Productions, Inc.

LETTER FROM THE PUBLISHERS

It is with great pride and pleasure that we bring you this **Third Annual International Edition of FILM DIRECTORS: A Complete Guide.** There are over 1400 *working* domestic and international directors—190 of them listed here for the first time—and thousands of additions and changes to the listings. We feel this is, without a doubt, the most complete reference work on directors ever.

In addition to using the listing and index sections of this book to answer the questions of who directed what and what was directed by whom, we hope that you will enjoy reading the six interviews in the special section, *From The Director's Chair.* These interviews by Michael Singer and photographs by Toris Von Wolfe were commissioned expressly for this book. We have chosen these directors as we feel that each has made a special contribution to the world of filmmaking. We hope that you will find their views and viewpoints interesting.

We look forward to your comments—pro or con. It is very satisfying to know that in just a few short years, what began as an idea has now become a standard reference book found in every production office in Hollywood and New York, not to mention around the world.

Thank you for your support.

Joan E. Vietor and Ralph S. Singleton
Publishers

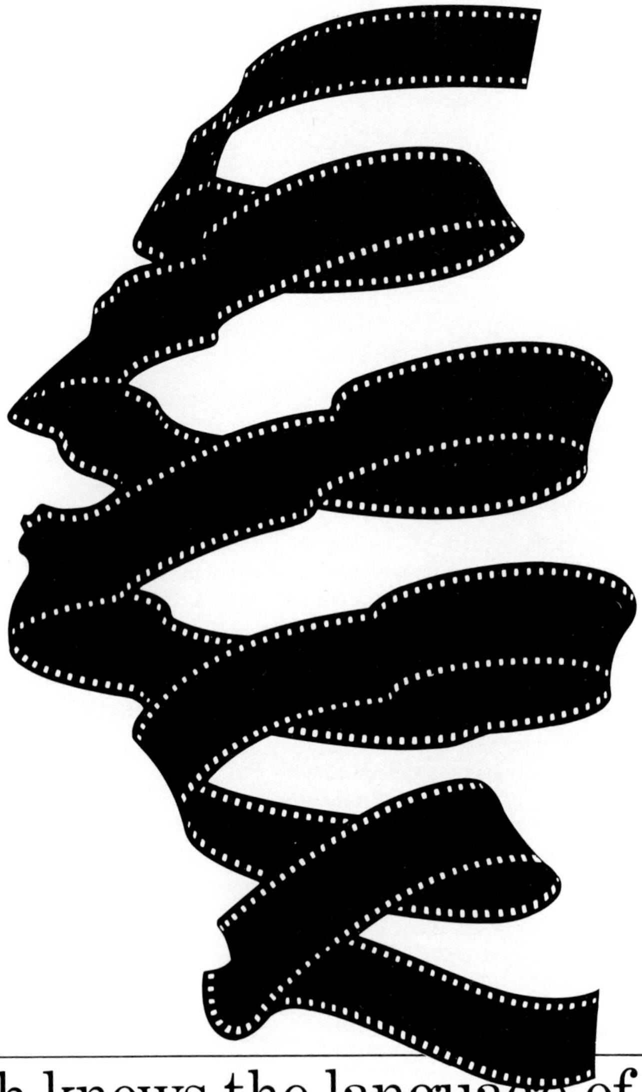

TABLE OF CONTENTS

INTRODUCTION

One year and 190 new director listings later, we present the Third Annual International Edition of **FILM DIRECTORS: A Complete Guide**, which includes feature and telefeature credits for over 1400 domestic and international filmmakers. Once again, we state the intention of this book—to provide an easy, practical and comprehensive reference to living film directors and their work.

Among our features are:

- An alphabetical listing of directors by name and a concise rundown of their credits by year.
- FROM THE DIRECTOR'S CHAIR, a special section highlighting six prominent directors, each representing different styles and approaches to moviemaking. These interviews are done by the editor especially for this book.
- A cross-referenced index of over 12,000 film titles in alphabetical order followed by the names of their directors. This will help those who remember the title of a film, but not its director.
- Academy and Emmy Award nominees and winners among the directors listed in this book.

Some words of explanation about the listings:

DIRECTORS—The listings herein are selective by necessity, as the inclusion of every living person who ever made a full-length film would inflate the guide to encyclopaedic proportions. Selecting is not an easy task, and we are—as always—open to suggestions and requests. Although the listed directors are primarily active, also included are some retired greats, such as Frank Capra, Rouben Mamoulian and Henry Hathaway out of sheer respect for their places in film history. Foreign directors included are those whose films have had some distribution and recognition in the United States. We've made an even greater effort this year to recognize several independent filmmakers working outside of the studio system as some of them may one day be *running* the studios.

The reader should be reminded that because we list only full-length features and telefeatures, a director whose last credit in the book is ten years old could be one of the many who actively work in episodic television.

Birthdates, birthplaces and contacts have been provided whenever possible, but it's well known—this year more than ever, it seems—that both birthdates and agents are subject to change without notice.

FILMS—One of the great frustrations of collecting data for this book is what the editor flippantly calls the "Spanish-Bulgarian Syndrome." That is, just when a director's credits appear to finally be complete, some obscure title materializes on T.V. at 2:15 A.M. on a Tuesday night and, *voila*, we find that it was directed by the same filmmaker in 1965, a Spanish-Bulgarian co-production which was only released theatrically in Sofia, not Madrid, and certainly not the United States. Needless to say, we've attempted to make these credits as complete as possible.

The criteria for listed films, in terms of running times, are as follows:

Features: A running time of 60 minutes or longer. Exceptions have been made in certain unusual cases, such as Andy Warhol's films, which have been timed anywhere from 60 seconds to 24 hours. Although it pains us to exclude short subjects of fine quality, including such films would legitimately mean that we should accept episodic T.V. programs as well, which usually run from approximately 22 to 45 minutes in length without commercials.

Telefeatures: On commercial television, an air time of 90 minutes to 4-½ hours. This is not as eccentric as it might seem—without commercials, a 90 minute telefeature still runs approximately 72 minutes, and a 4-½ hour "mini-series" clocks in at about 3 hours and 45 minutes, which is the length of such long features as GONE WITH THE WIND and DOCTOR ZHIVAGO. On non-commercial television, air times of 60 minutes to 4 hours are acceptable because of the elimination of any advertising.

Television Mini-Series: On commercial television, an air time of 4-½ hours or longer, or 4 hours or more on non-commercial television.

Videotaped television dramas—many of which are now called "movies" by the networks—are not included. Although truly impressive work has been done on video—such as Anthony Page's THE MISSILES OF OCTOBER and Edward Zwick's SPECIAL BULLETIN—we feel obliged to live up to our title of ***FILM* DIRECTORS: A Complete Guide.**

TITLES—Films are often known by a multiplicity of titles in the course of international distribution. Since this is a U.S.-based book, American release titles are utilized, with alternate titles following in *italics,* e.g.

BUTCHER, BAKER, NIGHTMARE MAKER *NIGHT WARNING/MOMMA'S BOY* Royal American, 1981

In the case of films from England, Australia or other English-speaking foreign countries, a title in *italics* usually represents the original title in that country if different from its American release title, e.g.

THE ROAD WARRIOR *MAD MAX II* Warner Bros., 1982, Australian

For foreign films which were distributed in the United States, the American title is listed first, followed by the original foreign-language title, only if its meaning is substantially different from the English, e.g.

ALL SCREWED UP *TUTTO A POSTE E NIENTE IN ORDINE* New Line Cinema, 1974, Italian

Films that did not receive American distribution are generally listed under their original foreign-language titles, as are films which were actually released in the U.S. under those original titles, e.g.

LA BELLA DI ROMA Lux Film, 1955, Italian

or:

LA VIE CONTINUE Triumph/Columbia, 1982, French

DISTRIBUTORS AND PRODUCTION COMPANIES—Original American distributors of feature films are listed, although movies often change their distributors through the course of time. For foreign films that received no U.S. distribution, the original distributors or production companies in their respective countries are included whenever possible.

Telefeatures and television mini-series are identified with the names of their production companies rather than the networks on which they aired.

Production companies are also listed for features which have not yet found distributors.

YEAR OF RELEASE—This is often extremely hard to determine. Usually, a foreign film is released in the United States a year or two (sometimes more) after its initial appearance in its own country. Therefore, for the sake of accuracy, the *original* year of release is provided rather than the American release date. Nevertheless, there are often differences of opinion as to when certain films, domestic *and* foreign, were first exhibited. The dates herein may be at variance with other sources. Also, release dates for films not yet released are projections.

COUNTRY OF ORIGIN—These are the years of incredibly complex international co-production deals. How does one explain that a film made in England with an American director, French producer and international cast, but registered in Panama for tax purposes is, therefore, a Panamanian film? We have opted for realism based upon the nationalities of production personnel, and geographic locations of participating companies.

Once again, we would like to thank the staffs of the UCLA Theatre Arts Library and the Academy of Motion Picture Arts & Sciences Margaret Herrick Library, for their fine and helpful service.

It's been particularly heartening to see a response to this book not only from members of the motion picture communities in Los Angeles and New York, but from all over the world as well. There are fragile binds connecting the global family, but a love of film is definitely one of them. Also, the suggestions, corrections and additions sent in by readers have helped immensely in the compilation of this new edition. Once again we've included insert cards for that very purpose, and we urge you to use them. We appreciate and seek your contributions.

Michael Singer
Los Angeles
December 1984

FROM THE

DIRECTOR'S

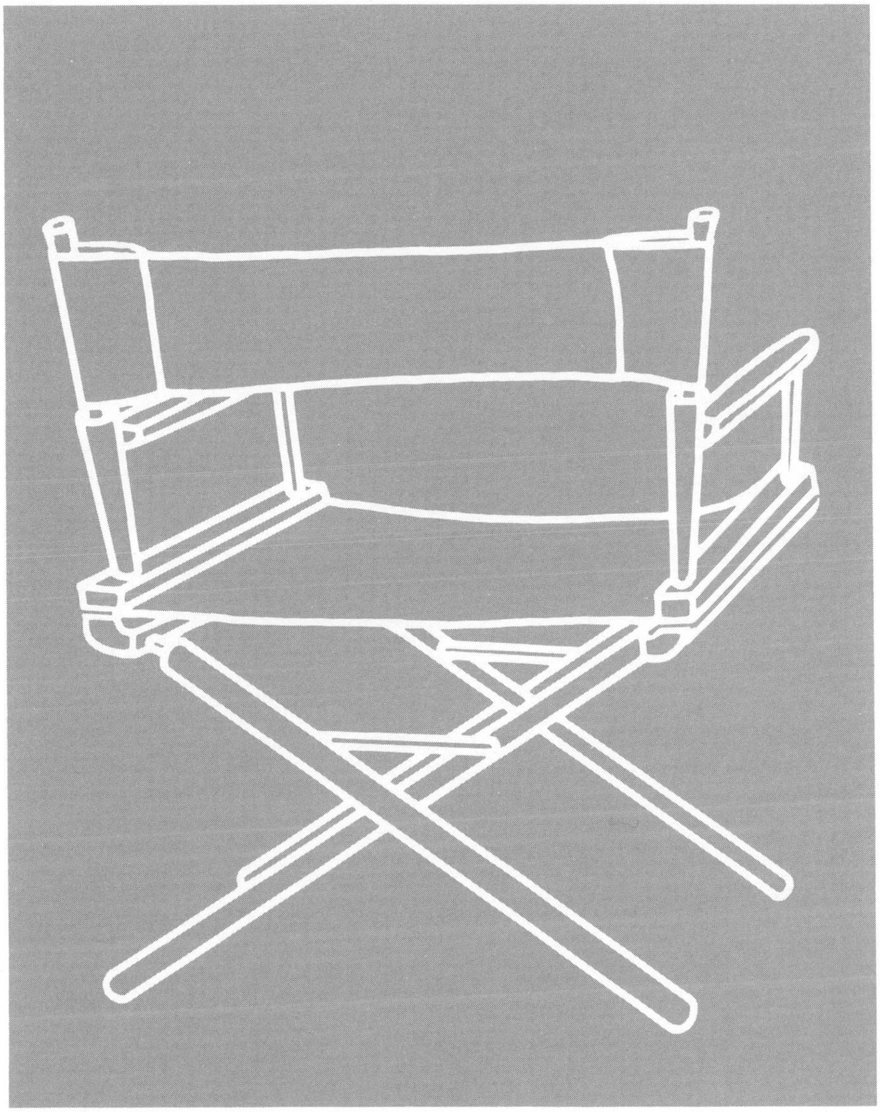

CHAIR

Toris Von Wolfe

J O H N B A D H A M

Visceral excitement, pungent dramatics, seamless technique—these are the hallmarks of John Badham's films, both for television and the big screen. Beginning his career at Universal Television at a time when such colleagues as Steven Spielberg and Michael Ritchie were also learning their craft, Badham's second feature—the influential blockbuster *SATURDAY NIGHT FEVER*—placed him solidly in the ranks of America's Most Wanted directors list. He pursued widely different venues with *DRACULA* and *WHOSE LIFE IS IT ANYWAY?* before directing two of 1983's biggest commercial hits, *BLUE THUNDER* and *WARGAMES.*

Following in Badham's tradition of combining breathtaking action with distinct touches of humanity is his latest film, *AMERICAN FLYER,* based on a script by noted screenwriter/playwright Steven (*BREAKING AWAY*) Tesich.

Michael Singer: *AMERICAN FLYER* had been circulating the studios for quite some time. How did it come to you or how did you come to it?

JOHN BADHAM: It came to me from Warner Bros. I had expressed a lot of interest in the subject matter, and I'm a big fan of Steven Tesich. I like the way he draws human beings and thought that it would be exciting to tell this story, which is a very personal relationship between two brothers set against the background of the largest bicycle race in the United States.

I assume that the elements are different enough so that people won't have a sense of *déjà-vu* watching another Steve Tesich bicycle race movie à la *BREAKING AWAY.*

You won't think you're seeing the same movie, or even a similar movie. The differences are really quite enormous. The Coors Classic that we filmed is a major world class race that traverses almost 1500 miles up and down the Rocky Mountains, and this bears only vague relationship to the rather small local race that was depicted in *BREAKING AWAY.*

Who play the brothers?

The actors are relatively new—to films, anyway. Kevin Costner plays the older brother and David Grant, the younger brother. They're both tremendously talented actors. There is also a wonderful appeal in having actors who are unknown to the audience. You discover them as you're watching the movie. It's like meeting a new friend.

What lured you into filmmaking in the first place? How about a brief chronology of John Badham's life and times?

I was born in England, and my mother remarried an American who brought us to the United States when I was about five. I was raised in Alabama, where he lived. I went to Yale as an undergraduate—I had been involved with theatre in high school, and got involved again at Yale. My mother had been an actress. She had studied at the Royal Academy in London and had a radio and television talk show in Birmingham, Alabama, when I was growing up. So my interest in theatre continued while I was an undergraduate, and then I went to the Yale Drama School as a director. I think I started out wanting to be an actor, but sometime during my Yale career found out that I was not very good, and that maybe I could get involved in something where at least I could meet some girls . . . I noticed that there were always girls surrounding those guys who were directing, so it looked like a good opportunity. I took a Master's Degree from the school as a theatre director, but by that point I had developed an interest in film. After graduating, instead of going to New York or applying to a college somewhere to teach, I came to California . . . largely on the strength of the fact that my sister Mary, who was nine years old and playing in the backyard in Alabama, had been discovered to star in *TO KILL A MOCKINGBIRD,* for which she got an Academy Award nomination. I thought, what the hell. She knows some people out there. Maybe I should go there and see what's going on. So I came out. After about four months of looking around Los Angeles for a job, I would have taken *any* kind of a job, even pumping gas.

Finally, feeling like somebody crawling across the desert trying to find an oasis, I took a job in the Universal mailroom. I found myself there with a lot of people who also had Master's Degrees and said they wanted to be directors and producers. There was some guy in there named Walter Hill who wanted to be a director, and some red-headed guy named Mike Medavoy who wanted to run a studio, and several others who have become producers over the years. We sort of fanned out of the mailroom as we found other jobs in other parts of the studio. Medavoy and I went into the casting department and trained as casting directors. I was a casting director on shows like *The Chrysler Theatre, Run For Your Life* and various half-hour shows. I eventually made friends with a terrific producer named William Sackheim, and became his assistant and then associate producer. Eventually, I started directing little things for him. And when I say little, I mean *little*—like inserts of ashtrays. The first shot I ever did with a professional crew was an insert of a transistor radio hanging from a rifle in a police car. I was petrified. I had more anxiety over that little insert than you can imagine. And the biggest compliment was that they let me do another insert!

Over a period of a year, I did more and more complicated things and finally another producer, David Levinson, agreed to let me direct an episode of a series called *The Senator,* which was part of *The Bold Ones* series. It was a very good beginning to my directing career because the show was so prestigious. Afterwards, I did a lot of television—hour shows, half-hour shows, and finally movies of the week.

At a time when T.V. movies were as similar as apples on a fruitstand, you made two—*The Law* and *The Gun*—which really stood out. Did you specifically look for material on television which would rise above the norm?

I think I learned from various people the clear lesson that, if you're interested in doing bigger and better things, you'd better have very good material. No matter how good a director you think you are, if you don't have wonderful scripts to start with you're never going to be able to distinguish yourself. That kept me away from lots and lots of movies or television shows that would have just kind of added to a mediocre credit list. I tried early on not to work just to be working, and to save my money so if I didn't work for a month or two, my family wouldn't scream and the creditors wouldn't bang down my front door. That was a very good decision, because I avoided doing a lot of turkey movies of the week.

You also seemed, aesthetically, to be not so much directing for television as for *film*. Were you conscious of that at the time?

I think I was just conscious of trying to make the most exciting piece of work that I could, whether I was doing a half-hour or an hour or a two-hour show.

Do you think that television is just about the best training ground for a newcomer?

I don't know if it's the best training ground, but it's a damn sight better than anything else that I know of. I see a terrible mistake being made constantly by beginning directors who have some writing talent. They get to the position in the movie business where they're able to get a chance to direct. And they get into deep trouble right away because they don't have any real training or background. You know, you can *read* all the books you want and *see* all the movies you want and *talk* to all the directors you want, but until you get out on the floor it's a mind boggler unlike anything you've ever seen. The responsibilities are enormous. If you start out doing an hour or a half-hour television show, the risks are much less. First of all, you can get through it a lot easier. Doing a lot of those shows is like operating a well-oiled machine. A director can barely know what he's doing and get through it. It may not be great, but he can get through it. Directing a full-length feature, however, is much, much harder. The fact is, the beaches are littered with the bodies of first-time feature directors, some of whom are friends of mine who have a hard time getting another directing job. These directors should have learned their craft in television before jumping in with the big boys.

It seems that, more and more, young writers and directors are turning up their noses at television.

Well, I can tell you that at Universal on any given day at the time I was there, Steven Spielberg, Richard Donner, Michael Ritchie, Jeannôt Szwarc and myself would be directing shows. We were all learning our craft and getting to a place where we were really in a position to do features.

Do you have any mentors who have in some way influenced your work?

Anybody who tells you they're *not* influenced by past or current directors is probably fibbing. It's almost impossible not to be influenced. Me, I take the attitude that if it's a good shot and I can use it, I'll steal it. I have no shame. My goal is to make the best movie possible. Whatever it takes, I'll do. I'm not ashamed to admit that I looked at *BULLITT* any number of times to study the car chase, and see what I could learn about shooting action. Even when I was doing *BLUE THUNDER* I would go back to *BULLITT* and look at it. I'm not ashamed to admit that Michael Ritchie's techniques of documentary filmmaking that you see in *DOWNHILL RACER* and *THE CANDIDATE* are techniques that I admire tremendously and learned from him.

I'd like to talk about some of your features. When you were shooting *SATURDAY NIGHT FEVER,* did you have any idea that you were creating a cultural icon of the Seventies?

Nobody had any intention of making cultural icons. No one knew that we were going to unleash upon the world a major new star. Everyone was hoping that we'd make a good little picture. The initial budget was $2.5 million, and even in 1977 that was a real tough New York picture to make for so little money. We were going with a relatively unknown director, a relatively unknown star and material culled from the pages of New York Magazine. We were blessed with five new songs from *The Bee Gees*, who at the time had gone into a kind of decline and hadn't really done anything for a while. They were viewed by the brass at Paramount as not being very good songs and having nothing to do with disco. I had never been in a disco up to two weeks before we started shooting the film. My experience with dance was my mother sending me to dance class when I was in grammar school. It was all very new to me. Before the movie was released, Paramount was scared to death of the profanity and begged the producer, Robert Stigwood, to delete most of it. Stigwood, bless him, wouldn't alter a single frame of the film. By the end of the first weekend of release, we knew we had a pretty nice hit going, and it never stopped. It was like *The Little Engine That Could,* just chugging and chugging, on and on. And before you knew it, we had a $300 million worldwide gross.

Would you make *WHOSE LIFE IS IT ANYWAY?* again exactly as you made it?

What I would do differently are some things that I wanted to do originally. First of all, I wanted to get the actors and myself to work for scale. I wanted to make it at an economic level where it really didn't matter how well or badly it did, because the economic risk would have been small enough so that if it had a small audience, it really wouldn't have mattered. On the other hand, MGM was trying its best to re-establish itself as a major studio and not appear as if they had to do only low-budget shows. I would hate like hell to have to give up the most magnificent set I ever had built for me (until the time of the *WARGAMES* set), but I guess I could have made it work in a real hospital in a practical situation.

Watching *WARGAMES* again on cable, it was apparent that couched within a very entertaining framework was one of the most potent anti-nuke messages seen in a feature film. Yet, people tend to think of it as more of straight entertainment than as a "message" film.

Well, it's interesting how when something serious intrudes into what up until that point had been an entertaining film, the serious aspects are overlooked. People tend to dismiss it, thinking, "It's just an action film." We thought that if we made the film entertaining we could slip in a little seriousness at the end. But when people talk about the film they don't view it with the same gravity as some of the other nuclear-themed films that appeared at the time. But, of course, nobody saw those films, so how could they have gotten the message that was put forth so seriously?

Toris Von Wolfe

R A N D A   H A I N E S

The Emmy Award winning ABC Theatre presentation of *SOMETHING ABOUT AMELIA* represented the first respectable effort in American film to come to grips with one of society's last taboos, incest. It also marked the very first network telefeature directed by Randa Haines, who had previously helmed two PBS films and such episodic programs as *Hill Street Blues*. Beginning her career as a New York stage actress, Haines moved into filmmaking first as a script supervisor and later as a writer before taking on the greater responsibilities of directing. Selecting her projects with care and discrimination, she made a dramatic impression on the industry with her unflinching but delicate direction of *SOMETHING ABOUT AMELIA*.

Haines' latest project is the feature adaptation of Mark Medoff's heralded play *CHILDREN OF A LESSER GOD*.

MICHAEL SINGER: Why did you decide to quit acting and go into film production?

RANDA HAINES: My acting career was a long period of frustration. To be the ingenue in those days you had to be the blonde, petite, all-American girl. I just didn't fit into that at all, so the only parts I got were these poetic, abstract off-Broadway types who could be dark and mysterious-looking and taller than the leading man. I got a job acting at the School of Visual Arts where they hired actors to work with the directing students, and I found myself kind of moving to their side of the room. Around that time I got an acting interview for a tiny little picture, and again I was wrong for the part. But I did tell them that I was interested in learning about filmmaking, and they said, "Gee, we were just thinking about hiring our first employee." So they hired me. It was a very small company where I got to do everything. I answered the phones, opened the mail, cut the sound effects, bought the props, and was exposed to a wide variety of filmmaking situations. Business got slow and they were going to have to lay me off, so somebody I knew got a job on a low-budget feature and they needed a script supervisor. So off I went on this little film shot in the Catskills. I always found myself one step ahead of the director in figuring things out. After that, I got another job on a low-budget feature and I worked as a non-union production manager a little bit. But I specialized in script supervision, got into the union and did that for almost ten years. About six years into working as a script supervisor, I began making suggestions very discreetly to the directors I was working with. Then I began to want to say those things out loud to see if it would work for me. People were always coming up to me and saying, "You should be a director." I'd say, "Okay . . . how do we do it?" I couldn't figure out a way to make it happen.

This was still at a time when women directors were few and far between?

Yes, I had never met one or even heard of one. Also, very few people moved up from crew positions to directing. But somewhere in those years I heard about the Directing Workshop for Women at the American Film Institute. The first year just about everybody in that program was a movie star, so I didn't think it was a real strong possibility. But somebody convinced me to apply. I wrote a letter describing the situation that I was in—a major support element of a lot of directors, but never getting a chance to say things out loud. I think I wrote a very passionate letter, and somehow I slipped in as a token unknown among many Oscar-winning classmates. Within two weeks of being notified, I packed up my life and moved to L.A., with my script supervisor bank account in my hand. I said okay, let's roll the dice. The only way to make a move is to strike out, take a chance and go all the way. I came out and participated in that program, which at the time had no real instruction. It was just, "Here's a thousand dollars, here's some very inadequate videotape equipment, go do what you want to do." A thousand dollars, of course, just barely pays for the bagels in the morning. I knew that to get people to work for free you have to treat them really well and make them a part of something. I also saw that the equipment was inadequate and so I rented a lot more. I really invested my whole bank account in the project, figuring that it was my best shot.

And it turned out well?

Yes, it turned out very professionally and also, it was a piece of material that was very difficult—a novel by Doris Lessing. Very internal, very challenging kind of material to dramatize. It impressed a lot of people and led to some writing work—*Family* and other television shows. Then I wanted to make directing a full-time effort, and that's what I did for the next couple of years. It was that tape and that energy that led to my first job on public television.

Which was?

UNDER THIS SKY, a 90-minute historical epic for $250,000. A suicide mission, something we could never have duplicated again. The luck in every moment of it, to manage to come in on that kind of budget. The film was set in 1860's Kansas and we shot it in Rhode Island in the middle of the winter. It doesn't look anything like Kansas, but somehow we made it work. One of the reviews said something about the "John Ford exteriors." How did I do that? Behind every tree there's a little New England cottage and a little lake, so we had to shoot at very low angles to avoid all that.

Do you think PBS was just about the only place at the time that would be willing to take a chance on you as, first of all, a neophyte director; and second of all, a woman director?

I suppose. I know other people managed to get their foot in the door some other way, but that was the way that presented itself to me. They did want a woman to direct the film, so I think it was a very special circumstance. I was in a very narrow field of competitors, and when the executive producer saw the piece that I had done for the Directing Workshop for Women, she thought that it had exactly the feeling that she wanted.

You followed with another film for PBS in 1979?

Yes, for the *American Short Story* series—*THE JILTING OF GRANNY WEATHERALL*, which was based on a Katherine Anne Porter story that I loved. When I read a script, what pulls me into it is not so much the genre or the subject matter, but if it's about people with complex psychological makeup who are involved with complicated relationships. *THE JILTING OF GRANNY WEATHERALL* was really about secrets of the heart. That's the kind of material that I really care about.

You never had any doubt that you were going to be successful, did you?

Oh, that's not true. I have had my periods of doubt. I've never said to myself, "I'm a woman, I can't do that," but just gone ahead and done it anyway. I think that's actually something I like about myself, because I'm always questioning and always driving myself crazy. But at the same time, that's never stopped me from doing things. But careerwise, after doing *UNDER THIS SKY* and *THE JILTING OF GRANNY WEATHERALL*, I came back to L.A. with the latter, which was a much better selling tool for me than the first one because of the nature of the material. And then two years went by in which I did not work. During those two years there was a *lot* of doubt.

You were between a rock and a hard place. You wanted to work but couldn't take a step back to do anything else but direct. What does a person do during two years of not working?

I was always busy, somehow. Somehow I managed to sustain a real level of energy and commitment despite this parallel of exhaustion and a feeling of my spirit cracking. Maybe if my tastes were different it all would have happened more easily. I don't regret any of that time now because the kind of work I've done since has been the kind of work I wanted to do. And the job that I finally got was the *creme de la creme* of television, *Hill Street Blues*. Mostly, what you encounter in trying to make these breaks from one plateau to the next is that people—though they may respect your abilities—don't have the imagination or the faith or the ability to take the leap, that if you've done X kind of films you could also do Y kind of films. Mostly they say, "Gee, we love your film, but there's no chicken in it. Our film stars a chicken, and we don't think you can direct a chicken." So here was *Hill Street Blues*, as far away as you could get from *THE JILTING OF GRANNY WEATHERALL*, with this huge cast, enormous pace, action, a visual style that was light years away from the other film. And here were a group of people who said, "gee, here's someone with talent . . . we bet she could adapt to our style and do our show." I just sat down and made a study of the show, looked at its style, got a feeling for it, hung around the set to get to know the actors a little bit, went in and did it. And it worked out very well. In three years I did four *Hill Streets*.

During that period, did you find that you were accepted on the set as a woman director, or were there still barriers?

Well, I think I have always tried to put blinders on a little bit about that. If you feel people aren't responding to you on the set because you didn't do your homework, or because they don't like the way you're shooting, or because you're not giving actors enough direction, you can take their responses as feedback and work on those problems. But if you feel that they're not working for you because you're a woman, what can you do about that? When I look back on it I know there might have been a couple of incidents, but there were really very few, even in taking my blinders off.

Was *SOMETHING ABOUT AMELIA* a project that you developed or was it something that was brought to you?

It was developed by a woman named Deborah Aal, a wonderful, talented person who was then working for Leonard Goldberg. The project was her idea and it took her about 2½ years to get it developed. She was one of the people whom I met during the two years I didn't work. She filed me away in her mind and now, years later, she had this project and I came back into her thoughts. In the meantime, I had moved way ahead from where I had been, so it all worked out. When the script was sent to me, I was a little apprehensive—I thought that the material might have been exploitative and sensationalized. But by page two, I realized just how good the writing was. It was tense, so much complexity beneath the surface of the dialogue, unlike a lot of television where the characters talk directly about what's going on. So I called back right after I finished it and said—I know this sounds corny—"This is terrific and *I'm* the person to direct it."

Weren't you afraid that network pressures would force you in directions you didn't want to take?

The quality of the script indicated to me that everyone knew this was a special project. Standards and Practices, of course, was very involved, but we never got frantic phone calls after dailies. We had no major problem. When the rough cut was finished they were incredibly enthusiastic.

You went into the film knowing that it was a special project. This was your first network movie, an ABC Theatre project and, of course, the theme was so delicate. Couldn't that have been overwhelming?

Of course, one thinks about the big view. There was a lot of responsibility, but the bigger responsibility was to the story. It ultimately narrows down to just the one family depicted in the film. I wasn't telling the story of everyone in the world who was ever in such a situation. We could only talk in terms of this daughter and this father and this family and this story. You can't direct it thinking that you're going to make the definitive film on incest in contemporary American life. You just try to make the story as truthful as it can possibly be, which is what you do with any story.

Were you at all apprehensive about casting Ted Danson as the father?

No, I think we felt that it worked to our advantage. Everybody knows what the story is about tuning in, so there are already twenty thousand strikes against that character. Casting the character with an actor who everybody has warm feelings about—because of his role in *Cheers*—is a real advantage. I did not want the father to be a villain. I thought he was a much more complex character, and as much as the audience would be capable of, I wanted them to feel compassion for him. Whatever despicable things he has done, by his own actions he has destroyed his own life and lost everything that meant anything to him. Plus, I also knew that Ted Danson was a really wonderful actor and could bring much to the role.

Did you expect the incredible effect that *SOMETHING ABOUT AMELIA* had on the American public and press?

No. I knew that we were going to have the hotline numbers at the end of the show, but I never really envisioned 60 million people watching the show in one night and tens of thousands of phone calls pouring in.

In essence, the film altered public perception of incest and helped remove the stigma from victims.

Television has such incredible power and people working in it do not often acknowledge the responsibility they have. It can open people's eyes and affect their points of view. And some of the choices that were made on the show affected the way people look at incest—not just that they can acknowledge that it's there, but that they can look at it without the kind of horror that prevents them from acting.

Is television work behind you now?

I want to work in features, and I'm

Randa Haines continued on page 16

Toris Von Wolfe

GREGORY NAVA

A film of poetry, magic and moving social drama, *EL NORTE* opens a door to a world rarely explored in such depth—the Indian cultures of the Americas—as it depicts the heartrending journey to the U.S. of a Guatemalan brother and sister fleeing political oppression in their own land. Critically praised, an official U.S. entry to the 1984 Cannes Film Festival, and the most successful Spanish language film ever released north of the border (*EL NORTE* is bilingual, with Indian dialects and English also spoken), it was directed by Gregory Nava, produced by Anna Thomas and co-written by both. The fact that collaborators Nava and Thomas are also husband and wife only fueled, it seems, *EL NORTE*'s artistic cohesiveness.

Together, they have redefined independent filmmaking, placing it squarely before the eyes of the press and public not only with *EL NORTE,* but their two previous efforts as well—Nava's *THE CONFESSIONS OF AMANS* and Thomas' *THE HAUNTING OF M.*

MICHAEL SINGER: What in your background prepared you for a career as a film director?

GREGORY NAVA: I grew up in a generation that very much loved the movies, and I did as well. From a very early age I was interested in getting ahold of my parents' movie camera and making movies. My relatives are Mexican on my father's side and Basque on my mother's side. The Basque side of the family has always taken hundreds of pictures going way back. And they got into home movies very early on, back to 1939. I look at these old single-strip color home movies, and they have a magical quality. Someone once said that one day, home movies are going to be studied like folk art. My brother was also interested in film, so he and I got together to make our first film—the history of the world. We started with a grand theme, and everything has been downhill ever since. But my brother didn't really like it too much, so I bought his camera and started making my own films. I started going to a theatre which opened in San Diego called the Unicorn. Since San Diego had not been hit too much by the wave of European films, they went through almost an entire backlog of the classics of both foreign and American cinema on double bills that would change every week. I saw all these movies by Bergman, Resnais, Godard, John Ford, Hitchcock, Satyajit Ray, Akira Kurosawa, Sergei Eisenstein. I was in ninth or tenth grade at the time.

Did you study film in school?

Yes, I went to the UCLA film school. The first 16mm film that I made there was titled *THE JOURNAL OF DIEGO RODRIGUEZ SILVA,* which was loosely based on the life of Garcia Lorca. It was a half-hour long and in black and white. I filmed it in Mexico all by myself, and found out something very important—you must do extraordinary things with very limited means if you're going to accomplish anything at all. If you're going to find anything, or do anything, or impress anybody or achieve what you want to achieve, you are going to be expected to do miracles. People said, "Why don't you shoot it here and use some adobe buildings around Los Angeles." But having been to Mexico, I knew that if I tried to shoot that story in Los Angeles it would look like junk. I could have a big crew and better equipment, but it wouldn't look as good. And who cares what's *behind* the camera? The only thing that matters is what's in *front* of the camera. It's better to go down to Mexico with a Bolex and shoot in Guanajuato and get something really extraordinary. *DIEGO RODRIGUEZ* was a tremendously successful student film—it won the National Student Film Festival Award for best dramatic film of the year in 1972. When people watch student films at UCLA at the end of a term, they watch them for an entire week, from eight in the morning till eight at night for five days straight. All the films look like Los Angeles because they've all been shot here. So when *DIEGO RODRIGUEZ* was shown, it looked amazing because it had been shot somewhere else. Latin America is a magnificent place, and Central Mexico is incredible. Those billowing clouds and fantastic landscapes and extraordinary cities with mindboggling architecture. The only thing people look at when they see a movie is what you have put in front of the lens.

Did you study anything else at UCLA besides film to round out your education?

My feeling is that everything is relevant to film. I took a tremendous number of courses outside the film department. One year, in addition to my film course, I took Mayan Archaeology. Pre-Columbian civilization, with my background, has been a lifelong interest. And many of the more striking visual concepts in *EL NORTE* began to develop from studying Mayan archaeology and civilization at UCLA at a time when a lot of film students thought I was nuts for doing that. The best visual ideas I ever have for films come not from other filmmaking or from other cinematography, but from painting and studying the arts of other societies and other cultures. In essence painting is particularly inspiring because you have—up to a certain period in history—the greatest minds of the world applying themselves to executing what in films is only one frame.

So the success of *DIEGO RODRIGUEZ* inspired you to pursue full-length filmmaking?

Right. The reaction to *DIEGO RODRIGUEZ* confirmed the ideas I had while making it. When I came to make my first very low-budget feature, which was about a wandering scholar in the Middle Ages, we shot it in Segovia, Spain.

This was *THE CONFESSIONS OF AMANS*?

Yes. It was 88 minutes long and shot in 1973, but it wasn't finished until 1976 because we needed more money, which we finally got with a grant from the American Film Institute. Even though it won the Best First Feature Prize at the Chicago Film Festival in 1976, there was a very big lull between *THE CONFESSIONS OF AMANS* and *EL NORTE.* It was very well reviewed, but nothing really happened. So at that point, Anna and I got an agent and started writing screenplays. Then, Anna was able to raise the budget to direct *THE HAUNTING OF M,* for which I did the cinematography.

In terms of what you said before about being influenced by art, did this continue with your work on *THE HAUNTING OF M*?

For *THE CONFESSIONS OF AMANS*, I took all my visual cues from medieval art—the way the space is organized and the way compositions are envisioned. I didn't want to make a film which looked at the middle ages from our perspective, which is the way they're generally done. I wanted to make a film as though it had been conceived by a medieval mind. This was a real breakthrough in terms of our visual style, which we then extended in *THE HAUNTING OF M.* Just to give you an example, when you look at medieval painting and you see portraits of people, they are never portrayed—or rarely—in a three-quarter or frontal view. Most of the portraits are in profile. So in *THE CONFESSIONS OF AMANS*, I used a tremendous number of profile close-ups. I fell in love with them. I also used a lot of them in shooting *THE HAUNTING OF M* and *EL NORTE.* It is a very striking and magnificent way of looking at the human face. It is also true of Mayan art that the face is conceived of in profile, so again, when I was designing the visuals for *EL NORTE*, I wanted to make a film truly Mayan in its visual conception. Again, I believe very strongly in looking outside film to find new visual ideas and concepts. But when you find new ways to express them, you always have to take your key from the story. For me, the visual research that goes into a film is very important. I've become a strong advocate of storyboarding a film, that is, figuring all the shots and cinematic concepts before going in to shoot it. That's not to say that you don't change things in the course of shooting, but the clearer you are on what your concepts are going to be for each scene, the more remarkable your film can be. It's very hard to be brilliant five minutes before you shoot—so many things are happening. One thing in *EL NORTE* that many people have commented on is the transition between the sequence in which Enrique is killing the soldier, to a shot of the father's decapitated head, to the shot of the full moon, to a full frame shot of the funeral drum. That's a classic case of something which can only be figured out with storyboards before the shooting starts.

Can you tell me how you collaborate with Anna [Thomas] on her projects and vice versa?

Working on *THE HAUNTING OF M* with Anna was very important for me. We work very, very well together. That film was Anna's vision. I feel I contributed to it and enhanced it. I always tried to key on her feelings about what she was trying to express. Our movies are so much better because Anna and I worked on them together. There's so much of her in *EL NORTE.* It is probably one of the greatest producing efforts in the history of film. She's also a fantastic director, and that's the avenue she wants to pursue.

I know from talking with Anna that filming *EL NORTE* was an incredibly challenging experience.

What we had to do to capture this film, to really tell it . . . well, there's nothing in the world that looks like the Mayan highlands. We had to shoot it there. We had to find that world. It's hard to get there and it's dangerous, but nothing else was going to give us that look. We shot in Chiapas, Central Mexico, the Mexican-U.S. border, San Diego, Los Angeles. Two different countries with essentially two completely different casts and crews on over a hundred locations. There were over eighty speaking parts, a two hour and twenty minute film with 139 scenes with the kind of budget that we had. I mean, what an unbelievable job of producing Anna did!

What about the origins of the film?

I mentioned that my family is Mexican on my father's side and Basque on my mother's. The Basque side emigrated to Southern California in the 1890's, and I have a lot of relatives from my father's side in Tijuana. So they're both settled on the border. The inspiration for *EL NORTE* comes from my experiences as a kid on the border. I speak Spanish, and as a child I wondered who lives in those "lost cities" across the border. A child can't explain this incredible cultural contrast. There's no natural border there. Nowhere else in the world do the first and third world share a common border as do the United States and Mexico. It's an image not only of the Americas, but of what's happening in the world. There's no place where the movement of the third world into the first is more graphic and more on the line than the border at Tijuana.

I remember the first time I drove from Los Angeles to Tijuana, coming down the freeway and suddenly seeing hills crowded with small, odd-colored buildings and church steeples. I realized that from a freeway in the United States I was looking at another *world.*

You're absolutely right. Visually, it's an astonishing transition. That world has always been very important to me. From an early age, I traveled a lot in Mexico. To a certain extent, *EL NORTE* came from a need and a desire to deal with that part of me. Latin America is going through an epic period in its history. It's a world where the dream is as real as reality. That's the first thing that strikes you when you go there. I've always been interested in dreams and dream technique. That really started for me when I was a sophomore in high school and visited Central Mexico with my parents, leaving the border areas for the first time. On that particular trip I started reading the dream realist literature of Latin America—Carlos Fuentes, Gabriel Garcia Marquez, Vargas Llosa, Borges. And most of all, in talking about *EL NORTE*, the Guatemalan writer Miguel Angel Asturias.

That doesn't surprise me. A few days after seeing *EL NORTE* for the first time, I saw a performance of Asturias' play *Soluna* at UCLA, which dealt with so many of the same themes. At the time I was glad that I had been introduced to Guatemalan folkloric and mystical themes by *EL NORTE*, which helped me to understand the play.

Well, everybody who sees *EL NORTE* talks about the influence from Gabriel Garcia Marquez. Of course, I do love his books and they're a real inspiration, but the real central inspiration for *EL NORTE* in terms of dream realism is Asturias, who was the first of that group to win a Nobel Prize. The dream realism that you find in the literature and life of Latin America is so amazing. What I wanted to do was make this film about Latin America from a Latin American point of view, which is part of me as well. And to tell it in a dream realist way, because if you do that, you capture all the richness and complexities of the culture. You can't tell this story in a neo-realist way. That may be fine for Italy after the war, but those styles developed to deal—rightly so—with those people's problems at that point in history. When people heard that a film was being made about Latin American social problems, they thought it would be neo-realist or a docudrama, but that's wrong for *EL NORTE*. It misses the half of the story that's going to make everything else make sense, especially when you're dealing with Indian people—that's the way they *think*. They don't make any distinction between their waking life and their dreaming life. It's a style and a way of doing films that I'm going to continue, because I think that it's something to

Gregory Nava continued on page 16

Toris Von Wolfe

M I C H A E L   S C H U L T Z

One of the few Black American directors consistently employed by Hollywood, Michael Schultz has displayed a versatility throughout his career that defies categorization. Working from a background in classical theatre, Schultz's first two films were the independently produced dramas, *TOGETHER FOR DAYS* and *HONEYBABY, HONEYBABY*. He then eased expertly into the funky urban settings of *COOLEY HIGH* and *CAR WASH* before directing Richard Pryor in two of his first starring features, *GREASED LIGHTNING* and *WHICH WAY IS UP?* Schultz temporarily moved away from ethnic concerns with *SGT. PEPPER'S LONELY HEARTS CLUB BAND* and *SCAVENGER HUNT*, but returned with the features *BUSTING LOOSE*, again starring Richard Pryor, *CARBON COPY*, and the television movies *BENNY'S PLACE* and *FOR US, THE LIVING*, the latter a deeply moving and highly praised biography of martyred civil rights leader Medgar Evers.

Schultz's latest project, *THE LAST DRAGON*, was shot for Motown Productions under a cloak of secrecy and is due for release in early 1985.

MICHAEL SINGER: There's been speculation that *THE LAST DRAGON* is anything from a kung fu movie to a fantasy film, but I have a feeling that it's neither of the two. I'm wondering if you once again return to an urban setting, which you seem quite comfortable with.

MICHAEL SCHULTZ: The setting is New York City. It's a contemporary urban fairy tale. Or, if you will, a musical fantasy. It is called *THE LAST DRAGON* because the lead character, whose name is Leroy Greene, is a young kid who wants to be Bruce Lee. There is an element of kung fu in this movie, but it's not a kung fu movie. It's a movie about a young man who finds who he really is, finding himself through various trials, like the trials of Hercules. It's very contemporary and laced with music. I won't call it a musical, but much of the film is driven by the Motown beat. And it's a love story.

Are these all original songs, or did you use any Motown classics?

No, it's all original music. We toyed with the idea of using at least one classic but discarded it because we want the film to have a totally fresh feel to it.

Music seems to play an important role in your films, particularly the constant underscoring of *CAR WASH*. You obviously love music. Do you actively seek projects that will allow use to make extensive use of music?

Sometimes. It really depends on the subject matter. I seek projects first and foremost out of the subject matter, usually with a narrative line that has something that, I feel, is valuable to say. I do love music and it's fun to work with.

***SGT. PEPPER'S LONELY HEARTS CLUB BAND* was one of the last musicals in which people were actually singing to each other.**

It was a tremendously underrated film and will probably come back around again sometime. A lot of people loved it, but all of the critics, almost, roundly hated it.

How badly do you react to negative responses from the press? I see that you didn't waste much time getting onto another project after *SGT. PEPPER*. It was certainly not your *HEAVEN'S GATE*.

Actually, I took a long rest, much longer than normal, because at that point I had directed four features back to back. So I turned down a lot of projects just because I wanted a normal life . . . watch my kids grow up a little bit. Then I thought, better get another project going because I'll forget how to do it! No, critics do not really affect me. I was outraged by some of the critical responses to that picture simply because a lot of them were personal attacks on [producer] Robert Stigwood rather than the picture itself. Other than that, the audience will determine. Critics hated *FLASHDANCE*, for example. One of the problems with *SGT. PEPPER* is that everybody had grown up to the music of *The Beatles*, and *The Bee Gees* did not fit their idea of successors to *The Beatles*. *FLASHDANCE*, though, had all original music so audiences had no such similar problems.

If you had to do it all over again, would you have done it differently? Or did you pretty much make the movie you wanted to make?

I think I made the movie I wanted to make. Stigwood had a very strong story concept, but outside of that, I had tremendous freedom to do whatever I wanted. But after the picture got out and we saw the audiences' responses, we noticed that the two segments that were the most successful, musically, were *Earth, Wind and Fire's* rendition of *Got To Get You Into My Life* and Billy Preston's *Get Back*. They brought the house down. And what was different was that we were being extremely faithful to how the music was produced with all the other songs except those two. Those two artists wanted to do it their way. If I had to do it all over again I'd have all new and individual interpretations of *The Beatles'* classics.

You're one of the very few filmmakers who makes films on Black subjects which are essentially serious, even if they're comedies like *CARBON COPY*. How important is this to you as a moviemaker?

It is very important. When I came to Hollywood, my background and reputation were all heavy drama, political statements and very impactful material. I had never really delved into comedy. I've always felt that all material, whether comic or tragic—in order to have value—should relate to something that we're about, the way we hope the world should be. And when it comes to Black material, a significant part of the human family in this country has had no real representation in the media. I'd just like to add to the quality of life on all our parts, Black and White and everything in between . . . if there's a good story to be told.

Such as the story of Medgar Evers in *FOR US, THE LIVING*, which was a rare piece of cinematic Black history. I'm almost amazed that you got it made in the first place.

It wasn't easy. The torch carrier for

that project was Ken Rotcop, a very committed person who happened to be Jewish. He tried to get the project made for seven years. He would just not give up. He had met Medgar Evers' wife, a magnificent woman who had gone through the first of three brutal political assassinations in a very close timespan. Eventually, he got the Corporation for Public Broadcasting to put up some money for it. I was not the original director, by the way. They had come to me first, but I was busy directing another film, and they hired someone else. Then they had problems, so I agreed to come to the rescue because I thought it was the kind of material that the world needed to know more about.

You must be very glad now that you were able to do it.

Oh yes, it was a terrific experience. We shot it in Atlanta. The city was extremely cooperative in giving us locations and helping us with extras. We shot it in 17 days at a killing pace.

Before *THE LAST DRAGON*, your previous two films were both for television. Are there certain projects which you think are best suited for T.V., and that you would actually prefer to make for the small tube rather than the big screen? Or would you prefer to stay with features?

It really doesn't make that much difference to me. Television requires tighter schedules and money, and that's the only thing that I don't like about it. That is counterbalanced by the fact that television offers more latitude in dealing with topical subjects that feature producers feel might be too soft for theatres. From my standpoint, it's all the same. You have heard stories of how difficult it was to get projects produced like *TERMS OF ENDEARMENT* or *THE CHINA SYNDROME* or *ONE FLEW OVER THE CUCKOO'S NEST*. Those kinds of projects, now today more than ever, studios feel are too soft for theatrical audiences in light of escapist, blockbuster competition. But it's all horse puckey. Right now we're heading into what I call a real errant period of teen movies and blockbusters. Everything outside of that is very difficult to get produced.

You seem to veer from very different kinds of projects in tone and sensibility. It's difficult to type you. How do you see yourself?

I consider this first ten-year period my development stage. I wanted to explore as much as I could—unfortunately, I couldn't get a shot at really dramatic material, so I decided to try as many kinds of films as I could so that I could learn as much as possible. I think I'm ready to move on now.

Do you hope to return in any way to your classical theatre roots?

As far as film goes?

Or theatre.

Definitely yes. I've been away from the theatre for too long. I shot *THE LAST DRAGON* in New York, so I was back in my milieu. I realized how much I miss doing theatre. One of my earlier goals—which I abandoned because I kept working so much—was to alternate one film and one play a year. Now I'd like to get back on track and start incorporating some theatre into my schedule. It would be great fun to have a live audience there. When theatre is good, it is unforgettable. And when it's bad . . . it's horrible.

Randa Haines continued

developing *CHILDREN OF A LESSER GOD* and other projects, but I don't believe in closing any doors. The problem with having done *SOMETHING ABOUT AMELIA* is that projects like that come along every ten years in television. Other things have been offered to me that haven't interested me as much, not just because of the subject matter, but because of the way the stories are told. I haven't yet come across a script that has excited me as much as *AMELIA* but wherever you find the material and the opportunity to tell a story, that's where you'll tell it.

Gregory Nava continued

work at breaking down the false barrier that exists between people's waking and dreaming lives. And certainly, film is the medium that has traditionally been thought of as doing that, isn't it? People talk about Hollywood as a "dream factory." And going to a movie is like dreaming—the lights get dark and the images come up before you like a dream. The relationship between the dream and cinema is fascinating. It affects and touches the audience deeply, and I think in that realm we find the true power of cinema. In that realm we find the essence of drama itself. I wanted to make a film that would be a cultural journey: telling the story of *all* the Americas. I wanted it to refer back to the pre-Columbian era, and also to the future, to the way the Americas are changing.

Toris Von Wolfe

A N N A   T H O M A S

The necessities of independent filmmaking can breed moviemakers who can handle practically any task. Anna Thomas functioned in several capacities while working on Gregory Nava's *THE CONFESSIONS OF AMANS* before writing and directing her own much-praised effort, *THE HAUNTING OF M.* On *EL NORTE,* she collaborated with Nava on the screenplay and then took on the massive task of producing the film, which was not only one of the most logistically ambitious independent efforts of all time, but a production fraught with enormous difficulties—such as kidnapping the production manager and the exposed stock and then holding them for ransom!

MICHAEL SINGER: The logistics of producing *EL NORTE* must have been staggering.

ANNA THOMAS: It was very complicated, because it was like shooting two features back to back. We had a whole shoot in Mexico, and then a shoot in the United States. Overall there were thirteen shooting weeks. We had something like 100 locations spread through different parts of Southern Mexico to Central Mexico to the border between Mexico and the United States, San Diego and then to Los Angeles. I was involved with a lot of specific location scouting and a lot of decisions that had to do with the ultimate look of the film. But it's truly Greg's vision.

Can you tell me about some of the hair-raising experiences you had shooting in Mexico? At one point I understand your production manager was kidnapped.

Our exposed stock was seized and our production manager was taken and held for the better part of the day. It was late that night when she was finally released. Then we had to negotiate an extortion payment to get back our stock; quite a large sum was paid in bundles of cash in a parking lot in Mexico City at night, to guys who had sub-machine guns and that's how we retrieved our negative. Of course, we had to leave Mexico with our Mexican shoot not completed and find ways later to finish it.

Who was responsible?

Well, it's hard to say, because when you're talking to people who have guns you don't ask too many questions . . . it's a different dynamic of conversation. Apparently—and I believe this was so—they were members of the Mexican secret police. I mean, what you have to do to make a movie!

Was it a politically motivated act, or purely rapacious?

I think it was a little of both, a nice, thick stew of the two of them mixed together. Politics definitely had something to do with it, but they were not going to let an opportunity like that slip by to skim off whatever they could. The idea was to shut the film down and while shutting it down, get whatever they could. I don't want to paint an entirely black picture of working in Mexico. There were a lot of Mexican people who helped us a lot and were very wonderful. But the situation in Mexico, especially at that time, was very volatile and sensitive. Ultimately, no matter who's helping you—and we were dealing with some people who were very well-connected—in the final analysis, if you're doing something that a strong element in the government does not want to see done, it doesn't matter who's been cooperating with you until then. They have very direct ways of dealing with you.

Officially, the present government of Mexico is sympathetic to the plight of the Guatemalan refugees.

Officially yes, the government is sympathetic to the guerilla movements in Central America, but unofficially they have allowed the Guatemalan army to cross the border, go into the refugee camps in Chiapas and massacre people. Really, the situation depicted in *EL NORTE* is the discontent of people. A scene of peasants being shot by armed soldiers is something that's a very threatening image to any government in Latin America, and certainly the government in Mexico. I think they have a lot of well-founded fears that a similar type of explosive unrest could really take hold in certain parts of Mexico. So these are things that cut through official policy and administrations. In a country where so many people are so poor and so few are very rich, there's always a lot of paranoia.

Where did you and Gregory find your stars, David Villalpando and Zaide Silvia Gutierrez?

It was a long search. Greg and I spent a long time here, in Mexico, even in Guatemala, through agencies, unions, theatre groups, recommendations. You do what you have to do. It's very difficult to find good actors who are young, who look like Indians, who are professionally trained and have the kind of capabilities to do a really complex, difficult role. I think we found the only two people in the world who could play the roles—we just had to look for them until we found them, which was ultimately in Mexico City. David we saw in a play, and Zaide we found through a union.

When did you start making movies?

Although I did student films while at UCLA, it really started when I began working with Greg on *THE CONFESSIONS OF AMANS.* It was the first thing I worked on that actually went before the public. As far as I'm concerned that's when it starts to count, and any filmmaker who says they're doing something only for themselves or only for their peer group of other filmmakers is lying, basically, whether they're doing it consciously or unconsciously.

And yet there are degrees of compromise that a filmmaker is willing to make for the public. You haven't seemed to compromise any personal vision in that effort to get your films before audiences.

I think that the amazing thing about *EL NORTE* is that we finally managed to make a film without compromising at all what we wanted to do and how we wanted to do it, and saw it become a commercial success. On *THE HAUNTING OF M,* which is the film that I directed, it was also a film that was not really compromised in any sense—I mean, I wasn't trying to make a film that would fit somebody's idea of what they wanted to sell and what they wanted to buy—but it was also not as completely successful commercially as I would have liked. It makes me very sad that it did not reach bigger audiences in this country, because I saw that it was able to when handled properly in a few markets where it was publicized with a little bit of money and effort. In San Francisco, for example, it was a hit. It didn't have enormous runs like *EL NORTE* has been having, but it was a good solid hit.

The film had a supernatural theme, didn't it?

Yes, it's a ghost story. Not a horror story, but a real ghost story. I love ghost stories, and I love the idea of the kinds of things you can communicate with that concept. The sense of the past and the force that the past exerts on us are very interesting to me.

I recall reading in the reviews that the period recreation, for such a low-budgeted film, was astonishing.

The look and the mood of *THE HAUNTING OF M* were, I think, very successful. And what goes into that? Sometimes things that are surprisingly simple. It's true that fashion and style are different for every period, but these things in movies tend to always be filtered through our own sense of what's stylish and nice and wonderful. So you look at a movie from the 1930's that was set in, say, the 1860's, and it looks like a 1930's movie set in the 1860's. They're always influenced by the style of the day. And what we tried to do on *THE HAUNTING OF M* was go back to the original period and take our cues, very often, from impressionist paintings of that period. Instead of trying to create something from a 1970's or 1980's sensibility looking back, it's really important to try to sink yourself into that period and take on the world view of somebody in that time. The lighting, the look, the composition, the way the film was set up, was very much taken from impressionist paintings. The costumes that we used were costumes that were used before, so they had the look of real clothing. The hair styles were done with a tremendous amount of care. The way people moved and spoke was attended to. Also, it was shot on real locations, not sets.

Where was it filmed?

In Scotland, in places that had been inhabited in those times and were restored to the way they were. All of these things give a feeling of much greater texture and much greater sense of period. And they're not necessarily things requiring a much higher budget. It's a very false concept that you cannot make a period film without a vast budget. Much more of the problem is coming to understand that period, knowing how to make it come alive and feel right without overloading it with things like pinafores and old bicycles which can make it look strained. You can overload too much period detail. You have to choose the right detail when you're getting things. You don't want to crowd your frame with a lot of bric-a-brac. Everything that you put in there may be authentic, but the way you put it in may be false to the situations that you're representing.

I heard *THE HAUNTING OF M* compared with Henry James and *The Turn of the Screw*, and I'm wondering if those are specious comparisons or if you were influenced by it.

Not *Turn of the Screw* necessarily, but Henry James in general, yes. I'm a great fan of Henry James. I like that very thoughtful, introspective, character-oriented type of literature. So in a sense I was influenced, although other things were probably even more direct influences. Like the works of Isak Dinesen, for example, which I think are wonderful.

Was Gregory involved with *THE HAUNTING OF M*?

Yes, he was the cinematographer. We work together differently every time. On *THE CONFESSIONS OF AMANS*, I worked with him on the script. He wrote the original story, and then I worked on the production—it's difficult to say in what capacity, because there were only three people on the crew! He was the director, and it was his movie, and I just helped in a lot of different ways. On *THE HAUNTING OF M*, I wrote and directed it, and he was the cinematographer and did a fantastic job. And then on *EL NORTE*, he directed and I produced, and we wrote the screenplay together.

I want to ask you about your commitment to independent filmmaking as a force of creative freedom. In the wake of *EL NORTE*'s success, I imagine that you've been besieged by offers from the studios.

Well, besieged is not a word I would use, but we've had a lot of interest.

How do you feel about a possible shift from independent to studio filmmaking?

We've been asked many times, even before *EL NORTE* and all this commercial success, whether either of us would think about going to the studios. I'll just say what I always said: it just depends on the project. There are some films that cannot be made through the studio system, like *EL NORTE*. Everybody we've talked to since then at the studios admit that wonderful as they think it is, happy as they are that it's a success, they never would have made *EL NORTE*. There are other films that can be made through the studio system and work out very successfully. In fact, there are projects that *should* be done through the studio system. If it's the type of story that can be done within the demands of that system, if it's the type of story that requires the kind of budget that only the studio system can provide, then fine. If I had to make a prediction right now, I would say that before I give it all up to write mystery novels in a villa by the Adriatic, I'll probably do some of both.

Toris Von Wolfe

A R T H U R   H I L L E R

One of Hollywood's most actively employed major filmmakers, Arthur Hiller has skillfully worked with an extraordinary range of genres. A listing of his films brings forth some truly impressive credits—his two collaborations with Paddy Chayefsky on *THE AMERICANIZATION OF EMILY* and *THE HOSPITAL*; the Neil Simon scripted *THE OUT-OF-TOWNERS* and *PLAZA SUITE*; the hugely successful *LOVE STORY*, for which he received an Academy Award nomination; and the very popular late 1970's comedies, *SILVER STREAK* and *THE IN-LAWS*.

Working in a solid tradition of craftsmanship and respect for what he calls the "blueprint" of the screenplay, Hiller's most recent effort is *TEACHERS*, for him a typical blend of comedy, drama and social concerns featuring strong performances and a deep commitment to the human condition.

MICHAEL SINGER: You've worked in a great range of genres, excluding horror or science fiction films. . . .

ARTHUR HILLER: No, that's my uncomfortable genre.

Well, you seem to be holding out very nicely on the human front. Whether comedies or dramas, the human element seems to be primary in your films. Is that what drew you to filmmaking in the first place?

Yes, no question, in the sense that I came to film from television and I came to television from radio. My work in radio was originally as a director of a public affairs program. When I first started, I was working on talk shows. Because of my interest in drama and my love of theatre, I started to do social dramas on radio dealing with civic or social issues. That came from my interest in people. I'm a great believer in the affirmation of the human spirit.

***TEACHERS* ends with such an affirmation.**

Yes, and that message has been in a few films that I've done. That you have to be in there fighting. It's not enough to see a problem. Once you realize what the problem is you have to try and do something about it. At the end of *HOSPITAL*, there's a phrase that says, "You've got to piss right smack into the wind." Also, in a sense, *MAN OF LA MANCHA* bears the same message.

***POPI*, as well . . . .**

Yes, the struggle of this man to raise his kids, as he said, "To be high in their shoes." It could easily have just been a film about the ghetto, but it wasn't. It was about coming *out* of the ghetto mentality, to think of themselves as being able to do more.

You've worked with some great writers, and you have been referred to as a writer's director. I don't know if that's the right phrase . . . .

The phrase I use is that I drop to my knees in front of the good writer. I feel that they get less credit than they deserve, in films at least. I'm terribly dependent on a good writer.

Would you be more comfortable being described as an interpreter rather than an auteur?

I really don't like either of those phrases.

Well, I do think of you as working in the time-honored tradition of a William Wyler or Lewis Milestone . . . .

I guess my favorites come from that tradition . . . David Lean and Fred Zinnemann. Sometimes people ask me if I have a style. And I think back and ask, what style does Lean have? Well, his style is *excellence*, that's all. He does each picture in the best way to bring that material to the screen. It just depends on what the material needs to best present it. For instance, in *TEACHERS*, there were more cuts than in any film I've ever done. It just lent itself to lots of cuts. A lot of other films, like *HOSPITAL*, could have had six pages in one shot. And yet, it's constantly in motion with a lot of movement and that semi-documentary feel.

Do you work closely with writers during production?

It doesn't happen very often. By the time you get to production, the writer feels that he or she has done the work and is spending a lot of time with minimal results. They're happy to let you go ahead and do it. My life would be easiest if the writers were on the set all the time, because a picture changes. All those creative juices come together, and out of it comes something new and different. It grows and shapes itself just by nature of the actors' contributions, or backgrounds. And those changes, if the writer is there, can be helped in the right directions. And even if there aren't any changes, at least the writer is aware why *you* have made certain changes and what prompted them.

You went from radio to television to features. What are the best avenues to directing these days, in your opinion?

I think the film schools are good. By the same token, if young film students come in to see me for advice, I ask if they've ever made a film. If they say no, I forget about them. Because if they really want to be a director, then somehow they've gotten ahold of an 8mm camera and shot 10 minutes somewhere. That's a good way to learn. I remember judging a student film festival one year. I saw a film by a nine-year-old that showed inventiveness and thought about what he was doing. Now it's true also that that particular student had a teacher who was interested in film and excited the kids. But I feel if they show that kind of interest, that kind of desire, than that's the way to learn. You learn in film school, you learn by observing on a set. Also, you have to be lucky. You really do. I'm not saying that you don't have to be good. But if you're in the right place at the right time, you're going to get the chance that twenty other people who are equally talented don't get.

I have a two part question for you. A, what were you thinking about when *you* were nine-years-old, and B, what was your lucky break?

Well, I can't remember what I was thinking about when I was nine. I was loving theatre already. My parents had started a little theatre group in Edmonton, Canada, where we lived. And when I was eight or nine years old, I was helping to paint the sets or do whatever a child that age could do. I think my interest deep down was always the theatre, but when I finished high school, through a series of circumstances . . . there was a professor from the University of Ohio who was up at the University of Alberta, where I was a student, who was teaching teachers how to teach drama. And he taught them by putting them in a play. They had to play all the parts, build the sets, do the costumes, find the props. He was short a couple of actors, so he went to the high school drama teacher and he asked who the best actors were. I ended up playing Donald, the Black servant, in *YOU CAN'T TAKE IT WITH YOU.* And from that, I was offered a drama scholarship at the University of Ohio! Well, at that time I just said no, because acting was what you did on weekends . . . it was not what you did as a life's work. Then off I went to World War II, came back and studied psychology at the university. One day, as I studied, I realized that what I was really interested in was communication. So I walked into the headquarters of the Canadian Broadcasting Corporation, up to the information desk and said, "Who do I see about a job?" They asked what kind of a job, so I said, "Well, I want to be a director." The receptionist told me to call Mr. Doyle, who was the manager of the network. I said fine, went home, phoned Mr. Doyle. His secretary said the name was Boyle, not Doyle, and what did I want to see him about? I told her, and she said, "Well, you can't see him. But you can see his associate, Mr. Palmer." So I went to see Palmer and told him that I wanted to be a director, mentioning that I was completing a Master's Degree and needed residence, and preferred to work there. He took me to meet the supervisor of public affairs, and we had what I thought was a very pleasant hour-and-a-half conversation. Well, later I realized that he was pumping me. How do I feel about this particular issue, how do I feel about this social problem, what do I read, etc. And he suggested that I apply for a job that he had available. I joined 64 other people, and three weeks later I was working. He was looking for somebody with a social science background and some experience in radio. I had worked during the summertime as an announcer in a small station where I lived. So the luck part was there. When I walked up to that desk, suppose the receptionist had said to me, "Why don't you go to the personnel office?" I could still be sitting there waiting my turn! Fortunately, she told me to call Mr. Doyle. The series of events just go together.

That social thread has wound itself down throughout your career.

I wish it had stayed there a little more. I've let it slip away a little. If I had my preference, I would be doing that all the time. But I like making movies and you can't always incorporate that.

Your strongest films have had those very powerful social concerns, though. *THE AMERICANIZATION OF EMILY*, for example.

My favorite. But you see, again, you're talking about the writer. Paddy Chayefsky. As I've often said, the only genius I've worked with. It's phenomenal. You couldn't go wrong with Paddy's material. I might have had some disagreements with Paddy. We had an argument on *HOSPITAL* where he was so angry with me he went into his office and didn't come out for four hours. Two days later he walked by when I was on the set, said, "You were right," and just kept walking. Basically, when he spoke I listened. When a genius speaks you pay attention. But I'm a big boy. When I disagreed, I disagreed. When you direct you have to go with your feelings. That doesn't mean you shouldn't take advice, it doesn't mean you shouldn't listen, but your feelings have to come through. If not, it won't be your film.

You've been involved with a couple of fairly well publicized shoots where you've had serious clashes with other important personnel. How do you get through it?

I don't know. Sometimes you wonder how you get through. If you have a feeling of responsibility, a respect for your fellow creative artists and the other people who are working . . . if you take on a project, you should give what you're supposed to give to that project. You can't give up. And that's what keeps you going.

How personally do you take criticism of your films?

It hurts. I've often said that when you start a picture, you're all gung ho and ready to gamble and take big chances because you believe in it. The closer it gets to the release of that picture, the more you want it to succeed, the more you care, and if the milkman says he didn't like a scene, you go into panic. You just want everybody to love it.

If the milkman does tell you he didn't like a scene, or worse than that, several critics and a couple of studio executives tell you they don't like your picture, how do you get the strength and courage to get back at it again?

It's hard. It does affect you and it does hurt. When I did *MAN OF LA MANCHA*, I had very high hopes. We felt very strongly that we had done something special and wonderful. It was adequately received and did good business, but not what I thought was going to happen. That threw me into a depression for about eight months, and I didn't work because I thought it was my fault. Here I had a play that was famous around the world, a terrific cast, United Artists was very supportive—so I could only blame myself. It took about eight months for me to figure out that *MAN OF LA MANCHA* was a play that shouldn't have been adapted for film. When you're in a darkened theatre with a surrealist set, and Don Quixote says, "That's not a kitchen scullery maid, that's a princess," you make the change in your head. But when Sophia Loren is standing there twenty feet tall on a 70mm screen, it's too real. You put too much pressure on the actor to make you believe what's going on.

Some of your most successful films have been comedies—*THE OUT-OF-TOWNERS, SILVER STREAK, THE IN-LAWS*—is it harder directing comedy?

I guess it must be in the sense there are obviously fewer good comedy directors than any other genre, and yet I don't feel that. If you get food actors with a comedy sense, your life is very easy. In other words, you're not playing for the laugh. You're playing an honest character in an honest situation, and because they have that good comedy sense, it just brings it to the humor quite naturally.

You seem to never stop working. Do you live for movies?

Yes. I love making movies.

Do you feel somewhat incomplete if you're not directing?

I do. My favorite time is the shooting time. I've been trying desperately not to work for a couple of months, but it's *very* hard.

DIRECTORS

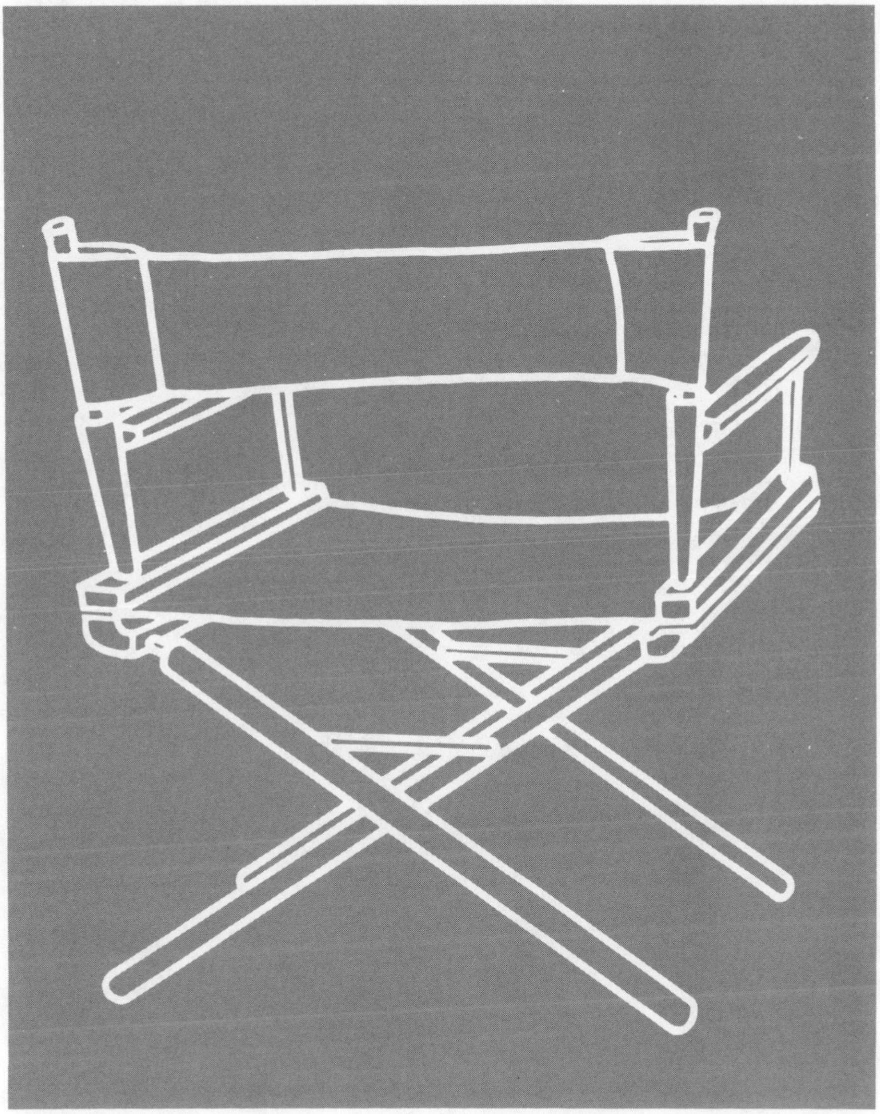

LISTINGS

Shooting on Location Can Be Tough
When You're Not Familiar with the Turf
New York State
Makes You Feel Like One of the Gang
Dept. of Commerce, Office of Motion Picture/TV Development
230 Park Ave., N.Y., NY 10169, Rm. 864 (212) 309-0540

KEY TO ABBREVIATIONS

(TF)	=	TELEFEATURE Motion pictures made for television with an on-air running time of 1½ hours to 4½ hours on commercial television; or 1 hour to 4 hours on non-commercial television.
(CTF)	=	CABLE TELEFEATURE Motion pictures made for cable television with an on-air running time of 1 hour to 4 hours.
(MS)	=	MINISERIES Motion pictures made for television with an on-air running time of 4½ hours and more on commercial television; or 4 hours or more on non-commercial television.
(CMS)	=	CABLE MINISERIES Motion pictures made for cable television with an on-air running time of 4 hours or more.
(FD)	=	FEATURE DOCUMENTARY Documentary films made for theatrical distribution of feature length (1 or more hours).
(TD)	=	TELEVISION DOCUMENTARY Documentary films made for television of feature length (1½ hours or more on commercial television, 1 hour or more on non-commercial television).
(CTD)	=	CABLE TELEVISION DOCUMENTARY Documentary films made for cable television of feature length (1 or more hours).
(AF)	=	ANIMATED FEATURE
(ATF)	=	ANIMATED TELEFEATURE

KEY TO SYMBOLS

*	after a director's name denotes membership in the Directors Guild of America.
★	after a film title denotes a directorial Academy Award nomination.
★★	after a film title denotes directorial Academy Award win.
☆	after a film title denotes directorial Emmy Award nomination.
☆☆	after a film title denotes directorial Emmy Award win.

A

PAUL AARON*

Agent: John Gaines, APA - Los Angeles, 273-0744

A DIFFERENT STORY   Avco Embassy, 1978
A FORCE OF ONE   American Cinema, 1979
THE MIRACLE WORKER (TF)   Katz-Gallin Productions/Half-Pint Productions, 1979
THIN ICE (TF)   CBS Entertainment, 1981
MAID IN AMERICA (TF)   CBS Entertainment, 1982
DEADLY FORCE   Embassy, 1983
WHEN SHE SAYS NO (TF)   I&C Productions/Jozak-Decade Enterprises, 1984
FREE SPIRIT   Orion, 1985

GEORGE ABBOTT

b. June 25, 1887 - Forestville, New York
Business: 1270 Avenue of the Americas, New York, NY

WHY BRING THAT UP?   1929
HALF-WAY TO HEAVEN   1929
MANSLAUGHTER   1930
THE SEA GOD   1930
STOLEN HEAVEN   Paramount, 1931
SECRETS OF A SECRETARY   Paramount, 1931
MY SIN   1931
THE CHEAT   1931
TOO MANY GIRLS   RKO Radio, 1940
THE PAJAMA GAME   co-director with Stanley Donen, Warner Bros., 1957
DAMN YANKEES   co-director with Stanley Donen, Warner Bros., 1958

ROBERT J. ABEL*

b. March 10, 1937 - Cleveland, Ohio
Business: Robert Abel & Associates, 953 Highland Avenue, Hollywood, CA 90038, 213/462-8100
Attorney: Sam Halpern, Bartman, Brown & Halpern, 1880 Century Park East - Suite 1015, Los Angeles, CA 90067, 213/552-1093

ELVIS ON TOUR (FD)   co-director with Pierre Adidge, MGM, 1972
LET THE GOOD TIMES ROLL (FD)   co-director with Sidney Levin, Columbia, 1973

JIM ABRAHAMS*

Business Manager: Abrahams Boy, Inc., 11777 San Vicente Blvd - Suite 600, Los Angeles, CA 90049, 213/820-1942

AIRPLANE!   co-director with David Zucker & Jerry Zucker, Paramount, 1980
TOP SECRET!   co-director with David Zucker & Jerry Zucker, Paramount, 1984

E D W A R D   A B R O M S *

Home: 1866 Marlowe Street, Thousand Oaks, CA 91360
Agent: Skip Nicholson, Skip Nicholson Agency, Inc. - Sherman Oaks, 818/906-2700

THE IMPOSTER (TF) Warner Bros. TV, 1975

D A V I D   A C O M B A

Agent: Jack Rapke, CAA - Los Angeles, 213/277-4545

SLIPSTREAM 1973, Canadian
HANK WILLIAMS: THE SHOW HE NEVER GAVE Simcon/Film Consortium of Canada, 1982, Canadian

A L   A D A M S O N

Business: Independent-International Pictures, 223 State Highway 18, East Brunswick, NJ, 201/249-8982

TWO TICKETS TO TERROR Victor Adamson, 1964
GUN RIDERS 1969
BLOOD OF DRACULA'S CASTLE Crown International, 1969
SATAN'S SADISTS Independent-International, 1970
HELL'S BLOODY DEVILS *THE FAKERS* Independent-International, 1970
FIVE BLOODY GRAVES Independent-International, 1971
HORROR OF THE BLOOD MONSTERS Independent-International, 1971
THE FEMALE BUNCH Dalia, 1971
LAST OF THE COMANCHEROS Independent-International, 1971
BLOOD OF GHASTLY HORROR Independent-International, 1972
THE BRAIN OF BLOOD Hemisphere, 1972
DOOMSDAY VOYAGE Futurama International, 1972
DRACULA VS. FRANKENSTEIN Independent-International, 1973
THE DYNAMITE BROTHERS Cinemation, 1974
GIRLS FOR RENT Independent-International, 1974
THE NAUGHTY STEWARDESSES Independent-International, 1975
STUD BROWN Cinemation, 1975
BLAZING STEWARDESSES Independent-International, 1975
JESSIE'S GIRLS Manson International, 1976
BLACK HEAT Independent-International, 1976
CINDERELLA 2000 Independent-International, 1977
BLACK SAMURAI BLLJ International, 1977
SUNSET COVE Cal-Am Artists, 1978
DEATH DIMENSION Movietime, 1978
NURSE SHERRI Independent-International, 1978
FREEZE BOMB Movietime, 1980
BLACK HEAT Independent-International, 1981
CARNIVAL MAGIC Krypton Corporation, 1982

P I E R R E   A D I D G E

JOE COCKER/MAD DOGS & ENGLISHMEN (FD) MGM, 1971
ELVIS ON TOUR (FD) co-director with Robert J. Abel, MGM, 1972

L O U   A D L E R *

Contact: Directors Guild of America - Los Angeles, 213/656-1220

UP IN SMOKE Paramount, 1978
LADIES AND GENTLEMEN...THE FABULOUS STAINS Paramount, 1982

C H A R L I E   A H E A R N

WILD STYLE First Run Features, 1983

MOUSTAPHA AKKAD

b. Syria
Office: Twickenham Studios, St. Margarets, Middlesex, England

MOHAMMAD, MESSENGER OF GOD *THE MESSAGE* Tarik, 1977, Lebanese-British
LION OF THE DESERT United Film Distribution, 1981, Libyan-British

ALAN ALDA*

b. January 28, 1936 - New York, New York
Agent: Martin Bauer Agency - Beverly Hills, 213/275-2421

THE FOUR SEASONS Universal, 1981

ADELL ALDRICH*

b. June 11, 1943 - Los Angeles, California
Business: The Aldrich Company, 606 N. Larchmont Blvd., Los Angeles, CA 90004, 213/462-6511
Agent: Dick Berman, TMI - Los Angeles, 213/273-4000

DADDY, I DON'T LIKE IT LIKE THIS (TF) CBS Entertainment, 1978
THE KID FROM LEFT FIELD (TF) Gary Coleman Productions/Deena Silver-Kramer's Movie Company, 1979

TOMAS GUTIERREZ ALEA

(See Tomas GUTIERREZ ALEA)

COREY ALLEN*

b. June 29, 1934 - Cleveland, Ohio
Agent: Ron Leif, Contemporary-Korman Artists - Beverly Hills, 213/278-8250

PINOCCHIO EUE, 1971
SEE THE MAN RUN (TF) Universal TV, 1971
CRY RAPE! (TF) Leonard Freeman Productions, 1973
YESTERDAY'S CHILD (TF) co-director with Bob Rosenbaum, Paramount TV, 1977
THUNDER AND LIGHTNING 20th Century-Fox, 1978
AVALANCHE New World, 1979
STONE (TF) Stephen J. Cannell Productions/Universal TV, 1979
THE MAN IN THE SANTA CLAUS SUIT (TF) Dick Clark Productions, 1979
THE RETURN OF FRANK CANNON (TF) QM Productions, 1980
MURDER, SHE WROTE: THE MURDER OF SHERLOCK HOLMES (TF) Universal TV, 1984

IRWIN ALLEN*

b. June 12, 1916 - New York, New York
Agent: Stan Kamen/Jerry Katzman, William Morris Agency - Beverly Hills, 213/274-7451

THE SEA AROUND US (FD) RKO Radio, 1951
THE ANIMAL WORLD (FD) Warner Bros., 1956
THE STORY OF MANKIND Warner Bros., 1957
THE LOST WORLD 20th Century-Fox, 1960
VOYAGE TO THE BOTTOM OF THE SEA 20th Century-Fox, 1961
FIVE WEEKS IN A BALLOON 20th Century-Fox, 1962
CITY BENEATH THE SEA (TF) 20th Century-Fox TV/Motion Pictures International, 1971
THE TOWERING INFERNO action sequences only, 20th Century-Fox, 1974
THE SWARM Warner Bros., 1978
BEYOND THE POSEIDON ADVENTURE Warner Bros., 1979

WOODY ALLEN*

(Allen Stewart Konigsberg)

b. December 1, 1935 - Brooklyn, New York
Personal Manager: Jack Rollins/Charles Joffe, 130 West 57th Street, New York, NY, 212/582-1940

WHAT'S UP, TIGER LILY? American International, 1966
TAKE THE MONEY AND RUN Cinerama Releasing Corporation, 1969
BANANAS United Artists, 1971
EVERYTHING YOU ALWAYS WANTED TO KNOW ABOUT SEX* (*BUT WERE AFRAID TO ASK) United Artists, 1972
SLEEPER United Artists, 1973
LOVE AND DEATH United Artists, 1975
ANNIE HALL ★★ United Artists, 1977
INTERIORS ★ United Artists, 1978
MANHATTAN United Artists, 1979
STARDUST MEMORIES United Artists, 1980
A MIDSUMMER NIGHT'S SEX COMEDY Orion/Warner Bros., 1982
ZELIG Orion/Warner Bros., 1983
BROADWAY DANNY ROSE Orion, 1983
THE PURPLE ROSE OF CAIRO Orion, 1985
HANNAH AND HER SISTERS Orion, 1985

NESTOR ALMENDROS

b. 1930 - Barcelona, Spain

IMPROPER CONDUCT (FD) co-director with Orlando Jimenez - Leal, Cinevista/Promovision International, 1984, French

PAUL ALMOND*

b. April 26, 1931 - Montreal, Quebec, Canada
Business: Quest Film Productions, Ltd., 1272 Redpath Drive, Montreal, Quebec H3G 2K1, Canada, 514/849-7921

BACKFIRE Anglo Amalgamated, 1962, British
THE DARK DID NOT CONQUER (TF) CBC, 1963, Canadian
JOURNEY TO THE CENTRE (TF) CBC, 1963, Canadian
ISABEL Paramount, 1968, Canadian
ACT OF THE HEART Universal, 1970, Canadian
JOURNEY EPOH, 1972, Canadian
EVERY PERSON IS CRAZY (TF) CBC, 1979, Canadian
FINAL ASSIGNMENT Almi Cinema 5, 1980, Canadian
UPS AND DOWNS JAD International 1983, Canadian

JOHN A. ALONZO*

b. 1934 - Dallas, Texas
Agent: Skip Nicholson, Skip Nicholson Agency, Inc. - Sherman Oaks, 818/906-2700
Business: John A. Alonzo Productions, 12301 Wilshire Blvd., Suite 203, Los Angeles, CA 90025, 213/820-8872

FM Universal, 1978
CHAMPIONS...A LOVE STORY (TF) Warner Bros. TV, 1979
PORTRAIT OF A STRIPPER (TF) Moonlight Productions/Filmways, 1979
BELLE STARR (TF) Entheos Unlimited Productions/Hanna-Barbera Productions, 1980
BLINDED BY THE LIGHT (TF) Time-Life Films, 1980

EMMETT ALSTON

NEW YEAR'S EVIL Cannon, 1981
DEADLY WARRIORS Amritraj Productions, 1985

ROBERT ALTMAN*

b. February 20, 1925 - Kansas City, Missouri
Business: Sandcastle 5 Productions, 128 Central Park South - Suite 4B, New York, NY 10019, 212/582-2970
Attorney: Eric Weissman, 9601 Wilshire Blvd., Los Angeles, CA, 213/858-7888
Business Manager: James W. Quinn, 11755 Addison Street, North Hollywood, CA 91607, 213/509-0259

THE DELINQUENTS United Artists, 1957
THE JAMES DEAN STORY (FD) co-director with George W. George; Warner Bros., 1957
NIGHTMARE IN CHICAGO (TF) MCA-TV, 1964
COUNTDOWN Warner Bros., 1968
THAT COLD DAY IN THE PARK Commonwealth United, 1969, Canadian-U.S.
M*A*S*H ★ 20th Century-Fox, 1970
BREWSTER McCLOUD MGM, 1970
McCABE & MRS. MILLER Warner Bros., 1971
IMAGES Columbia, 1972, Irish
THE LONG GOODBYE United Artists, 1973
THIEVES LIKE US United Artists, 1974
CALIFORNIA SPLIT Columbia, 1974
NASHVILLE ★ Paramount, 1976
BUFFALO BILL AND THE INDIANS or SITTING BULL'S HISTORY LESSON United Artists, 1976
3 WOMEN 20th Century-Fox, 1977
A WEDDING 20th Century-Fox, 1978
A PERFECT COUPLE 20th Century-Fox, 1979
QUINTET 20th Century-Fox, 1979
HEALTH 20th Century-Fox, 1980
POPEYE Paramount, 1980
COME BACK TO THE 5 & DIME JIMMY DEAN, JIMMY DEAN Cinecom International, 1982
STREAMERS United Artists Classics, 1983
SECRET HONOR Sandcastle 5, 1984
O.C. AND STIGGS MGM/UA, 1985

JOE ALVES*

b. May 21, 1938 - San Leandro, California
Home: 4176 Rosario Road, Woodland Hills, CA 91364, 818/346-4624
Agent: Peter Rawley, ICM - Los Angeles, 213/550-4000

JAWS 3-D Universal, 1983

ROD AMATEAU*

b. December 20, 1923 - New York, New York
Home: 133½ S. Linden Drive, Beverly Hills, CA 90212, 213/274-3865
Agent: Martin Baum, CAA - Los Angeles, 213/277-4545

THE BUSHWHACKERS Realart, 1951
MONSOON United Artists, 1952
PUSSYCAT, PUSSYCAT, I LOVE YOU United Artists, 1970, British
THE STATUE Cinerama Releasing Corporation, 1971, British
WHERE DOES IT HURT? American Internationl, 1972, British
DRIVE IN Columbia, 1976
THE SENIORS Cinema Shares International, 1978
HITLER'S SON 1978, British
UNCOMMON VALOR (TF) Brademan-Self Productions/Sunn Classic, 1983
HIGH SCHOOL U.S.A. (TF) Hill-Mandelker Films, 1983
LOVELINES Tri-Star, 1984

LINDSAY ANDERSON

b. April 17, 1923 - Bangalore, India
Address: 9 Stirling Mansions, Canfield Gardens, London W1, England

THIS SPORTING LIFE Continental, 1962, British
IF... Paramount, 1969, British
O LUCKY MAN! Warner Bros., 1973, British

LINDSAY ANDERSON —continued

IN CELEBRATION American Film Theatre, 1975, British-Canadian
BRITTANIA HOSPITAL United Artists Classics, 1982, British

MICHAEL ANDERSON*

b. January 30, 1920 - London, England
Address: 1 Park Lane - Suite 609, 211 St. Patrick, Toronto, Canada, 416/977-8530
Agent: ICM - Los Angeles, 213/550-4000

PRIVATE ANGELO co-director with Peter Ustinov, Associated British Picture Corporation, 1949, British
WATERFRONT WOMEN *WATERFRONT* Rank, 1950, British
HELL IS SOLD OUT Eros, 1951, British
NIGHT WAS OUR FRIEND Monarch, 1951, British
WILL ANY GENTLEMAN? Associated British Picture Corporation, 1953, British
THE HOUSE OF THE ARROW Associated British Picture Corporation, 1953, British
THE DAM BUSTERS Warner Bros., 1955, British
1984 Columbia, 1956, British
AROUND THE WORLD IN 80 DAYS ★ United Artists, 1956
BATTLE HELL *YANGTSE INCIDENT* DCA, 1957, British
CHASE A CROOKED SHADOW Warner Bros., 1958, British
SHAKE HANDS WITH THE DEVIL United Artists, 1959, British
THE WRECK OF THE MARY DEARE MGM, 1959
ALL THE FINE YOUNG CANNIBALS MGM, 1960
THE NAKED EDGE United Artists, 1961
FLIGHT FROM ASHIYA United Artists, 1964
WILD AND WONDERFUL Universal, 1964
OPERATION CROSSBOW MGM, 1965, British-Italian
THE QUILLER MEMORANDUM Paramount, 1966, British
THE SHOES OF THE FISHERMAN MGM, 1968
POPE JOAN Columbia, 1972, British
DOC SAVAGE, THE MAN OF BRONZE Warner Bros., 1975
CONDUCT UNBECOMING Allied Artists, 1975, British
LOGAN'S RUN MGM/United Artists, 1975
ORCA Paramount, 1976
DOMINIQUE Sword and Sworcery Productions, 1979, British
THE MARTIAN CHRONICLES (TF) Charles Fries Productions/Stonehenge Productions, 1980
MURDER BY PHONE New World, 1983, Canadian
SECOND TIME LUCKY United International Pictures, 1984, New Zealand-Australian

KEN ANNAKIN*

b. August 10, 1914 - Beverley, England
Agent: The Cooper Agency - Los Angeles, 213/277-8422

HOLIDAY CAMP Universal, 1947, British
MIRANDA Eagle-Lion, 1948, British
BROKEN JOURNEY Eagle-Lion, 1948, British
HERE COME THE HUGGETTS General Film Distributors, 1948, British
QUARTET co-director with Ralph Smart, Harold French & Arthur Crabtree, Eagle-Lion, 1948, British
VOTE FOR HUGGETT General Film Distributors, 1949, British
THE HUGGETTS ABROAD General Film Distributors, 1949, British
LANDFALL Associated British Picture Corporation, 1949, British
TRIO co-director with Harold French, Paramount, 1950, British
HOTEL SAHARA United Artists, 1951, British
THE STORY OF ROBIN HOOD co-director with Alex Bryce, RKO Radio, 1952, U.S.-British
OUTPOST IN MALAYA *THE PLANTER'S WIFE* United Artists, 1952, British
THE SWORD AND THE ROSE RKO Radio, 1953, U.S.-British
DOUBLE CONFESSION Stratford, 1953, British
YOU KNOW WHAT SAILORS ARE United Artists, 1954, British
LAND OF FURY *THE SEEKERS* Universal, 1955, British
LOSER TAKES ALL British Lion, 1956, British
VALUE FOR MONEY Rank, 1957, British
THREE MEN IN A BOAT DCA, 1958, British
ACROSS THE BRIDGE Rank, 1958, British

KEN ANNAKIN*—continued

THIRD MAN ON THE MOUNTAIN Buena Vista, 1959, U.S.-British
ELEPHANT GUN *NOR THE MOON BY NIGHT* Lopert, 1959, British
SWISS FAMILY ROBINSON Buena Vista, 1960
THE HELLIONS Columbia, 1962, British
A COMING-OUT PARTY *VERY IMPORTANT PERSON* Union, 1962, British
THE FAST LADY Rank, 1962, British
CROOKS ANONYMOUS Allied Artists, 1962, British
THE LONGEST DAY co-director with Andrew Marton & Bernhard Wicki, 20th Century-Fox, 1962
THOSE MAGNIFICENT MEN IN THEIR FLYING MACHINES 20th Century-Fox, 1965, British
BATTLE OF THE BULGE Warner Bros., 1965
UNDERWORLD INFORMERS *THE INFORMERS* Continental, 1966, British
THE LONG DUEL Paramount, 1967, British
THE BIGGEST BUNDLE OF THEM ALL MGM, 1968, U.S.-Italian
THOSE DARING YOUNG MEN IN THEIR JAUNTY JALOPIES Paramount, 1969, British-Italian-French
CALL OF THE WILD Constantin, 1975, West German-Spanish
PAPER TIGER Joseph E. Levine Presents, 1976, British
MURDER AT THE MARDI GRAS (TF) The Jozak Company/Paramount TV, 1978
HAROLD ROBBINS' THE PIRATE (TF) Howard W. Koch Productions/Warner Bros. TV, 1978
THE 5TH MUSKETEER Columbia, 1979, Austrian
INSTITUTE FOR REVENGE (TF) Gold-Driskill Productions/Columbia TV, 1979
CHEAPER TO KEEP HER American Cinema, 1980
THE PIRATE MOVIE 20th Century-Fox, 1982, Australian

JEAN-JACQUES ANNAUD

b. October 1, 1943 - Jurisy, France
Agent: Jeff Berg, ICM - Los Angeles, 213/550-1440

BLACK AND WHITE IN COLOR *LA VICTOIRE EN CHANTANT* Allied Artists, 1978, French-Ivory Coast-Swiss
COUP DE TETE *HOTHEAD* Quartet, 1980, French
QUEST FOR FIRE 20th Century-Fox, 1982, Canadian-French

JOSEPH ANTHONY

b. May 24, 1912 - Milwaukee, Wisconsin

THE RAINMAKER Paramount, 1956
THE MATCHMAKER Paramount, 1958
CAREER Paramount, 1959
ALL IN A NIGHT'S WORK Paramount, 1961
CONQUERED CITY American International, 1966, Italian
TOMORROW Filmgroup, 1972

LOU ANTONIO*

b. January 23, 1934 - Oklahoma City, Oklahoma
Agent: Triad Artists, Inc. - Los Angeles, 213/556-2727

SOMEONE I TOUCHED (TF) Charles Fries Productions, 1975
LANIGAN'S RABBI (TF) Universal TV, 1976
RICH MAN, POOR MAN - BOOK II (TF) Universal TV, 1976
THE GIRL IN THE EMPTY GRAVE (TF) NBC-TV, 1977
SOMETHING FOR JOEY (TF) ☆ MTM Productions, 1977
THE CRITICAL LIST (TF) MTM Productions, 1978
A REAL AMERICAN HERO (TF) Bing Crosby Productions, 1978
BREAKING UP IS HARD TO DO (TF) Green-Epstein Productions/Columbia TV, 1979
SILENT VICTORY: THE KITTY O'NEILL STORY (TF) ☆ Channing-Debin-Locke Company, 1979
THE CONTENDER (TF) co-director with Harry Falk, Universal TV, 1980
WE'RE FIGHTING BACK (TF) Highgate Pictures, 1981
THE STAR MAKER (TF) Channing-Debin-Locke Company/Carson Productions, 1981

LOU ANTONIO*—continued

SOMETHING SO RIGHT (TF) List-Estrin Productions/Tisch-Avnet Television, 1982
BETWEEN FRIENDS (CTF) HBO Premiere Films/Marian Rees Associates/Robert Cooper Films III/List-Estrin Productions, 1983, U.S.-Canadian
A GOOD SPORT (TF) Ralph Waite Productions/Warner Bros. TV, 1984
THREESOME (TF) CBS Entertainment, 1984
REARVIEW MIRROR (TF) Simon-Asher Entertainment/Sunn Classic Pictures, 1984

MICHELANGELO ANTONIONI

b. September 29, 1912 - Ferrara, Italy
Contact: Ministry of Tourism & Education, Via Della Ferratella, No. 51, 00184 Rome, Italy, 06/7732

STORY OF A LOVE AFFAIR New Yorker, 1950, Italian
I VINTI Film Costellazione, 1953, Italian
LA SIGNORA SENZA CAMELIE 1953, Italian
LOVE IN THE CITY co-director with Federico Fellini, Alberto Lattuada, Carlo Lizzani, Francesco Maselli & Dino Risi, Italian Films Export, 1953, Italian
LE AMICHE Trion Falcine/Titanus, 1955, Italian
IL GRIDO Astor, 1957, Italian
L'AVVENTURA Janus, 1961, Italian
LA NOTTE Lopert, 1961, Italian-French
L'ECLISSE Times, 1962, Italian-French
RED DESERT Rizzoli, 1965, Italian-French
I TRE VOLTI co-director, 1965, Italian
BLOW-UP ★ Premier, 1966, British-Italian
ZABRISKIE POINT MGM, 1970
CHUNG KUO (FD) Golan Productions 1972, Italian
THE PASSENGER *PROFESSIONE: REPORTER* MGM/United Artists, 1975, Italian-French-Spanish-U.S.
IL MISTERO DI OVERWALD Sacis, 1981, Italian
IDENTIFICATION OF A WOMAN Iter Film/Gaumont, 1982, Italian-French

MICHAEL APTED*

b. February 10, 1941 - Aylesbury, England
Agent: Michael Marcus, CAA - Los Angeles, 213/277-4545
Messages: 213/850-2631
Business Manager: Gary G. Cohen, 3520 Ocean Park Blvd. - Suite 100, Santa Monica, CA, 213/452-0123

THE TRIPLE ECHO Altura, 1973, British
STARDUST Columbia, 1975, British
STRONGER THAN THE SUN (TF) BBC, 1977, British
THE SQUEEZE Warner Bros., 1977, British
AGATHA Warner Bros., 1979, British
COAL MINER'S DAUGHTER Universal, 1980
CONTINENTAL DIVIDE Universal, 1981
KIPPERBANG *P'TANG, YANG, KIPPERBANG* MGM/UA Classics, 1983
GORKY PARK Orion, 1983
FIRSTBORN Paramount, 1984

DARIO ARGENTO

b. 1943 - Italy
Contact: Ministry of Tourism & Education, Via Della Ferratella, No. 51, 00184 Rome, Italy, 06/7732

THE BIRD WITH THE CRYSTAL PLUMAGE UMC, 1970, Italian-West German
CAT O'NINE TAILS National General, 1971, Italian-West German-French
FOUR FLIES ON GREY VELVET Paramount, 1972, Italian-French
LE CINQUE GIORNATE Seda Spettacoli, 1973, Italian
DEEP RED Howard Mahler Films, 1976, Italian
SUSPIRIA International Classics, 1977, Italian
INFERNO 20th Century-Fox, 1981, Italian
UNSANE *TENEBRAE* Bedford Entertainment/Film Gallery, 1982, Italian
PHENOMENA Titanus, 1985, Italian

ALAN ARKIN*

b. March 26, 1934 - New York, New York
Agent: ICM - Los Angeles, 213/550-4000
Business Manager: Saul B. Schneider - New York City, 212/489-0990

LITTLE MURDERS 20th Century-Fox, 1970
FIRE SALE 20th Century-Fox, 1977

ALLAN ARKUSH*

Home: 14134 Chandler Blvd., Van Nuys, CA 91401, 818/784-4830
Agent: Martin Caan, William Morris Agency - Beverly Hills, 213/274-7451

HOLLYWOOD BOULEVARD co-director with Joe Dante, New World, 1976
DEATHSPORT co-director with Henry Suso, New World, 1978
ROCK 'N' ROLL HIGH SCHOOL New World, 1979
HEARTBEEPS Universal, 1981
GET CRAZY Embassy, 1983

GEORGE ARMITAGE*

Agent: Mickey Freiberg, The Artists Agency - Los Angeles, 213/277-7779

PRIVATE DUTY NURSES New World, 1972
HIT MAN MGM, 1973
VIGILANTE FORCE United Artists, 1976
HOT ROD (TF) ABC Circle Films, 1979

GILLIAN ARMSTRONG

Address: c/o M&L Casting Consultants, 49 Darlinghurst Road, Kings Cross, NSW, 2011, Australia, 02/358-3111

THE SINGER AND THE DANCER Gillian Armstrong Productions, 1976, Australian
MY BRILLIANT CAREER Analysis, 1980, Australian
STARSTRUCK Cinecom International, 1982, Australian
MRS. SOFFEL MGM/UA, 1984

GWEN ARNER*

Home: 223 33rd Street, Hermosa Beach, CA 90254, 213/376-3875
Agent: Arnold Rifkin, Triad Artists, Inc. - Los Angeles, 213/556-2727

MY CHAMPION Shochiku, 1981, Japanese-U.S.
MOTHER'S DAY ON WALTON'S MOUNTAIN (TF) Lorimar Productions/ Amanda Productions, 1982

JACK ARNOLD*

b. October 14, 1916 - New Haven, Connecticut
Home: 4860 Nomad Drive, Woodland Hills, CA 91364, 818/703-8324
Agent: Abby Greshler, Diamond Artists Ltd. - Los Angeles, 213/278-8146

GIRLS IN THE NIGHT Universal, 1953
IT CAME FROM OUTER SPACE Universal, 1953
THE GLASS WEB Universal, 1953
THE CREATURE FROM THE BLACK LAGOON Universal, 1954
REVENGE OF THE CREATURE Universal, 1955
THE MAN FROM BITTER RIDGE Universal, 1955
TARANTULA Universal, 1955
OUTSIDE THE LAW Universal, 1956
RED SUNDOWN Universal, 1956
THE INCREDIBLE SHRINKING MAN Universal, 1957
THE TATTERED DRESS Universal, 1957
MAN IN THE SHADOW Universal, 1958
THE LADY TAKES A FLYER Universal, 1958
THE SPACE CHILDREN Paramount, 1958
MONSTER ON THE CAMPUS Universal, 1958
THE MOUSE THAT ROARED Columbia, 1959, British

JACK ARNOLD*—continued

NO NAME ON THE BULLET Universal, 1959
BACHELOR IN PARADISE MGM, 1961
THE LIVELY SET Universal, 1964
A GLOBAL AFFAIR MGM, 1964
HELLO DOWN THERE Paramount, 1969
BLACK EYE Warner Bros., 1974
THE GAMES GIRLS PLAY General Films, 1975
BOSS NIGGER Dimension, 1975
THE SWISS CONSPIRACY SJ International, 1977
SEX AND THE MARRIED WOMAN (TF) Universal TV, 1977
MARILYN: THE UNTOLD STORY (TF) co-director with John Flynn & Lawrence Schiller, Lawrence Schiller Productions, 1980

KAREN ARTHUR*

Agent: Peter Rawley, ICM - Los Angeles, 213/550-4165

LEGACY Kino International, 1976
THE MAFU CAGE Clouds Productions, 1979
CHARLESTON (TF) Robert Stigwood Productions/RSO, Inc., 1979
RETURN TO EDEN (MS) McElroy & McElroy/Hanna-Barbera Australia Productions, 1983, Australian
VICTIMS FOR VICTIMS (TF) Daniel L. Paulson - Loehr Spivey Productions/ Orion TV, 1984

HAL ASHBY*

b. 1936 - Ogden, Utah
Contact: Directors Guild of America - Los Angeles, 213/656-1220

THE LANDLORD United Artists, 1970
HAROLD AND MAUDE Paramount, 1971
THE LAST DETAIL Columbia, 1973
SHAMPOO Columbia, 1975
BOUND FOR GLORY United Artists, 1976
COMING HOME ★ United Artists, 1978
BEING THERE United Artists, 1979
SECOND HAND HEARTS Paramount, 1981
LOOKIN' TO GET OUT Paramount, 1982
LET'S SPEND THE NIGHT TOGETHER (FD) Embassy, 1983
THE SLUGGER'S WIFE Columbia, 1985

WILLIAM ASHER*

b. 1919
Agent: Fred Whitehead, ICM - Los Angeles, 213/550-4000

LEATHER GLOVES co-director with Richard Quine, Columbia, 1948
THE SHADOW ON THE WINDOW Columbia, 1956
THE 27TH DAY Columbia, 1956
BEACH PARTY American International, 1963
JOHNNY COOL United Artists, 1963
MUSCLE BEACH PARTY American International, 1963
BIKINI BEACH American International, 1964
BEACH BLANKET BINGO American International, 1965
HOW TO STUFF A WILD BIKINI American International, 1965
FIREBALL 500 American International, 1966
BUTCHER, BAKER, NIGHTMARE MAKER *NIGHT WARNING/MOMMA'S BOY* Comworld, 1981

JOHN ASTIN*

b. March 30, 1930 - Baltimore, Maryland
Home: P.O. Box 385, Beverly Hills, CA 90213
Agent: CAA - Los Angeles, 213/277-4545

OPERATION PETTICOAT (TF) Universal TV, 1977
ROSSETTI AND RYAN: MEN WHO LOVE WOMEN (TF) Universal TV, 1977

RICHARD ATTENBOROUGH*

b. August 29, 1923 - Cambridge, England
Business: Beaver Lodge, Richmond Green, Surrey, England, 01/940-7234
Agent: John Redway & Associates - London, 01/637-1612

OH! WHAT A LOVELY WAR Paramount, 1969, British
YOUNG WINSTON Columbia, 1972, British
A BRIDGE TOO FAR United Artists, 1977, British
MAGIC 20th Century-Fox, 1978
GANDHI ★★ Columbia, 1982, British-Indian
A CHORUS LINE Embassy, 1985

DANIEL ATTIAS*

Home: 6220 Temple Hill Drive, Los Angeles, CA 90068, 213/467-2841
Agent: David Gersh, The Gersh Agency - Beverly Hills, 213/274-6611

SILVER BULLET Paramount, 1985

RAY AUSTIN*

b. December 5, 1932 - London, England
Home: 8855 Hollywood Blvd., Los Angeles, CA 90068, 213/652-4400
Agent: Tom Chasin, ICM - Los Angeles, 213/550-4000
Business Manager: David G. Licht, 9171 Wilshire Blvd., Los Angeles, CA 90069, 213/278-1920

IT'S THE ONLY WAY TO GO Hallelujah, 1970, British
FUN AND GAMES 1971, British
THE VIRGIN WITCH Joseph Brenner Associates, 1972, British
HOUSE OF THE LIVING DEAD 1973, British
TALES OF THE GOLD MONKEY (TF) Universal TV/Belisarius Productions, 1982
THE RETURN OF THE MAN FROM U.N.C.L.E. (TF) Michael Sloan Productions/Viacom Productions, 1983
THE ZANY ADVENTURES OF ROBIN HOOD (TF) Bobka Productions/ Charles Fries Entertainment, 1984

IGOR AUZINS

Address: June Cann Management, 283 Alfred Street North, North Sydney, NSW, 2060, Australia, 02/922-3066

ALL AT SEA (TF) 1977, Australian
HIGH ROLLING Hexagon Productions, 1977, Australian
THE NIGHT NURSE (TF) Reg Grundy Organization, 1978, Australian
WATER UNDER THE BRIDGE (TF) Shotton Productions, 1980, Australian
TAURUS RISING (MS) 1982, Australian
WE OF THE NEVER NEVER Triumph/Columbia, 1983, Australian
COOLANGATTA GOLD Michael Edgley International/Hoyts Theatres, 1984, Australian

ARAM AVAKIAN*

Agent: Fred Milstein, William Morris Agency - New York City, 212/586-5100

LAD: A DOG co-director with Leslie H. Martinson, Warner Bros., 1961
END OF THE ROAD Allied Artists, 1970
COPS AND ROBBERS United Artists, 1973
11 HARROWHOUSE 20th Century-Fox, 1974, British

HOWARD (HIKMET) AVEDIS

Business: Hickmar Productions, The Burbank Studios, 4000 Warner Blvd., Burbank, CA 91522, 818/954-5104

THE STEPMOTHER Crown International, 1973
THE TEACHER Crown International, 1974
DR. MINX Dimension, 1975
THE SPECIALIST Crown International, 1975

HOWARD (HIKMET) AVEDIS —continued

SCORCHY American International, 1976
TEXAS DETOUR Cinema Shares International, 1978
THE FIFTH FLOOR Film Ventures International, 1980
SEPARATE WAYS Crown International, 1981
MORTUARY Artists Releasing Corporation/Film Ventures International, 1983
THEY'RE PLAYING WITH FIRE New World, 1984

HY AVERBACK*

b. 1925
Agent: Ron Meyer, CAA - Los Angeles, 213/277-4545

CHAMBER OF HORRORS Warner Bros., 1966
WHERE WERE YOU WHEN THE LIGHTS WENT OUT? MGM, 1968
I LOVE YOU, ALICE B. TOKLAS Warner Bros., 1968
THE GREAT BANK ROBBERY Warner Bros., 1969
SUPPOSE THEY GAVE A WAR AND NOBODY CAME? Cinerama Releasing Corporation, 1970
RICHIE BROCKELMAN: MISSING 24 HOURS (TF) Universal TV, 1976
THE LOVE BOAT II (TF) Aaron Spelling Productions, 1977
MAGNIFICENT MAGNET OF SANTA MESA (TF) Columbia TV, 1977
THE NEW MAVERICK (TF) Cherokee Productions/Warner Bros. TV, 1978
A GUIDE FOR THE MARRIED WOMAN (TF) 20th Century-Fox TV, 1978
PEARL (TF) Silliphant-Konigsberg Productions/Warner Bros. TV, 1978
THE NIGHT RIDER (TF) Stephen J. Cannell Productions/Universal TV, 1979
SHE'S IN THE ARMY NOW (TF) ABC Circle Films, 1981
THE GIRL, THE GOLD WATCH AND DYNAMITE (TF) Fellows-Keegan Company/Paramount TV, 1981
WHERE THE BOYS ARE Tri-Star, 1984

JOHN G. AVILDSEN*

b. 1937 - Chicago, Illinois
Home: 45 East 89th Street - Suite 37A, New York, NY 10028, 212/534-5891
Agent: Martin Bauer Agency, Beverly Hills - 213/275-2421

TURN ON TO LOVE Haven International, 1969
GUESS WHAT WE LEARNED IN SCHOOL TODAY? Cannon, 1970
JOE Cannon, 1970
CRY UNCLE! Cambist, 1971
OKAY BILL Four Star Excelsior, 1971
THE STOOLIE Jama, 1972
SAVE THE TIGER Paramount, 1973
FORE PLAY co-director with Bruce Malmuth & Robert McCarty, Cinema National, 1975
W.W. AND THE DIXIE DANCEKINGS 20th Century-Fox, 1975
ROCKY ** United Artists, 1976
SLOW DANCING IN THE BIG CITY United Artists, 1978
THE FORMULA MGM/United Artists, 1980
NEIGHBORS Columbia, 1982
A NIGHT IN HEAVEN 20th Century-Fox, 1983
THE KARATE KID Columbia, 1984

TOM AVILDSEN*

Home: 7501 Topeka Drive, Reseda, CA 91335
Agent: Marvin Moss Agency - Los Angeles, 213/274-8483

THINGS ARE TOUGH ALL OVER Columbia, 1982

GEORGE AXELROD*

b. June 9, 1922 - New York, New York
Agent: Irving Paul Lazar - Beverly Hills, 213/275-6153

LORD LOVE A DUCK United Artists, 1966
THE SECRET LIFE OF AN AMERICAN WIFE 20th Century-Fox, 1968

B

HECTOR BABENCO

b. Argentina
Contact: Conselho Nacional de Cinema, Rua Mayrink Veiga 28, Rio de Janeiro, Brazil, 2/233-8329

KING OF THE NIGHT 1975, Brazilian
LUCIO FLAVIO Unifilm/Embrafilme, 1978, Brazilian
PIXOTE Unifilm/Embrafilme, 1981, Brazilian
KISS OF THE SPIDER WOMAN MGM/UA, 1985, Brazilian-U.S.

RANDALL BADAT*

Agent: Tony Ludwig, CAA - Los Angeles, 213/277-4545

SURF II Arista, 1983

JOHN BADHAM*

b. 1939 - England
Agent: Triad Artists, Inc. - Los Angeles, 213/556-2727

THE IMPATIENT HEART (TF) Universal TV, 1971
ISN'T IT SHOCKING? (TF) ABC Circle Films, 1973
THE LAW (TF) Universal TV, 1974
THE GUN (TF) Universal TV, 1974
REFLECTIONS OF MURDER (TF) ABC Circle Films, 1974
THE GODCHILD (TF) MGM TV, 1974
THE KEEGANS (TF) Universal TV, 1976
THE BINGO LONG TRAVELING ALL STARS AND MOTOR KINGS Universal, 1976
SATURDAY NIGHT FEVER Paramount, 1977
DRACULA Universal, 1979
WHOSE LIFE IS IT ANYWAY? MGM/United Artists, 1981
BLUE THUNDER Columbia, 1983
WARGAMES MGM/UA, 1983
AMERICAN FLYER Warner Bros., 1985

REZA BADIYI*

b. April 17, 1936 - Iran
Agent: Geoff Brandt, APA - Los Angeles, 213/273-0744

DEATH OF A STRANGER Delta Commerz, 1972, West German-Israeli
THE EYES OF CHARLES SAND (TF) Warner Bros. TV, 1972
TRADER HORN MGM, 1973
THE BIG BLACK PILL (TF) Filmways/NBC Entertainment, 1981
OF MICE AND MEN (TF) Of Mice and Men Productions, 1981
WHITE WATER REBELS (TF) CBS Entertainment, 1983
MURDER ONE, DANCER 0 (TF) Mickey Productions, 1983
POLICEWOMAN CENTERFOLD (TF) Moonlight Productions, 1983

MAX BAER, JR.*

b. December 4, 1937 - Oakland, California
Home: 10433 Wilshire Blvd., Los Angeles, CA 90024, 213/470-2808
Personal Manager: Roger Camras - Los Angeles, 213/470-2808

THE WILD McCULLOCHS American International, 1975
ODE TO BILLY JOE Warner Bros., 1976
HOMETOWN, U.S.A. Film Ventures International, 1979

CHUCK BAIL*

Home: 1421 Morningside Drive, Burbank, CA 91506
Agent: Craig Rumar, F.A.M.E. - Los Angeles, 213/556-8071

BLACK SAMSON Warner Bros., 1974
CLEOPATRA JONES AND THE CASINO OF GOLD Warner Bros., 1975
GUMBALL RALLY Warner Bros., 1976

PATRICK BAILEY

b. April 17, 1947 - Crawfordsville, Indiana
Home: 14401 Villa Woods Place, Pacific Palisades, CA 90272, 213/454-0351
Agent: Rick Ray, Triad Artists, Inc. - Los Angeles, 213/556-2727

DOOR TO DOOR Shapiro Entertainment, 1984

GRAHAM BAKER*

Home: 2706 La Cuesta Drive, Los Angeles, CA 90046
Messages: 213/874-1441
Agent: Michael Marcus, CAA - Los Angeles, 213/277-4545

THE FINAL CONFLICT 20th Century-Fox, 1981
IMPULSE 20th Century Fox, 1984

ROY WARD BAKER

b. 1916 - London, England
Home: 2 St. Alban's Grove, London W8, England, 01/937-3964
Agent: Michael Whitehall, Leading Artists, 60 St. James Street, London SW1, England, 01/491-4400

THE OCTOBER MAN Eagle-Lion, 1947, British
THE WEAKER SEX Eagle-Lion, 1948, British
PAPER ORCHID 1949, British
OPERATION DISASTER *MORNING DEPARTURE* Universal, 1950, British
HIGHLY DANGEROUS Lippert, 1951, British
I'LL NEVER FORGET YOU *THE HOUSE IN THE SQUARE* 20th Century-Fox, 1951, British
DON'T BOTHER TO KNOCK 20th Century-Fox, 1952
NIGHT WITHOUT SLEEP 20th Century-Fox, 1952
INFERNO 20th Century-Fox, 1953
PASSAGE HOME 1955, British
JACQUELINE Rank, 1956, British
TIGER IN SMOKE 1956, British
THE ONE THAT GOT AWAY Rank, 1958, British
A NIGHT TO REMEMBER Rank, 1958, British
THE SINGER NOT THE SONG Warner Bros., 1962, British
FLAME IN THE STREETS Atlantic Pictures, 1962, British
THE VALIANT co-director with Giorgio Capitani, United Artists, 1962, British-Italian
TWO LEFT FEET 1963, British
FIVE MILLION YEARS TO EARTH *QUARTERMASS AND THE PIT* 20th Century-Fox, 1968, British
THE ANNIVERSARY 20th Century-Fox, 1968, British
THE SPY KILLER (TF) Halsan Productions, 1969
FOREIGN EXCHANGE (TF) Halsan Productions, 1970
MOON ZERO TWO Warner Bros., 1970, British
THE VAMPIRE LOVERS American International, 1970, British
THE SCARS OF DRACULA American Continental, 1971, British

ROY WARD BAKER —continued

DR. JEKYLL AND SISTER HYDE American International, 1972, British
ASYLUM Cinerama Releasing Corporation, 1972, British
THE VAULT OF HORROR Cinerama Releasing Corporation, 1973, British
AND NOW THE SCREAMING STARTS Cinerama Releasing Corporation, 1973, British
THE 7 BROTHERS MEET DRACULA *THE LEGEND OF THE SEVEN GOLDEN VAMPIRES* Dynamite Entertainment, 1979, British
THE MONSTER CLUB ITC, 1981, British
THE FLAME TREES OF THIKA (MS) London Films Ltd./Consolidated Productions Ltd., 1982, British
THE MASKS OF DEATH (TF) Tyburn Productions, 1985, British

RALPH BAKSHI*

b. October 26, 1938 - Haifa, Palestine
Business Manager: Gang, Tyre & Brown, 6400 Sunset Blvd., Los Angeles, CA 90028, 213/463-4863

FRITZ THE CAT (AF) American International, 1972
HEAVY TRAFFIC (AF) American International, 1973
COONSKIN (AF) Bryanston, 1974
WIZARDS (AF) 20th Century-Fox, 1977
THE LORD OF THE RINGS (AF) United Artists, 1978
AMERICAN POP (AF) Paramount, 1981
HEY GOOD LOOKIN' (AF) Warner Bros., 1982
FIRE AND ICE (AF) 20th Century-Fox, 1983

FERDINANDO BALDI

Contact: Ministry of Tourism & Education, Via Della Ferratella, No. 51, 00184 Rome, Italy, 06/7732

DAVID AND GOLIATH co-director with Richard Pottier, Allied Artists, 1960, Italian
DUEL OF CHAMPIONS co-director with Terence Young, Medallion, 1961, Italian-Spanish
IL PISTOLERO DELL'AVE MARIA BRCSRL, 1970, Italian-Spanish
BLINDMAN 20th Century-Fox, 1972, Italian
CARAMBOLA B.R.C./Aetoscin, 1974, Italian
GET MEAN Cee Note, 1976, Italian
NOVE OSPITI PER UN DELITTO Overseas, 1976, Italian
MY NAME IS TRINITY 1976, Italian
THE SICILIAN CONNECTION Joseph Green Pictures, 1977, Italian
L'INQUILINA DEL PIANO DI SOPRA Fair Film, 1977, Italian
LA SELVAGGIA *GEOMETRA PRINETTI SEL VAGGIAMENTEOSVALDO* Interfilm, 1978, Italian
LA RAGAZZA DEL VAGONE LETTO 1979, Italian
COMIN' AT YA Filmways, 1981, U.S.-Spanish
TREASURE OF THE FOUR CROWNS Cannon, 1983, U.S.-Spanish

PETER BALDWIN*

Agent: Frank Cooper, The Cooper Agency - Los Angeles, 213/277-8422

THE HARLEM GLOBETROTTERS ON GILLIGAN'S ISLAND (TF) Sherwood Schwartz Productions, 1981
THE BRADY GIRLS GET MARRIED (TF) Sherwood Schwartz Productions, 1981

CARROLL BALLARD

THE BLACK STALLION United Artists, 1979
NEVER CRY WOLF Buena Vista, 1983

ANNE BANCROFT*
(Anna Maria Louise Italiano)

b. September 17, 1931 - Bronx, New York
Business: Brooksfilms Limited, 20th Century Fox, P.O. Box 900, Beverly Hills, CA 90213, 213/203-1375

FATSO 20th Century-Fox, 1980

ALBERT BAND*
(Alfredo Antonini)

b. May 7, 1924 - Paris, France
Home: 8115 Amor Road, Los Angeles, CA 90046
Messages: 213/859-0034
Business: Empire International, 948 N. Fairfax Avenue, Los Angeles, CA 90046, 213/656-6610

THE YOUNG GUNS Allied Artists, 1956
I BURY THE LIVING United Artists, 1958
FACE OF FIRE Allied Artists, 1959
THE AVENGER Medallion, 1962, Italian-French
MASSACRO AL GRANDE CANYON Metra Film, 1965, Italian
THE TRAMPLERS Embassy, 1966, Italian
DRACULA'S DOG Crown International, 1978
SHE CAME TO THE VALLEY RGV Pictures, 1979

CHARLES BAND

Business: Empire International, 948 N. Fairfax Avenue, Los Angeles, CA 90046, 213/656-6610

CRASH Group 1, 1977
THE ALCHEMIST Ideal, 1980
PARASITE Embassy, 1982
METALSTORM: THE DESTRUCTION OF JARED-SYN Universal, 1983
RAGEWAR Empire International, 1984
THE DUNGEONMASTER co-director, Empire International, 1985
TRANCERS Empire International, 1985

RICHARD L. BARE*

b. 1909 - Turlock, California
Home: 700 Harbor Island Drive, Newport Beach, CA 92660, 714/675-6269

SMART GIRLS DON'T TALK Warner Bros., 1948
FLAXY MARTIN Warner Bros., 1949
THE HOUSE ACROSS THE STREET Warner Bros., 1949
THIS SIDE OF THE LAW Warner Bros., 1950
RETURN OF THE FRONTIERSMAN Warner Bros., 1950
PRISONERS OF THE CASBAH Columbia, 1953
THE OUTLANDERS Warner Bros., 1956
THE STORM RIDERS Warner Bros., 1956
BORDER SHOWDOWN Warner Bros., 1956
THE TRAVELLERS Warner Bros., 1957
SHOOT-OUT AT MEDICINE BEND Warner Bros., 1957
GIRL ON THE RUN Warner Bros., 1958
THIS REBEL BREED Warner Bros., 1960
WICKED, WICKED MGM, 1973

BRUNO BARRETO

Contact: Conselho Nacional de Cinema, Rua Mayrink Veiga 28, Rio de Janeiro, Brazil, 2/233-8329

DONA FLOR AND HER TWO HUSBANDS New Yorker, 1977, Brazilian
AMADA AMANTE 1979, Brazilian
AMOR BANDIDO Atlantic Releasing Corporation, 1982, Brazilian
GABRIELA MGM/UA Classics, 1983, Brazilian-Italian
THE KISS 1984, Brazilian

CHUCK BARRIS*

b. June 3 - Philadelphia, Pennsylvania
Home: 9100 Wilshire Blvd., Suite 411E, Beverly Hills, CA 90212, 213/278-9550

THE GONG SHOW MOVIE Universal, 1980

ARTHUR BARRON

THE WRIGHT BROTHERS (TF) PBS-TV, 1971
JEREMY United Artists, 1973
BROTHERS Warner Bros., 1977

STEVE BARRON

Contact: British Academy of Film & Television Arts, 195 Piccadilly, London W1, England, 01/734-0022

ELECTRIC DREAMS MGM/UA, 1984, British

ZELDA BARRON

Contact: British Academy of Film & Television Arts, 195 Piccadilly, London W1, England, 01/734-0022

SECRET PLACES TLC Films/20th Century Fox, 1984, British

PAUL BARTEL*

b. August 6, 1938 - Brooklyn, New York
Messages: 213/650-8878
Agent: Peter Rawley, ICM - Los Angeles, 213/550-4165

PRIVATE PARTS MGM, 1972
DEATH RACE 2000 New World, 1975
CANNONBALL New World, 1976
EATING RAOUL 20th Century-Fox International Classics, 1982
NOT FOR PUBLICATION Samuel Goldwyn Company, 1984
LUST IN THE DUST New World, 1985

HALL BARTLETT*

b. November 27, 1922 - Kansas City, Missouri
Home: 861 Stone Canyon Road, Los Angeles, CA 90024, 213/476-3916
Business: Hall Bartlett Films, Inc., 9200 Sunset Blvd. - Suite 908, Los Angeles, CA 90069, 213/278-8883

UNCHAINED Warner Bros., 1955
DRANGO co-director with Jules Bricken, United Artists, 1957
ZERO HOUR Paramount, 1957
ALL THE YOUNG MEN Columbia, 1960
THE CARETAKERS United Artists, 1963
CHANGES Cinerama Releasing Corporation, 1969
THE WILD PACK *THE SANDPIT GENERALS/THE DEFIANT* American International, 1972
JONATHAN LIVINGSTON SEAGULL Paramount, 1973
THE CHILDREN OF SANCHEZ Lone Star, 1978, U.S.-Mexican
LOVE IS FOREVER (TF) Michael Landon-Hall Bartlett Films/NBC-TV/20th Century-Fox TV, 1983

WILLIAM S. BARTMAN*

Home: 5517 Corteen Place, North Hollywood, CA 91607, 818/656-2541
Agent: Herb Tobias, Herb Tobias & Associates - Los Angeles, 213/277-6211

O'HARA'S WIFE Davis-Panzer Productions, 1982

HAL BARWOOD

b. Hanover, New Hampshire
Contact: Writers Guild of America - Los Angeles, 213/550-1000

BIOHAZARD 20th Century Fox, 1985

FRED BARZYK*

Home: 12 Brook Street, Chelmsford, MA 01824, 617/256-4868
Business: Creative Television Associates, Inc., 1380 Soldiers Field Road, Brighton, MA 02135, 617/783-2103

BETWEEN TIME & TIMBUKTU (TF) PBS, 1974
THE PHANTOM OF THE OPEN HEARTH (TF) co-director with David R. Loxton, WNET-13 Television Laboratory/WGBH New Television Workshop, 1976
CHARLIE SMITH AND THE FRITTER TREE (TF) co-director with David R. Loxton, WNET-13 Television Laboratory/WGBH New Television Workshop, 1978
THE LATHE OF HEAVEN (TF) co-director with David R. Loxton, WNET-13 Television Laboratory/Taurus Film, 1980
COUNTDOWN TO LOOKING GLASS (CTF) L & B Productions/Primedia Productions, 1984

JULES BASS

Business: Rankin-Bass Productions, Inc., 1 East 53rd Street, New York, NY 10022, 212/759-7721

MAD MONSTER PARTY (AF) Embassy, 1967
THE WACKY WORLD OF MOTHER GOOSE (AF) 1968
THE HOBBIT (ATF) co-director with Arthur Rankin, Jr., Rankin-Bass Productions, 1977
RUDOLPH AND FROSTY (ATF) co-director with Arthur Rankin Jr., Rankin-Bass Productions, 1979
THE RETURN OF THE KING (ATF) co-director with Arthur Rankin, Jr., Rankin-Bass Productions, 1979
THE LAST UNICORN (AF) co-director with Arthur Rankin, Jr., Jensen Farley Pictures, 1982
THE FLIGHT OF THE DRAGONS (ATF) co-director with Arthur Rankin, Jr., Rankin-Bass Productions, 1983
THE WIND IN THE WILLOWS (ATF) co-director with Arthur Rankin, Jr., Rankin-Bass Productions, 1983

SAUL BASS*

b. May 8, 1920 - New York, New York
Business: Saul Bass/Herb Yager & Associates, 7039 Sunset Blvd., Los Angeles, CA 90028, 213/466-9701

PHASE IV Paramount, 1974

LAWRENCE BASSOFF

WEEKEND PASS Crown International, 1984

MICHAL BAT-ADAM

Contract: Israel Film Centre, Ministry of Industry & Trade, 30 Agron Street, P.O. Box 299, Jerusalem 94190, Israel, 02/210433

EACH OTHER *MOMENTS* Franklin Media, 1979, Israeli-French
THE THIN LINE New Yorker, 1980, Israeli
YOUNG LOVE GUY Film Productions Ltd., 1983, Israeli

DAVID BEAIRD

OCTAVIA International Film Marketing, 1984
PARTY ANIMAL International Film Marketing, 1984

ROBERT B. BEAN*

Business: 212/628-0500

MADE FOR EACH OTHER 20th Century-Fox, 1971

CHRIS BEARDE*

Home: 2000 Avenue of the Stars, Los Angeles, CA 90067, 213/277-0800, ext. 306 (east)
Agent: Tom Chasin, ICM - Los Angeles, 213/550-4000

HYSTERICAL Embassy, 1983

ALAN BEATTIE

DELUSION New Line Cinema, 1981
THE HOUSE WHERE DEATH LIVES New American, 1984

WARREN BEATTY*

b. March 30, 1937 - Richmond, Virginia
Agent: William Morris Agency - Beverly Hills, 213/274-7451

HEAVEN CAN WAIT ★ co-director with Buck Henry, Paramount, 1978
REDS ★★ Paramount, 1981

GABRIELLE BEAUMONT*

Home: 3456 Alana Drive, Sherman Oaks, CA 91403, 818/906-0579
Agent: Joan Scott, Writers & Artists Agency - Los Angeles, 213/820-2240
Business Manager: Burton Merrill, Individual Productions, Inc., 4260 Arcola Avenue, Toluca Lake, CA 91602, 818/763-6903

THE GODSEND Cannon, 1980, British
DEATH OF A CENTERFOLD: THE DOROTHY STRATTEN STORY (TF) Wilcox Productions/MGM TV, 1981
SECRETS OF A MOTHER AND DAUGHTER (TF) The Shpetner Company, 1983
GONE ARE THE DAYES (CTF) Walt Disney Productions, 1984

HAROLD BECKER*

Agent: Stan Kamen, William Morris Agency - Beverly Hills, 213/274-7451

THE RAGMAN'S DAUGHTER Penelope Films, 1972, British
THE ONION FIELD Avco Embassy, 1979
THE BLACK MARBLE Avco Embassy, 1980
TAPS 20th Century-Fox, 1981
VISIONQUEST Warner Bros., 1985

TERRY BEDFORD*

Home: 9 Roderick Road, London NW3, England, 01/267-3220
Agent: Michael Marcus, CAA - Los Angeles, 213/277-4545
Business Manager: Paul E. Esposito, Jennie & Co., 127 West 79th Street, New York, NY 10024, 212/595-5200

SLAYGROUND Universal/AFD, 1983, British

JEAN-JACQUES BEINEIX

Contact: French Film Office, 745 Fifth Avenue, New York, NY 10151, 212/832-8860

DIVA United Artists Classics, 1982, French
THE MOON IN THE GUTTER Triumph/Columbia, 1983, French-Italian

EARL BELLAMY*

b. March 11, 1917 - Minneapolis, Minnesota
Agent: Herb Tobias & Associates - Los Angeles, 213/277-6211
Business Manager: Fred Barman, Los Angeles, 213/276-6666

SEMINOLE UPRISING Columbia, 1955
BLACKJACK KETCHUM, DESPERADO Columbia, 1956
TOUGHEST GUN IN TOMBSTONE United Artists, 1958
STAGECOACH TO DANCERS' ROCK Universal, 1962
FLUFFY Universal, 1965
INCIDENT AT PHANTOM HILL Universal, 1966
GUNPOINT Universal, 1966
MUNSTER, GO HOME Universal, 1966
THREE GUNS FOR TEXAS co-director with David Lowell Rich & Paul Stanley, Universal, 1968
BACKTRACK Universal, 1969
THE PIGEON (TF) Thomas-Spelling Productions, 1969
DESPERATE MISSION (TF) 20th Century-Fox TV, 1971
THE TRACKERS (TF) Aaron Spelling Productions, 1971
SEVEN ALONE Doty-Dayton, 1975
SIDECAR RACERS Universal, 1975, Australian
PART 2 WALKING TALL American International, 1975
AGAINST A CROOKED SKY Doty-Dayton, 1975
FLOOD! (TF) Irwin Allen Productions/20th Century-Fox TV, 1976
FIRE! (TF) Irwin Allen Productions/20th Century-Fox TV, 1977
SIDEWINDER ONE Avco Embassy, 1977
SPEEDTRAP First Artists, 1978
DESPERATE WOMEN (TF) Lorimar Productions, 1978
THE CASTAWAYS OF GILLIGAN'S ISLAND (TF) Sherwood Schwartz Productions, 1979
VALENTINE MAGIC ON LOVE ISLAND (TF) Dick Clark Productions/PKO/Osmond Television, 1980
MAGNUM THRUST Shenandoah Films, 1981

DONALD BELLISARIO*

Home: 6311 Heather Drive, Hollywood, CA 90068, 213/463-3059
Business: Universal Studios, 100 Universal City Plaza, Universal City, CA 91608, 818/508-2131
Agent: Bob Broder, Broder-Kurland Agency - Los Angeles, 213/274-8291

AIRWOLF (TF) Belisarius Productions/Universal TV, 1984

MARCO BELLOCCHIO

b. November 9, 1939 - Piacenza, Italy
Contact: Ministry of Tourism & Education, Via Della Ferratella, No. 51, 00184 Rome, Italy, 06/7732

FIST IN HIS POCKET Peppercorn-Wormser, 1965, Italian
CHINA IS NEAR Royal Films International, 1967, Italian
AMORE E RABBIA co-director, 1969, Italian
NEL NOME DEL PADRE 1972, Italian
SBATTI IL MOSTRO IN PRIMA PAGINA 1972, Italian
FIT TO BE UNTIED co-director, 1974, Italian
MATTA DA SLEGARE 11 Marzo Cinematografica, 1975, Italian
VICTORY MARCH Summit Features, 1976, Italian-French
LES YEUX FERTILES 1977; French-Italian
IL GABBIANO (TF) RAI, 1977, Italian
LA MACCHINA CINEMA 1978, Italian
LEAP INTO THE VOID Summit Features, 1979, Italian
THE EYES, THE MOUTH Triumph/Columbia, 1983, Italian-French
HENRY IV Orion Classics, 1984, Italian

JERRY BELSON*

Agent: Jack Rapke, CAA - Los Angeles, 213/277-4545

JEKYLL AND HYDE...TOGETHER AGAIN Paramount, 1982

JACK BENDER*

Agent: Arnold Rifkin, Triad Artists, Inc. - Los Angeles, 213/556-2727

IN LOVE WITH AN OLDER WOMAN (TF) Pound Ridge Productions/Charles Fries Productions, 1982
TWO KINDS OF LOVE (TF) CBS Entertainment, 1983
SHATTERED VOWS (TF) Bertinelli-Pequod Productions, 1984

LASLO BENEDEK*

b. March 5, 1907 - Budapest, Hungary
Home: 70 Bank Street, New York, NY 10014

THE KISSING BANDIT MGM, 1948
PORT OF NEW YORK Eagle- Lion, 1949
DEATH OF A SALESMAN Columbia, 1951
THE WILD ONE Columbia, 1954
BENGAL BRIGADE Columbia, 1954
KINDER, MUTTER UND EIN GENERAL 1955, West German
AFFAIR IN HAVANA Allied Artists, 1957
MALAGA Warner Bros., 1959, British
RECOURSE EN GRACE 1960, French
NAMU, THE KILLER WHALE United Artists, 1966
DARING GAME Paramount, 1968
THE NIGHT VISITOR UMC, 1971
ASSAULT ON AGATHON Nine Network, 1976

RICHARD BENJAMIN*

b. May 22, 1938 - New York, New York
Agent: Phil Gersh, The Gersh Agency - Beverly Hills, 213/274-6611

MY FAVORITE YEAR MGM/UA, 1982
RACING WITH THE MOON Paramount, 1984
CITY HEAT Warner Bros., 1984

RICHARD BENNER*

Home: 228 West 4th Street, Apt. 4, New York, NY 10014, 212/929-1067
Business Manager: Stephen Detasnady, Rigrod & Surpin, 1880 Century Park East, Los Angeles, CA 90067, 213/552-1808

OUTRAGEOUS! Cinema 5, 1977, Canadian
HAPPY BIRTHDAY GEMINI United Artists, 1980, U.S.-Canadian

RICHARD C. BENNETT*

Home: 17136 Index Street, Granada Hills, CA 91344, 818/363-3381
Agent: Ronald Leif, Contemporary-Korman Artists - Beverly Hills, 213/278-8250

HARPER VALLEY PTA April Fools, 1978
THE ESCAPE OF A ONE-TON PET (TF) Tomorrow Entertainment, 1978

ROBERT BENTON*

b. September 29, 1932 - Waxahachie, Texas
Agent: Sam Cohn, ICM - New York City, 212/556-6810

BAD COMPANY Paramount, 1972
THE LATE SHOW Warner Bros., 1976
KRAMER VS. KRAMER ★★ Columbia, 1979
STILL OF THE NIGHT MGM/UA, 1982
PLACES IN THE HEART Tri-Star, 1984

LUCA BERCOVICI

Agent: Artists Group, Ltd. - Los Angeles, 213/552-1100

GHOULIES Empire International, 1985

BRUCE BERESFORD*

b. 1940 - Australia
Home: Flat 5, 8 Sloane Gardens, London SW7, England, 01/730-1427
Flat 13, 3 Marathon Road, Darling Point, Sydney NSW, Australia 2027, 01/328-7854
Agent: Len Hirshan, William Morris Agency - Beverly Hills, 213/274-7451

THE ADVENTURES OF BARRY McKENZIE Double Head Productions, 1972, Australian
BARRY McKENZIE HOLDS HIS OWN Satori, 1974, Australian
DON'S PARTY Satori, 1976, Australian
THE GETTING OF WISDOM Atlantic Releasing Corporation, 1977, Australian
MONEY MOVERS South Australian Film Corporation, 1978, Australian
BREAKER MORANT New World/Quartet, 1980, Australian
THE CLUB South Australian Film Corporation, 1981, Australian
PUBERTY BLUES Universal Classics, 1982, Australian
TENDER MERCIES ★ Universal/AFD, 1983
KING DAVID Paramount, 1985, U.S.-British

ANDREW BERGMAN*

Home: 881 Seventh Avenue - Suite 834, New York, NY 10019, 212/582-9215
Agent: Lee Rosenberg, Triad Artists, Inc. - Los Angeles, 213/556-2727

SO FINE Warner Bros., 1981

INGMAR BERGMAN

(Ernst Ingmar Bergman)

b. July 14, 1918 - Uppsala, Sweden
Contact: Swedish Film Institute, P.O. Box 27126, S-10252 Stockholm, Sweden, 08/630510

CRISIS Svensk Filmindustri, 1945, Swedish
IT RAINS ON OUR LOVE Sveriges Folkbiografer, 1946, Swedish
THE LAND OF DESIRE Sveriges Folkbiografer, 1947, Swedish
NIGHT IS MY FUTURE Terrafilm, 1948, Swedish
PORT OF CALL Janus, 1948, Swedish
THE DEVIL'S WANTON Terrafilm, 1949, Swedish
THREE STRANGE LOVES *THIRST* Janus, 1949, Swedish
TO JOY Janus, 1950, Swedish
THIS CAN'T HAPPEN HERE Svensk Filmindustri, 1951, Swedish
ILLICIT INTERLUDE *SOMMARLEK* Janus, 1951, Swedish
SECRETS OF WOMEN Janus, 1952, Swedish
MONIKA Janus, 1953, Swedish
SAWDUST AND TINSEL *THE NAKED NIGHT* Janus, 1953, Swedish
A LESSON IN LOVE Janus, 1954, Swedish
DREAMS Janus, 1955, Swedish
SMILES OF A SUMMER NIGHT Janus, 1955, Swedish
THE SEVENTH SEAL Janus, 1957, Swedish
WILD STRAWBERRIES Janus, 1957, Swedish
SO CLOSE TO LIFE Janus, 1958, Swedish
THE MAGICIAN Janus, 1958, Swedish
THE VIRGIN SPRING Janus, 1960, Swedish
THE DEVIL'S EYE Janus, 1960, Swedish
THROUGH A GLASS DARKLY Janus, 1961, Swedish
WINTER LIGHT Janus, 1962, Swedish
THE SILENCE Janus, 1963, Swedish
ALL THESE WOMEN Janus, 1964, Swedish
PERSONA United Artists, 1966, Swedish
HOUR OF THE WOLF United Artists, 1968, Swedish
SHAME United Artists, 1968, Swedish
FARO DOCUMENT (TD) 1969, Swedish
THE RITUAL Janus, 1969, Swedish, originally made for television
THE PASSION OF ANNA United Artists, 1969, Swedish

INGMAR BERGMAN —continued

THE TOUCH Cinerama Releasing Corporation, 1971, Swedish, originally made for television
CRIES AND WHISPERS ★ New World, 1972, Swedish
SCENES FROM A MARRIAGE Cinema 5, 1973, Swedish, originally made for television
THE MAGIC FLUTE Surrogate, 1975, Swedish, originally made for television
FACE TO FACE ★ Paramount, 1976, Swedish
THE SERPENT'S EGG Paramount, 1978, West German
AUTUMN SONATA New World, 1978, West German
FROM THE LIFE OF THE MARIONETTES Universal/AFD, 1980, West German
FARO DOCUMENT 1979 (TD) Cinematograph, 1979, Swedish
FANNY AND ALEXANDER ★ Embassy, 1983, Swedish-French-West German
AFTER THE REHEARSAL Triumph/Columbia, 1983, Swedish-West German, originally made for television

DAVID BERLATSKY*

Home: 3261 W. Norton Avenue, Apt. 4, Los Angeles, CA 90046, 213/656-0714
Agent: Larry Becsey, TMI - Los Angeles, 213/273-4000

THE FARMER Columbia, 1977

TED BERMAN

Business: Walt Disney Productions, 500 S. Buena Vista Street, Burbank, CA 91521, 818/845-3141

THE FOX AND THE HOUND (AF) co-director with Art Stevens & Richard Rich, Buena Vista, 1981
THE BLACK CAULDRON (AF) co-director with Art Stevens & Richard Rich, Buena Vista, 1986

ARMYAN BERNSTEIN*

Agent: Michael Ovitz, CAA - Los Angeles, 213/277-4545
Business: Flying Barzini Brothers, 9021 Melrose Ave., Los Angeles, CA 90069, 213/278-4260

WINDY CITY Warner Bros., 1984

WALTER BERNSTEIN*

b. August 29, 1929 - Chicago, Illinois
Home: 320 Central Park West, New York, NY 10025, 212/724-1821
Agent: Sam Cohn, ICM - New York City, 212/556-6810

LITTLE MISS MARKER Universal, 1980

CLAUDE BERRI
(Claude Langmann)

b. July 1, 1934 - Paris, France
Contact: French Film Office, 745 Fifth Avenue, New York, NY 10151, 212/832-8860

LE BAISERS co-director, 1964, French
LE CHANCE ET L'AMOUR co-director, 1964, French
THE TWO OF US *LE VIEL HOMME ET L'ENFANT* Cinema 5, 1968, French
MARRY ME! MARRY ME! *MAZEL TOV OU LE MARIAGE* Allied Artists, 1969, French
THE MAN WITH CONNECTIONS *LE PISTONNE* Columbia, 1970, French
LE CINEMA DU PAPA Columbia, 1971, French
LE SEX SHOP Peppercorn-Wormser, 1973, French
MALE OF THE CENTURY Joseph Green Pictures, 1975, French
THE FIRST TIME EDP, 1976, French
ONE WILD MOMENT Quartet/Films Incorporated, 1978, French
A NOUS DEUX AMLF, 1979, French

CLAUDE BERRI —continued

JE VOUS AIME Renn Films/FR3/Cinevog, 1980, French
LE MAITRE D'ECOLE AMLF, 1981, French
TCHAO PANTIN European International, 1983, French

JOHN BERRY*

b. 1917 - New York, New York
Home: 299 West 12th Street, New York, NY 10014, 212/929-7134

MISS SUSIE SLAGLE'S Paramount, 1945
FROM THIS DAY FORWARD RKO Radio, 1946
CROSS MY HEART Paramount, 1946
CASBAH Universal, 1948
TENSION MGM, 1949
HE RAN ALL THE WAY United Artists, 1951
C'EST ARRIVE A PARIS 1952, French
CA VA BARDER 1954, French
JE SUIS UN SENTIMENTAL 1955, French
PANTALOONS *DON JUAN* United Motion Picture Organizations, 1956, French-Spanish
OH, QUE MAMBO 1958, French
TAMANGO Valiant, 1959, French
MAYA MGM, 1966
A TOUT CASSER 1967, French
CLAUDINE 20th Century-Fox, 1974
THIEVES Paramount, 1977
SPARROW 1978
THE BAD NEWS BEARS GO TO JAPAN Paramount, 1978
ANGEL ON MY SHOULDER (TF) Mace Neufeld Productions/Barney Rosenzweig Productions/Beowulf Productions, 1980
SISTER, SISTER (TF) 20th Century-Fox TV, 1982
HONEYBOY (TF) Fan Fares Inc. Productions/Estrada Productions, 1982

BERNARDO BERTOLUCCI

b. March 16, 1940 - Parma, Italy
Contact: Ministry of Tourism & Education, Via Della Ferratella, No. 51, 00184 Rome, Italy, 06/7732

LA COMMARE SECCA 1962, Italian
BEFORE THE REVOLUTION New Yorker, 1964, Italian
PARTNER New Yorker, 1968, Italian
AMORE E RABBIA co-director, 1969, Italian
THE SPIDER'S STRATAGEM New Yorker, 1970, Italian
THE CONFORMIST Paramount, 1971, Italian-French-West German
LAST TANGO IN PARIS ★ United Artists, 1973, Italian-French
1900 Paramount, 1977, Italian
LUNA 20th Century-Fox, 1979, Italian-U.S.
TRAGEDY OF A RIDICULOUS MAN The Ladd Company/Warner Bros., 1982, Italian

JAMES BESHEARS

HOMEWORK Jensen-Farley Pictures, 1982

LUC BESSON

Contact: French Film Office, 745 Fifth Avenue, New York, NY 10151, 212/832-8860

LE DERNIER COMBAT Gaumont/Les Films du Loup/Constantin Alexandrof Productions, 1983, French
SUBWAY Gaumont, 1985, French

JONATHAN BETUEL*

Contact: Directors Guild of America - Los Angeles, 213/656-1220

MY SCIENCE PROJECT Buena Vista, 1985

EDWARD BIANCHI*

Home: 36 Gramercy Park East, New York, NY 10003, 212/228-3668
Agent: Michael Black, ICM - Los Angeles, 213/550-4000

THE FAN Paramount, 1981

KATHRYN BIGELOW

THE LOVELESS co-director with Monty Montgomery, Atlantic Releasing Corporation, 1981

TONY BILL*

b. August 23, 1940 - San Diego, California
Business: Tony Bill Productions, 73 Market Street, Venice, CA 90291, 213/396-5937
Agent: Robinson, Luttrell & Associates - Beverly Hills, 213/275-6114

MY BODYGUARD 20th Century-Fox, 1980
SIX WEEKS Universal, 1982
LOVE THY NEIGHBOR (TF) Patricia Nardo Productions/20th Century Fox TV, 1984

KEVIN BILLINGTON

b. 1933 - England
Agent: Merrily Kane Agency - Beverly Hills, 213/550-8874
Home: Court House Films, 52 Tottenham Street, London W1, England, 01/636-1275

INTERLUDE Columbia, 1968, British
THE RISE AND RISE OF MICHAEL RIMMER Warner Bros., 1970, British
THE LIGHT AT THE EDGE OF THE WORLD National General, 1971, U.S.-Spanish
VOICES Hemdale, 1973, British
AND NO ONE COULD SAVE HER (TF) Associated London Films, 1973, British
ECHOES OF THE SIXTIES (TD) ALA Productions, 1979
THE GOOD SOLDIER (TF) Granada TV, 1983, British
REFLECTIONS (TF) Court House Films/Film Four International, 1984, British

BRUCE BILSON*

b. May 19, 1928 - New York, New York
Agent: The Cooper Agency - Los Angeles, 213/277-8422
Business: Downwind Enterprises, 4444 Radford Avenue, North Hollywood, CA 91607

THE GIRL WHO CAME GIFT-WRAPPED (TF) Spelling-Goldberg Productions, 1974
DEAD MAN ON THE RUN (TF) Sweeney-Finnegan Productions, 1975
THE NEW DAUGHTERS OF JOSHUA CABE (TF) Spelling-Goldberg Productions, 1976
BJ & THE BEAR (TF) Universal TV, 1978
THE NORTH AVENUE IRREGULARS Buena Vista, 1979
DALLAS COWBOYS CHEERLEADERS (TF) Aubrey-Hammer Productions, 1979
PLEASURE COVE (TF) Lou Shaw Productions/David Gerber Company/Columbia TV, 1979
THE GHOSTS OF BUXLEY HALL (TF) Walt Disney Productions, 1980
CHATTANOOGA CHOO CHOO April Fools, 1984
FINDER OF LOST LOVES (TF) Aaron Spelling Productions, 1984

JOHN BINDER*

Contact: Directors Guild of America - Los Angeles, 213/656-1220

UFORIA Universal, 1984

MACK BING*

Agent: Eisenbach-Greene, Inc. - Los Angeles, 213/659-3420

ALL THE LOVING COUPLES U-M, 1969
GABRIELLA 1974

PATRICIA BIRCH*

Agent: ICM - Los Angeles, 213/550-4000

GREASE 2 Paramount, 1982

STEWART BIRD

HOME FREE ALL Almi Classics, 1984

BILL BIXBY*

b. January 22, 1934 - San Francisco, California
Personal Manager: Paul Brandon - Los Angeles, 213/273-6173

THE BARBARY COAST (TF) Paramount TV, 1975
THREE ON A DATE (TF) ABC Circle Films, 1978

NOEL BLACK*

b. 1937 - Chicago, Illinois
Agent: Tom Chasin, ICM - Los Angeles, 213/550-4000

TRILOGY: THE AMERICAN BOY (TF) ABC Stage 67, 1968
PRETTY POISON 20th Century-Fox, 1968
COVER ME BABE 20th Century-Fox, 1970
JENNIFER ON MY MIND United Artists, 1971
MULLIGAN'S STEW (TF) Paramount TV, 1977
MIRRORS First American, 1978
A MAN, A WOMAN AND A BANK Avco Embassy, 1979, Canadian
THE GOLDEN HONEYMOON (TF) Learning in Focus, 1980
THE OTHER VICTIM (TF) Shpetner Company, 1981
PRIME SUSPECT (TF) Tisch-Avnet Television, 1982
THE ELECTRIC GRANDMOTHER (TF) Highgate Pictures, 1982
HAPPY ENDINGS (TF) Motown Productions, 1983
PRIVATE SCHOOL Universal, 1983
QUARTERBACK PRINCESS (TF) CBS Entertainment, 1983

LES BLAIR

Home: 63 Oakfield Road, London N4 4LD, England, 01/340-8261

NUMBER ONE Mark Forstater Productions, 1984, British

MICHAEL BLAKEMORE

Contact: Directors Guild of Great Britain, 56 Whitfield Street, London W1, England, 01/580-2256

PRIVATES ON PARADE Orion Classics, 1983, British

LES BLANK

b. November 27, 1935 - Tampa, Florida
Business: Flower Films, 10341 San Pablo Avenue, El Cerrito, CA 94530, 415/525-0942

DRY WOOD AND HOT PEPPER (FD) Flower Films, 1973
A POEM IS A NAKED PERSON (FD) Skyhill Films/Flower Films, 1974
CHULAS FRONTERAS (FD) Brazos Films, 1976
ALWAYS FOR PLEASURE (FD) Flower Films, 1978
BURDEN OF DREAMS (FD) Flower Films, 1982
IN HEAVEN THERE IS NO BEER? (FD) Flower Films, 1984

WILLIAM PETER BLATTY*

b. 1928 - New York, New York
Home: 23712 Malibu Colony, Malibu, CA 90265, 213/456-5081
Messages: 213/456-3317
Agent: Tony Fantozzi, CAA - Los Angeles, 213/277-4545

THE NINTH CONFIGURATION Warner Bros., 1979 - re-released under title TWINKLE, TWINKLE 'KILLER' KANE by United Film Distribution in 1980

COREY BLECHMAN

Contact: Writers Guild of America - Los Angeles, 213/550-1000

THE THREE WISHES OF BILLY GRIER (TF) I & C Productions, 1984

JEFF BLECKNER*

Home: 4815 Dunman Avenue, Woodland Hills, CA 91364, 818/887-5938
Agent: Paul Heller, ICM - Los Angeles, 213/550-4311

RYAN'S FOUR (TF) Fair Dinkum Inc./Groverton Productions/Paramount TV, 1983
WHEN YOUR LOVER LEAVES (TF) Major H Productions, 1983
CONCEALED ENEMIES (TF) WGBH-Boston/Goldcrest Films and Television/Comworld Productions, 1984, U.S.-British

BERTRAND BLIER

b. March 11, 1939 - Paris, France
Contact: French Film Office, 745 Fifth Avenue, New York, NY 10151, 212/832-8860

HITLER? CONNAIS PAS! 1963, French
SI J'ETAIS UN ESPION 1967, French
GOING PLACES *LES VALSEUSES* Cinema 5, 1974, French
FEMMES FATALES *CALMOS* New Line Cinema, 1976, French
GET OUT YOUR HANDKERCHIEFS New Line Cinema, 1978, French
BUFFET FROID Parafrance, 1979, French
BEAU PERE New Line Cinema, 1981, French
MY BEST FRIEND'S GIRL European International, 1983, French
SEPARATE ROOMS *NOTRE HISTOIRE* Spectrafilm, 1984, French

JEFFREY BLOOM*

Agent: Arnold Rifkin, Triad Artists, Inc. - Los Angeles, 213/556-2727

DOGPOUND SHUFFLE Paramount, 1974, Canadian
THE STICK UP Trident-Barber, 1978, British
BLOOD BEACH Jerry Gross Organization, 1981
JEALOUSY (TF) Charles Fries Productions/Alan Sacks Productions, 1983

GEORGE BLOOMFIELD*

b. Montreal, Quebec, Canada
Home: Admiral Road 50, Toronto, Ontario M5R215, Canada, 416/967-0826

JENNY Cinerama Releasing Corporation, 1970
TO KILL A CLOWN 20th Century-Fox, 1972
CHILD UNDER A LEAF Cinema National, 1975, Canadian
LOVE ON THE NOSE (TF) CBC, 1978, Canadian
NELLIE McCLUNG (TF) CBC, 1978, Canadian
RIEL CBC/Green River Productions, 1979, Canadian
NOTHING PERSONAL American International, 1980 Canadian
DOUBLE NEGATIVE Best Film and Video, 1981, Canadian

DON BLUTH

Business: Don Bluth Productions, 12229 Ventura Blvd., Studio City, CA 91604, 818/506-5440

THE SECRET OF NIMH (AF) MGM/UA, 1982

BUDD BOETTICHER*

(Oscar Boetticher, Jr.)

b. July 29, 1916 - Chicago, Illinois
Contact: Directors Guild of America - Los Angeles, 213/656-1220

ONE MYSTERIOUS NIGHT Columbia, 1944
THE MISSING JUROR Columbia, 1944
A GUY, A GAL AND A PAL Columbia, 1945
ESCAPE IN THE FOG Columbia, 1945
YOUTH ON TRIAL Columbia, 1945
THE FLEET THAT CAME TO STAY Paramount, 1946
ASSIGNED TO DANGER Eagle-Lion, 1948
BEHIND LOCKED DOORS Eagle-Lion, 1948
THE WOLF HUNTERS Monogram, 1949
BLACK MIDNIGHT Monogram, 1949
KILLER SHARK Monogram, 1950
THE BULLFIGHTER AND THE LADY Republic, 1951
THE SWORD OF D'ARTAGNAN Universal, 1951
THE CIMARRON KID Universal, 1951
RED BALL EXPRESS Universal, 1952
BRONCO BUSTER Universal, 1952
HORIZONS WEST Universal, 1952
CITY BENEATH THE SEA Universal, 1953
SEMINOLE Universal, 1953
THE MAN FROM THE ALAMO Universal, 1953
EAST OF SUMATRA Universal, 1953
WINGS OF THE HAWK Universal, 1953
THE MAGNIFICENT MATADOR 20th Century-Fox, 1955
THE KILLER IS LOOSE United Artists, 1956
SEVEN MEN FROM NOW Warner Bros., 1956
THE TALL T Columbia, 1957
DECISION AT SUNDOWN Columbia, 1957
BUCHANAN RIDES ALONE Columbia, 1958
RIDE LONESOME Columbia, 1959
WESTBOUND Warner Bros., 1959
COMANCHE STATION Columbia, 1960
THE RISE AND FALL OF LEGS DIAMOND Warner Bros., 1960
A TIME FOR DYING Etoile, 1971
ARRUZA (FD) Avco Embassy, 1972
LUSITANO (FD) Boetticher Productions, 1985

PAUL BOGART*

b. November 21, 1919 - New York, New York
Business: Tiber Productions, Inc., 760 N. La Cienega Blvd., Los Angeles, CA 90069, 213/652-0222
Agent: Michael Marcus, CAA - Los Angeles, 213/277-4545

MARLOWE MGM, 1969
HALLS OF ANGER United Artists, 1970

PAUL BOGART*—continued

SKIN GAME Warner Bros., 1971
IN SEARCH OF AMERICA (TF) Four Star Productions, 1971
CLASS OF '44 Warner Bros., 1973
CANCEL MY RESERVATION Warner Bros., 1974
TELL ME WHERE IT HURTS (TF) Tomorrow Entertainment, 1974
MR. RICCO MGM, 1975
WINNER TAKE ALL (TF) The Jozak Company, 1975
THE THREE SISTERS NTA, 1977
OH, GOD! YOU DEVIL Warner Bros., 1984

PETER BOGDANOVICH

b. July 30, 1939 - Kingston, New York

TARGETS Paramount, 1968
DIRECTED BY JOHN FORD (FD) American Film Institute, 1971
THE LAST PICTURE SHOW ★ Columbia, 1971
WHAT'S UP, DOC? Warner Bros., 1972
PAPER MOON Paramount, 1973
DAISY MILLER Paramount, 1974
AT LONG LAST LOVE 20th Century-Fox, 1975
NICKELODEON Columbia, 1976
SAINT JACK New World, 1979
THEY ALL LAUGHED United Artists Classics, 1982
MASK Universal, 1985

CLIFFORD BOLE*

Agent: Shapiro-Lichtman Agency - Los Angeles, 213/557-2244
Business Manager: Brad Marer & Associates - Los Angeles, 213/278-6690

T.J. HOOKER (TF) Spelling-Goldberg Productions, 1982

ROBERT BOLT

b. August 15, 1924 - Sale, England
Contact: British Academy of Film & Television Arts, 195 Piccadilly, London W1, England, 01/734-0022

LADY CAROLINE LAMB United Artists, 1973, British

SERGEI BONDARCHUK

b. September 25, 1920 - Belozersk, Ukraine, U.S.S.R.
Contact: State Committee of Cinematography of the U.S.S.R., Council of Ministers, 7 Maly Gnesdnikovsky Pereulok, Moscow, U.S.S.R., 7 095/229-9912

FATE OF A MAN Lopert, 1961, Soviet
WAR AND PEACE Continental, 1968, Soviet
WATERLOO Paramount, 1971, Italian-Soviet
THEY FOUGHT FOR THEIR MOTHERLAND Mosfilm, 1974, Soviet
THE STEPPE IFEX Film/Sovexport film, 1977, Soviet
RED BELLS: MEXICO IN FLAMES Mosfilm/Conacite-2/RAI/Vides International/Cinefin, 1982, Soviet-Mexican-Italian
RED BELLS: I'VE SEEN THE BIRTH OF THE NEW WORLD Mosfilm/Conacite-2/Vides International, 1983, Soviet-Mexican-Italian

PETER BONERZ*

Agent: Laurie Perlman, CAA - Los Angeles, 213/277-4545

NOBODY'S PERFEKT Columbia, 1981

JOHN BOORMAN*

b. January 18, 1933 - Shepperton, Middlesex, England
Business Manager: Edgar F. Gross, International Business Management - Los Angeles, 213/277-4455

HAVING A WILD WEEKEND *CATCH US IF YOU CAN* Warner Bros., 1965, British
POINT BLANK MGM, 1967
HELL IN THE PACIFIC Cinerama Releasing Corporation, 1968
LEO THE LAST United Artists, 1970, British
DELIVERANCE ★ Warner Bros., 1972
ZARDOZ 20th Century-Fox, 1974, British
THE HERETIC: EXORCIST II Warner Bros., 1977
EXCALIBUR Orion/Warner Bros., 1981, British-Irish
THE EMERALD FOREST Embassy, 1985, British

ROBERT BORIS

Agent: Rand Holston, CAA - Los Angeles, 213/277-4545

OXFORD BLUES MGM/UA, 1984, British

PHILLIP BORSOS

Agent: Michael Marcus, CAA - Los Angeles, 213/277-4545

THE GREY FOX United Artists Classics, 1983, Canadian
THE MEAN SEASON Orion, 1985

JOHN BOULTING

b. November 21, 1913 - Bray, Buckinghamshire, England
Business: Charter Film Productions Ltd., 8A Glebe Place, London 5W351B, England, 01/352-6838

JOURNEY TOGETHER RKO Radio, 1945, British
YOUNG SCARFACE *BRIGHTON ROCK* Mayer-Kingsley, 1947, British
SEVEN DAYS TO NOON Mayer-Kingsley, 1950, British
THE MAGIC BOX Rank, 1952, British
CREST OF THE WAVE *SEAGULLS OVER SORRENTO* co-director with Roy Boulting, MGM, 1954, British
PRIVATE'S PROGRESS DCA, 1956, British
LUCKY JIM Kingsley International, 1957, British
I'M ALL RIGHT, JACK Columbia, 1960, British
THE RISK *SUSPECT* co-director with Roy Boulting, Kingsley International, 1961, British
HEAVEN'S ABOVE! Janus, 1963, British
ROTTEN TO THE CORE Cinema 5, 1965, British

ROY BOULTING*

b. November 21, 1913 - Bray, Buckinghamshire, England
Business: Charter Film Productions Ltd., 8A Glebe Place, London 5W351B, England, 01/352-6838
Agent: John Redway & Associates - London, 01/637-1612 or Martin Baum, CAA - Los Angeles, 213/277-4545

TRUNK CRIME Angelo, 1939, British
INQUEST Grand National, 1939, British
PASTOR HALL United Artists, 1940, British
THUNDER ROCK English Films, 1942, British
DESERT VICTORY (FD) Army Film Unit, 1943, British
TUNISIAN VICTORY (FD) co-director with Frank Capra, Army Film Unit, 1943, British
BURMA VICTORY (FD) Army Film Unit, 1945, British
THE OUTSIDER *THE GUINEA PIG* Pathe, 1948, British
FAME IS THE SPUR Two Cities, 1949, British
HIGH TREASON Rank, 1951, British
SAILOR OF THE KING *SINGLE-HANDED* 20th Century-Fox, 1953, British

ROY BOULTING*—continued

CREST OF THE WAVE *SEAGULLS OVER SORRENTO* co-director with John Boulting, MGM, 1954
JOSEPHINE AND MEN 1955, British
RUN FOR THE SUN United Artists, 1956, British
BROTHERS IN LAW British Lion, 1957, British
HAPPY IS THE BRIDE Kassler, 1959, British
MAN IN A COCKED HAT *CARLTON-BROWNE OF THE F.O.* co-director with Jeffrey Dell, Show Corporation, 1960, British
A FRENCH MISTRESS Films Around the World, 1960, British
THE RISK *SUSPECT* co-director with John Boulting, Kingsley International, 1961, British
THE FAMILY WAY Warner Bros., 1967, British
TWISTED NERVE National General, 1969, British
THERE'S A GIRL IN MY SOUP Columbia, 1970, British
UNDERCOVERS HERO *SOFT BEDS AND HARD BATTLES* United Artists, 1975, British
THE LAST WORD The Samuel Goldwyn Company, 1979

JENNY BOWEN

STREET MUSIC Specialty, 1982
ANIMAL BEHAVIOR The Rasmussen Company/The Sundance Institute, 1985

GEORGE BOWERS*

Contact: Directors Guild of America - Los Angeles, 213/656-1220

THE HEARSE Crown International, 1980
BODY AND SOUL Cannon, 1982
MY TUTOR Crown International, 1983

BILL BRAME*

b. June 28, 1928
Home: 1111 Heatherside Drive, Pasadena, CA 91105, 818/795-6389

CYCLE SAVAGES Trans American, 1970
JIVE TURKEY Goldstone, 1976

MARLON BRANDO*

b. April 3, 1924 - Omaha, Nebraska
Contact: Directors Guild of America - Los Angeles, 213/656-1220

ONE-EYED JACKS Paramount, 1961

CHARLES BRAVERMAN*

Agent: Bob Crestani/Mike Simpson, William Morris Agency - Beverly Hills, 213/274-7451
Business: Crossover Programming Company, 1237 7th Street, Santa Monica, CA 90401, 213/451-9762

HIT AND RUN *REVENGE SQUAD* Comworld, 1982

ROBERT BRESSON

b. September 25, 1907 - Bromont-Lamothe, France
Contact: French Film Office, 745 Fifth Avenue, New York, NY 10151, 212/832-8860

LES AFFAIRES PUBLIQUE Arc Films, 1934, French
LES ANGES DU PECHE Synops/Roland Tual, 1943, French
THE LADIES OF THE PARK Brandon, 1945, French
DIARY OF A COUNTRY PRIEST Brandon, 1950, French
A MAN ESCAPED Continental, 1956, French
PICKPOCKET New Yorker, 1959, French
THE TRIAL OF JOAN OF ARC Pathe Contemporary, 1962, French

ROBERT BRESSON —continued

AU HASARD, BALTHAZAR Cinema Ventures, 1966, French
MOUCHETTE 1967, French
UNE FEMME DOUCE New Yorker, 1969, French
FOUR NIGHTS OF A DREAMER New Yorker, 1972, French
LANCELOT OF THE LAKE New Yorker, 1975, French-Italian
LE DIABLE PROBABLEMENT Gaumont, 1977, French
L'ARGENT (MONEY) Cinecom International, 1983, French-Swiss

MARTIN BREST*

b. 1951 - New York, New York
Agent: Jack Rapke, CAA - Los Angeles, 213/277-4545

HOT TOMORROWS American Film Institute, 1977
GOING IN STYLE Warner Bros., 1979
BEVERLY HILLS COP Paramount, 1984

MARSHALL BRICKMAN*

Business Manager: Bernstein & Freedman, 228 West 55th Street, New York, NY 10019

SIMON Orion/Warner Bros., 1980
LOVESICK The Ladd Company/Warner Bros., 1983

PAUL BRICKMAN*

Agent: Triad Artists, Inc - Los Angeles, 213/556-2727

RISKY BUSINESS The Geffen Company/Warner Bros., 1983

ALAN BRIDGES

b. September 28, 1928 - Liverpool, England
Home: The Old Manor Farm, Church Street, Sunbury-on-Thames, Middlesex TW16 6RG, England, Tel.: 76-80166
Agent: John Redway & Associates - London, 01/637-1612

ACT OF MURDER Warner-Pathe/Anglo-Amalgamated, 1964, British
INVASION Warner-Pathe/Anglo-Amalgamated, 1966, British
THE LIE 1970, British
THE HIRELING Columbia, 1973, British
BRIEF ENCOUNTER (TF) Carlo Ponti Productions/Cecil Clarke Productions, 1974, British
OUT OF SEASON Athenaeum, 1975, British
AGE OF INNOCENCE Rank, 1977, British-Canadian
LA PETITE FILLE EN VELOURS BLEU Warner-Columbia, 1978, French
RAIN ON THE ROOF (TF) London Weekend TV, 1980, British
VERY LIKE A WHALE Black Lion, 1981, British
THE RETURN OF THE SOLDIER Golden Communications, 1982, British
PUDDN'HEAD WILSON (TF) The Great Amwell Company/Nebraska ETV Network/Taurus Film, 1984, U.S.-West German
THE SHOOTING PARTY European Classics, 1984, British

BEAU BRIDGES*

(Lloyd Vernet Bridges III)

b. December 9, 1941 - Los Angeles, California
Agent: Jack Rapke, CAA - Los Angeles, 213/277-4545

THE KID FROM NOWHERE (TF) Cates-Bridges Company, telefeature, 1982

JAMES BRIDGES*

b. February 3, 1936 - Paris, Arkansas
Agent: Michael Ovitz, CAA - Los Angeles, 213/277-4545
Business Manager: Ron Koblin - Beverly Hills, 213/854-4420

THE BABY MAKER National General, 1970
THE PAPER CHASE 20th Century-Fox, 1973
9/30/55 *SEPTEMBER 30, 1955* Universal, 1977
THE CHINA SYNDROME Columbia, 1979
URBAN COWBOY Paramount, 1980
MIKE'S MURDER The Ladd Company/Warner Bros., 1984
PERFECT! Columbia, 1985

BURT BRINCKERHOFF*

b. October 25, 1936
Agent: Fred Westheimer, William Morris Agency - Beverly Hills, 213/274-7451

TWO BROTHERS (TF) KCET-TV, 1976
DOGS R.C. Riddell, 1977
ACAPULCO GOLD R.C. Riddell, 1978
THE CRACKER FACTORY (TF) Roger Gimbel Productions/EMI TV, 1979
CAN YOU HEAR THE LAUGHTER? THE STORY OF FREDDIE PRINZE (TF) Roger Gimbel Productions/EMI TV, 1979
MOTHER AND DAUGHTER - THE LOVING WAR (TF) Edgar J. Scherick Associates, 1980
BRAVE NEW WORLD (TF) Universal TV, 1980
THE DAY THE WOMEN GOT EVEN (TF) Otto Salaman Productions/PKO, 1980
BORN TO BE SOLD (TF) Ron Samuels Productions, 1981

JOHN BRODERICK

THE WARRIOR AND THE SORCERESS New World, 1984

KEVIN BRODIE*

Home: 32752 Pacific Coast Highway, Malibu, CA 90265, 213/506-4280
Business: Ice Corporation, 6051 Case Street, North Hollywood, CA 91606, 818/760-6745

MUGSY'S GIRLS Shapiro Entertainment/Spectrum Cinema/Ice Corporation, 1984

HUGH BRODY

Contact: British Academy of Film & Television Arts, 195 Piccadilly, London WI, England, 01/734-0022

1919 Spectrafilm, 1985, British

REX BROMFIELD

Business: Bromfilms, Inc., 1237 Howe Street, Vancouver, British Columbia, Canada

LOVE AT FIRST SIGHT Movietown, 1977, Canadian
TULIPS co-director with Mark Warren & Al Waxman under the collective pseudonym of Stan Ferris, Avco Embassy, 1981, Canadian
MELANIE Jensen Farley Pictures, 1983, Canadian

PETER BROOK

b. March 21, 1925 - London, England
Address: c/o C.I.C.T., 9 Rue du Cirque, Paris 8, France

THE BEGGAR'S OPERA Warner Bros., 1953, British
MODERATO CANTABILE Royal International, 1963, French-Italian
LORD OF THE FLIES Continental, 1963, British

PETER BROOK —continued

THE PERSECUTION AND ASSASINATION OF JEAN-PAUL MARAT AS PERFORMED BY THE INMATES OF THE ASYLUM OF CHARENTON UNDER THE DIRECTION OF THE MARQUIS DE SADE United Artists, 1967, British
TELL ME LIES Continental, 1968, British
KING LEAR Altura, 1971, British-Danish
MEETINGS WITH REMARKABLE MEN Libra, 1979, British
LA TRAGEDIE DE CARMEN MK2/Alby Films/Antenne-2, 1983, French

ADAM BROOKS

ALMOST YOU TLC Films/20th Century Fox, 1984

ALBERT BROOKS*

b. July 22, 1947 - Los Angeles, California
Business Manager: Gelfand & Macnow - Los Angeles, 213/553-1707

REAL LIFE Paramount, 1979
MODERN ROMANCE Columbia, 1981
LOST IN AMERICA The Geffen Company/Warner Bros., 1985

BOB BROOKS*

Business: BFCS Ltd., 59 North Wharf Street, London W2, England, 01/402-5561
Agent: Anthony Jones, A.D. Peters Ltd., 10 Buckingham Street, London WC2, England, 01/839-2556

THE KNOWLEDGE (TF) 1979, British
TATTOO 20th Century-Fox, 1981

JAMES L. BROOKS*

b. May 9, 1940 - Brooklyn, New York
Business: 20th Century Fox, P.O. Box 900, Beverly Hills, CA 91403, 213/277-2211

TERMS OF ENDEARMENT ★★ Paramount, 1983

JOSEPH BROOKS*

Business: Chancery Lane Films, Inc., 41-A East 74th Street, New York NY 10021, 212/759-8720

YOU LIGHT UP MY LIFE Columbia, 1977
IF EVER I SEE YOU AGAIN Columbia, 1978
HEADIN' FOR BROADWAY 20th Century-Fox, 1980
INVITATION TO THE WEDDING Chancery Lane Films, 1984, British

MEL BROOKS
(Melvin Kaminsky)

b. 1926 - New York, New York
Business: Brooksfilms Limited, 20th Century Fox, P.O. Box 900, Beverly Hills, CA 90213, 213/203-1375

THE PRODUCERS Avco Embassy, 1968
THE TWELVE CHAIRS UMC, 1970
BLAZING SADDLES Warner Bros., 1973
YOUNG FRANKENSTEIN 20th Century-Fox, 1974
SILENT MOVIE 20th Century-Fox, 1976
HIGH ANXIETY 20th Century-Fox, 1977
HISTORY OF THE WORLD, PART I 20th Century-Fox, 1981

RICHARD BROOKS*

b. May 18, 1912 - Philadelphia, Pennsylvania
Attorney: Gerald Lipsky - Beverly Hills, 213/878-4100

CRISIS MGM, 1950
THE LIGHT TOUCH MGM, 1951
DEADLINE - U.S.A. MGM, 1952
BATTLE CIRCUS MGM, 1953
TAKE THE HIGH GROUND MGM, 1953
FLAME AND THE FLESH MGM, 1954
THE LAST TIME I SAW PARIS MGM, 1954
THE BLACKBOARD JUNGLE MGM, 1955
THE LAST HUNT MGM, 1956
THE CATERED AFFAIR MGM, 1956
SOMETHING OF VALUE MGM, 1957
CAT ON A HOT TIN ROOF ★ MGM, 1958
THE BROTHERS KARAMAZOV MGM, 1958
ELMER GANTRY United Artists, 1960
SWEET BIRD OF YOUTH MGM, 1962
LORD JIM Columbia, 1964
THE PROFESSIONALS ★ Columbia, 1966
IN COLD BLOOD ★ Columbia, 1967
THE HAPPY ENDING United Artists, 1969
$ *DOLLARS* Columbia, 1971
BITE THE BULLET Columbia, 1975
LOOKING FOR MR. GOODBAR Paramount, 1977
WRONG IS RIGHT Columbia, 1982
THE FEVER MGM/UA, 1985

BARRY BROWN*

Messages: 213/340-2184

THE WAY WE LIVE NOW United Artists, 1970
CLOUD DANCER Blossom, 1980

GEORG STANFORD BROWN*

b. June 24 - Havana, Cuba
Agent: ICM - Los Angeles, 213/550-4000
Personal Manager: Jules Sharr, Jules Sharr Enterprises - Los Angeles, 213/278-1981

ROOTS: THE NEXT GENERATIONS (MS) co-director with John Erman, Charles Dubin & Lloyd Richards, Wolper Productions, 1979
GRAMBLING'S WHITE TIGER (TF) Jenner-Wallach Productions/Inter Planetary Productions, 1981

JIM BROWN

WASN'T THAT A TIME! (FD) United Artists Classics, 1982
HARD TRAVELIN' (TD) Ginger Group/Harold Leventhal Management, 1984
MUSICAL PASSAGE (FD) Films Inc., 1984

KIRK BROWNING*

b. May 28, 1921 - New York, New York
Home: 80 Central Park West, New York, NY 10023
Messages: 212/595-6474

BIG BLONDE (TF) PBS-TV, 1980

FRANCO BRUSATI

Contact: Ministry of Tourism & Education, Via Della Ferratella, No. 51, 00184 Rome, Italy, 06/7732

BREAD AND CHOCOLATE World Northal, 1978, Italian
TO FORGET VENICE Quartet, 1980, Italian-French
THE GOOD SOLDIER Gaumont, 1982, Italian

LARRY BUCHANAN*

Home: 5440 Lindley Avenue, Encino, CA 91316, 818/344-0976

FREE, WHITE AND 21 American International, 1963
UNDER AGE Falcon International, 1964
THE TRIAL OF LEE HARVEY OSWALD Falcon International, 1964
ZONTAR - THE THING FROM VENUS American International, 1966
CREATURE OF DESTRUCTION American International, 1967
HELL RAIDERS American International, 1968
MARS NEEDS WOMEN American International, 1968
STRAWBERRIES NEED RAIN 1970
A BULLET FOR PRETTY BOY American International, 1970
GOODBYE, NORMA JEAN Stirling Gold, 1976
HUGHES AND HARLOW: ANGELS IN HELL Pro International, 1978
THE LOCH NESS HORROR Omni-Leisure International, 1982
DOWN ON US Omni-Leisure International, 1984

MARK BUNTZMAN

EXTERMINATOR 2 Cannon, 1984

JUAN BUÑUEL

b. November 9, 1934 - Paris, France
Home: 6, Rue Leneveux, Paris 75014, France, Tel.: 540 53 94
Agent: Anne Alvarez Correa, 18, Rue Troyon, Paris 75017, France, Tel.: 755 80 85

AU RENDEZ-VOUS DE LA MORT JOYEUSE United Artists, 1972, French
LA FEMME AUX BOTTES ROUGES UGC/CFDC, 1974, French-Spanish
LEONOR CIC, 1975, French-Italian-Spanish

DEREK BURBIDGE

Agent: Zoetrope Ltd., Zoetrope House, 93 Union Road, London SW4 6JD, England, 01/720-8513
Contact: Directors Guild of Great Britain, 56 Whitfield Street, London W1, England, 01/580-9592

URGH! A MUSIC WAR (FD) Filmways, 1982
MEN WITHOUT WOMEN (FD) 1983

STUART BURGE

b. January 15, 1918 - Brentwood, England
Contact: Directors Guild of Great Britain, 56 Whitfield Street, London W1, England, 01/580-9592

THERE WAS A CROOKED MAN United Artists, 1962, British
UNCLE VANYA Arthur Cantor, 1963, British
OTHELLO Warner Bros., 1967, British
THE MIKADO Warner Bros., 1967, British
JULIUS CAESAR American International, 1971, British

MARTYN BURKE

Business: 113 N. San Vicente Blvd., Beverly Hills, CA 90211, 213/655-4115
Agent: Cheryl Peterson, CAA - Los Angeles, 213/277-4545

THE CLOWN MURDERS Canadian
POWER PLAY Magnum International Pictures/Cowry Film Productions, 1978, Canadian-British
THE LAST CHASE Crown International, 1981, Canadian

JAMES BURROWS*

b. December 30, 1940 - Los Angeles, California
Agent: Bob Broder, Broder-Kurland Agency - Los Angeles, 213/274-8921

MORE THAN FRIENDS (TF) Reiner-Mishkin Productions/Columbia TV, 1978
PARTNERS Paramount, 1982

WILLIAM J. BUSHNELL, JR.*

Home: 11972 Sunshine Terrace Drive, Los Angeles, CA 90068, 213/469-1517
Business: Los Angeles Actors' Theatre, 1089 N. Oxford Avenue, Los Angeles, CA 90029, 213/464-5603
Personal Manager: Harvey Shotz, The Shotz Group - Los Angeles, 213/659-4030

PRISONERS 1973
THE FOUR DEUCES Avco Embassy, 1974

ROBERT BUTLER*

b. November 17, 1927 - Los Angeles, California
Agent: Jim Wiatt, ICM - Los Angeles, 213/550-4273

THE COMPUTER WORE TENNIS SHOES Buena Vista, 1970
THE BAREFOOT EXECUTIVE Buena Vista, 1971
SCANDALOUS JOHN Buena Vista, 1971
DEATH TAKES A HOLIDAY (TF) Universal TV, 1971
NOW YOU SEE HIM, NOW YOU DON'T Buena Vista, 1972
THE BLUE KNIGHT (TF) ☆ Lorimar Productions, 1973
THE ULTIMATE THRILL General Cinema, 1974
STRANGE NEW WORLD (TF) Warner Brothers TV, 1975
DARK VICTORY (TF) Universal TV, 1976
JAMES DEAN (TF) The Jozak Company, 1976
MAYDAY AT 40,000 FEET (TF) Andrew J. Fenady Associates/Warner Brothers TV, 1976
IN THE GLITTER PALACE (TF) The Writer's Company/Columbia TV, 1977
HOT LEAD AND COLD FEET Buena Vista, 1978
A QUESTION OF GUILT (TF) Lorimar Productions, 1978
LACY AND THE MISSISSIPPI QUEEN (TF) Lawrence Gordon Productions/Paramount TV, 1978
NIGHT OF THE JUGGLER Columbia, 1980
UNDERGROUND ACES Filmways, 1981
UP THE CREEK Orion, 1983
CONCRETE BEAT (TF) Picturemaker Productions/Viacom, 1984

JOHN BYRUM*

b. March 14, 1947 - Evanston, Illinois
Agent: Rick Nicita, CAA - Los Angeles, 213/277-4545
Business Manager: Bob Colbert, Guild Management - Los Angeles, 213/277-9711

INSERTS United Artists, 1976, British
HEART BEAT Orion/Warner Bros., 1980
THE RAZOR'S EDGE Columbia, 1984

C

JAMES CAAN *

b. March 26, 1939 - Bronx, New York
Agent: Martin Baum, CAA - Los Angeles, 213/277-4545
Business Manager: Licker & Pines, 9025 Wilshire Blvd., Beverly Hills, CA 90211, 213/858-1276

HIDE IN PLAIN SIGHT MGM/United Artists, 1980

MICHAEL CACOYANNIS

b. June 11, 1922 - Cyprus
Contact: Greek Film Centre, Panepistimiou Street, Athens 134, Greece, 1/363-4586

WINDFALL IN ATHENS Audio Brandon, 1953, Greek
STELLA Milas Films, 1955, Greek
THE FINAL LIE Finos Films, 1958, Greek
OUR LAST SPRING Cacoyannis, 1959, Greek
A GIRL IN BLACK Kingsley International, 1959, Greek
THE WASTREL Lux/Tiberia, 1960, Italian
ELECTRA Lopert, 1962, Greek
ZORBA THE GREEK ★ International Classics, 1964, Greek
THE DAY THE FISH CAME OUT 20th Century-Fox, 1967, British-Greek
THE TROJAN WOMEN Cinerama Releasing Corporation, 1971, U.S.-Greek
THE STORY OF JACOB AND JOSEPH (TF) Screen Gems/Columbia TV, 1974
ATTILA '74 (FD) 1975, Greek
IPHIGENIA Cinema 5, 1977, Greek

MICHAEL CAFFEY *

Agent: Shapiro-Lichtman Agency - Los Angeles, 213/557-2244

SEVEN IN DARKNESS (TF) Paramount TV, 1969
THE SILENT GUN (TF) Paramount TV, 1969
THE DEVIL AND MISS SARAH (TF) Universal TV, 1971
THE HANGED MAN (TF) Fenady Associates/Bing Crosby Productions, 1974

CHRIS CAIN *

Agent: Fred Specktor, CAA - Los Angeles, 213/277-4545
Business: 5901 Clover Heights, Malibu, CA 90265, 213/457-3261

BROTHER, MY SONG Eagle International, 1976
GRAND JURY CCF, 1976
THE BUZZARD CCF, 1976
SIXTH AND MAIN National Cinema, 1977
THE STONE BOY TLC Films/20th Century Fox, 1984
THAT WAS THEN, THIS IS NOW Media Ventures/Allan Belkin Productions, 1985

JAMES CAMERON*

Agent: Bloom, Levy & Schorr Associates - Los Angeles, 213/659-6160

PIRHANA II - THE SPAWNING Saturn International, 1983, Italian-U.S.
THE TERMINATOR Orion, 1984

DOUGLAS CAMFIELD

b. London, England
Agent: London Management - London, 01/734-4192

IVANHOE (TF) Norman Rosemont Productions/Columbia TV, 1982, U.S.-British

DONALD CAMMELL*

Agent: Steve Reuther, William Morris Agency - Beverly Hills, 213/274-7451

PERFORMANCE co-director with Nicolas Roeg, Warner Bros., 1970, British
DEMON SEED MGM/United Artists, 1977

JOE CAMP*

b. April 20, 1939 - St. Louis, Missouri
Business: Mulberry Square Productions, 10300 N. Central Expressway, Dallas, Texas 75231, 214/369-2430

BENJI Mulberry Square, 1974
HAWMPS Mulberry Square, 1976
FOR THE LOVE OF BENJI Mulberry Square, 1978
THE DOUBLE McGUFFIN Mulberry Square, 1979
OH HEAVENLY DOG 20th Century-Fox, 1980

NORMAN CAMPBELL*

Home: 20 George Henry Blvd., Willowdale, Ontario M2J 1E2, Canada, 416/494-8576
Agent: Lee Gabler, ICM - Los Angeles, 213/550-4000

THE MAGIC SHOW Producers Distributing Company, 1983, Canadian

MICHAEL CAMPUS*

Home: 2121 Kress Street, Los Angeles, CA 90046, 213/656-2648
Agent: Ron Mardigian, William Morris Agency - Beverly Hills, 213/274-7451
Business Manager: Licker & Pines, 9025 Wilshire Blvd., Beverly Hills, CA 90211, 213/858-1276

Z.P.G. Paramount, 1972
THE MACK Cinerama Releasing Corporation, 1973
THE EDUCATION OF SONNY CARSON Paramount, 1974
THE PASSOVER PLOT Atlas, 1977, U.S.-Israeli

FRANK CAPRA*

b. May 18, 1897 - Palermo, Sicily
Home: P.O. Box 98, La Quinta, CA 92253

THE STRONG MAN First National, 1926
LONG PANTS First National, 1927
FOR THE LOVE OF MIKE First National, 1927
THAT CERTAIN THING Columbia, 1928
SO THIS IS LOVE Columbia, 1928
THE MATINEE IDOL Columbia, 1928
THE WAY OF THE STRONG Columbia, 1928
SAY IT WITH SABLES Columbia, 1928
SUBMARINE Columbia, 1928
THE POWER OF THE PRESS Columbia, 1928
THE YOUNGER GENERATION Columbia, 1929
THE DONOVAN AFFAIR Columbia, 1929

FRANK CAPRA*—continued

FLIGHT Columbia, 1929
LADIES OF LEISURE Columbia, 1930
RAIN OR SHINE Columbia, 1930
DIRIGIBLE Columbia, 1931
THE MIRACLE WOMAN Columbia, 1931
PLATINUM BLONDE Columbia, 1931
FORBIDDEN Columbia, 1932
AMERICAN MADNESS Columbia, 1932
THE BITTER TEA OF GENERAL YEN Columbia, 1933
LADY FOR A DAY ★ Columbia, 1933
IT HAPPENED ONE NIGHT ★★ Columbia, 1934
BROADWAY BILL Columbia, 1934
MR. DEEDS GOES TO TOWN ★★ Columbia, 1936
LOST HORIZON Columbia, 1937
YOU CAN'T TAKE IT WITH YOU ★★ Columbia, 1938
MR. SMITH GOES TO WASHINGTON ★ Columbia, 1939
MEET JOHN DOE Warner Bros., 1941
PRELUDE TO WAR (FD) U.S. Army, 1942
THE NAZIS STRIKE (FD) co-director with Anatole Litvak, U.S. Army, 1942
DIVIDE AND CONQUER (FD) co-director with Anatole Litvak, U.S. Army, 1943
BATTLE OF BRITAIN (FD) co-director, U.S. Army, 1943
BATTLE OF CHINA (FD) co-director with Anatole Litvak, U.S. Army, 1943
THE NEGRO SOLDIER (FD) U.S. Army, 1944
TUNISIAN VICTORY (FD) co-director with Roy Boulting, Army Film Unit, 1944, British
ARSENIC AND OLD LACE Warner Bros., 1944
KNOW YOUR ENEMY: JAPAN (FD) co-director with Joris Ivens, 1945
TWO DOWN AND ONE TO GO (FD) 1945
IT'S A WONDERFUL LIFE ★ RKO Radio, 1946
STATE OF THE UNION MGM, 1948
RIDING HIGH Paramount, 1950
HERE COMES THE GROOM Paramount, 1951
A HOLE IN THE HEAD United Artists, 1959
POCKETFUL OF MIRACLES United Artists, 1961

LAMAR CARD

b. September 8, 1942-Lookout Mountain, Tennessee
Business: 7318 Woodrow Wilson Drive, Los Angeles, CA 90046 213/851-1128

THE CLONES Premiere International, 1977
SUPERVAN New World, 1980
DISCO FEVER Group I, 1982

JACK CARDIFF

b. September 18, 1914 - Yarmouth, England
Agent: Eric L'Epine Smith, 10 Wyndham Place, London WI, England, 01/724-0739

WEB OF EVIDENCE *BEYOND THIS PLACE* Allied Artists, 1959, British
INTENT TO KILL 20th Century-Fox, 1959, British
HOLIDAY IN SPAIN 1960, British
SCENT OF MYSTERY Todd, 1960, British
SONS AND LOVERS ★ 20th Century-Fox, 1960, British
MY GEISHA Paramount, 1962
THE LION 20th Century-Fox, 1962, British
THE LONG SHIPS Columbia, 1964, British-Yugoslavian
YOUNG CASSIDY MGM, 1965, British
THE LIQUIDATOR MGM, 1966, British
DARK OF THE SUN *THE MERCENARIES* MGM, 1968, British
THE GIRL ON A MOTORCYCLE *NAKED UNDER LEATHER* Claridge, 1968, British-French
PENNY GOLD Scotia-Barber, 1973, British
THE MUTATIONS Columbia, 1974, British

J.S. CARDONE

THUNDER ALLEY Cannon, 1985

JOHN ''BUD'' CARDOS*

Home: 19116 Enadia Way, Reseda, CA 91335, 818/343-4077
Agent: Craig Rumar, F.A.M.E. - Los Angeles, 213/556-8071

SOUL SOLDIER *THE RED, WHITE AND BLACK* Fanfare, 1972
KINGDOM OF THE SPIDERS Dimension, 1977
THE DARK Film Ventures International, 1979
THE DAY TIME ENDED Compass International, 1979
NIGHT SHADOWS *MUTANT* Artists Releasing Corporation/Film Ventures International, 1984

GILLES CARLE

b. 1929 - Maniwaki, Quebec, Canada
Contact: Association des Realisateurs, 1406 Beaudry Street, Montreal, Quebec H2L 4K4, Canada, 514/843-7770

LA VIE HEUREUSE DE LÉOPOLD Z NFB, 1965, Canadian
PLACE A OLIVIER GUIMOND Onyx Films, 1966, Canadian
PLACE AUX JEROLAS Onyx Films, 1967, Canadian
LE VIOL D'UNE JEUNE FILLE DOUCE Onyx-Fournier, 1968, Canadian
RED Onyx Films/SMA, 1970, Canadian
LES MALES Onyx Films/France Films, 1970, Canadian
LES CHEVALIERS COFCI/ORTF, 1972, Canadian
LE VRAIE NATURE DE BERNADETTE Les Productions Carle-Lamy, 1972, Canadian
LES CORPS CELESTES Les Productions Carle-Lamy, 1973, Canadian
LA MORT D'UN BUCHERON Les Productions Carle-Lamy, 1973, Canadian
LA TETE DE NORMANDE ST. ONGE Les Productions Carle-Lamy, 1975, Canadian
THE ANGEL AND THE WOMAN RSL Productions, 1977, Canadian
NORMANDE Fred Baker Films, 1979, Canadian
FANTASTICA Les Productions du Verseau/El Productions, 1980, Canadian-French
THE PLOUFFE FAMILY ICC/Cine-London Productions, 1981, Canadian
THE GREAT CHESS MOVIE (FD) co-director with Camille Coudari, 1982, Canadian
MARIA CHAPDELAINE Astral Film Productions/Radio Canada/TFI, 1983, Canadian-French
THE CRIME OF OVIDE PLOUFFE 1984, Canadian

LEWIS JOHN CARLINO*

b. January 1, 1932 - New York, New York
Agent: Martin Baum, CAA - Los Angeles, 213/277-4545

THE SAILOR WHO FELL FROM GRACE WITH THE SEA Avco Embassy, 1976, British
THE GREAT SANTINI *THE ACE* Orion/Warner Bros., 1980
CLASS Orion, 1983

JOHN CARPENTER*

b. January 16, 1948 - Carthage, New York
Agent: David Gersh, The Gersh Agency - Beverly Hills, 213/274-6611

DARK STAR Jack H. Harris Enterprises, 1974
ASSAULT ON PRECINCT 13 Turtle Releasing Corporation, 1976
HALLOWEEN Compass International, 1978
SOMEONE IS WATCHING ME (TF) Warner Bros. TV, 1978
ELVIS (TF) Dick Clark Productions, 1979
THE FOG Avco Embassy, 1981
THE THING Universal, 1982
CHRISTINE Columbia, 1983
STARMAN Columbia, 1984

STEPHEN CARPENTER

THE DORM THAT DRIPPED BLOOD *PRANKS* co-director with Jeffrey Obrow, Artists Releasing Corporation/Film Ventures International, 1982
THE POWER co-director with Jeffrey Obrow, Artists Releasing Corporation/Film Ventures International, 1983

DAVID CARRADINE

b. December 8, 1936 - Hollywood, California

YOU AND ME Filmmakers International, 1975
AMERICANA Crown International, 1983

MICHAEL CARRERAS

b. 1927 - London, England
Contact: British Academy of Film & Television Arts, 195 Piccadilly, London W1, England, 01/734-0022

THE STEEL BAYONET United Artists, 1958, British
PASSPORT TO CHINA *VISA TO CANTON* Columbia, 1961, British
THE SAVAGE GUNS MGM, 1962, Spanish-U.S.
MANIAC Columbia, 1963, British
WHAT A CRAZY WORLD Warner-Pathe, 1963, British
THE CURSE OF THE MUMMY'S TOMB Columbia, 1965, British
PREHISTORIC WOMEN *SLAVE GIRLS* 20th Century-Fox, 1967, British
THE LOST CONTINENT 20th Century-Fox, 1968, British
CALL HIM MR. SHATTER Avco Embassy, 1975, British-Hong Kong

LARRY CARROLL

SWORDKILL Albert Band International/Empire International, 1984

THOMAS CARTER*

Agent: ICM - Los Angeles, 213/550-4000

TRAUMA CENTER (TF) Glen A. Larson Productions/Jeremac Productions/20th Century-Fox TV, 1983
CALL TO GLORY (TF) Tisch-Avnet Productions/Paramount TV, 1984
MIAMI VICE (TF) The Michael Mann Company/Universal TV, 1984

STEVE CARVER*

b. April 5, 1945 - Brooklyn, New York
Home: 1010 Pacific Avenue, Venice, CA 90291, 213/396-9905

THE ARENA New World, 1974
BIG BAD MAMA New World, 1974
CAPONE 20th Century-Fox, 1975
DRUM United Artists, 1976
FAST CHARLIE...THE MOONBEAM RIDER Universal, 1979
STEEL *LOOK DOWN AND DIE* World Northal, 1980
AN EYE FOR AN EYE Avco Embassy, 1981
LONE WOLF McQUADE Orion, 1983
ROAD TRIP Mt. Olympus Productions, 1985

JOHN CASSAVETES*

b. December 9, 1929 - New York, New York
Agent: ICM - Los Angeles, 213/550-4000

SHADOWS Lion International, 1961
TOO LATE BLUES Paramount, 1962
A CHILD IS WAITING United Artists, 1963
FACES Continental, 1968
HUSBANDS Columbia, 1970
MINNIE AND MOSKOWITZ Universal, 1971

JOHN CASSAVETES*—continued

A WOMAN UNDER THE INFLUENCE ★ Faces International, 1974
THE KILLING OF A CHINESE BOOKIE Faces International, 1976
OPENING NIGHT Faces International, 1979
GLORIA Columbia, 1980
LOVE STREAMS Cannon, 1984
BIG TROUBLE Columbia, 1985

NICK CASTLE*

Home: 8458 Ridpath Drive, Los Angeles, CA 90046, 213/656-2470
Personal Manager: Harry Ufland, Ufland-Roth Productions, 20th Century Fox, 10201 W. Pico Blvd., Executive Building Room 246, Los Angeles, CA 90035, 213/203-1295
Business Manager: Roy Skaff, Skaff & Kutcher, 17835 Ventura Blvd. - Suite 210, Encino, CA 91316, 213/344-4335

TAG New World, 1982
THE LAST STARFIGHTER Universal, 1984

GILBERT CATES*

b. June 6, 1934 - New York, New York
Business: Cates Brothers Company, 9200 Sunset Blvd., Los Angeles, CA 90069, 213/273-7773 or: 119 West 57th Street, New York, NY 10019, 212/765-1300
Agent: Jim Wiatt, ICM - Los Angeles, 213/550-4000

RINGS AROUND THE WORLD (FD) Columbia, 1967
I NEVER SANG FOR MY FATHER Columbia, 1970
TO ALL MY FRIENDS ON SHORE (TF) Jemmin & Jamel Productions, 1972
SUMMER WISHES, WINTER DREAMS Columbia, 1973
THE AFFAIR (TF) Spelling-Goldberg Productions, 1973
ONE SUMMER LOVE *DRAGONFLY* American International, 1976
JOHNNY, WE HARDLY KNEW YE (TF) Talent Associates/Jamel Productions, 1977
THE PROMISE Universal, 1979
THE LAST MARRIED COUPLE IN AMERICA Universal, 1980
OH, GOD! BOOK II Warner Bros., 1980
COUNTRY GOLD (TF) CBS Entertainment, 1982
HOBSON'S CHOICE (TF) CBS Entertainment, 1983
BURNING RAGE (TF) Gilbert Cates Productions, 1984

JOSEPH CATES*

b. 1924
Business: Cates Brothers Company, 9200 Sunset Blvd., Los Angeles, CA 90069, 213/273-7773 or: 119 West 57th Street, New York, NY 10019, 212/765-1300

GIRL OF THE NIGHT Warner Bros., 1960
WHO KILLED TEDDY BEAR? Magna, 1965
FAT SPY Magna, 1966

LILIANA CAVANI

b. January 12, 1936 - Capri, Italy
Contact: Ministry of Tourism & Education, Via Della Ferratella, No. 51, 00184 Rome, Italy, 06/7732

FRANCESCO D'ASSISI (TF) 1966, Italian
GALILEO Fenice Cinematografica/Rizzoli Film/Kinozenter, 1968, Italian-Bulgarian
I CANNIBALI 1969, Italian
L'OSPITE 1971, Italian
THE NIGHT PORTER Avco Embassy, 1974, Italian
MILAREPA Lotar Film, 1974, Italian
BEYOND GOOD AND EVIL International Showcase, 1977, Italian-French-West German
LA PELLE Triumph/Columbia, 1981, Italian-French
THE SECRET BEYOND THE DOOR Gaumont, 1982, Italian

JAMES CELLAN-JONES*

b. England
Home: 19 Cumberland Road, Kew, Surrey 13731, England, 01/940-8742
Agent: William Morris Agency - Beverly Hills, 213/274-7451

THE NELSON AFFAIR *A BEQUEST TO THE NATION* Universal, 1973, British
CAESAR AND CLEOPATRA (TF) NBC-TV, 1976, U.S.-British
SCHOOL PLAY (TF) BBC, 1979, British
THE DAY CHRIST DIED (TF) Martin Manulis Productions/20th Century-Fox TV, 1980
THE KINGFISHER (TF) 1982, British
SLEEPS SIX (TF) BBC, 1984, British

CLAUDE CHABROL

b. June 24, 1930 - Paris, France
Contact: French Film Office, 745 Fifth Avenue, New York, NY 10151, 212/832-8860

LE BEAU SERGE United Motion Picture Organization, 1958, French
THE COUSINS Films Around the World, 1959, French
LEDA *WEB OF PASSION/A DOUBLE TOUR* Times, 1959, French
LES BONNES FEMMES Robert Hakim, 1960, French-Italian
LES GODELUREAUX 1961, French
SEVEN CAPITAL SINS co-director with Jean-Luc Godard, Roger Vadim, Sylvaine Dhomme, Edouard Molinaro, Philippe De Broca, Jacques Demy, Marie-Jose Nat, Dominique Paturel, Jean-Marc Tennberg & Perrette Pradier, Embassy, 1962, French-Italian
L'OEIL DU MALIN 1962, French-Italian
OPHELIA New Line Cinema, 1962, French-Italian
LANDRU Embassy, 1963, French-Italian
LES PLUS BELLES ESCROQUERIES DU MONDE co-director, 1964, French-Italian-Japanese
LE TIGRE AIME LA CHAIR FRAICHE 1964, French-Italian
PARIS VU PAR... co-director, 1964, French
MARIE-CHANTAL CONTRE LE DOCTEUR KHA 1965, French-Italian-Moroccan
LE TIGRE SE PARFUME A LA DYNAMITE 1965, French-Spanish-Italian
LA LIGNE DE DEMARCATION 1966, French
THE CHAMPAGNE MURDERS *LE SCANDALE* Universal, 1967, French
LA ROUTE DE CORINTHE 1967, French-Italian-West German
LES BICHES VGC, 1968, French-Italian
LA FEMME INFIDELE Allied Artists, 1968, French-Italian
THIS MAN MUST DIE Allied Artists, 1969, French-Italian
LE BOUCHER Cinerama Releasing Corporation, 1969, French-Italian
LA RUPTURE New Line Cinema, 1970, French-Italian-Belgian
JUST BEFORE NIGHTFALL Libra, 1971, French-Italian
TEN DAYS' WONDER Levitt-Pickman, 1971, French
HIGH HEELS *DOCTEUR POPAUL* 1972, French-Italian
WEDDING IN BLOOD New Line Cinema, 1973, French-Italian
DE GREY - LE BANC DE DESOLATION (TF) 1973, French
THE NADA GANG *NADA* New Line Cinema, 1974, French-Italian
UNE PARTIE DE PLAISIR Joseph Green Pictures, 1975, French
DIRTY HANDS *LES INNOCENTS AUX MAIN SALES* New Line Cinema, 1975, French-Italian-West German
LES MAGICIENS 1975, French
FOLIES BOURGEOISES FFCM, 1976, French-Italian-West German
ALICE OU LA DERNIERE FUGUE Filmel-PHPG, 1977, French
LES LIENS DE SANG Filmcorp, 1978, Canadian-French
VIOLETTE *VIOLETTE NOZIERE* New Yorker, 1978, French
SPLINTERED 1980, French
LE CHEVAL D'ORGEUIL Planfilm, 1980, French
LES FANTOMES DU CHAPELIER Gaumont, 1982, French
THE BLOOD OF OTHERS (CMS) HBO Premiere Films/ICC/Filmax Productions, 1984, Canadian-French
POULET AU VINAIGRE MK2 Difussion, 1985, French

DON CHAFFEY*

b. August 5, 1917 - England
Home: 7020 La Presa Drive, Los Angeles, CA 90068, 213/851-0391
Agent: Ronald Leif, Contemporary-Korman Artists - Beverly Hills, 213/278-8250
Business Manager: Paul Gilbert, Oppenheim, Appel & Dixon - Los Angeles, 213/277-0400

THE MYSTERIOUS POACHER General Film Distributors, 1950, British
THE CASE OF THE MISSING SCENE General Film Distributors, 1951, British
SKID KIDS Associated British Film Distributors/Children's Film Foundation, 1953, British
TIME IS MY ENEMY Independent Film Distributors, 1954, British
THE SECRET TENT British Lion, 1956, British
THE GIRL IN THE PICTURE Eros, 1957, British
THE FLESH IS WEAK DCA, 1957, British
A QUESTION OF ADULTERY Eros, 1958, British
THE MAN UPSTAIRS Kingsley International, 1958, British
DANGER WITHIN British Lion, 1959, British
DENTIST IN THE CHAIR Ajay, 1960, British
LIES MY FATHER TOLD ME Eire, 1960, British
NEARLY A NASTY ACCIDENT Brittania, 1961, British
GREYFRIARS BOBBY Buena Vista, 1961, U.S.-British
A MATTER OF WHO Herts Lion, 1962, British
THE PRINCE AND THE PAUPER Buena Vista, 1962, U.S.-British
THE WEBSTER BOY RFI, 1963, British
THE HORSE WITHOUT A HEAD Buena Vista, 1963, British
JASON AND THE ARGONAUTS Columbia, 1963, British
THEY ALL DIED LAUGHING *A JOLLY BAD FELLOW* Continental, 1963, British
THE THREE LIVES OF THOMASINA Buena Vista, 1963, British-U.S.
THE CROOKED ROAD 7 Arts, 1965, British-Yugoslavian
ONE MILLION YEARS B.C. 20th Century-Fox, 1967, British
THE VIKING QUEEN American International, 1967, British
A TWIST OF SAND United Artists, 1968, British
CREATURES THE WORLD FORGOT Columbia, 1971, British
CLINIC XCLUSIVE Doverton, 1972, British
CHARLEY-ONE-EYE Paramount, 1973, British
THE TERROR OF SHEBA *PERSECUTION* Blueberry Hill, 1974, British
THE FOURTH WISH South Australian Film Corporation, 1975, Australian
HARNESS FEVER Walt Disney Productions, 1976, Australian
RIDE A WILD PONY *BORN TO RUN* Buena Vista, 1976, U.S.-Australian
SURF Trans-Atlantic Enterprises, 1977
PETE'S DRAGON Buena Vista, 1977
SHIMMERING LIGHT (TF) Australian Broadcasting Commission/Trans-Atlantic Enterprises, 1978, Australian
THE MAGIC OF LASSIE International Picture Show, 1978
THE GIFT OF LOVE (TF) Osmond Productions, 1978
C.H.O.M.P.S. American International, 1979
CASINO (TF) Trellis Productions/Aaron Spelling Productions, 1980

EVERETT CHAMBERS*

b. August 19, 1926 - Montrose, California
Business Manager: Arthur Gage, 1277 Sunset Plaza Drive, Los Angeles, CA 90069, 213/652-4118

RUN ACROSS THE RIVER Omat Corporation, 1959
THE LOLLIPOP COVER Continental, 1964

MATTHEW CHAPMAN

b. September 2, 1950
Address: 38 Portland Road, London W11, England

HUSSY Watchgrove Ltd., 1980, British
STRANGERS KISS Orion Classics, 1984

MICHAEL CHAPMAN*

Personal Manager: Keith Addis, Keith Addis & Associates - Beverly Hills, 213/655-6103

ALL THE RIGHT MOVES 20th Century-Fox, 1983
THE CLAN OF THE CAVE BEAR Warner Bros., 1985

DOUGLAS CHEEK*

Contact: Directors Guild of America - New York City, 212/581-0370

C.H.U.D. New World, 1984

MARVIN J. CHOMSKY*

b. May 23, 1929 - New York, New York
Agent: Len Hirshan, William Morris Agency - Beverly Hills, 213/274-7451
Business Manager: David B. Cohen, Plant, Cohen & Co., 9777 Wilshire Blvd., Beverly Hills, CA 90212, 213/278-6171

ASSAULT ON THE WAYNE (TF) Paramount TV, 1971
MONGO'S BACK IN TOWN (TF) Bob Banner Associates, 1971
EVEL KNIEVEL Fanfare, 1972
FIREBALL FORWARD (TF) 20th Century-Fox TV, 1972
FAMILY FLIGHT (TF) Universal TV, 1972
FEMALE ARTILLERY (TF) Universal TV, 1973
THE MAGICIAN (TF) Paramount TV, 1973
MRS. SUNDANCE (TF) 20th Century-Fox TV, 1974
THE FBI STORY: THE FBI VERSUS ALVIN KARPIS, PUBLIC ENEMY NUMBER ONE (TF) QM Productions/Warner Bros. TV, 1974
ATTACK ON TERROR: THE FBI VS. THE KU KLUX KLAN (TF) QM Productions, 1975
MACKINTOSH AND T.J. Penland, 1975
LIVE A LITTLE, STEAL A LOT *MURPH THE SURF* American International, 1975
KATE McSHANE (TF) Paramount TV, 1975
BRINK'S: THE GREAT ROBBERY (TF) QM Productions/Warner Bros. TV, 1976
A MATTER OF WIFE...AND DEATH (TF) Columbia TV, 1976
LAW AND ORDER (TF) Paramount TV, 1976
ROOTS (MS) ☆ co-director with David Greene, John Erman & Gilbert Moses, Wolper Productions, 1977
LITTLE LADIES OF THE NIGHT (TF) Spelling-Goldberg Productions, 1977
DANGER IN PARADISE (TF) Filmways, 1977
HOLOCAUST (MS) ☆☆ Titus Productions, 1978
GOOD LUCK, MISS WYCKOFF Bel Air/Gradison, 1979
HOLLOW IMAGE (TF) Titus Productions, 1979
DOCTOR FRANKEN (TF) co-director with Jeff Lieberman, Titus Productions/Janus Productions 1980
ATTICA (TF) ☆☆ ABC Circle Films, 1980
KING CRAB (TF) Titus Productions, 1980
EVITA PERON (TF) Hartwest Productions/Zephyr Productions, 1981
MY BODY, MY CHILD (TF) Titus Productions, 1982
INSIDE THE THIRD REICH (TF) ☆☆ ABC Circle Films, 1982
I WAS A MAIL ORDER BRIDE (TF) Jaffe Productions/Tuxedo Limited Productions/MGM TV, 1982
TANK Universal, 1984
NAIROBI FAIR (TF) Robert Halmi Productions, 1984
ROBERT F. KENNEDY AND HIS TIMES (MS) Chris-Rose Productions/Columbia TV, 1985

THOMAS CHONG*

b. Edmonton, Canada
Business: C&C Brown Productions, Columbia Plaza, Burbank, CA 91505 213/954-3162

THE NEXT CHEECH & CHONG MOVIE Universal, 1980
CHEECH & CHONG'S NICE DREAMS Columbia, 1981
CHEECH & CHONG: STILL SMOKIN Paramount, 1983
CHEECH & CHONG'S THE CORSICAN BROTHERS Orion, 1984

ROGER CHRISTIAN

Contact: British Academy of Film & Television Arts, 195 Piccadilly, London W1, England, 01/734-0022

THE SENDER Paramount, 1982, U.S.-British
2084 VTC/Rediffusion Films, 1985, British

BYRON CHUDNOW*

Home: 918 S. Westgate Avenue - Suite 4, Los Angeles, CA 90049, 213/820-1066

THE DOBERMAN GANG Dimension, 1973
THE DARING DOBERMANS Dimension, 1973
THE AMAZING DOBERMANS Golden, 1976

MATT CIMBER

(Matteo Ottaviano)

SINGLE ROOM FURNISHED Crown International, 1968
CALLIOPE Moonstone, 1971
THE BLACK SIX Cinemation, 1974
THE CANDY TANGERINE MAN Moonstone, 1975
GEMINI AFFAIR Moonstone, 1975
LADY COCOA Dimension, 1975
THE WITCH WHO CAME FROM THE SEA Moonstone, 1976
BUTTERFLY Analysis, 1981
FAKE OUT Analysis, 1983
A TIME TO DIE Almi Films, 1983
HUNDRA Film Ventures International, 1984, Spanish
YELLOW HAIR AND THE FORTRESS OF GOLD Crown International, 1984, Spanish
RIGGED Cinestar Films, 1985

MICHAEL CIMINO*

b. 1943
Agent: Sue Mengers, ICM - Los Angeles, 213/550-4000
Attorney: Barry Hirsch, Armstrong, Hendler & Hirsch - Los Angeles, 213/553-0305

THUNDERBOLT AND LIGHTFOOT United Artists, 1974
THE DEER HUNTER ★★ Universal, 1978
HEAVEN'S GATE United Artists, 1980
YEAR OF THE DRAGON MGM/UA, 1985

RICHARD CIUPKA

Home: 71 Cornwall Street, Town of Mount Royal, Montreal, Quebec H3P 1M6, Canada, 514/738-9996

CURTAINS directed under pseudonym of Jonathan Stryker, Jensen Farley Pictures, 1983, Canadian

BOB CLARK*

b. 1941 - New Orleans, Louisiana
Business: Brandywine Productions, 287A Park Avenue, Long Beach, CA 90803, 213/438-6851
Agent: Michael Marcus, CAA - Los Angeles, 213/277-4545
Business Manager: Harold Cohen - New York City, 212/550-0570

DEATHDREAM 1972, Canadian
CHILDREN SHOULDN'T PLAY WITH DEAD THINGS Gemini Film, 1972, Canadian
DEATH OF NIGHT Europix International, 1974, Canadian
BLACK CHRISTMAS *SILENT NIGHT, EVIL NIGHT/STRANGER IN THE HOUSE* Warner Bros., 1975, Canadian
BREAKING POINT 20th Century-Fox, 1976, Canadian
MURDER BY DECREE Avco Embassy, 1979, Canadian-British

BOB CLARK*—continued

TRIBUTE 20th Century-Fox, 1980, U.S.-Canadian
PORKY'S 20th Century-Fox, 1982, U.S.-Canadian
PORKY'S II: THE NEXT DAY 20th Century-Fox, 1983, U.S.-Canadian
A CHRISTMAS STORY MGM/UA, 1983, Canadian
RHINESTONE 20th Century Fox, 1984
TURK 182 20th Century Fox, 1985

BRUCE CLARK

NAKED ANGELS Favorite, 1969
THE SKI BUM Avco Embassy, 1971
HAMMER United Artists, 1972
GALAXY OF TERROR New World, 1981

FRANK C. CLARK

BEYOND THE REEF Universal, 1981

GREYDON CLARK

TOM Four Star International, 1973
BLACK SHAMPOO Dimension, 1976
THE BAD BUNCH Dimension, 1976
SATAN'S CHEERLEADERS World Amusement, 1977
HI-RIDERS Dimension, 1978
ANGELS BRIGADE Arista, 1980
WITHOUT WARNING Filmways, 1980
THE RETURN 1981
JOYSTICKS Jensen Farley Pictures, 1982
WACKO Jensen Farley Pictures, 1983
FINAL JUSTICE Arista, 1984

JAMES B. CLARK*

Home: 10051-5 Valley Circle Blvd., Chatsworth, CA 91311, 818/998-0962

UNDER FIRE 20th Century-Fox, 1957
SIERRA BARON 20th Century-Fox, 1958
VILLA! 20th Century-Fox, 1958
THE SAD HORSE 20th Century-Fox, 1959
A DOG OF FLANDERS 20th Century-Fox, 1960
ONE FOOT IN HELL 20th Century-Fox, 1960
THE BIG SHOW 20th Century-Fox, 1961, U.S.-West German
MISTY 20th Century-Fox, 1961
FLIPPER MGM, 1963
DRUMS OF AFRICA MGM, 1963
ISLAND OF THE BLUE DOLPHINS 20th Century-Fox, 1964
AND NOW MIGUEL Paramount, 1966
MY SIDE OF THE MOUNTAIN Paramount, 1969
THE LITTLE ARK National General, 1972

RON CLARK

Contact: Writers Guild of America, West - Los Angeles, 213/550-1000

THE FUNNY FARM New World, 1983, Canadian

JAMES KENELM CLARKE

Contact: British Academy of Film & Television Arts, 195 Piccadilly, London W1, England, 01/734-0022

FUNNY MONEY Cannon, 1983, British
YELLOW PAGES Richmond Productions, 1985

SHIRLEY CLARKE

b. 1925 - New York, New York
Business: UCLA Theatre Arts Department, 405 Hilgard Avenue, Los Angeles, CA 90024, 213/825-5761

DANCE IN THE SUN 1953
IN PARIS PARKS 1954
BULLFIGHT 1955
A MOMENT OF LOVE 1957
THE SKYSCRAPER co-director with Willard Van Dyke, 1958
LOOPS 1958
BRIDGES-GO-ROUND 1959
A SCARY TIME 1960
THE CONNECTION Films Around the World, 1962
THE COOL WORLD Cinema 5, 1964
PORTRAIT OF JASON (FD) Film-Makers, 1967

JAMES CLAVELL*

b. October 10, 1924 - Sydney, Australia
Agent: CAA - Los Angeles, 213/277-4545

FIVE GATES TO HELL 20th Century-Fox, 1959
WALK LIKE A DRAGON Paramount, 1960
TO SIR, WITH LOVE Columbia, 1967, British
THE SWEET AND THE BITTER Monarch, 1968, British
WHERE'S JACK? Paramount, 1969, British
THE LAST VALLEY Cinerama Releasing Corporation, 1971, British

WILLIAM F. CLAXTON*

b. October 22, 1914 - California
Home: 1065 Napoli Drive, Pacific Palisades, CA 90272, 213/454-3246
Agent: Ron Leif, Contemporary-Korman Artists - Beverly Hills, 213/278-8250

HALF PAST MIDNIGHT 20th Century-Fox, 1948
TUCSON 20th Century-Fox, 1949
ALL THAT I HAVE Family Films, 1951
STAGECOACH TO FURY 20th Century-Fox, 1956
THE QUIET GUN 20th Century-Fox, 1957
YOUNG AND DANGEROUS 20th Century-Fox, 1957
ROCKABILLY BABY 20th Century-Fox, 1957
GOD IS MY PARTNER 20th Century-Fox, 1957
DESIRE IN THE DUST 20th Century-Fox, 1960
YOUNG JESSE JAMES 20th Century-Fox, 1960
LAW OF THE LAWLESS Paramount, 1963
STAGE TO THUNDER ROCK Paramount, 1964
NIGHT OF THE LEPUS MGM, 1972

JACK CLAYTON*

b. 1921 - Brighton, England
Home: Heron's Flight, Highfield Park, Marlow, Buckinghamshire, England
Agent: Stan Kamen, William Morris Agency - Beverly Hills, 213/274-7451

ROOM AT THE TOP ★ Continental, 1959, British
THE INNOCENTS 20th Century-Fox, 1962, British
THE PUMPKIN EATER Royal International, 1964, British
OUR MOTHER'S HOUSE MGM, 1967, British
THE GREAT GATSBY Paramount, 1974
SOMETHING WICKED THIS WAY COMES Buena Vista, 1983

TOM CLEGG

Contact: British Academy of Film & Television Arts, 195 Piccadilly, London W1, England, 01/734-0022

LOVE IS A SPLENDID ILLUSION Schulman, 1970, British
SWEENEY 2 EMI, 1978, British
McVICAR Crown International, 1981, British

TOM CLEGG —continued

G'OLE! (FD) Warner Bros., 1983, British
THE INSIDE MAN Producers Enterprises/Nordisk Tonefilm/Terra Film International, 1984, British-Swedish
MOUNTBATTEN - THE LAST VICEROY (MS) George Walker TV Productions/Mobil Corporation, 1985, British

DICK CLEMENT*

b. September 5, 1937 - West Cliff-on-Sea, England
Home: 9700 Yoakum Drive, Beverly Hills, CA 90210, 213/276-4916
Business: Witzend Productions, 1600 N. Highland Avenue, Hollywood, CA 90028, 213/462-6185

OTLEY Columbia, 1969, British
A SEVERED HEAD Columbia, 1971, British
CATCH ME A SPY Rank, 1971, British
KEEP YOUR FINGERS CROSSED 1971, British
PORRIDGE ITC, 1979, British
BULLSHOT! HandMade Films, 1983, British

RENÉ CLEMENT

b. March 18, 1913 - Bordeaux, France
Contact: French Film Office, 745 Fifth Avenue, New York, NY 10151, 212/832-8860

LA BATAILLE DU RAIL 1946, French
LE PERE TRANQUILLE 1946, French
LES MAUDITS 1947, French
THE WALLS OF MALAPAGA Films International of America, 1949, Italian-French
LE CHÂTEAU DE VERRE 1950, French-Italian
FORBIDDEN GAMES Times, 1952, French
LOVERS, HAPPY LOVERS! *MONSIEUR RIPOIS/KNAVE OF HEARTS* 20th Century-Fox, 1954, French-British
GERVAISE Continental, 1956, French
THIS ANGRY AGE Columbia, 1958, Italian-French
PURPLE NOON Times, 1960, French-Italian
QUELLE JOIE DE VIVRE 1961, French-Italian
THE DAY AND THE HOUR MGM, 1962, French-Italian
JOY HOUSE *LES FELINS* MGM, 1964, French
IS PARIS BURNING? Paramount, 1966, French-U.S.
RIDER ON THE RAIN Avco Embassy, 1970, French-Italian
THE DEADLY TRAP *LA MAISON SOUS LES ARBRES* National General, 1971, French-Italian
...AND HOPE TO DIE *LA COURSE DU LIEVRE A TRAVERS LES CHAMPS* 20th Century-Fox, 1972, French
LA BABY-SITTER Titanus, 1975, Italian-French-Monacan

GRAEME CLIFFORD*

Agent: Lou Pitt, ICM - Los Angeles, 213/550-4000

FRANCES Universal/AFD, 1982
BURKE AND WILLS Michael Edgley Productions/Hoyts Theatres, 1985, Australian

PETER CLIFTON

Contact: British Academy of Film & Television Arts, 195 Piccadilly, London W1, England, 01/734-0022

POPCORN (FD) Sherpix, 1969, U.S.-Australian
SUPERSTARS IN FILM CONCERT (FD) National Cinema, 1971, British
THE SONG REMAINS THE SAME (FD) co-director with Joe Massot, Warner Bros., 1976, British
SWEET SOUL MUSIC (FD) 1977, British
THE LONDON ROCK & ROLL SHOW (FD) 1978, British
ROCK CITY *SOUND OF THE CITY: LONDON 1964-73 (FD)* Columbia, 1981, British

ROBERT CLOUSE*

Home: 454 Hotsprings Road, Santa Barbara, CA 93158, 805/969-4624
Agent: David Wardlow, ICM - Los Angeles, 213/550-4000

DARKER THAN AMBER National General, 1970
DREAMS OF GLASS Universal, 1970
ENTER THE DRAGON Warner Bros., 1973, U.S.-Hong Kong
BLACK BELT JONES Warner Bros., 1974
GOLDEN NEEDLES American International, 1974
THE ULTIMATE WARRIOR Warner Bros., 1976
THE AMSTERDAM KILL Columbia, 1978, U.S.-Hong Kong
THE PACK Warner Bros., 1978
GAME OF DEATH Columbia, 1979, U.S.-Hong Kong
THE OMEGA CONNECTION (TF) NBC-TV, 1979
THE KIDS WHO KNEW TOO MUCH (TF) Walt Disney Productions, 1980
THE BIG BRAWL Warner Bros., 1980
FORCE: FIVE American Cinema, 1981
NIGHT EYES *THE RATS* Warner Bros., 1983, Canadian
DARK WARRIOR Arista, 1984
GYMKATA MGM/UA, 1985

LEWIS COATES
(Luigi Cozzi)

Contact: Ministry of Tourism & Education, Via Della Ferratella, No. 51, 00184 Rome, Italy, 06/7732

LA PORTIERA NUDA CIA Cinematografica, 1975, Italian
L'ASSASSINO E COSTRETTO AD UCCIDERE ANCORA Albione Cinematografica/GIT International, 1976, Italian
DEDICATO A UNA STELLA Euro, 1978, Italian
STARCRASH New World, 1979, Italian
ALIEN CONTAMINATION Cannon, 1980, Italian-West German
HERCULES MGM/UA/Cannon, 1983, Italian
THE ADVENTURES OF HERCULES II Cannon, 1983, Italian

PETER COE

b. April 18, 1929 - London, England
Contact: British Academy of Film & Television Arts, 195 Piccadilly, London W1, England, 01/734-0022

LOCK UP YOUR DAUGHTERS Columbia, 1969, British

JOEL COEN

BLOOD SIMPLE Circle Releasing Corporation, 1984

ANNETTE COHEN

Home: 77 Roxborough Drive, Toronto, Ontario M4W 1X2, Canada, 416/364-4193 or 416/920-3745

LOVE co-director with Nancy Dowd, Liv Ullmann & Mai Zetterling, Velvet Films, 1982, Canadian

HOWARD R. COHEN

Agent: The Sy Fischer Company - Los Angeles, 213/557-0388

SATURDAY THE 14TH New World, 1981
SPACE RAIDERS New World, 1983

LARRY COHEN*

b. July 15, 1945 - New York, New York
Home: 2111 Coldwater Canyon Blvd., Beverly Hills, CA 90210, 213/550-7942
Personal Manager: The Robert Littman Company - Los Angeles, 213/278-1572
Attorney: Skip Brittenham, Ziffren, Brittenham & Gullen, 2049 Century Park East, Los Angeles, CA 90067, 213/552-3388

BONE Jack H. Harris Enterprises, 1972
BLACK CAESAR American International, 1973
HELL UP IN HARLEM American International, 1973
IT'S ALIVE Warner Bros., 1974
DEMON *GOD TOLD ME TO* New World, 1977
IT LIVES AGAIN Warner Bros., 1978
THE PRIVATE FILES OF J. EDGAR HOOVER American International, 1978
FULL MOON HIGH Filmways, 1981
Q United Film Distribution, 1982
BLIND ALLEY Hemdale, 1985
SPECIAL EFFECTS New Line Cinema, 1985
THE STUFF New World, 1985

ROB COHEN*

b. April 12, 1949 - Cornwall-on-the-Hudson, New York
Home: 1383 Miller Place, Los Angeles, CA 90069, 213/654-6289
Messages: 213/954-6635
Agent: Jack Rapke, CAA - Los Angeles, 213/277-4545

A SMALL CIRCLE OF FRIENDS United Artists, 1980
SCANDALOUS Orion, 1984

HARLEY COKLISS

b. February 11, 1945 - San Diego, California
Address: 25 Milman Road, London NW6, England, 01/960-6769
Agent: Duncan Heath Associates - London, 01/937-9898

THAT SUMMER Columbia, 1979, British
BATTLETRUCK *WARLORDS OF THE 21ST CENTURY* New World, 1982, U.S.-New Zealand
BLACK MOON RISING New World, 1985

RICHARD A. COLLA*

b. April 18, 1918 - Milwaukee, Wisconsin
Agent: Fred Westheimer, William Morris Agency - Beverly Hills, 213/274-7451

THE WORLD IS WATCHING (TF) Universal TV, 1969
ZIGZAG MGM, 1970
McCLOUD: WHO KILLED MISS U.S.A.? (TF) Universal TV, 1970
THE OTHER MAN (TF) Universal TV, 1970
SARGE: THE BADGE OR THE CROSS (TF) Universal TV, 1971
THE PRIEST KILLER (TF) Universal TV, 1971
FUZZ United Artists, 1972
TENAFLY (TF) Universal TV, 1973
THE QUESTOR TAPES (TF) Universal TV, 1974
LIVE AGAIN, DIE AGAIN (TF) Universal TV, 1974
THE TRIBE (TF) Universal TV, 1974
THE UFO INCIDENT (TF) Universal TV, 1975
OLLY OLLY OXEN FREE Sanrio, 1978
BATTLESTAR GALACTICA Universal, 1979
DON'T LOOK BACK (TF) TBA Productions/Satie Productions/TRISEME, 1981

ROBERT COLLECTOR

Contact: Writers Guild of America - Los Angeles, 213/550-1000

RED HEAT TAT Filmproductions/Aida United GMBH/International Screen, 1984, West German-U.S.

JAMES F. COLLIER*

Home: 11345 Brill Drive, Studio City, CA 91604, 818/986-1374

FOR PETE'S SAKE! World Wide, 1966
HIS LAND World Wide, 1967
TWO A PENNY World Wide, 1970, British
CATCH A PEBBLE World Wide, 1971, British
TIME TO RUN World Wide, 1972
THE HIDING PLACE World Wide, 1975
JONI World Wide, 1980
THE PRODIGAL World Wide, 1984

ROBERT COLLINS*

Agent: Bill Haber, CAA - Los Angeles, 213/277-4545

SERPICO: THE DEADLY GAME (TF) Dino De Laurentiis Productions/Paramount TV, 1976
THE LIFE AND ASSASSINATION OF THE KINGFISH (TF) Tomorrow Entertainment, 1977
WALK PROUD Universal, 1979
GIDEON'S TRUMPET (TF) Gideon Productions, 1980
SAVAGE HARVEST 20th Century-Fox, 1981
OUR FAMILY BUSINESS (TF) Lorimar Productions, 1981
MONEY ON THE SIDE (TF) Green-Epstein Productions/Hal Landers Productions/Columbia TV, 1982

LUIGI COMENCINI

b. June 8, 1916 - Salo, Brescia, Italy
Contact: Ministry of Tourism & Education, Via Della Ferratella, No. 51, 00184 Rome, Italy, 06/7732

PROIBITO RUBARE Lux Film, 1948, Italian
L'IMPERATORE DI CAPRI Lux Film, 1949, Italian
PERSIANE CHIUSE Rovere Film, 1951, Italian
HEIDI United Artists, 1952, Swiss
LA TRATTA DELLA BIANCHE Excelsa/Ponti/Dino De Laurentiis Cinematografica, 1952, Italian
BREAD, LOVE AND DREAMS Italian Film Export, 1953, Italian
LA VALIGIA DEI SOGNI Mambretti, 1954, Italian
FRISKY *PANE, AMORE E GELOSIA* DCA, 1954, Italian
LA BELLA DI ROMA Lux Film, 1955, Italian
LA FINESTRA SUL LUNA PARK Noria Film, 1957, Italian
MARITI IN CITTA Oscar Film/Morino Film, 1957, Italian
MOGLI PERICOLOSE Morino/Tempo Film, 1958, Italian
UND DAS AM MONTAGMORGEN 1959, West German
LA CORPRESE DELL'AMORE Morino/Tempo Film, 1959, Italian
EVERYBODY GO HOME! Royal Films International, 1960, Italian-French
A CAVALLO DELLA TIGRE Alfredo Bini, 1961, Italian
IL COMMISSARIO Dino De Laurentiis Cinematografica, 1962, Italian
BEBO'S GIRL Continental, 1963, Italian-French
TRE NOTTE D'AMORE co-director with Renato Costellani & Franco Rossi, Jolly Film/Cormoran Film, 1964, Italian-French
LA MIA SIGNORINA co-director, Dino De Laurentiis Cinematografica, 1964, Italian
BAMBOLE! co-director with Dino Risi, Franco Rossi & Mauro Bolognini, Royal Films International, 1965, Italian
IL COMPAGNO DON CAMILLO Rizzoli Film/Francoriz/Omnia Film, 1965, Italian-West German
LA BUGIARDA Ultra Film/Consortium Pathe/Tecisa, 1965, Italian-French-Spanish
INCOMPRESO 1966, Italian
ITALIAN SECRET SERVICE 1968, Italian
INFANZIA, VOCAZIONE E PRIME ESPERIENZE DI GIACOMO CASANOVA - VENEZIANO 1969, Italian
SENZA SAPERE NULLA DI LEI Rizzoli Film, 1969, Italian
LO SCOPONE SCIENTIFICO De Laurentiis, 1972, Italian
LE AVVENTURE DI PINOCCHIO RAI/ORTF/Bavaria Film, 1972, Italian-French-West German
DELITTO D'AMORE Documento Film, 1974, Italian
MIO DIO COME SONO CADUTA IN BASSO Dean Film, 1974, Italian
LA DONNA DELLA DOMENICA Prinex Italiana/Fox-Lira, 1975, Italian

LUIGI COMENCINI —continued

SUNDAY WOMAN 20th Century-Fox, 1976, Italian-French
LA GODURIA co-director, 1976, Italian
BASTA CHE NON SI SAPPIA IN GIRO co-director with Nanni Loy & Luigi Magni, Medusa, 1976, Italian
SIGNORE E SIGNORI BUONANOTTE co-director with Nanni Loy, Luigi Magni, Mario Monicelli & Ettore Scola, Titanus, 1976, Italian
QUELLE STRANE OCCASIONI co-director, Cineriz, 1977, Italian
TILL MARRIAGE US DO PART Franklin Media, 1977, Italian
TRA MOGLIE E MARITO 1977, Italian
L'AMORE IN ITALIA (TF) 1978, Italian
IL GATTO United Artists, 1978, Italian
TRAFFIC JAM *L'INGORGO* New Image, 1979, Italian-French-Spanish
THEY ALL LOVED HIM Medusa, 1980, Italian
VOLTATI EUGENIO Gaumont, 1981, Italian-French
CERCASI GESU Intercontinental/Nouvelle Cinevog, 1982, Italian-French
IL MATRIMONIO DI CATERINA (TF) 1982, Italian
CUORE (MS) RAI/Difilm/Antenne-2, 1984, Italian-French

RICHARD COMPTON*

Agent: John Gaines, APA - Los Angeles, 213/273-0744
Business Manager: Fred Altman - Beverly Hills, 213/278-4201

ANGELS DIE HARD New World, 1970
WELCOME HOME, SOLDIER BOYS 20th Century-Fox, 1972
MACON COUNTY LINE American International, 1974
RETURN TO MACON COUNTY American International, 1975
MANIAC New World, 1977
DEADMAN'S CURVE (TF) Roger Gimbel Productions/EMI TV, 1978
RAVAGES Columbia, 1979
WILD TIMES (TF) Metromedia Producers Corporation/Rattlesnake Productions, 1980

KEVIN CONNOR*

b. July 14, 1940 - London, England
Business Manager: Burton Merrill, Individual Productions, 4260 Arcola Avenue, Toluca Lake, CA 91602, 818/763-6903

FROM BEYOND THE GRAVE Howard Mahler Films, 1975, British
THE LAND THAT TIME FORGOT American International, 1975, British
AT THE EARTH'S CORE American International, 1976, British
DIRTY KNIGHTS' WORK *A CHOICE OF WEAPONS* Gamma III, 1976, British
THE PEOPLE THAT TIME FORGOT American International, 1977, British
WARLORDS OF ATLANTIS Columbia, 1978, British
ARABIAN ADVENTURE AFD, 1979, British
MOTEL HELL United Artists, 1980
GOLIATH AWAITS (TF) Larry White Productions/Hugh Benson Productions/ Columbia TV, 1981
THE HOUSE WHERE EVIL DWELLS MGM/UA, 1982, U.S.-Japanese
MASTER OF THE GAME (MS) co-director with Harvey Hart, Rosemont Productions, 1984
MISTRAL'S DAUGHTER (MS) co-director with Douglas Hickox, Steve Krantz Productions/R.T.L. Productions/Antenne-2, 1984, U.S.-French

WILLIAM CONRAD*

b. September 27, 1920 - Louisville, Kentucky
Home: P.O. Box 5289, Sherman Oaks, CA 91413, 818/343-5638
Agent: Rowland Perkins, CAA - Los Angeles, 213/277-4545

THE MAN FROM GALVESTON Warner Bros., 1964
TWO ON A GUILLOTINE Warner Bros., 1965
MY BLOOD RUNS COLD Warner Bros., 1965
BRAINSTORM Warner Bros., 1965
SIDE SHOW (TF) Krofft Entertainment, 1981

JAMES L. CONWAY

b. October 27, 1950 - New York, New York
Agent: Triad Artists, Inc. - Los Angeles, 213/556-2727

IN SEARCH OF NOAH'S ARK Sunn Classic, 1976
THE LINCOLN CONSPIRACY Sunn Classic, 1977
THE INCREDIBLE ROCKY MOUNTAIN RACE (TF) Sunn Classic Productions, 1977
THE LAST OF THE MOHICANS (TF) Sunn Classic Productions, 1977
BEYOND AND BACK Sunn Classic, 1978
DONNER PASS: THE ROAD TO SURVIVAL (TF) Sunn Classic Productions, 1978
GREATEST HEROES OF THE BIBLE (MS) Sunn Classic Productions, 1978
THE FALL OF THE HOUSE OF USHER Sunn Classic, 1979
HANGAR 18 Sunn Classic, 1980
THE LEGEND OF SLEEPY HOLLOW (TF) Sunn Classic, 1980
EARTHBOUND Taft International, 1981
NASHVILLE GRAB (TF) Taft International, 1981
THE BOOGENS Jensen Farley Pictures, 1981
THE PRESIDENT MUST DIE Jensen Farley Pictures, 1981

BRUCE COOK

THE CENSUS TAKER Argentum Productions, 1984

FIELDER COOK *

b. March 9, 1923 - Atlanta, Georgia
Home: 10585 Bradbury Road, Los Angeles, CA 90064
Messages: 213/838-0500
Agent: Triad Artists, Inc. - Los Angeles, 213/556-2727
Business Manager: Mortimer Leavy, Colton Weissberg, 505 Park Avenue, New York, NY 10022, 212/371-4350

PATTERNS United Artists, 1956
HOME IS THE HERO Showcorporation, 1961, Irish
A BIG HAND FOR THE LITTLE LADY Warner Bros., 1966
HOW TO SAVE A MARRIAGE AND RUIN YOUR LIFE Columbia, 1968
PRUDENCE AND THE PILL 20th Century-Fox, 1968, British
SAM HILL: WHO KILLED THE MYSTERIOUS MR. FOSTER? (TF) Universal TV, 1971
GOODBYE, RAGGEDY ANN (TF) Metromedia Producers Corporation, 1971
THE HOMECOMING (TF) ☆ Lorimar Productions, 1971
THE HANDS OF CORMAC JOYCE (TF) Crawford Productions/Foote, Cone & Belding, 1972
EAGLE IN A CAGE National General, 1972, British-Yugoslavian
MIRACLE ON 34TH STREET (TF) 20th Century-Fox TV, 1973
FROM THE MIXED-UP FILES OF MRS. BASIL E. FRANKWEILER *THE HIDEAWAYS* Cinema 5, 1973
THAT WAS THE WEST THAT WAS (TF) Universal TV, 1974
MILES TO GO BEFORE I SLEEP (TF) Tomorrow Entertainment, 1975
THE RIVALRY (TF) NBC-TV, 1975
VALLEY FORGE (TF) Clarion Productions/Columbia TV, 1975
BEAUTY AND THE BEAST (TF) Palms Films Ltd., 1976, British
JUDGE HORTON AND THE SCOTTSBORO BOYS (TF) ☆ Tomorrow Entertainment, 1976
A LOVE AFFAIR: THE ELEANOR AND LOU GEHRIG STORY (TF) Charles Fries Productions/Stonehenge Productions, 1977
TOO FAR TO GO (TF) Sea Cliff Productions, 1979
I KNOW WHY THE CAGED BIRD SINGS (TF) Tomorrow Entertainment, 1979
GAUGUIN THE SAVAGE (TF) Nephi Productions, 1980
FAMILY REUNION (TF) Creative Projects Inc./Columbia TV, 1981
WILL THERE REALLY BE A MORNING? (TF) Jaffe-Blakely Films/Sama Productions/Orion TV, 1983
WHY ME? (TF) Lorimar Productions, 1984

ALAN COOKE*

b. April 29, 1935 - London, England
Home: 7670 Woodrow Wilson Drive, Los Angeles, CA 90046, 213/851-7761
Agent: Martin Shapiro, Shapiro-Lichtman Agency - Los Angeles, 213/557-2244

FLAT TWO Anglo-Amalgamated, 1962, British
THE MIND OF MR. SOAMES Columbia, 1970, British
THE RIGHT PROSPECTUS (TF) BBC-TV, 1972, British
BLODWEN HOME FROM RACHEL'S MARRIAGE (TF) BBC-TV, 1976, British
THE HUNCHBACK OF NOTRE DAME (TF) BBC-TV, 1978, British
RENOIR, MY FATHER (TF) BBC-TV, 1979, British
COVER (MS) ITC, 1980, British
NADIA (TF) Dave Bell Productions/Tribune Entertainment Company/Jadran Film, 1984, U.S.-Yugoslavian

MARTHA COOLIDGE*

b. August 17, 1946 - New Haven, Connecticut
Agent: William Morris Agency - Beverly Hills, 213/274-7451

NOT A PRETTY PICTURE Films Incorporated, 1976
VALLEY GIRL Atlantic Releasing Corporation, 1983
JOY OF SEX Paramount, 1984
THE CITY GIRL Moon Pictures, 1984
REAL GENIUS Tri-Star, 1985

HAL COOPER*

Home: 2651 Hutton Drive, Beverly Hills, CA 90210, 213/271-8602
Agent: Major Talent Agency - Los Angeles, 213/820-5841

MILLION DOLLAR INFIELD (TF) CBS Entertainment, 1982

JACKIE COOPER*

b. September 15, 1921 - Los Angeles, California
Agent: Bill Haber, CAA - Los Angeles, 213/277-4545

STAND UP AND BE COUNTED Columbia, 1971
HAVING BABIES III (TF) The Jozak Company/Paramount TV, 1978
PERFECT GENTLEMEN (TF) Paramount TV, 1978
RAINBOW (TF) Ten-Four Productions, 1978
SEX AND THE SINGLE PARENT (TF) Time-Life Productions, 1979
MARATHON (TF) Alan Landsburg Productions, 1980
WHITE MAMA (TF) Tomorrow Entertainment, 1980
RODEO GIRL (TF) Steckler Productions/Marble Arch Productions, 1980
LEAVE 'EM LAUGHING (TF) Julian Fowles Productions/Charles Fries Productions, 1981
ROSIE: THE ROSEMARY CLOONEY STORY (TF) Charles Fries Productions/ Alan Sacks Productions, 1982
GO FOR THE GOLD Go for the Gold Productions, 1984
GLITTER (TF) Aaron Spelling Productions, 1984
THE NIGHT THEY SAVED CHRISTMAS (TF) Robert Halmi Productions, 1984

STUART COOPER

b. 1942 - Hoboken, New Jersey
Agent: ICM, 22 Grafton Street, London, England

LITTLE MALCOLM AND HIS STRUGGLE AGAINST THE EUNUCHS Multicetera Investments, 1974, British
OVERLORD 1975, British
THE DISAPPEARANCE Levitt-Pickman, 1977, Canadian
A.D. - ANNO DOMINI (MS) Procter & Gamble Productions/International Film Productions, 1985, U.S.-Italian

FRANCIS FORD COPPOLA*

b. April 7, 1939 - Detroit, Michigan
Business: American Zoetrope, Sentinel Building, 916 Kearny Street, San Francisco, CA 94133, 415/789-7500

TONIGHT FOR SURE Premier Pictures, 1961
DEMENTIA 13 American International, 1963
YOU'RE A BIG BOY NOW 7 Arts, 1966
FINIAN'S RAINBOW Warner Bros., 1968
THE RAIN PEOPLE Warner Bros., 1969
THE GODFATHER ★ Paramount, 1972
THE CONVERSATION Paramount, 1974
THE GODFATHER, PART II ★★ Paramount, 1974
APOCALYPSE NOW ★ United Artists, 1979
ONE FROM THE HEART Columbia, 1982
THE OUTSIDERS Warner Bros., 1983
RUMBLE FISH Universal, 1983
THE COTTON CLUB Orion, 1984

SERGIO CORBUCCI

b. December 6, 1927 - Rome, Italy
Contact: Ministry of Tourism & Education, Via Della Ferratella, No. 51, 00184 Rome, Italy, 06/7732

SALVATE MIA FIGLIA Lauro, 1951, Italian
LA PECCATRICE DELL'ISOLA Audax Film, 1953, Italian
TWO COLONELS Comet, 1961, Italian
DUEL OF THE TITANS *ROMOLO E REMO* Paramount, 1961, Italian
GOLIATH AND THE VAMPIRES *MACISTE CONTRO IL VAMPIRO* co-director with Giacomo Gentilomo, American International, 1961, Italian
THE SLAVE *IL FIGLIO DI SPARTACUS* MGM, 1962, Italian
IL PIU CORTO GIORNO Titanus, 1963, Italian
MINNESOTA CLAY Harlequin International, 1965, Italian-Spanish-French
DJANGO BRC, 1966, Italian
NAVAJO JOE *UN DOLLARO A TESTA* United Artists, 1966, Italian-Spanish
JOHNNY ORO Sanson, 1966, Italian
THE HELLBENDERS Embassy, 1966, Italian-Spanish
BERSAGLIO MOBILE Rizzoli Film, 1967, Italian
IL GRANDE SILENZIO Adelphia Cinematografica, 1967, Italian
THE MERCENARY United Artists, 1969, Italian-Spanish
GLI SPECIALISTI Adelphia Cinematografica, 1969, Italian
COMPAÑEROS *VAMOS A MATAR COMPAÑEROS* Cinerama Releasing Corporation, 1971, Spanish-Italian-West German
VIVA LA MUERTE...TUA! Tritone Filmind, 1971, Italian
CHE C'ENTRIAMO NOI CON LA RIVOLUZIONE? Fair Film, 1972, Italian
LA BANDA J & S - CRONACA CRIMINALE DEL FAR-WEST Roberto Loyola Cinematografica/Orfeo/Terra Film Kunst 1973, Italian-Spanish-Monacan
IL BESTIONE C.C. Champion, Inc., 1974, Italian-French
BLUFF - STORIE DI TRUFFE E DI IMBRAGLIONE Cineriz, 1975, Italian
UN GENIO, DUE COMPARI, UN POLLO Titanus, 1975, Italian-French-West German
DE CHE SEGNO SEI? PIC, 1976, Italian
IL SIGNOR ROBINSON - MONSTRUOSA STORIA D'AMORE E D'AVVENTURE United Artists, 1976, Italian
TRE TIGRI CONTRA TRE TIGRI Italian International Film, 1977, Italian
ECCO NOI PER ESEMPIO CIDIF, 1977, Italian
LA MAZZETTA United Artists, 1978, Italian
GIALLO NAPOLETANO CIDIF, 1979, Italian
ATTI ATROCISSIMA DE AMORE E DI VENDETTA 1979, Italian
PARI E DISPARI CIDIF, 1979, Italian
I DON'T UNDERSTAND YOU ANYMORE Capital, 1980, Italian
I'M GETTING MYSELF A YACHT Capital, 1981, Italian
CHI TROVO UN AMICO, TROVA UN TESORO CEIAD, 1981, Italian
SUPER FUZZ Avco Embassy, 1981, Italian
MY DARLING, MY DEAREST PLM Film, 1982, Italian
THREE WISE KINGS PLM Film, 1982, Italian
COUNT TACCHIA DAC/Adige, 1982, Italian
SING SING Columbia, 1983, Italian
QUESTO E QUELLO CIDIF, 1983, Italian
A TU PER TU DAC, 1984, Italian

NICHOLAS COREA*

b. April 7, 1943 - St. Louis, Missouri
Agent: The Richland Agency - Los Angeles, 213/553-1257

THE ARCHER: FUGITIVE FROM THE EMPIRE (TF) Mad-Dog Productions/ Universal TV, 1981

ROGER CORMAN

b. April 5, 1926 - Los Angeles, California
Business: New Horizons, 119 N. San Vicente Blvd., Beverly Hills, CA 213/651-2374

FIVE GUNS WEST American International, 1955
THE APACHE WOMAN American International, 1955
THE DAY THE WORLD ENDED American International, 1956
SWAMP WOMAN Woolner Brothers, 1956
THE OKLAHOMA WOMAN American International, 1956
THE GUNSLINGER ARC, 1956
IT CONQUERED THE WORLD American International, 1956
NOT OF THIS EARTH Allied Artists, 1957
THE UNDEAD American International, 1957
NAKED PARADISE American International, 1957
ATTACK OF THE CRAB MONSTERS Allied Artists, 1957
ROCK ALL NIGHT American International, 1957
TEENAGE DOLL Allied Artists, 1957
CARNIVAL ROCK Howco, 1957
SORORITY GIRL American International, 1957
THE VIKING WOMEN AND THE SEA SERPENT American International, 1957
WAR OF THE SATELLITES Allied Artists, 1958
THE SHE GODS OF SHARK REEF American International, 1958
MACHINE GUN KELLY American International, 1958
TEENAGE CAVEMAN American International, 1958
I, MOBSTER 20th Century-Fox, 1959
A BUCKET OF BLOOD American International, 1959
THE WASP WOMAN American International, 1959
SKI TROOP ATTACK Filmgroup; 1960
THE HOUSE OF USHER American International, 1960
THE LITTLE SHOP OF HORRORS Filmgroup, 1960
THE LAST WOMAN ON EARTH Filmgroup, 1960
CREATURE FROM THE HAUNTED SEA Filmgroup, 1961
ATLAS Filmgroup, 1961
THE PIT AND THE PENDULUM American International, 1961
THE INTRUDER *I HATE YOUR GUTS* Pathe American, 1962
THE PREMATURE BURIAL American International, 1962
TALES OF TERROR American International, 1962
TOWER OF LONDON American International, 1962
THE RAVEN American International, 1963
THE TERROR American International, 1963
"X" - THE MAN WITH THE X-RAY EYES American International, 1963
THE HAUNTED PALACE American International, 1963
THE YOUNG RACERS American International, 1963
THE SECRET INVASION United Artists, 1964
THE MASQUE OF THE RED DEATH American International, 1964, British-U.S.
THE TOMB OF LIGEIA American International, 1965
THE WILD ANGELS American International, 1966
THE ST. VALENTINE'S DAY MASSACRE 20th Century-Fox, 1967
THE TRIP American International, 1967
TARGET: HARRY directed under pseudonym of Harry Neill, ABC Pictures International, 1968
BLOODY MAMA American International, 1970
GAS-S-S-S! . . .OR IT BECAME NECESSARY TO DESTROY THE WORLD IN ORDER TO SAVE IT! American International, 1970
VON RICHTOFEN AND BROWN United Artists, 1971

HUBERT CORNFIELD

b. February 9, 1929 - Istanbul, Turkey

SUDDEN DANGER United Artists, 1955
LURE OF THE SWAMP 20th Century-Fox, 1957

HUBERT CORNFIELD —continued

PLUNDER ROAD 20th Century-Fox, 1957
THE THIRD VOICE 20th Century-Fox, 1959
ANGEL BABY co-director with Paul Wendkos, Allied Artists, 1961
PRESSURE POINT United Artists, 1962
THE NIGHT OF THE FOLLOWING DAY Universal, 1969
LES GRAND MOYENS Fox, 1976, French

EUGENE CORR

Contact: Writers Guild of America - Los Angeles, 213/550-1000

OVER-UNDER, SIDEWAYS-DOWN co-director with Steve Wax & Peter Gessner, Steve Wax/Cine-Manifest Productions, 1977
DESERT BLOOM Columbia, 1985

WILLIAM H. COSBY, JR.*

b. July 12, 1937 - Philadelphia, Pennsylvania
Agent: William Morris Agency - Beverly Hills, 213/274-7451
Business: Jemmin, Inc., 1900 Avenue of the Stars, Suite 1900, Los Angeles, CA 90067, 213/553-7674

BILL COSBY, HIMSELF 20th Century-Fox International Classics, 1983

DON COSCARELLI*

b. February 17, 1954 - Tripoli, Libya
Business: Coscarelli Corporation, 15445 Ventura Blvd. - Suite 10, Sherman Oaks, CA 91413, 818/784-8822

JIM - THE WORLD'S GREATEST Universal, 1976
KENNY AND COMPANY 20th Century-Fox, 1976
PHANTASM Avco Embassy, 1979
THE BEASTMASTER MGM/UA, 1982

GEORGE PAN COSMATOS*

Home: 2910 Seaview Road, Victoria, British Columbia V8N 1L1, Canada, 604/721-1675
Agent: Peter Meyer, William Morris Agency - Beverly Hills, 213/274-7451

MASSACRE IN ROME *RAPPRESAGLIA* National General, 1973, Italian-French
THE CASSANDRA CROSSING Avco Embassy, 1977, British-Italian-West German
RESTLESS Joseph Brenner Associates, 1978
ESCAPE TO ATHENA AFD, 1979, British
OF UNKNOWN ORIGIN Warner Bros., 1983, Canadian
RAMBO: FIRST BLOOD PART II Tri-Star, 1985

COSTA-GAVRAS

(See Costa GAVRAS)

JACK COUFFER*

Agent: Ben Benjamin, ICM - Los Angeles, 213/550-4153

NIKKI, WILD DOG OF THE NORTH Buena Vista, 1961, U.S.-Canadian
RING OF BRIGHT WATER Cinerama Releasing Corporation, 1969, British
LIVING FREE Columbia, 1972, British
THE DARWIN ADVENTURE 20th Century-Fox, 1972, British
THE LAST GIRAFFE (TF) Westfall Productions, 1979

JEROME COURTLAND*

b. December 27, 1926 - Knoxville, Tennessee
Agent; Herb Tobias & Associates - Los Angeles, 213/277-6211

RUN, COUGAR, RUN Buena Vista, 1972
DIAMONDS ON WHEELS Buena Vista, 1972, U.S.-British
THE SKY TRAP (TF) Walt Disney Productions, 1979

RAOUL COUTARD

b. September 16, 1924 - Paris, France
Contact: French Film Office, 745 Fifth Avenue, New York, NY 10151, 213/832-8860

HOA-BINH Transvue, 1971, French
LA LEGION SAUTE SUR KOLWEZI Bela Productions/FR3, 1980, French
S.A.S. A SAN SALVADOR UGC, 1982, French-West German

ALEX COX

REPO MAN Universal, 1984

NELL COX*

Home: 793 Lexington Avenue, New York, NY 10021, 212/980-8848
Agent: Steve White, The Cooper Agency - Los Angeles, 213/277-8422

LIZA'S PIONEER DIARY (TF) Nell Cox Films, 1976
THE ROOMMATE Rubicon Film Productions, 1985

PAUL COX

Agent: Roberta Kent, S.T.E. Representation - Los Angeles, 213/550-3982
Agent: Cameron's Management, 120 Victoria Street, Kings Cross, NSW, 2011, Australia, 02/358-6433

ILLUMINATIONS Illumination Film Productions, 1976, Australian
INSIDE LOOKING OUT Illumination Film Productions, 1977, Australian
LONELY HEARTS The Samuel Goldwyn Company, 1982, Australian
MAN OF FLOWERS Spectrafilm, 1983, Australian
MY FIRST WIFE Spectrafilm, 1984, Australian

WILLIAM CRAIN*

b. June 20, 1943
Business: P.O. Box 744, Beverly Hills, CA 90213
Agent: ICM - Los Angeles, 213/550-4000

BLACULA American International, 1972
DR. BLACK, MR. HYDE Dimension, 1976
THE WATTS MONSTER Dimension, 1979
THE KID FROM NOT-SO-BIG 1982
STANDING IN THE SHADOWS OF LOVE Brandenberg-Crain Productions, 1984

BARRY CRANE*

Business Manager: Brad Marer & Associates - Beverly Hills, 213/278-6690

THE HOUND OF THE BASKERVILLES (TF) Universal TV, 1972

PETER CRANE*

Home: 133 West 86th Street, New York, NY 10024, 212/595-0513
Agent: Ellen Glick, ICM - Los Angeles, 213/550-4000

COVER UP Glen A. Larson Productions/20th Century Fox TV, 1984

WES CRAVEN*

b. August 2, 1949 - Cleveland, Ohio
Business: Wesismore, Inc., 2309 Glynden Avenue, Venice, CA 90241, 213/397-4645
Agent: Marvin Moss Agency - Los Angeles, 213/274-8483

LAST HOUSE ON THE LEFT Hallmark Releasing Corporation, 1973
THE HILLS HAVE EYES Vanguard, 1977
STRANGER IN OUR HOUSE (TF) Inter Planetary Pictures/Finnegan Associates, 1978
DEADLY BLESSING United Artists, 1981
SWAMP THING Avco Embassy, 1982
INVITATION TO HELL (TF) Moonlight Productions II, 1984
A NIGHTMARE ON ELM STREET New Line Cinema, 1984
THE HILLS HAVE EYES PART 2 Thorn EMI, 1985

RICHARD CRENNA*

b. November 30, 1926 - Los Angeles, California
Agent: CAA - Los Angeles, 213/277-4545
Business: Pendick Enterprises - Los Angeles, 213/277-0700

BETTER LATE THAN NEVER (TF) Ten-Four Productions, 1979

CHARLES CRICHTON

b. August 6, 1910 - Wallasey, England
Contact: British Academy of Film & Television Arts, 195 Piccadilly, London W1, England, 01/734-0022

FOR THOSE IN PERIL 1944, British
PAINTED BOATS 1945, British
DEAD OF NIGHT co-director with Alberto Cavalcanti, Basil Dearden & Robert Hamer, Universal, 1945, British
HUE AND CRY Fine Arts, 1947, British
AGAINST THE WIND Eagle Lion, 1948, British
ANOTHER SHORE Rank, 1948, British
TRAIN OF EVENTS co-director with Basil Dearden & Sidney Cole, Rank, 1949, British
DANCE HALL Rank, 1950, British
THE LAVENDER HILL MOB Universal, 1951, British
THE STRANGER IN BETWEEN *HUNTED* Universal, 1952, British
THE TITFIELD THUNDERBOLT Universal, 1953, British
THE LOVER LOTTERY Continental, 1953, British
THE DIVIDED HEART Republic, 1954, British
DECISION AGAINST TIME *THE MAN IN THE SKY* MGM, 1956, British
LAW AND DISORDER co-director with Henry Cornelius, Continental, 1958, British
FLOODS OF FEAR Universal, 1958, British
THE BATTLE OF THE SEXES Continental, 1959, British
THE BOY WHO STOLE A MILLION Paramount, 1960, British
THE THIRD SECRET 20th Century-Fox, 1964, British
HE WHO RIDES A TIGER Sigma III, 1966, British

MICHAEL CRICHTON*

b. October 23, 1942 - Chicago, Illinois
Agent: Michael Ovitz, CAA - Los Angeles, 213/277-4545

PURSUIT (TF) ABC Circle Films, 1972
WESTWORLD MGM, 1973
COMA MGM/United Artists, 1978
THE GREAT TRAIN ROBBERY United Artists, 1979, British
LOOKER The Ladd Company/Warner Bros., 1981
RUNAWAY Tri-Star, 1984

DONALD CROMBIE

Business: Forest Home Films, 141 Penhurst Street, Willoughby, NSW, 2068, Australia, 02/411-4972

WHO KILLED JENNY LANGBY? (TF) 1974, Australian
DO I HAVE TO KILL MY CHILD? (TF) 1976, Australian
CADDIE Atlantic Releasing Corporation, 1976, Australian
THE IRISHMAN Forest Home Films, 1978, Australian
CATHY'S CHILD CB Productions, 1979, Australian
THE KILLING OF ANGEL STREET Forest Home Films, 1981, Australian
KITTY AND THE BAGMAN Quartet/Films Incorporated, 1982, Australian
ROBBERY UNDER ARMS co-director with Ken Hannam, 1984, Australian

DAVID CRONENBERG

Home: 184 Cottingham Street, Toronto, Ontario M4V 7C7, Canada, 416/961-3432
Agent: Michael Marcus, CAA - Los Angeles, 213/277-4545

STEREO Emergent Films, 1969, Canadian
CRIMES OF THE FUTURE Emergent Films, 1970, Canadian
THEY CAME FROM WITHIN *SHIVERS* Trans-America, 1976, Canadian
RABID New World, 1977, Canadian
THE BROOD New World, 1979, Canadian
FAST COMPANY Topar, 1979, Canadian
SCANNERS Avco Embassy, 1981, Canadian
VIDEODROME Universal, 1983, Canadian
THE DEAD ZONE Paramount, 1983, Canadian

AVERY CROUNSE

EYES OF FIRE Elysian Pictures, 1984

DICK CROY

b. January 30, 1943 - Greensberg, Pennsylvania
Home: 955 Maltman Avenue, Los Angeles, CA 90026, 213/666-3239
Agent: Jim Heacock, Heacock Literary Agency, 1523 Sixth Street, Santa Monica, CA 90405, 213/393-6227

THE UNKNOWN FORCE (TF) International Television Films, 1977

ROBERT CULP*

b. August 16, 1930 - Berkeley, California
Home: 10880 Wilshire Blvd - Suite 2110, Los Angeles, CA 90024, 213/470-1315
Personal Manager: Hillard Elkins - Los Angeles, 213/858-6090

HICKEY AND BOGGS United Artists, 1972

SEAN S. CUNNINGHAM*

b. December 31, 1941 - New York, New York
Home: 60 Brett Road, Fairfield, CT 06430, 203/255-0666
Agent: Jeff Berg/Peter Rawley, ICM - Los Angeles, 213/550-4000

TOGETHER Hallmark Releasing Corporation, 1971
CASE OF THE FULL MOON MURDERS *CASE OF THE SMILING STIFFS/SEX ON THE GROOVE TUBE* co-director with Brad Talbot, Seaberg, 1974
HERE COME THE TIGERS American International, 1978
MANNY'S ORPHANS United Artists, 1979
FRIDAY THE 13TH Paramount, 1980
A STRANGER IS WATCHING MGM/United Artists, 1982
SPRING BREAK Columbia, 1983
THE NEW KIDS Columbia, 1985

DAN CURTIS*

b. August 12 - Bridgeport, Connecticut
Business: Dan Curtis Productions, 5555 Melrose Avenue, Hollywood, CA 90004, 213/468-5000 ext. 5728
Business Manager: Michael Rutman, Breslauer, Jacobson & Rutman - Los Angeles, 213/879-0167

HOUSE OF DARK SHADOWS MGM, 1970
NIGHT OF DARK SHADOWS MGM, 1971
THE NIGHT STRANGLER (TF) ABC Circle Films, 1973
THE NORLISS TAPES (TF) Metromedia Producers Corporation, 1973
SCREAM OF THE WOLF (TF) Metromedia Producers Corporation, 1974
DRACULA (TF) Universal TV/Dan Curtis Productions, 1974
MELVIN PURVIS: G-MAN (TF) American International TV, 1974
THE GREAT ICE RIP-OFF (TF) ABC Circle Films, 1974
TRILOGY OF TERROR (TF) ABC Circle Films, 1975
THE KANSAS CITY MASSACRE (TF) ABC Circle Films, 1975
BURNT OFFERINGS United Artists, 1976
CURSE OF THE BLACK WIDOW (TF) Dan Curtis Productions/ABC Circle Films, 1977
WHEN EVERY DAY WAS THE FOURTH OF JULY (TF) Dan Curtis Productions, 1978
THE LAST RIDE OF THE DALTON GANG (TF) NBC Productions/Dan Curtis Productions, 1979
MRS. R'S DAUGHTER (TF) NBC Productions/Dan Curtis Productions, 1979
THE LONG DAYS OF SUMMER (TF) Dan Curtis Productions, 1980
THE WINDS OF WAR (MS) ☆ Paramount TV/Dan Curtis Productions, 1983

D

MORTON DA COSTA*
(Morton Tecosky)

b. March 7, 1914 - Philadelphia, Pennsylvania
Home: 20 Dorethy Road, West Redding, CT 06896, 203/938-2438
Attorney: Morton L. Leavy, Colton, Weissberger, 505 Park Avenue, New York, NY 10022, 212/371-4350

AUNTIE MAME Warner Bros., 1958
THE MUSIC MAN Warner Bros., 1962
ISLAND OF LOVE Warner Bros., 1963

ROBERT DALVA*

b. April 14, 1942 - New York, New York
Home/Business: Dalva Films, 33 Walnut Avenue, Larkspur, CA 94939, 415/924-0164
Agent: Jim Berkus, Leading Artists - Beverly Hills, 213/858-1999

THE BLACK STALLION RETURNS MGM/UA, 1983

DAMIANO DAMIANI

b. July 23, 1922 - Pasiano, Italy
Contact: Ministry of Tourism & Education, Via Della Ferratella, No. 51, 00184 Rome, Italy, 06/7732

IL ROSSETTO Europa Cinematografica/Explorer Film/EFPC, 1960, Italian-French
IL SICARIO Europa Cinematografica/Galatea, 1961, Italian
ARTURO'S ISLAND MGM, 1962, Italian
LA RIMPATRIATA Galatea/22 Dicembre/Coronet, 1963, Italian-French
THE EMPTY CANVAS Embassy, 1964, Italian
LA STREGA IN AMORE Arco Film, 1966, Italian
MAFIA *IL GIORNO DELLA CIVETTA* American International, 1968, Italian
A BULLET FOR THE GENERAL *QUIEN SABE?* Avco Embassy, 1968, Italian-Spanish
UNA RAGAZZA PIUTTOSTO COMPLICATA Produzioni Filmena/Fono Roma, 1969, Italian
CONFESSIONS OF A POLICE CAPTAIN *CONFESSIONE DI UN COMMISSARIO* 1970, Italian
LA MOGLIE PIU BELLA Explorer '58, 1970, Italian
L'ISTRUTTORIA E CHUISA DIMENTICHI Fair Film, 1971, Italian
IL SORRISO DEL GRANDE TENTATORE Euro, 1972, Italian
GIROLIMONI - IL MOSTRO DI ROMA Dino De Laurentiis Cinematografica, 1972, Italian
THE DEVIL IS A WOMAN 20th Century-Fox, 1975, British-Italian
UN GENIO, DUE COMPARI, UN POLLO Rafran Cinematografica, 1975, Italian
I AM AFRAID Auro Cinematografica, 1977, Italian
GOODBYE AND AMEN Cineriz, 1978, Italian-French
UN UOMO IN GINOCCHIO Cineriz, 1979, Italian
TIME OF THE JACKALS Capital, 1980, Italian
AMITYVILLE II: THE POSSESSION Orion, 1982

DAMIANO DAMIANI —continued

LA PIOVRA (MS) SACIS, 1984, Italian
SICILIAN LOVE AFFAIR Intercapital, 1985, Italian

MEL DAMSKI*

b. July 21, 1946 - New York, New York
Agent: David Gersh, The Gersh Agency - Beverly Hills, 213/274-6611

LONG JOURNEY BACK (TF) Lorimar Productions, 1978
THE CHILD STEALER (TF) The Production Company/Columbia TV, 1979
A PERFECT MATCH (TF) Lorimar Productions, 1980
WORD OF HONOR (TF) Georgia Bay Productions, 1981
AMERICAN DREAM (TF) Mace Neufeld Productions/Viacom, 1981
FOR LADIES ONLY (TF) The Catalina Production Group/Viacom, 1981
THE LEGEND OF WALKS FAR WOMAN (TF) Roger Gimbel Productions/EMI TV/Raquel Welch Productions/Lee Levinson Productions, 1982
AN INVASION OF PRIVACY (TF) Dick Berg-Stonehenge Productions/Embassy TV, 1983
YELLOWBEARD Orion, 1983, British
ATTACK ON FEAR (TF) Tomorrow Entertainment, 1984
MISCHIEF 20th Century Fox, 1985

LAWRENCE DANE

HEAVENLY BODIES MGM/UA, 1985, Canadian

MARC DANIELS*

Agent: Fred Westheimer, William Morris Agency - Beverly Hills, 213/274-7451

SQUEEZE A FLOWER MGM-EMI, 1971, Australian
PLANET EARTH (TF) Warner Bros. TV, 1974
SPECIAL PEOPLE: BASED ON A TRUE STORY (TF) Joe Cates Productions/CTV Broadcasting Corporation, 1984, U.S. - Canadian
HE'S FIRED, SHE'S HIRED (TF) CBS, 1984

HERBERT DANSKA*

Business: Emerald City Productions, Inc. - New York City, 212/666-4735

SWEET LOVE, BITTER *IT WON'T RUB OFF, BABY* Peppercorn-Wormser, 1967
RIGHT ON! Leacock-Pennebaker, 1970

JOE DANTE*

Agent: David Gersh, The Gersh Agency - Beverly Hills, 213/274-6611

HOLLYWOOD BOULEVARD co-director with Allan Arkush, New World, 1976
PIRANHA New World, 1978
THE HOWLING Avco Embassy, 1980
TWILIGHT ZONE - THE MOVIE co-director with John Landis, Steven Spielberg & George Miller, Warner Bros., 1983
GREMLINS Warner Bros., 1984
EXPLORERS Paramount, 1985

RAY DANTON*

b. September 19, 1931 - New York, New York
Business Manager: Joel Rosenbaum - Encino, 818/872-0231

THE DEATHMASTER American International, 1972
CRYPT OF THE LIVING DEAD Atlas, 1973
PSYCHIC KILLER Avco Embassy, 1975

PHILIP D'ANTONI*

b. February 19, 1929 - New York, New York
Business: 8 East 63rd Street, New York, NY 10021, 212/688-4205

THE SEVEN UPS 20th Century-Fox, 1973

JOAN DARLING*

b. April 14, 1935 - Boston, Massachusetts
Agent: Ed Bondy, William Morris Agency - Beverly Hills, 213/274-7451

FIRST LOVE Paramount, 1977
WILLA (TF) co-director with Claudio Guzman, GJL Productions/Dove, Inc., 1979
THE CHECK IS IN THE MAIL Robert Kaufman Productions, 1984

JULES DASSIN*

b. December 12, 1911 - Middletown, Connecticut
Home: 25 Anagnostopoulou Street, Athens, Greece, 3/629-751
Agent: Sue Mengers, ICM - Los Angeles, 213/550-4000

NAZI AGENT MGM, 1942
THE AFFAIRS OF MARTHA MGM, 1942
REUNION IN FRANCE MGM, 1942
YOUNG IDEAS MGM, 1943
THE CANTERVILLE GHOST MGM, 1944
A LETTER FOR EVIE MGM, 1945
TWO SMART PEOPLE MGM, 1946
BRUTE FORCE Warner Bros., 1947
THE NAKED CITY Universal, 1948
THIEVES' HIGHWAY RKO Radio, 1949
NIGHT AND THE CITY 20th Century-Fox, 1950, British
RIFIFI Pathe, 1954, French
WHERE THE HOT WIND BLOWS *LA LOI* MGM, 1960, French-Italian
NEVER ON SUNDAY ★ Lopert, 1960, Greek
PHAEDRA Lopert, 1962, Greek-U.S.-French
TOPKAPI United Artists, 1964
10:30 P.M. SUMMER Lopert, 1966, U.S.-Spanish
SURVIVAL '67 United, 1968, U.S.-Israeli
UP TIGHT Paramount, 1968
PROMISE AT DAWN Avco Embassy, 1970, French-U.S.
A DREAM OF PASSION Avco Embassy, 1978, Greek-U.S.
CIRCLE OF TWO World Northal, 1981, Canadian

HERSCHEL DAUGHERTY*

Home: 925 Santa Fe Drive, Encinitas, CA 92024
Messages: 914/753-6470

THE LIGHT IN THE FOREST Buena Vista, 1958
THE RAIDERS Universal, 1963
WINCHESTER '73 (TF) Universal TV, 1967
THE VICTIM (TF) Universal TV, 1972
SHE CRIED "MURDER" (TF) Universal TV, 1973
TWICE IN A LIFETIME (TF) Martin Rackin Productions, 1974

BOAZ DAVIDSON

Business: Cannon Group, 6464 Sunset Blvd., Los Angeles, CA 90038, 213/469-8124

AZIT THE PARATROOPER DOG Liran Corporation, 1972, Israeli
CHARLIE AND A HALF Filmonde, 1973, Israeli
LUPO GOES TO NEW YORK Noah Films, 1977, Israeli
THE TZANANI FAMILY Noah Films, 1978, Israeli
LEMON POPSICLE Noah Films, 1981, Israeli
GOING STEADY (LEMON POPSICLE II) Noah Films, 1981, Israeli
SEED OF INNOCENCE *TEEN MOTHERS* Cannon, 1981
X-RAY *HOSPITAL MASSACRE* Cannon, 1981
HOT BUBBLEGUM (LEMON POPSICLE III) Noah Films, 1981, Israeli

BOAZ DAVIDSON —continued

THE LAST AMERICAN VIRGIN Cannon, 1982
PRIVATE POPSICLE (LEMON POPSICLE IV) Noah Films, 1982, Israeli-West German

GORDON DAVIDSON*

b. May 7, 1933 - New York, New York
Business: 135 N. Grand Avenue, Los Angeles, CA 90012, 213/972-7388
Agent: Ed Bondy, William Morris Agency - Beverly Hills, 213/274-7451

THE TRIAL OF THE CATONSVILLE NINE Cinema 5, 1972

MARTIN DAVIDSON*

b. November 7, 1939 - New York, New York
Agent: Jim Wiatt, ICM - Los Angeles, 213/550-4000

THE LORDS OF FLATBUSH co-director with Stephen Verona, Columbia, 1974
ALMOST SUMMER Universal, 1978
HERO AT LARGE MGM/United Artists, 1980
EDDIE AND THE CRUISERS Embassy, 1983

JOHN DAVIES

Office: Frontroom Productions, 79 Wardour Street London W1, England, 01/734-4603

ACCEPTABLE LEVELS (TF) Frontroom Productions/Channel Four, 1983, British
KIM (TF) London Films, 1984, British
COVER HER FACE (TF) Anglia TV Ltd., 1985, British

ANDREW DAVIS*

Attorney: Peter Dekom, Pollock, Bloom & Dekom, 9255 Sunset Blvd., Los Angeles, CA 90069, 213/278-8622

STONY ISLAND World Northal, 1980
THE FINAL TERROR Comworld, 1983
CODE OF SILENCE Orion, 1985

BARRY DAVIS

Contact: British Academy of Film & Television Arts, 195 Piccadilly, London W1, England, 01/734-0022

TELFORD'S CHANGE (TF) BBC Enterprises, 1979, British
OPPENHEIMER (MS) BBC-TV/WGBH-Boston, 1982, British-U.S.

DESMOND DAVIS

b. 1928 - London, England
Agent: John Redway & Associates - London, 01/637-1612

THE GIRL WITH GREEN EYES United Artists, 1964, British
TIME LOST AND TIME REMEMBERED *I WAS HAPPY HERE* Continental, 1966, British
THE UNCLE Lennart, 1966, British
SMASHING TIME Paramount, 1967, British
A NICE GIRL LIKE ME Avco Embassy, 1969, British
CLASH OF THE TITANS MGM/United Artists, 1981, British
THE SIGN OF FOUR Mapleton Films Ltd., 1983, British
THE COUNTRY GIRLS London Films Ltd./Channel Four, 1983, British
ORDEAL BY INNOCENCE Cannon, 1984, British
CAMILLE (TF) Rosemont Productions, 1984, U.S. - British

OSSIE DAVIS

b. December 18, 1917 - Cogdell, Georgia
Agent: The Artists Agency - Los Angeles, 213/277-7779

COTTON COMES TO HARLEM United Artists, 1970
BLACK GIRL Cinerama Releasing Corporation, 1972
KONGI'S HARVEST Tan Communications, 1973
GORDON'S WAR 20th Century-Fox, 1973
COUNTDOWN AT KUSINI Columbia, 1976, U.S.-Nigerian

PETER DAVIS

Home: 325 Central Park West, New York, NY 10025

HEARTS AND MINDS (FD) Warner Bros., 1975
MIDDLETOWN (TD) PBS, 1982

ANTHONY M. DAWSON

(Antonio Margheriti)

Contact: Ministry of Tourism & Education, Via Della Ferratella, No. 51, 00184 Rome, Italy, 06/7732

LIGHTNING BOLT Woolner Brothers, 1967, Italian
THE YOUNG, THE EVIL AND THE SAVAGE American International, 1968, Italian
DECAMERON 3 Starkiss Roma, 1972, Italian
LES DIABLESSES Planfilm, 1974, French-Italian-West German
TAKE A HARD RIDE 20th Century-Fox, 1975
THE STRANGER AND THE GUNFIGHTER Columbia, 1976, Italian-Hong Kong
HOUSE OF 1,000 PLEASURES Group 1, 1977, Italian
DEATH RAGE *CON LA RABBIA AGLI OCCHI* S.J. International, 1977, Italian
THE SQUEEZE *RIP OFF* Maverick International, 1978, Italian-U.S.
KILLER FISH Associated Film Distribution, 1979, Italian-Brazilian
THE LAST HUNTER *HUNTER OF THE APOCALYPSE* World Northal, 1980, Italian
CANNIBALS IN THE STREETS Almi Cinema 5, 1982, Italian-Spanish
THE HUNTERS OF THE GOLDEN COBRA *THE RAIDERS OF THE GOLDEN COBRA* World Northal, 1982, Italian
YOR, THE HUNTER FROM THE FUTURE Columbia, 1983, Italian-Turkish
JUNGLE RAIDERS Filman, 1984, Italian
CODENAME WILDGEESE Ascot Distribution, 1985, West German

ERNEST DAY

GREEN ICE Universal/AFD, 1981, British
WALTZ ACROSS TEXAS Atlantic Releasing Corporation, 1983

ROBERT DAY *

b. September 11, 1922 - Sheen, England
Agent: Bruce Vinokour/Ron Meyer, CAA - Los Angeles, 213/277-4545

THE GREEN MAN DCA, 1957, British
STRANGERS' MEETING Rank, 1957, British
THE HAUNTED STRANGLER *GRIP OF THE STRANGLER* MGM, 1958, British
CORRIDORS OF BLOOD MGM, 1958, British
FIRST MAN INTO SPACE MGM, 1959, British
LIFE IN EMERGENCY WARD 10 Eros, 1959, British
BOBBIKINS 20th Century-Fox, 1960, British
TWO-WAY STRETCH Showcorporation, 1960, British
TARZAN THE MAGNIFICENT Paramount, 1960, British
CALL ME GENIUS *THE REBEL* Continental, 1961, British
OPERATION SNATCH Continental, 1962, British
TARZAN'S THREE CHALLENGES MGM, 1963, British
SHE MGM, 1965, British

ROBERT DAY*—continued

TARZAN AND THE VALLEY OF GOLD American International, 1966, U.S.-Swiss
TARZAN AND THE GREAT RIVER Paramount, 1967
I THINK WE'RE BEING FOLLOWED 1967, British
THE HOUSE ON GREENAPPLE ROAD (TF) QM Productions, 1970
RITUAL OF EVIL (TF) Universal TV, 1970
BANYON (TF) Warner Bros. TV, 1971
IN BROAD DAYLIGHT (TF) Aaron Spelling Productions, 1971
MR. AND MRS. BO JO JONES (TF) 20th Century-Fox TV, 1971
THE RELUCTANT HEROES (TF) Aaron Spelling Productions, 1971
THE GREAT AMERICAN BEAUTY CONTEST (TF) ABC Circle Films, 1973
DEATH STALK (TF) Wolper Productions, 1975
THE TRIAL OF CHAPLAIN JENSEN (TF) 20th Century-Fox TV, 1975
SWITCH (TF) Universal TV, 1975
A HOME OF OUR OWN (TF) QM Productions, 1975
TWIN DETECTIVES (TF) Charles Fries Productions, 1976
KINGSTON: THE POWER PLAY (TF) Universal TV, 1976
HAVING BABIES (TF) The Jozak Company, 1976
BLACK MARKET BABY (TF) Brut Productions, 1977
LOGAN'S RUN (TF) Goff-Roberts-Steiner Productions/MGM TV, 1977
THE INITIATION OF SARAH (TF) Charles Fries Productions, 1978
THE GRASS IS ALWAYS GREENER OVER THE SEPTIC TANK (TF) Joe Hamilton Productions, 1978
MURDER BY NATURAL CAUSES (TF) Richard Levinson-William Link Productions, 1979
WALKING THROUGH THE FIRE (TF) Time-Life Films, 1979
THE MAN WITH BOGART'S FACE *SAM MARLOW, PRIVATE EYE* 20th Century-Fox, 1980
PETER AND PAUL (TF) Universal TV, 1981
SCRUPLES (TF) Lou-Step Productions/Warner Brothers TV, 1981
MARIAN ROSE WHITE (TF) Gerald Abrams Productions/Cypress Point Productions, 1982
RUNNING OUT (TF) CBS Entertainment, 1983
YOUR PLACE OR MINE (TF) Poolhouse Productions/Finnegan Associates, 1983
CHINA ROSE (TF) Robert Halmi Production, 1983
COOK & PEARY: THE RACE TO THE POLE (TF) Robert Halmi Productions, 1983
LADY FROM YESTERDAY (TF) Barry Weitz Films/Comworld Productions, 1984
HOLLYWOOD WIVES (MS) Aaron Spelling Productions, 1985

LYMAN DAYTON

Business: Lyman Dayton Productions, 10850 Riverside Drive, North Hollywood, CA 91602, 213/980-7202

BAKER'S HAWK Doty-Dayton, 1976
RIVALS World Entertainment, 1979
THE STRANGER AT JEFFERSON HIGH (TF) Lyman Dayton Productions, 1981
THE AVENGING Comworld, 1981
SOLO Dayton-Stewart Organization, 1984
THE RED FURY Dayton-Stewart Organization, 1985

EMILE de ANTONIO

b. 1920 - Scranton, Pennsylvania
Address: P.O. Box 1567, New York, NY 10017, 212/475-2630 or 212/674-5825

POINT OF ORDER (FD) Point, 1963
RUSH TO JUDGMENT (FD) Impact, 1967
AMERICA IS HARD TO SEE (FD) 1968
IN THE YEAR OF THE PIG (FD) Pathe Contemporary, 1969
MILLHOUSE: A WHITE COMEDY New Yorker, 1971
PAINTERS PAINTING (FD) New Yorker, 1973
UNDERGROUND (FD) co-director with Mary Lampson & Haskell Wexler, New Yorker, 1976
IN THE KING OF PRUSSIA Turin Film Corporation, 1983

WILLIAM DEAR*

Home: 408/625-3696
Agent: Joan Hyler, William Morris Agency - Beverly Hills, 213/274-7451
Attorney: Andy Rigrod, Rigrod & Surpin - Los Angeles, 213/552-1808

TIMERIDER Jensen Farley Pictures, 1983

JAMES DEARDEN

Contact: British Academy of Film & Television Arts, 195 Piccadilly, London W1, England, 01/734-0022

THE COLD ROOM (TF) Jethro Films/Mark Forstater Productions, 1984, British

GIANFRANCO deBOSIO

Contact: Ministry of Tourism & Education, Via Della Ferratella, No. 51, 00184 Rome, Italy, 06/7732

LA BETIA Titanus, 1972, Italian-Yugoslavian
MOSES THE LAWGIVER (MS) ATV, Ltd./ITC/RAI, 1975, British-Italian
MOSES Avco Embassy, 1976, British-Italian, feature film version of MOSES THE LAWGIVER

PHILIPPE de BROCA

b. March 15, 1933 - Paris, France
Contact: French Film Office, 745 Fifth Avenue, New York, NY 10151, 212/832-8860

LES JEUX DE L'AMOUR 1960, French
THE JOKER Lopert, 1961, French
THE FIVE DAY LOVER Kingsley International, 1961, French-Italian
SEVEN CAPITAL SINS co-director with Jean-Luc Godard, Roger Vadim, Sylvaine Dhomme, Edouard Molinaro, Claude Chabrol, Jacques Demy, Marie-Jose Nat, Dominique Paturel, Jean-Marc Tennberg & Perrette Pradier, Embassy, 1962, French-Italian
CARTOUCHE Embassy, 1962, French-Italian
LES VEINARDS co-director, 1962, French
THAT MAN FROM RIO Lopert, 1964, French-Italian
MALE COMPANION International Classics, 1966, French-Italian
UP TO HIS EARS *LES TRIBULATIONS D'UN CHINOIS EN CHINE* Lopert, 1966, French-Italian
THE KING OF HEARTS Lopert, 1967, French-Italian
THE OLDEST PROFESSION *LES PLUX VIEUX METIER DU MONDE* co-director with Franco Indovina, Mauro Bolognini, Michael Pfleghar, Claude Autant-Lara & Jean-Luc Godard, Goldstone, 1968, French-Italian-West German
THE DEVIL BY THE TAIL Lopert, 1969, French-Italian
GIVE HER THE MOON *LES CAPRICES DE MARIE* United Artists, 1970, French-Italian
TOUCH AND GO *LA ROUTE AU SOLEIL* Libra, 1971, French
LA POUDRE D' ESCAMPETTE COLUMBIA, 1971, French-Italian
CHERE LOUISE Warner-Columbia, 1972, French-Italian
LE MAGNIFIQUE Cine III, 1973, French
INCORRIGIBLE EDP, 1975, French
JULIE-POT-DE-COLLE Prodis, 1977, French
DEAR DETECTIVE *DEAR INSPECTOR* Cinema 5, 1978, French
LE CAVALEUR CCFC, 1979, French
PRACTICE MAKES PERFECT Quartet/Films Incorporation, 1980, French
JUPITER'S THIGH *ON A VOLE LA CRUISSE DE JUPITER* Quartet/Films Inc., 1980,French
PSY Ariane Films/Antenne-2, 1981, French
L'AFRICAIN Renn Productions, 1982, French
LOUISIANA (CTF) ICC/Antenne-2/Superchannel/CTV/Societe de Development de L'Industrie Cinematographique Canadienne, 1983, Canadian-French

FRANK de FELITTA*

b. August 3, 1921 - New York, New York
Home: 3008 Paulcrest Drive, Los Angeles, CA 90046, 213/654-1310
Agent: Michael Marcus, CAA - Los Angeles, 213/277-4545

TRAPPED (TF) Universal TV, 1973
THE TWO WORLDS OF JENNY LOGAN (TF) Joe Wizan TV Productions/ Charles Fries Productions, 1979
DARK NIGHT OF THE SCARECROW (TF) Joe Wizan TV Productions, 1981

PHILIP DeGUERE*

Agent: Marvin Moss Agency - Los Angeles, 213/274-8483

DR. STRANGE (TF) Universal TV, 1978

DONNA DEITCH

b. June 8, 1945 - San Francisco, California
Business: Desert Heart Productions, 1524 Cloverfield Blvd., Santa Monica, CA 90404, 213/829-0288

DESERT OF THE HEART Desert Heart Productions, 1984

DOM DE LUISE*

b. August 1, 1933 - Brooklyn, New York
Agent: Todd Smith CAA - Los Angeles, 213/277-4545

HOT STUFF Columbia, 1979

JONATHAN DEMME*

b. 1944 - Rockville Centre, New York
Agent: William Morris Agency - Beverly Hills, 213/274-7451
Business Manager: Lee Winkler, Global Business Management, 9000 Sunset Blvd. - Suite 1115, Los Angeles, CA 90069, 213/278-4141

CAGED HEAT New World, 1974
CRAZY MAMA New World, 1975
FIGHTING MAD 20th Century-Fox, 1976
CITIZENS BAND *HANDLE WITH CARE* Paramount, 1977
LAST EMBRACE United Artists, 1979
MELVIN AND HOWARD Universal, 1980
WHO AM I THIS TIME? (TF) Rubicon Film Productions, 1982
SWING SHIFT Warner Bros., 1983
STOP MAKING SENSE (FD) Cinecom International/Island Alive, 1984

PIERRE DeMORO

SAVANNAH SMILES Embassy, 1983
HELL HOLE Arkoff International Pictures, 1985

JACQUES DEMY*

b. June 5, 1931 - Pont-Chateau, France
Home: 86 Rue Daguerre, Paris 75014, France, 322-32-36
Agent: The Lantz Office - Los Angeles, 213/858-1144

LOLA Films Around the World, 1961, French
SEVEN CAPITAL SINS co-director with Jean-Luc Godard, Roger Vadim, Sylvaine Dhomme, Edouard Molinaro, Philippe de Broca, Claude Chabrol, Marie-Jose Nat, Dominique Paturel, Jean-Marc Tennberg & Perrette Pradier, Embassy, 1962, French-Italian
BAY OF THE ANGELS Pathe Contemporary, 1964, French
THE UMBRELLAS OF CHERBOURG Landau, 1964, French-West German
THE YOUNG GIRLS OF ROCHEFORT Warner Bros., 1968, French
MODEL SHOP Columbia, 1969

JACQUES DEMY*—continued

DONKEY SKIN Janus, 1971, French
THE PIED PIPER Paramount, 1972, British-West German
L'EVENEMENT LE PLUS IMPORTANT DEPUIS QUE L'HOMME A MARCHE SUR LA LUNE Lira Films/Roas Production, 1973, French-Italian
A SLIGHTLY PREGNANT MAN SJ International, 1977, French
LADY OSCAR Toho, 1978, Japanese-French
UN CHAMBRE EN VILLE UGC, 1982, French

BRIAN DE PALMA*

b. September 11, 1940 - Newark, New Jersey
Agent: Martin Bauer Agency - Beverly Hills, 213/275-2421
Business Manager: Richard Roemer, Roemer & Nadler, 605 Third Avenue, New York, NY 10158, 212/972-1100

MURDER A LA MOD Aries, 1968
GREETINGS Sigma III, 1968
THE WEDDING PARTY co-director with Wilford Leach & Cynthia Munroe, Powell Productions Plus/Ondine, 1969
DIONYSUS IN '69 co-director with Robert Fiore & Bruce Rubin, Sigma III, 1970
HI, MOM! Sigma III, 1970
GET TO KNOW YOUR RABBIT Warner Bros., 1972
SISTERS American International, 1973
PHANTOM OF THE PARADISE 20th Century-Fox, 1974
OBSESSION Columbia, 1976
CARRIE United Artists, 1976
THE FURY 20th Century-Fox, 1978
HOME MOVIES United Artists Classics, 1980
DRESSED TO KILL Filmways, 1980
BLOW OUT Filmways, 1981
SCARFACE Universal, 1983
BODY DOUBLE Columbia, 1984

FRANK DE PALMA

b. May 3, 1957 - Los Angeles, California
Home: 605 S. Detroit Street, Apt. 202, Los Angeles, CA 90036, 213/939-1245

FUTURE TENSE (CTF) Walt Disney Productions, 1983

JACQUES DERAY

(Jacques Deray Desrayaud)

b. February 19, 1929 - Lyons, France
Contact: French Film Office, 745 Fifth Avenue, New York, NY 10151, 212/832-8860

LE GIGOLO 1960, French
RIFIFI IN TOKYO MGM, 1961, French-Italian
PAR UN BEAU MATIN D'ETE 1964, French
SYMPHONY FOR A MASSACRE 7 Arts, 1965, French-Italian
THAT MAN GEORGE! *L'HOMME DE MARRAKECH* Allied Artists, 1966, French-Italian-Spanish
AVEC LA PEAU AUTRES 1967, French
THE SWIMMING POOL Avco Embassy, 1970, French-Italian
BORSALINO Paramount, 1970, French-Italian
DOUCEMENT LES BASSES! CIC, 1971, French
UN PEU DE SOLEIL DANS L'EAU FROIDE SNC, 1971, French
THE OUTSIDE MAN *UN HOMME EST MORT* United Artists, 1973, French-Italian
BORSALINO AND CO. Medusa, 1974, French-Italian
FLIC STORY Adel Productions/Lira Films/Mondial, 1975, French
LE GANG Warner-Columbia, 1977, French
UN PAPILLON SUR L'EPAULE Action Films, 1978, French
TROIS HOMMES A ABBATRE Adel Production/Films A2, 1980, French
LE MARGINAL Gaumont/Cerito Rene Chateau, 1983, French

JOHN DEREK*
(Derek Harris)

b. August 12, 1926 - Hollywood, California
Agent: Martin Baum, CAA - Los Angeles, 213/277-4545

ONCE BEFORE I DIE 7 Arts, 1967, U.S.-Filipino
A BOY...A GIRL Jack Hanson, 1968
CHILDISH THINGS Filmworld, 1969
AND ONCE UPON A TIME *FANTASIES* Joseph Brenner Associates, 1973
TARZAN, THE APE MAN MGM/United Artists, 1981
BOLERO Cannon, 1984

CALEB DESCHANEL*

b. September 21, 1944 - Philadelphia, Pennsylvania
Contact: Directors Guild of America - Los Angeles, 213/656-1220

THE ESCAPE ARTIST Orion/Warner Bros., 1982

TOM DeSIMONE

CHATTER-BOX American International, 1977
HELL NIGHT Compass International, 1981
THE CONCRETE JUNGLE Pentagon, 1982

ANDRE DE TOTH*
(Sasvrai Farkasfawi Tothfalusi Toth Endre Antai Mihaly)

b. 1910 - Mako, Hungary
Home: 3690 Barham Blvd., Burbank, CA 90068, 818/874-3548
Agent: Ronald Leif, Contemporary-Korman Artists - Beverly Hills, 213/278-8250

TOPRINI NASZ 1939, Hungarian
OT ORA 40 1939, Hungarian
KET LANY AZ UTCAN 1939, Hungarian
SEMMELWEIS 1939, Hungarian
HAT HET BOLDOGSAG 1939, Hungarian
BALALAIKA 1939, Hungarian
TOPRINI NASZ 1939, Hungarian
PASSPORT TO SUEZ Columbia, 1943
NONE SHALL ESCAPE Columbia, 1944
DARK WATERS United Artists, 1944
RAMROD United Artists, 1947
THE OTHER LOVER United Artists, 1947
PITFALL United Artists, 1948
SLATTERY'S HURRICANE 20th Century-Fox, 1949
MAN IN THE SADDLE Columbia, 1951
CARSON CITY Warner Bros., 1952
SPRINGFIELD RIFLE Warner Bros., 1952
LAST OF THE COMANCHES Columbia, 1952
HOUSE OF WAX Warner Bros., 1953
THE STRANGER WORE A GUN Columbia, 1953
THUNDER OVER THE PLAINS Warner Bros., 1953
RIDING SHOTGUN Warner Bros., 1954
THE CITY IS DARK Warner Bros., 1954
THE BOUNTY HUNTER Warner Bros., 1954
TANGANYIKA Universal, 1954
THE INDIAN FIGHTER United Artists, 1955
MONKEY ON MY BACK United Artists, 1957
HIDDEN FEAR United Artists, 1957
THE TWO-HEADED SPY Columbia, 1959
DAY OF THE OUTLAW United Artists, 1959
MAN ON A STRING Columbia, 1960
MORGAN THE PIRATE MGM, 1960, British
THE MONGOLS Colorama, 1961, Italian
GOLD FOR THE CAESARS Colorama, 1962, Italian
PLAY DIRTY United Artists, 1968, British

JOHN DEXTER

b. 1935 - England
Contact: British Academy of Film & Television Arts, 195 Piccadilly, London W1, England, 01/734-0022

THE VIRGIN SOLDIERS Columbia, 1970, British
PIGEONS *THE SIDELONG GLANCES OF A PIGEON KICKER* MGM, 1970
I WANT WHAT I WANT Cinerama Releasing Corporation, 1972, British

MAURY DEXTER *

b. 1927
Home: 1384 Camino Magenta, Thousand Oaks, CA 91360, 805/498-0540
Business Manager: Hank Tani - Thousand Oaks, 805/498-0540

THE HIGH POWERED RIFLE 20th Century-Fox, 1960
WALK TALL 20th Century-Fox, 1960
THE PURPLE HILLS 20th Century-Fox, 1961
WOMAN HUNT 20th Century-Fox, 1961
THE FIREBRAND 20th Century-Fox, 1962
AIR PATROL 20th Century-Fox, 1962
THE DAY MARS INVADED EARTH 20th Century-Fox, 1962
HOUSE OF THE DAMNED 20th Century-Fox, 1962
HARBOR LIGHTS 20th Century-Fox, 1963
THE YOUNG SWINGERS 20th Century-Fox, 1963
POLICE NURSE 20th Century-Fox, 1963
YOUNG GUNS OF TEXAS 20th Century-Fox, 1963
SURF PARTY 20th Century-Fox, 1963
RAIDERS FROM BENEATH THE SEA 20th Century-Fox, 1964
WILD ON THE BEACH 20th Century-Fox, 1965
THE NAKED BRIGADE Universal, 1965
MARYJANE American International, 1968
THE MINI-SKIRT MOB American International, 1968
BORN WILD American International, 1968
HELL'S BELLES American International, 1969

MICHAEL DINNER

Agent: Jack Rapke, CAA - Los Angeles, 213/277-4545

MISS LONELYHEARTS H. Jay Holman Productions/American Film Institute, 1983
HEAVEN HELP US Tri-Star, 1985

IVAN DIXON *

b. April 6, 1931 - New York, New York
Home: 3432 N. Marengo Avenue, Altadena, CA 91001, 213/681-1327

TROUBLE MAN 20th Century-Fox, 1972
THE SPOOK WHO SAT BY THE DOOR United Artists, 1973
LOVE IS NOT ENOUGH (TF) Universal TV, 1978

WHEELER DIXON

b. March 12, 1950, New Brunswick, New Jersey
Business: Deliniator Films, Inc., c/o Philip Hacker & Company, 1888 Century Park East, Los Angeles, CA 90067, 213/553-6588

THE GAMMA CHRONICLES (MS) Gold Key Entertainment, 1980

EDWARD DMYTRYK *

b. September 4, 1908 - Grand Forks, Canada
Agent: Kurt Frings - Beverly Hills, 213/274-8883

THE HAWK Herman Wohl, 1935
TELEVISION SPY Paramount, 1939
EMERGENCY SQUAD Paramount, 1940

EDWARD DMYTRYK*—continued

MYSTERY SEA RAIDERS Paramount, 1940
GOLDEN GLOVES Paramount, 1940
HER FIRST ROMANCE Monogram, 1940
THE DEVIL COMMANDS Columbia, 1941
UNDER AGE Columbia, 1941
SWEETHEART OF THE CAMPUS Columbia, 1941
THE BLONDE FROM SINGAPORE Columbia, 1941
CONFESSIONS OF BOSTON BLACKIE Columbia, 1941
SECRETS OF THE LONE WOLF Columbia, 1941
COUNTER ESPIONAGE Columbia, 1942
SEVEN MILES FROM ALCATRAZ RKO Radio, 1942
THE FALCON STRIKES BACK RKO Radio, 1943
HITLER'S CHILDREN RKO Radio, 1943
CAPTIVE WILD WOMAN Universal, 1943
BEHIND THE RISING SUN RKO Radio, 1943
TENDER COMRADE RKO Radio, 1943
MURDER MY SWEET RKO Radio, 1945
BACK TO BATAAN RKO Radio, 1945
TILL THE END OF TIME RKO Radio, 1945
CROSSFIRE ★ RKO Radio, 1947
SO WELL REMEMBERED RKO Radio, 1947
THE HIDDEN ROOM *OBSESSION* British Lion, 1949, British
GIVE US THIS DAY *SALT TO THE DEVIL* Eagle Lion, 1949, British
MUTINY Universal, 1952
THE SNIPER Columbia, 1952
EIGHT IRON MEN Columbia, 1952
THE JUGGLER Columbia, 1953
THE CAINE MUTINY Columbia, 1954
BROKEN LANCE 20th Century-Fox, 1954
THE END OF THE AFFAIR Columbia, 1954
SOLDIER OF FORTUNE 20th Century-Fox, 1955
THE LEFT HAND OF GOD 20th Century-Fox, 1955
THE MOUNTAIN Paramount, 1956
RAINTREE COUNTY MGM, 1957
THE YOUNG LIONS 20th Century-Fox, 1958
WARLOCK 20th Century-Fox, 1959
THE BLUE ANGEL 20th Century-Fox, 1959
WALK ON THE WILD SIDE Columbia, 1962
THE RELUCTANT SAINT Davis-Royal, 1962, Italian-U.S.
THE CARPETBAGGERS Paramount, 1963
WHERE LOVE HAS GONE Paramount, 1964
MIRAGE Universal, 1965
ALVAREZ KELLY Columbia, 1966
ANZIO Columbia, 1968, Italian
SHALAKO! Cinerama Releasing Corporation, 1968, British
BLUEBEARD Cinerama Releasing Corporation, 1972, Italian-French-West German
THE HUMAN FACTOR Bryanston, 1974, British-U.S.
HE IS MY BROTHER Atlantic Releasing Corporation, 1976

ROGER DONALDSON

Personal Manager: Harry Ufland, Ufland-Roth Productions, 20th Century Fox, 10201 W. Pico Blvd., Executive Building Room 246, Los Angeles, CA 90035, 213/203-1295

SLEEPING DOGS Aardvark Films 1977, New Zealand
SMASH PALACE Atlantic Releasing Corporation, 1981, New Zealand
THE BOUNTY Orion, 1984, British
MARIE MGM/UA, 1985

STANLEY DONEN*

b. April 13, 1924 - Columbia, South Carolina
Agent: Stan Kamen, William Morris Agency - Beverly Hills, 213/274-7451
Business Manager: Edward Traubner, Traubner & Flynn, 2049 Century Park East - Suite 2500, Los Angeles, CA 90067, 213/859-4221

ON THE TOWN co-director with Gene Kelly, MGM, 1949
ROYAL WEDDING MGM, 1951
SINGIN' IN THE RAIN co-director with Gene Kelly, MGM, 1952
LOVE IS BETTER THAN NONE MGM, 1952

STANLEY DONEN*—continued

FEARLESS FAGAN MGM, 1952
GIVE A GIRL A BREAK MGM, 1953
SEVEN BRIDES FOR SEVEN BROTHERS MGM, 1954
DEEP IN MY HEART MGM, 1954
IT'S ALWAYS FAIR WEATHER co-director with Gene Kelly, MGM, 1955
FUNNY FACE Paramount, 1957
THE PAJAMA GAME co-director with George Abbott, Warner Bros., 1957
KISS THEM FOR ME 20th Century-Fox, 1957
INDISCREET Warner Bros., 1958, British
DAMN YANKEES co-director with George Abbott, Warner Bros., 1958
ONCE MORE, WITH FEELING Columbia, 1960
SURPRISE PACKAGE Columbia, 1960
THE GRASS IS GREENER Universal, 1961
CHARADE Universal, 1964
ARABESQUE Universal, 1966, British-U.S.
TWO FOR THE ROAD 20th Century-Fox, 1967, British-U.S.
BEDAZZLED 20th Century-Fox, 1967, British
STAIRCASE 20th Century-Fox, 1969, British
THE LITTLE PRINCE Paramount, 1974, British
LUCKY LADY 20th Century-Fox, 1975
MOVIE MOVIE Warner Bros., 1978
SATURN 3 AFD, 1980
BLAME IT ON RIO 20th Century Fox, 1984

WALTER DONIGER*

b. July 1, 1917 - New York, New York
Home: 555 Huntley Drive, Los Angeles, CA 90048, 213/659-2787
Agent: Triad Artists, Inc. - Los Angeles, 213/556-2727

DUFFY OF SAN QUENTIN Warner Bros., 1953
THE STEEL CAGE United Artists, 1954
THE STEEL JUNGLE Warner Bros., 1955
UNWED MOTHER Allied Artists, 1958
HOUSE OF WOMEN Warner Bros., 1960
SAFE AT HOME! Columbia, 1962
MAD BULL co-director with Len Steckler, Steckler Productions/Filmways, 1977
KENTUCKY WOMAN Walter Doniger Productions/20th Century-Fox TV, 1983

TOM DONNELLY

Contact: Writers Guide of America - Los Angeles, 213/550-1000

QUICKSILVER Columbia, 1985

CLIVE DONNER*

b. January 21, 1926 - London, England
Agent: William Morris Agency - Beverly Hills, 213/274-7451

THE SECRET PLACE Rank, 1957, British
HEART OF A CHILD Rank, 1958, British
MARRIAGE OF CONVENIENCE Allied Artists, 1961, British
THE SINISTER MAN Allied Artists, 1961, British
SOME PEOPLE American International, 1962, British
THE GUEST *THE CARETAKER* Janus, 1963, British
NOTHING BUT THE BEST Royal Films International, 1964, British
WHAT'S NEW PUSSYCAT? United Artists, 1965, British
LUV Columbia, 1967
HERE WE GO ROUND THE MULBERRY BUSH Lopert, 1968, British
ALFRED THE GREAT MGM, 1969, British
OLD DRACULA *VAMPIRA* American International, 1975, British
ROGUE MALE (TF) BBC, 1976, British
SPECTRE (TF) 20th Century-Fox TV, 1977
THE THIEF OF BAGHDAD (TF) Palm Films Ltd., 1979, British
THE NUDE BOMB Universal, 1980
CHARLIE CHAN THE CURSE OF THE DRAGON QUEEN American Cinema, 1980
OLIVER TWIST (TF) Claridge Group Ltd./Grafton Films, 1982, British
THE SCARLET PIMPERNEL (TF) London Films Ltd., 1982, British

CLIVE DONNER*—continued

ARTHUR THE KING (TF) Martin Poll Productions/Comworld Productions/Jadran Film, 1983, U.S.-Yugoslavian
TO CATCH A KING (CTF) HBO Premiere Films/Entertainment Partners/Gaylord Productions, 1984
A CHRISTMAS CAROL (TF) Entertainment Partners Ltd., 1984, U.S.-British

RICHARD DONNER*

Agent: Michael Ovitz, CAA - Los Angeles, 213/277-4545
Business Manager: Gerald Breslauer, Breslauer, Jacobson & Rutman - Los Angeles, 213/879-0167

X-15 United Artists, 1961
SALT AND PEPPER United Artists, 1968, British
LOLA *TWINKY* American International, 1970, British-Italian
LUCAS TANNER (TF) Universal TV, 1974
SENIOR YEAR (TF) Universal TV, 1974
A SHADOW IN THE STREETS (TF) Playboy Productions, 1975
SARAH T. - PORTRAIT OF A TEENAGE ALCOHOLIC (TF) Universal TV, 1975
THE OMEN 20th Century-Fox, 1976
SUPERMAN Warner Bros., 1978, U.S.-British
INSIDE MOVES AFD, 1980
THE TOY Columbia, 1982
LADYHAWKE Warner Bros., 1985
GOONIES Warner Bros., 1985

TOM DONOVAN*

Business: Director's Service, Inc., 650 Park Avenue, New York, NY 10021, 212/737-6910
Attorney: Thomas H. Ryan - New York City, 212/355-7003

THE LAST BRIDE OF SALEM (TF) 20th Century-Fox TV, 1974
TRISTAN AND ISOLT Clar Productions, 1981, British

ROBERT DORNHELM

THE CHILDREN OF THEATRE STREET (FD) Peppercorn-Wormser, 1977
SHE DANCES ALONE Continental, 1982, U.S.-Austrian, British
DIGITAL DREAMS Ripple Productions Ltd., 1983
ECHO PARK Wien-Film Productions/Walter Shenson Films/Austrian Film Board, 1985, U.S.-Austrian

GORDON DOUGLAS*

b. December 5, 1909 - New York, New York
Home: 6600 West 6th Street, Los Angeles, CA 90048
Business Manager: Robert Stilwell, Ryder, Stilwell, Inc., P.O. Box 92920, Los Angeles, CA 90009, 213/937-5500

GENERAL SPANKY co-director with Fred Newmayer, MGM, 1936
ZENOBIA United Artists, 1939
SAPS AT SEA United Artists, 1940
ROAD SHOW co-director with Hal Roach & Hal Roach, Jr., United Artists, 1941
BROADWAY LIMITED United Artists, 1941
NIAGARA FALLS United Artists, 1941
THE DEVIL WITH HITLER RKO Radio, 1942
THE GREAT GILDERSLEEVE RKO Radio, 1942
GILDERSLEEVE'S BAD DAY RKO Radio, 1943
GILDERSLEEVE ON BROADWAY RKO Radio, 1943
GILDERSLEEVE'S GHOST RKO Radio, 1944
A NIGHT OF ADVENTURE RKO Radio, 1944
GIRL RUSH RKO Radio, 1944
THE FALCON IN HOLLYWOOD RKO Radio, 1944
ZOMBIES ON BROADWAY RKO Radio, 1945
FIRST YANK INTO TOKYO RKO Radio, 1945
DICK TRACY VS. CUEBALL RKO Radio, 1946

GORDON DOUGLAS*—continued

SAN QUENTIN RKO Radio, 1946
IF YOU KNEW SUSIE RKO Radio, 1948
THE BLACK ARROW Columbia, 1948
WALK A CROOKED MILE Columbia, 1948
MR. SOFT TOUCH co-director with Henry Levin, Columbia, 1949
THE DOOLINS OF OKLAHOMA Columbia, 1949
THE NEVADAN Columbia, 1950
FORTUNES OF CAPTAIN BLOOD Columbia, 1950
ROGUES OF SHERWOOD FOREST Columbia, 1950
KISS TOMORROW GOODBYE United Artists, 1950
BETWEEN MIDNIGHT AND DAWN Columbia, 1950
THE GREAT MISSOURI RAID Paramount, 1951
ONLY THE VALIANT Warner Bros., 1951
I WAS A COMMUNIST FOR THE FBI Warner Bros., 1951
COME FILL THE CUP Warner Bros., 1951
MARU MARU Warner Bros., 1952
THE IRON MISTRESS Warner Bros., 1952
SHE'S BACK ON BROADWAY Warner Bros., 1953
THE CHARGE AT FEATHER CREEK Warner Bros., 1953
SO THIS IS LOVE Warner Bros., 1953
THEM Warner Bros., 1954
YOUNG AT HEART Warner Bros., 1954
THE McCONNELL STORY Warner Bros., 1955
SINCERELY YOURS Warner Bros., 1955
SANTIAGO Warner Bros., 1956
THE BIG LAND Warner Bros., 1957
BOMBERS B-52 Warner Bros., 1957
FORT DOBBS Warner Bros., 1958
THE FIEND WHO WALKED THE WEST 20th Century-Fox, 1958
UP PERISCOPE Warner Bros., 1959
YELLOWSTONE KELLY Warner Bros., 1959
GOLD OF THE SEVEN SAINTS Warner Bros., 1961
THE SINS OF RACHEL CADE Warner Bros., 1961
CLAUDELLE INGLISH Warner Bros., 1961
FOLLOW THAT DREAM United Artists, 1962
CALL ME BWANA United Artists, 1963
ROBIN AND THE SEVEN HOODS Warner Bros., 1964
RIO CONCHOS 20th Century-Fox, 1964
SYLVIA Paramount, 1965
HARLOW Paramount, 1965
STAGECOACH 20th Century-Fox, 1966
WAY...WAY OUT! 20th Century-Fox, 1966
IN LIKE FLINT 20th Century-Fox, 1967
CHUKA Paramount, 1967
TONY ROME 20th Century-Fox, 1967
THE DETECTIVE 20th Century-Fox, 1968
LADY IN CEMENT 20th Century-Fox, 1968
SKULLDUGGERY Universal, 1970
BARQUERO United Artists, 1970
THEY CALL ME MISTER TIBBS! United Artists, 1970
SLAUGHTER'S BIG RIP-OFF American International, 1973
NEVADA SMITH (TF) Rackin-Hayes Productions/Paramount TV, 1975
VIVA KNIEVEL! Warner Bros., 1978

KIRK DOUGLAS*

(Issur Danielovitch)

b. December 9, 1916 - Amsterdam, New York
Business: The Bryna Company, 141 El Camino Drive, Beverly Hills, CA 90212, 213/274-5294
Agent: Fred Specktor, CAA - Los Angeles, 213/277-4545

SCALAWAG Paramount, 1973, U.S.-Italian
POSSE Paramount, 1975

NANCY DOWD

b. Framingham, Massachusetts
Agent: Cheryl Peterson, CAA - Los Angeles, 213/277-4545

LOVE co-director with Annette Cohen, Liv Ullmann & Mai Zetterling, Velvet Films, 1982, Canadian

KATHLEEN DOWDEY

November 13, 1949 - Washington, D.C.
Business: Five Point Films, Inc., 915 Highland View N.E., Suite B, Atlanta, GA 30306, 404/875-6076
Attorney: Peter Nichols, Weissman, Wolff, Bergman, Coleman & Schulman, 9601 Wilshire Blvd., Suite 825, Beverly Hills, CA 90210, 213/858-7888

A CELTIC TRILOGY (FD) First Run Features, 1979
BLUE HEAVEN Five Point Films, 1984

ROBERT DOWNEY

b. June, 1936
Business: 8497 Crescent Drive, Los Angeles, CA 90046
Attorney: Franklin, Wienrib, Rudell - New York City, 212/489-0680

BABO 73 1963
CHAFED ELBOWS Grove Press, 1965
NO MORE EXCUSES Rogosin, 1968
PUTNEY SWOPE Cinema 5, 1969
POUND United Artists, 1970
GREASER'S PALACE Greaser's Palace, 1972
MAD MAGAZINE PRESENTS UP THE ACADEMY Warner Brothers, 1980
MOONBEAM Analysis, 1984

STAN DRAGOTI*

Business: EUE-Screen Gems, 3701 Oak Street, Burbank, CA 91505, 213/843-3221
Agent: Fred Specktor, CAA - Los Angeles, 213/277-4545

DIRTY LITTLE BILLY Columbia, 1972
LOVE AT FIRST BITE American International, 1979
MR. MOM 20th Century-Fox, 1983
THE MAN WITH ONE RED SHOE 20th Century Fox, 1985

ARTHUR DREIFUSS*

b. March 25, 1908 - Frankfurt am Main, Germany
Home: 11407 Valley Spring Lane, Apt. 7, Studio City, CA 91604, 818/762-2070
Agent: George Michaud, George Michaud Agency - Encino, 818/981-6680

DOUBLE DEAL International Road Shows, 1939
MYSTERY IN SWING International Road Shows, 1940
MURDER ON LENOX AVENUE International Road Shows, 1941
SUNDAY SINNERS International Road Shows, 1941
REG'LAR FELLERS Producers Releasing Corporation, 1941
BABY FACE MORGAN Producers Releasing Corporation, 1942
THE BOSS OF BIG TOWN Producers Releasing Corporation, 1942
THE PAY-OFF Producers Releasing Corporation, 1942
SARONG GIRL Monogram, 1943
MELODY PARADE Monogram, 1943
CAMPUS RHYTHM Monogram, 1943
NEARLY EIGHTEEN Monogram, 1943
THE SULTAN'S DAUGHTER Monogram, 1944
EVER SINCE VENUS Columbia, 1944
EDDIE WAS A LADY Columbia, 1945
BOSTON BLACKIE BOOKED ON SUSPICION Columbia, 1945
BOSTON BLACKIE'S RENDEZVOUS Columbia, 1945
THE GAY SENORITA Columbia, 1945
PRISON SHIP Columbia, 1945
JUNIOR PROM Monogram, 1946
FREDDIE STEPS OUT Monogram, 1946

ARTHUR DREIFUSS*—continued

HIGH SCHOOL HERO Monogram, 1946
VACATION DAYS Monogram, 1947
BETTY CO-ED Columbia, 1947
LITTLE MISS BROADWAY Columbia, 1947
TWO BLONDES AND A REDHEAD Columbia, 1947
SWEET GENEVIEVE Columbia, 1947
GLAMOUR GIRL Columbia, 1948
MARY LOU Columbia, 1948
I SURRENDER DEAR Columbia, 1948
AN OLD-FASHIONED GIRL Eagle Lion, 1948
MANHATTAN ANGEL Columbia, 1948
ALL AMERICAN PRO Columbia, 1948
SHAMROCK HILL Eagle Lion, 1949
THERE'S A GIRL IN MY HEART Allied Artists, 1949
SECRET FILE Triangle, 1955, British-Dutch
ASSIGNMENT ABROAD Triangle, 1956, British-Dutch
LIFE BEGINS AT 17 Columbia, 1958
THE LAST BLITZKRIEG Columbia, 1959
JUKE BOX RHYTHM Columbia, 1959
THE QUARE FELLOW Astor, 1962, Irish-British
RIOT ON SUNSET STRIP American International, 1967
THE LOVE-INS Columbia, 1967
FOR SINGLES ONLY Columbia, 1968
A TIME TO SING MGM, 1968
THE YOUNG RUNAWAYS MGM, 1968

DAVID DRURY

Contact: British Academy of Film & Television Arts, 195 Piccadilly, London W1, England, 01/734-0022

FOREVER YOUNG 20th Century Fox (U.K.), 1984, British

CHARLES S. DUBIN*

b. February 1, 1919 - New York, New York
Home: 651 Lorna Lane, Los Angeles, CA 90049
Agent: Bill Haber, CAA - Los Angeles, 213/277-4545

MISTER ROCK & ROLL Paramount, 1957
TO DIE IN PARIS (TF) co-director with Allen Reisner, Universal TV, 1968
MURDER ONCE REMOVED (TF) Metromedia Productions, 1971
MURDOCK'S GANG (TF) Don Fedderson Productions, 1973
MOVING VIOLATION 20th Century-Fox, 1976
THE TENTH LEVEL (TF) CBS, Inc., 1976
THE DEADLY TRIANGLE (TF) Columbia TV, 1977
TOPPER (TF) Cosmo Productions/Robert A. Papazian Productions, 1979
ROOTS: THE NEXT GENERATIONS (MS) co-director with John Erman, Lloyd Richards & Georg Stanford Brown, Wolper Productions, 1979
THE GATHERING, PART II (TF) Hanna-Barbera Productions, 1979
THE MANIONS OF AMERICA (MS) co-director with Joseph Sargent, Roger Gimbel Productions/EMI TV/Argonaut Films Ltd., 1981
MY PALIKARI (TF) Center for TV in the Humanities, 1982

ROGER DUCHOWNY*

Home: 7532 Birdview Avenue, Malibu, CA 90265, 213/457-2404
Agent: Martin Shapiro, Shapiro-Lichtman Agency-Los Angeles, 213/557-2244

MURDER CAN HURT YOU! (TF) Aaron Spelling Productions, 1970

PETER JOHN DUFFELL

Home: 13 Stratford Grove, Putney, London, SW15 1NV, England, 01/785-9512
Agent: Merrily Kane Agency - Beverly Hills, 213/550-8874

PARTNERS IN CRIME Allied Artists, 1961, British
THE HOUSE THAT DRIPPED BLOOD Cinerama Releasing Corporation, 1971, British
ENGLAND MADE ME Cine Globe, 1973, British

PETER JOHN DUFFELL —continued

INSIDE OUT Warner Bros., 1976, British
CAUGHT ON A TRAIN (TF) BBC, 1980
EXPERIENCE PREFERRED, BUT NOT ESSENTIAL The Samuel Goldwyn Company, 1983, British
THE FAR PAVILIONS (CMS) Geoff Reeve & Associates/Goldcrest, 1984, British

MICHAEL DUGAN*

Home: 3822 E. First Street, Long Beach, CA 90803, 213/439-3370

MAUSOLEUM MPM, 1983

JOHN DUIGAN

Home Address: 57 Gipps Street, Balmain, NSW, 2041, Australia, 02/827-2756

THE FIRM MAN John Duigan Productions, 1975, Australian
THE TRESPASSERS Vega Film Productions, 1976, Australian
MOUTH TO MOUTH Vega Film Productions, 1978, Australian
DIMBOOLA Ko-An Productions, 1979, Australian
WINTER OF OUR DREAMS Satori, 1981, Australian
FAR EAST Filmco Australia, 1983, Australian
ONE NIGHT STAND Astra Film Productions/Hoyts-Edgely, 1984, Australian
STOP WATCH (TF) ACTF Productions, 1985, Australian

BILL DUKE*

Home: 2200 Broadview Terrace, Los Angeles, CA 90068, 213/851-3904
Agent: Kaplan-Stahler Agency - Beverly Hills, 213/653-4483

THE KILLING FLOOR (TF) Public Forum Productions/KERA-Dallas-Ft. Worth, 1984

DARYL DUKE*

b. Vancouver, Canada
Address: 4220 Evergreen Avenue, West Vancouver V7V 1H1, Canada, 604/987-5029
Agent: Jack Gilardi, ICM - Los Angeles, 213/550-4000

THE SASKATCHEWAN (TF) CBC, 1965, Canadian
THE PSYCHIATRIST: GOD BLESS THE CHILDREN (TF) Universal TV, 1970
PAYDAY Cinerama Releasing Corporation, 1972
HAPPINESS IS A WARM CLUE (TF) Universal TV, 1973
THE PRESIDENT'S PLANE IS MISSING (TF) ABC Circle Films, 1973
I HEARD THE OWL CALL MY NAME (TF) Tomorrow Entertainment, 1973
A CRY FOR HELP (TF) Universal TV, 1975
THEY ONLY COME OUT AT NIGHT (TF) MGM TV, 1975
GRIFFIN AND PHOENIX (TF) ABC Circle Films, 1976
THE SILENT PARTNER EMC Film/Aurora, 1979, Canadian
HARD FEELINGS Astral Bellevue, 1981, Canadian
THE THORN BIRDS (MS) ☆ David L. Wolper-Stan Margulies Productions/Edward Lewis Productions/Warner Brothers TV, 1983
THE NIGHTINGALE SAGA (TF) Cypress Point Productions, 1985

RUDY DURAND*

Business: Koala Productions, Ltd., 361 N. Canon Drive, Beverly Hills, CA 90212, 213/476-1649
Attorney: Greg Bautzer, Wyman, Rothman, Bautzer & Kuchel, 2049 Century Park East, Los Angeles, CA 90067, 213/550-8000

TILT Warner Bros., 1979

MARGUERITE DURAS

b. 1914 - Giadinh, French Indochina
Contact: French Film Office, 745 Fifth Avenue, New York, NY 10151, 212/832-8860

LA MUSICA co-director, 1966, French
DESTROY, SHE SAID 1969, French
JAUNE DE SOLEIL 1971, French
NATHALIE GRANGER Films Moliere, 1973, French
LA FEMMES DU GANGES Sunchild Productions, 1974, French
INDIA SONG Sunchild Productions/Films Armorial, 1975, French
DES JOURNEES ENTIERES DANS LES ARBRES 1976, French
SON NOM DE VENISE DANS CALCUTTA DESERT (FD) Cinema 9, 1976, French
BAXTER, VERA BAXTER Sunchild Productions, 1977, French
LE CAMION Films Moliere, 1977, French
LE NAVIRE NIGHT MK2/Gaumont/Les Films du Losange, 1979 French
AURELIA STEINER Hors Champ Diffusion, 1979, French
AGATHA ET LES LECTURES ILLIMITEES Hors Champ Diffusion, 1981, French
IL DIALOGO DI ROMA (FD) RAI/Lunga Cooperative, 1983, Italian

ROBERT DUVALL

b. January 5, 1931 - San Diego, California
Agent: Fred Specktor, CAA - Los Angeles, 213/277-4545
Personal Manager: 703/548-8100

WE'RE NOT THE JET SET (FD) 1975
ANGELO, MY LOVE Cinecom International, 1983

BOB DYLAN

(Robert Zimmerman)

b. May 24, 1941 - Duluth, Minnesota

RENALDO AND CLARA Circuit, 1978

E

CHARLES EASTMAN*

Messages: 213/376-0251
Agent: Michael Black/Jane Sindell, ICM - Los Angeles, 213/550-4000

THE ALL-AMERICAN BOY Warner Bros., 1973

CLINT EASTWOOD*

b. May 31, 1930 - San Francisco, California
Business: Malpaso Productions, 1900 Avenue of the Stars - Suite 2270, Los Angeles, CA 90067, 213/277-1900
Agent: Leonard Hirshan, William Morris Agency - Beverly Hills, 213/274-7451

PLAY MISTY FOR ME Universal, 1971
HIGH PLAINS DRIFTER Universal, 1972
BREEZY Universal, 1973
THE EIGER SANCTION Universal, 1974
THE OUTLAW JOSEY WALES Warner Bros., 1976
THE GAUNTLET Warner Bros., 1977
BRONCO BILLY Warner Bros., 1980
FIREFOX Warner Bros., 1982
HONKYTONK MAN Warner Bros., 1982
SUDDEN IMPACT Warner Bros., 1983
PALE RIDER Warner Bros., 1985

THOM EBERHARDT

SOLE SURVIVOR International Film Marketing, 1984
NIGHT OF THE COMET Atlantic Releasing Corporation, 1984

BLAKE EDWARDS*

b. July 26, 1922 - Tulsa, Oklahoma
Agent: Martin Baum, CAA - Los Angeles, 213/277-4545
Business: The Management Company, 1888 Century Park East, Suite 1616, Los Angeles, CA 90067, 213/553-6741

BRING YOUR SMILE ALONG Columbia, 1955
HE LAUGHED LAST Columbia, 1956
MISTER CORY MGM, 1957
THIS HAPPY FEELING Universal, 1958
THE PERFECT FURLOUGH Universal, 1959
OPERATION PETTICOAT Universal, 1959
HIGH TIME 20th Century-Fox, 1960
BREAKFAST AT TIFFANY'S Paramount, 1961
EXPERIMENT IN TERROR Warner Bros., 1962
DAYS OF WINE AND ROSES Warner Bros., 1962
THE PINK PANTHER United Artists, 1964
A SHOT IN THE DARK United Artists, 1964
THE GREAT RACE Warner Bros., 1965
WHAT DID YOU DO IN THE WAR, DADDY? United Artists, 1966
GUNN Warner Bros., 1967
THE PARTY United Artists, 1968
DARLING LILI Paramount, 1970
WILD ROVERS MGM, 1971
THE CAREY TREATMENT MGM, 1972
THE TAMARIND SEED Avco Embassy, 1974
RETURN OF THE PINK PANTHER United Artists, 1975, British
THE PINK PANTHER STRIKES AGAIN United Artists, 1976, British
REVENGE OF THE PINK PANTHER United Artists, 1978, British
10 Orion/Warner Bros., 1979
S.O.B. Paramount, 1981
VICTOR/VICTORIA MGM/United Artists, 1982
TRAIL OF THE PINK PANTHER MGM/UA, 1982
CURSE OF THE PINK PANTHER MGM/UA, 1983
THE MAN WHO LOVED WOMEN Columbia, 1983
MICKI & MAUDE Columbia, 1984

GEORGE EDWARDS

Agent: Artists Group, Ltd. - Los Angeles, 213/552-1100

THE ATTIC Atlantic Releasing Corporation, 1984

VINCENT EDWARDS*

(Vincent Edward Zoimo)

b. July 9, 1928 - New York, New York
Agent: Artists Group, Ltd. - Los Angeles, 213/552-1100

MANEATER Universal TV, 1973

JAN EGLESON

BILLY IN THE LOWLANDS Theatre Company of Boston, 1979
THE DARK END OF THE STREET First Run Features, 1981
THE LITTLE SISTER (TF) Shefida Productions, 1984
TRUE LOVE 1985

ROBERT ELFSTROM

THE NASHVILLE SOUND (FD) co-director with David Hoffman, 1970
JOHNNY CASH! THE MAN, HIS WORLD, HIS MUSIC (FD) Continental, 1970
PETE SEEGER...A SONG AND A STONE (FD) Theatre Exchange, 1972
THE GOSPEL ROAD 20th Century-Fox, 1973
MYSTERIES OF THE SEA (FD) co-director with Al Giddings, Polygram Pictures/Ocean Films Ltd., 1980
MOSES PENDLETON PRESENTS MOSES PENDLETON (FD) ABC Video Enterprises, 1982

LARRY ELIKANN*

b. July 4, 1923 - New York, New York
Business: The Larry Elikann Company, Inc., 100 S. Doheny Drive, Los Angeles, CA 90048, 213/271-4406
Agent: William Morris Agency - Beverly Hills, 213/274-7451

JOEY AND REDHAWK (TF) Daniel Wilson Productions, 1978
THE GREAT WALLENDAS (TF) Daniel Wilson Productions, 1978
CHARLIE AND THE GREAT BALLOON CHASE (TF) Daniel Wilson Productions, 1981
SPRAGGUE (TF) MF Productions/Lorimar Productions, 1984
POISON IVY (TF) NBC Productions, 1984

LANG ELLIOTT*

b. 1950 - Los Angeles, California
Home: P.O. Box 480708, Los Angeles, CA 90048, 213/874-3558
Agent: Donald Barskin, The Barskin Agency - North Hollywood, 818/985-2992
Business Manager: Myron Slobedien, Loeb & Loeb, 10100 Santa Monica Blvd. - Suite 2200, Los Angeles, CA 90067, 213/552-7765

THE PRIVATE EYES New World, 1980

ROBERT ENDERS

Agent: Peter Crouch Associates, 59 Frith Street, London W1, England, 01/734-2167

STEVIE First Artists, 1978, British

CY ENDFIELD

b. November, 1914 - South Africa
Contact: British Academy of Film & Television Arts, 195 Piccadilly, London W1, England, 01/734-0022

GENTLEMAN JOE PALOOKA Monogram, 1946
STORK BITES MAN United Artists, 1947, British
THE ARGYLE SECRETS Film Classics, 1948, British
JOE PALOOKA IN THE BIG FIGHT Monogram, 1949

CY ENDFIELD —continued

THE UNDERWORLD STORY United Artists, 1950
THE SOUND OF FURY United Artists, 1950
TARZAN'S SAVAGE FURY RKO Radio, 1952
COLONEL MARCH INVESTIGATES Criterion, 1953, British
THE MASTER PLAN directed under pseudonym of Hugh Raker, Astor, 1954, British
THE SECRET Eros, 1955, British
CHILD IN THE HOUSE Eros, 1956, British
HELL DRIVERS Rank, 1957, British
SEA FURY Lopert, 1958, British
JET STORM United Producers Organization, 1959, British
MYSTERIOUS ISLAND Columbia, 1961, British
HIDE AND SEEK Universal, 1964, British
ZULU Embassy, 1964, British
SANDS OF THE KALAHARI Paramount, 1965, British
DE SADE American International, 1969, U.S.-West German
UNIVERSAL SOLDIER Hemdale, 1971, British

GEORGE ENGLUND*

b. June 22, 1926 - Washington, D.C.
Home: 765 Brooktree Road, Pacific Palisades, CA 90272, 213/459-5820
Agent: Rowland Perkins, CAA - Los Angeles, 213/277-4545
Business Manager: Dave Flynn, Traubner & Flynn, 2049 Century Park East - Suite 2500, Los Angeles, CA 90067, 213/859-4221

THE UGLY AMERICAN Universal, 1963
SIGNPOST TO MURDER MGM, 1965
ZACHARIAH Cinerama Releasing Corporation, 1970
SNOW JOB Warner Bros., 1972
A CHRISTMAS TO REMEMBER (TF) George Englund Productions, 1978
DIXIE: CHANGING HABITS (TF) George Englund Productions, 1983
THE VEGAS STRIP WAR (TF) George Englund Productions, 1984

ROBERT ENRICO

b. April 13, 1931 - Lievin, France
Contact: French Film Office, 745 Fifth Avenue, New York, NY 10151, 212/832-8860

AU COEUR DE LA VIE 1962, French
LA BELLE VIE 1963, French
THE WISE GUYS Universal, 1965, French
THE LAST ADVENTURE *I TRE AVVENTURIERI* Universal, 1969, Italian-French
ZITA Regional, 1968, French
HO! 1968, French
UN PEU, BEAUCOUP, PASSIONEMENT CFDC, 1971, French
BOULEVARD DU RHUM Gaumont, 1971, French-Italian-West German
LES CAIDS Parafrance, 1972, French
LE COMPAGNON INDESIRABLE 1973, French
LE SECRET Cinema National, 1974, French
THE OLD GUN Surrogate, 1976, French-West German
COUP DE FOUDRE 1978, French
UN NEVEU SILENCIEUX MK2, 1979, French
L'EMPREINTE DES GEANTS Filmel/SNC/FR3/Rialto Film, 1979, French-West German
HEADS OR TAILS Castle Hill, 1980, French
FOR THOSE I LOVED 20th Century-Fox, 1983, Canadian-French

MARCELO EPSTEIN

BODY ROCK New World, 1984

JOHN ERMAN*

b. Chicago, Illinois
Agent: Bill Haber, CAA - Los Angeles, 213/277-4545
Business Manager: Plant & Cohen, 10900 Wilshire Blvd. - Suite 900, Los Angeles, CA 90024, 213/824-2200

MAKING IT 20th Century-Fox, 1971
ACE ELI AND RODGER OF THE SKIES directed under pseudonym of Bill Sampson, 20th Century-Fox, 1973
LETTERS FROM THREE LOVERS (TF) Spelling-Goldberg Productions, 1973
GREEN EYES (TF) ABC, 1977
ROOTS (MS) ☆ co-director with David Greene, Marvin J. Chomsky & Gilbert Moses, Wolper Productions, 1977
ALEXANDER: THE OTHER SIDE OF DAWN (TF) Douglas Cramer Productions, 1977
JUST ME & YOU (TF) Roger Gimbel Productions/EMI, 1978
ROOTS: THE NEXT GENERATIONS (MS) co-director with Charles S. Dubin, Lloyd Richards & Georg Stanford Brown, Wolper Productions, 1979
MY OLD MAN (TF) Zeitman-McNichol-Halmi Productions, 1979
MOVIOLA (MS) ☆ David L. Wolper-Stan Margulies Productions/Warner Bros. TV, 1980
THE LETTER (TF) Hajeno Productions/Warner Bros. TV, 1982
ELEANOR, FIRST LADY OF THE WORLD (TF) Murbill Productions/Embassy TV, 1982
ANOTHER WOMAN'S CHILD (TF) CBS Entertainment, 1983
WHO WILL LOVE MY CHILDREN? (TF) ☆☆ ABC Circle Films, 1983
A STREETCAR NAMED DESIRE (TF) ☆ Keith Barish Productions, 1984
THE ATLANTA CHILD MURDERS (TF) Mann-Rafshoon Productions/Finnegan Associates, 1985

RICHARD EYRE

Home: 4 St. Martin's Road, London SW9, England,01/733-6207
Agent: Peter Murphy, Spokesmen, 1 Craven Hill, London W2, England, 01/262-1011

THE PLOUGHMAN'S LUNCH Samuel Goldwyn Company, 1983, British
LOOSE CONNECTIONS Orion Classics, 1983, British
LAUGHTER HOUSE Film Four International, 1984, British

F

FERDINAND FAIRFAX

b. August 1, 1944 - London, England
Address: 62 Leathwaite Road, London SW11 6RS, England, 01/228-5339
Agent: Duncan Heath Associates: 162/170 Wardour Street, London W1, England, 01/439-1471

THE SPEED KING (TF) BBC, British
DANGER UXB (MS) Thames TV, 1979, British

FERDINAND FAIRFAX —continued

WINSTON CHURCHILL - THE WILDERNESS YEARS (MS) Southern Pictures Productions, 1983, British
NATE AND HAYES *SAVAGE ISLANDS* Paramount, 1983, New Zealand

HARRY FALK*

Agent: William Morris Agency - Beverly Hills, 213/274-7451

THREE'S A CROWD (TF) Screen Gems/Columbia TV, 1969
THE DEATH SQUAD (TF) Spelling-Goldberg Productions, 1974
MEN OF THE DRAGON (TF) Wolper Productions, 1974
THE ABDUCTION OF SAINT ANNE (TF) QM Productions, 1975
MANDRAKE (TF) Universal TV, 1979
CENTENNIAL (MS) co-director with Paul Krasny, Bernard McEveety & Virgil Vogel, Universal TV, 1980
THE NIGHT THE CITY SCREAMED (TF) David Gerber Company, 1980
THE CONTENDER (TF) co-director with Lou Antonio, Universal TV, 1980
THE SOPHISTICATED GENTS (TF) Daniel Wilson Productions, 1981
ADVICE TO THE LOVELORN (TF) Universal TV, 1981
HEAR NO EVIL (TF) Paul Pompian Productions/MGM TV, 1982
EMERALD POINT, N.A.S. (TF) Richard and Esther Shapiro Productions/20th Century-Fox TV, 1983

JAMAA FANAKA

WELCOME HOME, BROTHER CHARLES Crown International, 1975
EMMA MAE Pro-International, 1977
PENITENTIARY Jerry Gross Organization, 1980
PENITENTIARY II MGM/UA, 1982
STREETWARS Arista, 1984

JAMES FARGO*

b. August 4, 1938 - Republic, Washington
Agent: Martin Shapiro, Shapiro-Lichtman Agency - Los Angeles, 213/557-2244
Business Manager: Howard Bernstein, Kaufman & Bernstein, 1900 Avenue of the Stars, Los Angeles, CA 90067, 213/277-1900

THE ENFORCER Warner Bros., 1976
EVERY WHICH WAY BUT LOOSE Warner Bros., 1978
CARAVANS Universal, 1979, U.S.-Iranian
GAME FOR VULTURES New Line Cinema, 1980, British
FORCED VENGEANCE MGM/United Artists, 1982
VOYAGE OF THE ROCK ALIENS KGA/Inter Planetary Pictures/Curb Communications, 1984

FEDERICO FELLINI

b. January 20, 1920 - Rimini, Italy
Contact: Ministry of Tourism & Education, Via Della Ferratella, No. 51, 00184 Rome, Italy, 06/7732

VARIETY LIGHTS co-director with Alberto Lattuada, Pathe Contemporary, 1950, Italian
THE WHITE SHEIK Pathe Contemporary, 1952, Italian
I VITTELONI API Productions, 1953, Italian
LOVE IN THE CITY co-director with Michelangelo Antonioni, Alberto Lattuada, Carlo Lizzani, Francesco Maselli & Dino Risi, Italian Films Export, 1953, Italian
LA STRADA Trans-Lux, 1954, Italian
IL BIDONE Astor, 1955, Italian
NIGHTS OF CABIRIA Lopert, 1957, Italian
LA DOLCE VITA ★ Astor, 1960, Italian
BOCCACCIO '70 co-director with Luchino Visconti & Vittorio De Sica, Embassy, 1962, Italian
8½ ★ Embassy, 1963, Italian
JULIET OF THE SPIRITS Rizzoli, 1965, Italian-French-West German
SPIRITS OF THE DEAD *HISTOIRES EXTRAORDINAIRES* co-director with Roger Vadim & Louis Malle, American International, 1969, French-Italian
FELLINI SATYRICON ★ United Artists, 1970, Italian-French

FEDERICO FELLINI —continued

THE CLOWNS Levitt-Pickman, 1971, Italian-French-West German, originally made for television
FELLINI'S ROMA United Artists, 1972, Italian-French
AMARCORD ★ New World, 1974, Italian
CASANOVA *IL CASANOVA DI FEDERICO FELLINI* Universal, 1977, Italian
ORCHESTRA REHEARSAL New Yorker, 1979, Italian-West German, originally made for television
CITY OF WOMEN New Yorker, 1981, Italian-French
AND THE SHIP SAILS ON Triumph/Columbia, 1983, Italian-French

KERRY FELTHAM*

b. March 20, 1939 - Edmonton, Alberta, Canada
Home: 650 Las Lomas, Pacific Palisades, CA 90272, 213/454-6806
Agent: Michael Margules, Paul Kohner, Inc. - Los Angeles, 213/550-1060

THE GREAT CHICAGO CONSPIRACY CIRCUS New Line Cinema, 1970

GEORG J. FENADY*

b. July 2, 1930 - Toledo, Ohio
Home: 602 N. Cherokee, Los Angeles, CA 90004, 213/466-5001
Agent: Mark Lichtman, Shapiro-Lichtman Agency - Los Angeles, 213/557-2244
Business Manager: Mike Merrick - Los Angeles, 213/278-5354

ARNOLD Cinerama Releasing Corporation, 1974
TERROR IN THE WAX MUSEUM Cinerama Releasing Corporation, 1974
THE NIGHT THE BRIDGE FELL DOWN (TF) Irwin Allen Productions/Warner Bros. TV, 1983
CAVE-IN! (TF) Irwin Allen Productions/Warner Bros. TV, 1983

MICHAEL FERGUSON

Contact: British Academy of Film & Television Arts, 195 Piccadilly, London WI, England, 01/734-0022

THE GLORY BOYS (TF) Yorkshire TV/Alan Landsburg Productions, 1984, British-U.S.

ABEL FERRARA

DRILLER KILLER Rochelle Films, 1979
MS. 45 Rochelle Films, 1981
FEAR CITY 20th Century Fox, 1985

JOSE FERRER*
(Jose Vincente Ferrer de Otero y Cintron)

b. January 8, 1912 - Santurce, Puerto Rico
Business: 2 Penn Plaza - Suite 1825, New York, NY 10001, 212/947-9930

THE SHRIKE Universal, 1955
THE COCKLESHELL HEROES Columbia, 1956, British
THE GREAT MAN Universal, 1956
I ACCUSE! MGM, 1958
THE HIGH COST OF LOVING MGM, 1958
RETURN TO PEYTON PLACE 20th Century-Fox, 1961
STATE FAIR 20th Century-Fox, 1962

MEL FERRER

b. August 25, 1917 - Elberon, New Jersey

THE GIRL OF THE LIMBERLOST Columbia, 1945
VENDETTA RKO Radio, 1950
THE SECRET FURY RKO Radio, 1950
GREEN MANSIONS MGM, 1959
CABRIOLA Columbia, 1966, Spanish

MARCO FERRERI

b. May 11, 1928 - Milan, Italy
Contact: Ministry of Tourism & Education, Via Della Ferratella, No. 51, 00184 Rome, Italy, 06/7732

EL PISITO 1958, Spanish
LOS CHICOS 1959, Spanish
EL COCHECITO 1960, Spanish
LE ITALIANE E L'AMORE co-director with 11 others, Magic Film, 1961, Italian
THE CONJUGAL BED *UNA STORIA MODERNA: L'APE REGINA* Embassy, 1963, Italian-French
THE APE WOMAN Embassy, 1964, Italian
CONTROSESSO co-director with Franco Rossi, Jacques Romain, Gianni Puccini & Mino Guerrini, Adelphia Cinematografica/France Cinema Production, 1964, Italian-French
KISS THE OTHER SHEIK *OGGI, DOMANI E DOPODEMANI* co-director with Eduardo de Filippo & Luciano Salce, MGM, 1965, Italian-French
MARCIA NUNZIALE Sancro Film/Transinter Film, 1966, Italian-French
L'HAREM Sancro Film, 1967, Italian
THE MAN WITH THE BALLOONS Sigma III, 1968, French-Italian
DILLINGER E MORTO Pegaso Film, 1969, Italian
THE SEED OF MAN SRL, 1970, Italian
L'UDIENZA Vides, 1971, Italian
LIZA Horizon, 1972, French-Italian
LA GRANDE BOUFFE ABKCO, 1973, French-Italian
TOUCHEZ PAS LA FEMME BLANCHE 1974, French-Italian
THE LAST WOMAN Columbia, 1976, Italian-French
BYE BYE MONKEY Fida, 1978, Italian
CHIEDO ASILO Gaumont, 1979, Italian-French-Tahitian
NO CHILD'S LAND Sacis, 1980, Italian-French
TALES OF ORDINARY MADNESS Fred Baker Films, 1983, Italian-French

MARCO FERRERI —continued

THE STORY OF PIERA UGC, 1983, Italian-French-West German
IL FUTURO E DONNA Fasco Film, 1984, Italian

KEN FINKLEMAN*

Agent: Ron Mardigian, William Morris Agency - Beverly Hills, 213/274-7451

AIRPLANE II: THE SEQUEL Paramount, 1983
HEAD OFFICE Tri-Star, 1985

ALBERT FINNEY

b. May 9, 1936 - Salford, England
Agent: ICM - Los Angeles, 213/550-4000

CHARLIE BUBBLES Regional, 1968, British

SAM FIRSTENBERG

b. Israel

ONE MORE CHANCE Cannon, 1981
REVENGE OF THE NINJA MGM/UA/Cannon, 1983
NINJA III: THE DOMINATION Cannon, 1984
BREAKIN' 2 ELECTRIC BOOGALOO Tri-Star/Cannon, 1984

MICHAEL FIRTH

Contact: New Zealand Film Commission, P.O. Box 11-546, Wellington, New Zealand, 4/72-2360

OFF THE EDGE Pentacle, 1977, New Zealand
HEART OF THE STAG New World, 1984, New Zealand
SYLVIA Sylvia Productions Ltd., 1985, New Zealand

MAX FISCHER

Contact: Canadian Film & Television Association, 8 King Street, Toronto, Ontario M5C 1B5, Canada, 416/363-0296

THE LUCKY STAR Pickman Films, 1981, Canadian
THE MAN IN 5A Neighbour Film Inc., 1983, Canadian

BERND FISCHERAUER

Contact: German Film & TV Academy, Pommernallee 1, 1000 Berlin 19, West Germany, 030/303-6212

BLOOD AND HONOR: YOUTH UNDER HITLER (MS) Daniel Wilson Productions/SWF Baden Baden/Taurus Film, 1982, U.S.-West German

DAVID FISHELSON

CITY NEWS co-director with Zoe Zinman, Cinecom International, 1983

DAVID FISHER

b. April 21, 1948 - Nashville, Tennessee
Home: 14144 Dickens, Apt. 115, Sherman Oaks, CA 91423, 818/907-1368

LIAR'S MOON Crown International, 1982
TOY SOLDIERS New World, 1984

JACK FISK*

b. December 19, 1945 - Ipava, Illinois
Agent: Rick Nicita, CAA - Los Angeles, 213/277-4545

RAGGEDY MAN Universal, 1981
VIOLETS ARE BLUE Columbia, 1985

RICHARD FLEISCHER*

b. December 8, 1916 - Brooklyn, New York
Agent: Phil Gersh, The Gersh Agency - Beverly Hills, 213/274-6611

CHILD OF DIVORCE RKO Radio, 1946
BANJO RKO Radio, 1947
DESIGN FOR DEATH RKO Radio, 1948
SO THIS IS NEW YORK United Artists, 1948
BODYGUARD Columbia, 1948
MAKE MINE LAUGHS RKO Radio, 1949
THE CLAY PIGEON RKO Radio, 1949
FOLLOW ME QUIETLY RKO Radio, 1949
TRAPPED Eagle Lion, 1949
ARMORED CAR ROBBERY RKO Radio, 1950
THE NARROW MARGIN RKO Radio, 1952
THE HAPPY TIME Columbia, 1952
ARENA MGM, 1953
20,000 LEAGUES UNDER THE SEA Buena Vista, 1954
VIOLENT SATURDAY 20th Century-Fox, 1955
THE GIRL IN THE RED VELVET SWING 20th Century-Fox, 1955
BANDIDO United Artists, 1956
BETWEEN HEAVEN AND HELL 20th Century-Fox, 1956
THE VIKINGS United Artists, 1958
THESE THOUSAND HILLS 20th Century-Fox, 1959
COMPULSION 20th Century-Fox, 1959
CRACK IN THE MIRROR 20th Century-Fox, 1960
THE BIG GAMBLE 20th Century-Fox, 1961
BARABBAS Columbia, 1962, Italian
FANTASTIC VOYAGE 20th Century-Fox, 1966
DR. DOLITTLE 20th Century-Fox, 1967
THE BOSTON STRANGLER 20th Century-Fox, 1968
CHE! 20th Century-Fox, 1969
TORA! TORA! TORA! co-director with Kinji Fukasaku, 20th Century-Fox, 1970, U.S.-Japanese
10 RILLINGTON PLACE Columbia, 1971, British
SEE NO EVIL Columbia, 1971, British
THE LAST RUN MGM, 1971
THE NEW CENTURIONS Columbia, 1972
SOYLENT GREEN MGM, 1972
THE DON IS DEAD Universal, 1973
THE SPIKES GANG United Artists, 1974
MR. MAJESTYK United Artists, 1974
MANDINGO Paramount, 1975
THE INCREDIBLE SARAH Reader's Digest, 1976, British
CROSSED SWORDS *THE PRINCE AND THE PAUPER* Warner Bros., 1978, British
ASHANTI Columbia, 1970, Swiss-U.S.
THE JAZZ SINGER AFD, 1980
TOUGH ENOUGH 20th Century-Fox, 1983
AMITYVILLE 3-D Orion, 1983
CONAN THE DESTROYER Universal, 1984
RED SONJA MGM/UA, 1985

GORDON FLEMYNG

b. March 7, 1934 - Glasgow, Scotland
Home: 1 Albert Road, Wilmslow, Cheshire, England
Agent: Duncan Heath Associates, 162/170 Wardour Street, London W1, England, 01/439-1471

SOLD FOR SPARROW Schoenfield, 1962, British
FIVE TO ONE Allied Artists, 1963, British
JUST FOR FUN Columbia, 1963
DR. WHO AND THE DALEKS Continental, 1966, British

GORDON FLEMYNG —continued

DALEKS - INVASION EARTH 2150 A.D. Continental, 1966, British
THE SPLIT MGM, 1968
GREAT CATHERINE Warner Bros., 1968, British
THE LAST GRENADE Cinerama Releasing Corporation, 1970, British
A GOOD HUMAN STORY (TF) Granada TV, 1977, British
MIRAGE (TF) Granada TV, 1978, British

THEODORE J. FLICKER*

b. June 6, 1930 - Freehold, New Jersey
Business Manager: Marvin Freedman, Freedman, Kinzelberg & Broder, 1801 Avenue of the Stars, Los Angeles, CA 90067, 213/277-0700

THE TROUBLEMAKER Janus, 1964
THE PRESIDENT'S ANALYST Paramount, 1967
UP IN THE CELLAR American International, 1970
PLAYMATES (TF) ABC Circle Films, 1972
GUESS WHO'S SLEEPING IN MY BED? (TF) ABC Circle Films, 1973
JUST A LITTLE INCONVENIENCE (TF) Universal TV, 1977
JACOB TWO-TWO MEETS THE HOODED FANG Cinema Shares International, 1978, Canadian
LAST OF THE GOOD GUYS (TF) Columbia TV, 1978
WHERE THE LADIES GO (TF) Universal TV, 1980
SOGGY BOTTOM, U.S.A. Cinemax Marketing & Distribution, 1981

JOHN FLYNN*

Home: 574 Latimer Road, Santa Monica, CA 90402, 213/454-6850
Agent: Jack Gilardi/Jeff Berg, ICM - Los Angeles, 213/550-4000
Business Manager: Paul Shaw, 2800 Olympic Blvd. - Suite 202, Santa Monica, CA 90404, 213/829-6805

THE SERGEANT Warner Bros., 1968
THE JERUSALEM FILE MGM, 1972, U.S.-Israeli
THE OUTFIT MGM, 1974
ROLLING THUNDER American International, 1978
DEFIANCE American International, 1980
MARILYN: THE UNTOLD STORY (TF) co-director with Jack Arnold & Lawrence Schiller, Lawrence Schiller Productions, 1980
TOUCHED Lorimar Productions/Wildwoods Partners, 1983

LAWRENCE D. FOLDES

b. November 4, 1959 - Los Angeles, California
Business: Star Cinema Production Group, Inc., 6253 Hollywood Blvd. - Suite 922, Los Angeles, CA 90028, 213/463-2000
Attorney: Ronald G. Gabler, 2029 Century Park East - Suite 1690, Los Angeles, CA 90067, 213/553-8848

MALIBU HIGH Crown International, 1979
DON'T GO NEAR THE PARK Cannon, 1981
THE GREAT SKYCOPTER RESCUE Cannon, 1982
YOUNG WARRIORS Cannon, 1983

JAMES FOLEY

Agent: Rick Nicita, CAA - Los Angeles, 213/277-4545

RECKLESS MGM/UA, 1984

PETER FONDA*

b. February 23, 1939 - New York, New York
Home: Indian Hill Ranch, 38 Box 2024, Livingston, MO 59047, 406/222-3686
Business Manager: Lawrence J. Stern, Nanas, Stern, Biers & Company, 9434 Wilshire Blvd., - Beverly Hills, CA 90212, 213/273-2501

THE HIRED HAND Universal, 1971
IDAHO TRANSFER Cinemation, 1975
WANDA NEVADA United Artists, 1979

BRYAN FORBES*

b. July 22, 1926 - Stratford-Atte-Bow, England
Business: Pinewood Studios, Iver Heath, Bucks, England
Agent: David Wardlow, ICM - Los Angeles, 213/550-4000

WHISTLE DOWN THE WIND Pathe-America, 1962, British
THE L-SHAPED ROOM Columbia, 1963, British
SEANCE ON A WET AFTERNOON Artixo, 1964, British
KING RAT Columbia, 1965, British
THE WRONG BOX Columbia, 1966, British
THE WHISPERERS United Artists, 1967, British
DEADFALL 20th Century-Fox, 1968, British
THE MADWOMAN OF CHAILLOT Warner Bros., 1969, British
LONG AGO TOMORROW *THE RAGING MOON* Cinema 5, 1971, British
THE STEPFORD WIVES Columbia, 1975
THE SLIPPER AND THE ROSE: THE STORY OF CINDERELLA Universal, 1976, British
INTERNATIONAL VELVET MGM/United Artists, 1978, British
SUNDAY LOVERS co-director with Edouard Molinaro, Dino Risi & Gene Wilder, MGM/United Artists, 1981, U.S.-British-Italian-French
CHANDLERTOWN *PHILIP MARLOWE - PRIVATE EYE (CMS)* co-director with Peter Hunt, David Wickes & Sidney Hayers, HBO/David Wickes Television Ltd./London Weekend Television, 1983, British
BETTER LATE THAN NEVER Warner Bros., 1983, British
THE NAKED FACE Cannon, 1985

STEPHEN H. FOREMAN*

Messages: 212/242-4772
Agent: Jim Wiatt, ICM - Los Angeles, 213/550-4000

COUGAR! (TF) ABC Circle Films, 1984

MILOS FORMAN*

b. February 18, 1932 - Caslav, Czechoslovakia
Agent: Robert Lantz, The Lantz Office - New York City, 212/586-0200

COMPETITION Brandon, 1963, Czech
BLACK PETER Billings, 1964, Czech
LOVES OF A BLONDE Prominent, 1966, Czech
THE FIREMAN'S BALL Cinema 5, 1968, Czech
TAKING OFF Universal, 1971
VISIONS OF EIGHT (FD) co-director with Yuri Ozerov, Mai Zetterling, Arthur Penn, Michael Pfleghar, Kon Ichikawa, Claude Lelouch & John Schlesinger, Cinema 5, 1973
ONE FLEW OVER THE CUCKOO'S NEST ★★ United Artists, 1976
HAIR United Artists, 1979
RAGTIME Paramount, 1981
AMADEUS Orion, 1984

BILL FORSYTH*

b. Scotland
Address: 20 Winton Drive, Glasgow G12, Scotland
Contact: Directors Guild of America - Los Angeles, 213/656-1220

THAT SINKING FEELING The Samuel Goldwyn Company, 1979, Scottish
GREGORY'S GIRL The Samuel Goldwyn Company, 1982, Scottish
LOCAL HERO Warner Bros., 1983, British-Scottish
COMFORT AND JOY Universal, 1984, British-Scottish

BOB FOSSE*

b. June 23, 1927 - Chicago, Illinois
Home: 58 West 58th Street, New York, NY 10019, 212/759-7323
Agent: ICM - New York City, 212/556-5600

SWEET CHARITY Universal, 1969
CABARET ★★ Allied Artists, 1972
LENNY ★ United Artists, 1974
ALL THAT JAZZ ★ 20th Century-Fox, 1979
STAR 80 The Ladd Company/Warner Bros., 1983

ROBERT FOWLER*

Home: 3561 Canada Street, Los Angeles, CA 90065
Agent: Elliot Webb, ICM - Los Angeles, 213/550-4000

BELOW THE BELT Atlantic Releasing Corporation, 1980

WILLIAM A. FRAKER*

b. 1923 - Los Angeles, California
Home: 2572 Outpost Drive, Hollywood, CA 90068
Agent: Phil Gersh, The Gersh Agency - Beverly Hills, 213/274-6611

MONTE WALSH National General, 1970
A REFLECTION OF FEAR Columbia, 1973, British
THE LEGEND OF THE LONE RANGER Universal/AFD, 1981

FREDDIE FRANCIS

b. 1917 - London, England
Address: 58 Wheatlands, Heston Village, Middlesex, England

TWO AND TWO MAKE SIX Union, 1962, British
THE BRAIN *VENGEANCE* Garrick, 1962, British-West German
PARANOIAC Universal, 1964, British
NIGHTMARE Universal, 1964, British
THE EVIL OF FRANKENSTEIN Universal, 1964, British
TRAITOR'S GATE Columbia, 1964, British-West German
DR. TERROR'S HOUSE OF HORRORS Paramount, 1965, British
HYSTERIA MGM, 1965, British
THE SKULL Paramount, 1965, British
THE PSYCHOPATH Paramount, 1966, British
THE DEADLY BEES Paramount, 1967, British
THEY CAME FROM BEYOND SPACE Embassy, 1967, British
TORTURE GARDEN Columbia, 1968, British
DRACULA HAS RISEN FROM THE GRAVE Warner Bros., 1969, British
MUMSY, NANNY, SONNY & GIRLY *GIRLY* Cinerama Releasing Corporation, 1970, British
TROG Warner Bros., 1970, British
THE HAPPENING OF THE VAMPIRE 1971, European
TALES FROM THE CRYPT Cinerama Releasing Corporation, 1972, British
TALES THAT WITNESS MADNESS Paramount, 1973, British
THE CREEPING FLESH Columbia, 1973, British
SON OF DRACULA Cinemation, 1974, British
CRAZE Warner Bros., 1974, British
THE GHOUL Rank, 1974, British
LEGEND OF THE WEREWOLF Tyburn, 1975, British

KARL FRANCIS

Contact: Directors Guild of Great Britain, 56 Whitfield Street, London W1, England, 01/580-9592

THE MOUSE AND THE WOMAN Facelift, 1981, British
AND NOTHING BUT THE TRUTH *GIRO CITY* Castle Hill Productions, 1982, British

MELVIN FRANK*

b. August 13, 1913 - Chicago, Illinois
Home: 9171 Wilshire Blvd. - Suite 530, Beverly Hills, CA 90212
Agent: William Morris Agency - Beverly Hills, 213/274-7451

THE REFORMER AND THE REDHEAD co-director with Norman Panama, MGM, 1950
CALLAWAY WENT THATAWAY co-director with Norman Panama, MGM, 1951
STRICTLY DISHONORABLE co-director with Norman Panama, MGM, 1951
ABOVE AND BEYOND co-director with Norman Panama, MGM, 1952
KNOCK ON WOOD co-director with Norman Panama, Paramount, 1954
THE COURT JESTER co-director with Norman Panama, Paramount, 1956
THAT CERTAIN FEELING co-director with Norman Panama, Paramount, 1956
THE JAYHAWKERS Paramount, 1959
LI'L ABNER Paramount, 1959
THE FACTS OF LIFE United Artists, 1960
STRANGE BEDFELLOWS Universal, 1965
BUONA SERA, MRS. CAMPBELL United Artists, 1968
A TOUCH OF CLASS Avco Embassy, 1973, British
THE PRISONER OF SECOND AVENUE Warner Bros., 1975
THE DUCHESS AND THE DIRTWATER FOX 20th Century-Fox, 1976
LOST AND FOUND Columbia, 1979

JOHN FRANKENHEIMER*

b. February 19, 1930 - Malba, New York
Business: John Frankenheimer Productions, 2800 Olympic Blvd., Santa Monica, CA 90404, 213/829-0404
Agent: Jeff Berg/Peter Rawley, ICM - Los Angeles, 213/550-4205

THE YOUNG STRANGER Universal, 1957
THE YOUNG SAVAGES United Artists, 1961
ALL FALL DOWN MGM, 1962
BIRDMAN OF ALCATRAZ United Artists, 1962
THE MANCHURIAN CANDIDATE United Artists, 1962
SEVEN DAYS IN MAY Paramount, 1964
THE TRAIN United Artists, 1965, U.S.-French-Italian
SECONDS Paramount, 1966
GRAND PRIX MGM, 1966
THE FIXER MGM, 1968, British
THE EXTRAORDINARY SEAMAN MGM, 1969
THE GYPSY MOTHS MGM, 1969
I WALK THE LINE Columbia, 1970
THE HORSEMEN Columbia, 1971
THE ICEMAN COMETH American Film Theatre, 1973
IMPOSSIBLE OBJECT Valoria, 1973, French-Italian
99 AND 44/100% DEAD 20th Century-Fox, 1974
FRENCH CONNECTION II 20th Century-Fox, 1975
BLACK SUNDAY Paramount, 1976
PROPHECY Paramount, 1979
THE CHALLENGE Embassy, 1982
THE HOLCROFT COVENANT Thorn EMI/Landau Productions, 1985

RICHARD FRANKLIN*

b. July 15, 1948 - Melbourne, Australia
Business: Trans-Pacific Pictures, 9255 Sunset Blvd., Los Angeles, CA 90069, 213/278-8622
Agent: Dan Ostrott, Writers and Artists Agency - Los Angeles, 213/820-2240

BELINDA Aquarius, 1972, Australian
LOVELAND Illustrated, 1973, Australian
THE TRUE STORY OF ESKIMO NELL *DICK DOWN UNDER* Quest Films/Filmways Australasian Distributors, 1975, Australian
FANTASM Filmways Australasian, 1977, Australian
PATRICK Cinema Shares International, 1979, Australian
ROAD GAMES Avco Embassy, 1981, Australian
PSYCHO II Universal, 1983
CLOAK & DAGGER Universal, 1984

JAMES FRAWLEY*

Agent: Joan Hyler, William Morris Agency - Beverly Hills, 213/274-7451
Business: Maya Films Ltd., 9220 Sunset Blvd., Los Angeles, CA 90069, 213/656-5075

THE CHRISTIAN LICORICE STORE National General, 1971
KID BLUE 20th Century-Fox, 1973
DELANCEY STREET: THE CRISIS WITHIN (TF) Paramount TV, 1975
THE BIG BUS Paramount, 1976
THE MUPPET MOVIE AFD, 1979, British
THE GREAT AMERICAN TRAFFIC JAM (TF) Ten-Four Productions, 1980
THE OUTLAWS (TF) Limekiln and Templar Productions/Universal TV, 1984
WENDELL New World, 1985

STEPHEN FREARS

Agent: D.R.M., 28 Charing Cross Road, London WC2H ODB, England, 01/836-3903
Contact: Directors Guild of Great Britain, 56 Whitfield Street, London W1, England, 01/580-2256

GUMSHOE Columbia, 1971, British
ABEL'S WILL (TF) BBC, 1977, British
BLOODY KIDS (TF) Black Lion Films, 1980, British
SAIGON - YEAR OF THE CAT (TF) Thames TV, 1983, British
THE HIT Island Alive, 1984, British

HERB FREED

AWOL BFB, 1972
HAUNTS Intercontinental, 1977
BEYOND EVIL IFI-Scope III, 1980
GRADUATION DAY IFI-Scope III, 1981
TOMBOY Crown International, 1985

JERROLD FREEDMAN*

Agent: Tony Ludwig, CAA - Los Angeles, 213/277-4545
Business: Chesapeake Films, Inc., 9220 Sunset Blvd. - Suite 206, Los Angeles, CA 90069, 213/275-3138

KANSAS CITY BOMBER MGM, 1972
A COLD NIGHT'S DEATH (TF) ABC Circle Films, 1973
BLOOD SPORT (TF) Danny Thomas Productions, 1973
THE LAST ANGRY MAN (TF) Screen Gems/Columbia TV, 1974
SOME KIND OF MIRACLE (TF) Lorimar Productions, 1979
THIS MAN STANDS ALONE (TF) Roger Gimbel Productions/EMI TV/Abby Mann Productions, 1979
THE STREETS OF L.A. (TF) George Englund Productions, 1979
THE BOY WHO DRANK TOO MUCH (TF) MTM Enterprises, 1980
BORDERLINE AFD, 1980
THE VICTIMS (TF) Hajeno Productions/Warner Bros. TV, 1982
LEGS (TF) The Catalina Production Group/Radio City Music Hall Productions/Comworld Productions, 1983

JERROLD FREEDMAN*—continued

THE SEDUCTION OF GINA (TF) Bertinelli-Jaffee Productions, 1984
BEST KEPT SECRETS (TF) ABC Circle Films, 1984
SEDUCED (TF) Catalina Production Group/Comworld Productions, 1985

ROBERT FREEDMAN*

Contact: Directors Guild of America - Los Angeles, 213/656-1220

GOIN' ALL THE WAY Saturn International, 1982

VICTOR FRENCH*

b. December 4, 1934 - Santa Barbara, California
Business Manager: Traubner & Flynn, 2049 Century Park East, Suite 2500, Los Angeles, CA 90067, 213/277-3000

LITTLE HOUSE: LOOK BACK TO YESTERDAY (TF) NBC Productions/Ed Friendly Productions, 1983
LITTLE HOUSE: BLESS ALL THE DEAR CHILDREN (TF) NBC Productions/Ed Friendly Productions, 1984

RICK FRIEDBERG*

Agent: Robert Wunsch, The Wunsch Agency - Los Angeles, 213/278-1955
Business Manager: M. Kenneth Suddleson, Loeb & Loeb, 10100 Santa Monica Blvd., Los Angeles, CA 90067, 213/552-7781

PRAY TV *K-GOD* Filmways, 1980
OFF THE WALL Jensen Farley Pictures, 1983

DICK FRIEDENBERG

Agent: Writers & Artists Agency - Los Angeles, 213/820-2240

FRONTIER FREMONT Sunn Classic, 1976
THE DEERSLAYER (TF) Sunn Classic Productions, 1978
THE BERMUDA TRIANGLE Sunn Classic, 1979

WILLIAM FRIEDKIN*

b. August 29, 1939 - Chicago, Illinois
Agent: Tony Fantozzi, William Morris Agency - Beverly Hills, 213/274-7451

GOOD TIMES Columbia, 1967
THE BIRTHDAY PARTY Continental, 1968, British
THE NIGHT THEY RAIDED MINSKY'S United Artists, 1968
THE BOYS IN THE BAND National General, 1970
THE FRENCH CONNECTION ★★ 20th Century-Fox, 1971
THE EXORCIST ★ Warner Bros., 1973
SORCERER Universal/Paramount, 1977
THE BRINK'S JOB Universal, 1978
CRUISING United Artists, 1980
DEAL OF THE CENTURY Warner Bros., 1983
TO LIVE AND DIE IN L.A. SLM Productions, 1985

KIM HARLENE FRIEDMAN*

Business Manager: Marty Mickelson - Los Angeles, 213/858-1097

BEFORE AND AFTER (TF) The Konigsberg Company, 1979

WILLIAM FRUET

Home: 51 Olive Street, Toronto, Ontario M6G 1T7, Canada, 416/535-3569

WEDDING IN WHITE Avco Embassy, 1973, Canadian
THE HOUSE BY THE LAKE *DEATH WEEKEND* American International, 1977, Canadian
SEARCH AND DESTROY *STRIKING BACK* Film Ventures International, 1979
FUNERAL HOME *CRIES IN THE NIGHT* MPM, 1981, Canadian
BAKER COUNTY USA *TRAPPED* Jensen Farley Pctures, 1982
SPASMS Producers Distribution Company, 1983, Canadian
BEDROOM EYES RSL Films, 1984, Canadian
THE FOOLING MGM/UA, 1985, Canadian

ROY FRUMKES

b. July 22, 1944 - New York, New York
Business: Bat Track Productions, 166 West 83rd Street, New York, NY 10024, 212/873-6626

DOCUMENT OF THE DEAD (FD) Roy Frumkes Productions, 1980

ROBERT FUEST*

b. 1927 - London, England
Contact: Directors Guild of America - Los Angeles, 213/656-1220

JUST LIKE A WOMAN Monarch, 1966, British
AND SOON THE DARKNESS Levitt-Pickman, 1970, British
WUTHERING HEIGHTS American International, 1971, British
THE ABOMINABLE DR. PHIBES American International, 1971, British
DR. PHIBES RISES AGAIN American International, 1972, British
THE LAST DAYS OF MAN ON EARTH *THE FINAL PROGRAMME* New World, 1974, British
THE DEVIL'S RAIN Bryanston, 1975, U.S.-Mexican
REVENGE OF THE STEPFORD WIVES (TF) Edgar J. Scherick Productions, 1980
APHRODITE Atlantic Releasing Corporation, 1982, French

SAMUEL FULLER*

b. August 12, 1911 - Worcester, Massachusetts
Agent: ICM - Los Angeles, 213/550-4000

I SHOT JESSE JAMES Screen Guild, 1949
THE BARON OF ARIZONA Lippert, 1950
THE STEEL HELMET Lippert, 1951
FIXED BAYONETS! 20th Century-Fox, 1951
PARK ROW United Artists, 1952
PICKUP ON SOUTH STREET 20th Century-Fox, 1953
HELL AND HIGH WATER 20th Century-Fox, 1954
HOUSE OF BAMBOO 20th Century-Fox, 1955
RUN OF THE ARROW 20th Century-Fox, 1957
FORTY GUNS 20th Century-Fox, 1957
CHINA GATE 20th Century-Fox, 1957
VERBOTEN! Columbia, 1958
THE CRIMSON KIMONO Columbia, 1959
UNDERWORLD U.S.A. Columbia, 1961
MERRILL'S MARAUDERS Warner Bros., 1962
SHOCK CORRIDOR Allied Artists, 1963
THE NAKED KISS Allied Artists, 1964
SHARK! Heritage, 1970, U.S.-Mexican
DEAD PIGEON ON BEETHOVEN STREET Emerson, 1972, West German
THE BIG RED ONE United Artists, 1980
WHITE DOG Paramount, 1982
THIEVES AFTER DARK Parafrance, 1983, French

ALLEN FUNT*

b. 1914 - New York, New York
Contact: Directors Guild of America - New York City, 212/581-0370

WHAT DO YOU SAY TO A NAKED WOMAN? United Artists, 1970
MONEY TALKS United Artists, 1971

SIDNEY J. FURIE*

b. February 28, 1933 - Toronto, Canada
Business: Furie Productions, Inc., 9169 Sunset Blvd., Los Angeles, CA 90069
Agent: Paul Kohner, Inc. - Los Angeles, 213/550-1060

A DANGEROUS AGE Ajay, 1959, Canadian
A COOL SOUND FROM HELL 1959, Canadian
DR. BLOOD'S COFFIN United Artists, 1960, British
THE SNAKE WOMAN United Artists, 1960, British
NIGHT OF PASSION Astor, 1961, British
THREE ON A SPREE United Artists, 1961, British
WONDERFUL TO BE YOUNG! Paramount, 1961, British
THE BOYS Gala, 1962, British
THE LEATHER BOYS Allied Artists, 1964, British
SWINGERS' PARADISE American International, 1964, British
THE IPCRESS FILE Universal, 1965, British
THE APPALOOSA Universal, 1966
THE NAKED RUNNER Warner Bros., 1967, British
THE LAWYER Paramount, 1970
LITTLE FAUSS AND BIG HALSY Paramount, 1970
LADY SINGS THE BLUES Paramount, 1972
HIT! Paramount, 1973
SHEILA LEVINE IS DEAD AND LIVING IN NEW YORK Paramount, 1975
GABLE AND LOMBARD Universal, 1976
THE BOYS IN COMPANY C Columbia, 1978
THE ENTITY 20th Century-Fox, 1983
PURPLE HEARTS The Ladd Company/Warner Bros., 1984

G

PAL GABOR

Contact: Hungarofilm, 1054 Bathory utca lo., Budapest, Hungary, 36-1/31-7777

ANGI VERA New Yorker, 1979, Hungarian
BRADY'S ESCAPE *THE LONG RUN* Satori, 1984, U.S.-Hungarian

ALAN GADNEY

b. January 1, 1941 - Dayton, Ohio
Business: Festival Films, P.O. Box 10180, Glendale, CA 91209, 213/222-8626

WEST TEXAS American Media Productions/American Films Ltd., 1973
MOONCHILD Filmmakers Ltd./American Films Ltd., 1974

GEORGE GAGE*

Home: 31316 Broad Beach Road, Malibu, CA 90265, 213/457-1170
Personal Manager: Harry Ufland, Ufland-Roth Productions 20th Century Fox, 10201 W. Pico Blvd., Executive Building Room 246, Los Angeles, CA 90035, 213/203-1295

SKATEBOARD Universal, 1978
FLASHBURN Crown International, 1984

TIMOTHY GALFAS*

b. December 31, 1934 - Atlanta, Georgia
Agent: Lew Weitzman, Lew Weitzman & Associates - Sherman Oaks, 818/995-4400
Business Manager: Howard Bernstein, Kaufman & Bernstein, 1900 Avenue of the Stars, Los Angeles, CA 90067, 213/277-1900

BOGARD L-T Films, 1975
THE BLACK STREETFIGHTER New Line Cinema, 1976
REVENGE FOR A RAPE (TF) Albert S. Ruddy Productions, 1976
BLACK FIST Worldwide, 1977
MANEATERS ARE LOOSE! (TF) Mona Productions/Finnegan Associates, 1978
SUNNYSIDE American International, 1979

JOHN A. GALLAGHER

Business: BGW Film Projects Ltd., 1540 Broadway, Suite 705, New York, NY 10036, 212/840-8605
Home: 212/260-5917
Agent: The Ron Bernstein Agency, New York, 212/265-0750

BEACH HOUSE New Line Cinema, 1972

HERB GARDNER*

Contact: Directors Guild of America - New York City, 212/581-0370

THE GOODBYE PEOPLE Embassy, 1984

JACK GARFEIN*

b. July 2, 1930 - Mukacevo, Czechoslovakia
Business: Actors & Directors Lab, 412 West 42nd Street, New York, NY 10036, 212/695-5429

THE STRANGE ONE *END AS A MAN* Columbia, 1957
SOMETHING WILD United Artists, 1961

PATRICK GARLAND

b. 1936 - London, England
Agent: Spokesmen, Ltd., 1 Craven Hill, London W2, England
Contact: Directors Guild of Great Britain, 56 Whitfield Street, London W1, England, 01/580-9592

THE SNOW GOOSE (TF) NBC, 1971
A DOLL'S HOUSE Paramount, 1973, Canadian-U.S.

TONY GARNETT

Contact: British Academy of Film & Television Arts, 195 Piccadilly, London W1, England, 01/734-0022

PROSTITUTE Mainline Pictures, 1981, British
DEEP IN THE HEART *HANDGUN* Warner Bros., 1984

LILA GARRETT*

b. New York, New York
Home: 1356 Laurel Way, Beverly Hills, CA 90212, 213/274-8041
Agent: Rowland Perkins, CAA - Los Angeles, 213/277-4545

TERRACES (TF) Charles Fries Productions/Worldvision, 1977

COSTA GAVRAS*

(Konstantinos Gavras)

Home: 244 Rue St. Jacques, Paris 75005, France
Agent: Stan Kamen, William Morris Agency - Beverly Hills, 213/274-7451

THE SLEEPING CAR MURDERS 7 Arts, 1966, French
SHOCK TROOPS *UN HOMME DE TROP* United Artists, 1968, French-Italian
Z ★ Cinema 5, 1969, French-Algerian
THE CONFESSION Paramount, 1970, French
STATE OF SIEGE Cinema 5, 1973, French
SPECIAL SECTION Universal, 1975, French-Italian-West German
CLAIR DE FEMME Atlantic Releasing Corporation, 1979, French-Italian-West German
MISSING Universal, 1982
HANNA K. Universal Classics, 1983, French

THEODORE GERSHUNY

Contact: Writers Guild of America, East - New York City, 212/245-6180

LOVE, DEATH 1973
SILENT NIGHT, BLOODY NIGHT Cannon, 1974
SUGAR COOKIES Troma, 1977
DEATHOUSE Cannon, 1981

NICHOLAS GESSNER

SOMEONE BEHIND THE DOOR GSF, 1971, French
THE LITTLE GIRL WHO LIVES DOWN THE LANE American International, 1977, U.S.-Canadian-French
IT RAINED ALL NIGHT THE DAY I LEFT Caneuram/Israfilm/COFCI, 1981, Canadian-Israeli-French

STEVEN GETHERS*

b. June 8, 1922
Agent: Rowland Perkins/Fred Specktor, CAA - Los Angeles, 213/277-4545

BILLY: PORTRAIT OF A STREET KID (TF) Mark Carliner Productions, 1977
DAMIEN...THE LEPER PRIEST (TF) Tomorrow Entertainment, 1980
JACQUELINE BOUVIER KENNEDY (TF) ABC Circle Films, 1981
CONFESSIONS OF A MARRIED MAN (TF) Gloria Monty Productions/ Comworld Productions, 1983

JOE GIANNONE

MADMAN Jensen Farley Pictures, 1982

ALAN GIBSON

b. April 28, 1938 - Canada
Business: 55 Portland Road, London W11 4LR, England, 01/727-0354
Agent: Tim Stone, Stone-Masser Talent Agents - Los Angeles, 213/275-9599

GOODBYE GEMINI Cinerama Releasing Corporation, 1970, British
CRESCENDO Warner Bros., 1972, British
DRACULA TODAY *DRACULA A.D. 1972* Warner Bros., 1972, British
THE PLAYBOY OF THE WESTERN WORLD (TF) BBC, 1975, British
COUNT DRACULA AND HIS VAMPIRE BRIDE *SATANIC RITES OF DRACULA* Dynamite Entertainment, 1978, British
CHECKERED FLAG OR CRASH Universal, 1978
CHURCHILL AND THE GENERALS (TF) BBC/Le Vien International, 1979, British
A WOMAN CALLED GOLDA (TF) Harve Bennett Productions/Paramount TV, 1982
WITNESS FOR THE PROSECUTION (TF) Norman Rosemont Productions/ United Artists Productions, 1982, U.S.-British
HELEN KELLER - THE MIRACLE CONTINUES (TF) Castle Combe Productions/20th Century-Fox TV, 1984, U.S.-British
MARTIN'S DAY MGM/UA, 1985, British

BRIAN GIBSON

Home: 65 Greenhill, Hampstead High Street, London NW3, England
Agent: A.D. Peters Ltd., 10 Buckingham Street, London WC2, England

BREAKING GLASS Paramount, 1980, British

LEWIS GILBERT*

b. March 6, 1920 - London, England
Address: 17 Sheldrake Place, Duchess of Bedford Walk, London W8, England
Attorney: Norman Tyre, Gang, Tyre & Brown - Los Angeles, 213/463-4863

THE LITTLE BALLERINA General Film Distributors, 1947, British
ONCE A SINNER Butcher, 1950, British
WALL OF DEATH *THERE IS ANOTHER SIDE* Realart, 1951, British
THE SCARLET THREAD Butcher, 1951, British
HUNDRED HOUR HUNT *EMERGENCY CALL* Greshler, 1952, British
TIME GENTLEMEN PLEASE! Eros, 1952, British
THE SLASHER *COSH BOY* Lippert, 1953, British
JOHNNY ON THE RUN co-director with Vernon Harris, Associated British Film Distributors/Children's Film Foundation, 1953, British
BREAK TO FREEDOM *ALBERT R.N.* United Artists, 1953, British
THE GOOD DIE YOUNG United Artists, 1954, British

LEWIS GILBERT*—continued

THE SEA SHALL NOT HAVE THEM United Artists, 1954, British
CAST A DARK SHADOW DCA, 1955, British
REACH FOR THE SKY Rank, 1956, British
PARADISE LAGOON *THE ADMIRABLE CRICHTON* Columbia, 1957, British
CARVE HER NAME WITH PRIDE Lopert, 1958, British
A CRY FROM THE STREETS Tudor, 1959, British
FERRY TO HONG KONG 20th Century-Fox, 1959, British
SINK THE BISMARCK! 20th Century-Fox, 1960, British
SKYWATCH *LIGHT UP THE SKY* Continental, 1960, British
LOSS OF INNOCENCE *THE GREENGAGE SUMMER* Columbia, 1961, British
DAMN THE DEFIANT! *H.M.S. DEFIANT* Columbia, 1962, British
THE SEVENTH DAWN United Artists, 1964, U.S.-British
ALFIE Paramount, 1966, British
YOU ONLY LIVE TWICE United Artists, 1967, British
THE ADVENTURERS Paramount, 1970
FRIENDS Paramount, 1971, British-French
PAUL AND MICHELLE Paramount, 1974, British-French
OPERATION DAYBREAK Warner Bros., 1975, British
SEVEN NIGHTS IN JAPAN EMI, 1976, British-French
THE SPY WHO LOVED ME United Artists, 1977, British-U.S.
MOONRAKER United Artists, 1979, British-French
EDUCATING RITA Columbia, 1983, British
NOT QUITE JERUSALEM Acorn Pictures/Rank, 1985, British

DAVID GILER*

Contact: Directors Guild of America - Los Angeles, 213/656-1220

THE BLACK BIRD Columbia, 1975

STUART GILLARD

Agent: Century Artists - Beverly Hills, 213/273-4366

PARADISE Avco Embassy, 1982, Canadian

TERRY GILLIAM

b. November 22, 1940 - Minneapolis, Minnesota
Address: 51 South Hill Park, London NW3, England

MONTY PYTHON AND THE HOLY GRAIL co-director with Terry Jones, Cinema 5, 1974, British
JABBERWOCKY Cinema 5, 1977, British
TIME BANDITS Avco Embassy, 1981, British
BRAZIL Universal, 1985, British

FRANK D. GILROY*

b. October 13, 1925 - New York, New York
Agent: Ziegler, Diskant, Inc. - Los Angeles, 213/278-0700

DESPERATE CHARACTERS ITC, 1971
JOHN O'HARA'S GIBBSVILLE (TF) Columbia TV, 1975
THE TURNING POINT OF JIM MALLOY (TF) David Gerber Company/Columbia TV, 1975
FROM NOON TILL THREE United Artists, 1976
ONCE IN PARIS... Atlantic Releasing Corporation, 1978
REX STOUT'S NERO WOLFE (TF) Emmett Lavery, Jr. Productions/Paramount TV, 1979

PETER GIMBEL*

b. February 14, 1928 - New York, New York
Business: Blue Gander, Inc., 10 East 63rd Street, New York, N.Y. 10021, 212/753-9088
Agent: Robert Stein, Leading Artists - Beverly Hills 213/858-1999

BLUE WATER, WHITE DEATH (FD) co-director with James Lipscomb, National General, 1971

MILTON MOSES GINSBERG

COMING APART Kaleidoscope, 1969
THE WEREWOLF OF WASHINGTON Diplomat, 1973

BOB GIRALDI*

Contact: Directors Guild of America - New York City, 212/581-0370

NATIONAL LAMPOON'S MOVIE MADNESS co-director with Henry Jaglom, United Artists, 1982

BERNARD GIRARD*

b. 1930
Contact: Directors Guild of America - Los Angeles, 213/656-1220

THE GREEN-EYED BLONDE Warner Bros., 1957
RIDE OUT FOR REVENGE United Artists, 1958
AS YOUNG AS WE ARE Paramount, 1958
THE PARTY CRASHERS Paramount, 1958
A PUBLIC AFFAIR Parade, 1962
DEAD HEAT ON A MERRY-GO-ROUND Paramount, 1966
MAD ROOM Columbia, 1969
HUNTERS ARE FOR KILLING (TF) Cinema Center, 1970
THE HAPPINESS CAGE *THE MIND SNATCHERS* Cinerama Releasing Corporation, 1972
GONE WITH THE WEST International Cinefilm, 1975

DAVID GLADWELL

b. April 2, 1935 - Gloucester, England
Address: 8 Caldervale Road, London SW4, England
Contact: Directors Guild of Great Britain, 56 Whitfield Street, London W1, England, 01/580-9592

REQUIEM FOR A VILLAGE BFI Production Board, 1977, British
MEMOIRS OF A SURVIVOR EMI, 1982, British

PAUL MICHAEL GLASER*

b. Cambridge, Massachusetts
Agent: Ron Meyer, CAA - Los Angeles, 213/277-4545

AMAZONS (TF) ABC Circle Films, 1984

JOHN GLEN

b. May 15, 1932 - Sunbury on Thames, England
Address: 22 Wheelers Orchard, Chalfont Street, Peter, Buckinghamshire, England

FOR YOUR EYES ONLY United Artists, 1981, British
OCTOPUSSY MGM/UA, 1983, British
A VIEW TO A KILL MGM/UA, 1985, British

PETER GLENVILLE*

b. October 28, 1913 - London, England
Messages: 212/758-0800

THE PRISONER Columbia, 1955, British
ME AND THE COLONEL Columbia, 1958
SUMMER AND SMOKE Paramount, 1961
TERM OF TRIAL Warner Bros., 1963, British
BECKET ★ Paramount, 1964, British
HOTEL PARADISO MGM, 1966, British
THE COMEDIANS MGM, 1967, British

JIM GLICKENHAUS*

b. July 24, 1950 - New York, New York
Business: Glickenhaus Film, Inc., 1619 Broadway - Suite 303, New York, NY 10019, 212/265-1150
Agent: Sue Mengers, ICM - Los Angeles, 213/550-4264

THE ASTROLOGER Interstar, 1979
THE EXTERMINATOR Avco Embassy, 1980
THE SOLDIER Embassy, 1982
THE PROTECTOR Golden Communications, 1985, U.S.-Hong Kong

KURT GLOOR

b. November 8, 1942 - Zurich, Switzerland
Business: Filmproduktion AG, Spiegelgasse 27, CH-8001 Zurich, Switzerland, 47-87-66

DIE PLOTZLICHE EINSAMKEIT DES KONRAD STEINER Kurt Gloor Filmproduktion, 1975, Swiss
LEHMANNS LETZTER (TF) Swiss TV, 1977, Swiss
DER CHINESE (TF) Bavaria Filmproduktion Munich, 1978, West German
DER ERFINDER Kurt Gloor Filmproduktion, 1980, Swiss
MANN OHNE GEDACHTNIS Kurt Gloor Filmproducktion, 1984, Swiss

JEAN-LUC GODARD

b. December 3, 1930 - Paris, France
Contact: French Film Office, 745 Fifth Avenue, New York, NY 10151, 212/832-8860

BREATHLESS *A BOUT DE SOUFFLE* Films Around the World, 1960, French
A WOMAN IS A WOMAN Pathe Contemporary, 1961, French
SEVEN CAPITAL SINS co-director with Roger Vadim, Sylvaine Dhomme, Edouard Molinaro, Philippe De Broca, Claude Chabrol, Jacques Demy, Marie-Jose Nat, Dominique Paturel, Jean-Marc Tennberg & Perrette Pradier, Embassy, 1962, French-Italian
MY LIFE TO LIVE Pathe Contemporary, 1962, French
ROGOPAG co-director, 1962, French
LE PETIT SOLDAT West End, 1963, French
LES CARABINIERS West End, 1963, French
CONTEMPT *LE MEPRIS* Embassy, 1964, French-Italian
LES PLUS BELLES ESCROQUERIES DU MONDE co-director, 1964, French-Italian-Japanese
BAND OF OUTSIDERS Royal Films International, 1964, French
THE MARRIED WOMAN Royal Films International, 1964, French
SIX IN PARIS co-director, 1965, French
ALPHAVILLE Pathe Contemporary, 1965, French
PIERROT LE FOU Pathe Contemporary, 1965, French
MASCULINE FEMININE Royal Films International, 1966, French-Swedish
MADE IN U.S.A. Pathe Contemporary, 1966, French
TWO OR THREE THINGS I KNOW ABOUT HER New Line Cinema, 1967, French
THE OLDEST PROFESSION *LES PLUS VIEUX METIER DU MONDE* co-director with Franco Indovina, Mauro Bolognini, Philippe de Broca, Michael Pfleghar, Claude Autant-Lara, Goldstone, 1967, Italian-French-West German
FAR FROM VIETNAM (FD) co-director with Alain Resnais, William Klein, Agnes Varda, Joris Ivens & Claude Lelouch, New Yorker, 1967, French

JEAN-LUC GODARD —continued

LA CHINOISE Leacock-Pennebaker, 1967, French
WEEKEND Grove Press, 1968, French-Italian
UN FILM COMME LES AUTRES 1968, French
AMORE E RABBIA co-director, 1969, Italian-French
LE GAI SAVOIR EYR, 1969, French
ONE A.M. Leacock-Pennebaker, 1969, French
COMMUNICATIONS 1969, French
SYMPATHY FOR THE DEVIL–1 + 1 New Line Cinema, 1969, British
BRITISH SOUNDS/SEE YOU AT MAO (TF) Kestrel Productions, co-director with Jean-Pierre Gorin, 1969, British
WIND FROM THE EAST co-director with Jean-Pierre Gorin, New Line Cinema, 1969, French-Italian-West German
PRAVDA (FD) co-director with Jean-Pierre Gorin, 1969, French-Czech
LOTTE IN ITALIA (FD) co-director with Jean-Pierre Gorin, RAI, 1970, Italian
JUSQU'A LA VICTOIRE (FD) co-director with Jean-Pierre Gorin, 1970, French
VLADIMIR ET ROSA co-director with Jean-Pierre Gorin, 1971, French
TOUT VA BIEN co-director with Jean-Pierre Gorin, New Yorker, 1972, French-Italian
LETTER TO JANE: INVESTIGATION OF A STILL co-director with Jean-Pierre Gorin, New Yorker, 1972, French
MOI JE 1973, French
NUMERO DEUX Zoetrope, 1975, French
LA COMMUNICATION (TF) 1976, French
COMMENT CA VA 1976, French
ICI ET AILLEURS MK2 Diffusion, 1976, French
SUR ET SOUS LA COMMUNICATION INA, 1977, French
EVERY MAN FOR HIMSELF *SAUVE QUI PEUT LA VIE* New Yorker/Zoetrope, 1980, Swiss-French
PASSION United Artists Classics, 1983, French-Swiss
FIRST NAME: CARMEN Spectrafilm, 1983, French-Swiss
DETECTIVE AAA, 1985, French
JE VOUS SALVE MARIE Triumph/Columbia, 1985, French

JIM GODDARD

Home: 61 Holland Park, London W11 3SJ, 01/229-9123
Agent: Michael Marcus, CAA - Los Angeles, 213/277-4545

A TALE OF TWO CITIES (TF) Norman Rosemont Productions/Marble Arch Productions, 1980, U.S.-British
REILLY - ACE OF SPIES (MS) co-director with Martin Campbell, Euston Films Ltd., 1984
KENNEDY (MS) Central Independent Television Productions/Alan Landsburg Productions, 1983, British-U.S.
BONES Moving Picture Company, 1985, British
HITLER'S S.S. (TF) Colason Limited Productions, 1985

MENAHEM GOLAN

b. May 31, 1929 - Tiberias, Israel
Business: Cannon Group, 6464 Sunset Blvd. - Suite 1150, Hollywood, CA 90028, 213/469-8124

EL DORADO 1963, Israeli
TRUNK TO CAIRO American International, 1967, Israeli-West German
THE GIRL FROM THE DEAD SEA 1967, Israeli
TEVYE AND HIS SEVEN DAUGHTERS Noah Films, 1968, Israeli
FORTUNA Trans-American, 1969, Israeli
WHAT'S GOOD FOR THE GOOSE National Showmanship, 1969, British
MARGO Cannon, 1970, Israeli
LUPO! Cannon, 1970, Israeli
QUEEN OF THE ROAD Noah Films, 1970, Israeli
KATZ AND KARASSO Noah Films, 1971, Israeli
THE GREAT TELEPHONE ROBBERY Noah Films, 1972, Israeli
ESCAPE TO THE SUN Cinevision, 1972, Israeli-West German-French
KAZABLAN MGM, 1973, Israeli
LEPKE Warner Bros., 1975
DIAMONDS Avco Embassy, 1975, U.S.-Israeli-Swiss
THE AMBASSADOR Noah Films, 1976, Israeli
OPERATION THUNDERBOLT Cinema Shares International, 1978, Israeli
THE URANIUM CONSPIRACY Noah Films, 1978, Israeli-West German

MENAHEM GOLAN —continued

THE MAGICIAN OF LUBLIN Cannon, 1979, Israeli-West German-U.S.
THE APPLE Cannon, 1980, U.S.-West German
ENTER THE NINJA Cannon, 1981
OVER THE BROOKLYN BRIDGE MGM/UA/Cannon, 1984

JACK GOLD

b. June 28, 1930 - London, England
Home: 18 Avenue Road, London N6, England, 01/348-5482
Agent: ICM - Los Angeles, 213/550-4000

THE BOFORS GUN Universal, 1968, British
THE RECKONING Columbia, 1969, British
CATHOLICS (TF) Sidney Glazier Productions, 1973, British
WHO? Allied Artists, 1975, British-West German
MAN FRIDAY Avco Embassy, 1975, British
ACES HIGH Cinema Shares International, 1977, British
THE MEDUSA TOUCH Warner Bros., 1978, British
THE SAILOR'S RETURN Euston Films Ltd., 1978
THE NAKED CIVIL SERVANT (TF) Thames TV, 1978, British
CHARLIE MUFFIN Euston Films Ltd., 1980, British
LITTLE LORD FAUNTLEROY (TF) Norman Rosemont Productions, 1980, U.S.-British
PRAYING MANTIS Portman Productions/Channel Four, 1982, British
RED MONARCH Enigma Films/Goldcrest Films & Television Ltd., 1983, British
GOOD AND BAD AT GAMES (TF) Portman Quintet Productions, 1983, British
SAKHAROV (CTF) HBO Premiere Films/Titus Productions, 1984, U.S.-British
THE CHAIN Quintet Films, 1985, British

JAMES GOLDSTONE*

b. June 8, 1931 - Los Angeles, California
Agent: John Gaines, APA - Los Angeles, 213/273-0744

SCALPLOCK (TF) Columbia TV, 1966
CODE NAME: HERACLITUS (TF) Universal TV, 1967
IRONSIDE (TF) Universal TV, 1967
SHADOW OVER ELVERON (TF) Universal TV, 1968
JIGSAW Universal, 1968
A MAN CALLED GANNON Universal, 1969
WINNING Universal, 1969
A CLEAR AND PRESENT DANGER (TF) ☆ Universal TV, 1970
BROTHER JOHN Columbia, 1971
RED SKY AT MORNING Universal, 1971
CRY PANIC (TF) Spelling-Goldberg Productions, 1974
DR. MAX (TF) CBS, Inc., 1974
THINGS IN THEIR SEASON (TF) Tomorrow Entertainment, 1974
JOURNEY FROM DARKNESS (TF) Bob Banner Associates, 1975
ERIC (TF) Lorimar Productions, 1975
SWASHBUCKLER Universal, 1976
ROLLERCOASTER Universal, 1977
STUDS LONIGAN (MS) Lorimar Productions, 1979
WHEN TIME RAN OUT Warner Bros., 1980
KENT STATE (TF) ☆☆ Inter Planetary Productions/Osmond Communications, 1981
CHARLES & DIANA: A ROYAL LOVE STORY (TF) St. Lorraine Productions, 1982
CALAMITY JANE (TF) CBS Entertainment, 1983
RITA HAYWORTH: THE LOVE GODDESS (TF) The Susskind Co., 1983
SENTIMENTAL JOURNEY (TF) Lucille Ball Productions/Smith-Richmond Productions/20th Century Fox TV, 1984
THE SUN ALSO RISES (TF) Furia-Oringer Productions/20th Century Fox TV, 1984

BERT I. GORDON*

b. September 24, 1922 - Kenosha, Wisconsin
Agent: The Gersh Agency - Beverly Hills, 213/274-6611

KING DINOSAUR Lippert, 1955
BEGINNING OF THE END Republic, 1957
CYCLOPS American International, 1957
THE AMAZING COLOSSAL MAN American International, 1957
ATTACK OF THE PUPPET PEOPLE American International, 1958
WAR OF THE COLASSAL BEAST American International, 1958
THE SPIDER American International, 1958
THE BOY AND THE PIRATES United Artists, 1960
TORMENTED Allied Artists, 1960
THE MAGIC SWORD United Artists, 1962
VILLAGE OF THE GIANTS Embassy, 1965
PICTURE MOMMY DEAD Embassy, 1966
HOW TO SUCCEED WITH SEX Medford, 1970
NECROMANCY American International, 1972
THE MAD BOMBER Cinemation, 1973
THE POLICE CONNECTION *DETECTIVE GERONIMO* 1973
THE FOOD OF THE GODS American International, 1976
EMPIRE OF THE ANTS American International, 1977
THE COMING 1981
DOING IT 1984

MICHAEL GORDON*

b. September 6, 1909 - Baltimore, Maryland
Home: 259 N. Layton Drive, Los Angeles, CA 90049, 213/476-2024
Business: UCLA Theatre Arts Department, 405 Hilgard Avenue, Los Angeles, CA 90024, 213/825-5761
Business Manager: Lynn Schweidel - Los Angeles, 213/651-2197

BOSTON BLACKIE GOES HOLLYWOOD Columbia, 1942
UNDERGROUND AGENT Columbia, 1942
ONE DANGEROUS NIGHT Columbia, 1943
CRIME DOCTOR Columbia, 1943
THE WEB Universal, 1947
ANOTHER PART OF THE FOREST Universal, 1948
AN ACT OF MURDER Universal, 1948
THE LADY GAMBLES Universal, 1949
WOMAN IN HIDING Universal, 1950
CYRANO DE BERGERAC United Artists, 1950
I CAN GET IT FOR YOUR WHOLESALE 20th Century-Fox, 1951
THE SECRET OF CONVICT LAKE 20th Century-Fox, 1951
WHEREVER SHE GOES Mayer-Kingsley, 1953, Australian
PILLOW TALK Universal, 1959
PORTRAIT IN BLACK Universal, 1960
BOYS' NIGHT OUT MGM, 1962
FOR LOVE OR MONEY Universal, 1963
MOVE OVER, DARLING 20th Century-Fox, 1963
A VERY SPECIAL FAVOR Universal, 1965
TEXAS ACROSS THE RIVER Universal, 1966
THE IMPOSSIBLE YEARS MGM, 1968
HOW DO I LOVE THEE? Cinerama Releasing Corporation, 1970

BERRY GORDY*

Business: Motown Records Corporation, 6255 Sunset Blvd., Hollywood, CA 90028, 213/468-3600

MAHOGANY Paramount, 1975

CLAUDE GORETTA

b. June 23, 1929 - Geneva, Switzerland
Contact: Swiss Film Center, Muenstergasse 18, CH-8001 Zurich, Switzerland, 01/472-860

LE FOU 1970, Swiss
LE JOUR DES NOCES (TF) 1971, Swiss

CLAUDE GORETTA —continued

L'INVITATION Janus, 1973, Swiss
THE WONDERFUL CROOK *PAS SI MERCHANT QUE CA...* New Yorker, 1975, Swiss-French
THE LACEMAKER New Yorker, 1977, Swiss-French
LES CHEMINS DE L'EXIT OU LES DERNIERES ANNEES DE JEAN JACQUES ROUSSEAU (MS) TFI/SSR/Telecip/BBC/RTB/SRC/TV60, 1978, French
BONHEUR TOI-MEME Phenix Films/FR3, 1980, French
THE GIRL FROM LORRAINE *LA PROVINCIALE* New Yorker, 1981, French
THE DEATH OF MARIO RICCI New Line Showcase, 1983, Swiss-French

CARL GOTTLIEB*

b. March 18, 1938
Agent: Larry Grossman & Associates - Beverly Hills, 213/550-8127

CAVEMAN United Artists, 1981

LISA GOTTLIEB

Contact: Writers Guild of America - Los Angeles, 213/550-1000

I WAS A TEENAGE BOY Columbia, 1985

WILLIAM A. GRAHAM*

Home: 21510 Calle de Barco, Malibu, CA 90265
Agent: Fred Specktor, CAA - Los Angeles, 213/277-4545

THE DOOMSDAY FLIGHT (TF) Universal TV, 1966
THE OUTSIDER (TF) Universal TV, 1967
WATERHOLE #3 Paramount, 1967
CHANGE OF HABIT Universal, 1968
THE LEGEND OF CUSTER (TF) 20th Century-Fox, 1968
SUBMARINE X-1 United Artists, 1969, British
TRIAL RUN (TF) Universal TV, 1969
THEN CAME BRONSON (TF) Universal TV, 1969
THE INTRUDERS (TF) Universal TV, 1970
CONGRATULATIONS, IT'S A BOY! (TF) Aaron Spelling Productions, 1971
THIEF (TF) Metromedia Productions/Stonehenge Productions, 1971
MARRIAGE: YEAR ONE (TF) Universal TV, 1971
JIGSAW (TF) Universal TV, 1972
MAGIC CARPET (TF) Universal TV, 1972
HONKY Jack H. Harris Enterprises, 1972
COUNT YOUR BULLETS *CRY FOR ME, BILLY* Brut Productions, 1972
BIRDS OF PREY (TF) Tomorrow Entertainment, 1973
MR. INSIDE/MR. OUTSIDE (TF) D'Antoni Productions, 1973
POLICE STORY (TF) Screen Gems/Columbia TV, 1973
SHIRTS/SKINS (TF) MGM TV, 1973
WHERE THE LILIES BLOOM United Artists, 1974
TOGETHER BROTHERS 20th Century-Fox, 1974
GET CHRISTIE LOVE! (TF) Wolper Productions, 1974
LARRY (TF) Tomorrow Entertainment, 1974
TRAPPED BENEATH THE SEA (TF) ABC Circle Films, 1974
BEYOND THE BERMUDA TRIANGLE (TF) Playboy Productions, 1975
PERILOUS VOYAGE (TF) Universal TV, 1976
SHARK KILL (TF) D'Antoni-Weitz Productions, 1976
21 HOURS AT MUNICH (TF) Filmways, 1976
PART 2 SOUNDER Gamma III, 1976
MINSTREL MAN (TF) Roger Gimbel Productions/EMI TV, 1977
THE AMAZING HOWARD HUGHES (TF) Roger Gimbel Productions/EMI TV, 1977
CONTRACT ON CHERRY STREET (TF) Columbia TV, 1977
CINDY (TF) John Charles Walters Productions, 1978
ONE IN A MILLION: THE RON LeFLORE STORY (TF) Roger Gimbel Productions/EMI TV, 1978
AND I ALONE SURVIVED (TF) Jerry Leider-OJL Productions, 1978
TRANSPLANT (TF) Time-Life Productions, 1979
ORPHAN TRAIN (TF) Roger Gimbel Productions/EMI TV, 1979

WILLIAM A. GRAHAM*—continued

GUYANA TRAGEDY: THE STORY OF JIM JONES (TF) ☆ The Konigsberg Company, 1980
RAGE (TF) Diane Silver Productions/Charles Fries Productions, 1980
DEADLY ENCOUNTER (TF) Rober Gimbel Productions/EMI TV, 1982
M.A.D.D.: MOTHERS AGAINST DRUNK DRIVERS (TF) Universal TV, 1983
THE LAST NINJA (TF) Paramount TV, 1983
HARRY TRACY Quartet/Films Inc., 1983, Canadian
WOMEN OF SAN QUENTIN (TF) David Gerber Company/MGM-UA TV, 1983
THE CALENDAR GIRL MURDERS (TF) Tisch-Avnet Productions, 1984
SECRETS OF A MARRIED MAN (TF) ITC Productions, 1984

LEE GRANT*

(Lyova Rosenthal)

b. October 31, 1927 - New York, New York
Agent: Ed Bondy/Stan Kamen, William Morris Agency - Beverly Hills, 213/274-7451

TELL ME A RIDDLE Filmways, 1980
THE WILLMAR 8 (FD) California Newsreel, 1981
WHEN WOMEN KILL (CTD) HBO/Joseph Feury Productions, 1983
A MATTER OF SEX (TF) Willmar 8 Productions/Orion TV, 1984

ALEX GRASSHOFF*

b. December 10, 1930 - Boston, Massachusetts
Business: Grassco Productions, 10852 Burbank Blvd., North Hollywood, CA 91601, 818/506-7763
Agent: Michael Douroux, TMI - Los Angeles, 213/273-4000

YOUNG AMERICANS (FD) Columbia, 1967
JOURNEY TO THE OUTER LIMITS (FD) 1974
THE LAST DINOSAUR (TF) co-director with Tom Kotani, 1977, U.S.-Japanese
SMOKEY AND THE GOODTIME OUTLAWS Howco International, 1978
J.D. & THE SALT FLAT KID 1978
WACKY TAXI 1982

WALTER GRAUMAN*

b. March 17, 1922 - Milwaukee, Wisconsin
Home: 244 Barlock Avenue, Los Angeles, CA 90049, 213/472-3160
Messages: 818/954-6535
Agent: Bob Broder, Broder-Kurland Agency - Los Angeles, 213/274-8291
Business Manager: Anita DeThomas, DeThomas & Associates, 1801 Avenue of the Stars - Suite 825, Los Angeles, CA 90067, 213/277-4866

THE DISEMBODIED Allied Artists, 1957
LADY IN A CAGE United Artists, 1964
633 SQUADRON United Artists, 1964, British
A RAGE TO LIVE United Artists, 1965
I DEAL IN DANGER 20th Century-Fox, 1966
DAUGHTER OF THE MIND (TF) 20th Century-Fox, 1969
THE LAST ESCAPE United Artists, 1970
THE OLD MAN WHO CRIED WOLF (TF) Aaron Spelling Productions, 1970
CROWHAVEN FARM (TF) Aaron Spelling Productions, 1970
THE FORGOTTEN MAN (TF) Walter Grauman Productions, 1971
PAPER MAN (TF) 20th Century-Fox TV, 1971
THEY CALL IT MURDER (TF) 20th Century-Fox TV, 1971
DEAD MEN TELL NO TALES (TF) 20th Century-Fox TV, 1971
THE STREETS OF SAN FRANCISCO (TF) QM Productions, 1972
MANHUNTER (TF) QM Productions, 1974
FORCE FIVE (TF) Universal TV, 1975
MOST WANTED (TF) QM Productions, 1976
ARE YOU IN THE HOUSE ALONE? (TF) Charles Fries Productions, 1978
CRISIS IN MID-AIR (TF) CBS Entertainment, 1979
THE GOLDEN GATE MURDERS (TF) Universal TV, 1979
THE TOP OF THE HILL (TF) Fellows-Keegan Company/Paramount TV, 1980
TO RACE THE WIND (TF) Walter Grauman Productions, 1980
THE MEMORY OF EVA RYKER (TF) Irwin Allen Productions, 1980
PLEASURE PALACE (TF) Norman Rosemont Productions/Marble Arch Productions, 1980

WALTER GRAUMAN*—continued

JACQUELINE SUSANN'S VALLEY OF THE DOLLS 1981 (MS) 20th Century-Fox TV, 1981
BARE ESSENCE (MS) Warner Bros. TV, 1982
ILLUSIONS (TF) CBS Entertainment, 1983

MIKE GRAY*

Home: 20373 Everding Lane, Topanga, CA 90290
Agent: ICM - Los Angeles, 213/550-4000

WAVELENGTH New World, 1983

GUY GREEN*

b. 1913 - Somerset, England
Agent: Phil Gersh, The Gersh Agency - Beverly Hills, 213/274-6611

RIVER BEAT Lippert, 1954, British
POSTMARK FOR DANGER *PORTRAIT OF ALISON* RKO Radio, 1955, British
TEARS FOR SIMON *LOST* Republic, 1956, British
TRIPLE DECEPTION *HOUSE OF SECRETS* Rank, 1956, British
THE SNORKEL Columbia, 1958, British
DESERT PATROL *SEA OF SAND* Universal, 1958, British
S.O.S. PACIFIC Universal, 1960, British
THE ANGRY SILENCE Valiant, 1960, British
THE MARK Continental, 1961, British
LIGHT IN THE PIAZZA MGM, 1962
DIAMOND HEAD Columbia, 1963
A PATCH OF BLUE MGM, 1965
A MATTER OF INNOCENCE *PRETTY POLLY* Universal, 1968, British
THE MAGUS 20th Century-Fox, 1968, British
A WALK IN THE SPRING RAIN Columbia, 1970
LUTHER American Film Theatre, 1974
JACQUELINE SUSANN'S ONCE IS NOT ENOUGH Paramount, 1975
THE DEVIL'S ADVOCATE Geria Films, 1978, West German
JENNIFER: A WOMAN'S STORY (TF) Marble Arch Productions, 1979
THE INCREDIBLE JOURNEY OF DR. MEG LAUREL (TF) Columbia TV, 1979
JIMMY B. & ANDRE (TF) Georgia Bay Productions, 1980
INMATES: A LOVE STORY (TF) Henerson-Hirsch Productions/Finnegan Associates, 1981
ISABEL'S CHOICE (TF) Stuart Miller-Pantheon TV, 1981

WALON GREEN*

b. December 15, 1936 - Baltimore, Maryland
Home: 3089 Seahorse, Ventura, CA 93001, 805/642-2366
Personal Manager: Harry Ufland, Ufland-Roth Productions, 20th Century Fox, 10201 W. Pico Blvd., Executive Building Room 246, Los Angeles, CA 90035, 213/203-1295

SPREE co-director with Mitchell Leisen, United Producers, 1967
THE HELLSTROM CHRONICLE (FD) Cinema 5, 1971
THE SECRET LIFE OF PLANTS (FD) Paramount, 1978

PETER GREENAWAY

Contact: British Academy of Film & Television Arts, 195 Piccadilly, London W1, England, 01/734-0022

THE FALLS British Film Institute, 1980, British
ACT OF GOD British Film Institute, 1981, British
THE DRAUGHTMAN'S CONTRACT United Artists Classics, 1983, British
MODERN AMERICAN COMPOSERS 1: CAGE AND MONK (TD) Trans Atlantic Films/Channel Four, 1984, British
MODERN AMERICAN COMPOSERS 2: GLASS AND ASHLEY (TD) Trans Atlantic Films/Channel Four, 1984, British

DANFORD B. GREENE

Home: 558 E. Channel Road, Santa Monica, CA 90402, 213/459-2369
Agent: Phil Gersh, The Gersh Agency - Beverly Hills, 213/274-6611

THE SECRET DIARY OF SIGMUND FREUD TLC Films/20th Century Fox, 1984
MILITARY UNIVERSITY co-director with Herb Margolis, 20th Century Fox, 1985, U.S.-Yugoslavian

DAVID GREENE*

b. February 22, 1921 - Manchester, England
Business: David Greene Productions, Inc., 4225 Coldwater Canyon Blvd., Studio City, CA, 818/766-3457
Agent: Bill Haber, CAA - Los Angeles, 213/277-4545

THE SHUTTERED ROOM Warner Bros., 1966, British
SEBASTIAN Paramount, 1968, British
THE STRANGE AFFAIR Paramount, 1968, British
I START COUNTING United Artists, 1969, British
THE PEOPLE NEXT DOOR Avco Embassy, 1970
MADAME SIN (TF) ITC, 1971, British
GODSPELL Columbia, 1973
THE COUNT OF MONTE CRISTO (TF) Norman Rosemont Productions/ITC, 1975, U.S.-British
ELLERY QUEEN (TF) Universal TV, 1975
RICH MAN, POOR MAN (MS) co-director with Boris Sagal, Universal TV, 1976
ROOTS (MS) ☆☆ co-director with Marvin J. Chomsky, John Erman & Gilbert Moses, Wolper Productions, 1977
LUCAN (TF) MGM TV, 1977
THE TRIAL OF LEE HARVEY OSWALD (TF) Charles Fries Productions, 1977
GRAY LADY DOWN Universal, 1978
FRIENDLY FIRE (TF) ☆☆ Marble Arch Productions, 1979
A VACATION IN HELL (TF) David Greene Productions/Finnegan Associates, 1979
THE CHOICE (TF) David Greene Productions/Finnegan Associates, 1981
HARD COUNTRY Universal/AFD, 1981
WORLD WAR III (TF) Finnegan Associates/David Greene Productions, 1982
REHEARSAL FOR MURDER (TF) Levinson-Link Productions/Robert Papazian Productions, 1982
TAKE YOUR BEST SHOT (TF) Levinson-Link Productions/Robert Papazian Productions, 1982
GHOST DANCING (TF) Herbert Brodkin Productions/The Eugene O'Neill Memorial Theatre Center/Titus Productions, 1983
PROTOTYPE (TF) Levinson-Link Productions/Robert Papazian Productions, 1983
THE GUARDIAN (CTF) HBO Premiere Films/Robert Cooper Productions/Stanley Chase Productions, 1984, U.S.-Canadian
SWEET REVENGE (TF) David Greene Productions/Robert Papazian Productions, 1984
FATAL VISION (TF) NBC Productions, 1984

SPARKY GREENE*

b. November 13, 1948 - Chicago, Illinois
Business: Titan Films, 73 Market Street, Venice, CA 90291, 213/349-9319
Attorney: Harley Williams, Blanc, Gilburne, Peters, Williams & Johnston, 1900 Avenue of the Stars, Los Angeles, CA 90067, 213/552-2500

THE OASIS Titan Films, 1984

BUD GREENSPAN*

Business: Cappy Productions, 33 East 68th Street, New York, NY 10021, 212/249-1800

THE GLORY OF THEIR TIMES (TD) Cappy Productions, 1977
WILMA (TF) Cappy Productions, 1977

ROBERT GREENWALD*

b. August 28, 1945 - New York, New York
Home: 53 27th Avenue, Venice, CA 90291, 213/392-5663
Messages: 818/508-4896
Business: Moonlight Productions, 100 Universal City Plaza, Universal City, CA 91608, 818/508-4896

SHARON: PORTRAIT OF A MISTRESS (TF) Moonlight Productions/Paramount TV, 1977
KATIE: PORTRAIT OF A CENTERFOLD (TF) Moonlight Productions/Warner Bros. TV, 1978
FLATBED ANNIE & SWEETIE PIE: LADY TRUCKERS (TF) Moonlight Productions/Filmways, 1979
XANADU Universal, 1980
FORTY DAYS FOR DANNY (TF) Moonlight Productions/Filmways, 1982
IN THE CUSTODY OF STRANGERS (TF) Moonlight Productions/Filmways, 1982
THE BURNING BED (TF) Tisch-Avnet Productions, 1984

DAVID GREENWALT

Contact: Writers Guild of America - Los Angeles, 213/550-1000

SECRET ADMIRER Orion, 1985

COLIN GREGG

Office: Floor 2, 1/6 Falkenberg Court, London W1, England, 01/734-0632
Agent: Linda Seifert Associates, 8A Brunswick Gardens, London W8 4AJ, England, 01/229-5163

BEGGING THE RING (TF) BBC/Colin Gregg Films, 1978, British
THE TRESPASSER (TF) LWT/Polytel, 1981
REMEMBRANCE (TF) Channel Four/Film on Four, 1982, British
TO THE LIGHTHOUSE (TF) BBC/UMF/Colin Gregg Ltd., 1983, British

CHARLES B. GRIFFITH

Agent: Jim Preminger Agency - Los Angeles, 213/475-9491

EAT MY DUST New World, 1976
UP FROM THE DEPTHS New World, 1979
DR. HECKLE AND MR. HYPE Cannon, 1980
SMOKEY BITES THE DUST New World, 1981

MARK GRIFFITHS

Contact: Writers Guild of America - Los Angeles, 213/550-1000

RUNNING HOT New Line Cinema, 1984
HARDBODIES Columbia, 1984

ULU GROSBARD*

b. January 9, 1929 - Antwerp, Belgium
Home: 29 West 10th Street, New York, NY 10011
Agent: Sam Cohn, ICM - New York City, 212/556-5610

THE SUBJECT WAS ROSES MGM, 1968
WHO IS HARRY KELLERMAN AND WHY IS HE SAYING THOSE TERRIBLE THINGS ABOUT ME? National General, 1971
STRAIGHT TIME Warner Bros., 1978
TRUE CONFESSIONS United Artists, 1981
FALLING IN LOVE Paramount, 1984

ROBERT GUENETTE*

b. January 12, 1935 - Holyoke, Massachusetts
Business: 8489 West Third Street, Los Angeles, CA 90048 213/658-8450
Agent: Steve Waterman, ICM - Los Angeles, 213/550-4000

THE TREE Guenette, 1969
THE MYSTERIOUS MONSTERS Sunn Classic, 1976
THE AMAZING WORLD OF PSYCHIC PHENOMENA Sunn Classic, 1976
THE MAN WHO SAW TOMORROW Warner Bros., 1981

JAMES WILLIAM GUERCIO*

Home: Caribou Ranch, Nederland, Colorado 80466, 303/258-3215
Agent: Jeff Berg, ICM - Los Angeles, 213/550-4205

ELECTRA GLIDE IN BLUE United Artists, 1973

VAL GUEST

b. 1911 - London, England
Address: 11 Melina Place, London NW8, England, 01/286-5766
Agent: Tim Stone, Stone-Masser Talent Agents - Los Angeles, 213/275-9599 or Denis Selinger, ICM - London, 01/629-8080

MISS LONDON LTD. General Film Distributors, 1943, British
BEES IN PARADISE General Film Distributors, 1944, British
GIVE US THE MOON General Film Distributors, 1944, British
I'LL BE YOUR SWEETHEART General Film Distributors, 1945, British
JUST WILLIAM'S LUCK United Artists, 1947, British
WILLIAM COME TO TOWN United Artists, 1948, British
MURDER AT THE WINDMILL Grand National, 1949, British
MISS PILGRIM'S PROGRESS Grand National, 1950, British
THE BODY SAID NO Eros, 1950, British
MISTER DRAKE'S DUCK United Artists, 1951, British
PENNY PRINCESS Universal, 1952, British
LIFE WITH THE LYONS Exclusive, 1954, British
THE RUNAWAY BUS Eros, 1954, British
MEN OF SHERWOOD FOREST Astor, 1954, British
DANCE LITTLE LADY Renown, 1954, British
THEY CAN'T HANG ME Independent Film Distributors, 1955, British
THE LYONS IN PARIS Exclusive, 1955, British
BREAK IN THE CIRCLE 20th Century-Fox, 1955, British
THE CREEPING UNKNOWN *THE QUATERMASS EXPERIMENT* United Artists, 1955, British
IT'S A WONDERFUL WORLD Renown, 1956, British
THE WEAPON Republic, 1956, British
CARRY ON ADMIRAL Renown, 1957, British
ENEMY FROM SPACE *QUATERMASS II* United Artists, 1957, British
THE ABOMINABLE SNOWMAN OF THE HIMALAYAS 20th Century-Fox, 1957, British
THE CAMP ON BLOOD ISLAND Columbia, 1958, British
UP THE CREEK Dominant, 1958, British
FURTHER UP THE CREEK Warner Bros., 1958, British
EXPRESSO BONGO Continental, 1959, British
YESTERDAY'S ENEMY Columbia, 1959
LIFE IS A CIRCUS 1960, British
HELL IS A CITY Columbia, 1960, British
STOP ME BEFORE I KILL *THE FULL TREATMENT* Columbia, 1961, British
THE DAY THE EARTH CAUGHT FIRE Universal, 1962, British
JIGSAW Beverly, 1962, British
80,000 SUSPECTS Rank, 1963, British
CONTEST GIRL *THE BEAUTY JUNGLE* Continental, 1964, British
WHERE THE SPIES ARE MGM, 1965, British
CASINO ROYALE co-director with Ken Hughes, John Huston, Joseph McGrath & Robert Parrish, Columbia, 1967, British
ASSIGNMENT K Columbia, 1968, British
WHEN DINOSAURS RULED THE EARTH Warner Bros., 1969, British
TOOMORROW FRD, 1970, British
THE PERSUADERS 1971, British
AU PAIR GIRLS Cannon, 1972, British
CONFESSIONS OF A WINDOW CLEANER Columbia, 1974, British

VAL GUEST —continued

KILLER FORCE American International, 1975, British-Swiss
THE SHILLINGBURY BLOWERS *...AND THE BAND PLAYED ON* Inner Circle, 1980, British
DANGEROUS DAVIES - THE LAST DETECTIVE ITC/Inner Circle/ Maidenhead Films, 1980, British
THE BOYS IN BLUE MAM Ltd./Apollo Leisure Group, 1983, British

JOHN GUILLERMIN*

b. November 11, 1925 - London, England
Agent: Martin Baum, CAA - Los Angeles, 213/277-4545

TORMENT Adelphi, 1949, British
SMART ALEC Grand National, 1951, British
TWO ON THE TILES Grand National, 1951, British
FOUR DAYS Grand National, 1951, British
BACHELOR IN PARIS *SONG OF PARIS* Lippert, 1952, British
MISS ROBIN HOOD Associated British Film Distributors, 1952, British
OPERATION DIPLOMAT Butcher, 1953, British
ADVENTURE IN THE HOPFIELDS British Lion/Children's Film Foundation, 1954, British
THE CROWDED DAY Adelphi, 1954, British
DUST AND GOLD 1955, British
THUNDERSTORM Allied Artists, 1955, British
TOWN ON TRIAL Columbia, 1957, British
THE WHOLE TRUTH Columbia, 1958, British
I WAS MONTY'S DOUBLE NTA Pictures, 1958, British
TARZAN'S GREATEST ADVENTURE Paramount, 1959, British-U.S.
THE DAY THEY ROBBED THE BANK OF ENGLAND MGM, 1960, British
NEVER LET GO Rank, 1960, British
WALTZ OF THE TOREADORS Continental, 1962, British
TARZAN GOES TO INDIA MGM, 1962, British-U.S.-Swiss
GUNS AT BATASI 20th Century-Fox, 1964, British-U.S.
RAPTURE International Classics, 1965, British-French
THE BLUE MAX 20th Century-Fox, 1966, British, U.S.
P.J. Universal, 1968
HOUSE OF CARDS Universal, 1969
THE BRIDGE AT REMAGEN United Artists, 1969
EL CONDOR National General, 1970
SKYJACKED MGM, 1972
SHAFT IN AFRICA MGM, 1973
THE TOWERING INFERNO 20th Century-Fox, 1974
KING KONG Paramount, 1976
DEATH ON THE NILE Paramount, 1978, British
MR. PATMAN Film Consortium, 1980, Canadian
SHEENA Columbia, 1984

BILL GUNN

Contact: Writers Guild of America, East - New York City, 212/245-6180

STOP Warner Bros., 1970
GANJA & HESS Kelly-Jordan, 1973

TOMAS GUTIERREZ ALEA

b. December 11, 1928 - Havana, Cuba

EL MEGANO co-director, 1955, Cuban
ESTA TIERRA NUESTRA 1959, Cuban
ASEMBLEA GENERAL 1960, Cuban
MUERTE AL INVASOR co-director, 1961, Cuban
HISTORIAS DE LA REVOLUCION 1961, Cuban
LAS DOCE SILLAS 1962, Cuban
CUMBITE 1964, Cuban
LA MUERTE DE AN BUROCRATA 1966, Cuban
MEMORIES OF UNDERDEVELOPMENT Tricontinental, 1968, Cuban
UNA PELEA CUBANA CONTRA LOS DEMONIOS 1971, Cuban
EL ARTE DEL TOBACO 1974, Cuban
THE LAST SUPPER Tricontinental, 1976, Cuban

TOMAS GUTIERREZ ALEA —continued

LOS SOBREVIVIENTES ICAIC, 1979, Cuban
UP TO A POINT New Yorker, 1984, Cuban

ANDRE GUTTFREUND*

Contact: Directors Guild of America - Los Angeles, 212/656-1220

BREACH OF CONTRACT Atlantic Releasing Corporation, 1984

CLAUDIO GUZMAN*

Home: 9785 Drake Lane, Beverly Hills, CA 90210, 213/278-8816

ANTONIO Guzman Productions, 1973
LINDA LOVELACE FOR PRESIDENT General Film, 1975
WILLA (TF) co-director with Joan Darling, GJL Productions/Dove, Inc., 1979
THE HOSTAGE TOWER (TF) Jerry Leider Productions, 1980
FOR LOVERS ONLY (TF) Henerson-Hirsch Productions/Caesar's Palace Productions, 1982

STEVE GYLLENHAAL*

Home: 226 S. Norton, Los Angeles, CA 90006, 213/938-5211
Agent: Geoffrey Sanford, The Artists Agency - Los Angeles, 213/277-7779

A CERTAIN FURY Entertainment Events, 1985, Canadian

H

TAYLOR HACKFORD*

Agent: Fred Specktor, CAA - Los Angeles, 213/277-4545
Attorney: Stuart Benjamin, Wyman, Rothman, Bautzer & Kuchel, 2049 Century Park East, Los Angeles, CA 90067, 213/556-8000

THE IDOLMAKER United Artists, 1980
AN OFFICER AND A GENTLEMAN Paramount, 1982
AGAINST ALL ODDS Columbia, 1984
WHITE NIGHTS Columbia, 1985

RUSSELL HAGG

Agent: Writers and Artists Agency - Los Angeles, 213/820-2240

CASH & CO. (MS) co-director with George Miller, Homestead Films/Network Seven, 1975, Australian
TANDARRA (MS) co-director, Homestead Films/Network Seven, 1976, Australian

RUSSELL HAGG —continued

RAW DEAL Greater Union Film Distributors, 1977, Australian
TAXI (TF) Network Seven, 1979, Australian

PIERS HAGGARD

b. 1939 - Scotland
Home: 35 Digby Mansions, London W6, England, 01/741-0812
Agent: Douglas Rae Management, 28 Charing Cross Road, London W1, England, 01/836-3903

WEDDING NIGHT American International, 1970, Irish
THE BLOOD ON SATAN'S CLAW *SATAN'S SKIN* Cannon, 1971, British
THE QUATERMASS CONCLUSION Euston Films Ltd., 1979, British
THE FIENDISH PLOT OF DR. FU MANCHU Orion/Warner Bros., 1980, British
MRS. REINHARDT (TF) BBC/WNET-13, 1981, British-U.S.
VENOM Paramount, 1982, British
ROLLING HOME (TF) BBC, 1982, British
MARKS (TF) BBC, 1982, British
DESERT OF LIES (TF) BBC, 1983, British
WATERS OF THE MOON (TF) BBC, 1983, British

LARRY HAGMAN*

b. September 21, 1931 - Fort Worth, Texas
Business: MajLar Productions, Inc., 26 Malibu Colony, Malibu, CA 90265
Agent: William Morris Agency - Beverly Hills, 213/274-7451
Business Manager: Norman Marcus, Ernst & Whinney - Beverly Hills, 213/553-2800

BEWARE! THE BLOB *SON OF BLOB* Jack H. Harris Enterprises, 1972

STUART HAGMANN*

b. September 2, 1942 - Sturgeon Bay, Wisconsin
Business Manager: Howard M. Borris, 9401 Wilshire Blvd., Beverly Hills, 90212, 213/550-0111

THE STRAWBERRY STATEMENT MGM, 1970
BELIEVE IN ME MGM, 1971
SHE LIVES (TF) ABC Circle Films, 1973
TARANTULAS: THE DEADLY CARGO (TF) Alan Landsburg Productions, 1977

RANDA HAINES*

Agent: Bill Block, ICM - Los Angeles, 213/550-4000

UNDER THIS SKY (TF) Red Cloud Productions/PBS, 1979
THE JILTING OF GRANNY WEATHERALL (TF) Learning in Focus/American Short Story, 1980
SOMETHING ABOUT AMELIA (TF) ☆ Leonard Goldberg Productions, 1984

WILLIAM ''BILLY'' HALE*

Agent: William Morris Agency - Beverly Hills, 213/274-7451
Personal Manager: Martin Mickelson - Beverly Hills, 213/858-1097

HOW I SPENT MY SUMMER VACATION (TF) Universal TV, 1967
GUNFIGHT IN ABILENE Universal, 1967
JOURNEY TO SHILOH Universal, 1968
NIGHTMARE (TF) CBS, Inc., 1974
THE GREAT NIAGARA (TF) Playboy Productions, 1974
CROSSFIRE (TF) QM Productions, 1975
THE KILLER WHO WOULDN'T DIE (TF) Paramount TV, 1976
STALK THE WILD CHILD (TF) Charles Fries Productions, 1976
RED ALERT (TF) The Jozak Company/Paramount TV, 1977
S.O.S. TITANIC (TF) Roger Gimbel Productions/EMI TV/Argonaut Films Ltd., 1979, U.S.-British
MURDER IN TEXAS (TF) Dick Clark Productions/Billy Hale Films, 1981

WILLIAM "BILLY" HALE*—continued

ONE SHOE MAKES IT MURDER (TF) The Fellows-Keegan Company/Lorimar Productions, 1982
THE DEMON MURDER CASE (TF) Dick Clark Productions/Len Steckler Productions, 1983
LACE (MS) Lorimar Productions, 1984
LACE 2 (MS) Lorimar Productions, 1985

JACK HALEY, JR.*

b. October 25, 1933 - Los Angeles, California
Business: 213/655-1106

NORWOOD Paramount, 1970
THE LOVE MACHINE Columbia, 1971
THAT'S ENTERTAINMENT! (FD) MGM/United Artists, 1974
THAT'S ENTERTAINMENT, PART 2 (FD) co-director with Gene Kelly, MGM/United Artists, 1976
THAT'S DANCING! (FD) MGM/UA, 1985

H.B. HALICKI

b. Dunkirk, New York
Business: H.B. Halicki Productions, P.O. Box 2123, Gardena, CA 90247, 213/327-1744 or 213/770-1744

GONE IN 60 SECONDS H.B. Halicki International, 1974
THE JUNKMAN H.B. Halicki International, 1982
DEADLINE AUTO THEFT H.B. Halicki International, 1983

ADRIAN HALL*

Home: 176 Pleasant Street, Providence, RI 02906, 401/421-4219
Personal Manager: Marion Simon, Trinity Square Repertory Company, Providence, RI 02903, 401/521-1100

THE HOUSE OF MIRTH (TF) Cinelit Productions/WNET-13, 1981

PETER HALL

b. November 22, 1930 - Bury St. Edmunds, Suffolk, England
Address: The Wall House, Mongewall Park, Wallingford, Berkshire, England
Contact: Directors Guild of Great Britain, 56 Whitfield Street, London W1, England, 01/580-9592

WORK IS A FOUR LETTER WORD Universal, 1968, British
A MIDSUMMER NIGHT'S DREAM Eagle, 1968, British
PERFECT FRIDAY Chevron, 1970, British
THE HOMECOMING American Film Theatre, 1973, British
AKENFIELD (FD) Angle Films, 1975, British

DANIEL HALLER*

b. 1926 - Los Angeles, California
Home: 5364 Jed Smith Road, Hidden Hills, CA 91302, 818/888-7936
Agent: Irv Schechter, Irv Schechter Company - Beverly Hills, 213/278-8070

DIE, MONSTER, DIE! American International, 1965, U.S.-British
DEVIL'S ANGELS American International, 1967
THE WILD RACERS American International, 1968
PADDY Allied Artists, 1970, Irish
PIECES OF DREAMS United Artists, 1970
THE DUNWICH HORROR American International, 1970
THE DESPERATE MILES (TF) Universal TV, 1975
MY SWEET LADY (TF) Universal TV, 1976
BLACK BEAUTY (MS) Universal TV, 1978
LITTLE MO (TF) Mark VII Ltd./Worldvision, 1978
BUCK ROGERS IN THE 25TH CENTURY Universal, 1979
HIGH MIDNIGHT (TF) The Mirisch Corporation/Universal TV, 1979
GEORGIA PEACHES (TF) New World TV, 1980

DANIEL HALLER*—continued

FOLLOW THAT CAR New World, 1981
MICKEY SPILLANE'S MARGIN FOR MURDER (TF) Hamner Productions, 1981
KNIGHT RIDER (TF) Glen A. Larson Productions/Universal TV, 1982

DAVID HAMILTON

Contact: French Film Office, 745 Fifth Avenue, New York, NY 10151, 212/832-8860

BILITIS Topar, 1976, French
TENDRE COUSINES Crown International, 1980, French
LAURA, LES OMBRES DE L'ETE Les Films de L'Alma/CORA, 1979, French
PREMIERS DESIRS AMLF, 1983, French-West German
UN ETE A SAINT TROPEZ (FD) Fugio & Associates/JVC, 1983, French-Japanese
TATIANA UGC, 1984, French

GUY HAMILTON*

b. September, 1922 - Paris, France
Agent: London Management - London, 01/493-1610

THE RINGER British Lion, 1952, British
THE INTRUDER Associated Artists, 1953, British
AN INSPECTOR CALLS Associated Artists, 1954, British
THE COLDITZ STORY Republic, 1955, British
CHARLEY MOON British Lion, 1956, British
STOWAWAY GIRL *MANUELA* Paramount, 1957, British
THE DEVIL'S DISCIPLE United Artists, 1959, British
A TOUCH OF LARCENY Paramount, 1960, British
THE BEST OF ENEMIES Columbia, 1962, Italian-British
MAN IN THE MIDDLE 20th Century-Fox, 1964, British-U.S.
GOLDFINGER United Artists, 1964, British
THE PARTY'S OVER Allied Artists, 1966, British
FUNERAL IN BERLIN Paramount, 1966, British
BATTLE OF BRITAIN United Artists, 1969, British
DIAMONDS ARE FOREVER United Artists, 1971, British
LIVE AND LET DIE United Artists, 1973, British
THE MAN WITH THE GOLDEN GUN United Artists, 1974, British
FORCE 10 FROM NAVARONE American International, 1978
THE MIRROR CRACK'D AFD, 1980, British
EVIL UNDER THE SUN Universal/AFD, 1982, British
REMO: UNARMED AND DANGEROUS Orion, 1985

JOHN HANCOCK*

b. February 9, 1939 - Kansas City, Missouri
Home: 21531 Deerpath Lane, Malibu, CA 90265, 213/456-3627
Agent: ICM - Los Angeles, 213/550-4000

LET'S SCARE JESSICA TO DEATH Paramount, 1971
BANG THE DRUM SLOWLY Paramount, 1973
BABY BLUE MARINE Columbia, 1976
CALIFORNIA DREAMING American International, 1979

CURTIS HANSON

Agent: Leading Artists - Beverly Hills, 213/858-1999

THE AROUSERS Asseyev-Hanson, 1976
THE LITTLE DRAGONS Aurora, 1980
LOSIN' IT Embassy, 1983, Canadian-U.S.

JOHN HANSON

Business: New Front Films, 125 W. Richmond Avenue, Point Richmond, CA 94801, 415/231-0225
Agent: Scott Harris, Abrams, Harris & Goldberg - 213/859-0625

NORTHERN LIGHTS co-director with Rob Nilsson, Cine Manifest/New Front Films, 1978
WILDROSE New Front Films, 1984

JOSEPH C. HANWRIGHT*

Home: P.O. Box 2122, Ketchum, ID 83340, 208/726-3594

UNCLE JOE SHANNON United Artists, 1979

JOSEPH HARDY*

b. March 8, 1929 - Carlsbad, New Mexico
Agent: Bill Haber, CAA - Los Angeles, 213/277-4545

GREAT EXPECTATIONS (TF) Transcontinental Film Productions, 1974, British
A TREE GROWS IN BROOKLYN (TF) 20th Century-Fox TV, 1974
LAST HOURS BEFORE MORNING (TF) Charles Fries Productions/MGM TV, 1975
THE SILENCE (TF) Palomar Pictures International, 1975
JAMES AT 15 (TF) 20th Century-Fox TV, 1977
THE USERS (TF) Aaron Spelling Productions, 1978
LOVE'S SAVAGE FURY (TF) Aaron Spelling Productions, 1979
THE SEDUCTION OF MISS LEONA (TF) Edgar J. Scherick Associates, 1980
DREAM HOUSE (TF) Hill-Mandelker Films/Time-Life Productions, 1981
THE DAY THE BUBBLE BURST (TF) Tamara Productions/20th Century-Fox TV/The Production Company, 1982
NOT IN FRONT OF THE CHILDREN (TF) Tamtco Productions/The Edward S. Feldman Company, 1982
TWO MARRIAGES (TF) Lorimar Productions/Raven's Claw Productions, 1983

ROBIN HARDY

Contact: British Academy of Film & Television Arts, 195 Piccadilly, London W1, England, 01/734-0022

THE WICKER MAN Warner Bros., 1975, British

DAVID HARE

Contact: British Academy of Film & Television Arts, 195 Piccadilly, London W1, England, 01/734-0022

WETHERBY Film Four International/Zenith Productions/Greenpoint Films, 1985, British

DEAN HARGROVE*

b. July 27, 1938 - Iola, Kansas
Agent: Major Talent Agency - Los Angeles, 213/820-5841

THE MANCHU EAGLE CAPER MYSTERY United Artists, 1975
THE BIG RIP-OFF (TF) Universal TV, 1975
THE RETURN OF THE WORLD'S GREATEST DETECTIVE (TF) Universal TV, 1976
DEAR DETECTIVE (TF) CBS, 1979

CURTIS HARRINGTON*

b. September 17, 1928 - Los Angeles, California
Agent: The Sy Fischer Company - Los Angeles, 213/557-0388

NIGHT TIDE Universal, 1963
QUEEN OF BLOOD American International, 1966

CURTIS HARRINGTON*—continued

GAMES Universal, 1967
HOW AWFUL ABOUT ALLAN (TF) Aaron Spelling Productions, 1970
WHO SLEW AUNTIE ROO? American International, 1971, British
WHAT'S THE MATTER WITH HELEN? United Artists, 1971
THE CAT CREATURE (TF) Screen Gems/Columbia TV, 1973
KILLER BEES (TF) RSO Films, 1974
THE KILLING KIND Media Trend, 1974
THE DEAD DON'T DIE (TF) Douglas S. Cramer Productions, 1975
RUBY Dimension, 1977
DEVIL DOG: THE HOUND OF HELL (TF) Zeitman-Landers-Roberts Productions, 1978
MATA HARI Cannon, 1985

DENNY HARRIS

Business: Denny Harris of California, Inc., 12166 W. Olympic Blvd., Los Angeles, CA 90064, 213/826-6265

SILENT SCREAM American Cinema, 1980

FRANK HARRIS

KILLPOINT Crown International, 1984

HARRY HARRIS*

b. September 8, 1922 -Kansas City, Missouri
Agent: Ronald Leif, Contemporary-Korman Artists - Beverly Hills, 213/278-8250

THE RUNAWAYS (TF) Lorimar Productions, 1975
THE SWISS FAMILY ROBINSON (TF) Irwin Allen Productions/20th Century-Fox TV, 1975
RIVKIN: BOUNTY HUNTER (TF) Chiarascurio Productions/Ten-Four Productions, 1981
A DAY FOR THANKS ON WALTON'S MOUNTAIN (TF) Lorimar Productions/Amanda Productions, 1982

JAMES B. HARRIS*

b. August 3, 1928 - New York, New York
Business: James B. Harris Productions, 248½ Lasky Drive, Beverly Hills, CA 90212, 213/273-4270

THE BEDFORD INCIDENT Columbia, 1965
SOME CALL IT LOVING Cine Globe, 1973
FAST-WALKING Pickman Films, 1982

RICHARD HARRIS

b. October 1, 1932 - Limerick, Ireland
Agent: William Morris Agency - Beverly Hills, 213/274-7451

THE HERO *BLOOMFIELD* Avco Embassy, 1972, Israeli-British

KEN HARRISON

Agent: Rick Jaffa, William Morris Agency - Beverly Hills, 213/274-7451

1918 Cinecom International, 1985

BRUCE HART*

b. January 15, 1938 - New York, New York
Home: 200 West 86th Street, New York, NY 10024, 212/724-1948
Agent: David Kennedy, ICM - New York City, 212/556-5761
Business Manager: Scott Shukat, The Shukat Co., Ltd., 340 West 55th Street, New York, NY 10019, 212/582-7614

SOONER OR LATER (TF) Laughing Willow Company/NBC, 1979

DEREK HART

Contact: British Academy of Film & Television Arts, 195 Piccadilly, London W1, England, 01/734-0022

BACKSTAGE AT THE KIROV (FD) Armand Hammer Productions, 1983

HARVEY HART*

b. 1928 - Toronto, Canada
Home: 5 Sultan Street, Toronto, Ontario M5 I16, Canada, 416/960-2351
Agent: Bill Haber, CAA - Los Angeles, 213/277-4545
Business Manager: Marty Rosenthal, Kaufman & Bernstein, 1900 Avenue of the Stars - Suite 2270, Los Angeles, CA 90067, 213/277-1900

BUS RILEY'S BACK IN TOWN Universal, 1965
DARK INTRUDER Universal, 1965
SULLIVAN'S EMPIRE co-director with Thomas Carr, Universal, 1967
THE SWEET RIDE 20th Century-Fox, 1968
THE YOUNG LAWYERS (TF) Paramount TV, 1969
FORTUNE AND MEN'S EYES MGM, 1971, Canadian
MAHONEY'S ESTATE (TF) Topaz Productions, 1972, Canadian
THE PYX Cinerama Releasing Corporation, 1973, Canadian
CAN ELLEN BE SAVED? (TF) ABC Circle Films, 1974
MURDER OR MERCY (TF) QM Productions, 1974
PANIC ON THE 5:22 (TF) QM Productions, 1974
SHOOT Avco Embassy, 1976, Canadian
STREET KILLING (TF) ABC Circle Films, 1976
THE CITY (TF) QM Productions, 1977
GOLDENROD (TF) Talent Associates/Film Funding Ltd. of Canada, 1977, U.S.-Canadian
THE PRINCE OF CENTRAL PARK (TF) Lorimar Productions, 1977
CAPTAINS COURAGEOUS (TF) Norman Rosemont Productions, 1977
STANDING TALL (TF) QM Productions, 1978
W.E.B. (TF) NBC, 1978
LIKE NORMAL PEOPLE (TF) Christiana Productions/20th Century-Fox TV, 1979
THE ALIENS ARE COMING (TF) Woodruff Productions/QM Productions, 1980
JOHN STEINBECK'S EAST OF EDEN (MS) Mace Neufeld Productions, 1981
THE HIGH COUNTRY Crown International, 1981, Canadian
MASSARATI AND THE BRAIN (TF) Aaron Spelling Productions, 1982
BORN BEAUTIFUL (TF) Procter & Gamble Productions/Telecom Entertainment Inc., 1982
GETTING EVEN New World, 1983, Canadian
MASTER OF THE GAME (MS) co-director with Kevin Connor, Rosemont Productions, 1984

ANTHONY HARVEY*

b. June 3, 1931 - London, England
Agent: Fred Milstein, William Morris Agency - New York City, 212/586-5100

DUTCHMAN Continental, 1967, British
THE LION IN WINTER ★ Avco Embassy, 1968, British
THEY MIGHT BE GIANTS Universal, 1971
THE GLASS MENAGERIE (TF) Talent Associates, 1973
THE ABDICATION Warner Bros., 1974, British
THE DISAPPEARANCE OF AIMEE (TF) Tomorrow Entertainment, 1976
PLAYERS Paramount, 1979
EAGLE'S WING International Picture Show, 1980, British
RICHARD'S THINGS New World, 1981, British

ANTHONY HARVEY*—continued

THE PATRICIA NEAL STORY (TF) co-director with Anthony Page, Lawrence Schiller Productions, 1981
SVENGALI (TF) Robert Halmi Productions, 1983
THE ULTIMATE SOLUTION OF GRACE QUIGLEY Cannon, 1984

HENRY HATHAWAY*

b. March 13, 1898 - Sacramento, California
Home Address: 888 Sarbonne Road, Los Angeles, CA 90077, 213/472-3684

HERITAGE OF THE DESERT 1932
WILD HORSE MESA 1932
UNDER THE TONTO RIM 1933
SUNSET PASS 1933
MAN OF THE FOREST 1933
TO THE LAST MAN 1933
THE THUNDERING HERD 1933
THE LAST ROUND-UP 1934
COME ON MARINES! 1934
THE WITCHING HOUR Paramount, 1934
NOW AND FOREVER Paramount, 1934
THE LIVES OF A BENGAL LANCER ★ Paramount, 1935
PETER IBBETSON Paramount, 1935
THE TRAIL OF THE LONESOME PINE Paramount, 1936
GO WEST, YOUNG MAN Paramount, 1936
SOULS AT SEA Paramount, 1937
SPAWN OF THE NORTH Paramount, 1938
THE REAL GLORY United Artists, 1939
JOHNNY APOLLO 20th Century-Fox, 1940
BRIGHAM YOUNG, FRONTIERSMAN 20th Century-Fox, 1940
THE SHEPHERD OF THE HILLS Paramount, 1941
SUNDOWN United Artists, 1941
TEN GENTLEMEN FROM WEST POINT 20th Century-Fox, 1942
CHINA GIRL 20th Century-Fox, 1942
HOME IN INDIANA 20th Century-Fox, 1944
WING AND A PRAYER 20th Century-Fox, 1944
NOB HILL 20th Century-Fox, 1945
THE HOUSE ON 92ND STREET 20th Century-Fox, 1945
THE DARK CORNER 20th Century-Fox, 1946
13 RUE MADELEINE 20th Century-Fox, 1947
KISS OF DEATH 20th Century-Fox, 1947
CALL NORTHSIDE 777 20th Century-Fox, 1948
DOWN TO THE SEA IN SHIPS 20th Century-Fox, 1949
THE BLACK ROSE 20th Century-Fox, 1950, British-U.S.
YOU'RE IN THE NAVY NOW 20th Century-Fox, 1951
FOURTEEN HOURS 20th Century-Fox, 1951
RAWHIDE 20th Century-Fox, 1951
THE DESERT FOX 20th Century-Fox, 1951
DIPLOMATIC COURIER 20th Century-Fox, 1952
O. HENRY'S FULL HOUSE co-director with Howard Hawks, Henry King, Henry Koster & Jean Negulesco, 20th Century-Fox, 1952
NIAGARA 20th Century-Fox, 1953
WHITE WITCH DOCTOR 20th Century-Fox, 1953
PRINCE VALIANT 20th Century-Fox, 1954
GARDEN OF EVIL 20th Century-Fox, 1954
THE RACERS 20th Century-Fox, 1955
THE BOTTOM OF THE BOTTLE 20th Century-Fox, 1956
23 PACES TO BAKER STREET 20th Century-Fox, 1956, British-U.S.
LEGEND OF THE LOST United Artists, 1957
FROM HELL TO TEXAS 20th Century-Fox, 1958
WOMAN OBSESSED 20th Century-Fox, 1959
SEVEN THIEVES 20th Century-Fox, 1960
NORTH TO ALASKA 20th Century-Fox, 1960
HOW THE WEST WAS WON co-director with John Ford & George Marshall, MGM, 1963
CIRCUS WORLD Paramount, 1964
THE SONS OF KATIE ELDER Paramount, 1965
NEVADA SMITH Paramount, 1966
THE LAST SAFARI Paramount, 1967, British
FIVE CARD STUD Paramount, 1968
TRUE GRIT Paramount, 1969
RAID ON ROMMEL Universal, 1971

HENRY HATHAWAY*—continued

SHOOT-OUT Universal, 1971
HANGUP *SUPER DUDE* Universal, 1974

SIDNEY HAYERS*

b. Edinburgh, Scotland
Home: 10545 Wyton Drive, Los Angeles, CA 90024, 213/474-8984
Messages: 213/474-0945
Agent: Mark Lichtman, Shapiro-Lichtman Agency - Los Angeles, 213/557-2244
Business Manager: Susan Grode, 2049 Century Park East - Suite 1260, Los Angeles, CA 90067, 213/552-0592

VIOLENT MOMENT Anglo-Amalgamated, 1959, British
THE WHITE TRAP Anglo-Amalgamated, 1959, British
CIRCUS OF HORRORS American International, 1960, British
THE MALPAS MYSTERY Anglo-Amalgamated, 1960, British
ECHO OF BARBARA Rank, 1961, British
BURN, WITCH, BURN *NIGHT OF THE EAGLE* American International, 1962, British
THIS IS MY STREET Anglo-Amalgamated, 1963, British
THREE HATS FOR LISA Anglo-Amalgamated, 1963, British
THE TRAP Rank, 1966, British
FINDERS KEEPERS United Artists, 1967, British
THE SOUTHERN STAR Columbia, 1969, French-British
MISTER JERICO (TF) ITC, 1970, British
IN THE DEVIL'S GARDEN *ASSAULT* Hemisphere, 1971, British
THE FIRECHASERS Rank, 1971, British
INN OF THE FRIGHTENED PEOPLE *TERROR FROM UNDER THE HOUSE/ REVENGE* Hemisphere, 1973, British
DEADLY STRANGERS Fox-Rank, 1974, British
DIAGNOSIS: MURDER CIC, 1975, British
WHAT CHANGED CHARLEY FARTHING? Stirling Gold, 1976, British
ONE WAY Silhouette Film Productions, 1976
THE SEEKERS (TF) Universal TV, 1978
THE LAST CONVERTIBLE (MS) co-director with Jo Swerling, Jr. & Gus Trikonis, Roy Huggins Productions/Universal TV, 1979
CONDOMINIUM (TF) Universal TV, 1980
CHANDLERTOWN *PHILIP MARLOWE - PRIVATE EYE (CMS)* co-director with Bryan Forbes, Peter Hunt & David Wickes, HBO/David Wickes Television Ltd./London Weekend Television, 1983, British

JACK HAZAN

Contact: British Academy of Film & Television Arts, 195 Piccadilly, London W1, England, 01/734-0022

A BIGGER SPLASH Lagoon Associates, 1975, British
RUDE BOY co-director with David Mingay, Atlantic Releasing Corporation, 1980, British

AMY HECKERLING*

Home: 1282 Devon Drive, Los Angeles, CA 90024, 213/271-9908
Agent: David Gersh, The Gersh Agency - Beverly Hills, 213/274-6611

FAST TIMES AT RIDGEMONT HIGH Universal, 1982
JOHNNY DANGEROUSLY 20th Century Fox, 1984
NATIONAL LAMPOON'S EUROPEAN VACATION Warner Bros., 1985

RICHARD T. HEFFRON*

Messages: 213/457-5323
Agent: Fred Specktor, CAA - Los Angeles, 213/277-4545

DO YOU TAKE THIS STRANGER? (TF) Universal TV, 1971
FILLMORE (FD) 20th Century-Fox, 1972
TOMA (TF) Universal TV, 1973
OUTRAGE! (TF) ABC Circle Films, 1973
NEWMAN'S LAW Universal, 1974
THE MORNING AFTER (TF) Wolper Productions, 1974

RICHARD T. HEFFRON*—continued

THE ROCKFORD FILES (TF) Universal TV, 1974
THE CALIFORNIA KID (TF) Universal TV, 1974
LOCUSTS (TF) Paramount TV, 1974
I WILL FIGHT NO MORE FOREVER (TF) Wolper Productions, 1975
DEATH SCREAM (TF) RSO Films, 1975
TRACKDOWN United Artists, 1976
FUTUREWORLD American International, 1976
YOUNG JOE, THE FORGOTTEN KENNEDY (TF) ABC Circle Films, 1977
OUTLAW BLUES Warner Bros., 1977
SEE HOW SHE RUNS (TF) CLN Productions, 1978
TRUE GRIT: A FURTHER ADVENTURE (TF) Paramount TV, 1978
FOOLIN' AROUND Columbia, 1978
A RUMOR OF WAR (TF) Charles Fries Productions, 1980
A WHALE FOR THE KILLING (TF) Play Productions/Beowulf Productions, 1981
I, THE JURY 20th Century-Fox, 1982
A KILLER IN THE FAMILY (TF) Stan Margulies Productions/Sunn Classic Pictures, 1983
THE MYSTIC WARRIOR (MS) David L. Wolper-Stan Margulies Productions/Warner Bros. TV, 1984
V: THE FINAL BATTLE (TF) Blatt-Singer Productions/Warner Bros. TV, 1984
ANATOMY OF AN ILLNESS (TF) Hamner Productions/CBS Entertainment, 1984

JEROME HELLMAN*

b. September 4, 1928 - New York, New York
Business: Jerome Hellman Productions, 68 Malibu Colony Drive, Malibu, CA 90265, 213/456-3361

PROMISES IN THE DARK Orion/Warner Bros., 1979

MONTE HELLMAN*

b. July 12, 1932 - New York, New York
Business: Monte Hellman Films, 265 N. Robertson Blvd., Beverly Hills, CA 90211, 213/278-2944
Agent: Mike Simpson, William Morris Agency - Beverly Hills, 213/274-7451

BEAST FROM HAUNTED CAVE Allied Artists, 1959
BACK DOOR TO HELL 20th Century-Fox, 1964
FLIGHT TO FURY 1965
THE SHOOTING American International, 1966
RIDE IN THE WHIRLWIND American International, 1966
TWO-LANE BLACKTOP Universal, 1971
COCKFIGHTER *BORN TO KILL* New World, 1974
CHINA 9 LIBERTY 37 Titanus, 1978, Italian

GUNNAR HELLSTROM*

Home: 10816-¾ Lindbrook Drive, Los Angeles, CA 90024, 213/474-6749
Business: Artistfilm, Toro, 14900 Nynashamn, Sweden, 0752-31135
Agent: F.A.M.E. - Los Angeles, 213/656-7590

THE NAME OF THE GAME IS KILL (TF) Universal TV, 1968
MARK, I LOVE YOU (TF) The Aubrey Company, 1980
RASKENSTAM Sandrews, 1983, Swedish

HENRI HELMAN

Contact: French Film Office, 745 Fifth Avenue, New York, NY 10151, 212/832-8860

LE COEUR FROID Films Moliere, 1977, French
WHERE IS PARSIFAL? Tri-Star, 1984, British

DAVID HELPERN, JR.

I'M A STRANGER HERE MYSELF (FD) October Films, 1974
HOLLYWOOD ON TRIAL (FD) Lumiere, 1976
SOMETHING SHORT OF PARADISE American International, 1979

DAVID HEMMINGS*

b. November 18, 1941 - Guildfold, England
Agent: Tim Stone, Stone-Masser Talent Agents - Los Angeles, 213/275-9599

RUNNING SCARED Paramount, 1972, British
THE 14 MGM-EMI, 1973, British
JUST A GIGOLO United Artists Classics, 1978, West German
THE SURVIVOR Hemdale, 1981, Australian
TREASURE OF THE YANKEE ZEPHYR *RACE TO THE YANKEE ZEPHYR* Artists Releasing Corporation/Film Ventures International, 1984, New Zealand-British
THE KEY TO REBECCA (TF) Taft Entertainment TV/Castle Combe Productions, 1985, U.S.-British

FRANK HENENLOTTER

BASKET CASE Analysis, 1982

BUCK HENRY*

b. 1930 - New York, New York
Agent: ICM - Los Angeles, 213/550-4000

HEAVEN CAN WAIT ★ co-director with Warren Beatty, Paramount, 1978
FIRST FAMILY Warner Bros., 1980

JIM HENSON*

b. September 24, 1936 - Greenville, North Carolina
Business: 212/794-2400

THE GREAT MUPPET CAPER Universal/AFD, 1981, British
THE DARK CRYSTAL co-director with Frank Oz, Universal/AFD, 1982, British

MICHAEL HERZ

Business: Troma, Inc., 733 Ninth Avenue, New York, NY 10019, 212/757-4555

WAITRESS! co-director with Samuel Weil, Troma, 1982
STUCK ON YOU! co-director with Samuel Weil, Troma, 1983
THE FIRST TURN-ON! co-director with Samuel Weil, Troma, 1984
THE TOXIC AVENGER co-director with Samuel Weil, Troma, 1984

JOHN HERZFELD*

Agent: Jack Rapke, CAA - Los Angeles, 213/277-4545

TWO OF A KIND 20th Century-Fox, 1983

WERNER HERZOG

b. September 5, 1942 - Sachrang, Germany
Address: Neureutherstrasse 20, D-8000, Munich 13, West Germany
Contact: German Film & TV Academy, Pommernallee 1, 1000 Berlin 19, West Germany, 030/303-6212

DIE FLIEGENDEN ARZTE VON OSTAFRIKA 1968, West German
SIGNS OF LIFE Werner Herzog Filmproduktion, 1968, West German
BEHINDERTE ZUNKUFT 1970, West German
EVEN DWARFS STARTED SMALL New Line Cinema, 1971, West German
LAND OF SILENCE AND DARKNESS (FD) New Yorker, 1972, West German

WERNER HERZOG —continued

AGUIRRE, THE WRATH OF GOD New Yorker, 1973, West German-Mexican-Peruvian
THE MYSTERY OF KASPAR HAUSER *EVERY MAN FOR HIMSELF AND GOD AGAINST ALL* Cinema 5, 1974, West German
HEART OF GLASS New Yorker, 1976, West German
STROSZEK New Yorker, 1977, West German
FATA MORGANA New Yorker, 1978, West German
WOYZECK New Yorker, 1979, West German
NOSFERATU THE VAMPYRE 20th Century-Fox, 1979, West German-French-U.S.
GOD'S ANGRY MAN (TD) 1980, West German
FITZCARRALDO New World, 1982, West German
WHERE THE GREEN ANTS DREAM Orion Classics, 1984, West German

GORDON HESSLER*

b. 1930 - Berlin, Germany
Home: 8910 Holly Place, Los Angeles, CA 90046, 213/654-9890

THE WOMAN WHO WOULDN'T DIE *CATACOMBS* Warner Bros., 1965, British
THE OBLONG BOX American International, 1969, British
THE LAST SHOT YOU HEAR 20th Century-Fox, 1969, British
SCREAM AND SCREAM AGAIN American International, 1970, British
CRY OF THE BANSHEE American International, 1970, British
MURDERS IN THE RUE MORGUE American International, 1971, British
EMBASSY Hemdale, 1973, British
SCREAM, PRETTY PEGGY (TF) Universal TV, 1973
SKYWAY TO DEATH (TF) Universal TV, 1974
HITCHHIKE! (TF) Universal TV, 1974
A CRY IN THE WILDERNESS (TF) Universal TV, 1974
BETRAYAL (TF) Metromedia Productions, 1974
THE GOLDEN VOYAGE OF SINBAD Columbia, 1974, British
TRACCO DI VELENO IN UNA COPPA DI CHAMPAGNE Arden, 1975, Italian
THE STRANGE POSSESSION OF MRS. OLIVER (TF) The Shpetner Company, 1977
PUZZLE (TF) Australian Broadcasting Commission/Trans-Atlantic Enterprises, 1978, Australian
SECRETS OF THREE HUNGRY WIVES (TF) Penthouse Productions, 1978
KISS MEETS THE PHANTOM OF THE PARK (TF) Hanna-Barbera Productions/KISS Productions, 1978
BEGGERMAN, THIEF (TF) Universal TV, 1980
THE SECRET WAR OF JACKIE'S GIRLS (TF) Public Arts Productions/Penthouse Productions/Universal TV, 1980
ESCAPE FROM EL DIABLO Cinema Presentations International, 1983, U.S.-Spanish-British
PRAY FOR DEATH Trans World Entertainment, 1985

CHARLTON HESTON

b. October 4, 1923 - Evanston, Illinois
Agent: ICM - Los Angeles, 213/550-4000

ANTONY AND CLEOPATRA Rank, 1973, British-Spanish-Swiss
MOTHER LODE Agamemnon Films, 1982, Canadian

DOUGLAS HEYES*

Business Manager: Clarke Lilly Associates, 333 Apolena Avenue, Balboa Island, CA 92662, 714/833-3347

KITTEN WITH A WHIP Universal, 1964
BEAU GESTE Universal, 1966
THE LONELY PROFESSION (TF) Universal TV, 1969
POWDERKEG (TF) Filmways/Rodphi, 1969
DRIVE HARD, DRIVE FAST (TF) Universal TV, 1973
CAPTAINS AND THE KINGS (MS) co-director with Allen Reisner, Universal TV, 1976

DOUGLAS HEYES*—continued

ASPEN (MS) Universal TV, 1977
THE FRENCH ATLANTIC AFFAIR (TF) Aaron Spelling Productions/MGM TV, 1979

DOUGLAS HICKOX*

Home: The White House, Ferry Lane, Wargrave, Berkshire, England, 073/522-2965
Agent: Shapiro-Lichtman Agency - Los Angeles, 213/557-2244

IT'S ALL OVER TOWN British Lion, 1963, British
JUST FOR YOU Columbia, 1963, British
ENTERTAINING MR. SLOANE Continental, 1970, British
SITTING TARGET MGM, 1972, British
THEATRE OF BLOOD United Artists, 1973, British
BRANNIGAN United Artists, 1975, British
SKY RIDERS 20th Century-Fox, 1976
ZULU DAWN American Cinema, 1979, British
THE PHOENIX (TF) Mark Carliner Productions, 1981
THE HOUND OF THE BASKERVILLES Mapleton Films Ltd., 1983, British
THE MASTER OF BALLANTRAE (TF) Larry White-Hugh Benson Productions/HTV/Columbia TV, 1984, U.S.-British
MISTRAL'S DAUGHTER (MS) co-director with Kevin Connor, Steve Krantz Productions/R.T.L. Productions/Antenne-2, 1984, U.S.-French
BLACKOUT (CTF) HBO Premiere Films, 1985

COLIN HIGGINS*

Agent: Michael Ovitz, CAA - Los Angeles, 213/277-4545

FOUL PLAY Paramount, 1978
NINE TO FIVE 20th Century-Fox, 1980
THE BEST LITTLE WHOREHOUSE IN TEXAS Universal, 1982

GEORGE ROY HILL*

b. December 20, 1922 - Minneapolis, Minnesota
Business: Pan Arts Productions, 4000 Warner Blvd., Burbank, CA 91522, 818/954-6000
Agent: William Morris Agency - Beverly Hills, 213/274-7451

PERIOD OF ADJUSTMENT MGM, 1962
TOYS IN THE ATTIC United Artists, 1963
THE WORLD OF HENRY ORIENT United Artists, 1964
HAWAII United Artists, 1966
THOROUGHLY MODERN MILLIE Universal, 1967
BUTCH CASSIDY AND THE SUNDANCE KID ★ 20th Century-Fox, 1969
SLAUGHTERHOUSE-FIVE Universal, 1971
THE STING ★★ Universal, 1973
THE GREAT WALDO PEPPER Universal, 1975
SLAP SHOT Universal, 1977
A LITTLE ROMANCE Orion/Warner Bros., 1979, U.S.-French
THE WORLD ACCORDING TO GARP Warner Bros., 1982
THE LITTLE DRUMMER GIRL Warner Bros., 1984

JACK HILL*

b. January 28, 1933 - Los Angeles, California
Home: 22014 De La Osa Street, Woodland Hills, CA 91364, 818/346-0110
Agent: Robinson-Weintraub & Associates - Los Angeles, 213/653-5802

BLOOD BATH co-director with Stephanie Rothman, American International, 1966
PIT STOP Distributors International, 1969
THE BIG DOLL HOUSE New World, 1971
THE BIG BIRD CAGE New World, 1972
COFFY American International, 1973
FOXY BROWN American International, 1974
THE SWINGING CHEERLEADERS Centaur, 1974
SWITCHBLADE SISTERS Centaur, 1975

JAMES HILL*

b. 1919 - England
Home: 1 Abdale Road, London W12, England, 01/743-7208
Agent: The Lantz Office - Los Angeles, 213/858-1144

THE STOLEN PLANS Associated British Film Distributors/Children's Film Foundation, 1952, British
THE CLUE OF THE MISSING APE Associated British Film Distributors/ Children's Film Foundation, 1953, British
PERIL FOR THE GUY British Lion/Children's Film, Foundation, 1956, British
MYSTERY IN THE MINE Children's Film Foundation, 1959, British
THE KITCHEN British Lion, 1961, British
THE DOCK BRIEF MGM, 1962, British
LUNCH HOUR Bryanston, 1962, British
SEASIDE SWINGERS *EVERY DAY'S A HOLIDAY* Embassy, 1964, British
A STUDY IN TERROR Columbia, 1966, British
BORN FREE Columbia, 1966, British
THE CORRUPT ONES *THE PEKING MEDALLION* Warner Bros., 1967, West German-French-Italian
CAPTAIN NEMO AND THE UNDERWATER CITY MGM, 1970, British
AN ELEPHANT CALLED SLOWLY American Continental, 1971, British
BLACK BEAUTY Paramount, 1971, British-West German-Spanish
THE BELSTONE FOX *FREE SPIRIT* Cine III, 1973, British
CHRISTIAN THE LION *THE LION AT WORLD'S END* co-director with Bill Travers, Scotia American, 1974, British
THE WILD AND THE FREE (TF) BSR Productions/Marble Arch Productions, 1980
OWAIN GLYNDWR - PRINCE OF WALES (TF) OPIX/S4C, 1983, British
THE YOUNG VISITORS (TF) Channel Four, 1984, British

WALTER HILL*

b. January 10, 1942 - Long Beach, California
Agent: Jeff Berg, ICM - Los Angeles, 213/550-4205

HARD TIMES Columbia, 1975
THE DRIVER 20th Century-Fox, 1978
THE WARRIORS Paramount, 1979
THE LONG RIDERS United Artists, 1980
SOUTHERN COMFORT 20th Century-Fox, 1981
48 HRS. Paramount, 1982
STREETS OF FIRE Universal, 1984
BREWSTER'S MILLIONS Universal, 1985

ARTHUR HILLER*

b. November 22, 1923 - Edmonton, Alberta, Canada
Agent: The Gersh Agency - Beverly Hills, 213/274-6611

THE CARELESS YEARS United Artists, 1957
THE MIRACLE OF THE WHITE STALLIONS Buena Vista, 1963
THE WHEELER DEALERS MGM, 1963
THE AMERICANIZATION OF EMILY MGM, 1964
PROMISE HER ANYTHING Paramount, 1966
PENELOPE MGM, 1966
TOBRUK Universal, 1967
THE TIGER MAKES OUT Columbia, 1967
POPI United Artists, 1969
THE OUT-OF-TOWNERS Paramount, 1970
LOVE STORY ★ Paramount, 1970
PLAZA SUITE Paramount, 1971
THE HOSPITAL United Artists, 1971
MAN OF LA MANCHA United Artists, 1972, Italian-U.S.
THE CRAZY WORLD OF JULIUS VROODER 20th Century-Fox, 1974
THE MAN IN THE GLASS BOOTH American Film Theatre, 1975
W.C. FIELDS AND ME Universal, 1976
SILVER STREAK 20th Century-Fox, 1976
THE IN-LAWS Columbia, 1979
NIGHTWING Columbia, 1979
MAKING LOVE 20th Century-Fox, 1981
AUTHOR! AUTHOR! 20th Century-Fox, 1982
ROMANTIC COMEDY MGM/UA, 1983

ARTHUR HILLER*—continued

THE LONELY GUY Universal, 1984
TEACHERS MGM/UA, 1984

WILLIAM BYRON HILLMAN*

b. Chicago, Illinois
Home: P.O. Box 321, Tarzana, CA 91356, 818/705-3456
Agent: Scott Penney, Eisenbach, Greene, Inc. - Los Angeles, 213/659-3420

BETTA BETTA Commonwealth United, 1971
THE TRAIL RIDE Gulf States, 1973
THE PHOTOGRAPHER Avco Embassy, 1974
THE MAN FROM CLOVER GROVE American Cinema, 1977
THETUS Rachel's Releasing Corporation, 1979
DOUBLE EXPOSURE Crown International, 1982

JACK B. HIVELY

THE ADVENTURES OF HUCKLEBERRY FINN (TF) Sunn Classic Productions, 1981
CALIFORNIA GOLD RUSH (TF) Sunn Classic Productions, 1981

MIKE HODGES*

Home: 70 Elgin Crescent, London, England, 01/229-2578
Agent: Fraser & Dunlop, 91 Regent Street, London W1, England, 01/734-7311

GET CARTER MGM, 1971, British
PULP United Artists, 1972, British
THE TERMINAL MAN Warner Bros., 1974
FLASH GORDON Universal, 1980, British
MISSING PIECES (TF) Entheos Unlimited Productions/TTC, 1983
SQUARING THE CIRCLE (TF) TVS Ltd./Metromedia Producers Corporation/ Brittanic Film and TV Ltd., 1984, British-U.S.
MORONS FROM OUTER SPACE Universal, 1985, British
BURIED ALIVE Kidvant Films, 1985, British

JACK HOFSISS*

b. September 28, 1950 - Brooklyn, New York
Contact: Directors Guild of America - New York City, 212/581-0370

I'M DANCING AS FAST AS I CAN Paramount, 1982
FAMILY SECRETS (TF) Katz-Gallin/Half-Pint Productions/Karoger Productions, 1984

ROD HOLCOMB*

Messages: 213/794-0700
Agent: Elliot Webb, Artists Entertainment Agency - Beverly Hills, 213/557-2507

CAPTAIN AMERICA (TF) Universal TV, 1979
MIDNIGHT OFFERINGS (TF) Stephen J. Cannell Productions, 1981
THE GREATEST AMERICAN HERO (TF) Stephen J. Cannell Productions, 1981
THE QUEST (TF) Stephen J. Cannell Productions, 1982
THE A TEAM (TF) Stephen J. Cannell Productions, 1983
STITCHES Marcucci-Kerr Productions, 1984
THE RED-LIGHT STING (TF) J.E. Productions/Universal TV, 1984
NO MAN'S LAND (TF) Jadda Productions/Warner Bros. TV, 1984
THE CARTIER AFFAIR (TF) Hill-Mandelker Productions, 1984
TWO FATHERS (TF) A. Shane Company, 1985

ALLAN HOLZMAN

FORBIDDEN WORLD New World, 1982
OUT OF CONTROL New World, 1985

ELLIOTT HONG

KILL THE GOLDEN GOOSE Lone Star, 1979
THEY CALL ME BRUCE? *A FISTFUL OF CHOPSTICKS* Artists Releasing Corporation/Film Ventures International, 1982
HOT AND DEADLY Saturn International, 1983

TOBE HOOPER*

Agent: ICM - Los Angeles, 213/550-4000
Business Manager: Jim Jorgenson & Company, 1801 Avenue of the Stars, Los Angeles, CA 90067, 213/556-1370

THE TEXAS CHAINSAW MASSACRE Bryanston, 1974
EATEN ALIVE Virgo International, 1977
SALEM'S LOT (TF) Warner Bros. TV, 1979
THE FUNHOUSE Universal, 1981
POLTERGEIST MGM/UA, 1982
LIFEFORCE Tri-Star/Cannon, 1985, British

DENNIS HOPPER

b. May 17, 1936 - Dodge City, Kansas
Personal Manager: 213/656-7731
Agent: The Artists Agency - Los Angeles, 213/277-7779

EASY RIDER Columbia, 1969
THE LAST MOVIE Universal, 1971
OUT OF THE BLUE Discovery Films, 1982, Canadian

JERRY HOPPER*

b. July 29, 1907 - Guthrie, Oklahoma
Home: 815 Avenida Salvador, San Clemente, CA 92672

THE ATOMIC CITY Paramount, 1952
HURRICANE SMITH Paramount, 1952
PONY EXPRESS Paramount, 1953
ALASKA SEAS Paramount, 1954
SECRET OF THE INCAS Paramount, 1954
NAKED ALIBI Universal, 1954
SMOKE SIGNAL Universal, 1955
THE PRIVATE WAR OF MAJOR BENSON Universal, 1955
ONE DESIRE Universal, 1955
THE SQUARE JUNGLE Universal, 1956
NEVER SAY GOODBYE Universal, 1956
TOY TIGER Universal, 1956
THE MISSOURI TRAVELER Buena Vista, 1958
BLUEPRINT FOR MURDER Paramount, 1961
MADRON Four Star-Excelsior, 1970, U.S.-Israeli

JOHN HOUGH*

b. November 21, 1941 - London, England
Business: Shooting Star Film Productions Ltd., Stable Cottage, Pinewood Studios, Iver Heath, Bucks, England, 0753-651 700 Ext. 540
Agent: Joe Funicello, ICM - Los Angeles, 213/550-4000 or: John Redway & Associates - London, 01/637-1612

WOLFHEAD 1970, British
SUDDEN TERROR *EYEWITNESS* National General, 1971, British
THE PRACTICE 1971, British
TWINS OF EVIL Universal, 1972, British
TREASURE ISLAND National General, 1972, British-French-West German-Spanish
THE LEGEND OF HELL HOUSE 20th Century-Fox, 1974, British
DIRTY MARY CRAZY LARRY 20th Century-Fox, 1974
ESCAPE TO WITCH MOUNTAIN Buena Vista, 1975
RETURN FROM WITCH MOUNTAIN Buena Vista, 1978
BRASS TARGET MGM/United Artists, 1978
THE WATCHER IN THE WOODS Buena Vista, 1980

JOHN HOUGH*—continued

THE INCUBUS Artists Releasing Corporation/Film Ventures International, 1982, Canadian
TRIUMPHS OF A MAN CALLED HORSE Jensen Farley Pictures, 1983, U.S.-Mexican
THE BLACK ARROW (CTF) Walt Disney Productions, 1985, British-U.S.

ROBERT ''BOBBY'' HOUSTON

Contact: Writers Guild of America - Los Angeles, 213/550-1000

SHOGUN ASSASSIN director of U.S. version, New World, 1980, Japanese-U.S.
BAD MANNERS *GROWING PAINS* New World, 1984

CY HOWARD*

b. September 27, 1915 - Milwaukee, Wisconsin
Home: 10230 Sunset Blvd., Los Angeles, CA 90024, 213/276-2615

LOVERS AND OTHER STRANGERS Cinerama Releasing Corporation, 1970
EVERY LITTLE CROOK AND NANNY MGM, 1972
IT COULDN'T HAPPEN TO A NICER GUY (TF) The Jozak Company, 1974

NOEL HOWARD

b. December 25, 1920 - Paris, France
Home: 1264 N. Hayworth, Los Angeles, CA 90046

MARCO THE MAGNIFICENT co-director with Denys de la Patelliere, MGM, 1966, French-Afghanistani-Egyptian-Italian-Yugoslavian
D'OU VIENS TO JOHNNY Hoche Productions, French
DON'T YOU HEAR THE DOGS BARK? co-director with Francois Reichenbach, 1975, Mexican-French

RON HOWARD*

b. March 1, 1954 - Duncan, Oklahoma
Agent: TMI - Los Angeles, 213/273-4000

GRAND THEFT AUTO New World, 1978
COTTON CANDY (TF) Major H Productions, 1978
SKYWARD (TF) Major H-Anson Productions, 1980
THROUGH THE MAGIC PYRAMID (TF) Major H Productions, 1981
NIGHT SHIFT The Ladd Company/Warner Bros., 1982
SPLASH Buena Vista, 1984
COCOON 20th Century Fox, 1985

KING HU

(Hu Chin Ch'uan)

b. April 29, 1931 - Peking, China
Business: King Hu Film Productions, 10C Fa Po St., 2nd Floor, Yau Yat Cheun, Kowloon, Hong Kong, (3)81-8920, Cable: KINGSMOVIE

ETERNAL LOVE co-director, Shaw Brothers, 1963, Hong Kong
SONS OF THE GOOD EARTH Shaw Brothers, 1964, Hong Kong
COME DRINK WITH ME Union Film Company, 1966, Hong Kong
DRAGON GATE INN Union Film Company, 1967, Hong Kong
A TOUCH OF ZEN Union Film Company, 1968, Hong Kong
FOUR MOODS co-director, 1970, Hong Kong
THE FATE OF LEE KHAN King Hu Film Productions, 1973, Hong Kong
THE VALIANT ONES King Hu Film Productions, 1974, Hong Kong
RAINING ON THE MOUNTAIN King Hu Film Productions, 1977, Hong Kong
LEGEND OF THE MOUNTAIN King Hu Film Productions, 1978, Hong Kong
THE JUVENIZER King Hu Film Productions, 1981, Hong Kong
ALL THE KING'S MEN Sunny Overseas Corporation/CMPC, 1983, Hong Kong

TOM HUCKABEE

b. September 2, 1955 - Forth Worth, Texas
Business: Tiger Mountain Productions, Inc., 2488 Cheremoya Avenue, Hollywood, CA 90068, 213/463-3831

TAKING TIGER MOUNTAIN co-director with Kent Smith, Horizon, 1983

HUGH HUDSON

Office: Hudson Film Ltd., 11 Queen's Gate Place Mews, London SW7, England, 01/581-3133
Agent: Michael Ovitz, CAA - Los Angeles, 213/277-4545

CHARIOTS OF FIRE ★ The Ladd Company/Warner Bros., 1981, British
GREYSTOKE: THE LEGEND OF TARZAN, LORD OF THE APES Warner Bros., 1984, British-U.S.

ROY HUGGINS*

b. July 18, 1914 - Litelle, Washington
Business: Public Arts, Inc., 1928 Mandeville Canyon, Los Angeles, CA 90049, 213/476-7892

HANGMAN'S KNOT Columbia, 1952
THE YOUNG COUNTRY (TF) Universal TV, 1970

JOHN HUGHES*

Contact: Directors Guild of America - Chicago, 312/644-5050

SIXTEEN CANDLES Universal, 1984
THE BREAKFAST CLUB Universal, 1985
WEIRD SCIENCE Universal, 1985

KENNETH ''KEN'' HUGHES*

b. January 19, 1922 - Liverpool, England
Home: 950 N. Kings Road - Suite 364, Los Angeles, CA 90069, 213/654-2068
Agent: Eisenbach-Greene, Inc. - Los Angeles, 213/656-7126

WIDE BOY Realart, 1952, British
HEAT WAVE *THE HOUSE ACROSS THE LAKE* Lippert, 1954, British
BLACK 13 Archway, 1954, British
THE BRAIN MACHINE RKO Radio, 1955, British
THE CASE OF THE RED MONKEY *LITTLE RED MONKEY* Allied Artists, 1955, British
THE DEADLIEST SIN *CONFESSION* Allied Artists, 1955, British
THE ATOMIC MAN *TIMESLIP* Allied Artists, 1955, British
JOE MACBETH Columbia, 1956, British
WICKED AS THEY COME Columbia, 1957, British
THE LONG HAUL Columbia, 1957, British
JAZZ BOAT Columbia, 1960, British
IN THE NICK Columbia, 1960, British
THE TRIALS OF OSCAR WILDE Kingsley International, 1960, British
PLAY IT COOLER Columbia, 1961, British
THE SMALL WORLD OF SAMMY LEE 7 Arts, 1963, British
OF HUMAN BONDAGE MGM, 1964, British
ARRIVEDERCI, BABY! *DROP DEAD, DARLING* Paramount, 1966, British
CASINO ROYALE co-director with Val Guest, John Huston, Joseph McGrath & Robert Parrish, Columbia, 1967, British
CHITTY CHITTY BANG BANG United Artists, 1968, British
CROMWELL Columbia, 1970, British
THE INTERNECINE PROJECT Allied Artists, 1974, British
ALFIE DARLING *OH! ALFIE* 1975, British
SEXTETTE Crown International, 1978
NIGHT SCHOOL *TERROR EYES* Paramount, 1981

TERRY HUGHES

Contact: Directors Guild of Great Britain, 56 Whitfield Street, London W1, England, 01/580-9592

MONTY PYTHON LIVE AT THE HOLLYWOOD BOWL Columbia, 1982, British
SUNSET LIMOUSINE (TF) Witzend Productions/ITC, 1983
FOR LOVE OR MONEY (TF) Robert Papazian Productions/Henerson-Hirsch Productions, 1984

ANN HUI

b. 1947 - Manchuria, China
Contact: Hong Kong International Film Festival, 5th Floor, High Block City Hall, Edinburgh Place, Hong Kong, (3)72-1193

THE SECRET 1979, Hong Kong
THE SPOOKY BUNCH 1980, Hong Kong
THE STORY OF WOO VIET 1981, Hong Kong
BOAT PEOPLE Spectrafilm, 1983, Hong Kong
LOVE IN A FALLEN CITY Shaw Brothers, 1984, Hong Kong

DONALD HULETTE

b. November 29, 1937 - Los Angeles, California
Home: 8835 Crescent Drive, Los Angeles, CA 90046, 213/654-9649

BREAKER BREAKER American International, 1978
A GREAT RIDE Manson International, 1979
TENNESSEE STALLION Classic Productions, 1982
THE CAFE RACER Kodiac Films, 1985

PETER HUNT*

b. March 11, 1928 - London, England
Home: 2229 Roscomare Road, Los Angeles, CA 90077, 213/472-1911
Agent: Martin Shapiro, Shapiro-Lichtman Agency - Los Angeles, 213/557-2244

ON HER MAJESTY'S SECRET SERVICE United Artists, 1969, British
GOLD Allied Artists, 1974, British
SHOUT AT THE DEVIL American International, 1976, British
GULLIVER'S TRAVELS EMI, 1977, British-Belgian
THE BEASTS ARE ON THE STREETS (TF) Hanna-Barbera Productions, 1978
DEATH HUNT 20th Century-Fox, 1981
CHANDLERTOWN *PHILIP MARLOWE - PRIVATE EYE (CMS)* co-director with Bryan Forbes, Sidney Hayers & David Wickes, HBO/David Wickes Television Ltd./London Weekend Television, 1983, British
THE LAST DAYS OF POMPEII (MS) David Gerber Company/Columbia TV/ Centerpoint Films/RAI, 1984, U.S.-British-Italian
WILD GEESE II Universal, 1985, British

PETER H. HUNT*

b. December 19, 1938 - Pasadena, California
Agent: Robert Lantz, The Lantz Office - New York City, 212/751-2107 or: Bill Haber, CAA - Los Angeles, 213/277-4545

1776 Columbia, 1972
FLYING HIGH (TF) Mark Carliner Productions, 1978
BULLY Maturo Image, 1978
WHEN SHE WAS BAD... (TF) Ladd Productions/Henry Jaffe Enterprises, 1979
RENDEZVOUS HOTEL (TF) Mark Carliner Productions, 1979
LIFE ON THE MISSISSIPPI (TF) The Great Amwell Company/Nebraska ETV Network/WNET-13/Taurus Films, 1980
THE PRIVATE HISTORY OF A CAMPAIGN THAT FAILED (TF) The Great Amwell Company/Nebraska ETV Network/WNET-13, 1981
THE MYSTERIOUS STRANGER (TF) The Great Amwell Company/Nebraska ETV Network/WNET-13/MR Film/Taurus Films, 1982
SKEEZER (TF) Margie-Lee Enterprises/The Blue Marble Company/Marble Arch Productions, 1982

PETER H. HUNT*—continued

MASQUERADE (TF) Renee Valente Productions/Glen A. Larson Productions/ 20th Century-Fox TV, 1983
THE PARADE (TF) Hill-Mandelker Productions, 1984
SINS OF THE PAST (TF) Sinpast Entertainment Company Productions, 1984

TIM HUNTER*

Agent: Tina Nides, CAA - Los Angeles, 213/277-4545

TEX Buena Vista, 1982
SYLVESTER Columbia, 1985

HARRY HURWITZ

Contact: Writers Guild of America, West - Los Angeles, 213/550-1000

THE PROJECTIONIST Maron Films Limited, 1971
THE COMEBACK TRAIL Dynamite Entertainment/Rearguard Productions, 1971
RICHARD co-director with Lorees Yerby, Billings, 1972
CHAPLINESQUE, MY LIFE AND HARD TIMES Xanadu, 1972
FAIRY TALES directed under pseudonym of Harry Tampa, 1978
NOCTURNA directed under pseudonym of Harry Tampa, Compass International, 1979
SAFARI 3000 United Artists, 1982
THE ROSEBUD BEACH HOTEL Almi Pictures, 1985

WARIS HUSSEIN*

b. 1938 - Lucknow, India
Agent: Elliot Webb/Lee Gabler, Artists Entertainment Agency - Beverly Hills, 213/557-2507

THANK YOU ALL VERY MUCH *A TOUCH OF LOVE* Columbia, 1969, British
QUACKSER FORTUNE HAS A COUSIN IN THE BRONX UMC, 1970, British
MELODY *S.W.A.L.K.* Levitt-Pickman, 1971, British
THE POSSESSION OF JOEL DELANEY Paramount, 1972
HENRY VIII AND HIS SIX WIVES Levitt-Pickman, 1973, British
DIVORCE HIS/DIVORCE HERS (TF) World Film Services, 1973
AND BABY MAKES SIX (TF) Alan Landsburg Productions, 1979
DEATH PENALTY (TF) Brockway Productions/NBC Entertainment, 1980
THE HENDERSON MONSTER (TF) Titus Productions, 1980
BABY COMES HOME (TF) Alan Landsburg Productions, 1980
CALLIE & SON (TF) Rosilyn Heller Productions/Hemdale Presentations/City Films/Motown Pictures Co., 1981
COMING OUT OF THE ICE (TF) The Konigsberg Company, 1982
LITTLE GLORIA...HAPPY AT LAST (TF) Edgar J. Scherick Associates/ Metromedia Producers Corporation, 1982, U.S.-Canadian-British
PRINCESS DAISY (MS) NBC Productions/Steve Krantz Productions, 1983
THE WINTER OF OUR DISCONTENT (TF) Lorimar Productions, 1983
ARCH OF TRIUMPH (TF) Newland-Raynor Productions/HTV, 1985, U.S.-British

JIMMY HUSTON

Agent: Ben Conway & Associates - Los Angeles, 213/271-8133

DEATH RIVER Omni, 1977
DARK SUNDAY Intercontinental, 1978
BUCKSTONE COUNTY PRISON Film Ventures International, 1978
SEABO E.O. Corporation, 1978
FINAL EXAM MPM, 1981
THE SLEUTH SLAYER Private Eye Productions, 1984

JOHN HUSTON*

b. August 5, 1906 - Nevada, Montana
Agent: Paul Kohner, Inc. - Los Angeles, 213/550-1060
Business Manager: Jess S. Morgan & Company, 6420 Wilshire Blvd., Los Angeles, CA 90048, 213/651-1601

THE MALTESE FALCON Warner Bros., 1941
IN THIS OUR LIFE Warner Bros., 1942
ACROSS THE PACIFIC Warner Bros., 1942
THE TREASURE OF THE SIERRA MADRE ★★ Warner Bros., 1948
KEY LARGO Warner Bros., 1948
WE WERE STRANGERS Columbia, 1949
THE ASPHALT JUNGLE ★ MGM, 1950
THE RED BADGE OF COURAGE MGM, 1951
THE AFRICAN QUEEN ★ United Artists, 1952
MOULIN ROUGE ★ United Artists, 1952, British
BEAT THE DEVIL United Artists, 1954, British
MOBY DICK Warner Bros., 1956, British
HEAVEN KNOWS, MR. ALLISON 20th Century-Fox, 1957
THE BARBARIAN AND THE GEISHA 20th Century-Fox, 1958
THE ROOTS OF HEAVEN 20th Century-Fox, 1958
THE UNFORGIVEN United Artists, 1960
THE MISFITS United Artists, 1961
FREUD Universal, 1963
THE LIST OF ADRIAN MESSENGER Universal, 1963
NIGHT OF THE IGUANA MGM, 1964
THE BIBLE...In the Beginning 20th Century-Fox, 1966, Italian
REFLECTIONS IN A GOLDEN EYE Warner Bros., 1967
CASINO ROYALE co-director with Val Guest, Ken Hughes, Joseph McGrath & Robert Parrish, Columbia, 1967, British
A WALK WITH LOVE AND DEATH 20th Century-Fox, 1969, British
SINFUL DAVEY United Artists, 1969, British
THE KREMLIN LETTER 20th Century-Fox, 1970
FAT CITY Columbia, 1972
THE LIFE AND TIMES OF JUDGE ROY BEAN National General, 1973
THE MACKINTOSH MAN Warner Bros., 1973, U.S.-British
THE MAN WHO WOULD BE KING Allied Artists, 1975, British
WISE BLOOD New Line Cinema, 1979
PHOBIA Paramount, 1981, Canadian
VICTORY Paramount, 1981
ANNIE Columbia, 1982
UNDER THE VOLCANO Universal Classics, 1984
PRIZZI'S HONOR 20th Century Fox, 1985

BRIAN G. HUTTON*

b. 1935 - New York, New York
Agent: Martin Baum, CAA - Los Angeles, 213/277-4545

WILD SEED Universal, 1965
THE PAD (...AND HOW TO USE IT) Universal, 1966
SOL MADRID MGM, 1968
WHERE EAGLES DARE MGM, 1969, British
KELLY'S HEROES MGM, 1970, U.S.-Yugoslavian
X Y & ZEE *ZEE & CO.* Columbia, 1972, British
NIGHT WATCH Avco Embassy, 1973, British
THE FIRST DEADLY SIN Filmways, 1980
HIGH ROAD TO CHINA Warner Bros., 1983, U.S.-Yugoslavian

WILLARD HUYCK

Agent: Michael Marcus/Michael Ovitz - CAA, 213/277-4545

MESSIAH OF EVIL International Cinefilm, 1975
FRENCH POSTCARDS Paramount, 1979
BEST DEFENSE Paramount, 1984

USS Ticonderoga, built by Ingalls Shipbuilding Division of Litton Industries, Pascagoula, MS

PETER HYAMS*

b. July 26, 1943 - New York, New York
Agent: Leonard Hirshan, William Morris Agency - Beverly Hills, 213/274-7451

ROLLING MAN (TF) ABC Circle Films, 1972
GOODNIGHT MY LOVE (TF) ABC Circle Films, 1972
BUSTING United Artists, 1974
OUR TIME Warner Bros., 1974
PEEPER 20th Century-Fox, 1976
CAPRICORN ONE 20th Century-Fox, 1978
HANOVER STREET Columbia, 1979
OUTLAND The Ladd Company/Warner Bros., 1981
THE STAR CHAMBER 20th Century-Fox, 1983
2010 MGM/UA, 1984

I

KON ICHIKAWA

b. November 20, 1915 - Ise, Mie Prefecture, Japan
Contact: Directors Guild of Japan, Tsukada Building, 8-33 Udagawa-cho, Shibuya-ku, Tokyo 150, Japan, 3/461-4411

A GIRL AT DOJO TEMPLE 1946, Japanese
A FLOWER BLOOMS 1948, Japanese
365 NIGHTS 1948, Japanese
DESIGN OF A HUMAN BEING 1949, Japanese
ENDLESS PASSION 1949, Japanese
SANSHIRO AT GINZA 1950, Japanese
THE HOT MARSHLAND 1950, Japanese
PURSUIT AT DAWN 1950, Japanese
NIGHTSHADE FLOWER 1951, Japanese
THE LOVER 1951, Japanese
THE MAN WITHOUT NATIONALITY 1951, Japanese
STOLEN LOVE 1951, Japanese
RIVER SOLO FLOWS 1951, Japanese
WEDDING MARCH 1951, Japanese
MR. LUCKY 1952, Japanese
THE YOUNG GENERATION 1952, Japanese
THE WOMAN WHO TOUCHED THE LEGS 1952, Japanese
THIS WAY - THAT WAY 1952, Japanese
MR. POO 1953, Japanese
THE BLUE REVOLUTION 1953, Japanese
THE YOUTH OF HEIJI SENIGATA 1953, Japanese
THE LOVERS Toho, 1953, Japanese
ALL OF MYSELF 1954, Japanese
A BILLIONAIRE 1954, Japanese
TWELVE CHAPTERS ABOUT WOMEN 1954, Japanese
GHOST STORY OF YOUTH 1955, Japanese
THE HEART 1955, Japanese
THE BURMESE HARP *HARP OF BURMA* Brandon, 1956, Japanese
PUNISHMENT ROOM 1956, Japanese
BRIDGE OF JAPAN 1956, Japanese

KON ICHIKAWA —continued

THE CROWDED TRAIN 1957, Japanese
THE HOLE 1957, Japanese
THE MEN OF TOHOKU 1957, Japanese
ENJO 1958, Japanese
MONEY AND THREE BAD MEN 1958, Japanese
GOODBYE - GOOD DAY 1959, Japanese
ODD OBSESSION Harrison Pictures, 1959, Japanese
FIRES ON THE PLAIN 1959, Japanese
POLICE AND SMALL GANGSTERS 1959, Japanese
A GINZA VETERAN 1960, Japanese
BONCHI 1960, Japanese
A WOMAN'S TESTAMENT co-director, 1960, Japanese
HER BROTHER 1960, Japanese
TEN BLACK WOMEN 1961, Japanese
THE SIN 1962, Japanese
BEING TWO ISN'T EASY 1962, Japanese
AN ACTOR'S REVENGE *THE REVENGE OF UKENO-JO* 1963, Japanese
ALONE ON THE PACIFIC 1963, Japanese
MONEY TALKS 1964, Japanese
TOKYO OLYMPIAD (FD) American International, 1965, Japanese
THE TALE OF GENJI (MS) 1966, Japanese
TOPO GIGIO E SEI LADRI 1967, Italian
TO LOVE AGAIN 1971, Japanese
MATATABI co-director, 1973, Japanese
VISIONS OF EIGHT (FD) co-director with Yuri Ozerov, Mai Zetterling, Arthur Penn, Michael Pfleghar, Milos Forman, Claude Lelouch & John Schlesinger, Cinema 5, 1973
I AM A CAT 1975, Japanese
BETWEEN WIFE AND LADY co-director with Shiro Toyoda, 1976, Japanese
THE INUGAMI FAMILY 1976, Japanese
THE DEVIL'S SONG OF BALL 1977, Japanese
QUEEN BEE Toho, 1978, Japanese
THE DEVIL'S ISLAND 1978, Japanese
THE OLD CITY to KOTO Toho, 1980, Japanese
HINOTORI Toho, 1980, Japanese
KOFUKU 1982, Japanese
THE MAKIOKA SISTERS Toho, 1983, Japanese
FINE SNOW Toho, 1983, Japanese
THE HARP OF BURMA Toho, 1985, Japanese

ERIC IDLE*

Agent: Rosalie Swedlin/Rick Nicita, CAA - Los Angeles, 213/277-4545

ALL YOU NEED IS CASH (TF) co-director with Gary Weis, NBC, 1978, British

SHOHEI IMAMURA

b. 1926 - Tokyo, Japan
Contact: Directors Guild of Japan, Tsukada Building, 8-33 Udagawa-cho, Shibuya-ku, Tokyo 150, Japan, 3/461-4411

THE STOLEN DESIRE 1958, Japanese
LIGHTS OF NIGHT 1958, Japanese
THE ENDLESS DESIRE 1958, Japanese
MY SECOND BROTHER 1959, Japanese
PIGS AND BATTLESHIPS 1961, Japanese
THE INSECT WOMAN 1963, Japanese
INTENTIONS OF MURDER *UNHOLY DESIRE* 1964, Japanese
THE PORNOGRAPHER 1966, Japanese
A MAN VANISHES 1967, Japanese
THE PROFOUND DESIRE OF THE GODS 1968, Japanese
HISTORY OF POST-WAR JAPAN AS TOLD BY A BAR HOSTESS (FD) 1970, Japanese
KARAYUKI-SAN, THE MAKING OF A PROSTITUTE (FD) 1975, Japanese
VENGEANCE IS MINE Shochiku, 1979, Japanese
EIJANAIKA Shochiku, 1981, Japanese
THE BALLAD OF NARAYAMA Kino International/Janus, 1983, Japanese

JOHN IRVIN*

Home: 6 Lower Common South, London SW15, England
Messages: 01/789-1514
Agent: William Morris Agency - Beverly Hills, 213/274-7451

TINKER, TAILOR, SOLDIER, SPY (TF) BBC/Paramount TV, 1979, British
THE DOGS OF WAR United Artists, 1981, U.S.-British
GHOST STORY Universal, 1981
CHAMPIONS Embassy, 1983, British
TURTLE SUMMER Warner Bros., 1985, British

DAVID IRVING

GOOD-BYE, CRUEL WORLD Sharp Features, 1982

RICHARD IRVING*

b. February 13, 1917 - New York, New York
Business: Richard Irving, Inc., 492 S. Spalding Drive, Beverly Hills, CA 90212
Agent: Stephanie Rogers & Associates, 9100 Sunset Blvd., Los Angeles, CA 90069, 213/278-2015

PRESCRIPTION: MURDER (TF) Universal TV, 1968
ISTANBUL EXPRESS (TF) Universal TV, 1968
BREAKOUT (TF) Universal TV, 1970
RANSOM FOR A DEAD MAN (TF) Universal TV, 1971
CUTTER (TF) Universal TV, 1972
THE SIX-MILLION DOLLAR MAN (TF) Universal TV, 1973
THE ART OF CRIME (TF) Universal TV, 1975
EXO-MAN (TF) Universal TV, 1977
SEVENTH AVENUE (MS) co-director with Russ Mayberry, Universal TV, 1977
CLASS OF '65 (TF) Universal TV, 1978
THE JESSE OWENS STORY (TF) Harve Bennett Productions/Paramount TV, 1984

GERALD I. ISENBERG*

b. May 13, 1940 - Cambridge, Massachusetts
Home: 2208 Stradella Road, Los Angeles, CA 90077, 213/476-4146
Agent: ICM - Los Angeles, 213/550-4000

SEIZURE: THE STORY OF KATHY MORRIS (TF) The Jozak Company, 1980

NEIL ISRAEL*

Agent: Jack Rapke, CAA - Los Angeles, 213/277-4545

TUNNELVISION co-director with Brad Swirnoff, World Wide, 1976
AMERICATHON United Artists, 1979
BACHELOR PARTY 20th Century Fox, 1984
MOVING VIOLATIONS 20th Century Fox, 1985

JAMES IVORY*

b. June 7, 1928 - Berkeley, California
Home: 400 East 52nd Street, New York, NY 10022, 212/759-3694
Messages: 518/851-7808
Business: Merchant Ivory Productions, 250 West 57th Street - Suite 1913A, New York, NY 10019, 212/582-8049
Agent: Susan Smith Agency - Beverly Hills, 213/277-8464

THE HOUSEHOLDER Royal Films International, 1963, Indian-U.S.
SHAKESPEARE WALLAH Continental, 1966, Indian
THE GURU 20th Century-Fox, 1969, British-Indian
BOMBAY TALKIE Dia Films, 1970, Indian
SAVAGES Angelika, 1972

JAMES IVORY*—continued

HELEN - QUEEN OF THE NAUTCH GIRLS (FD) Merchant Ivory Productions, 1973, Indian
MAHATMA AND THE MAD BOY Merchant Ivory Productions, 1973, Indian
THE WILD PARTY American International, 1975
AUTOBIOGRAPHY OF A PRINCESS (TF) Merchant Ivory Productions, 1975
SWEET SOUNDS Merchant Ivory Productions, 1976
ROSELAND Cinema Shares International, 1977
THE 5:48 (TF) 1979
HULLABALOO OVER GEORGIA & BONNIE'S PICTURES Corinth, 1979
THE EUROPEANS Levitt-Pickman, 1979, British
JANE AUSTEN IN MANHATTAN Contemporary, 1980
QUARTET New World, 1981, British-French
HEAT AND DUST Universal Classics, 1983, British
THE BOSTONIANS Almi Pictures, 1984

J

LEWIS JACKSON

Contact: Writers Guild of America, East - New York City, 212/245-6180

YOU BETTER WATCH OUT Edward R. Pressman Productions, 1980

JOSEPH JACOBY

Agent: Shapiro-Lichtman Agency - Los Angeles, 213/557-2244

SHAME, SHAME, EVERBODY KNOWS HER NAME JER, 1970
HURRY UP OR I'LL BE THIRTY Avco Embassy, 1973
THE GREAT BANK HOAX *SHENANIGANS* Warner Bros., 1978

JUST JAECKIN

b. 1940
Contact: French Film Office, 745 Fifth Avenue, New York, NY 10151, 212/832-8860

EMMANUELLE Columbia, 1974, French
THE STORY OF O Allied Artists, 1975, French
THE FRENCH WOMAN *MADAME CLAUDE* Monarch 1979, French
THE LAST ROMANTIC LOVER New Line Cinema, 1980, French
GIRLS Caneuram Films, 1980, Canadian-French-Israeli
COLLECTIONS PRIVEES co-director with Shuji Terayama & Walerian Borowczyk, Jeudi Films/Toei/French Movies, 1979, French-Japanese
LADY CHATTERLEY'S LOVER Cannon, 1982, French-British
THE PERILS OF GWENDOLINE *GWENDOLINE* Samual Goldwyn Company, 1984, French

STANLEY JAFFE*

Contact: Directors Guild of America - Los Angeles, 213/656-1220

WITHOUT A TRACE 20th Century-Fox, 1983

HENRY JAGLOM*

b. January 26, 1941 - London, England
Business: International Rainbow Pictures, 933 N. La Brea Avenue, Hollywood, CA 90038, 213/851-4811

A SAFE PLACE Columbia, 1971
TRACKS Trio, 1977
SITTING DUCKS Speciality Films, 1980
NATIONAL LAMPOON'S MOVIE MADNESS co-director with Bob Giraldi, United Artists, 1981
CAN SHE BAKE A CHERRY PIE? World Wide Classics, 1983
ALWAYS International Rainbow Pictures, 1985

JERRY JAMESON*

b. Hollywood, California
Agent: William Morris Agency - Beverly Hills, 213/274-7451

BRUTE CORPS General Films, 1971
THE DIRT GANG American International, 1972
THE BAT PEOPLE American International, 1974
HEATWAVE! (TF) Universal TV, 1974
THE ELEVATOR (TF) Universal TV, 1974
HURRICANE (TF) Metromedia Productions, 1974
TERROR ON THE 40TH FLOOR (TF) Metromedia Productions, 1974
THE SECRET NIGHT CALLER (TF) Charles Fries Productions/Penthouse Productions, 1975
THE DEADLY TOWER (TF) MGM TV, 1975
THE LIVES OF JENNY DOLAN (TF) Ross Hunter Productions/Paramount TV, 1975
THE CALL OF THE WILD (TF) Charles Fries Productions, 1976
THE INVASION OF JOHNSON COUNTY (TF) Roy Huggins Productions/ Universal TV, 1976
AIRPORT '77 Universal, 1977
SUPERDOME (TF) ABC Circle Films, 1978
A FIRE IN THE SKY (TF) Bill Driskill Productions, 1978
RAISE THE TITANIC AFD, 1980, British-U.S.
HIGH NOON - PART II: THE RETURN OF WILL KANE (TF) Charles Fries Productions, 1980
STAND BY YOUR MAN (TF) Robert Papazian Productions/Peter Guber-Jon Peters Productions, 1981
KILLING AT HELL'S GATE (TF) CBS Entertainment, 1981
HOTLINE (TF) Wrather Entertainment International/Ron Samuels Productions, 1982
STARFLIGHT: THE PLANE THAT COULDN'T LAND (TF) Orgolini-Nelson Productions, 1983
COWBOY (TF) Bercovici-St. Johns Productions/MGM TV, 1983
THIS GIRL FOR HIRE (TF) Barney Rosenzweig Productions/Orion TV, 1983
LAST OF THE GREAT SURVIVORS (TF) CBS Entertainment, 1984
THE COWBOY AND THE BALLERINA (TF) Cowboy Productions, 1984

MIKLOS JANCSO

b. September 27, 1921 - Vac, Hungary
Contact: Hungarofilm, 1054 Bathory utca lo., Budapest, Hungary, 36-1/31-7777

THE BELLS HAVE GONE TO ROME Mafilm, 1958, Hungarian
THREE STARS co-director, Mafilm, 1960, Hungarian
CANTATA Studio Budapest, 1963, Hungarian
MY WAY HOME Mafilm, 1964, Hungarian
THE ROUND-UP Altura, 1965, Hungarian
THE RED AND THE WHITE Brandon, 1967, Hungarian-Soviet
SILENCE AND CRY Mafilm, 1967, Hungarian
THE CONFRONTATION Mafilm, 1969, Hungarian
WINTER WIND *SIROKKO* Marquise Film/Mafilm, 1969, French-Hungarian
LA PACIFISTA Cinematografia Lombarda, 1970, Italian-French-West German
AGNUS DEI Mafilm, 1971, Hungarian
LA TECNICA E IL RITO RAI, 1971, Italian
RED PSALM Mafilm, 1972, Hungarian
ROMA RIVUOLE CESARE RAI, 1973, Italian
SZERELEM, ELEKTRA Studio Hunnia, 1974, Hungarian
PRIVATE VICES - PUBLIC VIRTUE 1976, Italian-Yugoslavian
MASTERWORK 1977, Hungarian
HUNGARIAN RHAPSODY Studio Dialog/Hungarofilm, 1978, Hungarian
ALLEGRO BARBARO Mafilm, 1979, Hungarian
HEART OF A TYRANT Sacis, 1981, Italian-Hungarian
HUZSIKA (TD) Magyar TV, 1984, Hungarian

DEREK JARMAN

Contact: British Academy of Film & Television Arts, 195 Piccadilly, London W1, England, 01/734-0022

SEBASTIANE co-director with Paul Humfress, Discopat, 1977, British
JUBILEE Libra, 1979, British

DEREK JARMAN —continued

THE TEMPEST World Northal, 1980, British
IN THE SHADOW OF THE SUN ICA, 1981, British

JIM JARMUSCH

b. Akron, Ohio

PERMANENT VACATION Gray City, 1982
STRANGER THAN PARADISE Samuel Goldwyn Company, 1984

CHARLES JARROTT*

b. June 6, 1927 - London, England
Agent: Len Hirshan, William Morris Agency - Beverly Hills, 213/274-7451
Business Manager: Jess S. Morgan & Company, 6420 Wilshire Blvd., Los Angeles, CA 90048, 213/651-1601

ANNE OF THE THOUSAND DAYS Universal, 1969, British
MARY, QUEEN OF SCOTS Universal, 1971, British
LOST HORIZON Columbia, 1972
THE DOVE Paramount, 1974
THE LITTLEST HORSE THIEVES *ESCAPE FROM THE DARK* Buena Vista, 1977, U.S.-British
THE OTHER SIDE OF MIDNIGHT 20th Century-Fox, 1977
THE LAST FLIGHT OF NOAH'S ARK Buena Vista, 1980
CONDORMAN Buena Vista, 1981
THE AMATEUR 20th Century-Fox, 1981, Canadian
A MARRIED MAN (TF) London Weekend TV Productions/Lionhead Productions, 1984, British
THE BOY IN BLUE 20th Century Fox, 1985, Canadian

LIONEL JEFFRIES

b. 1926 - London, England
Agent: Denis Selinger, William Morris Agency - London, 01/734-9361

THE RAILWAY CHILDREN Universal, 1971, British
THE AMAZING MR. BLUNDEN Goldstone, 1972, British
BAXTER! National General, 1973, British
THE WATER BABIES Pethurst International/Film Polski, 1978, British-Polish
WOMBLING FREE Satori, 1979, British

NORMAN JEWISON*

b. July 21, 1926 - Toronto, Canada
Business: Knightsbridge Films, 18 Gloucester Street, Toronto, Ontario M4Y 1L5, Canada, 416/923-2787
Agent: William Morris Agency - Beverly Hills, 213/274-7451
Business Manager: Capell, Flekman, Coyne & Co. - Beverly Hills, 213/553-0310

40 POUNDS OF TROUBLE Universal, 1962
THE THRILL OF IT ALL Universal, 1963
SEND ME NO FLOWERS Universal, 1964
THE ART OF LOVE Universal, 1965
THE CINCINNATI KID MGM, 1965
THE RUSSIANS ARE COMING THE RUSSIANS ARE COMING United Artists, 1966
IN THE HEAT OF THE NIGHT ★ United Artists, 1967
THE THOMAS CROWN AFFAIR United Artists, 1968
GAILY, GAILY United Artists, 1969
FIDDLER ON THE ROOF ★ United Artists, 1971
JESUS CHRIST SUPERSTAR Universal, 1973
ROLLERBALL United Artists, 1975
F.I.S.T. United Artists, 1978
...AND JUSTICE FOR ALL Columbia, 1979
BEST FRIENDS Warner Bros., 1982
A SOLDIER'S STORY Columbia, 1984
AGNES OF GOD Columbia, 1985

ORLANDO JIMENEZ-LEAL

EL SUPER Columbia, 1979
IMPROPER CONDUCT (FD) co-director with Nestor Almendros, Cinevista/ Promovision International, 1984, French

ROBERT JIRAS

I AM THE CHEESE Libra Cinema 5, 1983

ALEXANDRO JODOROWSKY

Contact: Direccion General de Radio, Television y Cinematografica de la Secretaria de Gobernacion, Atletas 2, Country Club, Mexico City 7DF, Mexico, 905/544-9580

FANDO AND LIS Cannon, 1970, Mexican
EL TOPO ABKCO, 1971, Mexican
THE HOLY MOUNTAIN ABKCO, 1974, Mexican
TUSK Yank Films-Films 21, 1980, French

ROLAND JOFFÉ

b. England
Agent: Merrily Kane Agency - Beverly Hills, 213/550-8874

THE SPONGERS (TF) BBC, 1978, British
NO, MAMA, NO (TF) Thames TV, 1979, British
UNITED KINGDOM (TF) BBC, 1981, British
THE KILLING FIELDS Warner Bros., 1984, British

ALAN JOHNSON*

Agent: Jim Lenny, 9701 Wilshire Blvd., Beverly Hills, CA 90212, 213/271-2174

TO BE OR NOT TO BE 20th Century-Fox, 1983

JED JOHNSON

ANDY WARHOL'S BAD New World, 1977

KENNETH JOHNSON*

b. October 26, 1942 - Pine Bluff, Arkansas
Business: Universal Studios, 100 Universal City Plaza, Universal City, CA 91608, 818/508-3256
Attorney: Charles Silverberg, Silverberg, Rosen, Leon & Behr - Los Angeles, 213/277-4500

THE INCREDIBLE HULK (TF) Universal TV, 1977
SENIOR TRIP (TF) Kenneth Johnson Productions, 1981
V (TF) Kenneth Johnson Productions/Warner Bros. TV, 1983
HOT PURSUIT (TF) Kenneth Johnson Productions/NBC Productions, 1984

LAMONT JOHNSON*

b. 1920 - Stockton, California
Agent: John Gaines, APA - Los Angeles, 213/273-0744

THIN ICE 20th Century-Fox, 1961
A COVENANT WITH DEATH Warner Bros., 1966
KONA COAST Warner Bros., 1968
DEADLOCK (TF) Universal TV, 1969
THE MACKENZIE BREAK United Artists, 1970
MY SWEET CHARLIE (TF) ☆ Universal TV, 1970
A GUNFIGHT Paramount, 1971
THE GROUNDSTAR CONSPIRACY Universal, 1972, U.S.-Canadian

LAMONT JOHNSON*—continued

YOU'LL LIKE MY MOTHER Universal, 1972
THAT CERTAIN SUMMER (TF) ☆ Universal TV, 1972
THE LAST AMERICAN HERO 20th Century-Fox, 1973
VISIT TO A CHIEF'S SON United Artists, 1974
THE EXECUTION OF PRIVATE SLOVIK (TF) ☆ Universal TV, 1974
FEAR ON TRIAL (TF) ☆ Alan Landsburg Productions, 1975
LIPSTICK Paramount, 1976
ONE ON ONE Warner Bros., 1977
SOMEBODY KILLED HER HUSBAND Columbia, 1978
PAUL'S CASE (TF) Learning in Focus, 1979
OFF THE MINNESOTA STRIP (TF) Cherokee Productions/Universal TV, 1980
CATTLE ANNIE AND LITTLE BRITCHES Universal, 1981
CRISIS AT CENTRAL HIGH (TF) Time-Life Productions, 1981
ESCAPE FROM IRAN: THE CANADIAN CAPER (TF) Canamedia Productions, 1981, Canadian
DANGEROUS COMPANY (TF) The Dangerous Company/Finnegan Associates, 1982
LIFE OF THE PARTY: THE STORY OF BEATRICE (TF) Welch-Welch Productions/Columbia TV, 1982
SPACEHUNTER: ADVENTURES IN THE FORBIDDEN ZONE Columbia, 1983, Canadian-U.S.
ERNIE KOVACS: BETWEEN THE LAUGHTER (TF) ☆ ABC Circle Films, 1984
WALLENBERG (TF) Stonehenge Productions/Paramount TV, 1985

AMY JONES

SLUMBER PARTY MASSACRE Santa Fe, 1982
LOVE LETTERS New World, 1983

DAVID JONES

b. February 19, 1934 - Poole, Dorset, England
Address: 26 Fitzjohns Avenue, London NW3, England

BETRAYAL 20th Century-Fox International Classics, 1983, British

EUGENE S. JONES*

Home: 461 Bellagio Terrace, Los Angeles, CA 90049, 213/476-6375
Attorney: Royal E. Blakeman, Pryor, Cashman, Sherman & Flynn, 415 Park Avenue, New York, NY 10022, 212/421-4100

A FACE OF WAR (FD) Commonwealth, 1968
TWO MEN OF KARAMOJA *THE WILD AND THE BRAVE (FD)* Tomorrow Entertainment, 1974
HIGH ICE (TF) ESJ Productions, 1980

JAMES CELLAN JONES

(See James CELLAN-JONES)

L.Q. JONES*

Business: 2144 N. Cahuenga Blvd., Hollywood, CA 90068, 213/463-4426
Agent: Mike Greenfield, Charter Management - Los Angeles, 213/278-1690

A BOY AND HIS DOG Pacific Film Enterprises, 1975

ROBERT JONES

b. November 2, 1942 - Boston Massachusetts
Business: Still River Films, P.O. Box 929, Cambridge, MASS 02140
Agent: Jeff Thal, Fred Amsel & Associates - Beverly Hills, 213/855-1200

MISSION HILL Atlantic Releasing Corporation, 1983.

TERRY JONES

b. 1942 - Colwyn Bay, Wales
Business: Python Productions, 6/7 Cambridge Gate, London NW1, England, 01/487-4485
Contact: Directors Guild of Great Britain, 56 Whitfield Street, London W1, England, 01/580-9592

MONTY PYTHON AND THE HOLY GRAIL co-director with Terry Gilliam, Cinema 5, 1974, British
MONTY PYTHON'S LIFE OF BRIAN Orion/Warner Bros., 1979, British
MONTY PYTHON'S THE MEANING OF LIFE Universal, 1983, British

GLENN JORDAN*

Business Manager: Sydney Bash, Bash, Gesas & Company, 9401 Wilshire Blvd. - Suite 700, Beverly Hills, CA 90212, 213/278-7700
Agent: Bill Haber, CAA - Los Angeles, 213/277-4545

FRANKENSTEIN (TF) Dan Curtis Productions, 1973
THE PICTURE OF DORIAN GRAY (TF) Dan Curtis Productions, 1973
SHELL GAME (TF) Thoroughbred Productions, 1975
ONE OF MY WIVES IS MISSING (TF) Spelling-Goldberg Productions, 1975
DELTA COUNTY, U.S.A. (TF) Leonard Goldberg Productions/Paramount TV, 1977
SUNSHINE CHRISTMAS (TF) Universal TV, 1977
IN THE MATTER OF KAREN ANN QUINLAN (TF) Warren V. Bush Productions, 1977
THE DISPLACED PERSON (TF) Learning in Focus, 1977
LES MISERABLES (TF) ☆ Norman Rosemont Productions/ITV Entertainment, 1978
SON RISE: A MIRACLE OF LOVE (TF) Rothman-Wohl Productions/Filmways, 1979
THE FAMILY MAN (TF) Time-Life Productions, 1979
THE WOMEN'S ROOM (TF) Philip Mandelker Productions/Warner Bros. TV, 1980
NEIL SIMON'S ONLY WHEN I LAUGH Columbia, 1981
THE PRINCESS AND THE CABBIE (TF) Freyda Rothstein Productions/Time-Life Productions, 1981
LOIS GIBBS AND THE LOVE CANAL (TF) Moonlight Productions/Filmways, 1982
THE BUDDY SYSTEM 20th Century Fox, 1984
HEARTSOUNDS (TF) Embassy TV, 1984
MASS APPEAL Universal, 1984

NEIL JORDAN

Contact: Film Division - Department of Industry and Energy, Kildare Street, Dublin, Ireland, 1/78-9411

DANNY BOY *ANGEL* Triumph/Columbia, 1983, Irish
THE COMPANY OF WOLVES Cannon, 1984, British

NATHAN JURAN*

b. September 1, 1907 - Austria
Home: 623 Via Horquilla, Palos Verdes Estates, CA 90274

THE BLACK CASTLE Universal, 1952
GUNSMOKE Universal, 1953
LAW AND ORDER Universal, 1953
THE GOLDEN BLADE Universal, 1953
TUMBLEWEED Universal, 1953
HIGHWAY DRAGNET Allied Artists, 1954
DRUMS ACROSS THE RIVER Universal, 1954
THE CROOKED WEB Columbia, 1955
THE DEADLY MANTIS Universal, 1957
HELLCATS OF THE NAVY Columbia, 1957
TWENTY MILLION MILES TO EARTH Columbia, 1957
THE 7TH VOYAGE OF SINBAD Columbia, 1958
GOOD DAY FOR A HANGING Columbia, 1959
FLIGHT OF THE LOST BALLOON Woolner Brothers, 1961

NATHAN JURAN*—continued

JACK THE GIANT KILLER United Artists, 1962
SIEGE OF THE SAXONS Columbia, 1963, British
FIRST MEN IN THE MOON Columbia, 1964, British
EAST OF SUDAN Columbia, 1964, British
LAND RAIDERS Columbia, 1970
THE BOY WHO CRIED WEREWOLF Universal, 1973

PAUL JUSTMAN

GIMME AN F 20th Century Fox, 1984

CLAUDE JUTRA

b. March 11, 1930 - Montreal, Quebec, Canada
Contact: Association Des Realisateurs, 1406 Beaudry Street, Montreal, Quebec H2L 4K4, Canada, 514/843-7770

LES MAINS NETTES NFB, 1958, Canadian
LE NIGER - JEUNE REPUBLIQUE (FD) NFB, 1961, Canadian
A TOUT PRENDE Lopert, 1963, Canadian
COMMENT SAVOIR NFB, 1966, Canadian
WOW! NFB, 1969, Canadian
MON ONCLE ANTOINE NFB/Gendon Films Ltd., 1970, Canadian
KAMOURASKA New Line Cinema, 1974, Canadian
POUR LE MEILLEUR ET POUR LE PIRE 1975, Canadian
DREAMSPEAKER (TF) CBC, 1977, Canadian
ADA (TF) CBC, 1977, Canadian
SURFACING Arista, 1981, Canadian
BY DESIGN Atlantic Releasing Corporation, 1982, Canadian
LA DAME EN COULEUR Les Productions Pierre Lamy/National Film Board of Canada, 1984, Canadian

K

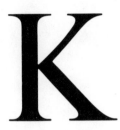

GEORGE KACZENDER

b. April 19, 1933 - Budapest, Hungary
Business: 2170 Century Park East - Suite 1608, Los Angeles, CA 90067, 213/203-0710
Agent: Scott Penney, Eisenbach-Greene, Inc. - Los Angeles, 213/659-3420

DON'T LET THE ANGELS FALL NFB, 1968, Canadian
THE GIRL IN BLUE *U-TURN* Cinerama Releasing Corporation, 1974, Canadian
IN PRAISE OF OLDER WOMEN Avco Embassy, 1978, Canadian
AGENCY Taft International, 1980, Canadian
YOUR TICKET IS NO LONGER VALID RSL Productions/Ambassador, 1981, Canadian
CHANEL SOLITAIRE United Film Distribution, 1981, French-British
FINISHING TOUCH 1982, Canadian

JEREMY PAUL KAGAN *

b. December 14, 1945 - Mt. Vernon, New York
Business: Our Own Company, c/o Pollock Bloom & Dekom, 9255 Sunset Blvd., Los Angeles, CA 90069, 213/278-8622
Agent: Triad Artists, Inc - Los Angeles, 213/556-2727

UNWED FATHER (TF) Wolper Productions, 1974
JUDGE DEE AND THE MONASTERY MURDERS (TF) ABC Circle Films, 1974
KATHERINE (TF) The Jozak Company, 1975
HEROES Universal, 1977
SCOTT JOPLIN Universal, 1977
THE BIG FIX Universal, 1978
THE CHOSEN 20th Century-Fox International Classics, 1982
THE STING II Universal, 1983
NATTY GANN Buena Vista, 1985

JEFF KANEW *

Home: 51 West 83rd Street, New York, NY 10024, 212/362-0522
Agent: William Morris Agency - New York City, 212/586-5100

BLACK RODEO (FD) Cinerama Releasing Corporation, 1972
NATURAL ENEMIES Cinema 5, 1979
EDDIE MACON'S RUN Universal, 1983
REVENGE OF THE NERDS 20th Century Fox, 1984
GOTCHA Universal, 1985

MAREK KANIEVSKA

Agent: Duncan Heath Associates, 162 Wardour Street, London W1, England, 01/439-1471
Contact: Directors Guild of Great Britain, 56 Whitfield Street, London W1, England, 01/580-9592

ANOTHER COUNTRY Orion Classics, 1984, British

GARSON KANIN*

b. November 24, 1912 - Rochester, New York
Business: TFT Corporation, 200 West 57th Street - Suite 1203, New York, NY 10019, 212/586-7850
Agent: William Morris Agency - New York City, 212/586-5100

A MAN TO REMEMBER RKO Radio, 1938
NEXT TIME I MARRY RKO Radio, 1938
THE GREAT MAN VOTES RKO Radio, 1939
BACHELOR MOTHER RKO Radio, 1939
MY FAVORITE WIFE RKO Radio, 1940
THEY KNEW WHAT THEY WANTED Columbia, 1940
TOM, DICK AND HARRY RKO Radio, 1941
THE TRUE GLORY co-director with Carol Reed, Columbia, 1945
WHERE IT'S AT United Artists, 1969
SOME KIND OF NUT United Artists, 1969

HAL KANTER*

b. December 18, 1918 - Savannah, Georgia
Agent: Marvin Moss Agency - Los Angeles, 213/274-8483

LOVING YOU Paramount, 1957
I MARRIED A WOMAN Universal, 1958
ONCE UPON A HORSE Universal, 1958
FOR THE LOVE OF IT (TF) Charles Fries Productions/Neila Productions, 1980

JONATHAN KAPLAN*

b. November 25, 1947 - Paris, France
Agent: William Morris Agency - Beverly Hills, 213/274-7451

THE STUDENT TEACHERS New World, 1973
THE SLAMS MGM, 1973
TRUCK TURNER American International, 1974
NIGHT CALL NURSES New World, 1974
WHITE LINE FEVER Columbia, 1975
MR. BILLION 20th Century-Fox, 1976
OVER THE EDGE Orion/Warner Bros., 1979
THE 11TH VICTIM (TF) Marty Katz Productions/Paramount TV, 1979
THE HUSTLER OF MUSCLE BEACH (TF) Furia-Oringer Productions, 1980
THE GENTLEMAN BANDIT (TF) Highgate Pictures, 1981
HEART LIKE A WHEEL 20th Century-Fox, 1983
GIRLS OF THE WHITE ORCHID (TF) Hill-Mandelker Films, 1983

NELLY KAPLAN

b. 1936 - Buenos Aires, Argentina
Business: Cythere Films, 18 Rue Marbeuf, 75000 Paris, France, 1/562-7901
Attorney: Eric Weissmann - Beverly Hills, 213/858-7888

GUSTAVE MOREAU (FD) Cythere Films, 1961, French
ABEL GANCE HIER ET DEMAIN (FD) Cythere Films, 1963, French
LE REGARD PICASSO (FD) Cythere Films, 1966, French
A VERY CURIOUS GIRL *LE FIANCEE DU PIRATE* Regional, 1970, French
PAPA LES PETITS BATEAUX Cythere Films, 1971, French
NEA *NEA - A YOUNG EMMANUELLE* Libra, 1976, French
CHARLES ET LUCIE Nu-Image, 1980, French
ABEL GANCE ET SON NAPOLEON (FD) Cythere Films, 1983, French

PHIL KARLSON*

(Philip Karlstein)

b. July 2, 1908 - Chicago, Illinois
Agent: The Gersh Agency - Beverly Hills, 213/274-6611

A WAVE, A WAC AND A MARINE Monogram, 1944
THERE GOES KELLY Monogram, 1945
G.I. HONEYMOON Monogram, 1945
THE SHANGHAI COBRA Monogram, 1945

PHIL KARLSON*—continued

DARK ALIBI Monogram, 1946
LIVE WIRES Monogram, 1946
THE MISSING LADY Monogram, 1946
SWING PARADE OF 1946 Monogram, 1946
BEHIND THE MASK Monogram, 1946
BOWERY BOMBSHELL Monogram, 1946
WIFE WANTED Monogram, 1946
BLACK GOLD Allied Artists, 1947
KILROY WAS HERE Monogram, 1947
LOUISIANA Monogram, 1947
ADVENTURES IN SILVERADO Columbia, 1948
ROCKY Monogram, 1948
THUNDERHOOF Columbia, 1948
THE LADIES OF THE CHORUS Columbia, 1948
DOWN MEMORY LANE Eagle Lion, 1949
THE BIG CAT Eagle Lion, 1949
THE IROQUOIS TRAIL United Artists, 1950
LORNA DOONE Columbia, 1951
THE TEXAS RANGERS Columbia, 1951
MASK OF THE AVENGER Columbia, 1951
SCANDAL SHEET Columbia, 1952
KANSAS CITY CONFIDENTIAL United Artists, 1952
THE BRIGAND Columbia, 1952
99 RIVER STREET United Artists, 1953
THEY RODE WEST Columbia, 1954
HELL'S ISLAND Paramount, 1955
TIGHT SPOT Columbia, 1955
FIVE AGAINST THE HOUSE Columbia, 1955
THE PHENIX CITY STORY Allied Artists, 1955
THE BROTHERS RICO Columbia, 1957
GUNMAN'S WALK Columbia, 1958
HELL TO ETERNITY Allied Artists, 1960
KEY WITNESS MGM, 1960
THE SECRET WAYS Universal, 1961
THE YOUNG DOCTORS United Artists, 1961
THE SCARFACE MOB Desilu, 1962
KID GALAHAD United Artists, 1962
RAMPAGE Warner Bros., 1963
THE SILENCERS Columbia, 1966
A TIME FOR KILLING Columbia, 1967
THE WRECKING CREW Columbia, 1968
HORNETS' NEST United Artists, 1970
BEN Cinerama Releasing Corporation, 1972
WALKING TALL Cinerama Releasing Corporation, 1973
FRAMED Paramount, 1974

ERIC KARSON*

Business: Karson-Higgins-Shaw Communications, Inc., 729 N. Seward Street, Hollywood, CA 90038, 213/461-3030

DIRT co-director with Cal Naylor, American Cinema, 1979
THE OCTAGON American Cinema, 1980

LAWRENCE KASDAN*

Attorney: Peter Benedek, Weissman, Wolff, Bergman, Coleman & Schulman - Beverly Hills, 213/858-7888

BODY HEAT The Ladd Company/Warner Bros., 1981
THE BIG CHILL Columbia, 1983
SILVERADO Columbia, 1985

MILTON KATSELAS*

b. December 22, 1933 - Pittsburg, Pennsylvania
Agent: Tom Chasin, ICM - Los Angeles, 213/550-4000
Business Manager: Jerry Wolff, Lehmann-Wolff Accountancy Corporation - Los Angeles, 213/475-0595

BUTTERFLIES ARE FREE Columbia, 1972
40 CARATS Columbia, 1973
REPORT TO THE COMMISSIONER United Artists, 1975
WHEN YOU COMIN' BACK, RED RYDER? Columbia, 1979
STRANGERS: THE STORY OF A MOTHER AND A DAUGHTER (TF) Chris-Rose Productions, 1979
THE RULES OF MARRIAGE (TF) Entheos Unlimited Productions/Brownstone Productions/20th Century-Fox TV, 1982

LEE H. KATZIN*

b. April 12, 1935 - Detroit, Michigan
Home: 13425 Java Drive, Beverly Hills, CA 90210, 213/278-7726
Agent: Ronald Leif, Contemporary-Korman Artists - Beverly Hills, 213/278-8250

HONDO AND THE APACHES MGM, 1967
HEAVEN WITH A GUN MGM, 1969
WHAT EVER HAPPENED TO AUNT ALICE? Cinerama Releasing Corporation, 1969
THE PHYNX Warner Bros., 1970
LE MANS National General, 1970
ALONG CAME A SPIDER (TF) 20th Century-Fox TV, 1970
THE SALZBURG CONNECTION 20th Century-Fox, 1972
VISIONS... (TF) CBS, Inc., 1972
THE VOYAGE OF THE YES (TF) Bing Crosby Productions, 1973
THE STRANGER (TF) Bing Crosby Productions, 1973
ORDEAL (TF) 20th Century-Fox TV, 1973
SAVAGES (TF) Spelling-Goldberg Productions, 1974
STRANGE HOMECOMING (TF) Alpine Productions/Worldvision, 1974
THE LAST SURVIVORS (TF) Bob Banner Associates, 1975
SKY HEI$T (TF) Warner Bros. TV, 1975
QUEST (TF) David Gerber Company/Columbia TV, 1976
THE MAN FROM ATLANTIS (TF) Solow Production Company, 1977
RELENTLESS (TF) CBS, Inc., 1977
THE BASTARD (TF) Universal TV, 1978
ZUMA BEACH (TF) Edgar J. Scherick Associates/Warner Bros. TV, 1978
TERROR OUT OF THE SKY (TF) Alan Landsburg Productions, 1978
REVENGE OF THE SAVAGE BEES (TF) 1979
SAMURAI (TF) Danny Thomas Productions/Universal TV, 1979
DEATH RAY 2000 (TF) Woodruff Productions/QM Productions, 1981
THE NEIGHBORHOOD (TF) David Gerber Company/Columbia TV, 1982
AUTOMAN (TF) Kushner-Locke Company/Glen A. Larson Productions/20th Century-Fox TV, 1983

JONATHAN KAUFER*

b. March 14, 1955 - Los Angeles, California
Agent: Lee Rosenberg, Triad Artists, Inc - Los Angeles, 213/556-2727

SOUP FOR ONE Warner Bros., 1982

CHARLES KAUFMAN

Contact: Writers Guild of America, West - Los Angeles 213/550-1000

THE SECRET DREAMS OF MONA Q Troma, 1977
MOTHER'S DAY United Film Distribution, 1980
WHEN NATURE CALLS Troma, 1984

PHILIP KAUFMAN*

b. October 23, 1936 - Chicago, Illinois
Agent: CAA - Los Angeles, 213/277-4545

GOLDSTEIN co-director with Benjamin Manaster, Altura, 1965
FEARLESS FRANK American International, 1969
THE GREAT NORTHFIELD, MINNESOTA RAID Universal, 1972
THE WHITE DAWN Paramount, 1974
INVASION OF THE BODY SNATCHERS United Artists, 1978
THE WANDERERS Orion/Warner Bros., 1979
THE RIGHT STUFF The Ladd Company/Warner Bros., 1983

ROBERT KAYLOR*

Agent: Randy Herron, Herb Tobias & Associates - Los Angeles, 213/277-6211

DERBY (FD) Cinerama Releasing Corporation, 1971
CARNY United Artists, 1980

ELIA KAZAN*

(Elia Kazanjoglou)

b. September 7, 1909 - Constantinople, Turkey
Home: 22 West 68th Street, New York, NY 10023
Messages: 212/496-0422

A TREE GROWS IN BROOKLYN 20th Century-Fox, 1945
SEA OF GRASS 20th Century-Fox, 1947
BOOMERANG! 20th Century-Fox, 1947
GENTLEMAN'S AGREEMENT ★★ 20th Century-Fox, 1947
PINKY 20th Century-Fox, 1949
PANIC IN THE STREETS 20th Century-Fox, 1950
A STREETCAR NAMED DESIRE ★ Warner Bros., 1951
VIVA ZAPATA! 20th Century-Fox, 1952
MAN ON A TIGHTROPE 20th Century-Fox, 1953
ON THE WATERFRONT ★★ Columbia, 1954
EAST OF EDEN ★ Warner Bros., 1955
BABY DOLL Warner Bros., 1956
A FACE IN THE CROWD Warner Bros., 1957
WILD RIVER 20th Century-Fox, 1960
SPLENDOR IN THE GRASS Warner Bros., 1961
AMERICA AMERICA ★ Warner Bros., 1963
THE ARRANGEMENT Warner Bros., 1969
THE VISITORS United Artists, 1972
THE LAST TYCOON Paramount, 1975

DON KEESLAR

BOG Marshall Films, 1978
THE CAPTURE OF GRIZZLY ADAMS (TF) Sunn Classic Productions, 1982

ASAAD KELADA*

Agent: Bob Broder, Broder-Kurland Agency - Los Angeles, 213/274-8921

THE FACTS OF LIFE GOES TO PARIS (TF) Embassy TV, 1982

FREDERICK KING KELLER

VAMPING Atlantic Releasing Corporation, 1984

BARNET KELLMAN*

Home: 718 Broadway, New York, NY 10003
Agent: Paul Martino, ICM - New York, 212/556-6820

KEY EXCHANGE TLC Films/20th Century Fox, 1985

GENE KELLY*

b. August 23, 1912 - Pittsburgh, Pennsylvania
Contact: Directors Guild of America - Los Angeles, 213/656-1220

ON THE TOWN co-director with Stanley Donen, MGM, 1949
SINGIN' IN THE RAIN co-director with Stanley Donen, MGM, 1952
IT'S ALWAYS FAIR WEATHER co-director with Stanley Donen, MGM, 1955
INVITATION TO THE DANCE MGM, 1956
THE HAPPY ROAD MGM, 1957
THE TUNNEL OF LOVE MGM, 1958
GIGOT 20th Century-Fox, 1962
A GUIDE FOR THE MARRIED MAN 20th Century-Fox, 1967
HELLO, DOLLY! 20th Century-Fox, 1969
THE CHEYENNE SOCIAL CLUB National General, 1970
THAT'S ENTERTAINMENT, PART 2 new sequences, MGM/United Artists, 1976

PATRICK KELLY*

Business: Kelly Pictures, Inc., Pier 62, West 23rd Street at 12th Avenue, New York, NY 10011, 212/929-6176

BEER Orion, 1985

BURT KENNEDY*

b. September 3, 1922 - Muskegon, Michigan
Home: 13138 Magnolia Blvd., Sherman Oaks, CA 91403, 818/986-8759
Attorney: Stan Karos, Ehrmann-Karos - Beverly Hills, 213/278-4011

THE CANADIANS 20th Century-Fox, 1961
MAIL ORDER BRIDE MGM, 1963
THE ROUNDERS MGM, 1965
THE MONEY TRAP MGM, 1966
RETURN OF THE SEVEN United Artists, 1966
WELCOME TO HARD TIMES MGM, 1967
THE WAR WAGON Universal, 1967
SUPPORT YOUR LOCAL SHERIFF United Artists, 1969
YOUNG BILLY YOUNG United Artists, 1969
THE GOOD GUYS AND THE BAD GUYS Warner Bros., 1969
DIRTY DINGUS MAGEE MGM, 1970
SUPPORT YOUR LOCAL GUNFIGHTER United Artists, 1971
HANNIE CAULDER Paramount, 1971, British
THE DESERTER Paramount, 1971, Italian-Yugoslavian
THE TRAIN ROBBERS Warner Bros., 1973
SHOOTOUT IN A ONE-DOG TOWN (TF) Hanna-Barbera Productions, 1974
SIDEKICKS (TF) Warner Bros. TV, 1974
ALL THE KIND STRANGERS (TF) Cinemation TV, 1974
THE KILLER INSIDE ME Warner Bros., 1976
HOW THE WEST WAS WON (MS) co-director with Daniel Mann, MGM TV, 1977
THE RHINEMANN EXCHANGE (MS) Universal TV, 1977
KATE BLISS & THE TICKER TAPE KID (TF) Aaron Spelling Productions, 1978
THE WILD WILD WEST REVISITED (TF) CBS Entertainment, 1979
THE CONCRETE COWBOYS (TF) Frankel Films, 1979
MORE WILD WILD WEST CBS Entertainment, 1980
WOLF LAKE *THE HONOR GUARD* Filmcorp Distribution, 1981, Canadian
TROUBLE AT THE ROYAL ROSE HBO/Brigade Productions, 1985

TOM KENNEDY

Agent: Mitch Kaplan, Kaplan-Stahler Agency - Beverly Hills, 213/653-4483

TIME WALKER New World, 1983

IRVIN KERSHNER*

b. April 29, 1923 - Philadelphia, Pennsylvania
Home: P.O. Box 232, Route 7 North, Kent, CT 06757, 203/927-4483
Agent: Michael Marcus, CAA - Los Angeles, 213/277-4545
Business Manager: Charles Silverberg, Silverberg, Rosen, Leon & Behr, 2029 Century Park East - Suite 1900, Los Angeles, CA 90067, 213/277-4500

STAKEOUT ON DOPE STREET Warner Bros., 1958
THE YOUNG CAPTIVES Paramount, 1959
THE HOODLUM PRIEST United Artists, 1961
A FACE IN THE RAIN Embassy, 1963
THE LUCK OF GINGER COFFEY Continental, 1964, Canadian
A FINE MADNESS Warner Bros., 1966
THE FLIM-FLAM MAN 20th Century-Fox, 1967
LOVING Columbia, 1970
UP THE SANDBOX National General, 1972
S*P*Y*S 20th Century-Fox, 1974, British-U.S.
THE RETURN OF A MAN CALLED HORSE United Artists, 1976
RAID ON ENTEBBE (TF) ☆ Edgar J. Scherick Associates/20th Century-Fox TV, 1977
EYES OF LAURA MARS Columbia, 1978
THE EMPIRE STRIKES BACK 20th Century-Fox, 1980
NEVER SAY NEVER AGAIN Warner Bros., 1983

BRUCE KESSLER*

b. March 23, 1936 - California
Home: 4444 Via Marina, Marina del Rey, CA 90291, 213/823-2394
Agent: The Cooper Agency - Los Angeles, 213/277-8422

ANGELS FROM HELL American International, 1968
KILLERS THREE American International, 1968
THE GAY DECEIVERS Fanfare, 1969
SIMON, KING OF WITCHES Fanfare, 1971
MURDER IN PEYTON PLACE (TF) 20th Century-Fox TV, 1977
THE TWO-FIVE (TF) Universal TV, 1978
DEATH MOON (TF) Roger Gimbel Productions/EMI TV, 1978
CRUISE INTO TERROR (TF) Aaron Spelling Productions, 1978

MICHAEL KIDD*

b. August 12, 1919 - Brooklyn, New York
Agent: William Morris Agency - Beverly Hills, 213/274-7451

MERRY ANDREW MGM, 1958

FRITZ KIERSCH

CHILDREN OF THE CORN New World, 1984
TUFF TURF New World, 1985

BRUCE KIMMEL*

b. December 8, 1947 - Los Angeles, California
Agent: Tim Stone, Stone-Masser Talent Agents - Los Angeles, 213/275-9599

THE FIRST NUDIE MUSICAL co-director with Mark Haggard, Paramount, 1976
SPACESHIP *THE CREATURE WASN'T NICE* Almi Cinema 5, 1982

ALLAN KING

b. 1930 - Vancouver, Canada
Home: 397 Carlton Street, Toronto, Ontario M5A 2M3, Canada, 416/964-7284

PEMBERTON VALLEY (FD) CBC, 1957, Canadian
A MATTER OF PRIDE (FD) CBC, 1961, Canadian
COMING OF AGE IN IBIZA *RUNNING AWAY BACKWARDS (FD)* CBC, 1964, Canadian

ALLAN KING —continued

WARRENDALE (FD) Grove Press, 1968, Canadian
A MARRIED COUPLE (FD) Aquarius, 1970, Canadian
COME ON CHILDREN (FD) Allan King Associates, 1972, Canadian
WHO HAS SEEN THE WIND Astral Bellevue, 1977, Canadian
MARIA (TF) CBC, 1977, Canadian
ONE-NIGHT STAND Janus, 1978, Canadian
SILENCE OF THE NORTH Universal, 1981, Canadian
READY FOR SLAUGHTER (TF) CBC, 1983, Canadian

RICHARD KINON*

Agent: Ellen Glick, ICM - Los Angeles, 213/550-4000

THE LOVE BOAT (TF) co-director with Alan Myerson, Douglas S. Cramer Productions, 1976
THE NEW LOVE BOAT (TF) Douglas S. Cramer Productions, 1977
ALOHA PARADISE (TF) Aaron Spelling Productions, 1981

EPHRAIM KISHON

Contact: Israel Film Centre, Ministry of Industry & Trade, 30 Agron Street, P.O. Box 299, Jerusalem 94190, Israel, 02/210433

SALLAH Palisades International, 1963, Israeli
THE BIG DIG Canal, 1969, Israeli
THE POLICEMAN Cinema 5, 1972, Israeli
ERVINKA 1974, Israeli
FOX IN THE CHICKEN COOP Hashu'alim Ltd., 1978, Israeli
THE MARRIAGE CONTRACT (TF) 1983, West German

ALF KJELLIN*

b. February 28, 1920 - Lund, Sweden
Home: 12630 Mulholland Drive, Beverly Hills, CA 90210, 213/273-6514
Agent: Neil Schanker, ICM - Los Angeles, 213/550-4000

GIRL IN THE RAIN 1955, Swedish
SEVENTEEN YEARS OLD 1957, Swedish
ENCOUNTERS AT DUSK 1957, Swedish
SWINGING AT THE CASTLE 1959, Swedish
ONLY A WAITER 1960, Swedish
PLEASURE GARDEN 1961, Swedish
SISKA 1962, Swedish
MIDAS RUN Cinerama Releasing Corporation, 1969
THE McMASTERS Chevron, 1970
THE DEADLY DREAM (TF) Universal TV, 1971
THE GIRLS OF HUNTINGTON HOUSE (TF) Lorimar Productions, 1973

ROBERT KLANE*

Agent: Ron Meyer, CAA - Los Angeles, 213/277-4545

THANK GOD IT'S FRIDAY Columbia, 1978

WILLIAM KLEIN

b. 1926 - New York, New York
Contact: French Film Office, 745 Fifth Avenue, New York, NY 10151, 212/832-8860

QUI ETES-VOUS POLLY MAGGOO? 1966, French
FAR FROM VIETNAM (FD) co-director with Jean-Luc Godard, Joris Ivens, Alain Resnais & Agnes Varda, New Yorker, 1967, French
MISTER FREEDOM 1969, French
FLOAT LIKE A BUTTERFLY - STING LIKE A BEE (FD) Delpire Advico/Films Paris-New York, 1969, French
FESTIVAL PANAFRICAIN (FD) 1969, French
ELDRIDGE CLEAVER (FD) 1970, French

WILLIAM KLEIN —continued

LE COUPLE TEMOIN Planfilm, 1977, French
THE FRENCH (FD) AAA, 1981, French

RANDAL KLEISER*

b. July 20, 1946
Agent: Michael Marcus, CAA - Los Angeles, 213/277-4545

ALL TOGETHER NOW (TF) RSO Films, 1975
DAWN: PORTRAIT OF A TEENAGE RUNAWAY (TF) Douglas S. Cramer Productions, 1976
THE BOY IN THE PLASTIC BUBBLE (TF) Spelling-Goldberg Productions, 1976
THE GATHERING (TF) ☆ Hanna-Barbera Productions, 1977
GREASE Paramount, 1978
THE BLUE LAGOON Columbia, 1980
SUMMER LOVERS Filmways, 1982
GRANDVIEW, U.S.A. Warner Bros., 1984

ROBERT KNIGHTS

Contact: Directors Guild of Great Britain, 56 Whitfield Street, London W1, England, 01/580-2256

TENDER IS THE NIGHT (CMS) Showtime/BBC, 1985, U.S.-British

MASAKI KOBAYASHI

b. February 14, 1916 - Hokkaido, Japan
Contact: Directors Guild of Japan, Tsukada Building, 8-33 Ugagawa-cho, Shibuya-ku, Tokyo 150, Japan, 3/461-4411

MY SON'S YOUTH 1952, Japanese
SINCERE HEART 1953, Japanese
ROOM WITH THICK WALLS 1953, Japanese
THREE LOVES 1954, Japanese
SOMEWHERE BENEATH THE WIDE SKY 1954, Japanese
BEAUTIFUL DAYS 1955, Japanese
THE FOUNTAINHEAD 1956, Japanese
I'LL BUY YOU 1956, Japanese
BLACK RIVER 1957, Japanese
THE HUMAN CONDITION, PART I (NO GREATER LOVE) Shochiku, 1959, Japanese
THE HUMAN CONDITION, PART II (ROAD TO ETERNITY) Shochiku, 1959, Japanese
THE HUMAN CONDITION, PART III (A SOLDIER'S PRAYER) Shochiku, 1961, Japanese
THE INHERITANCE Shochiku, 1962, Japanese
HARAKIRI *SEPPUKU* Toho, 1962, Japanese
KWAIDAN Continental, 1964, Japanese
REBELLION *SAMURAI REBELLION* Toho, 1967, Japanese
HYMN TO A TIRED MAN 1968, Japanese
INN OF EVIL 1971, Japanese
FOSSILS (MS) 1975, Japanese
GLOWING AUTUMN 1979, Japanese
TOKYO SAIBAN (FD) 1983, Japanese

HOWARD W. KOCH*

b. April 11, 1916 - New York, New York
Business: Koch-Kirkwood Productions, 4000 Warner Blvd., Burbank, CA 91505, 818/843-6000

SHIELD FOR MURDER co-director with Edmond O'Brien, United Artists, 1954
BIG HOUSE, U.S.A. United Artists, 1955
UNTAMED YOUTH Warner Bros., 1957
BOP GIRL United Artists, 1957
JUNGLE HEAT United Artists, 1957
THE GIRL IN BLACK STOCKINGS United Artists, 1957
FORT BOWIE United Artists, 1958

HOWARD W. KOCH*—continued

VIOLENT ROAD Warner Bros., 1958
FRANKENSTEIN - 1970 Allied Artists, 1958
ANDY HARDY COMES HOME MGM, 1958
THE LAST MILE United Artists, 1959
BORN RECKLESS Warner Bros., 1959
BADGE 373 Paramount, 1973

PANCHO KOHNER

b. January 7, 1939 - Los Angeles, California
Contact: Writers Guild of America, West - Los Angeles, 213/550-1000

THE BRIDGE IN THE JUNGLE United Artists, 1971, Mexican
MR. SYCAMORE Film Ventures International, 1975

JAMES KOMACK*

Agent: Jack Gilardi, William Morris Agency - Beverly Hills, 213/274-7451
Business Manager: Marvin "Dusty" Snyder, Oppenheim, Appel, Dixon & Co., 2029 Century Park East - Suite 1300, Los Angeles, CA 90067, 213/277-0400

PORKY'S REVENGE 20th Century Fox, 1985

ANDREI KONCHALOVSKY

(Andrei Mikhalkov-Konchalovsky)

b. August 20, 1937 - U.S.S.R.

A BOY AND A PIGEON Mosfilm, 1960, Soviet
THE FIRST TEACHER Mosfilm/Kirghizfilm, 1965, Soviet
ASYA'S HAPPINESS Mosfilm, 1967, Soviet
A NEST OF GENTRY Corinth, 1969, Soviet
UNCLE VANYA Mosfilm, 1971, Soviet
A LOVER'S ROMANCE Mosfilm, 1974, Soviet
SIBERIADE IFEX Film, 1979, Soviet
MARIA'S LOVERS Cannon, 1984

JACKIE KONG

THE BEING BFV Films, 1983
NIGHT PATROL New World, 1984

BARBARA KOPPLE*

Business: Cabin Creek Films, 58 East 11th Street, New York, NY 10003, 212/533-7157

HARLAN COUNTY, U.S.A. (FD) Cabin Creek Films, 1976
KEEPING ON (TF) Many Mansions Institute, 1983

JOHN KORTY*

b. July 22, 1936 - Lafayette, Indiana
Business: Korty Films, Inc., 200 Miller Avenue, Mill Valley, CA 94941, 415/383-6900

CRAZY QUILT Farallon, 1965
FUNNYMAN New Yorker, 1967
RIVERRUN Columbia, 1970
THE PEOPLE (TF) Metromedia Productions/American Zoetrope, 1972
GO ASK ALICE (TF) Metromedia Productions, 1973
CLASS OF '63 (TF) Metromedia Productions/Stonehenge Productions, 1973
SILENCE Cinema Financial of America, 1974
THE AUTOBIOGRAPHY OF MISS JANE PITTMAN (TF) ☆☆ Tomorrow Entertainment, 1974
ALEX & THE GYPSY 20th Century-Fox, 1976
FAREWELL TO MANZANAR (TF) Korty Films/Universal TV, 1976

JOHN KORTY*—continued

WHO ARE THE DE BOLTS?...AND WHERE DID THEY GET 19 KIDS? (FD) Pyramid Films, 1977
THE MUSIC ROOM (TF) Learning in Focus, 1977
FOREVER (TF) Roger Gimbel Productions/EMI TV, 1978
OLIVER'S STORY Paramount, 1979
A CHRISTMAS WITHOUT SNOW (TF) Korty Films/The Konigsberg Company, 1980
TWICE UPON A TIME (AF) co-director with Charles Swenson, The Ladd Company/Warner Bros., 1983
THE HAUNTING PASSION (TF) BSR Productions/ITC, 1983
SECOND SIGHT: A LOVE STORY (TF) Entheos Unlimited Productions/T.T.C. Enterprises, 1984
THE EWOK ADVENTURE (TF) Lucasfilm Ltd./Korty Films, 1984

HENRY KOSTER*

(Hermann Kosterlitz)

b. May 1, 1905 - Berlin, Germany
Home: 3101 Village 3, Camarillo, CA 93010

DAS ABENTEUER DER THEA ROLAND 1932, German
DAS HASSLICHE MADCHEN 1933, German
PETER 1934, Austrian-Hungarian
KLEINE MUTTI 1934, Austrian-Hungarian
KATHARINA DIE LETZTE 1935, Austrian
DAS TAGEBUCH DER GELIEBTEN 1936, Austrian-Italian
THREE SMART GIRLS Universal, 1936
100 MEN AND A GIRL Universal, 1937
THE RAGE OF PARIS Universal, 1938
THREE SMART GIRLS GROW UP Universal, 1939
FIRST LOVE Universal, 1939
SPRING PARADE Universal, 1940
IT STARTED WITH EVE Universal, 1941
BETWEEN US GIRLS Universal, 1942
MUSIC FOR MILLIONS MGM, 1944
TWO SISTERS FROM BOSTON MGM, 1946
THE UNFINISHED DANCE MGM, 1947
THE BISHOP'S WIFE ★ RKO Radio, 1947
THE LUCK OF THE IRISH 20th Century-Fox, 1948
COME TO THE STABLE 20th Century-Fox, 1949
THE INSPECTOR GENERAL Warner Bros., 1949
WABASH AVENUE 20th Century-Fox, 1950
MY BLUE HEAVEN 20th Century-Fox, 1950
HARVEY Universal, 1950
NO HIGHWAY IN THE SKY *NO HIGHWAY* 20th Century-Fox, 1951 British
MR. BELVEDERE RINGS THE BELL 20th Century-Fox, 1951
ELOPEMENT 20th Century-Fox, 1951
O. HENRY'S FULL HOUSE co-director with Henry Hathaway, Howard Hawks, Henry King & Jean Negulesco, 20th Century-Fox, 1952
STARS AND STRIPES FOREVER 20th Century-Fox, 1952
MY COUSIN RACHEL 20th Century-Fox, 1953
THE ROBE 20th Century-Fox, 1953
DESIREE 20th Century-Fox, 1954
A MAN CALLED PETER 20th Century-Fox, 1955
THE VIRGIN QUEEN 20th Century-Fox, 1955
GOOD MORNING, MISS DOVE 20th Century-Fox, 1955
D-DAY, THE SIXTH OF JUNE 20th Century-Fox, 1956
THE POWER AND THE PRIZE MGM, 1956
MY MAN GODFREY Universal, 1957
FRAULEIN 20th Century-Fox, 1958
THE NAKED MAJA United Artists, 1959
THE STORY OF RUTH 20th Century-Fox, 1960
FLOWER DRUM SONG Universal, 1961
MR. HOBBS TAKES A VACATION 20th Century-Fox, 1962
TAKE HER, SHE'S MINE 20th Century-Fox, 1963
DEAR BRIGITTE 20th Century-Fox, 1965
THE SINGING NUN MGM, 1966

TOM KOTANI

THE LAST DINOSAUR (TF) co-director with Alex Grasshoff, Rankin-Bass Productions, 1977, U.S.-Japanese
THE BERMUDA DEPTHS (TF) Rankin-Bass Productions, 1978
THE IVORY APE (TF) Rankin-Bass Productions, 1980, U.S.-Japanese
THE BUSHIDO BLADE Aquarius, 1982, U.S.-Japanese

TED KOTCHEFF*

b. April 7, 1931 - Toronto, Canada
Agent: Jeff Berg, ICM - Los Angeles, 213/550-4000

TIARA TAHITI Zenith International, 1962, British
LIFE AT THE TOP Columbia, 1965, British
TWO GENTLEMENT SHARING American International, 1969, British
OUTBACK *WAKE IN FRIGHT* United Artists, 1971, Australian
BILLY TWO HATS United Artists, 1972, British
THE APPRENTICESHIP OF DUDDY KRAVITZ Paramount, 1974 Canadian
FUN WITH DICK & JANE Columbia, 1977
WHO IS KILLING THE GREAT CHEFS OF EUROPE? Warner Bros., 1978
NORTH DALLAS FORTY Paramount, 1979
SPLIT IMAGE Orion, 1982
FIRST BLOOD Orion, 1982, Canadian
UNCOMMON VALOR Paramount, 1983
JOSHUA THEN AND NOW TLC Films/20th Century Fox, 1985, Canadian

YAPHET KOTTO

b. November 15, 1937 - New York, New York

THE LIMIT *TIME LIMIT/SPEED LIMIT 65* Cannon, 1972

JIM KOUF

Contact: Writers Guild of America - Los Angeles, 213/550-1000

MIRACLES Orion, 1985

BERNARD L. KOWALSKI*

b. August 2, 1929 - Brownsville, Texas
Home: 17524 Community Street, Northridge, CA 91324, 818/987-2433
Agent: Irv Schechter Company - Beverly Hills, 213/278-8070

HOT CAR GIRL Allied Artists, 1958
NIGHT OF THE BLOOD BEAST American International, 1958
THE GIANT LEECHES American International, 1959
KRAKATOA, EAST OF JAVA Cinerama Releasing Corporation, 1969
STILETTO Avco Embassy, 1969
MACHO CALLAHAN Avco Embassy, 1970
HUNTERS ARE FOR KILLING (TF) 1970
TERROR IN THE SKY (TF) Paramount TV, 1971
BLACK NOON (TF) Fenady Associates/Screen Gems, 1971
WOMEN IN CHAINS (TF) Paramount TV, 1972
TWO FOR THE MONEY (TF) Aaron Spelling Productions, 1972
THE WOMAN HUNTER (TF) Bing Crosby Productions, 1972
SHE CRIED MURDER (TF) 1973
Sssssss Universal, 1973
IN TANDEM (TF) D'Antoni Productions, 1974
FLIGHT TO HOLOCAUST (TF) Aycee Productions/First Artists, 1977
THE NATIVITY (TF) D'Angelo-Bullock-Allen Productions/20th Century-Fox TV, 1978
MARCIANO (TF) ABC Circle Films, 1979
B.A.D. CATS (TF) Aaron Spelling Productions, 1980
TURNOVER SMITH (TF) Wellington Productions, 1980
NIGHTSIDE (TF) Stephen J. Cannell Productions/Glen A. Larson Productions/ Universal TV, 1980

ROBERT KRAMER

b. June, 1939 - New York, New York
Contact: French Film Office, 745 Fifth Avenue, New York, NY 10151, 212/832-8860

FALN (FD) 1965
IN THE COUNTRY Newsreel, 1968
THE EDGE Film-Makers, 1968
PEOPLE'S WAR (FD) co-director, Newsreel, 1969
ICE New Yorker, 1970
MILESTONES co-director with John Douglas, Stone, 1975
SCENES FROM THE PORTUGUESE CLASS STRUGGLE (FD) 1977
GUNS S.N.D., 1980, French
BIRTH 1982, French
A TOUT ALLURE INA, 1982, French
UNSER NAZI 1984, West German
DIESEL Distributeurs Associes, 1985, French

STANLEY KRAMER*

b. September 23, 1913 - New York, New York
Business: Stanley Kramer Productions, P.O. Box 158, Bellevue, Washington 90889, 206/454-1785
Personal Manager: Roy Kaufman, 1900 Avenue of the Stars, Los Angeles, CA 90067, 213/277-1900

NOT AS A STRANGER United Artists, 1955
THE PRIDE AND THE PASSION United Artists, 1957
THE DEFIANT ONES ★ United Artists, 1958
ON THE BEACH United Artists, 1959
INHERIT THE WIND United Artists, 1960
JUDGMENT AT NUREMBERG ★ United Artists, 1961
IT'S A MAD, MAD, MAD, MAD WORLD United Artists, 1963
SHIP OF FOOLS Columbia, 1965
GUESS WHO'S COMING TO DINNER ★ Columbia, 1969
THE SECRET OF SANTA VITTORIA United Artists, 1969
R.P.M.* Columbia, 1970
BLESS THE BEASTS & CHILDREN Columbia, 1971
OKLAHOMA CRUDE Columbia, 1973
THE DOMINO PRINCIPLE Avco Embassy, 1977
THE RUNNER STUMBLES 20th Century-Fox, 1979

ALEXIS KRASILOVSKY

b. July 5, 1950
Home: 2045 Lake Shore Avenue, Los Angeles, CA 90039, 213/662-5746

BEALE STREET co-director, Real to Reel Productions, 1979

PAUL KRASNY*

b. August 8, 1935 - Cleveland, Ohio
Home: 3620 Goodland Drive, Studio City, CA 91604, 818/506-4200
Agent: Mark Lichtman, Shapiro-Lichtman Agency - Los Angeles, 213/557-2244

THE D.A.: CONSPIRACY TO KILL (TF) Universal TV/Mark VII Ltd., 1971
THE ADVENTURES OF NICK CARTER (TF) Universal TV, 1972
THE LETTERS (TF) co-director with Gene Nelson, ABC Circle Films, 1973
CHRISTINA International Amusements, 1974
BIG ROSE (TF) 20th Century-Fox TV, 1974
JOE PANTHER Artists Creation & Associates, 1976
CENTENNIAL (MS) co-director with Harry Falk, Bernard McEveety & Virgil Vogel, Universal TV, 1978
THE ISLANDER (TF) Universal TV, 1978
WHEN HELL WAS IN SESSION (TF) Aubrey-Hamner Productions, 1979
240-ROBERT (TF) Rosner TV/Filmways TV Productions, 1979
ALCATRAZ: THE WHOLE SHOCKING STORY (TF) Pierre Cossette Productions, 1980
FUGITIVE FAMILY (TF) Aubrey-Hamner Productions, 1980
TERROR AMONG US (TF) David Gerber Company, 1981

PAUL KRASNY*—continued

FLY AWAY HOME (TF) An Lac Productions/Warner Bros. TV, 1981
TIME BOMB (TF) Barry Weitz Films/Universal TV, 1984

JOHN KRISH

Contact: British Academy of Film & Television Arts, 195 Piccadilly, London W1, England, 01/734-0022

THE SALVAGE GANG Children's Film Foundation, 1958, British
THE WILD AFFAIR Goldstone, 1963, British
THE UNEARTHLY STRANGER American International, 1964, British
DECLINE AND FALL OF A BIRD WATCHER 20th Century-Fox, 1969, British
THE MAN WHO HAD POWER OVER WOMEN Avco Embassy, 1971, British
JESUS co-director with Peter Sykes, Warner Bros., 1979, British

WILLIAM KRONICK*

Home: 950 N. Kings Road, Los Angeles, CA 90069, 213/656-8150
Business: William Kronick Productions, 8489 W. Third Street, Los Angeles, CA 90048, 213/651-2810

THE 500-POUND JERK (TF) Wolper Productions, 1973
TO THE ENDS OF THE EARTH (TD) Armand Hammer Productions, 1984

JEREMY JOE KRONSBERG*

Home: P.O. Box 683, Malibu, CA 90265

GOING APE! Paramount, 1981

STANLEY KUBRICK*

b. July 26, 1928 - Bronx, New York
Contact: Directors Guild of Great Britian, 56 Whitfield Street, London W1, England, 01/580-9592
Attorney: Louis C. Blau, Loeb & Loeb, 10100 Santa Monica Blvd., Los Angeles, CA 90067, 213/552-7774

FEAR AND DESIRE Joseph Burstyn, Inc., 1954
KILLER'S KISS United Artists, 1955
THE KILLING United Artists, 1956
PATHS OF GLORY United Artists, 1957
SPARTACUS Universal, 1960
LOLITA MGM, 1962, British
DR. STRANGELOVE OR: HOW I LEARNED TO STOP WORRYING AND LOVE THE BOMB ★ Columbia,1964, British
2001: A SPACE ODYSSEY ★ MGM, 1968, British
A CLOCKWORK ORANGE ★ Warner Bros., 1971, British
BARRY LYNDON ★ Warner Bros., 1975, British
THE SHINING Warner Bros., 1980, British

ANDREW J. KUEHN*

Business: Kaleidoscope Films Ltd., 844 N. Seward Street, Hollywood, CA 90038, 213/465-1151

TERROR IN THE AISLES (FD) Universal, 1984

BUZZ KULIK*

b. 1923 - New York, New York
Agent: Hall Ross, William Morris Agency - Beverly Hills, 213/274-7451

THE EXPLOSIVE GENERATION United Artists, 1961
THE YELLOW CANARY 20th Century-Fox, 1963
READY FOR THE PEOPLE Warner Bros., 1964
WARNING SHOT Paramount, 1968
SERGEANT RYKER Universal, 1968

BUZZ KULIK*—continued

VILLA RIDES! Paramount, 1968
RIOT Paramount, 1969
VANISHED (TF) Universal TV, 1971
OWEN MARSHALL, COUNSELOR AT LAW (TF) Universal TV, 1971
BRIAN'S SONG (TF) ☆ Screen Gems/Columbia TV, 1971
TO FIND A MAN Columbia, 1972
INCIDENT ON A DARK STREET (TF) 20th Century-Fox TV, 1973
PIONEER WOMAN (TF) Filmways, 1973
SHAMUS Columbia, 1973
BAD RONALD (TF) Lorimar Productions, 1974
REMEMBER WHEN (TF) Danny Thomas Productions/The Raisin Company, 1974
CAGE WITHOUT A KEY (TF) Columbia TV, 1975
MATT HELM (TF) Columbia TV, 1975
BABE (TF) ☆ MGM TV, 1975
THE LINDBERGH KIDNAPPING CASE (TF) Columbia TV, 1976
COREY: FOR THE PEOPLE (TF) Columbia TV, 1977
KILL ME IF YOU CAN (TF) Columbia TV, 1977
ZIEGFELD: THE MAN AND HIS WOMEN (TF) Frankovich Productions/Columbia TV, 1978
FROM HERE TO ETERNITY (MS) Bennett-Katleman Productions/Columbia TV, 1979
THE HUNTER Paramount, 1980
SIDNEY SHELDON'S RAGE OF ANGELS *RAGE OF ANGELS (TF)* Furia-Oringer Productions/NBC Productions, 1983
GEORGE WASHINGTON (MS) David Gerber Company/MGM-UA TV, 1984

AKIRA KUROSAWA

b. March 23, 1910 - Tokyo, Japan
Contact: Directors Guild of Japan, Tsukada Building, 8-33 Udagawa-cho, Shibuya-ku, Tokyo 150, Japan, 3/461-4411

SANSHIRO SUGATA Toho, 1943, Japanese
THE MOST BEAUTIFUL Toho, 1944, Japanese
THOSE WHO TREAD ON THE TIGER'S TAIL Toho, 1945, Japanese
SANSHIRO SUGATA - PART TWO Toho, 1945, Japanese
NO REGRETS FOR OUR YOUTH Toho, 1946, Japanese
THOSE WHO MAKE TOMORROW Toho, 1946, Japanese
ONE WONDERFUL SUNDAY Toho, 1947, Japanese
DRUNKEN ANGEL Toho, 1948, Japanese
THE QUIET DUEL Daiei, 1949, Japanese
STRAY DOG Toho, 1949, Japanese
SCANDAL Shochiku, 1959, Japanese
RASHOMON RKO Radio, 1950, Japanese
THE IDIOT Shochiku, 1951, Japanese
IKIRU Brandon, 1952, Japanese
SEVEN SAMURAI Landmark Releasing, 1954, Japanese
I LIVE IN FEAR Brandon, 1955, Japanese
THE LOWER DEPTHS Brandon, 1957, Japanese
THRONE OF BLOOD *THE CASTLE OF THE SPIDER'S WEB* Brandon, 1957, Japanese
THE HIDDEN FORTRESS *THREE BAD MEN IN A HIDDEN FORTRESS* Toho, 1958, Japanese
THE BAD SLEEP WELL Toho, 1960, Japanese
YOJIMBO Seneca International, 1961, Japanese
SANJURO Toho, 1962, Japanese
HIGH AND LOW Continental, 1963, Japanese
RED BEARD Toho, 1965, Japanese
DODES'KA'DEN Janus, 1970, Japanese
DERSU UZALA New World, 1975, Soviet-Japanese
KAGEMUSHA: THE SHADOW WARRIOR 20th Century-Fox, 1980, Japanese
RAN Greenwich Films, 1985, Japanese

DIANE KURYS

Agent: Jeff Berg, ICM - Los Angeles, 213/550-4000

PEPPERMINT SODA *DIABOLO MENTHE* New Yorker, 1977, French
COCKTAIL MOLOTOV Putnam Square, 1980, French
ENTRE NOUS *COUP DE FOUDRE* United Artists Classics, 1983, French

KEN KWAPIS*

Home: 2307-½ Echo Park Avenue, Los Angeles, CA 90026, 213/660-9524
Agent: Patrick Faulstich, ICM - Los Angeles, 213/550-4000

SESAME STREET PRESENTS: FOLLOW THAT BIRD Warner Bros., 1985, Canadian

L

MORT LACHMAN*

Business: Mort Lachman & Associates, 4115 "B" Warner Blvd., Burbank, CA 91505, 818/769-6030
Agent: Bernie Weintraub, Robinson-Weintraub & Associates - Los Angeles, 213/653-5802

THE GIRL WHO COULDN'T LOSE (TF) ☆☆ Filmways, 1975

HARVEY LAIDMAN*

Agent: Louis Bershad, Century Artists Ltd. - Beverly Hills, 213/273-4366
Business Manager: Marvin Freedman, Freedman, Kinzelberg & Broder, 1801 Avenue of the Stars - Suite 911, Los Angeles, CA 90067, 213/277-0700

STEEL COWBOY (TF) Roger Gimbel Productions/EMI TV, 1978
THE BOY WHO LOVED TROLLS (TF) Q Productions, 1984

MARLENA LAIRD*

Home: 2729 Westshire Drive, Los Angeles, CA 90068, 213/465-6400
Agent: Irv Schechter Company - Beverly Hills, 213/278-8070

FRIENDSHIP, SECRETS AND LIES co-director with Ann Zane Shanks, Wittman-Riche Productions/Warner Bros. TV, 1979

FRANK LaLOGGIA

FEAR NO EVIL Avco Embassy, 1981

MARY LAMPSON

UNDERGROUND (FD) co-director with Emile de Antonio & Haskell Wexler, New Yorker, 1976
UNTIL SHE TALKS (TF) Alaska Street Productions, 1983

BURT LANCASTER*

b. November 2, 1913 - New York, New York
Agent: ICM - Los Angeles, 213/550-4000

THE MIDNIGHT MAN co-director with Roland Kibbee, Universal, 1974

JOHN LANDIS*

Agent: Michael Marcus, CAA - Los Angeles, 213/277-4545

SCHLOCK Jack H. Harris Enterprises, 1973
THE KENTUCKY FRIED MOVIE United Film Distribution, 1977
NATIONAL LAMPOON'S ANIMAL HOUSE Universal, 1978
THE BLUES BROTHERS Universal, 1980
AN AMERICAN WEREWOLF IN LONDON Universal, 1981
TWILIGHT ZONE - THE MOVIE co-director with Steven Spielberg, Joe Dante & George Miller, Warner Bros., 1983
TRADING PLACES Paramount, 1983
COMING SOON (CTD) Universal Pay TV, 1983
INTO THE NIGHT Universal, 1985

MICHAEL LANDON*

(Eugene Orowitz)

b. October 31, 1937 - Forest Hills, New York
Business Manager: Jay Eller, 1930 Century Park West - Suite 401, Los Angeles, CA 90067, 213/277-6408

IT'S GOOD TO BE ALIVE (TF) Metromedia Productions, 1974
LITTLE HOUSE ON THE PRAIRIE (TF) NBC Productions, 1974
THE LONELIEST RUNNER (TF) NBC Productions, 1976
KILLING STONE (TF) Universal TV, 1978
FATHER MURPHY (TF) NBC Productions, 1981
LITTLE HOUSE: THE LAST FAREWELL (TF) NBC Productions/Ed Friendly Productions, 1984
SAM'S SON Invictus Entertainment Corporation, 1984
HIGHWAY TO HEAVEN (TF) Michael Landon Productions, 1984

ALAN LANDSBURG*

b. May 10, 1933 - New York, New York
Home: 2204 N. Beverly Drive, Beverly Hills, CA 90210, 213/550-0081
Business: Alan Landsburg Productions, Inc., 1554 S. Sepulveda Blvd., Los Angeles, CA 90025, 213/473-9641

BLACK WATER GOLD (TF) Metromedia Productions, 1970

RICHARD LANG*

Agent: Herb Tobias & Associates - Los Angeles, 213/277-6211

FANTASY ISLAND (TF) Spelling-Goldberg Productions, 1977
THE HUNTED LADY (TF) QM Productions, 1977
NOWHERE TO RUN (TF) MTM Enterprises, 1978
NIGHT CRIES (TF) Charles Fries Productions, 1978
DR. SCORPION (TF) Universal TV, 1978
VEGA$ (TF) Aaron Spelling Productions, 1978
THE WORD (MS) Charles Fries Productions/Stonehenge Productions, 1978
THE MOUNTAIN MEN Columbia, 1980
A CHANGE OF SEASONS 20th Century-Fox, 1980
MATT HOUSTON (TF) Largo Productions/Aaron Spelling Productions, 1982
DON'T GO TO SLEEP (TF) Aaron Spelling Productions, 1982
SHOOTING STARS (TF) Aaron Spelling Productions, 1983
DARK MIRROR (TF) Aaron Spelling Productions, 1984
VELVET (TF) Aaron Spelling Productions, 1984

SIMON LANGTON

b. November 5, 1941 - Amersham, England
Home: 5 Arundel Court, Jubilee Place, London SW3 3TJ, England, 01/351-4733
Agent: Rosalie Swedlin, CAA - Los Angeles, 213/277-4545

SMILEY'S PEOPLE (MS) ☆ BBC/Paramount TV, 1982, British
THE LOST HONOR OF KATHRYN BECK (TF) Open Road Productions, 1984
ANNA KARENINA (TF) Rastar Productions/Colgems Productions, 1985

STAN LATHAN*

Agent: Michael Menchel, CAA - Los Angeles, 213/277-4545
Personal Manager: The Brillstein Company, 9200 Sunset Blvd., Suite 905, Los Angeles, CA 90069, 213/275-6135

SAVE THE CHILDREN (FD) Paramount, 1973
AMAZING GRACE United Artists, 1974
THE SKY IS GRAY (TF) Learning in Focus, 1980
DENMARK VESEY'S REBELLION (TF) WPBT-Miami, 1982
BEAT STREET Orion, 1984
BOOKER (TF) KQED-Frisco, 1984
GO TELL IT ON THE MOUNTAIN (TF) Learning in Focus, 1984

ALBERTO LATTUADA

b. November 13, 1914 - Milan, Italy
Address: Via N. Paganini, 7 Rome, Italy
Contact: Ministry of Tourism & Education, Via Della Ferratella, No. 51, 00184 Rome, Italy, 06/7732

GIACOMO L'IDEALISTA 1942, Italian
LA FRECCIA NEL FIANCO 1943, Italian
LA NOSTRA GUERRA 1943, Italian
IL BANDITO Lux Film, 1946, Italian
IL DELITTO DI GIOVANNI EPISCOPO Lux Film, 1947, Italian
SENZA PIETA Lux Film, 1948, Italian
LUCI DEL PO 1949, Italian
VARIETY LIGHTS co-director with Federico Fellini, Pathe Contemporary, 1950, Italian
ANNA Italian Films Export, 1951, Italian
IL CAPPOTTO Faro Film, 1952, Italian
LA LUPA Republic, 1953, Italian
LOVE IN THE CITY co-director, Italian Films Export, 1953, Italian
LA SPIAGGIA Titanus, 1954, Italian
SCUOLA ELEMENTARE Titanus/Societe General de Cinematographie, 1954, Italian-French
GUENDALINA Carlo Ponti/Les Films Marceau, 1957, Italian-French
TEMPEST Paramount, 1958, Italian-French-Yugoslavian
I DOLCI INGANNI Carlo Ponti/Titanus, 1960, Italian
LETTERA DI UNA NOVIZIA Champion/Euro International, 1960, Italian
L'IMPREVISTO Documento Film/Orsay Film, 1961, Italian-French
MAFIOSO Zenith International, 1962, Italian
LA STEPPA Zebra Film/Aera Film, 1962, Italian
LA MANDRAGOLA Arco Film/Lux Compagnie Cinematographie, 1965, Italian-French
MATCHLESS United Artists, 1966, Italian
DON GIOVANNI IN SICILIA Adelphia, 1967, Italian
FRAULEIN DOKTOR Paramount, 1969, Italian-Yugoslavian
L'AMICA Fair Film, 1969, Italian
VENGA A PRENDERE IL CAFFE DA NOI Mass Film, 1970, Italian
WHITE SISTER *BIANCO, ROSSO E...* Columbia, 1971, Italian-French-Spanish
SONO STATO IO Dear Film, 1973, Italian
LE FARO DA PADRE Clesi Cinematografica, 1974, Italian
LA BAMBINA 1974, Italian
CUORE DI CANE Italnoleggio, 1975, Italian
BRUCIATI DA COCENTE PASSIONE Cineriz, 1976, Italian
OH, SERAFINA Cineriz, 1976, Italian
COSI COME SEI CEIAD, 1978, Italian-Spanish
THE CRICKET PIC, 1979, Italian
THORN IN THE HEART 1981, Italian-French
CHRISTOPHER COLUMBUS (MS) RAI/Clesi Cinematografica/Antenne-2/Bavaria/Lorimar Productions, 1985, Italian-West German-U.S.

FRANK LAUGHLIN*

Home: 213/476-7262
Business Manager: c/o Pal-Mel Productions, 9350 Wilshire Blvd. - Suite 400, Beverly Hills, CA 90212, 213/869-0497

THE TRIAL OF BILLY JACK Taylor-Laughlin, 1974
THE MASTER GUNFIGHTER Taylor-Laughlin, 1975

MICHAEL LAUGHLIN

STRANGE BEHAVIOR *DEAD KIDS* World Northal, 1981, New Zealand-Australian
STRANGE INVADERS Orion, 1983, Canadian
MESMERIZED RKO/Challenge Corporation Services, 1985, New Zealand-Australian

TOM LAUGHLIN*

b. 1938 - Minneapolis, Minnesota
Business: National Student Film Corporation, 4024 Radford Avenue, Studio City, CA 91604, 818/394-0286

THE PROPER TIME Lopert, 1960
THE YOUNG SINNER United Screen Arts, 1965
BORN LOSERS directed under pseudonym of T.C. Frank, American International, 1967
BILLY JACK directed under pseudonym of T.C. Frank, Warner Bros., 1973
BILLY JACK GOES TO WASHINGTON Taylor-Laughlin, 1978

ARNOLD LAVEN*

b. February 23, 1922 - Chicago, Illinois
Agent: Ken Gross, The Literary Group - Los Angeles, 213/278-3350

WITHOUT WARNING United Artists, 1952
VICE SQUAD United Artists, 1953
DOWN THREE DARK STREETS United Artists, 1954
THE RACK MGM, 1956
THE MONSTER THAT CHALLENGED THE WORLD United Artists, 1957
SLAUGHTER ON TENTH AVENUE Universal, 1957
ANNA LUCASTA United Artists, 1958
GERONIMO United Artists, 1962
THE GLORY GUYS United Artists, 1965
ROUGH NIGHT IN JERICHO Universal, 1967
SAM WHISKEY United Artists, 1969

JOE LAYTON*

Personal Manager: Roy Gerber Associates, 9200 Sunset Blvd. - Suite 620, Los Angeles, CA 90069, 213/550-0100

RICHARD PRYOR LIVE ON THE SUNSET STRIP (FD) Columbia, 1982

ASHLEY LAZARUS

Contact: British Academy of Film & Television Arts, 195 Piccadilly, London W1, England, 01/734-0022

FOREVER YOUNG, FOREVER FREE *E'LOLLIPOP* Universal, 1976, British
GOLDEN RENDEZVOUS Rank, 1977, British

WILFORD LEACH

THE WEDDING PARTY co-director with Brian De Palma & Cynthia Munroe, Powell Productions Plus/Ondine, 1969
THE PIRATES OF PENZANCE Universal, 1983

PHILIP LEACOCK*

b. October 8, 1917 - London, England
Home: 914 Bienveneda Avenue, Pacific Palisades, CA 90272, 213/454-4188
Agent: Ronald Leif, Contemporary-Korman Artists - Beverly Hills, 213/278-8250

RIDERS OF THE NEW FOREST Crown, 1946, British
THE BRAVE DON'T CRY Mayer-Kingsley, 1952, British
ASSIGNMENT IN LONDON Associated Artists, 1953, British
THE LITTLE KIDNAPPERS *THE KIDNAPPERS* United Artists, 1954, British
ESCAPADE DCA, 1955, British
THE SPANISH GARDENER Rank, 1956, British
HIGH TIDE AT NOON Rank, 1957, British
INNOCENT SINNERS Rank, 1958, British
THE RABBIT TRAP United Artists, 1959
LET NO MAN WRITE MY EPITAPH Columbia, 1960
TAKE A GIANT STEP United Artists, 1960
HAND IN HAND Columbia, 1961, British
REACH FOR GLORY Royal Films International, 1962, British
13 WEST STREET Columbia, 1962
THE WAR LOVER Columbia, 1962, British
TAMAHINE MGM, 1964, British
ADAM'S WOMAN Warner Bros., 1970, Australian
THE BIRDMEN (TF) Universal TV, 1971
WHEN MICHAEL CALLS (TF) Palomar International, 1972
THE DAUGHTERS OF JOSHUA CABE (TF) Spelling-Goldberg Productions, 1972
BAFFLED! (TF) Arena Productions/ITC, 1973
THE GREAT MAN'S WHISKERS (TF) Universal TV, 1973
DYING ROOM ONLY (TF) Lorimar Productions, 1973
KEY WEST (TF) Warner Bros. TV, 1973
KILLER ON BOARD (TF) Lorimar Productions, 1977
WILD AND WOOLY (TF) Aaron Spelling Productions, 1978
THE CURSE OF KING TUT'S TOMB (TF) Stromberg-Kerby Productions/ Columbia TV/HTV West, 1980
ANGEL CITY (TF) Factor-Newland Productions, 1980
THE TWO LIVES OF CAROL LETNER (TF) Penthouse One Presentations, 1981
THE WILD WOMEN OF CHASTITY GULCH (TF) Aaron Spelling Productions, 1982

PAUL LEAF*

b. May 2, 1929 - New York, New York
Home: 924 23rd Street, Santa Monica, CA 90403, 213/829-2223
Agent: The Lantz Office - Los Angeles, 213/858-1144

TOP SECRET (TF) Jemmin, Inc./Sheldon Leonard Productions, 1978
SERGEANT MATLOVICH VS. THE U.S. AIR FORCE (TF) Tomorrow Entertainment, 1978

DAVID LEAN*

b. March 25, 1908 - Croydon, England
Agent: Dennis Van Thaal, London Management, 235/241 Regent Street, London W1, England, 01/493-1610
Contact: Directors Guild of Great Britain, 56 Whitfield Street, London W1, England, 01/580-9592

IN WHICH WE SERVE co-director with Noel Coward, Universal, 1942, British
THIS HAPPY BREED Universal, 1944, British
BLITHE SPIRIT United Artists, 1945, British
BRIEF ENCOUNTER Universal, 1946, British
GREAT EXPECTATIONS ★ Universal, 1947, British
OLIVER TWIST United Artists, 1948, British
ONE WOMAN'S STORY *THE PASSIONATE FRIENDS* Universal, 1949, British
MADELEINE Universal, 1950, British
BREAKING THE SOUND BARRIER *THE SOUND BARRIER* United Artists, 1952, British
HOBSON'S CHOICE United Artists, 1954, British
SUMMERTIME *SUMMER MADNESS* ★ United Artists, 1955, British
THE BRIDGE ON THE RIVER KWAI ★★ Columbia, 1957, British

DAVID LEAN*—continued

LAWRENCE OF ARABIA ★★ Columbia, 1962, British
DOCTOR ZHIVAGO ★ MGM, 1965, British
RYAN'S DAUGHTER MGM, 1970, British
A PASSAGE TO INDIA Columbia, 1984, British

NORMAN LEAR*

b. July 27, 1922 - New Haven, Connecticut
Business: TAT Communications, 1901 Avenue of the Stars - Suite 1600, Los Angeles, CA 90067, 213/553-3600

COLD TURKEY United Artists, 1971

JOANNA LEE*

Home: 135 S. Carmelina, Los Angeles, CA 90049, 213/270-3118
Agent: William Morris Agency - Beverly Hills, 213/274-7451
Business Manager: Anita deThomas & Associates, 1801 Avenue of the Stars, Los Angeles, CA 90067, 213/277-4866

MIRROR, MIRROR (TF) Christiana Productions, 1979
CHILDREN OF DIVORCE (TF) Christiana Productions/Marble Arch Productions, 1980

ROBERT LEEDS*

Agent: Brandon & Rodgers - Los Angeles, 213/273-6173

RETURN OF THE BEVERLY HILLBILLIES (TF) CBS, 1981

ERNEST LEHMAN

b. 1920 - New York, New York
Business Manager: Henry J. Bamberger, 2049 Century Park East, Los Angeles, CA 90067, 213/553-0581

PORTNOY'S COMPLAINT Warner Bros., 1972

DAVID LEIVICK

GOSPEL (FD) co-director with Frederick Ritzenberg, 20th Century-Fox, 1983

CLAUDE LELOUCH

b. October 30, 1937 - Paris, France
Address: 15 Avenue Hoche, 75008 Paris, France
Contact: French Film Office, 745 Fifth Avenue, New York, NY 10151, 212/832-8860

LE PROPRE DE L'HOMME 1960, French
L'AMOUR AVEC DES SI 1963, French
LA FEMME SPECTACLE 1964, French
TO BE A CROOK *UNE FILLE ET DES FUSILS* Comet, 1965, French
LES GRAND MOMENTS 1965, French
A MAN AND A WOMAN ★ Allied Artists, 1966, French
LIVE FOR LIFE United Artists, 1967, French
FAR FROM VIETNAM (FD) co-director with Jean-Luc Godard, Joris Ivens, William Klein, Alain Resnais & Agnes Varda, New Yorker, 1967, French
GRENOBLE (FD) co-director with Francois Reichenbach, United Producers of America, 1968, French
LIFE LOVE DEATH Lopert, 1969, French
LOVE IS A FUNNY THING *UN HOMME QUI ME PLAIT* United Artists, 1970, French-Italian
THE CROOK United Artists, 1971, French
SMIC, SMAC, SMOC GSF, 1971, French
MONEY MONEY MONEY *L'AVENTURE C'EST L'AVENTURE* GSF, 1972, French

CLAUDE LELOUCH —continued

HAPPY NEW YEAR *LA BONNE ANNEE* Avco Embassy, 1973, French-Italian
VISIONS OF EIGHT (FD) co-director with Yuri Ozerov, Mai Zetterling, Michael Pfleghar, Kon Ichikawa, Milos Forman & John Schlesinger, Cinema 5, 1973
AND NOW MY LOVE *TOUTE UNE VIE* Avco Embassy, 1975, French-Italian
MARIAGE 1975, French
CAT AND MOUSE Quartet, 1975, French
THE GOOD AND THE BAD Paramount, 1976, French
SECOND CHANCE *SI C'ETAIT A REFAIRE* United Artists Classics, 1976, French
ANOTHER MAN, ANOTHER CHANCE United Artists, 1977, U.S.-French
ROBERT ET ROBERT Quartet, 1978, French
A NOUS DEUX AMLF, 1979, French-Canadian
BOLERO *LES UNS ET LES AUTRES/WITHIN MEMORY* Double 13/Sharp Features, 1982, French
EDITH AND MARCEL Miramax, 1983, French
VIVA LA VIE UGC, 1984, French
PARTIR REVENIR UGC, 1985, French

JACK LEMMON*

b. February 8, 1925 - Boston, Massachusetts
Business: Jalem Productions, Inc., 141 El Camino - Suite 201, Beverly Hills, CA 90212, 213/278-7750
Agent: William Morris Agency - Beverly Hills, 213/274-7451
Business Manager: Marvin Freedman, Freedman, Kinzelberg & Broder, 1801 Avenue of the Stars - Suite 911, Los Angeles, CA 90067, 213/277-0700

KOTCH Cinerama Releasing Corporation, 1971

MALCOLM LEO*

b. October 9, 1944 - New York, New York
Home: 1938 N. Curson Avenue, Hollywood, CA 90028, 213/464-4448
Business: Malcolm Leo Productions, 6536 Sunset Blvd., Los Angeles, CA 90028, 213/464-5193
Agent: Michael Peretzian, William Morris Agency - Beverly Hills, 213/274-7451

HEROES OF ROCK AND ROLL (TD) co-director with Andrew Solt, ABC, 1979
THIS IS ELVIS (FD) co-director with Andrew Solt, Warner Bros., 1981
IT CAME FROM HOLLYWOOD (FD) co-director with Andrew Solt, Paramount, 1982

HERBERT B. LEONARD*

b. October 8, 1922
Home: 5300 Fulton Avenue, Van Nuys, CA 91401, 818/783-0457
Agent: ICM - Los Angeles, 213/550-4000

THE PERILS OF PAULINE Universal, 1967
GOING HOME MGM, 1971

JOHN LEONE*

Agent: William Morris Agency - Beverly Hills, 213/274-7451

THE GREAT SMOKEY ROADBLOCK *THE LAST OF THE COWBOYS* Dimension, 1978

SERGIO LEONE

b. January 3, 1929 - Rome, Italy
Contact: Ministry of Tourism & Education, Via Della Ferratella, No. 51, 00184 Rome, Italy, 06/7732

THE COLOSSUS OF RHODES MGM, 1960, Italian-French-Spanish
A FISTFUL OF DOLLARS United Artists, 1967, Italian-Spanish-West German

SERGIO LEONE —continued

FOR A FEW DOLLARS MORE United Artists, 1967, Italian-Spanish-West German
THE GOOD, THE BAD AND THE UGLY United Artists, 1968, Italian
ONCE UPON A TIME IN THE WEST Paramount, 1969, Italian-U.S.
DUCK! YOU SUCKER *FISTFUL OF DYNAMITE* United Artists, 1972, Italian-U.S.
ONCE UPON A TIME IN AMERICA The Ladd Company/Warner Bros., 1984, U.S.-Italian-Canadian

MERVYN LeROY *

b. October 15, 1900 - San Francisco, California
Business: Mervyn LeRoy Productions, 615 N. Camden Drive, Beverly Hills, CA 90210, 213/278-4441

NO PLACE TO GO First National, 1927
FLYING ROMEOS First National, 1928
HAROLD TEEN First National, 1928
OH KAY! First National, 1928
NAUGHTY BABY First National, 1929
HOT STUFF First National, 1929
BROADWAY BABIES First National, 1929
LITTLE JOHNNY JONES First National, 1929
PLAYING AROUND First National, 1929
SHOWGIRL IN HOLLYWOOD First National, 1930
NUMBERED MEN First National, 1930
TOP SPEED First National, 1930
LITTLE CAESAR First National, 1931
GENTLEMAN'S FATE First National, 1931
TOO YOUNG TO MARRY First National, 1931
BROAD MINDED First National, 1931
FIVE STAR FINAL First National, 1931
LOCAL BOY MAKES GOOD First National, 1931
TONIGHT OR NEVER United Artists, 1931
HIGH PRESSURE Warner Bros., 1932
TWO SECONDS First National, 1932
BIG CITY BLUES Warner Bros., 1932
THREE ON A MATCH First National, 1932
I AM A FUGITIVE FROM A CHAIN GANG Warner Bros., 1932
HARD TO HANDLE Warner Bros., 1933
ELMER THE GREAT First National, 1933
GOLD DIGGERS OF 1933 Warner Bros., 1933
TUGBOAT ANNIE MGM, 1933
THE WORLD CHANGES First National, 1933
HI, NELLIE! Warner Bros., 1934
HEAT LIGHTNING Warner Bros., 1934
HAPPINESS AHEAD First National, 1934
SWEET ADELINE Warner Bros., 1935
OIL FOR THE LAMPS OF CHINA Warner Bros., 1935
PAGE MISS GLORY Warner Bros., 1935
I FOUND STELLA PARISH First National, 1935
ANTHONY ADVERSE Warner Bros., 1936
THREE MEN ON A HORSE First National, 1936
THE KING AND THE CHORUS GIRL Warner Bros., 1937
THEY WON'T FORGET Warner Bros., 1937
FOOLS FOR SCANDAL Warner Bros., 1938
WATERLOO BRIDGE MGM, 1940
ESCAPE MGM, 1940
BLOSSOMS IN THE DUST MGM, 1941
UNHOLY PARTNERS MGM, 1941
JOHNNY EAGER MGM, 1941
RANDOM HARVEST ★ MGM, 1942
MADAME CURIE MGM, 1943
THIRTY SECONDS OVER TOKYO MGM, 1944
WITHOUT RESERVATIONS RKO Radio, 1946
HOMECOMING MGM, 1948
LITTLE WOMEN MGM, 1949
ANY NUMBER CAN PLAY MGM, 1949
EAST SIDE, WEST SIDE MGM, 1950
QUO VADIS MGM, 1951
LOVELY TO LOOK AT MGM, 1952
MILLION DOLLAR MERMAID MGM, 1952

MERVYN LeROY*—continued

LATIN LOVERS MGM, 1953
ROSE MARIE MGM, 1954
STRANGE LADY IN TOWN Warner Bros., 1955
MISTER ROBERTS co-director with John Ford, Warner Bros., 1955
THE BAD SEED Warner Bros., 1956
TOWARD THE UNKNOWN Warner Bros., 1956
NO TIME FOR SERGEANTS Warner Bros., 1958
HOME BEFORE DARK Warner Bros., 1958
THE FBI STORY Warner Bros., 1959
WAKE ME WHEN IT'S OVER 20th Century-Fox, 1960
THE DEVIL AT 4 O'CLOCK Columbia, 1961
A MAJORITY OF ONE Warner Bros., 1962
GYPSY Warner Bros., 1962
MARY, MARY Warner Bros., 1963
MOMENT TO MOMENT Universal, 1966

MARK L. LESTER*

Business: 7932 Mulholland Drive, Los Angeles, CA 90046, 213/876-8783
Agent: Tom Chasin, ICM - Los Angeles, 213/550-4000

STEEL ARENA L-T, 1973
TRUCK STOP WOMEN L-T, 1974
THE WAY HE WAS 1975
BOBBI JO AND THE OUTLAW American International, 1976
STUNTS New Line Cinema, 1977
GOLD OF THE AMAZON WOMEN (TF) Mi-Ka Productions, 1979
ROLLER BOOGIE United Artists, 1979
CLASS OF 1984 United Film Distribution, 1982, Canadian
FIRESTARTER Universal, 1984

RICHARD LESTER*

b. January 19, 1932 - Philadelphia, Pennsylvania
Messages: 213/892-4477
Business: Twickenham Film Studios, St. Margarets, Middlesex, England
Agent: Rick Nicita, CAA - Los Angeles, 213/277-4545

RING-A-DING RHYTHM *IT'S TRAD, DAD* Columbia, 1962, British
THE MOUSE ON THE MOON United Artists, 1963, British
A HARD DAY'S NIGHT United Artists, 1964, British
THE KNACK...AND HOW TO GET IT Lopert, 1965, British
HELP! United Artists, 1965, British
A FUNNY THING HAPPENED ON THE WAY TO THE FORUM United Artists, 1966, British
TEENAGE REBELLION *MONDO TEENO* co-director with Norman Herbert, Trans-American, 1967, British-U.S.
HOW I WON THE WAR United Artists, 1967, British
PETULIA Warner Bros., 1968, U.S.-British
THE BED SITTING ROOM United Artists, 1969, British
THE THREE MUSKETEERS *THE QUEEN'S DIAMONDS* 20th Century-Fox, 1974, British
JUGGERNAUT United Artists, 1974, British
THE FOUR MUSKETEERS *MILADY'S REVENGE* 20th Century-Fox, 1975, British
ROYAL FLASH 20th Century-Fox, 1976, British
ROBIN AND MARIAN Columbia, 1976, British
THE RITZ Warner Bros., 1976
BUTCH AND SUNDANCE: THE EARLY DAYS 20th Century-Fox, 1979
CUBA United Artists, 1979
SUPERMAN II Warner Bros., 1981, U.S.-British
SUPERMAN III Warner Bros., 1983, U.S.-British
FINDERS KEEPERS Warner Bros., 1984

WILLIAM A. LEVEY*

Home: 838 N. Doheny Drive, Apt. 904, Los Angeles, CA 90069, 213/273-3838
Agent: Peter Meyer, William Morris Agency - Beverly Hills, 213/274-7451

BLACKENSTEIN LFG, 1973
SLUMBER PARTY '57 Cannon, 1977
THE HAPPY HOOKER GOES TO WASHINGTON Cannon, 1977
SKATETOWN, U.S.A. Columbia, 1979

ALAN J. LEVI*

Home: 3951 Longridge Avenue, Sherman Oaks, CA 91423, 818/981-3417
Agent: Triad Artists, Inc. - Los Angeles, 213/556-2727

GEMINI MAN (TF) Universal TV, 1976
THE RETURN OF THE INCREDIBLE HULK (TF) Universal TV, 1977
GO WEST, YOUNG GIRL (TF) Bennett-Katleman Productions/Columbia TV, 1978
THE IMMIGRANTS (TF) Universal TV, 1978
THE LEGEND OF THE GOLDEN GUN (TF) Bennett-Katleman Productions/Columbia TV, 1979
SCRUPLES (TF) Lou-Step Productions/Warner Bros. TV, 1980
THE LAST SONG (TF) Ron Samuels Productions/Motown Pictures, 1980

PETER LEVIN*

Agent: David Gersh, The Gersh Agency - Beverly Hills, 213/274-6611

HEART IN HIDING (TF) Filmways, 1973
PALMERSTOWN, U.S.A. (TF) Haley-TAT Productions, 1980
THE COMEBACK KID (TF) ABC Circle Films, 1980
RAPE AND MARRIAGE: THE RIDEOUT CASE (TF) Stonehenge Productions/Blue Greene Productions/Lorimar Productions, 1980
THE MARVA COLLINS STORY (TF) NRW Features, 1981
WASHINGTON MISTRESS (TF) Lorimar Productions, 1982
THE ROYAL ROMANCE OF CHARLES AND DIANA (TF) Chrysalis-Yellen Productions, 1982
A DOCTOR'S STORY (TF) Embassy TV, 1984
A REASON TO LIVE (TF) Rastar Productions/Robert Papazian Productions, 1984

SIDNEY LEVIN*

Agent: Smith-Gosnell Agency - Malibu, 213/456-6641

LET THE GOOD TIMES ROLL (FD) co-director with Robert J. Abel, Columbia, 1973
THE GREAT BRAIN Osmond Distribution Company, 1978

BARRY LEVINSON*

Agent: Michael Ovitz, CAA - Los Angeles, 213/277-4545

DINER MGM/United Artists, 1982
THE NATURAL Tri-Star/Columbia, 1984

GENE LEVITT*

b. May 28, 1920 - New York, New York
Home: 315 Grand Canal, Balboa Island, CA 92662
Agent: Triad Artists, Inc. - Los Angeles, 213/556-2727
Business Manager: Henry J. Bamberger, 2049 Century Park East, Los Angeles, CA 90067, 213/553-0581

ANY SECOND NOW (TF) Universal TV, 1969
RUN A CROOKED MILE (TF) Universal TV, 1969
ALIAS SMITH AND JONES (TF) Universal TV, 1971
COOL MILLION (TF) Universal TV, 1972

GENE LEVITT*—continued

THE PHANTOM OF HOLLYWOOD MGM TV, 1974
SHE'LL BE SWEET (MS) Australian Broadcasting Commission/Trans-Atlantic Enterprises, 1979, Australian

EDMOND LEVY*

Home: 135 Central Park West, New York, NY 10023, 212/595-7666
Agent: Steve Weiss, William Morris Agency - Beverly Hills, 213/274-7451

MOM, THE WOLFMAN AND ME (TF) Time-Life Productions, 1981

RALPH LEVY*

Home: 206 McKenzie Street, Santa Fe, NM, 505/983-7545

BEDTIME STORY Universal, 1964
DO NOT DISTURB 20th Century-Fox, 1965

HERSCHELL GORDON LEWIS

LIVING VENUS Creative Services, 1960
THE ADVENTURES OF LUCKY PIERRE directed under the pseudonym of Lewis H. Gordon, 1961
DAUGHTER OF THE SUN directed under the pseudonym of Lewis H. Gordon, 1962
NATURE'S PLAYMATES directed under the pseudonym of Lewis H. Gordon, Dore Productions, 1962
BOIN-N-G directed under the pseudonym of Lewis H. Gordon, Box Office Spectaculars, 1963
BLOOD FEAST Box Office Spectaculars, 1963
GOLDILOCKS AND THE THREE BEARS *GOLDILOCKS' THREE CHICKS* directed under the pseudonym of Lewis H. Gordon, Dore Productions, 1963
BELL, BARE AND BEAUTIFUL directed under the pseudonym of Lewis H. Gordon, Griffith Productions, 1963
SCUM OF THE EARTH *DEVIL'S CAMERA* directed under the pseudonym of Lewis H. Gordon, Box Office Spectaculars, 1963
2000 MANIACS Box Office Spectaculars, 1964
MOONSHINE MOUNTAIN Herschell Gordon Lewis Productions, 1964
COLOR ME BLOOD RED Jacqueline Kay, Inc., 1965
MONSTER A GO-GO *TERROR AT HALFDAY* directed under the pseudonym of Sheldon Seymour, 1965
SIN, SUFFER AND REPENT director of additional scenes, 1965, British-U.S.
JIMMY, THE BOY WONDER Mayflower Pictures, 1966
ALLEY TRAMP directed under the pseudonym of Armand Parys, United Picture Organization, 1966
AN EYE FOR AN EYE Creative Film Enterprises, 1966
SANTA CLAUS VISITS THE LAND OF MOTHER GOOSE 1967
SUBURBAN ROULETTE Argent Film Productions, 1967
SOMETHING WEIRD Mayflower Pictures, 1967
A TASTE OF BLOOD Creative Film Enterprises, 1967
THE GRUESOME TWOSOME Mayflower Pictures, 1967
THE GIRL, THE BODY, AND THE PILL Creative Film Enterprises, 1967
BLAST-OFF GIRLS Creative Film Enterprises, 1967
THE ECSTASIES OF WOMEN directed under the pseudodym of Mark Hansen, United Pictures Organization, 1969
LINDA AND ABILENE directed under the pseudonym of Mark Hansen, United Pictures Organization, 1969
MISS NYMPHET'S ZAP-IN directed under the pseudonym of Sheldon Seymour, Mayflower Pictures, 1970
THE WIZARD OF GORE Mayflower Pictures, 1970
THIS STUFF'LL KILL YA! Ultima Productions, 1971
YEAR OF THE YAHOO! International Arts Corporation, 1972
BLACK LOVE directed under the pseudonym of R.L. Smith, Lewis Motion Picture Enterprises, 1972
THE GORE-GORE GIRLS Lewis Motion Picture Enterprises, 1972

J E R R Y   L E W I S *

(Joseph Levitch)

b. March 16, 1926 - Newark, New Jersey
Business: Jerry Lewis Films, Inc., 1888 Century Park East - Suite 830, Los Angeles, CA 90067, 213/552-2200
Agent: William Morris Agency - Beverly Hills, 213/274-7451

THE BELLBOY Paramount, 1960
THE LADIES' MAN Paramount, 1961
THE ERRAND BOY Paramount, 1962
THE NUTTY PROFESSOR Paramount, 1963
THE PATSY Paramount, 1964
THE FAMILY JEWELS Paramount, 1965
THREE ON A COUCH Columbia, 1966
THE BIG MOUTH Columbia, 1967
ONE MORE TIME United Artists, 1970, British
WHICH WAY TO THE FRONT? Warner Bros., 1970
HARDLY WORKING 20th Century-Fox, 1981
SMORGASBORD Warner Bros., 1983

R O B E R T   M .   L E W I S *

Agent: Triad Artists, Inc. - Los Angeles, 213/556-2727
Business Manager: Frank Rohner - Los Angeles, 213/274-6182

THE ASTRONAUT (TF) Universal TV, 1972
THE ALPHA CAPER (TF) Universal TV, 1973
MONEY TO BURN (TF) Universal TV, 1973
MESSAGE TO MY DAUGHTER (TF) Metromedia Productions, 1973
PRAY FOR THE WILDCATS (TF) ABC Circle Films, 1974
THE DAY THE EARTH MOVED (TF) ABC Circle Films, 1975
THE INVISIBLE MAN (TF) Universal TV, 1975
GUILTY OR INNOCENT: THE SAM SHEPPARD MURDER CASE (TF) Universal TV, 1975
NO ROOM TO RUN (TF) Australian Broadcasting Commission/Trans-Atlantic Enterprises, 1977, Australian
THE NIGHT THEY TOOK MISS BEAUTIFUL (TF) Don Kirshner Productions, 1977
RING OF PASSION (TF) 20th Century-Fox TV, 1980
S*H*E* (TF) Martin Bregman Productions, 1980
IF THINGS WERE DIFFERENT (TF) Bob Banner Associates, 1980
ESCAPE (TF) Henry Jaffe Enterprises, 1980
A PRIVATE BATTLE (TF) Procter & Gamble Productions/Robert Halmi Productions, 1980
FALLEN ANGEL (TF) Green-Epstein Productions/Columbia TV, 1981
THE MIRACLE OF KATHY MILLER (TF) Rothman-Wohl Productions/Universal TV, 1981
CHILD BRIDE OF SHORT CREEK (TF) Lawrence Schiller-Paul Monash Productions, 1981
DESPERATE LIVES (TF) Fellows-Keegan Company/Lorimar Productions, 1982
BETWEEN TWO BROTHERS (TF) Turman-Foster Company/Finnegan Associates, 1982
COMPUTERCIDE (TF) Anthony Wilson Productions, 1982
SUMMER GIRL (TF) Bruce Lansbury Productions/Roberta Haynes Productions/ Finnegan Associates, 1983
AGATHA CHRISTIE'S 'A CARIBBEAN MYSTERY' (TF) Stan Margulies Productions/Warner Bros. TV, 1983
AGATHA CHRISTIE'S 'SPARKLING CYANIDE' (TF) Stan Margulies Productions/Warner Bros. TV, 1983
FLIGHT 90: DISASTER ON THE POTOMAC (TF) Sheldon Pinchuk Productions/Finnegan Associates, 1984
CITY KILLER (TF) Stan Shpetner Productions, 1984

J E F F   L I E B E R M A N *

Agent: William Morris Agency - Beverly Hills, 213/274-7451

SQUIRM American International, 1976
BLUE SUNSHINE Cinema Shares International, 1979
DOCTOR FRANKEN (TF) co-director with Marvin Chomsky, Titus Productions/ Janus Productions, 1980
JUST BEFORE DAWN Picturmedia Limited, 1981

ROBERT LIEBERMAN*

Business: Harmony Pictures, 2242 Cahuenga Blvd., Los Angeles, CA 90068, 213/462-2121
Agent: Tom Chasin, ICM - Los Angeles, 213/550-4000

FIGHTING BACK (TF) MTM Enterprises, 1980
WILL: G. GORDON LIDDY (TF) A. Shane Company, 1982
TABLE FOR FIVE Warner Bros., 1983

PETER LILIENTHAL

Contact: German Film & TV Academy, Pommernallee 1, 1000 Berlin 19, West Germany, 030/303-6212

LA VICTORIA (FD) 1973, West German
ER HERRSCHT RUHE IM LAND Filmverlag Der Autoren, 1976, West German
DAVID Kino International, 1979, West German
THE UPRISING Kino International, 1981, El Salvador
DEAR MR. WONDERFUL Joachim von Vietinghoff Produktion/Westdeutscher Rundfunk/Sender Freis Berlin, 1982, West German
THE AUTOGRAPH Cine-International, 1984, West German-French

MICHAEL LINDSAY-HOGG*

b. May 5, 1940 - New York, New York
Contact: Directors Guild of America - Los Angeles, 213/656-1220

LET IT BE (FD) United Artists, 1970, British
NASTY HABITS Brut Productions, 1977, British
BRIDESHEAD REVISITED (MS) ☆ co-director with Charles Sturridge, Granada TV/WNET-13/NDR Hamburg, 1982, British-U.S.-West German
DOCTOR FISCHER OF GENEVA (TF) Consolidated Productions/BBC, 1984, British

ART LINSON*

b. Chicago, Illinois
Contact: Directors Guild of America - Los Angeles, 213/656-1220

WHERE THE BUFFALO ROAM Universal, 1980
THE WILD LIFE Universal, 1984

AARON LIPSTADT

Business: California SHO Films, Ltd., 8961 Sunset Blvd., Los Angeles, CA 90069, 213/276-6668

ANDROID Island Alive/New Realm, 1982
CITY LIMITS ShoFilms/Videoform Pictures, 1984

STEVEN LISBERGER*

b. April 1951 - Rye, New York
Agent: Jeff Berg, ICM - Los Angeles, 213/550-4205

ANIMALYMPICS Lisberger Studios, 1980 (AF)
TRON Buena Vista, 1982

DWIGHT LITTLE

KGB - THE SECRET WAR Spartan Distribution, 1984

LYNNE LITTMAN*

Home: 6620 Cahuenga Terrace, Los Angeles, CA 90068
Business: LDL Films, Inc., 8489 West Third Street, Los Angeles, CA 90048, 213/658-5177
Agent: Joan Hyler, William Morris Agency - Beverly Hills, 213/274-7451

TESTAMENT Paramount, 1983

CARLO LIZZANI

b. April 3, 1917 - Rome, Italy
Contact: Ministry of Tourism & Education, Via Della Ferratella, No. 51, 00184 Rome, Italy, 06/7732

ACHTUNG! BANDITI! Cooperativa Spettori Produtti Cinematografici, 1951, Italian
AI MARGINI DELLA METROPOLI Elios Film, 1953, Italian
LOVE IN THE CITY co-director, Italian Films Export, 1953
CRONACHE DI POVERI AMANTI Cooperative Spettori Produtti Cinematografici, 1954, Italian
LO SVITATO Galatea/ENIC, 1956, Italian
BEHIND THE GREAT WALL *LA MURAGLIA CINESE (FD)* Continental, 1958, Italian
ESTERINA Italia Prod. Film, 1959, Italian
IL GOBBO Dino De Laurentiis Cinematografica, 1960, Italian
IL CARABINIERE A CAVALLO Maxima Film, 1961, Italian
IL PROCESSO DI VERONA Duilio Cinematografica/Dino De Laurentiis Cinematografica, 1963, Italian
LA VITA AGRA Film Napoleon, 1964, Italian
AMORI PERICLOSI co-director with Giulio Questi & Alfredo Giannetti, Zebra Film/Fulco Film/Aera Film, 1964, Italian-French
LA CELESTINA P... R... Aston Film, 1965, Italian
THE DIRTY GAME *GUERRE SECRETE* co-director with Terence Young, Christian-Jaque & Werner Klinger, American International, 1966, French-Italian-West German
THRILLING co-director with Ettore Scola & Gian Luigi Polidori, Dino De Laurentiis Cinematografica, 1965, Italian
SVEGLIATI E UCCIDI Sanson Film/Castoro Film, 1966, Italian
THE HILLS RUN RED *UN FIUME DI DOLLARI* directed under pseudonym of Lee W. Beaver, United Artists, 1966, Italian
REQUIESCANT Castoro Film, 1967, Italian
THE VIOLENT FOUR *BANDITI A MILANO* Paramount, 1968, Italian
L'AMANTE DI GRAMIGNA Dino De Laurentiis Cinematografica, 1969, Italian
AMORE E RABBIA co-director with Bernardo Bertolucci, Pier Paolo Pasolini, Jean-Luc Godard & Marco Bellocchio, Castoro Film, 1969, Italian
BARBAGIA Dino De Laurentiis Cinematografica, 1969, Italian
ROMA BENE Castoro Film, 1971, Italian
TONINO NERA Dino De Laurentiis Cinematografica, 1972, Italian
CRAZY JOE Columbia, 1974, Italian-U.S.
THE LAST FOUR DAYS *MUSSOLINI - ULTIMO ATTO* Group 1, 1974, Italian
UOMINI MERCE 1976, Italian
SAN BABILA ORE 20: UN DELITTO INUTILE Agora, 1976, Italian
KLEINHOFF HOTEL Capitol, 1977, Italian
FONTAMARA Sacis, 1980, Italian
CASA DEL TAPPETO GIALLO Gaumont, 1983, Italian
ROME: THE IMAGE OF A CITY (FD) Transworld Film, 1983, Italian
NUCLEO ZERO Diamant Film/RAI, 1984, Italian

KENNETH LOACH

b. June 17, 1936 - Nuneaton, Warwickshire, England
Agent: Goodwin Associates, 19 London Street, London W2, England, 01/402-9137

POOR COW National General, 1968, British
KES United Artists, 1970, British
WEDNESDAY'S CHILD *FAMILY LIFE* Cinema 5, 1972, British
BLACK JACK Boyd's Company, 1979, British
THE GAMEKEEPER ATV, 1980, British
LOOKS AND SMILES Black Lion Films/Kestrel Films/MK2, 1981, British-French

TONY LO BIANCO*

b. New York, New York
Messages: 818/854-4240
Agent: Triad Artists, Inc. - Los Angeles, 213/556-2727

TOO SCARED TO SCREAM The Movie Store, 1984

JOSHUA LOGAN

b. October 5, 1908 - Texarkana, Texas
Business: 435 East 52nd Street, New York, NY 10022, 212/PL. 2-1910

I MET MY LOVE AGAIN co-director with Arthur Ripley, United Artists, 1938
PICNIC ★ Columbia, 1956
BUS STOP 20th Century-Fox, 1956
SAYONARA ★ Warner Bros., 1957
SOUTH PACIFIC Magna, 1958
TALL STORY Warner Bros., 1960
FANNY Warner Bros., 1961
ENSIGN PULVER Warner Bros., 1964
CAMELOT Warner Bros., 1967
PAINT YOUR WAGON Paramount, 1969

LOUIS LOMBARDO*

Home: 5455 Longridge Avenue, Van Nuys, CA 91401, 818/902-0422
Agent: Tony Ludwig, CAA - Los Angeles, 213/277-4545

RUSSIAN ROULETTE Avco Embassy, 1975, U.S.-Canadian

ULLI LOMMEL

b. West Germany
Business: New West Films, 1757 N. Curson Avenue, Hollywood, CA 90046, 213/876-1511
Publicity: Cassidy-Watson Associates, 1717 Vine Street, Hollywood, CA, 213/462-1739

TENDERNESS OF THE WOLVES Monument, 1973, West German
DER MANN VON OBERZALZBERG - ADOLF UND MARLENE Albatros Produktion/Trio Film, 1976, West German
BLANK GENERATION International Harmony, 1979, West German
COCAINE COWBOYS International Harmony, 1979, West German
THE BOOGEY MAN Jerry Gross Organization, 1980
A TASTE OF SIN Ambassador, 1983
BRAINWAVES MPM, 1983
THE DEVONSVILLE TERROR MPM, 1983
STRANGERS IN PARADISE New West, 1984

RICHARD LONCRAINE

b. October 20, 1946 - Cheltenham, England
Agent: Linda Seifert Associates, 8A Brunswick Gardens, London W8 4AJ, England, 01/229-5163

FLAME Goodtime Enterprises, 1975, British
THE HAUNTING OF JULIA *FULL CIRCLE* Discovery Films, 1977, British-Canadian
BLADE ON THE FEATHER (TF) London Weekend TV, 1980, British
BRIMSTONE AND TREACLE United Artists Classics, 1982, British
THE MISSIONARY Columbia, 1982, British

JERRY LONDON*

b. September 21, 1937 - Los Angeles, California
Business: London Films, c/o Finnegan Associates, 4225 Coldwater Canyon Blvd., Studio City, CA 91604, 818/985-0430
Agent: Bruce Vinokour, CAA - Los Angeles, 213/277-4545

KILLDOZER (TF) Universal TV, 1974
McNAUGHTON'S DAUGHTER (TF) Universal TV, 1976
COVER GIRLS (TF) Columbia TV, 1977
ARTHUR HAILEY'S WHEELS (MS) Universal TV, 1978
EVENING IN BYZANTIUM (TF) Universal TV, 1978
WOMEN IN WHITE (MS) NBC, 1979
SWAN SONG (TF) Renee Valente Productions/Topanga Services Ltd./20th Century-Fox TV, 1980
SHOGUN (MS) ★ Paramount TV/NBC Entertainment, 1980, U.S.-Japanese
FATHER FIGURE (TF) Finnegan Associates/Time-Life Productions, 1980
THE CHICAGO STORY (TF) Eric Bercovici Productions/MGM TV, 1981
THE ORDEAL OF BILL CARNEY (TF) Belle Company/Comworld Productions, 1981
THE GIFT OF LIFE (TF) CBS Entertainment, 1982
THE SCARLET AND THE BLACK (TF) Bill McCutchen Productions/ITC/RAI, 1983, U.S.-Italian
ARTHUR HAILEY'S HOTEL (TF) Aaron Spelling Productions, 1983
CHIEFS (MS) Highgate Pictures, 1983
ELLIS ISLAND (MS) Pantheon Pictures/Telepictures Productions, 1984, U.S.-British

JACK LORD*

(John Joseph Ryan)

b. December 30, 1928 - New York, New York
Home: 4999 Kahala Avenue, Honolulu, Hawaii 96816, 808/737-6060
Business: Lord & Lady Enterprises, Honolulu, Hawaii 96816, 808/734-8383
Business Manager: J. William Hayes, Executive Business Management, Inc., 132 S. Rodeo Drive, Beverly Hills, CA 90212, 213/858-2000

M STATION: HAWAII (TF) Lord & Lady Enterprises, 1980

EMIL LOTEANU

b. November 6, 1936 - Bukovina, U.S.S.R.
Contact: State Committee of Cinematography of the U.S.S.R., Council of Ministers, 7 Maly Gnesdikovsky Pereulok, Moscow, U.S.S.R., 7 095/229-9912

WAIT FOR US AT DAWN Moldovafilm, 1963, Soviet
RED MEADOWS Moldovafilm, 1966, Soviet
FRESCOS ON THE WHITE Moldovafilm, 1968, Soviet
THIS INSTANT Moldovafilm, 1969, Soviet
LAUTARY Moldovafilm, 1972, Soviet
MY WHITE CITY Moldovafilm, 1973, Soviet
INTO THE SUNSET Mosfilm, 1976, Soviet
THE SHOOTING PARTY Mosfilm, 1978, Soviet
ANNA PAVLOVA: A WOMAN FOR ALL TIME Cinema Development Corporation, 1985, Soviet-British-French

CHARLIE LOVENTHAL

THE FIRST TIME New Line Cinema, 1983

BERT LOVITT

PRINCE JACK LMF Productions, 1984

DICK LOWRY*

Home: 704 N. Gardner Avenue - Suite 5, Los Angeles, CA 90046, 213/653-6115
Agent: ICM - Los Angeles, 213/550-4000

OHMS (TF) Grant-Case-McGrath Enterprises, 1980
KENNY ROGERS AS THE GAMBLER (TF) Kragen & Co., 1980
THE JAYNE MANSFIELD STORY (TF) Alan Landsburg Productions, 1980
ANGEL DUSTED (TF) NRW Features, 1981
COWARD OF THE COUNTY (TF) Kraco Productions, 1981
A FEW DAYS IN WEASEL CREEK (TF) Hummingbird Productions/Warner Bros., 1981
RASCALS AND ROBBERS: THE SECRET ADVENTURES OF TOM SAWYER AND HUCKLEBERRY FINN (TF) CBS Entertainment, 1982
MISSING CHILDREN: A MOTHER'S STORY (TF) Kayden-Gleason Productions, 1982
LIVING PROOF: THE HANK WILLIAMS, JR. STORY (TF) Procter & Gamble Productions/Telecom Entertainment/Melpomene Productions, 1983
SMOKEY AND THE BANDIT PART 3 Universal, 1983
KENNY ROGERS AS THE GAMBLER - THE ADVENTURE CONTINUES (TF) Lion Share Productions, 1983
OFF SIDES (TF) Ten-Four Productions, 1984, filmed in 1980
WET GOLD (TF) Telepictures Productions, 1984
THE TOUGHEST MAN IN THE WORLD (TF) Guber-Peters Productions/ Centerpoint Productions, 1984

DAVID R. LOXTON*

Home: 935 Park Avenue, New York, NY 10028, 212/249-0538
Business: Television Laboratory, WNET-13, 356 West 58th Street, New York, NY 10019, 212/560-3192

THE PHANTOM OF THE OPEN HEARTH (TF) co-director with Fred Barzyk, WNET-13 Television Laboratory/WGBH New Television Workshop, 1976
CHARLIE SMITH AND THE FRITTER TREE (TF) co-director with Fred Barzyk, WNET-13 Television Laboratory/WGBH New Television Workshop, 1978
THE LATHE OF HEAVEN (TF) co-director with Fred Barzyk, WNET-13 Television Laboratory/Taurus Film, 1980

NANNI LOY

b. October 23, 1925 - Cagliari, Sardinia, Italy
Contact: Ministry of Tourism & Education, Via Della Ferratella, No. 51, 00184 Rome, Italy, 06/7732

PAROLA DI LADRO co-director with Gianni Puccini, Panal Film, 1957, Italian
IL MARITO co-director with Gianni Puccini, Fortuna Film/Chamartin, 1957, Italian-Spanish
AUDACE COLPO DEI SOLITI IGNOTI Titanus/Videss/SGC, 1959, Italian
UN GIORNO DA LEONI Lux Film/Vides/Galatea, 1961, Italian
THE FOUR DAYS OF NAPLES MGM, 1962, Italian
MADE IN ITALY Royal Films International, 1965, Italian-French
IL PADRE DI FAMILIGLIA Ultra/CFC/Marianne Productions, 1967, Italian-French
L'INFERNO DEL DESERTO 1969, Italian
ROSOLINO PATERNO SOLDATO Dino De Laurentiis Cinematografica, 1970, Italian
WHY *DETENUTO IN ATTESTA DI GUIDIZIO* Documento Film, 1971, Italian
SISTEMO L'AMERICA E TORNO Documento Film, 1973, Italian
LA GODURIA 1976, Italian
SIGNORE E SIGNORI BUONANOTTE co-director with Luigi Comencini, Luigi Magni, Mario Monicelli & Ettore Scola, Titanus, 1976, Italian
IL CAFFE E UN PIACERE...SE NON E BUONO CHE PLACERE E? 1978, Italian
INSIEME 1979, Italian
CAFE EXPRESS Summit Features, 1980, Italian
TESTA OR CROCE Filmauro, 1982, Italian
MI MANDA PICONE Italtoons/Wonder Movies, 1984, Italian

GEORGE LUCAS

b. January 14, 1944 - Modesto, California
Business: Lucasfilm Ltd., P.O. Box 668, San Anselmo, CA 94960

THX 1138 Warner Bros., 1971
AMERICAN GRAFFITI ★ Universal, 1973
STAR WARS ★ 20th Century-Fox, 1977

SIDNEY LUMET*

b. June 25, 1924 - Philadelphia, Pennsylvania
Agent: Sue Mengers, ICM - Los Angeles, 213/550-4264

TWELVE ANGRY MEN ★ United Artists, 1957
STAGE STRUCK RKO Radio, 1958
THAT KIND OF WOMAN Paramount, 1959
THE FUGITIVE KIND United Artists, 1960
A VIEW FROM THE BRIDGE Allied Artists, 1961, French-Italian
LONG DAY'S JOURNEY INTO NIGHT Embassy, 1962
FAIL SAFE Columbia, 1964
THE PAWNBROKER Landau/Allied Artists, 1965
THE HILL MGM, 1965, British
THE GROUP United Artists, 1965
THE DEADLY AFFAIR Columbia, 1967, British
BYE BYE BRAVERMAN Warner Bros., 1968
THE SEA GULL Warner Bros., 1968, British
THE APPOINTMENT MGM, 1969
LAST OF THE MOBILE HOT-SHOTS Warner Bros., 1970
KING: A FILMED RECORD...MONTGOMERY TO MEMPHIS (FED)
co-director with Joseph L. Mankiewicz, Maron Films Limited, 1970
THE ANDERSON TAPES Columbia, 1971
CHILD'S PLAY Paramount, 1972
THE OFFENSE United Artists, 1973, British
SERPICO Paramount, 1973
LOVIN' MOLLY Columbia, 1974
MURDER ON THE ORIENT EXPRESS Paramount, 1974, British
DOG DAY AFTERNOON ★ Warner Bros., 1975
NETWORK ★ MGM/United Artists, 1976
EQUUS United Artists, 1977, British
THE WIZ Universal, 1978
JUST TELL ME WHAT YOU WANT Columbia, 1980
PRINCE OF THE CITY Orion/Warner Bros., 1981
DEATHTRAP Warner Bros., 1982
THE VERDICT ★ 20th Century-Fox, 1982
DANIEL Paramount, 1983
GARBO TALKS MGM/UA, 1984

IDA LUPINO*

b. February 4, 1918 - London, England
Business Manager: David Martin, 205 S. Beverly Drive - Suite 214, Beverly Hills, CA 90212, 213/276-7071

OUTRAGE RKO Radio, 1950
HARD, FAST AND BEAUTIFUL RKO Radio, 1951
THE HITCH-HIKER RKO Radio, 1953
THE BIGAMIST Filmmakers, 1953
THE TROUBLE WITH ANGELS Columbia, 1966

TONY LURASCHI

THE OUTSIDER Paramount, 1980, U.S.-Irish

STEVEN LUSTGARDEN

b. August 1, 1951
Home: 404 N. Sierra Bonita, Apt. 203, Los Angeles, CA 90036, 213/655-0376

AMERICAN TABOO Motion Pictures International, 1983

WILLIAM LUSTIG

b. February 1, 1955 - Bronx, New York
Business: Magnum Motion Pictures, 45 West 60th Street, Suite 32E, New York, NY 10023, 212/582-3041
Attorney: Marc Chamlin, Phillips, Nizer, Benjamin, Krim & Ballon, 40 West 57th Street, New York, NY 10019, 212/977-9700

THE VIOLATION OF CLAUDIA Lustig Productions, 1977
MANIAC Analysis, 1981
VIGILANTE Artists Releasing Corporation/Film Ventures International, 1983

DAVID LYNCH*

Agent: Rick Nicita, CAA - Los Angeles, 213/277-4545

ERASERHEAD Libra, 1978
THE ELEPHANT MAN ★ Paramount, 1980, British-U.S.
DUNE Universal, 1984

PAUL LYNCH*

b. November 6, 1946
Business: Questcan, Inc., c/o Stan Nugit, 1460 Fourth Street, Santa Monica, CA 90401, 213/394-6996
Agent: David Gersh, The Gersh Agency - Beverly Hills, 213/274-6611
Attorney: Bruce Singman - Los Angeles, 213/276-2397

THE HARD PART BEGINS Cinepix, 1974, Canadian
BLOOD AND GUTS Ambassador, 1978, Canadian
PROM NIGHT Avco Embassy, 1980, Canadian
HUMONGOUS Avco Embassy, 1982, Canadian
CROSS-COUNTRY New World, 1983, Canadian
FLYING Brightstar Films, 1985, Canadian

ADRIAN LYNE*

Business Manager: Paul Esposito, Jennie & Co., 127 West 79th Street, New York, NY 10024, 212/595-5200

FOXES United Artists, 1980
FLASHDANCE Paramount, 1983
9½ WEEKS MGM/UA, 1985

M

ALEXANDER MACKENDRICK

b. 1912 - Boston, Massachusetts

TIGHT LITTLE ISLAND *WHISKEY GALORE!* Rank, 1949, British
THE MAN IN THE WHITE SUIT Rank, 1951, British
CRASH OF SILENCE *MANDY* Universal, 1952, British

ALEXANDER MACKENDRICK —continued

HIGH AND DRY *THE MAGGIE* Universal, 1954, British
THE LADYKILLERS Continental, 1956, British
SWEET SMELL OF SUCCESS United Artists, 1957
A BOY TEN FEET TALL *SAMMY GOING SOUTH* Paramount, 1963, British
A HIGH WIND IN JAMAICA 20th Century-Fox, 1965, British
DON'T MAKE WAVES MGM, 1967

JOHN MACKENZIE

b. Scotland
Home: 7 Clifton Hill, London NW8, England, 01/624-4233
Agent: Merrily Kane Agency - Beverly Hills, 213/550-8874

UNMAN, WITTERING & ZIGO Paramount, 1971, British
ONE BRIEF SUMMER Cinevision, 1972, British
MADE International Co-productions, 1975, British
A SENSE OF FREEDOM (TF) J. Isaacs Productions/STV, 1979, British
THE LONG GOOD FRIDAY Embassy, 1982, British
BEYOND THE LIMIT *THE HONORARY CONSUL* Paramount, 1983, British
THE AURA TVS Ltd./Tempest Films, 1985, British

LEE MADDEN*

Home: 16918 Marquez Avenue, Pacific Palisades, CA 90272, 213/454-6255

HELL'S ANGELS '69 American International, 1969
ANGEL UNCHAINED American International, 1970
THE MANHANDLERS Premiere, 1975
THE NIGHT GOD SCREAMED Cinemation, 1973
OUT OF THE DARKNESS *NIGHT CREATURES* Dimension, 1978
BENNY AND BUFORD Enfoque Films, 1984, Mexican

ALBERT MAGNOLI

PURPLE RAIN Warner Bros., 1984

DEZSO MAGYAR*

Home: 1539 Calmar Court, Los Angeles, CA 90024, 213/277-0537
Agent: John Ptak/David Schiff, William Morris Agency - Beverly Hills, 213/859-4346

RAPPACINI'S DAUGHTER (TF) Learning in Focus, 1980
SUMMER (TF) Cinelit Productions/WNET-13, 1981
KING OF AMERICA (TF) Center for Television in the Humanities, 1982

NORMAN MAILER

b. January 31, 1923 - Long Branch, New Jersey

WILD 90 Supreme Mix, 1968
BEYOND THE LAW Grove Press, 1968
MAIDSTONE Supreme Mix, 1971

DUSAN MAKAVEJEV

b. October 13, 1932 - Belgrade, Yugoslavia

MAN IS NOT A BIRD Grove Press, 1965, Yugoslavian
LOVE AFFAIR; OR THE CASE OF THE MISSING SWITCHBOARD OPERATOR Brandon, 1966, Yugoslavian
INNOCENCE UNPROTECTED Grove Press, 1968, Yugoslavian
WR - MYSTERIES OF THE ORGANISM Cinema 5, 1971, Yugoslavian
SWEET MOVIE Biograph, 1975, French-Canadian-West German
MONTENEGRO *MONTENEGRO, OR PIGS AND PEARLS* Atlantic Releasing Corporation, 1981, Swedish
THE COCA COLA KID Cinema Enterprises, 1985, Australian

TERRENCE MALICK*

b. October 30, 1944 - Waco, Texas
Agent: Ziegler, Diskant, Inc. - Los Angeles, 213/278-0070

BADLANDS Warner Bros., 1974
DAYS OF HEAVEN Paramount, 1978

LOUIS MALLE*

b. October 30, 1932 - Thumeries, France
Agent: Sam Cohn, ICM - New York City, 212/556-5600

FONTAINE DE VAUCLUSE 1953, French
STATION 307 1955, French
THE SILENT WORLD (FD) co-director with Jacques-Yves Cousteau, Columbia, 1956, French
FRANTIC *ASCENSEUR POUR L'ECHAFAUD* Times, 1957, French
THE LOVERS Zenith International, 1958, French
ZAZIE *ZAZIE DANS LE METRO* Astor, 1960, French
A VERY PRIVATE AFFAIR MGM, 1962, French-Italian
THE FIRE WITHIN Governor, 1963, French
VIVA MARIA! United Artists, 1965, French-Italian
THE THIEF OF PARIS *LE VOLEUR* Lopert, 1967, French-Italian
SPIRITS OF THE DEAD *HISTOIRES EXTRAORDINAIRES* co-director with Federico Fellini & Roger Vadim, American International, 1969, French-Italian
CALCUTTA (FD) 1969, French
PHANTOM INDIA (TD) Olympic, 1969, French
MURMUR OF THE HEART *LE SOUFFLE AU COEUR* Palomar, 1971, French
HUMAIN, TROP HUMAIN (FD) New Yorker, 1972, French
PLACE DE LA REPUBLIQUE (FD) NEF Diffusion, 1974, French
LACOMBE LUCIEN 20th Century-Fox, 1974, French-Italian-West German
BLACK MOON 20th Century-Fox, 1975, French
PRETTY BABY Paramount, 1978
ATLANTIC CITY ★ Paramount, 1981, Canadian-French
MY DINNER WITH ANDRE New Yorker, 1981
CRACKERS Universal, 1984
ALAMO BAY Tri-Star, 1985

BRUCE MALMUTH*

b. February 4, 1934 - New York, New York
Business: Soularview Productions, Inc., 9981 Robbins Drive, Beverly Hills, CA 90212, 213/277-4555

FORE PLAY co-director with John G. Avildsen & Robert McCarty, Cinema National, 1975
NIGHTHAWKS Universal, 1981
THE MAN WHO WASN'T THERE Paramount, 1983
WHERE ARE THE CHILDREN? Zev Braun Pictures, 1985

WILLIAM MALONE

SCARED TO DEATH Lone Star, 1982
TITAN FIND Comworld, 1985

ROUBEN MAMOULIAN*

b. October 8, 1897 - Tiflis, Georgia, Russia
Home: 1112 Schuyler Road, Beverly Hills, CA 90210

APPLAUSE Paramount, 1929
CITY STREETS Paramount, 1931
DR. JEKYLL AND MR. HYDE Paramount, 1932
LOVE ME TONIGHT Paramount, 1932
SONG OF SONGS Paramount, 1933
QUEEN CHRISTINA MGM, 1933
WE LIVE AGAIN United Artists, 1934
BECKY SHARP RKO Radio, 1935
THE GAY DESPERADO United Artists, 1936

ROUBEN MAMOULIAN*—continued

HIGH, WIDE, AND HANDSOME Paramount, 1937
GOLDEN BOY Columbia, 1939
THE MARK OF ZORRO 20th Century-Fox, 1940
BLOOD AND SAND 20th Century-Fox, 1941
RINGS ON HER FINGERS 20th Century-Fox, 1942
SUMMER HOLIDAY MGM, 1948
SILK STOCKINGS MGM, 1957

ROBERT MANDEL*

Agent: Jack Rapke, CAA - Los Angeles, 213/277-4545

INDEPENDENCE DAY Warner Bros., 1983
THE HAND ME DOWN KID (TF) Highgate Pictures, 1983
TOUCH AND GO Universal, 1985

JOSEPH MANDUKE*

Agent: Jerry Adler, Lew Weitzman & Associates - Sherman Oaks, 818/995-4400

JUMP Cannon, 1971
CORNBREAD, EARL AND ME American International, 1975
KID VENGEANCE Irwin Yablans, 1977, U.S.-Israeli
BEATLEMANIA American Cinema, 1981

FRANCIS MANKIEWICZ

Contact: Association des Realisateurs, 1406 Beaudry Street, Montreal, Quebec H2L 4K4, Canada, 514/843-7770

LE TEMPS D'UNE CHASSE Cinepix, 1973, Canadian
LES BONS DEBARRAS—GOOD RIDDANCE IFEX Film, 1981, Canadian
LES BEAUX SOUVENIRS National Film Board of Canada, 1982, Canadian

JOSEPH L. MANKIEWICZ*

b. February 11, 1909 - Wilkes-Barre, Pennsylvania
Agent: Ben Benjamin, William Morris Agency - New York City, 212/556-5652
Business Manager: Arthur B. Greene, 666 Fifth Avenue, New York, NY 10103, 212/246-1900

DRAGONWYCK 20th Century-Fox, 1946
SOMEWHERE IN THE NIGHT 20th Century-Fox, 1946
THE LATE GEORGE APLEY 20th Century-Fox, 1947
THE GHOST AND MRS. MUIR 20th Century-Fox, 1947
ESCAPE 20th Century-Fox, 1948
A LETTER TO THREE WIVES ★★ 20th Century-Fox, 1949
HOUSE OF STRANGERS 20th Century-Fox, 1949
NO WAY OUT 20th Century-Fox, 1950
ALL ABOUT EVE ★★ 20th Century-Fox, 1950
PEOPLE WILL TALK 20th Century-Fox, 1951
FIVE FINGERS ★ 20th Century-Fox, 1952
JULIUS CAESAR MGM, 1953
THE BAREFOOT CONTESSA United Artists, 1954, U.S.-Italian
GUYS AND DOLLS MGM, 1955
THE QUIET AMERICAN United Artists, 1958
SUDDENLY LAST SUMMER Columbia, 1960
CLEOPATRA 20th Century-Fox, 1963
THE HONEY POT United Artists, 1967, British-U.S.-Italian
THERE WAS A CROOKED MAN Warner Bros., 1970
KING: A FILMED RECORD...MONTGOMERY TO MEMPHIS (FD)
co-director with Sidney Lumet, Maron Films Limited, 1970
SLEUTH ★ 20th Century-Fox, 1972, British

TOM MANKIEWICZ*

b. June 1, 1942 - Los Angeles, California
Contact: Directors Guild of America - Los Angeles, 213/656-1220

HART TO HART (TF) Spelling-Goldberg Productions, 1979

ABBY MANN*

(Abraham Goodman)

b. 1927 - Philadelphia, Pennsylvania
Agent: Martin Baum, CAA - Los Angeles, 213/277-4545

KING (MS) ☆ Abby Mann Productions/Filmways, 1978

DANIEL MANN*

b. August 8, 1912 - New York, New York
Business Manager: The Berke Management Co. - Encino, 213/990-2631

COME BACK, LITTLE SHEBA Paramount, 1952
ABOUT MRS. LESLIE Paramount, 1954
THE ROSE TATTOO Paramount, 1955
I'LL CRY TOMORROW MGM, 1955
TEAHOUSE OF THE AUGUST MOON MGM, 1956
HOT SPELL Paramount, 1958
THE LAST ANGRY MAN Columbia, 1959
THE MOUNTAIN ROAD Columbia, 1960
BUTTERFIELD 8 MGM, 1960
ADA MGM, 1961
FIVE FINGER EXERCISE Columbia, 1962
WHO'S GOT THE ACTION? Paramount, 1962
WHO'S BEEN SLEEPING IN MY BED? Paramount, 1963
JUDITH Paramount, 1965, U.S.-British-Israeli
OUR MAN FLINT 20th Century-Fox, 1966
FOR LOVE OF IVY Cinerama Releasing Corporation, 1968
A DREAM OF KINGS National General, 1969
WILLARD Cinerama Releasing Corporation, 1971
THE REVENGERS National General, 1972, U.S.-Mexican
INTERVAL Avco Embassy, 1973, U.S.-Mexican
MAURIE *BIG MO* National General, 1973
LOST IN THE STARS American Film Theatre, 1974
JOURNEY INTO FEAR Stirling Gold, 1976, Canadian
HOW THE WEST WAS WON (MS) co-director with Burt Kennedy, MGM TV, 1977
MATILDA American International, 1978
PLAYING FOR TIME (TF) Syzygy Productions, 1980
THE DAY THE LOVING STOPPED (TF) Monash-Zeitman Productions, 1981

DELBERT MANN*

b. January 30, 1920 - Lawrence, Kansas
Agent: Leonard Hirshan, William Morris Agency - Beverly Hills, 213/274-7451

MARTY ★★ United Artists, 1965
THE BACHELOR PARTY United Artists, 1957
DESIRE UNDER THE ELMS Paramount, 1958
SEPARATE TABLES United Artists, 1959
MIDDLE OF THE NIGHT Columbia, 1959
THE DARK AT THE TOP OF THE STAIRS Warner Bros., 1960
THE OUTSIDER Universal, 1961
LOVER, COME BACK Universal, 1962
THAT TOUCH OF MINK Universal, 1962
A GATHERING OF EAGLES Universal, 1963
DEAR HEART Warner Bros., 1964
QUICK BEFORE IT MELTS MGM, 1965
MISTER BUDDWING MGM, 1966
FITZWILLY United Artists, 1967
HEIDI (TF) Omnibus Productions, 1968
THE PINK JUNGLE Universal, 1968
DAVID COPPERFIELD (TF) Omnibus Productions/Sagittarius Productions, 1970, British-U.S.

DELBERT MANN*—continued

KIDNAPPED American International, 1971, British
JANE EYRE (TF) Omnibus Productions/Sagittarius Productions, 1971, British-U.S.
SHE WAITS (TF) Metromedia Productions, 1972
NO PLACE TO RUN (TF) ABC Circle Films, 1972
THE MAN WITHOUT A COUNTRY (TF) Norman Rosemont Productions, 1973
A GIRL NAMED SOONER (TF) Frederick Brogger Associates/20th Century-Fox TV, 1975
BIRCH INTERVAL Gamma III, 1976
FRANCIS GARY POWERS: THE TRUE STORY OF THE U-2 SPY INCIDENT (TF) Charles Fries Productions, 1976
TELL ME MY NAME (TF) Talent Associates, 1977
BREAKING UP (TF) ☆ Time-Life Productions, 1978
LOVE'S DARK RIDE (TF) Mark VII Ltd./Worldvision, 1978
HOME TO STAY (TF) Time-Life Productions, 1978
THOU SHALT NOT COMMIT ADULTERY (TF) Edgar J. Scherick Associates, 1978
TORN BETWEEN TWO LOVERS (TF) Alan Landsburg Productions, 1979
ALL QUIET ON THE WESTERN FRONT (TF) ☆ Norman Rosemont Productions/Marble Arch Productions, 1979
TO FIND MY SON (TF) Green-Epstein Productions/Columbia TV, 1980
NIGHT CROSSING Buena Vista, 1982
BRONTE Charlotte Ltd. Partnership/Radio Telefis Eireann, 1983, U.S.-Irish
THE GIFT OF LOVE: A CHRISTMAS STORY (TF) Telecom Entertainment/Amanda Productions, 1983
LOVE LEADS THE WAY (CTF) Hawkins-Permut Productions, 1984

MICHAEL MANN*

Agent: Jeff Berg, ICM - Los Angeles, 213/550-4000

THE JERICHO MILE (TF) ABC Circle Films, 1979
THIEF United Artists, 1981
THE KEEP Paramount, 1983

RON MANN

POETRY IN MOTION (FD) Sphinx, 1983, Canadian
LISTEN TO THE CITY Spectrafilm, 1984, Canadian

TERRY MARCEL

b. 1942 - Oxford, England
Address: 4 Gaston Bell Close, Richmond, Surrey, England, 940-3310
Agent: Dick Blodgett, ICM - London, 01/629-8080
Contact: Directors Guild of Great Britain, 56 Whitfield Street, London W1, England, 01/580-9592

THERE GOES THE BRIDGE Vanguard, 1980, British
HAWK THE SLAYER ITC, 1980, British
PRISONERS OF THE LOST UNIVERSE (CTF) Marcel-Robertson Productions/Showtime, 1983, British

ALEX MARCH*

Contact: Directors Guild of America - Los Angeles, 213/656-1220

THE DANGEROUS DAYS OF KIOWA JONES (TF) MGM TV, 1966
PAPER LION United Artists, 1968
THE BIG BOUNCE Warner Bros., 1969
FIREHOUSE (TF) Metromedia Productions/Stonehenge Productions, 1972
MASTERMIND Goldstone, 1977

STUART MARGOLIN*

b. January 31 - Davenport, Iowa
Home: P.O. Box 478, Ganges, British Columbia VOS 1EO, Canada, 604/537-2961
Agent: Lou Pitt, ICM - Los Angeles, 213/550-4000
Business Manager: Bash, Gesas & Co., 9401 Wilshire Blvd. - Suite 700, Beverly Hills, CA 90212, 213/278-7700

SUDDENLY, LOVE (TF) Ross Hunter Productions, 1978
A SHINING SEASON (TF) Green-Epstein Productions/T-M Productions/ Columbia TV, 1979
BRET MAVERICK (TF) Comanche Productions/Warner Bros. TV, 1981
THE LONG SUMMER OF GEORGE ADAMS (TF) Warner Bros. TV, 1982
THE GLITTER DOME (CTF) HBO Premiere Films/Telepictures Productions/ Trincomali Productions, 1984, U.S.-Canadian

HERB MARGOLIS

MILITARY UNIVERSITY co-director with Danford B. Greene, 20th Century Fox, 1985, U.S.-Yugoslavian

PETER MARKLE

THE PERSONALS New World, 1982
HOT DOG...THE MOVIE MGM/UA, 1984
YOUNGBLOOD MGM/UA, 1985

ROBERT MARKOWITZ*

Home: 3037 Franklin Canyon Drive, Beverly Hills, CA 90210, 213/559-3934
Agent: Martin Caan, William Morris Agency - Beverly Hills, 213/859-4271

THE STORYTELLER (TF) Universal TV, 1977
THE DEADLIEST SEASON (TF) Titus Productions, 1977
VOICES MGM/United Artists, 1979
THE WALL (TF) Cinetex International/Time-Life Productions, 1982, U.S.-Polish
A LONG WAY HOME (TF) Alan Landsburg Productions, 1981
PRAY TV (TF) ABC Circle Films, 1982
PHANTOM OF THE OPERA (TF) Robert Halmi Productions, 1983
MY MOTHER'S SECRET LIFE (TF) Furia-Oringer Productions/ABC Circle Films, 1984

ARTHUR MARKS*

b. August 2, 1927 - Los Angeles, California
Personal Business: Arm Service Company, Inc., Arthur Productions Inc., P.O. Box 1305 Woodland Hills, CA 91365

CLASS OF '74 General Film Corporation, 1972
BONNIE'S KIDS General Film Corporation, 1973
THE ROOM MATES General Film Corporation, 1973
DETROIT 9000 General Film Corporation, 1973
A WOMAN FOR ALL MEN General Film Corporation, 1975
BUCKTOWN American International, 1975
FRIDAY FOSTER American International, 1975
J.D.'S REVENGE American International, 1976
THE MONKEY HUSTLE American International, 1976

RICHARD MARQUAND

b. Wales
Agent: Michael Marcus, CAA - Los Angeles, 213/277-4545

THE SEARCH FOR THE NILE (MS) BBC/Time-Life Productions, 1972, British
THE LEGACY Universal, 1979
BIRTH OF THE BEATLES (TF) Dick Clark Productions, 1979, British-U.S.
EYE OF THE NEEDLE United Artists, 1981, U.S.-British
RETURN OF THE JEDI 20th Century-Fox, 1983
UNTIL SEPTEMBER MGM/UA, 1984

GARRY MARSHALL*

Agent: Joel Cohen - The Sy Fischer Company - Los Angeles, 213/557-0388
Business Manager: Alexander Grant & Co. - Beverly Hills, 213/658-5595

YOUNG DOCTORS IN LOVE 20th Century-Fox, 1982
THE FLAMINGO KID 20th Century Fox, 1984

CHARLES MARTIN*

b. 1916 - Newark, New Jersey
Home: 304 S. Elm Drive, Beverly Hills, CA 90212
Messages: 213/277-5843

NO LEAVE TO LOVE MGM, 1946
MY DEAR SECRETARY United Artists, 1948
DEATH OF A SCOUNDREL RKO Radio, 1956
IF HE HOLLERS, LET HIM GO Cinerama Releasing Corporation, 1968
HOW TO SEDUCE A WOMAN Cenerama Releasing Corporation, 1974
ONE MAN JURY Cal-Am Artists, 1978
DEAD ON ARRIVAL Cinerama Shares International, 1979

LESLIE H. MARTINSON*

b. Boston, Massachusetts
Home: 2288 Coldwater Canyon Blvd., Beverly Hills, CA 90210, 213/271-4127
Agent: Shapiro-Lichtman Agency - Los Angeles, 213/550-2244

THE ATOMIC KID Republic, 1954
HOT ROD GIRL American International, 1956
HOT ROD RUMBLE Allied Artists, 1957
LAD: A DOG co-director with Aram Avakian, Warner Bros, 1961
PT 109 Warner Bros,. 1963
BLACK GOLD Warner Bros., 1963
F.B.I. CODE 98 Warner Bros., 1964
FOR THOSE WHO THINK YOUNG United Artists, 1964
BATMAN 20th Century-Fox, 1966
FATHOM 20th Century-Fox, 1967
THE CHALLENGERS (TF) Universal TV, 1970
MRS. POLLIFAX - SPY United Artists, 1971
HOW TO STEAL AN AIRPLANE (TF) Universal TV, 1971
ESCAPE FROM ANGOLA Doty-Dayton, 1976
CRUISE MISSILE Eichberg Film/Cinelux-Romano Film/Mundial Film/Cine-Luce/ Noble Productions/FPDC, 1978, West German-Spanish-U.S.-Iranian
RESCUE FROM GILLIGAN'S ISLAND (TF) Sherwood Schwartz Productions, 1978
THE KID WITH THE BROKEN HALO (TF) Satellite Productions, 1982
THE KID WITH THE 200 I.Q. (TF) Guillaume-Margo Productions/Zephyr Productions, 1983
THE FANTASTIC WORLD OF D.C. COLLINS (TF) Guillaume-Margo Productions/Zephyr Productions, 1984

ANDREW MARTON*

(Endre Marton)

b. January 26, 1904 - Budapest, Hungary
Home: 8856 Appian Way, Los Angeles, CA 90046, 213/654-1297
Agent: Paul Kohner, Inc. - Los Angeles, 213/271-5165

GYPSY COLT MGM, 1954
PRISONER OF WAR MGM, 1954
MEN OF THE FIGHTING LADY MGM, 1954
GREEN FIRE MGM, 1955
SEVEN WONDERS OF THE WORLD co-director, Stanley Warner Cinema Corporation, 1956
UNDERWATER WARRIOR MGM, 1958
THE LONGEST DAY co-director with Ken Annakin & Bernhard Wicki, 20th Century-Fox, 1962
IT HAPPENED IN ATHENS 20th Century-Fox, 1962
THE THIN RED LINE Allied Artists, 1964
CRACK IN THE WORLD Paramount, 1965, British
CLARENCE, THE CROSS-EYED LION MGM, 1965

ANDREW MARTON*—continued

AROUND THE WORLD UNDER THE SEA MGM, 1966
BIRDS DO IT Columbia, 1966
AFRICA - TEXAS STYLE! Paramount, 1967, British-U.S.

PAUL MASLANSKY*

b. November 23, 1933 - New York, New York
Business Manager: Leah Lynn Broidy - Los Angeles, 213/474-2795

SUGAR HILL American International, 1974

QUENTIN MASTERS*

b. July 12, 1946 - Australia
Agent: Cameron's Management, 120 Victoria Street, Potts Point, NSW, 2011, Australia, 02/358-6433

THUMB TRIPPING Avco Embassy, 1973
THE STUD Trans-American, 1978, British
THE PSI FACTOR 1981, British
A DANGEROUS SUMMER Filmco Ltd., 1982, Australian
MIDNITE SPARES Filmco Australia, 1983, Australian

NICO MASTORAKIS

Agent: The Artists Group - Los Angeles, 213/552-1100

THE NEXT ONE Allstar Productions, 1982, British-Greek
BLIND DATE New Line Cinema, 1984, British-Greek
SKYHIGH Forminx Corporation/Omega Productions, 1985

ARMAND MASTROIANNI

HE KNOWS YOU'RE ALONE MGM/United Artists 1980
THE CLAIRVOYANT *THE KILLING HOUR* 20th Century-Fox, 1982
THE SUPERNATURAL Republic Entertainment/Sandy/Howard Productions, 1985

VIVIAN MATALON*

Agent: Clifford Stevens, STE Representation Ltd. - New York City, 212/246-1030

PRIVATE CONTENTMENT (TF) WNET-13/South Carolina Educational TV, 1982

WALTER MATTHAU
(Walter Matuschanskavasky)

b. October 1, 1920 - New York, New York
Agent: William Morris Agency - Beverly Hills, 213/274-7451

GANGSTER STORY RCIP-States Rights, 1960

BURNY MATTINSON

Business: Walt Disney Productions, 500 S. Buena Vista Street, Burbank, CA 91521, 818/845-3141

BASIL OF BAKER STREET (AF) co-director with Dave Michener & John Musker, Buena Vista, 1987

RONALD F. MAXWELL*

b. January 3, 1947
Agent: Jeff Berg, ICM - Los Angeles, 213/550-4000

SEA MARKS (TF) PBS, 1976
VERNA: USO GIRL (TF) ☆ WNET-13, 1978
LITTLE DARLINGS Paramount, 1980
THE NIGHT THE LIGHTS WENT OUT IN GEORGIA Avco Embassy, 1981
KIDCO 20th Century-Fox, 1983

ELAINE MAY*

(Elaine Berlin)

b. April 21, 1932 - Philadelphia, Pennsylvania
Contact: Directors Guild of America - New York City, 212/581-0370

A NEW LEAF Paramount, 1971
THE HEARTBREAK KID 20th Century-Fox, 1972
MIKEY AND NICKY Paramount, 1977

RUSS MAYBERRY*

Agent: Sylvia Gold, ICM - Los Angeles, 213/550-4156

THE JESUS TRIP EMCO, 1971
PROBE (TF) Warner Bros. TV, 1972
A VERY MISSING PERSON (TF) Universal TV, 1972
FER-DE-LANCE (TF) Leslie Stevens Productions, 1974
SEVENTH AVENUE (MS) co-director with Richard Irving, Universal TV, 1977
STONESTREET: WHO KILLED THE CENTERFOLD MODEL? (TF) Universal TV, 1977
THE 3,000 MILE CHASE (TF) Universal TV, 1977
THE YOUNG RUNAWAYS (TF) NBC, 1978
THE MILLION DOLLAR DIXIE DELIVERY (TF) NBC, 1978
THE REBELS (MS) Universal TV, 1979
UNIDENTITIED FLYING ODDBALL Buena Vista, 1979
THE $5.20 AN HOUR DREAM (TF) Thompson-Sagal Productions/Big Deal Inc./Finnegan Associates, 1980
MARRIAGE IS ALIVE AND WELL (TF) Lorimar Productions, 1980
REUNION (TF) Barry Weitz Films, 1980
A MATTER OF LIFE AND DEATH (TF) Big Deal Inc./Raven's Claw Productions/Lorimar Productions, 1981
SIDNEY SHORR (TF) Hajeno Productions/Warner Bros. TV, 1981
THE FALL GUY (TF) Glen A. Larson Productions/20th Century-Fox TV, 1981
SIDE BY SIDE: THE TRUE STORY OF THE OSMOND FAMILY (TF) Osmond Productions/Comworld Productions, 1982
ROOSTER (TF) Glen A. Larson Productions/Tugboat Productions/20th Century-Fox TV, 1982
MANIMAL (TF) Glen A. Larson Productions/20th Century-Fox TV, 1983

TONY MAYLAM*

b. May 26, 1943 - London, England
Agent: APA - Los Angeles, 213/273-0744

WHITE ROCK (FD) EMI, 1977, British
THE RIDDLE OF THE SANDS Satori, 1979, British
THE BURNING Orion, 1982
THE SINS OF DORIAN GRAY (TF) Rankin-Bass Productions, 1983

ALBERT MAYSLES

b. November 26, 1926 - Brookline, Massachusetts

PSYCHIATRY IN RUSSIA (FD) 1955
YOUTH IN POLAND (FD) co-director with David Maysles, 1962
SHOWMAN (FD) co-director with David Maysles, 1962
WHAT'S HAPPENING: THE BEATLES IN THE USA (FD) co-director with David Maysles, 1964
MEET MARLON BRANDO (FD) co-director with David Maysles, 1965

ALBERT MAYSLES —continued

WITH LOVE FROM TRUMAN (FD) co-director with David Maysles, 1966
SALESMAN (FD) co-director with David Maysles & Charlotte Zwerin, Maysles Film, 1969
GIMME SHELTER (FD) co-director with David Maysles & Charlotte Zwerin, Cinema 5, 1971
CHRISTO'S VALLEY CURTAIN (FD) co-director with David Maysles & Ellen Giffard, 1972
GREY GARDENS (FD) co-director with David Maysles, Ellen Hovde & Muffie Meyer, 1975
RUNNING FENCE (FD) co-director with David Maysles & Charlotte Zwerin, 1977

DAVID MAYSLES

b. January 10, 1932 - Brookline, Massachusetts

YOUTH IN POLAND (FD) co-director with Albert Maysles, 1957
SHOWMAN (FD) co-director with Albert Maysles, 1962
WHAT'S HAPPENING: THE BEATLES IN THE USA (FD) co-director with Albert Maysles, 1964
MEET MARLON BRANDO (FD) co-director with Albert Maysles, 1965
WITH LOVE FROM TRUMAN (FD) co-director with Albert Maysles, 1966
SALESMAN (FD) co-director with Albert Maysles & Charlotte Zwerin, Maysles Film, 1969
GIMME SHELTER (FD) co-director with Albert Maysles & Charlotte Zwerin, Cinema 5, 1971
CHRISTO'S VALLEY CURTAIN (FD) co-director with Albert Maysles & Ellen Giffard, 1972
GREY GARDENS (FD) co-director with Albert Maysles, & Ellen Hovde & Muffie Meyer, 1975
RUNNING FENCE (FD) co-director with Albert Maysles & Charlotte Zwerin, 1977

PAUL MAZURSKY*

b. April 25, 1930 - Brooklyn, New York
Agent: ICM - Los Angeles, 213/550-4000
Business Manager: B. Francis, 3283 Beverly Drive, Beverly Hills, CA.

BOB & CAROL & TED & ALICE Columbia, 1969
ALEX IN WONDERLAND MGM, 1970
BLUME IN LOVE Warner Bros., 1973
HARRY AND TONTO 20th Century-Fox, 1974
NEXT STOP, GREENWICH VILLAGE 20th Century-Fox
AN UNMARRIED WOMAN 20th Century-Fox, 1978
WILLIE AND PHIL 20th Century-Fox, 1980
TEMPEST Columbia, 1982
MOSCOW ON THE HUDSON Columbia, 1984

JIM McBRIDE*

Contact: Directors Guild of America - Los Angeles, 213/656-1220

DAVID HOLZMAN'S DIARY Grove Press, 1967
MY GIRLFRIEND'S WEDDING 1968
GLEN AND RANDA UMC, 1971
A HARD DAY FOR ARCHIE *HOT TIMES* 1973, re-released under title MY EROTIC FANTASIES in 1974 with additional footage by another director
BREATHLESS Orion, 1983

ROBERT McCARTY

Home: 222 West 83rd Street, New York, NY 10024, 212/580-1034

I COULD NEVER HAVE SEX WITH A MAN WHO HAS SO LITTLE REGARD FOR MY HUSBAND Cinema 5, 1973
FORE PLAY co-director with John G. Avildsen & Bruce Malmuth, Cinema National, 1975

GEORGE McCOWAN

THE MONK (TF) Thomas-Spelling Productions, 1969
THE BALLAD OF ANDY CROCKER (TF) Thomas-Spelling Productions, 1969
CARTER'S ARMY (TF) Thomas-Spelling Productions, 1970
THE LOVE WAR (TF) Thomas-Spelling Productions, 1970
THE OVER-THE-HILL GANG RIDES AGAIN (TF) Thomas-Spelling Productions, 1970
RUN, SIMON, RUN (TF) Aaron Spelling Productions, 1970
LOVE, HATE, LOVE (TF) Aaron Spelling Productions, 1971
CANNON (TF) QM Productions, 1971
THE FACE OF FEAR (TF) QM Productions, 1971
IF TOMORROW COMES (TF) Aaron Spelling Productions, 1971
WELCOME HOME, JOHNNY BRISTOL (TF) Cinema Center, 1972
THE MAGNIFICENT SEVEN RIDE! United Artists, 1972
FROGS American International, 1972
MURDER ON FLIGHT 502 (TF) Spelling-Goldberg Productions, 1975
SHADOW OF THE HAWK Columbia, 1976, Canadian
SEPARATION (TF) CFTO-TV, 1978, Canadian
RETURN TO FANTASY ISLAND (TF) Spelling-Goldberg Productions, 1978
THE RETURN OF THE MOD SQUAD (TF) Thomas-Spelling Productions, 1979
THE SHAPE OF THINGS TO COME Film Ventures International, 1979, Canadian

DON McDOUGALL*

Home: 213/275-4578
Business Manager: R. Cohn - Los Angeles, 213/275-4577

ESCAPE TO MINDANAO (TF) Universal TV, 1968
WILD WOMEN (TF) Aaron Spelling Productions, 1970
THE AQUARIANS (TF) Ivan Tors Productions, 1975
THE HEIST (TF) Paramount TV, 1972
THE MARK OF ZORRO (TF) 20th Century-Fox TV, 1974
THE MISSING ARE DEADLY (TF) Lawrence Gordon Productions, 1975

RODDY McDOWALL

b. September 17, 1928 - London, England
Agent: William Morris Agency - Beverly Hills, 213/274-7451

TAM LIN *THE DEVILS'S WIDOW* American International, 1971

BERNARD McEVEETY*

Agent: Scott Penney, Eisenbach-Greene, Inc. - Los Angeles, 213/659-3420

RIDE BEYOND VENGEANCE Columbia, 1966
A STEP OUT OF LINE (TF) Cinema Center, 1971
THE BROTHERHOOD OF SATAN Columbia, 1971
KILLER BY NIGHT (TF) Cinema Center, 1972
NAPOLEON AND SAMANTHA Buena Vista, 1972
ONE LITTLE INDIAN Buena Vista, 1973
THE BEARS AND I Buena Vista, 1974
THE MACAHANS (TF) Albert S. Ruddy Productions/MGM TV, 1976
THE HOSTAGE HEART (TF) Andrew J. Fenady Associates/MGM TV, 1977
DONOVAN'S KID (TF) NBC, 1979
CENTENNIAL (MS) co-director with Harry Falk, Paul Krasny & Virgil Vogel, Universal TV, 1979
ROUGHNECKS (TF) Douglas Netter Productions/Metromedia Producers Corporations, 1980

VINCENT McEVEETY*

Home: 14561 Mulholland Drive, Los Angeles, CA 90077 213/783-4674
Agent: Shapiro-Lichtman Agency - Los Angeles, 213/557-2244

THIS SAVAGE LAND (TF) 1968
FIRECREEK Warner Bros., 1968
CUTTER'S TRAIL (TF) CBS Studio Center, 1970

VINCENT McEVEETY*—continued

THE MILLION DOLLAR DUCK Buena Vista, 1971
THE BISCUIT EATER Buena Vista, 1972
CHARLEY AND THE ANGEL Buena Vista, 1972
WONDER WOMAN (TF) Warner Bros. TV, 1974
SUPERDAD Buena Vista, 1972
THE CASTAWAY COWBOY Buena Vista, 1974
THE STRONGEST MAN IN THE WORLD Buena Vista, 1975
THE LAST DAY (TF) Paramount TV, 1975
THE TREASURE OF MATECUMBE Buena Vista, 1976
GUS Buena Vista, 1976
HERBIE GOES TO MONTE CARLO Buena Vista, 1976
THE APPLE DUMPLING GANG RIDES AGAIN Buena Vista, 1979
HERBIE GOES BANANAS Buena Vista, 1980
AMY Buena Vista, 1981
MCCLAIN'S LAW (TF) Eric Bercovici Productions/Epipsychidion Inc., 1982

DARREN McGAVIN*

b. May 7, 1922 - Spokane, Washington
Home: 8643 Holloway Plaza, Los Angeles, CA 90069, 213/855-0271
Agent: Jack Gilardi, ICM - Los Angeles, 213/550-4000

HAPPY MOTHER'S DAY - LOVE, GEORGE Cinema 5, 1973

PATRICK McGOOHAN*

b. May 19, 1928 - New York, New York
Contact: Directors Guild of America - Los Angeles, 213/656-1220

CATCH MY SOUL Cinerama Releasing Corporation, 1974

JOSEPH McGRATH

Business: McGrath and Mack, 10 Lower John Street, London W1, England, 01/437-4983
Agent: ICM - London, 01/629-8080

CASINO ROYALE co-director with Val Guest, Ken Hughes, John Huston & Robert Parrish, Columbia, 1967, British
30 IS A DANGEROUS AGE, CYNTHIA Columbia 1968, British
THE BLISS OF MRS. BLOSSOM Paramount, 1969, British
THE MAGIC CHRISTIAN Commonwealth United, 1970, British
DIGBY, THE BIGGEST DOG IN THE WORLD Cinerama Releasing Corporation, 1974, British
THE GREAT McGONAGALL Scotia American, 1975, British
I'M NOT FEELING MYSELF TONIGHT New Realm, 1976, British
THE STRANGE CASE OF THE END OF CIVILISATION AS WE KNOW IT (TF) Shearwater Films/London Weekend TV, 1978, British
RISING DAMP ITC 1980, British

THOMAS McGUANE*

Home: Hoffman Route, Livingston, Montana 59047
Agent: Jeff Berg, ICM - Los Angeles, 213/550-4000

92 IN THE SHADE United Artists, 1975

ANDREW V. McLAGLEN*

b. July 28, 1920 - London, England
Agent: Ronald Leif, Contemporary-Korman Artists - Beverly Hills, 213/278-8250

GUN THE MAN DOWN United Artists, 1956
MAN IN THE VAULT Universal, 1956
THE ABDUCTORS 20th Century-Fox, 1957
FRECKLES 20th Century-Fox, 1960
THE LITTLE SHEPHERD OF KINGDOM COME 20th Century-Fox, 1961
McLINTOCK! United Artists, 1963
SHENANDOAH Universal, 1965

ANDREW V. McLAGLEN*—continued

THE RARE BREED Universal, 1966
MONKEYS, GO HOME! Buena Vista, 1967
THE WAY WEST United Artists, 1967
THE BALLAD OF JOSIE Universal, 1968
THE DEVIL'S BRIGADE United Artists, 1968
BANDOLERO! 20th Century-Fox, 1968
HELLFIGHTERS Universal, 1969
THE UNDEFEATED 20th Century-Fox, 1969
CHISUM Warner Bros., 1970
ONE MORE TRAIN TO ROB Universal, 1971
FOOLS' PARADE Columbia, 1971
SOMETHING BIG National General, 1971
CAHILL, U.S. MARSHAL Warner Bros., 1973
MITCHELL Allied Artists, 1975
THE LOG OF THE BLACK PEARL (TF) Universal TV/Mark VII Ltd., 1975
STOWAWAY TO THE MOON (TF) 20th Century-Fox TV, 1975
BANJO HACKETT: ROAMIN' FREE (TF) Bruce Lansbury Productions/Columbia TV, 1976
THE LAST HARD MEN 20th Century-Fox, 1976
MURDER AT THE WORLD SERIES (TF) ABC Circle Films, 1977
THE FANTASTIC JOURNEY (TF) Bruce Lansbury Productions/Columbia TV, 1977
BREAKTHROUGH *SERGEANT STEINER* Maverick Pictures International, 1978, West German
THE WILD GEESE Allied Artists, 1979, British
ffolkes *NORTH SEA HIJACK* Universal, 1980, British
THE SEA WOLVES Paramount, 1981, British
THE SHADOW RIDERS (TF) The Pegasus Group Ltd./Columbia TV, 1982
THE BLUE AND THE GRAY (MS) Larry White-Lou Reda Productions/Columbia TV, 1982
TRAVIS McGEE (TF) Hajeno Productions/Warner Bros., TV, 1983
SAHARA MGM/UA/Cannon, 1984
THE DIRTY DOZEN: THE NEXT MISSION (TF) MGM-UA TV, 1985

MARY McMURRAY

Contact: British Academy of Film & Television Arts, 195 Piccadilly, London W1, England, 01/734-0022

THE ASSAM GARDEN The Moving Picture Company, 1985, British

JOHN McTIERNAN

Contact: Writers Guild of America - Los Angeles, 213/550-1000

NOMADS Elliott Kastner Productions, 1985

PETER MEDAK*

b. Budapest, Hungary
Home: 142 S. Bedford Drive, Beverly Hills, CA 90212
Agent: Jim Wiatt/Lou Pitt, ICM - Los Angeles, 213/550-4000
Business Manager: Fred Altman, Altman & Bemmel, 9229 Sunset Blvd., Los Angeles, CA, 213/278-4201

NEGATIVES Continental, 1968, British
A DAY IN THE DEATH OF JOE EGG Columbia, 1972, British
THE RULING CLASS Avco Embassy, 1972, British
THE THIRD GIRL FROM THE LEFT (TF) Playboy Productions, 1973
GHOST IN THE NOONDAY SUN Columbia, 1974, British
THE ODD JOB Columbia, 1978, British
THE CHANGELING AFD, 1980, Canadian
THE BABYSITTER (TF) Moonlight Productions/Filmways, 1980
ZORRO, THE GAY BLADE 20th Century-Fox, 1981
MISTRESS OF PARADISE (TF) Lorimar Productions, 1981
CRY FOR THE STRANGERS (TF) David Gerber Company/MGM TV, 1982

DON MEDFORD*

Home: 1956 S. Bently Avenue, Los Angeles, CA 90025, 213/473-3439
Agent: Irv Schechter Company - Beverly Hills, 213/278-8070

TO TRAP A SPY MGM, 1966
THE HUNTING PARTY United Artists, 1970
INCIDENT IN SAN FRANSISCO (TF) QM Productions, 1971
THE ORGANIZATION United Artists, 1971
THE NOVEMBER PLAN 1976
THE CLONE MASTER (TF) Mel Ferber Productions/Paramount TV, 1978
COACH OF THE YEAR (TF) A. Shane Company, 1980
SIZZLE (TF) Aaron Spelling Productions, 1981

CARY MEDOWAY

b. May 16, 1949 - Philadelphia, Pennsylvania
Agent: Shapiro-Lichtman Agency - Los Angeles, 213/550-2244

NEW KID IN TOWN Saturn International, 1984
THE HEAVENLY KID Orion, 1985

BILL MELENDEZ

Business: Bill Melendez Productions, 439 N. Larchmont Blvd., Los Angeles, CA 90004, 213/463-4101

A BOY NAMED CHARLIE BROWN (AF) National General, 1968
SNOOPY, COME HOME (AF) National General, 1972
DICK DEADEYE, OR DUTY DONE (AF) Intercontinental, 1976, British
RACE FOR YOUR LIFE, CHARLIE BROWN (AF) Paramount, 1978
BON VOYAGE, CHARLIE BROWN (AND DON'T COME BACK!) (AF) Paramount, 1980

GEORGE MENDELUK

Business: World Classic Pictures, 6263 Topia Drive, Malibu, CA 90265, 213/457-9911 or 213/457-5591

STONE COLD DEAD Dimension, 1979, Canadian
THE KIDNAPPING OF THE PRESIDENT Crown International, 1980, Canadian
DOIN' TIME The Ladd Company/Warner Bros., 1985
MEATBALLS III Dalco Productions, 1985, Canadian

KIETH MERRILL*

b. May 22, 1940 - Utah
Home: 11930 Rhus Ridge Road, Los Altos Hills, CA 94022, 415/941-8720

THE GREAT AMERICAN COWBOY (FD) Sun International, 1974
THREE WARRIORS United Artists, 1978
TAKE DOWN Buena Vista, 1979
WINDWALKER Pacific International, 1980
MR. KRUEGER'S CHRISTMAS (TF) Bonneville Productions, 1980
HARRY'S WAR Taft International, 1981
THE CHEROKEE TRAIL (TF) Walt Disney Productions, 1981

ALAN METTER*

Agent: Doug Warner, APA - Los Angeles, 213/273-0744
Business Manager: David Watkins, Kaufman-Eisenberg - Beverly Hills, 213/273-0744

GIRLS JUST WANT TO HAVE FUN New World, 1985

RADLEY METZGER

b. 1930

DARK ODYSSEY co-director with William Kyriaskys, ERA, 1961
DICTIONARY OF SEX 1964

RADLEY METZGER —continued

THE DIRTY GIRLS 1965
THE ALLEY CATS 1966
CARMEN, BABY Audubon, 1967, U.S.-Yugoslavian-West German
THERESE AND IASBELLE Audubon, 1968, West German-U.S.
CAMILLE 2000 Audubon, 1969, Italian
THE LICKERISH QUARTET Audubon, 1970, U.S.-Italian-West German
LITTLE MOTHER Audubon, 1972
SCORE Audubon, 1973
NAKED CAME THE STRANGER directed under pseudonym of Henry Paris, Catalyst, 1975
THE PRIVATE AFTERNOONS OF PAMELA MANN directed under pseudonym of Henry Paris, Hudson Valley, 1975
ESOTIKA, EROTIKA, PSICOTIKA FAB 1975, Italian-Monocan
THE PUNISHMENT OF ANNE 1975
THE IMAGE Audubon, 1976
THE OPENING OF MISTY BEETHOVEN directed under pseudonym of Henry Paris, Catalyst, 1976
BARBARA BROADCAST directed under pseudonym of Henry Paris, Crescent, 1977
MARASCHINO CHERRY directed under pseudonym of Henry Paris, 1978
THE CAT AND THE CANARY Quartet, 1978, British
THE TALE OF TIFFANY LUST directed under pseudonym of Henry Paris, Entertainment Ventures, 1981

NICHOLAS MEYER*

b. New York, New York
Home: 2109 Stanley Hills Drive, Los Angeles, CA 90046
Agent: William Morris Agency - Beverly Hills, 213/274-7451

TIME AFTER TIME Orion/Warner Bros., 1979
STAR TREK II: THE WRATH OF KHAN Paramount, 1982
THE DAY AFTER (TF) ☆ ABC Circle Films, 1983
VOLUNTEERS Tri-Star, 1985

RUSS MEYER*

b. March 21, 1922 - Oakland, California
Business RM Films International Inc., P.O. Box 3748, Hollywood, CA 90028, 213/466-7791

THE IMMORAL MR. TEAS Pedram, 1959
EVE AND THE HANDYMAN Eve, 1961
EROTICA Eve, 1961
THE IMMORAL WEST AND HOW IT WAS LOST Eve, 1961
EUROPE IN THE RAW Eve, 1963
HEAVENLY BODIES Eve, 1963
KISS ME QUICK! Eve, 1964
LORNA Eve, 1965
ROPE OF FLESH Eve, 1965
FANNY HILL: MEMOIRS OF A WOMAN OF PLEASURE Pan World, 1965, U.S.-West German
MOTOR PSYCHO Eve, 1965
FASTER PUSSYCAT, KILL! KILL! Eve, 1965
MONDO TOPLESS Eve, 1966
GOOD MORNING...AND GOODBYE Eve, 1967
COMMON LAW CABIN Eve, 1967
FINDERS KEEPERS, LOVERS WEEPERS Eve, 1968
RUSS MEYER'S VIXEN Eve, 1968
CHERRY, HARRY AND RAQUEL Eve, 1969
BEYOND THE VALLEY OF THE DOLLS 20th Century-Fox, 1970
THE SEVEN MINUTES 20th Century-Fox, 1971
SWEET SUZY! *BLACKSNAKE* Signal 166, 1975
SUPERVIXENS RM Films, 1975
RUSS MEYER'S UP! RM Films, 1976
BENEATH THE VALLEY OF THE ULTRAVIXENS RM Films, 1979
THE BREAST OF RUSS MEYER RM Films, 1983

RICHARD MICHAELS*

Agent: David Gersh, The Gersh Agency - Beverly Hills, 213/274-6611
Business Manager: David G. Licht, 9171 Wilshire Blvd., Beverly Hills, CA 90210, 213/278-1920

HOW COME NOBODY'S ON OUR SIDE? American Films Ltd., 1975
DEATH IS NOT THE END Libert Films International, 1976
ONCE AN EAGLE (MS) co-director with E.W. Swackhammer, Universal TV, 1976
CHARLIE COBB: NICE NIGHT FOR HANGING (TF) Universal TV, 1977
HAVING BABIES II (TF) The Jozak Company, 1977
LEAVE YESTERDAY BEHIND (TF) ABC Circle Films, 1978
MY HUSBAND IS MISSING (TF) Bob Banner Associates, 1978
...AND YOUR NAME IS JONAH (TF) Charles Fries Productions, 1979
HOMEWARD BOUND (TF) Tisch-Avner Productions, 1980
ONCE UPON A FAMILY (TF) Universal TV, 1980
THE PLUTONIUM INCIDENT (TF) Time-Life Productions, 1980
SCARED STRAIGHT! ANOTHER STORY (TF) Golcen West TV, 1980
BERLIN TUNNEL 21 (TF) Cypress Point Productions/Filmways, 1981
THE CHILDREN NOBODY WANTED (TF) Blatt-Singer Productions, 1981
BLUE SKIES AGAIN Warner Bros, 1983
ONE COOKS, THE OTHER DOESN'T (TF) Kaleidoscope Films Ltd./Lorimar Productions, 1983
SADAT (TF) Blatt-Singer Productions/Columbia TV, 1983
JESSIE (TF) Lindsay Wagner Productions/MGM-UA TV, 1984
SILENCE OF THE HEART (TF) David A. Simons Productions/Tisch-Avnet Productions, 1984

DAVE MICHENER

Business: Walt Disney Productions, 500 S. Buena Vista Street, Burbank, CA 91521, 818/845-3141

BASIL OF BAKER STREET (AF) co-director with Burny Mattinson & John Musker, Buena Vista, 1987

GEORGE MIHALKA

Home: 2030 Closse-Suite 4, Montreal, Quebec H3H 1Z9, Canada, 514/937-4740

MY BLOODY VALENTINE Paramount, 1981, Canadian
PICK-UP SUMMER *PINBALL SUMMER* Film Ventures International, 1981, Canadian
SCANDALE Vivafilm/Cine 360, 1982, Canadian

TED V. MIKELS

THE BLACK KLANSMAN 1966
THE UNDERTAKER AND HIS PALS 1966
THE ASTRO-ZOMBIES Gemini Films, 1969
THE CORPSE GRINDERS 1972
BLOOD ORGY OF THE SHE-DEVILS Gemini Films, 1973
THE DOLL SQUAD 1974
THE WORM EATERS New American, 1975
TEN VIOLENT WOMEN New American, 1982

NIKITA MIKHALKOV

b. U.S.S.R.
Contact: State Committee of Cinematography of the U.S.S.R., Council of Ministers, 7 Maly Gnesdiknovsky Pereulok, Moscow, U.S.S.R., 7 095/299-9912

AT HOME AMONG STRANGERS 1974, Soviet
A SLAVE OF LOVE Cinema 5, 1976, Soviet
AN UNFINISHED PIECE FOR PLAYER PIANO Corinth, 1977, Soviet
FIVE EVENINGS IFEX Film, 1979, Soviet
OBLOMOV IFEX Film, 1981, Soviet
FAMILY RELATIONS Mosfilm, 1983, Soviet
WITHOUT WITNESS IFEX FILM, 1984, Soviet

ANDREI MIKHALKOV-KONCHALOVSKY
(See Andrei KONCHALOVSKY)

CHRISTOPHER MILES

b. April 19, 1939 - London, England
Home: 49 Berkeley Square, London N1, England, 01/491-2625
Contact: Directors Guild of Great Britain, 56 Whitfield Street, London W1, 01/580-9592

UP JUMPED A SWAGMAN Anglo-Amalgamated/Warner-Pathe, 1966, British
THE VIRGIN AND THE GYPSY Chevron, 1970, British
TIME FOR LOVING Hemdale, 1972, British
THE MAIDS American Film Theatre, 1975, British-Canadian
THAT LUCKY TOUCH Allied Artists, 1975, British
PRIEST OF LOVE Filmways, 1981, British

JOHN MILIUS*

b. April 11, 1944 - St. Louis, Missouri
Agent: ICM - Los Angeles, 213/550-4000

DILLINGER American International, 1973
THE WIND AND THE LION MGM/United Artists, 1975
BIG WEDNESDAY Warner Bros., 1978
CONAN THE BARBARIAN Universal, 1982
RED DAWN MGM/UA, 1984

GAVIN MILLAR

Home: 16 Compton Terrace, London N1 2UN, England, 01/226-0210
Agent: Judy Daish Agency, 122 Wigmore Street, London W1, England, 01/486-5404
Contact: Directors Guild of Great Britain, 56 Whitfield Street, London W1, 01/580-9592

CREAM IN MY COFFEE (TF) London Weekend TV, 1980, British
INTENSIVE CARE (TF) BBC, 1982, British
STAN'S LAST NAME (TF) BBC, 1983, British
SECRETS The Samuel Goldwyn Company, 1983, British
THE WEATHER IN THE STREETS (TF) Rediffusion Films/BBC/Britannia TV, 1983, British
UNFAIR EXCHANGES (TF) BBC, 1984, British
DREAM CHILD Universal, 1985, British

STUART MILLAR *

b. 1929 - New York, New York
Home: 300 Central Park West - Suite 15G, New York, NY 10024, 212/873-5515

WHEN THE LEGENDS DIE 20th Century-Fox, 1972
ROOSTER COGBURN Universal, 1975

DAVID MILLER *

b. November 28, 1909 - Paterson, New Jersey
Home: 1843 Thayer Avenue, Los Angeles, CA 90025, 213/474-8542
Agent: The Gersh Agency - Beverly Hills, 213/274-6611

BILLY THE KID MGM, 1941
SUNDAY PUNCH MGM, 1942
FLYING TIGERS Republic, 1942
TOP O' THE MORNING Paramount, 1948
LOVE HAPPY United Artists, 1949
OUR VERY OWN RKO Radio, 1950
SATURDAY'S HERO Columbia, 1951
SUDDEN FEAR RKO Radio, 1952
TWIST OF FATE *THE BEAUTIFUL STRANGER* United Artists, 1954, British
DIANE MGM, 1956
THE OPPOSITE SEX MGM, 1956
THE STORY OF ESTHER COSTELLO Columbia, 1957
HAPPY ANNIVERSARY United Artists, 1959
MIDNIGHT LACE Universal, 1961
BACK STREET Universal, 1961
LONELY ARE THE BRAVE Universal, 1962
CAPTAIN NEWMAN, M.D. Universal, 1964
HAMMERHEAD Columbia, 1968, British
HAIL, HERO! National General, 1969
EXECUTIVE ACTION National General, 1973
BITTERSWEET LOVE Avco Embassy, 1976
LOVE FOR RENT (TF) Warren V. Bush Productions, 1979
THE BEST PLACE TO BE (TF) Ross Hunter Productions, 1979
GOLDIE AND THE BOXER (TF) Orenthal Productions/Columbia TV, 1979
GOLDIE AND THE BOXER GO TO HOLLYWOOD (TF) Orenthal Productions/Columbia TV, 1981

GEORGE MILLER *

b. March 3, 1945 - Brisbane, Australia
Contact: Directors Guild of America - Los Angeles, 213/656-1220
Business: Kennedy & Miller, Metro Theatre, 32 Orwell Street, Potts Point, NSW, 2011, Australia, 02/357-2322

MAD MAX American International, 1979, Australian
THE ROAD WARRIOR *MAD MAX II* Warner Bros., 1982, Australian
TWILIGHT ZONE - THE MOVIE co-director with John Landis, Steven Spielberg & Joe Dante, Warner Bros., 1983
MAD MAX III co-director with George Ogilvie, Warner Bros., 1985, Australian

GEORGE MILLER*

Address: 3 Reed Street, Albert Park, Victoria, 3206, Australia, 03/690-5663
Agent: Rosalie Swedlin, CAA - Los Angeles, 213/277-4545

CASH & CO. (MS) co-director with Russell Hagg, Homestead Films/Network Seven, 1975, Australian
AGAINST THE WIND (MS) co-director with Simon Wincer, Pegasus Productions, 1978, Australian
THE LAST OUTLAW (MS) co-director with Kevin Dobson, Network Seven/ Pegasus Productions, 1980, Australian
THE MAN FROM SNOWY RIVER 20th Century-Fox, 1982, Australian
ALL THE RIVERS RUN (CMS) co-director with Pino Amenta, Crawford Productions/Nine Network, 1984, Australian
THE AVIATOR MGM/UA, 1985
ANZACS (MS) co-director with John Dixon, Nine Network, 1985, Australian

JASON MILLER*

Contact: Directors Guild of America - Los Angeles, 213/656-1220

THAT CHAMPIONSHIP SEASON Cannon, 1982

JONATHAN MILLER

Contact: British Academy of Film & Television Arts, 195 Piccadilly, London W1, England, 01/734-0022

TAKE A GIRL LIKE YOU Columbia, 1970, British

MICHAEL MILLER*

Agent: David Gersh, The Gersh Agency - Beverly Hills, 213/274-6611
Business Manager: Henry Levine, Henry Levine & Associates, 9100 Wilshire Blvd. - Suite 517, Beverly Hills, CA 91210, 213/274-8691

STREET GIRLS New World, 1975
JACKSON COUNTY JAIL New World, 1976
OUTSIDE CHANCE (TF) New World Productions/Miller-Begun Productions, 1978
SILENT RAGE Columbia, 1982
NATIONAL LAMPOON'S CLASS REUNION 20th Century-Fox, 1983

ROBERT ELLIS MILLER*

b. July 18, 1932 - New York, New York
Agent: Paul Kohner, Inc. - Los Angeles, 213/550-1060
Business Manager: McGuire Management, 1901 Avenue of the Stars, Los Angeles, CA 90067, 213/277-5902

ANY WEDNESDAY Warner Bros., 1966
SWEET NOVEMBER Warner Bros., 1967
THE HEART IS A LONELY HUNTER Warner Bros., 1968
THE BUTTERCUP CHAIN Warner Bros., 1970, British
BIG TRUCK AND POOR CLARE Kastner-Ladd-Winkler/Pashanel-Topol-Gottesman, 1972, U.S.-Israeli
THE GIRL FROM PETROVKA Universal, 1974
JUST AN OLD SWEET SONG (TF) MTM Enterprises, 1976
ISHI: THE LAST OF HIS TRIBE (TF) Edward & Mildred Lewis Productions, 1978
THE BALTIMORE BULLET Avco Embassy, 1980
MADAME X (TF) Levenback-Riche Productions/Universal TV, 1981
REUBEN, REUBEN 20th Century-Fox International Classics, 1983
HER LIFE AS A MAN (TF) LS Entertainment, 1984

WALTER C. MILLER*

Home: 2401 Crest View Drive, Los Angeles, CA 90046, 213/656-2819

THE BORROWERS (TF) Walt DeFaria Productions/20th Century-Fox TV, 1973
CAN I SAVE MY CHILDREN? (TF) ☆ Stanley L. Colbert Co-Production Associates/20th Century-Fox TV, 1974

REGINALD MILLS

PETER RABBIT & TALES OF BEATRIX POTTER MGM, 1971, British

STEVE MINER

b. June 18, 1951 - Chicago, Illinois
Business: Steven C. Miner Films Inc., 11372 Second Street - Suite 103, Santa Monica, CA 90403, 213/393-0291
Agent: Mike Lynne, Blumenthal & Lynne, 488 Madison Avenue, New York, NY 10022, 212/758-0190

FRIDAY THE 13TH PART 2 Paramount, 1981
FRIDAY THE 13TH PART 3 Paramount, 1982

DAVID MINGAY

Contact: British Academy of Film & Television Arts, 195 Piccadilly, London W1, England, 01/734-0022

RUDE BOY co-director with Jack Hazan, Atlantic Releasing Corporation, 1980, British

VINCENTE MINNELLI*

b. February 28, 1910 - Chicago, Illinois
Home: 812 N. Crescent Drive, Beverly Hills, CA 90210, 213/276-8128
Agent: Paul Kohner, Inc. - Los Angeles, 213/550-1060
Business Manager: Nate Golden & Associates, 9601 Wilshire Blvd., Beverly Hills, CA 90210, 213/278-1103

CABIN IN THE SKY MGM, 1943
I DOOD IT MGM, 1943
MEET ME IN ST. LOUIS MGM, 1944
YOLANDA AND THE THIEF MGM, 1945
THE CLOCK MGM, 1945
ZIEGFELD FOLLIES MGM, 1946
TILL THE CLOUDS ROLL BY co-director with Richard Whorf, MGM, 1946
UNDERCURRENT MGM, 1946
THE PIRATE MGM, 1948
MADAME BOVARY MGM, 1949
FATHER OF THE BRIDE MGM, 1950
AN AMERICAN IN PARIS ★ MGM, 1951
FATHER'S LITTLE DIVIDEND MGM, 1951
THE BAD AND THE BEAUTIFUL MGM, 1952
THE STORY OF THREE LOVES MGM, 1953
THE BAND WAGON MGM, 1953
THE LONG, LONG TRAILER MGM, 1954
BRIGADOON MGM, 1954
THE COBWEB MGM, 1955
KISMET MGM, 1955
LUST FOR LIFE MGM, 1956
TEA AND SYMPATHY MGM, 1956
DESIGNING WOMAN MGM, 1957
GIGI ★ MGM, 1958
THE RELUCTANT DEBUTANTE MGM, 1958
SOME CAME RUNNING MGM, 1959
HOME FROM THE HILL MGM, 1960
BELLS ARE RINGING MGM, 1960
THE FOUR HORSEMEN OF THE APOCALYPSE MGM, 1962
TWO WEEKS IN ANOTHER TOWN MGM, 1962
THE COURTSHIP OF EDDIE'S FATHER MGM, 1963
GOODBYE, CHARLIE 20th Century-Fox, 1964

VINCENTE MINNELLI*—continued

THE SANDPIPER MGM, 1965
ON A CLEAR DAY YOU CAN SEE FOREVER Paramount, 1970
A MATTER OF TIME American International, 1976, U.S.-Italian

MOSHE MIZRAHI

Contact: French Film Office, 745 Fifth Avenue, New York NY 10151, 212/832-8860

LES STANCES A SOPHIE Prodis, 1971, French
I LOVE YOU ROSA Leisure Media, 1973, Israeli
THE HOUSE ON CHELOUCHE STREET Productions Unlimited, 1974, Israeli
DAUGHTERS! DAUGHTERS! Steinmann-Baxter, 1975, Israeli
RACHEL'S MAN Allied Artists, 1976, Israeli
MADAME ROSA *LA VIE DEVANT SOI* Atlantic Releasing Corporation, 1978, French
I SENT A LETTER TO MY LOVE *CHERE INCONNUE* Atlantic Releasing Corporation, 1980, French
LA VIE CONTINUE Triumph/Columbia, 1982, French
YOUTH 1983, French
THE CHILDREN'S WAR Stafford Productions, 1984

DAVID MOESSINGER*

Agent: Dan Richland, The Richland Agency - Los Angeles, 213/553-1257

MOBILE TWO (TF) Universal TV/Mark VII Ltd., 1975

EDOUARD MOLINARO

b. May 13, 1928 Bordeaux, France
Contact: French Film Office, 745 Fifth Avenue, New York, NY 10151, 212/832-8860

BACK TO THE WALL Ellis, 1958, French
DES FEMMES DISPARAISSENT 1959, French
UNE FILLE POUR L'ETE 1960, French
THE PASSION OF SLOW FIRE *LA MORT DE BELLE* Trans-Lux, 1961, French
SEVEN CAPITAL SINS co-director with Jean-Luc Godard, Roger Vadim, Sylvaine Dhomme, Philippe De Broca, Claude Chabrol, Jacques Demy, Marie-Jose Nat, Dominique Paturel, Jean-Marc Tennberg & Perrette Pradier, Embassy, 1962, French-Italian
LES ENNEMIS 1962, French
ARSENE LUPIN CONTRE ARSENE LUPIN 1962, French
UNE RAVISSANTE IDIOTE 1964, French
MALE HUNT Pathe Contemporary, 1965, French-Italian
QUAND PASSENT LES FAISANS 1965, French
TO COMMIT A MURDER *PEAU D'ESPION* Cinerama Releasing Corporation, 1967, French-Italian-West German
OSCAR 1968, French
HIBERNATUS 1969, French
MON ONCLE BENJAMIN 1969, French
LA LIBERTEEN CROUPE 1970, French
LES AVEUX LES PLUS DOUX MGM, 1971, French
LA MANDARINE Prodis, 1972, French-Italian
A PAIN IN THE A– *L'EMMERDEUR* Corwin-Mahler, 1973, French
LE GANG DES OTAGES Gaumont, 1973, French
L'IRONIE DU SORT CFDC, 1974, French
THE PINK TELEPHONE SJ International, 1975, French
DRACULA PERE ET FILS Gaumont, 1976, French
L'HOMME PRESSE AMLF, 1977, French
LA CAGE AUX FOLLES ★ United Artists, 1979, French-Italian
LA PITIE DANGEREUSE (TF) Christine Gouze-Renal Progefi/Antenne-2, 1979, French
CAUSE TOUJOURS...TU M'INTERESSES Albina Productions, 1979, French
SUNDAY LOVERS co-director with Bryan Forbes, Dino Risi & Gene Wilder, MGM/United Artists, 1981, U.S.-British-Italian-French
LA CAGE AUX FOLLES II United Artists, 1981, French-Italian
POUR 100 BRIQUES, T'AS PLUS RIEN! UGC, 1982, French

EDOUARD MOLINARO —continued

JUST THE WAY YOU ARE MGM/UA, 1984
L'AMOUR EN DOUCE Gaumont, 1985, French
PALACE Parafrance, 1985, French-West German

MARIO MONICELLI

b. May 16, 1915 - Tuscany, Italy
Address: Via del Babuino, 135 Rome, Italy
Contact: Ministry of Tourism & Education, Via Della Ferratella, No. 51, 00184 Rome, Italy, 06/7732

AL DIAVOLO LA CELEBRITA co-director with Steno, Produttori Associati, 1949, Italian
TOTO CERCA CASA co-director with Steno, ATA, 1949, Italian
VITA DA CANI co-director with Steno, ATA, 1950, Italian
E ARRIVATO IL CAVALIERE co-director with Steno, ATA/Excelsa Film, 1950, Italian
GUARDIE E LADRI co-director with Steno, Carlo Ponti/Dino De Laurentiis Cinematografica/Golden Film, 1951, Italian
TOTO E I RE DI ROMA co-director with Steno, Golden Film/Humanitas Film, 1952, Italian
LE INFIDELI co-director with Steno, Excelsa Film/Carlo Ponti/Dino De Laurentiis Cinematografica, 1953, Italian
PROIBITO Documento Film/UGC/Cormoran Film, 1954, Italian
TOTO E CAROLINA Rosa, 1955, Italian
UN EROE DEI NOSTRI TEMPI Titanus/Vides, 1955, Italian
DONATELLA Sud Film, 1956, Italian
THE TAILOR'S MAID *PADRI E FIGLI* Trans-Lux, 1957, Italian
IL MEDICO E LO STREGONE Royal Film/Francinex, 1957, Italian-French
BIG DEAL ON MADONNA STREET *I SOLITI IGNOTTI* United Motion Picture Organization, 1958, Italian
THE GREAT WAR United Artists, 1959, Italian
THE PASSIONATE THIEF Embassy, 1960, Italian
BOCCACCIO '70 co-director with Federico Fellini, Vittorio De Sica & Luchino Visconti, Embassy, 1962, Italian
THE ORGANIZER *I COMPAGNI* Continental, 1963, Italian-French-Yugoslavian
HIGH INFIDELITY co-director with Franco Rossi, Elio Petri & Luciano Salce, Magna, 1964, Italian-French
CASANOVA '70 Embassy, 1965, Italian-French
L'ARMATA BRANCALEONE Fair Film, 1966, Italian
THE QUEENS *LE FATE* co-director with Luciano Salce, Mauro Bolognini & Antonio Pietrangeli, Royal Films International, 1966, Italian-French
RAGAZZA CON LA PISTOLA Documento Film, 1968, Italian
CAPRICCIO ALL'ITALIANA co-director with Steno, Mauro Bolognini & Pier Paolo Pasolini, Dino De Laurentiis Cinematografica, 1968, Italian
TO'E MORTA LA NONNA Vides, 1969, Italian
LE COPPIE co-director with Alberto Sordi & Vittorio De Sica, Documento Film, 1970, Italian
BRANCALEONE ALLE CROCIATE Fair Film, 1970, Italian
LADY LIBERTY *MORTADELLA* United Artists, 1971, Italian
VOGLIAMO I COLONNELLI Dean Film, 1973, Italian
ROMANZO POPOLARE Capitolina, 1975, Italian
MY FRIENDS Allied Artists, 1975, Italian
CARO MICHELE Cineriz, 1976, Italian
SIGNORE E SIGNORI BUONANOTTE co-director with Luigi Comencini, Nanni Loy, Luigi Magni & Ettore Scola, Titanus, 1976, Italian
LA GODURIA co-director, 1976, Italian
UN BORGHESE PICCOLO PICCOLI Cineriz, 1977, Italian
VIVA ITALIA! *I NUOVI MOSTRI* co-director with Dino Risi & Ettore Scola, Cinema 5, 1978, Italian
LOVERS AND LIARS *TRAVELS WITH ANITA* Levitt-Pickman, 1979, Italian-French
HURRICANE ROSY United Artists, 1979, Italian-French-West German
CAMERA D'ALBERGO Filmauro/Nouvelle Cinevog, 1980, Italian-French
LE COPPIE co-director with Alberto Sordi, Documento Film, 1980, Italian
IL MARCHESE DEL GRILLO Opera/RAI, 1981, Italian-French
AMICI MIEI II Sacis, 1982, Italian
BERTOLDO BERTOLDINO E...CACASENO Gaumont, 1984, Italian
IL FU MATTIA PASCAL Sacis, 1985, Italian

GIULIANO MONTALDO

Contact: Ministry of Tourism & Education, Via Della Ferratella, No. 51, 00184 Rome, Italy, 06/7732

GRAND SLAM *AD OGNI COSTO* Paramount, 1968, Italian-Spanish-West German
MACHINE GUN McCAIN *GLI INTOCCABILI* Columbia, 1970, Italian
SACCO AND VANZETTI UMC, 1971, Italian
L'AGNESE UN A MORIRE Indipendenti Regionali, 1976, Italian
CLOSED CIRCUIT Filmalpha/RAI, 1977, Italian
IL GIOCATTOLO Titanus, 1979, Italian
MARCO POLO (MS) RAI/Franco Cristaldi Productions/Vincenzo Labella Productions, 1982, Italian

MONTY MONTGOMERY

THE LOVELESS co-director with Kathryn Bigelow, Atlantic Releasing Corporation, 1981

PATRICK MONTGOMERY

THE COMPLEAT BEATLES (FD) TeleCulture, 1984, originally released by MGM/UA Home Video in 1982

IRVING J. MOORE*

Agent: Ron Leif, Contemporary-Korman Artists - Beverly Hills, 213/278-8250

THE MAKING OF A MALE MODEL (TF) Aaron Spelling Productions, 1983

RICHARD MOORE*

b. October 4, 1925 - Jacksonville, Illinois
Home: 213/459-4593

CIRCLE OF IRON Avco Embassy, 1979

PHILIPPE MORA*

Agent: Leading Artists - Beverly Hills, 213/858-1999

TROUBLE IN MOLOPOLIS 1972, British
SWASTIKA (FD) Cinema 5, 1974, British
BROTHER, CAN YOU SPARE A DIME? (FD) Dimension, 1975, Canadian
MAD DOG *MAD DOG MORGAN* Cinema Shares International, 1976, Australian
THE BEAST WITHIN United Artists, 1982
THE RETURN OF CAPTAIN INVINCIBLE *LEGEND IN LEOTARDS* New World, 1983, Australian
A BREED APART Orion, 1983
THE HOWLING II Hemdale/United Film Production, 1985, British-U.S.

CHRISTOPHER MORAHAN

Home: 55 Winterbrook Road, London SE24 9HZ, England, 01/274-9087
Agent: Leading Artists, 60 St. James Street, London SW1, England, 01/491-4400

THE JEWEL IN THE CROWN (MS) co-director with Jim O'Brien, Granada TV, 1984, British
IN THE SECRET STATE Greenpoint Films, 1985, British

RICK MORANIS

Address: 95 Forest Heights Blvd., Willowdale, Ontario, Canada, 416/968-2939

STRANGE BREW co-director with Dave Thomas, MGM/UA, 1983, Canadian

JEANNE MOREAU

b. January 23, 1928 - Paris, France
Contact: French Film Office, 745 Fifth Avenue, New York, NY 10151, 212/832-8860

LUMIERE New World, 1976, French
L'ADOLESCENTE Landmark Releasing, 1979, French-West German

DAVID BURTON MORRIS

b. 1948 - Kansas City, Missouri
Agent: Bill Block, ICM - Los Angeles, 213/550-4000

LOOSE ENDS Twyman Films, 1975
PURPLE HAZE Triumph/Columbia, 1983

HOWARD MORRIS*

b. September 4, 1919 - New York, New York
Agent: Tom Korman, Contemporary-Korman Artists - Beverly Hills, 213/278-8250

WHO'S MINDING THE MINT? Columbia, 1967
WITH SIX YOU GET EGGROLL National General, 1968
DON'T DRINK THE WATER Avco Embassy, 1969
OH! BABY, BABY, BABY... (TF) Alan Landsburg Productions, 1974
GOIN' COCONUTS Osmond Distribution, 1978

PAUL MORRISSEY

b. 1939 - New York, New York
Contact: Writers Guild of America, West - Los Angeles, 213/550-1000

FLESH Warhol, 1968
TRASH Warhol, 1970
ANDY WARHOL'S WOMEN Warhol, 1971
HEAT Warhol, 1972
L'AMOUR co-director with Andy Warhol, Altura, 1973
ANDY WARHOL'S FRANKENSTEIN *FLESH FOR FRANKENSTEIN* Bryanston, 1974, Italian-French
ANDY WARHOL'S DRACULA *BLOOD FOR DRACULA* Bryanston, 1974, Italian-French
THE HOUND OF THE BASKERVILLES Atlantic Releasing Corporation, 1979, British
MADAME WANG'S 1981
FORTY-DEUCE Island Alive, 1982
MIXED BLOOD Sara Films, 1984, U.S.-French

GILBERT MOSES*

b. August 20, 1942 - Cleveland, Ohio
Agent: Irv Schechter & Company - Beverly Hills, 213/278-8070
Business: China Tee Company, c/o Cooper, Epstein & Horowitz, 9465 Wilshire Blvd., Beverly Hills, CA 90212, 213/278-1111

WILLIE DYNAMITE Universal, 1974
ROOTS (MS) ☆ co-director with Marvin J. Chomsky, John Erman & David Greene, Wolper Productions, 1977
THE GREATEST THING THAT ALMOST HAPPENED (TF) Charles Fries Productions, 1977
THE FISH THAT SAVED PITTSBURGH United Artists, 1979

HARRY MOSES*

Business: CBS News, 524 West 57th Street, New York, NY 10019, 212/975-1885
Agent: ICM - Los Angeles, 213/550-4000
Business Manager: Richard Leibner, N.S. Bienstock - New York City, 212/765-3040

THORNWELL (TF) MTM Enterprises, 1981

JOHN LLEWELLYN MOXEY*

b. 1920 - Burlingham, England
Personal Manager: Helen Kushnick, General Management Corporation - Beverly Hills, 213/274-8805

HORROR HOTEL *CITY OF THE DEAD* Trans-World, 1960, British
FOXHOLE IN CAIRO Paramount, 1961, British
DEATH TRAP Anglo-Amalgamated, 1962, British
THE 20,000 POUND KISS Anglo-Amalgamated, 1963, British
RICOCHET Warner-Pathe, 1963, British
DOWNFALL Embassy, 1964, British
FACE OF A STRANGER Warner-Pathe, 1964, British
STRANGLER'S WEB Embassy, 1965, British
PSYCHO-CIRCUS *CIRCUS OF FEAR* American International, 1967, British
THE TORMENTOR ITC, 1967, British
SAN FRANCISCO INTERNATIONAL AIRPORT (TF) Universal TV, 1970
THE HOUSE THAT WOULD NOT DIE (TF) Aaron Spelling Productions, 1970
ESCAPE (TF) Paramount TV, 1971
THE LAST CHILD (TF) Aaron Spelling Productions, 1971
A TASTE OF EVIL (TF) Aaron Spelling Productions, 1971
THE DEATH OF ME YET! (TF) Aaron Spelling Productions, 1971
THE NIGHT STALKER (TF) ABC, Inc., 1972
HARDCASE (TF) Hanna-Barbera Productions, 1972
THE BOUNTY MAN (TF) ABC Circle Films, 1972
HOME FOR THE HOLIDAYS (TF) ABC Circle Films, 1972
GENESIS II (TF) Warner Bros. TV, 1973
THE STRANGE AND DEADLY OCCURENCE (TF) Metromedia Productions, 1974
WHERE HAVE ALL THE PEOPLE GONE? (TF) Metromedia Productions, 1974
FOSTER AND LAURIE (TF) Charles Fries Productions, 1975
CHARLIE'S ANGELS (TF) Spelling-Goldberg Productions, 1976
CONSPIRACY OF TERROR (TF) Lorimar Productions, 1976
NIGHTMARE IN BADHAM COUNTY (TF) ABC Circle Films, 1976
SMASH-UP ON INTERSTATE 5 (TF) Filmways, 1976
PANIC IN ECHO PARK (TF) Edgar J. Scherick Associates, 1977
INTIMATE STRANGERS (TF) Charles Fries Productions, 1977
THE PRESIDENT'S MISTRESS (TF) Stephen Friedman/King's Road Productions, 1978
THE COURAGE AND THE PASSION (TF) David Gerber Company/Columbia TV, 1978
SANCTUARY OF FEAR (TF) Marble Arch Productions, 1979
THE POWER WITHIN (TF) Aaron Spelling Productions, 1979
THE SOLITARY MAN (TF) Universal TV, 1979
EBONY, IVORY AND JADE (TF) Frankel Films, 1979
THE CHILDREN OF AN LAC (TF) Charles Fries Productions, 1980
THE MATING SEASON (TF) Highgate Pictures, 1980
NO PLACE TO HIDE (TF) Metromedia Producers Corporation, 1981
THE VIOLATION OF SARAH McDAVID (TF) CBS Entertainment, 1981
KILLJOY (TF) Lorimar Productions, 1981
I, DESIRE (TF) Green-Epstein Productions/Columbia TV, 1982
THE CRADLE WILL FALL (TF) Cates Films Inc./Procter & Gamble Productions, 1983
THROUGH NAKED EYES (TF) Charles Fries Productions, 1983

ALLAN MOYLE*

Home: 49 Park Avenue, New York, NY 10016, 212/685-0823
Messages: 212/279-9321
Agent: Luis San Turjo, ICM - New York City, 212/556-5600

MONTREAL MAIN co-director with Frank Vitale & Maxine McGillivray, President Films/Canadian Film Development Corporation, 1978, Canadian
THE RUBBER GUN Schuman-Katzka, 1978, Canadian
TIMES SQUARE AFD, 1980

RUSSELL MULCAHY

Agent: John Ptak, William Morris Agency - Beverly Hills, 213/274-7451

DEREK AND CLIVE GET THE HORN (FD) Peter Cook Productions, 1981, British
RAZORBACK Warner Bros., 1984, Australian

ROBERT MULLIGAN*

b. August 23, 1925 - Bronx, New York
Agent: Stan Kamen, William Morris Agency - Beverly Hills, 213/274-7451

FEAR STRIKES OUT Paramount, 1957
THE RAT RACE Paramount, 1960
THE GREAT IMPOSTER Universal, 1961
COME SEPTEMBER Universal, 1961
THE SPIRAL ROAD Universal, 1962
TO KILL A MOCKINGBIRD ★ Universal, 1962
LOVE WITH THE PROPER STRANGER Paramount, 1964
BABY, THE RAIN MUST FALL Columbia, 1965
INSIDE DAISY CLOVER Warner Bros., 1966
UP THE DOWN STAIRCASE Warner Bros., 1967
THE STALKING MOON National General, 1969
THE PURSUIT OF HAPPINESS Columbia, 1971
SUMMER OF '42 Warner Bros., 1971
THE OTHER 20th Century-Fox, 1972
THE NICKEL RIDE 20th Century-Fox, 1975
BLOODBROTHERS Warner Bros., 1979
SAME TIME, NEXT YEAR Universal, 1979
KISS ME GOODBYE 20th Century-Fox, 1982

JIMMY T. MURAKAMI

Business: Murakami/Wolf/Swenson, Inc., 1463 Tamarind Avenue, Hollywood, CA 90028, 213/462-6473

BATTLE BEYOND THE STARS New World, 1979

WALTER MURCH

Contact: Writers Guild of America - Los Angeles, 213/550-1000

OZ Buena Vista, 1985

EDWARD MURPHY

RAW FORCE American Panorama, 1982
THE JUNGLE Media Home Entertainment/Jungle Production Corporation, 1985

GEOFF MURPHY

Contact: New Zealand Film Commission, P.O. Box 11-546, Wellington, New Zealand, 4/72-2360

WILDMAN New Zealand
GOODBYE PORK PIE The Samuel Goldwyn Company, 1981, New Zealand
UTU Pickman Films, 1983, New Zealand
THE QUIET EARTH Quiet Earth Productions, 1985, New Zealand

DON MURRAY

b. July 29, 1929 - Hollywood, California
Agent: F.A.M.E. - Los Angeles, 213/656-7590

THE CROSS AND THE SWITCHBLADE Dick Ross, 1970

JOHN MUSKER

Business: Walt Disney Productions, 500 S. Buena Vista Street, Burbank, CA 91521, 818/845-3141

BASIL OF BAKER STREET (AF) co-director with Burny Mattinson & Dave Michener, Buena Vista, 1987

FLOYD MUTRUX*

Contact: Directors Guild of America - Los Angeles, 213/656-1220

DUSTY AND SWEETS McGEE Warner Bros., 1971
ALOHA, BOBBY AND ROSE Columbia, 1975
AMERICAN HOT WAX Paramount, 1978
THE HOLLYWOOD KNIGHTS Columbia, 1980

ALAN MYERSON*

Agent: Scott Harris, Abrams, Harris, Goldberg - Los Angeles, 213/859-0625
Business Manager: Shapiro-West - Beverly Hills, 213/278-8896

STEELYARD BLUES Warner Bros., 1973
THE LOVE BOAT (TF) co-director with Richard Kinon, Douglas S. Cramer Productions, 1976
PRIVATE LESSONS Jensen Farley Pictures, 1981

N

ARTHUR H. NADEL*

Business: Filmation Studios, 18107 Sherman Way, Reseda, CA 91335, 818/345-7414
Attorney: Robert Kehr, Kehr, Siegel & Brifman - Los Angeles, 213/552-9681

CLAMBAKE United Artists, 1967
UNDERGROUND United Artists, 1970

IVAN NAGY*

b. January 23, 1938 - Budapest, Hungary
Home: 10128 Empyrean Way, Los Angeles, CA 90067, 213/552-4724
Agent: Jeff Cooper/Robby Wald, The Cooper Agency - Los Angeles, 213/277-8422

BAD CHARLESTON CHARLIE International Cinema, 1973
MONEY, MARBLES AND CHALK American International, 1973
FIVE MINUTES OF FREEDOM Cannon, 1973
DEADLY HERO Avco Embassy, 1976
MIND OVER MURDER (TF) Paramount TV, 1979
ONCE UPON A SPY (TF) David Gerber Company/Columbia TV, 1980
MIDNIGHT LACE (TF) Four R Productions/Universal TV, 1981

IVAN NAGY*—continued

A GUN IN THE HOUSE (TF) Channing-Debin-Locke Company, 1981
JANE DOE (TF) ITC, 1983
A TOUCH OF SCANDAL (TF) Doris M. Keating Productions/Columbia TV, 1984

MICHAEL NANKIN*

Messages: 213/981-0102
Agent: Linne Radmin, Henderson-Hogan - Beverly Hills, 213/274-7815

MIDNIGHT MADNESS co-director with David Wechter, Buena Vista, 1981

SILVIO NARIZZANO

b. February 8, 1928 - Montreal, Quebec, Canada
Home: 8400 De Longpre, Los Angeles, CA 90069, 213/654-9548
Agent: William Morris Agency - Beverly Hills, 213/274-7451

DIE! DIE! MY DARLING! *FANATIC* Columbia, 1965, British
GEORGY GIRL Columbia, 1967, British
BLUE Paramount, 1968, British
LOOT Cinevision, 1972, British
REDNECK International Amusements, 1975, British-Italian
THE SKY IS FALLING 1976, Canadian
WHY SHOOT THE TEACHER Quartet, 1977, Canadian
COME BACK, LITTLE SHEBA (TF) Granada TV, 1977, British
THE CLASS OF MISS MacMICHAEL Brut Productions, 1979, British
STAYING ON (TF) Granada TV, 1980, British
CHOICES 1981, Canadian

GREGORY NAVA

b. April 10, 1949 - San Diego, California
Agent: Jeff Berg, ICM, Los Angeles, 213/550-4000

THE CONFESSIONS OF AMANS Independent Productions, 1976
EL NORTE Cinecom International/Island Alive, 1984

CAL NAYLOR*

Home: 17606 Posetano Road, Pacific Palisades, CA 90272, 213/454-7229

DIRT co-director with Eric Karson, American Cinema, 1979

RONALD NEAME*

b. April 23, 1911 - London, England
Home: 2317 Kimridge Road, Beverly Hills, CA 90210
Agent: John Gaines, APA - Los Angeles, 213/273-0744

TAKE MY LIFE Eagle Lion, 1947, British
THE GOLDEN SALAMANDER Eagle Lion, 1950, British
THE PROMOTER *THE CARD* Universal, 1952, British
MAN WITH A MILLION *THE MILLION POUND NOTE* United Artists, 1954, British
THE MAN WHO NEVER WAS 20th Century-Fox, 1956, British
THE SEVENTH SIN MGM, 1957
WINDOM'S WAY Rank, 1958, British
THE HORSE'S MOUTH United Artists, 1959, British
TUNES OF GLORY Lopert, 1960, British
ESCAPE FROM ZAHRAIN Paramount, 1962
I COULD GO ON SINGING United Artists, 1963, British
THE CHALK GARDEN Universal, 1964, British
MISTER MOSES United Artists, 1965, British
A MAN COULD GET KILLED co-directed with Cliff Owen, Universal, 1966
GAMBIT Universal, 1966
THE PRIME OF MISS JEAN BRODIE 20th Century-Fox, 1969, British
SCROOGE National General, 1970, British
THE POSEIDON ADVENTURE 20th Century-Fox, 1972

RONALD NEAME*—continued

THE ODESSA FILE Columbia, 1974, British-West German
METEOR American International, 1979
HOPSCOTCH Avco Embassy, 1980
FIRST MONDAY IN OCTOBER Paramount, 1981

HAL NEEDHAM*

b. March 6, 1931 - Memphis, Tennessee
Business: 3518 Cahuenga Blvd. West, Hollywood, CA 90068, 213/876-8052
Agent: David Wardlow, ICM - Los Angeles, 213/550-4000

SMOKEY AND THE BANDIT Universal, 1977
HOOPER Warner Bros., 1978
THE VILLAIN Columbia, 1979
DEATH CAR ON THE FREEWAY (TF) Shpetner Productions, 1979
STUNTS UNLIMITED (TF) Lawrence Gordon Productions/Paramount TV, 1980
SMOKEY AND THE BANDIT, PART II Universal, 1980
THE CANNONBALL RUN 20th Century-Fox, 1981
MEGAFORCE 20th Century-Fox, 1982
STROKER ACE Universal, 1983
CANNONBALL RUN II Warner Bros., 1984

JEAN NEGULESCO*

b. February 29, 1900 - Craiova, Romania
Home: 20508 Mandel Street, Canoga Park, CA 91306, 818/998-2536
Business Manager: Harold B. Weiser - Canoga Park, 818/998-2536

SINGAPORE WOMAN Warner Bros., 1941
THE MASK OF DIMITRIOS Warner Bros., 1944
THE CONSPIRATORS Warner Bros., 1944
THREE STRANGERS Warner Bros., 1946
NOBODY LIVES FOREVER Warner Bros., 1946
HUMORESQUE Warner Bros., 1947
DEEP VALLEY Warner Bros., 1947
JOHNNY BELINDA ★ Warner Bros., 1948
ROAD HOUSE 20th Century-Fox, 1948
THE FORBIDDEN STREET *BRITANNIA MEWS* 20th Century-Fox, 1949
UNDER MY SKIN 20th Century-Fox, 1950
THREE CAME HOME 20th Century-Fox, 1950
THE MUDLARK 20th Century-Fox, 1950
TAKE CARE OF MY LITTLE GIRL 20th Century-Fox, 1951
PHONE CALL FROM A STRANGER 20th Century-Fox, 1952
LYDIA BAILEY 20th Century-Fox, 1952
LURE OF THE WILDERNESS 20th Century-Fox, 1952
O. HENRY'S FULL HOUSE co-director with Howard Hawks, Henry King & Henry Koster, 20th Century-Fox, 1952
TITANIC 20th Century-Fox, 1953
HOW TO MARRY A MILLIONAIRE 20th Century-Fox, 1953
SCANDAL AT SCOURIE MGM, 1953
THREE COINS IN THE FOUNTAIN 20th Century-Fox, 1954
A WOMAN'S WORLD 20th Century-Fox, 1954
DADDY LONG LEGS 20th Century-Fox, 1955
THE RAINS OF RANCHIPUR 20th Century-Fox, 1955
BOY ON A DOLPHIN 20th Century-Fox, 1957
THE GIFT OF LOVE 20th Century-Fox, 1958
A CERTAIN SMILE 20th Century-Fox, 1958
COUNT YOUR BLESSINGS MGM, 1959
THE BEST OF EVERYTHING 20th Century-Fox, 1959
JESSICA United Artists, 1962, U.S.-Italian-French
THE PLEASURE SEEKERS 20th Century-Fox, 1964
HELLO - GOODBYE 20th Century-Fox, 1970
THE INVINCIBLE SIX Continental, 1970, U.S.-Iranian

DAVID NELSON *

b. October 24, 1936 - New York, New York
Business: Western International Media, 8732 Sunset Blvd., Los Angeles, CA 90038, 213/659-5711

DEATH SCREAMS ABA Productions, 1981
LAST PLANE OUT New World, 1983
A RARE BREED New World, 1984

GARY NELSON *

Agent: Fred Specktor, CAA - Los Angeles, 213/277-4545

MOLLY AND LAWLESS JOHN Producers Distribution Corporation, 1972
SANTEE Crown International, 1973
THE GIRL ON THE LATE, LATE SHOW (TF) Screen Gems/Columbia TV, 1974
MEDICAL STORY (TF) David Gerber Company/Columbia TV, 1975
PANACHE (TF) Warner Bros. TV, 1976
WASHINGTON: BEHIND CLOSED DOORS (MS) ☆ Paramount TV, 1977
FREAKY FRIDAY Buena Vista, 1977
TO KILL A COP (TF) David Gerber Company/Columbia, TV, 1978
THE BLACK HOLE Buena Vista, 1979
THE PRIDE OF JESSE HALLAM (TF) The Konigsberg Company, 1981
SEVEN BRIDES FOR SEVEN BROTHERS (TF) David Gerber Company/MGM-UA TV, 1982
JIMMY THE KID New World, 1983
MURDER IN COWETA COUNTY (TF) Telecom Entertainment/The International Picture Show Co., 1983
MICKEY SPILLANE'S 'MURDER ME, MURDER YOU' (TF) Jay Bernstein Productions/Columbia TV, 1983
FOR LOVE AND HONOR (TF) David Gerber Company/MGM-UA TV, 1983

GENE NELSON *

(Gene Berg)

b. March 24, 1920 - Seattle, Washington
Home: 3431 Vinton Avenue, Los Angeles, CA 90034, 213/837-0484
Agent: Contemporary-Korman Artists - Beverly Hills, 213/278-8250

HAND OF DEATH 20th Century-Fox, 1962
HOOTENANNY HOOT MGM, 1962
KISSIN' COUSINS MGM, 1964
YOUR CHEATIN' HEART MGM, 1964
HARUM SCARUM MGM, 1965
THE COOL ONES Warner Bros., 1967
WAKE ME WHEN THE WAR IS OVER (TF) Thomas-Spelling Productions, 1969
THE LETTERS (TF) co-director with Paul Krasny, ABC Circle Films, 1973
THE BARON AND THE KID (TF) Telecom Entertainment, 1984

RALPH NELSON *

b. August 12, 1916 - New York, New York
Agent: ICM - Los Angeles, 213/550-4000
Business Manager: Howard Bernstein, Kaufman & Bernstein, 1900 Avenue of the Stars, Los Angeles, CA 90067, 213/277-1900

REQUIEM FOR A HEAVYWEIGHT Columbia, 1962
LILIES OF THE FIELD United Artists, 1963
SOLDIER IN THE RAIN Allied Artists, 1963
FATE IS THE HUNTER 20th Century-Fox, 1964
FATHER GOOSE Universal, 1964
ONCE A THIEF MGM, 1965
DUEL AT DIABLO United Artists, 1966
COUNTERPOINT Universal, 1968
CHARLY Cinerama Releasing Corporation, 1968
...tick...tick...tick... MGM, 1970
SOLDIER BLUE Avco Embassy, 1970
FLIGHT OF THE DOVES Columbia, 1971, British
THE WRATH OF GOD MGM, 1972

RALPH NELSON*—continued

THE WILBY CONSPIRACY United Artists, 1975, British
EMBRYO Cine Artists, 1976
A HERO AIN'T NOTHIN' BUT A SANDWICH New World, 1977
LADY OF THE HOUSE (TF) co-director with Vincent Sherman, Metromedia Productions, 1978
BECAUSE HE'S MY FRIEND (TF) Australian Broadcasting Commission/Trans-Atlantic Enterprises, 1979, Australian
CHRISTMAS LILIES OF THE FIELD (TF) Rainbow Productions/Osmond Productions, 1979
YOU CAN'T GO HOME AGAIN (TF) CBS Entertainment, 1979

AVI NESHER

Contact: Israel Film Centre, Ministry of Tourism & Trade, 30 Agron Street, P.O. Box 299, Jerusalem 94190, Israel, 02/210433

THE TROUPE *HALAHAKA* Eastways Productions, 1978, Israeli
DIZENGOFF 99 Shapira Films, 1979, Israeli
SHE Film Ventures International, 1984, Italian-U.S.
RAGE AND GLORY New Cinema, 1984, Israeli

MIKE NEWELL

b. 1942
Address: 30 Cantelowes Road, London NW1, England, 01/485-1584
Agent: Duncan Heath Associates, 57 Redliffe Road, London SW10, England

THE MAN IN THE IRON MASK (TF) Norman Rosemont Productions/ITC, 1977, U.S.-British
THE AWAKENING Orion/Warner Bros., 1980
BLOOD FEUD (TF) 20th Century-Fox TV/Glickman-Selznick Productions, 1983
BAD BLOOD Southern Pictures/New Zealand Film Commission, 1983, New Zealand
DANCE WITH A STRANGER Samuel Goldwyn Company, 1985, British

JOHN NEWLAND*

b. November 23, 1917 - Cincinnati, Ohio
Business: The Factor-Newland Production Corporation, 1438 Gower Street - Suite 250, Los Angeles, CA 90028, 213/467-1143
Agent: Herb Tobias & Associates - Los Angeles, 213/277-6211

THAT NIGHT Universal, 1957
THE VIOLATORS Universal, 1957
THE SPY WITH MY FACE MGM, 1966
MY LOVER, MY SON MGM, 1970, British
THE DEADLY HUNT (TF) Four Star International, 1971
CRAWLSPACE (TF) Titus Productions, 1972
DON'T BE AFRAID OF THE DARK (TF) Lorimar Productions, 1972
WHO FEARS THE DEVIL *THE LEGEND OF HILLBILLY JOHN* Jack H. Harris Enterprises, 1974
A SENSITIVE, PASSIONATE MAN (TF) Factor-Newland Production Corporation, 1977
OVERBOARD (TF) Factor-Newland Production Corporation, 1978
THE SUICIDE'S WIFE (TF) Factor-Newland Production Corporation, 1979

ANTHONY NEWLEY

b. September 24, 1931 - London, England
Agent: ICM - Los Angeles, 213/550-4000

CAN HIERONYMOUS MERKIN EVER FORGET MERCY HUMPPE AND FIND TRUE HAPPINESS? Regional, 1969, British
SUMMERTREE Columbia, 1971

PAUL NEWMAN*

b. January 26, 1925 - Cleveland, Ohio
Agent: Michael Ovitz, CAA - Los Angeles, 213/277-4545

RACHEL, RACHEL Warner Bros., 1968
SOMETIMES A GREAT NOTION *NEVER GIVE AN INCH* Universal, 1971
THE EFFECT OF GAMMA RAYS ON MAN-IN-THE-MOON MARIGOLDS 20th Century-Fox, 1973
THE SHADOW BOX (TF) ☆ The Shadow Box Film Company, 1980
HARRY & SON Orion, 1984

MIKE NICHOLS*

(Michael Igor Peschkowsky)

b. November 6, 1931 - Berlin, Germany
Agent: Sam Cohn, ICM - New York City, 212/556-6810
Attorney: Marvin B. Meyer, Rosenfeld, Meyer & Susman - Beverly Hills, 213/858-7700

WHO'S AFRAID OF VIRGINIA WOOLF? ★ Warner Bros., 1966
THE GRADUATE ★★ Avco Embassy, 1967
CATCH-22 Paramount, 1970
CARNAL KNOWLEDGE Avco Embassy, 1971
THE DAY OF THE DOLPHIN Avco Embassy, 1973
THE FORTUNE Columbia, 1975
GILDA LIVE (FD) Warner Bros., 1980
SILKWOOD ★ 20th Century-Fox, 1983

ALLAN NICHOLLS

Contact: Writers Guild of America, West - Los Angeles, 213/550-1000

DEAD RINGER Feature Films, 1982

JACK NICHOLSON*

b. April 22, 1937 - Neptune, New Jersey
Agent: Sandy Bresler, The Artists Agency - Los Angeles, 213/277-7779
Business Manager: Guild Management Corporation - Los Angeles, 213/277-9711

DRIVE, HE SAID Columbia, 1971
GOIN' SOUTH Paramount, 1979

PAUL NICOLAS

(Lutz Schaarwaechter)

BAD BLOOD *JULIE DARLING* Twin Continental, 1982, Canadian-West German
CHAINED HEAT Jensen Farley Pictures, 1983

GEORGE T. NIERENBERG

b. Roslyn Heights, New York

THE HOLLOW GTN Productions, 1975
NO MAPS ON MY TAPS (FD) GTN Productions, 1980
SAY AMEN, SOMEBODY (FD) United Artists Classics, 1983

ROB NILSSON

NORTHERN LIGHTS co-director with John Hanson, Cine-Manifest, 1979
ON THE EDGE Alliance Films, 1984
SIGNAL 7 1984

LEONARD NIMOY*

b. 1932 - Boston, Massachusetts
Agent: Merritt Blake, The Blake Agency - Beverly Hills, 213/278-6885

STAR TREK III: THE SEARCH FOR SPOCK Paramount, 1984

DON NORMAN

b. November 2, 1950 - New York, New York
Home: 1134 N. Ogden Drive, Los Angeles, CA 90046, 213/654-6911

A DEATH Venice Pictures, 1979
VT Marshfield Productions, 1980
RENNIE Horizons Productions, 1982
HORIZONS Horizons Productions, 1983

B.W.L. NORTON*

(William Lloyd Norton)

b. August 13, 1943 - California
Agent: John Ptak, William Morris Agency - Beverly Hills, 213/274-7451

CISCO PIKE Columbia, 1971
GARGOYLES (TF) Tomorrow Entertainment, 1972
MORE AMERICAN GRAFFITI Universal, 1979
BABY Buena Vista, 1985

NOEL NOSSECK*

Agent: Leading Artists - Beverly Hills, 213/858-1999

BEST FRIENDS Crown International, 1973
LAS VEGAS LADY Crown International, 1976
YOUNGBLOOD American International, 1978
DREAMER 20th Century-Fox, 1979
KING OF THE MOUNTAIN Universal, 1981
RETURN OF THE REBELS (TF) Moonlight Productions/Filmways, 1981
THE FIRST TIME (TF) Moonlight Productions, 1982
NIGHT PARTNERS (TF) Moonlight Productions II, 1983
SUMMER FANTASIES (TF) Moonlight Productions II, 1984

AMRAM NOWAK

THE CAFETERIA (TF) Amram Nowak Associates, 1984

PHILLIP NOYCE

Agent: Cameron's Management, 120 Victoria Street, Kings Cross, NSW, 2011, Australia, 02/358-6433

BACKROADS Cinema Ventures, 1978, Australian
NEWSFRONT New Yorker, 1979, Australian
HEATWAVE New Line Cinema, 1982, Australian

SIMON NUCHTERN

THE COWARDS Jaylo, 1970
WHAT DO I TELL THE BOYS AT THE STATION? August, 1972
THE BROAD COALITION August, 1972
TO HEX WITH SEX RAF Industries, 1975
THE BODYGUARD Aquarius, 1976
SILENT MADNESS Almi Pictures, 1984
NEW YORK NIGHTS International Talent Marketing, 1984
SAVAGE DAWN MAG Enterprises/Gregory Earls Productions, 1985

VICTOR NUÑEZ

GAL YOUNG UN Nuñez Films, 1979
A FLASH OF GREEN (TF) Nuñez Films, 1984

TREVOR NUNN

b. January 14, 1940 - Ipswich, Suffolk, England
Contact: Directors Guild of Great Britain, 56 Whitfield Street, London W1, England, 01/580-9592

HEDDA Brut Productions, 1975, British
LADY JANE Paramount, 1985, British

CHRISTIAN NYBY II*

b. June 1, 1941 - Glendale, California
Agent: Barry Perlman - Beverly Hills, 213/274-5999

THE RANGERS (TF) Universal TV/Mark VII Ltd., 1974
PINE CANYON IS BURNING (TF) Universal TV, 1977
RIPTIDE (TF) Stephen J. Cannell Productions, 1984

O

DAN O'BANNON

Agent: Morton Agency - Los Angeles, 213/824-4089

RETURN OF THE LIVING DEAD Orion, 1985

ARCH OBOLER

b. December 7, 1909 - Chicago, Illinois
Contact: Writers Guild of America, West - Los Angeles, 213/550-1000

BEWITCHED MGM, 1945
STRANGE HOLIDAY Producers Releasing Corporation, 1946
THE ARNELO AFFAIR MGM, 1947
FIVE Columbia, 1951
BWANA DEVIL United Artists, 1952
THE TWONKY United Artists, 1953
1 + 1: EXPLORING THE KINSEY REPORTS (FD) 1961, U.S.-Canadian
THE BUBBLE Oboler Films, 1967
DOMO ARIGATO (FD) Oboler Films, 1972

JIM O'BRIEN

Agent: Judy Daish Agency, 122 Wigmore Street, London W1H 9FE, England, 01/486-5404

THE JEWEL IN THE CROWN (MS) co-director with Christopher Morahan, Granada TV, 1984, British

JEFFREY OBROW

THE DORM THAT DRIPPED BLOOD *PRANKS* co-director with Stephen Carpenter, New Image Releasing, 1982
THE POWER co-director with Stephen Carpenter, Artists Releasing Corporation/ Film Ventures International, 1984

JACK O'CONNELL

GREENWICH VILLAGE STORY Lion International, 1963
REVOLUTION (FD) Lopert, 1968
SWEDISH FLY GIRLS *CHRISTA* American International, 1971, U.S.-Danish

JAMES O'CONNOLLY

Address: 61 Edith Grove, London SW10, England, 01/352-1242

THE HI-JACKERS Butcher, 1964, British
SMOKESCREEN Butcher, 1964, British
THE LITTLE ONES Columbia, 1965, British
BERSERK! Columbia, 1968, British
THE VALLEY OF GWANGI Warner Bros., 1969, British
SOPHIE'S PLACE *CROOKS AND CORONETS* Warner Bros., 1969, British
HORROR ON SNAPE ISLAND *BEYOND THE FOG* Fanfare, 1972, British
MISTRESS PAMELA Fanfare, 1974, British

PAT O'CONNOR

Contact: Film Division - Department of Industry and Energy, Kildare Street, Dublin, Ireland, 1/78-9411

CAL Warner Bros., 1984, Irish

MICHAEL O'DONOGHUE*

Agent: David Kennedy, ICM - New York City, 212/556-5600
Business Manager: Barry Secunda, Project X, 1619 Broadway - Suite 915, New York, NY 10019, 212/247-4790

MR. MIKE'S MONDO VIDEO New Line Cinema, 1979

GEORGE OGILVIE*

Contact: Australian Film Commission, 9229 W. Sunset Blvd., Los Angeles, CA 90069, 213/275-7074

MAD MAX III Co-director with George Miller, Warner Bros., 1985, Australian

GERRY O'HARA

b. 1924 - Boston, Lincolnshire, England
Address: 8 Broomhouse Road, London SW6, England, 01/736-7869
Agent: CCA, 29 Dawes Road, London SW6, England, 01/381-3551

MODELS, INC. *THAT KIND OF GIRL* Mutual, 1963, British
A GAME FOR THREE LOSERS Embassy, 1963, British
THE PLEASURE GIRLS Times, 1965, British
MAROC 7 Paramount, 1966, British
AMSTERDAM AFFAIR Lippert, 1968, British
FIDELIA 1970, British

GERRY O'HARA —continued

ALL THE RIGHT NOISES 20th Century-Fox, 1971, British
THE BRUTE Rank, 1976, British
LEOPARD IN THE SNOW New World, 1978, Canadian-British
THE BITCH Brent Walker Productions, 1979, British
FANNY HILL Playboy Enterprises, 1983, British

MICHAEL O'HERLIHY*

b. April 1, 1928 - Dublin, Ireland
Agent: Contemporary-Korman Artists - Beverly Hills, 213/278-8250

THE FIGHTING PRINCE OF DONEGAL Buena Vista, 1966, British-U.S.
THE ONE AND ONLY GENUINE, ORIGINAL FAMILY BAND Buena Vista, 1967
SMITH! Buena Vista, 1969
DEADLY HARVEST (TF) CBS, Inc., 1972
YOUNG PIONEERS (TF) ABC Circle Films, 1976
KISS ME, KILL ME (TF) Columbia TV, 1976
YOUNG PIONEERS' CHRISTMAS (TF) ABC Circle Films, 1976
PETER LUNDY AND THE MEDICINE HAT STALLION (TF) Ed Friendly Productions, 1977
BACKSTAIRS AT THE WHITE HOUSE (MS) Ed Friendly Productions, 1979
THE FLAME IS LOVE (TF) Ed Friendly Productions/Friendly-O'Herlihy Ltd., 1979
DALLAS COWBOYS CHEERLEADERS II (TF) Aubrey-Hamner Productions, 1980
DETOUR TO TERROR (TF) Orenthal Productions/Playboy Productions/Columbia TV, 1980
THE GREAT CASH GIVEAWAY GETAWAY (TF) Penthouse Productions/Cine Guarantors, Inc., 1980
CRY OF THE INNOCENT (TF) Tara Productions, 1980
DESPERATE VOYAGE (TF) Barry Weitz Films/Joe Wizan TV Productions, 1980
A TIME FOR MIRACLES (TF) ABC Circle Films, 1980
THE MILLION DOLLAR FACE (TF) Nephi-Hamner Productions, 1981
I MARRIED WYATT EARP (TF) Osmond TV Productions, 1983
TWO BY FORSYTH (TF) Tara Productions/ Mobil Corporation, 1984, U.S.-Irish

TOM O'HORGAN*

Contact: Directors Guild of America - New York City, 212/581-0370

FUTZ Commonwealth United, 1969
RHINOCEROS American Film Theatre, 1974

JOEL OLIANSKY*

b. October 11, 1935 - New York, New York
Agent: Triad Artists, Inc. - Los Angeles, 213/556-2727

THE COMPETITION Columbia, 1980

LAURENCE OLIVIER

b. May 22, 1907 - Dorking, England
Address: 33/34 Chancery Lane, London WC2, England
Agent: ICM - London, 01/629-8080

HENRY V Rank, 1945, British
HAMLET ★ Universal, 1946, British
RICHARD III Lopert, 1956, British
THE PRINCE AND THE SHOWGIRL Warner Bros., 1957, U.S.-British
THREE SISTERS American Film Theatre, 1970, British

ERMANNO OLMI

b. July 24, 1931 - Bergamo, Italy
Contact: Ministry of Tourism & Education, Via Della Ferratella, No. 51, 00184 Rome, Italy, 06/7732

IL TEMPO SI E FERMATO Sezione Cinema Edison Volta, 1959, Italian
THE SOUND OF TRUMPETS Janus, 1961, Italian
THE FIANCES Janus, 1963, Italian
AND THERE CAME A MAN Brandon, 1965, Italian
UN CERTO GIORNO Cinema Spa/Italnoleggio, 1968, Italian
I RECUPERANTI (TF) RAI/Produzione Palumbo, 1969, Italian
DURANTE L'ESTATE (TF) RAI, 1971, Italian
LA CIRCOSTANZA (TF) RAI/Italnoleggio, 1974, Italian
THE TREE OF WOODEN CLOGS New Yorker, 1979, Italian, originally made for television
KEEP WALKING RAI/Gaumont, 1983, Italian-French
CAMMINACAMMINA Grange Communications, 1983, Italian
MILANO '83 (FD) 1983, Italian

WILLIAM OLSEN

GETTING IT ON Comworld, 1983
SUMMERTIME BLUES Triad Entertainment Group, 1985

RON O'NEAL

b. September 1, 1937 - Utica, New York
Agent: 213/857-1234

SUPERFLY T.N.T. Paramount, 1973

ROBERT VINCENT O'NEIL

Agent: The Sy Fischer Company - Los Angeles, 213/557-0388

THE LOVING TOUCH Medford, 1970
BLOOD MANIA 1971
WONDER WOMEN 1973
PACO Cinema National, 1975
ANGEL New World, 1984
AVENGING ANGEL New World, 1985

MARCEL OPHULS

b. November 1, 1927 - Frankfurt-am-Main, Germany
Contact: French Film Office, 745 Fifth Avenue, New York, NY 10151, 212/832-8860

MATISSE 1960, French
LOVE AT TWENTY co-director with Francois Truffaut, Andrzej Wajda, Renzo Rossellini & Shintaro Ishihara, Embassy, 1962, French-Italian-Japanese-Polish-West German
BANANA PEEL Pathe Contemporary, 1965, French-Italian
FEU A VOLONTE 1965, French-Italian
MUNICH, OU LA PRIX POUR CENT ANS (TD) 1967, French
CLAVIGO (TF) 1970, French
THE HARVEST OF MY LAI (TD) 1970, French
AMERICA REVISITED (TD) 1971, French
ZWEI GANZE TAGE (TF) 1971, West German
THE SORROW AND THE PITY (FD) Cinema 5, 1972, French-Swiss-West German
A SENSE OF LOSS (FD) Cinema 5, 1972, U.S.-Swiss
THE MEMORY OF JUSTICE (FD) Paramount, 1976, British-West German
KORTNER GESCHICHTE (TD) 1980, West German
YORKTOWN, LE SANS D'UNE BETAILLE (TD) 1982, French

DOMINIC ORLANDO

CRY OF THE CITY Miami Gold Productions, 1985

JAMES ORR

Home: 59 Chelsea Avenue, Toronto, Ontario M6P 1B9, Canada, 416/535-6866 or: 1712 Courtney Avenue, Los Angeles, CA 90046, 213/851-4875

FUN PARK Filmline Productions, 1985, Canadian

NAGISA OSHIMA

b. March 31, 1932 - Kyoto, Japan
Contact: Directors Guild of Japan, Tsukada Building, 8-33 Udagawa-cho, Shibuya-ku, Tokyo 150, Japan, 3/461-4411

A TOWN OF LOVE AND HOPE Shochiku, 1959, Japanese
CRUEL STORY OF YOUTH Shochiku, 1960, Japanese
THE SUN'S BURIAL Shochiku, 1960, Japanese
NIGHT AND FOG IN JAPAN Shochiku, 1960, Japanese
THE CATCH Palace Productions/Taiho, 1961, Japanese
THE REVOLUTIONARY Toei, 1962, Japanese
A SMALL CHILD'S FIRST ADVENTURE Nissei Insurance Company, 1964, Japanese
IT'S ME HERE, BELLETT Society of Japanese Film Directors, 1964, Japanese
THE PLEASURES OF THE FLESH Sozosha/Shociku, 1965, Japanese
VIOLENCE AT NOON Sozosha/Shochiku, 1966, Japanese
BAND OF NINJA Sozosha/Art Theatre Guild, 1967, Japanese
A TREATISE IN JAPANESE BAWDY SONGS Sozosha/Shochiku, 1967, Japanese
JAPANESE SUMMER: DOUBLE SUICIDE Sozosha/Shochiku, 1967, Japanese
DEATH BY HANGING Grove Press, 1968, Japanese
THREE RESURRECTED DRUNKARDS Sozosha/Shochiku, 1968, Japanese
DIARY OF A SHINJUKU BURGLAR Grove Press, 1968, Japanese
BOY Grove Press, 1969, Japanese
THE CEREMONY New Yorker, 1974, Japanese
IN THE REALM OF THE SENSES Surrogate Releasing, 1977, Japanese
EMPIRE OF PASSION *CORRIDA OF LOVE* Barbary Coast, 1980, Japanese
MERRY CHRISTMAS, MR. LAWRENCE Universal, 1983, British-Japanese

SAM O'STEEN*

b. November 6, 1923
Personal Manager: Harry Ufland, Ufland-Roth Productions, 20th Century Fox, 10201 W. Pico Blvd., Executive Building Room 246, Los Angeles, CA 90035, 213/203-1295
Business Manager: Robert Morgan, Tucker, Morgan & Martindale - Los Angeles, 213/274-0891

A BRAND NEW LIFE (TF) Tomorrow Entertainment, 1973
I LOVE YOU, GOODBYE (TF) Tomorrow Entertainment, 1974
QUEEN OF THE STARDUST BALLROOM (TF) ☆ Tomorrow Entertainment, 1975
HIGH RISK (TF) Danny Thomas Productions/MGM TV, 1976
SPARKLE Warner Bros., 1976
LOOK WHAT'S HAPPENED TO ROSEMARY'S BABY (TF) Paramount TV, 1976
THE BEST LITTLE GIRL IN THE WORLD (TF) Aaron Spelling Productions, 1981

GERD OSWALD*

b. June 9, 1916 - Berlin, Germany
Home: 237A Spalding Drive, Beverly Hills, CA 90212, 213/553-7470

A KISS BEFORE DYING United Artists, 1956
THE BRASS LEGEND United Artists, 1956
CRIME OF PASSION United Artists, 1957
FURY AT SHOWDOWN United Artists, 1957
VALERIE United Artists, 1957
PARIS HOLIDAY United Artists, 1958
SCREAMING MIMI Columbia, 1958
AM TAG ALS DER REGEN KAM 1959, West German
BRAINWASHED Allied Artists, 1960, West German

GERD OSWALD*—continued

TEMPESTA SU CEYLON co-director with Giovanni Roccardi, FICIT/Rapid Film, 1963, Italian-French
AGENT FOR H.A.R.M. Universal, 1966
80 STEPS TO JONAH Warner Bros., 1969
BUNNY O'HARE American International, 1971
BIS ZUR BITTEREN NEIGE 1975, West German-Australian

GERARD OURY

(Max-Gerard Houry Tannenbaum)

b. April 29, 1919 - Paris, France
Contact: French Film Office, 745 Fifth Avenue, New York, NY 10151, 212/832-8860

LA MAIN CHAUDE Films de France, 1960, French
THE MENACE Warner Bros., 1961, French
CRIME DOES NOT PAY Embassy, 1962, French-Italian
THE SUCKER Royal Films International, 1966, French-Italian
DON'T LOOK NOW...WE'RE BEING SHOT AT *LA GRANDE VADROVILLE* Cinepix, 1966, French-British
THE BRAIN Paramount, 1969, French-Italian
DELUSIONS OF GRANDEUR Joseph Green Pictures, 1971, French
THE MAD ADVENTURES OF 'RABBI' JACOB 20th Century-Fox, 1974, French-Italian
LA CARAPATE Gaumont, 1978, French
LE COUP DU PARAPLUIE Gaumont, 1980, French
L'AS DES AS Gaumont/Cerito Rene Chateau, 1982, French-West German
LA VENGEANCE DU SERPENT A PLUMES AMLF, 1984, French

CLIFF OWEN

b. April 22, 1919 - London, England
Address: 20 Marlborough Place, London NW8, England
Contact: Directors Guild of Great Britain, 56 Whitfield Street, London W1, 01/580-9592

OFFBEAT 1961, British
A PRIZE OF ARMS British Lion, 1961, British
THE WRONG ARM OF THE LAW Continental, 1963, British
A MAN COULD GET KILLED co-director with Ronald Neame, Universal, 1966
THAT RIVIERA TOUCH Continental, 1966, British
WHAT HAPPENED AT CAMPO GRANDE? *THE MAGNIFICENT TWO* Alan Enterprises, 1967, British
THE VENGEANCE OF SHE 20th Century-Fox, 1968, British
STEPTOE AND SON MGM-EMI, 1972, British
OOH...YOU ARE AWFUL Lion International, 1973, British
NO SEX PLEASE - WE'RE BRITISH Columbia-Warner, 1973, British
THE BAWDY ADVENTURES OF TOM JONES Universal, 1975, British
GET CHARLIE TULLY 1976, British

DON OWEN

NOBODY WAVED GOODBYE Cinema 5, 1964, Canadian
THE ERNIE GAME CBC/National Film Board of Canada, 1967, Canadian
PARTNERS Astral Films, 1967, Canadian
UNFINISHED BUSINESS Zebra Films/National Film Board of Canada/CBC, 1984, Canadian

FRANK OZ

Business: ATV Studios, Elstree, Hertfordshire, England

THE DARK CRYSTAL co-director with Jim Henson, Universal/AFD, 1982, British
THE MUPPETS TAKE MANHATTAN Tri-Star/Columbia, 1984

P

ANTHONY PAGE*

b. September 21, 1935 - Bangalore, India
Agent: William Morris Agency - Beverly Hills, 213/274-7451
Business Manager: Richard M. Rosenthal - Los Angeles, 213/820-8585

INADMISSABLE EVIDENCE Paramount, 1968, British
ALPHA BETA Cine III, 1976, British
F. SCOTT FITZGERALD IN HOLLYWOOD (TF) Titus Productions, 1976
I NEVER PROMISED YOU A ROSE GARDEN New World, 1977
ABSOLUTION Enterprise Pictures, 1979, British
THE LADY VANISHES Rank, 1979, British

ANTHONY PAGE*—continued

THE PATRICIA NEAL STORY (TF) co-director with Anthony Harvey, Lawrence Schiller Productions, 1981
BILL (TF) Alan Landsburg Productions, 1981
JOHNNY BELINDA (TF) Dick Berg-Stonehenge Productions/Lorimar Productions, 1982
GRACE KELLY (TF) The Kota Company/Embassy TV, 1983
BILL: ON HIS OWN (TF) Alan Landsburg Productions, 1983
FORBIDDEN (CTF) HBO Premiere Films/Mark Forstater Productions/Clasart/Anthea Productions, 1985, U.S.-British-West German

ALAN J. PAKULA*

b. April 7, 1928 - New York, New York
Messages: 212/333-2973
Agent: Stan Kamen, William Morris Agency - Beverly Hills, 213/274-7451
Business: Gus Productions, 10889 Wilshire Blvd., Los Angeles, CA 90024, 213/208-3046

THE STERILE CUCKOO Paramount, 1969
KLUTE Warner Bros., 1971
LOVE AND PAIN AND THE WHOLE DAMNED THING Columbia, 1973, British-U.S.
THE PARALLAX VIEW Paramount, 1974
ALL THE PRESIDENT'S MEN ★ Warner Bros., 1976
COMES A HORSEMAN United Artists, 1978
STARTING OVER Paramount, 1979
ROLLOVER Orion/Warner Bros., 1981
SOPHIE'S CHOICE Universal/AFD, 1982
DREAM LOVER MGM/UA, 1985

TONY PALMER

Address: 4 Kensington Park Gardens, London W11, England
Contact: Directors Guild of Great Britain, 56 Whitfield Street, London W1, England, 01/580-9592

FAREWELL CREAM (FD) 1968, British
200 MOTELS co-director with Frank Zappa, United Artists, 1971, British
BIRD ON A WIRE (FD) EMI, 1974, British
A TIME THERE WAS *A PROFILE OF BENJAMIN BRITTEN (TD)* London Weekend TV, 1980, British
THE SPACE MOVIE (FD) International Harmony, 1980, British
WAGNER (MS) London Trust Productions/Richard Wagner Productions/Ladbroke Productions/Hungarofilm, 1983, British-Hungarian-Austrian

BRUCE PALTROW*

Business: MTM Enterprises, 4024 Radford Avenue, Studio City, CA 91604, 818/760-5000
Attorney: Ken Meyer, Rosenfeld, Meyer & Susman, 9601 Wilshire Blvd., Beverly Hills, 213/858-7700

A LITTLE SEX Universal, 1982

NORMAN PANAMA*

b. April 21, 1914 - Chicago, Illinois
Agent: Mitchell Kaplan, Kaplan-Stahler Agency - Los Angeles, 213/653-4483

THE REFORMER AND THE REDHEAD co-director with Melvin Frank, MGM, 1950
STRICTLY DISHONORABLE co-director with Melvin Frank, 1951
CALLAWAY WENT THATAWAY co-director with Melvin Frank, MGM, 1951
ABOVE AND BEYOND co-director with Melvin Frank, MGM, 1952
KNOCK ON WOOD co-director with Melvin Frank, Paramount, 1954
THE COURT JESTER co-director with Melvin Frank, Paramount, 1956
THAT CERTAIN FEELING co-director with Melvin Frank, Paramount, 1956
THE TRAP Paramount, 1959
THE ROAD TO HONG KONG United States, 1962
NOT WITH MY WIFE, YOU DON'T! Warner Bros., 1966

NORMAN PANAMA*—continued

HOW TO COMMIT MARRIAGE Cinerama Releasing Corporation, 1969
THE MALTESE BIPPY MGM, 1969
COFFEE, TEA OR ME? (TF) CBS, Inc., 1973
I WILL, I WILL...FOR NOW 20th Century-Fox, 1976
BARNABY AND ME Trans-Atlantic Enterprises, 1978

DOMONIC PARIS

DRACULA'S LAST RITES Cannon, 1980
SPLITZ Film Ventures International, 1984

HENRY PARIS

(see Radley METZGER)

JERRY PARIS*

b. July 25, 1925 - San Francisco, California
Agent: Roland Perkins, CAA - Los Angeles, 213/277-4545

DON'T RAISE THE BRIDGE - LOWER THE RIVER Columbia, 1968, British
NEVER A DULL MOMENT Buena Vista, 1968
HOW SWEET IT IS! National General, 1968
VIVA MAX! Commonwealth United, 1969
THE GRASSHOPPER National General, 1969
BUT I DON'T WANT TO GET MARRIED! (TF) Aaron Spelling Productions, 1970
THE FEMINIST AND THE FUZZ (TF) Screen Gems/Columbia TV, 1970
TWO ON A BENCH (TF) Universal TV, 1971
WHAT'S A NICE GIRL LIKE YOU...? Universal TV, 1971
STAR SPANGLED GIRL Paramount, 1971
CALL HER MOM (TF) Screen Gems/Columbia TV, 1972
EVIL ROY SLADE (TF) Universal TV, 1972
THE COUPLE TAKES A WIFE (TF) Universal TV, 1972
EVERY MAN NEEDS ONE (TF) ABC Circle Films, 1972
ONLY WITH MARRIED MEN (TF) Spelling-Goldberg Productions, 1974
HOW TO BREAK UP A HAPPY DIVORCE (TF) Charles Fries Productions, 1976
MAKE ME AN OFFER (TF) ABC Circle Films, 1980
LEO AND LOREE United Artists, 1980
POLICE ACADEMY II The Ladd Company, 1985

ALAN PARKER*

b. Feburary 14, 1944 - London, England
Business: The Alan Parker Film Company, Pinewood Studios, Iver Heath, Buckinghamshire, England
Agent: William Morris Agency - Beverly Hills, 213/274-7451

BUGSY MALONE Paramount, 1976, British
MIDNIGHT EXPRESS ★ Columbia, 1978, British
FAME MGM/United Artists, 1980
SHOOT THE MOON MGM/United Artists, 1982
PINK FLOYD - THE WALL MGM/UA, 1982, British
BIRDY Tri-Star, 1984

GORDON PARKS*

b. November 30, 1912 - Fort Scott, Kansas
Home: 860 U.N. Plaza, New York, NY 10017
Agent: ICM - Los Angeles, 213/550-4000

THE LEARNING TREE Warner Bros., 1969
SHAFT MGM, 1971
SHAFT'S BIG SCORE! MGM, 1972
THE SUPER COPS MGM, 1974
LEADBELLY Paramount, 1976
SUPER COPS (TF) MGM TV, 1976

EDWARD PARONE*

Agent: Mitch Kaplan, Kaplan-Stahler Agency - Beverly Hills, 213/653-4483

PROMISE HIM ANYTHING... (TF) ABC Circle Films, 1975
LETTERS FROM FRANK (TF) The Jozak Company/Cypress Point Productions, 1979

ROBERT PARRISH*

b. January 4, 1916 - Columbus, Georgia
Business Manager: Jess S. Morgan & Co., 6420 Wilshire Blvd., Los Angeles, CA 90048, 213/651-1601

CRY DANGER RKO Radio, 1951
THE MOB Columbia, 1951
THE SAN FRANCISCO STORY Warner Bros., 1952
ASSIGNMENT - PARIS Columbia, 1952
MY PAL GUS 20th Century-Fox, 1952
SHOOT FIRST *ROUGH SHOOT* United Artists, 1953, British
THE PURPLE PLAIN United Artists, 1954, British
LUCY GALLANT Paramount, 1955
FIRE DOWN BELOW Columbia, 1957
SADDLE THE WIND MGM, 1957
THE WONDERFUL COUNTRY United Artists, 1959
IN THE FRENCH STYLE Columbia, 1963, French-U.S.
UP FROM THE BEACH 20th Century-Fox, 1965
CASINO ROYALE co-director with Val Guest, Ken Hughes, John Huston & Joseph McGrath, Columbia, 1967, Columbia
THE BOBO Warner Bros., 1967, British
DUFFY Columbia, 1968, British
JOURNEY TO THE FAR SIDE OF THE SUN *DOPPELGANGER* Universal, 1969, British
A TOWN CALLED BASTARD *A TOWN CALLED HELL* Scotia International, 1971, British-Spanish
THE DESTRUCTORS *THE MARSEILLES CONTRACT* American International, 1974, British-French
MISSISSIPPI BLUES co-director with Bertrand Tavernier, Little Bear Productions/Odessa Films, 1984, French

MICHAEL PART

b. March 29, 1949 - Sheboygan, Wisconsin
Home: 5536 Carpenter Avenue, North Hollywood, CA 91607, 818/762-7278
Agent: Mike Rosen, Dade/Rosen/Lichtman - Los Angeles, 213/278-7074

STARBIRDS (ATF) 3B Productions Ltd., 1982, Japanese
REVENGE OF THE DEFENDERS (ATF) 3B Productions Ltd., 1982, Japanese
SHADOW WORLD (ATF) 3B Productions Ltd., 1983, Japanese
THE RAFT ADVENTURES OF HUCK AND JIM (ATF) 3B Productions Ltd., 1984, Japanese

GORAN PASKALJEVIC

THE BEACH GUARD IN WINTER Center FRZ, 1976, Yugoslavian
THE DOG THAT LIKED TRAINS Yugoslav Film Releasing, 1978, Yugoslavian
THE DAYS ARE PASSING Yugoslav Film Releasing, 1980
SPECIAL TREATMENT New Yorker, 1982, Yugoslavian
TWILIGHT TIME MGM/UA, 1983, U.S.-Yugoslavian

IVAN PASSER

b. July 10, 1983 - Prague, Czechoslovakia
Attorney: Egon Dumler - New York City, 212/PL. 9-4580

A BORING AFTERNOON 1965, Czech
INTIMATE LIGHTING Altura, 1965, Czech
BORN TO WIN United Artists, 1971
LAW AND DISORDER Columbia, 1974
CRIME AND PASSION American International, 1976
SILVER BEARS Columbia, 1978

IVAN PASSER —continued

CUTTER'S WAY *CUTTER AND BONE* United Artists Classics, 1981
CREATOR Universal, 1985

MICHAEL PATE

b. 1920 - Sydney, Australia
Business: Pisces Productions, 21 Bundarra Road, Bellevue Hill, NSW, 2023, Australia, 02/30-4208

TIM Satori, 1979, Australian

RAJU PATEL

IN THE SHADOW OF KILIMANJARO Intermedia Productions, 1984

SHARAD PATEL

b. India
Agent: Soren Fischer Associates, 14 Glebe House, Fitzroy Mews, London W1P 5DP, England, 01/437-6862

AMIN: THE RISE AND FALL *THE RISE AND FALL OF IDI AMIN* Twin Continental, 1983, British-Kenyan

STEVEN PAUL

b. May 16, 1958 - New York, New York
Business: Lance Entertainment Ltd., 8776 Sunset Blvd., Los Angeles, CA 90069, 213/652-9320

FALLING IN LOVE AGAIN International Picture Show Company, 1980
SLAPSTICK OF ANOTHER KIND *SLAPSTICK* Entertainment Releasing Corporation/International Film Marketing, 1983

DAVID PAULSEN *

Home: 15652 Woodfield Place, Sherman Oaks, CA 91403
Attorney: Frank Rohner & Associates, 9225 Sunset Blvd., Los Angeles, CA 90069, 213/274-6182

SAVAGE WEEKEND *THE UPSTATE MURDERS* Cannon, 1976
SCHIZOID Cannon, 1980

RICHARD PEARCE *

Home: 767 Paseo Miramar, Pacific Palisades, CA 90271
Agent: Martin Bauer Agency - Beverly Hills, 213/275-2421

THE GARDENER'S SON (TF) RIP/Filmhaus, 1977
SIEGE (TF) Titus Productions, 1978
NO OTHER LOVE (TF) Tisch-Avnet Productions, 1979
HEARTLAND Levitt-Pickman, 1979
THRESHOLD 20th Century-Fox International Classics, 1983, Canadian
SESSIONS (TF) Roger Gimbel Productions/EMI TV/Sarabande Productions, 1983
COUNTRY Buena Vista, 1984

SAM PECKINPAH *

b. February 21, 1925 - Fresno, California
Agent: Martin Baum, CAA - Los Angeles, 213/277-4545
Business Manager: Kip Dellinger - Los Angeles, 213/273-1410

THE DEADLY COMPANIONS Pathe-American, 1961
RIDE THE HIGH COUNTRY MGM, 1962
MAJOR DUNDEE Columbia, 1965
THE WILD BUNCH Warner Bros., 1969

SAM PECKINPAH*—continued

THE BALLAD OF CABLE HOGUE Warner Bros., 1970
STRAW DOGS Cinerama Releasing Corporation, 1972, British
THE GETAWAY National General, 1972
JUNIOR BONNER Cinerama Releasing Corporation, 1973
PAT GARRETT & BILLY THE KID MGM, 1973
BRING ME THE HEAD OF ALFREDO GARCIA United Artists, 1974
THE KILLER ELITE United Artists, 1975
CROSS OF IRON Avco Embassy, 1977, British-West German
CONVOY United Artists, 1978
THE OSTERMAN WEEKEND 20th Century-Fox, 1983

LARRY PEERCE*

b. Bronx, New York
Agent: Fred Specktor, CAA - Los Angeles, 213/277-4545

ONE POTATO, TWO POTATO Cinema 5, 1964
THE BIG T.N.T. SHOW (FD) American International, 1966
THE INCIDENT 20th Century-Fox, 1967
GOODBYE, COLUMBUS Paramount, 1969
THE SPORTING CLUB Avco Embassy, 1971
A SEPARATE PEACE Paramount, 1972
ASH WEDNESDAY Paramount, 1973
THE STRANGER WHO LOOKS LIKE ME (TF) Filmways, 1974
THE OTHER SIDE OF THE MOUNTAIN Universal, 1975
TWO-MINUTE WARNING Universal, 1976
THE OTHER SIDE OF THE MOUNTAIN - PART 2 Universal, 1978
THE BELL JAR Avco Embassy, 1979
WHY WOULD I LIE? MGM/United Artists, 1980
LOVE CHILD The Ladd Company/Warner Bros., 1982
I TAKE THESE MEN (TF) Lillian Gallo Productions/United Artists TV, 1983
HARD TO HOLD Universal, 1984

BARBARA PEETERS*

Business: The Big Movie Company, 4243 Bakeman Avenue, Studio City, CA 91602, 818/762-5883
Agent: Ronald Leif, Contemporary-Korman Artists, Beverly Hills, 213/278-8250

THE DARK SIDE OF TOMORROW co-director with Jacque Beerson, Able, 1970
BURY ME AN ANGEL New World, 1972
SUMMER SCHOOL TEACHERS New World, 1975
JUST THE TWO OF US Boxoffice International, 1975
STARHOPS First American, 1978
HUMANOIDS FROM THE DEEP New World, 1980

ARTHUR PENN*

b. September 27, 1922 - Philadelphia, Pennsylvania
Agent: Sam Cohn, ICM - New York City, 212/556-5600

THE LEFT HANDED GUN Warner Bros., 1958
THE MIRACLE WORKER ★ United Artists, 1962
MICKEY ONE Columbia, 1965
THE CHASE Columbia, 1966
BONNIE AND CLYDE ★ Warner Bros., 1967
ALICE'S RESTAURANT ★ United Artists, 1969
LITTLE BIG MAN National General, 1970
NIGHT MOVES Warner Bros., 1975
THE MISSOURI BREAKS United Artists, 1976
FOUR FRIENDS Filmways, 1981
TARGET Warner Bros., 1985

LEO PENN*

Agent: Herb Tobias & Associates - Los Angeles, 213/277-6211

QUARANTINED (TF) Paramount TV, 1970
TESTIMONY OF TWO MEN (MS) co-director with Larry Yust, Universal TV, 1977
THE DARK SECRET OF HARVEST HOME (TF) Universal TV, 1978
MURDER IN MUSIC CITY (TF) Frankel Films, 1979
HELLINGER'S LAW (TF) Universal TV, 1981

D.A. PENNEBAKER

(Don Alan Pennebaker)

b. 1930 - Evanston, Illinois
Business: Pennebaker Associates, 21 West 86th Street, New York, NY 10024, 212/496-9199

DON'T LOOK BACK (FD) Leacock-Pennebaker, 1967
MONTEREY POP (FD) Leacock-Pennebaker, 1967
COMPANY (FD) Pennebaker Associates, 1970
SWEET TORONTO *KEEP ON ROCKIN' (FD)* Pennebaker Associates, 1972
THE ENERGY WAR (TD) Pennebaker Associates/Corporation for Public Broadcasting, 1979
ELLIOTT CARTER (FD) Pennebaker Associates, 1980
TOWN BLOODY HALL (FD) co-director with Chris Hegedus, Pennebaker Associates, 1980
DeLOREAN (TD) Pennebaker Associates, 1981
ROCKABY (TD) co-director with Chris Hegedus Pennebaker Associates, 1983
ZIGGY STARDUST AND THE SPIDERS FROM MARS 20th Century-Fox International Classics/Miramax Films, 1983, filmed in 1973

EAGLE PENNELL

(Glenn Irwin Pinnell)

b. Texas

THE WHOLE SHOOTIN' MATCH First Run Features, 1979
LAST NIGHT AT THE ALAMO Cinecom International, 1983

GEORGE PEPPARD*

b. October 1, 1928 - Detroit, Michigan
Home: P.O. Box 1643, Beverly Hills, CA 90213, 213/652-6622
Agent: David Shapira & Associates - Sherman Oaks, 818/906-0322

FIVE DAYS FROM HOME Universal, 1977

ETIENNE PERIER

Contact: French Film Office, 745 Fifth Avenue, New York, NY 10151, 212/832-8860

BOBOSSE 1959, Belgian
MEURTRE EN 45 TOURS 1960, Belgian
BRIDGE TO THE SUN MGM, 1961, U.S.-French
SWORDSMAN OF SIENA MGM, 1962, Italian-French
DIS-MOI QUI TUER 1965, Belgian
DES GARCONS ET DES FILLES 1968, French
RUBLO DE LOS CARAS 1969, Spanish
WHEN EIGHT BELLS TOLL Cinerama Releasing Corporation, 1971, British
ZEPPELIN Warner Bros., 1971, British
A MURDER IS A MURDER...IS A MURDER Levitt-Pickman, 1972, French
LA MAIN A COUPER Planfilm 1974, French-Italian
THE INVESTIGATION *UN SI JOLI VILLAGE* Quartet/Films Inc., 1978, French
LA PART DU FEU Planfilm, 1978, French
LA CONFUSION DES SENTIMENTS (TF) Christine Gouze-Renel Progefi/FR3, 1979, French

FRANK PERRY*

b. 1930 - New York, New York
Home: 655 Park Avenue, New York, NY 10021, 212/535-2910
Business: Blackhawk Enterprises, 104 East 68th Street, New York, NY 10021, 212/535-2910
Agent: Michael Black/Sam Cohn, ICM - Los Angeles/New York 213/550-4000 or 212/556-5600

DAVID AND LISA ★ Continental, 1962
LADYBUG, LADYBUG United Artists, 1963
THE SWIMMER Columbia, 1968
LAST SUMMER Allied Artists, 1969
TRILOGY Allied Artists, 1969
DIARY OF A MAD HOUSEWIFE Universal, 1970
DOC United Artists, 1971
PLAY IT AS IT LAYS Universal, 1972
MAN ON A SWING Paramount, 1974
RANCHO DeLUXE United Artists, 1975
DUMMY (TF) The Konigsberg Company/Warner Bros. TV, 1979
SKAG (TF) ☆ NBC, 1980
MOMMIE DEAREST Paramount, 1981
MONSIGNOR 20th Century-Fox, 1982
COMPROMISING POSITIONS United Film Distribution, 1985

BILL PERSKY*

b. 1931 - New Haven, Connecticut
Agent: Ron Meyer, CAA - Los Angeles, 213/277-4545

ROLL, FREDDY, ROLL! (TF) ABC Circle Films, 1974
HOW TO PICK UP GIRLS! (TF) King-Hitzig Productions, 1978
SERIAL Paramount, 1980
WAIT TILL YOUR MOTHER GETS HOME (TF) Blue-Greene Productions/NBC Productions, 1983
TRACKDOWN: FINDING THE GOODBAR KILLER (TF) Grosso-Jacobson Productions, 1983
FOUND MONEY (TF) Cypress Point Productions/Warner Bros. TV, 1983

WOLFGANG PETERSEN

Agent: ICM - Los Angeles, 213/550-4000

THE CONSEQUENCE Libra, 1977, West German
BLACK AND WHITE LIKE DAY AND NIGHT New Yorker, 1978, West German
DAS BOOT (THE BOAT) ★ Triumph/Columbia, 1981, West German
THE NEVERENDING STORY Warner Bros., 1984, West German
ENEMY MINE 20th Century Fox, 1985

CHRIS PETIT

Contact: British Academy of Film & Television Arts, 195 Piccadilly, London W1, England, 01/732-0022

RADIO ON British Film Institute/Road Movies, 1979, British-West German
AN UNSUITABLE JOB FOR A WOMAN Boyd's Co., 1982, British
FLIGHT TO BERLIN Road Movies/British Film Institute/Channel Four, 1984, West German-British
CHINESE BOXES Chris Sievernich Productions/Palace Productions, 1984, West German-British

DANIEL PETRIE*

b. November 26, 1920 - Glace Bay, Nova Scotia, Canada
Agent: Fred Specktor, CAA - Los Angeles, 213/277-4545

THE BRAMBLE BUSH Warner Bros., 1960
A RAISIN IN THE SUN Columbia, 1961
THE MAIN ATTRACTION MGM, 1962
STOLEN HOURS United Artists, 1963

DANIEL PETRIE*—continued

THE IDOL Embassy, 1966, British
THE SPY WITH A COLD NOSE Embassy, 1966, British
SILENT NIGHT, LONELY NIGHT (TF) Universal TV, 1969
THE CITY (TF) Universal TV, 1971
A HOWLING IN THE WOODS (TF) Universal TV, 1971
MOON OF THE WOLF (TF) Filmways, 1972
HEC RAMSEY (TF) Universal TV/Mark VII Ltd., 1972
TROUBLE COMES TO TOWN (TF) ABC Circle Films, 1973
THE NEPTUNE FACTOR 20th Century-Fox, 1973, Canadian
MOUSEY (TF) Universal TV/Associated British Films, 1974, U.S.-British
THE GUN AND THE PULPIT (TF) Danny Thomas Productions, 1974
BUSTER AND BILLIE Columbia, 1974
RETURNING HOME (TF) Lorimar Productions/Samuel Goldwyn Productions, 1975
ELEANOR AND FRANKLIN (TF) ☆☆ Talent Associates, 1976
SYBIL (TF) Lorimar Productions, 1976
LIFEGUARD Paramount, 1976
ELEANOR AND FRANKLIN: THE WHITE HOUSE YEARS (TF) ☆☆ Talent Associates, 1977
THE QUINNS (TF) Daniel Wilson Productions, 1977
THE BETSY Allied Artists, 1978
RESURRECTION Universal, 1980
FORT APACHE, THE BRONX 20th Century-Fox, 1981
SIX PACK 20th Century-Fox, 1982
THE DOLLMAKER (TF) Finnegan Associates/IPC Films, Inc./Dollmaker Productions, 1984
THE BAY BOY Orion, 1984, Canadian-French

JOSEPH PEVNEY*

b. 1920 - New York, New York
Agent: Herb Tobias & Associates - Los Angeles, 213/277-6211
Business Manager: T.J. Smith - Granada Hills, 818/363-3341

SHAKEDOWN Universal, 1950
UNDERCOVER GIRL Universal, 1950
AIR CADET Universal, 1951
IRON MAN Universal, 1951
THE LADY FROM TEXAS Universal, 1951
THE STRANGE DOOR Universal, 1951
MEET DANNY WILSON Universal, 1952
FLESH AND FURY Universal, 1952
JUST ACROSS THE STREET Universal, 1952
BECAUSE OF YOU Universal, 1952
DESERT LEGION Universal, 1953
IT HAPPENS EVERY THURSDAY Universal, 1953
BACK TO GOD'S COUNTRY Universal, 1953
YANKEE PASHA Universal, 1954
PLAYGIRL Universal, 1954
THREE RING CIRCUS Paramount, 1954
SIX BRIDGES TO CROSS Universal, 1955
FOXFIRE Universal, 1955
FEMALE ON THE BEACH Universal, 1955
AWAY ALL BOATS Universal, 1956
CONGO CROSSING Universal, 1956
ISTANBUL Universal, 1956
TAMMY AND THE BACHELOR Universal, 1957
THE MIDNIGHT STORY Universal, 1957
MAN OF A THOUSAND FACES Universal, 1957
TWILIGHT FOR THE GODS Universal, 1958
TORPEDO RUN MGM, 1958
CASH McCALL Warner Bros., 1960
THE PLUNDERERS Allied Artists, 1960
THE CROWDED SKY Warner Bros., 1960
PORTRAIT OF A MOBSTER Warner Bros., 1961
THE NIGHT OF THE GRIZZLY Paramount, 1966
MY DARLING DAUGHTERS' ANNIVERSARY (TF) Universal TV, 1973
WHO IS THE BLACK DAHLIA? (TF) Douglas S. Cramer Productions, 1975
MYSTERIOUS ISLAND OF BEAUTIFUL WOMEN (TF) Alan Landsburg Productions, 1977
PRISONERS OF THE SEA McLane Enterprises, 1985

JOHN PEYSER*

b. August 10, 1916 - New York, New York
Home: 19721 Redwing Street, Woodland Hills, CA 91364, 818/884-7730
Agent: Martin Shapiro, Shapiro-Lichtman Agency - Los Angeles, 213/557-2244

UNDERSEA GIRL Allied Artists, 1958
THE MURDER MEN MGM, 1964
THE YOUNG WARRIORS Universal, 1967
HONEYMOON WITH A STRANGER (TF) 20th Century-Fox TV, 1969
MASSACRE HARBOR United Artists, 1970
CENTER FOLD GIRLS Dimension, 1974
STUNT SEVEN (TF) Martin Poll Productions, 1979

LEE PHILIPS*

Home: 11939 Gorham Avenue - Suite 104, Los Angeles, CA 90049, 213/820-7464
Agent: Martin Shapiro, Shapiro-Lichtman Agency - Los Angeles, 213/557-2244

GETTING AWAY FROM IT ALL (TF) Palomar Pictures International, 1972
THE GIRL MOST LIKELY TO... (TF) ABC Circle Films, 1973
THE STRANGER WITHIN (TF) Lorimar Productions, 1974
THE RED BADGE OF COURAGE (TF) 20th Century-Fox TV, 1974
SWEET HOSTAGE (TF) Brut Productions, 1975
LOUIS ARMSTRONG - CHICAGO STYLE (TF) Charles Fries Productions, 1975
JAMES A. MICHENER'S DYNASTY (TF) David Paradine TV, 1976
WANTED: THE SUNDANCE WOMAN (TF) 20th Century-Fox TV, 1976
THE SPELL (TF) Charles Fries Productions, 1977
THE WAR BETWEEN THE TATES (TF) Talent Associates, 1977
SPECIAL OLYMPICS (TF) Roger Gimbel Productions/EMI TV, 1978
THE COMEDY COMPANY (TF) Merrit Malloy-Jerry Adler Productions, 1978
SALVAGE (TF) Bennett-Katleman Productions/Columbia TV, 1979
VALENTINE (TF) Malloy-Philips Productions/Edward S. Feldman Company, 1979
HARDHAT AND LEGS (TF) Syzygy Productions, 1980
CRAZY TIMES (TF) Kayden-Gleason Productions/George Reeves Productions/ Warner Bros. TV, 1981
ON THE RIGHT TRACK 20th Century-Fox, 1981
A WEDDING ON WALTON'S MOUNTAIN (TF) Lorimar Productions/Amanda Productions, 1982
MAE WEST (TF) ★ Hill-Mandelker Films, 1982
GAMES MOTHER NEVER TAUGHT YOU (TF) CBS Entertainment, 1982
LOTTERY! (TF) Rosner TV Productions/Orion TV, 1983
HAPPY (TF) Bacchus Films Inc., 1983
SAMSON AND DELILAH (TF) Catalina Production Group/Comworld Productions, 1984
SPACE (MS) co-director with Joseph Sargent, Stonehenge Productions/ Paramount TV, 1985

CHARLES B. PIERCE

THE LEGEND OF BOGGY CREEK Howco International, 1973
BOOTLEGGERS Howco International, 1974
WINTERHAWK Howco International, 1975
THE WINDS OF AUTUMN Howco International, 1976
THE TOWN THAT DREADED SUNDOWN American International, 1977
GREYEAGLE American International, 1977
THE NORSEMEN American International, 1978
THE EVICTORS American International, 1979
SACRED GROUND Pacific International, 1983

FRANK PIERSON*

b. May 12, 1925 - New York, New York
Agent: Triad Artists, Inc. - Los Angeles, 213/556-2727

THE LOOKING GLASS WAR Columbia, 1970, British
THE NEON CEILING (TF) Universal TV, 1971
A STAR IS BORN Warner Bros., 1976
KING OF THE GYPSIES Paramount, 1978

HAROLD PINTER

b. October 10, 1930 - London, England
Home: 52 Campden Hill Square, London W8 England
Business: c/o ACTAC Ltd., 16 Cadogan Lane, London SW1, England, 01/235-2797

BUTLEY American Film Theatre, 1974, British

ERNEST PINTOFF*

b. December 15, 1931 - Watertown, Connecticut
Agent: Ronald Leif, Contemporary-Korman Artists - Beverly Hills, 213/278-8250

HARVEY MIDDLEMAN, FIREMAN Columbia, 1965
WHO KILLED MARY WHAT'S'ERNAME Cannon, 1971
DYNAMITE CHICKEN EYR, 1972
HUMAN FEELINGS (TF) Crestview Productions/Worldvision, 1978
JAGUAR LIVES American International, 1979
LUNCH WAGON *LUNCH WAGON GIRLS* Seymour Borde Associates, 1981
ST. HELENS Davis-Panzer Productions, 1981

AMOS POE

SUBWAY RIDERS Hep Pictures, 1981
ALPHABET CITY Atlantic Releasing Corporation, 1984

S. LEE POGOSTIN

Agent: Paul Kohner, Inc. - Los Angeles, 213/550-1060

HARD CONTRACT 20th Century-Fox, 1969

SIDNEY POITIER*

b. February 20, 1924 - Miami, Florida
Business: Verdon-Cedric Productions, Ltd., 9350 Wilshire Blvd., Beverly Hills, CA 90212, 213/274-7253
Agent: Martin Baum, CAA - Los Angeles, 213/277-4545

BUCK AND THE PREACHER Columbia, 1972
A WARM DECEMBER National General, 1973
UPTOWN SATURDAY NIGHT Warner Bros., 1974
LET'S DO IT AGAIN Warner Bros., 1975
A PIECE OF THE ACTION Warner Bros., 1977
STIR CRAZY Columbia, 1980
HANKY PANKY Columbia, 1982
FAST FORWARD Columbia, 1985

ROMAN POLANSKI

b. August 18, 1933 - Paris, France
Contact: French Film Office, 745 Fifth Avenue, New York, NY 10151, 212/832-8860

KNIFE IN THE WATER Kanawha, 1963, Polish
THE BEAUTIFUL SWINDLERS *LES PLUS BELLES ESCROQUERIES DU MONDE* co-director with Ugo Grigoretti, Claude Chabrol & Hiromichi Horikawa, Jack Ellis Films, 1964, French-Italian-Japanese-Dutch
REPULSION Royal Films International, 1965, British
CUL-DE-SAC Sigma III, 1966, British
THE FEARLESS VAMPIRE KILLERS, OR PARDON ME BUT YOUR TEETH ARE IN MY NECK *DANCE OF THE VAMPIRES* MGM, 1967, British
ROSEMARY'S BABY Paramount, 1968
MACBETH Columbia, 1971, British
WHAT? Avco Embassy, 1973, Italian-French-West German
CHINATOWN ★ Paramount, 1974
THE TENANT Paramount, 1976, French-U.S.
TESS ★ Columbia, 1980, French-British
PIRATES MGM/UA, 1985

BARRY POLLACK

COOL BREEZE MGM, 1972
THIS IS A HIJACK Fanfare, 1973

SYDNEY POLLACK*

b. July 1, 1934 - South Bend, Indiana
Business: Mirage Enterprises, 4000 Warner Blvd., Burbank, CA 91522, 818/954-1711
Agent: Michael Ovitz, CAA - Los Angeles, 213/277-4545
Attorney: Gary Hendler, Armstrong, Hendler & Hirsch - Los Angeles, 213/553-0305

THE SLENDER THREAD Paramount, 1965
THIS PROPERTY IS CONDEMNED Paramount, 1966
THE SCALPHUNTERS United Artists, 1968
CASTLE KEEP Columbia, 1969
THEY SHOOT HORSES, DON'T THEY? ★ Cinerama Releasing Corporation, 1969
JEREMIAH JOHNSON Warner Bros., 1972
THE WAY WE WERE Columbia, 1973
THE YAKUZA Warner Bros., 1975
3 DAYS OF THE CONDOR Paramount, 1975
BOBBY DEERFIELD Columbia, 1977
THE ELECTRIC HORSEMAN Columbia, 1979
ABSENCE OF MALICE Columbia, 1981
TOOTSIE ★ Columbia, 1982

ABRAHAM POLONSKY*

b. December 5, 1910 - New York, New York
Agent: The Gersh Agency - Beverly Hills, 213/274-6611
Attorney: Shanks, Davis & Remer - New York City, 212/986-0440

FORCE OF EVIL MGM, 1948
TELL THEM WILLIE BOY IS HERE Universal, 1969
ROMANCE OF A HORSETHIEF Allied Artists, 1971

GILLO PONTECORVO

b. November 19, 1919 - Pisa, Italy
Contact: Ministry of Tourism & Education, Via Della Ferratella, No. 51, 00184 Rome, Italy, 06/7732

DIE WINDROSE co-director, 1956, East German
LA GRANDE STRADA AZZURRA Ge-Si Malenotti/Play Art/Eichberg/Triglav Film, 1957, Italian-Yugoslavian
KAPO Vides/Zebra Film/Cineriz, 1960, Italian
BATTLE OF ALGIERS ★ Rizzoli, 1967, Italian-Algerian
BURNI *QUEIMADA!* United Artists, 1970, Italian-French
OPERATION OGRO CIDIF, 1979, Italian-Spanish-French

MAURIZIO PONZI

Contact: Ministry of Tourism & Education, Via Della Ferratella, No. 51, 00184 Rome, Italy, 06/7732

AURORA (TF) Roger Gimbel Productions/The Peregrine Producers Group/Sacis, 1984, U.S.-Italian

PETRU POPESCU

b. Romania
Agent: Lee Muhl, ICM - Los Angeles, 213/550-4000

DEATH OF AN ANGEL TLC Films/20th Century Fox, 1985

TED POST*

b. March 31, 1918 - Brooklyn, New York
Agent: ICM - Los Angeles, 213/550-4000
Business Manager: Norman Blumenthal, 3250 Ocean Park Blvd., Santa Monica, CA 90405

THE PEACEMAKER United Artists, 1956
THE LEGEND OF TOM DOOLEY Columbia, 1959
HANG 'EM HIGH United Artists, 1968
BENEATH THE PLANET OF THE APES 20th Century-Fox, 1970
NIGHT SLAVES (TF) Bing Crosby Productions, 1970
DR. COOK'S GARDEN (TF) Paramount TV, 1970
YUMA (TF) Aaron Spelling Productions, 1971
FIVE DESPERATE WOMEN (TF) Aaron Spelling Productions, 1971
DO NOT FOLD, SPINDLE OR MUTILATE (TF) Lee Rich Productions, 1971
THE BRAVOS (TF) Universal TV, 1972
SANDCASTLES (TF) Metromedia Productions, 1972
THE BABY Scotia International, 1973, British
THE HARRAD EXPERIMENT Cinerama Releasing Corporation, 1973
MAGNUM FORCE Warner Bros., 1973
WHIFFS 20th Century-Fox, 1975
GOOD GUYS WEAR BLACK American Cinema, 1978
GO TELL THE SPARTANS Avco Embassy, 1978
DIARY OF A TEENAGE HITCHHIKER (TF) The Shpetner Company, 1979
THE GIRLS IN THE OFFICE (TF) ABC Circle Films, 1979
NIGHTKILL (TF) Cine Artists, 1980
CAGNEY & LACEY (TF) Mace Neufeld Productions/Filmways, 1981

GERALD POTTERTON

Contact: Canadian Film & Television Association, 8 King Street, Toronto, Ontario M5C 1B5, Canada, 416/961-2288

THE RAINBOW BOYS 1975, Canadian
HEAVY METAL (AF) Columbia, 1981, Canadian

MICHAEL POWELL

b. September 30, 1905 - Canterbury, England
Contact: Directors Guild of Great Britain, 56 Whitfield Street, London W1, England, 01/580-2256

TWO CROWDED HOURS Fox, 1931, British
MY FRIEND THE KING Fox, 1931, British
RYNOX Ideal, 1931, British
THE RASP Fox, 1931, British
THE STAR REPORTER Fox, 1931, British
HOTEL SPLENDIDE Ideal, 1932, British
BORN LUCKY MGM, 1932, British
C.O.D. United Artists, 1932, British
HIS LORDSHIP United Artists, 1932, British
THE FIRE RAISERS Woolf & Freedman, 1933, British
THE NIGHT OF THE PARTY Gaumont, 1934, British
RED ENSIGN Gaumont, 1934, British
SOMETHING ALWAYS HAPPENS Warner Bros., 1934, British
THE GIRL IN THE CROWD First National, 1934, British
THE LOVE TEST Fox British, 1935, British
LAZYBONES Radio, 1935, British
SOME DAY Warner Bros., 1935, British
HER LAST AFFAIRE Producers Distributing Corporation, 1935, British
THE PRICE OF A SONG Fox British, 1935, British
THE PHANTOM LIGHT Gaumont, 1935, British
THE BROWN WALLET First National, 1936, British
CROWN VS. STEVENS Warner Bros., 1936, British
THE MAN BEHIND THE MASK MGM, 1936, British
THE EDGE OF THE WORLD British Independent Exhibitors' Distributors, 1937, British
U-BOAT 29 *THE SPY IN BLACK* Columbia, 1939, British
THE LION HAS WINGS co-director with Brian Desmond Hurst & Adrian Brunel, United Artists, 1939, British
THE THIEF OF BAGDAD co-director with Ludwig Berger & Tim Whelan, United Artists, 1940, British
CONTRABAND *BLACKOUT* Anglo-American, 1940, British
THE FORTY-NINTH PARALLEL *THE INVADERS* Columbia, 1941, British
ONE OF OUR AIRCRAFT IS MISSING co-director with Emeric Pressburger, United Artists, 1942, British
THE VOLUNTEER co-director with Emeric Pressburger, Anglo, 1943, British
COLONEL BLIMP *THE LIFE AND DEATH OF COLONEL BLIMP* co-director with Emeric Pressburger, GFO, 1943, British
A CANTERBURY TALE co-director with Emeric Pressburger, Eagle-Lion, 1944, British
I KNOW WHERE I'M GOING co-director with Emeric Pressburger, Universal, 1945, British
STAIRWAY TO HEAVEN *A MATTER OF LIFE AND DEATH* co-director with Emeric Pressburger, Universal, 1946, British
BLACK NARCISSUS co-director with Emeric Pressburger, Universal, 1947, British
THE RED SHOES co-director with Emeric Pressburger, Eagle-Lion, 1948, British
THE SMALL BACK ROOM *HOUR OF GLORY* co-director with Emeric Pressburger, Snader Productions, 1948, British
THE WILD HEART *GONE TO EARTH* co-director with Emeric Pressburger, RKO Radio, 1950, British
THE ELUSIVE PIMPERNEL co-director with Emeric Pressburger, British Lion, 1950, British
THE TALES OF HOFFMAN co-director with Emeric Pressburger, Lopert, 1951, British
OH ROSALINDA! co-director with Emeric Pressburger, Associated British Picture Corporatin, 1955, British
PURSUIT OF THE GRAF SPEE *THE BATTLE OF THE RIVER PLATE* co-director with Emeric Pressburger, Rank, 1956, British
NIGHT AMBUSH *ILL MET BY MOONLIGHT* co-director with Emeric Pressburger, Rank, 1957, British

MICHAEL POWELL —continued

HONEYMOON *LUNA DE MIEL* RKO Radio, 1958, Spanish
PEEPING TOM Astor, 1960, British
THE QUEEN'S GUARDS 20th Century-Fox, 1961, British
THEY'RE A WEIRD MOB Williamson/Powell, 1966, Australian
AGE OF CONSENT Columbia, 1970, Australian
THE TEMPEST 1974, Greek-British

TRISTRAM POWELL

Contact: Directors Guild of Great Britain, 56 Whitfield Street, London W1, England, 01/580-2256

THE GHOST WRITER (TF) WGBH-Boston/Malone-Gill Productions/BBC, 1984, U.S.-British

MICHAEL PREECE*

Home: 12233 Everglade Street, Mar Vista, CA 90066, 213/390-6414
Business: Charbridge Productions, 1901 Avenue of the Stars -Suite 840, Los Angeles, CA 90067, 213/277-9511
Agent: Herb Tobias & Associates - Los Angeles, 213/277-6211

THE PRIZE FIGHTER New World, 1979
PARADISE CONNECTION (TF) Woodruff Productions/QM Productions, 1979

OTTO PREMINGER*

b. December 5, 1906 - Vienna, Austria
Business: Sigma Productions, Inc., 129 East 64th Street, New York, NY 10021, 212/535-6001

DIE GROSSE LIEBE 1931, Austrian-German
UNDER YOUR SPELL 20th Century-Fox, 1936
DANGER - LOVE AT WORK 20th Century-Fox, 1937
MARGIN FOR ERROR 20th Century-Fox, 1943
IN THE MEANTIME, DARLING 20th Century-Fox, 1944
LAURA ★ 20th Century-Fox, 1944
A ROYAL SCANDAL 20th Century-Fox, 1945
FALLEN ANGEL 20th Century-Fox, 1945
CENTENNIAL SUMMER 20th Century-Fox, 1946
FOREVER AMBER 20th Century-Fox, 1947
DAISY KENYON 20th Century-Fox, 1947
THE FAN 20th Century-Fox, 1949
WHIRLPOOL 20th Century-Fox, 1950
WHERE THE SIDEWALK ENDS 20th Century-Fox, 1950
THE 13TH LETTER 20th Century-Fox, 1951
ANGEL FACE RKO Radio, 1953
THE MOON IS BLUE United Artists, 1953
RIVER OF NO RETURN 20th Century-Fox, 1954
CARMEN JONES 20th Century-Fox, 1955
THE MAN WITH THE GOLDEN ARM United Artists, 1955
THE COURT-MARTIAL OF BILLY MITCHELL Warner Bros., 1955
SAINT JOAN United Artists, 1957
BONJOUR TRISTESSE Columbia, 1958
PORGY AND BESS Columbia, 1959
ANATOMY OF A MURDER Columbia, 1959
EXODUS United Artists, 1960
ADVISE AND CONSENT Columbia, 1962
THE CARDINAL ★ Columbia, 1963
IN HARM'S WAY Paramount, 1964
BUNNY LAKE IS MISSING Columbia, 1965, British
HURRY SUNDOWN Paramount, 1967
SKIDOO Paramount, 1968
TELL ME THAT YOU LOVE ME, JUNIE MOON Paramount, 1970
SUCH GOOD FRIENDS Paramount, 1971
ROSEBUD United Artists, 1975
THE HUMAN FACTOR United Artists, 1979, British

MICHAEL PRESSMAN*

b. July 1, 1950 - New York, New York
Agent: Rick Nicita, CAA - Los Angeles, 213/277-4545
Business Manager: Bamberger Business Management, 2049 Century Park East, Los Angeles, CA 90067, 213/553-0581

THE GREAT TEXAS DYNAMITE CHASE New World, 1976
THE BAD NEWS BEARS IN BREAKING TRAINING Paramount, 1977
LIKE MOM, LIKE ME (TF) CBS Entertainment, 1978
BOULEVARD NIGHTS Warner Bros., 1979
THOSE LIPS, THOSE EYES United Artists, 1980
SOME KIND OF HERO Paramount, 1982
DOCTOR DETROIT Universal, 1983
THE IMPOSTER (TF) Gloria Monty Productions/Comworld Productions, 1984
PRIVATE SESSIONS (TF) Comworld Productions, 1985

HAROLD PRINCE

b. July 30, 1928
Business: 1270 Avenue of the Americas, New York, NY, 212/399-0960

SOMETHING FOR EVERYONE National General, 1970, British
A LITTLE NIGHT MUSIC New World, 1978, Austrian-U.S.

RICHARD PRYOR

b. December 1, 1940 - Peoria, Illinois
Attorney: Pollock, Bloom & Dekom - Los Angeles, 213/278-8622

RICHARD PRYOR HERE AND NOW (FD) Columbia, 1983

ALBERT PYUN

THE SWORD AND THE SORCERER Group 1, 1982
RADIOACTIVE DREAMS Esparza Productions/ITM Productions, 1984

Q

JOHN QUESTED

Business: Brent Walker Films, 9 Chesterfield Street, London WI, England

PHILADELPHIA, HERE I COME Irish
HERE ARE LADIES Arthur Cantor Films, 1971, Irish
LOOPHOLE MGM/United Artists, 1981, British

RICHARD QUINE*

b. November 12, 1920 - Detroit, Michigan
Agent: Martin Baum, CAA - Los Angeles, 213/277-4545

LEATHER GLOVES co-director with William Asher, Columbia 1948
SUNNY SIDE OF THE STREET Columbia, 1951
PURPLE HEART DIARY Columbia, 1951
SOUND OFF Columbia, 1952
RAINBOW 'ROUND MY SHOULDER Columbia, 1952
ALL ASHORE Columbia, 1953
SIREN OF BAGDAD Columbia, 1953
CRUISIN' DOWN THE RIVER Columbia, 1953
DRIVE A CROOKED ROAD Columbia, 1954
PUSHOVER Columbia, 1954
SO THIS IS PARIS Universal, 1955
MY SISTER EILEEN Universal, 1955
THE SOLID GOLD CADILLAC Columbia, 1956
FULL OF LIFE Columbia, 1957
OPERATION MAD BALL Columbia, 1957
BELL, BOOK AND CANDLE Columbia, 1958
IT HAPPENED TO JANE Columbia, 1959
STRANGERS WHEN WE MEET Columbia, 1960
THE WORLD OF SUZIE WONG Paramount, 1960
THE NOTORIOUS LANDLADY Columbia, 1962
PARIS WHEN IT SIZZLES Paramount, 1964
SEX AND THE SINGLE GIRL Warner Bros., 1965
HOW TO MURDER YOUR WIFE United Artists, 1965
SYNANON Columbia, 1965
OH DAD, POOR DAD, MOMMA'S HUNG YOU IN THE CLOSET AND I'M FEELING SO SAD Paramount, 1967
HOTEL Warner Bros., 1967
A TALENT FOR LOVING 1969
THE MOONSHINE WAR MGM, 1970
"W" Cinerama Releasing Corporation, 1974, British
THE SPECIALISTS (TF) Mark VII Ltd./Universal TV, 1975
THE PRISONER OF ZENDA Universal, 1979

ANTHONY QUINN

b. April 21, 1915 - Chihuahua, Mexico
Agent: William Morris Agency - Beverly Hills, 213/274-7451

THE BUCCANEER Paramount, 1959

JOSE QUINTERO*

Agent: The Lantz Office - New York City, 212/586-0200

THE ROMAN SPRING OF MRS. STONE Warner Bros., 1961

R

MICHAEL RADFORD

Home: 3B Pickering Mews, London W2, England, 01/727-3067
Agent: Linda Seifert Associates, 8A Brunswick Gardens, London W8 4AJ, England, 01/229-5163
Contact: Directors Guild of Great Britain, 56 Whitfield Street, London WI, England, 01/580-9592

VAN MORRISON IN IRELAND (FD) Caledonia-Angle Films, 1981, British
ANOTHER TIME, ANOTHER PLACE The Samuel Goldwyn Company, 1983, British
1984 Atlantic Releasing Corporation, 1984, British

MICHAEL RAE

LASERBLAST Irwin Yablans, 1978

MICHAEL RAEBURN

Home: 10 Spencer Park, London SW18, England, 01/874-0205
Agent: Tim Corrie, Fraser & Dunlop, 91 Regent Street, London W1, England, 01/734-7311

KILLING HEAT *THE GRASS IS SINGING* Satori, 1983, British-Swedish

BOB RAFELSON*

b. 1934 - New York, New York
Business: c/o Jolene Wolff 1400 N. Fuller Avenue, Hollywood, CA 90046, 213/851-2719
Agent: William Morris Agency - Beverly Hills, 213/274-7451

HEAD Columbia, 1968
FIVE EASY PIECES Columbia, 1970
THE KING OF MARVIN GARDENS Columbia, 1972
STAY HUNGRY United Artists, 1976
THE POSTMAN ALWAYS RINGS TWICE Paramount, 1981

STEWART RAFFILL*

Agent: Robert Littman, Leading Artists - Beverly Hills, 213/858-1999

THE TENDER WARRIOR Safari, 1971
THE ADVENTURES OF THE WILDERNESS FAMILY Pacific International, 1975
ACROSS THE GREAT DIVIDE Pacific International, 1976
THE SEA GYPSIES Warner Bros., 1978
HIGH RISK American Cinema, 1981
THE ICE PIRATES MGM/UA, 1983

ALAN RAFKIN*

Home: 1008 St. Bimini Circle, Palm Springs, CA, 619/323-4058
Personal Manager: The Brillstein Company - Los Angeles, 213/275-6135
Business Manager: Gelfand, Rennert & Feldman, 1880 Century Park East, Los Angeles, CA 90067, 213/553-1707

SKI PARTY American International, 1965
THE GHOST AND MR. CHICKEN Universal, 1966
THE RIDE TO HANGMAN'S TREE Universal, 1967
NOBODY'S PERFECT Universal, 1968
THE SHAKIEST GUN IN THE WEST Universal, 1968
ANGEL IN MY POCKET Universal, 1969
HOW TO FRAME A FIGG Universal, 1971
LET'S SWITCH (TF) Universal TV, 1975

SAM RAIMI

THE EVIL DEAD New Line Cinema, 1983
THE XYZ MURDERS Embassy, 1985

ALVIN RAKOFF

b. Toronto, Canada
Business: Jara Productions Ltd., 1 The Orchard, Chiswick, London W4 1JZ, England, 01/994-1269
Agent: John Redway & Associates, 16 Berners Street, London W1, England, 01/637-1612
Contact: Directors Guild of Great Britain, 56 Whitfield Street, London W1, England, 01/580-9592

PASSPORT TO SHAME British Lion, 1959, British
ON FRIDAY AT ELEVEN British Lion, 1961, West German-British
WORLD IN MY POCKET MGM, 1962, West German-French-Italian
THE COMEDY MAN Continental, 1964, British
CROSSPLOT United Artists, 1969, British
HOFFMAN Levitt-Pickman, 1971, British
SAY HELLO TO YESTERDAY Cinerama Releasing Corporation, 1971, British
THE ADVENTURES OF DON QUIXOTE (TF) Universal TV/BBC, 1973, U.S.-British
KING SOLOMON'S TREASURE Filmco Limited, 1978, Canadian
CITY ON FIRE! Avco Embassy, 1979, Canadian
DEATH SHIP Avco Embassy, 1980, Canadian
DIRTY TRICKS Avco Embassy, 1981, Canadian
A VOYAGE ROUND MY FATHER (TF) Thames TV/D.L. Taffner Ltd., 1983, British
THE FIRST OLYMPICS—ATHENS 1896 (MS) Larry White-Gary Allison Productions/Columbia TV, 1984

ALEXANDER RAMATI

Agent: Mike Zimring, William Morris Agency - Beverly Hills, 213/274-7451

THE ASSISI UNDERGROUND Cannon, 1985, Italian-British

HAROLD RAMIS*

Agent: Jack Rapke, CAA - Los Angeles, 213/277-4545
Business Manager: David B. Kahn, 111 W. Washington Street, Chicago, ILL 60602, 312/346-4321

CADDYSHACK Orion/Warner Bros., 1980
NATIONAL LAMPOON'S VACATION Warner Bros., 1983

ARTHUR RANKIN, JR.

Business: Rankin-Bass Productions, Inc., 1 East 53rd Street, New York, NY 10022, 212/759-7721

WILLY McBEAN AND HIS MAGIC MACHINE (AF) 1967
THE HOBBIT (ATF) co-director with Jules Bass, Rankin-Bass Productions, 1979
THE RETURN OF THE KING (ATF) co-director with Jules Bass, Rankin-Bass Productions, 1979
THE LAST UNICORN (AF) co-director with Jules Bass, Jensen Farley Pictures, 1982
THE FLIGHT OF THE DRAGONS (ATF) co-director with Jules Bass, Rankin-Bass Productions, 1983
THE WIND IN THE WILLOWS (ATF) co-director with Jules Bass, Rankin-Bass Productions, 1983

I.C. RAPOPORT*

Home: 559 Muskingum Avenue, Pacific Palisades, CA 90272, 213/454-3120
Agent: ICM - Los Angeles, 213/550-4301

THOU SHALT NOT KILL (TF) Edgar J. Scherick Associates/Warner Bros. TV, 1982

IRVING RAPPER*

b. 1898 - London, England
Home: 7250 Franklin Avenue, Los Angeles, CA 90046, 213/876-6000

SHINING VICTORY Warner Bros., 1941
ONE FOOT IN HEAVEN Warner Bros., 1941
THE GAY SISTERS Warner Bros., 1942
NOW, VOYAGER Warner Bros., 1942
THE ADVENTURES OF MARK TWAIN Warner Bros., 1944
THE CORN IS GREEN Warner Bros., 1945
RHAPSODY IN BLUE Warner Bros., 1945
DECEPTION Warner Bros., 1946
THE VOICE OF THE TURTLE Warner Bros., 1947
ANNA LUCASTA Columbia, 1949
THE GLASS MENAGERIE Warner Bros., 1950
ANOTHER MAN'S POISON United Artists, 1952, British
BAD FOR EACH OTHER Columbia, 1954
FOREVER FEMALE Paramount, 1954
STRANGE INTRUDER Allied Artists, 1956
THE BRAVE ONE Universal, 1956
MARJORIE MORNINGSTAR Warner Bros., 1958
THE MIRACLE Warner Bros., 1959
THE STORY OF JOSEPH AND HIS BRETHREN Colorama, 1960, Italian
PONTIUS PILATE US Films, 1962, Italian-French
THE CHRISTINE JORGENSEN STORY United Artists, 1970
BORN AGAIN Avco Embassy, 1978

STEVE RASH*

Home: 3742 Lower Mountain Road, Forest Grove, PA 18922, 215/794-5108

THE BUDDY HOLLY STORY Columbia, 1978
UNDER THE RAINBOW Orion/Warner Bros., 1981

SATYAJIT RAY

b. May 2, 1921 - Calcutta, India
Address: Flat 8, 1/1 Bishop Lefroy Road, Calcutta 20, India
Contact: Films Division, Ministry of Information & Broadcasting, 24 Dr G Beshmukh Marg, Bombay 40026, India, 36-1461

PATHER PANCHALI Harrison, 1955, Indian
APARAJITO Harrison, 1956, Indian
PARAS PATHAR 1957, Indian
THE MUSIC ROOM Harrison, 1958, Indian
THE WORLD OF APU Harrison, 1959, Indian

SATYAJIT RAY —continued

DEVI Harrison, 1960, Indian
RABINDRANATH TAGORE 1961, Indian
TWO DAUGHTERS Janus, 1961, Indian
KANCHENJUNGHA Harrison, 1962, Indian
ABHIJAN 1962, Indian
MAHANAGAR 1963, Indian
CHARULATA *THE LONELY WIFE* Trans-World, 1964, Indian
KAPURUSH-O-MAHAPURUSH 1966, Indian
NAYAK 1966, Indian
CHIRIAKHANA 1967, Indian
GOOPY GYNE BAGHA BYNE Purnima Pictures, 1968, Indian
DAYS AND NIGHTS IN THE FOREST Pathe Contemporary, 1970, Indian
THE ADVERSARY Audio Brandon, 1971, Indian
SIKKIM 1971, Indian
THE INNER EYE 1972, Indian
SIMABADDHA 1972, Indian
DISTANT THUNDER Cinema 5, 1973, Indian
SONAR KELLA 1974, Indian
BALA 1976, Indian
THE MIDDLEMAN Bauer International, 1976, Indian
THE CHESS PLAYERS Creative, 1977, Indian
JOI BABA FELUNATH 1978, Indian
HEERAK RAJAR DESHE 1979, Indian
THE ELEPHANT GOD R.D. Bansal & Company, 1979, Indian
THE KINGDOM OF DIAMONDS (TF) GOVWB, 1980, Indian
SADGATI 1982, Indian
THE HOME AND THE WORLD European Classics, 1984, Indian

ROBERT REDFORD*

b. August 17, 1937 - Santa Monica, California
Business: Wildwood Enterprises, Inc., 4000 Warner Blvd., Burbank, CA 91522, 818/954-3221
Agent: Michael Ovitz, CAA - Los Angeles, 213/277-4545

ORDINARY PEOPLE ★★ Paramount, 1980

JERRY REED

WHAT COMES AROUND Jerry Reed Productions, 1985

GEOFFREY REEVE

Business: Geoff Reeve Film and Television Ltd., 25 Jermyn Street, London SW1 6HR, England, 01/930-0123
Contact: Directors Guild of Great Britain, 56 Whitfield Street, London WI, England, 01/580-9592

PUPPET ON A CHAIN co-director with Don Sharp, Cinerama Releasing Corporation, 1972, British
CARAVAN TO VACCARES Bryanston, 1976, British-French

PATRICK REGAN*

b. January 23, 1939 - Los Angeles, California
Home: 3680 Will Rogers Station, Santa Monica, CA 90403
Messages: 213/393-2734
Business: Silver-Regan Productions, Laird Studios, 9336 W. Washington Blvd., Culver City, CA 90230, 213/559-0346

KISS DADDY GOODBYE Pendragon Film Ltd./Wrightwood Entertainment, 1981

GODFREY REGGIO

KOYAANISQATSI Island Alive/New Cinema, 1983

MARK REICHERT

UNION CITY Kinesis, 1980

FRANCOIS REICHENBACH

b. July 3, 1922 - Paris, France
Contact: French Film Office, 745 Fifth Avenue, New York, NY 10151, 212/832-8860

L'AMERIQUE INSOLITE (FD) 1960, French
UN COEUR GROS COMME CA (FD) 1961, French
LES AMOUREAUX DU "FRANCE" (FD) co-director with Pierre Grimblat, 1963, French
GRENOBLE (FD) co-director with Claude Lelouch, United Producers of America, 1968, French
MEXICO MEXICO (FD) 1969, French
ARTHUR RUBINSTEIN: LOVE OF LIFE (FD) co-director with Gerard Patris, New Yorker, 1970, French
L'INDISCRETE (FD) 1970, French
MEDICINE BALL CARAVAN (FD) Warner Bros., 1971, French-U.S.
YEHUDI MENUHIN - CHEMIN DE LUMIERE (FD) co-director with Bernard Gavoty, 1971, French
LA RAISON DU PLUS FOU Gaumont, 1973, French
JOHNNY HALLYDAY (FD) Prodis, 1972, French
LE HOLD-UP AU CRAYON (FD) Films du Prisme, 1973, French
CAN'T YOU HEAR THE DOGS BARK? co-director with Noel Howard, 1975, Mexican-French
SEX O'CLOCK USA (FD) 1976
ANOTHER WAY TO LOVE (FD) 1976
PELE (FD) Televisa, 1977, French-Mexican
HOUSTON, TEXAS (FD) Camera One/TFI/Prisme Films, 1980, French
FRANCOIS REICHENBACH'S JAPAN (FD) CIDIF, 1983, French

ALASTAIR REID*

b. July 21, 1939 - Edinburgh, Scotland
Address: The Old Stores, Curload, St. Gregory, Somerset, England, 082-369-645
Agent: Duncan Heath Associates, 162 Wardour Street, London W1, England, 01/439-1471

BABY LOVE Avco Embassy, 1969, British
THE NIGHT DIGGER MGM, 1971, British
SOMETHING TO HIDE 1971, British
THE FILE ON JILL HATCH (TF) WNET-13/BBC, 1983, U.S.-British

CARL REINER*

b. March 20, 1922 - Bronx, New York
Home: 714 N. Rodeo Drive, Beverly Hills, CA
Business Manager: George Shapiro, 141 El Camino Drive, Beverly Hills, CA 90212, 213/278-8896

ENTER LAUGHING Columbia, 1967
THE COMIC Columbia, 1969
WHERE'S POPPA? United Artists, 1970
THE ONE AND ONLY Paramount, 1978
OH, GOD! Warner Bros., 1978
THE JERK Universal, 1979
DEAD MEN DON'T WEAR PLAID Universal, 1979
THE MAN WITH TWO BRAINS Warner Bros., 1983
ALL OF ME Universal, 1984

ROB REINER*

b. 1947 - Beverly Hills, California
Agent: CAA - Los Angeles, 213/277-4545

THIS IS SPINAL TAP Embassy, 1984
THE SURE THING Embassy, 1985

ALLEN REISNER*

b. New York, New York
Home: 213/274-2844
Agent: Contemporary-Korman Artists - Beverly Hills, 213/278-8250

ST. LOUIS BLUES Paramount, 1958
ALL MINE TO GIVE *THE DAY THEY GAVE BABIES AWAY* Universal, 1958
TO DIE IN PARIS (TF) co-director with Charles Dubin, Universal TV, 1968
YOUR MONEY OR YOUR WIFE (TF) Brentwood Productions, 1972
CAPTAINS AND THE KINGS (MS) co-director with Douglas Heyes, Universal TV, 1976
MARY JANE HARPER CRIED LAST NIGHT (TF) Paramount TV, 1977
COPS AND ROBIN (TF) Paramount TV, 1978
THE LOVE TAPES (TF) Christiana Productions/MGM TV, 1980

KAREL REISZ*

b. July 21, 1926 - Ostrava, Czechoslovakia
Home: 11 Chalcot Gardens, England's Lane, London NW3, England, 01/722-6848
Agent: Sam Cohn, William Morris Agency - New York City, 213/556-5600

WE ARE THE LAMBETH BOYS Rank, 1958, British
SATURDAY NIGHT AND SUNDAY MORNING Continental, 1961, British
NIGHT MUST FALL Embassy, 1964, British
MORGAN! *MORGAN: A SUITABLE CASE FOR TREATMENT* Cinema 5, 1966, British
ISADORA *THE LOVES OF ISADORA* Universal, 1969, British
THE GAMBLER Paramount, 1974
WHO'LL STOP THE RAIN United Artists, 1978
THE FRENCH LIEUTENANT'S WOMAN United Artists, 1981, British
SWEET DREAMS Tri-Star, 1985

WOLFGANG REITHERMAN

Business: Walt Disney Productions, 500 S. Buena Vista Street, Burbank, CA 91521, 213/845-3141

101 DALMATIONS (AF) co-director with Hamilton S. Luke & Clyde Geronimi, Buena Vista, 1961
THE SWORD IN THE STONE (AF) Buena Vista, 1963
THE JUNGLE BOOK (AF) Buena Vista, 1967
THE ARISTOCATS (AF) Buena Vista, 1970
ROBIN HOOD (AF) Buena Vista, 1973
THE RESCUERS (AF) Buena Vista, 1977

IVAN REITMAN*

b. October 26, 1946 - Czechoslovakia
Agent: Michael Ovitz, CAA - Los Angeles, 213/277-4545

FOXY LADY Ivan Reitman Productions, 1971, Canadian
CANNIBAL GIRLS American International, 1973, Canadian
MEATBALLS Paramount, 1979, Canadian
STRIPES Columbia, 1981
GHOSTBUSTERS Columbia, 1984

ALAIN RESNAIS

b. June 3, 1922 - Vannes, France
Address: 70 rue des Plantes, 75014 Paris, France
Contact: French Film Office, 745 Fifth Avenue, New York, NY 10151, 212/832-8860

HIROSHIMA, MON AMOUR Zenith, 1959, French
LAST YEAR AT MARIENBAD Astor, 1961, French-Italian
MURIEL Lopert, 1963, French-Italian
LA GUERRE EST FINIE Brandon, 1966, French-Swedish
FAR FROM VIETNAM co-director with Jean-Luc Godard, William Klein, Claude Lelouch, Agnes Varda & Joris Ivens, New Yorker, 1967, French
JE T'AIME, JE T'AIME New Yorker, 1968, French-Spanish
STAVISKY Cinemation, 1974, French
PROVIDENCE Cinema 5, 1977, French-Swiss
MON ONCLE D'AMERIQUE New World, 1980, French
LIFE IS A BED OF ROSES *LA VIE EST UN ROMAN* Spectrafilm, 1983, French
L'AMOUR A MORT Roissy Film, 1984, French

BURT REYNOLDS*

b. February 11, 1936 - Waycross, Georgia
Business: Burt Reynolds Productions, 8730 Sunset Blvd. - Suite 201, Los Angeles, CA 90069, 213/652-6005
Agent: ICM - Los Angeles, 213/550-4000
Business Manager: Global Business Management - Beverly Hills, 213/278-4141

GATOR United Artists, 1976
THE END United Artists, 1978
SHARKY'S MACHINE Orion/Warner Bros., 1982
STICK Universal, 1985

GENE REYNOLDS*

Agent: Leonard Hanzer, Major Talent Agency - Los Angeles, 213/820-5841

IN DEFENSE OF KIDS (TF) MTM Enterprises, 1983

KEVIN REYNOLDS*

b. January 17, 1952 - San Antonio, Texas
Business: Windmill Films, Inc., 5201 Lake Jackson, Waco, TX 76710, 213/506-1690
Agent: Mike Simpson, William Morris Agency - Beverly Hills, 213/274-7451

FANDANGO Warner Bros., 1984

DAVID LOWELL RICH*

b. August 31, 1920 - New York, New York
Home: 465 Loring Avenue, Los Angeles, CA 90024, 213/279-1783
Agent: William Morris Agency - Beverly Hills, 213/274-7451
Business Manager: Wade Hansen, Boulder Brook, Inc., 3223 Laurel Canyon Blvd., Studio City, CA 91604, 818/273-9050

NO TIME TO BE YOUNG Columbia, 1957
SENIOR PROM Columbia, 1958
HEY BOY! HEY GIRL! Columbia, 1959
HAVE ROCKET, WILL TRAVEL Columbia, 1959
SEE HOW THEY RUN (TF) Universal TV, 1964
MADAME X Universal, 1966
THE PLAINSMAN Universal, 1966
ROSIE! Universal, 1967
WINGS OF FIRE (TF) Universal TV, 1967
THE BORGIA STICK (TF) Universal TV, 1967
A LOVELY WAY TO DIE Universal, 1968
THREE GUNS FOR TEXAS co-director with Paul Stanley & Earl Bellamy, Universal, 1968
MARCUS WELBY, M.D. (TF) Universal TV, 1969
EYE TO THE CAT Universal, 1969
THE MASK OF SHEBA (TF) MGM TV, 1970
BERLIN AFFAIR (TF) Universal TV, 1970
THE SHERIFF (TF) Screen Gems/Columbia TV, 1971
ASSIGNMENT: MUNICH (TF) MGM TV, 1972
LIEUTENANT SCHUSTER'S WIFE (TF) Universal TV, 1972
ALL MY DARLING DAUGHTERS (TF) Universal TV, 1972
THAT MAN BOLT co-director with Henry Levin, Universal, 1972
THE JUDGE AND JAKE WYLER (TF) Universal TV, 1972
SET THIS TOWN ON FIRE (TF) Universal TV, 1973
THE HORROR AT 37,000 FEET (TF) CBS, Inc., 1973
BROCK'S LAST CASE (TF) Talent Associates/Universal TV, 1973
CRIME CLUB (TF) CBS, Inc., 1973
BEG, BORROW...OR STEAL (TF) Universal TV, 1973
SATAN'S SCHOOL FOR GIRLS (TF) Spelling-Goldberg Productions, 1973
RUNAWAY! (TF) Universal TV, 1973
DEATH RACE (TF) Universal TV, 1973
THE CHADWICK FAMILY (TF) Universal TV, 1974
THE SEX SYMBOL (TF) Screen Gems/Columbia, 1974
ALOHA MEANS GOODBYE (TF) Universal TV, 1974
THE DAUGHTERS OF JOSHUA CABE RETURN (TF) Spelling-Goldberg Productions, 1975
ADVENTURES OF THE QUEEN (TF) 20th Century-Fox TV, 1975
YOU LIE SO DEEP, MY LOVE (TF) Universal TV, 1975
BRIDGER (TF) Universal TV, 1976
THE SECRET LIFE OF JOHN CHAPMAN (TF) The Jozak Company, 1976
THE STORY OF DAVID (TF) co-director with Alex Segal, Mildred Freed Alberg Productions/Columbia TV, 1976
SST - DEATH FLIGHT (TF) ABC Circle Films, 1977
RANSOM FOR ALICE! (TF) Universal TV, 1977
TELETHON (TF) ABC Circle Films, 1977
THE DEFECTION OF SIMAS KUDIRKA (TF) ☆☆ The Jozak Company/Paramount TV, 1978
A FAMILY UPSIDE DOWN (TF) Ross Hunter-Jacques Mapes Film/Paramount TV, 1978
LITTLE WOMEN (TF) Universal TV, 1978
THE CONCORDE - AIRPORT '79 Universal, 1979
NURSE (TF) Robert Halmi Productions, 1980
ENOLA GAY (TF) The Production Company/Viacom, 1980
CHU CHU AND THE PHILLY FLASH 20th Century-Fox, 1981
THURSDAY'S CHILD (TF) The Catalina Production Group/Viacom, 1983
THE FIGHTER (TF) Martin Manulis Productions/The Catalina Production Group, 1983

DAVID LOWELL RICH*—continued

I WANT TO LIVE (TF) United Artists Corporation, 1983
THE SKY'S THE LIMIT (TF) Palance-Levy Productions, 1984
HIS MISTRESS (TF) David L. Wolper Productions/Warner Bros. TV, 1984

JOHN RICH*

b. July 6, 1925 - Rockaway Beach, New York
Agent: Leonard Hanzer, Major Talent Agency - Los Angeles, 213/820-5841
Business Manager: Marvin Freedman, Freedman, Kinzelberg & Broder, 1801 Avenue of the Stars - Suite 911, Los Angeles, CA 90067, 213/277-0700
Attorney: Arnold Burk, Gang, Tyre & Brown - Los Angeles, 213/557-7777

WIVES AND LOVERS Paramount, 1963
THE NEW INTERNS Columbia, 1964
ROUSTABOUT Paramount, 1964
BOEING BOEING Paramount, 1965
EASY COME, EASY GO Paramount, 1967

RICHARD RICH

Business: Walt Disney Productions, 500 S. Buena Vista Street, Burbank, CA 91521, 213/845-3141

THE FOX AND THE HOUND (AF) co-director with Art Stevens & Ted Berman, Buena Vista, 1981
THE BLACK CAULDRON (AF) co-director with Art Stevens & Ted Berman, Buena Vista, 1986

DICK RICHARDS*

b. 1936
Agent: Stan Kamen, William Morris Agency - Beverly Hills, 213/274-7451

THE CULPEPPER CATTLE CO. 20th Century-Fox, 1972
RAFFERTY AND THE GOLD DUST TWINS Warner Bros., 1975
FAREWELL, MY LOVELY Avco Embassy, 1975
MARCH OR DIE Columbia, 1977, British
DEATH VALLEY Universal, 1981
MAN, WOMAN AND CHILD Paramount, 1983

LLOYD RICHARDS*

Home: 90 York Square, New Haven, CT 06511, 203/865-2933
Messages: 203/436-1586

ROOTS: THE NEXT GENERATIONS (MS) co-director with John Erman, Charles S. Dubin & Georg Stanford Brown, Wolper Productions, 1979

TONY RICHARDSON*

(Cecil Antonio Richardson)

b. June 5, 1928 - Shipley, England
Business: 1478 N. Kings Road, Los Angeles, CA 90069, 213/656-5314

LOOK BACK IN ANGER Warner Bros., 1958, British
THE ENTERTAINER Continental, 1960, British
SANCTUARY 20th Century-Fox, 1961
A TASTE OF HONEY Continental, 1962, British
THE LONELINESS OF THE LONG DISTANCE RUNNER Continental, 1962, British
TOM JONES ★★ Lopert, 1963, British
THE LOVED ONE MGM, 1965
MADEMOISELLE Lopert, 1966, French-British
THE SAILOR FROM GIBRALTER Lopert, 1967, British
THE CHARGE OF THE LIGHT BRIGADE United Artists, 1968, British
LAUGHTER IN THE DARK Lopert, 1969, British-French
HAMLET Columbia, 1969, British
NED KELLY United Artists, 1970, British
A DELICATE BALANCE American Film Theatre, 1973

TONY RICHARDSON*—continued

DEAD CERT United Artists, 1973, British
JOSEPH ANDREWS Paramount, 1977, British
A DEATH IN CANAAN (TF) Chris-Rose Productions/Warner Bros. TV, 1978
THE BORDER Universal, 1982
THE HOTEL NEW HAMPSHIRE Orion, 1984

WILLIAM RICHERT

Contact: Writers Guild of America, West - Los Angeles, 213/550-1000

FIRST POSITION (FD) Roninfilm, 1973
WINTER KILLS Avco Embassy, 1979
THE AMERICAN SUCCESS CO. *SUCCESS* Columbia, 1979, West German-U.S.

ANTHONY RICHMOND*

b. July 7, 1942 - London, England
Contact: Directors Guild of America - Los Angeles, 213/656-1220

DEJA VU Cannon, 1985, British

W.D. RICHTER*

Agent: Shapiro-Lichtman Agency - Los Angeles, 213/557-2244

THE ADVENTURES OF BUCKAROO BANZAI: ACROSS THE 8TH DIMENSION 20th Century Fox, 1984

TOM RICKMAN

Agent: Michael Marcus, CAA - Los Angeles, 213/277-4545

THE RIVER RAT Paramount, 1984

DINO RISI

b. December 23, 1917 - Milan, Italy
Contact: Ministry of Tourism & Education, Via Della Ferratella, No. 51, 00184 Rome, Italy, 06/7732

VACANZE COL GANGSTER Mambretti Film, 1952, Italian
VIALE DELLA SPERANZA Mambretti Film/ENIC, 1953, Italian
LOVE IN THE CITY co-director with Michelangelo Antonioni, Federico Fellini, Alberto Lattuada, Carlo Lizzani & Francesco Maselli, Italian Films Export, 1953, Italian
IL SEGNO DI VENERE Titanus, 1955, Italian
SCANDAL IN SORRENTO *PANE, AMORE E...* DCA, 1955, Italian
POOR BUT BEAUTIFUL Trans-Lux, 1956, Italian-French
LA NONNA SABELLA Titanus/Franco-London Films, 1957, Italian-French
BELLE MA POVERE Titanus, 1957, Italian
VENEZIA, LA LUNA E TU Titanus/Societe Generale de Cinematographie, 1958, Italian-French
POVERI MILLIONARI Titanus, 1958, Italian
IL VEDOVO Paneuropa/Cino Del Duca, 1959, Italian
LOVE AND LARCENY *IL MATTATORE* Major Film, 1960, Italian-French
UN AMORE A ROMA CEI Incom/Fair Film/Laetitia Film/Les Films Cocinor/Alpha Film, 1960, Italian-French-West German
A PORTE CHIUSE Fair Film/Cinematografica Rire/Societe Generale de Cinematographie/Ultra Film/Lyre Film/Roxy Film, 1960, Italian-French-West German
UNA VITA DIFFICILE Dino De Laurentiis Cinematografica, 1961, Italian
LA MARCIA SU ROMA Fair Film/Orsay Films, 1962, Italian-French
THE EASY LIFE *IL SORPASSO* Embassy, 1962, Italian
IL GIOVEDI Dino De Laurentiis Cinematografica/Center Film, 1963, Italian
15 FROM ROME *I MOSTRI* McAbee, 1963, Italian-French
IL GAUCHO Fair Film/Clemente Lococo, 1964, Italian-Argentinian
BAMBOLE! co-director with Luigi Comencini, Franco Rossi & Mauro Bolognini, Royal Films International, 1965, Italian

DINO RISI —continued

I COMPLESSI co-director with Franco Rossi & Luigi Filippo D'Amico, Documento Film/SPCE, 1965, Italian-French
WEEKEND, ITALIAN STYLE *L'OMBRELLONE* Marvin Films, 1965, Italian-French-Spanish
I NOSTRI MARITI co-director with Luigi Filippo D'Amico & Luigi Zampa, Documento Film, 1966, Italian
TREASURE OF SAN GENNARO *OPERAZIONE SAN GENNARO* Paramount, 1966, Italian-French-West German
THE TIGER AND THE PUSSYCAT *IL TIGRE* Embassy, 1967, Italian-U.S.
THE PROPHET Joseph Green Pictures, 1967, Italian
STRAZIAMI DA MI BACI SAZIAMI FIDA Cinematografica/Productions Jacques Roitfeld, 1968, Italian-French
VEDO NUDO Dean Film/Jupiter Generale Cinematografica, 1969, Italian
IL GIOVANE NORMALE Dean Film/Italnoleggio, 1969, Italian
THE PRIEST'S WIFE Warner Bros., 1970, Italian-French
NOI DONNE SIAMO FATTE COSI Apollo International Film, 1971, Italian
IN NOME DEL POPOLO ITALIANO Apollo International Film, 1972, Italian
MORDI E FUGGI C.C. Champion/Les Films Concordia, 1973, Italian-French
HOW FUNNY CAN SEX BE? *SESSOMATTO* In-Frame, 1973, Italian
TELEFONI BIANCHI Dean Film, 1975, Italian
SCENT OF A WOMAN 20th Century-Fox, 1976, Italian
ANIMA PERSA Dean Film/Les Productions Fox Europe, 1977, Italian-French
LA STANZA DEL VESCOVO Merope Film/Carlton Film Export/Societe Nouvelle Prodis, 1977, Italian-French
VIVA ITALIA! *I NUOVI MOSTRI* co-director with Mario Monicelli & Ettore Scola, Cinema 6, 1978, Italian
PRIMO AMORE Dean Film, 1978, Italian
CARO PAPA Dean Film/AMLF/Prospect Film, 1979, Italian-French-Canadian
SUNDAY LOVERS co-director with Bryan Forbes, Edouard Molinaro & Gene Wilder, MGM/United Artists, 1980, U.S.-British-Italian-French
SONO FOTOGENICO Dean Film/Marceau Cocinor, 1980, Italian-French
GHOST OF LOVE Dean Film/AMLF/Roxy Film, 1981, Italian-French-West German
SESSO E VOLENTIERI Dean Film, 1982, Italian
LA VITA CONTINUA (MS) RAI, 1984, Italian
LE BON ROI DAGOBERT Gaumount, 1984, French-Italian
SCENO DI GUERRA Titanus, 1985, Italian

MICHAEL RITCHIE*

b. 1938 - Waukesha, Wisconsin
Business: Miracle Pictures, 22 Miller Avenue, Mill Valley, CA 94941, 415/383-2564
Business Manager: Marvin Freedman, Freedman, Kinzelberg & Broder, 1801 Avenue of the Stars - Suite 911, Los Angeles, CA 90067, 213/277-0700

THE OUTSIDER (TF) Universal TV, 1967
THE SOUND OF ANGER (TF) Universal TV, 1968
DOWNHILL RACER Paramount, 1969
PRIME CUT National General, 1972
THE CANDIDATE Warner Bros., 1972
SMILE United Artists, 1975
THE BAD NEWS BEARS Paramount, 1976
SEMI-TOUGH United Artists, 1978
AN ALMOST PERFECT AFFAIR Paramount, 1979
THE ISLAND Universal, 1980
DIVINE MADNESS (FD) The Ladd Company/Warner Bros., 1980
THE SURVIVORS Columbia, 1983
FLETCH Universal, 1985

MARTIN RITT*

b. March 2, 1920 - New York, New York
Agent: George Chasin, ICM - Los Angeles, 213/550-4000

EDGE OF THE CITY MGM, 1957
NO DOWN PAYMENT 20th Century-Fox, 1957
THE LONG HOT SUMMER MGM, 1958
THE BLACK ORCHID Paramount, 1959
THE SOUND AND THE FURY 20th Century-Fox, 1959
FIVE BRANDED WOMEN Paramount, 1960, Italian-Yugoslavian-U.S.

MARTIN RITT*—continued

PARIS BLUES United Artists, 1961
HEMINGWAY'S ADVENTURES OF A YOUNG MAN 20th Century-Fox, 1962
HUD ★ Paramount, 1963
THE OUTRAGE MGM, 1964
THE SPY WHO CAME IN FROM THE COLD Paramount, 1965, British
HOMBRE 20th Century-Fox, 1967
THE BROTHERHOOD Paramount, 1968
THE MOLLY MAGUIRES Paramount, 1970
THE GREAT WHITE HOPE 20th Century-Fox, 1970
SOUNDER 20th Century-Fox, 1972
PETE N' TILLIE Universal, 1972
CONRACK 20th Century-Fox, 1974
THE FRONT Columbia, 1976
CASEY'S SHADOW Columbia, 1978
NORMA RAE 20th Century-Fox, 1979
BACK ROADS Warner Bros., 1981
CROSS CREEK Universal/AFD, 1983

FREDERICK RITZENBERG

GOSPEL (FD) co-director with David Leivick, 20th Century-Fox, 1983

JOAN RIVERS*

b. 1937 - New York, New York
Personal Manager: Katz-Gallin-Morey Enterprises, 9255 Sunset Blvd. - Suite 1115, Los Angeles, CA 90069, 213/273-4210

RABBIT TEST Avco Embassy, 1978

JACQUES RIVETTE

b. March 1, 1978 - Rouen, France
Address: 20 Boulevard de la Bastille, 75012 Paris, France

AUX QUATRE COINS 1950, French
LE QUADRILLE 1950, French
LE DIVERTISSEMENT 1952, French
LE COUP DE BERGER 1956, French
PARIS BELONGS TO US 1961, French
THE NUN Altura, 1966, French
JEAN RENOIR, LE PATRON (FD) 1966, French
L'AMOUR FOU 1968, French
OUT 1: SPECTRE Sunchild Productions, 1974, French
CELINE AND JULIE GO BOATING 1974, French
DUELLE Valoria, 1976, French
NOROIT Sunchild Productions, 1976, French
MERRY-GO-ROUND 1979, French
LE PONT DU NORD Gerik Distribution, 1981, French
PARIS S'EN VA 1981, French
LOVE ON THE GROUND Spectrafilm, 1984, French
HURLEVENT AMLF, 1985, French

ALAIN ROBBE-GRILLET

b. August 18, 1922 - Brest, France
Home: 18 Boulevard Maillot, 92200 Neuilly, France, 1/722-3122

L'IMMORTELLE Grove Press, 1963, French
TRANS-EUROP-EXPRESS Trans-American, 1967, French
THE MAN WHO LIES Grove Press, 1968, French-Czech
L'EDEN ET APRES Como Films, 1971, French-Czech-Tunisian
GLISSMENTS PROGRESSIFS DU PLAISIR SNETC, 1974, French
LE JEU AVEC LE FEU Arcadie Productions, 1975, Italian-French
LA BELLE CAPTIVE Argos Films, 1983, French

SEYMOUR ROBBIE*

Home: 9980 Liebe Drive, Beverly Hills, CA 90210, 213/274-6713
Agent: Sylvia Gold, ICM - Los Angeles, 213/550-4000

C.C. AND COMPANY Avco Embassy, 1970
MARCO Cinerama Releasing Corporation, 1974

JEROME ROBBINS*

(Jerome Rabinowitz)

b. October 11, 1918 - Weehawken, New Jersey
Business: New York City Ballet, 1 Lincoln Plaza, New York, NY, 212/870-5656

WEST SIDE STORY ★★ co-director with Robert Wise, United Artists, 1961

MATTHEW ROBBINS*

b. New York
Contact: Directors Guild of America - Los Angeles, 213/656-1220

CORVETTE SUMMER MGM/United Artists, 1978
DRAGONSLAYER Paramount, 1981, U.S.-British
FAIR IS FAIR Tri-Star, 1985

MIKE ROBE

Contact: Writers Guild of America - Los Angeles, 213/550-1000

WITH INTENT TO KILL (TF) London Productions, 1984

YVES ROBERT

b. June 19, 1920 - Saumur, France
Contact: French Film Office, 745 Fifth Avenue, New York, NY 10151, 212/832-8860

LES HOMMES NE PENSENT QU'A CA 1954, French
SIGNE ARSENE LUPIN 1959, French
LA FAMILLE FENOUILLARD 1961, French
LA GUERRE DES BOUTONS LGE, 1962, French
BEBERT ET L'OMNIBUS 1963, French
LES COPAINS 1964, French
MONNAIRE DE SINGE 1965, French
VERY HAPPY ALEXANDER *ALEXANDER* Cinema 5, 1968, French
CLERAMBARD 1969, French
THE TALL BLOND MAN WITH ONE BLACK SHOE Cinema 5, 1972, French
SALUT L'ARTISTE Exxel, 1973, French
RETURN OF THE TALL BLOND MAN WITH ONE BLACK SHOE Lanir Releasing, 1974, French
PARDON MON AFFAIRE *AN ELEPHANT CA TROMPE ENORMEMENT* First Artists, 1976, French
PARDON MON AFFAIRE, TOO! *NOUS IRONS TOUS AU PARADIS* First Artists, 1977, French
COURAGE FUYONS Gaumont, 1979, French
LE JUMEAU AAA, 1984, French

ALAN ROBERTS

Contact: Writers Guild of America, West - Los Angeles, 213/550-1000

THE ZODIAC COUPLES co-director with Bob Stein, SAE, 1970
PANORAMA BLUE Ellman Film Enterprises, 1974
YOUNG LADY CHATTERLEY PRO International, 1977
THE HAPPY HOOKER GOES HOLLYWOOD Cannon, 1980
FLASHDANCE FEVER Shapiro Entertainment, 1983
YOUNG LADY CHATTERLEY II Park Lane Productions/Playboy Features, 1984

CLIFF ROBERTSON*

b. September 9, 1925 - La Jolla, California
Agent: Michael Black, ICM - Los Angeles, 213/550-4000

J.W. COOP Columbia, 1972
THE PILOT Summit Features, 1981

HUGH A. ROBERTSON

Home: 208A Terrace Vale Road, Good Wood Park, Trinidad, West Indies, 809/637-5994
Business: Sharc Productions, Ltd., 1 Valleton Avenue, Maraval, Trinidad, West Indies, 809/622-6580
Agent: Ron Mutchnick - Los Angeles, 213/659-3294

MELINDA MGM, 1972
BIM Sharc Productions, 1976, West Indian

JOHN ROBINS*

Home: 18203 Coastline Drive, Apt. 4, Malibu, CA 90265, 213/454-0859
Business: The Compromise Picture Corporation, 1880 Century Park East, Suite 500, Los Angeles, CA 90067

HOT RESORT Cannon, 1985

JOHN MARK ROBINSON

ROADHOUSE 66 Atlantic Releasing Corporation, 1984

FRANC RODDAM*

b. April 29 - Stockton, England
Agent: Spokesmen, Ltd., 1 Craven Hill, London W2, England
Contact: Directors Guild of America - Los Angeles, 213/656-1220

DUMMY (TF) ATV Network, 1977, British
QUADROPHENIA World Northal, 1979, British
THE LORDS OF DISCIPLINE Paramount, 1983
THE BRIDE Columbia, 1985, British

NICOLAS ROEG*

b. December 15, 1928 - London, England
Home: 2 Oxford-Cambridge Mansions, Old Marylebone Road, London NW1, England, 01/262-8612
Agent: Robert Littman, Leading Artists - Beverly Hills, 213/858-1999

PERFORMANCE co-director with Donald Cammell, Warner Bros., 1970, British
WALKABOUT 20th Century-Fox, 1971, British-Australian
DON'T LOOK NOW Paramount, 1974, British-Italian
THE MAN WHO FELL TO EARTH Cinema 5, 1976, British
BAD TIMING/A SENSUAL OBSESSION World Northal, 1980, British
EUREKA MGM/UA Classics, 1984, British
INSIGNIFICANCE Island Alive, 1985, British

MICHAEL ROEMER

b. January 1, 1928 - Berlin, Germany

A TOUCH OF THE TIMES 1949
THE INFERNO *CORTILE CASCINO, ITALY (FD)* co-director with Robert M. Young Film Productions, 1962
NOTHING BUT A MAN co-director with Robert M. Young, Cinema 5, 1965
DYING (TD) WGBH-Boston, 1976
PILGRIM, FAREWELL Post Mills Productions, 1980
HAUNTED (TF) Post Mills Productions/WGBH-Boston, 1984

LIONEL ROGOSIN

b. 1924 - New York, New York

ON THE BOWERY (FD) Film Representations, 1957
COME BACK, AFRICA (FD) Rogosin, 1959
GOOD TIMES, WONDERFUL TIMES (FD) Rogosin, 1966
BLACK ROOTS (FD) Rogosin, 1970
BLACK FANTASY (FD) Impact, 1972
WOODCUTTERS OF THE DEEP SOUTH (FD) Rogosin, 1973

ERIC ROHMER

(Jean-Marie Maurice Scherer)

b. April 4, 1920 - Nancy, France
Business: 26 Avenue Pierre-ler-de-Serbie, 75116, Paris, France
Contact: French Film Office, 745 Fifth Avenue, New York, NY 10151, 212/832-8860

LE SIGNE DU LION 1959, French
LA CARRIERE DE SUZANNE Films du Losange, 1963, French
PARIS VU PAR... co-director, 1965, French
LA COLLECTIONNEUSE Pathe Contemporary, 1967, French
MY NIGHT AT MAUD'S Pathe Contemporary, 1970, French
CLAIRE'S KNEE *L'AMOUR, L'APRES-MIDI* Columbia, 1971, French
CHLOE IN THE AFTERNOON Columbia, 1972, French
THE MARQUISE OF O... New Line Cinema, 1976, French-West German
PERCEVAL *PERCEVAL LE GALLOIS* New Yorker, 1978, French
THE AVIATOR'S WIFE New Yorker, 1981, French
LE BEAU MARIAGE United Artists Classics, 1982, French
PAULINE AT THE BEACH Orion Classics, 1983, French
FULL MOON IN PARIS *LES NUITS DE LA PLEINE LUNE* Orion Classics, 1984, French

SUTTON ROLEY*

Home: 777 Arden Road, Pasadena, CA 91106, 213/449-2491

SWEET, SWEET RACHEL (TF) ABC, Inc., 1971
THE LONERS Fanfare, 1972
SNATCHED (TF) ABC Circle Films, 1973
SATAN'S TRIANGLE (TF) Danny Thomas Productions, 1975
CHOSEN SURVIVORS Columbia, 1974

EDDIE ROMERO

b. 1924 - Negros Oriental, Philippines
Contact: Philippine Motion Picture Producers Association, 514 Burke Building, Escolta Manila, Philippines, 2/48-7731

THE DAY OF THE TRUMPET 1957, U.S.-Filipino
THE RAIDERS OF LEYTE GULF Hemisphere, 1963, Filipino-U.S.
MORO WITCH DOCTOR 20th Century-Fox, 1964, Filipino-U.S.
THE KIDNAPPERS *MAN ON THE RUN* 1964
THE WALLS OF HELL co-director with Gerardo De Leon, Hemisphere, 1964, U.S.-Filipino
THE RAVAGERS Hemisphere, 1965, U.S.-Filipino
BEAST OF BLOOD Marvin Films, 1971, U.S.-Filipino
BLACK MAMA, WHITE MAMA American International, 1973, U.S.-Filipino
BEYOND ATLANTIS Dimension, 1973, U.S.-Filipino
SAVAGE SISTERS American International, 1974, U.S.-Filipino
THE WOMAN HUNT New World, 1975, U.S.-Filipino
SUDDEN DEATH Topar, 1977, U.S.-Filipino
AGUILA Bancom Audiovision Corporation, 1980, Filipino
DESIRE Hemisphere, 1983, Filipino
GANITO KAMI NOON, PAANO KAYO NGAYON? 1983, Filipino

GEORGE A. ROMERO

Business: Laurel Entertainment Inc., 928 Broadway, New York, NY 10010, 212/674-3800

NIGHT OF THE LIVING DEAD Continental, 1968
THERE'S ALWAYS VANILLA Cambist, 1972
THE CRAZIES *CODE NAME: TRIXIE* Cambist, 1972
HUNGRY WIVES Jack H. Harris Enterprises, 1973
MARTIN Libra, 1978
DAWN OF THE DEAD United Film Distribution, 1979
KNIGHTRIDERS United Film Distribution, 1981
CREEPSHOW Warner Bros., 1982
DAY OF THE DEAD United Film Distribution, 1985

CONRAD ROOKS

CHAPPAQUA Regional, 1968
SIDDHARTHA Columbia, 1973

LES ROSE

Home: 17 Maple Avenue, Toronto, Ontario, Canada, 415/960-1829
Agent: Jeanine Edwards/Fifi Oscard - New York City, 212/764-1100

THREE CARD MONTE Arista, 1977, Canadian
TITLE SHOT Arista, 1979, Canadian
HOG WILD Avco Embassy, 1980, Canadian
GAS Paramount, 1981, Canadian
GORDON PINSENT AND THE LIFE AND TIMES OF EDWIN ALONZO BOYD (TF) Poundmaker Productions, 1982, Canadian
DRASTIC MEASURES Lauron Productions, 1985, Canadian

MICKEY ROSE

Contact: Robinson-Weintraub Associates - Los Angeles, 213/653-5802

STUDENT BODIES Paramount, 1981

MARTIN ROSEN

WATERSHIP DOWN (AF) Avco Embassy, 1978, British
THE PLAGUE DOGS (AF) Nepenthe Productions, 1982, British

ROBERT L. ROSEN

b. January 7, 1937 - Palm Springs, California
Attorney: Marty Weiss, 12301 Wilshire Blvd., Suite 203, Los Angeles, CA 90025, 213/820-8872

COURAGE New World, 1984

STUART ROSENBERG*

b. New York, New York
Agent: William Morris Agency - Beverly Hills, 213/274-7451

MURDER, INC. co-director with Burt Balaban, 20th Century-Fox, 1960
QUESTION 7 De Rochemont, 1961, U.S.-West German
FAME IS THE NAME OF THE GAME (TF) Universal TV, 1966
ASYLUM FOR A SPY (TF) Universal TV, 1967
COOL HAND LUKE Warner Bros., 1967
THE APRIL FOOLS National General, 1969
MOVE 20th Century-Fox, 1970
WUSA Paramount, 1970
POCKET MONEY National General, 1972
THE LAUGHING POLICEMAN 20th Century-Fox, 1973
THE DROWNING POOL Warner Bros., 1975
VOYAGE OF THE DAMNED Avco Embassy, 1977, British

STUART ROSENBERG*—continued

LOVE AND BULLETS AFD, 1979
THE AMITYVILLE HORROR American International, 1979
BRUBAKER 20th Century-Fox, 1980
THE POPE OF GREENWICH VILLAGE MGM/UA, 1984

RALPH ROSENBLUM*

Home: 344 West 84th Street, New York, NY 10024, 212/595-7975
Agent: The Gersh Agency - Beverly Hills, 213/274-6611

THE GREATEST MAN IN THE WORLD (TF) Learning in Focus, 1979
ANY FRIEND OF NICHOLAS NICKLEBY IS A FRIEND OF MINE (TF) Rubicon Productions, 1982

RICK ROSENTHAL*

Agent: The Gersh Agency - Beverly Hills, 213/274-6611
Business: Whitewater Films, Inc., 7471 Melrose Avenue, Suite 17, Los Angeles, CA 90046, 213/658-8775

HALLOWEEN II Universal, 1981
BAD BOYS Universal/AFD, 1983
AMERICAN DREAMER Warner Bros., 1984

ROBERT J. ROSENTHAL

Contact: Writers Guild of America, West - Los Angeles, 213/550-1000

MALIBU BEACH Crown International, 1978
ZAPPED! Embassy, 1982

FRANCESCO ROSI

b. November 15, 1922 - Naples, Italy
Contact: Ministry of Tourism & Education, Via Della Ferratella, No. 51, 00184 Rome, Italy 06/7732

LA SFIDA Lux/Vices/Suevia Film, 1958, Italian-Spanish
I MAGLIARI Vides/Titanus, 1959, Italian
SALVATORE GIULIANO CCM Films, 1962, Italian-French
LE MANI SULLA CITTA Galatea Film, 1963, Italian
THE MOMENT OF TRUTH Rizzoli, 1965, Italian-Spanish
MORE THAN A MIRACLE *C'ERA UNA VOLTA* MGM, 1967, Italian-French
UOMINI CONTRO Prima Cinematografica/Jadran Film, 1970, Italian-Yugoslavian
THE MATTEI AFFAIR Paramount, 1973, Italian
LUCKY LUCIANO Avco Embassy, 1974, Italian
IL CONTESTO 1975, Italian
CADAVERI ECCELENTI United Artists, 1976, Italian-French
EBOLI *CHRIST STOPPED AT EBOLI* Franklin Media, 1980, Italian-French
THREE BROTHERS New World, 1981, Italian
BIZET'S CARMEN *CARMEN* Triumph/Columbia, 1984, Italian-French

MARK ROSMAN

THE HOUSE ON SORORITY ROW Artists Releasing Corporation/Film Ventures International, 1983

HERBERT ROSS*

b. May 13, 1927 - New York, New York
Agent: Michael Ovitz/Cheryl Peterson, CAA - Los Angeles, 213/277-4545

GOODBYE, MR. CHIPS MGM, 1969, British
THE OWL AND THE PUSSYCAT Columbia, 1970
T.R. BASKIN Paramount, 1971
PLAY IT AGAIN, SAM Paramount, 1972
THE LAST OF SHEILA Warner Bros., 1973
FUNNY LADY Columbia, 1975

HERBERT ROSS*—continued

THE SUNSHINE BOYS MGM/United Artists, 1975
THE SEVEN-PER-CENT SOLUTION Universal, 1976, British
THE TURNING POINT ★ 20th Century-Fox, 1977
THE GOODBYE GIRL Warner Bros., 1977
CALIFORNIA SUITE Columbia, 1978
NIJINSKY Paramount, 1980
PENNIES FROM HEAVEN MGM/United Artists, 1981
I OUGHT TO BE IN PICTURES 20th Century-Fox, 1982
MAX DUGAN RETURNS 20th Century-Fox, 1983
FOOTLOOSE Paramount, 1984
PROTOCOL Warner Bros., 1984

BOBBY ROTH*

Home: 7957 Fareholm Drive, Los Angeles, CA 90068, 213/851-9702
Messages: 818/508-3397
Agent: Arnold Rifkin, Triad Artists, Inc. - Los Angeles, 213/556-2727

INDEPENDENCE DAY Unifilm, 1977
THE BOSS' SON Circle Associates, 1980
CIRCLE OF POWER *MYSTIQUE/BRAINWASH/THE NAKED WEEKEND* Televicine, 1983
HEARTBREAKERS Orion, 1984

STEPHANIE ROTHMAN

Home: P.O. Box 491016, Los Angeles, CA 90049

BLOOD BATH co-director with Jack Hill, American International, 1966
IT'S A BIKINI WORLD American International, 1967
THE STUDENT NURSES New World, 1970
THE VELVET VAMPIRE New World, 1971
GROUP MARRIAGE Dimension, 1972
TERMINAL ISLAND Dimension, 1973
THE WORKING GIRLS Dimension, 1974

RUSSELL ROUSE*

b. April 3, 1915 - New York, New York
Attorney: Covey & Covey - Los Angeles, 213/272-0074

THE WELL co-director with Leo Popkins, United Artists, 1951
THE THIEF United Artists, 1952
WICKED WOMAN United Artists, 1954
NEW YORK CONFIDENTIAL Warner Bros., 1955
THE FASTEST GUN ALIVE MGM, 1956
HOUSE OF NUMBERS Columbia, 1957
THUNDER IN THE SUN Paramount, 1959
A HOUSE IS NOT A HOME Embassy, 1964
THE OSCAR Embassy, 1966
THE CAPER OF THE GOLDEN BULLS Embassy, 1967

JOSEPH RUBEN*

Home: 2680 Woodstock Road, Los Angeles, CA 90405, 213/392-9006
Agent: John Ptak, William Morris Agency - Beverly Hills, 213/274-7451

THE SISTER-IN-LAW Crown International, 1975
THE POM-POM GIRLS Crown International, 1976
JOYRIDE American International, 1977
OUR WINNING SEASON American International, 1978
GORP American International, 1980
DREAMSCAPE 20th Century Fox, 1984

ALAN RUDOLPH*

Agent: Sue Mengers/Jim Wiatt, ICM - Los Angeles, 213/550-4000
Business Manager: William Goldstein - Los Angeles, 213/783-7671

PREMONITION TransVue, 1972
WELCOME TO L.A. United Artists/Lions Gate, 1977
REMEMBER MY NAME Columbia/Lagoon Associates, 1979
ROADIE United Artists, 1980
ENDANGERED SPECIES MGM/UA, 1982
RETURN ENGAGEMENT (FD) Island Alive, 1983
CHOOSE ME Island Alive/New Cinema, 1984
SONGWRITER Tri-Star, 1984

RICHARD RUSH*

b. 1930
Agent: Jack Gilardi, ICM - Los Angeles, 213/550-4000

TOO SOON TO LOVE Universal, 1960
OF LOVE AND DESIRE 20th Century-Fox, 1963
FICKLE FINGER OF FATE Pro International, 1967
THUNDER ALLEY American International, 1967
HELL'S ANGELS ON WHEELS American International, 1967
A MAN CALLED DAGGER MGM, 1968
PSYCH-OUT American International, 1968
THE SAVAGE SEVEN American International, 1968
GETTING STRAIGHT Columbia, 1970
FREEBIE AND THE BEAN Warner Bros., 1974
THE STUNT MAN ★ 20th Century-Fox, 1980

KEN RUSSELL*

b. July 3, 1927 - Southampton, England
Agent: Peter Rawley, ICM - Los Angeles, 213/550-4000

FRENCH DRESSING Warner-Pathe, 1963, British
BILLION DOLLAR BRAIN United Artists, 1967, British
DANTE'S INFERNO (TF) BBC, 1967, British
SONG OF SUMMER (TF) BBC, 1968, British
THE DANCE OF THE SEVEN VEILS (TF) BBC, 1970, British
WOMEN IN LOVE ★ United Artists, 1970, British
THE MUSIC LOVERS United Artists, 1971, British
THE DEVILS Warner Bros., 1971, British
THE BOY FRIEND MGM, 1971, British
SAVAGE MESSIAH MGM, 1972, British
MAHLER Mayfair, 1974, British
TOMMY Columbia, 1975, British
LISZTOMANIA Warner Bros., 1975, British
VALENTINO United Artists, 1977, British
CLOUDS OF GLORY *WILLIAM AND DOROTHY (TF)* Granada TV, 1978, British
ALTERED STATES Warner Bros., 1980
CRIMES OF PASSION New World, 1984

MARK RYDELL*

b. March 23, 1934
Agent: William Morris Agency - Beverly Hills, 213/274-7451

THE FOX Claridge, 1968
THE REIVERS National General, 1969
THE COWBOYS Warner Bros., 1972
CINDERELLA LIBERTY 20th Century-Fox, 1974
HARRY AND WALTER GO TO NEW YORK Columbia, 1976
THE ROSE 20th Century-Fox, 1979
ON GOLDEN POND ★ Universal/AFD, 1981
THE RIVER Universal, 1984

S

WILLIAM SACHS

Agent: Shapiro-Lichtman Agency - Los Angeles, 231/557-2244

SECRETS OF THE GODS Film Ventures International, 1976
THERE IS NO THIRTEEN Film Ventures International, 1977
THE INCREDIBLE MELTING MAN American International, 1977
VAN NUYS BLVD. Crown International, 1979
GALAXINA Crown International, 1980
HOT SUMMER Cannon, 1985

ALAN SACKS

Contact: Writers Guild of America, West - Los Angeles, 213/550-1000

DU BEAT-E-O H-Z-H Presentation, 1984

HENRI SAFRAN

Contact: Mitch Consultancy, 98 Bay Road, Waverton, NSW, 2060, Australia, 02/922-6566

TROUBLE SHOOTER (MS) 1975, Australian
SOFTLY SOFTLY (MS) 1975, Australian
ELEPHANT BOY 1975, Australian
LOVE STORY (MS) 1976, Australian
STORM BOY South Australian Film Corporation, 1976, Australian
NORMAN LOVES ROSE Atlantic Releasing Corporation, 1981, Australian
THE WILD DUCK Orion, 1983, Australian
PRINCE AND THE GREAT RACE *BUSH CHRISTMAS* Quartet/Films Inc., 1983, Australian

GENE SAKS*

b. November 8, 1921 - New York, New York
Agent: John Planco, William Morris Agency - New York City, 212/586-5100
Business Manager: Wallin, Simon, Black & Co., 1350 Avenue of the Americas, New York, NY 10019

BAREFOOT IN THE PARK Paramount, 1966
THE ODD COUPLE Paramount, 1968
CACTUS FLOWER Columbia, 1969
LAST OF THE RED HOT LOVERS Paramount, 1972
MAME Warner Bros., 1974

LUCIANO SALCE

b. September 22, 1922 - Italy
Contact: Ministry of Tourism & Education, Via Della Ferratella, No. 51, 00184 Rome, Italy, 06/7732

LA PILLOLE DE ERCOLE Maxima Film/Dino De Laurentiis Cinematografica, 1960, Italian
IL FEDERALE Dino De Laurentiis Cinematografica, 1961, Italian
CRAZY DESIRE *LA VOGLIA MATTA* Embassy, 1962, Italian
LA CUCCAGNA CIRAC/Agliani Cinematografica, 1962, Italian
THE HOURS OF LOVE Cinema 5, 1963, Italian
THE LITTLE NUNS Embassy, 1963, Italian
HIGH INFIDELITY co-director with Mario Monicelli, Franco Rossi & Elio Petri, Magna, 1964, Italian-French
KISS THE OTHER SHEIK *OGGI, DOMANI E DOPODOMANI* co-director with Marco Ferreri & Eduardo de Filippo, MGM, 1965, Italian-French
SLALOM Fair Film/Cocinor/Copro Film, 1965, Italian-French-British
EL GRECO 20th Century-Fox, 1966, Italian-French
THE QUEENS *LE FATE* co-director with Mario Monicelli, Mauro Bolognini, & Antonio Pietrangeli, Royal Films International, 1966, Italian-French
TI HO SPOSATO PER ALLEGRIA Fair Film, 1967, Italian
LA PECORA NERA Fair Film, 1969, Italian
COLPO DI STATO Vides, 1969, Italian
IL PROF. DR. GUIDO TERSILLI, PRIMARIO DELLA CLINICA VILLA CELESTE, CONVENZIONATA CON LE MUTUE San Marco, 1969, Italian
BASTA GUARDARLA Fair Film, 1971, Italian
IL PROVINCIALE Fair Film, 1971, Italian
IO E LUI Dino De Laurentiis Cinematografica, 1973, Italian
TRAGICO FANTOZZI Cineriz, 1975, Italian
IL SECONDO TRAGICO FANTOZZI Cineriz, 1976, Italian
LA PRESIDENTESSA Gold Film, 1976, Italian
L'ANATRA ALL'ARANCIA Cineriz, 1976, Italian
ITALIANO COME ME 1977, Italian
IL...BELPAESE 77 Cinematografica, 1977, Italian
DOVE VAI IN VACANZA? co-director with Mauro Bolognini & Alberto Sordi, Cineriz, 1978, Italian
PROFESSOR KRANZ TEDESCO DI GERMANIA Gold Film, 1979, Italian-Brazilian
RIAVANTI...MARSCH I PAC, 1980, Italian
RAG. ARTURO DE FANTI BANCARIO PRECARIO PAC, 1980, Italian
THE INNOCENTS ABROAD (TF) Nebraska ETV Network/The Great Amwell Company/WNET-13, 1983

JAMES SALTER

Agent: Ziegler, Diskant, Inc. - Los Angeles, 213/278-0700

THREE United Artists, 1969, British

PAUL SALTZMAN

WHEN WE FIRST MET (CTF) Learning Corporation of America, 1984

DENIS SANDERS*

b. January 21, 1929 - New York, New York
Home: 5033 Campanile Drive, San Diego, CA 92115, 714/583-8803
Business: SRS Productions, 4224 Ellenita Avenue, Tarzana, CA 91356, 818/873-3171

CRIME AND PUNISHMENT, U.S.A. Allied Artists, 1959
WAR HUNT United Artists, 1961
ONE MAN'S WAY United Artists, 1964
SHOCK TREATMENT 20th Century-Fox, 1964
ELVIS - THAT'S THE WAY IT IS (FD) MGM, 1970
SOUL TO SOUL (FD) Cinerama Releasing Corporation, 1971
INVASION OF THE BEE GIRLS Centaur, 1973

JAY SANDRICH*

b. February 24, 1932 - Los Angeles, California
Home: 1 North Star - Suite 205, Marina del Rey, CA 90291, 213/392-7357
Agent: Michael Ovitz/Ron Meyer, CAA - Los Angeles, 213/277-4545
Business Manager: Bill Broder, Freedman, Kinzelberg & Broder, 1801 Avenue of the Stars - Suite 911, Los Angeles, CA 90067, 231/277-0700

THE CROOKED HEARTS (TF) Lorimar Productions, 1972
WHAT ARE BEST FRIENDS FOR? (TF) ABC Circle Films, 1973
NEIL SIMON'S SEEMS LIKE OLD TIMES Columbia, 1980
THE LONELY HEARTS (TF) Lorimar Productions, 1984

JONATHAN SANGER*

Business Manager: Freedman, Kinzelberg & Broder - Los Angeles, 213/277-0700

EMERALD MGM/UA, 1985

JIMMY SANGSTER*

b. December 2, 1927 - England
Agent: Shapiro-Lichtman Agency - Los Angeles, 213/557-2244

THE HORROR OF FRANKENSTEIN Levitt-Pickman, 1970, British
LUST FOR A VAMPIRE American Continental, 1971, British
FEAR IN THE NIGHT International Co-Productions, 1972, British

DERAN SARAFIAN

THE FALLING Film Ventures International, 1985

RICHARD C. SARAFIAN*

b. April 28, 1932 - New York, New York
Agent: Jack Gilardi, ICM - Los Angeles, 213/550-4000
Business Manager: John Mitchell, Nanas, Stern & Biers, 9454 Wilshire Blvd., Los Angeles, CA 90048, 213/275-2701

TERROR AT BLACK FALLS Beckman, 1962
ANDY Universal, 1965
SHADOW ON THE LAND (TF) Screen Gems/Columbia TV, 1968
RUN WILD, RUN FREE Columbia, 1969, British
FRAGMENT OF FEAR Columbia, 1971, British
MAN IN THE WILDERNESS Warner Bros., 1971
VANISHING POINT 20th Century-Fox, 1971
LOLLY-MADONNA XXX MGM, 1973
THE MAN WHO LOVED CAT DANCING MGM, 1973
ONE OF OUR OWN (TF) Universal TV, 1975
THE NEXT MAN Allied Artists, 1976
A KILLING AFFAIR (TF) Columbia TV, 1977
SUNBURN Paramount, 1979, U.S.-British
DISASTER ON THE COASTLINER (TF) Moonlight Productions/Filmways, 1979
THE GOLDEN MOMENT: AN OLYMPIC LOVE STORY (TF) Don Ohlmeyer Productions/Telepictures Corporation, 1980
THE GANGSTER CHRONICLES (TF) Universal TV, 1981
SPLENDOR IN THE GRASS (TF) Katz-Gallin Productions/Half-Pint Productions/Warner Bros. TV, 1981
THE BEAR Embassy, 1984

JOSEPH SARGENT*
(Giuseppe Danielle Sorgente)

b. July 25, 1925 - Jersey City, New Jersey
Agent: Shapiro-Lichtman Agency - Los Angeles, 213/557-2244
Business: Joseph Sargent Productions, 5746 Sunset Blvd., Hollywood, CA 90028, 213/462-7111

ONE SPY TOO MANY MGM, 1966
THE HELL WITH HEROES Universal, 1968
THE SUNSHINE PATRIOT (TF) Universal TV, 1968
THE IMMORTAL (TF) Paramount TV, 1969
COLOSSUS: THE FORBIN PROJECT Universal, 1970
TRIBES (TF) ☆ 20th Century-Fox, 1970
MAYBE I'LL COME HOME IN THE SPRING (TF) Metromedia Productions, 1971
LONGSTREET (TF) Paramount TV, 1971
MAN ON A STRING (TF) Screen Gems/Columbia TV, 1972
THE MAN Paramount, 1972
THE MARCUS-NELSON MURDERS (TF) ☆☆ Universal TV, 1973
THE MAN WHO DIED TWICE (TF) Cinema Center, 1973
SUNSHINE (TF) Universal TV, 1973
WHITE LIGHTNING United Artists, 1973
THE TAKING OF PELHAM 1-2-3 United Artists, 1974
HUSTLING (TF) Filmways, 1975
FRIENDLY PERSUASION (TF) International TV Productions/Allied Artists, 1975
THE NIGHT THAT PANICKED AMERICA (TF) Paramount TV, 1975
MacARTHUR Universal, 1977
GOLDENGIRL Avco Embassy, 1979
AMBER WAVES (TF) ☆ Time-Life Productions, 1980
COAST TO COAST Paramount, 1980
FREEDOM (TF) Hill-Mandelker Films, 1981
THE MANIONS OF AMERICA (MS) co-director with Charles S. Dubin, Roger Gimbel Productions/EMI TV/Argonaut Films Ltd., 1981
TOMORROW'S CHILD (TF) 20th Century-Fox TV, 1982
NIGHTMARES Universal, 1983
CHOICES OF THE HEART (TF) Katz-Gallin/Half-Pint Productions, 1983
MEMORIAL DAY (TF) Charles Fries Productions, 1983
TERRIBLE JOE MORAN (TF) Robert Halmi Productions, 1984
SPACE (MS) co-director with Lee Philips, Stonehenge Productions/Paramount TV, 1985

MICHAEL SARNE

b. August 6, 1939 - London, England
Address: 13 Airlie Gardens, London W8, England

LA ROUTE DE ST. TROPEZ 1966, French
JOANNA 20th Century-Fox, 1968, British
MYRA BRECKINRIDGE 20th Century-Fox, 1970
VERA VERAO Relevo Productions, 1975, Brazilian
INTIMIDADE Relevo Productions, 1976, Brazilian
THE PUNK 1978, British

PETER SASDY

b. Budapest, Hungary
Agent: Jack Gilardi, ICM - Los Angeles, 213/550-4000

TASTE THE BLOOD OF DRACULA Warner Bros., 1970, British
COUNTESS DRACULA 20th Century-Fox, 1972, British
HANDS OF THE RIPPER Universal, 1972, British
DOOMWATCH Avco Embassy, 1972, British
NOTHING BUT THE NIGHT Cinema Systems, 1975, British
THE DEVIL WITHIN HER *I DON'T WANT TO BE BORN* 20th Century-Fox, 1976, British
WELCOME TO BLOOD CITY EMI, 1977 British
THE LONELY LADY Universal, 1983

RON SATLOF*

Agent: David Shapira & Associates - Beverly Hills, 213/278-2742

BENNY & BARNEY: LAS VEGAS UNDERCOVER (TF) Universal TV, 1977
WAIKIKI (TF) Aaron Spelling Productions, 1980
THE MURDER THAT WOULDN'T DIE (TF) Universal TV, 1980
HUNTER (TF) Stephen J. Cannell Productions, 1984

CARLOS SAURA

b. January 4, 1932 - Huesca, Spain
Contact: Direccion General del Libro y de la Cinematografia, Ministerio de Cultura, Paseo de la Castellana 109, Madrid 16, Spain, 1/455-5000

CUENCA 1959, Spanish
LOS GOLFOS 1962, Spanish
LLANTO POR UN BANDITO 1964, Spanish
THE HUNT Trans-Lux, 1966, Spanish
PEPPERMINT FRAPPE Elias Querejeta Productions, 1967, Spanish
STRESS ES TRES TRES Elias Querejeta Productions, 1968, Spanish
HONEYCOMB *LA MADRIGUERA* CineGlobe, 1969, Spanish
THE GARDEN OF DELIGHTS Perry/Fleetwood, 1970, Spanish
ANA Y LOS LOBOS 1973, Spanish
COUSIN ANGELICA New Yorker, 1974, Spanish
CRIA! *CRIA CUERVOS* Jason Allen, 1976, Spanish
ELISA, VIDA MIA Elias Querejeta Productions, 1977, Spanish
LOS OJOS VENDADOS Elias Querejeta Productions, 1978, Spanish
MAMA CUMPLE CIEN ANOS Elias Querejeta Productions/Films Moliere/ Pierson Productions, 1979, Spanish-French
DEPRISA, DEPRISA Films Moliere, 1981, Spanish-French
SWEET HOURS New Yorker, 1982, Spanish
ANTONIETA Gaumont/Conacine/Nuevo Cine, 1982, French-Mexican
CARMEN Orion Classics, 1983, Spanish
LOS ZANCOS Emiliano Piedra Productions, 1984, Spanish

CLAUDE SAUTET

b. February 23, 1924 - Montrouge, France
Contact: French Film Office, 745 Fifth Avenue, New York, NY 10151, 212/832-8860

BONJOUR SOURIRE Vox, 1955, French
THE BIG RISK United Artists, 1960, French-Italian
L'ARME A GAUCHE 1965, French
THE THINGS OF LIFE Columbia, 1970, French
MAX ET LES FERRAILLEURS CFDC, 1971, French
CESAR AND ROSALIE Cinema 5, 1972, French-Italian-West German
VINCENT, FRANCOIS, PAUL AND THE OTHERS Joseph Green Pictures, 1974, French-Italian
MADO Joseph Green Pictures, 1976, French
A SIMPLE STORY Quartet, 1979, French
UN MAUVAIS FIL Sara Films/Antenne-2, 1980, French
GARCON Sara Film/Renn Productions, 1983, French

TELLY SAVALAS*

b. 1926 - Garden City, New Jersey
Agent: Jack Gilardi, ICM - Los Angeles, 213/550-4000
Business: 100 Universal City Plaza, Universal City, CA 91608, 818/985-4321
Business Manager: Tucker, Morgan, Martindale, 9200 Sunset Blvd. - Suite 418, Los Angeles, CA 90069, 213/274-0981

BEYOND REASON Goldfarb Distributors, 1982

PHILIP SAVILLE

b. London, England
Agent: Douglas Rae Management, 23 Charing Cross Road, London WC2, England, 01/836-3903
Contact: Directors Guild of Great Britain, 56 Whitfield Street, London W1, England, 01/580-2256

STOP THE WORLD - I WANT TO GET OFF Warner Bros., 1966, British
OEDIPUS THE KING Regional, 1968, British
THE RAINBIRDS (TF) BBC, 1970, British
SECRETS Lone Star, 1971, British
GANGSTERS (TF) BBC, 1975, British
THOSE GLORY, GLORY DAYS (TF) Channel Four/Enigma Films, 1983, British
SHADEY Larkspur Productions/Otto Plaschkes Productions/Film Four International, 1985, British

JOHN SAYLES*

Contact: Directors Guild of America - New York City, 212/581-0370

RETURN OF THE SECAUCUS SEVEN Libra/Specialty Films, 1980
LIANNA United Artists Classics, 1983
BABY IT'S YOU Paramount, 1983
THE BROTHER FROM ANOTHER PLANET Cinecom International, 1984

JOSEPH L. SCANLAN*

Home: 14004 Palawan Way, Apt. 314, Marina del Rey, CA 90292, 213/822-0318
Agent: Nancy Blaylock, The Gersh Agency - Beverly Hills, 231/274-6611

SPRING FEVER Comworld, 1983, Canadian

ALLEN SCHAAF

b. December 6, 1942 - San Francisco, California
Business: Tenth Street Production Group, Inc., 147 10th Street, San Francisco, CA 94103, 415/621-3395

DRACULA'S DISCIPLE Tenth Street Production Group, 1984

GEORGE SCHAEFER*

b. December 16, 1920 - Wallingford, Connecticut
Home: 1040 Woodland Drive, Beverly Hills, CA 90210, 213/274-6017
Business: Schaefer-Karpf Productions - Studio City 818/506-6655
Agent: Rowland Perkins, CAA - Los Angeles, 213/277-4545

MACBETH British Lion, 1961, British
PENDULUM Columbia, 1969
GENERATION Avco Embassy, 1969
DOCTOR'S WIVES Columbia, 1971
A WAR OF CHILDREN (TF) ☆ Tomorrow Entertainment, 1972
F. SCOTT FITZGERALD AND "THE LAST OF THE BELLES" (TF) Titus Productions, 1974
ONCE UPON A SCOUNDREL Image International, 1974, U.S.-Mexican
IN THIS HOUSE OF BREDE (TF) Tomorrow Entertainment, 1975
AMELIA EARHART (TF) Universal TV, 1976
THE GIRL CALLED HATTER FOX (TF) Roger Gimbel Productions/EMI TV, 1978
FIRST YOU CRY (TF) MTM Enterprises, 1978
AN ENEMY OF THE PEOPLE Warner Bros., 1978
WHO'LL SAVE OUR CHILDREN? (TF) Time-Life Productions, 1978
BLIND AMBITION (TF) Time-Life Productions, 1979
MAYFLOWER: THE PILGRIMS' ADVENTURE (TF) Syzygy Productions, 1979
THE BUNKER (TF) Time-Life Productions/SFP France/Antenne-2, 1981, U.S.-French
A PIANO FOR MRS. CIMINO (TF) Roger Gimbel Productions/EMI TV, 1982

GEORGE SCHAEFER*—continued

RIGHT OF WAY (CTF) HBO Premiere Films, Schaefer-Karpf Productions/Post-Newsweek Video, 1983
CHILDREN IN THE CROSSFIRE (TF) Schaefer-Karpf Productions/Prendergast-Brittcadia Productions/Gaylord Production Company, 1984

FRANKLIN J. SCHAFFNER*

b. May 30, 1920 - Tokyo, Japan
Agent: CAA - Los Angeles, 213/277-4545

THE STRIPPER 20th Century-Fox, 1962
THE BEST MAN Unitd Artists, 1964
THE WAR LORD Universal, 1965
THE DOUBLE MAN Warner Bros., 1968, British
PLANET OF THE APES 20th Century-Fox, 1968
PATTON ★★ 20th Century-Fox, 1970
NICHOLAS AND ALEXANDRA Columbia, 1971, British
PAPILLON Allied Artists, 1973
ISLANDS IN THE STREAM Paramount, 1977
THE BOYS FROM BRAZIL 20th Century-Fox, 1978
SPHINX Orion/Warner Bros., 1981
YES, GIORGIO MGM/UA, 1982

DON SCHAIN*

Home: 1817 N. Fuller Avenue, Los Angeles, CA 90046
Business: Derio Productions, Inc., 7942 Mulholland Drive, Los Angeles, CA 90046, 213/851-8140

GINGER Joseph Brenner Associates, 1971
THE ADBUCTORS Joseph Brenner Associates, 1972
A PLACE CALLED TODAY Avco Embassy, 1972
GIRLS ARE FOR LOVING Continental, 1973
TOO HOT TO HANDLE Derio Productions, 1978

JERRY SCHATZBERG*

b. New York, New York
Agent: William Morris Agency - New York City, 212/586-5100
Business Manager: Herb Bard, Bard & Kass, 551 Fifth Avenue, New York, NY 10176, 212/599-2880

PUZZLE OF A DOWNFALL CHILD Universal, 1970
PANIC IN NEEDLE PARK 20th Century-Fox, 1971
SCARECROW Warner Bros., 1973
SWEET REVENGE *DANDY, THE ALL-AMERICAN GIRL* MGM/United Artists, 1976
THE SEDUCTION OF JOE TYNAN Universal, 1979
HONEYSUCKLE ROSE Warner Bros., 1980
MISUNDERSTOOD MGM/UA, 1984
NO SMALL AFFAIR Columbia, 1984

ROBERT SCHEERER*

b. Santa Barbara, California
Agent: The Cooper Agency - Los Angeles, 213/277-8422

HANS BRINKER (TF) NBC, 1969
ADAM AT SIX A.M. National General, 1970
THE WORLD'S GREATEST ATHLETE Buena Vista, 1973
POOR DEVIL (TF) Paramount TV, 1973
TARGET RISK (TF) Universal TV, 1975
IT HAPPENED AT LAKEWOOD MANOR (TF) Alan Landsburg Productions, 1977
HAPPILY EVER AFTER (TF) Tri-Media II, Inc./Hamel-Somers Entertainment, 1978
HOW TO BEAT THE HIGH COST OF LIVING American International, 1980

MAXIMILIAN SCHELL

b. December 8, 1930 - Vienna, Austria
Agent: ICM - Los Angeles, 213/550-4000

FIRST LOVE UMC, 1970, Swiss-West German
THE PEDESTRIAN Cinerama Releasing Corporation, 1974, West German-Swiss-Israeli
END OF THE GAME 20th Century-Fox, 1976, West German-Italian
TALES FROM THE VIENNA WOODS Cinema 5, 1979, Austrian-West German
MARLENE (FD) Oko Film/Karel Dirka Productions, 1984, West German

HENNING SCHELLERUP

THE BLACK BUNCH Entertainment Pyramid, 9173
SWEET JESUS, PREACHER MAN MGM, 1973
THE BLACK ALLEYCATS Entertainment Pyramid, 1974
THE TIME MACHINE (TF) Sunn Classic Productions, 1978
IN SEARCH OF HISTORIC JESUS Sunn Classic, 1979
BEYOND DEATH'S DOOR Sunn Classic, 1979
THE LEGEND OF SLEEPY HOLLOW Sunn Classic, 1979
THE ADVENTURES OF NELLIE BLY(TF) Sunn Classic, 1981
CAMP-FIRE GIRLS Rainbow Spectrum Film Co., 1984

FRED SCHEPISI*

b. December 26, 1939 - Melbourne, Australia
Contact: Directors Guild of America - Los Angeles, 213/656-1220

LIBIDO co-director with John B. Murray, Tim Burstall & David Baker, Producers & Directors Guild of Australia, 1973, Australian
THE DEVIL'S PLAYGROUND Entertainment Marketing, 1976, Australian
THE CHANT OF JIMMIE BLACKSMITH New Yorker, 1978, Australian
BARBAROSA Universal/AFD, 1982
ICEMAN Universal, 1984
PLENTY 20th Century Fox, 1985, British

LAWRENCE J. SCHILLER*

b. December 28, 1936, New York, New York
Home: P.O. Box 5784, Sherman Oaks, CA 91413, 818/906-0926
Agent: Jeff Berg, ICM - Los Angeles, 213/550-4000

THE LEXINGTON EXPERIENCE (FD) Corda, 1971
THE AMERICAN DREAMER (FD) co-director with L.M. Kit Carson, EYR, 1971
HEY, I'M ALIVE! (TF) Charles Fries Productions/Worldvision, 1975
MARILYN: THE UNTOLD STORY (TF) co-director with Jack Arnold & John Flynn, Lawrence Schiller Productions, 1980
THE EXECUTIONER'S SONG (TF) Film Communications Inc., 1982

TOM SCHILLER*

Agent: Mike Hamilburg, Mitchell J. Hamilburg Agency, 292 S. La Cienega Blvd., Los Angeles, CA 90211, 213/657-1501

NOTHING LASTS FOREVER MGM/UA Classics, 1984

GEORGE SCHLATTER*

b. December 31, 1931
Business: Schlatter Productions, 8321 Beverly Blvd., Los Angeles, CA 90048, 213/655-1400
Agent: Tony Fantozzi, William Morris Agency - Beverly Hills, 213/274-7451

NORMAN...IS THAT YOU? MGM/United Artists, 1976

JOHN SCHLESINGER *

b. February 16, 1926 - London, England
Home: 10 Victoria Road, London W8 5RD, England, 01/937-3983
Agent: Stan Kamen, William Morris Agency - Beverly Hills, 213/274-7451

A KIND OF LOVING Continental, 1962 British
BILLY LIAR Continental, 1963, British
DARLING ★ Embassy, 1965, British
FAR FROM THE MADDING CROWD MGM, 1967, British
MIDNIGHT COWBOY ★★ United Artists, 1969
SUNDAY BLOODY SUNDAY ★ United Artists, 1970, British
VISIONS OF EIGHT (FD) co-director with Yuri Ozerov, Mai Zetterling, Arthur Penn, Michael Pfleghar, Kon Ickikawa, Milos Forman & Claude Lelouch, Cinema 5, 1973
THE DAY OF THE LOCUST Paramount, 1975
MARATHON MAN Paramount, 1976
YANKS Universal, 1979, British
HONKY TONK FREEWAY Universal/AFD, 1981
AN ENGLISHMAN ABROAD (TF) BBC, 1983, British
THE FALCON AND THE SNOWMAN Orion, 1985

VOLKER SCHLONDORFF

b. 1939 - Wiesbaden, Germany
Contact: German Film & TV Academy, Pommernallee 1, 1000 Berlin 19, West Germany, 030/303-6212

YOUNG TORLESS Kanawha, 1966, West German-French
A DEGREE OF MURDER Universal, 1967, West German
MICHAEL KOHLHAAS Columbia, 1969, West German
THE SUDDEN WEALTH OF THE POOR PEOPLE OF KOMBACK New Yorker, 1970, West German
BAAL (TF) Hessischer Rundfunk/Bayerischer Rundfunk/Hallelujah Film, 1970, West German
DIE MORAL DER RUTH HALBFASS Hallelujah Film/Hessischer Rundfunk, 1971, West German
A FREE WOMAN *STROHFEUER* New Yorker, 1971, West German
UBERNACHTUNG IN TIROL (TF) Hessischer Rundfunk, 1974, West German
GEORGINAS GRUNDE (TF) West Deutscher Rundfunk/ORTF, 1975, West German-Austrian
THE LOST HONOR OF KATHARINA BLUM co-director with Margaretha Von Trotta, New World, 1975, West German
COUP DE GRACE Cinema 5, 1976, West German
NUR ZUM SPASS - NUR ZUM SPIEL (TD) Kaleidoskop Valeska Gert/Bioskop Film, 1977
DEUTSCHLAND IM HERBST (FD) co-director, Filmverlag der Autoren/Hallelujah Film/Kairos Film, 1978, West German
THE TIN DRUM New World, 1980, West German
CIRCLE OF DECEIT *DIE FALSCHUNG* United Artists Classics, 1982, West German-French
KRIEG UND FRIEDEN (FD) co-director with Heinrich Boll, Alexander Kluge, Stefan Aust, Axel Engstfeld, TeleCulture, 1983, West German
SWANN IN LOVE Orion Classics, 1984, French-West German

JULIAN SCHLOSSBERG

NO NUKES (FD) co-director with Danny Goldberg & Anthony Potenza, Warner Bros., 1980
GOING HOLLYWOOD - THE 30'S (FD) Castle Hill Productions, 1984

DAVID SCHMOELLER

Agent: Shapiro-Lichtman Agency - Los Angeles, 213/557-2244

TOURIST TRAP Compass International, 1979
THE SEDUCTION Avco Embassy, 1981

ROBERT A. SCHNITZER

NO PLACE TO HIDE American Films Ltd., 1975
THE PREMONITION Avco Embassy, 1976

PAUL SCHRADER*

b. July 22, 1946 - Grand Rapids, Michigan
Agent: Jeff Berg, ICM - Los Angeles, 213/550-4000

BLUE COLLAR Universal, 1978
HARDCORE Columbia, 1979
AMERICAN GIGOLO Paramount, 1980
CAT PEOPLE Universal, 1982
MISHIMA Warner Bros., 1985, Japanese-U.S.

BARBET SCHROEDER

b. August 26, 1941 - Teheran, Iran
Business: Les Films du Losange, 26 Avenue Pierre de Serbie, Paris 75116, France, 720-5412

MORE Cinema 5, 1969, Luxembourg
THE VALLEY *OBSCURED BY CLOUDS* Lagoon Associates, 1972, French
IDI AMIN DADA *GENERAL IDI AMIN DADA (FD)* Tinc, 1974, French
MAITRESSE Tinc, 1976, French
KOKO, A TALKING GORILLA (FD) New Yorker, 1978, French
LES TRICHEURS Films du Galatee, 1983, French-West German

CARL SCHULTZ

Contact: Australian Film Commission, 9229 W. Sunset Blvd., Los Angeles, CA 90069, 213/275-7074

THE TICHBORNE AFFAIR (TF) Australian Broadcasting Commission, 1977, Australian
BLUE FIN Roadshow Distributors, 1978, Australian
RIDE ON STRANGER (TF) Australian Broadcasting Commission, 1979, Australian
CAREFUL HE MIGHT HEAR YOU TLC Films/20th Century Fox, 1983, Australian

MICHAEL SCHULTZ*

b. Milwaukee, Wisconsin
Business: Crystalite Productions, Inc. P.O. Box 1940, Santa Monica, CA 90406, 213/459-8552
Agent: Lou Pitt, ICM - Los Angeles, 213/550-4000

TOGETHER FOR DAYS Olas, 1973
HONEYBABY, HONEYBABY Kelly-Jordan, 1974
COOLEY HIGH American International, 1975
CAR WASH Universal, 1976
GREASED LIGHTNING Warner Bros, 1977
WHICH WAY IS UP? Universal, 1978
SGT. PEPPER'S LONELY HEARTS CLUB BAND Universal, 1978
SCAVENGER HUNT 20th Century-Fox, 1979
CARBON COPY Avco Embassy, 1981
BENNY's PLACE (TF) Titus Productions, 1982
FOR US, THE LIVING (TF) Charles Fries Productions, 1983
THE JERK, TOO (TF) 40 Share Productions/Universal TV, 1984
THE LAST DRAGON Tri-Star, 1985

JOEL SCHUMACHER*

b. 1942 - New York, New York
Agent: Martin Bauer Agency - Beverly Hills, 213/275-2421

THE VIRGINIA HILL STORY (TF) RSO Films, 1974
AMATEUR NIGHT AT THE DIXIE BAR & GRILL (TF) Motown/Universal TV, 1979
THE INCREDIBLE SHRINKING WOMAN Universal, 1981
D.C. CAB Universal, 1983
ST. ELMO'S FIRE Columbia, 1985

ARNOLD SCHWARTZMAN

GENOCIDE (FD) Simon Wiesenthal Center, 1982

ETTORE SCOLA

b. May 10, 1931 - Trevico, Italy
Contact: Ministry of Tourism & Education, Via Della Ferratella, No. 51, 00184 Rome, Italy, 06/7732

LET'S TALK ABOUT WOMEN *SE PERMETTE, PARLIAMO DI DONNE* Embassy, 1964, Italian-French
LA CONGIUNTURA Fair Film/Les Films Concordia, 1965, Italian-French
THRILLING co-director, 1966, Italian
THE DEVIL IN LOVE *L'ARCIDIAVOLO* Warner Bros, 1966, Italian
RIUSCIRANNO I NOSTRI EROI A TROVARE L'AMICO MISTERIOSAMENTE SCOMPARSO IN AFRICA? Documento Film, 1968, Italian
IL COMMISSARIO PEPE Dean Film, 1969, Italian
THE PIZZA TRIANGLE *DRAMMA DELLA GELOSIA - TUTTI I PARTICOLARI INCRONICA* Warner Bros., 1970, Italian-Spanish
MY NAME IS ROCCO PAPALEO Rumson, 1971, Italian
LA PIU BELLA SERATA DELLA MIA VITA Dino De Laurentiis Cinematografica, 1972, Italian
TREVICO-TORINO...VIAGGIO NEL FIAT NAM 1973, Italian
WE ALL LOVED EACH OTHER SO MUCH Cinema 5, 1975, Italian
DOWN AND DIRTY *BRUTTI, SPORCHI E CATTIVI* New Line Cinema, 1976, Italian
SIGNORE E SIGNORI BUONANOTTE co-director with Luigi Comencini, Nanni Loy, Luigi Magni & Mario Monicelli, Titanus, 1976, Italian
A SPECIAL DAY Cinema 5, 1977, Italian
VIVA ITALIA! *I NUOVI MOSTRI* co-director with Mario Monicelli & Dino Risi, Cinema 5, 1978, Italian
CHE SI DICE A ROMA 1979, Italian
LA TERRAZZA United Artists, 1980, Italian-French
PASSIONE D'AMORE Putnam Square, 1982, Italian-French
LA NUIT DE VARENNES Triumph/Columbia, 1982, French-Italian
LE BAL Almi Classics, 1983, French-Italian-Algerian
MACARONI Filmauro, 1985, Italian

MARTIN SCORSESE*

b. November 17, 1942 - Flushing, New York
Personal Manager: Harry Ufland, Ufland-Roth Productions, 20th Century Fox, 10201 W. Pico Blvd., Executive Building Room 246, Los Angeles, CA 90035, 213/203-1295

WHO'S THAT KNOCKING AT MY DOOR? Joseph Brenner Associates, 1968
BOXCAR BERTHA American International, 1972
MEAN STREETS Warner Bros., 1973
ALICE DOESN'T LIVE HERE ANYMORE Warner Bros., 1974
ITALIANAMERICAN (FD) 1974
TAXI DRIVER Columbia, 1976
NEW YORK, NEW YORK United Artists, 1977
AMERICAN BOY (FD) 1978
THE LAST WALTZ United Artists, 1978
RAGING BULL ★ United Artists, 1978
THE KING OF COMEDY 20th Century-Fox, 1983
AFTER HOURS The Geffen Company/Warner Bros., 1985

GEORGE C. SCOTT*

b. October 18, 1927 - Wise, Virginia
Agent: Jane Deacy Agency - New York City, 212/752-4865
Business Manager: Becker & London - New York City, 212/541-7070

RAGE Warner Bros., 1972
THE SAVAGE IS LOOSE Campbell Devon, 1974

OZ SCOTT*

Agent: Dennis Brady/Paul Yamamoto, William Morris Agency - Beverly Hills, 213/274-7451

BUSTIN' LOOSE Universal, 1981
DREAMLAND co-director with Nancy Baker & Joel Schulman, First Run Features, 1983

RIDLEY SCOTT*

b. England
Agent: Michael Marcus, CAA - Los Angeles, 213/277-4545

THE DUELLISTS Paramount, 1978, British
ALIEN 20th Century-Fox, 1979, U.S.-British
BLADE RUNNER The Ladd Company/Warner Bros., 1982
LEGEND Universal, 1985, British-U.S.

TONY SCOTT

b. England
Agent: Leading Artists - Beverly Hills, 213/858-1999

THE HUNGER MGM/UA, 1983, British

ARTHUR ALLAN SEIDELMAN*

b. New York, New York
Agent: Joe Rosenberg, Writers & Artists Agency - Los Angeles, 213/820-2240
.Business: Entertainment Professionals, Inc. 1015 Gayley Avenue - Suite 1149, Los Angeles, CA 90024, 213/208-6183

CHILDREN OF RAGE LSF, 1975, U.S.-Israeli
ECHOES Entertainment Professionals, 1983

SUSAN SEIDELMAN

SMITHEREENS New Line Cinema, 1982
DESPERATELY SEEKING SUSAN Orion, 1985

ARNAUD SELIGNAC

DREAM ONE Columbia, 1984, British-French

JACK M. SELL

b. September 15, 1954 - Albany, Georgia
Business: Sell Pictures, Inc. 9701 Wilshire Blvd., Beverly Hills, CA 90212, 213/659-2332
Attorney: Charles Biggam, 180 N. La Salle, Chicago, ILL 60601, 312/236-9119

THE PSYCHOTRONIC MAN International Harmony, 1980
OUTTAKES Sell Pictures, 1984

CHARLES E. SELLIER, JR.

Agent: John Schallert - Los Angeles, 213/276-2044

SMOOTH MOVES Comworld, 1984
SILENT NIGHT, DEADLY NIGHT Tri-Star, 1984

OUSMENE SEMBENE

b. January 8, 1923 - Ziguinchor, Senegal

BLACK GIRL *LA NOIRE DE...* New Yorker, 1965, Senegalese
MANDABI Grove Press, 1968, Senegalese
TAUW 1970, Senegalese
EMITAI New Yorker, 1973, Senegalese
XALA New Yorker, 1974, Senegalese
CEDDO New Yorker, 1977, Senegalese

RALPH SENENSKY*

b. May 1, 1923 - Mason City, Iowa
Agent: Shapiro-Lichtman Agency - Los Angeles, 213/557-2244

A DREAM FOR CHRISTMAS (TF) Lorimar Productions, 1973
THE FAMILY KOVACK (TF) Playboy Productions, 1974
DEATH CRUISE (TF) Spelling-Goldberg Productions, 1974
THE FAMILY NOBODY WANTED (TF) Universal TV, 1975
THE NEW ADVENTURES OF HEIDI (TF) Pierre Cossette Enterprises, 1978
DYNASTY (TF) Aaron Spelling Productions/Fox-Cat Productions, 1981

NICHOLAS SGARRO*

Agent: Louis Bershad, Century Artists Ltd. - Beverly Hills, 213/272-4366

THE HAPPY HOOKER Cannon, 1975
THE MAN WITH THE POWER (TF) Universal TV, 1977

KRISHNA SHAH*

b. May 10, 1938 - India
Home: P.O. Box 64515, Los Angeles, CA 90064

RIVALS Avco Embassy, 1972
THE RIVER NIGER Cine Artists, 1976
SHALIMAR Judson Productions/Laxmi Productions, 1978, U.S.-Indian
CINEMA-CINEMA (FD) Shahab Ahmed Productions, 1980, Indian
HARD ROCK ZOMBIES Patel-Shah Film Company, 1984
A NIGHT AT THE DRIVE-IN 1984

LINA SHANKLIN

SUMMERSPELL Lina Shanklin Film, 1983

ANN ZANE SHANKS*

Home: 2237 N. New Hampshire, Los Angeles, CA 90027, 213/660-0121
Personal Manager: John Schulman, Weissman, Wolff, Bergman, Coleman, & Schulman - Beverly Hills, 213/858-7888
Business Manager: Al Rudick, Lazaron & Company - Beverly Hills, 213/273-8900

FRIENDSHIPS, SECRETS AND LIES (TF) co-director with Marlena Laird, Wittman-Riche Productions/Warner Bros. TV. 1979

ALAN SHAPIRO

Contact: Writers Guild of America - Los Angeles, 213/550-1000

TIGER TOWN (CTF) Thompson Street Pictures, 1983

KEN SHAPIRO*

b. 1943 - New Jersey
Home: 2044 Stanley Hills Drive, Los Angeles, CA 90046 213/654-7471

THE GROOVE TUBE Levitt-Pickman, 1974
MODERN PROBLEMS 20th Century-Fox, 1981

MELVIN SHAPIRO

SAMMY STOPS THE WORLD (FD) Elkins, 1979

JIM SHARMAN

Contact: M&L Casting Consultants, 49 Darlinghurst Road, Kings Cross, NSW, 2100, Australia, 02/358-3111

SHIRLEY THOMPSON VERSUS THE ALIENS Kolossal Piktures, 1972, Australian
SUMMER OF SECRETS Greater Union Film Distribution, 1976, Australian
THE ROCKY HORROR PICTURE SHOW 20th Century-Fox, 1976, British
THE NIGHT THE PROWLER International Harmony, 1978, Australian
SHOCK TREATMENT 20th Century-Fox, 1981, British

ALAN SHARP

Contact: Writers Guild of America - Los Angeles, 213/550-1000

LITTLE TREASURE Tri-Star, 1985

DON SHARP

b. April, 1922 - Hobart, Tasmania
Home: 80 Castelnau, Barnes, London SW13 9EX, England, 01/748-4333
Agent: Denis Selinger, ICM - London, 01/629-8080

THE GOLDEN AIRLINER British Lion/Children's Film Foundation, 1955, British
THE ADVENTURES OF HAL 5 Children's Film Foundation, 1958, British
THE IN-BETWEEN AGE *THE GOLDEN DISC* Allied Artists, 1958, British
THE PROFESSIONALS American International, 1960, British
LINDA British Lion, 1961, British
IT'S ALL HAPPENING *THE DREAM MAKER* Universal, 1963, British
KISS OF THE VAMPIRE Universal, 1963, British
THE DEVIL-SHIP PIRATES Columbia, 1964, British
WITCHCRAFT 20th Century-Fox, 1964, British
THE FACE OF FU MANCHU 7 Arts, 1965, British
CURSE OF THE FLY 20th Century-Fox, 1965, British
RASPUTIN - THE MAD MONK *I KILLED RASPUTIN* 20th Century-Fox, 1966, British-French-Italian
BANG, BANG, YOU'RE DEAD! *OUR MAN IN MARRAKESH* American International, 1966, British
THE BRIDES OF FU MANCHU 7 Arts, 1966, British
THOSE FANTASTIC FLYING FOOLS *BLAST OFF/JULES VERNE'S ROCKET TO THE MOON* American International, 1967, British
TASTE OF EXCITEMENT Crispin, 1968, British
THE VIOLENT ENEMY 1969, British
PUPPET ON A CHAIN co-director with Geoffrey Reeve, Cinerama Releasing Corporation, 1972, British
THE DEATH WHEELERS *PSYCHOMANIA* Scotia International, 1973, British
DARK PLACES Cinerama Releasing Corporation, 1974, British
HENNESSY American International, 1975, British
CALLAN Cinema National, 1975, British
THE FOUR FEATHERS (TF) Norman Rosemont Productions/Trident Films Ltd., 1978, U.S.-British
THE 39 STEPS International Picture Show Company, 1978, British
BEAR ISLAND Taft International, 1980, Canadian-British
WHAT WAITS BELOW Spartan Distribution, 1984
A WOMAN OF SUBSTANCE (MS) Artemis Portman Productions, 1984, British

IAN SHARP

b. November 13, 1946 - Clitheroe, Lancashire, England
Home: 22 Westbere Road, London NW2, England
Agent: Duncan Heath Associates - London, 01/937-9898
Contact: Directors Guild of Great Britain, 56 Whitfield Street, London W1, England, 01/580-9592

THE MUSIC MACHINE Norfolk International Pictures/Target International Pictures, 1979, British
THE FINAL OPTION *WHO DARES WINS* MGM/UA, 1983, British
ROBIN OF SHERWOOD (TF) HTV/Goldcrest Films & Television, 1983, British

MELVILLE SHAVELSON*

b. April 1, 1917 - Brooklyn, New York
Business Manager: Freedman, Kinzelberg & Broder, 1801 Avenue of the Stars - Suite 911, Los Angeles, CA 90067, 213/277-0700
Agent: Ron Mardigian, William Morris Agency - Beverly Hills, 213/274-7451

THE SEVEN LITTLE FOYS Paramount, 1955
BEAU JAMES Paramount, 1957
HOUSEBOAT Paramount, 1958
THE FIVE PENNIES Paramount, 1959
IT STARTED IN NAPLES Paramount, 1960
ON THE DOUBLE Paramount, 1961
THE PIDGEON THAT TOOK ROME Paramount, 1962
A NEW KIND OF LOVE Paramount, 1963
CAST A GIANT SHADOW United Artists, 1966
YOURS, MINE AND OURS United Artists, 1968
THE WAR BETWEEN MEN AND WOMEN National General, 1972
MIXED COMPANY United Artists, 1974
THE LEGEND OF VALENTINO (TF) Spelling-Goldberg Productions 1975
THE GREAT HOUDINIS (TF) ABC Circle Films, 1976
IKE (MS) co-director with Boris Sagal, ABC Circle Films, 1979
THE OTHER WOMAN (TF) CBS Entertainmant, 1983

JACK SHEA*

b. August 1, 1928 - New York, New York
Agent: Len Hanzer, Major Talent Agency - Los Angeles, 213/820-5841
Business Manager: Freedman, Kinzelberg & Broder, 1801 Avenue of the Stars - Suite 911, Los Angeles, CA 90067, 213/277-0700

DAYTON'S DEVILS Commonwealth United, 1968
THE MONITORS Commonwealth United, 1969

DONALD SHEBIB

b. 1938 - Toronto, Canada
Address: 312 Wright Avenue, Toronto, Ontario M6R 1L9, Canada, 416/536-8969

GOIN' DOWN THE ROAD Chevron, 1970, Canadian
RIP-OFF Alliance, 1971, Canadian
BETWEEN FRIENDS Eudon Productions, 1973, Canadian
SECOND WIND Health and Entertainment Corporation of America, 1976, Canadian
THE FIGHTING MEN (TF) CBC, 1977, Canadian
FISH HAWK Avco Embassy, 1981, Canadian
HEARTACHES MPM, 1982, Canadian
RUNNING BRAVE directed under pseudonym of D.S. Everett, Buena Vista, 1983, Canadian

RIKI SHELACH

Contact: Israel Film Centre, Ministry of Industry & Trade, 30 Agron Street, P.O. Box 299, Jerusalem 94190, Israel, 02/210433

THE LAST WINTER Triumph/Columbia, 1983, Israeli

JAMES SHELDON*
(James Schleifer)

b. November 12 - New York, New York
Home: 9428 Lloydcrest Drive, Beverly Hills, CA 90210, 213/275-2210
Agent: Ronald Leif, Contemporary-Korman Artists - Beverly Hills, 213/278-8250

GIDGET GROWS UP (TF) Screen Gems/Columbia TV, 1969
WITH THIS RING (TF) The Jozak Company/Paramount TV, 1978
THE GOSSIP COLUMNIST (TF) Universal TV, 1980

SIDNEY SHELDON*

b. February 11, 1917 - Chicago, Illinois
Agent: Mike Rosenfeld/Bill Haber/Rowland Perkins, CAA - Los Angeles, 213/277-4545
Business Manager: Gerald Breslauer, Breslauer, Jacobson & Rutman - Los Angeles, 213/879-0167

DREAM WIFE MGM, 1953
THE BUSTER KEATON STORY Paramount, 1957

JACK SHER*

b. March 16, 1913 - Minneapolis, Minnesota
Home: 9520 Dalegrove Drive, Beverly Hills, CA 90210, 213/273-2091
Agent: Chasman & Strick Associates, 6725 Sunset Blvd., Hollywood, CA 90028, 213/463-1115

FOUR GIRLS IN TOWN Universal, 1957
KATHY O' Universal, 1958
THE WILD AND THE INNOCENT Universal, 1959
THE THREE WORLDS OF GULLIVER Columbia, 1960, British
LOVE IN A GOLDFISH BOWL Paramount, 1961

EDWIN SHERIN*

b. January 15, 1930 - Danville, Pennsylvania
Business: Hartman Theatre, 307 Atlantic Street, Stamford, CT 06901, 203/324-6781
Agent: William Morris Agency - New York City, 212/586-5100

VALDEZ IS COMING United Artists, 1971
MY OLD MAN'S PLACE *GLORY BOY* Cinerama Releasing Corporation, 1972

GARY A. SHERMAN*

Home: 4501 Cedros, Apt. 328, Sherman Oaks, CA 91403, 818/907-5950
Agent: John Gaines, APA - Los Angeles, 213/273-0744
Business Manager: Jim Jorgensen & Company, 1801 Avenue of the Stars - Suite 235, Los Angeles, CA 90067, 213/556-1730

RAW MEAT *DEATH LINE* American International, 1973
DEAD AND BURIED Avco Embassy, 1981
VICE SQUAD Avco Embassy, 1982
MYSTERIOUS TWO (TF) Alan Landsburg Productions, 1982

GEORGE SHERMAN*

b. July 14, 1908 - New York, New York
Personal Manager: Cleo Ronson, Ronsher Productions, 4314 Marina City Drive, Marina del Rey, CA 90291, 213/821-0693

WILD HORSE RODEO Republic, 1938
THE PURPLE VIGILANTES Republic, 1938
OUTLAWS OF SONORA Republic, 1938
RIDERS OF THE BLACK HILLS Republic, 1938
PALS OF THE SADDLE Republic, 1938
OVERLAND STAGE RAIDERS Republic, 1938

GEORGE SHERMAN*—continued

RHYTHM OF THE SADDLE Republic, 1938
SANTA FE STAMPEDE Republic, 1938
RED RIVER RANGE Republic, 1938
MEXICALI ROSE Republic, 1939
THE NIGHT RIDERS Republic, 1939
THREE TEXAS STEERS Republic, 1939
WYOMING OUTLAW Republic, 1939
COLORADO SUNSET Republic, 1939
NEW FRONTIER Republic, 1939
COWBOYS FROM TEXAS Republic, 1939
THE KANSAS TERRORS Republic, 1939
ROVIN' TUMBLEWEEDS Republic, 1939
SOUTH OF THE BORDER Republic, 1939
GHOST VALLEY RAIDERS Republic, 1940
ONE MAN'S LAW Republic, 1940
THE TULSA KID Republic, 1940
TEXAS TERRORS Republic, 1940
COVERED WAGON DAYS Republic, 1940
ROCKY MOUNTAIN RANGERS Republic, 1940
UNDER TEXAS SKIES Republic, 1940
THE TRAIL BLAZERS Republic, 1940
LONE STAR RAIDERS Republic, 1940
FRONTIER VENGEANCE Republic, 1940
WYOMING WILDCAT Republic, 1941
THE PHANTOM COWBOY Republic, 1941
TWO GUN SHERIFF Republic, 1941
DESERT BANDIT Republic, 1941
KANSAS CYCLONE Republic, 1941
DEATH VALLEY OUTLAWS Republic, 1941
A MISSOURI OUTLAW Republic, 1941
CITADEL OF CRIME Republic, 1941
THE APACHE KID Republic, 1941
ARIZONA TERRORS Republic, 1942
STAGECOACH EXPRESS Republic, 1942
JESSE JAMES JR. Republic, 1942
THE CYCLONE KID Republic, 1942
THE SOMBRERO KID Republic, 1942
X MARKS THE SPOT Republic, 1942
LONDON BLACKOUT MURDERS Republic, 1942
THE PURPLE V Republic, 1943
THE MANTRAP Republic, 1943
THE WEST SIDE KID Republic, 1943
MYSTERY BROADCAST Republic, 1943
THE LADY AND THE MONSTER Republic, 1944
STORM OVER LISBON Republic, 1944
THE CRIME DOCTOR'S COURAGE Columbia, 1945
THE GENTLEMAN MISBEHAVES Columbia, 1946
RENEGADES Columbia, 1946
TALK ABOUT A LADY Columbia, 1946
THE BANDIT OF SHERWOOD FOREST co-director with Henry Levin, Columbia, 1946
PERSONALITY KID Columbia, 1947
SECRETS OF THE WHISTLER Columbia, 1947
LAST OF THE REDMEN Columbia, 1947
RELENTLESS Columbia, 1948
BLACK BART Universal, 1948
RIVER LADY Universal, 1948
LARCENY Universal, 1948
RED CANYON Universal, 1949
CALAMITY JANE AND SAM BASS Universal, 1949
YES SIR, THAT'S MY BABY Universal, 1949
SWORD IN THE DESERT Universal, 1949
SPY HUNT Universal, 1950
THE SLEEPING CITY Universal, 1950
FEUDIN', FUSSIN' AND A-FIGHTIN' Universal, 1950
COMANCHE TERRITORY Universal, 1950
TOMAHAWK Universal, 1951
TARGET UNKNOWN Universal, 1951
THE RAGING TIDE Universal, 1951
THE GOLDEN HORDE Universal, 1951
STEEL TOWN Universal, 1952
AGAINST ALL FLAGS Universal, 1952
THE BATTLE AT APACHE PASS Universal, 1952

GEORGE SHERMAN*—continued

BACK AT THE FRONT Universal, 1952
THE LONE HAND Universal, 1953
WAR ARROW Universal, 1953
VEILS OF BAGDAD Universal, 1953
BORDER RIVER Universal, 1954
DAWN AT SOCORRO Universal, 1954
CHIEF CRAZY HORSE Universal, 1955
COUNT THREE AND PRAY Universal, 1955
THE TREASURE OF PANCHO VILLA Universal, 1955
COMANCHE Universal, 1956
REPRISAL! Columbia, 1956
THE HARD MAN Columbia, 1957
THE LAST OF THE FAST GUNS Universal, 1958
TEN DAYS TO TULARA United Artists, 1958
THE SON OF ROBIN HOOD 20th Century-Fox, 1959
THE FLYING FONTAINES Columbia, 1959
HELL BENT FOR LEATHER Universal, 1960
FOR THE LOVE OF MIKE 20th Century-Fox, 1960
THE ENEMY GENERAL Columbia, 1960
THE WIZARD OF BAGHDAD 20th Century-Fox, 1960
THE FIERCEST HEART 20th Century-Fox, 1961
PANIC BUTTON Gorton, 1964
MURIETA Warner Bros., 1965, Spanish
SMOKY 20th Century-Fox, 1966
BIG JAKE National General, 1971

VINCENT SHERMAN*

b. July 16, 1906 - Vienna, Georgia
Home: 6355 Sycamore Meadows Drive, Malibu, CA 90265, 213/457-2229
Agent: Martin Baum, CAA - Los Angeles, 213/277-4545

THE RETURN OF DOCTOR X Warner Bros., 1939
SATURDAY'S CHILDREN Warner Bros., 1940
THE MAN WHO TALKED TOO MUCH Warner Bros., 1940
FLIGHT FROM DESTINY Warner Bros., 1941
UNDERGROUND Warner Bros., 1941
ALL THROUGH THE NIGHT Warner Bros., 1942
THE HARD WAY Warner Bros., 1942
OLD ACQUAINTANCE Warner Bros., 1943
IN OUR TIME Warner Bros., 1944
MR. SKEFFINGTON Warner Bros., 1945
PILLOW TO POST Warner Bros., 1945
NORA PRENTISS Warner Bros., 1947
THE UNFAITHFUL Warner Bros., 1947
THE ADVENTURES OF DON JUAN Warner Bros., 1949
THE HASTY HEART Warner Bros., 1949
BACKFIRE Warner Bros., 1950
THE DAMNED DON'T CRY Warner Bros., 1950
HARRIET CRAIG Columbia, 1950
GOODBYE, MY FANCY Warner Bros., 1951
LONE STAR MGM, 1952
AFFAIR IN TRINIDAD Columbia, 1952
DIFENDO IL MIO AMORE 1956, Italian
THE GARMENT JUNGLE Columbia, 1957
THE NAKED EARTH 20th Century-Fox, 1959
THE YOUNG PHILADELPHIANS Warner Bros., 1959
ICE PALACE Warner Bros., 1960
A FEVER IN THE BLOOD Warner Bros., 1961
THE SECOND TIME AROUND 20th Century-Fox, 1961
THE YOUNG REBEL *CERVANTES* American International, 1968, Italian-Spanish-French
THE LAST HURRAH (TF) O'Connor-Becker Productions/Columbia TV, 1977
LADY OF THE HOUSE (TF) co-director with Ralph Nelson, Metromedia Productions, 1978
WOMEN AT WEST POINT (TF) Green-Epstein Productions/Alan Sacks Productions, 1979
BOGIE: THE LAST HERO (TF) Charles Fries Productions, 1980
THE DREAM MERCHANTS (TF) Columbia TV, 1980
TROUBLE IN HIGH TIMBER COUNTRY (TF) Witt-Thomas Productions/Warner Bros. TV, 1980

PETER SHILLINGFORD

b. London, England
Home: Shillingford & Company, 1120 N. Clark Street, Los Angeles, CA 90069, 213/659-4736

TODAY MEXICO - TOMORROW THE WORLD Shillingford & Company/Rank, 1970, British
THE MAKING OF 'STAR WARS' (TD) co-director, Lucasfilm/20th Century-Fox TV, 1977
THE ENGLISH ABROAD Shillingford & Company, 1979, British

KANETO SHINDO

b. April 22, 1922 - Hiroshima Prefecture, Japan
Contact: Directors Guild of Japan, Tsukada Building, 8-33 Udagawa-cho, Shibuya-ku, Tokyo 150, Japan, 3/461-4411

STORY OF MY LOVING WIFE 1951, Japanese
AVALANCHE 1952, Japanese
CHILDREN OF THE ATOM BOMB 1952, Japanese
EPITOME 1953, Japanese
A LIFE OF A WOMAN 1953, Japanese
GUTTER 1954, Japanese
WOLVES 1955, Japanese
SILVER DOUBLE SUICIDE 1956, Japanese
BANK OF DEPARTURE 1956, Japanese
AN ACTRESS 1956, Japanese
GUYS OF THE SEA 1957, Japanese
SORROW IS ONLY FOR WOMEN 1957, Japanese
DAI GO FUKURYU-MARU 1959, Japanese
THE WORLD'S BEST BRIDE 1959, Japanese
GRAFFITI BLACKBOARD 1959, Japanese
THE ISLAND Zenith International, 1960, Japanese
HUMAN BEING 1962, Japanese
MOTHER 1962, Japanese
ONIBABA Toho, 1964, Japanese
A SCOUNDREL 1965, Japanese
INSTINCT 1966, Japanese
MONUMENT OF TOTSUSEKI 1966, Japanese
FOUR SEASONS OF TATESHINA 1966, Japanese
ORIGIN OF SEX 1967, Japanese
A BLACK CAT IN THE BUSH 1968, Japanese
STRONG WOMAN AND WEAK MAN 1968, Japanese
HEAT HAZE 1969, Japanese
TENTACLES 1970, Japanese
NAKED 19-YEAR-OLD 1970, Japanese
IRON RING 1972, Japanese
A PAEAN 1972, Japanese
HEART 1973, Japanese
MY WAY 1974, Japanese
LIFE OF A FILM DIRECTOR: RECORD OF KENJI MIZOGUCHI (FD) 1975, Japanese
LIFE OF CHIKUZAN 1977, Japanese
HOKUSAI, UKIYOE MASTER 1982, Japanese
THE HORIZON Toho, 1984, Japanese

MASAHIRO SHINODA

b. March 9, 1931 - Gifu Prefecture, Japan
Address: 1-11-16 Kita-Senzoku, Ota-ku, Tokyo, Japan

ONE WAY TICKET TO LOVE 1960, Japanese
DRY LAKE 1960, Japanese
MY FACE RED IN THE SUNSET 1961, Japanese
EPITAPH TO MY LOVE 1961, Japanese
SHAMISEN AND MOTORCYCLE 1961, Japanese
OUR MARRIAGE 1962, Japanese
GLORY ON THE SUMMIT: BURNING YOUTH 1962, Japanese
TEARS ON THE LION'S MANE 1962, Japanese
PALE FLOWER 1963, Japanese
ASSASSINATION Toho, 1964, Japanese
WITH BEAUTY AND SORROW 1965, Japanese

MASAHIRO SHINODA —continued

SAMURAI SPY 1965, Japanese
PUNISHMENT ISLAND 1966, Japanese
CLOUDS AT SUNSET 1967, Japanese
DOUBLE SUICIDE Toho, 1969, Japanese
THE SCANDALOUS ADVENTURES OF BURAIKAN Toho, 1970, Japanese
SILENCE 1971, Japanese
SAPPORO WINTER OLYMPIC GAMES (FD) 1972, Japanese
THE PETRIFIED FOREST 1973, Japanese
HIMIKO 1974, Japanese
UNDER THE CHERRY BLOSSOMS 1975, Japanese
NIHON-MARU SHIP (FD) 1976, Japanese
SADO'S ONDEKO-ZA (FD) 1976, Japanese
THE BALLAD OF ORIN 1977, Japanese
DEMON POND 1979, Japanese
DEVIL'S ISLAND 1980, Japanese
MacARTHUR'S CHILDREN Herald Classics, 1984, Japanese

JACK SHOLDER

ALONE IN THE DARK New Line Cinema, 1982

SIG SHORE

Contact: Writers Guild of America, East - New York City, 212/245-6180

THAT'S THE WAY OF THE WORLD *SHINING STAR* United Artists, 1975
THE ACT Artists Releasing Corporation/Film Ventures International, 1984

CHARLES SHYER*

Agent: Jeff Berg, ICM - Los Angeles, 213/550-4000

IRRECONCILABLE DIFFERENCES Warner Bros., 1984

ANDY SIDARIS*

b. February 20, 1932 - Chicago, Illinois
Home: 1891 Carla Ridge, Beverly Hills, CA 90210, 213/275-6282

THE RACING SCENE (FD) Filmways, 1970
SEVEN American International, 1979
MALIBU EXPRESS The Sidaris Company, 1984

GEORGE SIDNEY*

b. October 4, 1916 - Long Island City, New York
Home: 910 N. Rexford Drive, Beverly Hills, CA 90210

FREE AND EASY MGM, 1941
PACIFIC RENDEZVOUS MGM, 1942
PILOT NO. 5 MGM, 1943
THOUSANDS CHEER MGM, 1943
BATHING BEAUTY MGM, 1944
ANCHORS AWEIGH MGM, 1945
THE HARVEY GIRLS MGM, 1946
HOLIDAY IN MEXICO MGM, 1946
CASS TIMBERLANE MGM, 1947
THE THREE MUSKETEERS MGM, 1948
THE RED DANUBE MGM, 1949
KEY TO THE CITY MGM, 1950
ANNIE GET YOUR GUN MGM, 1950
SHOW BOAT MGM, 1951
SCARAMOUCHE MGM, 1952
YOUNG BESS MGM, 1953
KISS ME KATE MGM, 1953
JUPITER'S DARLING MGM, 1955
THE EDDY DUCHIN STORY Columbia, 1956
JEANNE EAGELS Columbia, 1957

GEORGE SIDNEY*—continued

PAL JOEY Columbia, 1957
WHO WAS THAT LADY? Columbia, 1960
PEPE Columbia, 1960
BYE BYE BIRDIE Columbia, 1963
A TICKLISH AFFAIR MGM, 1963
VIVA LAS VEGAS MGM, 1964
THE SWINGER Paramount, 1966
HALF A SIXPENCE Paramount, 1968, British

DON SIEGEL*

b. October 26, 1912 - Chicago, Illinois
Agent: Len Hirshan - William Morris Agency - Beverly Hills, 213/274-7451
Business Manager: Manny Flekman, Flekman, Carlswell & Company, 9171 Wilshire Blvd. - Suite 530, Beverly Hills, CA 90210, 213/274-5847

THE VERDICT Warner Bros., 1946
NIGHT UNTO NIGHT Warner Bros., 1949
THE BIG STEAL RKO Radio, 1949
DUEL AT SILVER CREEK Universal, 1952
NO TIME FOR FLOWERS RKO Radio, 1952
COUNT THE HOURS RKO Radio, 1953
CHINA VENTURE Columbia, 1953
RIOT IN CELL BLOCK 11 Allied Artists, 1954
PRIVATE HELL 36 Filmmakers, 1954
AN ANNAPOLIS STORY Allied Artists, 1955
INVASION OF THE BODY SNATCHERS Allied Artists, 1956
CRIME IN THE STREETS Allied Artists, 1956
BABY FACE NELSON Allied Artists, 1957
SPANISH AFFAIR Paramount, 1958, Spanish
THE LINEUP Columbia, 1958
THE GUN RUNNERS United Artists, 1958
HOUND DOG MAN 20th Century-Fox, 1959
EDGE OF ETERNITY Columbia, 1959
FLAMING STAR 20th Century-Fox, 1960
HELL IS FOR HEROES Paramount, 1962
THE KILLERS Universal, 1964
THE HANGED MAN (TF) Universal TV, 1964
STRANGER ON THE RUN (TF) Universal TV, 1967
MADIGAN Universal, 1968
COOGAN'S BLUFF Universal, 1968
DEATH OF A GUNFIGHTER co-director with Robert Totten, both directed under pseudonym of Allen Smithee, Universal, 1969
TWO MULES FOR SISTER SARA Universal, 1970, U.S.-Mexican
THE BEGUILED Universal, 1971
DIRTY HARRY Warner Bros., 1972
CHARLEY VARRICK Universal, 1973
THE BLACK WINDMILL Universal, 1974, British
THE SHOOTIST Paramount, 1976
TELEFON MGM/United Artists, 1977
ESCAPE FROM ALCATRAZ Paramount, 1979
ROUGH CUT Paramount, 1980
JINXED MGM/UA, 1982

ROBERT J. SIEGEL*

Contact: Directors Guild of America - New York City, 212/581-0370

PARADES Cinerama Releasing Corporation, 1972

JAMES SIGNORELLI*

Contact: Directors Guild of America - New York City, 212/581-0370

EASY MONEY Orion, 1983

JOEL SILBERG

(Yoel Zilberg)

Business: Cannon Group, 6464 Sunset Blvd., Los Angeles, CA 90038, 213/469-8124

THE RABBI AND THE SHIKSE Roll Films, 1976, Israeli
MILLIONAIRE IN TROUBLE Shapira Films, 1978, Israeli
MARRIAGE, TEL AVIV STYLE Noah Films, 1979, Israeli
MY MOTHER THE GENERAL Noah Films, 1981, Israeli
BREAKDANCIN' MGM/UA/Cannon, 1984

JOAN MICKLIN SILVER*

b. May 24, 1935 - Omaha, Nebraska
Business: Midwest Film Productions, 600 Madison Avenue, New York, NY 10022, 212/355-0282
Agent: Arlene Donovan, ICM - New York City, 212/556-5600

HESTER STREET Midwest Film Productions, 1975
BETWEEN THE LINES Midwest Film Productions, 1977
HEAD OVER HEELS United Artists, 1979, re-released in newly edited version by United Artists Classics in 1982 under title CHILLY SCENES OF WINTER
HOW TO BE A PERFECT PERSON (TF) Highgate Pictures, 1984
FINNEGAN, BEGIN AGAIN (CTF) HBO Premiere Films/Zenith Productions/ Jennie & Co. Film Productions, 1985, U.S. - British

MARISA SILVER

OLD ENOUGH Orion Classics, 1984

RAPHAEL D. SILVER*

Business: Midwest Film Productions, 600 Madison Avenue, New York, NY 10022, 212/355-0282

ON THE YARD Midwest Film Productions, 1979

ELLIOT SILVERSTEIN*

b. 1927 - Boston, Massachusetts
Agent: Harold Cohen, Associated Management - Los Angeles, 213/275-9057

BELLE SOMMARS Columbia, 1962
CAT BALLOU Columbia, 1965
THE HAPPENING Columbia, 1967
A MAN CALLED HORSE National General, 1970
DEADLY HONEYMOON *NIGHTMARE HONEYMOON* MGM, 1974
THE CAR Universal, 1977

FRANCIS SIMON

THE CHICKEN CHRONICLES Avco Embassy, 1977

ANTHONY SIMMONS

Business: West One Film Producers Ltd., 2 Lower James Street, London W1R 3PN, England, 01/437-7015
Agent: Hatton & Baker, 18 Jermyn Street, London WI, England, 01/439-2971

YOUR MONEY OR YOUR WIFE Rank, 1960, British
FOUR IN THE MORNING West One, 1965, British
THE OPTIMISTS *THE OPTIMISTS OF NINE ELMS* Paramount, 1973, British
BLACK JOY Hemdale, 1977, British

FRANK SINATRA*

b. December 12, 1915 - Hoboken, New Jersey
Contact: Directors Guild of America - Los Angeles, 213/656-1220

NONE BUT THE BRAVE Warner Bros., 1964, U.S.-Japanese

ANDREW SINCLAIR

Contact: British Academy of Film & Television Arts, 195 Piccadilly, London W1, England, 01/732-0022

THE BREAKING OF BUMBO Timon/ABPC, 1971, British
UNDER MILK WOOD Altura, 1973, British
BLUE BLOOD Mallard Productions, 1975, British

GERALD SETH SINDELL

b. April 15, 1944 - Cleveland, Ohio
Home: 9566 Yoakum Drive, Beverly Hills, CA 90210, 213/275-3353
Attorney: Steve Burkow, Pollock, Bloom & Dekom, 9255 Sunset Blvd., Los Angeles, CA 90069, 213/278-8622

DOUBLE-STOP World Entertainment, 1967
HARPY (TF) Cinema Center 100, 1970
TEENAGER National Cinema, 1974
H.O.T.S. Derio Productions, 1979

ALEXANDER SINGER*

b. 1932 - New York, New York
Agent: ICM - Los Angeles, 213/550-4000

A COLD WIND IN AUGUST Lopert, 1961
PSYCHE 59 Royal Films International, 1964, British
LOVE HAS MANY FACES Columbia, 1965
CAPTAIN APACHE Scotia International, 1971, British
GLASS HOUSES Columbia, 1972
THE FIRST 36 HOURS OF DR. DURANT (TF) Columbia TV, 1975
TIME TRAVELERS (TF) Irwin Allen Productions/20th Century-Fox TV, 1976
THE MILLION DOLLAR RIP-OFF (TF) Charles Fries Productions, 1976
HUNTERS OF THE REEF (TF) Writers Company Productions/Paramount TV, 1978
THE RETURN OF MARCUS WELBY, M.D. (TF) Marstar Productions/ Universal TV, 1984

HAL SITOWITZ*

Agent: Triad Artists, Inc. - Los Angeles, 213/556-2727

A LAST CRY FOR HELP (TF) Myrt-Hal Productions/Viacom, 1979

VILGOT SJOMAN

(David Harald Vilgot Sjoman)

b. December 2, 1924 - Stockholm, Sweden
Contact: Swedish Film Institute, P.O. Box 27126, 102 52 Stockholm, Sweden, 08/63-0510

THE SWEDISH MISTRESS 1962, Swedish
491 Peppercorn-Wormser, 1964, Swedish
THE DRESS 1964, Swedish
STIMULANTIA co-director, 1965, Swedish
MY SISTER, MY LOVE *SYSKONBADD 1782* Sigma III, 1966, Swedish
I AM CURIOUS (YELLOW) Grove Press, 1967, Swedish
I AM CURIOUS (BLUE) Grove Press, 1968, Swedish
YOU'RE LYING Grove Press, 1969, Swedish
BLUSHING CHARLIE 1970, Swedish
TILL SEX DO US PART *TROLL* Astro, 1971, Swedish
THE KARLSSON BROTHERS 1972, Swedish

VILGOT SJOMAN —continued

A HANDFUL OF LOVE 1974, Swedish
THE GARAGE 1975, Swedish
TABU Svensk Filminstitut, 1977, Swedish
LINUS AND THE MYSTERIOUS RED BRICK HOUSE Svensk Filmindustri, 1979, Swedish
I AM BLUSHING 1982, Swedish

JERZY SKOLIMOWSKI

b. May 5, 1938 - Warsaw, Poland
Agent: Robert Littman, Leading Artists - Beverly Hills, 213/858-1999

IDENTIFICATION MARKS: NONE New Yorker, 1964, Polish
WALKOVER New Yorker, 1965, Polish
BARRIER Film Polski, 1966, Polish
LE DEPART Pathe Contemporary, 1967, Belgian
HANDS UP! 1967, Polish
DIALOGUE co-director, 1968, Czech
THE ADVENTURES OF GIRARD United Artists, 1969, British-Swiss
DEEP END Paramount, 1971, British-West German
KING, QUEEN, KNAVE Avco Embassy, 1972, West German-British
THE SHOUT Films Inc., 1979, British
MOONLIGHTING Universal Classics, 1982, British
SUCCESS IS THE BEST REVENGE Triumph/Columbia, 1984, British
THE LIGHTSHIP Warner Bros., 1985, U.S.-West German

LANE SLATE*

Contact: Directors Guild of America - Los Angeles, 213/656-1220

CLAY PIGEON co-director with Tom Stern, MGM, 1971
DEADLY GAME (TF) MGM TV, 1977

JACK SMIGHT*

b. March 9, 1926 - Minneapolis, Minnesota
Agent: Leading Artists - Beverly Hills, 213/858-1999

I'D RATHER BE RICH Universal, 1964
THE THIRD DAY Warner Bros., 1965
HARPER Warner Bros., 1966
KALEIDOSCOPE Warner Bros., 1966, British
THE SECRET WAR OF HARRY FRIGG Universal, 1968
NO WAY TO TREAT A LADY Paramount, 1968
STRATEGY OF TERROR Universal, 1969
THE ILLUSTRATED MAN Warner Bros., 1969
RABBIT, RUN Warner Bros., 1970
THE TRAVELING EXECUTIONER MGM, 1970
THE SCREAMING WOMAN (TF) Universal TV, 1972
BANACEK: DETOUR TO NOWHERE (TF) Universal TV, 1972
THE LONGEST NIGHT (TF) Universal TV, 1972
PARTNERS IN CRIME (TF) Universal TV, 1973
DOUBLE INDEMNITY (TF) Universal TV, 1973
LINDA (TF) Universal TV, 1973
FRANKENSTEIN: THE TRUE STORY (TF) Universal TV, 1973
AIRPORT 1975 Universal, 1974
MIDWAY Universal, 1976
DAMNATION ALLEY 20th Century-Fox, 1977
ROLL OF THUNDER, HEAR MY CRY (TF) Tomorrow Entertainment, 1978
FAST BREAK Columbia, 1979
LOVING COUPLES 20th Century-Fox, 1980
REMEMBRANCE OF LOVE (TF) Doris Quinlan Productions/Comworld Productions, 1982

CLIVE A. SMITH

Contact: Canadian Film & Television Association, 8 King Street, Toronto, Ontario M5C 1B5, Canada, 416/363-0296

ROCK & RULE (AF) MGM/UA, 1983, Canadian
RING OF POWER 1984, Canadian

HOWARD SMITH

Business: The Village Voice, 842 Broadway, New York, NY 10003, 212/475-3300

MARJOE (FD) co-director with Sarah Kernochan, Cinema 5, 1972
GIZMO! (FD) New Line Cinema, 1977

KENT SMITH

TAKING TIGER MOUNTAIN co-director with Tom Huckabee, Horizon, 1983

MARK S. SOBEL*

b. June 10, 1956 - Toronto, Ontario, Canada
Business: Cinecan Film Productions, P.O. Box 8601, Universal City, CA 91608, 818/763-5428

ACCESS CODE Intercontinental Releasing, 1984

ALFRED SOLE*

Home: 1641 N. Kings Road, Los Angeles, CA 90069, 213/656-9347
Agent: David Gersh, The Gersh Agency - Beverly Hills, 213/274-6611

ALICE, SWEET ALICE *COMMUNION/HOLY TERROR* Allied Artists, 1977
TANYA'S ISLAND IFEX Film/Fred Baker Films, 1981, Canadian
PANDEMONIUM MGM/UA, 1982

ANDREW SOLT*

b. December 13, 1947 - London, England
Home: 1252 Shadybrook Drive, Beverly Hills, CA 90210
Business: Andrew Solt Productions, 9113 Sunset Blvd., Los Angeles, CA 90064, 213/276-9522
Agent: William Morris Agency - Beverly Hills, 213/274-7451

HEROES OF ROCK AND ROLL (TD) co-director with Malcolm Leo, ABC, 1979
THIS IS ELVIS (FD) co-director with Malcolm Leo, Warner Bros., 1981
IT CAME FROM HOLLYWOOD (FD) co-director with Malcolm Leo, Paramount, 1982

SUSAN SONTAG

DUET FOR CANNIBALS Grove Press, 1969, Swedish
BROTHER CARL New Yorker, 1972, Swedish
PROMISED LANDS (FD) New Yorker, 1974, French

JIM SOTOS*

(Dimitri Sotirakis)

b. September 17, 1935 - New York, New York
Contact: Directors Guild of America - Los Angeles, 213/656-1220

THE LAST VICTIM Howard Mahler Films, 1975
FORCED ENTRY Century International, 1980
SWEET SIXTEEN Century International, 1982
HOT MOVES Cardinal Releasing, 1984

LARRY G. SPANGLER

THE SOUL OF NIGGER CHARLEY Paramount, 1973
A KNIFE FOR THE LADIES Bryanston, 1974
THE LIFE AND TIMES OF XAVIERA HOLLANDER Mature, 1974
JOSHUA Lone Star, 1976
SILENT SENTENCE Intercontinental, 1983

TERESA SPARKS

b. June 27, 1952 - Kentucky
Business: Shine Productions, 8871 Cynthia Street, Los Angeles, CA 90069, 213/659-7539

OVER THE SUMMER Shine Productions, 1984

PENELOPE SPHEERIS

THE DECLINE OF WESTERN CIVILIZATION (FD) Spheeris Films Inc., 1981
SUBURBIA *THE WILD SIDE* New World, 1984
NO APPARENT MOTIVE New World, 1985

STEVEN SPIELBERG*

b. December 18, 1947 - Cincinnati, Ohio
Agent: ICM - Los Angeles, 213/550-4000

NIGHT GALLERY (TF) co-director with Boris Sagal & Barry Shear, Universal TV, 1969
DUEL (TF) Universal TV, 1971
SOMETHING EVIL (TF) Belford Productions/CBS International, 1972
SAVAGE (TF) Universal TV, 1973
THE SUGARLAND EXPRESS Universal, 1974
JAWS Universal, 1975
CLOSE ENCOUNTERS OF THE THIRD KIND ★ Columbia, 1977
1941 Universal/Columbia, 1979
RAIDERS OF THE LOST ARK ★ Paramount, 1981
E.T. THE EXTRA-TERRESTRIAL ★ Universal, 1982
TWILIGHT ZONE - THE MOVIE co-director with John Landis, Joe Dante & George Miller, Warner Bros., 1983
INDIANA JONES AND THE TEMPLE OF DOOM Paramount, 1984

ROGER SPOTTISWOODE*

Home: 2451 Holly Drive, Los Angeles, CA 90068, 213/469-6679
Agent: Fred Specktor, CAA - Los Angeles, 213/277-4545
Business Manager: Jay Trulman, Jay Trulman Accountancy Corporation, 1930 Century Park West - Suite 3000, Los Angeles, CA 90067, 213/553-7300

TERROR TRAIN 20th Century-Fox, 1980, Canadian
THE PURSUIT OF D.B. COOPER Universal, 1982
THE RENEGADES (TF) Lawrence Gordon Productions/Paramount TV, 1982
UNDER FIRE Orion, 1983

G.D. SPRADLIN

Agent: The Mishkin Agency - Los Angeles, 213/274-5261

THE ONLY WAY HOME Regional, 1972

ROBIN SPRY

b. 1939 - Toronto, Canada
Home: 5330 Durocher, Montreal, Quebec H2V 3Y1, Canada, 514/277-1503

PROLOGUE Vaudeo, 1969, Canadian
ACTION: THE OCTOBER CRISIS (FD) 1974, Canadian
ONE MAN National Film Board of Canada, 1977, Canadian
DRYING UP THE STREETS CBC, 1978, Canadian

ROBIN SPRY —continued

DON'T FORGET - JE ME SOUVIENS (TF) CBC, 1979, Canadian
HIT AND RUN Agora Productions, 1981, Canadian
SUZANNE 20th Century-Fox, 1982, Canadian
STRESS AND EMOTIONS 1984, Canadian

RAYMOND ST. JACQUES

(James Arthur Johnson)

b. 1930 - Hartford, Connecticut
Agent: Contemporary-Korman Artists - Beverly Hills, 213/278-8250

BOOK OF NUMBERS Avco Embassy, 1973

CHRISTOPHER ST. JOHN

TOP OF THE HEAP Fanfare, 1972

SYLVESTER STALLONE*

b. July 6, 1946 - New York, New York
Agent: Ron Meyer, CAA - Los Angeles, 213/277-4545
Personal Manager: Herb Nanas Organization - Beverly Hills, 213/858-7049

PARADISE ALLEY Universal, 1978
ROCKY II United Artists, 1979
ROCKY III MGM/UA, 1982
STAYING ALIVE Paramount, 1983

PAUL STANLEY*

Agent: David Shapira & Associates - Beverly Hills, 213/278-2742

CRY TOUGH United Artists, 1959
THREE GUNS FOR TEXAS co-director with David Lowell Rich & Earl Bellamy, Universal, 1968
SOLE SURVIVOR (TF) Cinema Center, 1969
RIVER OF MYSTERY (TF) Universal TV, 1971
NICKY'S WORLD (TF) Tomorrow Entertainment, 1974
CRISIS IN SUN VALLEY (TF) Columbia TV, 1978
THE ULTIMATE IMPOSTER (TF) Universal TV, 1979

RINGO STARR

(Richard Starkey)

b. July 7, 1940 - Liverpool, England
Business: Wobble Music Ltd., 17 Berkeley Street, London W1, England

BORN TO BOOGIE (FD) MGM-EMI, 1972, British

JACK STARRETT

b. November 2, 1936 - Refugio, Texas
Agent: Stone-Masser Talent Agents - Los Angeles, 213/275-9599

RUN, ANGEL, RUN! Fanfare, 1969
THE LOSERS Fanfare, 1970
CRY BLOOD, APACHE Golden Eagle International, 1970
NIGHT CHASE (TF) Cinema Center, 1970
THE STRANGE VENGEANCE OF ROSALIE 20th Century-Fox, 1972
SLAUGHTER American International, 1972
CLEOPATRA JONES Warner Bros., 1973
GRAVY TRAIN *THE DION BROTHERS* Columbia, 1974
RACE WITH THE DEVIL 20th Century-Fox, 1975
A SMALL TOWN IN TEXAS American International, 1976
FINAL CHAPTER - WALKING TALL American International, 1977
ROGER & HARRY: THE MITERA TARGET (TF) Bruce Lansbury Productions/ Columbia TV, 1977

JACK STARRETT —continued

NOWHERE TO HIDE (TF) Mark Carliner Productions/Viacom, 1977
THADDEUS ROSE AND EDDIE (TF) CBS, Inc., 1978
BIG BOB JOHNSON AND HIS FANTASTIC SPEED CIRCUS (TF) Playboy Productions/Paramount TV, 1978
MR. HORN (TF) Lorimar Productions, 1979
SURVIVAL OF DANA (TF) EMI TV, 1979
KISS MY GRITS *A TEXAS LEGEND/SUMMER HEAT* Ambassador, 1982

RAY DENNIS STECKLER

WILD GUITAR Fairway International, 1962
THE INCREDIBLY STRANGE CREATURES WHO STOPPED LIVING AND BECAME MIXED-UP ZOMBIES Fairway International, 1962
THE THRILL KILLERS 1964
RAT PFINK A-BOO-BOO 1964
SCREAM OF THE BUTTERFLY 1965
SINTHIA, THE DEVIL'S DOLL
LEMON GROVE KIDS MEET THE MONSTERS
THE HOLLYWOOD STRANGLER MEETS THE SKID ROW SLASHER 1984

JEFF STEIN

THE KIDS ARE ALRIGHT (FD) New World, 1979, British

DAVID STEINBERG*

Agent: Stan Kamen, William Morris Agency - Beverly Hills, 213/274-7451
Business Manager: Neal Levin, Neal Levin Company - Beverly Hills, 213/858-8300

PATERNITY Paramount, 1981
GOING BERSERK Universal, 1983, Canadian

DANIEL STEINMANN

SAVAGE STREETS MPM, 1984

LEONARD B. STERN*

b. December 23, 1923 - New York, New York
Agent: William Morris Agency - Beverly Hills, 213/274-7451
Business Manager: Gerwin, Jamner & Pariser - Los Angeles, 213/652-0222

ONCE UPON A DEAD MAN (TF) Universal TV, 1971
THE SNOOP SISTERS (TF) Universal TV, 1972
JUST YOU AND ME, KID Columbia, 1979

SANDOR STERN*

b. July 13, 1936 - Timmins, Ontario, Canada
Home: 474 Peck Drive, Beverly Hills, CA 90212
Messages: 213/275-0180
Agent: Elliot Webb, Artists Entertainment Agency - Beverly Hills, 213/557-2507

THE SEEDING OF SARAH BURNS (TF) Michael Klein Productions, 1979
MUGGABLE MARY: STREET COP (TF) CBS Entertainment, 1982
MEMORIES NEVER DIE (TF) Groverton Productions/Scholastic Productions/ Universal TV, 1982
PASSIONS (TF) Carson Productions Group Ltd./Wizan TV Enterprises, 1984

STEVEN HILLARD STERN*

b. November 1, 1937 - Ontario, Canada
Home: 4321 Clear Valley Drive, Encino, CA 91436, 818/788-3607
Agent: John Gaines, APA - Los Angeles, 213/273-0744

B.S. I LOVE YOU 20th Century-Fox, 1971
NEITHER BY DAY NOR BY NIGHT Motion Pictures International, 1972, U.S.-Israeli
THE HARRAD SUMMER Cinerama Releasing Corporation, 1974
ESCAPE FROM BOGEN COUNTY (TF) Paramount TV, 1977
THE GHOST OF FLIGHT 401 (TF) Paramount TV, 1978
DOCTORS' PRIVATE LIVES (TF) David Gerber Company/Columbia TV, 1978
GETTING MARRIED (TF) Paramount TV, 1978
FAST FRIENDS (TF) Columbia TV, 1979
ANATOMY OF A SEDUCTION (TF) Moonlight Productions/Filmways, 1979
YOUNG LOVE, FIRST LOVE (TF) Lorimar Productions, 1979
RUNNING Columbia, 1979, Canadian-U.S.
PORTRAIT OF AN ESCORT (TF) Moonlight Productions/Filmways, 1980
THE DEVIL AND MAX DEVLIN Buena Vista, 1981
MIRACLE ON ICE (TF) Moonlight Productions/Filmways, 1981
A SMALL KILLING (TF) Orgolini-Nelson Productions/Motown Productions, 1982
THE AMBUSH MURDERS (TF) David Goldsmith Productions/Charles Fries Productions, 1982
PORTRAIT OF A SHOWGIRL (TF) Hamner Productions, 1982
NOT JUST ANOTHER AFFAIR (TF) Ten-Four Productions, 1982
FORBIDDEN LOVE (TF) Gross-Weston Productions, 1982
RONA JAFFE'S MAZES AND MONSTERS McDermott Productions/Procter & Gamble Productions, 1982
BABY SISTER (TF) Moonlight Productions II, 1983
STILL THE BEAVER (TF) Bud Austin Productions/Universal TV, 1983
AN UNCOMMON LOVE (TF) Beechwood Productions/Lorimar Productions, 1983
GETTING PHYSICAL (TF) CBS Entertainment, 1984
DRAW! (CTF) HBO Premiere Films/Astral Film Productions/Bryna Company, 1984, U.S.-Canadian
OBSESSIVE LOVE (TF) Onza Inc./Moonlight Productions, 1984
THE PARK IS MINE (CTF) HBO Premiere Films/Astral Film Productions/ICC, 1985, U.S.-Canadian

ART STEVENS

Business: Walt Disney Productions, 500 S. Buena Vista Street, Burbank, CA 91521, 213/845-3141

THE FOX AND THE HOUND (AF) co-director with Ted Berman & Richard Rich, Buena Vista, 1981
THE BLACK CAULDRON (AF) co-director with Ted Berman & Richard Rich, Buena Vista, 1986

DAVID STEVENS

Contact: Australian Film Commission, 9229 Sunset Blvd., Los Angeles, CA 90069, 213/275-7074

NUMBER 96 (MS) 1974, Australian
THE JOHN SULLIVAN STORY (TF) Crawford Productions/Nine Network/ Australian Film Commission, 1979, Australian
THE SULLIVANS (MS) co-director with Simon Wincer, 1980, Australian
A TOWN LIKE ALICE (MS) Seven Network/Victorian Film Corporation, 1981, Australian
THE CLINIC Film House/Generation Films, 1982, Australian
UNDERCOVER Filmco, 1983, Australian
WOMEN OF THE SUN (MS) co-director with Stephen Wallace, James Ricketson & Geoffrey Nottage, Generation Films, 1983, Australian

GEORGE STEVENS, JR.*

Business: New Liberty Productions, American Film Institute, John F. Kennedy Center, Washington, D.C. 20566, 202/828-4020

AMERICA AT THE MOVIES (FD) American Film Institute, 1976
GEORGE STEVENS: A FILMMAKER'S JOURNEY (FD) Creative Film Center, 1984

LESLIE STEVENS*

b. February 3, 1924 - Washington, D.C.
Business: Leslie Stevens Productions, 1107 Glendon Avenue, Los Angeles, CA 90024, 213/479-2770

PRIVATE PROPERTY Citation, 1960
INCUBUS 1961
HERO'S ISLAND United Artists, 1962
DELLA Four Star, 1964
FANFARE FOR A DEATH SCENE Four Star, 1967
I LOVE A MYSTERY (TF) Universal TV, 1973

ROBERT STEVENSON*

b. 1905 - London, England
Business: Walt Disney Productions, 500 S. Buena Vista Street, Burbank, CA 91521, 213/845-3141

HAPPILY EVER AFTER Gaumont, 1932, British
FALLING FOR YOU Woolf & Freedman, 1933, British
JACK OF ALL TRADES Gaumont, 1936, British
NINE DAYS A QUEEN *TUDOR ROSE* Gaumont, 1936, British
THE MAN WHO LIVED AGAIN *THE MAN WHO CHANGED HIS MIND* Gaumont, 1936, British
KING SOLOMON'S MINES Gaumont, 1937, British
NON-STOP NEW YORK General Film Distributors, 1937, British
TO THE VICTOR *OWD BOB* Gaumont, 1938, British
THE WARE CASE Associated British Film Distributors, 1939, British
A YOUNG MAN'S FANCY Associated British Film Distributors, 1939, British
RETURN TO YESTERDAY Associated British Film Distributors, 1939, British
TOM BROWN'S SCHOOLDAYS RKO Radio, 1940
BACK STREET Universal, 1941
JOAN OF PARIS RKO Radio, 1942
FOREVER AND A DAY co-director with Rene Clair, Edmund Goulding, Cedric Hardwicke, Frank Lloyd, Victor Saville & Herbert Wilcox, RKO Radio, 1943
JANE EYRE RKO Radio, 1944
DISHONORED LADY United Artists, 1947
TO THE ENDS OF THE EARTH RKO Radio, 1948
THE WOMAN ON PIER 13 *I MARRIED A COMMUNIST* RKO Radio, 1949
WALK SOFTLY, STRANGER RKO Radio, 1950
MY FORBIDDEN PAST RKO Radio, 1951
THE LAS VEGAS STORY RKO Radio, 1952
JOHNNY TREMAIN Buena Vista, 1957
OLD YELLER Buena Vista, 1957
DARBY O'GILL AND THE LITTLE PEOPLE Buena Vista, 1959
KIDNAPPED Buena Vista, 1960, British-U.S.
THE ABSENT-MINDED PROFESSOR Buena Vista, 1960
IN SEARCH OF THE CASTAWAYS Buena Vista, 1962, British-U.S.
SON OF FLUBBER Buena Vista, 1963
THE MISADVENTURES OF MERLIN JONES Buena Vista, 1964
MARY POPPINS ★ Buena Vista, 1964
THE MONKEY'S UNCLE Buena Vista, 1965
THAT DARN CAT Buena Vista, 1965
THE GNOME-MOBILE Buena Vista, 1967
BLACKBEARD'S GHOST Buena Vista, 1968
THE LOVE BUG Buena Vista, 1969
BEDKNOBS AND BROOMSTICKS Buena Vista, 1971
HERBIE RIDES AGAIN Buena Vista, 1974
THE ISLAND AT THE TOP OF THE WORLD Buena Vista, 1974
ONE OF OUR DINOSAURS IS MISSING Buena Vista, 1975, U.S.-British
THE SHAGGY D.A. Buena Vista, 1976

DOUGLAS DAY STEWART

Agent: Martin Bauer Agency - Beverly Hills, 213/275-2421

THIEF OF HEARTS Paramount, 1984

LARRY STEWART*

Agent: Irv Schechter & Company - Beverly Hills, 213/278-8070

THE INITIATION New World, 1984

JOHN STIX

FAMILY BUSINESS (TF) Screenscope Inc./South Carolina Educational TV Network, 1983

ANDREW L. STONE*

b. July 16, 1902 - Oakland, California
Home: 10478 Wyton Drive, Los Angeles, CA 90024, 213/279-2497
Agent: Calder Agency - Los Angeles, 213/845-7434

SOMBRAS DE GLORIA Sono Arts, 1930
HELL'S HEADQUARTERS Capitol, 1932
THE GIRL SAID NO Grand National, 1937
STOLEN HEAVEN Paramount, 1938
SAY IT IN FRENCH Paramount, 1938
THE GREAT VICTOR HERBERT Paramount, 1939
THERE'S MAGIC IN MUSIC Paramount, 1941
STORMY WEATHER 20th Century-Fox, 1943
HI DIDDLE DIDDLE RKO Radio, 1943
SENSATIONS OF 1945 United Artists, 1944
BEDSIDE MANNER United Artists, 1945
THE BACHELOR'S DAUGHTER United Artists, 1946
FUN ON A WEEKEND United Artists, 1947
HIGHWAY 301 Warner Bros., 1950
CONFIDENCE GIRL United Artists, 1951
THE STEEL TRAP 20th Century-Fox, 1952
A BLUEPRINT FOR MURDER 20th Century-Fox, 1953
THE NIGHT HOLDS TERROR Columbia, 1955
JULIE MGM, 1956
CRY TERROR! MGM, 1958
THE DECKS RAN RED MGM, 1958
THE LAST VOYAGE MGM, 1960
RING OF FIRE MGM, 1961
THE PASSWORD IS COURAGE MGM, 1963, British
NEVER PUT IT IN WRITING Allied Artists, 1964, British
THE SECRET OF MY SUCCESS MGM, 1965, British
SONG OF NORWAY Cinerama Releasing Corporation, 1970
THE GREAT WALTZ MGM, 1972

OLIVER STONE*

b. November 15, 1946 - New York, New York
Home: P.O. Box 43, Sagadonack, NY 11962, 516/537-3749
Business Manager: Licker & Pines, 9025 Wilshire Blvd., Beverly Hills, CA 90211, 213/858-1276

SEIZURE Cinerama Releasing Corporation, 1974, Canadian
THE HAND Orion/Warner Bros., 1981

BARBRA STREISAND*

b. 1942 - New York, New York
Agent: William Morris Agency - Beverly Hills, 213/274-7451

YENTL MGM/UA, 1983

JOSEPH STRICK*

b. July 6, 1923 - Braddock, Pennsylvania
Home: 266 River Road, Grandview, NY 10960, 914/359-9527
Business: Trans-Lux Corporation, 625 Madison Avenue, New York, NY 10022, 212/751-3110

THE SAVAGE EYE co-director with Ben Maddow & Sidney Meyers, Trans-Lux, 1959
THE BALCONY Continental, 1963
THE HECKLERS (TF) 1966, British
ULYSSES Continental, 1967
TROPIC OF CANCER Paramount, 1970
ROAD MOVIE Grove Press, 1974
A PORTRAIT OF THE ARTIST AS A YOUNG MAN Howard Mahler Films, 1979

BRIAN STUART

SORCERESS New World, 1982

MEL STUART*

b. September 2, 1928
Home: 11508 Thurston Circle, Los Angeles, CA 90049, 213/476-2634
Agent: The Richland Agency - Los Angeles, 213/553-1257

THE MAKING OF THE PRESIDENT (TD) David Wolper Productions, 1960
THE MAKING OF THE PRESIDENT (TD) David Wolper Productions, 1964
FOUR DAYS IN NOVEMBER (TD) David Wolper Productions, 1965
CHINA: ROOTS OF MADNESS (TD) David Wolper Productions, 1967
RISE AND FALL OF THE THIRD REICH (TD) David Wolper Productions, 1968
THE MAKING OF THE PRESIDENT (TD) David Wolper Productions, 1968
IF IT'S TUESDAY, THIS MUST BE BELGIUM United Artists, 1969
I LOVE MY WIFE Universal, 1970
WILLY WONKA AND THE CHOCOLATE FACTORY Paramount, 1971, British
ONE IS A LONELY NUMBER MGM, 1972
WATTSTAX (FD) Columbia, 1973
BRENDA STARR (TF) Wolper Productions, 1976
LIFE GOES TO THE MOVIES (TD) David Wolper Productions, 1976
OSCAR GOES TO WAR (TD) David Wolper Productions, 1977
MEAN DOG BLUES American International, 1978
RUBY AND OSWALD (TF) Alan Landsburg Productions, 1978
THE TRIANGLE FACTORY FIRE SCANDAL (TF) Alan Landsburg Productions/Don Kirshner Productions, 1979
THE CHISHOLMS (MS) Alan Landsburg Productions, 1979
THE WHITE LIONS Alan Landsburg Productions, 1979
SOPHIA LOREN: HER OWN STORY (TF) Roger Gimbel Productions/EMI TV, 1980

JOHN STURGES*

b. January 3, 1911 - Oak Park, Illinois
Agent: William Morris Agency - Beverly Hills, 213/274-7451
Business: The Alpha Corporation, 13063 Ventura Blvd., Suite 202, North Hollywood, CA 91604, 818/788-5750

THUNDERBOLT co-director with William Wyler, Monogram, 1945
THE MAN WHO DARED Columbia, 1946
SHADOWED Columbia, 1946
ALIAS MR. TWILIGHT Columbia, 1946
FOR THE LOVE OF RUSTY Columbia, 1947
KEEPER OF THE BEES Columbia, 1947
BEST MAN WINS Columbia, 1948
THE SIGN OF THE RAM Columbia, 1948
THE WALKING HILLS Columbia, 1949
THE CAPTURE RKO Radio, 1950
MYSTERY STREET MGM, 1950
RIGHT CROSS MGM, 1950
THE MAGNIFICENT YANKEE MGM, 1950

JOHN STURGES*—continued

KIND LADY MGM, 1951
THE PEOPLE AGAINST O'HARA MGM, 1951
IT'S A BIG COUNTRY co-director with Charles Vidor, Richard Thorpe, Don Hartman, Don Weis, Clarence Brown & William Wellman, MGM, 1952
THE GIRL IN WHITE MGM, 1952
JEOPARDY MGM, 1953
FAST COMPANY MGM, 1953
ESCAPE FROM FORT BRAVO MGM, 1953
BAD DAY AT BLACK ROCK ★ MGM, 1955
UNDERWATER! RKO Radio, 1955
THE SCARLET COAT MGM, 1955
BACKLASH MGM, 1956
GUNFIGHT AT THE O.K. CORRAL Paramount, 1957
THE LAW AND JAKE WADE MGM, 1958
THE OLD MAN AND THE SEA Warner Bros., 1958
LAST TRAIN FROM GUN HILL Paramount, 1959
NEVER SO FEW MGM, 1959
THE MAGNIFICENT SEVEN United Artists, 1960
BY LOVE POSSESSED United Artists, 1961
SERGEANTS 3 United Artists, 1962
A GIRL NAMED TAMIKO Paramount, 1963
THE GREAT ESCAPE United Artists, 1963
THE SATAN BUG United Artists, 1965
THE HALLELUJAH TRAIL United Artists, 1965
HOUR OF THE GUN United Artists, 1967
ICE STATION ZEBRA MGM, 1968
MAROONED Columbia, 1969
JOE KIDD Universal, 1972
CHINO *THE VALDEZ HORSES* Intercontinental, 1973, Italian-Spanish-French
McQ Warner Bros., 1974
THE EAGLE HAS LANDED Columbia, 1977, British

CHARLES STURRIDGE

Agent: Michael Marcus, CAA - Los Angeles, 213/277-4545
Contact: British Academy of Film & Television Arts, 195 Piccadilly, London W1, England, 01/732-0022

BRIDESHEAD REVISITED (MS) ☆ co-director with Michael Lindsay-Hogg, Granada TV/WNET-13/NDR Hamburg, 1982, British-U.S.-West German
RUNNERS The Samuel Goldwyn Company, 1983, British

JEREMY SUMMERS

Agent: Eric L'Epine Smith - London, 01/724-0759

DEPTH CHARGE British Lion, 1960, British
CROOKS IN CLOISTERS Warner-Pathe, 1964, British
FERRY CROSS THE MERSEY United Artists, 1965, British
SAN FERRY ANN British Lion, 1966, British
DATELINE DIAMONDS Rank, 1966, British
HOUSE OF 1,000 DOLLS American International, 1967, British
FIVE GOLDEN DRAGONS Warner-Pathe, 1968, British
THE VENGEANCE OF FU MANCHU Warner Bros., 1968, British
FALLEN HERO (TF) Granada TV, 1979, British
TOURIST (TF) Castle Combe Productions/Paramount TV, 1980
A KIND OF LOVING (TF) Granada TV, 1981, British

E.W. SWACKHAMER*

Agent: Shapiro-Lichtman Agency - Los Angeles, 213/557-2244

IN NAME ONLY (TF) Screen Gems/Columbia TV, 1969
MAN AND BOY Levitt-Pickman, 1972
GIDGET GETS MARRIED (TF) Screen Gems/Columbia TV, 1972
DEATH SENTENCE (TF) Spelling-Goldberg Productions, 1974
DEATH AT LOVE HOUSE (TF) Spelling-Goldberg Productions, 1976
ONCE AN EAGLE (MS) co-director with Richard Michaels, Universal TV, 1976
QUINCY, M.E. (TF) Glen A. Larson Productions/Universal TV, 1976
NIGHT TERROR (TF) Charles Fries Productions, 1977

E.W. SWACKHAMER*—continued

SPIDER-MAN (TF) Charles Fries Productions, 1977
THE DAIN CURSE (MS) ☆ Martin Poll Productions, 1978
THE WINDS OF KITTY HAWK (TF) Charles Fries Productions, 1978
VAMPIRE (TF) MTM Enterprises, 1979
THE DEATH OF OCEAN VIEW PARK (TF) Furia-Oringer Productions/Playboy Productions, 1979
REWARD (TF) Jerry Adler Productions/Espirit Enterprises/Lorimar Productions, 1980
TENSPEED AND BROWNSHOE (TF) Stephen J. Cannell Productions, 1980
THE OKLAHOMA CITY DOLLS (TF) IKE Productions/Columbia TV, 1981
LONGSHOT GG Productions, 1981
COCAINE AND BLUE EYES (TF) Orenthal Productions/Columbia TV, 1983
MALIBU (TF) Hamner Productions/Columbia TV, 1983
CARPOOL (TF) Charles Fries Productions/Cherryhill Productions, 1983
THE ROUSTERS (TF) Stephen J. Cannell Productions, 1983

BOB SWAIM

Contact: French Film Office, 745 Fifth Avenue, New York, NY 10151, 212/832-8860

LA NUIT DE SAINT-GERMAIN-DES-PRES Filmologies, 1977, French
LA BALANCE Spectrafilm, 1982, French

CHARLES SWENSON

Business: Murakami/Wolf/Swenson, Inc., 1463 Tamarind Avenue, Hollywood, CA 90028, 213/462-6473

DIRTY DUCK (AF) New World, 1977
THE MOUSE AND HIS CHILD (AF) co-director with Fred Wolf, Sanrio, 1977
TWICE UPON A TIME (AF) co-director with John Korty, The Ladd Company/Warner Bros., 1983

JO SWERLING, JR.*

b. June 18, 1931 - Los Angeles, California
Home: 5400 Jed Smith Road, Hidden Hills, CA 91302, 818/888-7231
Messages: 213/465-5800
Agent: Sam Adams, Triad Artists, Inc., - Los Angeles, 213/556-2727

THE LAST CONVERTIBLE (MS) co-director with Sidney Hayers & Gus Trikonis, Roy Huggins Productions/Universal TV, 1979

DAVID SWIFT*

b. 1919 - Minneapolis, Minnesota
Business Manager: Peter Dekom, Pollock, Bloom & Dekom, 9255 Sunset Blvd., Los Angeles, CA 90069, 213/278-8622

POLLYANNA Buena Vista, 1960
THE PARENT TRAP Buena Vista, 1961
THE INTERNS Columbia, 1962
LOVE IS A BALL United Artists, 1962
UNDER THE YUM YUM TREE Columbia, 1963
GOOD NEIGHBOR SAM Columbia, 1964
HOW TO SUCCEED IN BUSINESS WITHOUT REALLY TRYING United Artists, 1967

SAUL SWIMMER

FORCE OF IMPULSE Sutton, 1961
MRS. BROWN, YOU'VE GOT A LOVELY DAUGHTER MGM, 1968, British
COMETOGETHER Allied Artists, 1971, U.S.-Italian
THE CONCERT FOR BANGLADESH (FD) 20th Century-Fox, 1972
THE BLACK PEARL Diamond, 1977
WE WILL ROCK YOU (FD) Mobilevision/Yellowbill, 1983, Canadian

BRAD SWIRNOFF

Contact: Writers Guild of America, West - Los Angeles, 213/550-1000

TUNNELVISION co-director with Neil Israel, World Wide, 1976
AMERICAN RASPBERRY Cannon, 1980

HANS-JURGEN SYBERBERG

b. December 8, 1935 - Germany
Contact: German Film & TV Academy, Pommernallee 1, 1000 Berlin 19, West Germany, 030/303-6212

FUNFTER AKT, SIEBTE SZENE. FRITZ KORTNER PROBT KABALE UND LIEBE (FD) 1965, West German
ROMY. ANATOMIE EINES GESICHT (FD) 1965, West German
FRITZ KORTNER SPRICHT MONOLOGE FUR EINE SCHALLPLATTE (FD) 1966, West German
DIE GRAFFEN POCCI - EINIGE KAPITEL ZUR GESCHICHTE EINER FAMILIE (FD) 1967, West German
SCARABEA - WIENVIEL ERDE BRAUCHT DER MENSCH? 1968, West German
SEX-BUSINESS - MADE IN PASSING (FD) 1969, West German
SAN DOMINGO 1970, West German
NACH MEINEM LETZEN UMZUG 1970, West German
THEODOR HIERNEIS ODER: WIE MAN EHEM. HOFKOCH WIRD 1972, West German
LUDWIG: REQUIEM FOR A VIRGIN KING Zoetrope, 1972, West German
KARL MAY 7MS Film Gesellschaft, 1974, West German
WINIFRED WAGNER (FD) *WINIFRED WAGNER UND DIE GESCHICHTE DES HAUSES WAHNFRIED VON 1914-1975* Bauer International, 1978, West German
HITLER: A FILM FROM GERMANY Zoetrope, 1980, West German
PARSIFAL Triumph/Columbia, 1981, French-West German

PETER SYKES

b. June 17, 1939 - Melbourne, Australia
Address: 66 Highgate Hill - No. 6, London NW19, England, 01/272-1664

THE COMMITTEE Planet, 1968, British
DEMONS OF THE MIND MGM-EMI, 1972, British
THE HOUSE IN NIGHTMARE PARK MGM-EMI, 1973, British
STEPTOE AND SON RIDE AGAIN MGM-EMI, 1973, British
LEGEND OF SPIDER FOREST *VENOM* New Line Cinema, 1974, British
TO THE DEVIL A DAUGHTER EMI, 1976, British
CRAZY HOUSE Constellation, 1977, British
JESUS co-director with John Krish, Warner Bros., 1979, British
THE SEARCH FOR ALEXANDER THE GREAT (MS) Time-Life Productions/ Video Arts TV Productions, 1981, U.S.-British

PAUL SYLBERT*

Home: 52 East 64th Street - Suite 3, New York, NY 10021, 212/308-9078

THE STEAGLE Avco Embassy, 1971

ISTVAN SZABO

b. February 18, 1938 - Budapest, Hungary
Agent: Carole Dowling, William Morris Agency - New York City, 212/903-1182

AGE OF ILLUSIONS Brandon, 1964, Hungarian
FATHER Continental, 1966, Hungarian
LOVE FILM Mafilm, 1970, Hungarian
25, FIREMAN'S STREET Unifilm, 1970, Hungarian
PREMIERE (TF) Hungarian TV, 1974, Hungarian
BUDAPEST TALES Hunnia Studios, 1976, Hungarian
CONFIDENCE Mafilm, 1979, Hungarian
THE GREEN BIRD Teleculture, 1979, West German
MEPHISTO Analysis, 1980, Hungarian-West German

ISTVAN SZABO —continued

SALVE POUR UNE BUFLE NOIR Procinex/Objektiv Studios, 1985, French-Hungarian
COLONEL REDL Manfred Durniok Film/ZDF/OFR, 1985, West German-Austrian

JEANNOT SZWARC*

b. November 21, 1939 - Paris, France
Business: Terpsichore Productions, 10100 Santa Monica Blvd., Los Angeles, CA 90067, 213/553-8200
Agent: Shapiro-Lichtman Agency - Los Angeles, 213/557-2244

NIGHT OF TERROR (TF) Paramount TV, 1972
THE WEEKEND SUN (TF) Paramount TV, 1972
THE DEVIL'S DAUGHTER (TF) Paramount TV, 1973
YOU'LL NEVER SEE ME AGAIN (TF) Universal TV, 1973
LISA, BRIGHT AND DARK (TF) Bob Banner Associates, 1973
A SUMMER WITHOUT BOYS (TF) Playboy Productions, 1973
THE SMALL MIRACLE (TF) FCB Productions/Alan Landsburg Productions, 1973
EXTREME CLOSE-UP National General, 1973
CRIME CLUB (TF) Universal TV, 1975
BUG Paramount, 1975
CODE NAME: DIAMOND HEAD (TF) QM Productions, 1977
JAWS 2 Universal, 1978
SOMEWHERE IN TIME Universal, 1980
ENIGMA Embassy, 1982, British-French
SUPERGIRL Warner Bros., 1984, British
SANTA CLAUS - THE MOVIE Tri-Star, 1985, U.S.-British

T

JEAN-CHARLES TACCHELLA

b. September 23, 1925 - Cherbourg, France
Home: 8 bis Boulevard de Lesseps, Versailles 78000, France, 3/950-4764
Agent: Jean-Paul Faure, Agence IPF, 2 Rue Jules Chaplain, Paris, France, 325-5163

VOYAGE TO GRAND TARTARIE New Line Cinema, 1973, French
COUSIN COUSINE Libra, 1975, French
THE BLUE COUNTRY Quartet, 1977, French
IT'S A LONG TIME THAT I'VE LOVED YOU *SOUPCON* Durham/Pike, 1979, French
CROQUE LA VIE Prodis, 1981, French
ESCALIER C Films 7, 1984, French

GENE TAFT*

Contact: Directors Guild of America - Los Angeles, 213/656-1220

BLAME IT ON THE NIGHT Tri-Star, 1984

HARRY TAMPA
(See Harry HURWITZ)

WILLIAM TANNEN*
Home: 129 Fraser Avenue, Santa Monica, CA 90405, 213/392-3222
Business: The Film Consortium, 9165 Sunset Blvd., Los Angeles, CA 90069, 213/550-0190

FLASHPOINT Tri-Star, 1984

ALAIN TANNER
b. December 6, 1929 - Geneva, Switzerland
Contact: Swiss Film Center, Muenstergasse 18, CH-8001 Zurich, Switzerland, 01/472-860

LES APPRENTIS (FD) 1964, Swiss
UNE VILLE A CHANDIGARH 1966, Swiss
CHARLES, DEAD OR ALIVE New Yorker, 1969, Swiss-French
LA SALAMANDRE New Yorker, 1971, Swiss
LA RETOUR D'AFRIQUE Alain Tanner/Groupe 5, 1973, Swiss
THE MIDDLE OF THE WORLD New Yorker, 1974, Swiss
JONAH WHO WILL BE 25 IN THE YEAR 2000 New Yorker, 1976, Swiss
MESSIDOR New Yorker, 1979, Swiss-French
LIGHT YEARS AWAY New Yorker, 1981, Swiss-French
IN THE WHITE CITY Gray City, 1983, Swiss
NO MAN'S LAND MK2/Filmograph, 1985, French-Swiss

DANIEL TARADASH*
b. January 29, 1913 - Louisville, Kentucky
Agent: Ben Benjamin, ICM - Los Angeles, 213/550-4000

STORM CENTER Columbia, 1956

ANDREI TARKOVSKY
b. April 4, 1932 - Moscow, U.S.S.R.

THE ROLLER AND THE VIOLIN Mosfilm, 1960, Soviet
MY NAME IS IVAN Shore International, 1962, Soviet
ANDREI RUBLEV Columbia, 1968, Soviet
SOLARIS Mosfilm, 1972, Soviet
THE MIRROR Mosfilm, 1974, Soviet
STALKER New Yorker/Media Transactions Corporation, 1979, Soviet
NOSTALGHIA Grange Communications, 1983, Italian-Soviet

BERTRAND TAVERNIER
b. April 25, 1941 - Lyons, France
Contact: French Film Office, 745 Fifth Avenue, New York, NY 10151, 212/832-8860

LES BAISERS co-director, 1963, French
LA CHANCE ET L'AMOUR co-director, 1964, French
THE CLOCKMAKER OF ST. PAUL Joseph Green Pictures, 1974, French
LET JOY REIGN SUPREME *QUE LA FETE COMMENCE...* SJ International, 1975, French
THE JUDGE AND THE ASSASSIN Libra, 1976, French
SPOILED CHILDREN Corinth, 1977, French
FEMMES FATALES 1979, French
DEATH WATCH Quartet, 1980, French-West German
A WEEK'S VACATION *UNE SEMAINE DE VACANCES* Biograph, 1982, French
COUP DE TORCHON *CLEAN SLATE* Biograph/Quartet/Films Inc./The Frank Moreno Company, 1982, French
MISSISSIPPI BLUES co-director with Robert Parrish, Little Bear Productions/Odessa Films, 1984, French
A SUNDAY IN THE COUNTRY MGM/UA Classics, 1984, French

PAOLO TAVIANI

b. 1931 - San Miniato, Italy
Contact: Ministry of Culture & Education, Via Della Ferratella, No. 51, 00184 Rome, Italy, 06/7732

UN UOMO DA BRUCIARE co-director with Vittorio Taviani & Valentino Orsini, Moira Film/Ager Film/Sancro Film, 1963, Italian
I FUORILEGGE DEL METRAIMONIO co-director with Vittorio Taviani & Valentino Orsini, Ager Film/Filmcoop/D'errico Film, 1963, Italian
SOVVERSIVI co-director with Vittorio Taviani, Ager Film, 1967, Italian
SOTTO IL SEGNO DELLO SCORPIONE co-director with Vittorio Taviani, Ager Film, 1969, Italian
SAN MICHELE AVEVA UN GALLO (TF) co-director with Vittorio Taviani, Igor Film/RAI, 1971, Italian
ALLONSANFAN co-director with Vittorio Taviani, Italtoons/Wonder Movies, 1974, Italian
PADRE PADRONE co-director with Vittorio Taviani, New Yorker, 1977, Italian, originally made for television
THE MEADOW co-director with Vittorio Taviani, New Yorker, 1979, Italian-French
THE NIGHT OF THE SHOOTING STARS *LA NOTTE DI SAN LORENZO* co-director with Vittorio Taviani, United Artists Classics, 1981, Italian
XAOS co-director with Vittorio Taviani, Sacis, 1984, Italian

VITTORIO TAVIANI

b. 1929 - San Miniato, Italy
Contact: Ministry of Culture & Education, Via Della Ferratella, No. 51, 00184 Rome, Italy, 06/7732

UN UOMO DA BRUCIARE co-director with Paolo Taviani & Valentino Orsini, Moira Film/Ager Film/Sancro Film, 1963, Italian
I FUORILEGGE DEL METRAIMONIO co-director with Paolo Taviani & Valentino Orsini, Ager Film/Filmcoop/D'errico Film, 1963, Italian
SOVVERSIVI co-director with Paolo Taviani, Ager Film, 1967, Italian
SOTTO IL SEGNO DELLO SCORPIONE co-director with Paolo Taviani, Ager Film, 1969, Italian
SAN MICHELE AVEVA UN GALLO (TF) co-director with Paolo Taviani, Igor Film/RAI, 1971, Italian
ALLONSANFAN co-director with Paolo Taviani, Italtoons/Wonder Movies, 1974, Italian
PADRE PADRONE co-director with Paolo Taviani, New Yorker, 1977, Italian, originally made for television
THE MEADOW co-director with Paolo Taviani, New Yorker, 1979, Italian-French
THE NIGHT OF THE SHOOTING STARS *LA NOTTE DI SAN LORENZO* co-director with Paolo Taviani, United Artists Classics, 1981, Italian
XAOS co-director with Paolo Taviani, Sacis, 1984, Italian

DON TAYLOR*

b. December 13, 1920 - Freeport, Pennsylvania
Agent: The Gersh Agency - Beverly Hills, 213/274-6611

EVERTHING'S DUCKY Columbia, 1961
RIDE THE WILD SURF Columbia, 1964
JACK OF DIAMONDS MGM, 1967, U.S.-West German
SOMETHING FOR A LONELY MAN (TF) Universal TV, 1968
THE FIVE MAN ARMY MGM, 1970, Italian
WILD WOMEN (TF) Aaron Spelling Productions, 1970
ESCAPE FROM THE PLANET OF THE APES 20th Century-Fox, 1971
HEAT OF ANGER (TF) Metromedia Productions, 1972
TOM SAWYER United Artists, 1973
NIGHT GAMES (TF) Paramount TV, 1974
HONKY TONK (TF) MGM TV, 1974
ECHOES OF A SUMMER Cine Artists, 1976, U.S.-Canadian
THE MAN-HUNTER (TF) Universal TV, 1976
THE GREAT SCOUT AND CATHOUSE THURSDAY American International, 1976
A CIRCLE OF CHILDREN (TF) Edgar J. Scherick Associates/20th Century-Fox TV, 1977

DON TAYLOR*—continued

THE ISLAND OF DR. MOREAU American International, 1977
DAMIEN - OMEN II 20th Century-Fox, 1978
THE GIFT (TF) The Jozak Company/Cypress Point Productions/Paramount TV, 1979
THE FINAL COUNTDOWN United Artists, 1980
THE PROMISE OF LOVE (TF) Pierre Cossette Productions, 1980
BROKEN PROMISE (TF) 1981
RED FLAG: THE ULTIMATE GAME (TF) Marble Arch Productions, 1981
DROP-OUT FATHER (TF) CBS Entertainment, 1982
LISTEN TO YOUR HEART (TF) CBS Entertainment, 1983
SEPTEMBER GUN (TF) QM Productions/Taft Entertainment/Brademan-Self Productions, 1983
HE'S NOT YOUR SON (TF) CBS Entertainment, 1984
MY WICKED, WICKED WAYS: THE LEGEND OF ERROL FLYNN (TF) CBS Entertainment, 1985

JUD TAYLOR*

b. February 25, 1940
Agent: CAA - Los Angeles, 213/277-4545

FADE-IN Paramount, 1968
WEEKEND OF TERROR (TF) Paramount TV, 1970
SUDDENLY SINGLE (TF) Chris-Rose Productions, 1971
REVENGE (TF) Mark Carliner Productions, 1971
THE ROOKIES (TF) Aaron Spelling Productions, 1972
SAY GOODBYE, MAGGIE COLE (TF) Spelling-Goldberg Productions, 1972
HAWKINS ON MURDER (TF) Arena-Leda Productions/MGM TV, 1973
WINTER KILL (TF) Andy Griffith Enterprises/MGM TV, 1974
THE DISAPPEARANCE OF FLIGHT 412 (TF) Cinemobile Productions, 1975
SEARCH FOR THE GODS (TF) Warner Bros. TV, 1975
FUTURE COP (TF) Paramount TV, 1976
RETURN TO EARTH (TF) King-Hitzig Productions, 1976
WOMAN OF THE YEAR (TF) MGM TV, 1976
TAIL GUNNER JOE (TF) ☆ Universal TV, 1977
MARY WHITE (TF) Radnitz/Mattel Productions, 1977
CHRISTMAS MIRACLE IN CAUFIELD, U.S.A. (TF) 20th Century-Fox TV, 1977
THE LAST TENANT (TF) Titus Productions, 1978
LOVEY: A CIRCLE OF CHILDREN, PART II (TF) Time-Life Productions, 1978
FLESH AND BLOOD (TF) The Jozak Company/Cypress Point Productions/Paramount TV, 1979
CITY IN FEAR (TF) directed under pseudonym of Allen Smithee, Trans World International, 1980
ACT OF LOVE (TF) Cypress Point Productions/Paramount TV, 1980
MURDER AT CRESTRIDGE (TF) Jaffe-Taylor Productions, 1981
A QUESTION OF HONOR (TF) Roger Gimbel Productions/EMI TV/Sonny Grosso Productions, 1982
PACKIN' IT IN (TF) Roger Gimbel Productions/Thorn EMI TV/Jones-Reiker Ink Corporation, 1983
LICENSE TO KILL (TF) Marian Rees Associates/D. Petrie Productions, 1984

ROBERT TAYLOR

THE NINE LIVES OF FRITZ THE CAT (AF) American International, 1974
HEIDI'S SONG (AF) Paramount, 1982

LEWIS TEAGUE*

Agent: The Gersh Agency - Beverly Hills, 213/274-6611

DIRTY O'NEIL co-director with Howard Freen, American International, 1974
THE LADY IN RED New World, 1979
ALLIGATOR Group 1, 1980
FIGHTING BACK Paramount, 1982
CUJO Warner Bros., 1983
STEPHEN KING'S CAT'S EYE *CAT'S EYE* MGM/UA, 1985

JULIEN TEMPLE

Contact: Directors Guild of Great Britian, 56 Whitfield Street, London W1, England, 01/580-9592

THE GREAT ROCK 'N' ROLL SWINDLE Kendon Films/Matrix Best/Virgin Records, 1980, British
THE SECRET POLICEMAN'S OTHER BALL (FD) Miramax, 1981, British
IT'S ALL TRUE (TF) Island Pictures/BBC, 1983, British

JOAN TEWKESBURY*

b. 1937 - Redlands, California
Agent: Robert Lantz/Marion Rosenberg, The Lantz Office - Los Angeles, 213/858-1144

OLD BOYFRIENDS Avco Embassy, 1979
THE TENTH MONTH (TF) Joe Hamilton Productions, 1979
THE ACORN PEOPLE (TF) Rollins-Joffe-Morra-Brezner Productions, 1980

PETER TEWKSBURY

b. 1924

SUNDAY IN NEW YORK MGM, 1964
EMIL AND THE DETECTIVES Buena Vista, 1964
DOCTOR, YOU'VE GOT TO BE KIDDING MGM, 1967
STAY AWAY, JOE MGM, 1968
THE TROUBLE WITH GIRLS MGM, 1969
SECOND CHANCE (TF) Metromedia Productions, 1972

ANNA THOMAS

b. July 12, 1948 - Stuttgart, West Germany
Agent: Jeff Berg, ICM - Los Angeles, 213/550-4000

THE HAUNTING OF M Independent Productions, 1981

DAVE THOMAS

Address: 18 Saintfield, Don Mills, Ontario M3C 2M5, 416/487-8296

STRANGE BREW co-director with Rick Moranis, MGM/UA, 1983, Canadian

GERALD THOMAS

b. December 10, 1920 - Hull, England
Business: Pinewood Studios, Iver Heath, Buckinghamshire, England, IVER 651700
Contact: Directors Guild of Great Britain, 56 Whitfield Street, London W1, England, 01/580-9592

CIRCUS FRIENDS British Lion/Children's Film Foundation, 1956, British
TIMELOCK DCA, 1957, British
THE CIRCLE *THE VICIOUS CIRCLE* Kassler, 1957, British
THE DUKE WORE JEANS Anglo-Amalgamated, 1958, British
CHAIN OF EVENTS British Lion, 1958, British
CARRY ON SERGEANT Governor, 1958, British
CARRY ON NURSE Governor, 1959, British
PLEASE TURN OVER Columbia, 1959, British
WATCH YOUR STERN Magna, 1960, British
BEWARE OF CHILDREN *NO KIDDING* American International, 1960, British
CARRY ON CONSTABLE Governor, 1960, British
ROOMMATES *RAISING THE WIND* Herts-Lion International, 1961, British
CARRY ON REGARDLESS Anglo-Amalgamated, 1961, British
A SOLITARY CHILD British Lion, 1961, British
TWICE ROUND THE DAFFODILS Anglo-Amalgamated, 1962, British
CARRY ON CRUISING Governor, 1962, British
THE SWINGIN' MAIDEN *THE IRON MAIDEN* Columbia, 1962, British
NURSE ON WHEELS Janus, 1963, British
CARRY ON CABBY Anglo-Amalgamated/Warner-Pathe, 1963, British
CARRY ON JACK Anglo-Amalgamated/Warner-Pathe, 1964, British

GERALD THOMAS —continued

CARRY ON SPYING Governor, 1964, British
CARRY ON CLEO Governor, 1964, British
THE BIG JOB Anglo-Amalgamated/Warner-Pathe, 1966, British
CARRY ON COWBOY Anglo-Amalgamated/Warner-Pathe, 1966, British
CARRY ON SCREAMING Anglo-Amalgamated/Warner-Pathe, 1966, British
FOLLOW THAT CAMEL Schoenfeld Film Distributing, 1967, British
CARRY ON DOCTOR Rank, 1968, British
CARRY ON...UP THE KHYBER Rank, 1969, British
CARRY ON CAMPING Rank, 1969, British
CARRY ON UP THE JUNGLE Rank, 1970, British
CARRY ON AGAIN, DOCTOR Rank, 1970, British
CARRY ON AT YOUR CONVENIENCE Rank, 1971, British
CARRY ON HENRY Rank, 1971, British
CARRY ON LOVING Rank, 1971, British
CARRY ON ABROAD Rank, 1972, British
CARRY ON MATRON Rank, 1972, British
BLESS THIS HOUSE Rank, 1973, British
CARRY ON BEHIND Rank, 1976, British
CARRY ON ENGLAND Rank, 1976, British
CARRY ON EMMANUELLE Rank, 1978, British
THAT'S CARRY ON Rank, 1978, British

RALPH THOMAS

b. August 10, 1915 - Hull, England
Home: 20 Hyde Park Gardens Mews, London W2, England, 01/262-6402
Agent: Denis Selinger, ICM - London, 01/629-8080
Contact: Directors Guild of Great Britain, 56 Whitfield Street, London W1, England, 01/580-9592

HELTER SKELTER General Film Distributors, 1949, British
ONCE UPON A DREAM General Film Distributors, 1949, British
TRAVELLER'S JOY General Film Distributors, 1949, British
THE CLOUDED YELLOW General Film Distributors, 1950, British
ISLAND RESCUE *APPOINTMENT WITH VENUS* Universal, 1951, British
THE ASSASSIN *THE VENETIAN BIRD* United Artists, 1952, British
THE DOG AND THE DIAMONDS Associated British Film Distributors/ Children's Film Foundation, 1953, British
A DAY TO REMEMBER Republic, 1953, British
DOCTOR IN THE HOUSE Republic, 1954, British
MAD ABOUT MEN General Film Distributors, 1954, British
DOCTOR AT SEA Republic, 1955, British
ABOVE US THE WAVES Republic, 1955, British
THE IRON PETTICOAT MGM, 1956, British
CHECKPOINT Rank, 1956, British
DOCTOR AT LARGE Universal, 1957, British
CAMPBELL'S KINGDOM Rank, 1957, British
A TALE OF TWO CITIES Rank, 1958, British
THE WIND CANNOT READ 20th Century-Fox, 1958, British
THE 39 STEPS 20th Century-Fox, 1959, British
UPSTAIRS AND DOWNSTAIRS 20th Century-Fox, 1959, British
CONSPIRACY OF HEARTS Paramount, 1960, British
DOCTOR IN LOVE Governor, 1960, British
NO LOVE FOR JOHNNIE Embassy, 1961, British
NO, MY DARLING DAUGHTER Zenith, 1961, British
A PAIR OF BRIEFS Rank, 1962, British
YOUNG AND WILLING *THE WILD AND THE WILLING* Universal, 1962, British
DOCTOR IN DISTRESS Governor, 1963, British
AGENT 8 3/4 *HOT ENOUGH FOR JUNE* Continental, 1963, British
McGUIRE, GO HOME! *THE HIGH BRIGHT SUN* Continental, 1964, British
CARNABY, M.D. *DOCTOR IN CLOVER* Continental, 1965, British
DEADLIER THAN THE MALE Universal, 1966, British
SOME GIRLS DO United Artists, 1968, British
THE HIGH COMMISSIONER *NOBODY RUNS FOREVER* Cinerama Releasing Corporation, 1968, British
DOCTOR IN TROUBLE Rank, 1970, British
PERCY MGM, 1971, British
QUEST FOR LOVE Rank, 1971, British
IT'S A 2'6" ABOVE THE GROUND WORLD British Lion, 1972, British
THE LOVE BAN 1973, British

RALPH THOMAS —continued

IT'S NOT THE SIZE THAT COUNTS *PERCY'S PROGRESS* Joseph Brenner Associates, 1974, British
A NIGHTINGALE SANG IN BERKELEY SQUARE S. Benjamin Fisz Productions/Nightingale Productions, 1980, British

RALPH L. THOMAS

Address: 365 Markham Street, Toronto, Ontario M6G 2K8, England, 416/922-8700

TYLER (TF) CBC, 1977, Canadian
CEMENTHEAD (TF) CBC, 1978, Canadian
A PAID VACATION (TF) CBC, 1979, Canadian
AMBUSH AT IROQUOIS POINT (TF) CBC, 1979, Canadian
TICKET TO HEAVEN United Artists Classics, 1981, Canadian
THE TERRY FOX STORY (CTF) HBO Premiere Films/Robert Cooper Films II, 1983, Canadian

J. LEE THOMPSON*

b. 1914 - Bristol, England
Home: 21932 W. Pacific Coast Highway, Malibu, CA 90265
Agent: ICM - Los Angeles, 213/550-4000

MURDER WITHOUT CRIME Associated British Picture Corporation, 1950, British
THE YELLOW BALLOON Allied Artists, 1952, British
THE WEAK AND THE WICKED Allied Artists, 1954, British
COCKTAILS IN THE KITCHEN *FOR BETTER OR WORSE* Associated British Picture Corporation, 1954, British
AS LONG AS THEY'RE HAPPY Rank, 1955, British
AN ALLIGATOR NAMED DAISY Rank, 1955, British
BLONDE SINNER *YIELD TO THE NIGHT* Allied Artists, 1956, British
THE GOOD COMPANIONS Rank, 1957, British
WOMAN IN A DRESSING GOWN Warner Bros., 1957, British
DESERT ATTACK *ICE COLD IN ALEX* 20th Century-Fox, 1958 British
NO TREES IN THE STREET Associated British Picture Corporation, 1959, British
TIGER BAY Continental, 1959, British
FLAME OVER INDIA *NORTH WEST FRONTIER* 20th Century-Fox, 1959, British
I AIM AT THE STARS Columbia, 1960, U.S.-West German
THE GUNS OF NAVARONE ★ Columbia, 1961, U.S.-British
CAPE FEAR Universal, 1962
TARAS BULBA United Artists, 1962
KINGS OF THE SUN United Artists, 1963
WHAT A WAY TO GO! 20th Century-Fox, 1964
JOHN GOLDFARB, PLEASE COME HOME 20th Century-Fox, 1965
RETURN FROM THE ASHES United Artists, 1965, British-U.S.
EYE OF THE DEVIL MGM, 1967, British
BEFORE WINTER COMES Columbia, 1969, British
THE CHAIRMAN 20th Century-Fox, 1969, British
MACKENNA'S GOLD Columbia, 1969
BROTHERLY LOVE *COUNTRY DANCE* MGM, 1970, British
CONQUEST OF THE PLANET OF THE APES 20th Century-Fox, 1972
A GREAT AMERICAN TRAGEDY (TF) Metromedia Productions, 1972
BATTLE FOR THE PLANET OF THE APES 20th Century-Fox, 1973
HUCKLEBERRY FINN United Artists, 1974
THE BLUE KNIGHT (TF) Lorimar Productions, 1975
THE REINCARNATION OF PETER PROUD American International, 1975
ST. IVES Warner Bros., 1976
WIDOW (TF) Lorimar Productions, 1976
THE WHITE BUFFALO United Artists, 1977
THE GREEK TYCOON Universal, 1978
THE PASSAGE United Artists, 1979, British
CABOBLANCO Avco Embassy, 1981
HAPPY BIRTHDAY TO ME Columbia, 1981, Canadian
CODE RED (TF) Irwin Allen Productions/Columbia TV, 1981
10 TO MIDNIGHT Cannon, 1983
THE EVIL THAT MEN DO Tri-Star, 1984
THE AMBASSADOR MGM/UA/Cannon, 1984

ROBERT C. THOMPSON*

b. May 31, 1937 - Palmyra, New York
Home: 4536 Mary Ellen Avenue, Sherman Oaks, CA 91423, 818/995-0273
Messages: 818/501-3714
Agent: Debee Klein, Irv Schechter Company - Beverly Hills, 213/278-8070
Business Manager: Platt, Blue & Lucove, 23047 Ventura Blvd., Woodland Hills, CA, 818/883-7296

BUD AND LOU (TF) Bob Banner Associates, 1978

JERRY THORPE*

b. 1930
Home: 865 S. Bundy Drive, Los Angeles, CA 90049
Business: Blinn-Thorpe Productions, 4024 Radford Avenue, Studio City, CA 91604, 818/760-5201
Agent: Leonard Hanzer, Major Talent Agency - Los Angeles, 213/820-5841

THE VENETIAN AFFAIR MGM, 1968
DAY OF THE EVIL GUN MGM, 1968
DIAL HOT LINE (TF) Universal TV, 1970
LOCK, STOCK AND BARREL (TF) Universal TV, 1971
THE CABLE CAR MURDER (TF) Warner Bros. TV, 1971
KUNG FU (TF) Warner Bros. TV, 1972
COMPANY OF KILLERS *THE PROTECTORS* Universal, 1972
SMILE JENNY, YOU'RE DEAD (TF) Warner Bros. TV, 1974
THE DARK SIDE OF INNOCENCE (TF) Warner Bros. TV, 1976
I WANT TO KEEP MY BABY (TF) CBS, Inc., 1976
THE POSSESSED (TF) Warner Bros. TV, 1977
STICKIN' TOGETHER (TF) Blinn-Thorpe Productions/Viacom, 1978
A QUESTION OF LOVE (TF) Viacom, 1978
THE LAZARUS SYNDROME (TF) Blinn-Thorpe Productions/Viacom, 1979
ALL GOD'S CHILDREN (TF) Blinn-Thorpe Productions/Viacom, 1980
HAPPY ENDINGS (TF) Blinn-Thorpe Productions, 1983

ERIC TILL*

Home: 62 Chaplin Crescent, Toronto, Ontario M5P 1A3, Canada, 416/488-4068
Agent: Charles Hunt, Oscard Associates - New York City, 212/764-1100

A GREAT BIG THING Argofilms, 1967, British
HOT MILLIONS MGM, 1968, British
THE WALKING STICK MGM, 1970, British
A FAN'S NOTES Warner Bros., 1972, Canadian
BETHUNE (TF) CBC, 1977, Canadian
ALL THINGS BRIGHT AND BEAUTIFUL *IT SHOULDN'T HAPPEN TO A VET* World Northal, 1978, British
WILD HORSE HANK Film Consortium of Canada, 1979, Canadian
AN AMERICAN CHRISTMAS CAROL (TF) ABC, 1979
MARY AND JOSEPH: A STORY OF FAITH (TF) Lorimar Productions/CIP-Europaische Treuhand AG, 1979, U.S.-West German
IMPROPER CHANNELS Crown International, 1981, Canadian
IF YOU COULD SEE WHAT I HEAR Jensen Farley Pictures, 1982, Canadian

JAMES TOBACK

Home: 11 East 87th Street, New York, NY 10028, 212/427-5606
Agent: Jeff Berg, ICM - Los Angeles, 213/550-4000
Business Manager: David Kaufman, Kaufman & Nachbar, 100 Merrick Road, Rockville Centre, NY, 516/536-5760

FINGERS Brut Productions, 1978
LOVE AND MONEY Paramount, 1982
EXPOSED MGM/UA, 1983

BURT TOPPER*

b. July 31, 1928 - New York, New York
Business: 213/651-1320
Home: 8447 Wilshire Blvd., Apt. #102, Beverly Hills, CA 90211, 213/823-6434

HELL SQUAD American International, 1958
TANK COMMANDOS American International, 1959
THE DIARY OF A HIGH SCHOOL BRIDE American International, 1959
WAR IS HELL Allied Artists, 1964
THE STRANGLER Allied Artists, 1964
THE DEVIL'S 8 American International, 1968
THE HARD RIDE American International, 1971
THE DAY THE LORD GOT BUSTED American, 1976

ROBERT TOTTEN*

b. February 5, 1937 - Los Angeles, California
Home: 13819 Riverside Drive, Sherman Oaks, CA 91403, 818/788-4242
Agent: Herb Tobias & Associates - Los Angeles, 213/277-6211

THE QUICK AND THE DEAD Beckman, 1963
DEATH OF A GUNFIGHTER co-director with Don Siegel, both directed under pseudonym of Allen Smithee, Universal, 1967
THE WILD COUNTRY Buena Vista, 1971
THE RED PONY (TF) Universal TV/Omnibus Productions, 1973
HUCKLEBERRY FINN (TF) ABC Circle Films, 1975
PONY EXPRESS RIDER Doty-Dayton, 1976
THE SACKETTS (TF) Douglas Netter Enterprises/M.B. Scott Productions/ Shalako Enterprises, 1979

ROBERT TOWNE*

Contact: Directors Guild of America - Los Angeles, 213/656-1220

PERSONAL BEST The Geffen Company/Warner Bros., 1982

BUD TOWNSEND*

Home: 5917 Blairstone Drive, Culver City, CA 90230, 213/870-1559
Agent: The Gersh Agency - Beverly Hills, 213/274-6611

NIGHTMARE IN WAX Crown International, 1969
THE FOLKS AT RED WOLF INN *TERROR HOUSE* Scope III, 1972
ALICE IN WONDERLAND General National Enterprises, 1976
COACH Crown International, 1978
ECSTASY Playboy Enterprises, 1984

PAT TOWNSEND

Business: Crown International Pictures, 292 S. La Cienega Blvd., Beverly Hills, CA 90211, 213/657-6700

THE BEACH GIRLS Crown International, 1982

JEAN-CLAUDE TRAMONT*

Agent: Michael Black, ICM - Los Angeles, 213/550-4000

LE POINT DE MIRE Warner-Columbia, 1977, French
ALL NIGHT LONG Universal, 1981

JESUS SALVADOR TREVINO*

Home: 2358 Yorkshire Drive, Los Angeles, CA 90065
Messages: 213/256-8408

RAICES DE SANGRE Azteca, 1979, Mexican
SEGUIN (TF) KCET, 1982

GUS TRIKONIS*

b. New York, New York
Agent: Herb Tobias & Associates - Los Angeles, 213/277-6211

FIVE THE HARD WAY Fantascope, 1969
THE SWINGING BARMAIDS Premiere, 1975
SUPERCOCK Hagen-Wayne, 1975
NASHVILLE GIRL New World, 1976
MOONSHINE COUNTY EXPRESS New World, 1977
NEW GIRL IN TOWN New World, 1977
THE EVIL New World, 1978
THE DARKER SIDE OF TERROR (TF) Shaner-Ramrus Productions/Bob Banner Associates, 1979
SHE'S DRESSED TO KILL (TF) Grant-Case-McGrath Enterprises/Barry Weitz Films, 1979
THE LAST CONVERTIBLE (MS) co-director with Sidney Hayers & Jo Swerling, Jr., Roy Huggins Productions/Universal TV, 1979
FLAMINGO ROAD (TF) MF Productions/Lorimar Productions, 1980
TOUCHED BY LOVE Columbia, 1980
ELVIS AND THE BEAUTY QUEEN (TF) David Gerber Company/Columbia TV, 1981
TAKE THIS JOB AND SHOVE IT Avco Embassy, 1981
TWIRL (TF) Charles Fries Productions, 1981
MISS ALL-AMERICAN BEAUTY (TF) Marian Rees Associates, 1982
DEMPSEY (TF) Charles Fries Productions, 1983
DANCE OF THE DWARFS Dove, Inc., 1983
FIRST AFFAIR (TF) CBS Entertainment, 1983

JAN TROELL

b. July 23, 1931 - Limhamn, Skane, Sweden
Contact: Swedish Film Institute, P.O. Box 27126, 102 52 Stockholm, Sweden, 08/63-0510

4 X 4 co-director, 1965, Swedish-Finnish-Norwegian-Danish
HERE'S YOUR LIFE Brandon, 1966, Swedish
EENY, MEENY, MINY, MO *WHO SAW HIM DIE?* Svensk Filmindustri, 1968, Swedish
THE EMIGRANTS *UTVANDRARNA* ★ Warner Bros., 1972, Swedish
THE NEW LAND *NYBYGGARNA* Warner Bros., 1973, Swedish
ZANDY'S BRIDE Warner Bros., 1974
BANG! Svensk Filminstitut, 1977, Swedish
HURRICANE Paramount, 1979
THE FLIGHT OF THE EAGLE Summit Features, 1982, Swedish-West German-Norwegian

DOUGLAS TRUMBULL*

Business: Brock/Trumbull, 1335 Maxella Avenue, Venice, CA 90291, 213/823-0433

SILENT RUNNING Universal, 1972
BRAINSTORM MGM/UA, 1983

SLAVA TSUKERMAN

b. Moscow, U.S.S.R.
Telephone: (212) 620-0110

LIQUID SKY Cinevista, 1983

MICHAEL TUCHNER*

b. June 24, 1934 - Berlin, Germany
Agent: Mike Marcus, CAA - Los Angeles, 213/277-4545 or Douglas Rae Management - London, 01/836-3903

VILLAIN MGM, 1971, British
FEAR IS THE KEY Paramount, 1973, British
MR. QUILP Avco Embassy, 1975, British

MICHAEL TUCHNER*—continued

BAR MITZVAH BOY (TF) BBC, 1976, British
THE LIKELY LADS EMI, 1976, British
SUMMER OF MY GERMAN SOLDIER (TF) Highgate Productions, 1978
HAYWIRE (TF) Pando Productions/Warner Bros. TV, 1980
THE HUNCHBACK OF NOTRE DAME (TF) Norman Rosemont Productions/ Columbia TV, 1982, U.S.-British
PAROLE (TF) RSO Films, 1982
TRENCHCOAT Buena Vista, 1983
ADAM (TF) Alan Landsburg Productions, 1983

RICHARD TUGGLE

b. August 8, 1948 - Coral Gables, Florida
Agent: Martin Bauer Agency - Beverly Hills, 213/275-2321

TIGHTROPE Warner Bros., 1984

SANDY TUNG

BROKEN PROMISE *A MARRIAGE* Cinecom International, 1983

SOPHIA TURKIEWICZ

Contact: Australian Film Commission, 9229 Sunset Blvd., Los Angeles, CA 90069, 213/275-7074

SILVER CITY Samuel Goldwyn Company, 1984, Australian

ROSE MARIE TURKO

b. April 14, 1951 - Orleans, France
Address: Turko Films, 2019½ S. Beverly Glen Blvd., Los Angeles, CA 90025, 213/475-5714

SCARRED *STREET LOVE* Seymour Borde & Associates, 1983
THE DUNGEONMASTER co-director, Empire International, 1985

LAWRENCE TURMAN*

b. 1926 - Los Angeles, California
Business Manager: Kaufman-Eisenberg, 9301 Wilshire Blvd., Beverly Hills, CA 90210, 213/850-1580

MARRIAGE OF A YOUNG STOCKBROKER 20th Century-Fox, 1971
SECOND THOUGHTS Universal, 1983

U

LIV ULLMANN

b. December 16, 1939 - Tokyo, Japan
Agent: Paul Kohner, Inc. - Los Angeles, 213/550-1060

LOVE co-director with Annette Cohen, Nancy Dowd & Mai Zetterling, Velvet Films, 1982, Canadian

PETER USTINOV*

b. April 16, 1921 - London, England
Home: Rue de Silly, 91200 Boulogne, France, 1/603-8753
Agent: Steve Kenis, William Morris Agency - London, 01/734-9361

SCHOOL FOR SECRETS General Film Distributors, 1946, British
VICE VERSA General Film Distributors, 1948, British
PRIVATE ANGELO co-director with Michael Anderson, Associated British Picture Corporation, 1949, British
ROMANOFF AND JULIET Universal, 1961
BILLY BUDD Allied Artists, 1962, British
LADY L MGM, 1966, U.S.-Italian-French
HAMMERSMITH IS OUT Cinerama Releasing Corporation, 1972
MEMED Peter Ustinov Productions Ltd./Jadran Films, 1984, British-Yugoslavian

JAMIE UYS

Contact: Department of Interior, Civitas Building, Struben Street, Pretoria 0002, South Africa, 12/48-2551

DINGAKA Embassy, 1965, South African
AFTER YOU, COMRADE Continental, 1967, South African
LOST IN THE DESERT Columbia-Warner, 1971, South African
BEAUTIFUL PEOPLE *ANIMALS ARE BEAUTIFUL PEOPLE (FD)* Warner Bros., 1974, South African
THE GODS MUST BE CRAZY TLC Films/20th Century-Fox, 1979, Botswana
BEAUTIFUL PEOPLE II (FD) 1983, South African

V

ROGER VADIM
(Roger Vadim Plemiannikov)

b. January 26, 1928 - Paris, France
Agent: Leading Artists - Beverly Hills, 213/858-1999

AND GOD CREATED WOMAN Kingsley International, 1956, French
NO SUN IN VENICE *SAIT-ON JAMAIS?* Kingsley International, 1957, French-Italian
THE NIGHT HEAVEN FELL *LES BIJOUTIERS DU CLAIR DE LUNES* Kingsley International, 1957, French-Italian
LES LIAISONS DANGEREUSES Astor, 1959, French-Italian
BLOOD AND ROSES *ET MOURIR DE PLAISIR* Paramount, 1960, Italian
PLEASE, NOT NOW! *LA BRIDE SUR LE COU* 20th Century-Fox, 1961, French
SEVEN CAPITAL SINS co-director with Jean-Luc Godard, Sylvaine Dhomme, Edouard Molinaro, Philippe De Broca, Claude Chabrol, Jacques Demy, Marie-Jose Nat, Dominique Paturel, Jean-Marc Tennberg & Perrette Pradier, Embassy, 1962, French-Italian
LOVE ON A PILLOW *LE REPOS DU GUERRIER* Royal Films International, 1962, French-Italian
OF FLESH AND BLOOD *LES GRANDS CHEMINS* Times, 1963, French-Italian
VICE AND VIRTUE MGM, 1963, French
NUTTY, NAUGHTY CHATEAU *CHATEAU EN SUEDE* Lopert, 1963 French-Italian
CIRCLE OF LOVE *LA RONDE* Continental, 1964, French
THE GAME IS OVER *LA CUREE* Royal Films International, 1966, French-Italian
SPIRITS OF THE DEAD *HISTOIRES EXTRAORDINAIRES* co-director with Federico Fellini & Louis Malle, American International, 1968, Italian-French
BARBARELLA Paramount, 1968, Italian-French
PRETTY MAIDS ALL IN A ROW MGM, 1971
HELLE Cocinor, 1972, French
MS. DON JUAN *DON JUAN ETAIT UNE FEMME* Scotia American, 1973, French
CHARLOTTE *LA JEUNE FILLE ASSASSINEE* Gamma III, 1974, French
UNE FEMME FIDELE FFCM, 1976, French
NIGHT GAMES Avco Embassy, 1980, French
THE HOT TOUCH Astral Bellevue, 1981, Canadian
SURPRISE PARTY Uranium Films, 1982, French
COME BACK Comeci, 1983, French

LUIS VALDEZ*

Contact: Directors Guild of America - Los Angeles, 213/656-1220

ZOOT SUIT Universal, 1981

BRUCE VAN DUSEN

COLD FEET Cinecom International, 1984

BUDDY VAN HORN*

Home: 4409 Ponca Avenue, Toluca Lake, CA 91602
Messages: 213/462-2301

ANY WHICH WAY YOU CAN Warner Bros., 1980

KEES VAN OOSTRUM

b. July 5, 1954 - Amsterdam, Netherlands
Attorney: Peter Nichols, Weissman, Wolff, Bergman, Coleman & Schulman, 9665 Wilshire Blvd., Suite 900, Beverly Hills, CA 90212, 213/858-7888

MISSING PERSONS: FOUR TRUE STORIES (CTD) Dave Bell Associates, 1984
BITTER HERBS VNF, 1985, Dutch

MELVIN VAN PEEBLES*

b. 1932 - Chicago, Illinois
Home: 353 West 56th Street, Apt. 10F, New York, NY 10019, 212/489-6570

THE STORY OF A THREE-DAY PASS Sigma III, 1968, French
WATERMELON MAN Columbia, 1970
SWEET SWEETBACK'S BAADASSSSSS SONG Cinemation, 1971

NORMAN THADDEUS VANE

Contact: Writers Guild of America - Los Angeles, 213/550-1000

FRIGHTMARE Saturn International, 1983
THE BLACK ROOM co-director with Elly Kenner, CI Films, 1984

AGNES VARDA

b. May 30, 1928 - Brussels, Belgium
Home: 354 Indiana Avenue, Venice, CA, 213/392-7700

LA POINTE COURTE 1954, French
CLEO FROM 5 TO 7 Zenith, 1962, French
LE BONHEUR Clover, 1965, French
LES CREATURES New Yorker, 1966, French-Swedish
FAR FROM VIETNAM (FD) co-director with Jean-Luc Godard, Claude Lelouch, Alain Resnais, William Klein & Joris Ivens, New Yorker, 1967, French
LIONS LOVE Raab, 1969
NAUSICAA (TF) 1970, French
DAGUERREOTYPES (FD) 1975, French
ONE SINGS, THE OTHER DOESN'T Cinema 5, 1977, French
MUR MURS (FD) Cine-Tamaris, 1981, French
DOCUMENTEUR: AN EMOTION PICTURE Cine-Tamaris, 1981, French

FRANCIS VEBER

Agent: Rosalie Swedlin, CAA - Los Angeles, 213/277-4545

THE TOY Show Biz Company, 1976, French
LE CHEVRE European International, 1981, French
LES COMPERES European International, 1983, French

MIKE VEJAR*

Contact: Directors Guild of America - Los Angeles, 213/656-1220

HAWAIIAN HEAT (TF) James D. Parriott Productions/Universal TV, 1984

MICHAEL VENTURA

Contact: Writers Guild of America - Los Angeles, 213/550-1000

"I'M ALMOST NOT CRAZY..." JOHN CASSAVETES: THE MAN AND HIS WORK (FD) Cannon, 1984

PAUL VERHOEVEN

Business: Riverside Pictures B.V., Koningslaan 17, 1075 AA Amsterdam, Netherlands, 20/640-401
Agent: Marion Rosenberg, The Lantz Office - Los Angeles, 213/858-1144

WAT ZIEN IK Rob Houwer Film, 1972, Dutch
TURKISH DELIGHT Cinemation, 1974, Dutch
KEETJE TIPPEL Cinema National, 1976, Dutch
SOLDIER OF ORANGE The Samuel Goldwyn Company, 1979, Dutch
SPETTERS The Samuel Goldwyn Company, 1981, Dutch
THE 4TH MAN Spectrafilm, 1983, Dutch
FLESH AND BLOOD Orion, 1985

HENRI VERNEUIL

(Achod Malakian)

b. October 15, 1920 - Rodosto, Turkey
Business: V. Films, 12 Bis Rue Keppler, 75016 Paris, France, 723-5068

LA TABLE AUX CREVES 1951, French
BRELAN D'AS 1952, French
FORBIDDEN FRUIT Films Around the World, 1952, French
LE BOULANGER DE VALORGUE 1953, French
CARNAVAL 1953, French
THE MOST WANTED MAN IN THE WORLD *ENNEMI PUBLIC NO. 1* Astor, 1953, French-Italian
THE SHEEP HAS FIVE LEGS United Motion Picture Organization, 1954, French
LES AMANTS DU TAGE 1955, French
DES GENS SANS IMPORTANCE 1955, French
PARIS-PALACE-HOTEL 1956, French
WHAT PRICE MURDER *UNE MANCHE ET LA BELLE* United Motion Picture Organization, 1957, French
MAXIME Interworld, 1958, French
THE BIG CHIEF Continental, 1959, French-Italian
THE COW AND I *LA VACHE ET LE PRISONNIER* Zenith, 1959, French-West German
L'AFFAIRE D'UNE NUIT 1960, French
LA FRANCAISE ET L'AMOUR co-director, 1960, French
LE PRESIDENT 1961, French-Italian
THE LIONS ARE LOOSE Franco-London, 1961, French-Italian
A MONKEY IN WINTER MGM, 1962, French
ANY NUMBER CAN WIN *MELODIE EN SOUS-SOL* MGM, 1963, French
GREED IN THE SUN MGM, 1964, French
WEEKEND AT DUNKIRK *WEEKEND A ZUYDCOOTE* 20th Century-Fox, 1965, French-Italian
THE 25TH HOUR MGM, 1967, French-Italian-Yugoslavian
GUNS FOR SAN SEBASTIAN *LA BATAILLE DE SAN SEBASTIAN* MGM, 1968, French-Italian-Mexican
THE SICILIAN CLAN 20th Century-Fox, 1970, French
THE BURGLARS Columbia, 1972, French-Italian
THE SERPENT *NIGHT FLIGHT TO MOSCOW* Avco Embassy, 1973, French-Italian-West German
THE NIGHT CALLER *PEUR SUR LA VILLE* Columbia, 1975, French-Italian
LE CORPS DE MON ENNEMI AMLF, 1976, French
I... COMME ICARE V Films/SFP/Antenne-2, 1979, French
MILLE MILLIARDS DE DOLLARS V Films/Films A2, 1982, French
LES MORFALOUS AAA, 1984, French

STEPHEN F. VERONA*

b. September 11, 1940 - Illinois
Home: 1251 Stone Canyon Road, Los Angeles, CA 90024
Messages: 213/476-7387

THE LORDS OF FLATBUSH co-director with Martin Davidson, Columbia, 1974
PIPE DREAMS Avco Embassy, 1976
BOARDWALK Atlantic Releasing Corporation, 1979
TALKING WALLS Drummond Productions, 1984

DANIEL VIGNE

Contact: French Film Office, 745 Fifth Avenue, New York, NY 10151, 212/832-8860

LES HOMMES Cocinor, 1973, French-Italian
THE RETURN OF MARTIN GUERRE European International, 1983, French

CHUCK VINCENT

b. Garden City, Michigan
Business: Platinum Pictures, 264 West 35th Street, New York, NY 10001, 212/244-1518

BLUE SUMMER Monarch, 1971
WHILE THE CAT'S AWAY Monarch, 1971
THE APPOINTMENT New Line Cinema, 1971
MRS. BARRINGTON Monarch, 1972
LETCHER Command, 1974
HEAVY LOAD Command, 1975
AMERICAN TICKLER Platinum Pictures, 1976
BANG BANG *PORN FLAKES* Platinum Pictures, 1976
FAREWELL SCARLET Command, 1976
VISIONS Platinum Pictures, 1977
DIRTY LILLY Bunnco, 1978
HOT T-SHIRTS Cannon, 1979
BAD PENNY Platinum Pictures, 1979
JACK AND JILL Platinum Pictures, 1980
SUMMER CAMP Seymour Borde & Associates, 1981
BON APPETIT Distribpix, 1981
MISBEHAVIN' Distribpix, 1981
THAT LUCKY STIFF Distribpix, 1981
C.O.D. Lone Star, 1982
GAMES WOMEN PLAY Platinum Pictures, 1982
ROOMMATES Platinum Pictures, 1982
THIS LADY IS A TRAMP Bunnco, 1982
DIRTY LOOKS Platinum Pictures, 1983
PUSS 'N BOOTS Platinum Pictures, 1983
JACK AND JILL II Platinum Pictures, 1984
PREPPIES Platinum Pictures, 1984
HOLLYWOOD HOT TUBS Seymour Borde & Associates, 1984
HOUSE OF THE RISING SUN Platinum Pictures, 1985

VIRGIL W. VOGEL*

b. Peoria, Illinois
Agent: David Shapira & Associates - Beverly Hills, 213/278-2742
Business Manager: Lester Stein, 10350 Santa Monica Blvd., Suite 350, Los Angeles, CA 90025, 213/553-9709

THE MOLE PEOPLE Universal, 1956
THE KETTLES ON OLD McDONALD'S FARM Universal, 1957
THE LAND UNKNOWN Universal, 1957
THE SWORD OF ALI BABA Universal, 1965
THE RETURN OF JOE FORRESTER (TF) Columbia TV, 1975
THE DEPUTIES (TF) 1976
LAW OF THE LAND (TF) QM Productions, 1976
CENTENNIAL (MS) co-director with Paul Krasny, Harry Falk & Bernard McEveety, Universal TV, 1978

VIRGIL W. VOGEL*—continued

POWER (TF) co-director with Barry Shear, David Gerber Company/Columbia TV, 1980
PORTRAIT OF A REBEL: MARGARET SANGER (TF) Marvin Minoff Productions/David Paradine TV, 1980
BEULAH LAND (MS) co-director with Harry Falk, David Gerber Company/Columbia TV, 1980
TODAY'S FBI (TF) David Gerber Company, 1981

W

DANIEL WACHSMANN

Contact: Israel Film Centre, Ministry of Industry & Trade, 30 Agron Street, P.O. Box 299, Jerusalem 94190, Israel, 02/210433

TRANSIT Jacob Goldwasser Productions, 1979, Israeli
HOT WIND *HAMSIN* Hemdale, 1982, Israeli

MICHAEL WADLEIGH*

Contact: Directors Guild of America - Los Angeles, 213/656-1220

WOODSTOCK (FD) Warner Bros., 1970
WOLFEN Orion/Warner Bros., 1981

JANE WAGNER*

b. February 2, 1935 - Morristown, Tennessee
Home: 213/275-5161
Agent: Ron Mardigian/Stan Kamen, William Morris Agency - Beverly Hills, 213/274-7451

MOMENT BY MOMENT Universal, 1978

RALPH WAITE*

b. June 22, 1928 - White Plains, New York
Agent: Ron Meyer, CAA - Los Angeles, 213/277-4545
Business Manager: Global Business Management, 9000 Sunset Blvd. - Suite 1115, Los Angeles, CA 90069, 213/278-4141

ON THE NICKEL Rose's Park, 1980

ANDRZEJ WAJDA

b. March 6, 1926 - Suwalki, Poland
Contact: French Film Office, 745 Fifth Avenue, New York, NY 10151, 212/832-8860

A GENERATION WFF Wroclaw, 1954, Polish
JE VAIS VERS LE SOLEIL WFD Warsaw, 1955, French-Polish
KANAL Frankel, 1957, Polish
ASHES AND DIAMONDS Janus, 1958, Polish
LOTNA KADR Unit, 1959, Polish
INNOCENT SORCERERS KADR Unit, 1960, Polish
SAMSON Droga-KADR Unit, 1961, Polish
SIBERIAN LADY MACBETH Avala Film, 1961, Polish
LOVE AT TWENTY co-director with Francois Truffaut, Renzo Rossellini, Shintaro Ishihara & Marcel Ophuls, Embassy, 1962, French-Italian-Japanese-Polish-West German
ASHES 1965, Polish
GATES TO PARADISE 1967, British
EVERYTHING FOR SALE New Yorker, 1968, Polish
HUNTING FLIES 1969, Polish
LANDSCAPE AFTER BATTLE New Yorker, 1970, Polish
THE BIRCH-WOOD 1971, Polish
PILATUS UND ANDERE (TF) 1972, West German
THE WEDDING Film Polski, 1972, Polish
THE PROMISED LAND Film Polski, 1974, Polish
SHADOW LINE 1976, Polish
MAN OF MARBLE New Yorker, 1977, Polish
WITHOUT ANESTHETIC New Yorker, 1979, Polish
THE GIRLS FROM WILKO 1979, Polish-French
THE CONDUCTOR Film Polski, 1980, Polish
ROUGH TREATMENT Film Polski, 1980, Polish
MAN OF IRON United Artists Classics, 1981, Polish
DANTON Triumph/Columbia, 1983, French-Polish
A LOVE IN GERMANY Triumph/Columbia, 1983, West German-French

DORIAN WALKER

MAKING THE GRADE MGM/UA/Cannon, 1984

NANCY WALKER*

b. May 10, 1922 - Philadelphia, Pennsylvania
Agent: Tom Korman, Contemporary-Korman Artists - Beverly Hills, 213/278-8250

CAN'T STOP THE MUSIC AFD, 1980

PETER WALKER

Address: 23 Down Street - Flat 4, Mayfair, London W1, England, 01/493-7440
Contact: Directors Guild of Great Britain, 56 Whitfield Street, London W1, England, 01/580-9592

STRIP POKER Miracle, 1969, British
COOL IT CAROL! Miracle, 1970, British
MAN OF VIOLENCE Miracle, 1971, British
THE FLESH AND BLOOD SHOW Tigon, 1972, British
THE FOUR DIMENSIONS OF GRETA Hemdale, 1972, British
TIFFANY JONES Hemdale, 1973, British
HOUSE OF WHIPCORD Miracle, 1974, British
FRIGHTMARE Miracle, 1975, British
HOUSE OF MORTAL SIN Miracle, 1976, British
THE COMBACK Enterprise, 1978, British
HOME BEFORE MIDNIGHT Heritage/EMI, 1979, British
HOUSE OF THE LONG SHADOWS MGM/UA/Cannon, 1983, British

TOMMY LEE WALLACE*

Agent: David Gersh, The Gersh Agency - Beverly Hills, 213/274-6611

HALLOWEEN III: SEASON OF THE WITCH Universal, 1982
HANAUMA BAY Hanauma Bay Productions, 1985

HERB WALLERSTEIN*

Home: 23701 Mariano Street, Woodland Hills, CA 91367
Agent: Lew Sherrell Agency - Los Angeles, 213/461-9955

SNOWBEAST (TF) Douglas Cramer Productions, 1977

FRED WALTON*

Contact: Directors Guild of America - Los Angeles, 213/656-1220

WHEN A STRANGER CALLS Columbia, 1979
HADLEY'S REBELLION American Film Distributors, 1984

SAM WANAMAKER*

b. June 14, 1919 - Chicago, Illinois
Agent: Ed Limato, William Morris Agency - Beverly Hills, 213/274-7451

THE FILE ON THE GOLDEN GOOSE United Artists, 1969, British
THE EXECUTIONER Columbia, 1970, British
CATLOW MGM, 1971, U.S.-Spanish
SINBAD AND THE EYE OF THE TIGER Columbia, 1977, British
MY KIDNAPPER, MY LOVE (TF) Roger Gimbel Productions/EMI TV, 1980
THE KILLING OF RANDY WEBSTER (TF) Roger Gimbel Productions/EMI TV, 1981

WAYNE WANG

A MAN, A WOMAN, AND A KILLER co-director with Rick Schmidt, 1975
CHAN IS MISSING New Yorker, 1982
DIM SUM CIM Productions, 1984

DAVID S. WARD*

b. October 25, 1945
Home: 246 21st Street, Santa Monica, CA 90402
Agent: Jeff Berg, ICM - Los Angeles, 213/550-4000

CANNERY ROW MGM/United Artists, 1981

CLYDE WARE*

b. December 22, 1934 - West Virginia
Home: 1252 N. Laurel Avenue, Los Angeles, CA 90046, 213/650-8205
Agent: CAA - Los Angeles, 213/277-4545
Business Manager: Jerry Sutter - Beverly Hills, 213/272-4243

NO DRUMS, NO BUGLES Cinerama Releasing Corporation, 1971
THE STORY OF PRETTY BOY FLOYD (TF) Universal TV, 1974
THE HATFIELDS AND THE McCOYS (TF) Charles Fries Productions, 1975
THREE HUNDRED MILES FOR STEPHANIE (TF) Edward S. Feldman Company/Yellow Ribbon Productions/PKO, 1981

ANDY WARHOL
(Andrew Warhola)

b. August 6, 1927 - McKeesport, Pennsylvania
Agent: c/o Leo Castelli Gallery, 4 East 77th Street, New York, NY 10021

KISS Film-Makers, 1963
EAT Film-Makers, 1963
SLEEP Film-Makers, 1963
HAIRCUT Film-Makers, 1963
TARZAN AND JANE REGAINED...SORT OF co-director, Film-Makers, 1964
DANCE MOVIE Film-Makers, 1964
BLOW JOB Film-Makers, 1964
BATMAN DRACULA Film-Makers, 1964
SALOME AND DELILAH Film-Makers, 1964
SOAP OPERA co-director, Film-Makers, 1964
COUCH Film-Makers, 1964
13 MOST BEAUTIFUL WOMEN Film-Makers, 1964
HARLOT Film-Makers, 1964
THE LIFE OF JUANITA CASTRO Film-Makers, 1965
EMPIRE Film-Makers, 1965
POOR LITTLE RICH GIRL Film-Makers, 1965
SCREEN TEST Film-Makers, 1965
VINYL Film-Makers, 1965
BEAUTY #2 Film-Makers, 1965
BITCH Film-Makers, 1965
PRISON Film-Makers, 1965
SPACE Film-Makers, 1965
THE CLOSET Film-Makers, 1965
HENRY GELDZAHLER Film-Makers, 1965
TAYLOR MEAD'S ASS Film-Makers, 1965
FACE Film-Makers, 1965
MY HUSTLER Film-Makers, 1965
CAMP Film-Makers, 1965
SUICIDE Film-Makers, 1965
DRUNK Film-Makers, 1965
OUTER AND INNER SPACE Film-Makers, 1966
HEDY *HEDY THE SHOPLIFTER* Film-Makers, 1966
PAUL SWAN Film-Makers, 1966
MORE MILK, EVETTE *LANA TURNER* Film-Makers, 1965
THE VELVET UNDERGROUND AND NICO Film-Makers, 1966
KITCHEN Film-Makers, 1966
LUPE Film-Makers, 1966
EATING TOO FAST Film-Makers, 1966
THE CHELSEA GIRLS Film-Makers, 1966
I, A MAN Film-Makers, 1967
BIKE BOY Film-Makers, 1967
NUDE RESTAURANT Film-Makers, 1967
FOUR STARS *24-HOUR MOVIE* Film-Makers, 1967
IMITATION OF CHRIST Film-Makers, 1967
THE LOVES OF ONDINE Warhol, 1968
LONESOME COWBOYS Sherpix, 1968
BLUE MOVIE *FUCK* Factory, 1969
WOMEN IN REVOLT Warhol, 1972
L'AMOUR co-director with Paul Morrissey, Altura, 1973

CHARLES MARQUIS WARREN*

b. December 16, 1917 - Baltimore, Maryland
Home: 1130 Tower Road, Beverly Hills, CA 90210
Agent: Evarts Ziegler, Ziegler, Diskant, Inc. - Los Angeles, 213/278-0070

LITTLE BIG HORN Lippert, 1951
HELLGATE Lippert, 1952
ARROWHEAD Paramount, 1953
FLIGHT TO TANGIER Paramount, 1953
SEVEN ANGRY MEN Allied Artists, 1955
TENSION AT TABLE ROCK Universal, 1956
THE BLACK WHIP 20th Century-Fox, 1956
TROOPER HOOK United Artists, 1957
BACK FROM THE DEAD 20th Century-Fox, 1957
THE UNKNOWN TERROR 20th Century-Fox, 1957
COPPER SKY 20th Century-Fox, 1957

CHARLES MARQUIS WARREN*—continued

RIDE A VIOLENT MILE 20th Century-Fox, 1957
DESERT HELL 20th Century-Fox, 1958
CATTLE EMPIRE 20th Century-Fox, 1958
BLOOD ARROW 20th Century-Fox, 1958
CHARRO! National General, 1969

MARK WARREN*

Business Manager: Sheila Lane Reed, 211 S. Beverly Drive, Beverly Hills, CA 90212, 213/273-3442

COME BACK CHARLESTON BLUE Warner Bros., 1972
TULIPS co-director with Rex Bromfield & Al Waxman, all directed under pseudonym of Stan Ferris, Avco Embassy, 1981, Canadian
THE KINKY COACHES AND THE POM-POM PUSSYCATS *CRUNCH* Summa Vista, 1981, Canadian

JOHN WATERS

b. Baltimore, Maryland

MONDO TRASHO Film-Makers, 1970
PINK FLAMINGOS Saliva Films, 1974
FEMALE TROUBLE New Line Cinema, 1975
DESPERATE LIVING New Line Cinema, 1977
POLYESTER New Line Cinema, 1981

PETER WATKINS

b. October 29, 1935 - Norbiton, England
Contact: Swedish Film Institute, Film House, Box 27126, 102 52 Stockholm, Sweden

CULLODEN (TF) BBC, 1964, British
THE WAR GAME Pathe Contemporary, 1966, British
PRIVILEGE Universal, 1967, British
GLADIATORS 1969, Swedish
PUNISHMENT PARK Sherpix, 1971, British
EDVARD MUNCH New Yorker, 1974, Swedish-Norwegian
70-TALETS Manniskor, 1975, Swedish
FALLEN 1975, Swedish
EVENING LAND Panorama-ASA, 1977, Danish

JOHN WATSON

DEATHSTALKER New World, 1983, U.S.-Argentinian

PAUL WATSON

Contact: British Academy of Film & Television Arts, 195 Piccadilly, London W1, England, 01/732-0022

THE ROTHKO CONSPIRACY (TF) BBC/Lionheart TV, 1983, British

ROY WATTS

HAMBONE AND HILLIE New World, 1984

PETER WEBB

Contact: Directors Guild of Great Britain, 56 Whitfield Street, London W1, England, 01/580-9592

GIVE MY REGARDS TO BROAD STREET 20th Century Fox, 1984, British

NICHOLAS WEBSTER*

b. July 24 - Spokane, Washington
Home: 4135 Fulton Avenue, Sherman Oaks, CA 91403, 818/784-5690

GONE ARE THE DAYS! *PURLIE VICTORIOUS* Trans-Lux, 1963
SANTA CLAUS CONQUERS THE MARTIANS Embassy, 1964
MISSION MARS Allied Artists, 1968
NO LONGER ALONE World Wide, 1978, British

DAVID WECHTER*

b. June 27, 1956 - Los Angeles, California
Home: 4508 Farmdale Avenue, North Hollywood, CA 91602, 818/762-6585
Agent: Stu Miller, APA - Los Angeles, 213/273-0744

MIDNIGHT MADNESS co-director with Michael Nankin, Buena Vista, 1980

STEPHEN WEEKS

b. 1948
Address: Penhow Castle, Nr. Newport, Gwent., Penhow 400800, England

GAWAIN AND THE GREEN KNIGHT United Artists, 1972, British
I, MONSTER Cannon, 1974, British
CLASH OF THE SWORDS Cannon, 1984, British

SAMUEL WEIL

Business: Troma, Inc., 733 Ninth Avenue, New York, NY 10019, 212/757-4555

SQUEEZE PLAY! Troma, 1980
WAITRESS! co-director with Michael Herz, Troma, 1982
STUCK ON YOU! co-director with Michael Herz, Troma, 1983
THE FIRST TURN-ON! co-director with Michael Herz, Troma, 1984
THE TOXIC AVENGER co-director with Michael Herz, Troma, 1984

CLAUDIA WEILL*

b. 1947 - New York, New York
Business: Cyclops Films, Inc., 1697 Broadway, New York, NY 10019, 212/265-1375

THE OTHER HALF OF THE SKY: A CHINA MEMOIR (FD) co-director with Shirley MacLaine, 1975
GIRLFRIENDS Warner Bros., 1978
IT'S MY TURN Columbia, 1980
JOHNNY BULL (TF) Titus Productions, 1985

PETER WEIR

b. August 8, 1944 - Sydney, Australia
Business: McElroy & McElroy, 1-3 Atchison Street, St. Leonards, NSW, 2065, Australia, 02/438-4555
Agent: William Morris Agency - Beverly Hills, 213/274-7451

THREE TO GO co-director with Brian Hannant & Oliver Howes, Commonwealth Film Unit Production, 1971, Australian
THE CARS THAT EAT PEOPLE *THE CARS THAT ATE PARIS* New Line Cinema, 1974, Australian
PICNIC AT HANGING ROCK Atlantic Releasing Corporation, 1975, Australian
THE PLUMBER Barbary Coast, 1978, Australian, originally made for television
THE LAST WAVE World Northal, 1978, Australian
GALLIPOLI Paramount, 1981, Australian
THE YEAR OF LIVING DANGEROUSLY MGM/UA, 1983, Australian
WITNESS Paramount, 1985

DON WEIS*

b. May 13, 1922 - Milwaukee, Wisconsin
Agent: Irving Salkow Agency - Beverly Hills, 213/276-3141

BANNERLINE MGM, 1951
IT'S A BIG COUNTRY co-director with Charles Vidor, Richard Thorpe, John Sturges, Don Hartman, Clarence Brown & William Wellman, MGM, 1951
JUST THIS ONCE MGM, 1952
YOU FOR ME MGM, 1952
I LOVE MELVIN MGM, 1953
REMAINS TO BE SEEN MGM, 1953
A SLIGHT CASE OF LARCENY MGM, 1953
THE AFFAIRS OF DOBIE GILLIS MGM, 1953
HALF A HERO MGM, 1953
THE ADVENTURES OF HAJJI BABA 20th Century-Fox, 1954
RIDE THE HIGH IRON Columbia, 1957
MR. PHARAOH AND HIS CLEOPATRA 1959
THE GENE KRUPA STORY Columbia, 1960
CRITIC'S CHOICE Warner Bros., 1963
LOOKING FOR LOVE MGM, 1964
PAJAMA PARTY American International, 1964
BILLIE United Artists, 1965
THE GHOST IN THE INVISIBLE BIKINI American International, 1966
THE KING'S PIRATE Universal, 1967
THE LONGEST 100 MILES (TF) Universal TV, 1967
NOW YOU SEE IT, NOW YOU DON'T (TF) Universal TV, 1968
DID YOU HEAR THE ONE ABOUT THE TRAVELING SALESLADY? Universal, 1968
DEADLOCK (TF) Universal TV, 1969
THE MILLIONAIRE (TF) Don Fedderson Productions, 1978
ZERO TO SIXTY First Artists, 1978
THE MUNSTERS' REVENGE (TF) Universal TV, 1981

GARY WEIS

JIMI HENDRIX (FD) co-director with Joe Boyd & John Head, Warner Bros., 1973
ALL YOU NEED IS CASH (TF) co-director with Eric Idle, Rutles Corps Productions, 1978, British
80 BLOCKS FROM TIFFANY'S (FD) Above Average Productions, 1980
WHOLLY MOSES Columbia, 1980
YOUNG LUST RSO Films, 1982
MARLEY (FD) Island Alive, 1985

ORSON WELLES

b. May 6, 1916 - Kenosha, Wisconsin

CITIZEN KANE RKO Radio, 1941
THE MAGNIFICENT AMBERSONS RKO Radio, 1942
THE STRANGER RKO Radio, 1946
THE LADY FROM SHANGHAI Columbia, 1948
MACBETH Republic, 1948
OTHELLO United Artists, 1952, U.S.-Italian
MR. ARKADIN Warner Bros., 1955, Spanish-Swiss
TOUCH OF EVIL Universal, 1958
THE TRIAL Astor, 1963, French-Italian-West German
CHIMES AT MIDNIGHT *FALSTAFF* Peppercorn-Wormser, 1967, Spanish-Swiss
THE IMMORTAL STORY Altura, 1969, French, originally made for television
THE OTHER SIDE OF THE WIND 1972, unfinished
F FOR FAKE Specialty, 1977, French-Iranian-West German

WIM WENDERS*

b. 1945 - Dusseldorf, West Germany
Agent: Paul Kohner, Inc. - Los Angeles, 213/550-1060
Business Manager: Jess S. Morgan & Company, 6420 Wilshire Blvd., Los Angeles, CA 90048, 213/651-1601

SUMMER IN THE CITY (DEDICATED TO THE KINKS) 1970, West German
THE GOALIE'S ANXIETY AT THE PENALTY KICK Bauer International, 1972, West German
THE SCARLET LETTER Bauer International, 1973, West German-Spanish
ALICE IN THE CITIES New Yorker, 1974, West German
THE WRONG MOVE New Yorker, 1975, West German
KINGS OF THE ROAD Bauer International, 1976, West German
THE AMERICAN FRIEND New Yorker, 1977, West German-French
LIGHTNING OVER WATER *NICK'S MOVIE* co-director with Nicholas Ray, Pari Films, 1980, West German-Swiss-U.S.
THE STATE OF THINGS Gray City, 1982, U.S.-West German-Portuguese
HAMMETT Orion/Warner Bros., 1982
PARIS, TEXAS TLC Films/20th Century Fox, 1984, West German-French

PAUL WENDKOS*

b. September 20, 1922 - Philadelphia, Pennsylvania
Home: 19706 Pacific Coast Highway, Malibu, CA 90265
Agent: Fred Specktor, CAA - Los Angeles, 213/277-4545

THE BURGLAR Columbia, 1957
THE CASE AGAINST BROOKLYN Columbia, 1958
TARAWA BEACHHEAD Columbia, 1958
GIDGET Columbia, 1959
FACE OF A FUGITIVE Columbia, 1959
BATTLE OF THE CORAL SEA Columbia, 1959
BECAUSE THEY'RE YOUNG Columbia, 1960
GIDGET GOES HAWAIIAN Columbia, 1961
ANGEL BABY Allied Artists, 1961
TEMPLE OF THE SWINGING DOLL 20th Century-Fox, 1961
GIDGET GOES TO ROME Columbia, 1963
RECOIL Lion, 1963
JOHNNY TIGER Universal, 1966
ATTACK ON THE IRON COAST United Artists, 1968, U.S.-British
HAWAII FIVE-O (TF) Leonard Freeman Productions, 1968
GUNS OF THE MAGNIFICENT SEVEN United Artists, 1969
FEAR NO EVIL (TF) Universal TV, 1969
CANNON FOR CORDOBA United Artists, 1970
THE BROTHERHOOD OF THE BELL (TF) Cinema Center, 1970
THE MEPHISTO WALTZ 20th Century-Fox, 1971
TRAVIS LOGAN, D.A. (TF) QM Productions, 1971
A TATTERED WEB (TF) Metromedia Productions, 1971
A LITTLE GAME (TF) Universal TV, 1971
A DEATH OF INNOCENCE (TF) Mark Carliner Productions, 1971
THE DELPHI BUREAU (TF) Warner Bros. TV, 1972
THE FAMILY RICO (TF) CBS, Inc., 1972
HAUNTS OF THE VERY RICH (TF) ABC Circle Films, 1972
FOOTSTEPS (TF) Metromedia Productions, 1972
THE STRANGERS IN 7A (TF) Palomar Pictures International, 1972
HONOR THY FATHER (TF) Metromedia Productions, 1973
TERROR ON THE BEACH (TF) 20th Century-Fox TV, 1973
THE UNDERGROUND MAN (TF) Paramount TV, 1974
THE LEGEND OF LIZZIE BORDEN (TF) Paramount TV, 1975
DEATH AMONG FRIENDS (TF) Douglas S. Cramer Productions/Warner Bros. TV, 1975
SPECIAL DELIVERY American International, 1976
THE DEATH OF RICHIE (TF) Henry Jaffe Enterprises, 1977
SECRETS (TF) The Jozak Company, 1977
GOOD AGAINST EVIL (TF) Frankel-Bolen Productions/20th Century-Fox TV, 1977
HAROLD ROBBINS' 79 PARK AVENUE (MS) Universal TV, 1978
BETRAYAL (TF) Roger Gimbel Productions/EMI TV, 1978
A WOMAN CALLED MOSES (TF) Henry Jaffe Enterprises, 1978
THE ORDEAL OF PATTY HEARST (TF) Finnegan Associates/David Paradine TV, 1979
ACT OF VIOLENCE (TF) Emmett G. Lavery, Jr. Productions/Paramount TV, 1979

PAUL WENDKOS*—continued

THE ORDEAL OF DR. MUDD (TF) BSR Productions/Marble Arch Productions, 1980
A CRY FOR LOVE (TF) Charles Fries Productions/Alan Sacks Productions, 1980
THE FIVE OF ME (TF) Jack Farren Productions/Factor-Newland Production Corporation, 1981
GOLDEN GATE (TF) Lin Bolen Productions/Warner Bros. TV, 1981
FARRELL FOR THE PEOPLE (TF) InterMedia Entertainment/TAL Productions/ MGM-UA TV, 1982
COCAINE: ONE MAN'S SEDUCTION (TF) Charles Fries Productions/David Goldsmith Productions, 1983
INTIMATE AGONY (TF) Henerson-Hirsch Productions/Robert Papazian Productions, 1983
BOONE (TF) Lorimar Productions, 1983
CELEBRITY (MS) NBC Productions, 1984
SCORNED AND SWINDLED (TF) Cypress Point Productions, 1984
THE EXECUTION (TF) Newland-Raynor Productions/Comworld Productions, 1985
THE BAD SEED (TF) Hajeno Productions/Warner Bros. TV, 1985

JEFF WERNER*

Home: 4212 Teesdale Avenue, Studio City, CA 91604, 818/769-8651
Messages: 213/464-3511
Agent: Melinda Jason, The Artists Agency - Los Angeles, 213/277-7779

CHEERLEADERS' WILD WEEKEND Dimension, 1979
DIE LAUGHING Orion/Warner Bros., 1980

PETER WERNER*

b. January 17, 1947 - New York, New York
Home: 359 20th Street, Santa Monica, CA 90402, 213/395-4383
Agent: Leading Artists - Beverly Hills, 213/858-1999

FINDHORD (FD) Moving Pictures, 1976
BATTERED (TF) Henry Jaffe Enterprises, 1978
AUNT MARY (TF) Henry Jaffe Enterprises, 1979
DON'T CRY, IT'S ONLY THUNDER Sanrio, 1981, U.S.-Japanese
HARD KNOX (TF) A. Shane Company, 1984
I MARRIED A CENTERFOLD (TF) Moonlight II Productions, 1984
PRISONERS 20th Century Fox, 1984, New Zealand
SINS OF THE FATHER (TF) Fries Entertainment, 1985

LINA WERTMULLER

(Arcangela Felice Assunta Wertmuller von Elgg Spanol von Braueich)

b. August 14, 1928 - Rome, Italy
Contact: Ministry of Tourism & Education, Via Della Ferratella, No. 51, 00184 Rome, Italy, 06/7732

I BALISCHI 22 Dicembre/Galatea, 1963, Italian
LET'S TALK ABOUT MEN *QUESTA VOLTA PARLIAMO DI UOMINI* Allied Artists, 1965, Italian
RITA LA ZANZARA Mondial, 1966, Italian
NON STUZZICATE LA ZANZARA Mondial, 1967, Italian
THE SEDUCTION OF MIMI *MIMI METALLURGICO FERITO NELL'ONORE* New Line Cinema, 1972, Italian
LOVE AND ANARCHY *FILM D'AMORE E D'ANARCHIA* Peppercorn-Wormser, 1973, Italian
ALL SCREWED UP *TUTTO A POSTE E NIENTE IN ORDINE* New Line Cinema, 1974, Italian
SWEPT AWAY BY AN UNUSUAL DESTINY IN THE BLUE SEA OF AUGUST Cinema 5, 1974, Italian
SEVEN BEAUTIES *PASQUALINO SETTEBELLEZZE* ★ Cinema 5, 1976, Italian
THE END OF THE WORLD IN OUR USUAL BED IN A NIGHT FULL OF RAIN Warner Bros., 1978, Italian-U.S.

LINA WERTMULLER —continued

BLOOD FEUD *FATTO DI SANGUE FRA DUE UOMINI PER CAUSA DI UNA VEDOVA (SI SOSPETTANO MOVENTI POLITICI)* AFD, 1980, Italian
A JOKE OF DESTINY lying in wait around the corner like a street bandit Samuel Goldwyn Company, 1983, Italian
SOTTO, SOTTO Triumph/Columbia, 1984, Italian

ERIC WESTON*

Agent: Artists Group, Ltd. - Los Angeles, 213/552-1100

THEY WENT THAT-A-WAY AND THAT-A-WAY International Picture Show Company, 1979
EVILSPEAK The Frank Moreno Company, 1982
MARVIN AND TIGE *LIKE FATHER AND SON* 20th Century-Fox International Classics, 1983
DREAMS OF GOLD co-director with John Agras, Hemdale, 1985

HASKELL WEXLER*

b. 1926 - Chicago, Illinois
Home: 3659 Las Flores Canyon Road, Malibu, CA 90265, 213/456-3438

MEDIUM COOL Paramount, 1969
BRAZIL: A REPORT ON TORTURE (FD) co-director with Saul Landau, 1971
INTRODUCTION TO THE ENEMY (FD) co-director, 1974
UNDERGROUND (FD) co-director with Emile De Antonio & Mary Lampson, New Yorker, 1976
BUS II (FD) co-director with Bonnie Bass Parker & Tom Tyson, 1983

CLAUDE WHATHAM

Address: Camp House, Camp, Miserden, Stroud, Gloucestershire, England

THAT'LL BE THE DAY EMI, 1974, British
ALL CREATURES GREAT AND SMALL (TF) Talent Associates/EMI TV, 1975, British
SWALLOWS AND AMAZONS LDS, 1977, British
SWEET WILLIAM Kendon Films, 1980, British
HOODWINK CB Films, 1981, Australian
MURDER IS EASY (TF) David L. Wolper-Stan Margulies Productions/Warner Bros. TV, 1982

JIM WHEAT

Business: New Empire Films, 650 N. Bronson - Suite 144, Los Angeles, CA 90004, 213/461-8535

LIES co-director with Ken Wheat, New Empire, 1983

KEN WHEAT

Business: New Empire Films, 650 N. Bronson - Suite 144, Los Angeles, CA 90004, 213/461-8535

LIES co-director with Jim Wheat, New Empire, 1983

WILLIAM WIARD*

Agent: Triad Artists, Inc. - Los Angeles, 213/556-2727

SCOTT FREE (TF) Cherokee Productions/Universal TV, 1976
SKI LIFT TO DEATH (TF) The Jozak Company/Paramount TV, 1982
THE GIRL, THE GOLD WATCH AND EVERYTHING (TF) Fellows-Keegan Company/Paramount TV, 1980
TOM HORN Warner Bros., 1980
THIS HOUSE POSSESSED (TF) Mandy Productions, 1981
HELP WANTED: MALE (TF) QM Productions/Brademan-Self Productions, 1982

WILLIAM WIARD*—continued

FANTASIES (TF) Mandy Productions, 1982
DEADLY LESSONS (TF) Leonard Goldberg Productions, 1983

DAVID WICKES

Business: David Wickes Television Ltd., Twickenham Film Studios, St. Margaret's, Twickenham, Middlesex TW1 2AW, England, 01/892-4477
Agent: John Redway & Associates, 16 Berners Street, London W1, England, 01/637-1612

SWEENEY EMI, 1977, British
SILVER DREAM RACER Almi Cinema 5, 1980, British
CHANDLERTOWN *PHILIP MARLOWE - PRIVATE EYE* co-director with Sidney Hayers, Bryan Forbes & Peter Hunt, HBO/David Wickes Television Ltd./ London Weekend Television, 1983, British

BERNHARD WICKI*

b. October 28, 1919 - St. Polten, Austria
Home: Weissgerberstrasse 2, Munich 23, West Germany, 009-36-12-684 or: Restelbergstrase 60, 8 Zurich, Switzerland, 00411-361-37-45
Agent: Alexander Agency, William Morris Organization, 80 Lamontstrasse, 8 Munich, West Germany, 089-47-60-81

WARUM SIND SIE GEGEN UNS? 1958, West German
THE BRIDGE Allied Artists, 1959, West German
DAS WUNDER DES MALACHIAS 1961, West German
THE LONGEST DAY co-director with Ken Annakin & Andrew Marton, 20th Century-Fox, 1962
THE VISIT 20th Century-Fox, 1964, West German-Italian-French-U.S.
MORITURI *THE SABOTEUR, CODE NAME "MORITURI"* 20th Century-Fox, 1965
TRANSIT 1966, West German
QUADRIGA co-director, 1967, West German
DAS FALSCHE GEWICHT 1971, West German
DIE EROBERUNG DER ZITADELLE Scorpion Film, 1977, West German

BO WIDERBERG

b. June 8, 1930 - Malmo, Sweden
Contact: Swedish Film Institute, P.O. Box 27126, 102 52 Stockholm, Sweden, 08/63-0510

THE BABY CARRIAGE Europa Film, 1962, Swedish
RAVEN'S END New Yorker, 1963, Swedish
LOVE 65 Europa Film, 1965, Swedish
THIRTY TIMES YOUR MONEY Europa Film, 1965, Swedish
ELVIRA MADIGAN Cinema 5, 1967, Swedish
THE WHITE GAME co-director, 1968, Swedish
ADALEN '31 Paramount, 1971, Swedish-U.S.
JOE HILL Paramount, 1971, Swedish-U.S.
FIMPEN 1974, Swedish
MAN ON THE ROOF Cinema 5, 1977, Swedish
VICTORIA 1979, Swedish-West German
GRISFESTEN Nordiskfilm/Svensk Filmindustri/TV2/Drakfilm/Svenska Filminstitut, 1983, Swedish-Danish

KEN WIEDERHORN*

Agent: William Morris Agency - Beverly Hills, 213/274-7451

SHOCK WAVES Joseph Brenner Associates, 1977
KING FRAT Mad Makers, 1979
EYES OF A STRANGER Warner Bros., 1981
MEATBALLS PART II Tri-Star, 1984

ROBERT WIEMER

Business: Tigerfilm, Inc., 204 East 60th Street, New York, NY 10022, 212/319-8360

ANNA TO THE INFINITE POWER Tigerfilm, 1983
SOMEWHERE, TOMORROW Comworld, 1984

CORNEL WILDE*

b. October 13, 1915 - New York, New York
Home: 10450 Wilshire Blvd., Los Angeles, CA 90024, 213/474-3589
Business Manager: Jess S. Morgan & Company, 6420 Wilshire Blvd., Los Angeles, CA 90048, 213/651-1601

STORM FEAR United Artists, 1956
THE DEVIL'S HAIRPIN Paramount, 1957
MARACAIBO Paramount, 1958
THE SWORD OF LANCELOT *LANCELOT AND GUINEVERE* Universal, 1963, British
THE NAKED PREY Paramount, 1966, U.S.-South African
BEACH RED United Artists, 1967
NO BLADE OF GRASS MGM, 1970, British
SHARK'S TREASURE United Artists, 1975

BILLY WILDER*

(Samuel Wilder)

b. June 22, 1906 - Vienna, Austria
Agent: Paul Kohner, Inc. - Los Angeles, 213/550-1060
Business Manager: Equitable Investment Corporation - Los Angeles, 213/469-2975

MAUVAISE GRAINE co-director with Alexander Esway, 1933, German
THE MAJOR AND THE MINOR Paramount, 1942
FIVE GRAVES TO CAIRO Paramount, 1943
DOUBLE INDEMNITY ★ Paramount, 1944
THE LOST WEEKEND ★★ Paramount, 1945
THE EMPEROR WALTZ Paramount, 1948
A FOREIGN AFFAIR Paramount, 1948
SUNSET BOULEVARD ★★ Paramount, 1950
THE BIG CARNIVAL *ACE IN THE HOLE* Paramount, 1951
STALAG 17 ★ Paramount, 1953
SABRINA ★ Paramount, 1954
THE SEVEN YEAR ITCH 20th Century-Fox, 1955
THE SPIRIT OF ST. LOUIS Warner Bros., 1957
LOVE IN THE AFTERNOON Allied Artists, 1957
WITNESS FOR THE PROSECUTION ★ United Artists, 1958
SOME LIKE IT HOT ★ United Artists, 1959
THE APARTMENT ★★ United Artists, 1960
ONE, TWO, THREE United Artists, 1961
IRMA LA DOUCE United Artists, 1963
KISS ME, STUPID Lopert, 1964
THE FORTUNE COOKIE United Artists, 1966
THE PRIVATE LIFE OF SHERLOCK HOLMES United Artists, 1970, U.S.-British
AVANTI! United Artists, 1972, U.S.-Italian
THE FRONT PAGE Universal, 1974
FEDORA United Artists, 1979, West German-French
BUDDY BUDDY MGM/United Artists, 1981

GENE WILDER*

(Jerry Silberman)

b. June 11, 1935 - Milwaukee, Wisconsin
Business: 9350 Wilshire Blvd. - Suite 400, Beverly Hills, CA 90212, 213/277-2211

THE ADVENTURE OF SHERLOCK HOLMES' SMARTER BROTHER 20th Century-Fox, 1975
THE WORLD'S GREATEST LOVER 20th Century-Fox, 1977

GENE WILDER*—continued

SUNDAY LOVERS co-director with Bryan Forbes, Edouard Molinaro & Dino Risi, MGM/United Artists, 1981, U.S.-British-French-Italian
THE WOMAN IN RED Orion, 1984

GORDON WILES*

Home: 17123 Adlon Road, Encino, CA 91436, 818/788-2536

GINGER IN THE MORNING National Film, 1974

OSCAR WILLIAMS*

b. May 20, 1944 - St. Croix, Virgin Islands
Home: 856 S. St. Andrews Place, Los Angeles, CA 90005, 213/387-6487
Agent: Stephanie Rogers & Associates - Los Angeles, 213/278-2015

THE FINAL COMEDOWN New World, 1972
FIVE ON THE BLACK HAND SIDE United Artists, 1973
HOT POTATO Warner Bros., 1976

PAUL WILLIAMS*

b. 1944 - New York, New York
Messages: 213/457-3946
Agent: Robert Littman, Leading Artists - Beverly Hills, 213/858-1999

OUT OF IT United Artists, 1969
THE REVOLUTIONARY United Artists, 1970
DEALING: OR THE BERKELEY-TO-BOSTON FORTY-BRICK LOST-BAG BLUES Warner Bros., 1972
NUNZIO Universal, 1978
MISS RIGHT NIR, 1981, Italian

RICHARD WILLIAMS*

b. March 19, 1933 - Toronto, Canada
Home: 3193 Wade Street, Los Angeles, CA 90066, 213/391-0315
Business: Richard Williams Animation, 13 Soho Square, London W1V 5FB, England, 01/437-4455
Richard Williams Animation, 3193 Cahuenga Blvd. West, Hollywood, CA 90068, 213/851-8060

RAGGEDY ANN AND ANDY (AF) 20th Century-Fox, 1977

FRED WILLIAMSON

b. March 5, 1938 - Gary, Indiana
Business: Po' Boy Productions, 5907 W. Pico Blvd., West Los Angeles, CA 90035, 213/855-1285

ADIOS AMIGO Atlas, 1976
MEAN JOHNNY BARROWS Atlas, 1976
DEATH JOURNEY Atlas, 1976
NO WAY BACK Atlas, 1976
MR. MEAN Lone Star/Po' Boy, 1977, Italian-U.S.
ONE DOWN TWO TO GO Almi Films, 1982
THE LAST FIGHT Marvin Films, 1983
THE BIG SCORE Almi Distribution, 1983

GORDON WILLIS*

Business Manager: Ron Taft - New York City, 212/586-8844

WINDOWS United Artists, 1979

HUGH WILSON*

Personal Manager: The Brillstein Company - Los Angeles, 213/275-6135
Business Manager: John Mucci & Associates - Los Angeles, 213/273-1301

POLICE ACADEMY The Ladd Company/Warner Bros., 1984
RUSTLER'S RHAPSODY Paramount, 1985

RICHARD WILSON*

b. December 25, 1915 - McKeesport, Pennsylvania
Home: 501 Ocean Front, Santa Monica, CA 90402, 213/395-0012
Agent: Harold Greene, Eisenbach-Greene, Inc. - Los Angeles, 213/659-3420
Attorney: Gunther Schiff - Beverly Hills, 213/278-2752

MAN WITH THE GUN United Artists, 1955
THE BIG BOODLE United Artists, 1957
RAW WIND IN EDEN Universal, 1958
AL CAPONE Allied Artists, 1959
PAY OR DIE Allied Artists, 1960
WALL OF NOISE Warner Bros., 1963
INVITATION TO A GUNFIGHTER United Artists, 1964
THREE IN THE ATTIC American International, 1968

SIMON WINCER

Business: Michael Edgley International, 190 Exhibition Street, Melbourne, Victoria 3000, Australia, 03/63-5108

TANDARRA (MS) 1976, Australian
THE SULLIVANS (MS) co-director with David Stevens, 1976, Australian
AGAINST THE WIND (MS) co-director with George Miller, Pegasus Productions, 1978, Australian
THE DAY AFTER HALLOWEEN *SNAPSHOT* Group 1, 1979, Australian
HARLEQUIN New Image, 1980, Australian
PHAR LAP 20th Century-Fox, 1983, Australian

HARRY WINER*

Agent: Daniel Richland, The Richland Agency - Los Angeles, 213/553-1257

ONE OF A KIND (TF) ABC, 1982
PAPER DOLLS (TF) Mandy Productions/MGM-UA TV, 1984
SINGLE BARS, SINGLE WOMEN (TF) Carsey-Werner Productions/Sunn Classic Pictures, 1984

MICHAEL WINNER*

b. 1935 - London, England
Business: Scimitar Films, Ltd., 6-8 Sackville Street, London W1X 1DD, England, 01/734-8385
Contact: Directors Guild of Great Britain, 56 Whitfield Street, London W1, England, 01/580-9592

CLIMB UP THE WALL New Realm, 1960, British
SHOOT TO KILL New Realm, 1960, British
OLD MAC Carlyle, 1961, British
SOME LIKE IT COOL Carlyle, 1961, British
OUT OF THE SHADOW New Realm, 1961, British
PLAY IT COOL Allied Artists, 1962, British
THE COOL MIKADO United Artists, 1962, British
WEST 11 Warner-Pathe, 1963, British
THE GIRL GETTERS *THE SYSTEM* American International, 1964, British
YOU MUST BE JOKING! Columbia, 1965, British
THE JOKERS Universal, 1967, British
I'LL NEVER FORGET WHAT'S 'IS NAME Regional, 1968, British
HANNIBAL BROOKS United Artists, 1969, British
THE GAMES 20th Century-Fox, 1970, British
LAWMAN United Artists, 1971
CHATO'S LAND United Artists, 1972
THE NIGHTCOMERS Avco Embassy, 1972, British

MICHAEL WINNER*—continued

THE MECHANIC United Artists, 1972
SCORPIO United Artists, 1973
THE STONE KILLER Columbia, 1973
DEATH WISH Paramount, 1974
WON TON TON, THE DOG WHO SAVED HOLLYWOOD Paramount, 1976
THE SENTINEL Universal, 1977
THE BIG SLEEP United Artists, 1978, British
FIREPOWER AFD, 1979, British
DEATH WISH II Filmways, 1982
THE WICKED LADY MGM/UA/Cannon, 1983, British
SCREAM FOR HELP Lorimar Distribution International, 1984

DAVID WINTERS*

Business: D. W. Productions - Beverly Hills, 213/858-0363
Business Manager: Ron Comins, 2235 Gloaming Way, Beverly Hills, CA 90210, 213/276-8832

WELCOME TO MY NIGHTMARE (FD) Warner Bros., 1976
RACQUET Cal-Am Artists, 1979
JAYNE MANSFIELD - AN AMERICAN TRAGEDY 1981
THE LAST HORROR FILM *FANATIC* Twin Continental, 1983
MISSION KILL Goldfarb Distributors, 1984

FRANZ PETER WIRTH

Contact: Filmforderungsantalt des Offentlichenrechts, Budapester Strasse 41, P.O. Box 301/87, 1000 Berlin 31, West Germany, 49 30/261-6006

INSEL DER ROSEN (TF) Suddeutscher Rundfunk, 1976, West German
BUDDENBROOKS (MS) Taurus Film/Hessisher Rundfunk/TF-1/Film Polski, 1984, West German-French-Polish

HERBERT WISE*

Home: 13 Despard Road, London N19 5NP, England, 01/272-5047
Agent: Tim Corrie, Fraser & Dunlop Ltd., 91 Regent Street, London W1, England, 01/734-7311

TO HAVE AND TO HOLD Warner-Pathe, 1963, British
THE LOVERS! British Lion, 1973, British
THE GATHERING STORM (TF) BBC/Clarion Productions/Levien Productions, 1974, British
SKOKIE (TF) ☆ Titus Productions, 1981
POPE JOHN PAUL II (TF) Alvin Cooperman-Judith DePaul Productions/Taft Entertainment Company, 1984
REUNION AT FAIRBOROUGH (CTF) HBO Premiere Films/Alan Wagner Productions/Alan King Productions/Columbia TV, 1985

ROBERT WISE*

b. September 10, 1914 - Winchester, Indiana
Business: Robert Wise Productions, Sunset Gower Studios, 1438 N. Gower Street, Hollywood, CA 90028, 213/461-3864
Agent: The Gersh Agency - Beverly Hills, 213/274-7451

THE CURSE OF THE CAT PEOPLE co-director with Gunther von Fritsch, RKO Radio, 1944
MADEMOISELLE FIFI RKO Radio, 1944
THE BODY SNATCHER RKO Radio, 1945
A GAME OF DEATH RKO Radio, 1945
CRIMINAL COURT RKO Radio, 1946
BORN TO KILL RKO Radio, 1947
MYSTERY IN MEXICO RKO Radio, 1948
BLOOD ON THE MOON RKO Radio, 1948
THE SET-UP RKO Radio, 1949
TWO FLAGS WEST 20th Century-Fox, 1950
THREE SECRETS Warner Bros., 1950
THE HOUSE ON TELEGRAPH HILL 20th Century-Fox, 1951
THE DAY THE EARTH STOOD STILL 20th Century-Fox, 1951

ROBERT WISE*—continued

THE CAPTIVE CITY United Artists, 1952
SOMETHING FOR THE BIRDS MGM, 1952
THE DESERT RATS 20th Century-Fox, 1953
DESTINATION GOBI 20th Century-Fox, 1953
SO BIG Warner Bros., 1953
EXECUTIVE SUITE MGM, 1954
HELEN OF TROY Warner Bros., 1955, Italian-French
TRIBUTE TO A BAD MAN MGM, 1956
SOMEBODY UP THERE LIKES ME MGM, 1957
THIS COULD BE THE NIGHT MGM, 1957
UNTIL THEY SAIL MGM, 1957
RUN SILENT, RUN DEEP United Artists, 1958
I WANT TO LIVE! ★ United Artists, 1958
ODDS AGAINST TOMORROW United Artists, 1959
WEST SIDE STORY ★★ co-director with Jerome Robbins, United Artists, 1961
TWO FOR THE SEESAW United Artists, 1962
THE HAUNTING MGM, 1963, British-U.S.
THE SOUND OF MUSIC ★★ 20th Century-Fox, 1965
THE SAND PEBBLES 20th Century-Fox, 1966
STAR! *THOSE WERE THE HAPPY TIMES* 20th Century-Fox, 1968
THE ANDROMEDA STRAIN Universal, 1971
TWO PEOPLE Universal, 1973
THE HINDENBURG Universal, 1975
AUDREY ROSE United Artists, 1977
STAR TREK - THE MOTION PICTURE Paramount, 1979

FREDERICK WISEMAN

b. January 1, 1930 - Boston, Massachusetts
Home/Business: Zipporah Films, Inc., 1 Richdale Avenue - Suite 4, Cambridge, MASS 02140, 617/576-3603

TITICUT FOLLIES (FD) Zipporah Films, 1967
HIGH SCHOOL (FD) Zipporah Films, 1968
LAW AND ORDER (FD) Zipporah Films, 1969
HOSPITAL (FD) Zipporah Films, 1970
BASIC TRAINING (FD) Zipporah Films, 1971
ESSENE (FD) Zipporah Films, 1972
JUVENILE COURT (FD) Zipporah Films, 1973
PRIMATE (FD) Zipporah Films, 1974
WELFARE (FD) Zipporah Films, 1975
MEAT (FD) Zipporah Films, 1976
CANAL ZONE (FD) Zipporah Films, 1977
SINAI FIELD MISSION (FD) Zipporah Films, 1978
MANOEUVRE (FD) Zipporah Films, 1979
MODEL (FD) Zipporah Films, 1980
SERAPHITA'S DIARY Zipporah Films, 1982
THE STORE (FD) Zipporah Films, 1983

WILLIAM WITNEY*

b. May 15, 1910 - Lawton, Oklahoma
Agent: Lew Deuser, Armstrong-Deuser Agency - Beverly Hills, 213/553-8611

THE TRIGGER TRIO Republic, 1937
HI-YO SILVER co-director with John English, Republic, 1940
HEROES OF THE SADDLE Republic, 1940
OUTLAWS OF PINE RIDGE Republic, 1942
THE YUKON PATROL co-director with John English, Republic, 1942
HELLDORADO Republic, 1946
APACHE ROSE Republic, 1947
BELLS OF SAN ANGELO Republic, 1947
SPRINGTIME IN THE SIERRAS Republic, 1947
ON THE SPANISH TRAIL Republic, 1947
THE GAY RANCHERO Republic, 1948
UNDER CALIFORNIA SKIES Republic, 1948
EYES OF TEXAS Republic, 1948
THE FAR FRONTIER Republic, 1949
THE LAST MUSKETEER Republic, 1952
THE OUTCAST Republic, 1954
HEADLINE HUNTERS Republic, 1955

WILLIAM WITNEY*—continued

CITY OF SHADOWS Republic, 1955
A STRANGE ADVENTURE Republic, 1956
PANAMA SAL Republic, 1957
YOUNG AND WILD Republic, 1958
JUVENILE JUNGLE Republic, 1958
THE COOL AND THE CRAZY American International, 1958
THE BONNIE PARKER STORY American International, 1958
PARATROOP COMMAND American International, 1959
SECRET OF THE PURPLE REEF 20th Century-Fox, 1960
MASTER OF THE WORLD American International, 1961
THE LONG ROPE 20th Century-Fox, 1961
APACHE RIFLES 20th Century-Fox, 1964
THE GIRLS ON THE BEACH Paramount, 1965
ARIZONA RAIDERS Columbia, 1965
FORTY GUNS TO APACHE PASS Columbia, 1967
I ESCAPED FROM DEVIL'S ISLAND United Artists, 1973
DARKTOWN STRUTTERS *GET DOWN AND BOOGIE* New World, 1975

PETER WITTMAN

PLAY DEAD Aquarius, 1981
ELLIE R.S. Releasing, 1984

IRA WOHL

Contact: Directors Guild of Great Britain, 56 Whitfield Street, London W1, England, 01/580-2256

BEST BOY (FD) IFEX Film, 1980

DAN WOLMAN

b. October 28, 1941 - Jerusalem, Israel
Contact: Israel Film Centre, Ministry of Industry & Trade, 30 Agron Street, P.O. Box 299, Jerusalem 94190, Israel, 02/210433

THE MORNING BEFORE SLEEP Toda Films, 1969, Israeli
THE DREAMER Cannon, 1970, Israeli
FLOCH Aldan Films/Floch Ltd., 1972, Israeli
MY MICHAEL Alfred Plaine, 1976, Israeli
HIDE AND SEEK 1980, Israeli
NANA MGM/UA/Cannon, 1983, Italian-U.S.
BABY LOVE (LEMON POPSICLE V) Noah Films, 1983, Israeli
SOLDIER OF THE NIGHT Cannon, 1983, Israeli
UP YOUR ANCHOR (LEMON POPSICLE VI) Noah Films, 1984, Israeli

JOANNE WOODWARD*

b. 1930 - Thomasville, Georgia
Agent: CAA - Los Angeles, 213/277-4545

COME ALONG WITH ME (TF) Rubicon Productions, 1982

CASPER WREDE

Contact: British Academy of Film & Television Arts, 195 Piccadilly, London W1, England, 01/734-0022

PRIVATE POTTER MGM, 1964, British
ONE DAY IN THE LIFE OF IVAN DENISOVICH Cinerama Releasing Corporation, 1971, British-Norwegian
THE TERRORISTS *RANSOM* 20th Century-Fox, 1975, British

TOM WRIGHT*

Home: 213/248-0993
Agent: Tony Ludwig, CAA - Los Angeles, 213/277-4545

TORCHLIGHT Film Ventures International, 1984, U.S.-Mexican

DONALD WRYE*

Agent: John Ptak, William Morris Agency - Beverly Hills, 213/274-7451

THE MAN WHO COULD TALK TO KIDS (TF) Tomorrow Entertainment, 1973
BORN INNOCENT (TF) Tomorrow Entertainment, 1974
DEATH BE NOT PROUD (TF) Good Housekeeping Productions/Westfall Productions, 1975
THE ENTERTAINER (TF) RSO Films, 1976
IT HAPPENED ONE CHRISTMAS (TF) Universal TV, 1977
ICE CASTLES Columbia, 1979
THE HOUSE OF GOD *H.O.G.* United Artists, 1981
FIRE ON THE MOUNTAIN (TF) Bonnard Productions, 1982
DIVORCE WARS: A LOVE STORY (TF) Wrye-Konigsberg Films/Warner Bros. TV, 1982
THE FACE OF RAGE (TF) Hal Sitowitz Productions/Viacom, 1983
HEART OF STEEL (TF) Beowulf Productions, 1983

TRACY KEENAN WYNN*

b. February 28, 1945 - Los Angeles, California
Agent: ICM - Los Angeles, 213/550-4000

HIT LADY (TF) Spelling-Goldberg Productions, 1974

JIM WYNORSKI

b. August 14, 1950 - Long Island, New York
Business: Henry Plitt Productions, 1925 Century Park East - Suite 300, Los Angeles, CA 90067, 213/553-5307

THE LOST EMPIRE JGM Enterprises, 1984

Y

PETER YATES*

b. July 24, 1929 - Aldershot, England
Business: Tempest Productions, 1775 Broadway - Suite 621, New York, NY 10019, 212/974-1158
Agent: Tom Chasin, ICM - Los Angeles, 213/550-4000

SUMMER HOLIDAY American International, 1963, British
ONE WAY PENDULUM Lopert, 1964, British
ROBBERY Avco Embassy, 1967, British
BULLITT Warner Bros., 1968
JOHN AND MARY 20th Century-Fox, 1969
MURPHY'S WAR Paramount, 1971, British
THE HOT ROCK 20th Century-Fox, 1972
THE FRIENDS OF EDDIE COYLE Paramount, 1973
FOR PETE'S SAKE Columbia, 1974
MOTHER, JUGS AND SPEED 20th Century-Fox, 1976
THE DEEP Columbia, 1977
BREAKING AWAY ★ 20th Century-Fox, 1979
EYEWITNESS 20th Century-Fox, 1981
KRULL Columbia, 1983, U.S.-British
THE DRESSER ★ Columbia, 1983, British
ELENI Warner Bros., 1985

LINDA YELLEN*

Business: Chrysalis-Yellen Productions, 421 Hudson Street, Suite 303, New York, NY 10014, 212/675-5566
Home: 3 Sheridan Square, New York, NY 10014, 212/929-6674

COME OUT, COME OUT! 1969
LOOKING UP Levitt-Pickman, 1977
JACOBO TIMERMAN: PRISONER WITHOUT A NAME, CELL WITHOUT A NUMBER (TF) Chrysalis-Yellen Productions, 1983

BUD YORKIN*

(Alan David Yorkin)

b. February 22, 1926 - Washington, Pennsylvania
Business: Bud Yorkin Productions, 1901 Avenue of the Stars, Suite 1600, Los Angeles, CA 90067, 213/557-2323
Agent: Martin Baum, CAA - Los Angeles, 213/277-4545

COME BLOW YOUR HORN Paramount, 1963
NEVER TOO LATE Warner Bros., 1965
DIVORCE AMERICAN STYLE Columbia, 1967
INSPECTOR CLOUSEAU United Artists, 1968, British
START THE REVOLUTION WITHOUT ME Warner Bros., 1970, British
THE THIEF WHO CAME TO DINNER Warner Bros., 1972
TWICE IN A LIFETIME The Yorkin Company, 1985

YAKY YOSHA

Business: Yaky Yosha Ltd., 29 Lilienblum Street, Tel Aviv 65133, Israel, 03/659108

SHALOM Yaky Yosha Ltd., 1973, Israeli
ROCKINGHORSE Sus-Etz, 1978, Israeli
THE VULTURE New Yorker, 1981, Israeli
DEAD END STREET Lelo Motza Ltd., 1982, Israeli
SUNSTROKE Shapira Films, 1984, Israeli

FREDDIE YOUNG

b. 1902 - England
Address: 3 Roehampton Close, London SW15, England
Agent: London Management, 235/241 Regent Street, London W1, England, 01/493-1610
Contact: British Academy of Film & Television Arts, 195 Piccadilly, London W1, England, 01/734-0022

ARTHUR'S HALLOWED GROUND Enigma Productions/Goldcrest Films & Television, 1983, British

JEFFREY YOUNG*

Contact: Directors Guild of America - New York City, 212/581-0370

BEEN DOWN SO LONG IT LOOKS LIKE UP TO ME Paramount, 1971

ROBERT M. YOUNG*

b. November 22, 1924 - New York, New York
Home: 125 West 76th Street, New York, NY 10023, 212/724-0209
Business: Bobwin Associates, Inc., 245 West 55th Street, New York, NY 10019, 212/757-4580
Agent: Sam Cohn, ICM - New York City, 212/556-6810

THE INFERNO *CORTILE CASCINO, ITALY (FD)* co-director with Michael Roemer, Robert M. Young Film Productions, 1962
NOTHING BUT A MAN co-director with Michael Roemer, Cinema 5, 1965
ALAMBRISTA! Bobwin/Films Haus, 1977
SHORT EYES The Film League, 1978
RICH KIDS United Artists, 1979
ONE-TRICK PONY Warner Bros., 1980
THE BALLAD OF GREGORIO CORTEZ Embassy, 1983
SAVING GRACE Embassy, 1985

ROGER YOUNG*

Home: 213/506-6687
Agent: Broder-Kurland Agency - Los Angeles, 213/274-8921

BITTER HARVEST (TF) ☆ Charles Fries Productions, 1981
AN INNOCENT LOVE (TF) Steve Binder Productions, 1982
DREAMS DON'T DIE (TF) Hill-Mandelker Films, 1982
TWO OF A KIND (TF) Lorimar Productions, 1982
HARDCASTLE AND McCORMICK (TF) Stephen J. Cannell Productions, 1983
LASSITER Warner Bros., 1984
GULAG (CTF) Lorimar Productions/HBO Premiere Films, 1985

TERENCE YOUNG*

b. June 20, 1915 - Shanghai, China
Agent: Kurt Frings - Beverly Hills, 213/274-8881

MEN OF ARNHEM (FD) co-director with Brian Desmond Hurst, Army Film Unit, 1944, British
CORRIDOR OF MIRRORS Universal, 1948, British
ONE NIGHT WITH YOU Universal, 1948, British
WOMAN HATER Universal, 1948, British
THEY WERE NOT DIVIDED General Film Distributors, 1950, British
VALLEY OF THE EAGLES Lippert, 1951, British

TERENCE YOUNG*—continued

THE FRIGHTENED BRIDE *THE TALL HEADLINES* Beverly, 1952, British
PARATROOPER *THE RED BERET* Columbia, 1953, British
THAT LADY 20th Century-Fox, 1954, British
STORM OVER THE NILE co-director with Zoltan Korda, Columbia, 1955, British
SAFARI Columbia, 1956, British
ZARAK Columbia, 1956, British
ACTION OF THE TIGER MGM, 1957, British
TANK FORCE *NO TIME TO DIE* Columbia, 1958, British
SERIOUS CHARGE Eros, 1959, British
BLACK TIGHTS Magna, 1960, French
PLAYGIRL AFTER DARK *TOO HOT TO HANDLE* Topaz, 1960, British
DUEL OF CHAMPIONS co-director with Ferdinando Baldi, Medallion, 1961, Italian-Spanish
DR. NO United Artists, 1962, British
FROM RUSSIA WITH LOVE United Artists, 1963, British
THE AMOROUS ADVENTURES OF MOLL FLANDERS Paramount, 1965, British
THUNDERBALL United Artists, 1965, British
THE DIRTY GAME *GUERRE SECRETE* co-director with Christian-Jaque, Carlo Lizzani & Werner Klinger, American International, 1966, French-Italian-West German
TRIPLE CROSS Warner Bros., 1966, British-French
THE POPPY IS ALSO A FLOWER Comet, 1966, European
WAIT UNTIL DARK Warner Bros., 1967
L'AVVENTURIERO Arco Film, 1967, Italian
MAYERLING MGM, 1969, British-French
THE CHRISTMAS TREE Continental, 1969, French-Italian
COLD SWEAT *DE LA PART DES COPAINS* Emerson, 1970, French
RED SUN National General, 1972, French-Italian-Spanish
THE VALACHI PAPERS *JOE VALACHI: I SEGRETI DI COSA NOSTRA* Columbia, 1972, Italian-French
WAR GODDESS *LE GUERRIERE DEL SNO NUDA* American International, 1973, Italian
THE KLANSMAN Paramount, 1974
SIDNEY SHELDON'S BLOODLINE Paramount, 1979
INCHON! MGM/UA, 1982, South Korean
THE JIGSAW MAN United Film Distribution, 1984, British

LARRY YUST*

Agent: Ben Benjamin, ICM - Los Angeles, 213/550-4000

TRICK BABY Universal, 1973
HOMEBODIES Avco Embassy, 1974
TESTIMONY OF TWO MEN (TF) co-director with Leo Penn, Universal TV, 1977

Z

KRZYSZTOF ZANUSSI

b. July 17, 1939 - Warsaw, Poland
Contact: Ministry of Culture and Fine Arts (Central Board of Cinematography), 21/23 Krakowskie Przedmiescie, 00-0071 Warsaw, Poland, 26-7489

THE STRUCTURE OF CRYSTALS 1969, Polish
MOUNTAINS AT DUSK (TF) 1970, Polish
DIE ROLLE (TF) 1971, West German
FAMILY LIFE 1971, Polish
BEHIND THE WALL 1971, Polish
HYPOTHESIS (TF) 1972, Polish
ILLUMINATION 1973, Polish
THE CATAMOUNT KILLING 1974
NIGHT DUTY (TF) 1975, Polish
A WOMAN'S DECISION Tinc, 1975, Polish
CAMOUFLAGE Libra, 1977, Polish
THE SPIRAL 1978, Polish
WAYS IN THE NIGHT TeleCulture, 1980, West German
THE CONSTANT FACTOR New Yorker, 1980, Polish
CONTRACT New Yorker, 1981, Polish
FROM A FAR COUNTRY (POPE JOHN PAUL II) (TF) Trans World Film/ITC/RAI/Film Polski, 1981, British-Italian-Polish
IMPERATIV (TF) TeleCulture, 1982, West German
THE UNAPPROACHABLE TeleCulture, 1982, West German
BLAUBART (TF) Westdeutscher Rundfunk/DRS, 1984, West German-Swiss
THE YEAR OF THE QUIET SUN TeleCulture, 1984, Polish-West German-U.S.

FRANK ZAPPA

b. December 21, 1940 - Baltimore, Maryland

200 MOTELS co-director with Tony Palmer, United Artists, 1971, British
BABY SNAKES Intercontinental Absurdities, 1979

FRANCO ZEFFIRELLI*

b. February 12, 1923 - Florence, Italy
Agent: William Morris Agency - Beverly Hills, 213/274-7451

CAMPING 1957, Italian
LA BOHEME Warner Bros., 1965, Swiss
FLORENCE - DAYS OF DESTRUCTION (FD) 1966, Italian
THE TAMING OF THE SHREW Columbia, 1967, Italian-British
ROMEO AND JULIET ★ Paramount, 1968, Italian-British
BROTHER SUN SISTER MOON Paramount, 1973, Italian-British
JESUS OF NAZARETH (MS) Sir Lew Grade Productions/ITC, 1978, British-Italian
THE CHAMP MGM/United Artists, 1979
ENDLESS LOVE Universal, 1981
I PAGLIACCI (TF) 1981, Italian
LA TRAVIATA Universal Classics, 1982, Italian

ROBERT ZEMECKIS*

b. 1952 - Chicago, Illinois
Agent: Jack Rapke, CAA - Los Angeles, 213/277-4545

I WANNA HOLD YOUR HAND Universal, 1977
USED CARS Columbia, 1980
ROMANCING THE STONE 20th Century Fox, 1984
BACK TO THE FUTURE Universal, 1985

MAI ZETTERLING

b. May 24, 1925 - Vasteras, Sweden
Agent: Douglas Rae Management - London, 01/836-3903

LOVING COUPLES Prominent, 1964, Swedish
NIGHT GAMES Mondial, 1966, Swedish
DOCTOR GLAS 20th Century-Fox, 1968, Danish
THE GIRLS New Line Cinema, 1969, Swedish
VINCENT THE DUTCHMAN 1972, Swedish
VISIONS OF EIGHT (FD) co-director with Yuri Ozerov, Arthur Penn, Michael Pfleghar, Kon Ichikawa, Milos Forman, Claude Lelouch & John Schlesinger, Cinema 5, 1973
WE HAVE MANY NAMES 1976, Swedish
STOCKHOLM (TD) 1977, Canadian
LOVE co-director with Annette Cohen, Nancy Dowd & Liv Ullmann, Velvet Films, 1982, Canadian
SCRUBBERS Orion Classics, 1983, British

HOWARD ZIEFF*

b. 1943 - Los Angeles, California
Agent: Michael Ovitz/Ron Meyer, CAA - Los Angeles, 213/277-4545

SLITHER MGM, 1973
HEARTS OF THE WEST MGM/United Artists, 1975
HOUSE CALLS Universal, 1978
THE MAIN EVENT Warner Bros., 1979
PRIVATE BENJAMIN Warner Bros., 1980
UNFAITHFULLY YOURS 20th Century Fox, 1984

RAFAL ZIELINSKI

Contact: Canadian Film & Television Association, 8 King Street, Toronto, Ontario M5C 1B5, Canada, 416/363-0296

HEY BABE! Rafal Productions/Canadian Film Development Corporation/L'Institut Quebecois du Cinema/Famous Players Ltd., 1980, Canadian
SCREWBALLS New World, 1983, Canadian

VERNON ZIMMERMAN*

Business Manager: Eric Weissman - Beverly Hills, 213/858-7888

DEADHEAD MILES Paramount, 1971
UNHOLY ROLLERS American International, 1972
FADE TO BLACK American Cinema, 1980

ZOE ZINMAN

CITY NEWS co-director with David Fishelson, Cinecom International, 1983

FRED ZINNEMANN*

b. April 29, 1907 - Vienna, Austria
Office: 128 Mount Street, London W1, England, 01/499-8810
Agent: Stan Kamen, William Morris Agency - Beverly Hills, 213/274-7451

THE WAVE (FD) co-director with Emilio Gomez Muriel, Strand, 1935, Mexican
KID GLOVE KILLER MGM, 1942
EYES IN THE NIGHT MGM, 1942
THE SEVENTH CROSS MGM, 1944
LITTLE MR. JIM MGM, 1946
MY BROTHER TALKS TO HORSES MGM, 1947
THE SEARCH ★ MGM, 1948, U.S.-Swiss
ACT OF VIOLENCE MGM, 1949
THE MEN Columbia, 1950
TERESA MGM, 1951
HIGH NOON ★ United Artists, 1952
THE MEMBER OF THE WEDDING Columbia, 1953
FROM HERE TO ETERNITY ★★ Columbia, 1953
OKLAHOMA! Magna, 1955
A HATFUL OF RAIN 20th Century-Fox, 1957
THE NUN'S STORY ★ Warner Bros., 1959
THE SUNDOWNERS ★ Warner Bros., 1960
BEHOLD A PALE HORSE Columbia, 1964
A MAN FOR ALL SEASONS ★★ Columbia, 1966, British
THE DAY OF THE JACKAL Universal, 1973, British-French
JULIA ★ 20th Century-Fox, 1977
FIVE DAYS ONE SUMMER The Ladd Company/Warner Bros., 1982, British

PETER ZINNER

b. July 24, 1919 - Vienna, Austria

THE SALAMANDER ITC, 1981, British-Italian-U.S.

FABRICE ZIOLKOWSKI

b. January 28, 1954 - Charleville, France
Business: McCarroll-Ziolkowski Productions, 1131 Sanborn Avenue, Los Angeles, CA 90029, 213/661-0944

L.A.X. McCarroll-Ziolkowski Productions, 1980

JOSEPH ZITO

b. May 14, 1946 - New York, New York
Home: 11637 Spy Glass Drive, Porter Ranch, CA 91326, 818/366-3536

ABDUCTION United Film Distribution, 1981
THE PROWLER Sandhurst Corporation, 1982
FRIDAY THE 13TH - THE FINAL CHAPTER Paramount, 1984
MISSING IN ACTION Cannon, 1984

DAVID ZUCKER*

Business Manager: Terry Shagin, Shagin & Hyman, 11777 San Vicente Blvd., Los Angeles, CA 90049, 213/820-7717

AIRPLANE! co-director with Jim Abrahams & Jerry Zucker, Paramount, 1980
TOP SECRET! co-director with Jim Abrahams & Jerry Zucker, Paramount, 1984

JERRY ZUCKER*

Business Manager: Shagin & Hyman, 11777 San Vicente Blvd., Los Angeles, CA 90049, 213/820-7717

AIRPLANE! co-director with Jim Abrahams & David Zucker, Paramount, 1980
TOP SECRET! co-director with Jim Abrahams & David Zucker, Paramount, 1984

ALBERT ZUGSMITH*

b. April 24, 1910 - Atlantic City, New Jersey
Home: 1210 N. Wetherly Drive, Los Angeles, CA 90069, 213/275-8221
Messages: 213/276-6627
Agent: Peter Miller - Peter Miller Agency - New York City, 212/221-8329

COLLEGE CONFIDENTIAL Universal, 1960
SEX KITTENS GO TO COLLEGE Allied Artists, 1960
THE PRIVATE LIVES OF ADAM AND EVE Universal, 1960
DONDI Allied Artists, 1961
CONFESSIONS OF AN OPIUM EATER *EVILS OF CHINATOWN* Allied Artists, 1962
THE INCREDIBLE SEX REVOLUTION 1965
MOVIE STAR AMERICAN STYLE OR LSD - I HATE YOU 1966
ON HER BED OF ROSES 1966
THE VERY FRIENDLY NEIGHBORS 1969
TWO ROSES AND A GOLDEN ROD 1969

FRANK ZUNIGA*

Home: 12050 Valleyheart Drive, Apt. 102, Studio City, CA 91604, 818/980-0987
Agent: Michael Douroux, TMI - Los Angeles, 213/273-4000

FURTHER ADVENTURES OF THE WILDERNESS FAMILY - PART 2 Pacific International, 1978
HEARTBREAKER Monarex/Emerson Film Enterprises, 1983
THE GOLDEN SEAL The Samuel Goldwyn Company, 1983
WHAT COLOR IS THE WIND Pisces Productions, 1984

CHARLOTTE ZWERIN*

Home: 43 Morton Street, New York, NY 10014, 212/989-4042

GIMME SHELTER (FD) co-director with Albert Maysles & David Maysles, Cinema 5, 1971
RUNNING FENCE (FD) co-director with Albert Maysles & David Maysles, 1977

EDWARD ZWICK*

Home: 309 Sumac Lane, Santa Monica, CA 90402, 213/459-5116
Agent: Jeff Berg, ICM - Los Angeles, 213/550-4000

PAPER DOLLS (TF) Leonard Goldberg Productions, 1982
HAVING IT ALL (TF) Hill-Mandelker Films, 1982

I N D E X

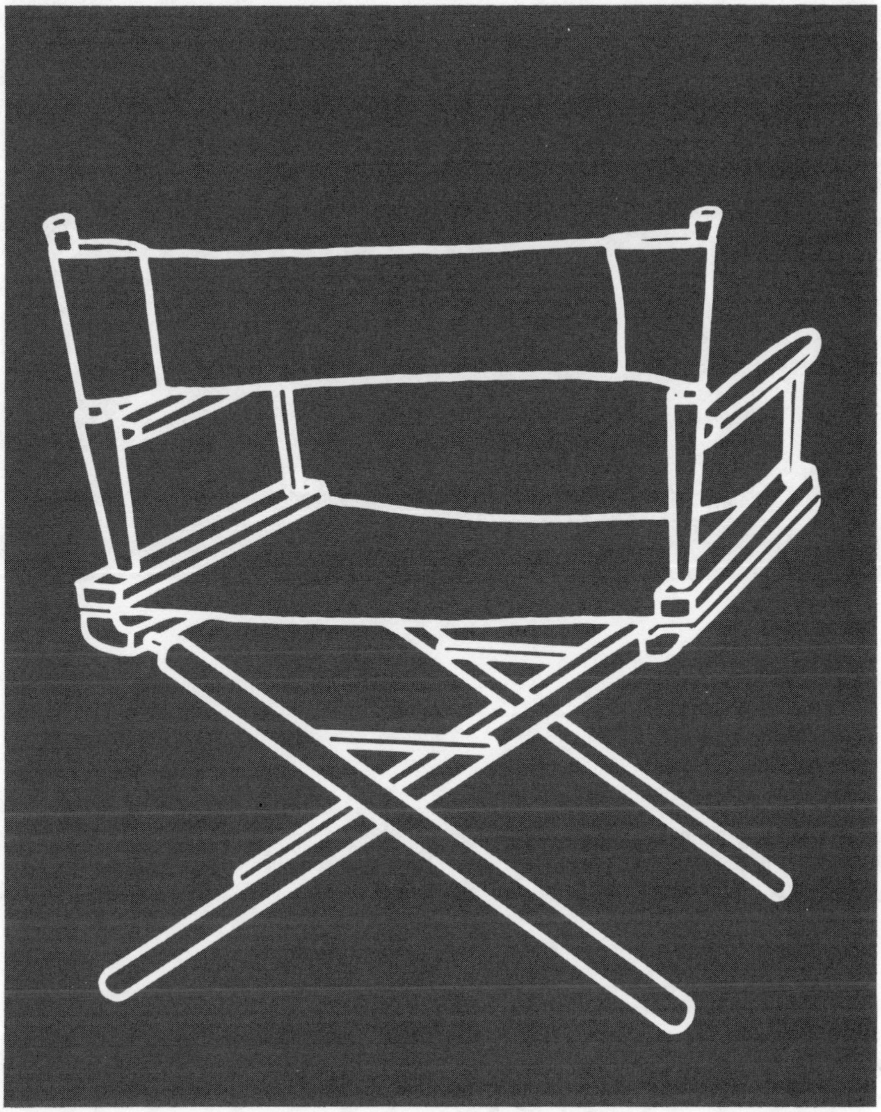

DIRECTORS • FILM TITLES • AGENTS • ADVERTISERS

Index of Directors

IN MEMORIAM

ROBERT ALDRICH	BYRON HASKIN
RICHARD BENEDICT	H. BRUCE HUMBERSTONE
THOROLD DICKINSON	WILLIAM KEIGHLEY
JACK DONOHUE	JOSEPH LOSEY
EDUARDO DE FILIPPO	ROBERT MOORE
CARL FOREMAN	TERRY O. MORSE
YILMAZ GUNEY	JOHN TRENT

FRANÇOIS TRUFFAUT

C

H

I

J

K

L

M

N

O

T

U

V

W

Y

Z

INDEX OF FILM TITLES

NOTE: This is *not* a title index to every film ever made, just to the films listed in this book.

ALFRED THE GREAT ... Clive Donner
ALIAS MR. TWILIGHT ... John Sturges
ALIAS SMITH AND JONES (TF) ... Gene Levitt
ALICE DOESN'T LIVE HERE ANYMORE ... Martin Scorsese
ALICE IN THE CITIES ... Wim Wenders
ALICE IN WONDERLAND ... Bud Townsend
ALICE OU LA DERNIERE FUGUE ... Claude Chabrol
ALICE, SWEET ALICE ... Alfred Sole
ALICE'S RESTAURANT ★ ... Arthur Penn
ALIEN ... Ridley Scott
ALIEN CONTAMINATION ... Lewis Coates
ALIENS ARE COMING, THE (TF) ... Harvey Hart
ALL ABOUT EVE ★★ ... Joseph L. Mankiewicz
ALL AMERICAN PRO ... Arthur Dreifuss
ALL ASHORE ... Richard Quine
ALL AT SEA (TF) ... Igor Auzins
ALL CREATURES GREAT AND SMALL (TF) ... Claude Whatham
ALL FALL DOWN ... John Frankenheimer
ALL GOD'S CHILDREN (TF) ... Jerry Thorpe
ALL IN A NIGHT'S WORK ... Joseph Anthony
ALL MINE TO GIVE ... Allen Reisner
ALL MY DARLING DAUGHTERS (TF) ... David Lowell Rich
ALL NIGHT LONG ... Jean-Claude Tramont
ALL OF ME ... Carl Reiner
ALL OF MYSELF ... Kon Ichikawa
ALL QUIET ON THE WESTERN FRONT (TF) ☆ ... Delbert Mann
ALL SCREWED UP ... Lina Wertmuller
ALL THAT I HAVE ... William F. Claxton
ALL THAT JAZZ ★ ... Bob Fosse
ALL THE FINE YOUNG CANNIBALS ... Michael Anderson
ALL THE KIND STRANGERS (TF) ... Burt Kennedy
ALL THE KING'S MEN ... King Hu
ALL THE LOVING COUPLES ... Mack Bing
ALL THE PRESIDENT'S MEN ★ ... Alan J. Pakula
ALL THE RIGHT MOVES ... Michael Chapman
ALL THE RIGHT NOISES ... Gerry O'Hara
ALL THE RIVERS RUN (CMS) ... George Miller
ALL THE YOUNG MEN ... Hall Bartlett
ALL THESE WOMEN ... Ingmar Bergman
ALL THINGS BRIGHT AND BEAUTIFUL ... Eric Till
ALL THROUGH THE NIGHT ... Vincent Sherman
ALL TOGETHER NOW (TF) ... Randal Kleiser
ALL YOU NEED IS CASH (TF) ... Eric Idle
ALL YOU NEED IS CASH (TF) ... Gary Weis
ALL-AMERICAN BOY, THE ... Charles Eastman
ALLEGRO BARBARO ... Miklos Jancso
ALLEY CATS, THE ... Radley Metzger
ALLEY TRAMP ... Herschell Gordon Lewis
ALLIGATOR ... Lewis Teague
ALLIGATOR NAMED DAISY, AN ... J. Lee Thompson
ALLONSANFAN ... Paolo Taviani
ALLONSANFAN ... Vittorio Taviani
ALMOST PERFECT AFFAIR, AN ... Michael Ritchie
ALMOST SUMMER ... Martin Davidson
ALMOST YOU ... Adam Brooks
ALOHA, BOBBY AND ROSE ... Floyd Mutrux
ALOHA MEANS GOODBYE (TF) ... David Lowell Rich
ALOHA PARADISE (TF) ... Richard Kinon
ALONE IN THE DARK ... Jack Sholder
ALONE ON THE PACIFIC ... Kon Ichikawa
ALONG CAME A SPIDER (TF) ... Lee H. Katzin
ALPHA BETA ... Anthony Page
ALPHA CAPER, THE (TF) ... Robert M. Lewis
ALPHABET CITY ... Amos Poe
ALPHAVILLE ... Jean-Luc Godard
ALTERED STATES ... Ken Russell
ALVAREZ KELLY ... Edward Dmytryk
ALWAYS ... Henry Jaglom
ALWAYS FOR PLEASURE (FD) ... Les Blank
AM TAG ALS DER REGEN KAM ... Gerd Oswald
AMADA AMANTE ... Bruno Barreto
AMADEUS ... Milos Forman
AMARCORD ★ ... Federico Fellini
AMATEUR NIGHT AT THE DIXIE BAR & GRILL (TF) ... Joel Schumacher
AMATEUR, THE ... Charles Jarrott
AMAZING COLOSSAL MAN, THE ... Bert I. Gordon
AMAZING DOBERMANS, THE ... Byron Chudnow
AMAZING GRACE ... Stan Lathan
AMAZING HOWARD HUGHES, THE (TF) ... William A. Graham
AMAZING MR. BLUNDEN, THE ... Lionel Jeffries
AMAZING WORLD OF PSYCHIC PHENOMENA, THE ... Robert Guenette
AMAZONS (TF) ... Paul Michael Glaser
AMBASSADOR, THE ... Menahem Golan
AMBASSADOR, THE ... J. Lee Thompson
AMBER WAVES (TF) ☆ ... Joseph Sargent
AMBUSH AT IROQUOIS POINT (TF) ... Ralph L. Thomas
AMBUSH MURDERS, THE (TF) ... Steven Hillard Stern
AMELIA EARHART (TF) ... George Schaefer
AMERICA AMERICA ★ ... Elia Kazan
AMERICA AT THE MOVIES (FD) ... George Stevens, Jr.
AMERICA IS HARD TO SEE (FD) ... Emile de Antonio
AMERICA REVISITED (TD) ... Marcel Ophuls
AMERICAN BOY (FD) ... Martin Scorsese
AMERICAN CHRISTMAS CAROL, AN (TF) ... Eric Till
AMERICAN DREAM (TF) ... Mel Damski
AMERICAN DREAMER ... Rick Rosenthal
AMERICAN DREAMER, THE (FD) ... Lawrence J. Schiller
AMERICAN FLYER ... John Badham
AMERICAN FRIEND, THE ... Wim Wenders
AMERICAN GIGOLO ... Paul Schrader
AMERICAN GRAFFITI ★ ... George Lucas
AMERICAN HOT WAX ... Floyd Mutrux
AMERICAN IN PARIS, AN ★ ... Vincente Minnelli
AMERICAN MADNESS ... Frank Capra
AMERICAN POP (AF) ... Ralph Bakshi
AMERICAN RASPBERRY ... Brad Swirnoff
AMERICAN SUCCESS CO., THE ... William Richert
AMERICAN TABOO ... Steven Lustgarden
AMERICAN TICKLER ... Chuck Vincent
AMERICAN WEREWOLF IN LONDON, AN ... John Landis
AMERICANA ... David Carradine
AMERICANIZATION OF EMILY, THE ... Arthur Hiller
AMERICATHON ... Neil Israel
AMICI MIEI II ... Mario Monicelli
AMIN: THE RISE AND FALL ... Sharad Patel
AMITYVILLE HORROR, THE ... Stuart Rosenberg
AMITYVILLE II: THE POSSESSION ... Damiano Damiani
AMITYVILLE 3-D ... Richard Fleischer
AMOR BANDIDO ... Bruno Barreto
AMORE E RABBIA ... Marco Bellocchio
AMORE E RABBIA ... Bernardo Bertolucci
AMORE E RABBIA ... Jean-Luc Godard
AMORE E RABBIA ... Carlo Lizzani
AMORI PERICLOSI ... Carlo Lizzani
AMOROUS ADVENTURES OF MOLL FLANDERS, THE ... Terence Young
AMSTERDAM AFFAIR ... Gerry O'Hara
AMSTERDAM KILL, THE ... Robert Clouse
AMY ... Vincent McEveety
AN ELEPHANT CA TROMPE ENORMEMENT ... Yves Robert
ANA Y LOS LOBOS ... Carlos Saura
ANATOMY OF A MURDER ... Otto Preminger
ANATOMY OF A SEDUCTION (TF) ... Steven Hillard Stern
ANATOMY OF AN ILLNESS (TF) ... Richard T. Heffron
ANCHORS AWEIGH ... George Sidney
AND BABY MAKES SIX (TF) ... Waris Hussein
AND GOD CREATED WOMAN ... Roger Vadim
...AND HOPE TO DIE ... René Clement
AND I ALONE SURVIVED (TF) ... William A. Graham
...AND JUSTICE FOR ALL ... Norman Jewison
AND NO ONE COULD SAVE HER (TF) ... Kevin Billington
AND NOTHING BUT THE TRUTH ... Karl Francis
AND NOW MIGUEL ... James B. Clark
AND NOW MY LOVE ... Claude Lelouch
AND NOW THE SCREAMING STARTS ... Roy Ward Baker
AND ONCE UPON A TIME ... John Derek
AND SOON THE DARKNESS ... Robert Fuest
...AND THE BAND PLAYED ON ... Val Guest
AND THE SHIP SAILS ON ... Federico Fellini
AND THERE CAME A MAN ... Ermanno Olmi
...AND YOUR NAME IS JONAH (TF) ... Richard Michaels
ANDERSON TAPES, THE ... Sidney Lumet
ANDREI RUBLEV ... Andrei Tarkovsky
ANDROID ... Aaron Lipstadt
ANDROMEDA STRAIN, THE ... Robert Wise
ANDY ... Richard C. Sarafian
ANDY HARDY COMES HOME ... Howard W. Koch
ANDY WARHOL'S BAD ... Jed Johnson
ANDY WARHOL'S DRACULA ... Paul Morrissey
ANDY WARHOL'S FRANKENSTEIN ... Paul Morrissey
ANDY WARHOL'S WOMEN ... Paul Morrissey
ANGEL ... Neil Jordan
ANGEL ... Robert Vincent O'Neil
ANGEL AND THE WOMAN, THE ... Gilles Carle
ANGEL BABY ... Hubert Cornfield
ANGEL BABY ... Paul Wendkos
ANGEL CITY (TF) ... Philip Leacock
ANGEL DUSTED (TF) ... Dick Lowry
ANGEL FACE ... Otto Preminger
ANGEL IN MY POCKET ... Alan Rafkin
ANGEL ON MY SHOULDER (TF) ... John Berry
ANGEL UNCHAINED ... Lee Madden
ANGELO, MY LOVE ... Robert Duvall
ANGELS BRIGADE ... Greydon Clark
ANGELS DIE HARD ... Richard Compton
ANGELS FROM HELL ... Bruce Kessler
ANGI VERA ... Pal Gabor
ANGRY SILENCE, THE ... Guy Green
ANIMA PERSA ... Dino Risi
ANIMAL BEHAVIOR ... Jenny Bowen
ANIMAL WORLD, THE (FD) ... Irwin Allen
ANIMALS ARE BEAUTIFUL PEOPLE (FD) ... Jamie Uys
ANIMALYMPICS ... Steven Lisberger
ANNA ... Alberto Lattuada
ANNA KARENINA (TF) ... Simon Langton
ANNA LUCASTA ... Arnold Laven
ANNA LUCASTA ... Irving Rapper
ANNA PAVLOVA: A WOMAN FOR ALL TIME ... Emil Loteanu
ANNA TO THE INFINITE POWER ... Robert Wiemer
ANNAPOLIS STORY, AN ... Don Siegel
ANNE OF THE THOUSAND DAYS ... Charles Jarrott
ANNIE ... John Huston
ANNIE GET YOUR GUN ... George Sidney
ANNIE HALL ★★ ... Woody Allen
ANNIVERSARY, THE ... Roy Ward Baker
ANOTHER COUNTRY ... Marek Kanievska
ANOTHER MAN, ANOTHER CHANCE ... Claude Lelouch
ANOTHER MAN'S POISON ... Irving Rapper
ANOTHER PART OF THE FOREST ... Michael Gordon
ANOTHER SHORE ... Charles Crichton
ANOTHER TIME, ANOTHER PLACE ... Michael Radford
ANOTHER WAY TO LOVE (FD) ... Francois Reichenbach
ANOTHER WOMAN'S CHILD (TF) ... John Erman
ANTHONY ADVERSE ... Mervyn Leroy
ANTONIETA ... Carlos Saura
ANTONIO ... Claudio Guzman
ANTONY AND CLEOPATRA ... Charlton Heston
ANY FRIEND OF NICHOLAS NICKLEBY IS A FRIEND OF MINE (TF) ... Ralph Rosenblum
ANY NUMBER CAN PLAY ... Mervyn Leroy
ANY NUMBER CAN WIN ... Henri Verneuil
ANY SECOND NOW (TF) ... Gene Levitt
ANY WEDNESDAY ... Robert Ellis Miller
ANY WHICH WAY YOU CAN ... Buddy Van Horn

ANZACS (MS) .... George Miller
ANZIO .... Edward Dmytryk
APACHE KID, THE .... George Sherman
APACHE RIFLES .... William Witney
APACHE ROSE .... William Witney
APACHE WOMAN, THE .... Roger Corman
APARAJITO .... Satyajit Ray
APARTMENT ★★, THE .... Billy Wilder
APE WOMAN, THE .... Marco Ferreri
APHRODITE .... Robert Fuest
APOCALYPSE NOW ★ ..... Francis Ford Coppola
APPALOOSA, THE .... Sidney J. Furie
APPLAUSE .... Rouben Mamoulian
APPLE, THE .... Menahem Golan
APPLE DUMPLING GANG RIDES AGAIN, THE .... Vincent McEveety
APPOINTMENT, THE .... Sidney Lumet
APPOINTMENT, THE .... Chuck Vincent
APPOINTMENT WITH VENUS .... Ralph Thomas
APPRENTICESHIP OF DUDDY KRAVITZ, THE .... Ted Kotcheff
APRIL FOOLS, THE .... Stuart Rosenberg
AQUARIANS, THE (TF) .... Don McDougall
ARABESQUE .... Stanley Donen
ARABIAN ADVENTURE .... Kevin Connor
ARCH OF TRIUMPH (TF) .... Waris Hussein
ARCHER: FUGITIVE FROM THE EMPIRE, THE (TF) .... Nicholas Corea
ARE YOU IN THE HOUSE ALONE? (TF) .... Walter Grauman
ARENA .... Richard Fleischer
ARENA, THE .... Steve Carver
ARGYLE SECRETS, THE .... Cy Endfield
ARISTOCATS, THE (AF) .... Wolfgang Reitherman
ARIZONA RAIDERS .... William Witney
ARIZONA TERRORS .... George Sherman
ARMORED CAR ROBBERY .... Richard Fleischer
ARNELO AFFAIR, THE .... Arch Oboler
ARNOLD .... Georg J. Fenady
AROUND THE WORLD IN 80 DAYS ★ .... Michael Anderson
AROUND THE WORLD UNDER THE SEA .... Andrew Marton
AROUSERS, THE .... Curtis Hanson
ARRANGEMENT, THE .... Elia Kazan
ARRIVEDERCI, BABY! .... Kenneth "Ken" Hughes
ARROWHEAD .... Charles Marquis Warren
ARRUZA (FD) .... Budd Boetticher
ARSENE LUPIN CONTRE ARSENE LUPIN .... Edouard Molinaro
ARSENIC AND OLD LACE .... Frank Capra
ART OF CRIME, THE (TF) .... Richard Irving
ART OF LOVE, THE .... Norman Jewison
ARTHUR HAILEY'S HOTEL (TF) .... Jerry London
ARTHUR HAILEY'S WHEELS (MS) .... Jerry London
ARTHUR RUBINSTEIN: LOVE OF LIFE (FD) .... Francois Reichenbach
ARTHUR THE KING (TF) .... Clive Donner
ARTHUR'S HALLOWED GROUND .... Freddie Young
ARTURO'S ISLAND .... Damiano Damiani
AS LONG AS THEY'RE HAPPY .... J. Lee Thompson
AS YOUNG AS WE ARE .... Bernard Girard
ASCENSEUR POUR L'ECHAFAUD .... Louis Malle
ASEMBLEA GENERAL .... Tomas Gutierrez Alea
ASH WEDNESDAY .... Larry Peerce
ASHANTI .... Richard Fleischer
ASHES .... Andrzej Wajda
ASHES AND DIAMONDS .... Andrzej Wajda
ASPEN (MS) .... Douglas Heyes
ASPHALT JUNGLE ★, THE .... John Huston
ASSAM GARDEN, THE .... Mary McMurray
ASSASSIN, THE .... Ralph Thomas
ASSASSINATION .... Masahiro Shinoda
ASSAULT .... Sidney Hayers
ASSAULT ON AGATHON .... Laslo Benedek
ASSAULT ON PRECINCT 13 .... John Carpenter
ASSAULT ON THE WAYNE (TF) .... Marvin J. Chomsky
ASSIGNED TO DANGER .... Budd Boetticher
ASSIGNMENT - PARIS .... Robert Parrish
ASSIGNMENT ABROAD .... Arthur Dreifuss
ASSIGNMENT IN LONDON .... Philip Leacock
ASSIGNMENT K .... Val Guest
ASSIGNMENT: INICH (TF) .... David Lowell Rich
ASSISI UNDERGROUND, THE .... Alexander Ramati
ASTROLOGER, THE .... Jim Glickenhaus
ASTRONAUT, THE (TF) .... Robert M. Lewis
ASTRO-ZOMBIES, THE .... Ted V. Mikels
ASYA'S HAPPINESS .... Andrei Konchalovsky
ASYLUM .... Roy Ward Baker
ASYLUM FOR A SPY (TF) .... Stuart Rosenberg
AT HOME AMONG STRANGERS .... Nikita Mikhalkov
AT LONG LAST LOVE .... Peter Bogdanovich
AT THE EARTH'S CORE .... Kevin Connor
ATLANTA CHILD MURDERS, THE (TF) .... John Erman
ATLANTIC CITY ★ .... Louis Malle
ATLAS .... Roger Corman
ATOMIC CITY, THE .... Jerry Hopper
ATOMIC KID, THE .... Leslie H. Martinson
ATOMIC MAN, THE ...... Kenneth "Ken" Hughes
ATTACK OF THE CRAB MONSTERS .... Roger Corman
ATTACK OF THE PUPPET PEOPLE .... Bert I. Gordon
ATTACK ON FEAR (TF) .... Mel Damski
ATTACK ON TERROR: THE FBI VS. THE KU KLUX KLAN (TF) .... Marvin J. Chomsky
ATTACK ON THE IRON COAST .... Paul Wendkos
ATTI ATROCISSIMA DE AMORE E DI VENDETTA .... Sergio Corbucci
ATTIC, THE .... George Edwards
ATTICA (TF) ☆☆ .... Marvin J. Chomsky
ATTILA '74 (FD) .... Michael Cacoyannis
AU COEUR DE LA VIE .... Robert Enrico
AU HASARD, BALTHAZAR .... Robert Bresson
AU PAIR GIRLS .... Val Guest
AU RENDEZ-VOUS DE LA MORT JOYEUSE .... Juan Buñuel
AUDACE COLPO DEI SOLITI IGNOTI .... Nanni Loy
AUDREY ROSE .... Robert Wise
AUNT MARY (TF) .... Peter Werner
AUNTIE MAME .... Morton Da Costa
AURA, THE .... John Mackenzie
AURELIA STEINER .... Marguerite Duras
AURORA (TF) .... Maurizio Ponzi
AUTHOR! AUTHOR! .... Arthur Hiller
AUTOBIOGRAPHY OF A PRINCESS (TF) .... James Ivory
AUTOBIOGRAPHY OF MISS JANE PITTMAN ☆☆, THE (TF) .... John Korty
AUTOGRAPH, THE .... Peter Lilienthal
AUTOMAN (TF) .... Lee H. Katzin
AUTUMN SONATA .... Ingmar Bergman
AUX QUATRE COINS .... Jacques Rivette
AVALANCHE .... Corey Allen
AVALANCHE .... Kaneto Shindo
AVANTI! .... Billy Wilder
AVEC LA PEAU AUTRES .... Jacques Deray
AVENGER, THE .... Albert Band
AVENGING ANGEL .... Robert Vincent O'Neil
AVENGING, THE .... Lyman Dayton
AVIATOR, THE .... George Miller
AVIATOR'S WIFE, THE .... Eric Rohmer
AWAKENING, THE .... Mike Newell
AWAY ALL BOATS .... Joseph Pevney
AWOL .... Herb Freed
AZIT THE PARATROOPER DOG .... Boaz Davidson

B

BAAL (TF) .... Volker Schlondorff
BABE (TF) ☆ .... Buzz Kulik
BABO 73 .... Robert Downey
BABY .... B.W.L. Norton
BABY, THE .... Ted Post
BABY BLUE MARINE .... John Hancock
BABY CARRIAGE, THE .... Bo Widerberg
BABY COMES HOME (TF) .... Waris Hussein
BABY DOLL .... Elia Kazan
BABY FACE MORGAN .... Arthur Dreifuss
BABY FACE NELSON .... Don Siegel
BABY IT'S YOU .... John Sayles
BABY LOVE .... Alastair Reid
BABY LOVE (LEMON POPSICLE V) .... Dan Wolman
BABY MAKER, THE .... James Bridges
BABY SISTER (TF) .... Steven Hillard Stern
BABY SNAKES .... Frank Zappa
BABY, THE RAIN MUST FALL .... Robert Mulligan
BABYSITTER, THE (TF) .... Peter Medak
BACHELOR IN PARADISE .... Jack Arnold
BACHELOR IN PARIS .... John Guillermin
BACHELOR MOTHER .... Garson Kanin
BACHELOR PARTY .... Neil Israel
BACHELOR PARTY, THE .... Delbert Mann
BACHELOR'S DAUGHTER, THE .... Andrew L. Stone
BACK AT THE FRONT .... George Sherman
BACK DOOR TO HELL .... Monte Hellman
BACK FROM THE DEAD .... Charles Marquis Warren
BACK ROADS .... Martin Ritt
BACK STREET .... David Miller
BACK STREET .... Robert Stevenson
BACK TO BATAAN .... Edward Dmytryk
BACK TO GOD'S COUNTRY .... Joseph Pevney
BACK TO THE FUTURE .... Robert Zemeckis
BACK TO THE WALL .... Edouard Molinaro
BACKFIRE .... Paul Almond
BACKFIRE .... Vincent Sherman
BACKLASH .... John Sturges
BACKROADS .... Phillip Noyce
BACKSTAGE AT THE KIROV (FD) .... Derek Hart
BACKSTAIRS AT THE WHITE HOUSE (MS) .... Michael O'Herlihy
BACKTRACK .... Earl Bellamy
BAD AND THE BEAUTIFUL, THE .... Vincente Minnelli
BAD BLOOD .... Mike Newell
BAD BLOOD .... Paul Nicolas
BAD BOYS .... Rick Rosenthal
BAD BUNCH, THE .... Greydon Clark
B.A.D. CATS (TF) .... Bernard L. Kowalski
BAD CHARLESTON CHARLIE .... Ivan Nagy
BAD COMPANY .... Robert Benton
BAD DAY AT BLACK ROCK ★ .... John Sturges
BAD FOR EACH OTHER .... Irving Rapper
BAD MANNERS .... Robert "Bobby" Houston
BAD NEWS BEARS GO TO JAPAN, THE .... John Berry
BAD NEWS BEARS IN BREAKING TRAINING, THE .... Michael Pressman
BAD NEWS BEARS, THE .... Michael Ritchie
BAD PENNY .... Chuck Vincent
BAD RONALD (TF) .... Buzz Kulik
BAD SEED, THE .... Mervyn Leroy
BAD SEED, THE .... Paul Wendkos
BAD SLEEP WELL, THE .... Akira Kurosawa
BAD TIMING/A SENSUAL OBSESSION .... Nicolas Roeg
BADGE 373 .... Howard W. Koch
BADLANDS .... Terrence Malick
BAFFLED! (TF) .... Philip Leacock
BAKER COUNTY USA .... William Fruet
BAKER'S HAWK .... Lyman Dayton
BALA .... Satyajit Ray
BALALAIKA .... Andre De Toth
BALCONY, THE .... Joseph Strick
BALLAD OF ANDY CROCKER, THE (TF) .... George McCowan
BALLAD OF CABLE HOGUE, THE .... Sam Peckinpah
BALLAD OF GREGORIO CORTEZ, THE .... Robert M. Young
BALLAD OF JOSIE, THE .... Andrew V. McLaglen
BALLAD OF NARAYAMA, THE .... Shohei Imamura
BALLAD OF ORIN, THE .... Masahiro Shinoda
BALTIMORE BULLET, THE .... Robert Ellis Miller
BAMBOLE! .... Luigi Comencini
BAMBOLE! .... Dino Risi
BANACEK: DETOUR TO NOWHERE (TF) .... Jack Smight
BANANA PEEL .... Marcel Ophuls
BANANAS .... Woody Allen
BAND OF NINJA .... Nagisa Oshima
BAND OF OUTSIDERS .... Jean-Luc Godard
BAND WAGON, THE .... Vincente Minnelli
BANDIDO .... Richard Fleischer
BANDIT OF SHERWOOD FOREST, THE .... George Sherman
BANDITI A MILANO .... Carlo Lizzani
BANDOLERO! .... Andrew V. McLaglen
BANG BANG .... Chuck Vincent
BANG, BANG, YOU'RE DEAD! .... Don Sharp
BANG THE DRUM SLOWLY .... John Hancock
BANG! .... Jan Troell
BANJO .... Richard Fleischer

BANJO HACKETT: ROAMIN' FREE (TF) ....Andrew V. McLaglen
BANK OF DEPARTURE ....Kaneto Shindo
BANNERLINE ....Don Weis
BANYON (TF) ....Robert Day
BAR MITZVAH BOY (TF) ....Michael Tuchner
BARABBAS ....Richard Fleischer
BARBAGIA ....Carlo Lizzani
BARBARA BROADCAST ....Radley Metzger
BARBARELLA ....Roger Vadim
BARBARIAN AND THE GEISHA, THE ....John Huston
BARBAROSA ....Fred Schepisi
BARBARY COAST, THE (TF) ....Bill Bixby
BARE ESSENCE (MS) ....Walter Grauman
BAREFOOT CONTESSA, THE ....Joseph L. Mankiewicz
BAREFOOT EXECUTIVE, THE ....Robert Butler
BAREFOOT IN THE PARK ....Gene Saks
BARNABY AND ME ....Norman Panama
BARON AND THE KID, THE (TF) ....Gene Nelson
BARON OF ARIZONA, THE ....Samuel Fuller
BARQUERO ....Gordon Douglas
BARRIER ....Jerzy Skolimowski
BARRY LYNDON ★ ....Stanley Kubrick
BARRY McKENZIE HOLDS HIS OWN ....Bruce Beresford
BASIC TRAINING (FD) ....Frederick Wiseman
BASIL OF BAKER STREET (AF) ....Burny Mattinson
BASIL OF BAKER STREET (AF) ....Dave Michener
BASIL OF BAKER STREET (AF) ....John Musker
BASKET CASE ....Frank Henenlotter
BASTA CHE NON SI SAPPIA IN GIRO ....Luigi Comencini
BASTA GUARDARLA ....Luciano Salce
BASTARD, THE (TF) ....Lee H. Katzin
BAT PEOPLE, THE ....Jerry Jameson
BATHING BEAUTY ....George Sidney
BATMAN ....Leslie H. Martinson
BATMAN DRACULA ....Andy Warhol
BATTERED (TF) ....Peter Werner
BATTLE AT APACHE PASS, THE ....George Sherman
BATTLE BEYOND THE STARS ....Jimmy T. Murakami
BATTLE CIRCUS ....Richard Brooks
BATTLE FOR THE PLANET OF THE APES ....J. Lee Thompson
BATTLE HELL ....Michael Anderson
BATTLE OF ALGIERS ★ ....Gillo Pontecorvo
BATTLE OF BRITAIN ....Guy Hamilton
BATTLE OF BRITAIN (FD) ....Frank Capra
BATTLE OF CHINA (FD) ....Frank Capra
BATTLE OF THE BULGE ....Ken Annakin
BATTLE OF THE CORAL SEA ....Paul Wendkos
BATTLE OF THE RIVER PLATE, THE ....Michael Powell
BATTLE OF THE SEXES, THE ....Charles Crichton
BATTLESTAR GALACTICA ....Richard A. Colla
BATTLETRUCK ....Harley Cokliss
BAWDY ADVENTURES OF TOM JONES, THE ....Cliff Owen
BAXTER, VERA BAXTER ....Marguerite Duras
BAXTER! ....Lionel Jeffries
BAY BOY, THE ....Daniel Petrie
BAY OF THE ANGELS ....Jacques Demy
BEACH BLANKET BINGO ....William Asher
BEACH GIRLS, THE ....Pat Townsend
BEACH GUARD IN WINTER, THE ....Goran Paskaljevic
BEACH HOUSE ....John A. Gallagher
BEACH PARTY ....William Asher
BEACH RED ....Cornel Wilde
BEALE STREET ....Alexis Krasilovsky
BEAR ISLAND ....Don Sharp
BEAR, THE ....Richard C. Sarafian
BEARS AND I, THE ....Bernard McEveety
BEAST FROM HAUNTED CAVE ....Monte Hellman
BEAST OF BLOOD ....Eddie Romero
BEAST WITHIN, THE ....Philippe Mora
BEASTMASTER, THE ....Don Coscarelli
BEASTS ARE ON THE STREETS, THE (TF) ....Peter Hunt
BEAT STREET ....Stan Lathan
BEAT THE DEVIL ....John Huston
BEATLEMANIA ....Joseph Manduke
BEAU GESTE ....Douglas Heyes
BEAU JAMES ....Melville Shavelson
BEAU PERE ....Bertrand Blier
BEAUTIFUL DAYS ....Masaki Kobayashi
BEAUTIFUL PEOPLE ....Jamie Uys
BEAUTIFUL PEOPLE II (FD) ....Jamie Uys
BEAUTIFUL STRANGER, THE ....David Miller
BEAUTIFUL SWINDLERS, THE ....Roman Polanski
BEAUTY #2 ....Andy Warhol
BEAUTY AND THE BEAST (TF) ....Fielder Cook
BEAUTY JUNGLE, THE ....Val Guest
BEBERT ET L'OMNIBUS ....Yves Robert
BEBO'S GIRL ....Luigi Comencini
BECAUSE HE'S MY FRIEND (TF) ....Ralph Nelson
BECAUSE OF YOU ....Joseph Pevney
BECAUSE THEY'RE YOUNG ....Paul Wendkos
BECKET ★ ....Peter Glenville
BECKY SHARP ....Rouben Mamoulian
BED SITTING ROOM, THE ....Richard Lester
BEDAZZLED ....Stanley Donen
BEDFORD INCIDENT, THE ....James B. Harris
BEDKNOBS AND BROOMSTICKS ....Robert Stevenson
BEDROOM EYES ....William Fruet
BEDSIDE MANNER ....Andrew L. Stone
BEDTIME STORY ....Ralph Levy
BEEN DOWN SO LONG IT LOOKS LIKE UP TO ME ....Jeffrey Young
BEER ....Patrick Kelly
BEES IN PARADISE ....Val Guest
BEFORE AND AFTER (TF) ....Kim Harlene Friedman
BEFORE THE REVOLUTION ....Bernardo Bertolucci
BEFORE WINTER COMES ....J. Lee Thompson
BEG, BORROW...OR STEAL (TF) ....David Lowell Rich
BEGGAR'S OPERA, THE ....Peter Brook
BEGGERMAN, THIEF (TF) ....Gordon Hessler
BEGGING THE RING (TF) ....Colin Gregg
BEGINNING OF THE END ....Bert I. Gordon
BEGUILED, THE ....Don Siegel
BEHIND LOCKED DOORS ....Budd Boetticher
BEHIND THE GREAT WALL ....Carlo Lizzani
BEHIND THE MASK ....Phil Karlson
BEHIND THE RISING SUN ....Edward Dmytryk
BEHIND THE WALL ....Krzysztof Zanussi
BEHINDERTE ZUNKUFT ....Werner Herzog
BEHOLD A PALE HORSE ....Fred Zinnemann
BEING, THE ....Jackie Kong
BEING THERE ....Hal Ashby
BEING TWO ISN'T EASY ....Kon Ichikawa
BELIEVE IN ME ....Stuart Hagmann
BELINDA ....Richard Franklin
BELL, BARE AND BEAUTIFUL ....Herschell Gordon Lewis
BELL, BOOK AND CANDLE ....Richard Quine
BELL JAR, THE ....Larry Peerce
BELLBOY, THE ....Jerry Lewis
BELLE MA POVERE ....Dino Risi
BELLE SOMMARS ....Elliot Silverstein
BELLE STARR (TF) ....John A. Alonzo
BELLS ARE RINGING ....Vincente Minnelli
BELLS HAVE GONE TO ROME, THE ....Miklos Jancso
BELLS OF SAN ANGELO ....William Witney
BELOW THE BELT ....Robert Fowler
BELSTONE FOX, THE ....James Hill
BEN ....Phil Karlson
BENEATH THE PLANET OF THE APES ....Ted Post
BENEATH THE VALLEY OF THE ULTRAVIXENS ....Russ Meyer
BENGAL BRIGADE ....Laslo Benedek
BENJI ....Joe Camp
BENNY & BARNEY: LAS VEGAS UNDERCOVER (TF) ....Ron Satlof
BENNY AND BUFORD ....Lee Madden
BENNY's PLACE (TF) ....Michael Schultz
BEQUEST TO THE NATION, A ....James Cellan-Jones
BERLIN AFFAIR (TF) ....David Lowell Rich
BERLIN TUNNEL 21 (TF) ....Richard Michaels
BERMUDA DEPTHS, THE (TF) ....Tom Kotani
BERMUDA TRIANGLE, THE .....Dick Friedenberg
BERSAGLIO MOBILE ....Sergio Corbucci
BERSERK! ....James O'Connolly
BERTOLDO BERTOLDINO E...CACASENO ....Mario Monicelli
BEST BOY (FD) ....Ira Wohl
BEST DEFENSE ....Willard Huyck
BEST FRIENDS ....Norman Jewison
BEST FRIENDS ....Noel Nosseck
BEST KEPT SECRETS (TF) ......Jerrold Freedman
BEST LITTLE GIRL IN THE WORLD, THE (TF) ....Sam O'Steen
BEST LITTLE WHOREHOUSE IN TEXAS, THE ....Colin Higgins
BEST MAN, THE ....Franklin J. Schaffner
BEST MAN WINS ....John Sturges
BEST OF ENEMIES, THE ....Guy Hamilton
BEST OF EVERYTHING, THE ....Jean Negulesco
BEST PLACE TO BE, THE (TF) ....David Miller
BETHUNE (TF) ....Eric Till
BETRAYAL ....David Jones
BETRAYAL (TF) ....Gordon Hessler
BETRAYAL (TF) ....Paul Wendkos
BETSY, THE ....Daniel Petrie
BETTA BETTA ....William Byron Hillman
BETTER LATE THAN NEVER ....Bryan Forbes
BETTER LATE THAN NEVER (TF) ....Richard Crenna
BETTY CO-ED ....Arthur Dreifuss
BETWEEN FRIENDS ....Donald Shebib
BETWEEN FRIENDS (CTF) ....Lou Antonio
BETWEEN HEAVEN AND HELL ....Richard Fleischer
BETWEEN MIDNIGHT AND DAWN ....Gordon Douglas
BETWEEN THE LINES ....Joan Micklin Silver
BETWEEN TIME & TIMBUKTU (TF) ....Fred Barzyk
BETWEEN TWO BROTHERS (TF) ....Robert M. Lewis
BETWEEN US GIRLS ....Henry Koster
BETWEEN WIFE AND LADY ....Kon Ichikawa
BEULAH LAND (MS) ....Virgil W. Vogel
BEVERLY HILLS COP ....Martin Brest
BEWARE OF CHILDREN ....Gerald Thomas
BEWARE! THE BLOB ....Larry Hagman
BEWITCHED ....Arch Oboler
BEYOND AND BACK ....James L. Conway
BEYOND ATLANTIS ....Eddie Romero
BEYOND DEATH'S DOOR ....Henning Schellerup
BEYOND EVIL ....Herb Freed
BEYOND GOOD AND EVIL ....Liliana Cavani
BEYOND REASON ....Telly Savalas
BEYOND THE BERMUDA TRIANGLE (TF) ....William A. Graham
BEYOND THE FOG ....James O'Connolly
BEYOND THE LAW ....Norman Mailer
BEYOND THE LIMIT ....John Mackenzie
BEYOND THE POSEIDON ADVENTURE ....Irwin Allen
BEYOND THE REEF ....Frank C. Clark
BEYOND THE VALLEY OF THE DOLLS ....Russ Meyer
BEYOND THIS PLACE ....Jack Cardiff
BIANCO, ROSSO E... ....Alberto Lattuada
BIBLE...IN THE BEGINNING, THE ....John Huston
BIG BAD MAMA ....Steve Carver
BIG BIRD CAGE, THE ....Jack Hill
BIG BLACK PILL, THE (TF) ....Reza Badiyi
BIG BLONDE (TF) ....Kirk Browning
BIG BOB JOHNSON AND HIS FANTASTIC SPEED CIRCUS (TF) ....Jack Starrett
BIG BOODLE, THE ....Richard Wilson
BIG BOUNCE, THE ....Alex March
BIG BRAWL, THE ....Robert Clouse
BIG BUS, THE ....James Frawley
BIG CARNIVAL, THE ....Billy Wilder
BIG CAT, THE ....Phil Karlson
BIG CHIEF, THE ....Henri Verneuil
BIG CHILL, THE ....Lawrence Kasdan
BIG CITY BLUES ....Mervyn Leroy
BIG DEAL ON MADONNA STREET ....Mario Monicelli
BIG DIG, THE ....Ephraim Kishon
BIG DOLL HOUSE, THE ....Jack Hill
BIG FIX, THE ....Jeremy Paul Kagan
BIG GAMBLE, THE ....Richard Fleischer
BIG HAND FOR THE LITTLE LADY, A ....Fielder Cook
BIG HOUSE, U.S.A. ....Howard W. Koch
BIG JAKE ....George Sherman
BIG JOB, THE ....Gerald Thomas

BIG LAND, THE ... Gordon Douglas
BIG MO ... Daniel Mann
BIG MOUTH, THE ... Jerry Lewis
BIG RED ONE, THE ... Samuel Fuller
BIG RIP-OFF, THE (TF) ... Dean Hargrove
BIG RISK, THE ... Claude Sautet
BIG ROSE (TF) ... Paul Krasny
BIG SCORE, THE ... Fred Williamson
BIG SHOW, THE ... James B. Clark
BIG SLEEP, THE ... Michael Winner
BIG STEAL, THE ... Don Siegel
BIG T.N.T. SHOW, THE (FD) ... Larry Peerce
BIG TROUBLE ... John Cassavetes
BIG TRUCK AND POOR CLARE ... Robert Ellis Miller
BIG WEDNESDAY ... John Milius
BIGAMIST, THE ... Ida Lupino
BIGGER SPLASH, A ... Jack Hazan
BIGGEST BUNDLE OF THEM ALL, THE ... Ken Annakin
BIKE BOY ... Andy Warhol
BIKINI BEACH ... William Asher
BILITIS ... David Hamilton
BILL (TF) ... Anthony Page
BILL COSBY, HIMSELF ... William H. Cosby, Jr.
BILL: ON HIS OWN (TF) ... Anthony Page
BILLIE ... Don Weis
BILLION DOLLAR BRAIN ... Ken Russell
BILLIONAIRE, A ... Kon Ichikawa
BILLY BUDD ... Peter Ustinov
BILLY IN THE LOWLANDS ... Jan Egleson
BILLY JACK ... Tom Laughlin
BILLY JACK GOES TO WASHINGTON ... Tom Laughlin
BILLY LIAR ... John Schlesinger
BILLY: PORTRAIT OF A STREET KID (TF) ... Steven Gethers
BILLY THE KID ... David Miller
BILLY TWO HATS ... Ted Kotcheff
BIM ... Hugh A. Robertson
BINGO LONG TRAVELING ALL STARS AND MOTOR KINGS, THE ... John Badham
BIOHAZARD ... Hal Barwood
BIRCH INTERVAL ... Delbert Mann
BIRCH-WOOD, THE ... Andrzej Wajda
BIRD ON A WIRE (FD) ... Tony Palmer
BIRD WITH THE CRYSTAL PLUMAGE, THE ... Dario Argento
BIRDMAN OF ALCATRAZ ... John Frankenheimer
BIRDMEN, THE (TF) ... Philip Leacock
BIRDS DO IT ... Andrew Marton
BIRDS OF PREY (TF) ... William A. Graham
BIRDY ... Alan Parker
BIRTH ... Robert Kramer
BIRTH OF THE BEATLES (TF) ... Richard Marquand
BIRTHDAY PARTY, THE ... William Friedkin
BIS ZUR BITTEREN NEIGE ... Gerd Oswald
BISCUIT EATER, THE ... Vincent McEveety
BISHOP'S WIFE ★, THE ... Henry Koster
BITCH ... Andy Warhol
BITCH, THE ... Gerry O'Hara
BITE THE BULLET ... Richard Brooks
BITTER HARVEST (TF) ☆ ... Roger Young
BITTER HERBS ... Kees Van Oostrum
BITTER TEA OF GENERAL YEN, THE ... Frank Capra
BITTERSWEET LOVE ... David Miller
BIZET'S CARMEN ... Francesco Rosi
BJ & THE BEAR (TF) ... Bruce Bilson
BLACK ALLEYCATS, THE ... Henning Schellerup
BLACK AND WHITE IN COLOR ... Jean-Jacques Annaud
BLACK AND WHITE LIKE DAY AND NIGHT ... Wolfgang Petersen
BLACK ARROW, THE (CTF) ... John Hough
BLACK ARROW, THE ... Gordon Douglas
BLACK BART ... George Sherman
BLACK BEAUTY ... James Hill
BLACK BEAUTY (MS) ... Daniel Haller
BLACK BELT JONES ... Robert Clouse
BLACK BIRD, THE ... David Giler
BLACK BUNCH, THE ... Henning Schellerup
BLACK CAESAR ... Larry Cohen
BLACK CASTLE, THE ... Nathan Juran
BLACK CAT IN THE BUSH, A ... Kaneto Shindo
BLACK CAULDRON, THE (AF) ... Ted Berman
BLACK CAULDRON, THE (AF) ... Richard Rich
BLACK CAULDRON, THE (AF) ... Art Stevens
BLACK CHRISTMAS ... Bob Clark
BLACK EYE ... Jack Arnold
BLACK FANTASY (FD) ... Lionel Rogosin
BLACK FIST ... Timothy Galfas
BLACK GIRL ... Ossie Davis
BLACK GIRL ... Ousmene Sembene
BLACK GOLD ... Phil Karlson
BLACK GOLD ... Leslie H. Martinson
BLACK HEAT ... Al Adamson
BLACK HEAT ... Al Adamson
BLACK HOLE, THE ... Gary Nelson
BLACK JACK ... Kenneth Loach
BLACK JOY ... Anthony Simmons
BLACK KLANSMAN, THE ... Ted V. Mikels
BLACK LOVE ... Herschell Gordon Lewis
BLACK MAMA, WHITE MAMA ... Eddie Romero
BLACK MARBLE, THE ... Harold Becker
BLACK MARKET BABY (TF) ... Robert Day
BLACK MIDNIGHT ... Budd Boetticher
BLACK MOON ... Louis Malle
BLACK MOON RISING ... Harley Cokliss
BLACK NARCISSUS ... Michael Powell
BLACK NOON (TF) ... Bernard L. Kowalski
BLACK ORCHID, THE ... Martin Ritt
BLACK PEARL, THE ... Saul Swimmer
BLACK PETER ... Milos Forman
BLACK RIVER ... Masaki Kobayashi
BLACK RODEO (FD) ... Jeff Kanew
BLACK ROOM, THE ... Norman Thaddeus Vane
BLACK ROOTS (FD) ... Lionel Rogosin
BLACK ROSE, THE ... Henry Hathaway
BLACK SAMSON ... Chuck Bail
BLACK SAMURAI ... Al Adamson
BLACK SHAMPOO ... Greydon Clark
BLACK SIX, THE ... Matt Cimber
BLACK STALLION RETURNS, THE ... Robert Dalva
BLACK STALLION, THE ... Carroll Ballard
BLACK STREETFIGHTER, THE ... Timothy Galfas
BLACK SUNDAY ... John Frankenheimer
BLACK 13 ... Kenneth "Ken" Hughes
BLACK TIGHTS ... Terence Young
BLACK WATER GOLD (TF) ... Alan Landsburg
BLACK WHIP, THE ... Charles Marquis Warren
BLACK WINDMILL, THE ... Don Siegel
BLACKBEARD'S GHOST ... Robert Stevenson
BLACKBOARD JUNGLE, THE ... Richard Brooks
BLACKENSTEIN ... William A. Levey
BLACKJACK KETCHUM, DESPERADO ... Earl Bellamy
BLACKOUT ... Michael Powell
BLACKOUT (CTF) ... Douglas Hickox
BLACKSNAKE ... Russ Meyer
BLACULA ... William Crain
BLADE ON THE FEATHER (TF) ... Richard Loncraine
BLADE RUNNER ... Ridley Scott
BLAME IT ON RIO ... Stanley Donen
BLAME IT ON THE NIGHT ... Gene Taft
BLANK GENERATION ... Ulli Lommel
BLAST OFF/JULES VERNE'S ROCKET TO THE MOON ... Don Sharp
BLAST-OFF GIRLS ... Herschell Gordon Lewis
BLAUBART (TF) ... Krzysztof Zanussi
BLAZING SADDLES ... Mel Brooks
BLAZING STEWARDESSES ... Al Adamson
BLESS THE BEASTS & CHILDREN ... Stanley Kramer
BLESS THIS HOUSE ... Gerald Thomas
BLIND ALLEY ... Larry Cohen
BLIND AMBITION (TF) ... George Schaefer
BLIND DATE ... Nico Mastorakis
BLINDED BY THE LIGHT (TF) ... John A. Alonzo
BLINDMAN ... Ferdinando Baldi
BLISS OF MRS. BLOSSOM, THE ... Joseph McGrath
BLITHE SPIRIT ... David Lean
BLODWEN HOME FROM RACHEL'S MARRIAGE (TF) ... Alan Cooke
BLONDE FROM SINGAPORE, THE ... Edward Dmytryk
BLONDE SINNER ... J. Lee Thompson
BLOOD AND GUTS ... Paul Lynch
BLOOD AND HONOR: YOUTH UNDER HITLER (MS) ... Bernd Fischerauer
BLOOD AND ROSES ... Roger Vadim
BLOOD AND SAND ... Rouben Mamoulian
BLOOD ARROW ... Charles Marquis Warren
BLOOD BATH ... Jack Hill
BLOOD BATH ... Stephanie Rothman
BLOOD BEACH ... Jeffrey Bloom
BLOOD FEAST ... Herschell Gordon Lewis
BLOOD FEUD ... Lina Wertmuller
BLOOD FEUD (TF) ... Mike Newell
BLOOD FOR DRACULA ... Paul Morrissey
BLOOD MANIA ... Robert Vincent O'Neil
BLOOD OF DRACULA'S CASTLE ... Al Adamson
BLOOD OF GHASTLY HORROR ... Al Adamson
BLOOD OF OTHERS, THE (CMS) ... Claude Chabrol
BLOOD ON SATAN'S CLAW, THE ... Piers Haggard
BLOOD ON THE MOON ... Robert Wise
BLOOD ORGY OF THE SHE-DEVILS ... Ted V. Mikels
BLOOD SIMPLE ... Joel Coen
BLOOD SPORT (TF) ... Jerrold Freedman
BLOODBROTHERS ... Robert Mulligan
BLOODY KIDS (TF) ... Stephen Frears
BLOODY MAMA ... Roger Corman
BLOOMFIELD ... Richard Harris
BLOSSOMS IN THE DUST ... Mervyn Leroy
BLOW JOB ... Andy Warhol
BLOW OUT ... Brian De Palma
BLOW-UP ★ ... Michelangelo Antonioni
BLUE ... Silvio Narizzano
BLUE AND THE GRAY, THE (MS) ... Andrew V. McLaglen
BLUE ANGEL, THE ... Edward Dmytryk
BLUE BLOOD ... Andrew Sinclair
BLUE COLLAR ... Paul Schrader
BLUE COUNTRY, THE ... Jean-Charles Tacchella
BLUE FIN ... Carl Schultz
BLUE HEAVEN ... Kathleen Dowdey
BLUE KNIGHT ☆, THE (TF) ... Robert Butler
BLUE KNIGHT, THE (TF) ... J. Lee Thompson
BLUE LAGOON, THE ... Randal Kleiser
BLUE MAX, THE ... John Guillermin
BLUE MOVIE ... Andy Warhol
BLUE REVOLUTION, THE ... Kon Ichikawa
BLUE SKIES AGAIN ... Richard Michaels
BLUE SUMMER ... Chuck Vincent
BLUE SUNSHINE ... Jeff Lieberman
BLUE THUNDER ... John Badham
BLUE WATER, WHITE DEATH (FD) ... Peter Gimbel
BLUEBEARD ... Edward Dmytryk
BLUEPRINT FOR MURDER ... Jerry Hopper
BLUEPRINT FOR MURDER, A ... Andrew L. Stone
BLUES BROTHERS, THE ... John Landis
BLUFF - STORIE DI TRUFFE E DI IMBRAGLIONE ... Sergio Corbucci
BLUME IN LOVE ... Paul Mazursky
BLUSHING CHARLIE ... Vilgot Sjoman
BOARDWALK ... Stephen F. Verona
BOAT PEOPLE ... Ann Hui
BOB & CAROL & TED & ALICE ... Paul Mazursky
BOBBI JO AND THE OUTLAW ... Mark L. Lester
BOBBIKINS ... Robert Day
BOBBY DEERFIELD ... Sydney Pollack
BOBO, THE ... Robert Parrish
BOBOSSE ... Etienne Perier
BOCCACCIO '70 ... Federico Fellini
BOCCACCIO '70 ... Mario Monicelli
BODY AND SOUL ... George Bowers
BODY DOUBLE ... Brian De Palma
BODY HEAT ... Lawrence Kasdan
BODY ROCK ... Marcelo Epstein
BODY SAID NO, THE ... Val Guest
BODY SNATCHER, THE ... Robert Wise
BODYGUARD ... Richard Fleischer
BODYGUARD, THE ... Simon Nuchtern
BOEING BOEING ... John Rich
BOFORS GUN, THE ... Jack Gold
BOG ... Don Keeslar
BOGARD ... Timothy Galfas
BOGIE: THE LAST HERO (TF) ... Vincent Sherman
BOIN-N-G ... Herschell Gordon Lewis
BOLERO ... John Derek
BOLERO ... Claude Lelouch
BOMBAY TALKIE ... James Ivory
BOMBERS B-52 ... Gordon Douglas
BON APPETIT ... Chuck Vincent

BON VOYAGE, CHARLIE BROWN (AND DON'T COME BACK!) (AF) ..... Bill Melendez
BONCHI ..... Kon Ichikawa
BONE ..... Larry Cohen
BONES ..... Jim Goddard
BONHEUR TOI-MEME ..... Claude Goretta
BONJOUR SOURIRE ..... Claude Sautet
BONJOUR TRISTESSE ..... Otto Preminger
BONNIE AND CLYDE ★ ..... Arthur Penn
BONNIE PARKER STORY, THE ..... William Witney
BONNIE'S KIDS ..... Arthur Marks
BOOGENS, THE ..... James L. Conway
BOOGEY MAN, THE ..... Ulli Lommel
BOOK OF NUMBERS ..... Raymond St.
BOOKER (TF) ..... Stan Lathan
BOOMERANG! ..... Elia Kazan
BOONE (TF) ..... Paul Wendkos
BOOTLEGGERS ..... Charles B. Pierce
BOP GIRL ..... Howard W. Koch
BORDER, THE ..... Tony Richardson
BORDER RIVER ..... George Sherman
BORDER SHOWDOWN ..... Richard L. Bare
BORDERLINE ..... Jerrold Freedman
BORGIA STICK, THE (TF) ..... David Lowell Rich
BORING AFTERNOON, A ..... Ivan Passer
BORN AGAIN ..... Irving Rapper
BORN BEAUTIFUL (TF) ..... Harvey Hart
BORN FREE ..... James Hill
BORN INNOCENT (TF) ..... Donald Wrye
BORN LOSERS ..... Tom Laughlin
BORN LUCKY ..... Michael Powell
BORN RECKLESS ..... Howard W. Koch
BORN TO BE SOLD (TF) ..... Burt Brinckerhoff
BORN TO BOOGIE (FD) ..... Ringo Starr
BORN TO KILL ..... Monte Hellman
BORN TO KILL ..... Robert Wise
BORN TO RUN ..... Don Chaffey
BORN TO WIN ..... Ivan Passer
BORN WILD ..... Maury Dexter
BORROWERS, THE (TF) ..... Walter C. Miller
BORSALINO ..... Jacques Deray
BORSALINO AND CO. ..... Jacques Deray
BOSS NIGGER ..... Jack Arnold
BOSS OF BIG TOWN, THE ..... Arthur Dreifuss
BOSS' SON, THE ..... Bobby Roth
BOSTON BLACKIE BOOKED ON SUSPICION ..... Arthur Dreifuss
BOSTON BLACKIE GOES HOLLYWOOD ..... Michael Gordon
BOSTON BLACKIE'S RENDEZVOUS ..... Arthur Dreifuss
BOSTON STRANGLER, THE ..... Richard Fleischer
BOSTONIANS, THE ..... James Ivory
BOTTOM OF THE BOTTLE, THE ..... Henry Hathaway
BOULEVARD DU RHUM ..... Robert Enrico
BOULEVARD NIGHTS ..... Michael Pressman
BOUND FOR GLORY ..... Hal Ashby
BOUNTY HUNTER, THE ..... Andre De Toth
BOUNTY MAN, THE (TF) ..... John Llewellyn Moxey
BOUNTY, THE ..... Roger Donaldson
BOWERY BOMBSHELL ..... Phil Karlson
BOXCAR BERTHA ..... Martin Scorsese
BOY ..... Nagisa Oshima
BOY AND A PIGEON, A ..... Andrei Konchalovsky
BOY AND HIS DOG, A ..... L.Q. Jones
BOY AND THE PIRATES, THE ..... Bert I. Gordon
BOY FRIEND, THE ..... Ken Russell
BOY IN BLUE, THE ..... Charles Jarrott
BOY IN THE PLASTIC BUBBLE, THE (TF) ..... Randal Kleiser
BOY NAMED CHARLIE BROWN, A (AF) ..... Bill Melendez
BOY ON A DOLPHIN ..... Jean Negulesco
BOY TEN FEET TALL, A ..... Alexander Mackendrick
BOY WHO CRIED WEREWOLF, THE ..... Nathan Juran
BOY WHO DRANK TOO MUCH, THE (TF) ..... Jerrold Freedman
BOY WHO LOVED TROLLS, THE (TF) ..... Harvey Laidman
BOY WHO STOLE A MILLION, THE ..... Charles Crichton
BOY...A GIRL, A ..... John Derek
BOYS, THE ..... Sidney J. Furie
BOYS FROM BRAZIL, THE ..... Franklin J. Schaffner
BOYS IN BLUE, THE ..... Val Guest
BOYS IN COMPANY C, THE ..... Sidney J. Furie
BOYS IN THE BAND, THE ..... William Friedkin
BOYS' NIGHT OUT ..... Michael Gordon
BRADY GIRLS GET MARRIED, THE (TF) ..... Peter Baldwin
BRADY'S ESCAPE ..... Pal Gabor
BRAIN, THE ..... Freddie Francis
BRAIN MACHINE, THE ..... Kenneth "Ken" Hughes
BRAIN OF BLOOD, THE ..... Al Adamson
BRAIN, THE ..... Gerard Oury
BRAINSTORM ..... William Conrad
BRAINSTORM ..... Douglas Trumbull
BRAINWASH ..... Bobby Roth
BRAINWASHED ..... Gerd Oswald
BRAINWAVES ..... Ulli Lommel
BRAMBLE BUSH, THE ..... Daniel Petrie
BRANCALEONE ALLE CROCIATE ..... Mario Monicelli
BRAND NEW LIFE, A (TF) ..... Sam O'Steen
BRANNIGAN ..... Douglas Hickox
BRASS LEGEND, THE ..... Gerd Oswald
BRASS TARGET ..... John Hough
BRAVE DON'T CRY, THE ..... Philip Leacock
BRAVE NEW WORLD (TF) ..... Burt Brinckerhoff
BRAVE ONE, THE ..... Irving Rapper
BRAVOS, THE (TF) ..... Ted Post
BRAZIL ..... Terry Gilliam
BRAZIL: A REPORT ON TORTURE (FD) ..... Haskell Wexler
BREACH OF CONTRACT ..... Andre Guttfreund
BREAD AND CHOCOLATE ..... Franco Brusati
BREAD, LOVE AND DREAMS ..... Luigi Comencini
BREAK IN THE CIRCLE ..... Val Guest
BREAK TO FREEDOM ..... Lewis Gilbert
BREAKDANCIN' ..... Joel Silberg
BREAKER BREAKER ..... Donald Hulette
BREAKER MORANT ..... Bruce Beresford
BREAKFAST AT TIFFANY'S ..... Blake Edwards
BREAKFAST CLUB, THE ..... John Hughes
BREAKIN' 2 ELECTRIC BOOGALOO ..... Sam Firstenberg
BREAKING AWAY ★ ..... Peter Yates
BREAKING GLASS ..... Brian Gibson
BREAKING OF BUMBO, THE ..... Andrew Sinclair
BREAKING POINT ..... Bob Clark
BREAKING THE SOUND BARRIER ..... David Lean
BREAKING UP (TF) ☆ ..... Delbert Mann
BREAKING UP IS HARD TO DO (TF) ..... Lou Antonio
BREAKOUT (TF) ..... Richard Irving
BREAKTHROUGH ..... Andrew V. McLaglen
BREAST OF RUSS MEYER, THE ..... Russ Meyer
BREATHLESS ..... Jean-Luc Godard
BREATHLESS ..... Jim McBride
BREED APART, A ..... Philippe Mora
BREEZY ..... Clint Eastwood
BRELAN D'AS ..... Henri Verneuil
BRENDA STARR (TF) ..... Mel Stuart
BRET MAVERICK (TF) ..... Stuart Margolin
BREWSTER McCLOUD ..... Robert Altman
BREWSTER'S MILLIONS ..... Walter Hill
BRIAN'S SONG (TF) ☆ ..... Buzz Kulik
BRIDE, THE ..... Franc Roddam
BRIDES OF FU MANCHU, THE ..... Don Sharp
BRIDESHEAD REVISITED (MS) ☆ ..... Michael Lindsay-Hogg
BRIDESHEAD REVISITED (MS) ☆ ..... Charles Sturridge
BRIDGE, THE ..... Bernhard Wicki
BRIDGE AT REMAGEN, THE ..... John Guillermin
BRIDGE IN THE JUNGLE, THE ..... Pancho Kohner
BRIDGE OF JAPAN ..... Kon Ichikawa
BRIDGE ON THE RIVER KWAI ★★, THE ..... David Lean
BRIDGE TO THE SUN ..... Etienne Perier
BRIDGE TOO FAR, A ..... Richard Attenborough
BRIDGER (TF) ..... David Lowell Rich
BRIDGES-GO-ROUND ..... Shirley Clarke
BRIEF ENCOUNTER ..... David Lean
BRIEF ENCOUNTER (TF) ..... Alan Bridges
BRIGADOON ..... Vincente Minnelli
BRIGAND, THE ..... Phil Karlson
BRIGHAM YOUNG, FRONTIERSMAN ..... Henry Hathaway
BRIGHTON ROCK ..... John Boulting
BRIMSTONE AND TREACLE ..... Richard Loncraine
BRING ME THE HEAD OF ALFREDO GARCIA ..... Sam Peckinpah
BRING YOUR SMILE ALONG ..... Blake Edwards
BRINK'S JOB, THE ..... William Friedkin
BRINK'S: THE GREAT ROBBERY (TF) ..... Marvin J. Chomsky
BRITANNIA MEWS ..... Jean Negulesco
BRITISH SOUNDS/SEE YOU AT MAO (TF) ..... Jean-Luc Godard
BRITTANIA HOSPITAL ..... Lindsay Anderson
BROAD COALITION, THE ..... Simon Nuchtern
BROAD MINDED ..... Mervyn Leroy
BROADWAY BABIES ..... Mervyn Leroy
BROADWAY BILL ..... Frank Capra
BROADWAY DANNY ROSE ..... Woody Allen
BROADWAY LIMITED ..... Gordon Douglas
BROCK'S LAST CASE (TF) ..... David Lowell Rich
BROKEN JOURNEY ..... Ken Annakin
BROKEN LANCE ..... Edward Dmytryk
BROKEN PROMISE ..... Sandy Tung
BROKEN PROMISE (TF) ..... Don Taylor
BRONCO BILLY ..... Clint Eastwood
BRONCO BUSTER ..... Budd Boetticher
BRONTE ..... Delbert Mann
BROOD, THE ..... David Cronenberg
BROTHER, CAN YOU SPARE A DIME? (FD) ..... Philippe Mora
BROTHER CARL ..... Susan Sontag
BROTHER FROM ANOTHER PLANET, THE ..... John Sayles
BROTHER JOHN ..... James Goldstone
BROTHER, MY SONG ..... Chris Cain
BROTHER SUN SISTER MOON ..... Franco Zeffirelli
BROTHERHOOD OF SATAN, THE ..... Bernard McEveety
BROTHERHOOD OF THE BELL, THE (TF) ..... Paul Wendkos
BROTHERHOOD, THE ..... Martin Ritt
BROTHERLY LOVE ..... J. Lee Thompson
BROTHERS ..... Arthur Barron
BROTHERS IN LAW ..... Roy Boulting
BROTHERS KARAMAZOV, THE ..... Richard Brooks
BROTHERS RICO, THE ..... Phil Karlson
BROWN WALLET, THE ..... Michael Powell
BRUBAKER ..... Stuart Rosenberg
BRUCIATI DA COCENTE PASSIONE ..... Alberto Lattuada
BRUTE CORPS ..... Jerry Jameson
BRUTE FORCE ..... Jules Dassin
BRUTE, THE ..... Gerry O'Hara
BRUTTI, SPORCHI E CATTIVI ..... Ettore Scola
B.S. I LOVE YOU ..... Steven Hillard Stern
BUBBLE, THE ..... Arch Oboler
BUCCANEER, THE ..... Anthony Quinn
BUCHANAN RIDES ALONE ..... Budd Boetticher
BUCK AND THE PREACHER ..... Sidney Poitier
BUCK ROGERS IN THE 25TH CENTURY ..... Daniel Haller
BUCKET OF BLOOD, A ..... Roger Corman
BUCKSTONE COUNTY PRISON ..... Jimmy Huston
BUCKTOWN ..... Arthur Marks
BUD AND LOU (TF) ..... Robert C. Thompson
BUDAPEST TALES ..... Istvan Szabo
BUDDENBROOKS (MS) ..... Franz Peter Wirth
BUDDY BUDDY ..... Billy Wilder
BUDDY HOLLY STORY, THE ..... Steve Rash
BUDDY SYSTEM, THE ..... Glenn Jordan
BUFFALO BILL AND THE INDIANS or SITTING BULL'S HISTORY LESSON ..... Robert Altman
BUFFET FROID ..... Bertrand Blier
BUG ..... Jeannot Szwarc
BUGSY MALONE ..... Alan Parker
BULLET FOR PRETTY BOY, A ..... Larry Buchanan
BULLET FOR THE GENERAL, A ..... Damiano Damiani
BULLFIGHT ..... Shirley Clarke
BULLFIGHTER AND THE LADY, THE ..... Budd Boetticher
BULLITT ..... Peter Yates
BULLSHOT! ..... Dick Clement
BULLY ..... Peter H. Hunt
BUNKER, THE (TF) ..... George Schaefer
BUNNY LAKE IS MISSING ..... Otto Preminger

BUNNY O'HARE ... Gerd Oswald
BUONA SERA, MRS. CAMPBELL ... Melvin Frank
BURDEN OF DREAMS (FD) ... Les Blank
BURGLAR, THE ... Paul Wendkos
BURGLARS, THE ... Henri Verneuil
BURIED ALIVE ... Mike Hodges
BURKE AND WILLS ... Graeme Clifford
BURMA VICTORY (FD) ... Roy Boulting
BURMESE HARP, THE ... Kon Ichikawa
BURN! ... Gillo Pontecorvo
BURN, WITCH, BURN ... Sidney Hayers
BURNING BED, THE (TF) ... Robert Greenwald
BURNING RAGE (TF) ... Gilbert Cates
BURNING, THE ... Tony Maylam
BURNT OFFERINGS ... Dan Curtis
BURY ME AN ANGEL ... Barbara Peeters
BUS II (FD) ... Haskell Wexler
BUS RILEY'S BACK IN TOWN ... Harvey Hart
BUS STOP ... Joshua Logan
BUSH CHRISTMAS ... Henri Safran
BUSHIDO BLADE, THE ... Tom Kotani
BUSHWHACKERS, THE ... Rod Amateau
BUSTER AND BILLIE ... Daniel Petrie
BUSTER KEATON STORY, THE ... Sidney Sheldon
BUSTIN' LOOSE ... Oz Scott
BUSTING ... Peter Hyams
BUT I DON'T WANT TO GET MARRIED! (TF) ... Jerry Paris
BUTCH AND SUNDANCE: THE EARLY DAYS ... Richard Lester
BUTCH CASSIDY AND THE SUNDANCE KID ★ ... George Roy Hill
BUTCHER, BAKER, NIGHTMARE MAKER ... William Asher
BUTLEY ... Harold Pinter
BUTTERCUP CHAIN, THE ... Robert Ellis Miller
BUTTERFIELD 8 ... Daniel Mann
BUTTERFLIES ARE FREE ... Milton Katselas
BUTTERFLY ... Matt Cimber
BUZZARD, THE ... Chris Cain
BWANA DEVIL ... Arch Oboler
BY DESIGN ... Claude Jutra
BY LOVE POSSESSED ... John Sturges
BYE BYE BIRDIE ... George Sidney
BYE BYE BRAVERMAN ... Sidney Lumet
BYE BYE MONKEY ... Marco Ferreri

C

CA VA BARDER ... John Berry
CABARET ★★ ... Bob Fosse
CABIN IN THE SKY ... Vincente Minnelli
CABLE CAR MURDER, THE (TF) ... Jerry Thorpe
CABOBLANCO ... J. Lee Thompson
CABRIOLA ... Mel Ferrer
CACTUS FLOWER ... Gene Saks
CADAVERI ECCELENTI ... Francesco Rosi
CADDIE ... Donald Crombie
CADDYSHACK ... Harold Ramis
CAESAR AND CLEOPATRA (TF) ... James Cellan-Jones
CAFE EXPRESS ... Nanni Loy
CAFE RACER, THE ... Donald Hulette
CAFETERIA, THE (TF) ... Amram Nowak
CAGE WITHOUT A KEY (TF) ... Buzz Kulik
CAGED HEAT ... Jonathan Demme
CAGNEY & LACEY (TF) ... Ted Post
CAHILL, U.S. MARSHAL ... Andrew V. McLaglen
CAINE MUTINY, THE ... Edward Dmytryk
CAL ... Pat O'Connor
CALAMITY JANE (TF) ... James Goldstone
CALAMITY JANE AND SAM BASS ... George Sherman
CALCUTTA (FD) ... Louis Malle
CALENDAR GIRL MURDERS, THE (TF) ... William A. Graham
CALIFORNIA DREAMING ... John Hancock
CALIFORNIA GOLD RUSH (TF) ... Jack B. Hively
CALIFORNIA KID, THE (TF) ... Richard T. Heffron
CALIFORNIA SPLIT ... Robert Altman
CALIFORNIA SUITE ... Herbert Ross
CALL HER MOM (TF) ... Jerry Paris
CALL HIM MR. SHATTER ... Michael Carreras
CALL ME BWANA ... Gordon Douglas
CALL ME GENIUS ... Robert Day
CALL NORTHSIDE 777 ... Henry Hathaway
CALL OF THE WILD ... Ken Annakin
CALL OF THE WILD, THE (TF) ... Jerry Jameson
CALL TO GLORY (TF) ... Thomas Carter
CALLAN ... Don Sharp
CALLAWAY WENT THATAWAY ... Melvin Frank
CALLAWAY WENT THATAWAY ... Norman Panama
CALLIE & SON (TF) ... Waris Hussein
CALLIOPE ... Matt Cimber
CALMOS ... Bertrand Blier
CAMELOT ... Joshua Logan
CAMERA D'ALBERGO ... Mario Monicelli
CAMILLE (TF) ... Desmond Davis
CAMILLE 2000 ... Radley Metzger
CAMMINACAMMINA ... Ermanno Olmi
CAMOUFLAGE ... Krzysztof Zanussi
CAMP ... Andy Warhol
CAMP ON BLOOD ISLAND, THE ... Val Guest
CAMPBELL'S KINGDOM ... Ralph Thomas
CAMP-FIRE GIRLS ... Henning Schellerup
CAMPING ... Franco Zeffirelli
CAMPUS RHYTHM ... Arthur Dreifuss
CAN ELLEN BE SAVED? (TF) ... Harvey Hart
CAN HIERONYMOUS MERKIN EVER FORGET MERCY HUMPPE AND FIND TRUE HAPPINESS? ... Anthony Newley
CAN I SAVE MY CHILDREN? (TF) ☆ ... Walter C. Miller
CAN SHE BAKE A CHERRY PIE? ... Henry Jaglom
CAN YOU HEAR THE LAUGHTER? THE STORY OF FREDDIE PRINZE (TF) ... Burt Brinckerhoff
CANADIANS, THE ... Burt Kennedy
CANAL ZONE (FD) ... Frederick Wiseman
CANCEL MY RESERVATION ... Paul Bogart
CANDIDATE, THE ... Michael Ritchie
CANDY TANGERINE MAN, THE ... Matt Cimber
CANNERY ROW ... David S. Ward
CANNIBAL GIRLS ... Ivan Reitman
CANNIBALS IN THE STREETS ... Anthony M. Dawson
CANNON (TF) ... George McCowan
CANNON FOR CORDOBA ... Paul Wendkos
CANNONBALL ... Paul Bartel
CANNONBALL RUN II ... Hal Needham
CANNONBALL RUN, THE ... Hal Needham
CAN'T STOP THE MUSIC ... Nancy Walker
CAN'T YOU HEAR THE DOGS BARK? ... Francois Reichenbach
CANTATA ... Miklos Jancso
CANTERBURY TALE, A ... Michael Powell
CANTERVILLE GHOST, THE ... Jules Dassin
CAPE FEAR ... J. Lee Thompson
CAPER OF THE GOLDEN BULLS, THE ... Russell Rouse
CAPONE ... Steve Carver
CAPRICCIO ALL'ITALIANA ... Mario Monicelli
CAPRICORN ONE ... Peter Hyams
CAPTAIN AMERICA (TF) ... Rod Holcomb
CAPTAIN APACHE ... Alexander Singer
CAPTAIN NEMO AND THE UNDERWATER CITY ... James Hill
CAPTAIN NEWMAN, M.D. ... David Miller
CAPTAINS AND THE KINGS (MS) ... Douglas Heyes
CAPTAINS AND THE KINGS (MS) ... Allen Reisner
CAPTAINS COURAGEOUS (TF) ... Harvey Hart
CAPTIVE CITY, THE ... Robert Wise
CAPTIVE WILD WOMAN ... Edward Dmytryk
CAPTURE OF GRIZZLY ADAMS, THE (TF) ... Don Keeslar
CAPTURE, THE ... John Sturges
CAR, THE ... Elliot Silverstein
CAR WASH ... Michael Schultz
CARAMBOLA ... Ferdinando Baldi
CARAVAN TO VACCARES ... Geoffrey Reeve
CARAVANS ... James Fargo
CARBON COPY ... Michael Schultz
CARD, THE ... Ronald Neame
CARDINAL ★, THE ... Otto Preminger
CAREER ... Joseph Anthony
CAREFUL HE MIGHT HEAR YOU ... Carl Schultz
CARELESS YEARS, THE ... Arthur Hiller
CARETAKER, THE ... Clive Donner
CARETAKERS, THE ... Hall Bartlett
CAREY TREATMENT, THE ... Blake Edwards
CARLTON-BROWNE OF THE F.O. ... Roy Boulting
CARMEN ... Francesco Rosi
CARMEN ... Carlos Saura
CARMEN, BABY ... Radley Metzger
CARMEN JONES ... Otto Preminger
CARNABY, M.D. ... Ralph Thomas
CARNAL KNOWLEDGE ... Mike Nichols
CARNAVAL ... Henri Verneuil
CARNIVAL MAGIC ... Al Adamson
CARNIVAL ROCK ... Roger Corman
CARNY ... Robert Kaylor
CARO MICHELE ... Mario Monicelli
CARO PAPA ... Dino Risi
CARPETBAGGERS, THE ... Edward Dmytryk
CARPOOL (TF) ... E.W. Swackhamer
CARRIE ... Brian De Palma
CARRY ON ABROAD ... Gerald Thomas
CARRY ON ADMIRAL ... Val Guest
CARRY ON AGAIN, DOCTOR ... Gerald Thomas
CARRY ON AT YOUR CONVENIENCE ... Gerald Thomas
CARRY ON BEHIND ... Gerald Thomas
CARRY ON CABBY ... Gerald Thomas
CARRY ON CAMPING ... Gerald Thomas
CARRY ON CLEO ... Gerald Thomas
CARRY ON CONSTABLE ... Gerald Thomas
CARRY ON COWBOY ... Gerald Thomas
CARRY ON CRUISING ... Gerald Thomas
CARRY ON DOCTOR ... Gerald Thomas
CARRY ON EMMANUELLE ... Gerald Thomas
CARRY ON ENGLAND ... Gerald Thomas
CARRY ON HENRY ... Gerald Thomas
CARRY ON JACK ... Gerald Thomas
CARRY ON LOVING ... Gerald Thomas
CARRY ON MATRON ... Gerald Thomas
CARRY ON NURSE ... Gerald Thomas
CARRY ON REGARDLESS ... Gerald Thomas
CARRY ON SCREAMING ... Gerald Thomas
CARRY ON SERGEANT ... Gerald Thomas
CARRY ON SPYING ... Gerald Thomas
CARRY ON UP THE JUNGLE ... Gerald Thomas
CARRY ON...UP THE KHYBER ... Gerald Thomas
CARS THAT ATE PARIS, THE ... Peter Weir
CARS THAT EAT PEOPLE, THE ... Peter Weir
CARSON CITY ... Andre De Toth
CARTER'S ARMY (TF) ... George McCowan
CARTIER AFFAIR, THE (TF) ... Rod Holcomb
CARTOUCHE ... Philippe de Broca
CARVE HER NAME WITH PRIDE ... Lewis Gilbert
CASA DEL TAPPETO GIALLO ... Carlo Lizzani
CASANOVA ... Federico Fellini
CASANOVA '70 ... Mario Monicelli
CASBAH ... John Berry
CASE AGAINST BROOKLYN, THE ... Paul Wendkos
CASE OF THE FULL MOON MURDERS ... Sean S. Cunningham
CASE OF THE MISSING SCENE, THE ... Don Chaffey
CASE OF THE RED MONKEY, THE ... Kenneth "Ken" Hughes
CASE OF THE SMILING STIFFS ... Sean S. Cunningham
CASEY'S SHADOW ... Martin Ritt
CASH & CO. (MS) ... Russell Hagg
CASH & CO. (MS) ... George Miller
CASH McCALL ... Joseph Pevney
CASINO (TF) ... Don Chaffey
CASINO ROYALE ... Val Guest
CASINO ROYALE ... Kenneth "Ken" Hughes
CASINO ROYALE ... John Huston
CASINO ROYALE ... Joseph McGrath
CASINO ROYALE ... Robert Parrish
CASS TIMBERLANE ... George Sidney
CASSANDRA CROSSING, THE ... George Pan Cosmatos
CAST A DARK SHADOW ... Lewis Gilbert
CAST A GIANT SHADOW ... Melville Shavelson
CASTAWAY COWBOY, THE ... Vincent McEveety
CASTAWAYS OF GILLIGAN'S ISLAND, THE (TF) ... Earl Bellamy
CASTLE KEEP ... Sydney Pollack

CASTLE OF THE SPIDER'S WEB, THE ... Akira Kurosawa
CAT AND MOUSE ... Claude Lelouch
CAT AND THE CANARY, THE ... Radley Metzger
CAT BALLOU ... Elliot Silverstein
CAT CREATURE, THE (TF) ... Curtis Harrington
CAT ON A HOT TIN ROOF ★ ... Richard Brooks
CAT O'NINE TAILS ... Dario Argento
CAT PEOPLE ... Paul Schrader
CATACOMBS ... Gordon Hessler
CATAMOUNT KILLING, THE ... Krzysztof Zanussi
CATCH, THE ... Nagisa Oshima
CATCH A PEBBLE ... James F. Collier
CATCH ME A SPY ... Dick Clement
CATCH MY SOUL ... Patrick McGoohan
CATCH US IF YOU CAN ... John Boorman
CATCH-22 ... Mike Nichols
CATERED AFFAIR, THE ... Richard Brooks
CATHOLICS (TF) ... Jack Gold
CATHY'S CHILD ... Donald Crombie
CATLOW ... Sam Wanamaker
CAT'S EYE ... Lewis Teague
CATTLE ANNIE AND LITTLE BRITCHES ... Lamont Johnson
CATTLE EMPIRE ... Charles Marquis Warren
CAUGHT ON A TRAIN (TF) ... Peter John Duffell
CAUSE TOUJOURS...TU M'INTERESSES ... Edouard Molinaro
CAVALLO DELLA TIGRE, A ... Luigi Comencini
CAVE-IN! (TF) ... Georg J. Fenady
CAVEMAN ... Carl Gottlieb
C.C. AND COMPANY ... Seymour Robbie
CEDDO ... Ousmene Sembene
CELEBRITY (MS) ... Paul Wendkos
CELINE AND JULIE GO BOATING ... Jacques Rivette
CELTIC TRILOGY, A (FD) ... Kathleen Dowdey
CEMENTHEAD (TF) ... Ralph L. Thomas
CENSUS TAKER, THE ... Bruce Cook
CENTENNIAL (MS) ... Harry Falk
CENTENNIAL (MS) ... Paul Krasny
CENTENNIAL (MS) ... Bernard McEveety
CENTENNIAL (MS) ... Virgil W. Vogel
CENTENNIAL SUMMER ... Otto Preminger
CENTER FOLD GIRLS ... John Peyser
C'ERA UNA VOLTA ... Francesco Rosi
CERCASI GESU ... Luigi Comencini
CEREMONY, THE ... Nagisa Oshima
CERTAIN FURY, A ... Steve Gyllenhaal
CERTAIN SMILE, A ... Jean Negulesco
CERVANTES ... Vincent Sherman
CESAR AND ROSALIE ... Claude Sautet
C'EST ARRIVE A PARIS ... John Berry
CHADWICK FAMILY, THE (TF) ... David Lowell Rich
CHAFED ELBOWS ... Robert Downey
CHAIN, THE ... Jack Gold
CHAIN OF EVENTS ... Gerald Thomas
CHAINED HEAT ... Paul Nicolas
CHAIRMAN, THE ... J. Lee Thompson
CHALK GARDEN, THE ... Ronald Neame
CHALLENGE, THE ... John Frankenheimer
CHALLENGERS, THE (TF) ... Leslie H. Martinson
CHAMBER OF HORRORS ... Hy Averback
CHAMP, THE ... Franco Zeffirelli
CHAMPAGNE MURDERS, THE ... Claude Chabrol
CHAMPIONS ... John Irvin
CHAMPIONS...A LOVE STORY (TF) ... John A. Alonzo
CHAN IS MISSING ... Wayne Wang
CHANDLERTOWN ... Bryan Forbes
CHANDLERTOWN ... Sidney Hayers
CHANDLERTOWN ... Peter Hunt
CHANDLERTOWN ... David Wickes
CHANEL SOLITAIRE ... George Kaczender
CHANGE OF HABIT ... William A. Graham
CHANGE OF SEASONS, A ... Richard Lang
CHANGELING, THE ... Peter Medak
CHANGES ... Hall Bartlett
CHANT OF JIMMIE BLACKSMITH, THE ... Fred Schepisi
CHAPLINESQUE, MY LIFE AND HARD TIMES ... Harry Hurwitz
CHAPPAQUA ... Conrad Rooks
CHARADE ... Stanley Donen
CHARGE AT FEATHER CREEK, THE ... Gordon Douglas
CHARGE OF THE LIGHT BRIGADE, THE ... Tony Richardson
CHARIOTS OF FIRE ★ ... Hugh Hudson
CHARLES & DIANA: A ROYAL LOVE STORY (TF) ... James Goldstone
CHARLES, DEAD OR ALIVE ... Alain Tanner
CHARLES ET LUCIE ... Nelly Kaplan
CHARLESTON (TF) ... Karen Arthur
CHARLEY AND THE ANGEL ... Vincent McEveety
CHARLEY MOON ... Guy Hamilton
CHARLEY VARRICK ... Don Siegel
CHARLEY-ONE-EYE ... Don Chaffey
CHARLIE AND A HALF ... Boaz Davidson
CHARLIE AND THE GREAT BALLOON CHASE (TF) ... Larry Elikann
CHARLIE BUBBLES ... Albert Finney
CHARLIE CHAN THE CURSE OF THE DRAGON QUEEN ... Clive Donner
CHARLIE COBB: NICE NIGHT FOR HANGING (TF) ... Richard Michaels
CHARLIE MUFFIN ... Jack Gold
CHARLIE SMITH AND THE FRITTER TREE (TF) ... Fred Barzyk
CHARLIE SMITH AND THE FRITTER TREE (TF) ... David R. Loxton
CHARLIE'S ANGELS (TF) ... John Llewellyn Moxey
CHARLOTTE ... Roger Vadim
CHARLY ... Ralph Nelson
CHARRO! ... Charles Marquis Warren
CHARULATA ... Satyajit Ray
CHASE A CROOKED SHADOW ... Michael Anderson
CHASE, THE ... Arthur Penn
CHATEAU EN SUEDE ... Roger Vadim
CHATO'S LAND ... Michael Winner
CHATTANOOGA CHOO CHOO ... Bruce Bilson
CHATTER-BOX ... Tom Desimone
CHE C'ENTRIAMO NOI CON LA RIVOLUZIONE? ... Sergio Corbucci
CHE SI DICE A ROMA ... Ettore Scola
CHE! ... Richard Fleischer
CHEAPER TO KEEP HER ... Ken Annakin
CHEAT, THE ... George Abbott
CHECK IS IN THE MAIL, THE ... Joan Darling
CHECKERED FLAG OR CRASH ... Alan Gibson
CHECKPOINT ... Ralph Thomas
CHEECH & CHONG: STILL SMOKIN ... Thomas Chong
CHEECH & CHONG'S NICE DREAMS ... Thomas Chong
CHEECH & CHONG'S THE CORSICAN BROTHERS ... Thomas Chong
CHEERLEADERS' WILD WEEKEND ... Jeff Werner
CHELSEA GIRLS, THE ... Andy Warhol
CHERE INCONNUE ... Moshe Mizrahi
CHERE LOUISE ... Philippe de Broca
CHEROKEE TRAIL, THE (TF) ... Kieth Merrill
CHERRY, HARRY AND RAQUEL ... Russ Meyer
CHESS PLAYERS, THE ... Satyajit Ray
CHEYENNE SOCIAL CLUB, THE ... Gene Kelly
CHI TROVO UN AMICO, TROVA UN TESORO ... Sergio Corbucci
CHICAGO STORY, THE (TF) ... Jerry London
CHICKEN CHRONICLES, THE ... Francis Simon
CHIEDO ASILO ... Marco Ferreri
CHIEF CRAZY HORSE ... George Sherman
CHIEFS (MS) ... Jerry London
CHILD BRIDE OF SHORT CREEK (TF) ... Robert M. Lewis
CHILD IN THE HOUSE ... Cy Endfield
CHILD IS WAITING, A ... John Cassavetes
CHILD OF DIVORCE ... Richard Fleischer
CHILD STEALER, THE (TF) ... Mel Damski
CHILD UNDER A LEAF ... George Bloomfield
CHILDISH THINGS ... John Derek
CHILDREN IN THE CROSSFIRE (TF) ... George Schaefer
CHILDREN NOBODY WANTED, THE (TF) ... Richard Michaels
CHILDREN OF AN LAC, THE (TF) ... John Llewellyn Moxey
CHILDREN OF DIVORCE (TF) ... Joanna Lee
CHILDREN OF RAGE ... Arthur Allan Seidelman
CHILDREN OF SANCHEZ, THE ... Hall Bartlett
CHILDREN OF THE ATOM BOMB ... Kaneto Shindo
CHILDREN OF THE CORN ... Fritz Kiersch
CHILDREN OF THEATRE STREET, THE (FD) ... Robert Dornhelm
CHILDREN SHOULDN'T PLAY WITH DEAD THINGS ... Bob Clark
CHILDREN'S WAR, THE ... Moshe Mizrahi
CHILD'S PLAY ... Sidney Lumet
CHIMES AT MIDNIGHT ... Orson Welles
CHINA GATE ... Samuel Fuller
CHINA GIRL ... Henry Hathaway
CHINA IS NEAR ... Marco Bellocchio
CHINA: ROOTS OF MADNESS (TD) ... Mel Stuart
CHINA ROSE (TF) ... Robert Day
CHINA SYNDROME, THE ... James Bridges
CHINA VENTURE ... Don Siegel
CHINA 9 LIBERTY 37 ... Monte Hellman
CHINATOWN ★ ... Roman Polanski
CHINESE BOXES ... Chris Petit
CHINO ... John Sturges
CHIRIAKHANA ... Satyajit Ray
CHISHOLMS, THE (MS) ... Mel Stuart
CHISUM ... Andrew V. McLaglen
CHITTY CHITTY BANG BANG ... Kenneth "Ken" Hughes
CHLOE IN THE AFTERNOON ... Eric Rohmer
CHOICE, THE (TF) ... David Greene
CHOICE OF WEAPONS, A ... Kevin Connor
CHOICES ... Silvio Narizzano
CHOICES OF THE HEART (TF) ... Joseph Sargent
C.H.O.M.P.S. ... Don Chaffey
CHOOSE ME ... Alan Rudolph
CHORUS LINE, A ... Richard Attenborough
CHOSEN SURVIVORS ... Sutton Roley
CHOSEN, THE ... Jeremy Paul Kagan
CHRIST STOPPED AT EBOLI ... Francesco Rosi
CHRISTA ... Jack O'Connell
CHRISTIAN LICORICE STORE, THE ... James Frawley
CHRISTIAN THE LION ... James Hill
CHRISTINA ... Paul Krasny
CHRISTINE ... John Carpenter
CHRISTINE JORGENSEN STORY, THE ... Irving Rapper
CHRISTMAS CAROL, A (TF) ... Clive Donner
CHRISTMAS LILIES OF THE FIELD (TF) ... Ralph Nelson
CHRISTMAS MIRACLE IN CAUFIELD, U.S.A. (TF) ... Jud Taylor
CHRISTMAS STORY, A ... Bob Clark
CHRISTMAS TO REMEMBER, A (TF) ... George Englund
CHRISTMAS TREE, THE ... Terence Young
CHRISTMAS WITHOUT SNOW, A (TF) ... John Korty
CHRISTOPHER COLUMBUS (MS) ... Alberto Lattuada
CHRISTO'S VALLEY CURTAIN (FD) ... Albert Maysles
CHRISTO'S VALLEY CURTAIN (FD) ... David Maysles
CHU CHU AND THE PHILLY FLASH ... David Lowell Rich
C.H.U.D. ... Douglas Cheek
CHUKA ... Gordon Douglas
CHULAS FRONTERAS (FD) ... Les Blank
CHUNG KUO (FD) ... Michelangelo Antonioni
CHURCHILL AND THE GENERALS (TF) ... Alan Gibson
CIMARRON KID, THE ... Budd Boetticher
CINCINNATI KID, THE ... Norman Jewison
CINDERELLA LIBERTY ... Mark Rydell
CINDERELLA 2000 ... Al Adamson
CINDY (TF) ... William A. Graham
CINEMA-CINEMA (FD) ... Krishna Shah
CIRCLE, THE ... Gerald Thomas
CIRCLE OF CHILDREN, A (TF) ... Don Taylor
CIRCLE OF DECEIT ... Volker Schlondorff
CIRCLE OF IRON ... Richard Moore
CIRCLE OF LOVE ... Roger Vadim
CIRCLE OF POWER ... Bobby Roth
CIRCLE OF TWO ... Jules Dassin
CIRCUS FRIENDS ... Gerald Thomas
CIRCUS OF FEAR ... John Llewellyn Moxey
CIRCUS OF HORRORS ... Sidney Hayers
CIRCUS WORLD ... Henry Hathaway
CISCO PIKE ... B.W.L. Norton
CITADEL OF CRIME ... George Sherman
CITIZEN KANE ... Orson Welles
CITIZENS BAND ... Jonathan Demme

CITY, THE (TF) ... Harvey Hart
CITY, THE (TF) ... Daniel Petrie
CITY BENEATH THE SEA ... Budd Boetticher
CITY BENEATH THE SEA (TF) ... Irwin Allen
CITY GIRL, THE ... Martha Coolidge
CITY HEAT ... Richard Benjamin
CITY IN FEAR (TF) ... Jud Taylor
CITY IS DARK, THE ... Andre De Toth
CITY KILLER (TF) ... Robert M. Lewis
CITY LIMITS ... Aaron Lipstadt
CITY NEWS ... David Fishelson
CITY NEWS ... Zoe Zinman
CITY OF SHADOWS ... William Witney
CITY OF THE DEAD ... John Llewellyn Moxey
CITY OF WOMEN ... Federico Fellini
CITY ON FIRE! ... Alvin Rakoff
CITY STREETS ... Rouben Mamoulian
CLAIR DE FEMME ... Costa-Gavras
CLAIRE'S KNEE ... Eric Rohmer
CLAIRVOYANT, THE ... Armand Mastroianni
CLAMBAKE ... Arthur H. Nadel
CLAN OF THE CAVE BEAR, THE ... Michael Chapman
CLARENCE, THE CROSS-EYED LION ... Andrew Marton
CLASH OF THE SWORDS ... Stephen Weeks
CLASH OF THE TITANS ... Desmond Davis
CLASS ... Lewis John Carlino
CLASS OF MISS MacMICHAEL, THE ... Silvio Narizzano
CLASS OF 1984 ... Mark L. Lester
CLASS OF '44 ... Paul Bogart
CLASS OF '63 (TF) ... John Korty
CLASS OF '65 (TF) ... Richard Irving
CLASS OF '74 ... Arthur Marks
CLAUDELLE INGLISH ... Gordon Douglas
CLAUDINE ... John Berry
CLAVIGO (TF) ... Marcel Ophuls
CLAY PIGEON ... Lane Slate
CLAY PIGEON, THE ... Richard Fleischer
CLEAN SLATE ... Bertrand Tavernier
CLEAR AND PRESENT DANGER ☆, A (TF) ... James Goldstone
CLEO FROM 5 TO 7 ... Agnes Varda
CLEOPATRA ... Joseph L. Mankiewicz
CLEOPATRA JONES ... Jack Starrett
CLEOPATRA JONES AND THE CASINO OF GOLD ... Chuck Bail
CLERAMBARD ... Yves Robert
CLIMB UP THE WALL ... Michael Winner
CLINIC, THE ... David Stevens
CLINIC XCLUSIVE ... Don Chaffey
CLOAK & DAGGER ... Richard Franklin
CLOCK, THE ... Vincente Minnelli
CLOCKMAKER OF ST. PAUL, THE ... Bertrand Tavernier
CLOCKWORK ORANGE ★, A ... Stanley Kubrick
CLONE MASTER, THE (TF) ... Don Medford
CLONES, THE ... Lamar Card
CLOSE ENCOUNTERS OF THE THIRD KIND ★ ... Steven Spielberg
CLOSED CIRCUIT ... Giuliano Montaldo
CLOSET, THE ... Andy Warhol
CLOUD DANCER ... Barry Brown
CLOUDED YELLOW, THE ... Ralph Thomas
CLOUDS AT SUNSET ... Masahiro Shinoda
CLOUDS OF GLORY ... Ken Russell
CLOWN MURDERS, THE ... Martyn Burke
CLOWNS, THE ... Federico Fellini
CLUB, THE ... Bruce Beresford
CLUE OF THE MISSING APE, THE ... James Hill
COACH ... Bud Townsend
COACH OF THE YEAR (TF) ... Don Medford
COAL MINER'S DAUGHTER ... Michael Apted
COAST TO COAST ... Joseph Sargent
COBWEB, THE ... Vincente Minnelli
COCA COLA KID, THE ... Dusan Makavejev
COCAINE AND BLUE EYES (TF) ... E.W. Swackhamer
COCAINE COWBOYS ... Ulli Lommel
COCAINE: ONE MAN'S SEDUCTION (TF) ... Paul Wendkos
COCKFIGHTER ... Monte Hellman
COCKLESHELL HEROES, THE ... Jose Ferrer
COCKTAIL MOLOTOV ... Diane Kurys
COCKTAILS IN THE KITCHEN ... J. Lee Thompson
COCOON ... Ron Howard
C.O.D. ... Michael Powell
C.O.D. ... Chuck Vincent
CODE NAME: DIAMOND HEAD (TF) ... Jeannot Szwarc
CODE NAME: HERACLITUS (TF) ... James Goldstone
CODE NAME: TRIXIE ... George A. Romero
CODE OF SILENCE ... Andrew Davis
CODE RED (TF) ... J. Lee Thompson
CODENAME WILDGEESE ... Anthony M. Dawson
COFFEE, TEA OR ME? (TF) ... Norman Panama
COFFY ... Jack Hill
COLD FEET ... Bruce Van Dusen
COLD NIGHT'S DEATH, A (TF) ... Jerrold Freedman
COLD ROOM, THE (TF) ... James Dearden
COLD SWEAT ... Terence Young
COLD TURKEY ... Norman Lear
COLD WIND IN AUGUST, A ... Alexander Singer
COLDITZ STORY, THE ... Guy Hamilton
COLLECTIONS PRIVEES ... Just Jaeckin
COLLEGE CONFIDENTIAL ... Albert Zugsmith
COLONEL BLIMP ... Michael Powell
COLONEL MARCH INVESTIGATES ... Cy Endfield
COLONEL REDL ... Istvan Szabo
COLOR ME BLOOD RED ... Herschell Gordon Lewis
COLORADO SUNSET ... George Sherman
COLOSSUS OF RHODES, THE ... Sergio Leone
COLOSSUS: THE FORBIN PROJECT ... Joseph Sargent
COLPO DI STATO ... Luciano Salce
COMA ... Michael Crichton
COMANCHE ... George Sherman
COMANCHE STATION ... Budd Boetticher
COMANCHE TERRITORY ... George Sherman
COMBACK, THE ... Peter Walker
COME ALONG WITH ME (TF) ... Joanne Woodward
COME BACK ... Roger Vadim
COME BACK, AFRICA (FD) ... Lionel Rogosin
COME BACK CHARLESTON BLUE ... Mark Warren
COME BACK, LITTLE SHEBA ... Daniel Mann
COME BACK, LITTLE SHEBA (TF) ... Silvio Narizzano
COME BACK TO THE 5 & DIME JIMMY DEAN, JIMMY DEAN ... Robert Altman
COME BLOW YOUR HORN ... Bud Yorkin
COME DRINK WITH ME ... King Hu
COME FILL THE CUP ... Gordon Douglas
COME ON CHILDREN (FD) ... Allan King
COME ON MARINES! ... Henry Hathaway
COME OUT, COME OUT! ... Linda Yellen
COME SEPTEMBER ... Robert Mulligan
COME TO THE STABLE ... Henry Koster
COMEBACK KID, THE (TF) ... Peter Levin
COMEBACK TRAIL, THE ... Harry Hurwitz
COMEDIANS, THE ... Peter Glenville
COMEDY COMPANY, THE (TF) ... Lee Philips
COMEDY MAN, THE ... Alvin Rakoff
COMES A HORSEMAN ... Alan J. Pakula
COMETOGETHER ... Saul Swimmer
COMFORT AND JOY ... Bill Forsyth
COMIC, THE ... Carl Reiner
COMIN' AT YA ... Ferdinando Baldi
COMING APART ... Milton Moses Ginsberg
COMING HOME ★ ... Hal Ashby
COMING OF AGE IN IBIZA ... Allan King
COMING OUT OF THE ICE (TF) ... Waris Hussein
COMING SOON (CTD) ... John Landis
COMING, THE ... Bert I. Gordon
COMING-OUT PARTY, A ... Ken Annakin
COMMENT CA VA ... Jean-Luc Godard
COMMENT SAVOIR ... Claude Jutra
COMMITTEE, THE ... Peter Sykes
COMMON LAW CABIN ... Russ Meyer
COMMUNICATIONS ... Jean-Luc Godard
COMMUNION/HOLY TERROR ... Alfred Sole
COMPAÑEROS ... Sergio Corbucci
COMPANY (FD) ... D.A. Pennebaker
COMPANY OF KILLERS ... Jerry Thorpe
COMPANY OF WOLVES, THE ... Neil Jordan
COMPETITION ... Milos Forman
COMPETITION, THE ... Joel Oliansky
COMPLEAT BEATLES, THE (FD) ... Patrick Montgomery
COMPROMISING POSITIONS ... Frank Perry
COMPULSION ... Richard Fleischer
COMPUTER WORE TENNIS SHOES, THE ... Robert Butler
COMPUTERCIDE (TF) ... Robert M. Lewis
CON LA RABBIA AGLI OCCHI ... Anthony M. Dawson
CONAN THE BARBARIAN ... John Milius
CONAN THE DESTROYER ... Richard Fleischer
CONCEALED ENEMIES (TF) ... Jeff Bleckner
CONCERT FOR BANGLADESH, THE (FD) ... Saul Swimmer
CONCORDE - AIRPORT '79, THE ... David Lowell Rich
CONCRETE BEAT (TF) ... Robert Butler
CONCRETE COWBOYS, THE (TF) ... Burt Kennedy
CONCRETE JUNGLE, THE ... Tom Desimone
CONDOMINIUM (TF) ... Sidney Hayers
CONDORMAN ... Charles Jarrott
CONDUCT UNBECOMING ... Michael Anderson
CONDUCTOR, THE ... Andrzej Wajda
CONFESSION ... Kenneth "Ken" Hughes
CONFESSION, THE ... Costa-Gavras
CONFESSIONE DI UN COMMISSARIO ... Damiano Damiani
CONFESSIONS OF A MARRIED MAN (TF) ... Steven Gethers
CONFESSIONS OF A POLICE CAPTAIN ... Damiano Damiani
CONFESSIONS OF A WINDOW CLEANER ... Val Guest
CONFESSIONS OF AMANS, THE ... Gregory Nava
CONFESSIONS OF AN OPIUM EATER ... Albert Zugsmith
CONFESSIONS OF BOSTON BLACKIE ... Edward Dmytryk
CONFIDENCE ... Istvan Szabo
CONFIDENCE GIRL ... Andrew L. Stone
CONFORMIST, THE ... Bernardo Bertolucci
CONFRONTATION, THE ... Miklos Jancso
CONGO CROSSING ... Joseph Pevney
CONGRATULATIONS, IT'S A BOY! (TF) ... William A. Graham
CONJUGAL BED, THE ... Marco Ferreri
CONNECTION, THE ... Shirley Clarke
CONQUERED CITY ... Joseph Anthony
CONQUEST OF THE PLANET OF THE APES ... J. Lee Thompson
CONRACK ... Martin Ritt
CONSEQUENCE, THE ... Wolfgang Petersen
CONSPIRACY OF HEARTS ... Ralph Thomas
CONSPIRACY OF TERROR (TF) ... John Llewellyn Moxey
CONSPIRATORS, THE ... Jean Negulesco
CONSTANT FACTOR, THE ... Krzysztof Zanussi
CONTEMPT ... Jean-Luc Godard
CONTENDER, THE (TF) ... Lou Antonio
CONTENDER, THE (TF) ... Harry Falk
CONTEST GIRL ... Val Guest
CONTINENTAL DIVIDE ... Michael Apted
CONTRABAND ... Michael Powell
CONTRACT ... Krzysztof Zanussi
CONTRACT ON CHERRY STREET (TF) ... William A. Graham
CONTROSESSO ... Marco Ferreri
CONVERSATION, THE ... Francis Ford Coppola
CONVOY ... Sam Peckinpah
COOGAN'S BLUFF ... Don Siegel
COOK & PEARY: THE RACE TO THE POLE (TF) ... Robert Day
COOL AND THE CRAZY, THE ... William Witney
COOL BREEZE ... Barry Pollack
COOL HAND LUKE ... Stuart Rosenberg
COOL IT CAROL! ... Peter Walker
COOL MIKADO, THE ... Michael Winner
COOL MILLION (TF) ... Gene Levitt
COOL ONES, THE ... Gene Nelson
COOL SOUND FROM HELL, A ... Sidney J. Furie
COOL WORLD, THE ... Shirley Clarke
COOLANGATTA GOLD ... Igor Auzins
COOLEY HIGH ... Michael Schultz
COONSKIN (AF) ... Ralph Bakshi
COPPER SKY ... Charles Marquis Warren
COPS AND ROBBERS ... Aram Avakian
COPS AND ROBIN (TF) ... Allen Reisner
COREY: FOR THE PEOPLE (TF) ... Buzz Kulik
CORN IS GREEN, THE ... Irving Rapper

CORNBREAD, EARL AND ME ... Joseph Manduke
CORPSE GRINDERS, THE ... Ted V. Mikels
CORRIDA OF LOVE ... Nagisa Oshima
CORRIDOR OF MIRRORS ... Terence Young
CORRIDORS OF BLOOD ... Robert Day
CORRUPT ONES, THE ... James Hill
CORTILE CASCINO, ITALY (FD) ... Michael Roemer
CORTILE CASCINO, ITALY (FD) ... Robert M. Young
CORVETTE SUMMER ... Matthew Robbins
COSH BOY ... Lewis Gilbert
COSI COME SEI ... Alberto Lattuada
COTTON CANDY (TF) ... Ron Howard
COTTON CLUB, THE ... Francis Ford Coppola
COTTON COMES TO HARLEM ... Ossie Davis
COUCH ... Andy Warhol
COUGAR! (TF) ... Stephen H. Foreman
COUNT DRACULA AND HIS VAMPIRE BRIDE ... Alan Gibson
COUNT OF MONTE CRISTO, THE (TF) ... David Greene
COUNT TACCHIA ... Sergio Corbucci
COUNT THE HOURS ... Don Siegel
COUNT THREE AND PRAY ... George Sherman
COUNT YOUR BLESSINGS ... Jean Negulesco
COUNT YOUR BULLETS ... William A. Graham
COUNTDOWN ... Robert Altman
COUNTDOWN AT KUSINI ... Ossie Davis
COUNTDOWN TO LOOKING GLASS (CTF) ... Fred Barzyk
COUNTER ESPIONAGE ... Edward Dmytryk
COUNTERPOINT ... Ralph Nelson
COUNTESS DRACULA ... Peter Sasdy
COUNTRY ... Richard Pearce
COUNTRY DANCE ... J. Lee Thompson
COUNTRY GIRLS, THE ... Desmond Davis
COUNTRY GOLD (TF) ... Gilbert Cates
COUP DE FOUDRE ... Robert Enrico
COUP DE FOUDRE ... Diane Kurys
COUP DE GRACE ... Volker Schlondorff
COUP DE TETE ... Jean-Jacques Annaud
COUP DE TORCHON ... Bertrand Tavernier
COUPLE TAKES A WIFE, THE (TF) ... Jerry Paris
COURAGE ... Robert L. Rosen
COURAGE AND THE PASSION, THE (TF) ... John Llewellyn Moxey
COURAGE FUYONS ... Yves Robert
COURT JESTER, THE ... Melvin Frank
COURT JESTER, THE ... Norman Panama
COURT-MARTIAL OF BILLY MITCHELL, THE ... Otto Preminger
COURTSHIP OF EDDIE'S FATHER, THE ... Vincente Minnelli
COUSIN ANGELICA ... Carlos Saura
COUSIN COUSINE ... Jean-Charles Tacchella
COUSINS, THE ... Claude Chabrol
COVENANT WITH DEATH, A ... Lamont Johnson
COVER (MS) ... Alan Cooke
COVER GIRLS (TF) ... Jerry London
COVER HER FACE (TF) ... John Davies
COVER ME BABE ... Noel Black
COVER UP ... Peter Crane
COVERED WAGON DAYS ... George Sherman
COW AND I, THE ... Henri Verneuil
COWARD OF THE COUNTY (TF) ... Dick Lowry
COWARDS, THE ... Simon Nuchtern
COWBOY (TF) ... Jerry Jameson
COWBOY AND THE BALLERINA, THE (TF) ... Jerry Jameson
COWBOYS FROM TEXAS ... George Sherman
COWBOYS, THE ... Mark Rydell
CRACK IN THE MIRROR ... Richard Fleischer
CRACK IN THE WORLD ... Andrew Marton
CRACKER FACTORY, THE (TF) ... Burt Brinckerhoff
CRACKERS ... Louis Malle
CRADLE WILL FALL, THE (TF) ... John Llewellyn Moxey
CRASH ... Charles Band
CRASH OF SILENCE ... Alexander Mackendrick
CRAWLSPACE (TF) ... John Newland
CRAZE ... Freddie Francis
CRAZIES, THE ... George A. Romero
CRAZY DESIRE ... Luciano Salce
CRAZY HOUSE ... Peter Sykes
CRAZY JOE ... Carlo Lizzani
CRAZY MAMA ... Jonathan Demme
CRAZY QUILT ... John Korty
CRAZY TIMES (TF) ... Lee Philips
CRAZY WORLD OF JULIUS VROODER, THE ... Arthur Hiller
CREAM IN MY COFFEE (TF) ... Gavin Millar
CREATOR ... Ivan Passer
CREATURE FROM THE BLACK LAGOON, THE ... Jack Arnold
CREATURE FROM THE HAUNTED SEA ... Roger Corman
CREATURE OF DESTRUCTION ... Larry Buchanan
CREATURE WASN'T NICE, THE ... Bruce Kimmel
CREATURES THE WORLD FORGOT ... Don Chaffey
CREEPING FLESH, THE ... Freddie Francis
CREEPING UNKNOWN, THE ... Val Guest
CREEPSHOW ... George A. Romero
CRESCENDO ... Alan Gibson
CREST OF THE WAVE ... John Boulting
CREST OF THE WAVE ... Roy Boulting
CRIA CUERVOS ... Carlos Saura
CRIA! ... Carlos Saura
CRICKET, THE ... Alberto Lattuada
CRIES AND WHISPERS ★ ... Ingmar Bergman
CRIES IN THE NIGHT ... William Fruet
CRIME AND PASSION ... Ivan Passer
CRIME AND PUNISHMENT, U.S.A. ... Denis Sanders
CRIME CLUB (TF) ... David Lowell Rich
CRIME CLUB (TF) ... Jeannot Szwarc
CRIME DOCTOR ... Michael Gordon
CRIME DOCTOR'S COURAGE, THE ... George Sherman
CRIME DOES NOT PAY ... Gerard Oury
CRIME IN THE STREETS ... Don Siegel
CRIME OF OVIDE PLOUFFE, THE ... Gilles Carle
CRIME OF PASSION ... Gerd Oswald
CRIMES OF PASSION ... Ken Russell
CRIMES OF THE FUTURE ... David Cronenberg
CRIMINAL COURT ... Robert Wise
CRIMSON KIMONO, THE ... Samuel Fuller
CRISIS ... Ingmar Bergman
CRISIS ... Richard Brooks
CRISIS AT CENTRAL HIGH (TF) ... Lamont Johnson
CRISIS IN MID-AIR (TF) ... Walter Grauman
CRISIS IN SUN VALLEY (TF) ... Paul Stanley
CRITICAL LIST, THE (TF) ... Lou Antonio
CRITIC'S CHOICE ... Don Weis
CROMWELL ... Kenneth "Ken" Hughes
CRONACHE DI POVERI AMANTI ... Carlo Lizzani
CROOK, THE ... Claude Lelouch
CROOKED HEARTS, THE (TF) ... Jay Sandrich
CROOKED ROAD, THE ... Don Chaffey
CROOKED WEB, THE ... Nathan Juran
CROOKS AND CORONETS ... James O'Connolly
CROOKS ANONYMOUS ... Ken Annakin
CROOKS IN CLOISTERS ... Jeremy Summers
CROQUE LA VIE ... Jean-Charles Tacchella
CROSS AND THE SWITCHBLADE, THE ... Don Murray
CROSS CREEK ... Martin Ritt
CROSS MY HEART ... John Berry
CROSS OF IRON ... Sam Peckinpah
CROSS-COUNTRY ... Paul Lynch
CROSSED SWORDS ... Richard Fleischer
CROSSFIRE (TF) ... William "Billy" Hale
CROSSFIRE ★ ... Edward Dmytryk
CROSSPLOT ... Alvin Rakoff
CROWDED DAY, THE ... John Guillermin
CROWDED SKY, THE ... Joseph Pevney
CROWDED TRAIN, THE ... Kon Ichikawa
CROWHAVEN FARM (TF) ... Walter Grauman
CROWN VS. STEVENS ... Michael Powell
CRUEL STORY OF YOUTH ... Nagisa Oshima
CRUISE INTO TERROR (TF) ... Bruce Kessler
CRUISE MISSILE ... Leslie H. Martinson
CRUISIN' DOWN THE RIVER ... Richard Quine
CRUISING ... William Friedkin
CRUNCH ... Mark Warren
CRY BLOOD, APACHE ... Jack Starrett
CRY DANGER ... Robert Parrish
CRY FOR HELP, A (TF) ... Daryl Duke
CRY FOR LOVE, A (TF) ... Paul Wendkos
CRY FOR ME, BILLY ... William A. Graham
CRY FOR THE STRANGERS (TF) ... Peter Medak
CRY FROM THE STREETS, A ... Lewis Gilbert
CRY IN THE WILDERNESS, A (TF) ... Gordon Hessler
CRY OF THE BANSHEE ... Gordon Hessler
CRY OF THE CITY ... Dominic Orlando
CRY OF THE INNOCENT (TF) ... Michael O'Herlihy
CRY PANIC (TF) ... James Goldstone
CRY RAPE! (TF) ... Corey Allen
CRY TERROR! ... Andrew L. Stone
CRY TOUGH ... Paul Stanley
CRY UNCLE! ... John G. Avildsen
CRYPT OF THE LIVING DEAD ... Ray Danton
CUBA ... Richard Lester
CUENCA ... Carlos Saura
CUJO ... Lewis Teague
CUL-DE-SAC ... Roman Polanski
CULLODEN (TF) ... Peter Watkins
CULPEPPER CATTLE CO., THE ... Dick Richards
CUMBITE ... Tomas Gutierrez Alea
CUORE (MS) ... Luigi Comencini
CUORE DI CANE ... Alberto Lattuada
CURSE OF KING TUT'S TOMB, THE (TF) ... Philip Leacock
CURSE OF THE BLACK WIDOW (TF) ... Dan Curtis
CURSE OF THE CAT PEOPLE, THE ... Robert Wise
CURSE OF THE FLY ... Don Sharp
CURSE OF THE MUMMY'S TOMB, THE ... Michael Carreras
CURSE OF THE PINK PANTHER ... Blake Edwards
CURTAINS ... Richard Ciupka
CUTTER (TF) ... Richard Irving
CUTTER AND BONE ... Ivan Passer
CUTTER'S TRAIL (TF) ... Vincent McEveety
CUTTER'S WAY ... Ivan Passer
CYCLE SAVAGES ... Bill Brame
CYCLONE KID, THE ... George Sherman
CYCLOPS ... Bert I. Gordon
CYRANO DE BERGERAC ... Michael Gordon

D

D.A.: CONSPIRACY TO KILL, THE (TF) ... Paul Krasny
DADDY, I DON'T LIKE IT LIKE THIS (TF) ... Adell Aldrich
DADDY LONG LEGS ... Jean Negulesco
DAGUERREOTYPES (FD) ... Agnes Varda
DAI GO FUKURYU-MARU ... Kaneto Shindo
DAIN CURSE ☆, THE (MS) ... E.W. Swackhamer
DAISY KENYON ... Otto Preminger
DAISY MILLER ... Peter Bogdanovich
DALEKS - INVASION EARTH 2150 A.D. ... Gordon Flemyng
DALLAS COWBOYS CHEERLEADERS (TF) ... Bruce Bilson
DALLAS COWBOYS CHEERLEADERS II (TF) ... Michael O'Herlihy
DAM BUSTERS, THE ... Michael Anderson
DAMIEN - OMEN II ... Don Taylor
DAMIEN...THE LEPER PRIEST (TF) ... Steven Gethers
DAMN THE DEFIANT! ... Lewis Gilbert
DAMN YANKEES ... George Abbott
DAMN YANKEES ... Stanley Donen
DAMNATION ALLEY ... Jack Smight
DAMNED DON'T CRY, THE ... Vincent Sherman
DANCE HALL ... Charles Crichton
DANCE IN THE SUN ... Shirley Clarke
DANCE LITTLE LADY ... Val Guest
DANCE MOVIE ... Andy Warhol
DANCE OF THE DWARFS ... Gus Trikonis
DANCE OF THE SEVEN VEILS, THE (TF) ... Ken Russell
DANCE OF THE VAMPIRES ... Roman Polanski
DANCE WITH A STRANGER ... Mike Newell
DANDY, THE ALL-AMERICAN GIRL ... Jerry Schatzberg
DANGER - LOVE AT WORK ... Otto Preminger
DANGER IN PARADISE (TF) ... Marvin J. Chomsky
DANGER UXB (MS) ... Ferdinand Fairfax
DANGER WITHIN ... Don Chaffey
DANGEROUS AGE, A ... Sidney J. Furie

DANGEROUS COMPANY (TF) ...... Lamont Johnson
DANGEROUS DAVIES - THE LAST DETECTIVE ...... Val Guest
DANGEROUS DAYS OF KIOWA JONES, THE (TF) ...... Alex March
DANGEROUS SUMMER, A ...... Quentin Masters
DANIEL ...... Sidney Lumet
DANNY BOY ...... Neil Jordan
DANTE'S INFERNO (TF) ...... Ken Russell
DANTON ...... Andrzej Wajda
DARBY O'GILL AND THE LITTLE PEOPLE ...... Robert Stevenson
DARING DOBERMANS, THE ...... Byron Chudnow
DARING GAME ...... Laslo Benedek
DARK ALIBI ...... Phil Karlson
DARK AT THE TOP OF THE STAIRS, THE ...... Delbert Mann
DARK CORNER, THE ...... Henry Hathaway
DARK CRYSTAL, THE ...... Jim Henson
DARK CRYSTAL, THE ...... Frank Oz
DARK DID NOT CONQUER, THE (TF) ...... Paul Almond
DARK END OF THE STREET, THE ...... Jan Egleson
DARK INTRUDER ...... Harvey Hart
DARK MIRROR (TF) ...... Richard Lang
DARK NIGHT OF THE SCARECROW (TF) ...... Frank de Felitta
DARK ODYSSEY ...... Radley Metzger
DARK OF THE SUN ...... Jack Cardiff
DARK PLACES ...... Don Sharp
DARK SECRET OF HARVEST HOME, THE (TF) ...... Leo Penn
DARK SIDE OF INNOCENCE, THE (TF) ...... Jerry Thorpe
DARK SIDE OF TOMORROW, THE ...... Barbara Peeters
DARK STAR ...... John Carpenter
DARK SUNDAY ...... Jimmy Huston
DARK, THE ...... John "Bud" Cardos
DARK VICTORY (TF) ...... Robert Butler
DARK WARRIOR ...... Robert Clouse
DARK WATERS ...... Andre De Toth
DARKER SIDE OF TERROR, THE (TF) ...... Gus Trikonis
DARKER THAN AMBER ...... Robert Clouse
DARKTOWN STRUTTERS ...... William Witney
DARLING ★ ...... John Schlesinger
DARLING LILI ...... Blake Edwards
DARWIN ADVENTURE, THE ...... Jack Couffer
DAS ABENTEUER DER THEA ROLAND ...... Henry Koster
DAS BOOT (THE BOAT) ★ ...... Wolfgang Petersen
DAS FALSCHE GEWICHT ...... Bernhard Wicki
DAS HASSLICHE MADCHEN ...... Henry Koster
DAS TAGEBUCH DER GELIEBTEN ...... Henry Koster
DAS WUNDER DES MALACHIAS ...... Bernhard Wicki
DATELINE DIAMONDS ...... Jeremy Summers
DAUGHTER OF THE MIND (TF) ...... Walter Grauman
DAUGHTER OF THE SUN ...... Herschell Gordon Lewis
DAUGHTERS OF JOSHUA CABE, THE (TF) ...... Philip Leacock
DAUGHTERS OF JOSHUA CABE RETURN, THE (TF) ...... David Lowell Rich
DAUGHTERS I DAUGHTERS I ...... Moshe Mizrahi
DAVID ...... Peter Lilienthal
DAVID AND GOLIATH ...... Ferdinando Baldi
DAVID AND LISA ★ ...... Frank Perry
DAVID COPPERFIELD (TF) ...... Delbert Mann
DAVID HOLZMAN'S DIARY ...... Jim McBride
DAWN AT SOCORRO ...... George Sherman
DAWN OF THE DEAD ...... George A. Romero
DAWN: PORTRAIT OF A TEENAGE RUNAWAY (TF) ...... Randal Kleiser
DAY AFTER ☆, THE (TF) ...... Nicholas Meyer
DAY AFTER HALLOWEEN, THE ...... Simon Wincer
DAY AND THE HOUR, THE ...... René Clement
DAY CHRIST DIED, THE (TF) ...... James Cellan-Jones
DAY FOR THANKS ON WALTON'S MOUNTAIN, A (TF) ...... Harry Harris
DAY IN THE DEATH OF JOE EGG, A ...... Peter Medak
DAY MARS INVADED EARTH, THE ...... Maury Dexter
DAY OF THE DEAD ...... George A. Romero
DAY OF THE DOLPHIN, THE ...... Mike Nichols
DAY OF THE EVIL GUN ...... Jerry Thorpe
DAY OF THE JACKAL, THE ...... Fred Zinnemann
DAY OF THE LOCUST, THE ...... John Schlesinger
DAY OF THE OUTLAW ...... Andre De Toth
DAY OF THE TRUMPET, THE ...... Eddie Romero
DAY THE BUBBLE BURST, THE (TF) ...... Joseph Hardy
DAY THE EARTH CAUGHT FIRE, THE ...... Val Guest
DAY THE EARTH MOVED, THE (TF) ...... Robert M. Lewis
DAY THE EARTH STOOD STILL, THE ...... Robert Wise
DAY THE FISH CAME OUT, THE ...... Michael Cacoyannis
DAY THE LORD GOT BUSTED, THE ...... Burt Topper
DAY THE LOVING STOPPED, THE (TF) ...... Daniel Mann
DAY THE WOMEN GOT EVEN, THE (TF) ...... Burt Brinckerhoff
DAY THE WORLD ENDED, THE ...... Roger Corman
DAY THEY GAVE BABIES AWAY, THE ...... Allen Reisner
DAY THEY ROBBED THE BANK OF ENGLAND, THE ...... John Guillermin
DAY TIME ENDED, THE ...... John "Bud" Cardos
DAY TO REMEMBER, A ...... Ralph Thomas
DAYS AND NIGHTS IN THE FOREST ...... Satyajit Ray
DAYS ARE PASSING, THE ...... Goran Paskaljevic
DAYS OF HEAVEN ...... Terrence Malick
DAYS OF WINE AND ROSES ...... Blake Edwards
DAYTON'S DEVILS ...... Jack Shea
D.C. CAB ...... Joel Schumacher
D-DAY, THE SIXTH OF JUNE ...... Henry Koster
DE CHE SEGNO SEI? ...... Sergio Corbucci
DE GREY - LE BANC DE DESOLATION (TF) ...... Claude Chabrol
DE LA PART DES COPAINS ...... Terence Young
DE SADE ...... Cy Endfield
DEAD AND BURIED ...... Gary A. Sherman
DEAD CERT ...... Tony Richardson
DEAD DON'T DIE, THE (TF) ...... Curtis Harrington
DEAD END STREET ...... Yaky Yosha
DEAD HEAT ON A MERRY-GO-ROUND ...... Bernard Girard
DEAD KIDS ...... Michael Laughlin
DEAD MAN ON THE RUN (TF) ...... Bruce Bilson
DEAD MEN DON'T WEAR PLAID ...... Carl Reiner
DEAD MEN TELL NO TALES (TF) ...... Walter Grauman
DEAD OF NIGHT ...... Charles Crichton
DEAD ON ARRIVAL ...... Charles Martin
DEAD PIGEON ON BEETHOVEN STREET ...... Samuel Fuller
DEAD RINGER ...... Allan Nicholls
DEAD ZONE, THE ...... David Cronenberg
DEADFALL ...... Bryan Forbes
DEADHEAD MILES ...... Vernon Zimmerman
DEADLIER THAN THE MALE ...... Ralph Thomas
DEADLIEST SEASON, THE (TF) ...... Robert Markowitz
DEADLIEST SIN, THE ...... Kenneth "Ken" Hughes
DEADLINE - U.S.A. ...... Richard Brooks
DEADLINE AUTO THEFT ...... H.B. Halicki
DEADLOCK (TF) ...... Lamont Johnson
DEADLOCK (TF) ...... Don Weis
DEADLY AFFAIR, THE ...... Sidney Lumet
DEADLY BEES, THE ...... Freddie Francis
DEADLY BLESSING ...... Wes Craven
DEADLY COMPANIONS, THE ...... Sam Peckinpah
DEADLY DREAM, THE (TF) ...... Alf Kjellin
DEADLY ENCOUNTER (TF) ...... William A. Graham
DEADLY FORCE ...... Paul Aaron
DEADLY GAME (TF) ...... Lane Slate
DEADLY HARVEST (TF) ...... Michael O'Herlihy
DEADLY HERO ...... Ivan Nagy
DEADLY HONEYMOON ...... Elliot Silverstein
DEADLY HUNT, THE (TF) ...... John Newland
DEADLY LESSONS (TF) ...... William Wiard
DEADLY MANTIS, THE ...... Nathan Juran
DEADLY STRANGERS ...... Sidney Hayers
DEADLY TOWER, THE (TF) ...... Jerry Jameson
DEADLY TRAP, THE ...... René Clement
DEADLY TRIANGLE, THE (TF) ...... Charles S. Dubin
DEADLY WARRIORS ...... Emmett Alston
DEADMAN'S CURVE (TF) ...... Richard Compton
DEAL OF THE CENTURY ...... William Friedkin
DEALING: OR THE BERKELEY-TO-BOSTON FORTY-BRICK LOST-BAG BLUES ...... Paul Williams
DEAR BRIGITTE ...... Henry Koster
DEAR DETECTIVE ...... Philippe de Broca
DEAR DETECTIVE (TF) ...... Dean Hargrove
DEAR HEART ...... Delbert Mann
DEAR INSPECTOR ...... Philippe de Broca
DEAR MR. WONDERFUL ...... Peter Lilienthal
DEATH, A ...... Don Norman
DEATH AMONG FRIENDS (TF) ...... Paul Wendkos
DEATH AT LOVE HOUSE (TF) ...... E.W. Swackhamer
DEATH BE NOT PROUD (TF) ...... Donald Wrye
DEATH BY HANGING ...... Nagisa Oshima
DEATH CAR ON THE FREEWAY (TF) ...... Hal Needham
DEATH CRUISE (TF) ...... Ralph Senensky
DEATH DIMENSION ...... Al Adamson
DEATH HUNT ...... Peter Hunt
DEATH IN CANAAN, A (TF) ...... Tony Richardson
DEATH IS NOT THE END ...... Richard Michaels
DEATH JOURNEY ...... Fred Williamson
DEATH LINE ...... Gary A. Sherman
DEATH MOON (TF) ...... Bruce Kessler
DEATH OF A CENTERFOLD: THE DOROTHY STRATTEN STORY (TF) ...... Gabrielle Beaumont
DEATH OF A GUNFIGHTER ...... Don Siegel
DEATH OF A GUNFIGHTER ...... Robert Totten
DEATH OF A SALESMAN ...... Laslo Benedek
DEATH OF A SCOUNDREL ...... Charles Martin
DEATH OF A STRANGER ...... Reza Badiyi
DEATH OF AN ANGEL ...... Petru Popescu
DEATH OF INNOCENCE, A (TF) ...... Paul Wendkos
DEATH OF MARIO RICCI, THE ...... Claude Goretta
DEATH OF ME YET I, THE (TF) ...... John Llewellyn Moxey
DEATH OF NIGHT ...... Bob Clark
DEATH OF OCEAN VIEW PARK, THE (TF) ...... E.W. Swackhamer
DEATH OF RICHIE, THE (TF) ...... Paul Wendkos
DEATH ON THE NILE ...... John Guillermin
DEATH PENALTY (TF) ...... Waris Hussein
DEATH RACE (TF) ...... David Lowell Rich
DEATH RACE 2000 ...... Paul Bartel
DEATH RAGE ...... Anthony M. Dawson
DEATH RAY 2000 (TF) ...... Lee H. Katzin
DEATH RIVER ...... Jimmy Huston
DEATH SCREAM (TF) ...... Richard T. Heffron
DEATH SCREAMS ...... David Nelson
DEATH SENTENCE (TF) ...... E.W. Swackhamer
DEATH SHIP ...... Alvin Rakoff
DEATH SQUAD, THE (TF) ...... Harry Falk
DEATH STALK (TF) ...... Robert Day
DEATH TAKES A HOLIDAY (TF) ...... Robert Butler
DEATH TRAP ...... John Llewellyn Moxey
DEATH VALLEY ...... Dick Richards
DEATH VALLEY OUTLAWS ...... George Sherman
DEATH WATCH ...... Bertrand Tavernier
DEATH WEEKEND ...... William Fruet
DEATH WHEELERS, THE ...... Don Sharp
DEATH WISH ...... Michael Winner
DEATH WISH II ...... Michael Winner
DEATHDREAM ...... Bob Clark
DEATHMASTER, THE ...... Ray Danton
DEATHOUSE ...... Theodore Gershuny
DEATHSPORT ...... Allan Arkush
DEATHSTALKER ...... John Watson
DEATHTRAP ...... Sidney Lumet
DECAMERON 3 ...... Anthony M. Dawson
DECEPTION ...... Irving Rapper
DECISION AGAINST TIME ...... Charles Crichton
DECISION AT SUNDOWN ...... Budd Boetticher
DECKS RAN RED, THE ...... Andrew L. Stone
DECLINE AND FALL OF A BIRD WATCHER ...... John Krish
DECLINE OF WESTERN CIVILIZATION, THE (FD) ...... Penelope Spheeris
DEDICATO A UNA STELLA ...... Lewis Coates
DEEP END ...... Jerzy Skolimowski
DEEP IN MY HEART ...... Stanley Donen

DEEP IN THE HEART .... Tony Garnett
DEEP RED .... Dario Argento
DEEP, THE .... Peter Yates
DEEP VALLEY .... Jean Negulesco
DEER HUNTER ★★, THE .... Michael Cimino
DEERSLAYER, THE (TF) .... Dick Friedenberg
DEFECTION OF SIMAS KUDIRKA ☆☆, THE (TF) .... David Lowell Rich
DEFIANCE .... John Flynn
DEFIANT ONES ★, THE .... Stanley Kramer
DEGREE OF MURDER, A .... Volker Schlondorff
DEJA VU .... Anthony Richmond
DELANCEY STREET: THE CRISIS WITHIN (TF) .... James Frawley
DELICATE BALANCE, A .... Tony Richardson
DELINQUENTS, THE .... Robert Altman
DELITTO D'AMORE .... Luigi Comencini
DELIVERANCE ★ .... John Boorman
DELLA .... Leslie Stevens
DeLOREAN (TD) .... D.A. Pennebaker
DELPHI BUREAU, THE (TF) .... Paul Wendkos
DELTA COUNTY, U.S.A. (TF) .... Glenn Jordan
DELUSION .... Alan Beattie
DELUSIONS OF GRANDEUR .... Gerard Oury
DEMENTIA 13 .... Francis Ford Coppola
DEMON .... Larry Cohen
DEMON MURDER CASE, THE (TF) .... William "Billy" Hale
DEMON POND .... Masahiro Shinoda
DEMON SEED .... Donald Cammell
DEMONS OF THE MIND .... Peter Sykes
DEMPSEY (TF) .... Gus Trikonis
DENMARK VESEY'S REBELLION (TF) .... Stan Lathan
DENTIST IN THE CHAIR .... Don Chaffey
DEPRISA, DEPRISA .... Carlos Saura
DEPTH CHARGE .... Jeremy Summers
DEPUTIES, THE (TF) .... Virgil W. Vogel
DER CHINESE (TF) .... Kurt Gloor
DER ERFINDER .... Kurt Gloor
DER MANN VON OBERZALZBERG - ADOLF UND MARLENE .... Ulli Lommel
DERBY (FD) .... Robert Kaylor
DEREK AND CLIVE GET THE HORN (FD) .... Russell Mulcahy
DERSU UZALA .... Akira Kurosawa
DES FEMMES DISPARAISSENT .... Edouard Molinaro
DES GARCONS ET DES FILLES .... Etienne Perier
DES GENS SANS IMPORTANCE .... Henri Verneuil
DES JOURNEES ENTIERES DANS LES ARBRES .... Marguerite Duras
DESERT ATTACK .... J. Lee Thompson
DESERT BANDIT .... George Sherman
DESERT BLOOM .... Eugene Corr
DESERT FOX, THE .... Henry Hathaway
DESERT HELL .... Charles Marquis Warren
DESERT LEGION .... Joseph Pevney
DESERT OF LIES (TF) .... Piers Haggard
DESERT OF THE HEART .... Donna Deitch
DESERT PATROL .... Guy Green
DESERT RATS, THE .... Robert Wise
DESERT VICTORY (FD) .... Roy Boulting
DESERTER, THE .... Burt Kennedy
DESIGN FOR DEATH .... Richard Fleischer
DESIGN OF A HUMAN BEING .... Kon Ichikawa
DESIGNING WOMAN .... Vincente Minnelli
DESIRE .... Eddie Romero
DESIRE IN THE DUST .... William F. Claxton
DESIRE UNDER THE ELMS .... Delbert Mann
DESIREE .... Henry Koster
DESPERATE CHARACTERS .... Frank D. Gilroy
DESPERATE LIVES (TF) .... Robert M. Lewis
DESPERATE LIVING .... John Waters
DESPERATE MILES, THE (TF) .... Daniel Haller
DESPERATE MISSION (TF) .... Earl Bellamy
DESPERATE VOYAGE (TF) .... Michael O'Herlihy
DESPERATE WOMEN (TF) .... Earl Bellamy
DESPERATELY SEEKING SUSAN .... Susan Seidelman
DESTINATION GOBI .... Robert Wise
DESTROY, SHE SAID .... Marguerite Duras
DESTRUCTORS, THE .... Robert Parrish
DETECTIVE .... Jean-Luc Godard
DETECTIVE GERONIMO .... Bert I. Gordon
DETECTIVE, THE .... Gordon Douglas
DETENUTO IN ATTESTA DI GUIDIZIO .... Nanni Loy
DETOUR TO TERROR (TF) .... Michael O'Herlihy
DETROIT 9000 .... Arthur Marks
DEUTSCHLAND IM HERBST (FD) .... Volker Schlondorff
DEVI .... Satyajit Ray
DEVIL AND MAX DEVLIN, THE .... Steven Hillard Stern
DEVIL AND MISS SARAH, THE (TF) .... Michael Caffey
DEVIL AT 4 O'CLOCK, THE .... Mervyn Leroy
DEVIL BY THE TAIL, THE .... Philippe de Broca
DEVIL COMMANDS, THE .... Edward Dmytryk
DEVIL DOG: THE HOUND OF HELL (TF) .... Curtis Harrington
DEVIL IN LOVE, THE .... Ettore Scola
DEVIL IS A WOMAN, THE .... Damiano Damiani
DEVIL WITH HITLER, THE .... Gordon Douglas
DEVIL WITHIN HER, THE .... Peter Sasdy
DEVIL'S ADVOCATE, THE .... Guy Green
DEVIL'S ANGELS .... Daniel Haller
DEVIL'S BRIGADE, THE .... Andrew V. McLaglen
DEVIL'S CAMERA .... Herschell Gordon Lewis
DEVIL'S DAUGHTER, THE (TF) .... Jeannot Szwarc
DEVIL'S DISCIPLE, THE .... Guy Hamilton
DEVIL'S EYE, THE .... Ingmar Bergman
DEVIL'S HAIRPIN, THE .... Cornel Wilde
DEVIL'S ISLAND .... Masahiro Shinoda
DEVIL'S ISLAND, THE .... Kon Ichikawa
DEVIL'S PLAYGROUND, THE .... Fred Schepisi
DEVIL'S RAIN, THE .... Robert Fuest
DEVIL'S SONG OF BALL, THE .... Kon Ichikawa
DEVILS, THE .... Ken Russell
DEVIL'S WANTON, THE .... Ingmar Bergman
DEVIL'S 8, THE .... Burt Topper
DEVIL-SHIP PIRATES, THE .... Don Sharp
DEVILS'S WIDOW, THE .... Roddy McDowall
DEVONSVILLE TERROR, THE .... Ulli Lommel
DIABOLO MENTHE .... Diane Kurys
DIAGNOSIS: MURDER .... Sidney Hayers
DIAL HOT LINE (TF) .... Jerry Thorpe
DIALOGUE .... Jerzy Skolimowski
DIAMOND HEAD .... Guy Green
DIAMONDS .... Menahem Golan
DIAMONDS ARE FOREVER .... Guy Hamilton
DIAMONDS ON WHEELS .... Jerome Courtland
DIANE .... David Miller
DIARY OF A COUNTRY PRIEST .... Robert Bresson
DIARY OF A HIGH SCHOOL BRIDE, THE .... Burt Topper
DIARY OF A MAD HOUSEWIFE .... Frank Perry
DIARY OF A SHINJUKU BURGLAR .... Nagisa Oshima
DIARY OF A TEENAGE HITCHHIKER (TF) .... Ted Post
DICK DEADEYE, OR DUTY DONE (AF) .... Bill Melendez
DICK DOWN UNDER .... Richard Franklin
DICK TRACY VS. CUEBALL .... Gordon Douglas
DICTIONARY OF SEX .... Radley Metzger
DID YOU HEAR THE ONE ABOUT THE TRAVELING SALESLADY? .... Don Weis
DIE EROBERUNG DER ZITADELLE .... Bernhard Wicki
DIE FALSCHUNG .... Volker Schlondorff
DIE FLIEGENDEN ARZTE VON OSTAFRIKA .... Werner Herzog
DIE GRAFFEN POCCI - EINIGE ITEL ZUR GESCHICHTE EINER FAMILIE (FD) .... Hans-Jurgen Syberberg
DIE GROSSE LIEBE .... Otto Preminger
DIE LAUGHING .... Jeff Werner
DIE, MONSTER, DIE! .... Daniel Haller
DIE MORAL DER RUTH HALBFASS .... Volker Schlondorff
DIE PLOTZLICHE EINSAMKEIT DES KONRAD STEINER .... Kurt Gloor
DIE ROLLE (TF) .... Krzysztof Zanussi
DIE WINDROSE .... Gillo Pontecorvo
DIE! DIE! MY DARLING! .... Silvio Narizzano
DIESEL .... Robert Kramer
DIFENDO IL MIO AMORE .... Vincent Sherman
DIFFERENT STORY, A .... Paul Aaron
DIGBY, THE BIGGEST DOG IN THE WORLD .... Joseph McGrath
DIGITAL DREAMS .... Robert Dornhelm
DILLINGER .... John Milius
DILLINGER E MORTO .... Marco Ferreri
DIM SUM .... Wayne Wang
DIMBOOLA .... John Duigan
DINER .... Barry Levinson
DINGAKA .... Jamie Uys
DION BROTHERS, THE .... Jack Starrett
DIONYSUS IN '69 .... Brian De Palma
DIPLOMATIC COURIER .... Henry Hathaway
DIRECTED BY JOHN FORD (FD) .... Peter Bogdanovich
DIRIGIBLE .... Frank Capra
DIRT .... Eric Karson
DIRT .... Cal Naylor
DIRT GANG, THE .... Jerry Jameson
DIRTY DINGUS MAGEE .... Burt Kennedy
DIRTY DOZEN: THE NEXT MISSION, THE (TF) .... Andrew V. McLaglen
DIRTY DUCK (AF) .... Charles Swenson
DIRTY GAME, THE .... Carlo Lizzani
DIRTY GAME, THE .... Terence Young
DIRTY GIRLS, THE .... Radley Metzger
DIRTY HANDS .... Claude Chabrol
DIRTY HARRY .... Don Siegel
DIRTY KNIGHTS' WORK .... Kevin Connor
DIRTY LILLY .... Chuck Vincent
DIRTY LITTLE BILLY .... Stan Dragoti
DIRTY LOOKS .... Chuck Vincent
DIRTY MARY CRAZY LARRY .... John Hough
DIRTY O'NEIL .... Lewis Teague
DIRTY TRICKS .... Alvin Rakoff
DISAPPEARANCE OF AIMEE, THE (TF) .... Anthony Harvey
DISAPPEARANCE OF FLIGHT 412, THE (TF) .... Jud Taylor
DISAPPEARANCE, THE .... Stuart Cooper
DISASTER ON THE COASTLINER (TF) .... Richard C. Sarafian
DISCO FEVER .... Lamar Card
DISEMBODIED, THE .... Walter Grauman
DISHONORED LADY .... Robert Stevenson
DIS-MOI QUI TUER .... Etienne Perier
DISPLACED PERSON, THE (TF) .... Glenn Jordan
DISTANT THUNDER .... Satyajit Ray
DIVA .... Jean-Jacques Beineix
DIVIDE AND CONQUER (FD) .... Frank Capra
DIVIDED HEART, THE .... Charles Crichton
DIVINE MADNESS (TF) .... Michael Ritchie
DIVORCE AMERICAN STYLE .... Bud Yorkin
DIVORCE HIS/DIVORCE HERS (TF) .... Waris Hussein
DIVORCE WARS: A LOVE STORY (TF) .... Donald Wrye
DIXIE: CHANGING HABITS (TF) .... George Englund
DIZENGOFF 99 .... Avi Nesher
DJANGO .... Sergio Corbucci
DO I HAVE TO KILL MY CHILD? (TF) .... Donald Crombie
DO NOT DISTURB .... Ralph Levy
DO NOT FOLD, SPINDLE OR MUTILATE (TF) .... Ted Post
DO YOU TAKE THIS STRANGER? (TF) .... Richard T. Heffron
DOBERMAN GANG, THE .... Byron Chudnow
DOC .... Frank Perry
DOC SAVAGE, THE MAN OF BRONZE .... Michael Anderson
DOCK BRIEF, THE .... James Hill
DOCTEUR POPAUL .... Claude Chabrol
DOCTOR AT LARGE .... Ralph Thomas
DOCTOR AT SEA .... Ralph Thomas
DOCTOR DETROIT .... Michael Pressman
DOCTOR FISCHER OF GENEVA (TF) .... Michael Lindsay-Hogg
DOCTOR FRANKEN (TF) .... Marvin J. Chomsky
DOCTOR FRANKEN (TF) .... Jeff Lieberman
DOCTOR GLAS .... Mai Zetterling
DOCTOR IN CLOVER .... Ralph Thomas
DOCTOR IN DISTRESS .... Ralph Thomas
DOCTOR IN LOVE .... Ralph Thomas
DOCTOR IN THE HOUSE .... Ralph Thomas
DOCTOR IN TROUBLE .... Ralph Thomas
DOCTOR, YOU'VE GOT TO BE KIDDING .... Peter Tewksbury
DOCTOR ZHIVAGO ★ .... David Lean
DOCTORS' PRIVATE LIVES (TF) .... Steven Hillard Stern
DOCTOR'S STORY, A (TF) .... Peter Levin
DOCTOR'S WIVES .... George Schaefer

Title	Director
DOCUMENT OF THE DEAD (FD)	Roy Frumkes
DOCUMENTEUR: AN EMOTION PICTURE	Agnes Varda
DODES'KA'DEN	Akira Kurosawa
DOG AND THE DIAMONDS, THE	Ralph Thomas
DOG DAY AFTERNOON ★	Sidney Lumet
DOG OF FLANDERS, A	James B. Clark
DOG THAT LIKED TRAINS, THE	Goran Paskaljevic
DOGPOUND SHUFFLE	Jeffrey Bloom
DOGS	Burt Brinckerhoff
DOGS OF WAR, THE	John Irvin
DOIN' TIME	George Mendeluk
DOING IT	Bert I. Gordon
DOLL SQUAD, THE	Ted V. Mikels
DOLLARS	Richard Brooks
DOLLMAKER, THE (TF)	Daniel Petrie
DOLL'S HOUSE, A	Patrick Garland
DOMINIQUE	Michael Anderson
DOMINO PRINCIPLE, THE	Stanley Kramer
DOMO ARIGATO (FD)	Arch Oboler
DON GIOVANNI IN SICILIA	Alberto Lattuada
DON IS DEAD, THE	Richard Fleischer
DON JUAN	John Berry
DON JUAN ETAIT UNE FEMME	Roger Vadim
DONA FLOR AND HER TWO HUSBANDS	Bruno Barreto
DONATELLA	Mario Monicelli
DONDI	Albert Zugsmith
DONKEY SKIN	Jacques Demy
DONNER PASS: THE ROAD TO SURVIVAL (TF)	James L. Conway
DONOVAN AFFAIR, THE	Frank Capra
DONOVAN'S KID (TF)	Bernard McEveety
DON'S PARTY	Bruce Beresford
DON'T BE AFRAID OF THE DARK (TF)	John Newland
DON'T BOTHER TO KNOCK	Roy Ward Baker
DON'T CRY, IT'S ONLY THUNDER	Peter Werner
DON'T DRINK THE WATER	Howard Morris
DON'T FORGET - JE ME SOUVIENS (TF)	Robin Spry
DON'T GO NEAR THE PARK	Lawrence D. Foldes
DON'T GO TO SLEEP (TF)	Richard Lang
DON'T LET THE ANGELS FALL	George Kaczender
DON'T LOOK BACK (FD)	D.A. Pennebaker
DON'T LOOK BACK (TF)	Richard A. Colla
DON'T LOOK NOW	Nicolas Roeg
DON'T LOOK NOW...WE'RE BEING SHOT AT	Gerard Oury
DON'T MAKE WAVES	Alexander Mackendrick
DON'T RAISE THE BRIDGE - LOWER THE RIVER	Jerry Paris
DON'T YOU HEAR THE DOGS BARK?	Noel Howard
DOOLINS OF OKLAHOMA, THE	Gordon Douglas
DOOMSDAY FLIGHT, THE (TF)	William A. Graham
DOOMSDAY VOYAGE	Al Adamson
DOOMWATCH	Peter Sasdy
DOOR TO DOOR	Patrick Bailey
DOPPELGANGER	Robert Parrish
DORM THAT DRIPPED BLOOD, THE	Stephen Carpenter
DORM THAT DRIPPED BLOOD, THE	Jeffrey Obrow
D'OU VIENS TO JOHNNY	Noel Howard
DOUBLE CONFESSION	Ken Annakin
DOUBLE DEAL	Arthur Dreifuss
DOUBLE EXPOSURE	William Byron Hillman
DOUBLE INDEMNITY (TF)	Jack Smight
DOUBLE INDEMNITY ★	Billy Wilder
DOUBLE McGUFFIN, THE	Joe Camp
DOUBLE MAN, THE	Franklin J. Schaffner
DOUBLE NEGATIVE	George Bloomfield
DOUBLE SUICIDE	Masahiro Shinoda
DOUBLE-STOP	Gerald Seth Sindell
DOUCEMENT LES BASSES !	Jacques Deray
DOVE, THE	Charles Jarrott
DOVE VAI IN VACANZA?	Luciano Salce
DOWN AND DIRTY	Ettore Scola
DOWN MEMORY LANE	Phil Karlson
DOWN ON US	Larry Buchanan
DOWN THREE DARK STREETS	Arnold Laven
DOWN TO THE SEA IN SHIPS	Henry Hathaway
DOWNFALL	John Llewellyn Moxey
DOWNHILL RACER	Michael Ritchie
DR. BLACK, MR. HYDE	William Crain
DR. BLOOD'S COFFIN	Sidney J. Furie
DR. COOK'S GARDEN (TF)	Ted Post
DR. DOLITTLE	Richard Fleischer
DR. HECKLE AND MR. HYPE	Charles B. Griffith
DR. JEKYLL AND MR. HYDE	Rouben Mamoulian
DR. JEKYLL AND SISTER HYDE	Roy Ward Baker
DR. MAX (TF)	James Goldstone
DR. MINX	Howard (Hikmet) Avedis
DR. NO	Terence Young
DR. PHIBES RISES AGAIN	Robert Fuest
DR. SCORPION (TF)	Richard Lang
DR. STRANGE (TF)	Philip De Guere
DR. STRANGELOVE OR: HOW I LEARNED TO STOP WORRYING AND LOVE THE BOMB ★	Stanley Kubrick
DR. TERROR'S HOUSE OF HORRORS	Freddie Francis
DR. WHO AND THE DALEKS	Gordon Flemyng
DRACULA	John Badham
DRACULA (TF)	Dan Curtis
DRACULA A.D. 1972	Alan Gibson
DRACULA HAS RISEN FROM THE GRAVE	Freddie Francis
DRACULA PERE ET FILS	Edouard Molinaro
DRACULA TODAY	Alan Gibson
DRACULA VS. FRANKENSTEIN	Al Adamson
DRACULA'S DISCIPLE	Allen Schaaf
DRACULA'S DOG	Albert Band
DRACULA'S LAST RITES	Domonic Paris
DRAGON GATE INN	King Hu
DRAGONFLY	Gilbert Cates
DRAGONSLAYER	Matthew Robbins
DRAGONWYCK	Joseph L. Mankiewicz
DRAMMA DELLA GELOSIA - TUTTI I PARTICOLARI INCRONICA	Ettore Scola
DRANGO	Hall Bartlett
DRASTIC MEASURES	Les Rose
DRAUGHTMAN'S CONTRACT, THE	Peter Greenaway
DRAW! (CTF)	Steven Hillard Stern
DREAM CHILD	Gavin Millar
DREAM FOR CHRISTMAS, A (TF)	Ralph Senensky
DREAM HOUSE (TF)	Joseph Hardy
DREAM LOVER	Alan J. Pakula
DREAM MAKER, THE	Don Sharp
DREAM MERCHANTS, THE (TF)	Vincent Sherman
DREAM OF KINGS, A	Daniel Mann
DREAM OF PASSION, A	Jules Dassin
DREAM ONE	Arnaud Selignac
DREAM WIFE	Sidney Sheldon
DREAMER	Noel Nosseck
DREAMER, THE	Dan Wolman
DREAMLAND	Oz Scott
DREAMS	Ingmar Bergman
DREAMS DON'T DIE (TF)	Roger Young
DREAMS OF GLASS	Robert Clouse
DREAMS OF GOLD	Eric Weston
DREAMSCAPE	Joseph Ruben
DREAMSPEAKER (TF)	Claude Jutra
DRESS, THE	Vilgot Sjoman
DRESSED TO KILL	Brian De Palma
DRESSER ★, THE	Peter Yates
DRILLER KILLER	Abel Ferrara
DRIVE A CROOKED ROAD	Richard Quine
DRIVE HARD, DRIVE FAST (TF)	Douglas Heyes
DRIVE, HE SAID	Jack Nicholson
DRIVE IN	Rod Amateau
DRIVER, THE	Walter Hill
DROP DEAD, DARLING	Kenneth "Ken" Hughes
DROP-OUT FATHER (TF)	Don Taylor
DROWNING POOL, THE	Stuart Rosenberg
DRUM	Steve Carver
DRUMS ACROSS THE RIVER	Nathan Juran
DRUMS OF AFRICA	James B. Clark
DRUNK	Andy Warhol
DRUNKEN ANGEL	Akira Kurosawa
DRY LAKE	Masahiro Shinoda
DRY WOOD AND HOT PEPPER (FD)	Les Blank
DRYING UP THE STREETS	Robin Spry
DU BEAT-E-O	Alan Sacks
DUCHESS AND THE DIRTWATER FOX, THE	Melvin Frank
DUCK ! YOU SUCKER	Sergio Leone
DUEL (TF)	Steven Spielberg
DUEL AT DIABLO	Ralph Nelson
DUEL AT SILVER CREEK	Don Siegel
DUEL OF CHAMPIONS	Ferdinando Baldi
DUEL OF CHAMPIONS	Terence Young
DUEL OF THE TITANS	Sergio Corbucci
DUELLE	Jacques Rivette
DUELLISTS, THE	Ridley Scott
DUET FOR CANNIBALS	Susan Sontag
DUFFY	Robert Parrish
DUFFY OF SAN QUENTIN	Walter Doniger
DUKE WORE JEANS, THE	Gerald Thomas
DUMMY (TF)	Frank Perry
DUMMY (TF)	Franc Roddam
DUNE	David Lynch
DUNGEONMASTER, THE	Charles Band
DUNGEONMASTER, THE	Rose Marie Turko
DUNWICH HORROR, THE	Daniel Haller
DURANTE L'ESTATE (TF)	Ermanno Olmi
DUST AND GOLD	John Guillermin
DUSTY AND SWEETS McGEE	Floyd Mutrux
DUTCHMAN	Anthony Harvey
DYING (TD)	Michael Roemer
DYING ROOM ONLY (TF)	Philip Leacock
DYNAMITE BROTHERS, THE	Al Adamson
DYNAMITE CHICKEN	Ernest Pintoff
DYNASTY (TF)	Ralph Senensky

E

Title	Director
E ARRIVATO IL CAVALIERE	Mario Monicelli
EACH OTHER	Michal Bat-Adam
EAGLE HAS LANDED, THE	John Sturges
EAGLE IN A CAGE	Fielder Cook
EAGLE'S WING	Anthony Harvey
EARTHBOUND	James L. Conway
EAST OF EDEN ★	Elia Kazan
EAST OF SUDAN	Nathan Juran
EAST OF SUMATRA	Budd Boetticher
EAST SIDE, WEST SIDE	Mervyn Leroy
EASY COME, EASY GO	John Rich
EASY LIFE, THE	Dino Risi
EASY MONEY	James Signorelli
EASY RIDER	Dennis Hopper
EAT	Andy Warhol
EAT MY DUST	Charles B. Griffith
EATEN ALIVE	Tobe Hooper
EATING RAOUL	Paul Bartel
EATING TOO FAST	Andy Warhol
EBOLI	Francesco Rosi
EBONY, IVORY AND JADE (TF)	John Llewellyn Moxey
ECCO NOI PER ESEMPIO	Sergio Corbucci
ECHO OF BARBARA	Sidney Hayers
ECHO PARK	Robert Dornhelm
ECHOES	Arthur Allan Seidelman
ECHOES OF A SUMMER	Don Taylor
ECHOES OF THE SIXTIES (TD)	Kevin Billington
ECSTASIES OF WOMEN, THE	Herschell Gordon Lewis
ECSTASY	Bud Townsend
EDDIE AND THE CRUISERS	Martin Davidson
EDDIE MACON'S RUN	Jeff Kanew
EDDIE WAS A LADY	Arthur Dreifuss
EDDY DUCHIN STORY, THE	George Sidney
EDGE OF ETERNITY	Don Siegel
EDGE OF THE CITY	Martin Ritt
EDGE OF THE WORLD, THE	Michael Powell
EDGE, THE	Robert Kramer
EDITH AND MARCEL	Claude Lelouch
EDUCATING RITA	Lewis Gilbert
EDUCATION OF SONNY CARSON, THE	Michael Campus
EDVARD MUNCH	Peter Watkins
EENY, MEENY, MINY, MO	Jan Troell
EFFECT OF GAMMA RAYS ON MAN-IN-THE-MOON MARIGOLDS, THE	Paul Newman
EIGER SANCTION, THE	Clint Eastwood
EIGHT IRON MEN	Edward Dmytryk
EIJANAIKA	Shohei Imamura
EL ARTE DEL TOBACO	Tomas Gutierrez Alea

EL COCHECITO ... Marco Ferreri
EL CONDOR ... John Guillermin
EL DORADO ... Menahem Golan
EL GRECO ... Luciano Salce
EL MEGANO ... Tomas Gutierrez Alea
EL NORTE ... Gregory Nava
EL PISITO ... Marco Ferreri
EL SUPER ... Orlando Jimenez-Leal
EL TOPO ... Alexandro Jodorowsky
ELDRIDGE CLEAVER (FD) ... William Klein
ELEANOR AND FRANKLIN (TF) ☆☆ ... Daniel Petrie
ELEANOR AND FRANKLIN: THE WHITE HOUSE YEARS (TF) ☆☆ ... Daniel Petrie
ELEANOR, FIRST LADY OF THE WORLD (TF) ... John Erman
ELECTRA ... Michael Cacoyannis
ELECTRA GLIDE IN BLUE ... James William Guercio
ELECTRIC DREAMS ... Steve Barron
ELECTRIC GRANDMOTHER, THE (TF) ... Noel Black
ELECTRIC HORSEMAN, THE ... Sydney Pollack
ELENI ... Peter Yates
ELEPHANT BOY ... Henri Safran
ELEPHANT CALLED SLOWLY, AN ... James Hill
ELEPHANT GOD, THE ... Satyajit Ray
ELEPHANT GUN ... Ken Annakin
ELEPHANT MAN ★, THE ... David Lynch
ELEVATOR, THE (TF) ... Jerry Jameson
ELISA, VIDA MIA ... Carlos Saura
ELLERY QUEEN (TF) ... David Greene
ELLIE ... Peter Wittman
ELLIOTT CARTER (FD) ... D.A. Pennebaker
ELLIS ISLAND (MS) ... Jerry London
ELMER GANTRY ... Richard Brooks
ELMER THE GREAT ... Mervyn Leroy
E'LOLLIPOP ... Ashley Lazarus
ELOPEMENT ... Henry Koster
ELUSIVE PIMPERNEL, THE ... Michael Powell
ELVIRA MADIGAN ... Bo Widerberg
ELVIS - THAT'S THE WAY IT IS (FD) ... Denis Sanders
ELVIS (TF) ... John Carpenter
ELVIS AND THE BEAUTY QUEEN (TF) ... Gus Trikonis
ELVIS ON TOUR (FD) ... Robert J. Abel
ELVIS ON TOUR (FD) ... Pierre Adidge
EMBASSY ... Gordon Hessler
EMBRYO ... Ralph Nelson
EMERALD ... Jonathan Sanger
EMERALD FOREST, THE ... John Boorman
EMERALD POINT, N.A.S. (TF) ... Harry Falk
EMERGENCY CALL ... Lewis Gilbert
EMERGENCY SQUAD ... Edward Dmytryk
EMIGRANTS, THE ... Jan Troell
EMIL AND THE DETECTIVES ... Peter Tewksbury
EMITAI ... Ousmene Sembene
EMMA MAE ... Jamaa Fanaka
EMMANUELLE ... Just Jaeckin
EMPEROR WALTZ, THE ... Billy Wilder
EMPIRE ... Andy Warhol
EMPIRE OF PASSION ... Nagisa Oshima
EMPIRE OF THE ANTS ... Bert I. Gordon
EMPIRE STRIKES BACK, THE ... Irvin Kershner
EMPTY CANVAS, THE ... Damiano Damiani
ENCOUNTERS AT DUSK ... Alf Kjellin
END AS A MAN ... Jack Garfein
END OF THE AFFAIR, THE ... Edward Dmytryk
END OF THE GAME ... Maximilian Schell
END OF THE ROAD ... Aram Avakian
END OF THE WORLD IN OUR USUAL BED IN A NIGHT FULL OF RAIN, THE ... Lina Wertmuller
END, THE ... Burt Reynolds
ENDANGERED SPECIES ... Alan Rudolph
ENDLESS DESIRE, THE ... Shohei Imamura
ENDLESS LOVE ... Franco Zeffirelli
ENDLESS PASSION ... Kon Ichikawa
ENEMY FROM SPACE ... Val Guest
ENEMY GENERAL, THE ... George Sherman
ENEMY MINE ... Wolfgang Petersen
ENEMY OF THE PEOPLE, AN ... George Schaefer
ENERGY WAR, THE (TD) ... D.A. Pennebaker
ENFORCER, THE ... James Fargo
ENGLAND MADE ME ... Peter John Duffell
ENGLISH ABROAD, THE ... Peter Shillingford
ENGLISHMAN ABROAD, AN (TF) ... John Schlesinger
ENIGMA ... Jeannot Szwarc
ENJO ... Kon Ichikawa
ENNEMI PUBLIC NO. 1 ... Henri Verneuil
ENOLA GAY (TF) ... David Lowell Rich
ENSIGN PULVER ... Joshua Logan
ENTER LAUGHING ... Carl Reiner
ENTER THE DRAGON ... Robert Clouse
ENTER THE NINJA ... Menahem Golan
ENTERTAINER, THE (TF) ... Donald Wrye
ENTERTAINER, THE ... Tony Richardson
ENTERTAINING MR. SLOANE ... Douglas Hickox
ENTITY, THE ... Sidney J. Furie
ENTRE NOUS ... Diane Kurys
EPITAPH TO MY LOVE ... Masahiro Shinoda
EPITOME ... Kaneto Shindo
EQUUS ... Sidney Lumet
ER HERRSCHT RUHE IM LAND ... Peter Lilienthal
ERASERHEAD ... David Lynch
ERIC (TF) ... James Goldstone
ERNIE GAME, THE ... Don Owen
ERNIE KOVACS: BETWEEN THE LAUGHTER (TF) ☆ ... Lamont Johnson
EROTICA ... Russ Meyer
ERRAND BOY, THE ... Jerry Lewis
ERVINKA ... Ephraim Kishon
ESCALIER C ... Jean-Charles Tacchella
ESCAPADE ... Philip Leacock
ESCAPE ... Mervyn Leroy
ESCAPE ... Joseph L. Mankiewicz
ESCAPE (TF) ... Robert M. Lewis
ESCAPE (TF) ... John Llewellyn Moxey
ESCAPE ARTIST, THE ... Caleb Deschanel
ESCAPE FROM ALCATRAZ ... Don Siegel
ESCAPE FROM ANGOLA ... Leslie H. Martinson
ESCAPE FROM BOGEN COUNTY (TF) ... Steven Hillard Stern
ESCAPE FROM EL DIABLO ... Gordon Hessler
ESCAPE FROM FORT BRAVO ... John Sturges
ESCAPE FROM IRAN: THE CANADIAN CAPER (TF) ... Lamont Johnson
ESCAPE FROM THE DARK ... Charles Jarrott
ESCAPE FROM THE PLANET OF THE APES ... Don Taylor
ESCAPE FROM ZAHRAIN ... Ronald Neame
ESCAPE IN THE FOG ... Budd Boetticher
ESCAPE OF A ONE-TON PET, THE (TF) ... Richard C. Bennett
ESCAPE TO ATHENA ... George Pan Cosmatos
ESCAPE TO MINDANAO (TF) ... Don McDougall
ESCAPE TO THE SUN ... Menahem Golan
ESCAPE TO WITCH MOUNTAIN ... John Hough
ESOTIKA, EROTIKA, PSICOTIKA FAB ... Radley Metzger
ESSENE (FD) ... Frederick Wiseman
ESTA TIERRA NUESTRA ... Tomas Gutierrez Alea
ESTERINA ... Carlo Lizzani
ET MOURIR DE PLAISIR ... Roger Vadim
E.T. THE EXTRA-TERRESTRIAL ★ ... Steven Spielberg
ETERNAL LOVE ... King Hu
EUREKA ... Nicolas Roeg
EUROPE IN THE RAW ... Russ Meyer
EUROPEANS, THE ... James Ivory
EVE AND THE HANDYMAN ... Russ Meyer
EVEL KNIEVEL ... Marvin J. Chomsky
EVEN DWARFS STARTED SMALL ... Werner Herzog
EVENING IN BYZANTIUM (TF) ... Jerry London
EVENING LAND ... Peter Watkins
EVER SINCE VENUS ... Arthur Dreifuss
EVERTHING'S DUCKY ... Don Taylor
EVERY DAY'S A HOLIDAY ... James Hill
EVERY LITTLE CROOK AND NANNY ... Cy Howard
EVERY MAN FOR HIMSELF ... Jean-Luc Godard
EVERY MAN FOR HIMSELF AND GOD AGAINST ALL ... Werner Herzog
EVERY MAN NEEDS ONE (TF) ... Jerry Paris
EVERY PERSON IS CRAZY (TF) ... Paul Almond
EVERY WHICH WAY BUT LOOSE ... James Fargo
EVERYBODY GO HOME! ... Luigi Comencini
EVERYTHING FOR SALE ... Andrzej Wajda
EVERYTHING YOU ALWAYS WANTED TO KNOW ABOUT SEX* (*BUT WERE AFRAID TO ASK) ... Woody Allen
EVICTORS, THE ... Charles B. Pierce
EVIL DEAD, THE ... Sam Raimi
EVIL OF FRANKENSTEIN, THE ... Freddie Francis
EVIL ROY SLADE (TF) ... Jerry Paris
EVIL THAT MEN DO, THE ... J. Lee Thompson
EVIL, THE ... Gus Trikonis
EVIL UNDER THE SUN ... Guy Hamilton
EVILS OF CHINATOWN ... Albert Zugsmith
EVILSPEAK ... Eric Weston
EVITA PERON (TF) ... Marvin J. Chomsky
EWOK ADVENTURE, THE (TF) ... John Korty
EXCALIBUR ... John Boorman
EXECUTION, THE (TF) ... Paul Wendkos
EXECUTION OF PRIVATE SLOVIK ☆, THE (TF) ... Lamont Johnson
EXECUTIONER, THE ... Sam Wanamaker
EXECUTIONER'S SONG, THE (TF) ... Lawrence J. Schiller
EXECUTIVE ACTION ... David Miller
EXECUTIVE SUITE ... Robert Wise
EXODUS ... Otto Preminger
EXO-MAN (TF) ... Richard Irving
EXORCIST ★, THE ... William Friedkin
EXPERIENCE PREFERRED, BUT NOT ESSENTIAL ... Peter John Duffell
EXPERIMENT IN TERROR ... Blake Edwards
EXPLORERS ... Joe Dante
EXPLOSIVE GENERATION, THE ... Buzz Kulik
EXPOSED ... James Toback
EXPRESSO BONGO ... Val Guest
EXTERMINATOR, THE ... Jim Glickenhaus
EXTERMINATOR 2 ... Mark Buntzman
EXTRAORDINARY SEAMAN, THE ... John Frankenheimer
EXTREME CLOSE-UP ... Jeannot Szwarc
EYE FOR AN EYE, AN ... Steve Carver
EYE FOR AN EYE, AN ... Herschell Gordon Lewis
EYE OF THE DEVIL ... J. Lee Thompson
EYE OF THE NEEDLE ... Richard Marquand
EYE TO THE CAT ... David Lowell Rich
EYES IN THE NIGHT ... Fred Zinnemann
EYES OF A STRANGER ... Ken Wiederhorn
EYES OF CHARLES SAND, THE (TF) ... Reza Badiyi
EYES OF FIRE ... Avery Crounse
EYES OF LAURA MARS ... Irvin Kershner
EYES OF TEXAS ... William Witney
EYES, THE MOUTH, THE ... Marco Bellocchio
EYEWITNESS ... John Hough
EYEWITNESS ... Peter Yates

F

F FOR FAKE ... Orson Welles
F. SCOTT FITZGERALD AND "THE LAST OF THE BELLES" (TF) ... George Schaefer
F. SCOTT FITZGERALD IN HOLLYWOOD (TF) ... Anthony Page
FACE ... Andy Warhol
FACE IN THE CROWD, A ... Elia Kazan
FACE IN THE RAIN, A ... Irvin Kershner
FACE OF A FUGITIVE ... Paul Wendkos
FACE OF A STRANGER ... John Llewellyn Moxey
FACE OF FEAR, THE (TF) ... George McCowan
FACE OF FIRE ... Albert Band
FACE OF FU MANCHU, THE ... Don Sharp
FACE OF RAGE, THE (TF) ... Donald Wrye
FACE OF WAR, A (FD) ... Eugene S. Jones
FACE TO FACE ★ ... Ingmar Bergman
FACES ... John Cassavetes
FACTS OF LIFE GOES TO PARIS, THE (TF) ... Asaad Kelada
FACTS OF LIFE, THE ... Melvin Frank
FADE TO BLACK ... Vernon Zimmerman
FADE-IN ... Jud Taylor
FAIL SAFE ... Sidney Lumet
FAIR IS FAIR ... Matthew Robbins
FAIRY TALES ... Harry Hurwitz
FAKE OUT ... Matt Cimber
FAKERS, THE ... Al Adamson

FALCON AND THE SNOWMAN, THE ... John Schlesinger
FALCON IN HOLLYWOOD, THE ... Gordon Douglas
FALCON STRIKES BACK, THE ... Edward Dmytryk
FALL GUY, THE (TF) ... Russ Mayberry
FALL OF THE HOUSE OF USHER, THE ... James L. Conway
FALLEN ... Peter Watkins
FALLEN ANGEL ... Otto Preminger
FALLEN ANGEL (TF) ... Robert M. Lewis
FALLEN HERO (TF) ... Jeremy Summers
FALLING, THE ... Deran Sarafian
FALLING FOR YOU ... Robert Stevenson
FALLING IN LOVE ... Ulu Grosbard
FALLING IN LOVE AGAIN ... Steven Paul
FALLS, THE ... Peter Greenaway
FALN (FD) ... Robert Kramer
FALSTAFF ... Orson Welles
FAME ... Alan Parker
FAME IS THE NAME OF THE GAME (TF) ... Stuart Rosenberg
FAME IS THE SPUR ... Roy Boulting
FAMILY BUSINESS (TF) ... John Stix
FAMILY FLIGHT (TF) ... Marvin J. Chomsky
FAMILY JEWELS, THE ... Jerry Lewis
FAMILY KOVACK, THE (TF) ... Ralph Senensky
FAMILY LIFE ... Kenneth Loach
FAMILY LIFE ... Krzysztof Zanussi
FAMILY MAN, THE (TF) ... Glenn Jordan
FAMILY NOBODY WANTED, THE (TF) ... Ralph Senensky
FAMILY RELATIONS ... Nikita Mikhalkov
FAMILY REUNION (TF) ... Fielder Cook
FAMILY RICO, THE (TF) ... Paul Wendkos
FAMILY SECRETS (TF) ... Jack Hofsiss
FAMILY UPSIDE DOWN, A (TF) ... David Lowell Rich
FAMILY WAY, THE ... Roy Boulting
FAN, THE ... Edward Bianchi
FAN, THE ... Otto Preminger
FANATIC ... Silvio Narizzano
FANATIC ... David Winters
FANDANGO ... Kevin Reynolds
FANDO AND LIS ... Alexandro Jodorowsky
FANFARE FOR A DEATH SCENE ... Leslie Stevens
FANNY ... Joshua Logan
FANNY AND ALEXANDER ★ ... Ingmar Bergman
FANNY HILL ... Gerry O'Hara
FANNY HILL: MEMOIRS OF A WOMAN OF PLEASURE ... Russ Meyer
FAN'S NOTES, A ... Eric Till
FANTASIES ... John Derek
FANTASIES (TF) ... William Wiard
FANTASM ... Richard Franklin
FANTASTIC JOURNEY, THE (TF) ... Andrew V. McLaglen
FANTASTIC VOYAGE ... Richard Fleischer
FANTASTIC WORLD OF D.C. COLLINS, THE (TF) ... Leslie H. Martinson
FANTASTICA ... Gilles Carle
FANTASY ISLAND (TF) ... Richard Lang
FAR EAST ... John Duigan
FAR FROM THE MADDING CROWD ... John Schlesinger
FAR FROM VIETNAM ... Alain Resnais
FAR FROM VIETNAM (FD) ... William Klein
FAR FROM VIETNAM (FD) ... Jean-Luc Godard
FAR FROM VIETNAM (FD) ... Claude Lelouch
FAR FROM VIETNAM (FD) ... Agnes Varda
FAR FRONTIER, THE ... William Witney
FAR PAVILIONS, THE (CMS) ... Peter John Duffell
FAREWELL CREAM (FD) ... Tony Palmer
FAREWELL, MY LOVELY ... Dick Richards
FAREWELL SCARLET ... Chuck Vincent
FAREWELL TO MANZANAR (TF) ... John Korty
FARMER, THE ... David Berlatsky
FARO DOCUMENT (TD) ... Ingmar Bergman
FARO DOCUMENT 1979 (TD) ... Ingmar Bergman
FARRELL FOR THE PEOPLE (TF) ... Paul Wendkos
FAST BREAK ... Jack Smight
FAST CHARLIE...THE MOONBEAM RIDER ... Steve Carver
FAST COMPANY ... David Cronenberg
FAST COMPANY ... John Sturges
FAST FORWARD ... Sidney Poitier
FAST FRIENDS (TF) ... Steven Hillard Stern
FAST LADY, THE ... Ken Annakin
FAST TIMES AT RIDGEMONT HIGH ... Amy Heckerling
FASTER PUSSYCAT, KILL! KILL! ... Russ Meyer
FASTEST GUN ALIVE, THE ... Russell Rouse
FAST-WALKING ... James B. Harris
FAT CITY ... John Huston
FAT SPY ... Joseph Cates
FATA MORGANA ... Werner Herzog
FATAL VISION (TF) ... David Greene
FATE IS THE HUNTER ... Ralph Nelson
FATE OF A MAN ... Sergei Bondarchuk
FATE OF LEE KHAN, THE ... King Hu
FATHER ... Istvan Szabo
FATHER FIGURE (TF) ... Jerry London
FATHER GOOSE ... Ralph Nelson
FATHER MURPHY (TF) ... Michael Landon
FATHER OF THE BRIDE ... Vincente Minnelli
FATHER'S LITTLE DIVIDEND ... Vincente Minnelli
FATHOM ... Leslie H. Martinson
FATSO ... Anne Bancroft
FATTO DI SANGUE FRA DUE UOMINI PER CAUSA DI UNA VEDOVA (SI SOSPETTANO MOVENTI POLITICI) ... Lina Wertmuller
F.B.I. CODE 98 ... Leslie H. Martinson
FBI STORY, THE ... Mervyn Leroy
FBI STORY: THE FBI VERSUS ALVIN KARPIS, PUBLIC ENEMY NUMBER ONE, THE (TF) ... Marvin J. Chomsky
FEAR AND DESIRE ... Stanley Kubrick
FEAR CITY ... Abel Ferrara
FEAR IN THE NIGHT ... Jimmy Sangster
FEAR IS THE KEY ... Michael Tuchner
FEAR NO EVIL ... Frank Laloggia
FEAR NO EVIL (TF) ... Paul Wendkos
FEAR ON TRIAL (TF) ☆ ... Lamont Johnson
FEAR STRIKES OUT ... Robert Mulligan
FEARLESS FAGAN ... Stanley Donen
FEARLESS FRANK ... Philip Kaufman
FEARLESS VAMPIRE KILLERS, OR PARDON ME BUT YOUR TEETH ARE IN MY NECK, THE ... Roman Polanski
FEDORA ... Billy Wilder
FELLINI SATYRICON ★ ... Federico Fellini
FELLINI'S ROMA ... Federico Fellini
FEMALE ARTILLERY (TF) ... Marvin J. Chomsky
FEMALE BUNCH, THE ... Al Adamson
FEMALE ON THE BEACH ... Joseph Pevney
FEMALE TROUBLE ... John Waters
FEMINIST AND THE FUZZ, THE (TF) ... Jerry Paris
FEMMES FATALES ... Bertrand Blier
FEMMES FATALES ... Bertrand Tavernier
FER-DE-LANCE (TF) ... Russ Mayberry
FERRY CROSS THE MERSEY ... Jeremy Summers
FERRY TO HONG KONG ... Lewis Gilbert
FESTIVAL PANAFRICAIN (FD) ... William Klein
FEU A VOLONTE ... Marcel Ophuls
FEUDIN', FUSSIN' AND A-FIGHTIN' ... George Sherman
FEVER IN THE BLOOD, A ... Vincent Sherman
FEVER, THE ... Richard Brooks
FEW DAYS IN WEASEL CREEK, A (TF) ... Dick Lowry
FFOLKES ... Andrew V. McLaglen
FIANCES, THE ... Ermanno Olmi
FICKLE FINGER OF FATE ... Richard Rush
FIDDLER ON THE ROOF ★ ... Norman Jewison
FIDELIA ... Gerry O'Hara
FIEND WHO WALKED THE WEST, THE ... Gordon Douglas
FIENDISH PLOT OF DR. FU MANCHU, THE ... Piers Haggard
FIERCEST HEART, THE ... George Sherman
FIFTH FLOOR, THE ... Howard (Hikmet) Avedis
FIGHTER, THE (TF) ... David Lowell Rich
FIGHTING BACK ... Lewis Teague
FIGHTING BACK (TF) ... Robert Lieberman
FIGHTING MAD ... Jonathan Demme
FIGHTING MEN, THE (TF) ... Donald Shebib
FIGHTING PRINCE OF DONEGAL, THE ... Michael O'Herlihy
FILE ON JILL HATCH, THE (TF) ... Alastair Reid
FILE ON THE GOLDEN GOOSE, THE ... Sam Wanamaker
FILLMORE (FD) ... Richard T. Heffron
FILM D'AMORE E D'ANARCHIA ... Lina Wertmuller
FIMPEN ... Bo Widerberg
FINAL ASSIGNMENT ... Paul Almond
FINAL CHAPTER - WALKING TALL ... Jack Starrett
FINAL COMEDOWN, THE ... Oscar Williams
FINAL CONFLICT, THE ... Graham Baker
FINAL COUNTDOWN, THE ... Don Taylor
FINAL EXAM ... Jimmy Huston
FINAL JUSTICE ... Greydon Clark
FINAL LIE, THE ... Michael Cacoyannis
FINAL OPTION, THE ... Ian Sharp
FINAL PROGRAMME, THE ... Robert Fuest
FINAL TERROR, THE ... Andrew Davis
FINDER OF LOST LOVES (TF) ... Bruce Bilson
FINDERS KEEPERS ... Sidney Hayers
FINDERS KEEPERS ... Richard Lester
FINDERS KEEPERS, LOVERS WEEPERS ... Russ Meyer
FINDHORD (FD) ... Peter Werner
FINE MADNESS, A ... Irvin Kershner
FINE SNOW ... Kon Ichikawa
FINGERS ... James Toback
FINIAN'S RAINBOW ... Francis Ford Coppola
FINISHING TOUCH ... George Kaczender
FINNEGAN, BEGIN AGAIN (CTF) ... Joan Micklin Silver
FIRE! (TF) ... Earl Bellamy
FIRE AND ICE (AF) ... Ralph Bakshi
FIRE DOWN BELOW ... Robert Parrish
FIRE IN THE SKY, A (TF) ... Jerry Jameson
FIRE ON THE MOUNTAIN (TF) ... Donald Wrye
FIRE RAISERS, THE ... Michael Powell
FIRE SALE ... Alan Arkin
FIRE WITHIN, THE ... Louis Malle
FIREBALL FORWARD (TF) ... Marvin J. Chomsky
FIREBALL 500 ... William Asher
FIREBRAND, THE ... Maury Dexter
FIRECHASERS, THE ... Sidney Hayers
FIRECREEK ... Vincent McEveety
FIREFOX ... Clint Eastwood
FIREHOUSE (TF) ... Alex March
FIREMAN'S BALL, THE ... Milos Forman
FIREPOWER ... Michael Winner
FIRES ON THE PLAIN ... Kon Ichikawa
FIRESTARTER ... Mark L. Lester
FIRM MAN, THE ... John Duigan
FIRST AFFAIR (TF) ... Gus Trikonis
FIRST BLOOD ... Ted Kotcheff
FIRST DEADLY SIN, THE ... Brian G. Hutton
FIRST FAMILY ... Buck Henry
FIRST LOVE ... Joan Darling
FIRST LOVE ... Henry Koster
FIRST LOVE ... Maximilian Schell
FIRST MAN INTO SPACE ... Robert Day
FIRST MEN IN THE MOON ... Nathan Juran
FIRST MONDAY IN OCTOBER ... Ronald Neame
FIRST NAME: CARMEN ... Jean-Luc Godard
FIRST NUDIE MUSICAL, THE ... Bruce Kimmel
FIRST OLYMPICS—ATHENS 1896, THE (MS) ... Alvin Rakoff
FIRST POSITION (FD) ... William Richert
FIRST TEACHER, THE ... Andrei Konchalovsky
FIRST TIME, THE (TF) ... Noel Nosseck
FIRST TIME, THE ... Claude Berri
FIRST TIME, THE ... Charlie Loventhal
FIRST TURN-ON!, THE ... Michael Herz
FIRST TURN-ON!, THE ... Samuel Weil
FIRST YANK INTO TOKYO ... Gordon Douglas
FIRST YOU CRY (TF) ... George Schaefer
FIRST 36 HOURS OF DR. DURANT, THE (TF) ... Alexander Singer
FIRSTBORN ... Michael Apted
FISH HAWK ... Donald Shebib
FISH THAT SAVED PITTSBURGH, THE ... Gilbert Moses
F.I.S.T. ... Norman Jewison
FIST IN HIS POCKET ... Marco Bellocchio
FISTFUL OF CHOPSTICKS, A ... Elliott Hong
FISTFUL OF DOLLARS, A ... Sergio Leone
FISTFUL OF DYNAMITE ... Sergio Leone
FIT TO BE UNTIED ... Marco Bellocchio
FITZCARRALDO ... Werner Herzog
FITZWILLY ... Delbert Mann
FIVE ... Arch Oboler
FIVE AGAINST THE HOUSE ... Phil Karlson
FIVE BLOODY GRAVES ... Al Adamson
FIVE BRANDED WOMEN ... Martin Ritt

FIVE CARD STUD .... Henry Hathaway
FIVE DAY LOVER, THE .... Philippe de Broca
FIVE DAYS FROM HOME .... George Peppard
FIVE DAYS ONE SUMMER .... Fred Zinnemann
FIVE DESPERATE WOMEN (TF) .... Ted Post
FIVE EASY PIECES .... Bob Rafelson
FIVE EVENINGS .... Nikita Mikhalkov
FIVE FINGER EXERCISE .... Daniel Mann
FIVE FINGERS ★ .... Joseph L. Mankiewicz
FIVE GATES TO HELL .... James Clavell
FIVE GOLDEN DRAGONS .... Jeremy Summers
FIVE GRAVES TO CAIRO .... Billy Wilder
FIVE GUNS WEST .... Roger Corman
FIVE MAN ARMY, THE .... Don Taylor
FIVE MILLION YEARS TO EARTH .... Roy Ward Baker
FIVE MINUTES OF FREEDOM .... Ivan Nagy
FIVE OF ME, THE (TF) .... Paul Wendkos
FIVE ON THE BLACK HAND SIDE .... Oscar Williams
FIVE PENNIES, THE .... Melville Shavelson
FIVE STAR FINAL .... Mervyn Leroy
FIVE THE HARD WAY .... Gus Trikonis
FIVE TO ONE .... Gordon Flemyng
FIVE WEEKS IN A BALLOON .... Irwin Allen
FIXED BAYONETS! .... Samuel Fuller
FIXER, THE .... John Frankenheimer
FLAME .... Richard Loncraine
FLAME AND THE FLESH .... Richard Brooks
FLAME IN THE STREETS .... Roy Ward Baker
FLAME IS LOVE, THE (TF) ...... Michael O'Herlihy
FLAME OVER INDIA .... J. Lee Thompson
FLAME TREES OF THIKA, THE (MS) .... Roy Ward Baker
FLAMING STAR .... Don Siegel
FLAMINGO KID, THE .... Garry Marshall
FLAMINGO ROAD (TF) .... Gus Trikonis
FLASH GORDON .... Mike Hodges
FLASH OF GREEN, A (TF) .... Victor Nuñez
FLASHBURN .... George Gage
FLASHDANCE .... Adrian Lyne
FLASHDANCE FEVER .... Alan Roberts
FLASHPOINT .... William Tannen
FLAT TWO .... Alan Cooke
FLATBED ANNIE & SWEETIE PIE: LADY TRUCKERS (TF) .... Robert Greenwald
FLAXY MARTIN .... Richard L. Bare
FLEET THAT CAME TO STAY, THE .... Budd Boetticher
FLESH .... Paul Morrissey
FLESH AND BLOOD .... Paul Verhoeven
FLESH AND BLOOD (TF) .... Jud Taylor
FLESH AND BLOOD SHOW, THE .... Peter Walker
FLESH AND FURY .... Joseph Pevney
FLESH FOR FRANKENSTEIN .... Paul Morrissey
FLESH IS WEAK, THE .... Don Chaffey
FLETCH .... Michael Ritchie
FLIC STORY .... Jacques Deray
FLIGHT .... Frank Capra
FLIGHT FROM ASHIYA .... Michael Anderson
FLIGHT FROM DESTINY .... Vincent Sherman
FLIGHT OF THE DOVES .... Ralph Nelson
FLIGHT OF THE DRAGONS, THE (ATF) .... Jules Bass
FLIGHT OF THE DRAGONS, THE (ATF) .... Arthur Rankin, Jr.
FLIGHT OF THE EAGLE, THE .... Jan Troell
FLIGHT OF THE LOST BALLOON .... Nathan Juran
FLIGHT TO BERLIN .... Chris Petit
FLIGHT TO FURY .... Monte Hellman
FLIGHT TO HOLOCAUST (TF) .... Bernard L. Kowalski
FLIGHT TO TANGIER ... Charles Marquis Warren
FLIGHT 90: DISASTER ON THE POTOMAC (TF) .... Robert M. Lewis
FLIM-FLAM MAN, THE .... Irvin Kershner
FLIPPER .... James B. Clark
FLOAT LIKE A BUTTERFLY - STING LIKE A BEE (FD) .... William Klein
FLOCH .... Dan Wolman
FLOOD! (TF) .... Earl Bellamy
FLOODS OF FEAR .... Charles Crichton
FLORENCE - DAYS OF DESTRUCTION (FD) .... Franco Zeffirelli
FLOWER BLOOMS, A .... Kon Ichikawa
FLOWER DRUM SONG .... Henry Koster
FLUFFY .... Earl Bellamy
FLY AWAY HOME (TF) .... Paul Krasny
FLYING .... Paul Lynch
FLYING FONTAINES, THE .... George Sherman
FLYING HIGH (TF) .... Peter H. Hunt
FLYING ROMEOS .... Mervyn Leroy
FLYING TIGERS .... David Miller
FM .... John A. Alonzo
FOG, THE .... John Carpenter
FOLIES BOURGEOISES .... Claude Chabrol
FOLKS AT RED WOLF INN, THE .... Bud Townsend
FOLLOW ME QUIETLY .... Richard Fleischer
FOLLOW THAT CAMEL .... Gerald Thomas
FOLLOW THAT CAR .... Daniel Haller
FOLLOW THAT DREAM .... Gordon Douglas
FONTAINE DE VAUCLUSE .... Louis Malle
FONTAMARA .... Carlo Lizzani
FOOD OF THE GODS, THE .... Bert I. Gordon
FOOLIN' AROUND .... Richard T. Heffron
FOOLING, THE .... William Fruet
FOOLS FOR SCANDAL .... Mervyn Leroy
FOOLS' PARADE .... Andrew V. McLaglen
FOOTLOOSE .... Herbert Ross
FOOTSTEPS (TF) .... Paul Wendkos
FOR A FEW DOLLARS MORE .... Sergio Leone
FOR BETTER OR WORSE .... J. Lee Thompson
FOR LADIES ONLY (TF) .... Mel Damski
FOR LOVE AND HONOR (TF) .... Gary Nelson
FOR LOVE OF IVY .... Daniel Mann
FOR LOVE OR MONEY .... Michael Gordon
FOR LOVE OR MONEY (TF) .... Terry Hughes
FOR LOVERS ONLY (TF) .... Claudio Guzman
FOR PETE'S SAKE .... Peter Yates
FOR PETE'S SAKE! .... James F. Collier
FOR SINGLES ONLY .... Arthur Dreifuss
FOR THE LOVE OF BENJI .... Joe Camp
FOR THE LOVE OF IT (TF) .... Hal Kanter
FOR THE LOVE OF MIKE .... Frank Capra
FOR THE LOVE OF MIKE .... George Sherman
FOR THE LOVE OF RUSTY .... John Sturges
FOR THOSE I LOVED .... Robert Enrico
FOR THOSE IN PERIL .... Charles Crichton
FOR THOSE WHO THINK YOUNG .... Leslie H. Martinson
FOR US, THE LIVING (TF) .... Michael Schultz
FOR YOUR EYES ONLY .... John Glen
FORBIDDEN .... Frank Capra
FORBIDDEN (CTF) .... Anthony Page
FORBIDDEN FRUIT .... Henri Verneuil
FORBIDDEN GAMES .... René Clement
FORBIDDEN LOVE (TF) .... Steven Hillard Stern
FORBIDDEN STREET, THE .... Jean Negulesco
FORBIDDEN WORLD .... Allan Holzman
FORCE: FIVE .... Robert Clouse
FORCE FIVE (TF) .... Walter Grauman
FORCE OF EVIL .... Abraham Polonsky
FORCE OF IMPULSE .... Saul Swimmer
FORCE OF ONE, A .... Paul Aaron
FORCE 10 FROM NAVARONE .... Guy Hamilton
FORCED ENTRY .... Jim Sotos
FORCED VENGEANCE .... James Fargo
FORE PLAY .... John G. Avildsen
FORE PLAY .... Robert McCarty
FORE PLAY .... Bruce Malmuth
FOREIGN AFFAIR, A .... Billy Wilder
FOREIGN EXCHANGE (TF) .... Roy Ward Baker
FOREVER (TF) .... John Korty
FOREVER AMBER .... Otto Preminger
FOREVER AND A DAY .... Robert Stevenson
FOREVER FEMALE .... Irving Rapper
FOREVER YOUNG .... David Drury
FOREVER YOUNG, FOREVER FREE .... Ashley Lazarus
FORGOTTEN MAN, THE (TF) .... Walter Grauman
FORMULA, THE .... John G. Avildsen
FORT APACHE, THE BRONX .... Daniel Petrie
FORT BOWIE .... Howard W. Koch
FORT DOBBS .... Gordon Douglas
FORTUNA .... Menahem Golan
FORTUNE AND MEN'S EYES .... Harvey Hart
FORTUNE COOKIE, THE .... Billy Wilder
FORTUNE, THE .... Mike Nichols
FORTUNES OF CAPTAIN BLOOD .... Gordon Douglas
FORTY DAYS FOR DANNY (TF) .... Robert Greenwald
FORTY GUNS .... Samuel Fuller
FORTY GUNS TO APACHE PASS .... William Witney
FORTY-DEUCE .... Paul Morrissey
FORTY-NINTH PARALLEL, THE .... Michael Powell
FOSSILS (MS) .... Masaki Kobayashi
FOSTER AND LAURIE (TF) .... John Llewellyn Moxey
FOUL PLAY .... Colin Higgins
FOUND MONEY (TF) .... Bill Persky
FOUNTAINHEAD, THE .... Masaki Kobayashi
FOUR DAYS .... John Guillermin
FOUR DAYS IN NOVEMBER (TD) .... Mel Stuart
FOUR DAYS OF NAPLES, THE .... Nanni Loy
FOUR DEUCES, THE ..... William J. Bushnell, Jr.
FOUR DIMENSIONS OF GRETA, THE .... Peter Walker
FOUR FEATHERS, THE (TF) .... Don Sharp
FOUR FLIES ON GREY VELVET .... Dario Argento
FOUR FRIENDS .... Arthur Penn
FOUR GIRLS IN TOWN .... Jack Sher
FOUR HORSEMEN OF THE APOCALYPSE, THE .... Vincente Minnelli
FOUR IN THE MORNING .... Anthony Simmons
FOUR MOODS .... King Hu
FOUR MUSKETEERS, THE .... Richard Lester
FOUR NIGHTS OF A DREAMER .... Robert Bresson
FOUR SEASONS OF TATESHINA .... Kaneto Shindo
FOUR SEASONS, THE .... Alan Alda
FOUR STARS .... Andy Warhol
FOURTEEN HOURS .... Henry Hathaway
FOURTH WISH, THE .... Don Chaffey
FOX AND THE HOUND, THE (AF) .... Ted Berman
FOX AND THE HOUND, THE (AF) .... Richard Rich
FOX AND THE HOUND, THE (AF) .... Art Stevens
FOX IN THE CHICKEN COOP .... Ephraim Kishon
FOX, THE .... Mark Rydell
FOXES .... Adrian Lyne
FOXFIRE .... Joseph Pevney
FOXHOLE IN CAIRO .... John Llewellyn Moxey
FOXY BROWN .... Jack Hill
FOXY LADY .... Ivan Reitman
FRAGMENT OF FEAR .... Richard C. Sarafian
FRAMED .... Phil Karlson
FRANCES .... Graeme Clifford
FRANCESCO D'ASSISI (TF) .... Liliana Cavani
FRANCIS GARY POWERS: THE TRUE STORY OF THE U-2 SPY INCIDENT (TF) .... Delbert Mann
FRANCOIS REICHENBACH'S JAPAN (FD) .... Francois Reichenbach
FRANKENSTEIN (TF) .... Glenn Jordan
FRANKENSTEIN - 1970 .... Howard W. Koch
FRANKENSTEIN: THE TRUE STORY (TF) .... Jack Smight
FRANTIC .... Louis Malle
FRAULEIN .... Henry Koster
FRAULEIN DOKTOR .... Alberto Lattuada
FREAKY FRIDAY .... Gary Nelson
FRECKLES .... Andrew V. McLaglen
FREDDIE STEPS OUT .... Arthur Dreifuss
FREE AND EASY .... George Sidney
FREE SPIRIT .... Paul Aaron
FREE SPIRIT .... James Hill
FREE, WHITE AND 21 .... Larry Buchanan
FREE WOMAN, A .... Volker Schlondorff
FREEBIE AND THE BEAN .... Richard Rush
FREEDOM (TF) .... Joseph Sargent
FREEZE BOMB .... Al Adamson
FRENCH, THE (FD) .... William Klein
FRENCH ATLANTIC AFFAIR, THE (TF) .... Douglas Heyes
FRENCH CONNECTION ★★, THE .... William Friedkin
FRENCH CONNECTION II ... John Frankenheimer
FRENCH DRESSING .... Ken Russell
FRENCH LIEUTENANT'S WOMAN, THE .... Karel Reisz
FRENCH MISTRESS, A .... Roy Boulting
FRENCH POSTCARDS .... Willard Huyck
FRENCH WOMAN, THE .... Just Jaeckin
FRESCOS ON THE WHITE .... Emil Loteanu
FREUD .... John Huston
FRIDAY FOSTER .... Arthur Marks
FRIDAY THE 13TH .... Sean S. Cunningham
FRIDAY THE 13TH PART 2 .... Steve Miner
FRIDAY THE 13TH PART 3 .... Steve Miner

FRIDAY THE 13TH - THE FINAL CHAPTER ... Joseph Zito
FRIENDLY FIRE (TF) ☆☆ ... David Greene
FRIENDLY PERSUASION (TF) ... Joseph Sargent
FRIENDS ... Lewis Gilbert
FRIENDS OF EDDIE COYLE, THE ... Peter Yates
FRIENDSHIP, SECRETS AND LIES ... Marlena Laird
FRIENDSHIPS, SECRETS AND LIES (TF) ... Ann Zane Shanks
FRIGHTENED BRIDE, THE ... Terence Young
FRIGHTMARE ... Norman Thaddeus Vane
FRIGHTMARE ... Peter Walker
FRISKY ... Luigi Comencini
FRITZ KORTNER SPRICHT MONOLOGE FUR EINE SCHALLPLATTE (FD) ... Hans-Jurgen Syberberg
FRITZ THE CAT (AF) ... Ralph Bakshi
FROGS ... George McCowan
FROM A FAR COUNTRY (POPE JOHN PAUL II) (TF) ... Krzysztof Zanussi
FROM BEYOND THE GRAVE ... Kevin Connor
FROM HELL TO TEXAS ... Henry Hathaway
FROM HERE TO ETERNITY (MS) ... Buzz Kulik
FROM HERE TO ETERNITY ★★ ... Fred Zinnemann
FROM NOON TILL THREE ... Frank D. Gilroy
FROM RUSSIA WITH LOVE ... Terence Young
FROM THE LIFE OF THE MARIONETTES ... Ingmar Bergman
FROM THE MIXED-UP FILES OF MRS. BASIL E. FRANKWEILER ... Fielder Cook
FROM THIS DAY FORWARD ... John Berry
FRONT PAGE, THE ... Billy Wilder
FRONT, THE ... Martin Ritt
FRONTIER FREMONT ... Dick Friedenberg
FRONTIER VENGEANCE ... George Sherman
FUCK ... Andy Warhol
FUGITIVE FAMILY (TF) ... Paul Krasny
FUGITIVE KIND, THE ... Sidney Lumet
FULL CIRCLE ... Richard Loncraine
FULL MOON HIGH ... Larry Cohen
FULL MOON IN PARIS ... Eric Rohmer
FULL OF LIFE ... Richard Quine
FULL TREATMENT, THE ... Val Guest
FUN AND GAMES ... Ray Austin
FUN ON A WEEKEND ... Andrew L. Stone
FUN PARK ... James Orr
FUN WITH DICK & JANE ... Ted Kotcheff
FUNERAL HOME ... William Fruet
FUNERAL IN BERLIN ... Guy Hamilton
FUNFTER AKT, SIEBTE SZENE. FRITZ KORTNER PROBT KABALE UND LIEBE (FD) ... Hans-Jurgen Syberberg
FUNHOUSE, THE ... Tobe Hooper
FUNNY FACE ... Stanley Donen
FUNNY FARM, THE ... Ron Clark
FUNNY LADY ... Herbert Ross
FUNNY MONEY ... James Kenelm Clarke
FUNNY THING HAPPENED ON THE WAY TO THE FORUM, A ... Richard Lester
FUNNYMAN ... John Korty
FURTHER ADVENTURES OF THE WILDERNESS FAMILY - PART 2 ... Frank Zuniga
FURTHER UP THE CREEK ... Val Guest
FURY AT SHOWDOWN ... Gerd Oswald
FURY, THE ... Brian De Palma
FUTURE COP (TF) ... Jud Taylor
FUTURE TENSE (CTF) ... Frank De Palma
FUTUREWORLD ... Richard T. Heffron
FUTZ ... Tom O'Horgan
FUZZ ... Richard A. Colla

G

GABLE AND LOMBARD ... Sidney J. Furie
GABRIELA ... Bruno Barreto
GABRIELLA ... Mack Bing
GAILY, GAILY ... Norman Jewison
GAL YOUNG UN ... Victor Nuñez
GALAXINA ... William Sachs
GALAXY OF TERROR ... Bruce Clark
GALILEO ... Liliana Cavani
GALLIPOLI ... Peter Weir
GAMBIT ... Ronald Neame
GAMBLER, THE ... Karel Reisz
GAME FOR THREE LOSERS, A ... Gerry O'Hara
GAME FOR VULTURES ... James Fargo
GAME IS OVER, THE ... Roger Vadim
GAME OF DEATH ... Robert Clouse
GAME OF DEATH, A ... Robert Wise
GAMEKEEPER, THE ... Kenneth Loach
GAMES ... Curtis Harrington
GAMES GIRLS PLAY, THE ... Jack Arnold
GAMES MOTHER NEVER TAUGHT YOU (TF) ... Lee Philips
GAMES, THE ... Michael Winner
GAMES WOMEN PLAY ... Chuck Vincent
GAMMA CHRONICLES, THE (MS) ... Wheeler Dixon
GANDHI ★★ ... Richard Attenborough
GANGSTER CHRONICLES, THE (TF) ... Richard C. Sarafian
GANGSTER STORY ... Walter Matthau
GANGSTERS (TF) ... Philip Saville
GANITO KAMI NOON, PAANO KAYO NGAYON? ... Eddie Romero
GANJA & HESS ... Bill Gunn
GARAGE, THE ... Vilgot Sjoman
GARBO TALKS ... Sidney Lumet
GARCON ... Claude Sautet
GARDEN OF DELIGHTS, THE ... Carlos Saura
GARDEN OF EVIL ... Henry Hathaway
GARDENER'S SON, THE (TF) ... Richard Pearce
GARGOYLES (TF) ... B.W.L. Norton
GARMENT JUNGLE, THE ... Vincent Sherman
GAS ... Les Rose
GAS-S-S-S! . . .OR IT BECAME NECESSARY TO DESTROY THE WORLD IN ORDER TO SAVE IT! ... Roger Corman
GATES TO PARADISE ... Andrzej Wajda
GATHERING ☆, THE (TF) ... Randal Kleiser
GATHERING OF EAGLES, A ... Delbert Mann
GATHERING, PART II, THE (TF) ... Charles S. Dubin
GATHERING STORM, THE (TF) ... Herbert Wise
GATOR ... Burt Reynolds
GAUGUIN THE SAVAGE (TF) ... Fielder Cook
GAUNTLET, THE ... Clint Eastwood
GAWAIN AND THE GREEN KNIGHT ... Stephen Weeks
GAY DECEIVERS, THE ... Bruce Kessler
GAY DESPERADO, THE ... Rouben Mamoulian
GAY RANCHERO, THE ... William Witney
GAY SENORITA, THE ... Arthur Dreifuss
GAY SISTERS, THE ... Irving Rapper
GEMINI AFFAIR ... Matt Cimber
GEMINI MAN (TF) ... Alan J. Levi
GENE KRUPA STORY, THE ... Don Weis
GENERAL IDI AMIN DADA (FD) ... Barbet Schroeder
GENERAL SPANKY ... Gordon Douglas
GENERATION ... George Schaefer
GENERATION, A ... Andrzej Wajda
GENESIS II (TF) ... John Llewellyn Moxey
GENOCIDE (FD) ... Arnold Schwartzman
GENTLEMAN BANDIT, THE (TF) ... Jonathan Kaplan
GENTLEMAN JOE PALOOKA ... Cy Endfield
GENTLEMAN MISBEHAVES, THE ... George Sherman
GENTLEMAN'S AGREEMENT ★★ ... Elia Kazan
GENTLEMAN'S FATE ... Mervyn Leroy
GEOMETRA PRINETTI SEL VAGGIAMENTEOSVALDO ... Ferdinando Baldi
GEORGE STEVENS: A FILMMAKER'S JOURNEY (FD) ... George Stevens, Jr.
GEORGE WASHINGTON (MS) ... Buzz Kulik
GEORGIA PEACHES (TF) ... Daniel Haller
GEORGINAS GRUNDE (TF) ... Volker Schlondorff
GEORGY GIRL ... Silvio Narizzano
GERONIMO ... Arnold Laven
GERVAISE ... René Clement
GET CARTER ... Mike Hodges
GET CHARLIE TULLY ... Cliff Owen
GET CHRISTIE LOVE! (TF) ... William A. Graham
GET CRAZY ... Allan Arkush
GET DOWN AND BOOGIE ... William Witney
GET MEAN ... Ferdinando Baldi
GET OUT YOUR HANDKERCHIEFS ... Bertrand Blier
GET TO KNOW YOUR RABBIT ... Brian De Palma
GETAWAY, THE ... Sam Peckinpah
GETTING AWAY FROM IT ALL (TF) ... Lee Philips
GETTING EVEN ... Harvey Hart
GETTING IT ON ... William Olsen
GETTING MARRIED (TF) ... Steven Hillard Stern
GETTING OF WISDOM, THE ... Bruce Beresford
GETTING PHYSICAL (TF) ... Steven Hillard Stern
GETTING STRAIGHT ... Richard Rush
GHOST AND MR. CHICKEN, THE ... Alan Rafkin
GHOST AND MRS. MUIR, THE ... Joseph L. Mankiewicz
GHOSTBUSTERS ... Ivan Reitman
GHOST DANCING (TF) ... David Greene
GHOST IN THE INVISIBLE BIKINI, THE ... Don Weis
GHOST IN THE NOONDAY SUN ... Peter Medak
GHOST OF FLIGHT 401, THE (TF) ... Steven Hillard Stern
GHOST OF LOVE ... Dino Risi
GHOST STORY ... John Irvin
GHOST STORY OF YOUTH ... Kon Ichikawa
GHOST VALLEY RAIDERS ... George Sherman
GHOST WRITER, THE (TF) ... Tristram Powell
GHOSTS OF BUXLEY HALL, THE (TF) ... Bruce Bilson
GHOUL, THE ... Freddie Francis
GHOULIES ... Luca Bercovici
G.I. HONEYMOON ... Phil Karlson
GIACOMO L'IDEALISTA ... Alberto Lattuada
GIALLO NAPOLETANO ... Sergio Corbucci
GIANT LEECHES, THE ... Bernard L. Kowalski
GIDEON'S TRUMPET (TF) ... Robert Collins
GIDGET ... Paul Wendkos
GIDGET GETS MARRIED (TF) ... E.W. Swackhamer
GIDGET GOES HAWAIIAN ... Paul Wendkos
GIDGET GOES TO ROME ... Paul Wendkos
GIDGET GROWS UP (TF) ... James Sheldon
GIFT, THE (TF) ... Don Taylor
GIFT OF LIFE, THE (TF) ... Jerry London
GIFT OF LOVE, THE (TF) ... Don Chaffey
GIFT OF LOVE: A CHRISTMAS STORY, THE (TF) ... Delbert Mann
GIFT OF LOVE, THE ... Jean Negulesco
GIGI ★ ... Vincente Minnelli
GIGOT ... Gene Kelly
GILDA LIVE (FD) ... Mike Nichols
GILDERSLEEVE ON BROADWAY ... Gordon Douglas
GILDERSLEEVE'S BAD DAY ... Gordon Douglas
GILDERSLEEVE'S GHOST ... Gordon Douglas
GIMME AN F ... Paul Justman
GIMME SHELTER (FD) ... Albert Maysles
GIMME SHELTER (FD) ... David Maysles
GIMME SHELTER (FD) ... Charlotte Zwerin
GINGER ... Don Schain
GINGER IN THE MORNING ... Gordon Wiles
GINZA VETERAN, A ... Kon Ichikawa
GIRL AT DOJO TEMPLE, A ... Kon Ichikawa
GIRL CALLED HATTER FOX, THE (TF) ... George Schaefer
GIRL FROM LORRAINE, THE ... Claude Goretta
GIRL FROM PETROVKA, THE ... Robert Ellis Miller
GIRL FROM THE DEAD SEA, THE ... Menahem Golan
GIRL GETTERS, THE ... Michael Winner
GIRL IN BLACK, A ... Michael Cacoyannis
GIRL IN BLACK STOCKINGS, THE ... Howard W. Koch
GIRL IN BLUE, THE ... George Kaczender
GIRL IN THE CROWD, THE ... Michael Powell
GIRL IN THE EMPTY GRAVE, THE (TF) ... Lou Antonio
GIRL IN THE PICTURE, THE ... Don Chaffey
GIRL IN THE RAIN ... Alf Kjellin
GIRL IN THE RED VELVET SWING, THE ... Richard Fleischer
GIRL IN WHITE, THE ... John Sturges
GIRL MOST LIKELY TO..., THE (TF) ... Lee Philips

GIRL NAMED SOONER, A (TF) ... Delbert Mann
GIRL NAMED TAMIKO, A ... John Sturges
GIRL OF THE LIMBERLOST, THE ... Mel Ferrer
GIRL OF THE NIGHT ... Joseph Cates
GIRL ON A MOTORCYCLE, THE ... Jack Cardiff
GIRL ON THE LATE, LATE SHOW, THE (TF) ... Gary Nelson
GIRL ON THE RUN ... Richard L. Bare
GIRL RUSH ... Gordon Douglas
GIRL SAID NO, THE ... Andrew L. Stone
GIRL, THE BODY, AND THE PILL, THE ... Herschell Gordon Lewis
GIRL, THE GOLD WATCH AND DYNAMITE, THE (TF) ... Hy Averback
GIRL, THE GOLD WATCH AND EVERYTHING, THE (TF) ... William Wiard
GIRL WHO CAME GIFT-WRAPPED, THE (TF) ... Bruce Bilson
GIRL WHO COULDN'T LOSE ☆☆, THE (TF) ... Mort Lachman
GIRL WITH GREEN EYES, THE ... Desmond Davis
GIRLFRIENDS ... Claudia Weill
GIRLS ... Just Jaeckin
GIRLS, THE ... Mai Zetterling
GIRLS ARE FOR LOVING ... Don Schain
GIRLS FOR RENT ... Al Adamson
GIRLS FROM WILKO, THE ... Andrzej Wajda
GIRLS IN THE NIGHT ... Jack Arnold
GIRLS IN THE OFFICE, THE (TF) ... Ted Post
GIRLS JUST WANT TO HAVE FUN ... Alan Metter
GIRLS OF HUNTINGTON HOUSE, THE (TF) ... Alf Kjellin
GIRLS OF THE WHITE ORCHID (TF) ... Jonathan Kaplan
GIRLS ON THE BEACH, THE ... William Witney
GIRLY ... Freddie Francis
GIRO CITY ... Karl Francis
GIROLIMONI - IL MOSTRO DI ROMA ... Damiano Damiani
GIVE A GIRL A BREAK ... Stanley Donen
GIVE HER THE MOON ... Philippe de Broca
GIVE MY REGARDS TO BROAD STREET ... Peter Webb
GIVE US THE MOON ... Val Guest
GIVE US THIS DAY ... Edward Dmytryk
GIZMO! (FD) ... Howard Smith
GLADIATORS ... Peter Watkins
GLAMOUR GIRL ... Arthur Dreifuss
GLASS HOUSES ... Alexander Singer
GLASS MENAGERIE, THE (TF) ... Anthony Harvey
GLASS MENAGERIE, THE ... Irving Rapper
GLASS WEB, THE ... Jack Arnold
GLEN AND RANDA ... Jim McBride
GLI INTOCCABILI ... Giuliano Montaldo
GLI SPECIALISTI ... Sergio Corbucci
GLISSMENTS PROGRESSIFS DU PLAISIR ... Alain Robbe-Grillet
GLITTER (TF) ... Jackie Cooper
GLITTER DOME, THE (CTF) ... Stuart Margolin
GLOBAL AFFAIR, A ... Jack Arnold
GLORIA ... John Cassavetes
GLORY BOY ... Edwin Sherin
GLORY BOYS, THE (TF) ... Michael Ferguson
GLORY GUYS, THE ... Arnold Laven
GLORY OF THEIR TIMES, THE (TD) ... Bud Greenspan
GLORY ON THE SUMMIT: BURNING YOUTH ... Masahiro Shinoda
GLOWING AUTUMN ... Masaki Kobayashi
GNOME-MOBILE, THE ... Robert Stevenson
GO ASK ALICE (TF) ... John Korty
GO FOR THE GOLD ... Jackie Cooper
GO TELL IT ON THE MOUNTAIN (TF) ... Stan Lathan
GO TELL THE SPARTANS ... Ted Post
GO WEST, YOUNG GIRL (TF) ... Alan J. Levi
GO WEST, YOUNG MAN ... Henry Hathaway
GOALIE'S ANXIETY AT THE PENALTY KICK, THE ... Wim Wenders
GOD IS MY PARTNER ... William F. Claxton
GOD TOLD ME TO ... Larry Cohen
GODCHILD, THE (TF) ... John Badham
GODFATHER ★, THE ... Francis Ford Coppola
GODFATHER, PART II ★★, THE ... Francis Ford Coppola
GOD'S ANGRY MAN (TD) ... Werner Herzog
GODS MUST BE CRAZY, THE ... Jamie Uys
GODSEND, THE ... Gabrielle Beaumont
GODSPELL ... David Greene
GOIN' ALL THE WAY ... Robert Freedman
GOIN' COCONUTS ... Howard Morris
GOIN' DOWN THE ROAD ... Donald Shebib
GOIN' SOUTH ... Jack Nicholson
GOING APE! ... Jeremy Joe Kronsberg
GOING BERSERK ... David Steinberg
GOING HOLLYWOOD - THE 30'S (FD) ... Julian Schlossberg
GOING HOME ... Herbert B. Leonard
GOING IN STYLE ... Martin Brest
GOING PLACES ... Bertrand Blier
GOING STEADY (LEMON POPSICLE II) ... Boaz Davidson
GOLD ... Peter Hunt
GOLD DIGGERS OF 1933 ... Mervyn Leroy
GOLD FOR THE CAESARS ... Andre De Toth
GOLD OF THE AMAZON WOMEN (TF) ... Mark L. Lester
GOLD OF THE SEVEN SAINTS ... Gordon Douglas
GOLDEN AIRLINER, THE ... Don Sharp
GOLDEN BLADE, THE ... Nathan Juran
GOLDEN BOY ... Rouben Mamoulian
GOLDEN DISC, THE ... Don Sharp
GOLDEN GATE (TF) ... Paul Wendkos
GOLDEN GATE MURDERS, THE (TF) ... Walter Grauman
GOLDEN GLOVES ... Edward Dmytryk
GOLDEN HONEYMOON, THE (TF) ... Noel Black
GOLDEN HORDE, THE ... George Sherman
GOLDEN MOMENT: AN OLYMPIC LOVE STORY, THE (TF) ... Richard C. Sarafian
GOLDEN NEEDLES ... Robert Clouse
GOLDEN RENDEZVOUS ... Ashley Lazarus
GOLDEN SALAMANDER, THE ... Ronald Neame
GOLDEN SEAL, THE ... Frank Zuniga
GOLDEN VOYAGE OF SINBAD, THE ... Gordon Hessler
GOLDENGIRL ... Joseph Sargent
GOLDENROD (TF) ... Harvey Hart
GOLDFINGER ... Guy Hamilton
GOLDIE AND THE BOXER (TF) ... David Miller
GOLDIE AND THE BOXER GO TO HOLLYWOOD (TF) ... David Miller
GOLDILOCKS AND THE THREE BEARS ... Herschell Gordon Lewis
GOLDILOCKS' THREE CHICKS ... Herschell Gordon Lewis
GOLDSTEIN ... Philip Kaufman
G'OLE! (FD) ... Tom Clegg
GOLIATH AND THE VAMPIRES ... Sergio Corbucci
GOLIATH AWAITS (TF) ... Kevin Connor
GONE ARE THE DAYES (CTF) ... Gabrielle Beaumont
GONE ARE THE DAYS! ... Nicholas Webster
GONE IN 60 SECONDS ... H.B. Halicki
GONE TO EARTH ... Michael Powell
GONE WITH THE WEST ... Bernard Girard
GONG SHOW MOVIE, THE ... Chuck Barris
GOOD AGAINST EVIL (TF) ... Paul Wendkos
GOOD AND BAD AT GAMES (TF) ... Jack Gold
GOOD AND THE BAD, THE ... Claude Lelouch
GOOD COMPANIONS, THE ... J. Lee Thompson
GOOD DAY FOR A HANGING ... Nathan Juran
GOOD DIE YOUNG, THE ... Lewis Gilbert
GOOD GUYS AND THE BAD GUYS, THE ... Burt Kennedy
GOOD GUYS WEAR BLACK ... Ted Post
GOOD HUMAN STORY, A (TF) ... Gordon Flemyng
GOOD LUCK, MISS WYCKOFF ... Marvin J. Chomsky
GOOD MORNING, MISS DOVE ... Henry Koster
GOOD MORNING...AND GOODBYE ... Russ Meyer
GOOD NEIGHBOR SAM ... David Swift
GOOD SOLDIER, THE (TF) ... Kevin Billington
GOOD SOLDIER, THE ... Franco Brusati
GOOD SPORT, A (TF) ... Lou Antonio
GOOD, THE BAD AND THE UGLY, THE ... Sergio Leone
GOOD TIMES ... William Friedkin
GOOD TIMES, WONDERFUL TIMES (FD) ... Lionel Rogosin
GOODBYE - GOOD DAY ... Kon Ichikawa
GOODBYE AND AMEN ... Damiano Damiani
GOODBYE, CHARLIE ... Vincente Minnelli
GOODBYE, COLUMBUS ... Larry Peerce
GOOD-BYE, CRUEL WORLD ... David Irving
GOODBYE GEMINI ... Alan Gibson
GOODBYE GIRL, THE ... Herbert Ross
GOODBYE, MR. CHIPS ... Herbert Ross
GOODBYE, MY FANCY ... Vincent Sherman
GOODBYE, NORMA JEAN ... Larry Buchanan
GOODBYE PEOPLE, THE ... Herb Gardner
GOODBYE PORK PIE ... Geoff Murphy
GOODBYE, RAGGEDY ANN (TF) ... Fielder Cook
GOODNIGHT MY LOVE (TF) ... Peter Hyams
GOONIES ... Richard Donner
GOOPY GYNE BAGHA BYNE ... Satyajit Ray
GORDON PINSENT AND THE LIFE AND TIMES OF EDWIN ALONZO BOYD (TF) ... Les Rose
GORDON'S WAR ... Ossie Davis
GORE-GORE GIRLS, THE ... Herschell Gordon Lewis
GORKY PARK ... Michael Apted
GORP ... Joseph Ruben
GOSPEL (FD) ... David Leivick
GOSPEL (FD) ... Frederick Ritzenberg
GOSPEL ROAD, THE ... Robert Elfstrom
GOSSIP COLUMNIST, THE (TF) ... James Sheldon
GOTCHA ... Jeff Kanew
GRACE KELLY (TF) ... Anthony Page
GRADUATE ★★, THE ... Mike Nichols
GRADUATION DAY ... Herb Freed
GRAFFITI BLACKBOARD ... Kaneto Shindo
GRAMBLING'S WHITE TIGER (TF) ... Georg Stanford Brown
GRAND JURY ... Chris Cain
GRAND PRIX ... John Frankenheimer
GRAND SLAM ... Giuliano Montaldo
GRAND THEFT AUTO ... Ron Howard
GRANDVIEW, U.S.A. ... Randal Kleiser
GRASS IS ALWAYS GREENER OVER THE SEPTIC TANK, THE (TF) ... Robert Day
GRASS IS GREENER, THE ... Stanley Donen
GRASS IS SINGING, THE ... Michael Raeburn
GRASSHOPPER, THE ... Jerry Paris
GRAVY TRAIN ... Jack Starrett
GRAY LADY DOWN ... David Greene
GREASE ... Randal Kleiser
GREASE 2 ... Patricia Birch
GREASED LIGHTNING ... Michael Schultz
GREASER'S PALACE ... Robert Downey
GREAT AMERICAN BEAUTY CONTEST, THE (TF) ... Robert Day
GREAT AMERICAN COWBOY, THE (FD) ... Kieth Merrill
GREAT AMERICAN TRAFFIC JAM, THE (TF) ... James Frawley
GREAT AMERICAN TRAGEDY, A (TF) ... J. Lee Thompson
GREAT BANK HOAX, THE ... Joseph Jacoby
GREAT BANK ROBBERY, THE ... Hy Averback
GREAT BIG THING, A ... Eric Till
GREAT BRAIN, THE ... Sidney Levin
GREAT CASH GIVEAWAY GETAWAY, THE (TF) ... Michael O'Herlihy
GREAT CATHERINE ... Gordon Flemyng
GREAT CHESS MOVIE, THE (FD) ... Gilles Carle
GREAT CHICAGO CONSPIRACY CIRCUS, THE ... Kerry Feltham
GREAT ESCAPE, THE ... John Sturges
GREAT EXPECTATIONS (TF) ... Joseph Hardy
GREAT EXPECTATIONS ★ ... David Lean
GREAT GATSBY, THE ... Jack Clayton
GREAT GILDERSLEEVE, THE ... Gordon Douglas
GREAT HOUDINIS, THE (TF) ... Melville Shavelson
GREAT ICE RIP-OFF, THE (TF) ... Dan Curtis
GREAT IMPOSTER, THE ... Robert Mulligan
GREAT McGONAGALL, THE ... Joseph McGrath
GREAT MAN, THE ... Jose Ferrer
GREAT MAN VOTES, THE ... Garson Kanin

GREAT MAN'S WHISKERS, THE (TF) ... Philip Leacock
GREAT MISSOURI RAID, THE ... Gordon Douglas
GREAT MUPPET CAPER, THE ... Jim Henson
GREAT NIAGARA, THE (TF) ... William "Billy" Hale
GREAT NORTHFIELD, MINNESOTA RAID, THE ... Philip Kaufman
GREAT RACE, THE ... Blake Edwards
GREAT RIDE, A ... Donald Hulette
GREAT ROCK 'N' ROLL SWINDLE, THE ... Julien Temple
GREAT SANTINI, THE ... Lewis John Carlino
GREAT SCOUT AND CATHOUSE THURSDAY, THE ... Don Taylor
GREAT SKYCOPTER RESCUE, THE ... Lawrence D. Foldes
GREAT SMOKEY ROADBLOCK, THE ... John Leone
GREAT TELEPHONE ROBBERY, THE ... Menahem Golan
GREAT TEXAS DYNAMITE CHASE, THE ... Michael Pressman
GREAT TRAIN ROBBERY, THE ... Michael Crichton
GREAT VICTOR HERBERT, THE ... Andrew L. Stone
GREAT WALDO PEPPER, THE ... George Roy Hill
GREAT WALLENDAS, THE (TF) ... Larry Elikann
GREAT WALTZ, THE ... Andrew L. Stone
GREAT WAR, THE ... Mario Monicelli
GREAT WHITE HOPE, THE ... Martin Ritt
GREATEST AMERICAN HERO, THE (TF) ... Rod Holcomb
GREATEST HEROES OF THE BIBLE (MS) ... James L. Conway
GREATEST MAN IN THE WORLD, THE (TF) ... Ralph Rosenblum
GREATEST THING THAT ALMOST HAPPENED, THE (TF) ... Gilbert Moses
GREED IN THE SUN ... Henri Verneuil
GREEK TYCOON, THE ... J. Lee Thompson
GREEN BIRD, THE ... Istvan Szabo
GREEN EYES (TF) ... John Erman
GREEN FIRE ... Andrew Marton
GREEN ICE ... Ernest Day
GREEN MAN, THE ... Robert Day
GREEN MANSIONS ... Mel Ferrer
GREEN-EYED BLONDE, THE ... Bernard Girard
GREENGAGE SUMMER, THE ... Lewis Gilbert
GREENWICH VILLAGE STORY ... Jack O'Connell
GREETINGS ... Brian De Palma
GREGORY'S GIRL ... Bill Forsyth
GREMLINS ... Joe Dante
GRENOBLE (FD) ... Claude Lelouch
GRENOBLE (FD) ... Francois Reichenbach
GREY FOX, THE ... Phillip Borsos
GREY GARDENS (FD) ... Albert Maysles
GREY GARDENS (FD) ... David Maysles
GREYEAGLE ... Charles B. Pierce
GREYFRIARS BOBBY ... Don Chaffey
GREYSTOKE: THE LEGEND OF TARZAN, LORD OF THE APES ... Hugh Hudson
GRIFFIN AND PHOENIX (TF) ... Daryl Duke
GRIP OF THE STRANGLER ... Robert Day
GRISFESTEN ... Bo Widerberg
GROOVE TUBE, THE ... Ken Shapiro
GROUNDSTAR CONSPIRACY, THE ... Lamont Johnson
GROUP MARRIAGE ... Stephanie Rothman
GROUP, THE ... Sidney Lumet
GROWING PAINS ... Robert "Bobby" Houston
GRUESOME TWOSOME, THE ... Herschell Gordon Lewis
GUARDIAN, THE (CTF) ... David Greene
GUARDIE E LADRI ... Mario Monicelli
GUENDALINA ... Alberto Lattuada
GUERRE SECRETE ... Carlo Lizzani
GUERRE SECRETE ... Terence Young
GUESS WHAT WE LEARNED IN SCHOOL TODAY? ... John G. Avildsen
GUESS WHO'S COMING TO DINNER ★ ... Stanley Kramer
GUESS WHO'S SLEEPING IN MY BED? (TF) ... Theodore J. Flicker
GUEST, THE ... Clive Donner
GUIDE FOR THE MARRIED MAN, A ... Gene Kelly
GUIDE FOR THE MARRIED WOMAN, A (TF) ... Hy Averback
GUILTY OR INNOCENT: THE SAM SHEPPARD MURDER CASE (TF) ... Robert M. Lewis
GUINEA PIG, THE ... Roy Boulting
GULAG (CTF) ... Roger Young
GULLIVER'S TRAVELS ... Peter Hunt
GUMBALL RALLY ... Chuck Bail
GUMSHOE ... Stephen Frears
GUN, THE (TF) ... John Badham
GUN AND THE PULPIT, THE (TF) ... Daniel Petrie
GUN IN THE HOUSE, A (TF) ... Ivan Nagy
GUN RIDERS ... Al Adamson
GUN RUNNERS, THE ... Don Siegel
GUN THE MAN DOWN ... Andrew V. McLaglen
GUNFIGHT, A ... Lamont Johnson
GUNFIGHT AT THE O.K. CORRAL ... John Sturges
GUNFIGHT IN ABILENE ... William "Billy" Hale
GUNMAN'S WALK ... Phil Karlson
GUNN ... Blake Edwards
GUNPOINT ... Earl Bellamy
GUNS ... Robert Kramer
GUNS AT BATASI ... John Guillermin
GUNS FOR SAN SEBASTIAN ... Henri Verneuil
GUNS OF NAVARONE ★, THE ... J. Lee Thompson
GUNS OF THE MAGNIFICENT SEVEN ... Paul Wendkos
GUNSLINGER, THE ... Roger Corman
GUNSMOKE ... Nathan Juran
GURU, THE ... James Ivory
GUS ... Vincent McEveety
GUSTAVE MOREAU (FD) ... Nelly Kaplan
GUTTER ... Kaneto Shindo
GUY, A GAL AND A PAL, A ... Budd Boetticher
GUYANA TRAGEDY: THE STORY OF JIM JONES (TF) ☆ ... William A. Graham
GUYS AND DOLLS ... Joseph L. Mankiewicz
GUYS OF THE SEA ... Kaneto Shindo
GWENDOLINE ... Just Jaeckin
GYMKATA ... Robert Clouse
GYPSY ... Mervyn Leroy
GYPSY COLT ... Andrew Marton
GYPSY MOTHS, THE ... John Frankenheimer

H

HADLEY'S REBELLION ... Fred Walton
HAIL, HERO! ... David Miller
HAIR ... Milos Forman
HAIRCUT ... Andy Warhol
HALAHAKA ... Avi Nesher
HALF A HERO ... Don Weis
HALF A SIXPENCE ... George Sidney
HALF PAST MIDNIGHT ... William F. Claxton
HALF-WAY TO HEAVEN ... George Abbott
HALLELUJAH TRAIL, THE ... John Sturges
HALLOWEEN ... John Carpenter
HALLOWEEN II ... Rick Rosenthal
HALLOWEEN III: SEASON OF THE WITCH ... Tommy Lee Wallace
HALLS OF ANGER ... Paul Bogart
HAMBONE AND HILLIE ... Roy Watts
HAMLET ... Tony Richardson
HAMLET ★ ... Laurence Olivier
HAMMER ... Bruce Clark
HAMMERHEAD ... David Miller
HAMMERSMITH IS OUT ... Peter Ustinov
HAMMETT ... Wim Wenders
HAMSIN ... Daniel Wachsmann
HANAUMA BAY ... Tommy Lee Wallace
HAND IN HAND ... Philip Leacock
HAND ME DOWN KID, THE (TF) ... Robert Mandel
HAND OF DEATH ... Gene Nelson
HAND, THE ... Oliver Stone
HANDFUL OF LOVE, A ... Vilgot Sjoman
HANDGUN ... Tony Garnett
HANDLE WITH CARE ... Jonathan Demme
HANDS OF CORMAC JOYCE, THE (TF) ... Fielder Cook
HANDS OF THE RIPPER ... Peter Sasdy
HANDS UP! ... Jerzy Skolimowski
HANG 'EM HIGH ... Ted Post
HANGAR 18 ... James L. Conway
HANGED MAN, THE (TF) ... Michael Caffey
HANGED MAN, THE (TF) ... Don Siegel
HANGMAN'S KNOT ... Roy Huggins
HANGUP ... Henry Hathaway
HANK WILLIAMS: THE SHOW HE NEVER GAVE ... David Acomba
HANKY PANKY ... Sidney Poitier
HANNA K. ... Costa-Gavras
HANNAH AND HER SISTERS ... Woody Allen
HANNIBAL BROOKS ... Michael Winner
HANNIE CAULDER ... Burt Kennedy
HANOVER STREET ... Peter Hyams
HANS BRINKER (TF) ... Robert Scheerer
HAPPENING OF THE VAMPIRE, THE ... Freddie Francis
HAPPENING, THE ... Elliot Silverstein
HAPPILY EVER AFTER ... Robert Stevenson
HAPPILY EVER AFTER (TF) ... Robert Scheerer
HAPPINESS AHEAD ... Mervyn Leroy
HAPPINESS CAGE, THE ... Bernard Girard
HAPPINESS IS A WARM CLUE (TF) ... Daryl Duke
HAPPY (TF) ... Lee Philips
HAPPY ANNIVERSARY ... David Miller
HAPPY BIRTHDAY GEMINI ... Richard Benner
HAPPY BIRTHDAY TO ME ... J. Lee Thompson
HAPPY ENDING, THE ... Richard Brooks
HAPPY ENDINGS (TF) ... Noel Black
HAPPY ENDINGS (TF) ... Jerry Thorpe
HAPPY HOOKER, THE ... Nicholas Sgarro
HAPPY HOOKER GOES HOLLYWOOD, THE ... Alan Roberts
HAPPY HOOKER GOES TO WASHINGTON, THE ... William A. Levey
HAPPY IS THE BRIDE ... Roy Boulting
HAPPY MOTHER'S DAY - LOVE, GEORGE ... Darren McGavin
HAPPY NEW YEAR ... Claude Lelouch
HAPPY ROAD, THE ... Gene Kelly
HAPPY TIME, THE ... Richard Fleischer
HARAKIRI ... Masaki Kobayashi
HARBOR LIGHTS ... Maury Dexter
HARD CONTRACT ... S. Lee Pogostin
HARD COUNTRY ... David Greene
HARD DAY FOR ARCHIE, A ... Jim McBride
HARD DAY'S NIGHT, A ... Richard Lester
HARD, FAST AND BEAUTIFUL ... Ida Lupino
HARD FEELINGS ... Daryl Duke
HARD KNOX (TF) ... Peter Werner
HARD MAN, THE ... George Sherman
HARD PART BEGINS, THE ... Paul Lynch
HARD RIDE, THE ... Burt Topper
HARD ROCK ZOMBIES ... Krishna Shah
HARD TIMES ... Walter Hill
HARD TO HANDLE ... Mervyn Leroy
HARD TO HOLD ... Larry Peerce
HARD TRAVELIN' (TD) ... Jim Brown
HARD WAY, THE ... Vincent Sherman
HARDBODIES ... Mark Griffiths
HARDCASE (TF) ... John Llewellyn Moxey
HARDCASTLE AND McCORMICK (TF) ... Roger Young
HARDCORE ... Paul Schrader
HARDHAT AND LEGS (TF) ... Lee Philips
HARDLY WORKING ... Jerry Lewis
HARLAN COUNTY, U.S.A. (FD) ... Barbara Kopple
HARLEM GLOBETROTTERS ON GILLIGAN'S ISLAND, THE (TF) ... Peter Baldwin
HARLEQUIN ... Simon Wincer
HARLOT ... Andy Warhol
HARLOW ... Gordon Douglas
HARNESS FEVER ... Don Chaffey
HAROLD AND MAUDE ... Hal Ashby
HAROLD ROBBINS' THE PIRATE (TF) ... Ken Annakin
HAROLD ROBBINS' 79 PARK AVENUE (MS) ... Paul Wendkos
HAROLD TEEN ... Mervyn Leroy
HARP OF BURMA, THE ... Kon Ichikawa
HARPER ... Jack Smight
HARPER VALLEY PTA ... Richard C. Bennett
HARPY (TF) ... Gerald Seth Sindell
HARRAD EXPERIMENT, THE ... Ted Post
HARRAD SUMMER, THE ... Steven Hillard Stern
HARRIET CRAIG ... Vincent Sherman
HARRY & SON ... Paul Newman

Title	Director
HARRY AND TONTO	Paul Mazursky
HARRY AND WALTER GO TO NEW YORK	Mark Rydell
HARRY TRACY	William A. Graham
HARRY'S WAR	Kieth Merrill
HART TO HART (TF)	Tom Mankiewicz
HARUM SCARUM	Gene Nelson
HARVEST OF MY LAI, THE (TD)	Marcel Ophuls
HARVEY	Henry Koster
HARVEY GIRLS, THE	George Sidney
HARVEY MIDDLEMAN, FIREMAN	Ernest Pintoff
HASTY HEART, THE	Vincent Sherman
HAT HET BOLDOGSAG	Andre De Toth
HATFIELDS AND THE McCOYS, THE (TF)	Clyde Ware
HATFUL OF RAIN, A	Fred Zinnemann
HAUNTED (TF)	Michael Roemer
HAUNTED PALACE, THE	Roger Corman
HAUNTED STRANGLER, THE	Robert Day
HAUNTING OF JULIA, THE	Richard Loncraine
HAUNTING OF M, THE	Anna Thomas
HAUNTING PASSION, THE (TF)	John Korty
HAUNTING, THE	Robert Wise
HAUNTS	Herb Freed
HAUNTS OF THE VERY RICH (TF)	Paul Wendkos
HAVE ROCKET, WILL TRAVEL	David Lowell Rich
HAVING A WILD WEEKEND	John Boorman
HAVING BABIES (TF)	Robert Day
HAVING BABIES II (TF)	Richard Michaels
HAVING BABIES III (TF)	Jackie Cooper
HAVING IT ALL (TF)	Edward Zwick
HAWAII	George Roy Hill
HAWAII FIVE-O (TF)	Paul Wendkos
HAWAIIAN HEAT (TF)	Mike Vejar
HAWK, THE	Edward Dmytryk
HAWK THE SLAYER	Terry Marcel
HAWKINS ON MURDER (TF)	Jud Taylor
HAWMPS	Joe Camp
HAYWIRE (TF)	Michael Tuchner
HE IS MY BROTHER	Edward Dmytryk
HE KNOWS YOU'RE ALONE	Armand Mastroianni
HE LAUGHED LAST	Blake Edwards
HE RAN ALL THE WAY	John Berry
HE WHO RIDES A TIGER	Charles Crichton
HEAD	Bob Rafelson
HEAD OFFICE	Ken Finkleman
HEAD OVER HEELS	Joan Micklin Silver
HEADIN' FOR BROADWAY	Joseph Brooks
HEADLINE HUNTERS	William Witney
HEADS OR TAILS	Robert Enrico
HEALTH	Robert Altman
HEAR NO EVIL (TF)	Harry Falk
HEARSE, THE	George Bowers
HEART	Kaneto Shindo
HEART, THE	Kon Ichikawa
HEART BEAT	John Byrum
HEART IN HIDING (TF)	Peter Levin
HEART IS A LONELY HUNTER, THE	Robert Ellis Miller
HEART LIKE A WHEEL	Jonathan Kaplan
HEART OF A CHILD	Clive Donner
HEART OF A TYRANT	Miklos Jancso
HEART OF GLASS	Werner Herzog
HEART OF STEEL (TF)	Donald Wrye
HEART OF THE STAG	Michael Firth
HEARTACHES	Donald Shebib
HEARTBEEPS	Allan Arkush
HEARTBREAK KID, THE	Elaine May
HEARTBREAKER	Frank Zuniga
HEARTBREAKERS	Bobby Roth
HEARTLAND	Richard Pearce
HEARTS AND MINDS (FD)	Peter Davis
HEARTS OF THE WEST	Howard Zieff
HEARTSOUNDS (TF)	Glenn Jordan
HEAT	Paul Morrissey
HEAT AND DUST	James Ivory
HEAT HAZE	Kaneto Shindo
HEAT LIGHTNING	Mervyn Leroy
HEAT OF ANGER (TF)	Don Taylor
HEAT WAVE	Kenneth "Ken" Hughes
HEATWAVE	Phillip Noyce
HEATWAVE! (TF)	Jerry Jameson
HEAVEN CAN WAIT ★	Warren Beatty
HEAVEN CAN WAIT ★	Buck Henry
HEAVEN HELP US	Michael Dinner
HEAVEN KNOWS, MR. ALLISON	John Huston
HEAVEN WITH A GUN	Lee H. Katzin
HEAVENLY BODIES	Lawrence Dane
HEAVENLY BODIES	Russ Meyer
HEAVENLY KID, THE	Cary Medoway
HEAVEN'S ABOVE!	John Boulting
HEAVEN'S GATE	Michael Cimino
HEAVY LOAD	Chuck Vincent
HEAVY METAL (AF)	Gerald Potterton
HEAVY TRAFFIC (AF)	Ralph Bakshi
HEC RAMSEY (TF)	Daniel Petrie
HECKLERS, THE (TF)	Joseph Strick
HEDDA	Trevor Nunn
HEDY	Andy Warhol
HEDY THE SHOPLIFTER	Andy Warhol
HEERAK RAJAR DESHE	Satyajit Ray
HEIDI	Luigi Comencini
HEIDI (TF)	Delbert Mann
HEIDI'S SONG (AF)	Robert Taylor
HEIST, THE (TF)	Don McDougall
HELEN - QUEEN OF THE NAUTCH GIRLS (FD)	James Ivory
HELEN KELLER - THE MIRACLE CONTINUES (TF)	Alan Gibson
HELEN OF TROY	Robert Wise
HELL AND HIGH WATER	Samuel Fuller
HELL BENT FOR LEATHER	George Sherman
HELL DRIVERS	Cy Endfield
HELL HOLE	Pierre DeMoro
HELL IN THE PACIFIC	John Boorman
HELL IS A CITY	Val Guest
HELL IS FOR HEROES	Don Siegel
HELL IS SOLD OUT	Michael Anderson
HELL NIGHT	Tom Desimone
HELL RAIDERS	Larry Buchanan
HELL SQUAD	Burt Topper
HELL TO ETERNITY	Phil Karlson
HELL UP IN HARLEM	Larry Cohen
HELL WITH HEROES, THE	Joseph Sargent
HELLBENDERS, THE	Sergio Corbucci
HELLCATS OF THE NAVY	Nathan Juran
HELLDORADO	William Witney
HELLE	Roger Vadim
HELLFIGHTERS	Andrew V. McLaglen
HELLGATE	Charles Marquis Warren
HELLINGER'S LAW (TF)	Leo Penn
HELLIONS, THE	Ken Annakin
HELLO - GOODBYE	Jean Negulesco
HELLO, DOLLY!	Gene Kelly
HELLO DOWN THERE	Jack Arnold
HELL'S ANGELS ON WHEELS	Richard Rush
HELL'S ANGELS '69	Lee Madden
HELL'S BELLES	Maury Dexter
HELL'S BLOODY DEVILS	Al Adamson
HELL'S HEADQUARTERS	Andrew L. Stone
HELL'S ISLAND	Phil Karlson
HELLSTROM CHRONICLE, THE (FD)	Walon Green
HELP WANTED: MALE (TF)	William Wiard
HELP!	Richard Lester
HELTER SKELTER	Ralph Thomas
HEMINGWAY'S ADVENTURES OF A YOUNG MAN	Martin Ritt
HENDERSON MONSTER, THE (TF)	Waris Hussein
HENNESSY	Don Sharp
HENRY GELDZAHLER	Andy Warhol
HENRY IV	Marco Bellocchio
HENRY V	Laurence Olivier
HENRY VIII AND HIS SIX WIVES	Waris Hussein
HER BROTHER	Kon Ichikawa
HER FIRST ROMANCE	Edward Dmytryk
HER LAST AFFAIRE	Michael Powell
HER LIFE AS A MAN (TF)	Robert Ellis Miller
HERBIE GOES BANANAS	Vincent McEveety
HERBIE GOES TO MONTE CARLO	Vincent McEveety
HERBIE RIDES AGAIN	Robert Stevenson
HERCULES	Lewis Coates
HERE ARE LADIES	John Quested
HERE COME THE HUGGETTS	Ken Annakin
HERE COME THE TIGERS	Sean S. Cunningham
HERE COMES THE GROOM	Frank Capra
HERE WE GO ROUND THE MULBERRY BUSH	Clive Donner
HERE'S YOUR LIFE	Jan Troell
HERETIC: EXORCIST II, THE	John Boorman
HERITAGE OF THE DESERT	Henry Hathaway
HERO, THE	Richard Harris
HERO AIN'T NOTHIN' BUT A SANDWICH, A	Ralph Nelson
HERO AT LARGE	Martin Davidson
HEROES	Jeremy Paul Kagan
HEROES OF ROCK AND ROLL (TD)	Malcolm Leo
HEROES OF ROCK AND ROLL (TD)	Andrew Solt
HEROES OF THE SADDLE	William Witney
HERO'S ISLAND	Leslie Stevens
HE'S FIRED, SHE'S HIRED (TF)	Marc Daniels
HE'S NOT YOUR SON (TF)	Don Taylor
HESTER STREET	Joan Micklin Silver
HEY BABE!	Rafal Zielinski
HEY BOY! HEY GIRL!	David Lowell Rich
HEY GOOD LOOKIN' (AF)	Ralph Bakshi
HEY, I'M ALIVE! (TF)	Lawrence J. Schiller
HI DIDDLE DIDDLE	Andrew L. Stone
HI, MOM!	Brian De Palma
HI, NELLIE!	Mervyn Leroy
HIBERNATUS	Edouard Molinaro
HICKEY AND BOGGS	Robert Culp
HIDDEN FEAR	Andre De Toth
HIDDEN FORTRESS, THE	Akira Kurosawa
HIDDEN ROOM, THE	Edward Dmytryk
HIDE AND SEEK	Cy Endfield
HIDE AND SEEK	Dan Wolman
HIDE IN PLAIN SIGHT	James Caan
HIDEAWAYS, THE	Fielder Cook
HIDING PLACE, THE	James F. Collier
HIGH AND DRY	Alexander Mackendrick
HIGH AND LOW	Akira Kurosawa
HIGH ANXIETY	Mel Brooks
HIGH BRIGHT SUN, THE	Ralph Thomas
HIGH COMMISSIONER, THE	Ralph Thomas
HIGH COST OF LOVING, THE	Jose Ferrer
HIGH COUNTRY, THE	Harvey Hart
HIGH HEELS	Claude Chabrol
HIGH ICE (TF)	Eugene S. Jones
HIGH INFIDELITY	Mario Monicelli
HIGH INFIDELITY	Luciano Salce
HIGH MIDNIGHT (TF)	Daniel Haller
HIGH NOON - PART II: THE RETURN OF WILL KANE (TF)	Jerry Jameson
HIGH NOON ★	Fred Zinnemann
HIGH PLAINS DRIFTER	Clint Eastwood
HIGH POWERED RIFLE, THE	Maury Dexter
HIGH PRESSURE	Mervyn Leroy
HIGH RISK	Stewart Raffill
HIGH RISK (TF)	Sam O'Steen
HIGH ROAD TO CHINA	Brian G. Hutton
HIGH ROLLING	Igor Auzins
HIGH SCHOOL (FD)	Frederick Wiseman
HIGH SCHOOL HERO	Arthur Dreifuss
HIGH SCHOOL U.S.A. (TF)	Rod Amateau
HIGH TIDE AT NOON	Philip Leacock
HIGH TIME	Blake Edwards
HIGH TREASON	Roy Boulting
HIGH, WIDE, AND HANDSOME	Rouben Mamoulian
HIGH WIND IN JAMAICA, A	Alexander Mackendrick
HIGHLY DANGEROUS	Roy Ward Baker
HIGHWAY DRAGNET	Nathan Juran
HIGHWAY TO HEAVEN (TF)	Michael Landon
HIGHWAY 301	Andrew L. Stone
HI-JACKERS, THE	James O'Connolly
HILL, THE	Sidney Lumet
HILLS HAVE EYES, THE	Wes Craven
HILLS HAVE EYES PART 2, THE	Wes Craven
HILLS RUN RED, THE	Carlo Lizzani
HIMIKO	Masahiro Shinoda
HINDENBURG, THE	Robert Wise
HINOTORI	Kon Ichikawa
HIRED HAND, THE	Peter Fonda
HIRELING, THE	Alan Bridges
HI-RIDERS	Greydon Clark
HIROSHIMA, MON AMOUR	Alain Resnais
HIS LAND	James F. Collier
HIS LORDSHIP	Michael Powell
HIS MISTRESS (TF)	David Lowell Rich
HISTOIRES EXTRAORDINAIRES	Federico Fellini
HISTOIRES EXTRAORDINAIRES	Louis Malle
HISTOIRES EXTRAORDINAIRES	Roger Vadim

HISTORIAS DE LA REVOLUCION ... Tomas Gutierrez Alea
HISTORY OF POST-WAR JAPAN AS TOLD BY A BAR HOSTESS (FD) ... Shohei Imamura
HISTORY OF THE WORLD, PART I ... Mel Brooks
HIT! ... Sidney J. Furie
HIT, THE ... Stephen Frears
HIT AND RUN ... Charles Braverman
HIT AND RUN ... Robin Spry
HIT LADY (TF) ... Tracy Keenan Wynn
HIT MAN ... George Armitage
HITCHHIKE! (TF) ... Gordon Hessler
HITCH-HIKER, THE ... Ida Lupino
HITLER: A FILM FROM GERMANY ... Hans-Jurgen Syberberg
HITLER? CONNAIS PAS! ... Bertrand Blier
HITLER'S CHILDREN ... Edward Dmytryk
HITLER'S SON ... Rod Amateau
HITLER'S S.S. (TF) ... Jim Goddard
HI-YO SILVER ... William Witney
H.M.S. DEFIANT ... Lewis Gilbert
HO! ... Robert Enrico
HOA-BINH ... Raoul Coutard
HOBBIT, THE (ATF) ... Jules Bass
HOBBIT, THE (ATF) ... Arthur Rankin, Jr.
HOBSON'S CHOICE ... David Lean
HOBSON'S CHOICE (TF) ... Gilbert Cates
HOFFMAN ... Alvin Rakoff
H.O.G. ... Donald Wrye
HOG WILD ... Les Rose
HOKUSAI, UKIYOE MASTER ... Kaneto Shindo
HOLCROFT COVENANT, THE ... John Frankenheimer
HOLE IN THE HEAD, A ... Frank Capra
HOLE, THE ... Kon Ichikawa
HOLIDAY CAMP ... Ken Annakin
HOLIDAY IN MEXICO ... George Sidney
HOLIDAY IN SPAIN ... Jack Cardiff
HOLLOW IMAGE (TF) ... Marvin J. Chomsky
HOLLOW, THE ... George T. Nierenberg
HOLLYWOOD BOULEVARD ... Allan Arkush
HOLLYWOOD BOULEVARD ... Joe Dante
HOLLYWOOD HOT TUBS ... Chuck Vincent
HOLLYWOOD KNIGHTS, THE ... Floyd Mutrux
HOLLYWOOD ON TRIAL (FD) ... David Helpern, Jr.
HOLLYWOOD STRANGLER MEETS THE SKID ROW SLASHER, THE ... Ray Dennis Steckler
HOLLYWOOD WIVES (MS) ... Robert Day
HOLOCAUST (MS) ☆☆ ... Marvin J. Chomsky
HOLY MOUNTAIN, THE ... Alexandro Jodorowsky
HOMBRE ... Martin Ritt
HOME AND THE WORLD, THE ... Satyajit Ray
HOME BEFORE DARK ... Mervyn Leroy
HOME BEFORE MIDNIGHT ... Peter Walker
HOME FOR THE HOLIDAYS (TF) ... John Llewellyn Moxey
HOME FREE ALL ... Stewart Bird
HOME FROM THE HILL ... Vincente Minnelli
HOME IN INDIANA ... Henry Hathaway
HOME IS THE HERO ... Fielder Cook
HOME MOVIES ... Brian De Palma
HOME OF OUR OWN, A (TF) ... Robert Day
HOME TO STAY (TF) ... Delbert Mann
HOMEBODIES ... Larry Yust
HOMECOMING ... Mervyn Leroy
HOMECOMING, THE (TF) ☆ ... Fielder Cook
HOMECOMING, THE ... Peter Hall
HOMETOWN, U.S.A. ... Max Baer, Jr.
HOMEWARD BOUND (TF) ... Richard Michaels
HOMEWORK ... James Beshears
HONDO AND THE APACHES ... Lee H. Katzin
HONEY POT, THE ... Joseph L. Mankiewicz
HONEYBABY, HONEYBABY ... Michael Schultz
HONEYBOY (TF) ... John Berry
HONEYCOMB ... Carlos Saura
HONEYMOON ... Michael Powell
HONEYMOON WITH A STRANGER (TF) ... John Peyser
HONEYSUCKLE ROSE ... Jerry Schatzberg
HONKY ... William A. Graham
HONKY TONK (TF) ... Don Taylor
HONKY TONK FREEWAY ... John Schlesinger
HONKYTONK MAN ... Clint Eastwood
HONOR GUARD, THE ... Burt Kennedy
HONOR THY FATHER (TF) ... Paul Wendkos
HONORARY CONSUL, THE ... John Mackenzie
HOODLUM PRIEST, THE ... Irvin Kershner
HOODWINK ... Claude Whatham
HOOPER ... Hal Needham
HOOTENANNY HOOT ... Gene Nelson
HOPSCOTCH ... Ronald Neame
HORIZON, THE ... Kaneto Shindo
HORIZONS ... Don Norman
HORIZONS WEST ... Budd Boetticher
HORNETS' NEST ... Phil Karlson
HORROR AT 37,000 FEET, THE (TF) ... David Lowell Rich
HORROR HOTEL ... John Llewellyn Moxey
HORROR OF FRANKENSTEIN, THE ... Jimmy Sangster
HORROR OF THE BLOOD MONSTERS ... Al Adamson
HORROR ON SNAPE ISLAND ... James O'Connolly
HORSE WITHOUT A HEAD, THE ... Don Chaffey
HORSEMEN, THE ... John Frankenheimer
HORSE'S MOUTH, THE ... Ronald Neame
HOSPITAL (FD) ... Frederick Wiseman
HOSPITAL MASSACRE ... Boaz Davidson
HOSPITAL, THE ... Arthur Hiller
HOSTAGE HEART, THE (TF) ... Bernard McEveety
HOSTAGE TOWER, THE (TF) ... Claudio Guzman
HOT AND DEADLY ... Elliott Hong
HOT BUBBLEGUM (LEMON POPSICLE III) ... Boaz Davidson
HOT CAR GIRL ... Bernard L. Kowalski
HOT DOG...THE MOVIE ... Peter Markle
HOT ENOUGH FOR JUNE ... Ralph Thomas
HOT LEAD AND COLD FEET ... Robert Butler
HOT MARSHLAND, THE ... Kon Ichikawa
HOT MILLIONS ... Eric Till
HOT MOVES ... Jim Sotos
HOT POTATO ... Oscar Williams
HOT PURSUIT (TF) ... Kenneth Johnson
HOT RESORT ... John Robins
HOT ROCK, THE ... Peter Yates
HOT ROD (TF) ... George Armitage
HOT ROD GIRL ... Leslie H. Martinson
HOT ROD RUMBLE ... Leslie H. Martinson
HOT SPELL ... Daniel Mann
HOT STUFF ... Dom De Luise
HOT STUFF ... Mervyn Leroy
HOT SUMMER ... William Sachs
HOT TIMES ... Jim McBride
HOT TOMORROWS ... Martin Brest
HOT TOUCH, THE ... Roger Vadim
HOT T-SHIRTS ... Chuck Vincent
HOT WIND ... Daniel Wachsmann
HOTEL ... Richard Quine
HOTEL NEW HAMPSHIRE, THE ... Tony Richardson
HOTEL PARADISO ... Peter Glenville
HOTEL SAHARA ... Ken Annakin
HOTEL SPLENDIDE ... Michael Powell
HOTHEAD ... Jean-Jacques Annaud
HOTLINE (TF) ... Jerry Jameson
H.O.T.S. ... Gerald Seth Sindell
HOUND DOG MAN ... Don Siegel
HOUND OF THE BASKERVILLES, THE (TF) ... Barry Crane
HOUND OF THE BASKERVILLES, THE ... Douglas Hickox
HOUND OF THE BASKERVILLES, THE ... Paul Morrissey
HOUR OF GLORY ... Michael Powell
HOUR OF THE GUN ... John Sturges
HOUR OF THE WOLF ... Ingmar Bergman
HOURS OF LOVE, THE ... Luciano Salce
HOUSE ACROSS THE LAKE, THE ... Kenneth "Ken" Hughes
HOUSE ACROSS THE STREET, THE ... Richard L. Bare
HOUSE BY THE LAKE, THE ... William Fruet
HOUSE CALLS ... Howard Zieff
HOUSE IN NIGHTMARE PARK, THE ... Peter Sykes
HOUSE IN THE SQUARE, THE ... Roy Ward Baker
HOUSE IS NOT A HOME, A ... Russell Rouse
HOUSE OF BAMBOO ... Samuel Fuller
HOUSE OF CARDS ... John Guillermin
HOUSE OF DARK SHADOWS ... Dan Curtis
HOUSE OF GOD, THE ... Donald Wrye
HOUSE OF MIRTH, THE (TF) ... Adrian Hall
HOUSE OF MORTAL SIN ... Peter Walker
HOUSE OF NUMBERS ... Russell Rouse
HOUSE OF SECRETS ... Guy Green
HOUSE OF STRANGERS ... Joseph L. Mankiewicz
HOUSE OF THE ARROW, THE ... Michael Anderson
HOUSE OF THE DAMNED ... Maury Dexter
HOUSE OF THE LIVING DEAD ... Ray Austin
HOUSE OF THE LONG SHADOWS ... Peter Walker
HOUSE OF THE RISING SUN ... Chuck Vincent
HOUSE OF USHER, THE ... Roger Corman
HOUSE OF WAX ... Andre De Toth
HOUSE OF WHIPCORD ... Peter Walker
HOUSE OF WOMEN ... Walter Doniger
HOUSE OF 1,000 DOLLS ... Jeremy Summers
HOUSE OF 1,000 PLEASURES ... Anthony M. Dawson
HOUSE ON CHELOUCHE STREET, THE ... Moshe Mizrahi
HOUSE ON GREENAPPLE ROAD, THE (TF) ... Robert Day
HOUSE ON SORORITY ROW, THE ... Mark Rosman
HOUSE ON TELEGRAPH HILL, THE ... Robert Wise
HOUSE ON 92ND STREET, THE ... Henry Hathaway
HOUSE THAT DRIPPED BLOOD, THE ... Peter John Duffell
HOUSE THAT WOULD NOT DIE, THE (TF) ... John Llewellyn Moxey
HOUSE WHERE DEATH LIVES, THE ... Alan Beattie
HOUSE WHERE EVIL DWELLS, THE ... Kevin Connor
HOUSEBOAT ... Melville Shavelson
HOUSEHOLDER, THE ... James Ivory
HOUSTON, TEXAS (FD) ... Francois Reichenbach
HOW AWFUL ABOUT ALLAN (TF) ... Curtis Harrington
HOW COME NOBODY'S ON OUR SIDE? ... Richard Michaels
HOW DO I LOVE THEE? ... Michael Gordon
HOW FUNNY CAN SEX BE? ... Dino Risi
HOW I SPENT MY SUMMER VACATION (TF) ... William "Billy" Hale
HOW I WON THE WAR ... Richard Lester
HOW SWEET IT IS! ... Jerry Paris
HOW THE WEST WAS WON ... Henry Hathaway
HOW THE WEST WAS WON (MS) ... Burt Kennedy
HOW THE WEST WAS WON (MS) ... Daniel Mann
HOW TO BE A PERFECT PERSON (TF) ... Joan Micklin Silver
HOW TO BEAT THE HIGH COST OF LIVING ... Robert Scheerer
HOW TO BREAK UP A HAPPY DIVORCE (TF) ... Jerry Paris
HOW TO COMMIT MARRIAGE ... Norman Panama
HOW TO FRAME A FIGG ... Alan Rafkin
HOW TO MARRY A MILLIONAIRE ... Jean Negulesco
HOW TO MURDER YOUR WIFE ... Richard Quine
HOW TO PICK UP GIRLS! (TF) ... Bill Persky
HOW TO SAVE A MARRIAGE AND RUIN YOUR LIFE ... Fielder Cook
HOW TO SEDUCE A WOMAN ... Charles Martin
HOW TO STEAL AN AIRPLANE (TF) ... Leslie H. Martinson
HOW TO STUFF A WILD BIKINI ... William Asher
HOW TO SUCCEED IN BUSINESS WITHOUT REALLY TRYING ... David Swift
HOW TO SUCCEED WITH SEX ... Bert I. Gordon
HOWLING II, THE ... Philippe Mora
HOWLING IN THE WOODS, A (TF) ... Daniel Petrie
HOWLING, THE ... Joe Dante
HUCKLEBERRY FINN ... J. Lee Thompson

HUCKLEBERRY FINN (TF) ... Robert Totten
HUD ★ ... Martin Ritt
HUE AND CRY ... Charles Crichton
HUGGETTS ABROAD, THE ... Ken Annakin
HUGHES AND HARLOW: ANGELS IN HELL ... Larry Buchanan
HULLABALOO OVER GEORGIA & BONNIE'S PICTURES ... James Ivory
HUMAIN, TROP HUMAIN (FD) ... Louis Malle
HUMAN BEING ... Kaneto Shindo
HUMAN CONDITION, PART I (NO GREATER LOVE), THE ... Masaki Kobayashi
HUMAN CONDITION, PART II (ROAD TO ETERNITY), THE ... Masaki Kobayashi
HUMAN CONDITION, PART III (A SOLDIER'S PRAYER), THE ... Masaki Kobayashi
HUMAN FACTOR, THE ... Edward Dmytryk
HUMAN FACTOR, THE ... Otto Preminger
HUMAN FEELINGS (TF) ... Ernest Pintoff
HUMANOIDS FROM THE DEEP ... Barbara Peeters
HUMONGOUS ... Paul Lynch
HUMORESQUE ... Jean Negulesco
HUNCHBACK OF NOTRE DAME, THE (TF) ... Alan Cooke
HUNCHBACK OF NOTRE DAME, THE (TF) ... Michael Tuchner
HUNDRA ... Matt Cimber
HUNDRED HOUR HUNT ... Lewis Gilbert
HUNGARIAN RHAPSODY ... Miklos Jancso
HUNGER, THE ... Tony Scott
HUNGRY WIVES ... George A. Romero
HUNT, THE ... Carlos Saura
HUNTED ... Charles Crichton
HUNTED LADY, THE (TF) ... Richard Lang
HUNTER (TF) ... Ron Satlof
HUNTER, THE ... Buzz Kulik
HUNTER OF THE APOCALYPSE ... Anthony M. Dawson
HUNTERS ARE FOR KILLING (TF) ... Bernard Girard
HUNTERS ARE FOR KILLING (TF) ... Bernard L. Kowalski
HUNTERS OF THE GOLDEN COBRA, THE ... Anthony M. Dawson
HUNTERS OF THE REEF (TF) ... Alexander Singer
HUNTING FLIES ... Andrzej Wajda
HUNTING PARTY, THE ... Don Medford
HURLEVENT ... Jacques Rivette
HURRICANE ... Jan Troell
HURRICANE (TF) ... Jerry Jameson
HURRICANE ROSY ... Mario Monicelli
HURRICANE SMITH ... Jerry Hopper
HURRY SUNDOWN ... Otto Preminger
HURRY UP OR I'LL BE THIRTY ... Joseph Jacoby
HUSBANDS ... John Cassavetes
HUSSY ... Matthew Chapman
HUSTLER OF MUSCLE BEACH, THE (TF) ... Jonathan Kaplan
HUSTLING (TF) ... Joseph Sargent
HUZSIKA (TD) ... Miklos Jancso
HYMN TO A TIRED MAN ... Masaki Kobayashi
HYPOTHESIS (TF) ... Krzysztof Zanussi
HYSTERIA ... Freddie Francis
HYSTERICAL ... Chris Bearde

I

I ACCUSE! ... Jose Ferrer
I, A MAN ... Andy Warhol
I AIM AT THE STARS ... J. Lee Thompson
I AM A CAT ... Kon Ichikawa
I AM A FUGITIVE FROM A CHAIN GANG ... Mervyn Leroy
I AM AFRAID ... Damiano Damiani
I AM BLUSHING ... Vilgot Sjoman
I AM CURIOUS (BLUE) ... Vilgot Sjoman
I AM CURIOUS (YELLOW) ... Vilgot Sjoman
I AM THE CHEESE ... Robert Jiras
I BALISCHI ... Lina Wertmuller
I BURY THE LIVING ... Albert Band
I CAN GET IT FOR YOUR WHOLESALE ... Michael Gordon
I CANNIBALI ... Liliana Cavani
I . . . COMME ICARE ... Henri Verneuil
I COMPAGNI ... Mario Monicelli
I COMPLESSI ... Dino Risi
I COULD GO ON SINGING ... Ronald Neame
I COULD NEVER HAVE SEX WITH A MAN WHO HAS SO LITTLE REGARD FOR MY HUSBAND ... Robert McCarty
I DEAL IN DANGER ... Walter Grauman
I, DESIRE (TF) ... John Llewellyn Moxey
I DOLCI INGANNI ... Alberto Lattuada
I DON'T UNDERSTAND YOU ANYMORE ... Sergio Corbucci
I DON'T WANT TO BE BORN ... Peter Sasdy
I DOOD IT ... Vincente Minnelli
I ESCAPED FROM DEVIL'S ISLAND ... William Witney
I FOUND STELLA PARISH ... Mervyn Leroy
I FUORILEGGE DEL METRAIMONIO ... Paolo Taviani
I FUORILEGGE DEL METRAIMONIO ... Vittorio Taviani
I HATE YOUR GUTS ... Roger Corman
I HEARD THE OWL CALL MY NAME (TF) ... Daryl Duke
I KILLED RASPUTIN ... Don Sharp
I KNOW WHERE I'M GOING ... Michael Powell
I KNOW WHY THE CAGED fBIRD SINGS (TF) ... Fielder Cook
I LIVE IN FEAR ... Akira Kurosawa
I LOVE A MYSTERY (TF) ... Leslie Stevens
I LOVE MELVIN ... Don Weis
I LOVE MY WIFE ... Mel Stuart
I LOVE YOU, ALICE B. TOKLAS ... Hy Averback
I LOVE YOU, GOODBYE (TF) ... Sam O'Steen
I LOVE YOU ROSA ... Moshe Mizrahi
I MAGLIARI ... Francesco Rosi
I MARRIED A CENTERFOLD (TF) ... Peter Werner
I MARRIED A COMMUNIST ... Robert Stevenson
I MARRIED A WOMAN ... Hal Kanter
I MARRIED WYATT EARP (TF) ... Michael O'Herlihy
I MET MY LOVE AGAIN ... Joshua Logan
I, MOBSTER ... Roger Corman
I, MONSTER ... Stephen Weeks
I MOSTRI ... Dino Risi
I NEVER PROMISED YOU A ROSE GARDEN ... Anthony Page
I NEVER SANG FOR MY FATHER ... Gilbert Cates
I NOSTRI MARITI ... Dino Risi
I NUOVI MOSTRI ... Mario Monicelli
I NUOVI MOSTRI ... Dino Risi
I NUOVI MOSTRI ... Ettore Scola
I OUGHT TO BE IN PICTURES ... Herbert Ross
I PAGLIACCI (TF) ... Franco Zeffirelli
I RECUPERANTI (TF) ... Ermanno Olmi
I SENT A LETTER TO MY LOVE ... Moshe Mizrahi
I SHOT JESSE JAMES ... Samuel Fuller
I SOLITI IGNOTTI ... Mario Monicelli
I START COUNTING ... David Greene
I SURRENDER DEAR ... Arthur Dreifuss
I TAKE THESE MEN (TF) ... Larry Peerce
I, THE JURY ... Richard T. Heffron
I THINK WE'RE BEING FOLLOWED ... Robert Day
I TRE AVVENTURIERI ... Robert Enrico
I TRE VOLTI ... Michelangelo Antonioni
I VINTI ... Michelangelo Antonioni
I VITTELONI ... Federico Fellini
I WALK THE LINE ... John Frankenheimer
I WANNA HOLD YOUR HAND ... Robert Zemeckis
I WANT TO KEEP MY BABY (TF) ... Jerry Thorpe
I WANT TO LIVE (TF) ... David Lowell Rich
I WANT TO LIVE! ★ ... Robert Wise
I WANT WHAT I WANT ... John Dexter
I WAS A COMMUNIST FOR THE FBI ... Gordon Douglas
I WAS A MAIL ORDER BRIDE (TF) ... Marvin J. Chomsky
I WAS A TEENAGE BOY ... Lisa Gottlieb
I WAS HAPPY HERE ... Desmond Davis
I WAS MONTY'S DOUBLE ... John Guillermin
I WILL FIGHT NO MORE FOREVER (TF) ... Richard T. Heffron
I WILL, I WILL...FOR NOW ... Norman Panama
ICE ... Robert Kramer
ICE CASTLES ... Donald Wrye
ICE COLD IN ALEX ... J. Lee Thompson
ICE PALACE ... Vincent Sherman
ICE PIRATES, THE ... Stewart Raffill
ICE STATION ZEBRA ... John Sturges
ICEMAN ... Fred Schepisi
ICEMAN COMETH, THE ... John Frankenheimer
ICI ET AILLEURS ... Jean-Luc Godard
I'D RATHER BE RICH ... Jack Smight
IDAHO TRANSFER ... Peter Fonda
IDENTIFICATION MARKS: NONE ... Jerzy Skolimowski
IDENTIFICATION OF A WOMAN ... Michelangelo Antonioni
IDI AMIN DADA ... Barbet Schroeder
IDIOT, THE ... Akira Kurosawa
IDOL, THE ... Daniel Petrie
IDOLMAKER, THE ... Taylor Hackford
IF... ... Lindsay Anderson
IF EVER I SEE YOU AGAIN ... Joseph Brooks
IF HE HOLLERS, LET HIM GO ... Charles Martin
IF IT'S TUESDAY, THIS MUST BE BELGIUM ... Mel Stuart
IF THINGS WERE DIFFERENT (TF) ... Robert M. Lewis
IF TOMORROW COMES (TF) ... George McCowan
IF YOU COULD SEE WHAT I HEAR ... Eric Till
IF YOU KNEW SUSIE ... Gordon Douglas
IKE (MS) ... Melville Shavelson
IKIRU ... Akira Kurosawa
IL BANDITO ... Alberto Lattuada
IL BESTIONE ... Sergio Corbucci
IL BIDONE ... Federico Fellini
IL CAFFE E UN PIACERE...SE NON E BUONO CHE PLACERE E? ... Nanni Loy
IL CAPPOTTO ... Alberto Lattuada
IL CARABINIERE A CAVALLO ... Carlo Lizzani
IL CASANOVA DI FEDERICO FELLINI ... Federico Fellini
IL COMMISSARIO ... Luigi Comencini
IL COMMISSARIO PEPE ... Ettore Scola
IL COMPAGNO DON CAMILLO ... Luigi Comencini
IL CONTESTO ... Francesco Rosi
IL DELITTO DI GIOVANNI EPISCOPO ... Alberto Lattuada
IL DIALOGO DI ROMA (FD) ... Marguerite Duras
IL FEDERALE ... Luciano Salce
IL FIGLIO DI SPARTACUS ... Sergio Corbucci
IL FU MATTIA PASCAL ... Mario Monicelli
IL FUTURO E DONNA ... Marco Ferreri
IL GABBIANO (TF) ... Marco Bellocchio
IL GATTO ... Luigi Comencini
IL GAUCHO ... Dino Risi
IL GIOCATTOLO ... Giuliano Montaldo
IL GIORNO DELLA CIVETTA ... Damiano Damiani
IL GIOVANE NORMALE ... Dino Risi
IL GIOVEDI ... Dino Risi
IL GOBBO ... Carlo Lizzani
IL GRANDE SILENZIO ... Sergio Corbucci
IL GRIDO ... Michelangelo Antonioni
IL MARCHESE DEL GRILLO ... Mario Monicelli
IL MARITO ... Nanni Loy
IL MATRIMONIO DI CATERINA (TF) ... Luigi Comencini
IL MATTATORE ... Dino Risi
IL MEDICO E LO STREGONE ... Mario Monicelli
IL MISTERO DI OVERWALD ... Michelangelo Antonioni
IL PADRE DI FAMILIGLIA ... Nanni Loy
IL PISTOLERO DELL'AVE MARIA ... Ferdinando Baldi
IL PIU CORTO GIORNO ... Sergio Corbucci
IL PROCESSO DI VERONA ... Carlo Lizzani
IL PROF. DR. GUIDO TERSILLI, PRIMARIO DELLA CLINICA VILLA CELESTE, CONVENZIONATA CON LE MUTUE ... Luciano Salce
IL PROVINCIALE ... Luciano Salce
IL ROSSETTO ... Damiano Damiani
IL SECONDO TRAGICO FANTOZZI ... Luciano Salce
IL SEGNO DI VENERE ... Dino Risi
IL SICARIO ... Damiano Damiani

IL SIGNOR ROBINSON - MONSTRUOSA STORIA D'AMORE E D'AVVENTURE ... Sergio Corbucci
IL SORPASSO ... Dino Risi
IL SORRISO DEL GRANDE TENTATORE ... Damiano Damiani
IL TEMPO SI E FERMATO ... Ermanno Olmi
IL TIGRE ... Dino Risi
IL VEDOVO ... Dino Risi
IL...BELPAESE ... Luciano Salce
I'LL BE YOUR SWEETHEART ... Val Guest
I'LL BUY YOU ... Masaki Kobayashi
I'LL CRY TOMORROW ... Daniel Mann
ILL MET BY MOONLIGHT ... Michael Powell
I'LL NEVER FORGET WHAT'S 'IS NAME ... Michael Winner
I'LL NEVER FORGET YOU ... Roy Ward Baker
ILLICIT INTERLUDE ... Ingmar Bergman
ILLUMINATION ... Krzysztof Zanussi
ILLUMINATIONS ... Paul Cox
ILLUSIONS (TF) ... Walter Grauman
ILLUSTRATED MAN, THE ... Jack Smight
I'M A STRANGER HERE MYSELF (FD) ... David Helpern, Jr.
I'M ALL RIGHT, JACK ... John Boulting
"I'M ALMOST NOT CRAZY..." JOHN CASSAVETES: THE MAN AND HIS WORK (FD) ... Michael Ventura
I'M DANCING AS FAST AS I CAN ... Jack Hofsiss
I'M GETTING MYSELF A YACHT ... Sergio Corbucci
I'M NOT FEELING MYSELF TONIGHT ... Joseph McGrath
IMAGE, THE ... Radley Metzger
IMAGES ... Robert Altman
IMITATION OF CHRIST ... Andy Warhol
IMMIGRANTS, THE (TF) ... Alan J. Levi
IMMORAL MR. TEAS, THE ... Russ Meyer
IMMORAL WEST AND HOW IT WAS LOST, THE ... Russ Meyer
IMMORTAL, THE (TF) ... Joseph Sargent
IMMORTAL STORY, THE ... Orson Welles
IMPATIENT HEART, THE (TF) ... John Badham
IMPERATIV (TF) ... Krzysztof Zanussi
IMPOSSIBLE OBJECT ... John Frankenheimer
IMPOSSIBLE YEARS, THE ... Michael Gordon
IMPOSTER, THE (TF) ... Edward Abroms
IMPOSTER, THE (TF) ... Michael Pressman
IMPROPER CHANNELS ... Eric Till
IMPROPER CONDUCT (FD) ... Nestor Almendros
IMPROPER CONDUCT (FD) ... Orlando Jimenez-Leal
IMPULSE ... Graham Baker
IN BROAD DAYLIGHT (TF) ... Robert Day
IN CELEBRATION ... Lindsay Anderson
IN COLD BLOOD ★ ... Richard Brooks
IN DEFENSE OF KIDS (TF) ... Gene Reynolds
IN HARM'S WAY ... Otto Preminger
IN HEAVEN THERE IS NO BEER? (FD) ... Les Blank
IN LIKE FLINT ... Gordon Douglas
IN LOVE WITH AN OLDER WOMAN (TF) ... Jack Bender
IN NAME ONLY (TF) ... E.W. Swackhamer
IN NOME DEL POPOLO ITALIANO ... Dino Risi
IN OUR TIME ... Vincent Sherman
IN PARIS PARKS ... Shirley Clarke
IN PRAISE OF OLDER WOMEN ... George Kaczender
IN SEARCH OF AMERICA (TF) ... Paul Bogart
IN SEARCH OF HISTORIC JESUS ... Henning Schellerup
IN SEARCH OF NOAH'S ARK ... James L. Conway
IN SEARCH OF THE CASTAWAYS ... Robert Stevenson
IN TANDEM (TF) ... Bernard L. Kowalski
IN THE COUNTRY ... Robert Kramer
IN THE CUSTODY OF STRANGERS (TF) ... Robert Greenwald
IN THE DEVIL'S GARDEN ... Sidney Hayers
IN THE FRENCH STYLE ... Robert Parrish
IN THE GLITTER PALACE (TF) ... Robert Butler
IN THE HEAT OF THE NIGHT ★ ... Norman Jewison
IN THE KING OF PRUSSIA ... Emile de Antonio
IN THE MATTER OF KAREN ANN QUINLAN (TF) ... Glenn Jordan
IN THE MEANTIME, DARLING ... Otto Preminger
IN THE NICK ... Kenneth "Ken" Hughes
IN THE REALM OF THE SENSES ... Nagisa Oshima
IN THE SECRET STATE ... Christopher Morahan
IN THE SHADOW OF KILIMANJARO ... Raju Patel
IN THE SHADOW OF THE SUN ... Derek Jarman
IN THE WHITE CITY ... Alain Tanner
IN THE YEAR OF THE PIG (FD) ... Emile de Antonio
IN THIS HOUSE OF BREDE (TF) ... George Schaefer
IN THIS OUR LIFE ... John Huston
IN WHICH WE SERVE ... David Lean
INADMISSABLE EVIDENCE ... Anthony Page
IN-BETWEEN AGE, THE ... Don Sharp
INCHON! ... Terence Young
INCIDENT AT PHANTOM HILL ... Earl Bellamy
INCIDENT IN SAN FRANSISCO (TF) ... Don Medford
INCIDENT ON A DARK STREET (TF) ... Buzz Kulik
INCIDENT, THE ... Larry Peerce
INCOMPRESO ... Luigi Comencini
INCORRIGIBLE ... Philippe de Broca
INCREDIBLE HULK, THE (TF) ... Kenneth Johnson
INCREDIBLE JOURNEY OF DR. MEG LAUREL, THE (TF) ... Guy Green
INCREDIBLE MELTING MAN, THE ... William Sachs
INCREDIBLE ROCKY MOUNTAIN RACE, THE (TF) ... James L. Conway
INCREDIBLE SARAH, THE ... Richard Fleischer
INCREDIBLE SEX REVOLUTION, THE ... Albert Zugsmith
INCREDIBLE SHRINKING MAN, THE ... Jack Arnold
INCREDIBLE SHRINKING WOMAN, THE ... Joel Schumacher
INCREDIBLY STRANGE CREATURES WHO STOPPED LIVING AND BECAME MIXED-UP ZOMBIES, THE ... Ray Dennis Steckler
INCUBUS ... Leslie Stevens
INCUBUS, THE ... John Hough
INDEPENDENCE DAY ... Robert Mandel
INDEPENDENCE DAY ... Bobby Roth
INDIA SONG ... Marguerite Duras
INDIAN FIGHTER, THE ... Andre De Toth
INDIANA JONES AND THE TEMPLE OF DOOM ... Steven Spielberg
INDISCREET ... Stanley Donen
INFANZIA, VOCAZIONE E PRIME ESPERIENZE DI GIACOMO CASANOVA - VENEZIANO ... Luigi Comencini
INFERNO ... Dario Argento
INFERNO ... Roy Ward Baker
INFERNO, THE ... Michael Roemer
INFERNO, THE ... Robert M. Young
INFORMERS, THE ... Ken Annakin
INHERIT THE WIND ... Stanley Kramer
INHERITANCE, THE ... Masaki Kobayashi
INITIATION OF SARAH, THE (TF) ... Robert Day
INITIATION, THE ... Larry Stewart
IN-LAWS, THE ... Arthur Hiller
INMATES: A LOVE STORY (TF) ... Guy Green
INN OF EVIL ... Masaki Kobayashi
INN OF THE FRIGHTENED PEOPLE ... Sidney Hayers
INNER EYE, THE ... Satyajit Ray
INNOCENCE UNPROTECTED ... Dusan Makavejev
INNOCENT LOVE, AN (TF) ... Roger Young
INNOCENT SINNERS ... Philip Leacock
INNOCENT SORCERERS ... Andrzej Wajda
INNOCENTS ABROAD, THE (TF) ... Luciano Salce
INNOCENTS, THE ... Jack Clayton
INQUEST ... Roy Boulting
INSECT WOMAN, THE ... Shohei Imamura
INSEL DER ROSEN (TF) ... Franz Peter Wirth
INSERTS ... John Byrum
INSIDE DAISY CLOVER ... Robert Mulligan
INSIDE LOOKING OUT ... Paul Cox
INSIDE MAN, THE ... Tom Clegg
INSIDE MOVES ... Richard Donner
INSIDE OUT ... Peter John Duffell
INSIDE THE THIRD REICH (TF) ☆☆ ... Marvin J. Chomsky
INSIEME ... Nanni Loy
INSIGNIFICANCE ... Nicolas Roeg
INSPECTOR CALLS, AN ... Guy Hamilton
INSPECTOR CLOUSEAU ... Bud Yorkin
INSPECTOR GENERAL, THE ... Henry Koster
INSTINCT ... Kaneto Shindo
INSTITUTE FOR REVENGE (TF) ... Ken Annakin
INTENSIVE CARE (TF) ... Gavin Millar
INTENT TO KILL ... Jack Cardiff
INTENTIONS OF MURDER ... Shohei Imamura
INTERIORS ★ ... Woody Allen
INTERLUDE ... Kevin Billington
INTERNATIONAL VELVET ... Bryan Forbes
INTERNECINE PROJECT, THE ... Kenneth "Ken" Hughes
INTERNS, THE ... David Swift
INTERVAL ... Daniel Mann
INTIMATE AGONY (TF) ... Paul Wendkos
INTIMATE LIGHTING ... Ivan Passer
INTIMATE STRANGERS (TF) ... John Llewellyn Moxey
INTIMIDADE ... Michael Sarne
INTO THE NIGHT ... John Landis
INTO THE SUNSET ... Emil Loteanu
INTRODUCTION TO THE ENEMY (FD) ... Haskell Wexler
INTRUDER, THE ... Roger Corman
INTRUDER, THE ... Guy Hamilton
INTRUDERS, THE (TF) ... William A. Graham
INUGAMI FAMILY, THE ... Kon Ichikawa
INVADERS, THE ... Michael Powell
INVASION ... Alan Bridges
INVASION OF JOHNSON COUNTY, THE (TF) ... Jerry Jameson
INVASION OF PRIVACY, AN (TF) ... Mel Damski
INVASION OF THE BEE GIRLS ... Denis Sanders
INVASION OF THE BODY SNATCHERS ... Philip Kaufman
INVASION OF THE BODY SNATCHERS ... Don Siegel
INVESTIGATION, THE ... Etienne Perier
INVINCIBLE SIX, THE ... Jean Negulesco
INVISIBLE MAN, THE (TF) ... Robert M. Lewis
INVITATION TO A GUNFIGHTER ... Richard Wilson
INVITATION TO HELL (TF) ... Wes Craven
INVITATION TO THE DANCE ... Gene Kelly
INVITATION TO THE WEDDING ... Joseph Brooks
IO E LUI ... Luciano Salce
IPCRESS FILE, THE ... Sidney J. Furie
IPHIGENIA ... Michael Cacoyannis
IRISHMAN, THE ... Donald Crombie
IRMA LA DOUCE ... Billy Wilder
IRON MAIDEN, THE ... Gerald Thomas
IRON MAN ... Joseph Pevney
IRON MISTRESS, THE ... Gordon Douglas
IRON PETTICOAT, THE ... Ralph Thomas
IRON RING ... Kaneto Shindo
IRONSIDE (TF) ... James Goldstone
IROQUOIS TRAIL, THE ... Phil Karlson
IRRECONCILABLE DIFFERENCES ... Charles Shyer
IS PARIS BURNING? ... René Clement
ISABEL ... Paul Almond
ISABEL'S CHOICE (TF) ... Guy Green
ISADORA ... Karel Reisz
ISHI: THE LAST OF HIS TRIBE (TF) ... Robert Ellis Miller
ISLAND AT THE TOP OF THE WORLD, THE ... Robert Stevenson
ISLAND OF DR. MOREAU, THE ... Don Taylor
ISLAND OF LOVE ... Morton Da Costa
ISLAND OF THE BLUE DOLPHINS ... James B. Clark
ISLAND RESCUE ... Ralph Thomas
ISLAND, THE ... Michael Ritchie
ISLAND, THE ... Kaneto Shindo
ISLANDER, THE (TF) ... Paul Krasny
ISLANDS IN THE STREAM ... Franklin J. Schaffner
ISN'T IT SHOCKING? (TF) ... John Badham

ISTANBUL .... Joseph Pevney
ISTANBUL EXPRESS (TF) .... Richard Irving
IT CAME FROM HOLLYWOOD (FD) .... Malcolm Leo
IT CAME FROM HOLLYWOOD (FD) .... Andrew Solt
IT CAME FROM OUTER SPACE .... Jack Arnold
IT CONQUERED THE WORLD .... Roger Corman
IT COULDN'T HAPPEN TO A NICER GUY (TF) .... Cy Howard
IT HAPPENED AT LAKEWOOD MANOR (TF) .... Robert Scheerer
IT HAPPENED IN ATHENS .... Andrew Marton
IT HAPPENED ONE CHRISTMAS (TF) .... Donald Wrye
IT HAPPENED ONE NIGHT ★★ .... Frank Capra
IT HAPPENED TO JANE .... Richard Quine
IT HAPPENS EVERY THURSDAY .... Joseph Pevney
IT LIVES AGAIN .... Larry Cohen
IT RAINED ALL NIGHT THE DAY I LEFT .... Nicholas Gessner
IT RAINS ON OUR LOVE .... Ingmar Bergman
IT SHOULDN'T HAPPEN TO A VET .... Eric Till
IT STARTED IN NAPLES .... Melville Shavelson
IT STARTED WITH EVE .... Henry Koster
IT WON'T RUB OFF, BABY .... Herbert Danska
ITALIAN SECRET SERVICE .... Luigi Comencini
ITALIANAMERICAN (FD) .... Martin Scorsese
ITALIANO COME ME .... Luciano Salce
IT'S A BIG COUNTRY .... John Sturges
IT'S A BIG COUNTRY .... Don Weis
IT'S A BIKINI WORLD .... Stephanie Rothman
IT'S A LONG TIME THAT I'VE LOVED YOU .... Jean-Charles Tacchella
IT'S A MAD, MAD, MAD, MAD WORLD .... Stanley Kramer
IT'S A WONDERFUL LIFE ★ .... Frank Capra
IT'S A WONDERFUL WORLD .... Val Guest
IT'S A 2'6" ABOVE THE GROUND WORLD .... Ralph Thomas
IT'S ALIVE .... Larry Cohen
IT'S ALL HAPPENING .... Don Sharp
IT'S ALL OVER TOWN .... Douglas Hickox
IT'S ALL TRUE (TF) .... Julien Temple
IT'S ALWAYS FAIR WEATHER .... Stanley Donen
IT'S ALWAYS FAIR WEATHER .... Gene Kelly
IT'S GOOD TO BE ALIVE (TF) .... Michael Landon
IT'S ME HERE, BELLETT .... Nagisa Oshima
IT'S MY TURN .... Claudia Weill
IT'S NOT THE SIZE THAT COUNTS .... Ralph Thomas
IT'S THE ONLY WAY TO GO .... Ray Austin
IT'S TRAD, DAD .... Richard Lester
IVANHOE (TF) .... Douglas Camfield
IVORY APE, THE (TF) .... Tom Kotani

J

JABBERWOCKY .... Terry Gilliam
JACK AND JILL .... Chuck Vincent
JACK AND JILL II .... Chuck Vincent
JACK OF ALL TRADES .... Robert Stevenson
JACK OF DIAMONDS .... Don Taylor
JACK THE GIANT KILLER .... Nathan Juran
JACKSON COUNTY JAIL .... Michael Miller
JACOB TWO-TWO MEETS THE HOODED FANG .... Theodore J. Flicker
JACOBO TIMERMAN: PRISONER WITHOUT A NAME, CELL WITHOUT A NUMBER (TF) .... Linda Yellen
JACQUELINE .... Roy Ward Baker
JACQUELINE BOUVIER KENNEDY (TF) .... Steven Gethers
JACQUELINE SUSANN'S ONCE IS NOT ENOUGH .... Guy Green
JACQUELINE SUSANN'S VALLEY OF THE DOLLS 1981 (MS) .... Walter Grauman
JAGUAR LIVES .... Ernest Pintoff
JAMES A. MICHENER'S DYNASTY (TF) .... Lee Philips
JAMES AT 15 (TF) .... Joseph Hardy
JAMES DEAN (TF) .... Robert Butler
JAMES DEAN STORY, THE (FD) .... Robert Altman
JANE AUSTEN IN MANHATTAN .... James Ivory
JANE DOE (TF) .... Ivan Nagy
JANE EYRE .... Robert Stevenson
JANE EYRE (TF) .... Delbert Mann
JAPANESE SUMMER: DOUBLE SUICIDE .... Nagisa Oshima
JASON AND THE ARGONAUTS .... Don Chaffey
JAUNE DE SOLEIL .... Marguerite Duras
JAWS .... Steven Spielberg
JAWS 2 .... Jeannot Szwarc
JAWS 3-D .... Joe Alves
JAYHAWKERS, THE .... Melvin Frank
JAYNE MANSFIELD - AN AMERICAN TRAGEDY .... David Winters
JAYNE MANSFIELD STORY, THE (TF) .... Dick Lowry
JAZZ BOAT .... Kenneth "Ken" Hughes
JAZZ SINGER, THE .... Richard Fleischer
J.D. & THE SALT FLAT KID .... Alex Grasshoff
J.D.'S REVENGE .... Arthur Marks
JE SUIS UN SENTIMENTAL .... John Berry
JE T'AIME, JE T'AIME .... Alain Resnais
JE VAIS VERS LE SOLEIL .... Andrzej Wajda
JE VOUS AIME .... Claude Berri
JE VOUS SALVE MARIE .... Jean-Luc Godard
JEALOUSY (TF) .... Jeffrey Bloom
JEAN RENOIR, LE PATRON (FD) .... Jacques Rivette
JEANNE EAGELS .... George Sidney
JEKYLL AND HYDE...TOGETHER AGAIN .... Jerry Belson
JENNIFER: A WOMAN'S STORY (TF) .... Guy Green
JENNIFER ON MY MIND .... Noel Black
JENNY .... George Bloomfield
JEOPARDY .... John Sturges
JEREMIAH JOHNSON .... Sydney Pollack
JEREMY .... Arthur Barron
JERICHO MILE, THE (TF) .... Michael Mann
JERK, THE .... Carl Reiner
JERK, TOO, THE (TF) .... Michael Schultz
JERUSALEM FILE, THE .... John Flynn
JESSE JAMES JR. .... George Sherman
JESSE OWENS STORY, THE (TF) .... Richard Irving
JESSICA .... Jean Negulesco
JESSIE (TF) .... Richard Michaels
JESSIE'S GIRLS .... Al Adamson
JESUS .... John Krish
JESUS .... Peter Sykes
JESUS CHRIST SUPERSTAR .... Norman Jewison
JESUS OF NAZARETH (MS) .... Franco Zeffirelli
JESUS TRIP, THE .... Russ Mayberry
JET STORM .... Cy Endfield
JEWEL IN THE CROWN, THE (MS) .... Christopher Morahan
JEWEL IN THE CROWN, THE (MS) .... Jim O'Brien
JIGSAW .... James Goldstone
JIGSAW .... Val Guest
JIGSAW (TF) .... William A. Graham
JIGSAW MAN, THE .... Terence Young
JILTING OF GRANNY WEATHERALL, THE (TF) .... Randa Haines
JIM - THE WORLD'S GREATEST .... Don Coscarelli
JIMI HENDRIX (FD) .... Gary Weis
JIMMY B. & ANDRE (TF) .... Guy Green
JIMMY, THE BOY WONDER .... Herschell Gordon Lewis
JIMMY THE KID .... Gary Nelson
JINXED .... Don Siegel
JIVE TURKEY .... Bill Brame
JOAN OF PARIS .... Robert Stevenson
JOANNA .... Michael Sarne
JOE .... John G. Avildsen
JOE COCKER/MAD DOGS & ENGLISHMEN (FD) .... Pierre Adidge
JOE HILL .... Bo Widerberg
JOE KIDD .... John Sturges
JOE MACBETH .... Kenneth "Ken" Hughes
JOE PALOOKA IN THE BIG FIGHT .... Cy Endfield
JOE PANTHER .... Paul Krasny
JOE VALACHI: I SEGRETI DI COSA NOSTRA .... Terence Young
JOEY AND REDHAWK (TF) .... Larry Elikann
JOHN AND MARY .... Peter Yates
JOHN GOLDFARB, PLEASE COME HOME .... J. Lee Thompson
JOHN O'HARA'S GIBBSVILLE (TF) .... Frank D. Gilroy
JOHN STEINBECK'S EAST OF EDEN (MS) .... Harvey Hart
JOHN SULLIVAN STORY, THE (TF) .... David Stevens
JOHNNY APOLLO .... Henry Hathaway
JOHNNY BELINDA (TF) .... Anthony Page
JOHNNY BELINDA ★ .... Jean Negulesco
JOHNNY BULL (TF) .... Claudia Weill
JOHNNY CASH I THE MAN, HIS WORLD, HIS MUSIC (FD) .... Robert Elfstrom
JOHNNY COOL .... William Asher
JOHNNY DANGEROUSLY .... Amy Heckerling
JOHNNY EAGER .... Mervyn Leroy
JOHNNY HALLYDAY (FD) .... Francois Reichenbach
JOHNNY ON THE RUN .... Lewis Gilbert
JOHNNY ORO .... Sergio Corbucci
JOHNNY TIGER .... Paul Wendkos
JOHNNY TREMAIN .... Robert Stevenson
JOHNNY, WE HARDLY KNEW YE (TF) .... Gilbert Cates
JOI BABA FELUNATH .... Satyajit Ray
JOKE OF DESTINY lying in wait around the corner like a street bandit, A .... Lina Wertmuller
JOKER, THE .... Philippe de Broca
JOKERS, THE .... Michael Winner
JOLLY BAD FELLOW, A .... Don Chaffey
JONAH WHO WILL BE 25 IN THE YEAR 2000 .... Alain Tanner
JONATHAN LIVINGSTON SEAGULL .... Hall Bartlett
JONI .... James F. Collier
JOSEPH ANDREWS .... Tony Richardson
JOSEPHINE AND MEN .... Roy Boulting
JOSHUA .... Larry G. Spangler
JOSHUA THEN AND NOW .... Ted Kotcheff
JOURNEY .... Paul Almond
JOURNEY FROM DARKNESS (TF) .... James Goldstone
JOURNEY INTO FEAR .... Daniel Mann
JOURNEY TO SHILOH .... William "Billy" Hale
JOURNEY TO THE CENTRE (TF) .... Paul Almond
JOURNEY TO THE FAR SIDE OF THE SUN .... Robert Parrish
JOURNEY TO THE OUTER LIMITS (FD) .... Alex Grasshoff
JOURNEY TOGETHER .... John Boulting
JOY HOUSE .... René Clement
JOY OF SEX .... Martha Coolidge
JOYRIDE .... Joseph Ruben
JOYSTICKS .... Greydon Clark
JUBILEE .... Derek Jarman
JUDGE AND JAKE WYLER, THE (TF) .... David Lowell Rich
JUDGE AND THE ASSASSIN, THE .... Bertrand Tavernier
JUDGE DEE AND THE MONASTERY MURDERS (TF) .... Jeremy Paul Kagan
JUDGE HORTON AND THE SCOTTSBORO BOYS (TF) ☆ .... Fielder Cook
JUDGMENT AT NUREMBERG ★ .... Stanley Kramer
JUDITH .... Daniel Mann
JUGGERNAUT .... Richard Lester
JUGGLER, THE .... Edward Dmytryk
JUKE BOX RHYTHM .... Arthur Dreifuss
JULIA ★ .... Fred Zinnemann
JULIE .... Andrew L. Stone
JULIE DARLING .... Paul Nicolas
JULIE-POT-DE-COLLE .... Philippe de Broca
JULIET OF THE SPIRITS .... Federico Fellini
JULIUS CAESAR .... Stuart Burge
JULIUS CAESAR .... Joseph L. Mankiewicz
JUMP .... Joseph Manduke
JUNGLE BOOK, THE (AF) .... Wolfgang Reitherman
JUNGLE HEAT .... Howard W. Koch
JUNGLE RAIDERS .... Anthony M. Dawson
JUNGLE, THE .... Edward Murphy
JUNIOR BONNER .... Sam Peckinpah
JUNIOR PROM .... Arthur Dreifuss
JUNKMAN, THE .... H.B. Halicki
JUPITER'S DARLING .... George Sidney

JUPITER'S THIGH ..... Philippe de Broca
JUSQU'A LA VICTOIRE (FD) ..... Jean-Luc Godard
JUST A GIGOLO ..... David Hemmings
JUST A LITTLE INCONVENIENCE (TF) ..... Theodore J. Flicker
JUST ACROSS THE STREET ..... Joseph Pevney
JUST AN OLD SWEET SONG (TF) ..... Robert Ellis Miller
JUST BEFORE DAWN ..... Jeff Lieberman
JUST BEFORE NIGHTFALL ..... Claude Chabrol
JUST FOR FUN ..... Gordon Flemyng
JUST FOR YOU ..... Douglas Hickox
JUST LIKE A WOMAN ..... Robert Fuest
JUST ME & YOU (TF) ..... John Erman
JUST TELL ME WHAT YOU WANT ..... Sidney Lumet
JUST THE TWO OF US ..... Barbara Peeters
JUST THE WAY YOU ARE ..... Edouard Molinaro
JUST THIS ONCE ..... Don Weis
JUST WILLIAM'S LUCK ..... Val Guest
JUST YOU AND ME, KID ..... Leonard B. Stern
JUVENILE COURT (FD) ..... Frederick Wiseman
JUVENILE JUNGLE ..... William Witney
JUVENIZER, THE ..... King Hu
J.W. COOP ..... Cliff Robertson

K

KAGEMUSHA: THE SHADOW WARRIOR ..... Akira Kurosawa
KALEIDOSCOPE ..... Jack Smight
KAMOURASKA ..... Claude Jutra
KANAL ..... Andrzej Wajda
KANCHENJUNGHA ..... Satyajit Ray
KANSAS CITY BOMBER ..... Jerrold Freedman
KANSAS CITY CONFIDENTIAL ..... Phil Karlson
KANSAS CITY MASSACRE, THE (TF) ..... Dan Curtis
KANSAS CYCLONE ..... George Sherman
KANSAS TERRORS, THE ..... George Sherman
KAPO ..... Gillo Pontecorvo
KAPURUSH-O-MAHAPURUSH ..... Satyajit Ray
KARATE KID, THE ..... John G. Avildsen
KARAYUKI-SAN, THE MAKING OF A PROSTITUTE (FD) ..... Shohei Imamura
KARL MAY ..... Hans-Jurgen Syberberg
KARLSSON BROTHERS, THE ..... Vilgot Sjoman
KATE BLISS & THE TICKER TAPE KID (TF) ..... Burt Kennedy
KATE McSHANE (TF) ..... Marvin J. Chomsky
KATHARINA DIE LETZTE ..... Henry Koster
KATHERINE (TF) ..... Jeremy Paul Kagan
KATHY O' ..... Jack Sher
KATIE: PORTRAIT OF A CENTERFOLD (TF) ..... Robert Greenwald
KATZ AND KARASSO ..... Menahem Golan
KAZABLAN ..... Menahem Golan
KEEGANS, THE (TF) ..... John Badham
KEEP ON ROCKIN' (FD) ..... D.A. Pennebaker
KEEP, THE ..... Michael Mann
KEEP WALKING ..... Ermanno Olmi
KEEP YOUR FINGERS CROSSED ..... Dick Clement
KEEPER OF THE BEES ..... John Sturges
KEEPING ON (TF) ..... Barbara Kopple
KEETJE TIPPEL ..... Paul Verhoeven
KELLY'S HEROES ..... Brian G. Hutton
KENNEDY (MS) ..... Jim Goddard
KENNY AND COMPANY ..... Don Coscarelli
KENNY ROGERS AS THE GAMBLER - THE ADVENTURE CONTINUES (TF) ..... Dick Lowry
KENNY ROGERS AS THE GAMBLER (TF) ..... Dick Lowry
KENT STATE (TF) ☆☆ ..... James Goldstone
KENTUCKY FRIED MOVIE, THE ..... John Landis
KENTUCKY WOMAN ..... Walter Doniger
KES ..... Kenneth Loach
KET LANY AZ UTCAN ..... Andre De Toth
KETTLES ON OLD McDONALD'S FARM, THE ..... Virgil W. Vogel
KEY EXCHANGE ..... Barnet Kellman
KEY LARGO ..... John Huston
KEY TO REBECCA, THE (TF) ..... David Hemmings
KEY TO THE CITY ..... George Sidney
KEY WEST (TF) ..... Philip Leacock
KEY WITNESS ..... Phil Karlson
KGB - THE SECRET WAR ..... Dwight Little
K-GOD ..... Rick Friedberg
KID BLUE ..... James Frawley
KID FROM LEFT FIELD, THE (TF) ..... Adell Aldrich
KID FROM NOT-SO-BIG, THE ..... William Crain
KID FROM NOWHERE, THE (TF) ..... Beau Bridges
KID GALAHAD ..... Phil Karlson
KID GLOVE KILLER ..... Fred Zinnemann
KID VENGEANCE ..... Joseph Manduke
KID WITH THE BROKEN HALO, THE (TF) ..... Leslie H. Martinson
KID WITH THE 200 I.Q., THE (TF) ..... Leslie H. Martinson
KIDCO ..... Ronald F. Maxwell
KIDNAPPED ..... Delbert Mann
KIDNAPPED ..... Robert Stevenson
KIDNAPPERS, THE ..... Eddie Romero
KIDNAPPERS, THE ..... Philip Leacock
KIDNAPPING OF THE PRESIDENT, THE ..... George Mendeluk
KIDS ARE ALRIGHT, THE (FD) ..... Jeff Stein
KIDS WHO KNEW TOO MUCH, THE (TF) ..... Robert Clouse
KILL ME IF YOU CAN (TF) ..... Buzz Kulik
KILL THE GOLDEN GOOSE ..... Elliott Hong
KILLDOZER (TF) ..... Jerry London
KILLER BEES (TF) ..... Curtis Harrington
KILLER BY NIGHT (TF) ..... Bernard McEveety
KILLER ELITE, THE ..... Sam Peckinpah
KILLER FISH ..... Anthony M. Dawson
KILLER FORCE ..... Val Guest
KILLER IN THE FAMILY, A (TF) ..... Richard T. Heffron
KILLER INSIDE ME, THE ..... Burt Kennedy
KILLER IS LOOSE, THE ..... Budd Boetticher
KILLER ON BOARD (TF) ..... Philip Leacock
KILLER SHARK ..... Budd Boetticher
KILLER WHO WOULDN'T DIE, THE (TF) ..... William "Billy" Hale
KILLER'S KISS ..... Stanley Kubrick
KILLERS, THE ..... Don Siegel
KILLERS THREE ..... Bruce Kessler
KILLING AFFAIR, A (TF) ..... Richard C. Sarafian
KILLING AT HELL'S GATE (TF) ..... Jerry Jameson
KILLING FIELDS, THE ..... Roland Joffé
KILLING FLOOR, THE (TF) ..... Bill Duke
KILLING HEAT ..... Michael Raeburn
KILLING HOUR, THE ..... Armand Mastroianni
KILLING KIND, THE ..... Curtis Harrington
KILLING OF A CHINESE BOOKIE, THE ..... John Cassavetes
KILLING OF ANGEL STREET, THE ..... Donald Crombie
KILLING OF RANDY WEBSTER, THE (TF) ..... Sam Wanamaker
KILLING STONE (TF) ..... Michael Landon
KILLING, THE ..... Stanley Kubrick
KILLJOY (TF) ..... John Llewellyn Moxey
KILLPOINT ..... Frank Harris
KILROY WAS HERE ..... Phil Karlson
KIM (TF) ..... John Davies
KIND LADY ..... John Sturges
KIND OF LOVING, A (TF) ..... Jeremy Summers
KIND OF LOVING, A ..... John Schlesinger
KINDER, MUTTER UND EIN GENERAL ..... Laslo Benedek
KING (MS) ☆ ..... Abby Mann
KING: A FILMED RECORD...MONTGOMERY TO MEMPHIS (FD) ..... Joseph L. Mankiewicz
KING: A FILMED RECORD...MONTGOMERY TO MEMPHIS (FD) ..... Sidney Lumet
KING AND THE CHORUS GIRL, THE ..... Mervyn Leroy
KING CRAB (TF) ..... Marvin J. Chomsky
KING DAVID ..... Bruce Beresford
KING DINOSAUR ..... Bert I. Gordon
KING FRAT ..... Ken Wiederhorn
KING KONG ..... John Guillermin
KING LEAR ..... Peter Brook
KING OF AMERICA (TF) ..... Dezso Magyar
KING OF COMEDY, THE ..... Martin Scorsese
KING OF HEARTS, THE ..... Philippe de Broca
KING OF MARVIN GARDENS, THE ..... Bob Rafelson
KING OF THE GYPSIES ..... Frank Pierson
KING OF THE MOUNTAIN ..... Noel Nosseck
KING OF THE NIGHT ..... Hector Babenco
KING, QUEEN, KNAVE ..... Jerzy Skolimowski
KING RAT ..... Bryan Forbes
KING SOLOMON'S MINES ..... Robert Stevenson
KING SOLOMON'S TREASURE ..... Alvin Rakoff
KINGDOM OF DIAMONDS, THE (TF) ..... Satyajit Ray
KINGDOM OF THE SPIDERS ..... John "Bud" Cardos
KINGFISHER, THE (TF) ..... James Cellan-Jones
KINGS OF THE ROAD ..... Wim Wenders
KINGS OF THE SUN ..... J. Lee Thompson
KING'S PIRATE, THE ..... Don Weis
KINGSTON: THE POWER PLAY (TF) ..... Robert Day
KINKY COACHES AND THE POM-POM PUSSYCATS, THE ..... Mark Warren
KIPPERBANG ..... Michael Apted
KISMET ..... Vincente Minnelli
KISS ..... Andy Warhol
KISS BEFORE DYING, A ..... Gerd Oswald
KISS DADDY GOODBYE ..... Patrick Regan
KISS ME GOODBYE ..... Robert Mulligan
KISS ME KATE ..... George Sidney
KISS ME, KILL ME (TF) ..... Michael O'Herlihy
KISS ME QUICK! ..... Russ Meyer
KISS ME, STUPID ..... Billy Wilder
KISS MEETS THE PHANTOM OF THE PARK (TF) ..... Gordon Hessler
KISS MY GRITS ..... Jack Starrett
KISS OF DEATH ..... Henry Hathaway
KISS OF THE SPIDER WOMAN ..... Hector Babenco
KISS OF THE VAMPIRE ..... Don Sharp
KISS, THE ..... Bruno Barreto
KISS THE OTHER SHEIK ..... Marco Ferreri
KISS THE OTHER SHEIK ..... Luciano Salce
KISS THEM FOR ME ..... Stanley Donen
KISS TOMORROW GOODBYE ..... Gordon Douglas
KISSIN' COUSINS ..... Gene Nelson
KISSING BANDIT, THE ..... Laslo Benedek
KITCHEN ..... Andy Warhol
KITCHEN, THE ..... James Hill
KITTEN WITH A WHIP ..... Douglas Heyes
KITTY AND THE BAGMAN ..... Donald Crombie
KLANSMAN, THE ..... Terence Young
KLEINE MUTTI ..... Henry Koster
KLEINHOFF HOTEL ..... Carlo Lizzani
KLUTE ..... Alan J. Pakula
KNACK...AND HOW TO GET IT, THE ..... Richard Lester
KNIFE FOR THE LADIES, A ..... Larry G. Spangler
KNIFE IN THE WATER ..... Roman Polanski
KNIGHT RIDER (TF) ..... Daniel Haller
KNIGHTRIDERS ..... George A. Romero
KNOCK ON WOOD ..... Melvin Frank
KNOCK ON WOOD ..... Norman Panama
KNOW YOUR ENEMY: JAPAN (FD) ..... Frank Capra
KNOWLEDGE, THE (TF) ..... Bob Brooks
KOFUKU ..... Kon Ichikawa
KOKO, A TALKING GORILLA (FD) ..... Barbet Schroeder
KONA COAST ..... Lamont Johnson
KONGI'S HARVEST ..... Ossie Davis
KORTNER GESCHICHTE (TD) ..... Marcel Ophuls
KOTCH ..... Jack Lemmon
KOYAANISQATSI ..... Godfrey Reggio
KRAKATOA, EAST OF JAVA ..... Bernard L. Kowalski
KRAMER VS. KRAMER ★★ ..... Robert Benton
KREMLIN LETTER, THE ..... John Huston
KRIEG UND FRIEDEN (FD) ..... Volker Schlondorff
KRULL ..... Peter Yates
KUNG FU (TF) ..... Jerry Thorpe
KWAIDAN ..... Masaki Kobayashi

L

LA BABY-SITTER ..... René Clement
LA BALANCE ..... Bob Swaim
LA BAMBINA ..... Alberto Lattuada
LA BANDA J & S - CRONACA CRIMINALE DEL FAR-WEST ..... Sergio Corbucci

LA BATAILLE DE SAN SEBASTIAN ... Henri Verneuil
LA BATAILLE DU RAIL ... René Clement
LA BELLA DI ROMA ... Luigi Comencini
LA BELLE CAPTIVE ... Alain Robbe-Grillet
LA BELLE VIE ... Robert Enrico
LA BETIA ... Gianfranco de Bosio
LA BOHEME ... Franco Zeffirelli
LA BONNE ANNEE ... Claude Lelouch
LA BRIDE SUR LE COU ... Roger Vadim
LA BUGIARDA ... Luigi Comencini
LA CAGE AUX FOLLES ★ ... Edouard Molinaro
LA CAGE AUX FOLLES II ... Edouard Molinaro
LA CARAPATE ... Gerard Oury
LA CARRIERE DE SUZANNE ... Eric Rohmer
LA CELESTINA P... R... ... Carlo Lizzani
LA CHANCE ET L'AMOUR ... Bertrand Tavernier
LA CHINOISE ... Jean-Luc Godard
LA CIRCOSTANZA (TF) ... Ermanno Olmi
LA COLLECTIONNEUSE ... Eric Rohmer
LA COMMARE SECCA ... Bernardo Bertolucci
LA COMMUNICATION (TF) ... Jean-Luc Godard
LA CONFUSION DES SENTIMENTS (TF) ... Etienne Perier
LA CONGIUNTURA ... Ettore Scola
LA CORPRESE DELL'AMORE ... Luigi Comencini
LA COURSE DU LIEVRE A TRAVERS LES CHAMPS ... René Clement
LA CUCCAGNA ... Luciano Salce
LA CUREE ... Roger Vadim
LA DAME EN COULEUR ... Claude Jutra
LA DOLCE VITA ★ ... Federico Fellini
LA DONNA DELLA DOMENICA ... Luigi Comencini
LA FAMILLE FENOUILLARD ... Yves Robert
LA FEMME AUX BOTTES ROUGES ... Juan Buñuel
LA FEMME INFIDELE ... Claude Chabrol
LA FEMME SPECTACLE ... Claude Lelouch
LA FEMMES DU GANGES ... Marguerite Duras
LA FINESTRA SUL LUNA PARK ... Luigi Comencini
LA FRANCAISE ET L'AMOUR ... Henri Verneuil
LA FRECCIA NEL FIANCO ... Alberto Lattuada
LA GODURIA ... Luigi Comencini
LA GODURIA ... Nanni Loy
LA GODURIA ... Mario Monicelli
LA GRANDE BOUFFE ... Marco Ferreri
LA GRANDE STRADA AZZURRA ... Gillo Pontecorvo
LA GRANDE VADROVILLE ... Gerard Oury
LA GUERRE DES BOUTONS ... Yves Robert
LA GUERRE EST FINIE ... Alain Resnais
LA JEUNE FILLE ASSASSINEE ... Roger Vadim
LA LEGION SAUTE SUR KOLWEZI ... Raoul Coutard
LA LIBERTEEN CROUPE ... Edouard Molinaro
LA LIGNE DE DEMARCATION ... Claude Chabrol
LA LOI ... Jules Dassin
LA LUPA ... Alberto Lattuada
LA MACCHINA CINEMA ... Marco Bellocchio
LA MADRIGUERA ... Carlos Saura
LA MAIN A COUPER ... Etienne Perier
LA MAIN CHAUDE ... Gerard Oury
LA MAISON SOUS LES ARBRES ... René Clement
LA MANDARINE ... Edouard Molinaro
LA MANDRAGOLA ... Alberto Lattuada
LA MARCIA SU ROMA ... Dino Risi
LA MAZZETTA ... Sergio Corbucci
LA MIA SIGNORINA ... Luigi Comencini
LA MOGLIE PIU BELLA ... Damiano Damiani
LA MORT DE BELLE ... Edouard Molinaro
LA MORT D'UN BUCHERON ... Gilles Carle
LA MUERTE DE AN BUROCRATA ... Tomas Gutierrez Alea
LA MURAGLIA CINESE (FD) ... Carlo Lizzani
LA MUSICA ... Marguerite Duras
LA NOIRE DE... ... Ousmene Sembene
LA NONNA SABELLA ... Dino Risi
LA NOSTRA GUERRA ... Alberto Lattuada
LA NOTTE ... Michelangelo Antonioni
LA NOTTE DI SAN LORENZO ... Paolo Taviani
LA NOTTE DI SAN LORENZO ... Vittorio Taviani
LA NUIT DE SAINT-GERMAIN-DES-PRES ... Bob Swaim
LA NUIT DE VARENNES ... Ettore Scola
LA PACIFISTA ... Miklos Jancso
LA PART DU FEU ... Etienne Perier
LA PECCATRICE DELL'ISOLA ... Sergio Corbucci
LA PECORA NERA ... Luciano Salce
LA PELLE ... Liliana Cavani
LA PETITE FILLE EN VELOURS BLEU ... Alan Bridges
LA PILLOLE DE ERCOLE ... Luciano Salce
LA PIOVRA (MS) ... Damiano Damiani
LA PITIE DANGEREUSE (TF) ... Edouard Molinaro
LA PIU BELLA SERATA DELLA MIA VITA ... Ettore Scola
LA POINTE COURTE ... Agnes Varda
LA PORTIERA NUDA ... Lewis Coates
LA POUDRE D' ESCAMPETTE ... Philippe de Broca
LA PRESIDENTESSA ... Luciano Salce
LA PROVINCIALE ... Claude Goretta
LA RAGAZZA DEL VAGONE LETTO ... Ferdinando Baldi
LA RAISON DU PLUS FOU ... Francois Reichenbach
LA RETOUR D'AFRIQUE ... Alain Tanner
LA RIMPATRIATA ... Damiano Damiani
LA RONDE ... Roger Vadim
LA ROUTE AU SOLEIL ... Philippe de Broca
LA ROUTE DE CORINTHE ... Claude Chabrol
LA ROUTE DE ST. TROPEZ ... Michael Sarne
LA RUPTURE ... Claude Chabrol
LA SALAMANDRE ... Alain Tanner
LA SELVAGGIA ... Ferdinando Baldi
LA SFIDA ... Francesco Rosi
LA SIGNORA SENZA CAMELIE ... Michelangelo Antonioni
LA SPIAGGIA ... Alberto Lattuada
LA STANZA DEL VESCOVO ... Dino Risi
LA STEPPA ... Alberto Lattuada
LA STRADA ... Federico Fellini
LA STREGA IN AMORE ... Damiano Damiani
LA TABLE AUX CREVES ... Henri Verneuil
LA TECNICA E IL RITO ... Miklos Jancso
LA TERRAZZA ... Ettore Scola
LA TETE DE NORMANDE ST. ONGE ... Gilles Carle
LA TRAGEDIE DE CARMEN ... Peter Brook
LA TRATTA DELLA BIANCHE ... Luigi Comencini
LA TRAVIATA ... Franco Zeffirelli
LA VACHE ET LE PRISONNIER ... Henri Verneuil
LA VALIGIA DEI SOGNI ... Luigi Comencini
LA VENGEANCE DU SERPENT A PLUMES ... Gerard Oury
LA VICTOIRE EN CHANTANT ... Jean-Jacques Annaud
LA VICTORIA (FD) ... Peter Lilienthal
LA VIE CONTINUE ... Moshe Mizrahi
LA VIE DEVANT SOI ... Moshe Mizrahi
LA VIE EST UN ROMAN ... Alain Resnais
LA VIE HEUREUSE DE LÉOPOLD Z ... Gilles Carle
LA VITA AGRA ... Carlo Lizzani
LA VITA CONTINUA (MS) ... Dino Risi
LA VOGLIA MATTA ... Luciano Salce
LACE (MS) ... William "Billy" Hale
LACE 2 (MS) ... William "Billy" Hale
LACEMAKER, THE ... Claude Goretta
LACOMBE LUCIEN ... Louis Malle
LACY AND THE MISSISSIPPI QUEEN (TF) ... Robert Butler
LAD: A DOG ... Aram Avakian
LAD: A DOG ... Leslie H. Martinson
LADIES AND GENTLEMEN...THE FABULOUS STAINS ... Lou Adler
LADIES' MAN, THE ... Jerry Lewis
LADIES OF LEISURE ... Frank Capra
LADIES OF THE CHORUS, THE ... Phil Karlson
LADIES OF THE PARK, THE ... Robert Bresson
L'ADOLESCENTE ... Jeanne Moreau
LADY AND THE MONSTER, THE ... George Sherman
LADY CAROLINE LAMB ... Robert Bolt
LADY CHATTERLEY'S LOVER ... Just Jaeckin
LADY COCOA ... Matt Cimber
LADY FOR A DAY ★ ... Frank Capra
LADY FROM SHANGHAI, THE ... Orson Welles
LADY FROM TEXAS, THE ... Joseph Pevney
LADY FROM YESTERDAY (TF) ... Robert Day
LADY GAMBLES, THE ... Michael Gordon
LADY IN A CAGE ... Walter Grauman
LADY IN CEMENT ... Gordon Douglas
LADY IN RED, THE ... Lewis Teague
LADY JANE ... Trevor Nunn
LADY L ... Peter Ustinov
LADY LIBERTY ... Mario Monicelli
LADY OF THE HOUSE (TF) ... Ralph Nelson
LADY OF THE HOUSE (TF) ... Vincent Sherman
LADY OSCAR ... Jacques Demy
LADY SINGS THE BLUES ... Sidney J. Furie
LADY TAKES A FLYER, THE ... Jack Arnold
LADY VANISHES, THE ... Anthony Page
LADYBUG, LADYBUG ... Frank Perry
LADYHAWKE ... Richard Donner
LADYKILLERS, THE ... Alexander Mackendrick
L'AFFAIRE D'UNE NUIT ... Henri Verneuil
L'AFRICAIN ... Philippe de Broca
L'AGNESE UN A MORIRE ... Giuliano Montaldo
L'AMANTE DI GRAMIGNA ... Carlo Lizzani
L'AMERIQUE INSOLITE (FD) ... Francois Reichenbach
L'AMICA ... Alberto Lattuada
L'AMORE IN ITALIA (TF) ... Luigi Comencini
L'AMOUR ... Paul Morrissey
L'AMOUR ... Andy Warhol
L'AMOUR A MORT ... Alain Resnais
L'AMOUR AVEC DES SI ... Claude Lelouch
L'AMOUR EN DOUCE ... Edouard Molinaro
L'AMOUR FOU ... Jacques Rivette
L'AMOUR, L'APRES-MIDI ... Eric Rohmer
LANA TURNER ... Andy Warhol
L'ANATRA ALL'ARANCIA ... Luciano Salce
LANCELOT AND GUINEVERE ... Cornel Wilde
LANCELOT OF THE LAKE ... Robert Bresson
LAND OF DESIRE, THE ... Ingmar Bergman
LAND OF FURY ... Ken Annakin
LAND OF SILENCE AND DARKNESS (FD) ... Werner Herzog
LAND RAIDERS ... Nathan Juran
LAND THAT TIME FORGOT, THE ... Kevin Connor
LAND UNKNOWN, THE ... Virgil W. Vogel
LANDFALL ... Ken Annakin
LANDLORD, THE ... Hal Ashby
LANDRU ... Claude Chabrol
LANDSCAPE AFTER BATTLE ... Andrzej Wajda
LANIGAN'S RABBI (TF) ... Lou Antonio
LARCENY ... George Sherman
L'ARCIDIAVOLO ... Ettore Scola
L'ARGENT (MONEY) ... Robert Bresson
L'ARMATA BRANCALEONE ... Mario Monicelli
L'ARME A GAUCHE ... Claude Sautet
LARRY (TF) ... William A. Graham
L'AS DES AS ... Gerard Oury
LAS DOCE SILLAS ... Tomas Gutierrez Alea
LAS VEGAS LADY ... Noel Nosseck
LAS VEGAS STORY, THE ... Robert Stevenson
LASERBLAST ... Michael Rae
L'ASSASSINO E COSTRETTO AD UCCIDERE ANCORA ... Lewis Coates
LASSITER ... Roger Young
LAST ADVENTURE, THE ... Robert Enrico
LAST AMERICAN HERO, THE ... Lamont Johnson
LAST AMERICAN VIRGIN, THE ... Boaz Davidson
LAST ANGRY MAN, THE (TF) ... Jerrold Freedman
LAST ANGRY MAN, THE ... Daniel Mann
LAST BLITZKRIEG, THE ... Arthur Dreifuss
LAST BRIDE OF SALEM, THE (TF) ... Tom Donovan
LAST CHASE, THE ... Martyn Burke
LAST CHILD, THE (TF) ... John Llewellyn Moxey
LAST CONVERTIBLE, THE (MS) ... Sidney Hayers
LAST CONVERTIBLE, THE (MS) ... Jo Swerling, Jr.
LAST CONVERTIBLE, THE (MS) ... Gus Trikonis
LAST CRY FOR HELP, A (TF) ... Hal Sitowitz
LAST DAY, THE (TF) ... Vincent McEveety
LAST DAYS OF MAN ON EARTH, THE ... Robert Fuest
LAST DAYS OF POMPEII, THE (MS) ... Peter Hunt
LAST DETAIL, THE ... Hal Ashby

LAST DINOSAUR, THE (TF) ... Alex Grasshoff
LAST DINOSAUR, THE (TF) ... Tom Kotani
LAST DRAGON, THE ... Michael Schultz
LAST EMBRACE ... Jonathan Demme
LAST ESCAPE, THE ... Walter Grauman
LAST FIGHT, THE ... Fred Williamson
LAST FLIGHT OF NOAH'S ARK, THE ... Charles Jarrott
LAST FOUR DAYS, THE ... Carlo Lizzani
LAST GIRAFFE, THE (TF) ... Jack Couffer
LAST GRENADE, THE ... Gordon Flemyng
LAST HARD MEN, THE ... Andrew V. McLaglen
LAST HORROR FILM, THE ... David Winters
LAST HOURS BEFORE MORNING (TF) ... Joseph Hardy
LAST HOUSE ON THE LEFT ... Wes Craven
LAST HUNT, THE ... Richard Brooks
LAST HUNTER, THE ... Anthony M. Dawson
LAST HURRAH, THE (TF) ... Vincent Sherman
LAST MARRIED COUPLE IN AMERICA, THE ... Gilbert Cates
LAST MILE, THE ... Howard W. Koch
LAST MOVIE, THE ... Dennis Hopper
LAST MUSKETEER, THE ... William Witney
LAST NIGHT AT THE ALAMO ... Eagle Pennell
LAST NINJA, THE (TF) ... William A. Graham
LAST OF SHEILA, THE ... Herbert Ross
LAST OF THE COMANCHEROS ... Al Adamson
LAST OF THE COMANCHES ... Andre De Toth
LAST OF THE COWBOYS, THE ... John Leone
LAST OF THE FAST GUNS, THE ... George Sherman
LAST OF THE GOOD GUYS (TF) ... Theodore J. Flicker
LAST OF THE GREAT SURVIVORS (TF) ... Jerry Jameson
LAST OF THE MOBILE HOT-SHOTS ... Sidney Lumet
LAST OF THE MOHICANS, THE (TF) ... James L. Conway
LAST OF THE RED HOT LOVERS ... Gene Saks
LAST OF THE REDMEN ... George Sherman
LAST OUTLAW, THE (MS) ... George Miller
LAST PICTURE SHOW ★, THE ... Peter Bogdanovich
LAST PLANE OUT ... David Nelson
LAST RIDE OF THE DALTON GANG, THE (TF) ... Dan Curtis
LAST ROMANTIC LOVER, THE ... Just Jaeckin
LAST ROUND-UP, THE ... Henry Hathaway
LAST RUN, THE ... Richard Fleischer
LAST SAFARI, THE ... Henry Hathaway
LAST SHOT YOU HEAR, THE ... Gordon Hessler
LAST SONG, THE (TF) ... Alan J. Levi
LAST STARFIGHTER, THE ... Nick Castle
LAST SUMMER ... Frank Perry
LAST SUPPER, THE ... Tomas Gutierrez Alea
LAST SURVIVORS, THE (TF) ... Lee H. Katzin
LAST TANGO IN PARIS ★ ... Bernardo Bertolucci
LAST TENANT, THE (TF) ... Jud Taylor
LAST TIME I SAW PARIS, THE ... Richard Brooks
LAST TRAIN FROM GUN HILL ... John Sturges
LAST TYCOON, THE ... Elia Kazan
LAST UNICORN, THE (AF) ... Jules Bass
LAST UNICORN, THE (AF) ... Arthur Rankin, Jr.
LAST VALLEY, THE ... James Clavell
LAST VICTIM, THE ... Jim Sotos
LAST VOYAGE, THE ... Andrew L. Stone
LAST WALTZ, THE ... Martin Scorsese
LAST WAVE, THE ... Peter Weir
LAST WINTER, THE ... Riki Shelach
LAST WOMAN ON EARTH, THE ... Roger Corman
LAST WOMAN, THE ... Marco Ferreri
LAST WORD, THE ... Roy Boulting
LAST YEAR AT MARIENBAD ... Alain Resnais
LATE GEORGE APLEY, THE ... Joseph L. Mankiewicz
LATE SHOW, THE ... Robert Benton
LATHE OF HEAVEN, THE (TF) ... Fred Barzyk
LATHE OF HEAVEN, THE (TF) ... David R. Loxton
LATIN LOVERS ... Mervyn Leroy
LAUGHING POLICEMAN, THE ... Stuart Rosenberg
LAUGHTER HOUSE ... Richard Eyre
LAUGHTER IN THE DARK ... Tony Richardson
LAURA ★ ... Otto Preminger
LAURA, LES OMBRES DE L'ETE ... David Hamilton
LAUTARY ... Emil Loteanu
LAVENDER HILL MOB, THE ... Charles Crichton
L'AVENTURE C'EST L'AVENTURE ... Claude Lelouch
L'AVVENTURA ... Michelangelo Antonioni
L'AVVENTURIERO ... Terence Young
LAW, THE (TF) ... John Badham
LAW AND DISORDER ... Charles Crichton
LAW AND DISORDER ... Ivan Passer
LAW AND JAKE WADE, THE ... John Sturges
LAW AND ORDER ... Nathan Juran
LAW AND ORDER (FD) ... Frederick Wiseman
LAW AND ORDER (TF) ... Marvin J. Chomsky
LAW OF THE LAND (TF) ... Virgil W. Vogel
LAW OF THE LAWLESS ... William F. Claxton
LAWMAN ... Michael Winner
LAWRENCE OF ARABIA ★★ ... David Lean
LAWYER, THE ... Sidney J. Furie
L.A.X. ... Fabrice Ziolkowski
LAZARUS SYNDROME, THE (TF) ... Jerry Thorpe
LAZYBONES ... Michael Powell
LE AMICHE ... Michelangelo Antonioni
LE AVVENTURE DI PINOCCHIO ... Luigi Comencini
LE BAISERS ... Claude Berri
LE BAL ... Ettore Scola
LE BEAU MARIAGE ... Eric Rohmer
LE BEAU SERGE ... Claude Chabrol
LE BON ROI DAGOBERT ... Dino Risi
LE BONHEUR ... Agnes Varda
LE BOUCHER ... Claude Chabrol
LE BOULANGER DE VALORGUE ... Henri Verneuil
LE CAMION ... Marguerite Duras
LE CAVALEUR ... Philippe de Broca
LE CHÂTEAU DE VERRE ... René Clement
LE CHANCE ET L'AMOUR ... Claude Berri
LE CHEVAL D'ORGEUIL ... Claude Chabrol
LE CHEVRE ... Francis Veber
LE CINEMA DU PAPA ... Claude Berri
LE CINQUE GIORNATE ... Dario Argento
LE COEUR FROID ... Henri Helman
LE COMPAGNON INDESIRABLE ... Robert Enrico
LE COPPIE ... Mario Monicelli
LE CORPS DE MON ENNEMI ... Henri Verneuil
LE COUP DE BERGER ... Jacques Rivette
LE COUP DU PARAPLUIE ... Gerard Oury
LE COUPLE TEMOIN ... William Klein
LE DEPART ... Jerzy Skolimowski
LE DERNIER COMBAT ... Luc Besson
LE DIABLE PROBABLEMENT ... Robert Bresson
LE DIVERTISSEMENT ... Jacques Rivette
LE FARO DA PADRE ... Alberto Lattuada
LE FATE ... Mario Monicelli
LE FATE ... Luciano Salce
LE FIANCEE DU PIRATE ... Nelly Kaplan
LE FOU ... Claude Goretta
LE GAI SAVOIR ... Jean-Luc Godard
LE GANG ... Jacques Deray
LE GANG DES OTAGES ... Edouard Molinaro
LE GIGOLO ... Jacques Deray
LE GUERRIERE DEL SNO NUDA ... Terence Young
LE HOLD-UP AU CRAYON (FD) ... Francois Reichenbach
LE INFIDELI ... Mario Monicelli
LE ITALIANE E L'AMORE ... Marco Ferreri
LE JEU AVEC LE FEU ... Alain Robbe-Grillet
LE JOUR DES NOCES (TF) ... Claude Goretta
LE JUMEAU ... Yves Robert
LE MAGNIFIQUE ... Philippe de Broca
LE MAITRE D'ECOLE ... Claude Berri
LE MANI SULLA CITTA ... Francesco Rosi
LE MANS ... Lee H. Katzin
LE MARGINAL ... Jacques Deray
LE MEPRIS ... Jean-Luc Godard
LE NAVIRE NIGHT ... Marguerite Duras
LE NIGER - JEUNE REPUBLIQUE (FD) ... Claude Jutra
LE PERE TRANQUILLE ... René Clement
LE PETIT SOLDAT ... Jean-Luc Godard
LE PISTONNE ... Claude Berri
LE POINT DE MIRE ... Jean-Claude Tramont
LE PONT DU NORD ... Jacques Rivette
LE PRESIDENT ... Henri Verneuil
LE PROPRE DE L'HOMME ... Claude Lelouch
LE QUADRILLE ... Jacques Rivette
LE REGARD PICASSO (FD) ... Nelly Kaplan
LE REPOS DU GUERRIER ... Roger Vadim
LE SCANDALE ... Claude Chabrol
LE SECRET ... Robert Enrico
LE SEX SHOP ... Claude Berri
LE SIGNE DU LION ... Eric Rohmer
LE SOUFFLE AU COEUR ... Louis Malle
LE TEMPS D'UNE CHASSE ... Francis Mankiewicz
LE TIGRE AIME LA CHAIR FRAICHE ... Claude Chabrol
LE TIGRE SE PARFUME À LA DYNAMITE ... Claude Chabrol
LE VIEL HOMME ET L'ENFANT ... Claude Berri
LE VIOL D'UNE JEUNE FILLE DOUCE ... Gilles Carle
LE VOLEUR ... Louis Malle
LE VRAIE NATURE DE BERNADETTE ... Gilles Carle
LEADBELLY ... Gordon Parks
LEAP INTO THE VOID ... Marco Bellocchio
LEARNING TREE, THE ... Gordon Parks
LEATHER BOYS, THE ... Sidney J. Furie
LEATHER GLOVES ... William Asher
LEATHER GLOVES ... Richard Quine
LEAVE 'EM LAUGHING (TF) ... Jackie Cooper
LEAVE YESTERDAY BEHIND (TF) ... Richard Michaels
L'ECLISSE ... Michelangelo Antonioni
LEDA ... Claude Chabrol
L'EDEN ET APRES ... Alain Robbe-Grillet
LEFT HAND OF GOD, THE ... Edward Dmytryk
LEFT HANDED GUN, THE ... Arthur Penn
LEGACY ... Karen Arthur
LEGACY, THE ... Richard Marquand
LEGEND ... Ridley Scott
LEGEND IN LEOTARDS ... Philippe Mora
LEGEND OF BOGGY CREEK, THE ... Charles B. Pierce
LEGEND OF CUSTER, THE (TF) ... William A. Graham
LEGEND OF HELL HOUSE, THE ... John Hough
LEGEND OF HILLBILLY JOHN, THE ... John Newland
LEGEND OF LIZZIE BORDEN, THE (TF) ... Paul Wendkos
LEGEND OF SLEEPY HOLLOW, THE (TF) ... James L. Conway
LEGEND OF SLEEPY HOLLOW, THE ... Henning Schellerup
LEGEND OF SPIDER FOREST ... Peter Sykes
LEGEND OF THE GOLDEN GUN, THE (TF) ... Alan J. Levi
LEGEND OF THE LONE RANGER, THE ... William A. Fraker
LEGEND OF THE LOST ... Henry Hathaway
LEGEND OF THE MOUNTAIN ... King Hu
LEGEND OF THE SEVEN GOLDEN VAMPIRES, THE ... Roy Ward Baker
LEGEND OF THE WEREWOLF ... Freddie Francis
LEGEND OF TOM DOOLEY, THE ... Ted Post
LEGEND OF VALENTINO, THE (TF) ... Melville Shavelson
LEGEND OF WALKS FAR WOMAN, THE (TF) ... Mel Damski
LEGS (TF) ... Jerrold Freedman
LEHMANNS LETZTER (TF) ... Kurt Gloor
L'EMMERDEUR ... Edouard Molinaro
LEMON GROVE KIDS MEET THE MONSTERS ... Ray Dennis Steckler
LEMON POPSICLE ... Boaz Davidson
L'EMPREINTE DES GEANTS ... Robert Enrico
LENNY ★ ... Bob Fosse
LEO AND LOREE ... Jerry Paris
LEO THE LAST ... John Boorman
LEONOR ... Juan Buñuel
LEOPARD IN THE SNOW ... Gerry O'Hara
LEPKE ... Menahem Golan
LES AFFAIRES PUBLIQUE ... Robert Bresson

LIVE AGAIN, DIE AGAIN (TF) ... Richard A. Colla
LIVE AND DIE IN L.A. ... William Friedkin
LIVE AND LET DIE ... Guy Hamilton
LIVE FOR LIFE ... Claude Lelouch
LIVE WIRES ... Phil Karlson
LIVELY SET, THE ... Jack Arnold
LIVES OF A BENGAL LANCER ★, THE ... Henry Hathaway
LIVES OF JENNY DOLAN, THE (TF) ... Jerry Jameson
LIVING FREE ... Jack Couffer
LIVING PROOF: THE HANK WILLIAMS, JR. STORY (TF) ... Dick Lowry
LIVING VENUS ... Herschell Gordon Lewis
LIZA ... Marco Ferreri
LIZA'S PIONEER DIARY (TF) ... Nell Cox
LLANTO POR UN BANDITO ... Carlos Saura
LO SCOPONE SCIENTIFICO ... Luigi Comencini
LO SVITATO ... Carlo Lizzani
LOCAL BOY MAKES GOOD ... Mervyn Leroy
LOCAL HERO ... Bill Forsyth
LOCH NESS HORROR, THE ... Larry Buchanan
LOCK, STOCK AND BARREL (TF) ... Jerry Thorpe
LOCK UP YOUR DAUGHTERS ... Peter Coe
LOCUSTS (TF) ... Richard T. Heffron
L'OEIL DU MALIN ... Claude Chabrol
LOG OF THE BLACK PEARL, THE (TF) ... Andrew V. McLaglen
LOGAN'S RUN ... Michael Anderson
LOGAN'S RUN (TF) ... Robert Day
LOIS GIBBS AND THE LOVE CANAL (TF) ... Glenn Jordan
LOLA ... Jacques Demy
LOLA ... Richard Donner
LOLITA ... Stanley Kubrick
LOLLIPOP COVER, THE ... Everett Chambers
LOLLY-MADONNA XXX ... Richard C. Sarafian
L'OMBRELLONE ... Dino Risi
LONDON BLACKOUT MURDERS ... George Sherman
LONDON ROCK & ROLL SHOW, THE (FD) ... Peter Clifton
LONE HAND, THE ... George Sherman
LONE STAR ... Vincent Sherman
LONE STAR RAIDERS ... George Sherman
LONE WOLF McQUADE ... Steve Carver
LONELIEST RUNNER, THE (TF) ... Michael Landon
LONELINESS OF THE LONG DISTANCE RUNNER, THE ... Tony Richardson
LONELY ARE THE BRAVE ... David Miller
LONELY GUY, THE ... Arthur Hiller
LONELY HEARTS ... Paul Cox
LONELY HEARTS, THE (TF) ... Jay Sandrich
LONELY LADY, THE ... Peter Sasdy
LONELY PROFESSION, THE (TF) ... Douglas Heyes
LONELY WIFE, THE ... Satyajit Ray
LONERS, THE ... Sutton Roley
LONESOME COWBOYS ... Andy Warhol
LONG AGO TOMORROW ... Bryan Forbes
LONG DAY'S JOURNEY INTO NIGHT ... Sidney Lumet
LONG DAYS OF SUMMER, THE (TF) ... Dan Curtis
LONG DUEL, THE ... Ken Annakin
LONG GOOD FRIDAY, THE ... John Mackenzie
LONG GOODBYE, THE ... Robert Altman
LONG HAUL, THE ... Kenneth "Ken" Hughes
LONG HOT SUMMER, THE ... Martin Ritt
LONG JOURNEY BACK (TF) ... Mel Damski
LONG, LONG TRAILER, THE ... Vincente Minnelli
LONG PANTS ... Frank Capra
LONG RIDERS, THE ... Walter Hill
LONG ROPE, THE ... William Witney
LONG RUN, THE ... Pal Gabor
LONG SHIPS, THE ... Jack Cardiff
LONG SUMMER OF GEORGE ADAMS, THE (TF) ... Stuart Margolin
LONG WAY HOME, A (TF) ... Robert Markowitz
LONGEST DAY, THE ... Ken Annakin
LONGEST DAY, THE ... Andrew Marton
LONGEST DAY, THE ... Bernhard Wicki
LONGEST NIGHT, THE (TF) ... Jack Smight
LONGEST 100 MILES, THE (TF) ... Don Weis
LONGSHOT ... E.W. Swackhamer
LONGSTREET (TF) ... Joseph Sargent
LOOK BACK IN ANGER ... Tony Richardson
LOOK DOWN AND DIE ... Steve Carver
LOOK WHAT'S HAPPENED TO ROSEMARY'S BABY (TF) ... Sam O'Steen
LOOKER ... Michael Crichton
LOOKIN' TO GET OUT ... Hal Ashby
LOOKING FOR LOVE ... Don Weis
LOOKING FOR MR. GOODBAR ... Richard Brooks
LOOKING GLASS WAR, THE ... Frank Pierson
LOOKING UP ... Linda Yellen
LOOKS AND SMILES ... Kenneth Loach
LOOPHOLE ... John Quested
LOOPS ... Shirley Clarke
LOOSE CONNECTIONS ... Richard Eyre
LOOSE ENDS ... David Burton Morris
LOOT ... Silvio Narizzano
LORD JIM ... Richard Brooks
LORD LOVE A DUCK ... George Axelrod
LORD OF THE FLIES ... Peter Brook
LORD OF THE RINGS, THE (AF) ... Ralph Bakshi
LORDS OF DISCIPLINE, THE ... Franc Roddam
LORDS OF FLATBUSH, THE ... Martin Davidson
LORDS OF FLATBUSH, THE ... Stephen F. Verona
LORNA ... Russ Meyer
LORNA DOONE ... Phil Karlson
LOS CHICOS ... Marco Ferreri
LOS GOLFOS ... Carlos Saura
LOS OJOS VENDADOS ... Carlos Saura
LOS SOBREVIVIENTES ... Tomas Gutierrez Alea
LOS ZANCOS ... Carlos Saura
LOSER TAKES ALL ... Ken Annakin
LOSERS, THE ... Jack Starrett
LOSIN' IT ... Curtis Hanson
L'OSPITE ... Liliana Cavani
LOSS OF INNOCENCE ... Lewis Gilbert
LOST ... Guy Green
LOST AND FOUND ... Melvin Frank
LOST CONTINENT, THE ... Michael Carreras
LOST EMPIRE, THE ... Jim Wynorski
LOST HONOR OF KATHARINA BLUM, THE ... Volker Schlondorff
LOST HONOR OF KATHRYN BECK, THE (TF) ... Simon Langton
LOST HORIZON ... Frank Capra
LOST HORIZON ... Charles Jarrott
LOST IN AMERICA ... Albert Brooks
LOST IN THE DESERT ... Jamie Uys
LOST IN THE STARS ... Daniel Mann
LOST WEEKEND ★★, THE ... Billy Wilder
LOST WORLD, THE ... Irwin Allen
LOTNA ... Andrzej Wajda
LOTTE IN ITALIA (FD) ... Jean-Luc Godard
LOTTERY! (TF) ... Lee Philips
LOUIS ARMSTRONG - CHICAGO STYLE (TF) ... Lee Philips
LOUISIANA ... Phil Karlson
LOUISIANA (CTF) ... Philippe de Broca
LOVE ... Annette Cohen
LOVE ... Nancy Dowd
LOVE ... Liv Ullmann
LOVE ... Mai Zetterling
LOVE AFFAIR: THE ELEANOR AND LOU GEHRIG STORY, A (TF) ... Fielder Cook
LOVE AFFAIR; OR THE CASE OF THE MISSING SWITCHBOARD OPERATOR ... Dusan Makavejev
LOVE AND ANARCHY ... Lina Wertmuller
LOVE AND BULLETS ... Stuart Rosenberg
LOVE AND DEATH ... Woody Allen
LOVE AND LARCENY ... Dino Risi
LOVE AND MONEY ... James Toback
LOVE AND PAIN AND THE WHOLE DAMNED THING ... Alan J. Pakula
LOVE AT FIRST BITE ... Stan Dragoti
LOVE AT FIRST SIGHT ... Rex Bromfield
LOVE AT TWENTY ... Marcel Ophuls
LOVE AT TWENTY ... Andrzej Wajda
LOVE BAN, THE ... Ralph Thomas
LOVE BOAT, THE (TF) ... Richard Kinon
LOVE BOAT, THE (TF) ... Alan Myerson
LOVE BOAT II, THE (TF) ... Hy Averback
LOVE BUG, THE ... Robert Stevenson
LOVE CHILD ... Larry Peerce
LOVE, DEATH ... Theodore Gershuny
LOVE FILM ... Istvan Szabo
LOVE FOR RENT (TF) ... David Miller
LOVE HAPPY ... David Miller
LOVE HAS MANY FACES ... Alexander Singer
LOVE, HATE, LOVE (TF) ... George McCowan
LOVE IN A FALLEN CITY ... Ann Hui
LOVE IN A GOLDFISH BOWL ... Jack Sher
LOVE IN GERMANY, A ... Andrzej Wajda
LOVE IN THE AFTERNOON ... Billy Wilder
LOVE IN THE CITY ... Michelangelo Antonioni
LOVE IN THE CITY ... Federico Fellini
LOVE IN THE CITY ... Alberto Lattuada
LOVE IN THE CITY ... Carlo Lizzani
LOVE IN THE CITY ... Dino Risi
LOVE IS A BALL ... David Swift
LOVE IS A FUNNY THING ... Claude Lelouch
LOVE IS A SPLENDID ILLUSION ... Tom Clegg
LOVE IS BETTER THAN NONE ... Stanley Donen
LOVE IS FOREVER (TF) ... Hall Bartlett
LOVE IS NOT ENOUGH (TF) ... Ivan Dixon
LOVE LEADS THE WAY (CTF) ... Delbert Mann
LOVE LETTERS ... Amy Jones
LOVE MACHINE, THE ... Jack Haley, Jr.
LOVE ME TONIGHT ... Rouben Mamoulian
LOVE ON A PILLOW ... Roger Vadim
LOVE ON THE GROUND ... Jacques Rivette
LOVE ON THE NOSE (TF) ... George Bloomfield
LOVE STORY (MS) ... Henri Safran
LOVE STORY ★ ... Arthur Hiller
LOVE STREAMS ... John Cassavetes
LOVE TAPES, THE (TF) ... Allen Reisner
LOVE TEST, THE ... Michael Powell
LOVE THY NEIGHBOR (TF) ... Tony Bill
LOVE WAR, THE (TF) ... George McCowan
LOVE WITH THE PROPER STRANGER ... Robert Mulligan
LOVE 65 ... Bo Widerberg
LOVED ONE, THE ... Tony Richardson
LOVE-INS, THE ... Arthur Dreifuss
LOVELAND ... Richard Franklin
LOVELESS, THE ... Kathryn Bigelow
LOVELESS, THE ... Monty Montgomery
LOVELINES ... Rod Amateau
LOVELY TO LOOK AT ... Mervyn Leroy
LOVELY WAY TO DIE, A ... David Lowell Rich
LOVER, COME BACK ... Delbert Mann
LOVER LOTTERY, THE ... Charles Crichton
LOVER, THE ... Kon Ichikawa
LOVERS AND LIARS ... Mario Monicelli
LOVERS AND OTHER STRANGERS ... Cy Howard
LOVERS, HAPPY LOVERS! ... René Clement
LOVER'S ROMANCE, A ... Andrei Konchalovsky
LOVERS, THE ... Kon Ichikawa
LOVERS, THE ... Louis Malle
LOVERS!, THE ... Herbert Wise
LOVE'S DARK RIDE (TF) ... Delbert Mann
LOVES OF A BLONDE ... Milos Forman
LOVES OF ISADORA, THE ... Karel Reisz
LOVES OF ONDINE, THE ... Andy Warhol
LOVE'S SAVAGE FURY (TF) ... Joseph Hardy
LOVESICK ... Marshall Brickman
LOVEY: A CIRCLE OF CHILDREN, PART II (TF) ... Jud Taylor
LOVIN' MOLLY ... Sidney Lumet
LOVING ... Irvin Kershner
LOVING COUPLES ... Jack Smight
LOVING COUPLES ... Mai Zetterling
LOVING TOUCH, THE ... Robert Vincent O'Neil
LOVING YOU ... Hal Kanter
LOWER DEPTHS, THE ... Akira Kurosawa
L-SHAPED ROOM, THE ... Bryan Forbes
LUCAN (TF) ... David Greene
LUCAS TANNER (TF) ... Richard Donner
LUCI DEL PO ... Alberto Lattuada
LUCIO FLAVIO ... Hector Babenco
LUCK OF GINGER COFFEY, THE ... Irvin Kershner
LUCK OF THE IRISH, THE ... Henry Koster
LUCKY JIM ... John Boulting
LUCKY LADY ... Stanley Donen
LUCKY LUCIANO ... Francesco Rosi
LUCKY STAR, THE ... Max Fischer
LUCY GALLANT ... Robert Parrish
L'UDIENZA ... Marco Ferreri
LUDWIG: REQUIEM FOR A VIRGIN KING ... Hans-Jurgen Syberberg
LUMIERE ... Jeanne Moreau
LUNA ... Bernardo Bertolucci
LUNA DE MIEL ... Michael Powell
LUNCH HOUR ... James Hill
LUNCH WAGON ... Ernest Pintoff
LUNCH WAGON GIRLS ... Ernest Pintoff
LUPE ... Andy Warhol

LUPO GOES TO NEW YORK ... Boaz Davidson
LUPO! ... Menahem Golan
LURE OF THE SWAMP ... Hubert Cornfield
LURE OF THE WILDERNESS ... Jean Negulesco
LUSITANO (FD) ... Budd Boetticher
LUST FOR A VAMPIRE ... Jimmy Sangster
LUST FOR LIFE ... Vincente Minnelli
LUST IN THE DUST ... Paul Bartel
LUTHER ... Guy Green
LUV ... Clive Donner
LYDIA BAILEY ... Jean Negulesco
LYONS IN PARIS, THE ... Val Guest

M

M STATION: HAWAII (TF) ... Jack Lord
MacARTHUR ... Joseph Sargent
MacARTHUR'S CHILDREN ... Masahiro Shinoda
McCABE & MRS. MILLER ... Robert Altman
McCLOUD: WHO KILLED MISS U.S.A.? (TF) ... Richard A. Colla
McCONNELL STORY, THE ... Gordon Douglas
McGUIRE, GO HOME! ... Ralph Thomas
McLINTOCK! ... Andrew V. McLaglen
McMASTERS, THE ... Alf Kjellin
McNAUGHTON'S DAUGHTER (TF) ... Jerry London
McQ ... John Sturges
McVICAR ... Tom Clegg
MACAHANS, THE (TF) ... Bernard McEveety
MACARONI ... Ettore Scola
MACBETH ... Roman Polanski
MACBETH ... George Schaefer
MACBETH ... Orson Welles
MACHINE GUN KELLY ... Roger Corman
MACHINE GUN McCAIN ... Giuliano Montaldo
MACHO CALLAHAN ... Bernard L. Kowalski
MACISTE CONTRO IL VAMPIRO ... Sergio Corbucci
MACK, THE ... Michael Campus
MACKENNA'S GOLD ... J. Lee Thompson
MACKENZIE BREAK, THE ... Lamont Johnson
MACKINTOSH AND T.J. ... Marvin J. Chomsky
MACKINTOSH MAN, THE ... John Huston
MACON COUNTY LINE ... Richard Compton
MAD ABOUT MEN ... Ralph Thomas
MAD ADVENTURES OF 'RABBI' JACOB, THE ... Gerard Oury
MAD BOMBER, THE ... Bert I. Gordon
MAD BULL ... Walter Doniger
MAD DOG ... Philippe Mora
MAD DOG MORGAN ... Philippe Mora
MAD MAGAZINE PRESENTS UP THE ACADEMY ... Robert Downey
MAD MAX ... George Miller
MAD MAX II ... George Miller
MAD MAX III ... George Miller
MAD MAX III ... George Ogilvie
MAD MONSTER PARTY (AF) ... Jules Bass
MAD ROOM ... Bernard Girard
MADAME BOVARY ... Vincente Minnelli
MADAME CLAUDE ... Just Jaeckin
MADAME CURIE ... Mervyn Leroy
MADAME ROSA ... Moshe Mizrahi
MADAME SIN (TF) ... David Greene
MADAME WANG'S ... Paul Morrissey
MADAME X ... David Lowell Rich
MADAME X (TF) ... Robert Ellis Miller
M.A.D.D.: MOTHERS AGAINST DRUNK DRIVERS (TF) ... William A. Graham
MADE ... John Mackenzie
MADE FOR EACH OTHER ... Robert B. Bean
MADE IN ITALY ... Nanni Loy
MADE IN U.S.A. ... Jean-Luc Godard
MADELEINE ... David Lean
MADEMOISELLE ... Tony Richardson
MADEMOISELLE FIFI ... Robert Wise
MADIGAN ... Don Siegel
MADMAN ... Joe Giannone
MADO ... Claude Sautet
MADRON ... Jerry Hopper
MADWOMAN OF CHAILLOT, THE ... Bryan Forbes
MAE WEST (TF) ★ ... Lee Philips
MAFIA ... Damiano Damiani
MAFIOSO ... Alberto Lattuada
MAFU CAGE, THE ... Karen Arthur
MAGGIE, THE ... Alexander Mackendrick
MAGIC ... Richard Attenborough
MAGIC BOX, THE ... John Boulting
MAGIC CARPET (TF) ... William A. Graham
MAGIC CHRISTIAN, THE ... Joseph McGrath
MAGIC FLUTE, THE ... Ingmar Bergman
MAGIC OF LASSIE, THE ... Don Chaffey
MAGIC SHOW, THE ... Norman Campbell
MAGIC SWORD, THE ... Bert I. Gordon
MAGICIAN, THE (TF) ... Marvin J. Chomsky
MAGICIAN OF LUBLIN, THE ... Menahem Golan
MAGICIAN, THE ... Ingmar Bergman
MAGNIFICENT AMBERSONS, THE ... Orson Welles
MAGNIFICENT MAGNET OF SANTA MESA (TF) ... Hy Averback
MAGNIFICENT MATADOR, THE ... Budd Boetticher
MAGNIFICENT SEVEN RIDE!, THE ... George McCowan
MAGNIFICENT SEVEN, THE ... John Sturges
MAGNIFICENT TWO, THE ... Cliff Owen
MAGNIFICENT YANKEE, THE ... John Sturges
MAGNUM FORCE ... Ted Post
MAGNUM THRUST ... Earl Bellamy
MAGUS, THE ... Guy Green
MAHANAGAR ... Satyajit Ray
MAHATMA AND THE MAD BOY ... James Ivory
MAHLER ... Ken Russell
MAHOGANY ... Berry Gordy
MAHONEY'S ESTATE (TF) ... Harvey Hart
MAID IN AMERICA (TF) ... Paul Aaron
MAIDS, THE ... Christopher Miles
MAIDSTONE ... Norman Mailer
MAIL ORDER BRIDE ... Burt Kennedy
MAIN ATTRACTION, THE ... Daniel Petrie
MAIN EVENT, THE ... Howard Zieff
MAITRESSE ... Barbet Schroeder
MAJOR AND THE MINOR, THE ... Billy Wilder
MAJOR DUNDEE ... Sam Peckinpah
MAJORITY OF ONE, A ... Mervyn Leroy
MAKE ME AN OFFER (TF) ... Jerry Paris
MAKE MINE LAUGHS ... Richard Fleischer
MAKING IT ... John Erman
MAKING LOVE ... Arthur Hiller
MAKING OF A MALE MODEL, THE (TF) ... Irving J. Moore
MAKING OF 'STAR WARS', THE (TD) ... Peter Shillingford
MAKING OF THE PRESIDENT (1), THE (TD) ... Mel Stuart
MAKING OF THE PRESIDENT (2), THE (TD) ... Mel Stuart
MAKING OF THE PRESIDENT (3), THE (TD) ... Mel Stuart
MAKING THE GRADE ... Dorian Walker
MAKIOKA SISTERS, THE ... Kon Ichikawa
MALAGA ... Laslo Benedek
MALE COMPANION ... Philippe de Broca
MALE HUNT ... Edouard Molinaro
MALE OF THE CENTURY ... Claude Berri
MALIBU (TF) ... E.W. Swackhamer
MALIBU BEACH ... Robert J. Rosenthal
MALIBU EXPRESS ... Andy Sidaris
MALIBU HIGH ... Lawrence D. Foldes
MALPAS MYSTERY, THE ... Sidney Hayers
MALTESE BIPPY, THE ... Norman Panama
MALTESE FALCON, THE ... John Huston
MAMA CUMPLE CIEN ANOS ... Carlos Saura
MAME ... Gene Saks
MAN, A WOMAN AND A BANK, A ... Noel Black
MAN, A WOMAN, AND A KILLER, A ... Wayne Wang
MAN AND A WOMAN ★, A ... Claude Lelouch
MAN AND BOY ... E.W. Swackhamer
MAN BEHIND THE MASK, THE ... Michael Powell
MAN CALLED DAGGER, A ... Richard Rush
MAN CALLED GANNON, A ... James Goldstone
MAN CALLED HORSE, A ... Elliot Silverstein
MAN CALLED PETER, A ... Henry Koster
MAN COULD GET KILLED, A ... Ronald Neame
MAN COULD GET KILLED, A ... Cliff Owen
MAN ESCAPED, A ... Robert Bresson
MAN FOR ALL SEASONS ★★, A ... Fred Zinnemann
MAN FRIDAY ... Jack Gold
MAN FROM ATLANTIS, THE (TF) ... Lee H. Katzin
MAN FROM BITTER RIDGE, THE ... Jack Arnold
MAN FROM CLOVER GROVE, THE ... William Byron Hillman
MAN FROM GALVESTON, THE ... William Conrad
MAN FROM SNOWY RIVER, THE ... George Miller
MAN FROM THE ALAMO, THE ... Budd Boetticher
MAN IN A COCKED HAT ... Roy Boulting
MAN IN THE GLASS BOOTH, THE ... Arthur Hiller
MAN IN THE IRON MASK, THE (TF) ... Mike Newell
MAN IN THE MIDDLE ... Guy Hamilton
MAN IN THE SADDLE ... Andre De Toth
MAN IN THE SANTA CLAUS SUIT, THE (TF) ... Corey Allen
MAN IN THE SHADOW ... Jack Arnold
MAN IN THE SKY, THE ... Charles Crichton
MAN IN THE VAULT ... Andrew V. McLaglen
MAN IN THE WHITE SUIT, THE ... Alexander Mackendrick
MAN IN THE WILDERNESS ... Richard C. Sarafian
MAN IN 5A, THE ... Max Fischer
MAN IS NOT A BIRD ... Dusan Makavejev
MAN OF A THOUSAND FACES ... Joseph Pevney
MAN OF FLOWERS ... Paul Cox
MAN OF IRON ... Andrzej Wajda
MAN OF LA MANCHA ... Arthur Hiller
MAN OF MARBLE ... Andrzej Wajda
MAN OF THE FOREST ... Henry Hathaway
MAN OF VIOLENCE ... Peter Walker
MAN ON A STRING ... Andre De Toth
MAN ON A STRING (TF) ... Joseph Sargent
MAN ON A SWING ... Frank Perry
MAN ON A TIGHTROPE ... Elia Kazan
MAN ON THE ROOF ... Bo Widerberg
MAN ON THE RUN ... Eddie Romero
MAN, THE ... Joseph Sargent
MAN TO REMEMBER, A ... Garson Kanin
MAN UPSTAIRS, THE ... Don Chaffey
MAN VANISHES, A ... Shohei Imamura
MAN WHO CHANGED HIS MIND, THE ... Robert Stevenson
MAN WHO COULD TALK TO KIDS, THE (TF) ... Donald Wrye
MAN WHO DARED, THE ... John Sturges
MAN WHO DIED TWICE, THE (TF) ... Joseph Sargent
MAN WHO FELL TO EARTH, THE ... Nicolas Roeg
MAN WHO HAD POWER OVER WOMEN, THE ... John Krish
MAN WHO LIES, THE ... Alain Robbe-Grillet
MAN WHO LIVED AGAIN, THE ... Robert Stevenson
MAN WHO LOVED CAT DANCING, THE ... Richard C. Sarafian
MAN WHO LOVED WOMEN, THE ... Blake Edwards
MAN WHO NEVER WAS, THE ... Ronald Neame
MAN WHO SAW TOMORROW, THE ... Robert Guenette
MAN WHO TALKED TOO MUCH, THE ... Vincent Sherman
MAN WHO WASN'T THERE, THE ... Bruce Malmuth
MAN WHO WOULD BE KING, THE ... John Huston
MAN WITH A MILLION ... Ronald Neame
MAN WITH BOGART'S FACE, THE ... Robert Day
MAN WITH CONNECTIONS, THE ... Claude Berri
MAN WITH ONE RED SHOE, THE ... Stan Dragoti
MAN WITH THE BALLOONS, THE ... Marco Ferreri
MAN WITH THE GOLDEN ARM, THE ... Otto Preminger
MAN WITH THE GOLDEN GUN, THE ... Guy Hamilton
MAN WITH THE GUN ... Richard Wilson
MAN WITH THE POWER, THE (TF) ... Nicholas Sgarro
MAN WITH TWO BRAINS, THE ... Carl Reiner

MAN WITHOUT A COUNTRY, THE (TF) ..... Delbert Mann
MAN WITHOUT NATIONALITY, THE ..... Kon Ichikawa
MAN, WOMAN AND CHILD ..... Dick Richards
MANCHU EAGLE CAPER MYSTERY, THE ..... Dean Hargrove
MANCHURIAN CANDIDATE, THE ..... John Frankenheimer
MANDABI ..... Ousmene Sembene
MANDINGO ..... Richard Fleischer
MANDRAKE (TF) ..... Harry Falk
MANDY ..... Alexander Mackendrick
MANEATER ..... Vincent Edwards
MANEATERS ARE LOOSE! (TF) ..... Timothy Galfas
MANHANDLERS, THE ..... Lee Madden
MANHATTAN ..... Woody Allen
MANHATTAN ANGEL ..... Arthur Dreifuss
MANHUNTER (TF) ..... Walter Grauman
MAN-HUNTER, THE (TF) ..... Don Taylor
MANIAC ..... Michael Carreras
MANIAC ..... Richard Compton
MANIAC ..... William Lustig
MANIMAL (TF) ..... Russ Mayberry
MANIONS OF AMERICA, THE (MS) ..... Charles S. Dubin
MANIONS OF AMERICA, THE (MS) ..... Joseph Sargent
MANN OHNE GEDACHTNIS ..... Kurt Gloor
MANNY'S ORPHANS ..... Sean S. Cunningham
MANOEUVRE (FD) ..... Frederick Wiseman
MANSLAUGHTER ..... George Abbott
MANTRAP, THE ..... George Sherman
MANUELA ..... Guy Hamilton
MARACAIBO ..... Cornel Wilde
MARASCHINO CHERRY ..... Radley Metzger
MARATHON (TF) ..... Jackie Cooper
MARATHON MAN ..... John Schlesinger
MARAT/SADE ..... Peter Brook
MARCH OR DIE ..... Dick Richards
MARCIA NUNZIALE ..... Marco Ferreri
MARCIANO (TF) ..... Bernard L. Kowalski
MARCO ..... Seymour Robbie
MARCO POLO (MS) ..... Giuliano Montaldo
MARCO THE MAGNIFICENT ..... Noel Howard
MARCUS WELBY, M.D. (TF) ..... David Lowell Rich
MARCUS-NELSON MURDERS ☆☆, THE (TF) ..... Joseph Sargent
MARGIN FOR ERROR ..... Otto Preminger
MARGO ..... Menahem Golan
MARIA (TF) ..... Allan King
MARIA CHAPDELAINE ..... Gilles Carle
MARIAGE ..... Claude Lelouch
MARIAN ROSE WHITE (TF) ..... Robert Day
MARIA'S LOVERS ..... Andrei Konchalovsky
MARIE ..... Roger Donaldson
MARIE-CHANTAL CONTRE LE DOCTEUR KHA ..... Claude Chabrol
MARILYN: THE UNTOLD STORY (TF) ..... Jack Arnold
MARILYN: THE UNTOLD STORY (TF) ..... John Flynn
MARILYN: THE UNTOLD STORY (TF) ..... Lawrence J. Schiller
MARITI IN CITTA ..... Luigi Comencini
MARJOE (FD) ..... Howard Smith
MARJORIE MORNINGSTAR ..... Irving Rapper
MARK, I LOVE YOU (TF) ..... Gunnar Hellstrom
MARK OF ZORRO, THE (TF) ..... Don McDougall
MARK OF ZORRO, THE ..... Rouben Mamoulian
MARK, THE ..... Guy Green
MARKS (TF) ..... Piers Haggard
MARLENE (FD) ..... Maximilian Schell
MARLEY (FD) ..... Gary Weis
MARLOWE ..... Paul Bogart
MAROC 7 ..... Gerry O'Hara
MAROONED ..... John Sturges
MARQUISE OF O..., THE ..... Eric Rohmer
MARRIAGE, A ..... Sandy Tung
MARRIAGE CONTRACT, THE (TF) ..... Ephraim Kishon
MARRIAGE IS ALIVE AND WELL (TF) ..... Russ Mayberry
MARRIAGE OF A YOUNG STOCKBROKER ..... Lawrence Turman
MARRIAGE OF CONVENIENCE ..... Clive Donner
MARRIAGE, TEL AVIV STYLE ..... Joel Silberg
MARRIAGE: YEAR ONE (TF) ..... William A. Graham
MARRIED COUPLE, A (FD) ..... Allan King
MARRIED MAN, A (TF) ..... Charles Jarrott
MARRIED WOMAN, THE ..... Jean-Luc Godard
MARRY ME! MARRY ME! ..... Claude Berri
MARS NEEDS WOMEN ..... Larry Buchanan
MARSEILLES CONTRACT, THE ..... Robert Parrish
MARTIAN CHRONICLES, THE (TF) ..... Michael Anderson
MARTIN ..... George A. Romero
MARTIN'S DAY ..... Alan Gibson
MARTY ★★ ..... Delbert Mann
MARU MARU ..... Gordon Douglas
MARVA COLLINS STORY, THE (TF) ..... Peter Levin
MARVIN AND TIGE ..... Eric Weston
MARY AND JOSEPH: A STORY OF FAITH (TF) ..... Eric Till
MARY JANE HARPER CRIED LAST NIGHT (TF) ..... Allen Reisner
MARY LOU ..... Arthur Dreifuss
MARY, MARY ..... Mervyn Leroy
MARY POPPINS ★ ..... Robert Stevenson
MARY, QUEEN OF SCOTS ..... Charles Jarrott
MARY WHITE (TF) ..... Jud Taylor
MARYJANE ..... Maury Dexter
MASCULINE FEMININE ..... Jean-Luc Godard
M*A*S*H ★ ..... Robert Altman
MASK ..... Peter Bogdanovich
MASK OF DIMITRIOS, THE ..... Jean Negulesco
MASK OF SHEBA, THE (TF) ..... David Lowell Rich
MASK OF THE AVENGER ..... Phil Karlson
MASKS OF DEATH, THE (TF) ..... Roy Ward Baker
MASQUE OF THE RED DEATH, THE ..... Roger Corman
MASQUERADE (TF) ..... Peter H. Hunt
MASS APPEAL ..... Glenn Jordan
MASSACRE HARBOR ..... John Peyser
MASSACRE IN ROME ..... George Pan Cosmatos
MASSACRO AL GRANDE CANYON ..... Albert Band
MASSARATI AND THE BRAIN (TF) ..... Harvey Hart
MASTER GUNFIGHTER, THE ..... Frank Laughlin
MASTER OF BALLANTRAE, THE (TF) ..... Douglas Hickox
MASTER OF THE GAME (MS) ..... Kevin Connor
MASTER OF THE GAME (MS) ..... Harvey Hart
MASTER OF THE WORLD ..... William Witney
MASTER PLAN, THE ..... Cy Endfield
MASTERMIND ..... Alex March
MASTERWORK ..... Miklos Jancso
MATA HARI ..... Curtis Harrington
MATATABI ..... Kon Ichikawa
MATCHLESS ..... Alberto Lattuada
MATCHMAKER, THE ..... Joseph Anthony
MATILDA ..... Daniel Mann
MATINEE IDOL, THE ..... Frank Capra
MATING SEASON, THE (TF) ..... John Llewellyn Moxey
MATISSE ..... Marcel Ophuls
MATT HELM (TF) ..... Buzz Kulik
MATT HOUSTON (TF) ..... Richard Lang
MATTA DA SLEGARE ..... Marco Bellocchio
MATTEI AFFAIR, THE ..... Francesco Rosi
MATTER OF INNOCENCE, A ..... Guy Green
MATTER OF LIFE AND DEATH, A (TF) ..... Russ Mayberry
MATTER OF LIFE AND DEATH, A ..... Michael Powell
MATTER OF PRIDE, A (FD) ..... Allan King
MATTER OF SEX, A (TF) ..... Lee Grant
MATTER OF TIME, A ..... Vincente Minnelli
MATTER OF WHO, A ..... Don Chaffey
MATTER OF WIFE...AND DEATH, A (TF) ..... Marvin J. Chomsky
MAURIE ..... Daniel Mann
MAUSOLEUM ..... Michael Dugan
MAUVAISE GRAINE ..... Billy Wilder
MAX DUGAN RETURNS ..... Herbert Ross
MAX ET LES FERRAILLEURS ..... Claude Sautet
MAXIME ..... Henri Verneuil
MAYA ..... John Berry
MAYBE I'LL COME HOME IN THE SPRING (TF) ..... Joseph Sargent
MAYDAY AT 40,000 FEET (TF) ..... Robert Butler
MAYERLING ..... Terence Young
MAYFLOWER: THE PILGRIMS' ADVENTURE (TF) ..... George Schaefer
MAZEL TOV OU LE MARIAGE ..... Claude Berri
MCCLAIN'S LAW (TF) ..... Vincent McEveety
ME AND THE COLONEL ..... Peter Glenville
MEADOW, THE ..... Paolo Taviani
MEADOW, THE ..... Vittorio Taviani
MEAN DOG BLUES ..... Mel Stuart
MEAN JOHNNY BARROWS ..... Fred Williamson
MEAN SEASON, THE ..... Phillip Borsos
MEAN STREETS ..... Martin Scorsese
MEAT (FD) ..... Frederick Wiseman
MEATBALLS ..... Ivan Reitman
MEATBALLS III ..... George Mendeluk
MEATBALLS PART II ..... Ken Wiederhorn
MECHANIC, THE ..... Michael Winner
MEDICAL STORY (TF) ..... Gary Nelson
MEDICINE BALL CARAVAN (FD) ..... Francois Reichenbach
MEDIUM COOL ..... Haskell Wexler
MEDUSA TOUCH, THE ..... Jack Gold
MEET DANNY WILSON ..... Joseph Pevney
MEET JOHN DOE ..... Frank Capra
MEET MARLON BRANDO (FD) ..... Albert Maysles
MEET MARLON BRANDO (FD) ..... David Maysles
MEET ME IN ST. LOUIS ..... Vincente Minnelli
MEETINGS WITH REMARKABLE MEN ..... Peter Brook
MEGAFORCE ..... Hal Needham
MELANIE ..... Rex Bromfield
MELINDA ..... Hugh A. Robertson
MELODIE EN SOUS-SOL ..... Henri Verneuil
MELODY ..... Waris Hussein
MELODY PARADE ..... Arthur Dreifuss
MELVIN AND HOWARD ..... Jonathan Demme
MELVIN PURVIS: G-MAN (TF) ..... Dan Curtis
MEMBER OF THE WEDDING, THE ..... Fred Zinnemann
MEMED ..... Peter Ustinov
MEMOIRS OF A SURVIVOR ..... David Gladwell
MEMORIAL DAY (TF) ..... Joseph Sargent
MEMORIES NEVER DIE (TF) ..... Sandor Stern
MEMORIES OF UNDER-DEVELOPMENT ..... Tomas Gutierrez Alea
MEMORY OF EVA RYKER, THE (TF) ..... Walter Grauman
MEMORY OF JUSTICE, THE (FD) ..... Marcel Ophuls
MEN OF ARNHEM (FD) ..... Terence Young
MEN OF SHERWOOD FOREST ..... Val Guest
MEN OF THE DRAGON (TF) ..... Harry Falk
MEN OF THE FIGHTING LADY ..... Andrew Marton
MEN OF TOHOKU, THE ..... Kon Ichikawa
MEN, THE ..... Fred Zinnemann
MEN WITHOUT WOMEN (FD) ..... Derek Burbidge
MENACE, THE ..... Gerard Oury
MEPHISTO ..... Istvan Szabo
MEPHISTO WALTZ, THE ..... Paul Wendkos
MERCENARIES, THE ..... Jack Cardiff
MERCENARY, THE ..... Sergio Corbucci
MERRILL'S MARAUDERS ..... Samuel Fuller
MERRY ANDREW ..... Michael Kidd
MERRY CHRISTMAS, MR. LAWRENCE ..... Nagisa Oshima
MERRY-GO-ROUND ..... Jacques Rivette
MESMERIZED ..... Michael Laughlin
MESSAGE, THE ..... Moustapha Akkad
MESSAGE TO MY DAUGHTER (TF) ..... Robert M. Lewis
MESSIAH OF EVIL ..... Willard Huyck
MESSIDOR ..... Alain Tanner
METALSTORM: THE DESTRUCTION OF JARED-SYN ..... Charles Band
METEOR ..... Ronald Neame
MEURTRE EN 45 TOURS ..... Etienne Perier
MEXICALI ROSE ..... George Sherman
MEXICO MEXICO (FD) ..... Francois Reichenbach
MI MANDA PICONE ..... Nanni Loy
MIAMI VICE (TF) ..... Thomas Carter
MICHAEL KOHLHAAS ..... Volker Schlondorff
MICKEY ONE ..... Arthur Penn
MICKEY SPILLANE'S MARGIN FOR MURDER (TF) ..... Daniel Haller
MICKEY SPILLANE'S 'MURDER ME, MURDER YOU' (TF) ..... Gary Nelson
MICKI & MAUDE ..... Blake Edwards

MIDAS RUN ... Alf Kjellin
MIDDLE OF THE NIGHT ... Delbert Mann
MIDDLE OF THE WORLD, THE ... Alain Tanner
MIDDLEMAN, THE ... Satyajit Ray
MIDDLETOWN (TD) ... Peter Davis
MIDNIGHT EXPRESS ★ ... Alan Parker
MIDNIGHT COWBOY ★★ ... John Schlesinger
MIDNIGHT LACE ... David Miller
MIDNIGHT LACE (TF) ... Ivan Nagy
MIDNIGHT MADNESS ... Michael Nankin
MIDNIGHT MADNESS ... David Wechter
MIDNIGHT MAN, THE ... Burt Lancaster
MIDNIGHT OFFERINGS (TF) ... Rod Holcomb
MIDNIGHT STORY, THE ... Joseph Pevney
MIDNITE SPARES ... Quentin Masters
MIDSUMMER NIGHT'S DREAM, A ... Peter Hall
MIDSUMMER NIGHT'S SEX COMEDY, A ... Woody Allen
MIDWAY ... Jack Smight
MIKADO, THE ... Stuart Burge
MIKE'S MURDER ... James Bridges
MIKEY AND NICKY ... Elaine May
MILADY'S REVENGE ... Richard Lester
MILANO '83 (FD) ... Ermanno Olmi
MILAREPA ... Liliana Cavani
MILES TO GO BEFORE I SLEEP (TF) ... Fielder Cook
MILESTONES ... Robert Kramer
MILITARY UNIVERSITY ... Danford B. Greene
MILITARY UNIVERSITY ... Herb Margolis
MILLE MILLIARDS DE DOLLARS ... Henri Verneuil
MILLHOUSE: A WHITE COMEDY ... Emile de Antonio
MILLION DOLLAR DIXIE DELIVERY, THE (TF) ... Russ Mayberry
MILLION DOLLAR DUCK, THE ... Vincent McEveety
MILLION DOLLAR FACE, THE (TF) ... Michael O'Herlihy
MILLION DOLLAR INFIELD (TF) ... Hal Cooper
MILLION DOLLAR MERMAID ... Mervyn Leroy
MILLION DOLLAR RIP-OFF, THE (TF) ... Alexander Singer
MILLION POUND NOTE, THE ... Ronald Neame
MILLIONAIRE, THE (TF) ... Don Weis
MILLIONAIRE IN TROUBLE ... Joel Silberg
MIMI METALLURGICO FERITO NELL'ONORE ... Lina Wertmuller
MIND OF MR. SOAMES, THE ... Alan Cooke
MIND OVER MURDER (TF) ... Ivan Nagy
MIND SNATCHERS, THE ... Bernard Girard
MINI-SKIRT MOB, THE ... Maury Dexter
MINNESOTA CLAY ... Sergio Corbucci
MINNIE AND MOSKOWITZ ... John Cassavetes
MINSTREL MAN (TF) ... William A. Graham
MIO DIO COME SONO CADUTA IN BASSO ... Luigi Comencini
MIRACLE OF KATHY MILLER, THE (TF) ... Robert M. Lewis
MIRACLE OF THE WHITE STALLIONS, THE ... Arthur Hiller
MIRACLE ON ICE (TF) ... Steven Hillard Stern
MIRACLE ON 34TH STREET (TF) ... Fielder Cook
MIRACLE, THE ... Irving Rapper
MIRACLE WOMAN, THE ... Frank Capra
MIRACLE WORKER, THE (TF) ... Paul Aaron
MIRACLE WORKER ★, THE ... Arthur Penn
MIRACLES ... Jim Kouf
MIRAGE ... Edward Dmytryk
MIRAGE (TF) ... Gordon Flemyng
MIRANDA ... Ken Annakin
MIRROR CRACK'D, THE ... Guy Hamilton
MIRROR, MIRROR (TF) ... Joanna Lee
MIRROR, THE ... Andrei Tarkovsky
MIRRORS ... Noel Black
MISADVENTURES OF MERLIN JONES, THE ... Robert Stevenson
MISBEHAVIN' ... Chuck Vincent
MISCHIEF ... Mel Damski
MISFITS, THE ... John Huston
MISHIMA ... Paul Schrader
MISS ALL-AMERICAN BEAUTY (TF) ... Gus Trikonis
MISS LONDON LTD. ... Val Guest
MISS LONELYHEARTS ... Michael Dinner
MISS NYMPHET'S ZAP-IN ... Herschell Gordon Lewis
MISS PILGRIM'S PROGRESS ... Val Guest
MISS RIGHT ... Paul Williams
MISS ROBIN HOOD ... John Guillermin
MISS SUSIE SLAGLE'S ... John Berry
MISSING ... Costa-Gavras
MISSING ARE DEADLY, THE (TF) ... Don McDougall
MISSING CHILDREN: A MOTHER'S STORY (TF) ... Dick Lowry
MISSING IN ACTION ... Joseph Zito
MISSING JUROR, THE ... Budd Boetticher
MISSING LADY, THE ... Phil Karlson
MISSING PERSONS: FOUR TRUE STORIES (CTD) ... Kees Van Oostrum
MISSING PIECES (TF) ... Mike Hodges
MISSION HILL ... Robert Jones
MISSION KILL ... David Winters
MISSION MARS ... Nicholas Webster
MISSIONARY, THE ... Richard Loncraine
MISSISSIPPI BLUES ... Robert Parrish
MISSISSIPPI BLUES ... Bertrand Tavernier
MISSOURI BREAKS, THE ... Arthur Penn
MISSOURI OUTLAW, A ... George Sherman
MISSOURI TRAVELER, THE ... Jerry Hopper
MISTER BUDDWING ... Delbert Mann
MISTER CORY ... Blake Edwards
MISTER DRAKE'S DUCK ... Val Guest
MISTER FREEDOM ... William Klein
MISTER JERICO (TF) ... Sidney Hayers
MISTER MOSES ... Ronald Neame
MISTER ROBERTS ... Mervyn Leroy
MISTER ROCK & ROLL ... Charles S. Dubin
MISTRAL'S DAUGHTER (MS) ... Kevin Connor
MISTRAL'S DAUGHTER (MS) ... Douglas Hickox
MISTRESS OF PARADISE (TF) ... Peter Medak
MISTRESS PAMELA ... James O'Connolly
MISTY ... James B. Clark
MISUNDERSTOOD ... Jerry Schatzberg
MITCHELL ... Andrew V. McLaglen
MIXED BLOOD ... Paul Morrissey
MIXED COMPANY ... Melville Shavelson
MOB, THE ... Robert Parrish
MOBILE TWO (TF) ... David Moessinger
MOBY DICK ... John Huston
MODEL (FD) ... Frederick Wiseman
MODEL SHOP ... Jacques Demy
MODELS, INC. ... Gerry O'Hara
MODERATO CANTABILE ... Peter Brook
MODERN AMERICAN COMPOSERS 1: CAGE AND MONK (TD) ... Peter Greenaway
MODERN AMERICAN COMPOSERS 2: GLASS AND ASHLEY (TD) ... Peter Greenaway
MODERN PROBLEMS ... Ken Shapiro
MODERN ROMANCE ... Albert Brooks
MOGLI PERICOLOSE ... Luigi Comencini
MOHAMMAD, MESSENGER OF GOD ... Moustapha Akkad
MOI JE ... Jean-Luc Godard
MOLE PEOPLE, THE ... Virgil W. Vogel
MOLLY AND LAWLESS JOHN ... Gary Nelson
MOLLY MAGUIRES, THE ... Martin Ritt
MOM, THE WOLFMAN AND ME (TF) ... Edmond Levy
MOMENT BY MOMENT ... Jane Wagner
MOMENT OF LOVE, A ... Shirley Clarke
MOMENT OF TRUTH, THE ... Francesco Rosi
MOMENT TO MOMENT ... Mervyn Leroy
MOMENTS ... Michal Bat-Adam
MOMMA'S BOY ... William Asher
MOMMIE DEAREST ... Frank Perry
MON ONCLE ANTOINE ... Claude Jutra
MON ONCLE BENJAMIN ... Edouard Molinaro
MON ONCLE D'AMERIQUE ... Alain Resnais
MONDO TEENO ... Richard Lester
MONDO TOPLESS ... Russ Meyer
MONDO TRASHO ... John Waters
MONEY AND THREE BAD MEN ... Kon Ichikawa
MONEY, MARBLES AND CHALK ... Ivan Nagy
MONEY MONEY MONEY ... Claude Lelouch
MONEY MOVERS ... Bruce Beresford
MONEY ON THE SIDE (TF) ... Robert Collins
MONEY TALKS ... Allen Funt
MONEY TALKS ... Kon Ichikawa
MONEY TO BURN (TF) ... Robert M. Lewis
MONEY TRAP, THE ... Burt Kennedy
MONGOLS, THE ... Andre De Toth
MONGO'S BACK IN TOWN (TF) ... Marvin J. Chomsky
MONIKA ... Ingmar Bergman
MONITORS, THE ... Jack Shea
MONK, THE (TF) ... George McCowan
MONKEY HUSTLE, THE ... Arthur Marks
MONKEY IN WINTER, A ... Henri Verneuil
MONKEY ON MY BACK ... Andre De Toth
MONKEYS, GO HOME! ... Andrew V. McLaglen
MONKEY'S UNCLE, THE ... Robert Stevenson
MONNAIRE DE SINGE ... Yves Robert
MONSIEUR RIPOIS/KNAVE OF HEARTS ... René Clement
MONSIGNOR ... Frank Perry
MONSOON ... Rod Amateau
MONSTER A GO-GO ... Herschell Gordon Lewis
MONSTER CLUB, THE ... Roy Ward Baker
MONSTER ON THE CAMPUS ... Jack Arnold
MONSTER THAT CHALLENGED THE WORLD, THE ... Arnold Laven
MONTE WALSH ... William A. Fraker
MONTENEGRO ... Dusan Makavejev
MONTENEGRO, OR PIGS AND PEARLS ... Dusan Makavejev
MONTEREY POP (FD) ... D.A. Pennebaker
MONTREAL MAIN ... Allan Moyle
MONTY PYTHON AND THE HOLY GRAIL ... Terry Gilliam
MONTY PYTHON AND THE HOLY GRAIL ... Terry Jones
MONTY PYTHON LIVE AT THE HOLLYWOOD BOWL ... Terry Hughes
MONTY PYTHON'S LIFE OF BRIAN ... Terry Jones
MONTY PYTHON'S THE MEANING OF LIFE ... Terry Jones
MONUMENT OF TOTSUSEKI ... Kaneto Shindo
MOON IN THE GUTTER, THE ... Jean-Jacques Beineix
MOON IS BLUE, THE ... Otto Preminger
MOON OF THE WOLF (TF) ... Daniel Petrie
MOON ZERO TWO ... Roy Ward Baker
MOONBEAM ... Robert Downey
MOONCHILD ... Alan Gadney
MOONLIGHTING ... Jerzy Skolimowski
MOONRAKER ... Lewis Gilbert
MOONSHINE COUNTY EXPRESS ... Gus Trikonis
MOONSHINE MOUNTAIN ... Herschell Gordon Lewis
MOONSHINE WAR, THE ... Richard Quine
MORDI E FUGGI ... Dino Risi
MORE ... Barbet Schroeder
MORE AMERICAN GRAFFITI ... B.W.L. Norton
MORE MILK, EVETTE ... Andy Warhol
MORE THAN A MIRACLE ... Francesco Rosi
MORE THAN FRIENDS (TF) ... James Burrows
MORE WILD WILD WEST ... Burt Kennedy
MORGAN: A SUITABLE CASE FOR TREATMENT ... Karel Reisz
MORGAN THE PIRATE ... Andre De Toth
MORGAN! ... Karel Reisz
MORITURI ... Bernhard Wicki
MORNING AFTER, THE (TF) ... Richard T. Heffron
MORNING BEFORE SLEEP, THE ... Dan Wolman
MORNING DEPARTURE ... Roy Ward Baker
MORO WITCH DOCTOR ... Eddie Romero
MORONS FROM OUTER SPACE ... Mike Hodges
MORTADELLA ... Mario Monicelli
MORTUARY ... Howard (Hikmet) Avedis
MOSCOW ON THE HUDSON ... Paul Mazursky
MOSES ... Gianfranco de Bosio
MOSES PENDLETON PRESENTS MOSES PENDLETON (FD) ... Robert Elfstrom
MOSES THE LAWGIVER (MS) ... Gianfranco de Bosio
MOST BEAUTIFUL, THE ... Akira Kurosawa
MOST WANTED (TF) ... Walter Grauman
MOST WANTED MAN IN THE WORLD, THE ... Henri Verneuil
MOTEL HELL ... Kevin Connor
MOTHER ... Kaneto Shindo

MOTHER AND DAUGHTER - THE LOVING WAR (TF) ... Burt Brinckerhoff
MOTHER, JUGS AND SPEED ... Peter Yates
MOTHER LODE ... Charlton Heston
MOTHER'S DAY ... Charles Kaufman
MOTHER'S DAY ON WALTON'S MOUNTAIN (TF) ... Gwen Arner
MOTOR PSYCHO ... Russ Meyer
MOUCHETTE ... Robert Bresson
MOULIN ROUGE ★ ... John Huston
MOUNTAIN MEN, THE ... Richard Lang
MOUNTAIN ROAD, THE ... Daniel Mann
MOUNTAIN, THE ... Edward Dmytryk
MOUNTAINS AT DUSK (TF) ... Krzysztof Zanussi
MOUNTBATTEN - THE LAST VICEROY (MS) ... Tom Clegg
MOUSE AND HIS CHILD, THE (AF) ... Charles Swenson
MOUSE AND THE WOMAN, THE ... Karl Francis
MOUSE ON THE MOON, THE ... Richard Lester
MOUSE THAT ROARED, THE ... Jack Arnold
MOUSEY (TF) ... Daniel Petrie
MOUTH TO MOUTH ... John Duigan
MOVE ... Stuart Rosenberg
MOVE OVER, DARLING ... Michael Gordon
MOVIE MOVIE ... Stanley Donen
MOVIE STAR AMERICAN STYLE OR LSD - I HATE YOU ... Albert Zugsmith
MOVING VIOLATION ... Charles S. Dubin
MOVING VIOLATIONS ... Neil Israel
MOVIOLA (MS) ☆ ... John Erman
MR. AND MRS. BO JO JONES (TF) ... Robert Day
MR. ARKADIN ... Orson Welles
MR. BELVEDERE RINGS THE BELL ... Henry Koster
MR. BILLION ... Jonathan Kaplan
MR. DEEDS GOES TO TOWN ★★ ... Frank Capra
MR. HOBBS TAKES A VACATION ... Henry Koster
MR. HORN (TF) ... Jack Starrett
MR. INSIDE/MR. OUTSIDE (TF) ... William A. Graham
MR. KRUEGER'S CHRISTMAS (TF) ... Kieth Merrill
MR. LUCKY ... Kon Ichikawa
MR. MAJESTYK ... Richard Fleischer
MR. MEAN ... Fred Williamson
MR. MIKE'S MONDO VIDEO ... Michael O'Donoghue
MR. MOM ... Stan Dragoti
MR. PATMAN ... John Guillermin
MR. PHARAOH AND HIS CLEOPATRA ... Don Weis
MR. POO ... Kon Ichikawa
MR. QUILP ... Michael Tuchner
MR. RICCO ... Paul Bogart
MR. SKEFFINGTON ... Vincent Sherman
MR. SMITH GOES TO WASHINGTON ★ ... Frank Capra
MR. SOFT TOUCH ... Gordon Douglas
MR. SYCAMORE ... Pancho Kohner
MRS. BARRINGTON ... Chuck Vincent
MRS. BROWN, YOU'VE GOT A LOVELY DAUGHTER ... Saul Swimmer
MRS. POLLIFAX - SPY ... Leslie H. Martinson
MRS. REINHARDT (TF) ... Piers Haggard
MRS. R'S DAUGHTER (TF) ... Dan Curtis
MRS. SOFFEL ... Gillian Armstrong
MRS. SUNDANCE (TF) ... Marvin J. Chomsky
MS. DON JUAN ... Roger Vadim
MS. 45 ... Abel Ferrara
MUDLARK, THE ... Jean Negulesco
MUERTE AL INVASOR ... Tomas Gutierrez Alea
MUGGABLE MARY: STREET COP (TF) ... Sandor Stern
MUGSY'S GIRLS ... Kevin Brodie
MULLIGAN'S STEW (TF) ... Noel Black
MUMSY, NANNY, SONNY & GIRLY ... Freddie Francis
MUNICH, OU LA PRIX POUR CENT ANS (TD) ... Marcel Ophuls
MUNSTER, GO HOME ... Earl Bellamy
MUNSTERS' REVENGE, THE (TF) ... Don Weis
MUPPET MOVIE, THE ... James Frawley
MUPPETS TAKE MANHATTAN, THE ... Frank Oz
MUR MURS (FD) ... Agnes Varda
MURDER A LA MOD ... Brian De Palma
MURDER AT CRESTRIDGE (TF) ... Jud Taylor
MURDER AT THE MARDI GRAS (TF) ... Ken Annakin
MURDER AT THE WINDMILL ... Val Guest
MURDER AT THE WORLD SERIES (TF) ... Andrew V. McLaglen
MURDER BY DECREE ... Bob Clark
MURDER BY NATURAL CAUSES (TF) ... Robert Day
MURDER BY PHONE ... Michael Anderson
MURDER CAN HURT YOU! (TF) ... Roger Duchowny
MURDER IN COWETA COUNTY (TF) ... Gary Nelson
MURDER IN MUSIC CITY (TF) ... Leo Penn
MURDER IN PEYTON PLACE (TF) ... Bruce Kessler
MURDER IN TEXAS (TF) ... William "Billy" Hale
MURDER, INC. ... Stuart Rosenberg
MURDER IS A MURDER...IS A MURDER, A ... Etienne Perier
MURDER IS EASY (TF) ... Claude Whatham
MURDER MEN, THE ... John Peyser
MURDER MY SWEET ... Edward Dmytryk
MURDER ON FLIGHT 502 (TF) ... George McCowan
MURDER ON LENOX AVENUE ... Arthur Dreifuss
MURDER ON THE ORIENT EXPRESS ... Sidney Lumet
MURDER ONCE REMOVED (TF) ... Charles S. Dubin
MURDER ONE, DANCER 0 (TF) ... Reza Badiyi
MURDER OR MERCY (TF) ... Harvey Hart
MURDER, SHE WROTE: THE MURDER OF SHERLOCK HOLMES (TF) ... Corey Allen
MURDER THAT WOULDN'T DIE, THE (TF) ... Ron Satlof
MURDER WITHOUT CRIME ... J. Lee Thompson
MURDERS IN THE RUE MORGUE ... Gordon Hessler
MURDOCK'S GANG (TF) ... Charles S. Dubin
MURIEL ... Alain Resnais
MURIETA ... George Sherman
MURMUR OF THE HEART ... Louis Malle
MURPH THE SURF ... Marvin J. Chomsky
MURPHY'S WAR ... Peter Yates
MUSCLE BEACH PARTY ... William Asher
MUSIC FOR MILLIONS ... Henry Koster
MUSIC LOVERS, THE ... Ken Russell
MUSIC MACHINE, THE ... Ian Sharp
MUSIC MAN, THE ... Morton Da Costa
MUSIC ROOM, THE (TF) ... John Korty
MUSIC ROOM, THE ... Satyajit Ray
MUSICAL PASSAGE (FD) ... Jim Brown
MUSSOLINI - ULTIMO ATTO ... Carlo Lizzani
MUTANT ... John "Bud" Cardos
MUTATIONS, THE ... Jack Cardiff
MUTINY ... Edward Dmytryk
MY BEST FRIEND'S GIRL ... Bertrand Blier
MY BLOOD RUNS COLD ... William Conrad
MY BLOODY VALENTINE ... George Mihalka
MY BLUE HEAVEN ... Henry Koster
MY BODY, MY CHILD (TF) ... Marvin J. Chomsky
MY BODYGUARD ... Tony Bill
MY BRILLIANT CAREER ... Gillian Armstrong
MY BROTHER TALKS TO HORSES ... Fred Zinnemann
MY CHAMPION ... Gwen Arner
MY COUSIN RACHEL ... Henry Koster
MY DARLING DAUGHTERS' ANNIVERSARY (TF) ... Joseph Pevney
MY DARLING, MY DEAREST ... Sergio Corbucci
MY DEAR SECRETARY ... Charles Martin
MY DINNER WITH ANDRE ... Louis Malle
MY FACE RED IN THE SUNSET ... Masahiro Shinoda
MY FAVORITE WIFE ... Garson Kanin
MY FAVORITE YEAR ... Richard Benjamin
MY FIRST WIFE ... Paul Cox
MY FORBIDDEN PAST ... Robert Stevenson
MY FRIEND THE KING ... Michael Powell
MY FRIENDS ... Mario Monicelli
MY GEISHA ... Jack Cardiff
MY GIRLFRIEND'S WEDDING ... Jim McBride
MY HUSBAND IS MISSING (TF) ... Richard Michaels
MY HUSTLER ... Andy Warhol
MY KIDNAPPER, MY LOVE (TF) ... Sam Wanamaker
MY LIFE TO LIVE ... Jean-Luc Godard
MY LOVER, MY SON ... John Newland
MY MAN GODFREY ... Henry Koster
MY MICHAEL ... Dan Wolman
MY MOTHER THE GENERAL ... Joel Silberg
MY MOTHER'S SECRET LIFE (TF) ... Robert Markowitz
MY NAME IS IVAN ... Andrei Tarkovsky
MY NAME IS ROCCO PAPALEO ... Ettore Scola
MY NAME IS TRINITY ... Ferdinando Baldi
MY NIGHT AT MAUD'S ... Eric Rohmer
MY OLD MAN (TF) ... John Erman
MY OLD MAN'S PLACE ... Edwin Sherin
MY PAL GUS ... Robert Parrish
MY PALIKARI (TF) ... Charles S. Dubin
MY SCIENCE PROJECT ... Jonathan Betuel
MY SECOND BROTHER ... Shohei Imamura
MY SIDE OF THE MOUNTAIN ... James B. Clark
MY SIN ... George Abbott
MY SISTER EILEEN ... Richard Quine
MY SISTER, MY LOVE ... Vilgot Sjoman
MY SON'S YOUTH ... Masaki Kobayashi
MY SWEET CHARLIE (TF) ☆ ... Lamont Johnson
MY SWEET LADY (TF) ... Daniel Haller
MY TUTOR ... George Bowers
MY WAY ... Kaneto Shindo
MY WAY HOME ... Miklos Jancso
MY WHITE CITY ... Emil Loteanu
MY WICKED, WICKED WAYS: THE LEGEND OF ERROL FLYNN (TF) ... Don Taylor
MYRA BRECKINRIDGE ... Michael Sarne
MYSTERIES OF THE SEA (FD) ... Robert Elfstrom
MYSTERIOUS ISLAND ... Cy Endfield
MYSTERIOUS ISLAND OF BEAUTIFUL WOMEN (TF) ... Joseph Pevney
MYSTERIOUS MONSTERS, THE ... Robert Guenette
MYSTERIOUS POACHER, THE ... Don Chaffey
MYSTERIOUS STRANGER, THE (TF) ... Peter H. Hunt
MYSTERIOUS TWO (TF) ... Gary A. Sherman
MYSTERY BROADCAST ... George Sherman
MYSTERY IN MEXICO ... Robert Wise
MYSTERY IN SWING ... Arthur Dreifuss
MYSTERY IN THE MINE ... James Hill
MYSTERY OF KASPAR HAUSER, THE ... Werner Herzog
MYSTERY SEA RAIDERS ... Edward Dmytryk
MYSTERY STREET ... John Sturges
MYSTIC WARRIOR, THE (MS) ... Richard T. Heffron
MYSTIQUE ... Bobby Roth

N

NACH MEINEM LETZEN UMZUG ... Hans-Jurgen Syberberg
NADA ... Claude Chabrol
NADA GANG, THE ... Claude Chabrol
NADIA (TF) ... Alan Cooke
NAIROBI FAIR (TF) ... Marvin J. Chomsky
NAKED ALIBI ... Jerry Hopper
NAKED ANGELS ... Bruce Clark
NAKED BRIGADE, THE ... Maury Dexter
NAKED CAME THE STRANGER ... Radley Metzger
NAKED CITY, THE ... Jules Dassin
NAKED CIVIL SERVANT, THE (TF) ... Jack Gold
NAKED EARTH, THE ... Vincent Sherman
NAKED EDGE, THE ... Michael Anderson
NAKED FACE, THE ... Bryan Forbes
NAKED KISS, THE ... Samuel Fuller
NAKED MAJA, THE ... Henry Koster
NAKED NIGHT, THE ... Ingmar Bergman
NAKED 19-YEAR-OLD ... Kaneto Shindo

NAKED PARADISE .... Roger Corman
NAKED PREY, THE .... Cornel Wilde
NAKED RUNNER, THE .... Sidney J. Furie
NAKED UNDER LEATHER .... Jack Cardiff
NAKED WEEKEND, THE .... Bobby Roth
NAME OF THE GAME IS KILL, THE (TF) .... Gunnar Hellstrom
NAMU, THE KILLER WHALE .... Laslo Benedek
NANA .... Dan Wolman
NAPOLEON AND SAMANTHA .... Bernard McEveety
NARROW MARGIN, THE .... Richard Fleischer
NASHVILLE ★ .... Robert Altman
NASHVILLE GIRL .... Gus Trikonis
NASHVILLE GRAB (TF) .... James L. Conway
NASHVILLE SOUND, THE (FD) .... Robert Elfstrom
NASTY HABITS .... Michael Lindsay-Hogg
NATE AND HAYES .... Ferdinand Fairfax
NATHALIE GRANGER .... Marguerite Duras
NATIONAL LAMPOON'S ANIMAL HOUSE .... John Landis
NATIONAL LAMPOON'S CLASS REUNION .... Michael Miller
NATIONAL LAMPOON'S EUROPEAN VACATION .... Amy Heckerling
NATIONAL LAMPOON'S MOVIE MADNESS .... Bob Giraldi
NATIONAL LAMPOON'S MOVIE MADNESS .... Henry Jaglom
NATIONAL LAMPOON'S VACATION .... Harold Ramis
NATIVITY, THE (TF) .... Bernard L. Kowalski
NATTY GANN .... Jeremy Paul Kagan
NATURAL ENEMIES .... Jeff Kanew
NATURAL, THE .... Barry Levinson
NATURE'S PLAYMATES .... Herschell Gordon Lewis
NAUGHTY BABY .... Mervyn Leroy
NAUGHTY STEWARDESSES, THE .... Al Adamson
NAUSICAA (TF) .... Agnes Varda
NAVAJO JOE .... Sergio Corbucci
NAYAK .... Satyajit Ray
NAZI AGENT .... Jules Dassin
NAZIS STRIKE, THE (FD) .... Frank Capra
NEA .... Nelly Kaplan
NEA - A YOUNG EMMANUELLE .... Nelly Kaplan
NEARLY A NASTY ACCIDENT .... Don Chaffey
NEARLY EIGHTEEN .... Arthur Dreifuss
NECROMANCY .... Bert I. Gordon
NED KELLY .... Tony Richardson
NEGATIVES .... Peter Medak
NEGRO SOLDIER, THE (FD) .... Frank Capra
NEIGHBORHOOD, THE (TF) .... Lee H. Katzin
NEIGHBORS .... John G. Avildsen
NEIL SIMON'S ONLY WHEN I LAUGH .... Glenn Jordan
NEIL SIMON'S SEEMS LIKE OLD TIMES .... Jay Sandrich
NEITHER BY DAY NOR BY NIGHT .... Steven Hillard Stern
NEL NOME DEL PADRE .... Marco Bellocchio
NELLIE McCLUNG (TF) .... George Bloomfield
NELSON AFFAIR, THE .... James Cellan-Jones
NEON CEILING, THE (TF) .... Frank Pierson
NEPTUNE FACTOR, THE .... Daniel Petrie
NEST OF GENTRY, A .... Andrei Konchalovsky
NETWORK ★ .... Sidney Lumet
NEVADA SMITH .... Henry Hathaway
NEVADA SMITH (TF) .... Gordon Douglas
NEVADAN, THE .... Gordon Douglas
NEVER A DULL MOMENT .... Jerry Paris
NEVER CRY WOLF .... Carroll Ballard
NEVER GIVE AN INCH .... Paul Newman
NEVER LET GO .... John Guillermin
NEVER ON SUNDAY ★ .... Jules Dassin
NEVER PUT IT IN WRITING .... Andrew L. Stone
NEVER SAY GOODBYE .... Jerry Hopper
NEVER SAY NEVER AGAIN .... Irvin Kershner
NEVER SO FEW .... John Sturges
NEVER TOO LATE .... Bud Yorkin
NEVERENDING STORY, THE .... Wolfgang Petersen
NEW ADVENTURES OF HEIDI, THE (TF) .... Ralph Senensky
NEW CENTURIONS, THE .... Richard Fleischer
NEW DAUGHTERS OF JOSHUA CABE, THE (TF) .... Bruce Bilson
NEW FRONTIER .... George Sherman
NEW GIRL IN TOWN .... Gus Trikonis
NEW INTERNS, THE .... John Rich
NEW KID IN TOWN .... Cary Medoway
NEW KIDS, THE .... Sean S. Cunningham
NEW KIND OF LOVE, A .... Melville Shavelson
NEW LAND, THE .... Jan Troell
NEW LEAF, A .... Elaine May
NEW LOVE BOAT, THE (TF) .... Richard Kinon
NEW MAVERICK, THE (TF) .... Hy Averback
NEW YEAR'S EVIL .... Emmett Alston
NEW YORK CONFIDENTIAL .... Russell Rouse
NEW YORK, NEW YORK .... Martin Scorsese
NEW YORK NIGHTS .... Simon Nuchtern
NEWMAN'S LAW .... Richard T. Heffron
NEWSFRONT .... Phillip Noyce
NEXT CHEECH & CHONG MOVIE, THE .... Thomas Chong
NEXT MAN, THE .... Richard C. Sarafian
NEXT ONE, THE .... Nico Mastorakis
NEXT STOP, GREENWICH VILLAGE .... Paul Mazursky
NEXT TIME I MARRY .... Garson Kanin
NIAGARA .... Henry Hathaway
NIAGARA FALLS .... Gordon Douglas
NICE GIRL LIKE ME, A .... Desmond Davis
NICHOLAS AND ALEXANDRA .... Franklin J. Schaffner
NICKEL RIDE, THE .... Robert Mulligan
NICKELODEON .... Peter Bogdanovich
NICK'S MOVIE .... Wim Wenders
NICKY'S WORLD (TF) .... Paul Stanley
NIGHT AMBUSH .... Michael Powell
NIGHT AND FOG IN JAPAN ...... Nagisa Oshima
NIGHT AND THE CITY .... Jules Dassin
NIGHT AT THE DRIVE-IN, A .... Krishna Shah
NIGHT CALL NURSES .... Jonathan Kaplan
NIGHT CALLER, THE .... Henri Verneuil
NIGHT CHASE (TF) .... Jack Starrett
NIGHT CREATURES .... Lee Madden
NIGHT CRIES (TF) .... Richard Lang
NIGHT CROSSING .... Delbert Mann
NIGHT DIGGER, THE .... Alastair Reid
NIGHT DUTY (TF) .... Krzysztof Zanussi
NIGHT EYES .... Robert Clouse
NIGHT FLIGHT TO MOSCOW .... Henri Verneuil
NIGHT GALLERY (TF) .... Steven Spielberg
NIGHT GAMES .... Roger Vadim
NIGHT GAMES .... Mai Zetterling
NIGHT GAMES (TF) .... Don Taylor
NIGHT GOD SCREAMED, THE .... Lee Madden
NIGHT HEAVEN FELL, THE .... Roger Vadim
NIGHT HOLDS TERROR, THE .... Andrew L. Stone
NIGHT IN HEAVEN, A .... John G. Avildsen
NIGHT IS MY FUTURE .... Ingmar Bergman
NIGHT MOVES .... Arthur Penn
NIGHT MUST FALL .... Karel Reisz
NIGHT NURSE, THE (TF) .... Igor Auzins
NIGHT OF ADVENTURE, A .... Gordon Douglas
NIGHT OF DARK SHADOWS .... Dan Curtis
NIGHT OF PASSION .... Sidney J. Furie
NIGHT OF TERROR (TF) .... Jeannot Szwarc
NIGHT OF THE BLOOD BEAST .... Bernard L. Kowalski
NIGHT OF THE COMET .... Thom Eberhardt
NIGHT OF THE EAGLE .... Sidney Hayers
NIGHT OF THE FOLLOWING DAY, THE .... Hubert Cornfield
NIGHT OF THE GRIZZLY, THE .... Joseph Pevney
NIGHT OF THE IGUANA .... John Huston
NIGHT OF THE JUGGLER .... Robert Butler
NIGHT OF THE LEPUS .... William F. Claxton
NIGHT OF THE LIVING DEAD .... George A. Romero
NIGHT OF THE PARTY, THE ...... Michael Powell
NIGHT OF THE SHOOTING STARS, THE .... Paolo Taviani
NIGHT OF THE SHOOTING STARS, THE .... Vittorio Taviani
NIGHT PARTNERS (TF) .... Noel Nosseck
NIGHT PATROL .... Jackie Kong
NIGHT PORTER, THE .... Liliana Cavani
NIGHT RIDER, THE (TF) .... Hy Averback
NIGHT RIDERS, THE .... George Sherman
NIGHT SCHOOL .... Kenneth "Ken" Hughes
NIGHT SHADOWS .... John "Bud" Cardos
NIGHT SHIFT .... Ron Howard
NIGHT SLAVES (TF) .... Ted Post
NIGHT STALKER, THE (TF) .... John Llewellyn Moxey
NIGHT STRANGLER, THE (TF) .... Dan Curtis
NIGHT TERROR (TF) .... E.W. Swackhamer
NIGHT THAT PANICKED AMERICA, THE (TF) .... Joseph Sargent
NIGHT THE BRIDGE FELL DOWN, THE (TF) .... Georg J. Fenady
NIGHT THE CITY SCREAMED, THE (TF) .... Harry Falk
NIGHT THE LIGHTS WENT OUT IN GEORGIA, THE ..... Ronald F. Maxwell
NIGHT THE PROWLER, THE .... Jim Sharman
NIGHT THEY RAIDED MINSKY'S, THE .... William Friedkin
NIGHT THEY SAVED CHRISTMAS, THE (TF) .... Jackie Cooper
NIGHT THEY TOOK MISS BEAUTIFUL, THE (TF) .... Robert M. Lewis
NIGHT TIDE .... Curtis Harrington
NIGHT TO REMEMBER, A .... Roy Ward Baker
NIGHT UNTO NIGHT .... Don Siegel
NIGHT VISITOR, THE .... Laslo Benedek
NIGHT WARNING .... William Asher
NIGHT WAS OUR FRIEND ..... Michael Anderson
NIGHT WATCH .... Brian G. Hutton
NIGHT WITHOUT SLEEP .... Roy Ward Baker
NIGHTCOMERS, THE .... Michael Winner
NIGHTHAWKS .... Bruce Malmuth
NIGHTINGALE SAGA, THE (TF) .... Daryl Duke
NIGHTINGALE SANG IN BERKELEY SQUARE, A .... Ralph Thomas
NIGHTKILL (TF) .... Ted Post
NIGHTMARE .... Freddie Francis
NIGHTMARE (TF) .... William "Billy" Hale
NIGHTMARE HONEYMOON .... Elliot Silverstein
NIGHTMARE IN BADHAM COUNTY (TF) .... John Llewellyn Moxey
NIGHTMARE IN CHICAGO (TF) .... Robert Altman
NIGHTMARE IN WAX .... Bud Townsend
NIGHTMARE ON ELM STREET, A .... Wes Craven
NIGHTMARES .... Joseph Sargent
NIGHTS OF CABIRIA .... Federico Fellini
NIGHTSHADE FLOWER .... Kon Ichikawa
NIGHTSIDE (TF) .... Bernard L. Kowalski
NIGHTWING .... Arthur Hiller
NIHON-MARU SHIP (FD) .... Masahiro Shinoda
NIJINSKY .... Herbert Ross
NIKKI, WILD DOG OF THE NORTH .... Jack Couffer
NINE DAYS A QUEEN .... Robert Stevenson
NINE LIVES OF FRITZ THE CAT, THE (AF) .... Robert Taylor
NINE TO FIVE .... Colin Higgins
NINJA III: THE DOMINATION .... Sam Firstenberg
NINTH CONFIGURATION, THE .... William Peter Blatty
NO APPARENT MOTIVE .... Penelope Spheeris
NO BLADE OF GRASS .... Cornel Wilde
NO CHILD'S LAND .... Marco Ferreri
NO DOWN PAYMENT .... Martin Ritt
NO DRUMS, NO BUGLES .... Clyde Ware
NO HIGHWAY .... Henry Koster
NO HIGHWAY IN THE SKY .... Henry Koster
NO KIDDING .... Gerald Thomas
NO LEAVE TO LOVE .... Charles Martin
NO LONGER ALONE .... Nicholas Webster
NO LOVE FOR JOHNNIE .... Ralph Thomas
NO, MAMA, NO (TF) .... Roland Joffé
NO MAN'S LAND .... Alain Tanner
NO MAN'S LAND (TF) .... Rod Holcomb
NO MAPS ON MY TAPS (FD) .... George T. Nierenberg
NO MORE EXCUSES .... Robert Downey
NO, MY DARLING DAUGHTER .... Ralph Thomas
NO NAME ON THE BULLET .... Jack Arnold
NO NUKES (FD) .... Julian Schlossberg
NO OTHER LOVE (TF) .... Richard Pearce
NO PLACE TO GO .... Mervyn Leroy
NO PLACE TO HIDE .... Robert A. Schnitzer
NO PLACE TO HIDE (TF) .... John Llewellyn Moxey
NO PLACE TO RUN (TF) .... Delbert Mann
NO REGRETS FOR OUR YOUTH .... Akira Kurosawa
NO ROOM TO RUN (TF) .... Robert M. Lewis
NO SEX PLEASE - WE'RE BRITISH .... Cliff Owen
NO SMALL AFFAIR .... Jerry Schatzberg
NO SUN IN VENICE .... Roger Vadim
NO TIME FOR FLOWERS .... Don Siegel
NO TIME FOR SERGEANTS .... Mervyn Leroy

NO TIME TO BE YOUNG ...... David Lowell Rich
NO TIME TO DIE .... Terence Young
NO TREES IN THE STREET .... J. Lee Thompson
NO WAY BACK .... Fred Williamson
NO WAY OUT .... Joseph L. Mankiewicz
NO WAY TO TREAT A LADY .... Jack Smight
NOB HILL .... Henry Hathaway
NOBODY LIVES FOREVER .... Jean Negulesco
NOBODY RUNS FOREVER .... Ralph Thomas
NOBODY WAVED GOODBYE .... Don Owen
NOBODY'S PERFECT .... Alan Rafkin
NOBODY'S PERFEKT .... Peter Bonerz
NOCTURNA .... Harry Hurwitz
NOI DONNE SIAMO FATTE COSI .... Dino Risi
NOMADS .... John McTiernan
NON STUZZICATE LA ZANZARA .... Lina Wertmuller
NONE BUT THE BRAVE .... Frank Sinatra
NONE SHALL ESCAPE .... Andre De Toth
NON-STOP NEW YORK .... Robert Stevenson
NOR THE MOON BY NIGHT .... Ken Annakin
NORA PRENTISS .... Vincent Sherman
NORLISS TAPES, THE (TF) .... Dan Curtis
NORMA RAE .... Martin Ritt
NORMAN LOVES ROSE .... Henri Safran
NORMANDE .... Gilles Carle
NORMAN...IS THAT YOU? .... George Schlatter
NOROIT .... Jacques Rivette
NORSEMEN, THE .... Charles B. Pierce
NORTH AVENUE IRREGULARS, THE .... Bruce Bilson
NORTH DALLAS FORTY .... Ted Kotcheff
NORTH SEA HIJACK .... Andrew V. McLaglen
NORTH TO ALASKA .... Henry Hathaway
NORTH WEST FRONTIER .... J. Lee Thompson
NORTHERN LIGHTS .... John Hanson
NORTHERN LIGHTS .... Rob Nilsson
NORWOOD .... Jack Haley, Jr.
NOSFERATU THE VAMPYRE .... Werner Herzog
NOSTALGHIA .... Andrei Tarkovsky
NOT A PRETTY PICTURE .... Martha Coolidge
NOT AS A STRANGER .... Stanley Kramer
NOT FOR PUBLICATION .... Paul Bartel
NOT IN FRONT OF THE CHILDREN (TF) .... Joseph Hardy
NOT JUST ANOTHER AFFAIR (TF) .... Steven Hillard Stern
NOT OF THIS EARTH .... Roger Corman
NOT QUITE JERUSALEM .... Lewis Gilbert
NOT WITH MY WIFE, YOU DON'T! .... Norman Panama
NOTHING BUT A MAN .... Michael Roemer
NOTHING BUT A MAN .... Robert M. Young
NOTHING BUT THE BEST .... Clive Donner
NOTHING BUT THE NIGHT .... Peter Sasdy
NOTHING LASTS FOREVER .... Tom Schiller
NOTHING PERSONAL .... George Bloomfield
NOTORIOUS LANDLADY, THE .... Richard Quine
NOTRE HISTOIRE .... Bertrand Blier
NOUS DEUX, A .... Claude Lelouch
NOUS IRONS TOUS AU PARADIS .... Yves Robert
NOVE OSPITI PER UN DELITTO .... Ferdinando Baldi
NOVEMBER PLAN, THE .... Don Medford
NOW AND FOREVER .... Henry Hathaway
NOW, VOYAGER .... Irving Rapper
NOW YOU SEE HIM, NOW YOU DON'T .... Robert Butler
NOW YOU SEE IT, NOW YOU DON'T (TF) .... Don Weis
NOWHERE TO HIDE (TF) .... Jack Starrett
NOWHERE TO RUN (TF) .... Richard Lang
NUCLEO ZERO .... Carlo Lizzani
NUDE BOMB, THE .... Clive Donner
NUDE RESTAURANT .... Andy Warhol
NUMBER ONE .... Les Blair
NUMBER 96 (MS) .... David Stevens
NUMBERED MEN .... Mervyn Leroy
NUMERO DEUX .... Jean-Luc Godard
NUN, THE .... Jacques Rivette
NUN'S STORY ★, THE .... Fred Zinnemann
NUNZIO .... Paul Williams
NUR ZUM SPASS - NUR ZUM SPIEL (TD) .... Volker Schlondorff
NURSE (TF) .... David Lowell Rich
NURSE ON WHEELS .... Gerald Thomas
NURSE SHERRI .... Al Adamson
NUTTY, NAUGHTY CHATEAU .... Roger Vadim
NUTTY PROFESSOR, THE .... Jerry Lewis
NYBYGGARNA .... Jan Troell

O

O. HENRY'S FULL HOUSE .... Henry Hathaway
O. HENRY'S FULL HOUSE .... Henry Koster
O. HENRY'S FULL HOUSE .... Jean Negulesco
O LUCKY MAN! .... Lindsay Anderson
OASIS, THE .... Sparky Greene
OBLOMOV .... Nikita Mikhalkov
OBLONG BOX, THE .... Gordon Hessler
OBSCURED BY CLOUDS .... Barbet Schroeder
OBSESSION .... Brian De Palma
OBSESSION .... Edward Dmytryk
OBSESSIVE LOVE (TF) .... Steven Hillard Stern
O.C. AND STIGGS .... Robert Altman
OCTAGON, THE .... Eric Karson
OCTAVIA .... David Beaird
OCTOBER MAN, THE .... Roy Ward Baker
OCTOPUSSY .... John Glen
ODD COUPLE, THE .... Gene Saks
ODD JOB, THE .... Peter Medak
ODD OBSESSION .... Kon Ichikawa
ODDS AGAINST TOMORROW .... Robert Wise
ODE TO BILLY JOE .... Max Baer, Jr.
ODESSA FILE, THE .... Ronald Neame
OEDIPUS THE KING .... Philip Saville
OF FLESH AND BLOOD .... Roger Vadim
OF HUMAN BONDAGE .... Kenneth "Ken" Hughes
OF LOVE AND DESIRE .... Richard Rush
OF MICE AND MEN (TF) .... Reza Badiyi
OF UNKNOWN ORIGIN .... George Pan Cosmatos
OFF SIDES (TF) .... Dick Lowry
OFF THE EDGE .... Michael Firth
OFF THE MINNESOTA STRIP (TF) .... Lamont Johnson
OFF THE WALL .... Rick Friedberg
OFFBEAT .... Cliff Owen
OFFENSE, THE .... Sidney Lumet
OFFICER AND A GENTLEMAN, AN .... Taylor Hackford
OGGI, DOMANI E DOPODOMANI .... Marco Ferreri
OGGI, DOMANI E DOPODOMANI .... Luciano Salce
OH! BABY, BABY, BABY... (TF) .... Howard Morris
OH DAD, POOR DAD, MOMMA'S HUNG YOU IN THE CLOSET AND I'M FEELING SO SAD .... Richard Quine
OH, GOD! BOOK II .... Gilbert Cates
OH, GOD! YOU DEVIL .... Paul Bogart
OH, GOD! .... Carl Reiner
OH HEAVENLY DOG .... Joe Camp
OH KAY! .... Mervyn Leroy
OH, QUE MAMBO .... John Berry
OH ROSALINDA! .... Michael Powell
OH, SERAFINA .... Alberto Lattuada
OH! ALFIE .... Kenneth "Ken" Hughes
OH! WHAT A LOVELY WAR .... Richard Attenborough
O'HARA'S WIFE .... William S. Bartman
OHMS (TF) .... Dick Lowry
OIL FOR THE LAMPS OF CHINA .... Mervyn Leroy
OKAY BILL .... John G. Avildsen
OKLAHOMA CITY DOLLS, THE (TF) .... E.W. Swackhamer
OKLAHOMA CRUDE .... Stanley Kramer
OKLAHOMA WOMAN, THE .... Roger Corman
OKLAHOMA! .... Fred Zinnemann
OLD ACQUAINTANCE .... Vincent Sherman
OLD BOYFRIENDS .... Joan Tewkesbury
OLD CITY to KOTO, THE .... Kon Ichikawa
OLD DRACULA .... Clive Donner
OLD ENOUGH .... Marisa Silver
OLD-FASHIONED GIRL, AN .... Arthur Dreifuss
OLD GUN, THE .... Robert Enrico
OLD MAC .... Michael Winner
OLD MAN AND THE SEA, THE .... John Sturges
OLD MAN WHO CRIED WOLF, THE (TF) .... Walter Grauman
OLD YELLER .... Robert Stevenson
OLDEST PROFESSION, THE .... Philippe de Broca
OLDEST PROFESSION, THE ..... Jean-Luc Godard
OLIVER TWIST .... David Lean
OLIVER TWIST (TF) .... Clive Donner
OLIVER'S STORY .... John Korty
OLLY OLLY OXEN FREE .... Richard A. Colla
OMEGA CONNECTION, THE (TF) .... Robert Clouse
OMEN, THE .... Richard Donner
ON A CLEAR DAY YOU CAN SEE FOREVER .... Vincente Minnelli
ON A VOLE LA CRUISSE DE JUPITER .... Philippe de Broca
ON FRIDAY AT ELEVEN .... Alvin Rakoff
ON GOLDEN POND ★ .... Mark Rydell
ON HER BED OF ROSES .... Albert Zugsmith
ON HER MAJESTY'S SECRET SERVICE .... Peter Hunt
ON THE BEACH .... Stanley Kramer
ON THE BOWERY (FD) .... Lionel Rogosin
ON THE DOUBLE .... Melville Shavelson
ON THE EDGE .... Rob Nilsson
ON THE NICKEL .... Ralph Waite
ON THE RIGHT TRACK .... Lee Philips
ON THE SPANISH TRAIL .... William Witney
ON THE TOWN .... Stanley Donen
ON THE TOWN .... Gene Kelly
ON THE WATERFRONT ★★ .... Elia Kazan
ON THE YARD .... Raphael D. Silver
ONCE A SINNER .... Lewis Gilbert
ONCE A THIEF .... Ralph Nelson
ONCE AN EAGLE (MS) .... Richard Michaels
ONCE AN EAGLE (MS) .... E.W. Swackhamer
ONCE BEFORE I DIE .... John Derek
ONCE IN PARIS... .... Frank D. Gilroy
ONCE MORE, WITH FEELING .... Stanley Donen
ONCE UPON A DEAD MAN (TF) .... Leonard B. Stern
ONCE UPON A DREAM .... Ralph Thomas
ONCE UPON A FAMILY (TF) ... Richard Michaels
ONCE UPON A HORSE .... Hal Kanter
ONCE UPON A SCOUNDREL .... George Schaefer
ONCE UPON A SPY (TF) .... Ivan Nagy
ONCE UPON A TIME IN AMERICA .... Sergio Leone
ONCE UPON A TIME IN THE WEST .... Sergio Leone
ONE A.M. .... Jean-Luc Godard
ONE AND ONLY GENUINE, ORIGINAL FAMILY BAND, THE .... Michael O'Herlihy
ONE AND ONLY, THE .... Carl Reiner
ONE BRIEF SUMMER .... John Mackenzie
ONE COOKS, THE OTHER DOESN'T (TF) .... Richard Michaels
ONE DANGEROUS NIGHT .... Michael Gordon
ONE DAY IN THE LIFE OF IVAN DENISOVICH .... Casper Wrede
ONE DESIRE .... Jerry Hopper
ONE DOWN TWO TO GO .... Fred Williamson
ONE FLEW OVER THE CUCKOO'S NEST ★★ .... Milos Forman
ONE FOOT IN HEAVEN .... Irving Rapper
ONE FOOT IN HELL .... James B. Clark
ONE FROM THE HEART ... Francis Ford Coppola
ONE IN A MILLION: THE RON LEFLORE STORY (TF) .... William A. Graham
ONE IS A LONELY NUMBER .... Mel Stuart
ONE LITTLE INDIAN .... Bernard McEveety
ONE MAN .... Robin Spry
ONE MAN JURY .... Charles Martin
ONE MAN'S LAW .... George Sherman
ONE MAN'S WAY .... Denis Sanders
ONE MILLION YEARS B.C. .... Don Chaffey
ONE MORE CHANCE .... Sam Firstenberg
ONE MORE TIME .... Jerry Lewis
ONE MORE TRAIN TO ROB .... Andrew V. McLaglen
ONE MYSTERIOUS NIGHT .... Budd Boetticher
ONE NIGHT STAND .... John Duigan
ONE NIGHT WITH YOU .... Terence Young
ONE OF A KIND (TF) .... Harry Winer
ONE OF MY WIVES IS MISSING (TF) .... Glenn Jordan
ONE OF OUR AIRCRAFT IS MISSING .... Michael Powell
ONE OF OUR DINOSAURS IS MISSING .... Robert Stevenson
ONE OF OUR OWN (TF) ...... Richard C. Sarafian
ONE ON ONE .... Lamont Johnson

ONE POTATO, TWO POTATO ... Larry Peerce
ONE SHOE MAKES IT MURDER (TF) ... William "Billy" Hale
ONE SINGS, THE OTHER DOESN'T ... Agnes Varda
ONE SPY TOO MANY ... Joseph Sargent
ONE SUMMER LOVE ... Gilbert Cates
ONE THAT GOT AWAY, THE ... Roy Ward Baker
ONE, TWO, THREE ... Billy Wilder
ONE WAY ... Sidney Hayers
ONE WAY PENDULUM ... Peter Yates
ONE WAY TICKET TO LOVE ... Masahiro Shinoda
ONE WILD MOMENT ... Claude Berri
ONE WOMAN'S STORY ... David Lean
ONE WONDERFUL SUNDAY ... Akira Kurosawa
ONE-EYED JACKS ... Marlon Brando
ONE-NIGHT STAND ... Allan King
ONE-TRICK PONY ... Robert M. Young
ONIBABA ... Kaneto Shindo
ONION FIELD, THE ... Harold Becker
ONLY A WAITER ... Alf Kjellin
ONLY THE VALIANT ... Gordon Douglas
ONLY WAY HOME, THE ... G.D. Spradlin
ONLY WITH MARRIED MEN (TF) ... Jerry Paris
OOH...YOU ARE AWFUL ... Cliff Owen
OPENING NIGHT ... John Cassavetes
OPENING OF MISTY BEETHOVEN, THE ... Radley Metzger
OPERATION CROSSBOW ... Michael Anderson
OPERATION DAYBREAK ... Lewis Gilbert
OPERATION DIPLOMAT ... John Guillermin
OPERATION DISASTER ... Roy Ward Baker
OPERATION MAD BALL ... Richard Quine
OPERATION OGRO ... Gillo Pontecorvo
OPERATION PETTICOAT ... Blake Edwards
OPERATION PETTICOAT (TF) ... John Astin
OPERATION SNATCH ... Robert Day
OPERATION THUNDERBOLT ... Menahem Golan
OPERAZIONE SAN GENNARO ... Dino Risi
OPHELIA ... Claude Chabrol
OPPENHEIMER (MS) ... Barry Davis
OPPOSITE SEX, THE ... David Miller
OPTIMISTS, THE ... Anthony Simmons
OPTIMISTS OF NINE ELMS, THE ... Anthony Simmons
ORCA ... Michael Anderson
ORCHESTRA REHEARSAL ... Federico Fellini
ORDEAL (TF) ... Lee H. Katzin
ORDEAL BY INNOCENCE ... Desmond Davis
ORDEAL OF BILL CARNEY, THE (TF) ... Jerry London
ORDEAL OF DR. MUDD, THE (TF) ... Paul Wendkos
ORDEAL OF PATTY HEARST, THE (TF) ... Paul Wendkos
ORDINARY PEOPLE ★★ ... Robert Redford
ORGANIZATION, THE ... Don Medford
ORGANIZER, THE ... Mario Monicelli
ORIGIN OF SEX ... Kaneto Shindo
ORPHAN TRAIN (TF) ... William A. Graham
OSCAR ... Edouard Molinaro
OSCAR GOES TO WAR (TD) ... Mel Stuart
OSCAR, THE ... Russell Rouse
OSTERMAN WEEKEND, THE ... Sam Peckinpah
OT ORA 40 ... Andre De Toth
OTHELLO ... Stuart Burge
OTHELLO ... Orson Welles
OTHER HALF OF THE SKY: A CHINA MEMOIR, THE (FD) ... Claudia Weill
OTHER LOVER, THE ... Andre De Toth
OTHER MAN, THE (TF) ... Richard A. Colla
OTHER SIDE OF MIDNIGHT, THE ... Charles Jarrott
OTHER SIDE OF THE MOUNTAIN - PART 2, THE ... Larry Peerce
OTHER SIDE OF THE MOUNTAIN, THE ... Larry Peerce
OTHER SIDE OF THE WIND, THE ... Orson Welles
OTHER, THE ... Robert Mulligan
OTHER VICTIM, THE (TF) ... Noel Black
OTHER WOMAN, THE (TF) ... Melville Shavelson
OTLEY ... Dick Clement
OUR FAMILY BUSINESS (TF) ... Robert Collins
OUR LAST SPRING ... Michael Cacoyannis
OUR MAN FLINT ... Daniel Mann
OUR MAN IN MARRAKESH ... Don Sharp
OUR MARRIAGE ... Masahiro Shinoda
OUR MOTHER'S HOUSE ... Jack Clayton
OUR TIME ... Peter Hyams
OUR VERY OWN ... David Miller
OUR WINNING SEASON ... Joseph Ruben
OUT OF CONTROL ... Allan Holzman
OUT OF IT ... Paul Williams
OUT OF SEASON ... Alan Bridges
OUT OF THE BLUE ... Dennis Hopper
OUT OF THE DARKNESS ... Lee Madden
OUT OF THE SHADOW ... Michael Winner
OUT 1: SPECTRE ... Jacques Rivette
OUTBACK ... Ted Kotcheff
OUTCAST, THE ... William Witney
OUTER AND INNER SPACE ... Andy Warhol
OUTFIT, THE ... John Flynn
OUTLAND ... Peter Hyams
OUTLANDERS, THE ... Richard L. Bare
OUTLAW BLUES ... Richard T. Heffron
OUTLAW JOSEY WALES, THE ... Clint Eastwood
OUTLAWS, THE (TF) ... James Frawley
OUTLAWS OF PINE RIDGE ... William Witney
OUTLAWS OF SONORA ... George Sherman
OUT-OF-TOWNERS, THE ... Arthur Hiller
OUTPOST IN MALAYA ... Ken Annakin
OUTRAGE ... Ida Lupino
OUTRAGE, THE ... Martin Ritt
OUTRAGE! (TF) ... Richard T. Heffron
OUTRAGEOUS! ... Richard Benner
OUTSIDE CHANCE (TF) ... Michael Miller
OUTSIDE MAN, THE ... Jacques Deray
OUTSIDE THE LAW ... Jack Arnold
OUTSIDER, THE ... Roy Boulting
OUTSIDER, THE (TF) ... William A. Graham
OUTSIDER, THE (TF) ... Michael Ritchie
OUTSIDER, THE ... Tony Luraschi
OUTSIDER, THE ... Delbert Mann
OUTSIDERS, THE ... Francis Ford Coppola
OUTTAKES ... Jack M. Sell
OVER THE BROOKLYN BRIDGE ... Menahem Golan
OVER THE EDGE ... Jonathan Kaplan
OVER THE SUMMER ... Teresa Sparks
OVERBOARD (TF) ... John Newland
OVERLAND STAGE RAIDERS ... George Sherman
OVERLORD ... Stuart Cooper
OVER-THE-HILL GANG RIDES AGAIN, THE (TF) ... George McCowan
OVER-UNDER, SIDEWAYS-DOWN ... Eugene Corr
OVER-UNDER, SIDEWAYS-DOWN ... Peter Gessner
OVER-UNDER, SIDEWAYS-DOWN ... Steve Wax
OWAIN GLYNDWR - PRINCE OF WALES (TF) ... James Hill
OWD BOB ... Robert Stevenson
OWEN MARSHALL, COUNSELOR AT LAW (TF) ... Buzz Kulik
OWL AND THE PUSSYCAT, THE ... Herbert Ross
OXFORD BLUES ... Robert Boris
OZ ... Walter Murch

P

PACIFIC RENDEZVOUS ... George Sidney
PACK, THE ... Robert Clouse
PACKIN' IT IN (TF) ... Jud Taylor
PACO ... Robert Vincent O'Neil
PAD (...AND HOW TO USE IT), THE ... Brian G. Hutton
PADDY ... Daniel Haller
PADRE PADRONE ... Paolo Taviani
PADRE PADRONE ... Vittorio Taviani
PADRI E FIGLI ... Mario Monicelli
PAEAN, A ... Kaneto Shindo
PAGE MISS GLORY ... Mervyn Leroy
PAID VACATION, A (TF) ... Ralph L. Thomas
PAIN IN THE A–, A ... Edouard Molinaro
PAINT YOUR WAGON ... Joshua Logan
PAINTED BOATS ... Charles Crichton
PAINTERS PAINTING (FD) ... Emile de Antonio
PAIR OF BRIEFS, A ... Ralph Thomas
PAJAMA GAME, THE ... George Abbott
PAJAMA GAME, THE ... Stanley Donen
PAJAMA PARTY ... Don Weis
PAL JOEY ... George Sidney
PALACE ... Edouard Molinaro
PALE FLOWER ... Masahiro Shinoda
PALE RIDER ... Clint Eastwood
PALMERSTOWN, U.S.A. (TF) ... Peter Levin
PALS OF THE SADDLE ... George Sherman
PANACHE (TF) ... Gary Nelson
PANAMA SAL ... William Witney
PANDEMONIUM ... Alfred Sole
PANE, AMORE E... ... Dino Risi
PANE, AMORE E GELOSIA ... Luigi Comencini
PANIC BUTTON ... George Sherman
PANIC IN ECHO PARK (TF) ... John Llewellyn Moxey
PANIC IN NEEDLE PARK ... Jerry Schatzberg
PANIC IN THE STREETS ... Elia Kazan
PANIC ON THE 5:22 (TF) ... Harvey Hart
PANORAMA BLUE ... Alan Roberts
PANTALOONS ... John Berry
PAPA LES PETITS BATEAUX ... Nelly Kaplan
PAPER CHASE, THE ... James Bridges
PAPER DOLLS (TF) ... Harry Winer
PAPER DOLLS (TF) ... Edward Zwick
PAPER LION ... Alex March
PAPER MAN (TF) ... Walter Grauman
PAPER MOON ... Peter Bogdanovich
PAPER ORCHID ... Roy Ward Baker
PAPER TIGER ... Ken Annakin
PAPILLON ... Franklin J. Schaffner
PAR UN BEAU MATIN D'ETE ... Jacques Deray
PARADE, THE (TF) ... Peter H. Hunt
PARADES ... Robert J. Siegel
PARADISE ... Stuart Gillard
PARADISE ALLEY ... Sylvester Stallone
PARADISE CONNECTION (TF) ... Michael Preece
PARADISE LAGOON ... Lewis Gilbert
PARALLAX VIEW, THE ... Alan J. Pakula
PARANOIAC ... Freddie Francis
PARAS PATHAR ... Satyajit Ray
PARASITE ... Charles Band
PARATROOP COMMAND ... William Witney
PARATROOPER ... Terence Young
PARDON MON AFFAIRE ... Yves Robert
PARDON MON AFFAIRE, TOO! ... Yves Robert
PARENT TRAP, THE ... David Swift
PARI E DISPARI ... Sergio Corbucci
PARIS BELONGS TO US ... Jacques Rivette
PARIS BLUES ... Martin Ritt
PARIS HOLIDAY ... Gerd Oswald
PARIS S'EN VA ... Jacques Rivette
PARIS, TEXAS ... Wim Wenders
PARIS VU PAR... ... Claude Chabrol
PARIS VU PAR... ... Eric Rohmer
PARIS WHEN IT SIZZLES ... Richard Quine
PARIS-PALACE-HOTEL ... Henri Verneuil
PARK IS MINE, THE (CTF) ... Steven Hillard Stern
PARK ROW ... Samuel Fuller
PAROLA DI LADRO ... Nanni Loy
PAROLE (TF) ... Michael Tuchner
PARSIFAL ... Hans-Jurgen Syberberg
PART 2 SOUNDER ... William A. Graham
PART 2 WALKING TALL ... Earl Bellamy
PARTIR REVENIR ... Claude Lelouch
PARTNER ... Bernardo Bertolucci
PARTNERS ... James Burrows
PARTNERS ... Andre Guttfreund
PARTNERS ... Don Owen
PARTNERS IN CRIME ... Peter John Duffell
PARTNERS IN CRIME (TF) ... Jack Smight
PARTY ANIMAL ... David Beaird
PARTY CRASHERS, THE ... Bernard Girard
PARTY, THE ... Blake Edwards
PARTY'S OVER, THE ... Guy Hamilton
PAS SI MERCHANT QUE CA... ... Claude Goretta
PASQUALINO SETTEBELLEZZE ★ ... Lina Wertmuller
PASSAGE HOME ... Roy Ward Baker
PASSAGE, THE ... J. Lee Thompson
PASSAGE TO INDIA, A ... David Lean
PASSENGER, THE ... Michelangelo Antonioni
PASSION ... Jean-Luc Godard
PASSION OF ANNA, THE ... Ingmar Bergman

PASSION OF SLOW FIRE, THE .... Edouard Molinaro
PASSIONATE FRIENDS, THE .... David Lean
PASSIONATE THIEF, THE .... Mario Monicelli
PASSIONE D'AMORE .... Ettore Scola
PASSIONS (TF) .... Sandor Stern
PASSOVER PLOT, THE .... Michael Campus
PASSPORT TO CHINA .... Michael Carreras
PASSPORT TO SHAME .... Alvin Rakoff
PASSPORT TO SUEZ .... Andre De Toth
PASSWORD IS COURAGE, THE .... Andrew L. Stone
PASTOR HALL .... Roy Boulting
PAT GARRETT & BILLY THE KID .... Sam Peckinpah
PATCH OF BLUE, A .... Guy Green
PATERNITY .... David Steinberg
PATHER PANCHALI .... Satyajit Ray
PATHS OF GLORY .... Stanley Kubrick
PATRICIA NEAL STORY, THE (TF) .... Anthony Harvey
PATRICIA NEAL STORY, THE (TF) .... Anthony Page
PATRICK .... Richard Franklin
PATSY, THE .... Jerry Lewis
PATTERNS .... Fielder Cook
PATTON ★★ .... Franklin J. Schaffner
PAUL AND MICHELLE .... Lewis Gilbert
PAUL SWAN .... Andy Warhol
PAULINE AT THE BEACH .... Eric Rohmer
PAUL'S CASE (TF) .... Lamont Johnson
PAWNBROKER, THE .... Sidney Lumet
PAY OR DIE .... Richard Wilson
PAYDAY .... Daryl Duke
PAY-OFF, THE .... Arthur Dreifuss
PEACEMAKER, THE .... Ted Post
PEARL (TF) .... Hy Averback
PEAU D'ESPION .... Edouard Molinaro
PEDESTRIAN, THE .... Maximilian Schell
PEEPER .... Peter Hyams
PEEPING TOM .... Michael Powell
PEKING MEDALLION, THE .... James Hill
PELE (FD) .... Francois Reichenbach
PEMBERTON VALLEY (FD) .... Allan King
PENDULUM .... George Schaefer
PENELOPE .... Arthur Hiller
PENITENTIARY .... Jamaa Fanaka
PENITENTIARY II .... Jamaa Fanaka
PENNIES FROM HEAVEN .... Herbert Ross
PENNY GOLD .... Jack Cardiff
PENNY PRINCESS .... Val Guest
PEOPLE, THE (TF) .... John Korty
PEOPLE AGAINST O'HARA, THE .... John Sturges
PEOPLE NEXT DOOR, THE .... David Greene
PEOPLE THAT TIME FORGOT, THE .... Kevin Connor
PEOPLE WILL TALK .... Joseph L. Mankiewicz
PEOPLE'S WAR (FD) .... Robert Kramer
PEPE .... George Sidney
PEPPERMINT FRAPPE .... Carlos Saura
PEPPERMINT SODA .... Diane Kurys
PERCEVAL .... Eric Rohmer
PERCEVAL LE GALLOIS .... Eric Rohmer
PERCY .... Ralph Thomas
PERCY'S PROGRESS .... Ralph Thomas
PERFECT! .... James Bridges
PERFECT COUPLE, A .... Robert Altman
PERFECT FRIDAY .... Peter Hall
PERFECT FURLOUGH, THE .... Blake Edwards
PERFECT GENTLEMEN (TF) .... Jackie Cooper
PERFECT MATCH, A (TF) .... Mel Damski
PERFORMANCE .... Donald Cammell
PERFORMANCE .... Nicolas Roeg
PERIL FOR THE GUY .... James Hill
PERILOUS VOYAGE (TF) .... William A. Graham
PERILS OF GWENDOLINE, THE .... Just Jaeckin
PERILS OF PAULINE, THE ... Herbert B. Leonard
PERIOD OF ADJUSTMENT .... George Roy Hill
PERMANENT VACATION .... Jim Jarmusch
PERSECUTION .... Don Chaffey
PERSECUTION AND ASSASINATION OF JEAN-PAUL MARAT AS PERFORMED BY THE INMATES OF THE ASYLUM OF CHARENTON UNDER THE DIRECTION OF THE MARQUIS DE SADE .... Peter Brook
PERSIANE CHIUSE .... Luigi Comencini
PERSONA .... Ingmar Bergman
PERSONAL BEST .... Robert Towne
PERSONALITY KID .... George Sherman
PERSONALS, THE .... Peter Markle
PERSUADERS, THE .... Val Guest
PETE N' TILLIE .... Martin Ritt
PETE SEEGER...A SONG AND A STONE (FD) .... Robert Elfstrom
PETER .... Henry Koster
PETER AND PAUL (TF) .... Robert Day
PETER IBBETSON .... Henry Hathaway
PETER LUNDY AND THE MEDICINE HAT STALLION (TF) .... Michael O'Herlihy
PETER RABBIT & TALES OF BEATRIX POTTER .... Reginald Mills
PETE'S DRAGON .... Don Chaffey
PETRIFIED FOREST, THE .... Masahiro Shinoda
PETULIA .... Richard Lester
PEUR SUR LA VILLE .... Henri Verneuil
PHAEDRA .... Jules Dassin
PHANTASM .... Don Coscarelli
PHANTOM COWBOY, THE .... George Sherman
PHANTOM INDIA (TD) .... Louis Malle
PHANTOM LIGHT, THE .... Michael Powell
PHANTOM OF HOLLYWOOD, THE .... Gene Levitt
PHANTOM OF THE OPEN HEARTH, THE (TF) .... Fred Barzyk
PHANTOM OF THE OPEN HEARTH, THE (TF) .... David R. Loxton
PHANTOM OF THE OPERA (TF) .... Robert Markowitz
PHANTOM OF THE PARADISE .... Brian De Palma
PHAR LAP .... Simon Wincer
PHASE IV .... Saul Bass
PHENIX CITY STORY, THE .... Phil Karlson
PHENOMENA .... Dario Argento
PHILADELPHIA, HERE I COME .... John Quested
PHILIP MARLOWE - PRIVATE EYE .... David Wickes
PHILIP MARLOWE - PRIVATE EYE (CMS) .... Bryan Forbes
PHILIP MARLOWE - PRIVATE EYE (CMS) .... Sidney Hayers
PHILIP MARLOWE - PRIVATE EYE (CMS) .... Peter Hunt
PHOBIA .... John Huston
PHOENIX, THE (TF) .... Douglas Hickox
PHONE CALL FROM A STRANGER .... Jean Negulesco
PHOTOGRAPHER, THE .... William Byron Hillman
PHYNX, THE .... Lee H. Katzin
PIANO FOR MRS. CIMINO, A (TF) .... George Schaefer
PICKPOCKET .... Robert Bresson
PICKUP ON SOUTH STREET .... Samuel Fuller
PICK-UP SUMMER .... George Mihalka
PICNIC ★ .... Joshua Logan
PICNIC AT HANGING ROCK .... Peter Weir
PICTURE MOMMY DEAD .... Bert I. Gordon
PICTURE OF DORIAN GRAY, THE (TF) .... Glenn Jordan
PIDGEON THAT TOOK ROME, THE .... Melville Shavelson
PIECE OF THE ACTION, A .... Sidney Poitier
PIECES OF DREAMS .... Daniel Haller
PIED PIPER, THE .... Jacques Demy
PIERROT LE FOU .... Jean-Luc Godard
PIGEON, THE (TF) .... Earl Bellamy
PIGEONS .... John Dexter
PIGS AND BATTLESHIPS .... Shohei Imamura
PILATUS UND ANDERE (TF) .... Andrzej Wajda
PILGRIM, FAREWELL .... Michael Roemer
PILLOW TALK .... Michael Gordon
PILLOW TO POST .... Vincent Sherman
PILOT, THE .... Cliff Robertson
PILOT NO. 5 .... George Sidney
PINBALL SUMMER .... George Mihalka
PINE CANYON IS BURNING (TF) .... Christian Nyby II
PINK FLAMINGOS .... John Waters
PINK FLOYD - THE WALL .... Alan Parker
PINK JUNGLE, THE .... Delbert Mann
PINK PANTHER STRIKES AGAIN, THE .... Blake Edwards
PINK PANTHER, THE .... Blake Edwards
PINK TELEPHONE, THE .... Edouard Molinaro
PINKY .... Elia Kazan
PINOCCHIO .... Corey Allen
PIONEER WOMAN (TF) .... Buzz Kulik
PIPE DREAMS .... Stephen F. Verona
PIRANHA .... Joe Dante
PIRATE MOVIE, THE .... Ken Annakin
PIRATE, THE .... Vincente Minnelli
PIRATES .... Roman Polanski
PIRATES OF PENZANCE, THE .... Wilford Leach
PIRHANA II - THE SPAWNING .... James Cameron
PIT AND THE PENDULUM, THE .... Roger Corman
PIT STOP .... Jack Hill
PITFALL .... Andre De Toth
PIXOTE .... Hector Babenco
PIZZA TRIANGLE, THE .... Ettore Scola
P.J. .... John Guillermin
PLACE A OLIVIER GUIMOND .... Gilles Carle
PLACE AUX JEROLAS .... Gilles Carle
PLACE CALLED TODAY, A .... Don Schain
PLACE DE LA REPUBLIQUE (FD) .... Louis Malle
PLACES IN THE HEART .... Robert Benton
PLAGUE DOGS, THE (AF) .... Martin Rosen
PLAINSMAN, THE .... David Lowell Rich
PLANET EARTH (TF) .... Marc Daniels
PLANET OF THE APES ...... Franklin J. Schaffner
PLANTER'S WIFE, THE .... Ken Annakin
PLATINUM BLONDE .... Frank Capra
PLAY DEAD .... Peter Wittman
PLAY DIRTY .... Andre De Toth
PLAY IT AGAIN, SAM .... Herbert Ross
PLAY IT AS IT LAYS .... Frank Perry
PLAY IT COOL .... Michael Winner
PLAY IT COOLER .... Kenneth "Ken" Hughes
PLAY MISTY FOR ME .... Clint Eastwood
PLAYBOY OF THE WESTERN WORLD, THE (TF) .... Alan Gibson
PLAYERS .... Anthony Harvey
PLAYGIRL .... Joseph Pevney
PLAYGIRL AFTER DARK .... Terence Young
PLAYING AROUND .... Mervyn Leroy
PLAYING FOR TIME (TF) .... Daniel Mann
PLAYMATES (TF) .... Theodore J. Flicker
PLAZA SUITE .... Arthur Hiller
PLEASE, NOT NOW! .... Roger Vadim
PLEASE TURN OVER .... Gerald Thomas
PLEASURE COVE (TF) .... Bruce Bilson
PLEASURE GARDEN .... Alf Kjellin
PLEASURE GIRLS, THE .... Gerry O'Hara
PLEASURE PALACE (TF) .... Walter Grauman
PLEASURE SEEKERS, THE .... Jean Negulesco
PLEASURES OF THE FLESH, THE .... Nagisa Oshima
PLENTY .... Fred Schepisi
PLOUFFE FAMILY, THE .... Gilles Carle
PLOUGHMAN'S LUNCH, THE .... Richard Eyre
PLUMBER, THE .... Peter Weir
PLUNDER ROAD .... Hubert Cornfield
PLUNDERERS, THE .... Joseph Pevney
PLUTONIUM INCIDENT, THE (TF) .... Richard Michaels
POCKET MONEY .... Stuart Rosenberg
POCKETFUL OF MIRACLES .... Frank Capra
POEM IS A NAKED PERSON, A (FD) .... Les Blank
POETRY IN MOTION (FD) .... Ron Mann
POINT BLANK .... John Boorman
POINT OF ORDER (FD) .... Emile de Antonio
POISON IVY (TF) .... Larry Elikann
POLICE ACADEMY .... Hugh Wilson
POLICE ACADEMY II .... Jerry Paris
POLICE AND SMALL GANGSTERS .... Kon Ichikawa
POLICE CONNECTION, THE .... Bert I. Gordon
POLICE NURSE .... Maury Dexter
POLICE STORY (TF) .... William A. Graham
POLICEMAN, THE .... Ephraim Kishon
POLICEWOMAN CENTERFOLD (TF) .... Reza Badiyi
POLTERGEIST .... Tobe Hooper
POLLYANNA .... David Swift
POLYESTER .... John Waters
POM-POM GIRLS, THE .... Joseph Ruben
PONTIUS PILATE .... Irving Rapper
PONY EXPRESS .... Jerry Hopper
PONY EXPRESS RIDER .... Robert Totten
POOR BUT BEAUTIFUL .... Dino Risi
POOR COW .... Kenneth Loach
POOR DEVIL (TF) .... Robert Scheerer
POOR LITTLE RICH GIRL .... Andy Warhol
POPCORN (FD) .... Peter Clifton
POPE JOAN .... Michael Anderson
POPE JOHN PAUL II (TF) .... Herbert Wise

POPE OF GREENWICH VILLAGE, THE .... Stuart Rosenberg
POPEYE .... Robert Altman
POPI .... Arthur Hiller
POPPY IS ALSO A FLOWER, THE .... Terence Young
PORGY AND BESS .... Otto Preminger
PORKY'S .... Bob Clark
PORKY'S REVENGE .... James Komack
PORKY'S II: THE NEXT DAY .... Bob Clark
PORN FLAKES .... Chuck Vincent
PORNOGRAPHER, THE .... Shohei Imamura
PORRIDGE .... Dick Clement
PORT OF CALL .... Ingmar Bergman
PORT OF NEW YORK .... Laslo Benedek
PORTE CHIUSE, A .... Dino Risi
PORTNOY'S COMPLAINT .... Ernest Lehman
PORTRAIT IN BLACK .... Michael Gordon
PORTRAIT OF A MOBSTER .... Joseph Pevney
PORTRAIT OF A REBEL: MARGARET SANGER (TF) .... Virgil W. Vogel
PORTRAIT OF A SHOWGIRL (TF) .... Steven Hillard Stern
PORTRAIT OF A STRIPPER (TF) .... John A. Alonzo
PORTRAIT OF ALISON .... Guy Green
PORTRAIT OF AN ESCORT (TF) .... Steven Hillard Stern
PORTRAIT OF JASON (FD) .... Shirley Clarke
PORTRAIT OF THE ARTIST AS A YOUNG MAN, A .... Joseph Strick
POSEIDON ADVENTURE, THE .... Ronald Neame
POSSE .... Kirk Douglas
POSSESSED, THE (TF) .... Jerry Thorpe
POSSESSION OF JOEL DELANEY, THE .... Waris Hussein
POSTMAN ALWAYS RINGS TWICE, THE .... Bob Rafelson
POSTMARK FOR DANGER .... Guy Green
POULET AU VINAIGRE .... Claude Chabrol
POUND .... Robert Downey
POUR LE MEILLEUR ET POUR LE PIRE .... Claude Jutra
POUR 100 BRIQUES, T'AS PLUS RIEN! .... Edouard Molinaro
POVERI MILLIONARI .... Dino Risi
POWDERKEG (TF) .... Douglas Heyes
POWER (TF) .... Virgil W. Vogel
POWER AND THE PRIZE, THE .... Henry Koster
POWER OF THE PRESS, THE .... Frank Capra
POWER PLAY .... Martyn Burke
POWER, THE .... Stephen Carpenter
POWER, THE .... Jeffrey Obrow
POWER WITHIN, THE (TF) .... John Llewellyn Moxey
PRACTICE MAKES PERFECT .... Philippe de Broca
PRACTICE, THE .... John Hough
PRANKS .... Stephen Carpenter
PRANKS .... Jeffrey Obrow
PRAVDA (FD) .... Jean-Luc Godard
PRAY FOR DEATH .... Gordon Hessler
PRAY FOR THE WILDCATS (TF) .... Robert M. Lewis
PRAY TV .... Rick Friedberg
PRAY TV (TF) .... Robert Markowitz
PRAYING MANTIS .... Jack Gold
PREHISTORIC WOMEN .... Michael Carreras
PRELUDE TO WAR (FD) .... Frank Capra
PREMATURE BURIAL, THE .... Roger Corman
PREMIERE (TF) .... Istvan Szabo
PREMIERS DESIRS .... David Hamilton
PREMONITION .... Alan Rudolph
PREMONITION, THE .... Robert A. Schnitzer
PREPPIES .... Chuck Vincent
PRESCRIPTION: MURDER (TF) .... Richard Irving
PRESIDENT MUST DIE, THE .... James L. Conway
PRESIDENT'S ANALYST, THE .... Theodore J. Flicker
PRESIDENT'S MISTRESS, THE (TF) .... John Llewellyn Moxey
PRESIDENT'S PLANE IS MISSING, THE (TF) .... Daryl Duke
PRESSURE POINT .... Hubert Cornfield
PRETTY BABY .... Louis Malle
PRETTY MAIDS ALL IN A ROW .... Roger Vadim
PRETTY POISON .... Noel Black
PRETTY POLLY .... Guy Green
PRICE OF A SONG, THE .... Michael Powell
PRIDE AND THE PASSION, THE .... Stanley Kramer
PRIDE OF JESSE HALLAM, THE (TF) .... Gary Nelson
PRIEST KILLER, THE (TF) .... Richard A. Colla
PRIEST OF LOVE .... Christopher Miles
PRIEST'S WIFE, THE .... Dino Risi
PRIMATE (FD) .... Frederick Wiseman
PRIME CUT .... Michael Ritchie
PRIME OF MISS JEAN BRODIE, THE .... Ronald Neame
PRIME SUSPECT (TF) .... Noel Black
PRIMO AMORE .... Dino Risi
PRINCE AND THE GREAT RACE .... Henri Safran
PRINCE AND THE PAUPER, THE .... Don Chaffey
PRINCE AND THE PAUPER, THE .... Richard Fleischer
PRINCE AND THE SHOWGIRL, THE .... Laurence Olivier
PRINCE JACK .... Bert Lovitt
PRINCE OF CENTRAL PARK, THE (TF) .... Harvey Hart
PRINCE OF THE CITY .... Sidney Lumet
PRINCE VALIANT .... Henry Hathaway
PRINCESS AND THE CABBIE, THE (TF) .... Glenn Jordan
PRINCESS DAISY (MS) .... Waris Hussein
PRISON .... Andy Warhol
PRISON SHIP .... Arthur Dreifuss
PRISONER OF SECOND AVENUE, THE .... Melvin Frank
PRISONER OF WAR .... Andrew Marton
PRISONER OF ZENDA, THE .... Richard Quine
PRISONER, THE .... Peter Glenville
PRISONERS .... William J. Bushnell, Jr.
PRISONERS .... Peter Werner
PRISONERS OF THE CASBAH .... Richard L. Bare
PRISONERS OF THE LOST UNIVERSE (CTF) .... Terry Marcel
PRISONERS OF THE SEA .... Joseph Pevney
PRIVATE AFTERNOONS OF PAMELA MANN, THE .... Radley Metzger
PRIVATE ANGELO .... Michael Anderson
PRIVATE ANGELO .... Peter Ustinov
PRIVATE BATTLE, A (TF) .... Robert M. Lewis
PRIVATE BENJAMIN .... Howard Zieff
PRIVATE CONTENTMENT (TF) .... Vivian Matalon
PRIVATE DUTY NURSES .... George Armitage
PRIVATE EYES, THE .... Lang Elliott
PRIVATE FILES OF J. EDGAR HOOVER, THE .... Larry Cohen
PRIVATE HELL 36 .... Don Siegel
PRIVATE HISTORY OF A CAMPAIGN THAT FAILED, THE (TF) .... Peter H. Hunt
PRIVATE LESSONS .... Alan Myerson
PRIVATE LIFE OF SHERLOCK HOLMES, THE .... Billy Wilder
PRIVATE LIVES OF ADAM AND EVE, THE .... Albert Zugsmith
PRIVATE PARTS .... Paul Bartel
PRIVATE POPSICLE (LEMON POPSICLE IV) .... Boaz Davidson
PRIVATE POTTER .... Casper Wrede
PRIVATE PROPERTY .... Leslie Stevens
PRIVATE SCHOOL .... Noel Black
PRIVATE SESSIONS (TF) .... Michael Pressman
PRIVATE VICES - PUBLIC VIRTUE .... Miklos Jancso
PRIVATE WAR OF MAJOR BENSON, THE .... Jerry Hopper
PRIVATES ON PARADE .... Michael Blakemore
PRIVATE'S PROGRESS .... John Boulting
PRIVILEGE .... Peter Watkins
PRIZE FIGHTER, THE .... Michael Preece
PRIZE OF ARMS, A .... Cliff Owen
PRIZZI'S HONOR .... John Huston
PROBE (TF) .... Russ Mayberry
PRODIGAL, THE .... James F. Collier
PRODUCERS, THE .... Mel Brooks
PROFESSIONALS ★, THE .... Richard Brooks
PROFESSIONALS, THE .... Don Sharp
PROFESSIONE: REPORTER .... Michelangelo Antonioni
PROFESSOR KRANZ TEDESCO DI GERMANIA .... Luciano Salce
PROFILE OF BENJAMIN BRITTEN, A (TD) .... Tony Palmer
PROFOUND DESIRE OF THE GODS, THE .... Shohei Imamura
PROIBITO .... Mario Monicelli
PROIBITO RUBARE .... Luigi Comencini
PROJECTIONIST, THE .... Harry Hurwitz
PROLOGUE .... Robin Spry
PROM NIGHT .... Paul Lynch
PROMISE AT DAWN .... Jules Dassin
PROMISE HER ANYTHING .... Arthur Hiller
PROMISE HIM ANYTHING... (TF) .... Edward Parone
PROMISE OF LOVE, THE (TF) .... Don Taylor
PROMISE, THE .... Gilbert Cates
PROMISED LAND, THE .... Andrzej Wajda
PROMISED LANDS (FD) .... Susan Sontag
PROMISES IN THE DARK .... Jerome Hellman
PROMOTER, THE .... Ronald Neame
PROPER TIME, THE .... Tom Laughlin
PROPHECY .... John Frankenheimer
PROPHET, THE .... Dino Risi
PROSTITUTE .... Tony Garnett
PROTECTOR, THE .... Jim Glickenhaus
PROTECTORS, THE .... Jerry Thorpe
PROTOCOL .... Herbert Ross
PROTOTYPE (TF) .... David Greene
PROVIDENCE .... Alain Resnais
PROWLER, THE .... Joseph Zito
PRUDENCE AND THE PILL .... Fielder Cook
PSI FACTOR, THE .... Quentin Masters
PSY .... Philippe de Broca
PSYCHE 59 .... Alexander Singer
PSYCHIATRIST: GOD BLESS THE CHILDREN, THE (TF) .... Daryl Duke
PSYCHIATRY IN RUSSIA (FD) .... Albert Maysles
PSYCHIC KILLER .... Ray Danton
PSYCHO II .... Richard Franklin
PSYCHO-CIRCUS .... John Llewellyn Moxey
PSYCHOMANIA .... Don Sharp
PSYCHOPATH, THE .... Freddie Francis
PSYCHOTRONIC MAN, THE .... Jack M. Sell
PSYCH-OUT .... Richard Rush
PT 109 .... Leslie H. Martinson
P'TANG, YANG, KIPPERBANG .... Michael Apted
PUBERTY BLUES .... Bruce Beresford
PUBLIC AFFAIR, A .... Bernard Girard
PUDDN'HEAD WILSON (TF) .... Alan Bridges
PULP .... Mike Hodges
PUMPKIN EATER, THE .... Jack Clayton
PUNISHMENT ISLAND .... Masahiro Shinoda
PUNISHMENT OF ANNE, THE .... Radley Metzger
PUNISHMENT PARK .... Peter Watkins
PUNISHMENT ROOM .... Kon Ichikawa
PUNK, THE .... Michael Sarne
PUPPET ON A CHAIN .... Geoffrey Reeve
PUPPET ON A CHAIN .... Don Sharp
PURLIE VICTORIOUS .... Nicholas Webster
PURPLE HAZE .... David Burton Morris
PURPLE HEART DIARY .... Richard Quine
PURPLE HEARTS .... Sidney J. Furie
PURPLE HILLS, THE .... Maury Dexter
PURPLE NOON .... René Clement
PURPLE PLAIN, THE .... Robert Parrish
PURPLE RAIN .... Albert Magnoli
PURPLE ROSE OF CAIRO, THE .... Woody Allen
PURPLE V, THE .... George Sherman
PURPLE VIGILANTES, THE .... George Sherman
PURSUIT (TF) .... Michael Crichton
PURSUIT AT DAWN .... Kon Ichikawa
PURSUIT OF D.B. COOPER, THE .... Roger Spottiswoode
PURSUIT OF HAPPINESS, THE .... Robert Mulligan
PURSUIT OF THE GRAF SPEE .... Michael Powell
PUSHOVER .... Richard Quine
PUSS 'N BOOTS .... Chuck Vincent
PUSSYCAT, PUSSYCAT, I LOVE YOU .... Rod Amateau
PUTNEY SWOPE .... Robert Downey
PUZZLE (TF) .... Gordon Hessler
PUZZLE OF A DOWNFALL CHILD .... Jerry Schatzberg
PYX, THE .... Harvey Hart

Q

Q ... Larry Cohen
QUACKSER FORTUNE HAS A COUSIN IN THE BRONX ... Waris Hussein
QUADRIGA ... Bernhard Wicki
QUADROPHENIA ... Franc Roddam
QUAND PASSENT LES FAISANS ... Edouard Molinaro
QUARANTINED (TF) ... Leo Penn
QUARE FELLOW, THE ... Arthur Dreifuss
QUARTERBACK PRINCESS (TF) ... Noel Black
QUARTERMASS AND THE PIT ... Roy Ward Baker
QUARTET ... Ken Annakin
QUARTET ... James Ivory
QUATERMASS CONCLUSION, THE ... Piers Haggard
QUATERMASS EXPERIMENT, THE ... Val Guest
QUATERMASS II ... Val Guest
QUE LA FETE COMMENCE... ... Bertrand Tavernier
QUEEN BEE ... Kon Ichikawa
QUEEN CHRISTINA ... Rouben Mamoulian
QUEEN OF BLOOD ... Curtis Harrington
QUEEN OF THE ROAD ... Menahem Golan
QUEEN OF THE STARDUST BALLROOM (TF) ☆ ... Sam O'Steen
QUEENS, THE ... Mario Monicelli
QUEENS, THE ... Luciano Salce
QUEEN'S DIAMONDS, THE ... Richard Lester
QUEEN'S GUARDS, THE ... Michael Powell
QUEIMADA! ... Gillo Pontecorvo
QUELLE JOIE DE VIVRE ... René Clement
QUELLE STRANE OCCASIONI ... Luigi Comencini
QUEST (TF) ... Lee H. Katzin
QUEST, THE (TF) ... Rod Holcomb
QUEST FOR FIRE ... Jean-Jacques Annaud
QUEST FOR LOVE ... Ralph Thomas
QUESTA VOLTA PARLIAMO DI UOMINI ... Lina Wertmuller
QUESTION OF ADULTERY, A ... Don Chaffey
QUESTION OF GUILT, A (TF) ... Robert Butler
QUESTION OF HONOR, A (TF) ... Jud Taylor
QUESTION OF LOVE, A (TF) ... Jerry Thorpe
QUESTION 7 ... Stuart Rosenberg
QUESTO E QUELLO ... Sergio Corbucci
QUESTOR TAPES, THE (TF) ... Richard A. Colla
QUI ETES-VOUS POLLY MAGGOO? ... William Klein
QUICK AND THE DEAD, THE ... Robert Totten
QUICK BEFORE IT MELTS ... Delbert Mann
QUICKSILVER ... Tom Donnelly
QUIEN SABE? ... Damiano Damiani
QUIET AMERICAN, THE ... Joseph L. Mankiewicz
QUIET DUEL, THE ... Akira Kurosawa
QUIET EARTH, THE ... Geoff Murphy
QUIET GUN, THE ... William F. Claxton
QUILLER MEMORANDUM, THE ... Michael Anderson
QUINCY, M.E. (TF) ... E.W. Swackhamer
QUINNS, THE (TF) ... Daniel Petrie
QUINTET ... Robert Altman
QUO VADIS ... Mervyn Leroy

R

RABBI AND THE SHIKSE, THE ... Joel Silberg
RABBIT, RUN ... Jack Smight
RABBIT TEST ... Joan Rivers
RABBIT TRAP, THE ... Philip Leacock
RABID ... David Cronenberg
RABINDRANATH TAGORE ... Satyajit Ray
RACE FOR YOUR LIFE, CHARLIE BROWN (AF) ... Bill Melendez
RACE TO THE YANKEE ZEPHYR ... David Hemmings
RACE WITH THE DEVIL ... Jack Starrett
RACERS, THE ... Henry Hathaway
RACHEL, RACHEL ... Paul Newman
RACHEL'S MAN ... Moshe Mizrahi
RACING SCENE, THE (FD) ... Andy Sidaris
RACING WITH THE MOON ... Richard Benjamin
RACK, THE ... Arnold Laven
RACQUET ... David Winters
RADIO ON ... Chris Petit
RADIOACTIVE DREAMS ... Albert Pyun
RAFFERTY AND THE GOLD DUST TWINS ... Dick Richards
RAFT ADVENTURES OF HUCK AND JIM, THE (ATF) ... Michael Part
RAG. ARTURO DE FANTI BANCARIO PRECARIO ... Luciano Salce
RAGAZZA CON LA PISTOLA ... Mario Monicelli
RAGE ... George C. Scott
RAGE (TF) ... William A. Graham
RAGE AND GLORY ... Avi Nesher
RAGE OF ANGELS ... Buzz Kulik
RAGE OF PARIS, THE ... Henry Koster
RAGE TO LIVE, A ... Walter Grauman
RAGEWAR ... Charles Band
RAGGEDY ANN AND ANDY (AF) ... Richard Williams
RAGGEDY MAN ... Jack Fisk
RAGING BULL ★ ... Martin Scorsese
RAGING MOON, THE ... Bryan Forbes
RAGING TIDE, THE ... George Sherman
RAGMAN'S DAUGHTER, THE ... Harold Becker
RAGTIME ... Milos Forman
RAICES DE SANGRE ... Jesus Salvador Trevino
RAID ON ENTEBBE (TF) ☆ ... Irvin Kershner
RAID ON ROMMEL ... Henry Hathaway
RAIDERS, THE ... Herschel Daugherty
RAIDERS FROM BENEATH THE SEA ... Maury Dexter
RAIDERS OF LEYTE GULF, THE ... Eddie Romero
RAIDERS OF THE GOLDEN COBRA, THE ... Anthony M. Dawson
RAIDERS OF THE LOST ARK ★ ... Steven Spielberg
RAILWAY CHILDREN, THE ... Lionel Jeffries
RAIN ON THE ROOF (TF) ... Alan Bridges
RAIN OR SHINE ... Frank Capra
RAIN PEOPLE, THE ... Francis Ford Coppola
RAINBIRDS, THE (TF) ... Philip Saville
RAINBOW (TF) ... Jackie Cooper
RAINBOW BOYS, THE ... Gerald Potterton
RAINBOW 'ROUND MY SHOULDER ... Richard Quine
RAINING ON THE MOUNTAIN ... King Hu
RAINMAKER, THE ... Joseph Anthony
RAINS OF RANCHIPUR, THE ... Jean Negulesco
RAINTREE COUNTY ... Edward Dmytryk
RAISE THE TITANIC ... Jerry Jameson
RAISIN IN THE SUN, A ... Daniel Petrie
RAISING THE WIND ... Gerald Thomas
RAMBO: FIRST BLOOD PART II ... George Pan Cosmatos
RAMPAGE ... Phil Karlson
RAMROD ... Andre De Toth
RAN ... Akira Kurosawa
RANCHO DeLUXE ... Frank Perry
RANDOM HARVEST ★ ... Mervyn Leroy
RANGERS, THE (TF) ... Christian Nyby II
RANSOM ... Casper Wrede
RANSOM FOR A DEAD MAN (TF) ... Richard Irving
RANSOM FOR ALICE! (TF) ... David Lowell Rich
RAPE AND MARRIAGE: THE RIDEOUT CASE (TF) ... Peter Levin
RAPPACINI'S DAUGHTER (TF) ... Dezso Magyar
RAPPRESAGLIA ... George Pan Cosmatos
RAPTURE ... John Guillermin
RARE BREED, A ... David Nelson
RARE BREED, THE ... Andrew V. McLaglen
RASCALS AND ROBBERS: THE SECRET ADVENTURES OF TOM SAWYER AND HUCKLEBERRY FINN (TF) ... Dick Lowry
RASHOMON ... Akira Kurosawa
RASKENSTAM ... Gunnar Hellstrom
RASP, THE ... Michael Powell
RASPUTIN - THE MAD MONK ... Don Sharp
RAT PFINK A-BOO-BOO ... Ray Dennis Steckler
RAT RACE, THE ... Robert Mulligan
RATS, THE ... Robert Clouse
RAVAGERS, THE ... Eddie Romero
RAVAGES ... Richard Compton
RAVEN, THE ... Roger Corman
RAVEN'S END ... Bo Widerberg
RAW DEAL ... Russell Hagg
RAW FORCE ... Edward Murphy
RAW MEAT ... Gary A. Sherman
RAW WIND IN EDEN ... Richard Wilson
RAWHIDE ... Henry Hathaway
RAZORBACK ... Russell Mulcahy
RAZOR'S EDGE, THE ... John Byrum
REACH FOR GLORY ... Philip Leacock
REACH FOR THE SKY ... Lewis Gilbert
READY FOR SLAUGHTER (TF) ... Allan King
READY FOR THE PEOPLE ... Buzz Kulik
REAL AMERICAN HERO, A (TF) ... Lou Antonio
REAL GENIUS ... Martha Coolidge
REAL GLORY, THE ... Henry Hathaway
REAL LIFE ... Albert Brooks
REARVIEW MIRROR (TF) ... Lou Antonio
REASON TO LIVE, A (TF) ... Peter Levin
REBEL, THE ... Robert Day
REBELLION ... Masaki Kobayashi
REBELS, THE (MS) ... Russ Mayberry
RECKLESS ... James Foley
RECKONING, THE ... Jack Gold
RECOIL ... Paul Wendkos
RECOURSE EN GRACE ... Laslo Benedek
RED ... Gilles Carle
RED ALERT (TF) ... William "Billy" Hale
RED AND THE WHITE, THE ... Miklos Jancso
RED BADGE OF COURAGE, THE (TF) ... Lee Philips
RED BADGE OF COURAGE, THE ... John Huston
RED BALL EXPRESS ... Budd Boetticher
RED BEARD ... Akira Kurosawa
RED BELLS: I'VE SEEN THE BIRTH OF THE NEW WORLD ... Sergei Bondarchuk
RED BELLS: MEXICO IN FLAMES ... Sergei Bondarchuk
RED BERET, THE ... Terence Young
RED CANYON ... George Sherman
RED DANUBE, THE ... George Sidney
RED DAWN ... John Milius
RED DESERT ... Michelangelo Antonioni
RED ENSIGN ... Michael Powell
RED FLAG: THE ULTIMATE GAME (TF) ... Don Taylor
RED FURY, THE ... Lyman Dayton
RED HEAT ... Robert Collector
RED MEADOWS ... Emil Loteanu
RED MONARCH ... Jack Gold
RED PONY, THE (TF) ... Robert Totten
RED PSALM ... Miklos Jancso
RED RIVER RANGE ... George Sherman
RED SHOES, THE ... Michael Powell
RED SKY AT MORNING ... James Goldstone
RED SONJA ... Richard Fleischer
RED SUN ... Terence Young
RED SUNDOWN ... Jack Arnold
RED, WHITE AND BLACK, THE ... John "Bud" Cardos
RED-LIGHT STING, THE (TF) ... Rod Holcomb
REDNECK ... Silvio Narizzano
REDS ★★ ... Warren Beatty
REFLECTION OF FEAR, A ... William A. Fraker
REFLECTIONS (TF) ... Kevin Billington
REFLECTIONS IN A GOLDEN EYE ... John Huston
REFLECTIONS OF MURDER (TF) ... John Badham
REFORMER AND THE REDHEAD, THE ... Melvin Frank
REFORMER AND THE REDHEAD, THE ... Norman Panama
REG'LAR FELLERS ... Arthur Dreifuss
REHEARSAL FOR MURDER (TF) ... David Greene
REILLY - ACE OF SPIES (MS) ... Jim Goddard
REINCARNATION OF PETER PROUD, THE ... J. Lee Thompson
REIVERS, THE ... Mark Rydell
RELENTLESS ... George Sherman
RELENTLESS (TF) ... Lee H. Katzin
RELUCTANT DEBUTANTE, THE ... Vincente Minnelli
RELUCTANT HEROES, THE (TF) ... Robert Day
RELUCTANT SAINT, THE ... Edward Dmytryk
REMAINS TO BE SEEN ... Don Weis

REMEMBER MY NAME ... Alan Rudolph
REMEMBER WHEN (TF) ... Buzz Kulik
REMEMBRANCE (TF) ... Colin Gregg
REMEMBRANCE OF LOVE (TF) ... Jack Smight
REMO: UNARMED AND DANGEROUS ... Guy Hamilton
RENALDO AND CLARA ... Bob Dylan
RENDEZVOUS HOTEL (TF) ... Peter H. Hunt
RENEGADES ... George Sherman
RENEGADES, THE (TF) ... Roger Spottiswoode
RENNIE ... Don Norman
RENOIR, MY FATHER (TF) ... Alan Cooke
REPO MAN ... Alex Cox
REPORT TO THE COMMISSIONER ... Milton Katselas
REPRISAL! ... George Sherman
REPULSION ... Roman Polanski
REQUIEM FOR A HEAVYWEIGHT ... Ralph Nelson
REQUIEM FOR A VILLAGE ... David Gladwell
REQUIESCANT ... Carlo Lizzani
RESCUE FROM GILLIGAN'S ISLAND (TF) ... Leslie H. Martinson
RESCUERS, THE (AF) ... Wolfgang Reitherman
RESTLESS ... George Pan Cosmatos
RESURRECTION ... Daniel Petrie
RETURN ENGAGEMENT (FD) ... Alan Rudolph
RETURN FROM THE ASHES ... J. Lee Thompson
RETURN FROM WITCH MOUNTAIN ... John Hough
RETURN OF A MAN CALLED HORSE, THE ... Irvin Kershner
RETURN OF CAPTAIN INVINCIBLE, THE ... Philippe Mora
RETURN OF DOCTOR X, THE ... Vincent Sherman
RETURN OF FRANK CANNON, THE (TF) ... Corey Allen
RETURN OF JOE FORRESTER, THE (TF) ... Virgil W. Vogel
RETURN OF MARCUS WELBY, M.D., THE (TF) ... Alexander Singer
RETURN OF MARTIN GUERRE, THE ... Daniel Vigne
RETURN OF THE BEVERLY HILLBILLIES (TF) ... Robert Leeds
RETURN OF THE FRONTIERSMAN ... Richard L. Bare
RETURN OF THE INCREDIBLE HULK, THE (TF) ... Alan J. Levi
RETURN OF THE JEDI ... Richard Marquand
RETURN OF THE KING, THE (ATF) ... Jules Bass
RETURN OF THE KING, THE (ATF) ... Arthur Rankin, Jr.
RETURN OF THE LIVING DEAD ... Dan O'Bannon
RETURN OF THE MAN FROM U.N.C.L.E., THE (TF) ... Ray Austin
RETURN OF THE MOD SQUAD, THE (TF) ... George McCowan
RETURN OF THE PINK PANTHER ... Blake Edwards
RETURN OF THE REBELS (TF) ... Noel Nosseck
RETURN OF THE SECAUCUS SEVEN ... John Sayles
RETURN OF THE SEVEN ... Burt Kennedy
RETURN OF THE SOLDIER, THE ... Alan Bridges
RETURN OF THE TALL BLOND MAN WITH ONE BLACK SHOE ... Yves Robert
RETURN OF THE WORLD'S GREATEST DETECTIVE, THE (TF) ... Dean Hargrove
RETURN, THE ... Greydon Clark
RETURN TO EARTH (TF) ... Jud Taylor
RETURN TO EDEN (MS) ... Karen Arthur
RETURN TO FANTASY ISLAND (TF) ... George McCowan
RETURN TO MACON COUNTY ... Richard Compton
RETURN TO PEYTON PLACE ... Jose Ferrer
RETURN TO YESTERDAY ... Robert Stevenson
RETURNING HOME (TF) ... Daniel Petrie
REUBEN, REUBEN ... Robert Ellis Miller
REUNION (TF) ... Russ Mayberry
REUNION AT FAIRBOROUGH (CTF) ... Herbert Wise
REUNION IN FRANCE ... Jules Dassin
REVENGE (TF) ... Jud Taylor
REVENGE FOR A RAPE (TF) ... Timothy Galfas
REVENGE OF THE CREATURE ... Jack Arnold
REVENGE OF THE DEFENDERS (ATF) ... Michael Part
REVENGE OF THE NERDS ... Jeff Kanew
REVENGE OF THE NINJA ... Sam Firstenberg
REVENGE OF THE PINK PANTHER ... Blake Edwards
REVENGE OF THE SAVAGE BEES (TF) ... Lee H. Katzin
REVENGE OF THE STEPFORD WIVES (TF) ... Robert Fuest
REVENGE OF UKENO-JO, THE ... Kon Ichikawa
REVENGE SQUAD ... Charles Braverman
REVENGERS, THE ... Daniel Mann
REVOLUTION (FD) ... Jack O'Connell
REVOLUTIONARY, THE ... Nagisa Oshima
REVOLUTIONARY, THE ... Paul Williams
REWARD (TF) ... E.W. Swackhamer
REX STOUT'S NERO WOLFE (TF) ... Frank D. Gilroy
RHAPSODY IN BLUE ... Irving Rapper
RHINEMANN EXCHANGE, THE (MS) ... Burt Kennedy
RHINESTONE ... Bob Clark
RHINOCEROS ... Tom O'Horgan
RHYTHM OF THE SADDLE ... George Sherman
RIAVANTI...MARSCH! ... Luciano Salce
RICH KIDS ... Robert M. Young
RICH MAN, POOR MAN - BOOK II (TF) ... Lou Antonio
RICH MAN, POOR MAN (MS) ... David Greene
RICHARD ... Harry Hurwitz
RICHARD III ... Laurence Olivier
RICHARD PRYOR HERE AND NOW (FD) ... Richard Pryor
RICHARD PRYOR LIVE ON THE SUNSET STRIP (FD) ... Joe Layton
RICHARD'S THINGS ... Anthony Harvey
RICHIE BROCKELMAN: MISSING 24 HOURS (TF) ... Hy Averback
RICOCHET ... John Llewellyn Moxey
RIDDLE OF THE SANDS, THE ... Tony Maylam
RIDE A VIOLENT MILE ... Charles Marquis Warren
RIDE A WILD PONY ... Don Chaffey
RIDE BEYOND VENGEANCE ... Bernard McEveety
RIDE IN THE WHIRLWIND ... Monte Hellman
RIDE LONESOME ... Budd Boetticher
RIDE ON STRANGER (TF) ... Carl Schultz
RIDE OUT FOR REVENGE ... Bernard Girard
RIDE THE HIGH COUNTRY ... Sam Peckinpah
RIDE THE HIGH IRON ... Don Weis
RIDE THE WILD SURF ... Don Taylor
RIDE TO HANGMAN'S TREE, THE ... Alan Rafkin
RIDER ON THE RAIN ... René Clement
RIDERS OF THE BLACK HILLS ... George Sherman
RIDERS OF THE NEW FOREST ... Philip Leacock
RIDING HIGH ... Frank Capra
RIDING SHOTGUN ... Andre De Toth
RIEL ... George Bloomfield
RIFIFI ... Jules Dassin
RIFIFI IN TOKYO ... Jacques Deray
RIGGED ... Matt Cimber
RIGHT CROSS ... John Sturges
RIGHT OF WAY (CTF) ... George Schaefer
RIGHT ON! ... Herbert Danska
RIGHT PROSPECTUS, THE (TF) ... Alan Cooke
RIGHT STUFF, THE ... Philip Kaufman
RING OF BRIGHT WATER ... Jack Couffer
RING OF FIRE ... Andrew L. Stone
RING OF PASSION (TF) ... Robert M. Lewis
RING OF POWER ... Clive A. Smith
RING-A-DING RHYTHM ... Richard Lester
RINGER, THE ... Guy Hamilton
RINGS AROUND THE WORLD (FD) ... Gilbert Cates
RINGS ON HER FINGERS ... Rouben Mamoulian
RIO CONCHOS ... Gordon Douglas
RIOT ... Buzz Kulik
RIOT IN CELL BLOCK 11 ... Don Siegel
RIOT ON SUNSET STRIP ... Arthur Dreifuss
RIP OFF ... Anthony M. Dawson
RIP-OFF ... Donald Shebib
RIPTIDE (TF) ... Christian Nyby II
RISE AND FALL OF IDI AMIN, THE ... Sharad Patel
RISE AND FALL OF LEGS DIAMOND, THE ... Budd Boetticher
RISE AND FALL OF THE THIRD REICH (TD) ... Mel Stuart
RISE AND RISE OF MICHAEL RIMMER, THE ... Kevin Billington
RISING DAMP ... Joseph McGrath
RISK, THE ... John Boulting
RISK, THE ... Roy Boulting
RISKY BUSINESS ... Paul Brickman
RITA HAYWORTH: THE LOVE GODDESS (TF) ... James Goldstone
RITA LA ZANZARA ... Lina Wertmuller
RITUAL OF EVIL (TF) ... Robert Day
RITUAL, THE ... Ingmar Bergman
RITZ, THE ... Richard Lester
RIUSCIRANNO I NOSTRI EROI A TROVARE L'AMICO MISTERIOSAMENTE SCOMPARSO IN AFRICA? ... Ettore Scola
RIVALRY, THE (TF) ... Fielder Cook
RIVALS ... Lyman Dayton
RIVALS ... Krishna Shah
RIVER BEAT ... Guy Green
RIVER LADY ... George Sherman
RIVER NIGER, THE ... Krishna Shah
RIVER OF MYSTERY (TF) ... Paul Stanley
RIVER OF NO RETURN ... Otto Preminger
RIVER RAT, THE ... Tom Rickman
RIVER SOLO FLOWS ... Kon Ichikawa
RIVER, THE ... Mark Rydell
RIVERRUN ... John Korty
RIVKIN: BOUNTY HUNTER (TF) ... Harry Harris
ROAD GAMES ... Richard Franklin
ROAD HOUSE ... Jean Negulesco
ROAD MOVIE ... Joseph Strick
ROAD SHOW ... Gordon Douglas
ROAD TO HONG KONG, THE ... Norman Panama
ROAD TRIP ... Steve Carver
ROAD WARRIOR, THE ... George Miller
ROADHOUSE 66 ... John Mark Robinson
ROADIE ... Alan Rudolph
ROBBERY ... Peter Yates
ROBBERY UNDER ARMS ... Donald Crombie
ROBE, THE ... Henry Koster
ROBERT ET ROBERT ... Claude Lelouch
ROBERT F. KENNEDY AND HIS TIMES (MS) ... Marvin J. Chomsky
ROBIN AND MARIAN ... Richard Lester
ROBIN AND THE SEVEN HOODS ... Gordon Douglas
ROBIN HOOD (AF) ... Wolfgang Reitherman
ROBIN OF SHERWOOD (TF) ... Ian Sharp
ROCK & RULE (AF) ... Clive A. Smith
ROCK ALL NIGHT ... Roger Corman
ROCK CITY ... Peter Clifton
ROCK 'N' ROLL HIGH SCHOOL ... Allan Arkush
ROCKABILLY BABY ... William F. Claxton
ROCKABY (TD) ... D.A. Pennebaker
ROCKFORD FILES, THE (TF) ... Richard T. Heffron
ROCKINGHORSE ... Yaky Yosha
ROCKY ... Phil Karlson
ROCKY ★★ ... John G. Avildsen
ROCKY II ... Sylvester Stallone
ROCKY III ... Sylvester Stallone
ROCKY HORROR PICTURE SHOW, THE ... Jim Sharman
ROCKY MOUNTAIN RANGERS ... George Sherman
RODEO GIRL (TF) ... Jackie Cooper
ROGER & HARRY: THE MITERA TARGET (TF) ... Jack Starrett
ROGOPAG ... Jean-Luc Godard
ROGUE MALE (TF) ... Clive Donner
ROGUES OF SHERWOOD FOREST ... Gordon Douglas
ROLL, FREDDY, ROLL! (TF) ... Bill Persky
ROLL OF THUNDER, HEAR MY CRY (TF) ... Jack Smight
ROLLER AND THE VIOLIN, THE ... Andrei Tarkovsky
ROLLER BOOGIE ... Mark L. Lester
ROLLERBALL ... Norman Jewison
ROLLERCOASTER ... James Goldstone
ROLLING HOME (TF) ... Piers Haggard
ROLLING MAN (TF) ... Peter Hyams
ROLLING THUNDER ... John Flynn

ROLLOVER ... Alan J. Pakula
ROMA BENE ... Carlo Lizzani
ROMA RIVUOLE CESARE ... Miklos Jancso
ROMAN SPRING OF MRS. STONE, THE ... Jose Quintero
ROMANCE OF A HORSETHIEF ... Abraham Polonsky
ROMANCING THE STONE ... Robert Zemeckis
ROMANOFF AND JULIET ... Peter Ustinov
ROMANTIC COMEDY ... Arthur Hiller
ROMANZO POPOLARE ... Mario Monicelli
ROME: THE IMAGE OF A CITY (FD) ... Carlo Lizzani
ROMEO AND JULIET ★ ... Franco Zeffirelli
ROMOLO E REMO ... Sergio Corbucci
ROMY. ANATOMIE EINES GESICHT (FD) ... Hans-Jurgen Syberberg
RONA JAFFE'S MAZES AND MONSTERS ... Steven Hillard Stern
ROOKIES, THE (TF) ... Jud Taylor
ROOM AT THE TOP ★ ... Jack Clayton
ROOM MATES, THE ... Arthur Marks
ROOM WITH THICK WALLS ... Masaki Kobayashi
ROOMMATE, THE ... Nell Cox
ROOMMATES ... Gerald Thomas
ROOMMATES ... Chuck Vincent
ROOSTER (TF) ... Russ Mayberry
ROOSTER COGBURN ... Stuart Millar
ROOTS (MS) ☆ ... Marvin J. Chomsky
ROOTS (MS) ☆ ... John Erman
ROOTS (MS) ☆ ... Gilbert Moses
ROOTS (MS) ☆☆ ... David Greene
ROOTS OF HEAVEN, THE ... John Huston
ROOTS: THE NEXT GENERATIONS (MS) ... Georg Stanford Brown
ROOTS: THE NEXT GENERATIONS (MS) ... Charles S. Dubin
ROOTS: THE NEXT GENERATIONS (MS) ... John Erman
ROOTS: THE NEXT GENERATIONS (MS) ... Lloyd Richards
ROPE OF FLESH ... Russ Meyer
ROSE MARIE ... Mervyn Leroy
ROSE TATTOO, THE ... Daniel Mann
ROSE, THE ... Mark Rydell
ROSEBUD ... Otto Preminger
ROSEBUD BEACH HOTEL, THE ... Harry Hurwitz
ROSELAND ... James Ivory
ROSEMARY'S BABY ... Roman Polanski
ROSIE: THE ROSEMARY CLOONEY STORY (TF) ... Jackie Cooper
ROSIE! ... David Lowell Rich
ROSOLINO PATERNO SOLDATO ... Nanni Loy
ROSSETTI AND RYAN: MEN WHO LOVE WOMEN (TF) ... John Astin
ROTHKO CONSPIRACY, THE (TF) ... Paul Watson
ROTTEN TO THE CORE ... John Boulting
ROUGH CUT ... Don Siegel
ROUGH NIGHT IN JERICHO ... Arnold Laven
ROUGH SHOOT ... Robert Parrish
ROUGH TREATMENT ... Andrzej Wajda
ROUGHNECKS (TF) ... Bernard McEveety
ROUNDERS, THE ... Burt Kennedy
ROUND-UP, THE ... Miklos Jancso
ROUSTABOUT ... John Rich
ROUSTERS, THE (TF) ... E.W. Swackhamer
ROVIN' TUMBLEWEEDS ... George Sherman
ROYAL FLASH ... Richard Lester
ROYAL ROMANCE OF CHARLES AND DIANA, THE (TF) ... Peter Levin
ROYAL SCANDAL, A ... Otto Preminger
ROYAL WEDDING ... Stanley Donen
R.P.M.* ... Stanley Kramer
RUBBER GUN, THE ... Allan Moyle
RUBLO DE LOS CARAS ... Etienne Perier
RUBY ... Curtis Harrington
RUBY AND OSWALD (TF) ... Mel Stuart
RUDE BOY ... Jack Hazan
RUDE BOY ... David Mingay
RUDOLPH AND FROSTY (ATF) ... Jules Bass
RULES OF MARRIAGE, THE (TF) ... Milton Katselas
RULING CLASS, THE ... Peter Medak
RUMBLE FISH ... Francis Ford Coppola
RUMOR OF WAR, A (TF) ... Richard T. Heffron
RUN A CROOKED MILE (TF) ... Gene Levitt
RUN ACROSS THE RIVER ... Everett Chambers
RUN, ANGEL, RUN! ... Jack Starrett
RUN, COUGAR, RUN ... Jerome Courtland
RUN FOR THE SUN ... Roy Boulting
RUN OF THE ARROW ... Samuel Fuller
RUN SILENT, RUN DEEP ... Robert Wise
RUN, SIMON, RUN (TF) ... George McCowan
RUN WILD, RUN FREE ... Richard C. Sarafian
RUNAWAY ... Michael Crichton
RUNAWAY BUS, THE ... Val Guest
RUNAWAY! (TF) ... David Lowell Rich
RUNAWAYS, THE (TF) ... Harry Harris
RUNNER STUMBLES, THE ... Stanley Kramer
RUNNERS ... Charles Sturridge
RUNNING ... Steven Hillard Stern
RUNNING AWAY BACKWARDS (FD) ... Allan King
RUNNING BRAVE ... Donald Shebib
RUNNING FENCE (FD) ... Albert Maysles
RUNNING FENCE (FD) ... David Maysles
RUNNING FENCE (FD) ... Charlotte Zwerin
RUNNING HOT ... Mark Griffiths
RUNNING OUT (TF) ... Robert Day
RUNNING SCARED ... David Hemmings
RUSH TO JUDGMENT (FD) ... Emile de Antonio
RUSS MEYER'S UP! ... Russ Meyer
RUSS MEYER'S VIXEN ... Russ Meyer
RUSSIAN ROULETTE ... Louis Lombardo
RUSSIANS ARE COMING THE RUSSIANS ARE COMING, THE ... Norman Jewison
RUSTLER'S RHAPSODY ... Hugh Wilson
RYAN'S DAUGHTER ... David Lean
RYAN'S FOUR (TF) ... Jeff Bleckner
RYNOX ... Michael Powell

S

SABOTEUR, CODE NAME "MORITURI", THE ... Bernhard Wicki
SABRINA ★ ... Billy Wilder
SACCO AND VANZETTI ... Giuliano Montaldo
SACKETTS, THE (TF) ... Robert Totten
SACRED GROUND ... Charles B. Pierce
SAD HORSE, THE ... James B. Clark
SADAT (TF) ... Richard Michaels
SADDLE THE WIND ... Robert Parrish
SADGATI ... Satyajit Ray
SADO'S ONDEKO-ZA (FD) ... Masahiro Shinoda
SAFARI ... Terence Young
SAFARI 3000 ... Harry Hurwitz
SAFE AT HOME! ... Walter Doniger
SAFE PLACE, A ... Henry Jaglom
SAHARA ... Andrew V. McLaglen
SAIGON - YEAR OF THE CAT (TF) ... Stephen Frears
SAILOR FROM GIBRALTER, THE ... Tony Richardson
SAILOR OF THE KING ... Roy Boulting
SAILOR WHO FELL FROM GRACE WITH THE SEA, THE ... Lewis John Carlino
SAILOR'S RETURN, THE ... Jack Gold
SAINT JACK ... Peter Bogdanovich
SAINT JOAN ... Otto Preminger
SAIT-ON JAMAIS? ... Roger Vadim
SAKHAROV (CTF) ... Jack Gold
SALAMANDER, THE ... Peter Zinner
SALEM'S LOT (TF) ... Tobe Hooper
SALESMAN (FD) ... Albert Maysles
SALESMAN (FD) ... David Maysles
SALLAH ... Ephraim Kishon
SALOME AND DELILAH ... Andy Warhol
SALT AND PEPPER ... Richard Donner
SALT TO THE DEVIL ... Edward Dmytryk
SALUT L'ARTISTE ... Yves Robert
SALVAGE (TF) ... Lee Philips
SALVAGE GANG, THE ... John Krish
SALVATE MIA FIGLIA ... Sergio Corbucci
SALVATORE GIULIANO ... Francesco Rosi
SALVE POUR UNE BUFLE NOIR ... Istvan Szabo
SALZBURG CONNECTION, THE ... Lee H. Katzin
SAM HILL: WHO KILLED THE MYSTERIOUS MR. FOSTER? (TF) ... Fielder Cook
SAM MARLOW, PRIVATE EYE ... Robert Day
SAM WHISKEY ... Arnold Laven
SAME TIME, NEXT YEAR ... Robert Mulligan
SAMMY GOING SOUTH ... Alexander Mackendrick
SAMMY STOPS THE WORLD (FD) ... Melvin Shapiro
SAM'S SON ... Michael Landon
SAMSON ... Andrzej Wajda
SAMSON AND DELILAH (TF) ... Lee Philips
SAMURAI (TF) ... Lee H. Katzin
SAMURAI REBELLION ... Masaki Kobayashi
SAMURAI SPY ... Masahiro Shinoda
SAN BABILA ORE 20: UN DELITTO INUTILE ... Carlo Lizzani
SAN DOMINGO ... Hans-Jurgen Syberberg
SAN FERRY ANN ... Jeremy Summers
SAN FRANCISCO INTERNATIONAL AIRPORT (TF) ... John Llewellyn Moxey
SAN FRANCISCO STORY, THE ... Robert Parrish
SAN MICHELE AVEVA UN GALLO (TF) ... Paolo Taviani
SAN MICHELE AVEVA UN GALLO (TF) ... Vittorio Taviani
SAN QUENTIN ... Gordon Douglas
SANCTUARY ... Tony Richardson
SANCTUARY OF FEAR (TF) ... John Llewellyn Moxey
SAND PEBBLES, THE ... Robert Wise
SANDCASTLES (TF) ... Ted Post
SANDPIPER, THE ... Vincente Minnelli
SANDPIT GENERALS / THE DEFIANT, THE ... Hall Bartlett
SANDS OF THE KALAHARI ... Cy Endfield
SANJURO ... Akira Kurosawa
SANSHIRO AT GINZA ... Kon Ichikawa
SANSHIRO SUGATA ... Akira Kurosawa
SANSHIRO SUGATA - PART TWO ... Akira Kurosawa
SANTA CLAUS - THE MOVIE ... Jeannot Szwarc
SANTA CLAUS CONQUERS THE MARTIANS ... Nicholas Webster
SANTA CLAUS VISITS THE LAND OF MOTHER GOOSE ... Herschell Gordon Lewis
SANTA FE STAMPEDE ... George Sherman
SANTEE ... Gary Nelson
SANTIAGO ... Gordon Douglas
SAPPORO WINTER OLYMPIC GAMES (FD) ... Masahiro Shinoda
SAPS AT SEA ... Gordon Douglas
SARAH T. - PORTRAIT OF A TEENAGE ALCOHOLIC (TF) ... Richard Donner
SARGE: THE BADGE OR THE CROSS (TF) ... Richard A. Colla
SARONG GIRL ... Arthur Dreifuss
S.A.S. A SAN SALVADOR ... Raoul Coutard
SASKATCHEWAN, THE (TF) ... Daryl Duke
SATAN BUG, THE ... John Sturges
SATANIC RITES OF DRACULA ... Alan Gibson
SATAN'S CHEERLEADERS ... Greydon Clark
SATAN'S SADISTS ... Al Adamson
SATAN'S SCHOOL FOR GIRLS (TF) ... David Lowell Rich
SATAN'S SKIN ... Piers Haggard
SATAN'S TRIANGLE (TF) ... Sutton Roley
SATURDAY NIGHT AND SUNDAY MORNING ... Karel Reisz
SATURDAY NIGHT FEVER ... John Badham
SATURDAY THE 14TH ... Howard R. Cohen
SATURDAY'S CHILDREN ... Vincent Sherman
SATURDAY'S HERO ... David Miller
SATURN 3 ... Stanley Donen
SAUVE QUI PEUT LA VIE ... Jean-Luc Godard
SAVAGE (TF) ... Steven Spielberg
SAVAGE DAWN ... Simon Nuchtern
SAVAGE EYE, THE ... Joseph Strick
SAVAGE GUNS, THE ... Michael Carreras
SAVAGE HARVEST ... Robert Collins
SAVAGE IS LOOSE, THE ... George C. Scott
SAVAGE ISLANDS ... Ferdinand Fairfax
SAVAGE MESSIAH ... Ken Russell
SAVAGE SEVEN, THE ... Richard Rush
SAVAGE SISTERS ... Eddie Romero
SAVAGE STREETS ... Daniel Steinmann
SAVAGE WEEKEND ... David Paulsen
SAVAGES ... James Ivory
SAVAGES (TF) ... Lee H. Katzin
SAVANNAH SMILES ... Pierre DeMoro
SAVE THE CHILDREN (FD) ... Stan Lathan
SAVE THE TIGER ... John G. Avildsen
SAVING GRACE ... Robert M. Young
SAWDUST AND TINSEL ... Ingmar Bergman

SAY AMEN, SOMEBODY (FD) ..... George T. Nierenberg
SAY GOODBYE, MAGGIE COLE (TF) ..... Jud Taylor
SAY HELLO TO YESTERDAY ..... Alvin Rakoff
SAY IT IN FRENCH ..... Andrew L. Stone
SAY IT WITH SABLES ..... Frank Capra
SAYONARA ★ ..... Joshua Logan
SBATTI IL MOSTRO IN PRIMA PAGINA ..... Marco Bellocchio
SCALAWAG ..... Kirk Douglas
SCALPHUNTERS, THE ..... Sydney Pollack
SCALPLOCK (TF) ..... James Goldstone
SCANDAL ..... Akira Kurosawa
SCANDAL AT SCOURIE ..... Jean Negulesco
SCANDAL IN SORRENTO ..... Dino Risi
SCANDAL SHEET ..... Phil Karlson
SCANDALE ..... George Mihalka
SCANDALOUS ..... Rob Cohen
SCANDALOUS ADVENTURES OF BURAIKAN, THE ..... Masahiro Shinoda
SCANDALOUS JOHN ..... Robert Butler
SCANNERS ..... David Cronenberg
SCARABEA - WIENVIEL ERDE BRAUCHT DER MENSCH? ..... Hans-Jurgen Syberberg
SCARAMOUCHE ..... George Sidney
SCARECROW ..... Jerry Schatzberg
SCARED STRAIGHT! ANOTHER STORY (TF) ..... Richard Michaels
SCARED TO DEATH ..... William Malone
SCARFACE ..... Brian De Palma
SCARFACE MOB, THE ..... Phil Karlson
SCARLET AND THE BLACK, THE (TF) ..... Jerry London
SCARLET COAT, THE ..... John Sturges
SCARLET LETTER, THE ..... Wim Wenders
SCARLET PIMPERNEL, THE (TF) ..... Clive Donner
SCARLET THREAD, THE ..... Lewis Gilbert
SCARRED ..... Rose Marie Turko
SCARS OF DRACULA, THE ..... Roy Ward Baker
SCARY TIME, A ..... Shirley Clarke
SCAVENGER HUNT ..... Michael Schultz
SCENES FROM A MARRIAGE ..... Ingmar Bergman
SCENES FROM THE PORTUGUESE CLASS STRUGGLE (FD) ..... Robert Kramer
SCENO DI GUERRA ..... Dino Risi
SCENT OF A WOMAN ..... Dino Risi
SCENT OF MYSTERY ..... Jack Cardiff
SCHIZOID ..... David Paulsen
SCHLOCK ..... John Landis
SCHOOL FOR SECRETS ..... Peter Ustinov
SCHOOL PLAY (TF) ..... James Cellan-Jones
SCORCHY ..... Howard (Hikmet) Avedis
SCORE ..... Radley Metzger
SCORNED AND SWINDLED (TF) ..... Paul Wendkos
SCORPIO ..... Michael Winner
SCOTT FREE (TF) ..... William Wiard
SCOTT JOPLIN ..... Jeremy Paul Kagan
SCOUNDREL, A ..... Kaneto Shindo
SCREAM AND SCREAM AGAIN ..... Gordon Hessler
SCREAM FOR HELP ..... Michael Winner
SCREAM OF THE BUTTERFLY ..... Ray Dennis Steckler
SCREAM OF THE WOLF (TF) ..... Dan Curtis
SCREAM, PRETTY PEGGY (TF) ..... Gordon Hessler
SCREAMING MIMI ..... Gerd Oswald
SCREAMING WOMAN, THE (TF) ..... Jack Smight
SCREEN TEST ..... Andy Warhol
SCREWBALLS ..... Rafal Zielinski
SCROOGE ..... Ronald Neame
SCRUBBERS ..... Mai Zetterling
SCRUPLES (TF) ..... Robert Day
SCRUPLES (TF) ..... Alan J. Levi
SCUM OF THE EARTH ..... Herschell Gordon Lewis
SCUOLA ELEMENTARE ..... Alberto Lattuada
SE PERMETTE, PARLIAMO DI DONNE ..... Ettore Scola
SEA AROUND US, THE (FD) ..... Irwin Allen
SEA FURY ..... Cy Endfield
SEA GOD, THE ..... George Abbott
SEA GULL, THE ..... Sidney Lumet
SEA GYPSIES, THE ..... Stewart Raffill
SEA MARKS (TF) ..... Ronald F. Maxwell
SEA OF GRASS ..... Elia Kazan
SEA OF SAND ..... Guy Green
SEA SHALL NOT HAVE THEM, THE ..... Lewis Gilbert
SEA WOLVES, THE ..... Andrew V. McLaglen
SEABO ..... Jimmy Huston
SEAGULLS OVER SORRENTO ..... John Boulting
SEAGULLS OVER SORRENTO ..... Roy Boulting
SEANCE ON A WET AFTERNOON ..... Bryan Forbes
SEARCH ★, THE ..... Fred Zinnemann
SEARCH AND DESTROY ..... William Fruet
SEARCH FOR ALEXANDER THE GREAT, THE (MS) ..... Peter Sykes
SEARCH FOR THE GODS (TF) ..... Jud Taylor
SEARCH FOR THE NILE, THE (MS) ..... Richard Marquand
SEASIDE SWINGERS ..... James Hill
SEBASTIAN ..... David Greene
SEBASTIANE ..... Derek Jarman
SECOND CHANCE ..... Claude Lelouch
SECOND CHANCE (TF) ..... Peter Tewksbury
SECOND HAND HEARTS ..... Hal Ashby
SECOND SIGHT: A LOVE STORY (TF) ..... John Korty
SECOND THOUGHTS ..... Lawrence Turman
SECOND TIME AROUND, THE ..... Vincent Sherman
SECOND TIME LUCKY ..... Michael Anderson
SECOND WIND ..... Donald Shebib
SECONDS ..... John Frankenheimer
SECRET, THE ..... Cy Endfield
SECRET, THE ..... Ann Hui
SECRET ADMIRER ..... David Greenwalt
SECRET BEYOND THE DOOR, THE ..... Liliana Cavani
SECRET DIARY OF SIGMUND FREUD, THE ..... Danford B. Greene
SECRET DREAMS OF MONA Q, THE ..... Charles Kaufman
SECRET FILE ..... Arthur Dreifuss
SECRET FURY, THE ..... Mel Ferrer
SECRET HONOR ..... Robert Altman
SECRET INVASION, THE ..... Roger Corman
SECRET LIFE OF AN AMERICAN WIFE, THE ..... George Axelrod
SECRET LIFE OF JOHN CHAPMAN, THE (TF) ..... David Lowell Rich
SECRET LIFE OF PLANTS, THE (FD) ..... Walon Green
SECRET NIGHT CALLER, THE (TF) ..... Jerry Jameson
SECRET OF CONVICT LAKE, THE ..... Michael Gordon
SECRET OF MY SUCCESS, THE ..... Andrew L. Stone
SECRET OF NIMH, THE (AF) ..... Don Bluth
SECRET OF SANTA VITTORIA, THE ..... Stanley Kramer
SECRET OF THE INCAS ..... Jerry Hopper
SECRET OF THE PURPLE REEF ..... William Witney
SECRET PLACE, THE ..... Clive Donner
SECRET PLACES ..... Zelda Barron
SECRET POLICEMAN'S OTHER BALL, THE (FD) ..... Julien Temple
SECRET TENT, THE ..... Don Chaffey
SECRET WAR OF HARRY FRIGG, THE ..... Jack Smight
SECRET WAR OF JACKIE'S GIRLS, THE (TF) ..... Gordon Hessler
SECRET WAYS, THE ..... Phil Karlson
SECRETS ..... Gavin Millar
SECRETS ..... Philip Saville
SECRETS (TF) ..... Paul Wendkos
SECRETS OF A MARRIED MAN (TF) ..... William A. Graham
SECRETS OF A MOTHER AND DAUGHTER (TF) ..... Gabrielle Beaumont
SECRETS OF A SECRETARY ..... George Abbott
SECRETS OF THE GODS ..... William Sachs
SECRETS OF THE LONE WOLF ..... Edward Dmytryk
SECRETS OF THE WHISTLER ..... George Sherman
SECRETS OF THREE HUNGRY WIVES (TF) ..... Gordon Hessler
SECRETS OF WOMEN ..... Ingmar Bergman
SEDUCED (TF) ..... Jerrold Freedman
SEDUCTION OF GINA, THE (TF) ..... Jerrold Freedman
SEDUCTION OF JOE TYNAN, THE ..... Jerry Schatzberg
SEDUCTION OF MIMI, THE ..... Lina Wertmuller
SEDUCTION OF MISS LEONA, THE (TF) ..... Joseph Hardy
SEDUCTION, THE ..... David Schmoeller
SEE HOW SHE RUNS (TF) ... Richard T. Heffron
SEE HOW THEY RUN (TF) ..... David Lowell Rich
SEE NO EVIL ..... Richard Fleischer
SEE THE MAN RUN (TF) ..... Corey Allen
SEED OF INNOCENCE ..... Boaz Davidson
SEED OF MAN, THE ..... Marco Ferreri
SEEDING OF SARAH BURNS, THE (TF) ..... Sandor Stern
SEEKERS, THE (TF) ..... Sidney Hayers
SEEKERS, THE ..... Ken Annakin
SEGUIN (TF) ..... Jesus Salvador Trevino
SEIZURE ..... Oliver Stone
SEIZURE: THE STORY OF KATHY MORRIS (TF) ..... Gerald I. Isenberg
SEMINOLE ..... Budd Boetticher
SEMINOLE UPRISING ..... Earl Bellamy
SEMI-TOUGH ..... Michael Ritchie
SEMMELWEIS ..... Andre De Toth
SEND ME NO FLOWERS ..... Norman Jewison
SENDER, THE ..... Roger Christian
SENIOR PROM ..... David Lowell Rich
SENIOR TRIP (TF) ..... Kenneth Johnson
SENIOR YEAR (TF) ..... Richard Donner
SENIORS, THE ..... Rod Amateau
SENSATIONS OF 1945 ..... Andrew L. Stone
SENSE OF FREEDOM, A (TF) ..... John Mackenzie
SENSE OF LOSS, A (FD) ..... Marcel Ophuls
SENSITIVE, PASSIONATE MAN, A (TF) ..... John Newland
SENTIMENTAL JOURNEY (TF) ..... James Goldstone
SENTINEL, THE ..... Michael Winner
SENZA PIETA ..... Alberto Lattuada
SENZA SAPERE NULLA DI LEI ..... Luigi Comencini
SEPARATE PEACE, A ..... Larry Peerce
SEPARATE ROOMS ..... Bertrand Blier
SEPARATE TABLES ..... Delbert Mann
SEPARATE WAYS ..... Howard (Hikmet) Avedis
SEPARATION (TF) ..... George McCowan
SEPPUKU ..... Masaki Kobayashi
SEPTEMBER GUN (TF) ..... Don Taylor
SEPTEMBER 30, 1955 ..... James Bridges
SERAPHITA'S DIARY ..... Frederick Wiseman
SERGEANT MATLOVICH VS. THE U.S. AIR FORCE (TF) ..... Paul Leaf
SERGEANT RYKER ..... Buzz Kulik
SERGEANT STEINER ..... Andrew V. McLaglen
SERGEANT, THE ..... John Flynn
SERGEANTS 3 ..... John Sturges
SERIAL ..... Bill Persky
SERIOUS CHARGE ..... Terence Young
SERPENT, THE ..... Henri Verneuil
SERPENT'S EGG, THE ..... Ingmar Bergman
SERPICO ..... Sidney Lumet
SERPICO: THE DEADLY GAME (TF) ..... Robert Collins
SESAME STREET PRESENTS: FOLLOW THAT BIRD ..... Ken Kwapis
SESSIONS (TF) ..... Richard Pearce
SESSO E VOLENTIERI ..... Dino Risi
SESSOMATTO ..... Dino Risi
SET THIS TOWN ON FIRE (TF) ..... David Lowell Rich
SET-UP, THE ..... Robert Wise
SEVEN ..... Andy Sidaris
SEVEN ALONE ..... Earl Bellamy
SEVEN ANGRY MEN .... Charles Marquis Warren
SEVEN BEAUTIES ..... Lina Wertmuller
SEVEN BRIDES FOR SEVEN BROTHERS ..... Stanley Donen
SEVEN BRIDES FOR SEVEN BROTHERS (TF) ..... Gary Nelson
SEVEN CAPITAL SINS ..... Philippe de Broca
SEVEN CAPITAL SINS ..... Claude Chabrol
SEVEN CAPITAL SINS ..... Jacques Demy
SEVEN CAPITAL SINS ..... Jean-Luc Godard
SEVEN CAPITAL SINS ..... Edouard Molinaro
SEVEN CAPITAL SINS ..... Roger Vadim
SEVEN DAYS IN MAY ..... John Frankenheimer
SEVEN DAYS TO NOON ..... John Boulting
SEVEN IN DARKNESS (TF) ..... Michael Caffey
SEVEN LITTLE FOYS, THE .... Melville Shavelson
SEVEN MEN FROM NOW ..... Budd Boetticher

SEVEN MILES FROM ALCATRAZ .... Edward Dmytryk
SEVEN MINUTES, THE .... Russ Meyer
SEVEN NIGHTS IN JAPAN .... Lewis Gilbert
SEVEN SAMURAI .... Akira Kurosawa
SEVEN THIEVES .... Henry Hathaway
SEVEN UPS, THE .... Philip D'Antoni
SEVEN WONDERS OF THE WORLD .... Andrew Marton
SEVEN YEAR ITCH, THE .... Billy Wilder
SEVEN-PER-CENT SOLUTION, THE .... Herbert Ross
SEVENTEEN YEARS OLD .... Alf Kjellin
SEVENTH AVENUE (MS) .... Richard Irving
SEVENTH AVENUE (MS) .... Russ Mayberry
SEVENTH CROSS, THE .... Fred Zinnemann
SEVENTH DAWN, THE .... Lewis Gilbert
SEVENTH SEAL, THE .... Ingmar Bergman
SEVENTH SIN, THE .... Ronald Neame
SEVERED HEAD, A .... Dick Clement
SEX AND THE MARRIED WOMAN (TF) .... Jack Arnold
SEX AND THE SINGLE GIRL .... Richard Quine
SEX AND THE SINGLE PARENT (TF) .... Jackie Cooper
SEX KITTENS GO TO COLLEGE .... Albert Zugsmith
SEX O'CLOCK USA (FD) .... Francois Reichenbach
SEX ON THE GROOVE TUBE .... Sean S. Cunningham
SEX SYMBOL, THE (TF) .... David Lowell Rich
SEX-BUSINESS - MADE IN PASSING (FD) .... Hans-Jurgen Syberberg
SEXTETTE .... Kenneth "Ken" Hughes
SGT. PEPPER'S LONELY HEARTS CLUB BAND .... Michael Schultz
SHADEY .... Philip Saville
SHADOW BOX ☆, THE (TF) .... Paul Newman
SHADOW IN THE STREETS, A (TF) .... Richard Donner
SHADOW LINE .... Andrzej Wajda
SHADOW OF THE HAWK .... George McCowan
SHADOW ON THE LAND (TF) .... Richard C. Sarafian
SHADOW ON THE WINDOW, THE .... William Asher
SHADOW OVER ELVERON (TF) .... James Goldstone
SHADOW RIDERS, THE (TF) .... Andrew V. McLaglen
SHADOW WORLD (ATF) .... Michael Part
SHADOWED .... John Sturges
SHADOWS .... John Cassavetes
SHAFT .... Gordon Parks
SHAFT IN AFRICA .... John Guillermin
SHAFT'S BIG SCORE! .... Gordon Parks
SHAGGY D.A., THE .... Robert Stevenson
SHAKE HANDS WITH THE DEVIL .... Michael Anderson
SHAKEDOWN .... Joseph Pevney
SHAKESPEARE WALLAH .... James Ivory
SHAKIEST GUN IN THE WEST, THE .... Alan Rafkin
SHALAKO! .... Edward Dmytryk
SHALIMAR .... Krishna Shah
SHALOM .... Yaky Yosha
SHAME .... Ingmar Bergman
SHAME, SHAME, EVERBODY KNOWS HER NAME .... Joseph Jacoby
SHAMISEN AND MOTORCYCLE .... Masahiro Shinoda
SHAMPOO .... Hal Ashby
SHAMROCK HILL .... Arthur Dreifuss
SHAMUS .... Buzz Kulik
SHANGHAI COBRA, THE .... Phil Karlson
SHAPE OF THINGS TO COME, THE .... George McCowan
SHARK KILL (TF) .... William A. Graham
SHARK! .... Samuel Fuller
SHARK'S TREASURE .... Cornel Wilde
SHARKY'S MACHINE .... Burt Reynolds
SHARON: PORTRAIT OF A MISTRESS (TF) .... Robert Greenwald
SHATTERED VOWS (TF) .... Jack Bender
SHE .... Robert Day
SHE .... Avi Nesher
S*H*E* (TF) .... Robert M. Lewis
SHE CAME TO THE VALLEY .... Albert Band
SHE CRIED "MURDER" (TF) .... Herschel Daugherty
SHE CRIED MURDER (TF) .... Bernard L. Kowalski
SHE DANCES ALONE .... Robert Dornhelm
SHE GODS OF SHARK REEF, THE .... Roger Corman
SHE LIVES (TF) .... Stuart Hagmann
SHE WAITS (TF) .... Delbert Mann
SHEENA .... John Guillermin
SHEEP HAS FIVE LEGS, THE .... Henri Verneuil
SHEILA LEVINE IS DEAD AND LIVING IN NEW YORK .... Sidney J. Furie
SHE'LL BE SWEET (MS) .... Gene Levitt
SHELL GAME (TF) .... Glenn Jordan
SHENANDOAH .... Andrew V. McLaglen
SHENANIGANS .... Joseph Jacoby
SHEPHERD OF THE HILLS, THE .... Henry Hathaway
SHERIFF, THE (TF) .... David Lowell Rich
SHE'S BACK ON BROADWAY .... Gordon Douglas
SHE'S DRESSED TO KILL (TF) .... Gus Trikonis
SHE'S IN THE ARMY NOW (TF) .... Hy Averback
SHIELD FOR MURDER .... Howard W. Koch
SHILLINGBURY BLOWERS, THE .... Val Guest
SHIMMERING LIGHT (TF) .... Don Chaffey
SHINING SEASON, A (TF) .... Stuart Margolin
SHINING STAR .... Sig Shore
SHINING, THE .... Stanley Kubrick
SHINING VICTORY .... Irving Rapper
SHIP OF FOOLS .... Stanley Kramer
SHIRLEY THOMPSON VERSUS THE ALIENS .... Jim Sharman
SHIRTS/SKINS (TF) .... William A. Graham
SHIVERS .... David Cronenberg
SHOCK CORRIDOR .... Samuel Fuller
SHOCK TREATMENT .... Denis Sanders
SHOCK TREATMENT .... Jim Sharman
SHOCK TROOPS .... Costa-Gavras
SHOCK WAVES .... Ken Wiederhorn
SHOES OF THE FISHERMAN, THE .... Michael Anderson
SHOGUN (MS) ★ .... Jerry London
SHOGUN ASSASSIN .... Robert "Bobby" Houston
SHOOT .... Harvey Hart
SHOOT FIRST .... Robert Parrish
SHOOT THE MOON .... Alan Parker
SHOOT TO KILL .... Michael Winner
SHOOTING PARTY, THE .... Alan Bridges
SHOOTING PARTY, THE .... Emil Loteanu
SHOOTING STARS (TF) .... Richard Lang
SHOOTING, THE .... Monte Hellman
SHOOTIST, THE .... Don Siegel
SHOOT-OUT .... Henry Hathaway
SHOOT-OUT AT MEDICINE BEND .... Richard L. Bare
SHOOTOUT IN A ONE-DOG TOWN (TF) .... Burt Kennedy
SHORT EYES .... Robert M. Young
SHOT IN THE DARK, A .... Blake Edwards
SHOUT AT THE DEVIL .... Peter Hunt
SHOUT, THE .... Jerzy Skolimowski
SHOW BOAT .... George Sidney
SHOWGIRL IN HOLLYWOOD .... Mervyn Leroy
SHOWMAN (FD) .... Albert Maysles
SHOWMAN (FD) .... David Maysles
SHRIKE, THE .... Jose Ferrer
SHUTTERED ROOM, THE .... David Greene
SI C'ETAIT A REFAIRE .... Claude Lelouch
SI J'ETAIS UN ESPION .... Bertrand Blier
SIBERIADE .... Andrei Konchalovsky
SIBERIAN LADY MACBETH .... Andrzej Wajda
SICILIAN CLAN, THE .... Henri Verneuil
SICILIAN CONNECTION, THE .... Ferdinando Baldi
SICILIAN LOVE AFFAIR .... Damiano Damiani
SIDDHARTHA .... Conrad Rooks
SIDE BY SIDE: THE TRUE STORY OF THE OSMOND FAMILY (TF) .... Russ Mayberry
SIDE SHOW (TF) .... William Conrad
SIDECAR RACERS .... Earl Bellamy
SIDEKICKS (TF) .... Burt Kennedy
SIDELONG GLANCES OF A PIGEON KICKER, THE .... John Dexter
SIDEWINDER ONE .... Earl Bellamy
SIDNEY SHELDON'S BLOODLINE .... Terence Young
SIDNEY SHELDON'S RAGE OF ANGELS (TF) .... Buzz Kulik
SIDNEY SHORR (TF) .... Russ Mayberry
SIEGE (TF) .... Richard Pearce
SIEGE OF THE SAXONS .... Nathan Juran
SIERRA BARON .... James B. Clark
SIGN OF FOUR, THE .... Desmond Davis
SIGN OF THE RAM, THE .... John Sturges
SIGNAL 7 .... Rob Nilsson
SIGNE ARSENE LUPIN .... Yves Robert
SIGNORE E SIGNORI BUONANOTTE .... Luigi Comencini
SIGNORE E SIGNORI BUONANOTTE .... Nanni Loy
SIGNORE E SIGNORI BUONANOTTE .... Mario Monicelli
SIGNORE E SIGNORI BUONANOTTE .... Ettore Scola
SIGNPOST TO MURDER .... George Englund
SIGNS OF LIFE .... Werner Herzog
SIKKIM .... Satyajit Ray
SILENCE .... John Korty
SILENCE .... Masahiro Shinoda
SILENCE, THE (TF) .... Joseph Hardy
SILENCE AND CRY .... Miklos Jancso
SILENCE OF THE HEART (TF) .... Richard Michaels
SILENCE OF THE NORTH .... Allan King
SILENCE, THE .... Ingmar Bergman
SILENCERS, THE .... Phil Karlson
SILENT GUN, THE (TF) .... Michael Caffey
SILENT MADNESS .... Simon Nuchtern
SILENT MOVIE .... Mel Brooks
SILENT NIGHT, BLOODY NIGHT .... Theodore Gershuny
SILENT NIGHT, DEADLY NIGHT .... Charles E. Sellier, Jr.
SILENT NIGHT, EVIL NIGHT .... Bob Clark
SILENT NIGHT, LONELY NIGHT (TF) .... Daniel Petrie
SILENT PARTNER, THE .... Daryl Duke
SILENT RAGE .... Michael Miller
SILENT RUNNING .... Douglas Trumbull
SILENT SCREAM .... Denny Harris
SILENT SENTENCE .... Larry G. Spangler
SILENT VICTORY: THE KITTY O'NEILL STORY (TF) ☆ .... Lou Antonio
SILENT WORLD, THE (FD) .... Louis Malle
SILK STOCKINGS .... Rouben Mamoulian
SILKWOOD ★ .... Mike Nichols
SILVER BEARS .... Ivan Passer
SILVER BULLET .... Daniel Attias
SILVER CITY .... Sophia Turkiewicz
SILVER DOUBLE SUICIDE .... Kaneto Shindo
SILVER DREAM RACER .... David Wickes
SILVER STREAK .... Arthur Hiller
SILVERADO .... Lawrence Kasdan
SIMABADDHA .... Satyajit Ray
SIMON .... Marshall Brickman
SIMON, KING OF WITCHES .... Bruce Kessler
SIMPLE STORY, A .... Claude Sautet
SIN, SUFFER AND REPENT .... Herschell Gordon Lewis
SIN, THE .... Kon Ichikawa
SINAI FIELD MISSION (FD) .... Frederick Wiseman
SINBAD AND THE EYE OF THE TIGER .... Sam Wanamaker
SINCERE HEART .... Masaki Kobayashi
SINCERELY YOURS .... Gordon Douglas
SINFUL DAVEY .... John Huston
SING SING .... Sergio Corbucci
SINGAPORE WOMAN .... Jean Negulesco
SINGER AND THE DANCER, THE .... Gillian Armstrong
SINGER NOT THE SONG, THE .... Roy Ward Baker
SINGIN' IN THE RAIN .... Stanley Donen
SINGIN' IN THE RAIN .... Gene Kelly
SINGING NUN, THE .... Henry Koster
SINGLE BARS, SINGLE WOMEN (TF) .... Harry Winer
SINGLE ROOM FURNISHED .... Matt Cimber
SINGLE-HANDED .... Roy Boulting
SINISTER MAN, THE .... Clive Donner
SINK THE BISMARCK! .... Lewis Gilbert
SINS OF DORIAN GRAY, THE (TF) .... Tony Maylam
SINS OF RACHEL CADE, THE .... Gordon Douglas
SINS OF THE FATHER (TF) .... Peter Werner
SINS OF THE PAST (TF) .... Peter H. Hunt
SINTHIA, THE DEVIL'S DOLL .... Ray Dennis Steckler

SIREN OF BAGDAD .... Richard Quine
SIROKKO .... Miklos Jancso
SISKA .... Alf Kjellin
SISTEMO L'AMERICA E
TORNO .... Nanni Loy
SISTER, SISTER (TF) .... John Berry
SISTER-IN-LAW, THE .... Joseph Ruben
SISTERS .... Brian De Palma
SITTING DUCKS .... Henry Jaglom
SITTING TARGET .... Douglas Hickox
SIX BRIDGES TO CROSS .... Joseph Pevney
SIX IN PARIS .... Jean-Luc Godard
SIX PACK .... Daniel Petrie
SIX WEEKS .... Tony Bill
SIX-MILLION DOLLAR
MAN, THE (TF) .... Richard Irving
SIXTEEN CANDLES .... John Hughes
SIXTH AND MAIN .... Chris Cain
SIZZLE (TF) .... Don Medford
SKAG (TF) ☆ .... Frank Perry
SKATEBOARD .... George Gage
SKATETOWN, U.S.A. .... William A. Levey
SKEEZER (TF) .... Peter H. Hunt
SKI BUM, THE .... Bruce Clark
SKI LIFT TO DEATH (TF) .... William Wiard
SKI PARTY .... Alan Rafkin
SKI TROOP ATTACK .... Roger Corman
SKID KIDS .... Don Chaffey
SKIDOO .... Otto Preminger
SKIN GAME .... Paul Bogart
SKOKIE (TF) ☆ .... Herbert Wise
SKULL, THE .... Freddie Francis
SKULLDUGGERY .... Gordon Douglas
SKY HEI$T (TF) .... Lee H. Katzin
SKY IS FALLING, THE .... Silvio Narizzano
SKY IS GRAY, THE (TF) .... Stan Lathan
SKY RIDERS .... Douglas Hickox
SKY TRAP, THE (TF) .... Jerome Courtland
SKYHIGH .... Nico Mastorakis
SKYJACKED .... John Guillermin
SKY'S THE LIMIT,
THE (TF) .... David Lowell Rich
SKYSCRAPER, THE .... Shirley Clarke
SKYWARD (TF) .... Ron Howard
SKYWATCH .... Lewis Gilbert
SKYWAY TO DEATH (TF) .... Gordon Hessler
SLALOM .... Luciano Salce
SLAMS, THE .... Jonathan Kaplan
SLAP SHOT .... George Roy Hill
SLAPSTICK .... Steven Paul
SLAPSTICK OF ANOTHER
KIND .... Steven Paul
SLASHER, THE .... Lewis Gilbert
SLATTERY'S HURRICANE .... Andre De Toth
SLAUGHTER .... Jack Starrett
SLAUGHTER ON TENTH
AVENUE .... Arnold Laven
SLAUGHTERHOUSE-FIVE .... George Roy Hill
SLAUGHTER'S BIG RIP-OFF ...... Gordon Douglas
SLAVE, THE .... Sergio Corbucci
SLAVE GIRLS .... Michael Carreras
SLAVE OF LOVE, A .... Nikita Mikhalkov
SLAYGROUND .... Terry Bedford
SLEEP .... Andy Warhol
SLEEPER .... Woody Allen
SLEEPING CAR MURDERS,
THE .... Costa-Gavras
SLEEPING CITY, THE .... George Sherman
SLEEPING DOGS .... Roger Donaldson
SLEEPS SIX (TF) .... James Cellan-Jones
SLENDER THREAD, THE .... Sydney Pollack
SLEUTH ★ .... Joseph L. Mankiewicz
SLEUTH SLAYER, THE .... Jimmy Huston
SLIGHT CASE OF LARCENY,
A .... Don Weis
SLIGHTLY PREGNANT MAN,
A .... Jacques Demy
SLIPPER AND THE ROSE: THE
STORY OF CINDERELLA,
THE .... Bryan Forbes
SLIPSTREAM .... David Acomba
SLITHER .... Howard Zieff
SLOW DANCING IN THE BIG
CITY .... John G. Avildsen
SLUGGER'S WIFE, THE .... Hal Ashby
SLUMBER PARTY
MASSACRE .... Amy Jones
SLUMBER PARTY '57 .... William A. Levey
SMALL BACK ROOM, THE .... Michael Powell
SMALL CHILD'S
FIRST ADVENTURE, A .... Nagisa Oshima
SMALL CIRCLE OF FRIENDS,
A .... Rob Cohen
SMALL KILLING, A (TF) ...... Steven Hillard Stern
SMALL MIRACLE, THE (TF) .... Jeannot Szwarc
SMALL TOWN IN TEXAS,
A .... Jack Starrett
SMALL WORLD OF SAMMY
LEE, THE .... Kenneth "Ken" Hughes
SMART ALEC .... John Guillermin
SMART GIRLS DON'T TALK ...... Richard L. Bare
SMASH PALACE .... Roger Donaldson
SMASHING TIME .... Desmond Davis
SMASH-UP ON INTERSTATE
5 (TF) .... John Llewellyn Moxey
SMIC, SMAC, SMOC .... Claude Lelouch
SMILE .... Michael Ritchie
SMILE JENNY, YOU'RE
DEAD (TF) .... Jerry Thorpe
SMILES OF A SUMMER
NIGHT .... Ingmar Bergman
SMILEY'S PEOPLE (MS) ☆ .... Simon Langton
SMITH! .... Michael O'Herlihy
SMITHEREENS .... Susan Seidelman
SMOKE SIGNAL .... Jerry Hopper
SMOKESCREEN .... James O'Connolly
SMOKEY AND THE BANDIT .... Hal Needham
SMOKEY AND THE BANDIT,
PART II .... Hal Needham
SMOKEY AND THE BANDIT
PART 3 .... Dick Lowry
SMOKEY AND THE
GOODTIME OUTLAWS .... Alex Grasshoff
SMOKEY BITES THE DUST ... Charles B. Griffith
SMOKY .... George Sherman
SMOOTH MOVES .... Charles E. Sellier, Jr.
SMORGASBORD .... Jerry Lewis
SNAKE WOMAN, THE .... Sidney J. Furie
SNAPSHOT .... Simon Wincer
SNATCHED (TF) .... Sutton Roley
SNIPER, THE .... Edward Dmytryk
SNOOP SISTERS, THE (TF) ..... Leonard B. Stern
SNOOPY, COME HOME (AF) .... Bill Melendez
SNORKEL, THE .... Guy Green
SNOW GOOSE, THE (TF) .... Patrick Garland
SNOW JOB .... George Englund
SNOWBEAST (TF) .... Herb Wallerstein
SO BIG .... Robert Wise
SO CLOSE TO LIFE .... Ingmar Bergman
SO FINE .... Andrew Bergman
SO THIS IS LOVE .... Frank Capra
SO THIS IS LOVE .... Gordon Douglas
SO THIS IS NEW YORK .... Richard Fleischer
SO THIS IS PARIS .... Richard Quine
SO WELL REMEMBERED .... Edward Dmytryk
SOAP OPERA .... Andy Warhol
S.O.B. .... Blake Edwards
SOFT BEDS AND HARD
BATTLES .... Roy Boulting
SOFTLY SOFTLY (MS) .... Henri Safran
SOGGY BOTTOM, U.S.A. ..... Theodore J. Flicker
SOL MADRID .... Brian G. Hutton
SOLARIS .... Andrei Tarkovsky
SOLD FOR SPARROW .... Gordon Flemyng
SOLDIER, THE .... Jim Glickenhaus
SOLDIER BLUE .... Ralph Nelson
SOLDIER IN THE RAIN .... Ralph Nelson
SOLDIER OF FORTUNE .... Edward Dmytryk
SOLDIER OF ORANGE .... Paul Verhoeven
SOLDIER OF THE NIGHT .... Dan Wolman
SOLDIER'S STORY, A .... Norman Jewison
SOLE SURVIVOR .... Thom Eberhardt
SOLE SURVIVOR (TF) .... Paul Stanley
SOLID GOLD CADILLAC,
THE .... Richard Quine
SOLITARY CHILD, A .... Gerald Thomas
SOLITARY MAN,
THE (TF) .... John Llewellyn Moxey
SOLO .... Lyman Dayton
SOMBRAS DE GLORIA .... Andrew L. Stone
SOMBRERO KID, THE .... George Sherman
SOME CALL IT LOVING .... James B. Harris
SOME CAME RUNNING .... Vincente Minnelli
SOME DAY .... Michael Powell
SOME GIRLS DO .... Ralph Thomas
SOME KIND OF HERO .... Michael Pressman
SOME KIND OF
MIRACLE (TF) .... Jerrold Freedman
SOME KIND OF NUT .... Garson Kanin
SOME LIKE IT COOL .... Michael Winner
SOME LIKE IT HOT ★ .... Billy Wilder
SOME PEOPLE .... Clive Donner
SOMEBODY KILLED HER
HUSBAND .... Lamont Johnson
SOMEBODY UP THERE LIKES
ME .... Robert Wise
SOMEONE BEHIND THE
DOOR .... Nicholas Gessner
SOMEONE I TOUCHED (TF) .... Lou Antonio
SOMEONE IS WATCHING
ME (TF) .... John Carpenter
SOMETHING ABOUT
AMELIA (TF) ☆ .... Randa Haines
SOMETHING ALWAYS
HAPPENS .... Michael Powell
SOMETHING BIG .... Andrew V. McLaglen
SOMETHING EVIL (TF) .... Steven Spielberg
SOMETHING FOR A LONELY
MAN (TF) .... Don Taylor
SOMETHING FOR
EVERYONE .... Harold Prince
SOMETHING FOR
JOEY (TF) ☆ .... Lou Antonio
SOMETHING FOR THE
BIRDS .... Robert Wise
SOMETHING OF VALUE .... Richard Brooks
SOMETHING SHORT OF
PARADISE .... David Helpern, Jr.
SOMETHING SO RIGHT (TF) .... Lou Antonio
SOMETHING TO HIDE .... Alastair Reid
SOMETHING WEIRD ..... Herschell Gordon Lewis
SOMETHING WICKED THIS
WAY COMES .... Jack Clayton
SOMETHING WILD .... Jack Garfein
SOMETIMES A GREAT
NOTION .... Paul Newman
SOMEWHERE BENEATH THE
WIDE SKY .... Masaki Kobayashi
SOMEWHERE IN THE
NIGHT .... Joseph L. Mankiewicz
SOMEWHERE IN TIME .... Jeannot Szwarc
SOMEWHERE, TOMORROW .... Robert Wiemer
SOMMARLEK .... Ingmar Bergman
SON NOM DE VENISE DANS
CALCUTTA DESERT (FD) ..... Marguerite Duras
SON OF BLOB .... Larry Hagman
SON OF DRACULA .... Freddie Francis
SON OF FLUBBER .... Robert Stevenson
SON OF ROBIN HOOD,
THE .... George Sherman
SON RISE: A MIRACLE OF
LOVE (TF) .... Glenn Jordan
SONAR KELLA .... Satyajit Ray
SONG OF NORWAY .... Andrew L. Stone
SONG OF PARIS .... John Guillermin
SONG OF SONGS .... Rouben Mamoulian
SONG OF SUMMER (TF) .... Ken Russell
SONG REMAINS THE
SAME, THE (FD) .... Peter Clifton
SONGWRITER .... Alan Rudolph
SONO FOTOGENICO .... Dino Risi
SONO STATO IO .... Alberto Lattuada
SONS AND LOVERS ★ .... Jack Cardiff
SONS OF KATIE ELDER,
THE .... Henry Hathaway
SONS OF THE GOOD
EARTH .... King Hu
SOONER OR LATER (TF) .... Bruce Hart
SOPHIA LOREN: HER OWN
STORY (TF) .... Mel Stuart
SOPHIE'S CHOICE .... Alan J. Pakula
SOPHIE'S PLACE .... James O'Connolly
SOPHISTICATED GENTS,
THE (TF) .... Harry Falk
SORCERER .... William Friedkin
SORCERESS .... Brian Stuart
SORORITY GIRL .... Roger Corman
SORROW AND THE PITY,
THE (FD) .... Marcel Ophuls
SORROW IS ONLY FOR
WOMEN .... Kaneto Shindo
S.O.S. PACIFIC .... Guy Green
S.O.S. TITANIC (TF) .... William "Billy" Hale
SOTTO IL SEGNO DELLO
SCORPIONE .... Paolo Taviani
SOTTO IL SEGNO DELLO
SCORPIONE .... Vittorio Taviani
SOTTO, SOTTO .... Lina Wertmuller
SOUL OF NIGGER CHARLEY,
THE .... Larry G. Spangler
SOUL SOLDIER .... John "Bud" Cardos
SOUL TO SOUL (FD) .... Denis Sanders
SOULS AT SEA .... Henry Hathaway
SOUND AND THE FURY,
THE .... Martin Ritt
SOUND BARRIER, THE .... David Lean
SOUND OF ANGER,
THE (TF) .... Michael Ritchie
SOUND OF FURY, THE .... Cy Endfield
SOUND OF MUSIC ★★,
THE .... Robert Wise

SOUND OF THE CITY: LONDON 1964-73 (FD) ... Peter Clifton
SOUND OF TRUMPETS, THE ... Ermanno Olmi
SOUND OFF ... Richard Quine
SOUNDER ... Martin Ritt
SOUP FOR ONE ... Jonathan Kaufer
SOUPCON ... Jean-Charles Tacchella
SOUTH OF THE BORDER ... George Sherman
SOUTH PACIFIC ... Joshua Logan
SOUTHERN COMFORT ... Walter Hill
SOUTHERN STAR, THE ... Sidney Hayers
SOVVERSIVI ... Paolo Taviani
SOVVERSIVI ... Vittorio Taviani
SOYLENT GREEN ... Richard Fleischer
SPACE ... Andy Warhol
SPACE (MS) ... Lee Philips
SPACE (MS) ... Joseph Sargent
SPACE CHILDREN, THE ... Jack Arnold
SPACE MOVIE, THE (FD) ... Tony Palmer
SPACE RAIDERS ... Howard R. Cohen
SPACEHUNTER: ADVENTURES IN THE FORBIDDEN ZONE ... Lamont Johnson
SPACESHIP ... Bruce Kimmel
SPANISH AFFAIR ... Don Siegel
SPANISH GARDENER, THE ... Philip Leacock
SPARKLE ... Sam O'Steen
SPARROW ... John Berry
SPARTACUS ... Stanley Kubrick
SPASMS ... William Fruet
SPAWN OF THE NORTH ... Henry Hathaway
SPECIAL DAY, A ... Ettore Scola
SPECIAL DELIVERY ... Paul Wendkos
SPECIAL EFFECTS ... Larry Cohen
SPECIAL OLYMPICS (TF) ... Lee Philips
SPECIAL PEOPLE BASED ON A TRUE STORY (TF) ... Marc Daniels
SPECIAL SECTION ... Costa-Gavras
SPECIAL TREATMENT ... Goran Paskaljevic
SPECIALIST, THE ... Howard (Hikmet) Avedis
SPECIALISTS, THE (TF) ... Richard Quine
SPECTRE (TF) ... Clive Donner
SPEED KING, THE (TF) ... Ferdinand Fairfax
SPEED LIMIT 65 ... Yaphet Kotto
SPEEDTRAP ... Earl Bellamy
SPELL, THE (TF) ... Lee Philips
SPETTERS ... Paul Verhoeven
SPHINX ... Franklin J. Schaffner
SPIDER, THE ... Bert I. Gordon
SPIDER-MAN (TF) ... E.W. Swackhamer
SPIDER'S STRATAGEM, THE ... Bernardo Bertolucci
SPIKES GANG, THE ... Richard Fleischer
SPIRAL ROAD, THE ... Robert Mulligan
SPIRAL, THE ... Krzysztof Zanussi
SPIRIT OF ST. LOUIS, THE ... Billy Wilder
SPIRITS OF THE DEAD ... Federico Fellini
SPIRITS OF THE DEAD ... Louis Malle
SPIRITS OF THE DEAD ... Roger Vadim
SPLASH ... Ron Howard
SPLENDOR IN THE GRASS ... Elia Kazan
SPLENDOR IN THE GRASS (TF) ... Richard C. Sarafian
SPLINTERED ... Claude Chabrol
SPLIT, THE ... Gordon Flemyng
SPLIT IMAGE ... Ted Kotcheff
SPLITZ ... Domonic Paris
SPOILED CHILDREN ... Bertrand Tavernier
SPONGERS, THE (TF) ... Roland Joffé
SPOOK WHO SAT BY THE DOOR, THE ... Ivan Dixon
SPOOKY BUNCH, THE ... Ann Hui
SPORTING CLUB, THE ... Larry Peerce
SPRAGGUE (TF) ... Larry Elikann
SPREE ... Walon Green
SPRING BREAK ... Sean S. Cunningham
SPRING FEVER ... Joseph L. Scanlan
SPRING PARADE ... Henry Koster
SPRINGFIELD RIFLE ... Andre De Toth
SPRINGTIME IN THE SIERRAS ... William Witney
SPY HUNT ... George Sherman
SPY IN BLACK, THE ... Michael Powell
SPY KILLER, THE (TF) ... Roy Ward Baker
SPY WHO CAME IN FROM THE COLD, THE ... Martin Ritt
SPY WHO LOVED ME, THE ... Lewis Gilbert
SPY WITH A COLD NOSE, THE ... Daniel Petrie
SPY WITH MY FACE, THE ... John Newland
S*P*Y*S ... Irvin Kershner
SQUARE JUNGLE, THE ... Jerry Hopper
SQUARING THE CIRCLE (TF) ... Mike Hodges
SQUEEZE, THE ... Michael Apted
SQUEEZE, THE ... Anthony M. Dawson
SQUEEZE A FLOWER ... Marc Daniels
SQUEEZE PLAY! ... Samuel Weil
SQUIRM ... Jeff Lieberman
Sssssss ... Bernard L. Kowalski
SST - DEATH FLIGHT (TF) ... David Lowell Rich
ST. ELMO'S FIRE ... Joel Schumacher
ST. HELENS ... Ernest Pintoff
ST. IVES ... J. Lee Thompson
ST. LOUIS BLUES ... Allen Reisner
ST. VALENTINE'S DAY MASSACRE, THE ... Roger Corman
STAGE STRUCK ... Sidney Lumet
STAGE TO THUNDER ROCK ... William F. Claxton
STAGECOACH ... Gordon Douglas
STAGECOACH EXPRESS ... George Sherman
STAGECOACH TO DANCERS' ROCK ... Earl Bellamy
STAGECOACH TO FURY ... William F. Claxton
STAIRCASE ... Stanley Donen
STAIRWAY TO HEAVEN ... Michael Powell
STAKEOUT ON DOPE STREET ... Irvin Kershner
STALAG 17 ★ ... Billy Wilder
STALK THE WILD CHILD (TF) ... William "Billy" Hale
STALKER ... Andrei Tarkovsky
STALKING MOON, THE ... Robert Mulligan
STAND BY YOUR MAN (TF) ... Jerry Jameson
STAND UP AND BE COUNTED ... Jackie Cooper
STANDING IN THE SHADOWS OF LOVE ... William Crain
STANDING TALL (TF) ... Harvey Hart
STAN'S LAST NAME (TF) ... Gavin Millar
STAR! ... Robert Wise
STAR CHAMBER, THE ... Peter Hyams
STAR IS BORN, A ... Frank Pierson
STAR MAKER, THE (TF) ... Lou Antonio
STAR REPORTER, THE ... Michael Powell
STAR SPANGLED GIRL ... Jerry Paris
STAR TREK - THE MOTION PICTURE ... Robert Wise
STAR TREK II: THE WRATH OF KHAN ... Nicholas Meyer
STAR TREK III: THE SEARCH FOR SPOCK ... Leonard Nimoy
STAR WARS ★ ... George Lucas
STAR 80 ... Bob Fosse
STARBIRDS (ATF) ... Michael Part
STARCRASH ... Lewis Coates
STARDUST ... Michael Apted
STARDUST MEMORIES ... Woody Allen
STARFLIGHT: THE PLANE THAT COULDN'T LAND (TF) ... Jerry Jameson
STARHOPS ... Barbara Peeters
STARMAN ... John Carpenter
STARS AND STRIPES FOREVER ... Henry Koster
STARSTRUCK ... Gillian Armstrong
START THE REVOLUTION WITHOUT ME ... Bud Yorkin
STARTING OVER ... Alan J. Pakula
STATE FAIR ... Jose Ferrer
STATE OF SIEGE ... Costa-Gavras
STATE OF THE UNION ... Frank Capra
STATE OF THINGS, THE ... Wim Wenders
STATION 307 ... Louis Malle
STATUE, THE ... Rod Amateau
STAVISKY ... Alain Resnais
STAY AWAY, JOE ... Peter Tewksbury
STAY HUNGRY ... Bob Rafelson
STAYING ALIVE ... Sylvester Stallone
STAYING ON (TF) ... Silvio Narizzano
STEAGLE, THE ... Paul Sylbert
STEEL ... Steve Carver
STEEL ARENA ... Mark L. Lester
STEEL BAYONET, THE ... Michael Carreras
STEEL CAGE, THE ... Walter Doniger
STEEL COWBOY (TF) ... Harvey Laidman
STEEL HELMET, THE ... Samuel Fuller
STEEL JUNGLE, THE ... Walter Doniger
STEEL TOWN ... George Sherman
STEEL TRAP, THE ... Andrew L. Stone
STEELYARD BLUES ... Alan Myerson
STELLA ... Michael Cacoyannis
STEP OUT OF LINE, A (TF) ... Bernard McEveety
STEPFORD WIVES, THE ... Bryan Forbes
STEPHEN KING'S CAT'S EYE ... Lewis Teague
STEPMOTHER, THE ... Howard (Hikmet) Avedis
STEPPE, THE ... Sergei Bondarchuk
STEPTOE AND SON ... Cliff Owen
STEPTOE AND SON RIDE AGAIN ... Peter Sykes
STEREO ... David Cronenberg
STERILE CUCKOO, THE ... Alan J. Pakula
STEVIE ... Robert Enders
STICK ... Burt Reynolds
STICK UP, THE ... Jeffrey Bloom
STICKIN' TOGETHER (TF) ... Jerry Thorpe
STILETTO ... Bernard L. Kowalski
STILL OF THE NIGHT ... Robert Benton
STILL THE BEAVER (TF) ... Steven Hillard Stern
STIMULANTIA ... Vilgot Sjoman
STING ★★, THE ... George Roy Hill
STING II, THE ... Jeremy Paul Kagan
STIR CRAZY ... Sidney Poitier
STITCHES ... Rod Holcomb
STOCKHOLM (TD) ... Mai Zetterling
STOLEN DESIRE, THE ... Shohei Imamura
STOLEN HEAVEN ... George Abbott
STOLEN HEAVEN ... Andrew L. Stone
STOLEN HOURS ... Daniel Petrie
STOLEN LOVE ... Kon Ichikawa
STOLEN PLANS, THE ... James Hill
STONE (TF) ... Corey Allen
STONE BOY, THE ... Chris Cain
STONE COLD DEAD ... George Mendeluk
STONE KILLER, THE ... Michael Winner
STONESTREET: WHO KILLED THE CENTERFOLD MODEL? (TF) ... Russ Mayberry
STONY ISLAND ... Andrew Davis
STOOLIE, THE ... John G. Avildsen
STOP ... Bill Gunn
STOP MAKING SENSE (FD) ... Jonathan Demme
STOP ME BEFORE I KILL ... Val Guest
STOP THE WORLD - I WANT TO GET OFF ... Philip Saville
STOP WATCH (TF) ... John Duigan
STORE, THE (FD) ... Frederick Wiseman
STORK BITES MAN ... Cy Endfield
STORM BOY ... Henri Safran
STORM CENTER ... Daniel Taradash
STORM FEAR ... Cornel Wilde
STORM OVER LISBON ... George Sherman
STORM OVER THE NILE ... Terence Young
STORM RIDERS, THE ... Richard L. Bare
STORMY WEATHER ... Andrew L. Stone
STORY OF A LOVE AFFAIR ... Michelangelo Antonioni
STORY OF A THREE-DAY PASS, THE ... Melvin Van Peebles
STORY OF DAVID, THE (TF) ... David Lowell Rich
STORY OF ESTHER COSTELLO, THE ... David Miller
STORY OF JACOB AND JOSEPH, THE (TF) ... Michael Cacoyannis
STORY OF JOSEPH AND HIS BRETHREN, THE ... Irving Rapper
STORY OF MANKIND, THE ... Irwin Allen
STORY OF MY LOVING WIFE ... Kaneto Shindo
STORY OF O, THE ... Just Jaeckin
STORY OF PIERA, THE ... Marco Ferreri
STORY OF PRETTY BOY FLOYD, THE (TF) ... Clyde Ware
STORY OF ROBIN HOOD, THE ... Ken Annakin
STORY OF RUTH, THE ... Henry Koster
STORY OF THREE LOVES, THE ... Vincente Minnelli
STORY OF WOO VIET, THE ... Ann Hui
STORYTELLER, THE (TF) ... Robert Markowitz
STOWAWAY GIRL ... Guy Hamilton
STOWAWAY TO THE MOON (TF) ... Andrew V. McLaglen
STRAIGHT TIME ... Ulu Grosbard
STRANGE ADVENTURE, A ... William Witney
STRANGE AFFAIR, THE ... David Greene
STRANGE AND DEADLY OCCURENCE, THE (TF) ... John Llewellyn Moxey
STRANGE BEDFELLOWS ... Melvin Frank
STRANGE BEHAVIOR ... Michael Laughlin
STRANGE BREW ... Rick Moranis
STRANGE BREW ... Dave Thomas
STRANGE CASE OF THE END OF CIVILISATION AS WE KNOW IT, THE (TF) ... Joseph McGrath

STRANGE DOOR, THE .... Joseph Pevney
STRANGE HOLIDAY .... Arch Oboler
STRANGE HOMECOMING (TF) .... Lee H. Katzin
STRANGE INTRUDER .... Irving Rapper
STRANGE INVADERS .... Michael Laughlin
STRANGE LADY IN TOWN .... Mervyn Leroy
STRANGE NEW WORLD (TF) .... Robert Butler
STRANGE ONE, THE .... Jack Garfein
STRANGE POSSESSION OF MRS. OLIVER, THE (TF) .... Gordon Hessler
STRANGE VENGEANCE OF ROSALIE, THE .... Jack Starrett
STRANGER, THE (TF) .... Lee H. Katzin
STRANGER, THE .... Orson Welles
STRANGER AND THE GUNFIGHTER, THE .... Anthony M. Dawson
STRANGER AT JEFFERSON HIGH, THE (TF) .... Lyman Dayton
STRANGER IN BETWEEN, THE .... Charles Crichton
STRANGER IN OUR HOUSE (TF) .... Wes Craven
STRANGER IN THE HOUSE .... Bob Clark
STRANGER IS WATCHING, A .... Sean S. Cunningham
STRANGER ON THE RUN (TF) .... Don Siegel
STRANGER THAN PARADISE .... Jim Jarmusch
STRANGER WHO LOOKS LIKE ME, THE (TF) .... Larry Peerce
STRANGER WITHIN, THE (TF) .... Lee Philips
STRANGER WORE A GUN, THE .... Andre De Toth
STRANGERS IN PARADISE .... Ulli Lommel
STRANGERS IN 7A, THE (TF) .... Paul Wendkos
STRANGERS KISS .... Matthew Chapman
STRANGERS' MEETING .... Robert Day
STRANGERS: THE STORY OF A MOTHER AND A DAUGHTER (TF) .... Milton Katselas
STRANGERS WHEN WE MEET .... Richard Quine
STRANGLER, THE .... Burt Topper
STRANGLER'S WEB .... John Llewellyn Moxey
STRATEGY OF TERROR .... Jack Smight
STRAW DOGS .... Sam Peckinpah
STRAWBERRIES NEED RAIN .... Larry Buchanan
STRAWBERRY STATEMENT, THE .... Stuart Hagmann
STRAY DOG .... Akira Kurosawa
STRAZIAMI DA MI BACI SAZIAMI .... Dino Risi
STREAMERS .... Robert Altman
STREET GIRLS .... Michael Miller
STREET KILLING (TF) .... Harvey Hart
STREET LOVE .... Rose Marie Turko
STREET MUSIC .... Jenny Bowen
STREETCAR NAMED DESIRE ☆, A(TF) .... John Erman
STREETCAR NAMED DESIRE ★, A .... Elia Kazan
STREETS OF FIRE .... Walter Hill
STREETS OF L.A., THE (TF) .... Jerrold Freedman
STREETS OF SAN FRANCISCO, THE (TF) .... Walter Grauman
STREETWARS .... Jamaa Fanaka
STRESS AND EMOTIONS .... Robin Spry
STRESS ES TRES TRES .... Carlos Saura
STRICTLY DISHONORABLE .... Melvin Frank
STRICTLY DISHONORABLE ...... Norman Panama
STRIKING BACK .... William Fruet
STRIP POKER .... Peter Walker
STRIPES .... Ivan Reitman
STRIPPER, THE .... Franklin J. Schaffner
STROHFEUER .... Volker Schlondorff
STROKER ACE .... Hal Needham
STRONG MAN, THE .... Frank Capra
STRONG WOMAN AND WEAK MAN .... Kaneto Shindo
STRONGER THAN THE SUN (TF) .... Michael Apted
STRONGEST MAN IN THE WORLD, THE .... Vincent McEveety
STROSZEK .... Werner Herzog
STRUCTURE OF CRYSTALS, THE .... Krzysztof Zanussi
STUCK ON YOU ! .... Michael Herz
STUCK ON YOU ! .... Samuel Weil
STUD, THE .... Quentin Masters
STUD BROWN .... Al Adamson
STUDENT BODIES .... Mickey Rose
STUDENT NURSES, THE ..... Stephanie Rothman
STUDENT TEACHERS, THE ...... Jonathan Kaplan
STUDS LONIGAN (MS) .... James Goldstone
STUDY IN TERROR, A .... James Hill
STUFF, THE .... Larry Cohen
STUNT MAN ★, THE .... Richard Rush
STUNT SEVEN (TF) .... John Peyser
STUNTS .... Mark L. Lester
STUNTS UNLIMITED (TF) .... Hal Needham
SUBJECT WAS ROSES, THE .... Ulu Grosbard
SUBMARINE .... Frank Capra
SUBMARINE X-1 .... William A. Graham
SUBURBAN ROULETTE .... Herschell Gordon Lewis
SUBURBIA .... Penelope Spheeris
SUBWAY .... Luc Besson
SUBWAY RIDERS .... Amos Poe
SUCCESS .... William Richert
SUCCESS IS THE BEST REVENGE .... Jerzy Skolimowski
SUCH GOOD FRIENDS .... Otto Preminger
SUCKER, THE .... Gerard Oury
SUDDEN DANGER .... Hubert Cornfield
SUDDEN DEATH .... Eddie Romero
SUDDEN FEAR .... David Miller
SUDDEN IMPACT .... Clint Eastwood
SUDDEN TERROR .... John Hough
SUDDEN WEALTH OF THE POOR PEOPLE OF KOMBACK, THE .... Volker Schlondorff
SUDDENLY LAST SUMMER .... Joseph L. Mankiewicz
SUDDENLY, LOVE (TF) .... Stuart Margolin
SUDDENLY SINGLE (TF) .... Jud Taylor
SUGAR COOKIES .... Theodore Gershuny
SUGAR HILL .... Paul Maslansky
SUGARLAND EXPRESS, THE .... Steven Spielberg
SUICIDE .... Andy Warhol
SUICIDE'S WIFE, THE (TF) .... John Newland
SULLIVANS, THE (MS) .... David Stevens
SULLIVANS, THE (MS) .... Simon Wincer
SULLIVAN'S EMPIRE .... Harvey Hart
SULTAN'S DAUGHTER, THE ...... Arthur Dreifuss
SUMMER (TF) .... Dezso Magyar
SUMMER AND SMOKE .... Peter Glenville
SUMMER CAMP .... Chuck Vincent
SUMMER FANTASIES (TF) .... Noel Nosseck
SUMMER GIRL (TF) .... Robert M. Lewis
SUMMER HOLIDAY .... Rouben Mamoulian
SUMMER HOLIDAY .... Peter Yates
SUMMER IN THE CITY (DEDICATED TO THE KINKS) .... Wim Wenders
SUMMER LOVERS .... Randal Kleiser
SUMMER MADNESS ★ .... David Lean
SUMMER OF MY GERMAN SOLDIER (TF) .... Michael Tuchner
SUMMER OF SECRETS .... Jim Sharman
SUMMER OF '42 .... Robert Mulligan
SUMMER SCHOOL TEACHERS .... Barbara Peeters
SUMMER WISHES, WINTER DREAMS .... Gilbert Cates
SUMMER WITHOUT BOYS, A (TF) .... Jeannot Szwarc
SUMMERSPELL .... Lina Shanklin
SUMMERTIME .... David Lean
SUMMERTIME BLUES .... William Olsen
SUMMERTREE .... Anthony Newley
SUN ALSO RISES, THE (TF) ... James Goldstone
SUNBURN .... Richard C. Sarafian
SUNDAY BLOODY SUNDAY ★ .... John Schlesinger
SUNDAY IN NEW YORK .... Peter Tewksbury
SUNDAY IN THE COUNTRY, A .... Bertrand Tavernier
SUNDAY LOVERS .... Bryan Forbes
SUNDAY LOVERS .... Edouard Molinaro
SUNDAY LOVERS .... Dino Risi
SUNDAY LOVERS .... Gene Wilder
SUNDAY PUNCH .... David Miller
SUNDAY SINNERS .... Arthur Dreifuss
SUNDAY WOMAN .... Luigi Comencini
SUNDOWN .... Henry Hathaway
SUNDOWNERS ★, THE .... Fred Zinnemann
SUNNY SIDE OF THE STREET .... Richard Quine
SUNNYSIDE .... Timothy Galfas
SUN'S BURIAL, THE .... Nagisa Oshima
SUNSET BOULEVARD ★★ .... Billy Wilder
SUNSET COVE .... Al Adamson
SUNSET LIMOUSINE (TF) .... Terry Hughes
SUNSET PASS .... Henry Hathaway
SUNSHINE (TF) .... Joseph Sargent
SUNSHINE BOYS, THE .... Herbert Ross
SUNSHINE CHRISTMAS (TF) .... Glenn Jordan
SUNSHINE PATRIOT, THE (TF) .... Joseph Sargent
SUNSTROKE .... Yaky Yosha
SUPER COPS (TF) .... Gordon Parks
SUPER COPS, THE .... Gordon Parks
SUPER DUDE .... Henry Hathaway
SUPER FUZZ .... Sergio Corbucci
SUPERCOCK .... Gus Trikonis
SUPERDAD .... Vincent McEveety
SUPERDOME (TF) .... Jerry Jameson
SUPERFLY T.N.T. .... Ron O'Neal
SUPERGIRL .... Jeannot Szwarc
SUPERMAN .... Richard Donner
SUPERMAN II .... Richard Lester
SUPERMAN III .... Richard Lester
SUPERNATURAL, THE .... Armand Mastroianni
SUPERSTARS IN FILM CONCERT (FD) .... Peter Clifton
SUPERVAN .... Lamar Card
SUPERVIXENS .... Russ Meyer
SUPPORT YOUR LOCAL GUNFIGHTER .... Burt Kennedy
SUPPORT YOUR LOCAL SHERIFF .... Burt Kennedy
SUPPOSE THEY GAVE A WAR AND NOBODY CAME? .... Hy Averback
SUR ET SOUS LA COMMUNICATION .... Jean-Luc Godard
SURE THING, THE .... Rob Reiner
SURF .... Don Chaffey
SURF II .... Randall Badat
SURF PARTY .... Maury Dexter
SURFACING .... Claude Jutra
SURPRISE PACKAGE .... Stanley Donen
SURPRISE PARTY .... Roger Vadim
SURVIVAL OF DANA (TF) .... Jack Starrett
SURVIVAL '67 .... Jules Dassin
SURVIVOR, THE .... David Hemmings
SURVIVORS, THE .... Michael Ritchie
SUSPECT .... John Boulting
SUSPECT .... Roy Boulting
SUSPIRIA .... Dario Argento
SUZANNE .... Robin Spry
SVEGLIATI E UCCIDI .... Carlo Lizzani
SVENGALI (TF) .... Anthony Harvey
S.W.A.L.K. .... Waris Hussein
SWALLOWS AND AMAZONS .... Claude Whatham
SWAMP THING .... Wes Craven
SWAMP WOMAN .... Roger Corman
SWAN SONG (TF) .... Jerry London
SWANN IN LOVE .... Volker Schlondorff
SWARM, THE .... Irwin Allen
SWASHBUCKLER .... James Goldstone
SWASTIKA (FD) .... Philippe Mora
SWEDISH FLY GIRLS .... Jack O'Connell
SWEDISH MISTRESS, THE .... Vilgot Sjoman
SWEENEY .... David Wickes
SWEENEY 2 .... Tom Clegg
SWEET ADELINE .... Mervyn Leroy
SWEET AND THE BITTER, THE .... James Clavell
SWEET BIRD OF YOUTH .... Richard Brooks
SWEET CHARITY .... Bob Fosse
SWEET DREAMS .... Karel Reisz
SWEET GENEVIEVE .... Arthur Dreifuss
SWEET HOSTAGE (TF) .... Lee Philips
SWEET HOURS .... Carlos Saura
SWEET JESUS, PREACHER MAN .... Henning Schellerup
SWEET LOVE, BITTER .... Herbert Danska
SWEET MOVIE .... Dusan Makavejev
SWEET NOVEMBER .... Robert Ellis Miller
SWEET REVENGE .... Jerry Schatzberg
SWEET REVENGE (TF) .... David Greene
SWEET RIDE, THE .... Harvey Hart
SWEET SIXTEEN .... Jim Sotos
SWEET SMELL OF SUCCESS .... Alexander Mackendrick
SWEET SOUL MUSIC (FD) .... Peter Clifton
SWEET SOUNDS .... James Ivory
SWEET SUZY ! .... Russ Meyer
SWEET, SWEET RACHEL (TF) .... Sutton Roley

SWEET SWEETBACK'S BAADASSSSSS SONG .... Melvin Van Peebles
SWEET TORONTO .... D.A. Pennebaker
SWEET WILLIAM .... Claude Whatham
SWEETHEART OF THE CAMPUS .... Edward Dmytryk
SWEPT AWAY BY AN UNUSUAL DESTINY IN THE BLUE SEA OF AUGUST .... Lina Wertmuller
SWIMMER, THE .... Frank Perry
SWIMMING POOL, THE .... Jacques Deray
SWING PARADE OF 1946 .... Phil Karlson
SWING SHIFT .... Jonathan Demme
SWINGER, THE .... George Sidney
SWINGERS' PARADISE .... Sidney J. Furie
SWINGIN' MAIDEN, THE .... Gerald Thomas
SWINGING AT THE CASTLE .... Alf Kjellin
SWINGING BARMAIDS, THE .... Gus Trikonis
SWINGING CHEERLEADERS, THE .... Jack Hill
SWISS CONSPIRACY, THE .... Jack Arnold
SWISS FAMILY ROBINSON .... Ken Annakin
SWISS FAMILY ROBINSON, THE (TF) .... Harry Harris
SWITCH (TF) .... Robert Day
SWITCHBLADE SISTERS .... Jack Hill
SWORD AND THE ROSE, THE .... Ken Annakin
SWORD AND THE SORCERER, THE .... Albert Pyun
SWORD IN THE DESERT .... George Sherman
SWORD IN THE STONE, THE (AF) .... Wolfgang Reitherman
SWORD OF ALI BABA, THE .... Virgil W. Vogel
SWORD OF D'ARTAGNAN, THE .... Budd Boetticher
SWORD OF LANCELOT, THE .... Cornel Wilde
SWORDKILL .... Larry Carroll
SWORDSMAN OF SIENA .... Etienne Perier
SYBIL (TF) .... Daniel Petrie
SYLVESTER .... Tim Hunter
SYLVIA .... Gordon Douglas
SYLVIA .... Michael Firth
SYMPATHY FOR THE DEVIL–1 + 1 .... Jean-Luc Godard
SYMPHONY FOR A MASSACRE .... Jacques Deray
SYNANON .... Richard Quine
SYSKONBADD 1782 .... Vilgot Sjoman
SYSTEM, THE .... Michael Winner
SZERELEM, ELEKTRA .... Miklos Jancso

T

TABLE FOR FIVE .... Robert Lieberman
TABU .... Vilgot Sjoman
TAG .... Nick Castle
TAIL GUNNER JOE (TF) ☆ .... Jud Taylor
TAILOR'S MAID, THE .... Mario Monicelli
TAKE A GIANT STEP .... Philip Leacock
TAKE A GIRL LIKE YOU .... Jonathan Miller
TAKE A HARD RIDE .... Anthony M. Dawson
TAKE CARE OF MY LITTLE GIRL .... Jean Negulesco
TAKE DOWN .... Kieth Merrill
TAKE HER, SHE'S MINE .... Henry Koster
TAKE MY LIFE .... Ronald Neame
TAKE THE HIGH GROUND .... Richard Brooks
TAKE THE MONEY AND RUN .... Woody Allen
TAKE THIS JOB AND SHOVE IT .... Gus Trikonis
TAKE YOUR BEST SHOT (TF) .... David Greene
TAKING OF PELHAM 1-2-3, THE .... Joseph Sargent
TAKING OFF .... Milos Forman
TAKING TIGER MOUNTAIN .... Tom Huckabee
TAKING TIGER MOUNTAIN .... Kent Smith
TALE OF GENJI, THE (MS) .... Kon Ichikawa
TALE OF TIFFANY LUST, THE .... Radley Metzger
TALE OF TWO CITIES, A (TF) .... Jim Goddard
TALE OF TWO CITIES, A .... Ralph Thomas
TALENT FOR LOVING, A .... Richard Quine
TALES FROM THE CRYPT .... Freddie Francis
TALES FROM THE VIENNA WOODS .... Maximilian Schell
TALES OF HOFFMAN, THE .... Michael Powell
TALES OF ORDINARY MADNESS .... Marco Ferreri
TALES OF TERROR .... Roger Corman
TALES OF THE GOLD MONKEY (TF) .... Ray Austin
TALES THAT WITNESS MADNESS .... Freddie Francis
TALK ABOUT A LADY .... George Sherman
TALKING WALLS .... Stephen F. Verona
TALL BLOND MAN WITH ONE BLACK SHOE, THE .... Yves Robert
TALL HEADLINES, THE .... Terence Young
TALL STORY .... Joshua Logan
TALL T, THE .... Budd Boetticher
TAM LIN .... Roddy McDowall
TAMAHINE .... Philip Leacock
TAMANGO .... John Berry
TAMARIND SEED, THE .... Blake Edwards
TAMING OF THE SHREW, THE .... Franco Zeffirelli
TAMMY AND THE BACHELOR .... Joseph Pevney
TANDARRA (MS) .... Russell Hagg
TANDARRA (MS) .... Simon Wincer
TANGANYIKA .... Andre De Toth
TANK .... Marvin J. Chomsky
TANK COMMANDOS .... Burt Topper
TANK FORCE .... Terence Young
TANYA'S ISLAND .... Alfred Sole
TAPS .... Harold Becker
TARANTULA .... Jack Arnold
TARANTULAS: THE DEADLY CARGO (TF) .... Stuart Hagmann
TARAS BULBA .... J. Lee Thompson
TARAWA BEACHHEAD .... Paul Wendkos
TARGET .... Arthur Penn
TARGET: HARRY .... Roger Corman
TARGET RISK (TF) .... Robert Scheerer
TARGET UNKNOWN .... George Sherman
TARGETS .... Peter Bogdanovich
TARZAN AND JANE REGAINED...SORT OF .... Andy Warhol
TARZAN AND THE GREAT RIVER .... Robert Day
TARZAN AND THE VALLEY OF GOLD .... Robert Day
TARZAN GOES TO INDIA .... John Guillermin
TARZAN, THE APE MAN .... John Derek
TARZAN THE MAGNIFICENT .... Robert Day
TARZAN'S GREATEST ADVENTURE .... John Guillermin
TARZAN'S SAVAGE FURY .... Cy Endfield
TARZAN'S THREE CHALLENGES .... Robert Day
TASTE OF BLOOD, A .... Herschell Gordon Lewis
TASTE OF EVIL, A (TF) .... John Llewellyn Moxey
TASTE OF EXCITEMENT .... Don Sharp
TASTE OF HONEY, A .... Tony Richardson
TASTE OF SIN, A .... Ulli Lommel
TASTE THE BLOOD OF DRACULA .... Peter Sasdy
TATIANA .... David Hamilton
TATTERED DRESS, THE .... Jack Arnold
TATTERED WEB, A (TF) .... Paul Wendkos
TATTOO .... Bob Brooks
TAURUS RISING (MS) .... Igor Auzins
TAUW .... Ousmene Sembene
TAXI (TF) .... Russell Hagg
TAXI DRIVER .... Martin Scorsese
TAYLOR MEAD'S ASS .... Andy Warhol
TCHAO PANTIN .... Claude Berri
TEA AND SYMPATHY .... Vincente Minnelli
TEACHER, THE .... Howard (Hikmet) Avedis
TEACHERS .... Arthur Hiller
TEAHOUSE OF THE AUGUST MOON .... Daniel Mann
TEARS FOR SIMON .... Guy Green
TEARS ON THE LION'S MANE .... Masahiro Shinoda
TEEN MOTHERS .... Boaz Davidson
TEENAGE CAVEMAN .... Roger Corman
TEENAGE DOLL .... Roger Corman
TEENAGE REBELLION .... Richard Lester
TEENAGER .... Gerald Seth Sindell
TELEFON .... Don Siegel
TELEFONI BIANCHI .... Dino Risi
TELETHON (TF) .... David Lowell Rich
TELEVISION SPY .... Edward Dmytryk
TELFORD'S CHANGE (TF) .... Barry Davis
TELL ME A RIDDLE .... Lee Grant
TELL ME LIES .... Peter Brook
TELL ME MY NAME (TF) .... Delbert Mann
TELL ME THAT YOU LOVE ME, JUNIE MOON .... Otto Preminger
TELL ME WHERE IT HURTS (TF) .... Paul Bogart
TELL THEM WILLIE BOY IS HERE .... Abraham Polonsky
TEMPEST .... Alberto Lattuada
TEMPEST .... Paul Mazursky
TEMPEST, THE .... Derek Jarman
TEMPEST, THE .... Michael Powell
TEMPESTA SU CEYLON .... Gerd Oswald
TEMPLE OF THE SWINGING DOLL .... Paul Wendkos
TEN BLACK WOMEN .... Kon Ichikawa
TEN DAYS TO TULARA .... George Sherman
TEN DAYS' WONDER .... Claude Chabrol
TEN GENTLEMEN FROM WEST POINT .... Henry Hathaway
TEN VIOLENT WOMEN .... Ted V. Mikels
TENAFLY (TF) .... Richard A. Colla
TENANT, THE .... Roman Polanski
TENDER COMRADE .... Edward Dmytryk
TENDER IS THE NIGHT (CMS) .... Robert Knights
TENDER MERCIES ★ .... Bruce Beresford
TENDER WARRIOR, THE .... Stewart Raffill
TENDERNESS OF THE WOLVES .... Ulli Lommel
TENDRE COUSINES .... David Hamilton
TENEBRAE .... Dario Argento
TENNESSEE STALLION .... Donald Hulette
TENSION .... John Berry
TENSION AT TABLE ROCK .... Charles Marquis Warren
TENSPEED AND BROWNSHOE (TF) .... E.W. Swackhamer
TENTACLES .... Kaneto Shindo
TENTH LEVEL, THE (TF) .... Charles S. Dubin
TENTH MONTH, THE (TF) .... Joan Tewkesbury
TERESA .... Fred Zinnemann
TERM OF TRIAL .... Peter Glenville
TERMINAL ISLAND .... Stephanie Rothman
TERMINAL MAN, THE .... Mike Hodges
TERMINATOR, THE .... James Cameron
TERMS OF ENDEARMENT .... James L. Brooks
TERRACES (TF) .... Lila Garrett
TERRIBLE JOE MORAN (TF) .... Joseph Sargent
TERROR AMONG US (TF) .... Paul Krasny
TERROR AT BLACK FALLS .... Richard C. Sarafian
TERROR AT HALFDAY .... Herschell Gordon Lewis
TERROR EYES .... Kenneth "Ken" Hughes
TERROR FROM UNDER THE HOUSE/REVENGE .... Sidney Hayers
TERROR HOUSE .... Bud Townsend
TERROR IN THE AISLES (FD) .... Andrew J. Kuehn
TERROR IN THE SKY (TF) .... Bernard L. Kowalski
TERROR IN THE WAX MUSEUM .... Georg J. Fenady
TERROR OF SHEBA, THE .... Don Chaffey
TERROR ON THE BEACH (TF) .... Paul Wendkos
TERROR ON THE 40TH FLOOR (TF) .... Jerry Jameson
TERROR OUT OF THE SKY (TF) .... Lee H. Katzin
TERROR, THE .... Roger Corman
TERROR TRAIN .... Roger Spottiswoode
TERRORISTS, THE .... Casper Wrede
TERRY FOX STORY, THE (CTF) .... Ralph L. Thomas
TESS ★ .... Roman Polanski
TESTA OR CROCE .... Nanni Loy
TESTAMENT .... Lynne Littman
TESTIMONY OF TWO MEN (MS) .... Leo Penn
TESTIMONY OF TWO MEN (TF) .... Larry Yust
TEVYE AND HIS SEVEN DAUGHTERS .... Menahem Golan
TEX .... Tim Hunter
TEXAS ACROSS THE RIVER .... Michael Gordon
TEXAS CHAINSAW MASSACRE, THE .... Tobe Hooper
TEXAS DETOUR .... Howard (Hikmet) Avedis
TEXAS LEGEND/SUMMER HEAT, A .... Jack Starrett

TEXAS RANGERS, THE ....Phil Karlson
TEXAS TERRORS ....George Sherman
THADDEUS ROSE AND
EDDIE (TF) ....Jack Starrett
THANK GOD IT'S FRIDAY ....Robert Klane
THANK YOU ALL VERY
MUCH ....Waris Hussein
THAT CERTAIN FEELING ....Melvin Frank
THAT CERTAIN FEELING ....Norman Panama
THAT CERTAIN
SUMMER (TF) ☆ ....Lamont Johnson
THAT CERTAIN THING ....Frank Capra
THAT CHAMPIONSHIP
SEASON ....Jason Miller
THAT COLD DAY IN THE
PARK ....Robert Altman
THAT DARN CAT ....Robert Stevenson
THAT KIND OF GIRL ....Gerry O'Hara
THAT KIND OF WOMAN............Sidney Lumet
THAT LADY ....Terence Young
THAT LUCKY STIFF..................Chuck Vincent
THAT LUCKY TOUCH ....Christopher Miles
THAT MAN BOLT.................David Lowell Rich
THAT MAN FROM RIO..........Philippe de Broca
THAT MAN GEORGE! ....Jacques Deray
THAT NIGHT...........................John Newland
THAT RIVIERA TOUCH ....Cliff Owen
THAT SINKING FEELING ....Bill Forsyth
THAT SUMMER ....Harley Cokliss
THAT TOUCH OF MINK ....Delbert Mann
THAT WAS THE WEST THAT
WAS (TF) ....Fielder Cook
THAT WAS THEN, THIS IS
NOW ....Chris Cain
THAT'LL BE THE DAY............Claude Whatham
THAT'S CARRY ON ....Gerald Thomas
THAT'S DANCING! (FD) ....Jack Haley, Jr.
THAT'S ENTERTAINMENT,
PART 2 ....Gene Kelly
THAT'S ENTERTAINMENT,
PART 2 (FD) ....Jack Haley, Jr.
THAT'S ENTERTAINMENT!
(FD)......................................Jack Haley, Jr.
THAT'S THE WAY OF THE
WORLD ....Sig Shore
THEATRE OF BLOOD ....Douglas Hickox
THEM ....Gordon Douglas
THEN CAME
BRONSON (TF) ....William A. Graham
THEODOR HIERNEIS ODER:
WIE MAN EHEM. HOFKOCH
WIRD ....Hans-Jurgen Syberberg
THERE GOES KELLY ....Phil Karlson
THERE GOES THE BRIDGE ....Terry Marcel
THERE IS ANOTHER SIDE ....Lewis Gilbert
THERE IS NO THIRTEEN ....William Sachs
THERE WAS A CROOKED
MAN ....Stuart Burge
THERE WAS A CROOKED
MAN..................Joseph L. Mankiewicz
THERE'S A GIRL IN MY
HEART ....Arthur Dreifuss
THERE'S A GIRL IN MY
SOUP.......................................Roy Boulting
THERE'S ALWAYS
VANILLA ....George A. Romero
THERE'S MAGIC IN MUSIC .... Andrew L. Stone
THERESE AND IASBELLE ....Radley Metzger
THESE THOUSAND HILLS ...... Richard Fleischer
THETUS ....William Byron Hillman
THEY ALL DIED LAUGHING..........Don Chaffey
THEY ALL LAUGHED ....Peter Bogdanovich
THEY ALL LOVED HIM ....Luigi Comencini
THEY CALL IT
MURDER (TF) ....Walter Grauman
THEY CALL ME MISTER
TIBBS! ....Gordon Douglas
THEY CALL ME BRUCE? ....Elliott Hong
THEY CAME FROM BEYOND
SPACE ....Freddie Francis
THEY CAME FROM
WITHIN ....David Cronenberg
THEY CAN'T HANG ME ....Val Guest
THEY FOUGHT FOR THEIR
MOTHERLAND.................Sergei Bondarchuk
THEY KNEW WHAT THEY
WANTED ....Garson Kanin
THEY MIGHT BE GIANTS ....Anthony Harvey
THEY ONLY COME OUT AT
NIGHT (TF)................................Daryl Duke
THEY RODE WEST ....Phil Karlson
THEY SHOOT HORSES, DON'T
THEY? ★..............................Sydney Pollack
THEY WENT THAT-A-WAY
AND THAT-A-WAY ....Eric Weston
THEY WERE NOT DIVIDED........Terence Young
THEY WON'T FORGET ....Mervyn Leroy
THEY'RE A WEIRD MOB ....Michael Powell
THEY'RE PLAYING WITH
FIRE........................Howard (Hikmet) Avedis
THIEF...Michael Mann
THIEF (TF) ....William A. Graham
THIEF, THE ....Russell Rouse
THIEF OF BAGDAD, THE...........Michael Powell
THIEF OF BAGHDAD,
THE (TF) ....Clive Donner
THIEF OF HEARTS...........Douglas Day Stewart
THIEF OF PARIS, THE ....Louis Malle
THIEF WHO CAME TO
DINNER, THE ....Bud Yorkin
THIEVES.......................................John Berry
THIEVES AFTER DARK ....Samuel Fuller
THIEVES' HIGHWAY ....Jules Dassin
THIEVES LIKE US ....Robert Altman
THIN ICE ....Lamont Johnson
THIN ICE (TF)..................................Paul Aaron
THIN LINE, THE ....Michal Bat-Adam
THIN RED LINE, THE ....Andrew Marton
THING, THE ....John Carpenter
THINGS ARE TOUGH ALL
OVER ....Tom Avildsen
THINGS IN THEIR
SEASON (TF) ....James Goldstone
THINGS OF LIFE, THE................Claude Sautet
THIRD DAY, THE.........................Jack Smight
THIRD GIRL FROM THE
LEFT, THE (TF) ....Peter Medak
THIRD MAN ON THE
MOUNTAIN ....Ken Annakin
THIRD SECRET, THE ....Charles Crichton
THIRD VOICE, THE ....Hubert Cornfield
THIRST ....Ingmar Bergman
THIRTY SECONDS OVER
TOKYO.....................................Mervyn Leroy
THIRTY TIMES YOUR
MONEY ....Bo Widerberg
THIS ANGRY AGE ....René Clement
THIS CAN'T HAPPEN HERE .....Ingmar Bergman
THIS COULD BE THE
NIGHT....................................Robert Wise
THIS GIRL FOR HIRE (TF)...........Jerry Jameson
THIS HAPPY BREED ....David Lean
THIS HAPPY FEELING................Blake Edwards
THIS HOUSE
POSSESSED (TF) ....William Wiard
THIS INSTANT ....Emil Loteanu
THIS IS A HIJACK ....Barry Pollack
THIS IS ELVIS (FD) ....Malcolm Leo
THIS IS ELVIS (FD) ....Andrew Solt
THIS IS MY STREET ....Sidney Hayers
THIS IS SPINAL TAP........................Rob Reiner
THIS LADY IS A TRAMP............Chuck Vincent
THIS MAN MUST DIE..............Claude Chabrol
THIS MAN STANDS
ALONE (TF) ....Jerrold Freedman
THIS PROPERTY IS
CONDEMNED ....Sydney Pollack
THIS REBEL BREED ....Richard L. Bare
THIS SAVAGE LAND (TF) ...... Vincent McEveety
THIS SIDE OF THE LAW..............Richard L. Bare
THIS SPORTING LIFE........... Lindsay Anderson
THIS STUFF'LL KILL
YA!........................Herschell Gordon Lewis
THIS WAY - THAT WAY ....Kon Ichikawa
THOMAS CROWN AFFAIR,
THE ....Norman Jewison
THORN BIRDS ☆, THE (MS).............Daryl Duke
THORN IN THE HEART ....Alberto Lattuada
THORNWELL (TF) ....Harry Moses
THOROUGHLY MODERN
MILLIE..................................George Roy Hill
THOSE DARING YOUNG MEN
IN THEIR JAUNTY
JALOPIES ....Ken Annakin
THOSE FANTASTIC FLYING
FOOLS ....Don Sharp
THOSE GLORY, GLORY
DAYS (TF) ....Philip Saville
THOSE LIPS, THOSE EYES....Michael Pressman
THOSE MAGNIFICENT MEN IN
THEIR FLYING
MACHINES ....Ken Annakin
THOSE WERE THE HAPPY
TIMES ....Robert Wise
THOSE WHO MAKE
TOMORROW........................Akira Kurosawa
THOSE WHO TREAD ON THE
TIGER'S TAIL ....Akira Kurosawa
THOU SHALT NOT COMMIT
ADULTERY (TF) ....Delbert Mann
THOU SHALT NOT
KILL (TF).....................................I.C. Rapoport
THOUSANDS CHEER ....George Sidney
THREE...James Salter
THREE BAD MEN IN A
HIDDEN FORTRESS ....Akira Kurosawa
THREE BROTHERS......................Francesco Rosi
THREE CAME HOME................Jean Negulesco
THREE CARD MONTE ....Les Rose
THREE COINS IN THE
FOUNTAIN ....Jean Negulesco
THREE GUNS FOR TEXAS.............Earl Bellamy
THREE GUNS FOR TEXAS.....David Lowell Rich
THREE GUNS FOR TEXAS............Paul Stanley
THREE HATS FOR LISA ....Sidney Hayers
THREE HUNDRED MILES FOR
STEPHANIE (TF) ....Clyde Ware
THREE IN THE ATTIC ....Richard Wilson
THREE LIVES OF
THOMASINA, THE ....Don Chaffey
THREE LOVES ....Masaki Kobayashi
THREE MEN IN A BOAT ....Ken Annakin
THREE MEN ON A HORSE ....Mervyn Leroy
THREE MUSKETEERS, THE ....Richard Lester
THREE MUSKETEERS, THE .... George Sidney
THREE ON A COUCH ....Jerry Lewis
THREE ON A DATE (TF) ....Bill Bixby
THREE ON A MATCH ....Mervyn Leroy
THREE ON A SPREE ....Sidney J. Furie
THREE RESURRECTED
DRUNKARDS ....Nagisa Oshima
THREE RING CIRCUS ....Joseph Pevney
THREE SECRETS ....Robert Wise
THREE SISTERS ....Laurence Olivier
THREE SISTERS, THE ....Paul Bogart
THREE SMART GIRLS ....Henry Koster
THREE SMART GIRLS GROW
UP ....Henry Koster
THREE STARS ....Miklos Jancso
THREE STRANGE LOVES.........Ingmar Bergman
THREE STRANGERS.................Jean Negulesco
THREE TEXAS STEERS ....George Sherman
THREE TO GO ....Peter Weir
THREE WARRIORS ....Kieth Merrill
THREE WISE KINGS ....Sergio Corbucci
THREE WISHES OF BILLY
GRIER, THE (TF) ....Corey Blechman
THREE WORLDS OF
GULLIVER, THE ....Jack Sher
THREE'S A CROWD (TF) ....Harry Falk
THREESOME (TF).........................Lou Antonio
THRESHOLD ....Richard Pearce
THRILL KILLERS, THE ....Ray Dennis Steckler
THRILL OF IT ALL, THE ....Norman Jewison
THRILLING...................................Carlo Lizzani
THRILLING....................................Ettore Scola
THRONE OF BLOOD ....Akira Kurosawa
THROUGH A GLASS
DARKLY ....Ingmar Bergman
THROUGH NAKED
EYES (TF) ....John Llewellyn Moxey
THROUGH THE MAGIC
PYRAMID (TF) ....Ron Howard
THUMB TRIPPING ....Quentin Masters
THUNDER ALLEY .........................J.S. Cardone
THUNDER ALLEY ....Richard Rush
THUNDER AND LIGHTNING............Corey Allen
THUNDER IN THE SUN.............Russell Rouse
THUNDER OVER THE
PLAINS ....Andre De Toth
THUNDER ROCK ....Roy Boulting
THUNDERBALL.........................Terence Young
THUNDERBOLT ....John Sturges
THUNDERBOLT AND
LIGHTFOOT ....Michael Cimino
THUNDERHOOF..............................Phil Karlson
THUNDERING HERD, THE........ Henry Hathaway
THUNDERSTORM ....John Guillermin
THURSDAY'S CHILD (TF) ......David Lowell Rich
THX 1138.................................George Lucas
TI HO SPOSATO PER
ALLEGRIA ....Luciano Salce
TIARA TAHITI ....Ted Kotcheff
TICHBORNE AFFAIR,
THE (TF) ....Carl Schultz
...tick...tick...tick... ....Ralph Nelson
TICKET TO HEAVEN ....Ralph L. Thomas
TICKLISH AFFAIR, A ....George Sidney
TIFFANY JONES..........................Peter Walker

TIGER AND THE PUSSYCAT, THE ... Dino Risi
TIGER BAY ... J. Lee Thompson
TIGER IN SMOKE ... Roy Ward Baker
TIGER MAKES OUT, THE ... Arthur Hiller
TIGER TOWN (CTF) ... Alan Shapiro
TIGHT LITTLE ISLAND ... Alexander Mackendrick
TIGHT SPOT ... Phil Karlson
TIGHTROPE ... Richard Tuggle
TILL MARRIAGE US DO PART ... Luigi Comencini
TILL SEX DO US PART ... Vilgot Sjoman
TILL THE CLOUDS ROLL BY ... Vincente Minnelli
TILL THE END OF TIME ... Edward Dmytryk
TILT ... Rudy Durand
TIM ... Michael Pate
TIME AFTER TIME ... Nicholas Meyer
TIME BANDITS ... Terry Gilliam
TIME BOMB (TF) ... Paul Krasny
TIME FOR DYING, A ... Budd Boetticher
TIME FOR KILLING, A ... Phil Karlson
TIME FOR LOVING ... Christopher Miles
TIME FOR MIRACLES, A (TF) ... Michael O'Herlihy
TIME GENTLEMEN PLEASE! ... Lewis Gilbert
TIME IS MY ENEMY ... Don Chaffey
TIME LIMIT ... Yaphet Kotto
TIME LOST AND TIME REMEMBERED ... Desmond Davis
TIME MACHINE, THE (TF) ... Henning Schellerup
TIME OF THE JACKALS ... Damiano Damiani
TIME THERE WAS, A ... Tony Palmer
TIME TO DIE, A ... Matt Cimber
TIME TO RUN ... James F. Collier
TIME TO SING, A ... Arthur Dreifuss
TIME TRAVELERS (TF) ... Alexander Singer
TIME WALKER ... Tom Kennedy
TIMELOCK ... Gerald Thomas
TIMERIDER ... William Dear
TIMES SQUARE ... Allan Moyle
TIMESLIP ... Kenneth "Ken" Hughes
TIN DRUM, THE ... Volker Schlondorff
TINKER, TAILOR, SOLDIER, SPY (TF) ... John Irvin
TITAN FIND ... William Malone
TITANIC ... Jean Negulesco
TITFIELD THUNDERBOLT, THE ... Charles Crichton
TITICUT FOLLIES (FD) ... Frederick Wiseman
TITLE SHOT ... Les Rose
T.J. HOOKER (TF) ... Clifford Bole
TO ALL MY FRIENDS ON SHORE (TF) ... Gilbert Cates
TO BE A CROOK ... Claude Lelouch
TO BE OR NOT TO BE ... Alan Johnson
TO CATCH A KING (CTF) ... Clive Donner
TO COMMIT A MURDER ... Edouard Molinaro
TO DIE IN PARIS (TF) ... Charles S. Dubin
TO DIE IN PARIS (TF) ... Allen Reisner
TO FIND A MAN ... Buzz Kulik
TO FIND MY SON (TF) ... Delbert Mann
TO FORGET VENICE ... Franco Brusati
TO HAVE AND TO HOLD ... Herbert Wise
TO HEX WITH SEX ... Simon Nuchtern
TO JOY ... Ingmar Bergman
TO KILL A CLOWN ... George Bloomfield
TO KILL A COP (TF) ... Gary Nelson
TO KILL A MOCKINGBIRD ★ ... Robert Mulligan
TO LIVE AND DIE IN L.A. ... William Friedkin
TO LOVE AGAIN ... Kon Ichikawa
TO RACE THE WIND (TF) ... Walter Grauman
TO SIR, WITH LOVE ... James Clavell
TO THE DEVIL A DAUGHTER ... Peter Sykes
TO THE ENDS OF THE EARTH ... Robert Stevenson
TO THE ENDS OF THE EARTH (FD) ... William Kronick
TO THE LAST MAN ... Henry Hathaway
TO THE LIGHTHOUSE (TF) ... Colin Gregg
TO THE VICTOR ... Robert Stevenson
TO TRAP A SPY ... Don Medford
TOBRUK ... Arthur Hiller
TODAY MEXICO - TOMORROW THE WORLD ... Peter Shillingford
TODAY'S FBI (TF) ... Virgil W. Vogel
TO'E MORTA LA NONNA ... Mario Monicelli
TOGETHER ... Sean S. Cunningham
TOGETHER BROTHERS ... William A. Graham
TOGETHER FOR DAYS ... Michael Schultz
TOKYO OLYMPIAD (FD) ... Kon Ichikawa
TOKYO SAIBAN (FD) ... Masaki Kobayashi
TOM ... Greydon Clark
TOM BROWN'S SCHOOLDAYS ... Robert Stevenson
TOM, DICK AND HARRY ... Garson Kanin
TOM HORN ... William Wiard
TOM JONES ★★ ... Tony Richardson
TOM SAWYER ... Don Taylor
TOMA (TF) ... Richard T. Heffron
TOMAHAWK ... George Sherman
TOMB OF LIGEIA, THE ... Roger Corman
TOMBOY ... Herb Freed
TOMMY ... Ken Russell
TOMORROW ... Joseph Anthony
TOMORROW'S CHILD (TF) ... Joseph Sargent
TONIGHT FOR SURE ... Francis Ford Coppola
TONIGHT OR NEVER ... Mervyn Leroy
TONINO NERA ... Carlo Lizzani
TONY ROME ... Gordon Douglas
TOO FAR TO GO (TF) ... Fielder Cook
TOO HOT TO HANDLE ... Don Schain
TOO HOT TO HANDLE ... Terence Young
TOO LATE BLUES ... John Cassavetes
TOO MANY GIRLS ... George Abbott
TOO SCARED TO SCREAM ... Tony Lo Bianco
TOO SOON TO LOVE ... Richard Rush
TOO YOUNG TO MARRY ... Mervyn Leroy
TOOMORROW ... Val Guest
TOOTSIE ★ ... Sydney Pollack
TOP O' THE MORNING ... David Miller
TOP OF THE HEAP ... Christopher St.
TOP OF THE HILL, THE (TF) ... Walter Grauman
TOP SECRET (TF) ... Paul Leaf
TOP SECRET! ... Jim Abrahams
TOP SECRET! ... David Zucker
TOP SECRET! ... Jerry Zucker
TOP SPEED ... Mervyn Leroy
TOPKAPI ... Jules Dassin
TOPO GIGIO E SEI LADRI ... Kon Ichikawa
TOPPER (TF) ... Charles S. Dubin
TOPRINI NASZ (1) ... Andre De Toth
TOPRINI NASZ (2) ... Andre DeToth
TORA! TORA! TORA! ... Richard Fleischer
TORCHLIGHT ... Tom Wright
TORMENT ... John Guillermin
TORMENTED ... Bert I. Gordon
TORMENTOR, THE ... John Llewellyn Moxey
TORN BETWEEN TWO LOVERS (TF) ... Delbert Mann
TORPEDO RUN ... Joseph Pevney
TORTURE GARDEN ... Freddie Francis
TOTO CERCA CASA ... Mario Monicelli
TOTO E CAROLINA ... Mario Monicelli
TOTO E I RE DI ROMA ... Mario Monicelli
TOUCH AND GO ... Philippe de Broca
TOUCH AND GO ... Robert Mandel
TOUCH OF CLASS, A ... Melvin Frank
TOUCH OF EVIL ... Orson Welles
TOUCH OF LARCENY, A ... Guy Hamilton
TOUCH OF LOVE, A ... Waris Hussein
TOUCH OF SCANDAL, A (TF) ... Ivan Nagy
TOUCH OF THE TIMES, A ... Michael Roemer
TOUCH OF ZEN, A ... King Hu
TOUCH, THE ... Ingmar Bergman
TOUCHED ... John Flynn
TOUCHED BY LOVE ... Gus Trikonis
TOUCHEZ PAS LA FEMME BLANCHE ... Marco Ferreri
TOUGH ENOUGH ... Richard Fleischer
TOUGHEST GUN IN TOMBSTONE ... Earl Bellamy
TOUGHEST MAN IN THE WORLD, THE (TF) ... Dick Lowry
TOURIST (TF) ... Jeremy Summers
TOURIST TRAP ... David Schmoeller
TOUT VA BIEN ... Jean-Luc Godard
TOUTE UNE VIE ... Claude Lelouch
TOWARD THE UNKNOWN ... Mervyn Leroy
TOWER OF LONDON ... Roger Corman
TOWERING INFERNO, THE ... Irwin Allen
TOWERING INFERNO, THE ... John Guillermin
TOWN BLOODY HALL (FD) ... D.A. Pennebaker
TOWN CALLED BASTARD, A ... Robert Parrish
TOWN CALLED HELL, A ... Robert Parrish
TOWN LIKE ALICE, A (MS) ... David Stevens
TOWN OF LOVE AND HOPE, A ... Nagisa Oshima
TOWN ON TRIAL ... John Guillermin
TOWN THAT DREADED SUNDOWN, THE ... Charles B. Pierce
TOXIC AVENGER, THE ... Michael Herz
TOXIC AVENGER, THE ... Samuel Weil
TOY SOLDIERS ... David Fisher
TOY, THE ... Richard Donner
TOY, THE ... Francis Veber
TOY TIGER ... Jerry Hopper
TOYS IN THE ATTIC ... George Roy Hill
T.R. BASKIN ... Herbert Ross
TRA MOGLIE E MARITO ... Luigi Comencini
TRACCO DI VELENO IN UNA COPPA DI CHAMPAGNE ... Gordon Hessler
TRACKDOWN ... Richard T. Heffron
TRACKDOWN: FINDING THE GOODBAR KILLER (TF) ... Bill Persky
TRACKERS, THE (TF) ... Earl Bellamy
TRACKS ... Henry Jaglom
TRADER HORN ... Reza Badiyi
TRADING PLACES ... John Landis
TRAFFIC JAM ... Luigi Comencini
TRAGEDY OF A RIDICULOUS MAN ... Bernardo Bertolucci
TRAGICO FANTOZZI ... Luciano Salce
TRAIL BLAZERS, THE ... George Sherman
TRAIL OF THE LONESOME PINE, THE ... Henry Hathaway
TRAIL OF THE PINK PANTHER ... Blake Edwards
TRAIL RIDE, THE ... William Byron Hillman
TRAIN, THE ... John Frankenheimer
TRAIN OF EVENTS ... Charles Crichton
TRAIN ROBBERS, THE ... Burt Kennedy
TRAITOR'S GATE ... Freddie Francis
TRAMPLERS, THE ... Albert Band
TRANCERS ... Charles Band
TRANS-EUROP-EXPRESS ... Alain Robbe-Grillet
TRANSIT ... Daniel Wachsmann
TRANSIT ... Bernhard Wicki
TRANSPLANT (TF) ... William A. Graham
TRAP, THE ... Sidney Hayers
TRAP, THE ... Norman Panama
TRAPPED ... Richard Fleischer
TRAPPED ... William Fruet
TRAPPED (TF) ... Frank de Felitta
TRAPPED BENEATH THE SEA (TF) ... William A. Graham
TRASH ... Paul Morrissey
TRAUMA CENTER (TF) ... Thomas Carter
TRAVELING EXECUTIONER, THE ... Jack Smight
TRAVELLER'S JOY ... Ralph Thomas
TRAVELLERS, THE ... Richard L. Bare
TRAVELS WITH ANITA ... Mario Monicelli
TRAVIS LOGAN, D.A. (TF) ... Paul Wendkos
TRAVIS McGEE (TF) ... Andrew V. McLaglen
TRE NOTTE D'AMORE ... Luigi Comencini
TRE TIGRI CONTRA TRE TIGRI ... Sergio Corbucci
TREASURE ISLAND ... John Hough
TREASURE OF MATECUMBE, THE ... Vincent McEveety
TREASURE OF PANCHO VILLA, THE ... George Sherman
TREASURE OF SAN GENNARO ... Dino Risi
TREASURE OF THE FOUR CROWNS ... Ferdinando Baldi
TREASURE OF THE SIERRA MADRE ★★, THE ... John Huston
TREASURE OF THE YANKEE ZEPHYR ... David Hemmings
TREATISE IN JAPANESE BAWDY SONGS, A ... Nagisa Oshima
TREE, THE ... Robert Guenette
TREE GROWS IN BROOKLYN, A (TF) ... Joseph Hardy
TREE GROWS IN BROOKLYN, A ... Elia Kazan
TREE OF WOODEN CLOGS, THE ... Ermanno Olmi
TRENCHCOAT ... Michael Tuchner
TRESPASSER, THE (TF) ... Colin Gregg
TRESPASSERS, THE ... John Duigan
TREVICO-TORINO...VIAGGIO NEL FIAT NAM ... Ettore Scola
TRIAL, THE ... Orson Welles
TRIAL OF BILLY JACK, THE ... Frank Laughlin
TRIAL OF CHAPLAIN JENSEN, THE (TF) ... Robert Day
TRIAL OF JOAN OF ARC, THE ... Robert Bresson
TRIAL OF LEE HARVEY OSWALD, THE (TF) ... David Greene
TRIAL OF LEE HARVEY OSWALD, THE ... Larry Buchanan

TRIAL OF THE CATONSVILLE NINE, THE ... Gordon Davidson
TRIAL RUN (TF) ... William A. Graham
TRIALS OF OSCAR WILDE, THE ... Kenneth "Ken" Hughes
TRIANGLE FACTORY FIRE SCANDAL, THE (TF) ... Mel Stuart
TRIBE, THE (TF) ... Richard A. Colla
TRIBES (TF) ☆ ... Joseph Sargent
TRIBUTE ... Bob Clark
TRIBUTE TO A BAD MAN ... Robert Wise
TRICK BABY ... Larry Yust
TRIGGER TRIO, THE ... William Witney
TRILOGY ... Frank Perry
TRILOGY OF TERROR (TF) ... Dan Curtis
TRILOGY: THE AMERICAN BOY (TF) ... Noel Black
TRIO ... Ken Annakin
TRIP, THE ... Roger Corman
TRIPLE CROSS ... Terence Young
TRIPLE DECEPTION ... Guy Green
TRIPLE ECHO, THE ... Michael Apted
TRISTAN AND ISOLT ... Tom Donovan
TRIUMPHS OF A MAN CALLED HORSE ... John Hough
TROG ... Freddie Francis
TROIS HOMMES A ABBATRE ... Jacques Deray
TROJAN WOMEN, THE ... Michael Cacoyannis
TROLL ... Vilgot Sjoman
TRON ... Steven Lisberger
TROOPER HOOK ... Charles Marquis Warren
TROPIC OF CANCER ... Joseph Strick
TROUBLE AT THE ROYAL ROSE ... Burt Kennedy
TROUBLE COMES TO TOWN (TF) ... Daniel Petrie
TROUBLE IN HIGH TIMBER COUNTRY (TF) ... Vincent Sherman
TROUBLE IN MOLOPOLIS ... Philippe Mora
TROUBLE MAN ... Ivan Dixon
TROUBLE SHOOTER (MS) ... Henri Safran
TROUBLE WITH ANGELS, THE ... Ida Lupino
TROUBLE WITH GIRLS, THE ... Peter Tewksbury
TROUBLEMAKER, THE ... Theodore J. Flicker
TROUPE, THE ... Avi Nesher
TRUCK STOP WOMEN ... Mark L. Lester
TRUCK TURNER ... Jonathan Kaplan
TRUE CONFESSIONS ... Ulu Grosbard
TRUE GLORY, THE ... Garson Kanin
TRUE GRIT ... Henry Hathaway
TRUE GRIT: A FURTHER ADVENTURE (TF) ... Richard T. Heffron
TRUE LOVE ... Jan Egleson
TRUE STORY OF ESKIMO NELL, THE ... Richard Franklin
TRUNK CRIME ... Roy Boulting
TRUNK TO CAIRO ... Menahem Golan
TU PER TU, A ... Sergio Corbucci
TUCSON ... William F. Claxton
TUDOR ROSE ... Robert Stevenson
TUFF TURF ... Fritz Kiersch
TUGBOAT ANNIE ... Mervyn Leroy
TULIPS ... Rex Bromfield
TULIPS ... Mark Warren
TULSA KID, THE ... George Sherman
TUMBLEWEED ... Nathan Juran
TUNES OF GLORY ... Ronald Neame
TUNISIAN VICTORY (FD) ... Roy Boulting
TUNISIAN VICTORY (FD) ... Frank Capra
TUNNEL OF LOVE, THE ... Gene Kelly
TUNNELVISION ... Neil Israel
TUNNELVISION ... Brad Swirnoff
TURK 182 ... Bob Clark
TURKISH DELIGHT ... Paul Verhoeven
TURN ON TO LOVE ... John G. Avildsen
TURNING POINT ★, THE ... Herbert Ross
TURNING POINT OF JIM MALLOY, THE (TF) ... Frank D. Gilroy
TURNOVER SMITH (TF) ... Bernard L. Kowalski
TURTLE SUMMER ... John Irvin
TUSK ... Alexandro Jodorowsky
TUTTO A POSTE E NIENTE IN ORDINE ... Lina Wertmuller
TWELVE ANGRY MEN ★ ... Sidney Lumet
TWELVE CHAIRS, THE ... Mel Brooks
TWELVE CHAPTERS ABOUT WOMEN ... Kon Ichikawa
TWENTY MILLION MILES TO EARTH ... Nathan Juran
TWICE IN A LIFETIME ... Bud Yorkin
TWICE IN A LIFETIME (TF) ... Herschel Daugherty
TWICE ROUND THE DAFFODILS ... Gerald Thomas
TWICE UPON A TIME (AF) ... John Korty
TWICE UPON A TIME (AF) ... Charles Swenson
TWILIGHT FOR THE GODS ... Joseph Pevney
TWILIGHT TIME ... Goran Paskaljevic
TWILIGHT ZONE - THE MOVIE ... Joe Dante
TWILIGHT ZONE - THE MOVIE ... John Landis
TWILIGHT ZONE - THE MOVIE ... George Miller
TWILIGHT ZONE - THE MOVIE ... Steven Spielberg
TWIN DETECTIVES (TF) ... Robert Day
TWINKY ... Richard Donner
TWINS OF EVIL ... John Hough
TWIRL (TF) ... Gus Trikonis
TWIST OF FATE ... David Miller
TWIST OF SAND, A ... Don Chaffey
TWISTED NERVE ... Roy Boulting
TWO A PENNY ... James F. Collier
TWO AND TWO MAKE SIX ... Freddie Francis
TWO BLONDES AND A REDHEAD ... Arthur Dreifuss
TWO BROTHERS (TF) ... Burt Brinckerhoff
TWO BY FORSYTH (TF) ... Michael O'Herlihy
TWO COLONELS ... Sergio Corbucci
TWO CROWDED HOURS ... Michael Powell
TWO DAUGHTERS ... Satyajit Ray
TWO DOWN AND ONE TO GO (FD) ... Frank Capra
TWO FATHERS (TF) ... Rod Holcomb
TWO FLAGS WEST ... Robert Wise
TWO FOR THE MONEY (TF) ... Bernard L. Kowalski
TWO FOR THE ROAD ... Stanley Donen
TWO FOR THE SEESAW ... Robert Wise
TWO GENTLEMENT SHARING ... Ted Kotcheff
TWO GUN SHERIFF ... George Sherman
TWO KINDS OF LOVE (TF) ... Jack Bender
TWO LEFT FEET ... Roy Ward Baker
TWO LIVES OF CAROL LETNER, THE (TF) ... Philip Leacock
TWO MARRIAGES (TF) ... Joseph Hardy
TWO MEN OF KARAMOJA ... Eugene S. Jones
TWO MULES FOR SISTER SARA ... Don Siegel
TWO OF A KIND ... John Herzfeld
TWO OF A KIND (TF) ... Roger Young
TWO OF US, THE ... Claude Berri
TWO ON A BENCH (TF) ... Jerry Paris
TWO ON A GUILLOTINE ... William Conrad
TWO ON THE TILES ... John Guillermin
TWO OR THREE THINGS I KNOW ABOUT HER ... Jean-Luc Godard
TWO PEOPLE ... Robert Wise
TWO ROSES AND A GOLDEN ROD ... Albert Zugsmith
TWO SECONDS ... Mervyn Leroy
TWO SISTERS FROM BOSTON ... Henry Koster
TWO SMART PEOPLE ... Jules Dassin
TWO TICKETS TO TERROR ... Al Adamson
TWO WEEKS IN ANOTHER TOWN ... Vincente Minnelli
TWO WORLDS OF JENNY LOGAN, THE (TF) ... Frank de Felitta
TWO-FIVE, THE (TF) ... Bruce Kessler
TWO-HEADED SPY, THE ... Andre De Toth
TWO-LANE BLACKTOP ... Monte Hellman
TWO-MINUTE WARNING ... Larry Peerce
TWONKY, THE ... Arch Oboler
TWO-WAY STRETCH ... Robert Day
TYLER (TF) ... Ralph L. Thomas
TZANANI FAMILY, THE ... Boaz Davidson

U

UBERNACHTUNG IN TIROL (TF) ... Volker Schlondorff
U-BOAT 29 ... Michael Powell
UFO INCIDENT, THE (TF) ... Richard A. Colla
UFORIA ... John Binder
UGLY AMERICAN, THE ... George Englund
ULTIMATE IMPOSTER, THE (TF) ... Paul Stanley
ULTIMATE SOLUTION OF GRACE QUIGLEY, THE ... Anthony Harvey
ULTIMATE THRILL, THE ... Robert Butler
ULTIMATE WARRIOR, THE ... Robert Clouse
ULYSSES ... Joseph Strick
UMBRELLAS OF CHERBOURG, THE ... Jacques Demy
UN AMORE A ROMA ... Dino Risi
UN BORGHESE PICCOLO PICCOLI ... Mario Monicelli
UN CERTO GIORNO ... Ermanno Olmi
UN CHAMBRE EN VILLE ... Jacques Demy
UN COEUR GROS COMME CA (FD) ... Francois Reichenbach
UN DOLLARO A TESTA ... Sergio Corbucci
UN EROE DEI NOSTRI TEMPI ... Mario Monicelli
UN ETE A SAINT TROPEZ (FD) ... David Hamilton
UN FILM COMME LES AUTRES ... Jean-Luc Godard
UN FIUME DI DOLLARI ... Carlo Lizzani
UN GENIO, DUE COMPARI, UN POLLO ... Sergio Corbucci
UN GENIO, DUE COMPARI, UN POLLO ... Damiano Damiani
UN GIORNO DA LEONI ... Nanni Loy
UN HOMME DE TROP ... Costa-Gavras
UN HOMME EST MORT ... Jacques Deray
UN HOMME QUI ME PLAIT ... Claude Lelouch
UN MAUVAIS FIL ... Claude Sautet
UN NEVEU SILENCIEUX ... Robert Enrico
UN PAPILLON SUR L'EPAULE ... Jacques Deray
UN PEU, BEAUCOUP, PASSIONEMENT ... Robert Enrico
UN PEU DE SOLEIL DANS L'EAU FROIDE ... Jacques Deray
UN SI JOLI VILLAGE ... Etienne Perier
UN UOMO DA BRUCIARE ... Paolo Taviani
UN UOMO DA BRUCIARE ... Vittorio Taviani
UN UOMO IN GINOCCHIO ... Damiano Damiani
UNA PELEA CUBANA CONTRA LOS DEMONIOS ... Tomas Gutierrez Alea
UNA RAGAZZA PIUTTOSTO COMPLICATA ... Damiano Damiani
UNA STORIA MODERNA: L'APE REGINA ... Marco Ferreri
UNA VITA DIFFICILE ... Dino Risi
UNAPPROACHABLE, THE ... Krzysztof Zanussi
UNARMED AND DANGEROUS ... Guy Hamilton
UNCHAINED ... Hall Bartlett
UNCLE JOE SHANNON ... Joseph C. Hanwright
UNCLE, THE ... Desmond Davis
UNCLE VANYA ... Stuart Burge
UNCLE VANYA ... Andrei Konchalovsky
UNCOMMON LOVE, AN (TF) ... Steven Hillard Stern
UNCOMMON VALOR ... Ted Kotcheff
UNCOMMON VALOR (TF) ... Rod Amateau
UND DAS AM MONTAGMORGEN ... Luigi Comencini
UNDEAD, THE ... Roger Corman
UNDEFEATED, THE ... Andrew V. McLaglen
UNDER AGE ... Larry Buchanan
UNDER AGE ... Edward Dmytryk
UNDER CALIFORNIA SKIES ... William Witney
UNDER FIRE ... James B. Clark
UNDER FIRE ... Roger Spottiswoode
UNDER MILK WOOD ... Andrew Sinclair
UNDER MY SKIN ... Jean Negulesco
UNDER TEXAS SKIES ... George Sherman
UNDER THE CHERRY BLOSSOMS ... Masahiro Shinoda
UNDER THE RAINBOW ... Steve Rash
UNDER THE TONTO RIM ... Henry Hathaway
UNDER THE VOLCANO ... John Huston
UNDER THE YUM YUM TREE ... David Swift
UNDER THIS SKY (TF) ... Randa Haines
UNDER YOUR SPELL ... Otto Preminger
UNDERCOVER ... David Stevens
UNDERCOVER GIRL ... Joseph Pevney
UNDERCOVERS HERO ... Roy Boulting
UNDERCURRENT ... Vincente Minnelli
UNDERGROUND ... Arthur H. Nadel
UNDERGROUND ... Vincent Sherman
UNDERGROUND (FD) ... Emile de Antonio
UNDERGROUND (FD) ... Mary Lampson
UNDERGROUND (FD) ... Haskell Wexler
UNDERGROUND ACES ... Robert Butler
UNDERGROUND AGENT ... Michael Gordon

UNDERGROUND MAN, THE (TF) .... Paul Wendkos
UNDERSEA GIRL .... John Peyser
UNDERTAKER AND HIS PALS, THE .... Ted V. Mikels
UNDERWATER! .... John Sturges
UNDERWATER WARRIOR .... Andrew Marton
UNDERWORLD INFORMERS .... Ken Annakin
UNDERWORLD STORY, THE .... Cy Endfield
UNDERWORLD U.S.A. .... Samuel Fuller
UNE FEMME DOUCE .... Robert Bresson
UNE FEMME FIDELE .... Roger Vadim
UNE FILLE ET DES FUSILS .... Claude Lelouch
UNE FILLE POUR L'ETE .... Edouard Molinaro
UNE MANCHE ET LA BELLE .... Henri Verneuil
UNE PARTIE DE PLAISIR .... Claude Chabrol
UNE RAVISSANTE IDIOTE .... Edouard Molinaro
UNE SEMAINE DE VACANCES .... Bertrand Tavernier
UNE VILLE A CHANDIGARH .... Alain Tanner
UNEARTHLY STRANGER, THE .... John Krish
UNFAIR EXCHANGES (TF) .... Gavin Millar
UNFAITHFUL, THE .... Vincent Sherman
UNFAITHFULLY YOURS .... Howard Zieff
UNFINISHED BUSINESS .... Don Owen
UNFINISHED DANCE, THE .... Henry Koster
UNFINISHED PIECE FOR PLAYER PIANO, AN .... Nikita Mikhalkov
UNFORGIVEN, THE .... John Huston
UNHOLY DESIRE .... Shohei Imamura
UNHOLY PARTNERS .... Mervyn Leroy
UNHOLY ROLLERS .... Vernon Zimmerman
UNIDENTITIED FLYING ODDBALL .... Russ Mayberry
UNION CITY .... Mark Reichert
UNITED KINGDOM (TF) .... Roland Joffé
UNIVERSAL SOLDIER .... Cy Endfield
UNKNOWN FORCE, THE (TF) .... Dick Croy
UNKNOWN TERROR, THE .... Charles Marquis Warren
UNMAN, WITTERING & ZIGO .... John Mackenzie
UNMARRIED WOMAN, AN .... Paul Mazursky
UNSANE .... Dario Argento
UNSER NAZI .... Robert Kramer
UNSUITABLE JOB FOR A WOMAN, AN .... Chris Petit
UNTAMED YOUTH .... Howard W. Koch
UNTIL SEPTEMBER .... Richard Marquand
UNTIL SHE TALKS (TF) .... Mary Lampson
UNTIL THEY SAIL .... Robert Wise
UNWED FATHER (TF) .... Jeremy Paul Kagan
UNWED MOTHER .... Walter Doniger
UOMINI CONTRO .... Francesco Rosi
UOMINI MERCE .... Carlo Lizzani
UP FROM THE BEACH .... Robert Parrish
UP FROM THE DEPTHS .... Charles B. Griffith
UP IN SMOKE .... Lou Adler
UP IN THE CELLAR .... Theodore J. Flicker
UP JUMPED A SWAGMAN .... Christopher Miles
UP PERISCOPE .... Gordon Douglas
UP THE CREEK .... Robert Butler
UP THE CREEK .... Val Guest
UP THE DOWN STAIRCASE .... Robert Mulligan
UP THE SANDBOX .... Irvin Kershner
UP TIGHT .... Jules Dassin
UP TO A POINT .... Tomas Gutierrez Alea
UP TO HIS EARS .... Philippe de Broca
UP YOUR ANCHOR (LEMON POPSICLE VI) .... Dan Wolman
UPRISING, THE .... Peter Lilienthal
UPS AND DOWNS .... Paul Almond
UPSTAIRS AND DOWNSTAIRS .... Ralph Thomas
UPSTATE MURDERS, THE .... David Paulsen
UPTOWN SATURDAY NIGHT .... Sidney Poitier
URANIUM CONSPIRACY, THE .... Menahem Golan
URBAN COWBOY .... James Bridges
URGH! A MUSIC WAR (FD) .... Derek Burbidge
USED CARS .... Robert Zemeckis
USERS, THE (TF) .... Joseph Hardy
UTU .... Geoff Murphy
U-TURN .... George Kaczender
UTVANDRARNA ★ .... Jan Troell

V

V (TF) .... Kenneth Johnson
V: THE FINAL BATTLE (TF) .... Richard T. Heffron
VACANZE COL GANGSTER .... Dino Risi
VACATION DAYS .... Arthur Dreifuss
VACATION IN HELL, A (TF) .... David Greene
VALACHI PAPERS, THE .... Terence Young
VALDEZ HORSES, THE .... John Sturges
VALDEZ IS COMING .... Edwin Sherin
VALENTINE (TF) .... Lee Philips
VALENTINE MAGIC ON LOVE ISLAND (TF) .... Earl Bellamy
VALENTINO .... Ken Russell
VALERIE .... Gerd Oswald
VALIANT ONES, THE .... King Hu
VALIANT, THE .... Roy Ward Baker
VALLEY, THE .... Barbet Schroeder
VALLEY FORGE (TF) .... Fielder Cook
VALLEY GIRL .... Martha Coolidge
VALLEY OF GWANGI, THE .... James O'Connolly
VALLEY OF THE EAGLES .... Terence Young
VALUE FOR MONEY .... Ken Annakin
VAMOS A MATAR COMPAÑEROS .... Sergio Corbucci
VAMPING .... Frederick King Keller
VAMPIRA .... Clive Donner
VAMPIRE (TF) .... E.W. Swackhamer
VAMPIRE LOVERS, THE .... Roy Ward Baker
VAN MORRISON IN IRELAND (FD) .... Michael Radford
VAN NUYS BLVD. .... William Sachs
VANISHED (TF) .... Buzz Kulik
VANISHING POINT .... Richard C. Sarafian
VARIETY LIGHTS .... Federico Fellini
VARIETY LIGHTS .... Alberto Lattuada
VAULT OF HORROR, THE .... Roy Ward Baker
VEDO NUDO .... Dino Risi
VEGA$ (TF) .... Richard Lang
VEGAS STRIP WAR, THE (TF) .... Richard Englund
VEILS OF BAGDAD .... George Sherman
VELVET (TF) .... Richard Lang
VELVET UNDERGROUND AND NICO, THE .... Andy Warhol
VELVET VAMPIRE, THE .... Stephanie Rothman
VENDETTA .... Mel Ferrer
VENETIAN AFFAIR, THE .... Jerry Thorpe
VENETIAN BIRD, THE .... Ralph Thomas
VENEZIA, LA LUNA E TU .... Dino Risi
VENGA A PRENDERE IL CAFFE DA NOI .... Alberto Lattuada
VENGEANCE .... Freddie Francis
VENGEANCE IS MINE .... Shohei Imamura
VENGEANCE OF FU MANCHU, THE .... Jeremy Summers
VENGEANCE OF SHE, THE .... Cliff Owen
VENOM .... Piers Haggard
VENOM .... Peter Sykes
VERA VERAO .... Michael Sarne
VERBOTEN! .... Samuel Fuller
VERDICT ★, THE .... Sidney Lumet
VERDICT, THE .... Don Siegel
VERNA: USO GIRL (TF) ☆ .... Ronald F. Maxwell
VERY CURIOUS GIRL, A .... Nelly Kaplan
VERY FRIENDLY NEIGHBORS, THE .... Albert Zugsmith
VERY HAPPY ALEXANDER .... Yves Robert
VERY IMPORTANT PERSON .... Ken Annakin
VERY LIKE A WHALE .... Alan Bridges
VERY MISSING PERSON, A (TF) .... Russ Mayberry
VERY PRIVATE AFFAIR, A .... Louis Malle
VERY SPECIAL FAVOR, A .... Michael Gordon
VIALE DELLA SPERANZA .... Dino Risi
VICE AND VIRTUE .... Roger Vadim
VICE SQUAD .... Gary A. Sherman
VICE SQUARD .... Arnold Laven
VICE VERSA .... Peter Ustinov
VICIOUS CIRCLE, THE .... Gerald Thomas
VICTIM, THE (TF) .... Herschel Daugherty
VICTIMS, THE (TF) .... Jerrold Freedman
VICTIMS FOR VICTIMS (TF) .... Karen Arthur
VICTORIA .... Bo Widerberg
VICTOR/VICTORIA .... Blake Edwards
VICTORY .... John Huston
VICTORY MARCH .... Marco Bellocchio
VIDEODROME .... David Cronenberg
VIEW FROM THE BRIDGE, A .... Sidney Lumet
VIEW TO A KILL, A .... John Glen
VIGILANTE .... William Lustig
VIGILANTE FORCE .... George Armitage
VIKING QUEEN, THE .... Don Chaffey
VIKING WOMEN AND THE SEA SERPENT, THE .... Roger Corman
VIKINGS, THE .... Richard Fleischer
VILLA! .... James B. Clark
VILLA RIDES! .... Buzz Kulik
VILLAGE OF THE GIANTS .... Bert I. Gordon
VILLAIN .... Michael Tuchner
VILLAIN, THE .... Hal Needham
VINCENT, FRANCOIS, PAUL AND THE OTHERS .... Claude Sautet
VINCENT THE DUTCHMAN .... Mai Zetterling
VINYL .... Andy Warhol
VIOLATION OF CLAUDIA, THE .... William Lustig
VIOLATION OF SARAH McDAVID, THE (TF) .... John Llewellyn Moxey
VIOLATORS, THE .... John Newland
VIOLENCE AT NOON .... Nagisa Oshima
VIOLENT ENEMY, THE .... Don Sharp
VIOLENT FOUR, THE .... Carlo Lizzani
VIOLENT MOMENT .... Sidney Hayers
VIOLENT ROAD .... Howard W. Koch
VIOLENT SATURDAY .... Richard Fleischer
VIOLETS ARE BLUE .... Jack Fisk
VIOLETTE .... Claude Chabrol
VIOLETTE NOZIERE .... Claude Chabrol
VIRGIN AND THE GYPSY, THE .... Christopher Miles
VIRGIN QUEEN, THE .... Henry Koster
VIRGIN SOLDIERS, THE .... John Dexter
VIRGIN SPRING, THE .... Ingmar Bergman
VIRGIN WITCH, THE .... Ray Austin
VIRGINIA HILL STORY, THE (TF) .... Joel Schumacher
VISA TO CANTON .... Michael Carreras
VISIONQUEST .... Harold Becker
VISIONS .... Chuck Vincent
VISIONS... (TF) .... Lee H. Katzin
VISIONS OF EIGHT (FD) .... Milos Forman
VISIONS OF EIGHT (FD) .... Kon Ichikawa
VISIONS OF EIGHT (FD) .... Claude Lelouch
VISIONS OF EIGHT (FD) .... John Schlesinger
VISIONS OF EIGHT (FD) .... Mai Zetterling
VISIT, THE .... Bernhard Wicki
VISIT TO A CHIEF'S SON .... Lamont Johnson
VISITORS, THE .... Elia Kazan
VITA DA CANI .... Mario Monicelli
VIVA ITALIA! .... Mario Monicelli
VIVA ITALIA! .... Ettore Scola
VIVA ITALIA! .... Dino Risi
VIVA KNIEVEL! .... Gordon Douglas
VIVA LA MUERTE...TUA! .... Sergio Corbucci
VIVA LA VIE .... Claude Lelouch
VIVA LAS VEGAS .... George Sidney
VIVA MARIA! .... Louis Malle
VIVA MAX! .... Jerry Paris
VIVA ZAPATA! .... Elia Kazan
VLADIMIR ET ROSA .... Jean-Luc Godard
VOGLIAMO I COLONNELLI .... Mario Monicelli
VOICE OF THE TURTLE, THE .... Irving Rapper
VOICES .... Kevin Billington
VOICES .... Robert Markowitz
VOLTATI EUGENIO .... Luigi Comencini
VOLUNTEER, THE .... Michael Powell
VOLUNTEERS .... Nicholas Meyer
VON RICHTOFEN AND BROWN .... Roger Corman
VOTE FOR HUGGETT .... Ken Annakin
VOYAGE OF THE DAMNED .... Stuart Rosenberg
VOYAGE OF THE ROCK ALIENS .... James Fargo
VOYAGE OF THE YES, THE (TF) .... Lee H. Katzin
VOYAGE ROUND MY FATHER, A (TF) .... Alvin Rakoff
VOYAGE TO GRAND TARTARIE .... Jean-Charles Tacchella
VOYAGE TO THE BOTTOM OF THE SEA .... Irwin Allen
VT .... Don Norman
VULTURE, THE .... Yaky Yosha

W

"W" .... Richard Quine
WABASH AVENUE .... Henry Koster
WACKO .... Greydon Clark
WACKY TAXI .... Alex Grasshoff

WACKY WORLD OF MOTHER GOOSE, THE (AF) .... Jules Bass
WAGNER (MS) .... Tony Palmer
WAIKIKI (TF) .... Ron Satlof
WAIT FOR US AT DAWN .... Emil Loteanu
WAIT TILL YOUR MOTHER GETS HOME (TF) .... Bill Persky
WAIT UNTIL DARK .... Terence Young
WAITRESS! .... Michael Herz
WAITRESS! .... Samuel Weil
WAKE IN FRIGHT .... Ted Kotcheff
WAKE ME WHEN IT'S OVER .... Mervyn Leroy
WAKE ME WHEN THE WAR IS OVER (TF) .... Gene Nelson
WALK A CROOKED MILE .... Gordon Douglas
WALK IN THE SPRING RAIN, A .... Guy Green
WALK LIKE A DRAGON .... James Clavell
WALK ON THE WILD SIDE .... Edward Dmytryk
WALK PROUD .... Robert Collins
WALK SOFTLY, STRANGER .... Robert Stevenson
WALK TALL .... Maury Dexter
WALK WITH LOVE AND DEATH, A .... John Huston
WALKABOUT .... Nicolas Roeg
WALKING HILLS, THE .... John Sturges
WALKING STICK, THE .... Eric Till
WALKING TALL .... Phil Karlson
WALKING THROUGH THE FIRE (TF) .... Robert Day
WALKOVER .... Jerzy Skolimowski
WALL, THE (TF) .... Robert Markowitz
WALL OF DEATH .... Lewis Gilbert
WALL OF NOISE .... Richard Wilson
WALLENBERG (TF) .... Lamont Johnson
WALLS OF HELL, THE .... Eddie Romero
WALLS OF MALAPAGA, THE .... René Clement
WALTZ ACROSS TEXAS .... Ernest Day
WALTZ OF THE TOREADORS .... John Guillermin
WANDA NEVADA .... Peter Fonda
WANDERERS, THE .... Philip Kaufman
WANTED: THE SUNDANCE WOMAN (TF) .... Lee Philips
WAR AND PEACE .... Sergei Bondarchuk
WAR ARROW .... George Sherman
WAR BETWEEN MEN AND WOMEN, THE .... Melville Shavelson
WAR BETWEEN THE TATES, THE (TF) .... Lee Philips
WAR GAME, THE .... Peter Watkins
WAR GODDESS .... Terence Young
WAR HUNT .... Denis Sanders
WAR IS HELL .... Burt Topper
WAR LORD, THE .... Franklin J. Schaffner
WAR LOVER, THE .... Philip Leacock
WAR OF CHILDREN ☆, A (TF) .... George Schaefer
WAR OF THE COLASSAL BEAST .... Bert I. Gordon
WAR OF THE SATELLITES .... Roger Corman
WAR WAGON, THE .... Burt Kennedy
WARE CASE, THE .... Robert Stevenson
WARGAMES .... John Badham
WARLOCK .... Edward Dmytryk
WARLORDS OF ATLANTIS .... Kevin Connor
WARLORDS OF THE 21ST CENTURY .... Harley Cokliss
WARM DECEMBER, A .... Sidney Poitier
WARNING SHOT .... Buzz Kulik
WARRENDALE (FD) .... Allan King
WARRIOR AND THE SORCERESS, THE .... John Broderick
WARRIORS, THE .... Walter Hill
WARUM SIND SIE GEGEN UNS? .... Bernhard Wicki
WASHINGTON: BEHIND CLOSED DOORS (MS) ☆ .... Gary Nelson
WASHINGTON MISTRESS (TF) .... Peter Levin
WASN'T THAT A TIME! (FD) .... Jim Brown
WASP WOMAN, THE .... Roger Corman
WASTREL, THE .... Michael Cacoyannis
WAT ZIEN IK .... Paul Verhoeven
WATCH YOUR STERN .... Gerald Thomas
WATCHER IN THE WOODS, THE .... John Hough
WATER BABIES, THE .... Lionel Jeffries
WATER UNDER THE BRIDGE (TF) .... Igor Auzins
WATERFRONT .... Michael Anderson
WATERFRONT WOMEN .... Michael Anderson
WATERHOLE #3 .... William A. Graham
WATERLOO .... Sergei Bondarchuk
WATERLOO BRIDGE .... Mervyn Leroy
WATERMELON MAN .... Melvin Van Peebles
WATERS OF THE MOON (TF) .... Piers Haggard
WATERSHIP DOWN (AF) .... Martin Rosen
WATTS MONSTER, THE .... William Crain
WATTSTAX (FD) .... Mel Stuart
WAVE, THE (FD) .... Fred Zinnemann
WAVE, A WAC AND A MARINE, A .... Phil Karlson
WAVELENGTH .... Mike Gray
WAY HE WAS, THE .... Mark L. Lester
WAY OF THE STRONG, THE .... Frank Capra
WAY WE LIVE NOW, THE .... Barry Brown
WAY WE WERE, THE .... Sydney Pollack
WAY WEST, THE .... Andrew V. McLaglen
WAYS IN THE NIGHT .... Krzysztof Zanussi
WAY...WAY OUT! .... Gordon Douglas
W.C. FIELDS AND ME .... Authur Hiller
WE ALL LOVED EACH OTHER SO MUCH .... Ettore Scola
WE ARE THE LAMBETH BOYS .... Karel Reisz
WE HAVE MANY NAMES .... Mai Zetterling
WE LIVE AGAIN .... Rouben Mamoulian
WE OF THE NEVER NEVER .... Igor Auzins
WE WERE STRANGERS .... John Huston
WE WILL ROCK YOU (FD) .... Saul Swimmer
WEAK AND THE WICKED, THE .... J. Lee Thompson
WEAKER SEX, THE .... Roy Ward Baker
WEAPON, THE .... Val Guest
WEATHER IN THE STREETS, THE (TF) .... Gavin Millar
W.E.B. (TF) .... Harvey Hart
WEB OF EVIDENCE .... Jack Cardiff
WEB OF PASSION/A DOUBLE TOUR .... Claude Chabrol
WEB, THE .... Michael Gordon
WEBSTER BOY, THE .... Don Chaffey
WEDDING, A .... Robert Altman
WEDDING, THE .... Andrzej Wajda
WEDDING IN BLOOD .... Claude Chabrol
WEDDING IN WHITE .... William Fruet
WEDDING MARCH .... Kon Ichikawa
WEDDING NIGHT .... Piers Haggard
WEDDING ON WALTON'S MOUNTAIN, A (TF) .... Lee Philips
WEDDING PARTY, THE .... Brian De Palma
WEDDING PARTY, THE .... Wilford Leach
WEDNESDAY'S CHILD .... Kenneth Loach
WEEKEND .... Jean-Luc Godard
WEEKEND A ZUYDCOOTE .... Henri Verneuil
WEEKEND AT DUNKIRK .... Henri Verneuil
WEEKEND, ITALIAN STYLE .... Dino Risi
WEEKEND OF TERROR (TF) .... Jud Taylor
WEEKEND PASS .... Lawrence Bassoff
WEEKEND SUN, THE (TF) .... Jeannot Szwarc
WEEK'S VACATION, A .... Bertrand Tavernier
WEIRD SCIENCE .... John Hughes
WELCOME HOME, BROTHER CHARLES .... Jamaa Fanaka
WELCOME HOME, JOHNNY BRISTOL (TF) .... George McCowan
WELCOME HOME, SOLDIER BOYS .... Richard Compton
WELCOME TO BLOOD CITY .... Peter Sasdy
WELCOME TO HARD TIMES .... Burt Kennedy
WELCOME TO L.A. .... Alan Rudolph
WELCOME TO MY NIGHTMARE (FD) .... David Winters
WELFARE (FD) .... Frederick Wiseman
WELL, THE .... Russell Rouse
WENDELL .... James Frawley
WE'RE FIGHTING BACK (TF) .... Lou Antonio
WE'RE NOT THE JET SET (FD) .... Robert Duvall
WEREWOLF OF WASHINGTON, THE .... Milton Moses Ginsberg
WEST SIDE KID, THE .... George Sherman
WEST SIDE STORY ★★ .... Jerome Robbins
WEST SIDE STORY ★★ .... Robert Wise
WEST TEXAS .... Alan Gadney
WEST 11 .... Michael Winner
WESTBOUND .... Budd Boetticher
WESTWORLD .... Michael Crichton
WET GOLD (TF) .... Dick Lowry
WETHERBY .... David Hare
WHALE FOR THE KILLING, A (TF) .... Richard T. Heffron
WHAT? .... Roman Polanski
WHAT A CRAZY WORLD .... Michael Carreras
WHAT A WAY TO GO! .... J. Lee Thompson
WHAT ARE BEST FRIENDS FOR? (TF) .... Jay Sandrich
WHAT CHANGED CHARLEY FARTHING? .... Sidney Hayers
WHAT COLOR IS THE WIND .... Frank Zuniga
WHAT COMES AROUND .... Jerry Reed
WHAT DID YOU DO IN THE WAR, DADDY? .... Blake Edwards
WHAT DO I TELL THE BOYS AT THE STATION? .... Simon Nuchtern
WHAT DO YOU SAY TO A NAKED WOMAN? .... Allen Funt
WHAT EVER HAPPENED TO AUNT ALICE? .... Lee H. Katzin
WHAT HAPPENED AT CAMPO GRANDE? .... Cliff Owen
WHAT PRICE MURDER .... Henri Verneuil
WHAT WAITS BELOW .... Don Sharp
WHAT'S A NICE GIRL LIKE YOU...? .... Jerry Paris
WHAT'S GOOD FOR THE GOOSE .... Menahem Golan
WHAT'S HAPPENING: THE BEATLES IN THE USA (FD) .... Albert Maysles
WHAT'S HAPPENING: THE BEATLES IN THE USA (FD) .... David Maysles
WHAT'S NEW PUSSYCAT? .... Clive Donner
WHAT'S THE MATTER WITH HELEN? .... Curtis Harrington
WHAT'S UP, DOC? .... Peter Bogdanovich
WHAT'S UP, TIGER LILY? .... Woody Allen
WHEELER DEALERS, THE .... Authur Hiller
WHEN A STRANGER CALLS .... Fred Walton
WHEN DINOSAURS RULED THE EARTH .... Val Guest
WHEN EIGHT BELLS TOLL .... Etienne Perier
WHEN EVERY DAY WAS THE FOURTH OF JULY (TF) .... Dan Curtis
WHEN HELL WAS IN SESSION (TF) .... Paul Krasny
WHEN MICHAEL CALLS (TF) .... Philip Leacock
WHEN NATURE CALLS .... Charles Kaufman
WHEN SHE SAYS NO (TF) .... Paul Aaron
WHEN SHE WAS BAD... (TF) .... Peter H. Hunt
WHEN THE LEGENDS DIE .... Stuart Millar
WHEN TIME RAN OUT .... James Goldstone
WHEN WE FIRST MET (CTF) .... Paul Saltzman
WHEN WOMEN KILL (CTD) .... Lee Grant
WHEN YOU COMIN' BACK, RED RYDER? .... Milton Katselas
WHEN YOUR LOVER LEAVES (TF) .... Jeff Bleckner
WHERE ARE THE CHILDREN? .... Bruce Malmuth
WHERE DOES IT HURT? .... Rod Amateau
WHERE EAGLES DARE .... Brian G. Hutton
WHERE HAVE ALL THE PEOPLE GONE? (TF) .... John Llewellyn Moxey
WHERE IS PARSIFAL? .... Henri Helman
WHERE IT'S AT .... Garson Kanin
WHERE LOVE HAS GONE .... Edward Dmytryk
WHERE THE BOYS ARE .... Hy Averback
WHERE THE BUFFALO ROAM .... Art Linson
WHERE THE GREEN ANTS DREAM .... Werner Herzog
WHERE THE HOT WIND BLOWS .... Jules Dassin
WHERE THE LADIES GO (TF) .... Theodore J. Flicker
WHERE THE LILIES BLOOM .... William A. Graham
WHERE THE SIDEWALK ENDS .... Otto Preminger
WHERE THE SPIES ARE .... Val Guest
WHERE WERE YOU WHEN THE LIGHTS WENT OUT? .... Hy Averback
WHERE'S JACK? .... James Clavell
WHERE'S POPPA? .... Carl Reiner
WHEREVER SHE GOES .... Michael Gordon
WHICH WAY IS UP? .... Michael Schultz

WHICH WAY TO THE FRONT? ...... Jerry Lewis
WHIFFS ...... Ted Post
WHILE THE CAT'S AWAY ...... Chuck Vincent
WHIRLPOOL ...... Otto Preminger
WHISKEY GALORE! ...... Alexander Mackendrick
WHISPERERS, THE ...... Bryan Forbes
WHISTLE DOWN THE WIND ...... Bryan Forbes
WHITE BUFFALO, THE ...... J. Lee Thompson
WHITE DAWN, THE ...... Philip Kaufman
WHITE DOG ...... Samuel Fuller
WHITE GAME, THE ...... Bo Widerberg
WHITE LIGHTNING ...... Joseph Sargent
WHITE LINE FEVER ...... Jonathan Kaplan
WHITE LIONS, THE ...... Mel Stuart
WHITE MAMA (TF) ...... Jackie Cooper
WHITE NIGHTS ...... Taylor Hackford
WHITE ROCK (FD) ...... Tony Maylam
WHITE SHEIK, THE ...... Federico Fellini
WHITE SISTER ...... Alberto Lattuada
WHITE TRAP, THE ...... Sidney Hayers
WHITE WATER REBELS (TF) ...... Reza Badiyi
WHITE WITCH DOCTOR ...... Henry Hathaway
WHO? ...... Jack Gold
WHO AM I THIS TIME? (TF) ...... Jonathan Demme
WHO ARE THE DE BOLTS?...AND WHERE DID THEY GET 19 KIDS? (FD) ...... John Korty
WHO DARES WINS ...... Ian Sharp
WHO FEARS THE DEVIL ...... John Newland
WHO HAS SEEN THE WIND ...... Allan King
WHO IS HARRY KELLERMAN AND WHY IS HE SAYING THOSE TERRIBLE THINGS ABOUT ME? ...... Ulu Grosbard
WHO IS KILLING THE GREAT CHEFS OF EUROPE? ...... Ted Kotcheff
WHO IS THE BLACK DAHLIA? (TF) ...... Joseph Pevney
WHO KILLED JENNY LANGBY? (TF) ...... Donald Crombie
WHO KILLED MARY WHAT'S'ERNAME ...... Ernest Pintoff
WHO KILLED TEDDY BEAR? ...... Joseph Cates
WHO SAW HIM DIE? ...... Jan Troell
WHO SLEW AUNTIE ROO? ...... Curtis Harrington
WHO WAS THAT LADY? ...... George Sidney
WHO WILL LOVE MY CHILDREN? (TF) ☆☆ ...... John Erman
WHOLE SHOOTIN' MATCH, THE ...... Eagle Pennell
WHOLE TRUTH, THE ...... John Guillermin
WHO'LL SAVE OUR CHILDREN? (TF) ...... George Schaefer
WHO'LL STOP THE RAIN ...... Karel Reisz
WHOLLY MOSES ...... Gary Weis
WHO'S AFRAID OF VIRGINIA WOOLF? ★ ...... Mike Nichols
WHO'S BEEN SLEEPING IN MY BED? ...... Daniel Mann
WHO'S GOT THE ACTION? ...... Daniel Mann
WHO'S MINDING THE MINT? ...... Howard Morris
WHO'S THAT KNOCKING AT MY DOOR? ...... Martin Scorsese
WHOSE LIFE IS IT ANYWAY? ...... John Badham
WHY ...... Nanni Loy
WHY BRING THAT UP? ...... George Abbott
WHY ME? (TF) ...... Fielder Cook
WHY SHOOT THE TEACHER ...... Silvio Narizzano
WHY WOULD I LIE? ...... Larry Peerce
WICKED AS THEY COME ...... Kenneth "Ken" Hughes
WICKED LADY, THE ...... Michael Winner
WICKED, WICKED ...... Richard L. Bare
WICKED WOMAN ...... Russell Rouse
WICKER MAN, THE ...... Robin Hardy
WIDE BOY ...... Kenneth "Ken" Hughes
WIDOW (TF) ...... J. Lee Thompson
WIFE WANTED ...... Phil Karlson
WILBY CONSPIRACY, THE ...... Ralph Nelson
WILD AFFAIR, THE ...... John Krish
WILD AND THE BRAVE, THE (FD) ...... Eugene S. Jones
WILD AND THE FREE, THE (TF) ...... James Hill
WILD AND THE INNOCENT, THE ...... Jack Sher
WILD AND THE WILLING, THE ...... Ralph Thomas
WILD AND WONDERFUL ...... Michael Anderson
WILD AND WOOLY (TF) ...... Philip Leacock
WILD ANGELS, THE ...... Roger Corman
WILD BUNCH, THE ...... Sam Peckinpah
WILD COUNTRY, THE ...... Robert Totten
WILD DUCK, THE ...... Henri Safran
WILD GEESE II ...... Peter Hunt
WILD GEESE, THE ...... Andrew V. McLaglen
WILD GUITAR ...... Ray Dennis Steckler
WILD HEART, THE ...... Michael Powell
WILD HORSE HANK ...... Eric Till
WILD HORSE MESA ...... Henry Hathaway
WILD HORSE RODEO ...... George Sherman
WILD LIFE, THE ...... Art Linson
WILD McCULLOCHS, THE ...... Max Baer, Jr.
WILD ON THE BEACH ...... Maury Dexter
WILD ONE, THE ...... Laslo Benedek
WILD PACK, THE ...... Hall Bartlett
WILD PARTY, THE ...... James Ivory
WILD RACERS, THE ...... Daniel Haller
WILD RIVER ...... Elia Kazan
WILD ROVERS ...... Blake Edwards
WILD SEED ...... Brian G. Hutton
WILD SIDE, THE ...... Penelope Spheeris
WILD STRAWBERRIES ...... Ingmar Bergman
WILD STYLE ...... Charlie Ahearn
WILD TIMES (TF) ...... Richard Compton
WILD WILD WEST REVISITED, THE (TF) ...... Burt Kennedy
WILD WOMEN (TF) ...... Don McDougall
WILD WOMEN (TF) ...... Don Taylor
WILD WOMEN OF CHASTITY GULCH, THE (TF) ...... Philip Leacock
WILD 90 ...... Norman Mailer
WILDMAN ...... Geoff Murphy
WILDROSE ...... John Hanson
WILL ANY GENTLEMAN? ...... Michael Anderson
WILL: G. GORDON LIDDY (TF) ...... Robert Lieberman
WILL THERE REALLY BE A MORNING? (TF) ...... Fielder Cook
WILLA (TF) ...... Joan Darling
WILLA (TF) ...... Claudio Guzman
WILLARD ...... Daniel Mann
WILLIAM AND DOROTHY (TF) ...... Ken Russell
WILLIAM COME TO TOWN ...... Val Guest
WILLIE AND PHIL ...... Paul Mazursky
WILLIE DYNAMITE ...... Gilbert Moses
WILLMAR 8, THE (FD) ...... Lee Grant
WILLY McBEAN AND HIS MAGIC MACHINE (AF) ...... Arthur Rankin, Jr.
WILLY WONKA AND THE CHOCOLATE FACTORY ...... Mel Stuart
WILMA (TF) ...... Bud Greenspan
WINCHESTER '73 (TF) ...... Herschel Daugherty
WIND AND THE LION, THE ...... John Milius
WIND CANNOT READ, THE ...... Ralph Thomas
WIND FROM THE EAST ...... Jean-Luc Godard
WIND IN THE WILLOWS, THE (ATF) ...... Jules Bass
WIND IN THE WILLOWS, THE (ATF) ...... Arthur Rankin, Jr.
WINDFALL IN ATHENS ...... Michael Cacoyannis
WINDOM'S WAY ...... Ronald Neame
WINDOWS ...... Gordon Willis
WINDS OF AUTUMN, THE ...... Charles B. Pierce
WINDS OF KITTY HAWK, THE (TF) ...... E.W. Swackhamer
WINDS OF WAR ☆, THE (MS) ...... Dan Curtis
WINDWALKER ...... Kieth Merrill
WINDY CITY ...... Armyan Bernstein
WING AND A PRAYER ...... Henry Hathaway
WINGS OF FIRE (TF) ...... David Lowell Rich
WINGS OF THE HAWK ...... Budd Boetticher
WINIFRED WAGNER (FD) ...... Hans-Jurgen Syberberg
WINIFRED WAGNER UND DIE GESCHICHTE DES HAUSES WAHNFRIED VON 1914-1975 ...... Hans-Jurgen Syberberg
WINNER TAKE ALL (TF) ...... Paul Bogart
WINNING ...... James Goldstone
WINSTON CHURCHILL - THE WILDERNESS YEARS (MS) ...... Ferdinand Fairfax
WINTER KILL (TF) ...... Jud Taylor
WINTER KILLS ...... William Richert
WINTER LIGHT ...... Ingmar Bergman
WINTER OF OUR DISCONTENT, THE (TF) ...... Waris Hussein
WINTER OF OUR DREAMS ...... John Duigan
WINTER WIND ...... Miklos Jancso
WINTERHAWK ...... Charles B. Pierce
WISE BLOOD ...... John Huston
WISE GUYS, THE ...... Robert Enrico
WITCH WHO CAME FROM THE SEA, THE ...... Matt Cimber
WITCHCRAFT ...... Don Sharp
WITCHING HOUR, THE ...... Henry Hathaway
WITH BEAUTY AND SORROW ...... Masahiro Shinoda
WITH INTENT TO KILL (TF) ...... Mike Robe
WITH LOVE FROM TRUMAN (FD) ...... Albert Maysles
WITH LOVE FROM TRUMAN (FD) ...... David Maysles
WITH SIX YOU GET EGGROLL ...... Howard Morris
WITH THIS RING (TF) ...... James Sheldon
WITHOUT A TRACE ...... Stanley Jaffe
WITHOUT ANESTHETIC ...... Andrzej Wajda
WITHOUT RESERVATIONS ...... Mervyn Leroy
WITHOUT WARNING ...... Greydon Clark
WITHOUT WARNING ...... Arnold Laven
WITHOUT WITNESS ...... Nikita Mikhalkov
WITNESS ...... Peter Weir
WITNESS FOR THE PROSECUTION (TF) ...... Alan Gibson
WITNESS FOR THE PROSECUTION ★ ...... Billy Wilder
WIVES AND LOVERS ...... John Rich
WIZ, THE ...... Sidney Lumet
WIZARD OF BAGHDAD, THE ...... George Sherman
WIZARD OF GORE, THE ...... Herschell Gordon Lewis
WIZARDS (AF) ...... Ralph Bakshi
WOLF HUNTERS, THE ...... Budd Boetticher
WOLF LAKE ...... Burt Kennedy
WOLFEN ...... Michael Wadleigh
WOLFHEAD ...... John Hough
WOLVES ...... Kaneto Shindo
WOMAN CALLED GOLDA, A (TF) ...... Alan Gibson
WOMAN CALLED MOSES, A (TF) ...... Paul Wendkos
WOMAN FOR ALL MEN, A ...... Arthur Marks
WOMAN HATER ...... Terence Young
WOMAN HUNT ...... Maury Dexter
WOMAN HUNT, THE ...... Eddie Romero
WOMAN HUNTER, THE (TF) ...... Bernard L. Kowalski
WOMAN IN A DRESSING GOWN ...... J. Lee Thompson
WOMAN IN HIDING ...... Michael Gordon
WOMAN IN RED, THE ...... Gene Wilder
WOMAN IS A WOMAN, A ...... Jean-Luc Godard
WOMAN OBSESSED ...... Henry Hathaway
WOMAN OF SUBSTANCE, A (MS) ...... Don Sharp
WOMAN OF THE YEAR (TF) ...... Jud Taylor
WOMAN ON PIER 13, THE ...... Robert Stevenson
WOMAN UNDER THE INFLUENCE ★, A ...... John Cassavetes
WOMAN WHO TOUCHED THE LEGS, THE ...... Kon Ichikawa
WOMAN WHO WOULDN'T DIE, THE ...... Gordon Hessler
WOMAN'S DECISION, A ...... Krzysztof Zanussi
WOMAN'S TESTAMENT, A ...... Kon Ichikawa
WOMAN'S WORLD, A ...... Jean Negulesco
WOMBLING FREE ...... Lionel Jeffries
WOMEN AT WEST POINT (TF) ...... Vincent Sherman
WOMEN IN CHAINS (TF) ...... Bernard L. Kowalski
WOMEN IN LOVE ★ ...... Ken Russell
WOMEN IN REVOLT ...... Andy Warhol
WOMEN IN WHITE (MS) ...... Jerry London
WOMEN OF SAN QUENTIN (TF) ...... William A. Graham
WOMEN OF THE SUN (MS) ...... David Stevens
WOMEN'S ROOM, THE (TF) ...... Glenn Jordan
WON TON TON, THE DOG WHO SAVED HOLLYWOOD ...... Michael Winner
WONDER WOMAN (TF) ...... Vincent McEveety
WONDER WOMEN ...... Robert Vincent O'Neil
WONDERFUL COUNTRY, THE ...... Robert Parrish
WONDERFUL CROOK, THE ...... Claude Goretta
WONDERFUL TO BE YOUNG! ...... Sidney J. Furie

WOODCUTTERS OF THE DEEP SOUTH (FD) ... Lionel Rogosin
WOODSTOCK (FD) ... Michael Wadleigh
WORD, THE (MS) ... Richard Lang
WORD OF HONOR (TF) ... Mel Damski
WORK IS A FOUR LETTER WORD ... Peter Hall
WORKING GIRLS, THE ... Stephanie Rothman
WORLD ACCORDING TO GARP, THE ... George Roy Hill
WORLD CHANGES, THE ... Mervyn Leroy
WORLD IN MY POCKET ... Alvin Rakoff
WORLD IS WATCHING, THE (TF) ... Richard A. Colla
WORLD OF APU, THE ... Satyajit Ray
WORLD OF HENRY ORIENT, THE ... George Roy Hill
WORLD OF SUZIE WONG, THE ... Richard Quine
WORLD WAR III (TF) ... David Greene
WORLD'S BEST BRIDE, THE ... Kaneto Shindo
WORLD'S GREATEST ATHLETE, THE ... Robert Scheerer
WORLD'S GREATEST LOVER, THE ... Gene Wilder
WORM EATERS, THE ... Ted V. Mikels
WOW! ... Claude Jutra
WOYZECK ... Werner Herzog
WR - MYSTERIES OF THE ORGANISM ... Dusan Makavejev
WRATH OF GOD, THE ... Ralph Nelson
WRECK OF THE MARY DEARE, THE ... Michael Anderson
WRECKING CREW, THE ... Phil Karlson
WRIGHT BROTHERS, THE (TF) ... Arthur Barron
WRONG ARM OF THE LAW, THE ... Cliff Owen
WRONG BOX, THE ... Bryan Forbes
WRONG IS RIGHT ... Richard Brooks
WRONG MOVE, THE ... Wim Wenders
WUSA ... Stuart Rosenberg
WUTHERING HEIGHTS ... Robert Fuest
W.W. AND THE DIXIE DANCEKINGS ... John G. Avildsen
WYOMING OUTLAW ... George Sherman
WYOMING WILDCAT ... George Sherman

X

"X" - THE MAN WITH THE X-RAY EYES ... Roger Corman
X MARKS THE SPOT ... George Sherman
X Y & ZEE ... Brian G. Hutton
XALA ... Ousmene Sembene
XANADU ... Robert Greenwald
XAOS ... Paolo Taviani
XAOS ... Vittorio Taviani
X-RAY ... Boaz Davidson
XYZ MURDERS, THE ... Sam Raimi
X-15 ... Richard Donner

Y

YAKUZA, THE ... Sydney Pollack
YANGTSE INCIDENT ... Michael Anderson
YANKEE PASHA ... Joseph Pevney
YANKS ... John Schlesinger
YEAR OF LIVING DANGEROUSLY, THE ... Peter Weir
YEAR OF THE DRAGON ... Michael Cimino
YEAR OF THE QUIET SUN, THE ... Krzysztof Zanussi
YEAR OF THE YAHOO! ... Herschell Gordon Lewis
YEHUDI MENUHIN - CHEMIN DE LUMIERE (FD) ... Francois Reichenbach
YELLOW BALLOON, THE ... J. Lee Thompson
YELLOW CANARY, THE ... Buzz Kulik
YELLOW HAIR AND THE FORTRESS OF GOLD ... Matt Cimber
YELLOW PAGES ... James Kenelm Clarke
YELLOWBEARD ... Mel Damski
YELLOWSTONE KELLY ... Gordon Douglas
YENTL ... Barbra Streisand
YES, GIORGIO ... Franklin J. Schaffner
YES SIR, THAT'S MY BABY ... George Sherman
YESTERDAY'S CHILD (TF) ... Corey Allen
YESTERDAY'S ENEMY ... Val Guest
YIELD TO THE NIGHT ... J. Lee Thompson
YOJIMBO ... Akira Kurosawa
YOLANDA AND THE THIEF ... Vincente Minnelli
YOR, THE HUNTER FROM THE FUTURE ... Anthony M. Dawson
YORKTOWN, LE SANS D'UNE BETAILLE (TD) ... Marcel Ophuls
YOU AND ME ... David Carradine
YOU BETTER WATCH OUT ... Lewis Jackson
YOU CAN'T GO HOME AGAIN (TF) ... Ralph Nelson
YOU CAN'T TAKE IT WITH YOU ★★ ... Frank Capra
YOU FOR ME ... Don Weis
YOU KNOW WHAT SAILORS ARE ... Ken Annakin
YOU LIE SO DEEP, MY LOVE (TF) ... David Lowell Rich
YOU LIGHT UP MY LIFE ... Joseph Brooks
YOU MUST BE JOKING! ... Michael Winner
YOU ONLY LIVE TWICE ... Lewis Gilbert
YOU'LL LIKE MY MOTHER ... Lamont Johnson
YOU'LL NEVER SEE ME AGAIN (TF) ... Jeannot Szwarc
YOUNG AMERICANS (FD) ... Alex Grasshoff
YOUNG AND DANGEROUS ... William F. Claxton
YOUNG AND WILD ... William Witney
YOUNG AND WILLING ... Ralph Thomas
YOUNG AT HEART ... Gordon Douglas
YOUNG BESS ... George Sidney
YOUNG BILLY YOUNG ... Burt Kennedy
YOUNG CAPTIVES, THE ... Irvin Kershner
YOUNG CASSIDY ... Jack Cardiff
YOUNG COUNTRY, THE (TF) ... Roy Huggins
YOUNG DOCTORS IN LOVE ... Garry Marshall
YOUNG DOCTORS, THE ... Phil Karlson
YOUNG FRANKENSTEIN ... Mel Brooks
YOUNG GENERATION, THE ... Kon Ichikawa
YOUNG GIRLS OF ROCHEFORT, THE ... Jacques Demy
YOUNG GUNS OF TEXAS ... Maury Dexter
YOUNG GUNS, THE ... Albert Band
YOUNG IDEAS ... Jules Dassin
YOUNG JESSE JAMES ... William F. Claxton
YOUNG JOE, THE FORGOTTEN KENNEDY (TF) ... Richard T. Heffron
YOUNG LADY CHATTERLEY ... Alan Roberts
YOUNG LADY CHATTERLEY II ... Alan Roberts
YOUNG LAWYERS, THE (TF) ... Harvey Hart
YOUNG LIONS, THE ... Edward Dmytryk
YOUNG LOVE ... Michal Bat-Adam
YOUNG LOVE, FIRST LOVE (TF) ... Steven Hillard Stern
YOUNG LUST ... Gary Weis
YOUNG MAN'S FANCY, A ... Robert Stevenson
YOUNG PHILADELPHIANS, THE ... Vincent Sherman
YOUNG PIONEERS (TF) ... Michael O'Herlihy
YOUNG PIONEERS' CHRISTMAS (TF) ... Michael O'Herlihy
YOUNG RACERS, THE ... Roger Corman
YOUNG REBEL, THE ... Vincent Sherman
YOUNG RUNAWAYS, THE (TF) ... Russ Mayberry
YOUNG RUNAWAYS, THE ... Arthur Dreifuss
YOUNG SAVAGES, THE ... John Frankenheimer
YOUNG SCARFACE ... John Boulting
YOUNG SINNER, THE ... Tom Laughlin
YOUNG STRANGER, THE ... John Frankenheimer
YOUNG SWINGERS, THE ... Maury Dexter
YOUNG, THE EVIL AND THE SAVAGE, THE ... Anthony M. Dawson
YOUNG TORLESS ... Volker Schlondorff
YOUNG VISITORS, THE (TF) ... James Hill
YOUNG WARRIORS ... Lawrence D. Foldes
YOUNG WARRIORS, THE ... John Peyser
YOUNG WINSTON ... Richard Attenborough
YOUNGBLOOD ... Peter Markle
YOUNGBLOOD ... Noel Nosseck
YOUNGER GENERATION, THE ... Frank Capra
YOUR CHEATIN' HEART ... Gene Nelson
YOUR MONEY OR YOUR WIFE ... Anthony Simmons
YOUR MONEY OR YOUR WIFE (TF) ... Allen Reisner
YOUR PLACE OR MINE (TF) ... Robert Day
YOUR TICKET IS NO LONGER VALID ... George Kaczender
YOU'RE A BIG BOY NOW ... Francis Ford Coppola
YOU'RE IN THE NAVY NOW ... Henry Hathaway
YOU'RE LYING ... Vilgot Sjoman
YOURS, MINE AND OURS ... Melville Shavelson
YOUTH ... Moshe Mizrahi
YOUTH IN POLAND (FD) ... Albert Maysles
YOUTH IN POLAND (FD) ... David Maysles
YOUTH OF HEIJI SENIGATA, THE ... Kon Ichikawa
YOUTH ON TRIAL ... Budd Boetticher
YUKON PATROL, THE ... William Witney
YUMA (TF) ... Ted Post

Z

Z ★ ... Costa-Gavras
ZABRISKIE POINT ... Michelangelo Antonioni
ZACHARIAH ... George Englund
ZANDY'S BRIDE ... Jan Troell
ZANY ADVENTURES OF ROBIN HOOD, THE (TF) ... Ray Austin
ZAPPED! ... Robert J. Rosenthal
ZARAK ... Terence Young
ZARDOZ ... John Boorman
ZAZIE ... Louis Malle
ZAZIE DANS LE METRO ... Louis Malle
ZEE & CO. ... Brian G. Hutton
ZELIG ... Woody Allen
ZENOBIA ... Gordon Douglas
ZEPPELIN ... Etienne Perier
ZERO HOUR ... Hall Bartlett
ZERO TO SIXTY ... Don Weis
ZIEGFELD FOLLIES ... Vincente Minnelli
ZIEGFELD: THE MAN AND HIS WOMEN (TF) ... Buzz Kulik
ZIGGY STARDUST AND THE SPIDERS FROM MARS ... D.A. Pennebaker
ZIGZAG ... Richard A. Colla
ZITA ... Robert Enrico
ZODIAC COUPLES, THE ... Alan Roberts
ZOMBIES ON BROADWAY ... Gordon Douglas
ZONTAR - THE THING FROM VENUS ... Larry Buchanan
ZOOT SUIT ... Luis Valdez
ZORBA THE GREEK ★ ... Michael Cacoyannis
ZORRO, THE GAY BLADE ... Peter Medak
Z.P.G. ... Michael Campus
ZULU ... Cy Endfield
ZULU DAWN ... Douglas Hickox
ZUMA BEACH (TF) ... Lee H. Katzin
ZWEI GANZE TAGE (TF) ... Marcel Ophuls

INDEX OF AGENTS/MANAGERS

A

ABRAMS RUBALOFF & ASSOCIATES
8075 W. Third Street, Suite 303
Los Angeles, CA 90048
213/935-1700

ADAMS, RAY & ROSENBERG
(See TRIAD ARTISTS, INC.)

AGENCY FOR THE PERFORMING ARTS, INC., (APA)
9000 Sunset Blvd., 12th Floor
Los Angeles, CA 90069
213/273-0744

7630 Biscayne Blvd.
Miami, FL 33188
305/758-8731

120 West 57th Street
New York, NY 10019
212/582-1500

BUDDY ALTONI TALENT AGENCY
P.O. Box 1022
Newport Beach, CA 92660
714/851-1711
Mr. Buddy Altoni

CARLOS ALVARADO AGENCY
8820 Sunset Blvd., Suites A & B
Los Angeles, CA 90028
213/652-0272
Mr. Carlos Alvarado
Ms. Monalee Schilling

FRED AMSEL & ASSOCIATES, INC.
291 S. La Cienega Blvd., Suite 3
Beverly Hills, CA 90211
213/855-1200
Mr. Fred Amsel

THE ARTISTS AGENCY
10000 Santa Monica Blvd.
Los Angeles, CA 90067
213/277-7779
Mr. Mickey Frieberg

ARTISTS CAREER MANAGEMENT
9157 Sunset Blvd., Suite 206
Los Angeles, CA 90069
213/278-9157
Mr. Edgar Small

THE ARTISTS GROUP, LTD.
1930 Century Park West
Suite 303
Los Angeles, CA 90067
213/552-1100
Mr. Hal Stalmaster
Mr. Mark Harris
Mr. Arnold Soloway

HOWARD J. ASKENASE
217 Glen Airy Drive
Los Angeles, CA 90068
213/464-4114

B

BARSKIN AGENCY
11240 Magnolia Blvd., Suite 202
No. Hollywood, CA 91601
818/985-2992
Mr. Doovid Barskin

BAUMAN & HILLER
9220 Sunset Blvd., Suite 202
Los Angeles, CA 90069
213/271-5601

250 W. 57th Street, Suite 803
New York, NY 10019
212/757-0098

BEAKEL & JENNINGS AGENCY
427 N. Canon Drive, Suite 205
Beverly Hills, CA 90210
213/274-5418
Mr. Walter Beakel
Mr. Tom Jennings

GEORGE BEAUME
3 Quai Maiaquais
Paris 75006, France
325-2759
Mr. George Beaume

BERKUS, COSAY, HANDLEY & STEIN
(See LEADING ARTISTS, INC.)

BLAKE-GLENN AGENCY
409 N. Camden Drive
Beverly Hills, CA 90210
213/278-6885

BLOOM, LEVY & SHORR ASSOCIATES
800 S. Robertson Blvd., Suite 9
Los Angeles, CA 90035
213/659-6160

HARRY BLOOM AGENCY
8833 Sunset Blvd., Suite 202
Los Angeles, CA 90069
213/659-5985

J. MICHAEL BLOOM LTD.
9200 Sunset Blvd., Suite 1210
Los Angeles, CA 90069
213/275-6800

400 Madison Avenue 20th Floor
New York, NY 10017
212/932-6900

PAUL BRANDON & ASSOC.
9046 Sunset Blvd.
Los Angeles, CA 90069
213/273-6173

BERNIE BRILLSTEIN & CO.
9200 Sunset Blvd., Suite 428
Los Angeles, CA 90069
213/275-6135
Mr. Bernie Brillstein

BRODER/KURLAND AGENCY
9046 Sunset Blvd., Suite 202
Los Angeles, CA 90069
213/274-8291
Mr. Bob Broder

C

CAREY-PHELPS-COLVIN
1407 N. La Brea Avenue
Los Angeles, CA 90028
213/874-7780

CENTURY ARTISTS, LTD.
9744 Wilshire Blvd., Suite 206
Beverly Hills, CA 90212
213/273-4366
Mr. Louis Bershad

CHARTER MANAGEMENT
9000 Sunset Blvd., Suite 1112
Los Angeles, CA 90069
213/278-1690

CHASIN-PARK-CITRON
(See INTERNATIONAL CREATIVE MANAGEMENT)

CHASMAN & STRICK ASSOCIATES
6725 Sunset Blvd., Suite 506
Los Angeles, CA 90028
213/463-1115
Ms. Tanya Chasman
Ms. Shirley Strick

COLEMAN-ROSENBERG
667 Madison Avenue
New York, NY 10021
212/838-0734

KINGSLEY COLTON & ASSOCIATES
16661 Ventura Blvd., Suite 400
Encino, CA 91436
818/788-6043

POLLY CONNELL & ASSOCIATES
4605 Lankershim Blvd.
Suite 213
North Hollywood, CA 91602
818/985-6266
Ms. Polly Connell

CONTEMPORARY-KORMAN ARTISTS
132 Lasky Drive
Beverly Hills, CA 90212
213/278-8250
Mr. Ronald Leif

BEN CONWAY & ASSOCIATES, INC.
999 N. Doheny Drive, Suite 403
Los Angeles, CA 90069
213/271-8133
Mr. Ben Conway

THE COOPER AGENCY
1900 Avenue of the Stars
Suite 2535
Los Angeles, CA 90067
213/277-8422
Mr. Frank Cooper

CREATIVE ARTISTS AGENCY (CAA)
1888 Century Park East
14th Floor
Los Angeles, CA 90067
213/277-4545

LIL CUMBER ATTRACTIONS AGENCY
6515 Sunset Blvd., Suite 300A
Hollywood, CA 90028
213/469-1919

CURTIS-BROWN, LTD.
575 Madison Avenue
New York, NY
212/755-4200

D

DADE/ROSEN ASSOCIATES
9172 Sunset Blvd., Suite 2
Los Angeles, CA 90069
213/278-7077
Mr. Mike Rosen

DAVID, HUNTER, KIMBLE, PARSEGHIAN & RIFKIN
(See TRIAD ARTISTS, INC.)

DENNIS, KARG, DENNIS & CO.
470 S. San Vicente Blvd.
Los Angeles, CA 90048
213/651-1700

DIAMOND ARTISTS, LTD.
9200 Sunset Blvd., Suite 909
Los Angeles, CA 90069
213/278-8146
Mr. Abby Greshler

E

EISENBACH-GREENE, INC.
760 N. La Cienega Blvd.
Los Angeles, CA 90069
213/659-3420

F

JACK FIELDS & ASSOCIATES
9255 Sunset Blvd., Suite 1105
Los Angeles, CA 90069
213/278-1333

FILM ARTISTS ASSOCIATES
9200 Sunset Blvd., Suite 431
Los Angeles, CA 90069
213/275-6193

FILM ARTISTS MANAGEMENT ENTERPRISES (F.A.M.E.)
1800 Avenue of the Stars
Los Angeles, CA 90067
213/556-8071

THE SY FISCHER COMPANY
10960 Wilshire Blvd. Suite 924
Los Angeles, CA 90024
213/208-0455
Ms. Diane Cairns
Mr. Lew Weitzman

KURT FRINGS AGENCY, INC.
415 N. Crescent Drive
Beverly Hills, CA 90210
213/274-8881
Mr. Kurt Frings

G

THE GAGE GROUP
9229 Sunset Blvd., Suite 306
Los Angeles, CA 90069
213/859-8777

1650 Broadway
New York, NY 10019
212/541-5250

DALE GARRICK INTERNATIONAL AGENCY
8831 Sunset Blvd., Suite 402
Los Angeles, CA 90069
213/657-2661
Mr. Dale Garrick

GELFAND, RENNERT & FELDMAN
1880 Century Park East
Suite 900
Los Angeles, CA 90067
213/553-1707

GENERAL MANAGEMENT CORP.
9000 Sunset Blvd., Suite 400
Los Angeles, CA 90069
213/274-8805
Ms. Helen Kushnick

ROY GERBER & ASSOCIATES
9200 Sunset Blvd., Suite 620
Los Angeles, CA 90069
213/550-0100

THE GERSH AGENCY
222 N. Canon Drive, Suite 201
Beverly Hills, CA 90210
213/274-6611
Mr. Phil Gersh

J. CARTER GIBSON
9000 Sunset Blvd., Suite 811
Los Angeles, CA 90069
213/274-8813

PHILLIP B. GITTLEMAN
1221 N. Kings Road-PH405
Los Angeles, CA 90069
213/656-9215

GOLDFARB-LEWIS AGENCY
8733 Sunset Blvd., Suite 202
Los Angeles, CA 90069
213/659-5955

GOTLER AGENCY
9100 Sunset Blvd., Suite 360
Los Angeles, CA 90069
213/273-2811
Mr. Joel Gotler

IVAN GREEN AGENCY
1888 Century Park East
Suite 908
Los Angeles, CA 90067
213/277-1541
Mr. Ivan Green

LARRY GROSSMAN & ASSOCIATES
211 S. Beverly Drive, Suite 206
Beverly Hills, CA 90212
213/550-8127

H

REECE HALSEY AGENCY
8733 Sunset Blvd., Suite 101
Los Angeles, CA 90069
213/652-2409

ERIK HANSTEEN
9701 Wilshire Blvd., Suite 800
Beverly Hills, CA 90212
213/271-5666
Ms. Dorris Halsey

JAMES HARPER
13063 Ventura Blvd.
Studio City, CA 91604
818/872-0944
Mr. James Harper

HENDERSON/HOGAN AGENCY, INC.
247 S. Beverly Drive, Suite 102
Beverly Hills, CA 90212
213/274-7815
Ms. Lynne Radmin

200 57th Street
New York, NY 10019
212/765-5190

HESSELTINE-BAKER ASSOCIATES
165 W. 46th St., Suite 409
New York, NY 10019
212/921-4460

ROBERT G. HUSSONG AGENCY
721 N. La Brea Ave., Suite 201
Los Angeles, CA 90038
213/655-2534

I

GEORGE INGERSOLL AGENCY
6513 Hollywood Blvd., Suite 217
Los Angeles, CA 90028
213/874-6434
Mr. George Ingersoll

INTERNATIONAL CREATIVE MANAGEMENT (ICM)
8899 Beverly Blvd.
Los Angeles, CA 90048
213/550-4000

22 Champs-Elysee
Paris 75008, France
723-9066

40 West 57th St.
New York, NY 10019
212/556-5600

38 Via Siacci
Rome 75008, Italy
806-041

22 Grafton Street
London W1 England
01-629-8080

K

MERRILY KANE AGENCY
9171 Wilshire Blvd., Suite 310
Beverly Hills, CA 90210
213/550-8874

KAPLAN-STAHLER AGENCY
119 N. San Vicente Blvd.
Beverly Hills, CA 90211
213/653-4483

PARTRICIA KARLAN AGENCY
3815 W. Olive Ave., Suite 202
Burbank, CA 91505
818/954-8848

PAUL KOHNER, INC.
9169 Sunset Boulevard
Los Angeles, CA 90069
213/550-1060
Mr. Paul Kohner

BKM MANAGEMENT, INC.
9076 St. Ives Drive
Los Angeles, CA 90059
213/550-7358
Mr. Barry Krost

L

THE CANDACE LAKE OFFICE
1103 Glendon Avenue
Los Angeles, CA 90024
213/824-9706
Ms. Candace Lake

THE LANTZ OFFICE, INC.
9255 Sunset Blvd., Suite 505
Los Angeles, CA 90069
213/858-1144

888 Seventh Avenue
New York, NY 10106
212/586-0200
Mr. Robert Lantz

IRVING PAUL LAZAR AGENCY
211 S. Beverly Drive, Suite 110
Beverly Hills, CA 90212
213/275-6153
Mr. Irving Paul Lazar

One East 66th Street
New York, NY 10021
212/355-1177

LEADING ARTISTS, INC.
1900 Avenue of the Stars
Suite 1530
Los Angeles, CA 90067
213/277-9090

JACK LENNY & ASSOCIATES
9701 Wilshire Blvd., Suite 800
Beverly Hills, CA 90212
213/271-2174

140 W. 58th Street
New York, NY 10019
212/582-0270

LITKE/GROSSBART MANAGEMENT
8500 Wilshire Blvd., Suite 506
Beverly Hills, CA 90211
213/657-5562
Mr. Marty Litke
Mr. Jack Grossbart

ROBERT LITTMAN COMPANY, INC.
(See LEADING ARTISTS, INC)

STERLING LORD AGENCY
660 Madison Avenue
New York, NY 10021
212/751-2533

LUND AGENCY
6515 Sunset Blvd., Suite 204
Los Angeles, CA 90028
213/466-8280
Mr. Reginald Lund

GRACE LYONS AGENCY
204 S. Beverly Drive, Suite 102
Beverly Hills, CA 90212
213/652-5290

M

MAJOR TALENT AGENCY
11812 San Vicente Blvd.
Suite 510
Los Angeles, CA 90049
213/820-5841

CHRISTOPHER MANN, LTD.
39 Davies Street
London, WI England
01/493-2810
Mr. Christopher Mann

MCCARTT, ORECK & BARRETT
9200 Sunset Blvd., Suite 1009
Los Angeles, CA 90069
213/278-6243

JAMES MCHUGH AGENCY
8150 Beverly Blvd., Suite 303
Los Angeles, CA 90048
213/651-2770

FRED MESSENGER AGENCY
8235 Santa Monica Blvd.
Suite 315
Los Angeles, CA 90046
213/654-3800
Mr. Fred Messenger

GEORGE MICHAUD AGENCY
4950 Densmore Avenue, Suite 1
Encino, CA 91436
818/981-6680
Mr. Arthur Dreifuss

MILLER AGENCY
4425 Riverside Dr., Suite 200
Burbank, CA 91505
818/849-2363
Mr. Tommy Miller

WILLIAM MORRIS AGENCY
151 South El Camino Dr.
Beverly Hills, CA 90212
213/274-7451

1350 Avenue of the Americas
New York, NY 10019
212/586-5100

2325 Crestmoore Road
Nashville, TN 37215
615/385-0310

147-149 Wardour Street
London, WI England
01/734-9361

Lamonstrasse 9
Munich 27, Germany
47/608-1234

Via Giosuè Carducci, 10
00187 Rome, Italy
48-6961

MARVIN MOSS, INC.
9200 Sunset Blvd., Suite 601
Los Angeles, CA 90069
213/278-8483
Mr. Marvin Moss

N

SKIP NICHOLSON AGENCY, INC.
13701 Riverside Drive
Suite 314
Sherman Oaks, CA 91423
818/906-2700

NOVEMBER NINTH MANAGEMENT
9021 Melrose Ave., Suite 301
Los Angeles, CA 90069
213/652-9800

O

FIFI OSCARD AGENCY
19 West 44th Street
New York, NY 10036
212/764-1100
Ms. Fifi Oscard,
Mr. Charles Hunt

P

ANTHONY JONES PETERS
London 01-839-2556
Mr. Anthony Jones Peters

PICKMAN COMPANY, INC.
9025 Wilshire Blvd., Suite 214
Beverly Hills, CA 90212
213/273-8273
Mr. Milton Pickman

PROGRESSIVE ARTISTS AGENCY
400 S. Beverly Drive
Beverly Hills, CA 90212
213/553-8561

R

RAPER ENTERPRISES
9441 Wilshire Blvd., Suite 620D
Beverly Hills, CA 90212
213/273-7704

RICHLAND AGENCY
1888 Avenue of the Stars
Los Angeles, CA 90067
213/553-1257
Mr. Dan Richland
Mr. Joe Richland

THE ROBERTS COMPANY
427 N. Canon Drive
Beverly Hills, CA 90210
213/275-9384

FLORA ROBERTS AGENCY
157 West 57th St.
New York, NY 10022
212/355-4165

ROBINSON-LUTTRELL ASSOCIATES
141 El Camino Drive
Beverly Hills, CA 90212
213/275-6114
Mr. Bill Robinson

ROBINSON-WEINTRAUB & ASSOCIATES
554 S. San Vicente Blvd.
Suite 3
Los Angeles, CA 90048
213/652-5802

STEPHANIE ROGERS & ASSOCIATES
9100 Sunset Blvd., Suite 340
Los Angeles, CA 90069
213/278-2015
Ms. Stephanie Rogers

ROLLINS-JOFFE
Paramount Studios
5555 Melrose Avenue
Los Angeles, CA 90038
213/462-6677

130 W. 57th St.
New York, NY
212/582-1940
Mr. Jack Rollins
Mr. Charles Joffe

JACK ROSE AGENCY
6430 Sunset Blvd., Suite 1203
Los Angeles, CA 90028
213/461-4911 or 213/463-7300
Mr. Jack Rose

HOWARD ROTHBERG
P.O. Box 10657
9701 Wilshire Blvd.
Beverly Hills, CA 90213
213/273-9100

S

SACKHEIM AGENCY
9301 Wilshire Blvd., Suite 606
Beverly Hills, CA 90210
213/858-0606

IRVING SALKOW AGENCY
9350 Wilshire Blvd., Suite 214
Beverly Hills, CA 90210
213/276-3141
Mr. Irving Salkow

SANFORD-BECKETT & ASSOCIATES
1015 Gayley Avenue - Suite 301
Los Angeles, CA 90024
213/208-2100
Mr. Geoffrey Sanford
Ms. Brenda Beckett

IRV SCHECHTER & CO.
9300 Wilshire Blvd., Suite 410
Beverly Hills, CA 90212
213/278-8070
Mr. Irv Schechter

DON SCHWARTZ & ASSOCIATES
8721 Sunset Blvd., Suite 200
Los Angeles, CA 90069
213/657-8910
Ms. Anita Haeggstrom

SELECTED ARTISTS AGENCY
12711 Ventura Blvd., Suite 460
Studio City, CA 91604
818/763-9731
Ms. Flo Joseph

DAVID SHAPIRA & ASSOCIATES, LTD.
15301 Ventura Blvd., Suite 345
Sherman Oaks, CA 91403
818/906-0322
Mr. David Shapira

SHAPIRO-LICHTMAN AGENCY
2049 Century Park East
Suite 1320
Los Angeles, CA 90067
213/557-2244

SHAPIRO/WEST
141 El Camino Drive, Suite 295
Beverly Hills, CA 90212
213/278-8896
Mr. George Shapiro

SHARP ENTERPRISES, INC.
9145 Sunset Blvd., Suite 228
Los Angeles, CA 90069
213/278-1981
Mr. Jules Sharr

LEW SHERRELL AGENCY, LTD.
7060 Hollywood Blvd., Suite 610
Los Angeles, CA 90028
213/461-9955

SMITH-FRIEDMAN & ASSOCIATES
9869 Santa Monica Blvd.
Suite 207
Beverly Hills, CA 90212
213/277-8464
Ms. Susan Smith

CRAYTON SMITH-RAY GOSNELL AGENCY
3872 Las Flores Cyn. #2
Malibu, CA 90265
213/456-6641
Mr. Crayton Smith
Mr. Ray Gosnell

STE REPRESENTATION, LTD.
211 S. Beverly Dr., Suite 201
Beverly Hills, CA 90212
213/550-3982
Mr. David Eidenberg

888 Seventh Avenue
New York, NY 10019
212/246-1030
Mr. Clifford Stevens

CHARLES H. STERN AGENCY, INC.
9220 Sunset Blvd., Suite 218
Los Angeles, CA 90069
213/273-6890
Mr. Charles H. Stern

STONE-MASSER AGENCY
1052 Carol Drive
Los Angeles, CA 90069
213/275-9599

H. N. SWANSON, INC.
8523 Sunset Boulevard
Los Angeles, CA 90069
213/652-5385

T

TALENT MANAGEMENT INTERNATIONAL
6380 Wilshire Blvd., Suite 910
Los Angeles, CA 90048
213/273-4000
Mr. Lawrence Becksey

HERB TOBIAS & ASSOCIATES
1901 Avenue of the Stars
Suite 840
Los Angeles, CA 90067
213/277-6211
Mr. Herb Tobias

TRIAD ARTISTS, INC.
10100 Santa Monica Blvd.
16th Floor
Los Angeles, CA 90067
213/556-2727

165 West 46th Street
New York, NY 10036
212/869-2880

TWENTIETH CENTURY ARTISTS
13727 Ventura Blvd., Suite 211
Studio City, CA 91604
818/990-8580
Ms. Diane Davis

U

UFLAND/ROTH PRODUCTIONS
c/o 20th Century Fox
P.O. Box 900
Beverly Hills, CA 90213
213/203-1295
Mr. Harry Ufland

W

ELLIOT WAX & ASSOCIATES
9255 Sunset Blvd., Suite 612
Los Angeles, CA 90069
213/273-8217
Mr. Elliot Wax

PHILIP WELTMAN
425 S. Beverly Drive
Beverly Hills, CA 90212
213/556-2081

SYLVIA WOSK AGENCY
439 S. La Cienega Blvd.
Los Angeles, CA 90048
213/274-8063

WRITERS & ARTISTS AGENCY
11726 San Vicente Blvd.
Suite 300
Los Angeles, CA 90049
213/820-2240
Ms. Joan Scott

Z

ZIEGLER, DISKANT, INC.
9255 Sunset Blvd., Suite 1112
Los Angeles, CA 90069
213/278-0070
Mr. Martin Hurwitz

INDEX OF ADVERTISERS

A special thanks to our new and continued advertisers whose support allowed us to bring you this **Third Annual International Edition of FILM DIRECTORS: A Complete Guide.**

FEELING LEFT OUT???

The 1986 Fourth International Edition of FILM DIRECTORS: A Complete Guide will be published in January 1986. We update our records continuously during the year. If you are a director and you qualify to be listed (please read the introduction for qualifications), then send us your information as soon as possible. Our editorial deadline is August 31, 1985. **PLEASE DO NOT WAIT UNTIL THEN.** Our computer **loves** getting up-dated information all year long.

Send all listing information to:

FILM DIRECTORS: A Complete Guide
Lone Eagle Publishing
9903 Santa Monica Blvd. - Suite 204
Beverly Hills, CA 90212
Phone: 213/471-8066 or 213/277-9616

Or, just fill out the post-paid tear-out card in the front of the book and drop in the mail. We'll send you the information form.

EDITOR/COMPILER

MICHAEL SINGER, 32, has worked in motion pictures for twelve years as a writer, publicist, producer's aide, director's assistant, story analyst, researcher and journalist.

A native of New York City, he now resides in Los Angeles.